The Treasury of Precious Instructions: Essential Teachings of the Eight Practice Lineages of Tibet

Volume 3: Kadam
Part 1

The Tsadra Foundation Series
published by Snow Lion, an imprint of Shambhala Publications

Tsadra Foundation is a US-based nonprofit organization that contributes to the ongoing development of wisdom and compassion in Western minds by advancing the combined study and practice of Tibetan Buddhism.

Taking its inspiration from the nineteenth-century nonsectarian Tibetan Buddhist scholar and meditation master Jamgön Kongtrul Lodrö Taye, Tsadra Foundation is named after his hermitage in eastern Tibet, Tsadra Rinchen Drak. The Foundation's various program areas reflect his values of excellence in both scholarship and contemplative practice, and the recognition of their mutual complementarity.

Tsadra Foundation envisions a flourishing community of Western contemplatives and scholar-practitioners who are fully trained in the traditions of Tibetan Buddhism. It is our conviction that, grounded in wisdom and compassion, these individuals will actively enrich the world through their openness and excellence.

This publication is a part of Tsadra Foundation's Translation Program, which aims to make authentic and authoritative texts from the Tibetan traditions available in English. The Foundation is honored to present the work of its fellows and grantees, individuals of confirmed contemplative and intellectual integrity; however, their views do not necessarily reflect those of the Foundation.

Tsadra Foundation is delighted to collaborate with Shambhala Publications in making these important texts available in the English language.

Kadam

Stages of the Path, Mind Training, and Esoteric Practice

Part 1

The Treasury of Precious Instructions:
Essential Teachings of the Eight Practice Lineages of Tibet
Volume 3

Compiled by Jamgön Kongtrul Lodrö Taye

translated by
Artemus B. Engle

Snow Lion

Snow Lion
An imprint of Shambhala Publications, Inc.
2129 13th Street
Boulder, Colorado 80302
www.shambhala.com

9 8 7 6 5 4 3 2 1

First Edition
Printed in the United States of America

Shambhala Publications makes every effort to print on acid-free, recycled paper.
Snow Lion is distributed worldwide by Penguin Random House, Inc., and its subsidiaries.

LIBRARY OF CONGRESS CATALOGING-IN-PUBLICATION DATA
Names: Kong-sprul Blo-gros-mtha'-yas, 1813–1899 author. | Engle, Artemus B., 1948– translator. | Kong-sprul Blo-gros-mtha'-yas, 1813–1899. Gdams ngag mdzod.
Title: Kadam: stages of the path, mind training, and esoteric practice. Part one / compiled by Jamgön Kongtrul Lodrö Taye; translated by Artemus B. Engle.
Other titles: Gdams ngag mdzod. English
Description: Boulder: Shambhala, 2024. | Series: The Treasury of Precious Instructions: Essential Teachings of the Eight Practice Lineages of Tibet; volume 3 | Includes bibliographical references and index.
Identifiers: LCCN 2023001263 | ISBN 9781559395052 (hardback)
Subjects: LCSH: Spiritual life—Buddhism. | Blo-sbyong. | Buddhism—China—Tibet Autonomous Region.
Classification: LCC BQ7805 .K6513 2024 | DDC 294.3/444—dc23/eng/20230206
LC record available at https://lccn.loc.gov/2023001263

Contents

Part Three: The Instruction Lineage

Foreword

In his vast work *The Treasury of Precious Instructions* (*gDams ngag rin po che'i mdzod*), Jamgön Kongtrul Lodrö Taye, that most eminent of Tibetan Buddhist masters, collected all the empowerments, instructions, and practices of the eight great chariots of the practice lineages. Not only that, but he himself received the complete transmissions for all the practices, accomplished them including the retreats, and preserved them in his own mind stream. He then passed on the transmissions to his own students and all who requested them.

The Treasury of Precious Instructions exemplifies how Jamgön Kongtrul Lodrö Taye's whole life was dedicated to teaching and spreading the dharma, whether it be sūtra or mantra, *kama* or *terma*, old or new translation school, free of sectarian bias. Without his supreme efforts, many traditions of Tibetan Buddhism would have been lost.

The teachings of the Buddha have now spread throughout the Western world, and there is a growing need for major texts to be translated into English so that Western dharma students and scholars have access to these essential teachings. I was, therefore, delighted to hear that having successfully published a translation in ten volumes of Jamgön Kongtrul Lodrö Taye's *The Treasury of Knowledge* (*Shes bya kun khyab mdzod*), the Tsadra Foundation has embarked on a second major project, the translation of *The Treasury of Precious Instructions*, and I would like to express my gratitude to them.

May their work be of benefit to countless sentient beings.

His Holiness the Seventeenth Karmapa, Ogyen Trinley Dorje
Bodhgaya
February 21, 2016

Series Introduction

THE *TREASURY of Precious Instructions* (*gDams ngag rin po che'i mdzod*) is the fourth of the five great treasuries compiled or composed by Jamgön Kongtrul Lodrö Taye (1813–1900), also known as Karma Ngawang Yönten Gyatso, among many other names. Kongtrul was one of the greatest Buddhist masters of Tibet. His accomplishments were so vast and varied that it is impossible to do them justice here. The reader is referred to an excellent short biography in the introduction to the first translated volume of another of his great works, *The Treasury of Knowledge*, or the lengthy *Autobiography of Jamgön Kongtrul*. Even if his achievements had consisted solely of his literary output represented in these five treasuries, it would be difficult to comprehend his level of scholarship.

Unlike *The Treasury of Knowledge*, which is Kongtrul's own composition, his other four treasuries may be considered anthologies. Kongtrul's stated mission was to collect and preserve without bias the teachings and practices of all the lineages of Tibetan Buddhism, particularly those that were in danger of disappearing. The English publication of *The Treasury of Knowledge* in ten volumes and the forthcoming translations of this *Treasury of Precious Instructions* in some eighteen volumes can attest to the success of his endeavor, perhaps even beyond what he had imagined.

The Treasury of Precious Instructions is, in some ways, the epitome of Kongtrul's intention. He first conceived of the project around 1870, as always in close consultation with his spiritual friend and mentor Jamyang Khyentse Wangpo (1820–1892). The two of them, along with other great masters, such as Chokgyur Dechen Lingpa, Mipam Gyatso, and Ponlop Loter Wangpo, were active in an eclectic trend in which the preservation of the texts of Tibetan Buddhism was paramount.[1] It was with Khyentse's encouragement and collaboration that Kongtrul had created *The Treasury of Knowledge*—his incredible summation of all that was to be known—and compiled the anthologies of *The Treasury of Kagyu Mantra* and *The Treasury of Precious Hidden Teachings*. This next treasury expanded the scope by aiming to collect in one place the most important instructions of *all* the main practice lineages.

Kongtrul employed a scheme for organizing the vast array of teachings that flourished, or floundered, in Tibet during his time into the eight great chariots of the practice lineages (*sgrub brgyud shing rta chen po brgyad*), or eight lineages that are vehicles of attainment. He based this on a much earlier text by Sherap Özer (Prajñārasmi, 1518–1584).[2] The structure and contents of that early text indicate that the seeds of the so-called nonsectarian movement (*ris med*) of the nineteenth century in eastern Tibet had already been planted and just needed cultivation. The organizing principle of the scheme was to trace the lineages of the instructions for religious practice that had come into Tibet from India. This boiled down to eight "charioteers"—individuals who could be identified as the conduits between India and Tibet and who were therefore the sources of the practice lineages, all equally valid in terms of origin and comparable in terms of practice. This scheme of eight practice lineages became a kind of paradigm for the nonsectarian approach championed by Kongtrul and his colleagues.[3]

The Treasury of Precious Instructions implements this scheme in a tangible way by collecting the crucial texts and organizing them around those eight lineages. These may be summarized as follows:

1. The Nyingma tradition derives from the transmissions of Padmasambhava and Vimalamitra during the eighth century, along with the former's illustrious twenty-five disciples (*rje 'bangs nyer lnga*) headed by the sovereign Trisong Detsen.
2. The Kadam tradition derives from Atiśa (982–1054) and his Tibetan disciples headed by Dromtön Gyalwai Jungne (1004–1063).
3. The Sakya tradition, emphasizing the system known as the "Path with Its Result," derives from Virūpa, Ḍombi Heruka, and other mahāsiddhas, and passes through Gayadhara and his Tibetan disciple Drokmi Lotsāwa Śākya Yeshe (992–1072).
4. The Marpa Kagyu tradition derives from the Indian masters Saraha, Tilopa, Naropa, and Maitrīpa, as well as the Tibetan Marpa Chökyi Lodrö (1000?–1081?).
5. The Shangpa Kagyu tradition derives from the ḍākinī Niguma

and her Tibetan disciple Khyungpo Naljor Tsultrim Gönpo of Shang.

6. Pacification and Severance derive from Pa Dampa Sangye (d. 1117) and his Tibetan successor, Machik Lapkyi Drönma (ca. 1055–1143).
7. The Six-Branch Yoga of the *Kālacakra Tantra* derives from Somanātha and his Tibetan disciple Gyijo Lotsāwa Dawai Özer during the eleventh century and was maintained preeminently through the lineages associated with Zhalu and Jonang.
8. The Approach and Attainment of the Three Vajras derives from the revelations of the deity Vajrayoginī, compiled by the Tibetan master Orgyenpa Rinchen Pal (1230–1309) during his travels in Oḍḍiyāna.

The very structure of *The Treasury* thus stands as a statement of the nonsectarian approach. With all these teachings gathered together and set side by side—and each one authenticated by its identification with a direct lineage traced back to the source of Buddhism (India)—maintaining a sectarian attitude would be next to impossible. Or at least that must have been Kongtrul's hope. In explaining his purpose for the collection, he states:

> Generally speaking, in each of the eight great mainstream lineages of accomplishment there exists such a profound and vast range of authentic sources from the sūtra and tantra traditions, and such limitless cycles of scriptures and pith instructions, that no one could compile everything.[4]

Nevertheless, he made a good start in *The Treasury of Precious Instructions*, which he kept expanding over the years until at least 1887. The woodblocks for the original printing—carved at Palpung Monastery, where Kongtrul resided in his nearby retreat center—took up ten volumes. An edition of this is currently available in twelve volumes as the Kundeling printing, published in 1971–1972.[5] With the addition of several missing texts, an expanded and altered version was published in eighteen volumes in 1979–1981 by Dilgo Khyentse Rinpoche. Finally, in 1999 the most complete version became available in the edition published by Shechen Monastery, which is the basis for the current translations.[6] The structure of this enhanced edition, of course, still centers on the eight lineages, as follows:

1. Nyingma (Ancient Tradition), volumes 1 and 2;
2. Kadampa (Transmitted Precepts and Instructions Lineage), volumes 3 and 4;
3. Sakya, or Lamdre (Path with Its Result), volumes 5 and 6;
4. Marpa Kagyu (Precept Lineage of Marpa), volumes 7 through 10;
5. Shangpa Kagyu (Precept Lineage of Shang), volumes 11 and 12;
6. Zhije (Pacification), volume 13, and Chöd (Severance), volume 14;
7. Jordruk (Six Yogas [of Kālacakra]), volume 15; and
8. Dorje Sumgyi Nyendrup (Approach and Attainment of Three Vajras, also called after its founder Orgyenpa), volume 15.

Volumes 16 and 17 are devoted to various other cycles of instruction. Volume 18 mainly consists of the *One Hundred and Eight Teaching Manuals of Jonang*, a prototype and inspiration for Kongtrul's eclectic anthology, and also includes his catalog to the whole *Treasury*.

Translator's Introduction

THIS CURRENT VOLUME, volume 3, and the next, volume 4, of *The Treasury of Precious Instructions* are dedicated to a collection of spiritual literature identified with the Kadam tradition of Tibetan Buddhism. This lineage arose from the visit to and twelve-year stay in Tibet by the Indian master Dīpaṃkara Śrījñāna, better known by the popular epithet Atiśa, who traveled there in the middle of the eleventh century C.E.

Atiśa was born in 982 C.E. into what is described as the royal family of a region referred to as Zahor by Tibetans, which is thought to be located in the northeast region of the South Asian continent in what is now Bangladesh. At the time, this area was under the sway of the Pāla dynasty. Biographies describe Atiśa, whose childhood name was Candragarbha, as having developed an interest in Buddhism at a relatively young age. He was introduced to tantric practice by an Indian master named Rāhulagupta and remained a layperson until the age of twenty-nine. After deciding that his spiritual efforts would be most effective if he were to become a Buddhist monk, he took ordination and was given the name Dīpaṃkara Śrījñāna. For several years following this event, Atiśa undertook to study the full range of Buddhist doctrine and religious literature. Some years later, in his early thirties, he traveled to Sumatra, known at the time as Suvarṇadvīpa, or the Isle of Gold, to study with a Buddhist teacher referred to by Tibetans as Lama Serlingpa, which means "the guru from the Isle of Gold." Atiśa sought out this teacher, a renowned master of Mahāyāna spiritual practices, in order to receive instruction on the topic of enlightenment mind, or bodhicitta, which is the spiritual attitude that is the entry point for the path that leads to the attainment of supreme buddhahood. He remained in Sumatra for a period of twelve years receiving instruction from this teacher. Later, Atiśa often remarked to his Tibetan disciples that Lama Serlingpa was the most revered among all of his one hundred and fifty-seven spiritual teachers, because it was this figure who enabled him to gain some mastery of the crucially important attitude of enlightenment mind.

After returning to India, Atiśa continued to study with one of Lama Serlingpa's disciples, Ratnākaraśānti, and is said to have begun carrying out activities in support of the Buddhist teaching. It was during this period that he was invited to become a resident scholar at Vikramaśīla Monastery, a religious center established in the late eighth or early ninth century C.E. by the Pāla monarch Dharmapāla that continued to enjoy the patronage of his successors. Biographical accounts state that it was a Pāla monarch of the time, possibly Neyapāla, who conferred upon Dīpaṃkara Śrījñāna the epithet Atiśa, which means "preeminent one," in recognition of his outstanding qualities among the learned scholars at Vikramaśīla.

At the end of the tenth century C.E., the Tibetan rulers in the western region of Ngari had become active in seeking to promote the development of Buddhism in their kingdom. One monarch, Lha Lama Yeshe Ö,[1] who had become an ordained monk himself and abdicated his rule, was instrumental in sponsoring young scholars' travel to India to study Buddhism with the aim of returning to their homeland in order to continue translating important Indian Buddhist works into Tibetan. Some of the Tibetans who studied at Vikramaśīla Monastery were the ones who recommended to their patrons that Atiśa be invited to Tibet to help promote Buddhism in their homeland. Lha Lama Jangchup Ö,[2] the great nephew of Yeshe Ö, is the figure who first sought to invite Atiśa to Tibet, an effort that did not succeed initially. Nevertheless, eventually Atiśa did accept the Tibetan invitation and arrived at Tholing,[3] the capital of the Ngari kingdom, in the year 1042. Although it had originally been agreed that he would only spend three years in Tibet, Atiśa lived out the remainder of his life in this northern land, passing away in 1054 at the age of seventy-two at Nyethang, which lies nearby Lhasa in a southwesterly direction.

One year prior to the end of the original three-year period, one of Atiśa's translators, Naktso Lotsāwa,[4] urged his Tibetan colleagues to request teachings from the master. This led Jangchup Ö, who had become a disciple of Atiśa, to formally request a Mahāyāna teaching that would dispel mistaken views that were prevalent among Tibetans and would address the key elements of both sūtra and tantra doctrine. This act resulted in the composition of Atiśa's most widely known composition, *A Lamp for the Path to Enlightenment*,[5] which is also the first treatise that appears in this volume. A verse text of just sixty-eight verses, it is recognized as the root text for the influential system of instruction known as The Stages of the Path for the Three Types of Person, a body of teachings that has spawned an enormous quantity of commentarial literature over subsequent centuries. Elements of this system of instruction are addressed in all the works contained in the first of five categories of Kadam literature.

While Atiśa met with and taught a significant number of well-known Tibetan scholars of the day, it was not until the original three-year period for Atiśa's stay was about to end that the individual who was to become his most influential Tibetan disciple, Drom Tönpa Gyalwai Jungne,[6] met the master. Tradition holds that the deity Tārā had prophesied to Atiśa that he would meet an *upāsaka*, or lay disciple, in Tibet and that this individual would be instrumental in ensuring the success of his efforts on behalf of the Buddha's teaching there. Indeed, Drom Tönpa is referred to as the patriarch of the Kadam tradition, and it is his efforts that played the largest role in establishing Atiśa's legacy in Tibet. After meeting his teacher, Drom Tönpa arranged for Atiśa to travel to other regions of Tibet where he continued to teach. It was these efforts that resulted in the extension of Atiśa's stay in Tibet.

The two syllables that make up the name of the Kadam tradition are nouns; *ka*, which means "word" in the sense of the discourses of the Buddha, and *dam*, which means "instruction" in the sense of a teacher's oral explanations on how to put those canonical teachings into practice. While historical works record several interpretations of this name, the most widely cited one states that the followers of the Kadam lineage were referred to by this term because they believed that not even a single letter of the Buddha's "word" contained in the three baskets of his teachings could be discarded and that, if properly understood, they would all be recognized as supreme forms of "instruction" that contribute to and promote the attainment of the ultimate goal of buddhahood. This notion is illustrated in the following lines that are attributed to Drom Tönpa:

> The marvelous word contained in the three baskets
> is richly filled with instruction for the three types of person.
> True meaning will be gained by anyone who counts
> the Kadam tradition's precious golden prayer beads.[7]

The Tibetan tradition established more than three centuries later at the end of the fourteenth century by Je Tsongkhapa also placed great importance on the Kadam teachings that have come to be known by the name Lamrim, or Stages of the Path. Indeed, Tsongkhapa's followers, who are known most widely as adherents of the Geluk,[8] or "virtuous system," are also referred to as the "new Kadampas." The two Kadam volumes contain a number of works by Je Tsongkhapa and several important religious figures who were his followers.

Jamgön Kongtrul's catalog[9] to *The Treasury of Precious Instructions* classifies the Kadam literature into five categories: (1) treatise,[10] (2) instruction,[11] (3) esoteric instruction,[12] (4) ancillary works,[13] and (5) associated works.[14] It also asserts that the first three of these categories are related to three Kadam lineages that were established by three students of Atiśa's principal disciple, Drom Tönpa Gyalwai Jungne, who were known as the "Three Brothers"—namely, Potowa Rinchen Sel,[15] Chengawa Tsultrim Bar,[16] and Puchungwa Zhönu Gyaltsen.[17] While these three individuals were important early Kadam figures and the names for the first two categories do correspond to distinct Kadam lineages, this explanation of the nature of the first three categories is somewhat misleading. Moreover, the third category, called "esoteric instruction," in fact refers to the esoteric Kadam lineage of Sixteen Drops,[18] which I do not believe Tibetan historical literature has ever been described by this name. It would be more accurate to describe them as being made up of three separate bodies of Kadam instruction, each of which is represented by a particular "root text." These representative works are (1) Atiśa's *Lamp for the Path to Enlightenment*, (2) the aphorisms of the instruction known as the Seven-Point Mind Training, and (3) Atiśa's *Bodhisattva's Jewel Garland*, respectively, and they are the first three texts that appear in volume 3.

Atiśa's *Lamp for the Path to Enlightenment* is the root text for the Kadam teaching that in recent times has come to be known as Lamrim, or Stages of the Path. During the original Kadam period, this system of instruction was also referred by such names as the Supreme Path and the Stages of the Teaching. The second category of Kadam literature is devoted to the genre of Mahāyāna teachings known as Lojong, or Mind Training. While the "root text" for this category is an annotated version of the aphorisms to the specific Lojong teaching known as Seven-Point Mind Training, the second category of Kadam literature includes a wide range of works associated with the Lojong tradition as a whole. The third root text, Atiśa's *Bodhisattva's Jewel Garland*, is meant to represent the esoteric Kadam instruction known as the Sixteen Drops, despite the fact that it does not make any direct reference to that teaching. Nevertheless, as explained below, there is a justification for linking it with teaching on the Sixteen Drops. The editors did not assign any root text to the final two of the five categories of Kadam literature—that is, ancillary works and associated works, respectively.

1. The Treatise Lineage

Volume 3 of *The Treasury of Precious Instructions* contains ten works that are associated with Atiśa's *Lamp for the Path to Enlightenment*, the representative work for this first category. While authorship of the first of the ten, titled *The Brilliant Illumination of the Path to Enlightenment*, is attributed to Jamgön Kongtrul, the colophon explains that it was "composed by extracting essential elements from the writings of excellent spiritual teachers." In fact, it is largely a truncated version of a commentary to Atiśa's root text written by the Paṇchen Losang Chökyi Gyaltsen, to which Jamgön Kongtrul added several passages from Je Tsongkhapa's *Great Treatise on the Stages of the Path to Enlightenment*[19] and a single passage from his *Shorter Treatise on the Stages of the Path to Enlightenment*.[20] It should also be noted that the Tibetan version of this commentary does not provide the individual verses from Atiśa's root text on their own, prior to explaining their meaning. Rather, the words that make up the root verses are simply woven into the language that forms the prose text. Nevertheless, for the convenience of the reader, the root verses have been added to the English translation of the commentary at the beginning of each passage in which they are being explained, with the individual words of the verses placed in italics in the prose explanations.

Jamgön Kongtrul's catalog to the overall *Treasury of Precious Instructions* states that he intended to include a Lamrim work by the second Shamar Tokden Khachö Wangpo,[21] which he described as a "Lamrim text written according to the system of Gampopa [Sönam Rinchen]." The illustrious Kagyu master Gampopa had been a student of the Kadam teacher Jayulwa Zhönu Ö[22] before he sought out the great yogi Milarepa as his principal spiritual teacher. Gampopa himself wrote a well-known treatise that combines the Kadam Lamrim instructions with elements of the Kagyu Mahāmudrā doctrine. However, Tokden Khachö Wangpo's work was not included in any of the published editions of *The Treasury of Precious Instructions*.

In addition to Jamgön Kongtrul's commentary to *A Lamp for the Path to Enlightenment*, the first category of Kadam texts includes three prose commentaries that address the entirety of the Lamrim system of practice: the

Third Dalai Lama, Sönam Gyatso's *Nectar That Is Like Highly Refined Gold*; the Fourth Paṇchen Lama, Losang Chökyi Gyaltsen's *Easy Path That Leads to Omniscience*; and Jetsun Tāranātha's *Essence of Nectar*. Sönam Gyatso's work is one of the earliest Lamrim works composed by a Geluk master other than Je Tsongkhapa. It is organized around a Lamrim verse text composed by Je Tsongkhapa, known variously by such popular names as *A Compendium of the Stages of the Path*[23] and *The Song of Spiritual Realization*.[24] This poem is also included among the ten Lamrim works in volume 3 under the title *A Verse Compendium of the Spiritual Practices of the Stages of the Path to Enlightenment*.

Losang Chökyi Gyaltsen's *Easy Path* is another well-known Geluk Lamrim commentary. As the colophon notes, its origin can be traced to an oral teaching that the Paṇchen Lama gave at Tashi Lhunpo Monastery in which he presented the Lamrim instructions as they were preserved in a Geluk tradition known as the Wensa Oral Transmission Lineage.[25] Using notes that were taken down by disciples who attended the teaching, Losang Chökyi Gyaltsen edited the material into its current written form.

Tāranātha's Lamrim text is the second longest composition in this first of the two Kadam volumes. The instructions are presented in the framework of sixty-four meditation topics. This structure is the most distinctive feature of the treatise, which the author meant as an outline for a practitioner to use in his or her effort to cultivate the overall system of practice. While the explanations themselves are deliberately presented in an abbreviated manner, Tāranātha makes the following statement regarding the methodology underlying his text:

> This work is an instruction manual that addresses how to meditate in the sense of the manner in which to direct the mind as one reflects on the various individual topics. Explanations of the doctrinal meanings that one must understand in order to bring them to mind as the subject matter for reflection should be sought out from other writings composed by the former spiritual masters of this tradition.

The five remaining works in this first category of Kadam literature address specific elements of the Lamrim tradition. Of these, chapter 6, titled *The Flower Cluster of Spiritual Attainments*, is a short poem by Je Tsongkhapa written in the genre of verses of supplication,[26] which, in this case, are addressed to the lineage masters of a so-called "near," or short, lineage that is made up of three beings: Vajradhara, Mañjughoṣa, and Tsongkhapa's contemporary, a yogi known popularly as Lama Umapa but who is referred to in the poem by his spiritual name Pawo Dorje. This lineage reflects a tradition that originated when Je Tsongkhapa, initially through the assistance of Lama Umapa, gained the ability to communicate directly with the divine figure Mañjughoṣa, also known as Mañjuśrī. Verses 4 and 5 of the text that is contained here do not appear in Je Tsongkhapa's original composition; rather, they represent later figures in a lineage that primarily constitutes an esoteric body of instruction on right view and that was originally propagated from teacher to disciple only through direct oral communication.

Although the title of chapter 9, a work by Jamyang Khyentse Wangpo titled *An Essential Summary of the Method of Practice in the System of the Stages of the Path to Enlightenment*, seems to address the overall system of Lamrim practice, it is mainly devoted to the topic of the six preliminary practices,[27] a devotional exercise that is meant to be carried out at the beginning of each meditation session on the Lamrim instruction. This topic is also addressed in some detail both in Sönam Gyatso's *Nectar That Is Like Highly Refined Gold* and Paṇchen Losang Chökyi Gyaltsen's *Easy Path*. The only main topic of instruction that Jamyang Khyentse Wangpo's work touches on is that of how to rely upon a spiritual teacher.

The next two works in this first category each provide explanations on carrying out the ritual for generating enlightenment mind and accepting the bodhisattva vow. Both texts indicate that, depending on the nature of the disciples, separate rituals can be carried out at different times in order to confer only the aspirational form of enlightenment mind and not the active form of enlightenment mind. Alternatively, both forms of enlightenment mind can be received sequentially during one and the same overall ceremony.

Chapter 11, titled *A Guidebook for the Path to Great Awakening* and composed by Jamgön Kongtrul, addresses the ritual ceremony based largely upon material presented in Śāntideva's *Entry into the Conduct That Leads to Enlightenment*[28] and describes it as the system that has been propagated in the Lineage of the Profound View. This name refers to a lineage of masters associated with the Madhyamaka, or Middle Way school, that was established by Nāgārjuna.

Chapter 12, titled *The Excellent Path of the Bodhisattvas* and composed by Jamyang Khyentse Wangpo, takes up the same topic as the preceding work; however, this treatise presents the ritual according to the System of Great Vastness,[29] a lineage that is more commonly known as the Lineage of Extensive Conduct.[30] This tradition is identified with the Yogācāra school of Mahāyāna Buddhism that was founded by Ārya Asaṅga. The principal resource for this second presentation is the morality chapter of Asaṅga's *Stage of a Bodhisattva*.

Both Jamgön Kongtrul and Jamyang Khyentse Wangpo refer to these two systems as being distinct from one another in a variety of significant ways, including the person who confers the vow, the person who receives the vow, the nature of the ritual in which the vow is received, the particular precepts that are accepted in the ritual, and the method by which transgressions of the vows can be remedied. An opposing viewpoint maintains that the two systems should not be regarded as distinct in any meaningful way. The early Kadam master Sharawa Yönten Drak[31] mentions these same five purported differences in his treatise on the stages of the path[32] and argues that they do not represent substantive differences. Je Tsongkhapa also addresses this controversy in his commentary on bodhisattva morality titled *A Guidebook for the Path to Enlightenment*[33] and concurs with Sharawa that these two historical Indian systems for generating the bodhisattva vow should not be considered distinct in any meaningful way. In fact, his work formulates a system of practice that combines the views presented in the two traditions.

The final work in this first category of Kadam literature, Chenga Lodrö Gyaltsen's *Opening the Door to the Dharma*, is the longest text contained in volume 3. This text is placed at the end of the first Kadam volume in the Tibetan edition of *The Treasury of Precious Instructions*. Although it occurs after the introduction of several works that form part of the second category of texts—that is, those associated with the Instruction Lineage—Jamgön Kongtrul's catalog clearly indicates that Chenga Lodrö Gyaltsen's work is meant to be included in the Treatise Lineage. Therefore, we have moved the text in this English translation to chapter 13 in order to include it among the other works associated with the general topic of The Stages of the Path to Enlightenment and Atiśa's root text, *A Lamp for Path to Enlightenment*.

Chenga Lodrö Gyaltsen's entire composition is devoted to the topic of "mentally abandoning this life."[34] While this goal is typically associated with the spiritual practice of a so-called lesser person[35]—a term that is generally thought of as referring to a novice—the discussion is actually directed toward those Buddhist practitioners who are capable of following the strict and austere lifestyle of a Buddhist contemplative ascetic. It is also tacitly understood that this type of practitioner is one who seeks the ultimate Mahāyāna goal of supreme enlightenment rather than simply a favorable samsaric rebirth. As evidence that the author was a committed follower of the recently formed Geluk school who studied with a number of Je Tsongkhapa's direct disciples, Chenga Lodrö Gyaltsen refers to himself as "a dharma teacher who has placed on the crown of his head the dust under the feet of the omniscient and precious lord, the spiritual father who was from the Shar Tsongkha region, and his spiritual sons." Nevertheless, in addition to many early Kadam teachers, his work cites passages from the writings of numerous spiritual figures from virtually all the major historical Tibetan traditions.

After providing a somewhat lengthy introductory section that sets out to describe and illustrate what is meant by the act of "mentally abandoning this life," Chenga Lodrö Gyaltsen refers to a text[36] composed by the Kagyu master Tsangpa Gyare Yeshe Dorje,[37] which identifies seven defining attributes,[38] or character traits, that a true dharma practitioner needs to possess and then lists eleven precepts or commitments[39] that such individuals should also be willing to adopt in order to overcome attachment to this life. After listing the commitments, Chenga Lodrö Gyaltsen presents instructions on nineteen distinct topics that he recognizes as conforming to these commitments. The style or methodology consists of citing multiple passages—mostly, but not exclusively, from the writings of Tibetan masters. These quotations are typically not more than a few verses or a short paragraph, often from just two or three masters but sometimes more, for each point. There are also citations from various sūtras, most notably the *Sūtra Encouraging a Superior Attitude*.[40] Another feature of this work is the numerous annotations that offer brief historical details about the religious figures referenced in the text. One exception is a passage from the *Sūtra Encouraging a Superior Attitude*, in which the annotations serve to explain virtually every expression that appears in a passage describing the faults of being attached to gain and honor,[41] the very antithesis of the goal of mentally abandoning this life.

2. The Instruction Lineage

As noted earlier, although the second category of Kadam literature is purported to be identified with the so-called Instruction Lineage that originated with the early Kadam teacher Chengawa Tsultrim Bar, in reality it is devoted to literature associated with systems of instruction known as Lojong,[42] or Mind Training. While some examples of Indian Lojong texts were known from the earliest period of the Kadam tradition, Atiśa himself seems to have only taught the key elements of this form of spiritual practice orally and to a very limited number of disciples, among whom Drom Tönpa was the most prominent figure.

Perhaps the most influential and complete example of Mind Training practice is a teaching that came to be known as the Seven-Point Mind Training.[43] Although it did not exist in written form during the earliest Kadam period, Atiśa is nonetheless regarded as having been its source. According to tradition, Chekawa Yeshe Dorje[44] is responsible for having made the decision to teach it more openly and perhaps is even responsible for systematizing the instructions into seven sections. While there are a number of different written editions of the root text for this system of practice—no less than six appear in volumes 3 and 4 of *The Treasury of Precious Instructions*, either as stand-alone works or embedded in commentaries—the version that was selected as the primary text for this second category of Kadam literature was extracted from a commentary on the Seven-Point Mind Training composed by the important fourteenth-century Tibetan teacher Gyalse Tokme Zangpo.[45] Annotations were added to the aphorisms, perhaps by Jamgön Kongtrul himself, principally to identify which portions of the text correspond to each of the overall instruction's seven sections. Despite its original source, Jamgön Kongtrul's catalog to *The Treasury of Precious Instructions* refers to this text as having been "created"[46] by Chekawa Yeshe Dorje.

As for the group of works chosen to illustrate this second category of Kadam instruction, the majority were selected from an important collection of Mind Training texts known popularly in Tibetan as *Lojong Gyatsa*,[47] or *The Hundredfold Collection on Mind Training*. Geshe Thupten Jinpa has produced an English translation of this entire volume published under the title *Mind Training: The Great Collection*. Permission was obtained to use his translations of the twenty-eight titles from this collection that appear in volumes 3 and 4 of *The Treasury of Precious Instructions*. Chapter 14 of volume 3, titled *A Listing of the Mahāyāna Works on Mind Training*, identifies the specific works[48] from *The Hundredfold Collection on Mind Training* works that were chosen by the editors to be included in *The Treasury of Precious Instructions*.

The first two of the Mind Training texts that were selected from *The Hundredfold Collection* are early works of a biographical nature that describe different periods in Atiśa's life. Of these, the first is a verse text that addresses the early years of his youth and describes the manner in which he first began to pursue the dharma. The second, written in mixed prose and verse, describes his journey to Sumatra to meet and receive instructions from the spiritual teacher known as Lama Serlingpa. A third work that addresses an incident in Atiśa's life is item fourteen in chapter 14's listing of texts, which is titled *Two Yoginīs' Admonition to Atiśa to Train His Mind.* This text contains a very brief description of a vision-like experience in which Atiśa encounters two semi-divine female figures, identified as emanations of the deities Tārā and Bṛkutī, who appear in the sky while he was visiting Bodhgaya, the holy site of the Buddha's enlightenment. He observes them discussing how anyone who wishes to achieve enlightenment quickly must cultivate an esoteric method of cultivating enlightenment mind. The practice is a tantric form of meditation that is described in the next work, item fifteen entitled *Kusulu's Accumulation Mind Training.* Several other selections from *The Hundredfold Collection* explicitly state that the instruction contained in them was given to Atiśa by one or another of his spiritual teachers.

Items three and four of chapter 14, which appear near the end of volume 3 in *The Treasury of Precious Instructions,* contain separate versions of the root text to the Seven-Point Mind Training; one is an annotated version of the aphorisms with the second containing just the root text. Item five, the first work that appears in volume 4, which is titled simply *A Commentary on the Seven-Point Mind Training,* was compiled by Chekawa's principal disciple Se Jilbuwa Chökyi Gyaltsen.[49] This important and influential text is one of the earliest written commentaries on the teaching. The next two titles, items six and seven, are well-known Indian Mind Training works that were both composed by the Indian master Dharmarakṣita, one of Atiśa's three principal teachers on Lojong practice—namely, *The Wheel of Sharp Weapons* and *The Peacock's Neutralizing of Poison.*

The above-referenced Tibetan edition of *The Hundredfold Collection on Mind Training* includes a catalog/table of contents[50] at the beginning of the volume. A noteworthy feature of this tabulation is that in a number of instances, a series of texts is grouped together under a single, separate title page. This attribute is mirrored in the Mind Training works included in *The Treasury of Precious Instructions.* For instance, items eight through twelve in the listing of volume 3's chapter 14 appear in volume 4 grouped together under the single title *Melodies of an Adamantine Song: A Chanting Meditation on Mind Training.*[51] The section title for this series of texts is derived from the first item,[52] which contains the descriptive phrase "adamantine song of chanting meditation,"[53] and thus it can be understood as referring specifically to this work. Item nine, a text in four sections titled *Stages of the Heroic Mind*, is a verse composition that mainly addresses instructions that relate to two practices that are central to the Mind Training tradition—namely, the Equality and Exchange between Oneself and Others,[54] and Giving and Taking.[55] Item ten, referred to by the descriptive name *A Mind Training Teaching That Serlingpa Taught to Jowo Atiśa for the Purpose of Taming Inhabitants of a Borderland*, is a composition made up of ten verses that describe key elements of Mind Training practice. It should be noted that item twenty-seven, which has no formal title but ends with a statement that is virtually identical to the descriptive title of this text, is in fact a prose commentary on these verses. Items eleven and twelve are two short prose texts that were committed to writing by an unnamed Tibetan author or authors as a record of Mind Training instructions that were transmitted orally by lineage holders. The former is titled *A Teaching on Taking Afflictions onto the Path* and the latter is simply identified as *Guru Yoga*.

A second example in which a series of texts is grouped together under a section title applies to items eleven through nineteen. These works are combined together under the title *Instructions on the Purification of Evil Deeds*.[56] One reason for grouping these texts together may be that some of the instructions are not identified by any specific name. This is particularly true of the initial practice that is presented at the beginning of this second group of texts. While Geshe Jinpa assigns it the name of the section title,[57] the listing in chapter 14 does not mention it as a separate work nor is it identified explicitly in the corresponding series of texts in volume 4 of *The Treasury of Precious Instructions*. This quite short instruction is simply described in the body of the text as a practice that conveys a great blessing and has the ability to purify such great evil deeds as the creation of discord within a religious community.[58] We have included the instruction at the beginning of item thirteen, which is titled *A Mahāyāna System of Practice for Eliminating Grudges*. The subject matter of items fourteen and fifteen—titled *Two Yoginīs' Admonition to Atiśa to Train His Mind* and *Kusulu's Accumulation Mind Training*, respectively—were addressed above. Item fifteen, titled *Mind Training Taking Joys and Pains onto the Path*, is a short prose commentary that is devoted to a single verse attributed to the Indian master Śākyaśrībhadra, who came to Tibet in 1203 and taught there for a decade before returning to India. The prose commentary, no doubt by a Tibetan author, is distinguished by its reference to elements of tantric practice in which the practitioner identifies him- or herself with a buddha's three bodies. Item fourteen, titled *Sumpa Lotsāwa's Ear-Lineage*[59] *Mind Training*, is a relatively short prose text that is based on another vision-like experience, similar to the one experienced by Atiśa that is described in item thirteen, in which the Tibetan Sumpa Lotsāwa, while making a pilgrimage to Bodhgaya, witnesses two female figures discussing four essential maxims relating to spiritual practice. Explanations of these maxims are addressed in the prose text. Item fifteen, *Bodhisattva Samantabhadra's Mind Training*, derives its name from a description of the nature in which bodhisattvas must develop an "expansive mind,"[60] an expression that is meant to indicate the manner in which a bodhisattva must generate an attitude that is dedicated to the welfare of all sentient beings. After referring to how Buddha Śākyamuni and the three bodhisattvas Avalokiteśvara, Vajrapāṇi, and Mañjuśrī developed such a mind, the text praises the extraordinary manner in which Samantabhadra did so. The text also addresses the necessity of developing both a "resolute mind"[61] that is unwavering in the face of hardships and a "diamond-like mind"[62] that relies on an understanding of emptiness in order to combine the elements of wisdom and means. The final work in this section, titled *Eight-Sessions Mind Training*, is attributed to Drom Tönpa, who is said to have received the teaching from Atiśa. After describing its lineage and a few general comments about the nature of Mind Training practice, the text describes how to practice elements of this system in relation to these eight topics: food, breath, taking on beings' suffering, flesh and blood, torma oblations, the four elements, a wish-fulfilling jewel, and the moment of death.

The remaining selections from *The Hundredfold Collection on Mind Training*—namely, items twenty through twenty-eight from the chapter 14 listing—also are grouped within a single section heading in that source that is titled *Mind Training That Removes Obstacles*; however, for reasons that are not clear this heading does not appear as a separate title page[63] in volume 4 of *The Treasury of Precious Instructions*. Rather, the names of items twenty through twenty-eight are simply presented consecutively, wherever they may occur in the middle of a particular folio. With the exception of Chekawa's commentary to the *Eight Verses on Mind Training*, these are somewhat less familiar works by both Indian and Tibetan masters. For example, items twenty and twenty-one—titled *A Mahāyāna Mind Training That Dispels Obstacles* and *A Mahāyāna Mind Training for Averting Future*

Abandonment of the Practice, respectively—are related works that likely were composed by a single Tibetan author of unknown identity. In some instances, the authorship is fairly well established, such as items twenty-three, twenty-four, twenty-five, and twenty-seven, which were either composed in their entirety or contain essential elements of instruction by such figures as the Tibetan Kadam master Chim Namkha Drak and the Indian masters Virvapa, Atiśa, and Serlingpa, respectively. Another case, item twenty-two is a work that, despite the name *Atiśa's Seven-Point Mind Training*, was probably written by some unidentified figure. Likewise, item twenty-eight, titled *A Mahāyāna Mind Training*, is another Seven-Point Mind Training text of uncertain authorship. Item twenty-six, titled *A Commentary on the Eight Verses on Mind Training* and attributed to Chekawa Yeshe Dorje, is noteworthy in that it is an early explanation of the famous Mind Training root text by the Kadampa master Langri Tangpa Dorje Senge.[64]

The final five entries in this category of Kadam works do not appear in the chapter 14 listing, as they do not form part of the aforementioned *Hundredfold Collection on Mind Training*. These include Gyalse Tokme Zangpo's fourteenth-century commentary, identified by the title *The Seven-Point Mind Training Instruction Composed by Gyalse Tokme Zangpo Pel*; Jamyang Khyentse Wangpo's *Seeds of Benefit and Happiness*, which mainly discusses the same six preliminary practices[65] that he explained in his earlier work in the first category of Kadam works that appears in volume 3[66] and three separate Lojong works by Jamgön Kongtrul; his commentary titled *A Guidebook for the Path to Enlightenment: An Instruction Manual on the Mahāyāna Seven-Point Mind Training Composed for Ease of Practice by Persons of Lesser Proficiency*; a supplication prayer to the lineage masters of this tradition titled *Dispelling the Torment of Faith*; and a Mind Training aspirational prayer titled *Entry Point for the Ocean of Enlightenment Mind*.[67]

3. The Esoteric Instruction Lineage

The root text for the third category of Kadam works is Atiśa's *Bodhisattva's Jewel Garland*, a relatively short poem of twenty-six verses, which addresses a range of fundamental Mahāyāna spiritual practices. While it also appears as the first text in *The Hundredfold Collection on Mind Training*, it does not mention such key Mind Training practices as the Equality and Exchange between Oneself and Others or Giving and Taking, presumably because Atiśa did not teach these practices openly. Nor does it make explicit reference to any esoteric Kadam practices. Nevertheless, this composition is recognized as the root text for another treatise titled *The Jewel Garland of Dialogues*,[68] an extraordinary and lengthy work consisting of twenty-three chapters written almost entirely in verse that records verbal exchanges principally between Atiśa and Drom Tönpa on a wide range of topics, including many that are central to the practices of the Sixteen Drops. While this longer work describes many visionary experiences and makes reference to various elements of esoteric practice, it too makes no explicit reference to the practice known as the Sixteen Drops.

In any case, volume 4 of *The Treasury of Precious Instructions* contains three works that make up this third category of Kadam teachings, all of which are devoted to the teaching known as the Sixteen Drops. The various forms of meditation and mantra recitation that make up the Sixteen Drops represent the quintessential form of esoteric instruction within the Kadam tradition. All of the practices are said to be subsumed within five recollections that were articulated by Tārā in a statement she addressed to Drom Tönpa, whom she addresses as Avalokiteśvara, indicating that he is to be regarded as an emanation of the deity. The five recollections are: recalling the lamas as the object of refuge, recalling all beings as one's fathers and mothers, recalling emptiness as the mind's ultimate nature, recalling one's body as a deity's form, and recalling one's speech as mantra recitation. Each of the sixteen stages of practice is made up of a range of divine visualizations and related devotional exercises, starting with the Drop of the Outer Inconceivable Array, in which the practitioner visualizes a divine realm within which one generates oneself as a form of Avalokiteśvara called Jinasāgara[69] and reflects on spiritual qualities that are said to resemble those described in the *Kāraṇḍavyūha Sūtra*.[70] These meditations progress through the remaining stages in which each successive drop, consisting of a divine realm and its related deity, is generated inside the heart of the preceding drop's deity, culminating with the final Drop of Enlightenment. The overall practice is described as encompassing all the elements of the three trainings and the four categories of tantra. Several commentaries also state that this practice is informed by instruction on the completion stage of Highest Yoga Tantra as taught by Buddha Jñānapāda in his divinely inspired oral instruction titled *Meditation on the Reality of the Two Stages*.[71]

The first of the three works devoted to the Sixteen Drops, authored by Jamgön Kongtrul and titled *An Ornament of Compassion's Transcendent Play*, is made up of two parts: a sādhana ritual that devotees can use to carry out the practice and a manual that a lama can use to confer the empowerment or consecration ritual[72] upon qualified disciples. This empowerment ritual is a requirement for disciples to undertake the practice, which includes elements of many forms of Buddhist tantra practice, in particular the generation and completion stages that are unique to Highest Yoga Tantra. The remaining two works, which address the spiritual exercises themselves, are both described in their titles as "essential summaries of the practice." The first of the two, titled *An Essential Summary of the Method of Practicing the Meditation and Mantra Recitation of the Sixteen Drops*, was composed by the Geluk lama Gungtang Könchok Tenpe Drönme.[73] It is a ritual text composed in verse with a short prose introduction and occasional brief explanatory notes interspersed throughout. The second explanatory text, titled *An Essential Summary on the Stages of a Profound Oral Instruction on the Kadam Teaching Known as the "Sixteen Drops That Confer the Supreme Boon of the Two Spiritual Attainments"* was composed by Jamyang Khyentse Wangpo. It is a more expanded presentation of the practice that also includes the relevant forms of recitation. The author states in the colophon that the work was compiled on the basis of memorial notes[74] taken at an oral teaching by the Geluk lama Könchok Tenpa Rapgye[75] at Tashi Lhunpo Monastery.

4. Ancillary Works

This fourth category of Kadam writings, which has no root text, is made up of four works. The first, titled *The Permission Rituals for the Four Deities That Are the Untainted Root Practice of the Kadam Tradition and That Were Extracted from "The Jewel Mine of Sādhana Rituals,"* contains four brief rituals for each of the four principal Kadam deities: Buddha Śākyamuni, Avalokiteśvara, Tārā, and Acala. As the title indicates, all four rituals have been extracted from a much larger collection of sādhana rituals compiled by Tāranātha that is titled *The Jewel Mine of an Ocean of Tutelary Deities' Sādhana Rituals.*[76] At the conclusion of the first ritual devoted to Buddha Śākyamuni, the text also repeats language that Tāranātha expresses in his source work, which is that the first three liturgies are not true permission rituals[77] but rather merely "methods for conferring an oral transmission"[78] that enable practitioners to perform the sādhana[79] of the particular deity that is addressed in the opening portion of the text. He further asserts that the fourth ritual, devoted to the deity Acala, is both an oral transmission for reciting the deity's mantra and a genuine permission ritual. To emphasize this point, he declares that later collections of ritual texts have improperly represented the first three to be true permission rituals when they are not. The principal issue seems to be that the first three rituals devoted to Śākyamuni, Avalokiteśvara, and Tārā, respectively, do not include formal invocations by the officiating lama of the deity's body, speech, and mind. The colophon of the text that appears in *The Treasury of Precious Instructions* further states that the editor has inserted additional words of clarification.

The second text, titled *A Collection of the Essence of the Sūtra and Tantra Paths: A Written Account of an Oral Teaching on the Practice of the Four Kadam Deities,* is a commentary on spiritual practices that relate directly to the four deities addressed in the first work. The colophon identifies the work as a record of memorial notes[80] that was compiled by Jamgön Kongtrul from an oral teaching given by Jamyang Khyentse Wangpo at Palpung Thupten Chökor Ling Monastery.[81] He further states that he also consulted the writings of Nyukla Paṇchen Ngawang Drakpa,[82] Jamgön Kunga Sönam,[83] and Jetsun Kunga Drölchok.[84]

The instructions for all four deities include a sādhana ritual for the deity, followed by meditation on the relative and ultimate forms of enlightenment mind. In the case of the Tārā section, in particular, the instruction is presented in the context of the five recollections that were mentioned earlier. The portion of the text devoted to the deity Acala includes a special section of instruction on the six practices of tummo, or psychic heat; dream yoga; illusory body; clear-light meditation; powa, or transference yoga; and meditation on the intermediate state, or bardo, all of which are associated with Highest Yoga Tantra.

The third work in this section is a well-known poem by Je Tsongkhapa titled *The Three Principal Elements of the Path,*[85] which consists of fourteen verses. It was originally written as a letter that Je Tsongkhapa sent to one of his earliest disciples named Tsako Wönpo Ngawang Drakpa,[86] who had returned to his native region of Gyalrong in eastern Tibet. The three topics addressed in the poem are the spiritual attitudes of renunciation,[87] enlightenment mind,[88] and right view.[89] The instruction related to these topics is considered to have been received by Je Tsongkhapa directly from Mañjughoṣa, and thus the work is identified with the lineage addressed in the supplication prayer titled *The Flower Cluster of Spiritual Attainments,* which appears in chapter 6 of volume 3.

The fourth and final work in this section, titled *The Entry Point to*

Liberation for Fortunate Beings: A Brief Word Commentary on "The Three Principal Elements of the Path," was composed by Jamgön Kongtrul. The expression "word commentary"[90] indicates that it is a work in the genre that explains the actual wording of a particular text rather than elaborating in any extensive way on the import of the subject matter that is being addressed. Jamgön Kongtrul states in the colophon that his work stems from a teaching on the root text that he received from Jamyang Khyentse Wangpo. He further notes that the teaching was based on the commentaries to the poem written by the Fifth Dalai Lama, Ngawang Losang Gyatso and the Fifth Paṇchen Lama, Losang Yeshe. He states that he wrote this commentary because he felt that this was an important instruction that needed to be included in *The Treasury of Precious Instructions*. He further notes that he used the language found in Ngulchu Dharmabhadra's commentary[91] on Tsongkhapa's poem to write his own treatise. This last point is reminiscent of Jamgön Kongtrul's commentary on Atiśa's *Lamp for the Path*, in that in both instances he incorporated the language of an existing work into his own composition.

Associated Works

The fifth and final category of Kadam works can be thought of as being made up of two groups of works. The first four texts are loosely related to the general topic of right view, while the latter four are devotional in nature. Of the first four, the first two are works by the Fourth Paṇchen Lama, Losang Chökyi Gyaltsen[92] on the topic of Mahāmudrā, or the Great Seal, as taught in the Geluk tradition of Je Tsongkhapa and his followers. The first of these, titled *A Guidebook for the Path to the Victorious One's State: A Root Text on the Great Seal of the Precious Genden Lineage*, presents the instruction in verse form. The second, titled *The Lamp of Utmost Brightness: An Extensive Explanation of the Root Text on the Great Seal according to the System of the Precious Genden Lineage*, is an autocommentary on that root text. Prior to Paṇchen Losang Chökyi Gyaltsen, this body of Geluk instruction had not been committed to writing and was only taught in a restricted manner to a few select disciples.

While the Geluk version of the Great Seal teaching includes the main features of earlier Kagyu traditions, it is considered to contain instruction that is unique to Je Tsongkhapa on the nature of ultimate reality or emptiness, particularly that of the mind itself, which represents one aspect of the

Great Seal. A second aspect of the Great Seal is identified as the mind that perceives this emptiness. In addition, the root text notes that there are two versions of the teaching, one that is limited to Mahāyāna sūtra doctrine and a second that is based upon the esoteric doctrine of Highest Yoga Tantra, especially that of the Ārya Nāgārjuna system of the Guhyasamāja tradition.

The Paṇchen Lama only devotes a few lines of the root text to the tantric form of the Great Seal, describing it as "the clear light of great bliss[93] that arises / through carrying out such skillful means / as piercing the vital points[94] of the adamantine body" that is made up of psychic channels, vital airs, and subtle drops. The root text cites the *Sevenfold Collection of Siddhi Texts*[95] and the *Trilogy on the Essence*[96] as the principal Indian source texts for this instruction, and identifies Saraha, Nāgārjuna, Naropa, and Maitrīpa as its main exponents.

However, the main body of the text is limited to the sūtra form of the Great Seal, which is identified with the explicit teachings of the *Perfection of Wisdom Sūtras* on the topic of emptiness or the nature of ultimate reality. This material is also divided into two parts: instruction for meditating one-pointedly on the mind's relative truth nature of clarity and awareness in order to develop quiescence[97] and instruction on how to realize the mind's ultimate-truth nature of emptiness. He describes the overall system as one that "pursues the view on the basis of meditation," which means to initially pursue quiescence and, after having attained that state, to seek to gain a realization of the correct view of emptiness. This is contrasted with the more conventional approach that "pursues meditation on the basis of the view," which means to begin by developing a correct conceptual understanding of emptiness through relying upon correct forms of reasoning and then making that understanding the meditation object for cultivating quiescence, followed by the practice of insight,[98] and ultimately the union of quiescence and insight.[99]

Of the next two works in this section, the first is a brief overview of the practice of quiescence, along with a description of the topic of insight according to the tenets of the Indian Middle Way and Mind Only schools, respectively, that is attributed to the sixteenth-century Sakya scholar Mangtö Ludrup Gyatso.[100] Titled *The Essence of Nectar: An Instruction Manual on the Middle Way View That Conforms to the Treatises of the Two Great Champions*,[101] the work is actually an excerpt from a larger text[102] by Ludrup Gyatso that was selected by Jamyang Khyentse Wangpo[103] as a concise presentation of this author's views on the just-mentioned topics. As the title also suggests, the discussion includes citations from authoritative Indian treatises and canonical texts that support the explanations that are presented.

The last of the first four works is also devoted to the topic of correct view in that it is a treatise by Jamgön Kongtrul on the doctrine known as *zhentong*, or "emptiness of the other." A somewhat brief overview of this doctrine, it is titled *The Immaculate Light Rays of the Adamantine Moon: An Instruction Manual on the Great Middle Way View That Is the Emptiness of Other.*[104]

As noted above, the remaining four works in this fifth and last category of Kadam literature are principally devotional in nature. The subject matter of the first among them is explicitly described in its title: *The Ocean of Auspicious Renown: A Ritual for Honoring and Making Supplication to the Lamas of the Kadampa Lineage, of Which Lord Atiśa Is the Principal Figure.*[105] The final three works are related to the protector class of deities. All three were extracted from the same collection of sādhanas and permission rituals compiled by Tāranātha that was mentioned earlier.[106] The title of the first of these clearly indicates its topic, as well as the source text from which it was extracted: *A Sādhana for the Five-Deity Form of White Jambhala together with Its Permission Ritual, Which Were Extracted from the Jewel Mine of Tutelary Deities' Sādhana Rituals.*[107]

The final two works, also extracts from Tāranātha's collection of rituals, are devoted to a form of the protector deity Kartarīdhara,[108] which is a form of the protector Mahākāla. The first of the two, described as containing both a sādhana ritual and a permission ritual, is titled *Destroyer of All Wickedness: A Sādhana and Permission Ritual for Protector Kartarīdhara, Defender of the Teaching*. By contrast, the second work, titled *A Sādhana for the Solitary-Hero Form of Kartarīdhara, together with a Method for Conferring an Oral Transmission*, only contains a sādhana ritual for Kartarīdhara, along with a description of a method for conferring an oral transmission[109] of that sādhana ritual.

The Kadam tradition did not survive as a distinct Tibetan Buddhist institution much beyond the fifteenth century C.E. All the historical lineages of its unique teaching systems that are still viable today were eventually absorbed into one or another of the four principal Tibetan schools that are active in the modern era—namely, Nyingma, Sakya, Kagyu, and Geluk. Many of the original Kadam monastic seats, such as Radreng, Narthang, and Gyama Rinchen Gang, also came under the control of Geluk monastic institutions. With a series of notable exceptions, even the bulk of the writings by early Kadam figures were not readily available until the fairly recent discovery of some thirty handwritten volumes that had been in the possession of the Dalai Lama's private library at Drepung Monastery.

It is also evident that the editors of *The Treasury of Precious Instructions* did not intend to provide a historical record of Kadampa literature. Only a few of the writings in volume 3 and 4 were even written by Kadam masters. The ones that were are limited to the three "root texts" that appear as the first three items in volume 3, which can be attributed to Atiśa himself, and several of the Mind Training texts that are spread out in both volumes 3 and 4. Rather, the principal aim of Jamyang Khyentse Wangpo and Jamgön Kongtrul seems to have been to bring together works associated with three distinct Kadam teachings that continue to exert a significant influence on Tibetan Buddhism and that therefore represent the main legacy of the Kadam tradition. The three teachings are addressed in the first three of the five categories of literature that were discussed above: the instruction that is most widely known today as Lamrim, or Stages of the Path, the Lojong, or Mind Training, teachings, and the esoteric practice known as the Sixteen Drops. In my estimation, this first aim was effectively achieved.

While the makeup of the first three categories of Kadam-related writings is fairly straightforward, I don't believe the same can be said for the final two. The main purpose of these sections seems to have been twofold: to present liturgical works associated with the principal deities that were worshiped in the Kadam tradition and to include several examples of important Geluk writings by such figures as Je Tsongkhapa and the Paṇchen Lama, Losang Chökyi Gyaltsen. Regarding the devotional material, both the fourth and fifth categories contain ritual texts devoted to the principal deities worshiped by followers of the Kadam tradition. As noted above, all the rituals were extracted from an anthology of sādhanas and permission rituals compiled by Tāranātha. While the decision to include this devotional material is understandable, the same cannot be said for the choice of Je Tsongkhapa's *Three Principal Elements of the Path* and the Paṇchen Lama's two Mahāmudrā works. None of these three has any direct link with the teachings propagated within the Kadam tradition. The only explicit reason that Jamgön Kongtrul provides for their inclusion is that he considers Je Tsongkhapa's *Three Principal Elements of the Path* to be an important example of the literature of the New Kadam tradition. While this can be interpreted as an acknowledgment that the Geluk school is something of an heir to the teachings of the original Kadam tradition, one can also easily argue that, despite this fact, neither Je Tsongkhapa's poem nor the Paṇchen Lama's two Mahāmudrā works have any direct link with the teachings propagated within the original Kadam tradition.

Technical Note

In Tibetan canonical references in the bibliography and notes, I have numbered the volumes of the Derge Kangyur and Tengyur editions according to the lettering system in the catalog published by the Tohoku Imperial University. In the case of the Kangyur, each of the first seven of the collection's nine sections begins with *ka*—hence, volume 1—and none of the sections contains more than thirty volumes. Although the final two sections—which are dedicated to a lengthy Kālacakra commentary and a collection of dhāraṇī mantras and maṅgala (auspicious) verses, respectively—have a different lettering system, none of those works are referenced in this volume of *The Treasury of Precious Instructions*. The case of the Tengyur is a bit more complicated. The first section of the Tengyur, called *bstod tshogs* (works of praise), contains a single volume listed as volume 1, *ka*. The second section, *rgyud* (tantra), which is the largest of the entire corpus, contains seventy-eight volumes that begin with volume 1, *ka*, and then follows the system of adding the vowel *i* to the thirty Tibetan consonants for volumes 31–60 and the vowel *u* for volume 61 down to *tshu* for the final volume 78. The remainder of the collection contains 134 volumes, which are organized into fifteen sections. The first fourteen of these, which range from *shes phyin* (perfection of wisdom) to *sna tshogs* (miscellaneous works), are designated consecutively from volume 1, *ka*, for the first volume of the *shes phyin* section to volume 133, *po*, for the final volume of the *sna tshogs* section. The last section, *Jo bo'i chos 'byung* (teachings associated with Lord Atiśa), is made up of a single volume of 219 folios and does not seem to have a letter designation. The two Tibetan *dkar chag* (catalog) volumes at the end are named Lakṣmī and Śrī, respectively.

PART ONE

Three Root Texts for the Treatise, Instruction, and Esoteric Instruction Lineages

1. {1} A Lamp for the Path to Enlightenment

A Mahāyāna Scripture on the Stages of the Path[1]

Atiśa

{2} The Sanskrit title: *Bodhipathapradīpam*
The Tibetan title: *Byang chub lam gyi sgron ma*

Homage to the bodhisattva Mañjuśrī, appearing as a divine youth.

Having bowed with great respect to all the victors
of the three times, to their dharma, and to the sangha,
I shall explain *A Lamp for the Path to Enlightenment*
at the request of my excellent disciple Jangchup Ö. (1)

Through being lesser, middling, or supreme,
three types of person are to be understood.
I shall write individual descriptions
that clarify their defining attributes. (2)

One who by various means
seeks only the happiness
of samsara for him- or herself
is known as a lesser person. (3)

Turned away from the happiness of samsaric existence
with a nature that avoids evil deeds,
one who seeks only peace for him- or herself
is said to be a middling person. (4)

One who, through the suffering
of his or her own continuum, truly desires
to terminate completely all the suffering
of others is a supreme person. (5)

I shall explain to those excellent beings
who seek supreme enlightenment
the correct methods
that the gurus have taught. (6)

Facing a painting of the perfect Buddha, and the like,
a caitya shrine, and a holy dharma scripture,[2]
perform acts of worship with flowers, incense,
and other objects, according to your means. (7)

Also perform the sevenfold worship declared
in the *Prayer for Excellent Spiritual Conduct.*
With an irreversible mind that is maintained {3}
until you reach the seat of enlightenment (8)

and with devout faith in the Three Jewels,
and after placing your knees upon the ground
and joining your palms together,
first go for refuge three times. (9)

Following that, preceded by the attitude
of loving-kindness toward all sentient beings,
examine the entire world of beings who suffer
in the three lower realms, through birth, and so forth,
and by falling downward when they die, and so forth. (10)

Then, with the desire to liberate the world
from the suffering of suffering,
suffering, and the causes of suffering,
generate the enlightenment mind
that makes an irreversible pledge. (11)

The good qualities of having generated
the aspirational mind in this way
are declared by Maitreya
in the *Gaṇḍavyūha Sūtra*. (12)

That practitioner should read sūtras or hear them
from a guru and learn the limitless good qualities
of the mind directed toward complete enlightenment.
To maintain that mind, it should be generated repeatedly. (13)

Among the descriptions of this mind's merit
that are found in the *Sūtra on Vīradatta's Queries*,
I shall write here just three verses
as a summary. (14)

If the merit of enlightenment mind
were to become form,
after completely filling the realm of space,
there would be an excess of even more. (15)

Between a person who would give
to the guardians of the world
buddha fields filled with excellent jewels
equal in number to the sand grains of the Ganges {4} (16)

and a person who, having joined the palms together,
would turn his or her mind to enlightenment,
this latter act of worship is superior
and one that has no limit.[3] (17)

After having generated the aspirational enlightenment mind,
you should cause it to develop through many exertions;
and, in order to recall it even in other rebirths,
you should also observe the precepts as they have been taught. (18)

Without the vow whose nature is active enlightenment mind,
the correct aspiration will not become stronger.

Therefore, one who desires to strengthen the vow to attain
complete enlightenment must diligently adopt this vow. (19)

A person who always maintains another vow—
that is, one of the seven types of prātimokṣa discipline—
has the good fortune to develop the vow
of a bodhisattva; otherwise, he or she does not. (20)

Among the seven types of prātimokṣa vow
that were taught by the Tathāgata,
the glory of chaste conduct is the best,
which is understood to be the bhikṣu[4] vow. (21)

By means of the ritual that is explained
in the morality chapter of *The Stage of a Bodhisattva*,
you should accept the vow from an excellent guru
who possesses the proper attributes. (22)

One who is skilled in the ritual for the vow,
who possesses a nature that abides in the vow,
who is able to confer the vow, and is compassionate
is understood to be an excellent guru. (23)

If, after striving at this,
you cannot find such a guru,
I shall describe a different ritual
for receiving the vow. (24)

Regarding this, I shall write here clearly
how Mañjuśrī generated enlightenment mind
at a former time when he was Ambarāja, as declared
in the *Mañjuśrībuddhakṣetrālaṃkāra Sūtra*. (25)

I generate the mind intent upon complete enlightenment
in the presence of the lords.
I invite the entire world of beings
to liberate them from samsara. (26)

I shall not develop malice,
or a rancorous mind, or envy,
or stinginess {5} from this day forward
until I achieve enlightenment. (27)

I shall practice chaste conduct,
I shall abandon sensory pleasures and evil deeds,
and I shall train myself as the buddhas did
by joyfully observing the vow of morality. (28)

I shall not strive here to attain
enlightenment in a swift manner.
I shall remain until the furthest end of time
for the sake of even a single sentient being. (29)

I shall purify a buddha field
that is immeasurable and inconceivable.
I shall cause my name to be celebrated
throughout the ten directions. (30)

I shall cause my deeds of body and speech
to become pure in every way.
I shall also cause my mental deeds to become pure
and I shall not perform any bad deeds.[5] (31)

By abiding in the vow whose nature is active enlightenment mind—
the cause that brings purity to your own body, speech, and mind—
and training yourself well in the threefold training of morality,
you will become one who greatly reveres the threefold training of
morality. (32)

Therefore, by striving for purity of the vow in the restraint
of a being who seeks pure and complete enlightenment,
the accumulations for complete enlightenment
will be brought to fulfillment. (33)

All the buddhas agree that the cause
for completing the accumulations,

whose natures are merit and wisdom,
is to develop supernatural knowledge. (34)

Just as a bird that has not grown feathers
cannot fly into the sky, one who lacks
the power of supernatural knowledge
cannot accomplish the welfare of beings. (35)

The merit gained in a day and a night
by one who possesses supernatural knowledge
is not gained even in a hundred births
by one who lacks supernatural knowledge. (36)

One who desires to complete quickly
the accumulations that bring perfect enlightenment
will achieve supernatural knowledge
through exertion, not by idleness. (37)

One who has not attained quiescence
will not develop supernatural knowledge;
therefore, exert yourself repeatedly
in order to achieve quiescence. (38)

One in whom the essential limbs {6} for quiescence
are absent may practice meditation zealously,
but he or she will not achieve one-pointed concentration
even after thousands of years. (39)

Therefore, one who is well established in the essential limbs
taught in the *Chapter on the Requisites for One-Pointed Concentration*
should fix the mind on any one
of the many virtuous meditation objects. (40)

Once a meditator has attained quiescence,
he or she will also achieve supernatural knowledge.
However, without the practice of perfection of wisdom,
the obscurations cannot be destroyed. (41)

Therefore, in order to abandon entirely the obscurations
of the mental afflictions and to that which needs to be known,
one should meditate continually on the practice of
perfection of wisdom that is accompanied by means. (42)

Because both wisdom without means
and means without wisdom
were declared to be bondage,
do not abandon either of them. (43)

In order to remove uncertainty about
what wisdom is and what means are,
I shall explain the distinguishing characteristics
of means and wisdom. (44)

Excluding the perfection of wisdom,
all the other virtuous qualities[6]
of the perfection of generosity, and the rest,
were declared by the victors to be means. (45)

One who meditates upon wisdom
with a nature influenced by cultivation[7] of means
will attain enlightenment quickly,
not by meditating on selflessness alone. (46)

Wisdom is explained to be the knowledge
of emptiness regarding an essential nature,
which realizes the nonorigination
of the heaps, constituents, and bases. (47)

It is not reasonable for an existent thing to arise;
it is also not for a nonexistent one, like a sky-flower.
Nor can that which is both come into existence
because then both errors would follow. (48)

Entities do not arise from themselves;
they also do not from something different than themselves,

or from something that is both, or without a cause.
Therefore, they lack an inherent essence. (49)

Alternatively, when all entities are examined
with regard to being a unity or a multiplicity,
because no {7} inherent nature can be perceived,
it is determined that they lack a real essence. (50)

The reasons in *The Seventy Verses on Emptiness*,
as well as *The Root Verses on the Middle Way*, and the rest,
explain how the emptiness of a real essence
is proven in relation to entities. (51)

Because the treatise would become too lengthy,
I have not expounded on this subject here.
Just the established tenets have been presented
so that they might be contemplated. (52)

Therefore, this very meditation on the selflessness
that is the nonapprehension of an essence
in relation to the totality of entities
is meditation upon wisdom. (53)

Just as with all entities, regarding which
wisdom does not see an essence,
meditate in a nonconceptual manner on that very wisdom
that has been analyzed with discerning awareness. (54)

This existence, which arises from conceptual thought,
has the nature of conceptual thought.
Therefore, the complete abandonment
of conceptualization is supreme nirvana. (55)

Moreover, the Bhagavān declared this in the following manner:
"Conceptual thought is the great ignorance
that causes one to fall into the ocean of samsara.
One who abides in the concentration that is free
of conceptual thought shines like the stainless sky."[8] (56)

The *Avikalpapraveśadhāraṇī Sūtra* also declares:
"Once a victor's offspring has developed
a nonconceptual attitude toward this true dharma
and gone beyond concepts that are difficult to transcend,
he or she will in due course attain freedom from conception."[9] (57)

Having ascertained the unoriginated
and insubstantial nature of all entities
on the basis of scripture and reasoning,
one should meditate free of conception. (58)

After meditating on reality in this way
and successively achieving Heat, and the rest,
Joy, and the rest, will be attained,
and a buddha's enlightenment will not be far off. (59)

Through the activities of pacifying and prospering, and the rest,
which are gained through the power of mantra,
as well as the power of achieving the vase of fortune, and so forth,
and the eight great spiritual attainments, and the like, (60)

if you wish to complete with ease
{8} the requisites for enlightenment
and you wish to engage in the Secret Mantra practice
taught in the Kriyā, Caryā, and other tantras, (61)

you should please a genuine lama in every way,
by honoring, giving jewels, and the like,
by following instructions, and so forth,
in order to receive the teacher's initiation. (62)

By receiving the complete teacher's initiation
through having pleased the lama,
you become one whose nature has been purified of all bad deeds
and one who is fit to pursue the spiritual attainments. (63)

One who observes chaste conduct should not receive
the secret and wisdom consecrations,

because this is emphatically forbidden
in the *Ādibuddha Mahātantra*. (64)

If one who is observing the austerity
of chaste conduct were to receive those initiations,
the vow of austerity would be ruined
through having engaged in a forbidden act. (65)

That practitioner of austerity will incur
a transgression that is an extreme defeat
and, by falling into the lower realms,
will also not gain any spiritual attainments. (66)

One who has been consecrated as a teacher
is permitted to hear and teach all the tantras
and to perform fire offerings, acts of worship, and the like.
There is also no offense for one who has knowledge of reality. (67)

The elder Dīpaṃkara Śrī, who learned
the teachings expressed in sūtras and other scriptures,
composed this brief explanation of the path to enlightenment
at the request of Jangchup Ö. (68)

This concludes *A Lamp for the Path to Enlightenment*, composed by the great teacher Dīpaṃkara Śrījñāna. It was translated, edited, and established in its final form by the Indian master Dīpaṃkara Śrījñāna and the translator Gelong Gewe Lodrö.

2. The Root Text of the Mahāyāna Instruction Known as "The Seven-Point Mind Training"[1]

Gyalse Tokme Zangpo

oṃ[2] *svasti*[3]

(Although there are many different ways in which the various forms of Mahāyāna instruction known as Mind Training are taught, the spiritual teacher Chekawa's[4] system does so in seven points: (1) a presentation of the preliminary teachings that are the foundation of the practice, (2) the main practice of cultivating enlightenment mind, {9} (3) turning adversity into the path to enlightenment, (4) a concise presentation of what to practice throughout one's lifetime, (5) the standard for having mastered the training, (6) the Mind Training commitments, and (7) the Mind Training precepts.

With regard to the first point, the root text declares:)

First, train yourself in the preliminaries.

(This point is made up of three topics: meditating on (1) the difficulty of obtaining leisure and fortune, (2) impermanence in the form of death, and (3) the faults of samsara.

The second point, the main practice of cultivating enlightenment mind, is made up of two topics: (1) ultimate enlightenment mind and (2) conventional enlightenment mind. The first topic contains three parts: (1) preparation, (2) main practice, and (3) post-meditative practice.

The first part is further made up of (1) taking refuge and generating enlightenment mind, (2) making supplication to the spiritual teacher and tutelary deity, (3) carrying out the seven-limb devotional practice, (4) straightening the posture of your body, and (5) keeping count of twenty-one breaths without becoming confused.

With regard to the second part,[5] the root text declares:)

> Reflect that entities are like objects in a dream.
> Investigate the mind's ultimate nature of lacking origination.
> Release the antidote, as well, into its own ultimate state.
> Place the mind in the storehouse state that is the path's essence.

(With regard to the third part, the root text declares:)

> Between meditation sessions, act as an illusory person.

(The second topic, meditating on conventional enlightenment mind, is made up of two parts: (1) meditative absorption and (2) post-meditative practice.

With regard to the first part, the root text declares:)

> Cultivate the two exercises of giving and taking alternately.
> Mount these two on your breath.

(With regard to the second part,[6] the root text declares:)

> There are three objects, three poisons, and three roots of virtue.
> In all activities, train yourself with verbal expressions.
> The order for the practice of taking starts with yourself.

(With regard to the third point—transforming adversity into the path to enlightenment—the root text declares:)

> When the vessel[7] and its contents[8] are filled with evil,
> transform adversity into the path to enlightenment.

(This point is made up of two topics: transforming adversity through (1) thought and (2) action.

The first of these also has two parts: transforming adversity on the basis of (1) conventional enlightenment mind and (2) ultimate enlightenment mind.

With regard to the first part, the root text declares:)

> Place all the blame on one.
> Meditate on the great kindness of all beings.

(As relates to the second part,[9] the root text declares:)

> The emptiness practice of meditating on erring appearances
> as a buddha's four bodies is the unsurpassed form of protection.

(With regard to the second topic, transforming adversity through action, the root text declares:)

> The fourfold practice is the supreme method.

([The four practices are] collecting the accumulations, purifying yourself of evil deeds, making offerings to malevolent spirits, and making offerings to dharma protectors. With regard to this topic, the root text also declares:)

> Use what is encountered suddenly in your meditation practice.

(As the fourth point, a concise presentation of what to practice throughout one's lifetime, the root text declares:)

> A summary of the instruction's essence
> is to apply yourself to the five powers. {10}

(The five powers are intention, repeated practice, the white seed, repudiation, and aspirational prayer. The root text also declares:)

> The Mahāyāna instruction for passing away
> is the same five powers and attention to posture.

(For the fifth point, a presentation of the standard for having attained mastery, the root text declares:)

> All dharma is based on a single aim.
> Accept the most important of the two witnesses (—that is, between oneself and others).
> Always maintain solely a happy mind.
> If you can maintain the practice even when distracted, you have become proficient.

(For the sixth point, a presentation of the Mind Training commitments, the root text declares:)

(1) Always train yourself in the three general principles, (which are not to violate any precepts that you have accepted, not to be reckless, and not to fall into partiality).
(2) Change your aspiration but keep the same demeanor.
(3) Don't call anyone a deficient person.
(4) Don't think adversely of others in any way.
(5) Abandon first whichever mental affliction is strongest.
(6) Relinquish all expectation of a reward.
(7) Get rid of food that contains poison.
(8) Don't maintain a steadfast character.
(9) Don't engage in spiteful quarreling.
(10) Don't lie in wait on a narrow path.
(11) Don't strike a vulnerable point.
(12) Don't place the load of a dzo onto an ox.
(13) Don't try to be the fastest.
(14) Don't engage in misguided rituals.
(15) Don't turn a god into a demon.
(16) Don't seek misery as a means to happiness.

(For the seventh point, the Mind Training precepts, the root text declares:)

(1) Do all spiritual practices with one attitude.
(2) All erring distress should be met with one remedy.
(3) Two actions are to be done, one at the beginning and one at the end.
(4) Be forbearing when either of the two occur (—that is, the two of prosperity and adversity.)
(5) Safeguard the two even when your life is at risk (—that is, the general dharma commitments and the commitments that pertain to the Mind Training practice.)
(6) Train yourself in the three that are difficult (—which are the difficult acts of recalling, overcoming, and terminating mental afflictions when they arise.)
(7) Acquire the three principal causes (—which are to meet with an excellent lama, to engage in the practice properly, and to obtain all the resources that are necessary to cultivate a dharma practice.)
(8) Cultivate the three in an unimpaired form (—that is, devotion and respect toward one's lama, zealous exertion in cultivating the Mind Training practice, and observance of the moral precepts.)

(9) Maintain the three that should never be lacking (—that is, a virtuous body, speech, and mind.)
(10) Train yourself impartially toward all objects.
(11) Value everything by practicing comprehensively and with a deep-seated proficiency.
(12) Meditate constantly with regard to special beings.
(13) Don't depend upon favorable conditions.
(14) On this occasion, {11} practice what is most important.
(15) Don't engage in mistaken understanding (—that is, [1] mistaken patience, [2] mistaken aspiration, [3] mistaken enjoyments, [4] mistaken compassion, [5] mistake interests, and [6] mistaken rejoicing.)
(16) Don't be sporadic.
(17) Train decisively.
(18) Free yourself with the two qualities of deliberation and reflection.
(19) Don't be boastful.
(20) Don't be irascible.
(21) Don't be capricious.
(22) Don't yearn for recognition.

(The root text states that training yourself well in these precepts)

transforms the five rampant degeneracies
into the path to enlightenment.

(As a statement of the instruction's origin, the root text declares:)

This instruction, a quintessential elixir . . . was handed down by Serlingpa.[10]

(Having successfully trained himself well in this instruction, the great lord of practitioners Chekawa praised it with these words:)

With an abundance of devotion
awakened by residual karma from past spiritual practice,
I sought the instruction that removes apprehension of a self,
ignoring hardship and expressions of disapproval.
Now, I can die with no regrets.

(Although there are a number of root texts on this teaching that vary in length and arrange the aphorisms in different ways, the version presented here accords exactly with the collection of aphorisms that are cited in Gyalse Tokme Rinpoche's[11] instruction manual. May auspiciousness abound!)

3. Bodhisattva's Jewel Garland

A Root Text of Mahāyāna Instruction from the Precious Kadam Scripture[1]

Atiśa

Translated by Thupten Jinpa

Sanskrit title: *Bodhisattvamaṇevalī*

Homage to great compassion.
Homage to the teachers.
Homage to the faith divinities.

Discard all lingering doubts,
and strive with dedication in your practice.
Thoroughly relinquish sloth, mental dullness, and laziness,
and strive always with joyful perseverance. (1)

With mindfulness, vigilance, and conscientiousness,
constantly guard the gateways of your senses.
Again and again, three times both day and night,
examine the flow of your thoughts. (2)

Reveal your own shortcomings,
but do not seek out others' errors.

Shambhala Publications gratefully acknowledges Wisdom Publications for their generous permission to reprint Thupten Jinpa's translations first published in *Mind Training: The Great Collection*, which constitute chapters 3, 15, 16, 17, and 18 in this volume.

Conceal your own good qualities,
but proclaim those of others. (3)

Forsake wealth and ministrations;
at all times relinquish gain and fame. {12}
Have modest desires, be easily satisfied,
and reciprocate kindness. (4)

Cultivate love and compassion,
and stabilize your awakening mind.
Relinquish the ten negative actions,
and always reinforce your faith.[2] (5)

Destroy anger and conceit,
and be endowed with humility.
Relinquish wrong livelihood,
and be sustained by ethical livelihood. (6)

Forsake material possessions,
embellish yourself with the wealth of the noble ones.
Avoid all trifling distractions,
and reside in the solitude of wilderness. (7)

Abandon frivolous words;
constantly guard your speech.
When you see your teachers and preceptors,[3]
reverently generate the wish to serve. (8)

Wise beings with dharma eyes
and beginners on the path as well—
recognize them as your spiritual teachers.
In fact when you see any sentient being,
view them as your parent, your child, or your grandchild. (9)

Renounce negative friendships,
and rely on a spiritual friend.
Dispel hostility and unpleasantness,[4]
and venture forth to where happiness lies. (10)

Abandon attachment to all things
and abide free of desire.
Attachment fails to bring even the higher realms;
in fact, it kills the life of true liberation. (11)

When you encounter the causes of happiness,
in these always persevere.
Whichever task you take up first,
address this task primarily.
In this way, you ensure the success of both tasks,
where otherwise you accomplish neither. (12)

Since you take no pleasure in negative deeds,
when a thought of self-importance arises,
at that instant deflate your pride
and recall your teacher's instructions. (13)

When discouraged thoughts arise,
uplift your mind
and meditate on the emptiness of both.[3]
When objects of attraction or aversion appear,
view them as you would illusions and apparitions. (14)

When you hear unpleasant words,
view them as mere echoes.
When injuries afflict your body, {13}
see them as the fruits of past deeds. (15)

Dwell utterly in solitude, beyond town limits.
Like the carcass of a wild animal,
hide yourself away in the forest
and live free of attachment. (16)

Always remain firm in your commitment.
When a hint of procrastination and laziness arises,
at that instant enumerate your flaws
and recall the essence of spiritual conduct. (17)

However, if you do encounter others,
speak peacefully and truthfully.
Do not grimace or frown,
but always maintain a smile. (18)

In general, when you see others,
be free of miserliness and delight in giving;
relinquish all thoughts of envy. (19)

To help soothe others' minds,
forsake all disputation
and be endowed with forbearance. (20)

Be free of flattery and fickleness in friendship;
be steadfast and reliable at all times.
Do not disparage others,
but always abide with a respectful demeanor. (21)

When giving advice,
maintain compassion and altruism.
Never defame the teachings.
Whatever practices you admire,
with aspiration and the ten spiritual deeds,
strive diligently, dividing day and night.[6] (22)

Whatever virtues you gather through the three times,
dedicate them toward the unexcelled great awakening.
Disperse your merit to all sentient beings,
and utter the peerless aspiration prayers
of the seven limbs at all times. (23)

If you proceed thus, you'll swiftly perfect merit and wisdom
and eliminate the two defilements.[7]
Since your human existence will be meaningful,
you'll attain the unexcelled enlightenment. (24)

The wealth of faith, the wealth of morality,
the wealth of giving, the wealth of learning,

the wealth of conscience, the wealth of shame,
and the wealth of insight—these are the seven riches. (25)

These precious and excellent jewels
are the seven inexhaustible riches.[8]
Do not speak of these to those not human.
Among others guard your speech;
when alone guard your mind. (26)

{14} This concludes the *Bodhisattva's Jewel Garland* composed by the Indian abbot Dīpaṃkara Śrījñāna.

PART TWO

THE TREATISE LINEAGE

4. {16} The Brilliant Illumination of the Path to Enlightenment

A Commentary That Summarizes the Essence of A Lamp for the Path to Enlightenment[1]

Jamgön Kongtrul

I pay homage with great respect to the feet of my lama whose essential nature is one with the King of the Śākyas.[2]

His hundredfold merit formed the flowers of major marks that possess
filaments of beautiful secondary signs;
he reveals liberation's path to the three lineages' followers with the
drum-like sound of a speech having sixty qualities;
his transcendent awareness is a sky-like mirror on whose surface the
reflections of all knowable objects appear unmistakably—
I recall with heartfelt gratitude the incomparable kindness of our
supreme Master[3] and pray to be sustained by his compassion.

Those who have entered the path and who have attained the stages,
from developing the supreme mind until the continuum's endpoint,[4]
as well as the jewel-like supreme mind from which their spiritual
transformation arises—
may the hundred petals of the mind that has faith and devotion toward
the spheres of the sun and moon
that are the excellent speech with its threefold virtues that teach these
very topics become manifest in all my future lives.

I pay homage to Lord Atiśa, a son of the victors,
whose limitless miraculous displays taught unerringly

the path to liberation in the country known as the Snowy Land
and who is a towering victory banner renowned throughout the three
spheres.

With confident faith,[5] I wear as a crown the pearl garland
of those who uphold his[6] lineage in the old and new traditions,[7]
which teach the Buddha's word as personal instruction,[8]
strung on the golden thread of their liberating spiritual deeds.

This pristine treatise,[9] which resembles pure lapis lazuli
and is the common treasure of the Snowy Land's people, is the foundation.
It brings detachment from samsara merely by being heard
and {17} attainment of the ultimate aim by being practiced.

Though this system of teaching as renowned as the sun and moon
has been thoroughly explained by many great beings, I shall present,
as a small measure of concentrated nectar, a word commentary
that easily fills the small pitchers of intellect like myself.

I shall explain here *A Lamp for the Path to Enlightenment*, which is a compendium of the key points taught in all of the Victor's discourses. It constitutes the system that incorporates instruction formulated by the two great champions,[10] Nāgārjuna and Asaṅga, the spiritual tradition for supreme beings that are seeking to reach the state that is the knowledge of all modes, and it is a comprehensive summary of all the stages of spiritual practice that are to be carried out by the three types of person. It is made up of two parts: (1) how the instruction should be taught and (2) the meaning of the actual instruction.

I. How the Instruction Should Be Taught

The learned scholars of Vikramaśīla Monastery[11] regarded three preliminary topics as being of great importance: (1) a presentation of the greatness of the teaching's originator to show that the teaching derives from an authoritative source, (2) a presentation of the greatness of the teaching to generate respect for the instruction, and (3) the manner in which to listen to and explain the teaching that possesses the two qualities of greatness. In keeping with this view, I shall also provide a brief explanation of these three topics here.

A. The Greatness of the Teaching's Originator

The author[12] of this treatise, the great paṇḍita[13] known as Jowo Je[14] and also Glorious Atiśa,[15] was a bodhisattva of this fortunate era who knowingly took birth in a great family of the kṣatriya caste[16] that lived in the country of Zahor.[17] After attaining all the spiritual qualities associated with the scriptural form of the dharma that is characterized by possessing wide learning in the discourses of the three baskets and all the spiritual qualities associated with the cognitional form of the dharma that arises through having correctly practiced those scriptural teachings, he defeated non-Buddhist heretics who were proponents of inferior doctrines in religious debates on three separate occasions at the Mahābodhi temple in Vajrāsana.[18] In this and a variety of other ways, he accomplished extensive activities on behalf of the Buddha's teaching in both India and Tibet. In particular, after traveling to Tibet, he turned the wheel of the profound and extensive aspects of the dharma in limitless ways. Through a variety of activities, including the composition of this very treatise, he restored traditions of the Victor's teaching that had been lost and promulgated traditions that still existed in a diminished form. In this way, all his activities served, directly or indirectly, to lead beings onto the unerring paths that result in the attainment of an elevated status[19] and the highest good.[20] As Naktso Lotsāwa's[21] *Praise in Eighty Verses* states:

> If the Lord had not come to Tibet,
> all would have remained spiritually blind.
> Because you, with your vast knowledge, did come,
> the sun of transcendent awareness arose in Tibet.[22]

B. The Greatness of the Teaching

The treatise that is a compendium of the essence of all the discourses of the Muni, who is the sole lamp for all of the three spheres, contains the path systems of the two great champions,[23] is a body of instruction that merges three lineage rivers,[24] is a great path that leads to an elevated status and the highest good, is the key that unlocks all the sūtras and the commentaries that explain their underlying thought, is the roadway that was traversed by all the learned scholars and realized adepts of India and Tibet, and teaches in an all-inclusive manner the spiritual practices that are undertaken by the three types of person. It is titled *A Lamp for the Path to Enlightenment*. This is true because its subject matter is all-inclusive in that it contains all the key elements of both the sūtra and tantra teaching systems, because it is easy to practice in that it principally teaches the methods for spiritually taming sentient beings, and because it is superior to other teaching systems in that it is adorned with the instruction of the two lamas[25] who were knowledgeable in the teaching systems of the two great champions.[26]

C. The Manner in Which to Listen to and Explain the Teaching That Possesses the Two Qualities of Greatness

This topic is made up of the manner in which to listen to the teaching, the manner in which to explain the teaching, and the acts that are to be done by the teacher and the disciples together at the conclusion of a teaching session. {19} A detailed explanation of these points should be learned from the manner in which they are taught in the instruction manuals on the teaching system known as The Stages of the Path to Enlightenment.

II. The Meaning of the Actual Instruction

The topic is made up of four sections: (1) the meaning of the treatise's name, (2) the translator's statement of homage, (3) the meaning of the treatise, and (4) the meaning of the concluding portion.[27]

A. The Meaning of the Treatise's Name

Among the four great languages of India, the Land of Āryas, the title of this treatise in the Sanskrit language is *Bodhipathapradīpa*, which has been translated into the Tibetan language as *Jangchup Lamgyi Drönma*. Further, the word *bodhi* means "enlightenment,"[28] *patha* means "path," and *pradīpa* means "lamp." [Hence, the title can be rendered in English as *A Lamp for the Path to Enlightenment*.]

Regarding these terms, the transcendent awareness of a buddha, whose nature is that of having perfected the elimination of all the abandonments and the attainment of all the realizations, is the state of enlightenment because it is a state in which the two classes of obscurations, along with their traces, have been eliminated[29] in their entirety and because it is the ultimate form of knowledge that realizes[30] all entities—both the mode of being that represents their true ultimate nature[31] and the mode of being that represents the full range of their diversity.[32]

This text is called a "lamp" because it is a treatise that eliminates the darkness represented by the obstacles to the path that leads to that enlightenment—namely, lack of knowledge, mistaken understanding, and doubt regarding this path—and it illuminates the nature of the ten stages and the five paths.

The original Sanskrit title is stated at the beginning of a treatise that has been translated into Tibetan for such reasons as the following: to make known the authoritative source of the teaching, to engender appreciation and gratitude toward the Tibetan translators and Indian paṇḍitas, as well as the Tibetan royal patrons and ministers, all of whom were essential in making the translations possible, and to implant karmic traces of respect for the Sanskrit language in the minds of those who learn the text.

B. The Translator's Statement of Homage

The translator's statement "Homage to the bodhisattva Mañjuśrī appearing as a divine youth" is placed at the beginning of his translation for such reasons as the following: First, while, in a general sense, this treatise is a commentary that explains the views of the Victor that are contained in the entire body of his discourses, the statement of homage makes known that it is principally a teaching on the doctrine contained in the Mahāyāna abhidharma[33] collection. Second, the statement of homage is also meant to promote the successful completion of the effort to translate the treatise.

C. The Meaning of the Treatise

This topic is made up of three parts: (1) the statement of homage and a declaration of the intent to explain the subject matter, (2) an explanation of the main portion of the text, and (3) the cause that led to the composition of this treatise.

1. The Statement of Homage and a Declaration of the Intent to Explain the Subject Matter

> **Having bowed with great respect to all the victors**
> **of the three times, to their dharma, and to the sangha,**

I shall explain *A Lamp for the Path to Enlightenment* at the request of my excellent disciple Jangchup Ö. (1)

The entities to whom homage is paid at the outset of the composition of the treatise {20} are these three: *all* the buddhas *of* the ten directions and *the three times*, who are *victors* in the sense that they have defeated both the evil qualities[34] that are the cause of all adversity and the result of that evil, namely, the host of Māra's army[35]; *their dharma*, which includes the collection of discourses that contain the doctrine[36] that was taught by the buddhas of the three times, as well as the dharma in the sense of the spiritual practice[37] that implements the instruction taught in those discourses and the dharma in the sense of the attainments[38] that are brought into being by meditating upon the instruction taught in those discourses; and the *sangha*, who are referred to by that term because having attained the faith born of insight[39] toward the refuge object,[40] as well as all forms of virtue, they possess strong aspiration for that refuge object and for virtue and cannot be separated from them.[41] Moreover, the sangha is made up of the eight types of spiritual beings who are either pursuing any of the four fruits of the path[42] or abiding in one of them, as well as those who are abiding in the stages of both the pratyekabuddha and the bodhisattva paths.

The act of bowing to these three objects is done *with* a *great respect* that is mental in nature, through perceiving the spiritual qualities that qualify them as being the source in which to take refuge, and with a great respect that is physical and verbal in nature through those outer expressions of reverence that are engendered by that mental aspect. This act of homage is done in order to overcome obstructive spirits and other obstacles so that the composition can be brought to completion, as well as to conform to the honorable behavior carried out by genuine spiritual beings and to instruct those of us who are later Buddhist followers so that we too might carry out such a practice.

If you ask what will be done after *having bowed*, the answer is that an extraordinary act is to be carried out, which can be understood as follows: Jangchup Ö was a dharma king in the sense that he was the lord of the Buddhist teaching for all of Tibet; he was a being who had taken birth within the spiritual lineage of bodhisattvas; he had taken ordination as a bhikṣu; he possessed irreversible faith in the Three Jewels, as well as the large eyes of wisdom that perceive the sūtra and tantra teachings; and he put forth many efforts in order to bring Lord Atiśa to Tibet. Jangchup Ö pleased Atiśa with every kind of agreeable object and the master regarded his *disciple* as one who was *excellent* in that he had generated the extraordinary attitude.[43] The royal monk[44] *Jangchup* Ö informed Lord Atiśa that because many ill-considered views had been put forth in Tibet about the Buddha's teaching, what was needed most at this time was genuine spiritual instruction that would greatly promote the teaching as a whole. Therefore, *at the request* of Jangchup Ö, who asked Atiśa to compose a treatise that was brief in words but included the meaning of the entire Mahāyāna tradition and that represented the understanding that the master himself had developed through his own practice, the Lord declared, "*I shall explain* a treatise whose title indicates that it resembles a *lamp*, in that it will shed light on the nature of {21} the *path* that leads *to* the attainment of unsurpassed *enlightenment*." This declaration of the intent to explain a lamp for the Buddha's teaching was made in order to promote the successful completion of the act of composing it.

2. An Explanation of the Main Portion of the Text

This section is made up of two parts: (1) a brief presentation of the nature of the three types of person and (2) an explanation of the defining attributes of their respective paths.

a. A Brief Presentation of the Nature of the Three Types of Person

> **Through being lesser, middling, or supreme,**
> **three types of person are to be understood.**
> **I shall write individual descriptions**
> **that clarify their defining attributes. (2)**

Regarding the line from the verse addressed above that states "I shall explain *A Lamp for the Path to Enlightenment*," if you ask, "What is the nature of the path to enlightenment?" speaking generally, the term *person* is one that can be applied to any and all sentient beings. However, in the present context the original Sanskrit equivalent for "person," which is *puruṣa*,[45] also means an individual who can accomplish a particular aim or one who has a particular ability. Therefore, the term *person* here should be understood to mean an individual who has the ability to accomplish a spiritual aim that relates to future lives and beyond.

Moreover, it can be said that a true human being is one who possesses a mind that investigates to a significant extent the spiritual practice that will benefit future lives and beyond. In the context of what is being taught here, an individual who merely seeks what pertains to this life would not be called a true human being or a true person. As the *Udder* declares:

> Evil is abandoned through fear of being reborn in the lower realms
> in one's next life.
> The desire for liberation engendered by recalling samsara's faults
> moves one to practice the three trainings in accord with the
> doctrine of the Four Truths.
> Enlightenment mind is cultivated through fear of the
> shortcomings of the Hīnayāna.
> Such are the valid types of human conduct;
> what, other than these, makes one a true human being?[46]

The path that leads to unsurpassed enlightenment is made up of three elements: the path for *lesser* persons, which brings attainment of an elevated status;[47] the path for *middling* persons, which brings attainment of the highest good that is common to both the Hīnayāna and the Mahāyāna traditions; and the path for *supreme* persons, which leads to buddhahood. Therefore, it should *be understood* that the path for the *three types of person* is also threefold in nature.

The author also states, "*I shall write . . . descriptions* of those three paths *that clarify their defining attributes* by illustrating their respective natures in an easily understood manner and in a manner that provides distinct explanations of their *individual* natures and characteristics."

At this point, as an incidental topic, the following is a brief explanation of the overall structure of the path. All buddhas who initially generate the aspiration to attain enlightenment, who collect the two accumulations during the intermediate period that is represented by the path, {22} and who finally attain true and complete enlightenment do so solely for the sake of sentient beings. Therefore, all the dharma that was taught was also meant solely as a means of accomplishing the welfare of sentient beings. As such, the object to be achieved—which is to say, the aim of sentient beings—is twofold: the temporary goal of an elevated status and the ultimate goal of the highest good. Moreover, the totality of everything that the Buddha taught in relation to accomplishing the first goal is included within the doctrine that represents the dharma that is held in common with the person of lesser capacity because the superior form of a lesser person is one who is not greatly concerned about this life but rather is desirous of attaining the excellence of rebirth in a higher realm[48] and therefore undertakes to cultivate the causes that will bring about that result. The ultimate goal of the highest good has two forms: the liberation that is merely one's own deliverance from samsara and the omniscience of buddhahood. Everything that the Buddha taught in relation to the Śrāvakayāna (Vehicle of Listeners) and the Pratyekabuddhayāna (Vehicle of Solitary Realizers) is included either within doctrine that pertains to the actual middling person or a person whose practice is held in common with that middling person because a middling person is an individual who develops aversion for all of samsaric existence and then strives to attain the liberation that consists of deliverance from samsaric existence for his or her own personal benefit. The method of pursuing this goal consists of practicing the three trainings.

There are two methods for pursuing the ultimate goal of omniscience: that of the Pāramitāyāna (Vehicle of the Perfections) and that of the Mantrayāna (Vehicle of Mantra). These two methods are included within doctrine that pertains to a great person because a great person is an individual who is governed by great compassion and strives to achieve buddhahood in order to put an end to all of sentient beings' suffering. To that end he or she cultivates such practices as the six perfections[49] and the two stages[50] of Highest Yoga Tantra.

Moreover, these points are taught in the root text beginning with the next verse, which declares: "One who by various means / seeks only the happiness / of samsara for him- or herself / is known as a lesser person" and succeeding verses, since among the elements of the paths that relate to these three types of person, both those of the Pāramitāyāna and the Mantrayāna are presented in the verses that appear below.

The expression "three types of person" is mentioned in numerous works, such as the *Collection of Determinations*[51] and *A Commentary on "The Treasury of Higher Learning."*[52] Regarding the lesser person, {23} there are two forms: an individual who is most concerned about this life and an individual who is most concerned about future lives. In this treatise, the latter type is the one that is meant and should further be recognized as an individual who has undertaken to practice the unerring method for achieving an elevated status.

Even though the three types of person were described in the manner that was presented earlier, because the path that is associated with the great person also includes the paths that are associated with the two other types of person, Ācārya Aśvaghoṣa declared that the latter two paths are in fact subordinate elements of the Mahāyāna path.[53] Therefore, here[54] several elements that are held in common with the path of the lesser person (who merely considers the happiness of samsaric existence as the goal to be achieved) and the path of the middling person (who merely considers liberation from samsara for his or her own benefit as the goal to be achieved) are regarded as forms of practice that are to be carried out prior to the actual path of a great person, and as such they are categorized as subordinate elements of the principal effort to train oneself in the path of a great person.

Moreover, the reason for making this distinction can be understood as follows: The sole entry point for the Mahāyāna path is the act of generating the aspiration to achieve supreme enlightenment, as a verse from the treatise *Entry into the Conduct That Leads to Enlightenment* declares:

> As soon as enlightenment mind has arisen,
> a wretch that is bound in the prison of samsaric existence
> is instantly called a spiritual offspring of the sugatas,[55]
> and becomes worthy of veneration by the world of gods and men.[56]

Thus, when this attitude has arisen in someone's mind, that person gains the appellation "enlightenment being"[57] and enters the ranks of Mahāyānists. However, if that attitude should be lost, then that individual will have left the ranks of Mahāyānists. For this reason, those who wish to enter the Mahāyāna path must strive in many ways to generate that attitude. Moreover, *The Compendium of Training*[58] and *Entry into the Conduct That Leads to Enlightenment* both state that in order to generate that attitude, you must first develop enthusiasm for gaining the benefits of generating it through meditating on those benefits, and you must also carry out the seven-limb devotional practice, together with the act of taking refuge.

The benefits that are described in this manner can be classified into two types: temporary and ultimate benefits. The first type is twofold: to avoid falling into the unhappy migratory states and to be reborn in the happy migratory states. If you develop that enlightenment mind, the causes for being reborn in the lower realms that you accumulated previously will be eliminated and you will not continue to accumulate new ones in the future.

{24} Also, the causes that you accumulated for being reborn in the happy migratory states in the future, through being influenced by that enlightenment mind, will increase greatly in their effectiveness, and the new causes that you create, through having been motivated by that mind, will become inexhaustible. The ultimate goals of liberation and omniscience also will easily be attained on the basis of that enlightenment mind.

If you do not initially develop an uncontrived aspiration to gain the temporary and ultimate benefits of enlightenment mind, you may declare, "I shall strive to generate enlightenment mind because those benefits come about by generating enlightenment mind." However, such a statement will be nothing more than mere words. Therefore, before attempting to generate enlightenment mind, you must meditate on the attitudes that are held in common with lesser and intermediate persons so that you can develop the aspiration to gain the two forms of benefit. After you have generated the aspiration to gain the two benefits in this way, when you meditate on the enlightenment mind that gives rise to these benefits, you must develop the loving-kindness and compassion that are the root causes of that mind. Regarding that, an individual whose body hairs do not stand on end when contemplating the manner in which he or she personally must wander in samsara bereft of happiness and tormented by suffering will not find it unbearable that other sentient beings are bereft of happiness and tormented by suffering. As a verse from the treatise *Entry into the Conduct That Leads to Enlightenment* declares:

> Even in their dreams, this wish
> has not arisen previously in those very beings,
> even as their own aim. How, then, could it occur
> as an aim that relates to others?[59]

Therefore, when you are training yourself in the instructions for a lesser person, you contemplate the way in which you would be harmed by the suffering of the lower realms, and when you are training yourself in the instructions for a middling person, you contemplate the way in which the higher states also constitute forms of suffering and a lack of genuine forms of happiness. Following that, using the forms of experiential awareness that you developed in relation to yourself to meditate on the similar forms of suffering that are experienced by sentient beings who are regarded as close relations, those prior methods of practice become the causes by which you develop loving-kindness and compassion. Therefore, since enlightenment mind arises through that loving-kindness and compassion, cultivation of the attitudes that are held in common with the practices for lesser and middling persons constitutes the means of developing an uncontrived form of enlightenment mind.

Similarly, in connection with the instructions that relate to those two types of person, the many ways in which you strive to accumulate merit and purify yourself of obstacles by means of such practices as taking refuge and reflecting on the nature of karma and its results {25} represent the method for training your mind in the preliminary exercises for developing enlightenment mind and form one or another element of the seven-limb devotional practice, together with the act of taking refuge. Therefore, those practices, too, should be understood to constitute part of the method for developing that enlightenment mind.

It is important to recognize how, in this system of practice, the body of teachings that relate to lesser and middle persons form an element of the process for developing enlightenment mind, because if you fail to recognize this, those teachings will become part of a path that is distinct from and unrelated to the path for a great person. Accordingly, with this understanding you should make every effort to develop within your mental continuum an uncontrived form of the aspiration to attain enlightenment. Following that, in order to make that mind firm, after first carrying out the unique form of taking refuge, you should take part in the ritual for generating the aspirational form of enlightenment mind. Having taken hold of the aspirational mind in this ritual act, you should train yourself in the precepts that relate to it. Then you should train your mind so that you develop the desire to cultivate the practices that relate to the six perfections and the four principles for attracting a following.[60] When you gain a heartfelt desire to cultivate these practices, you should adopt a pure form of the bodhisattva vow that is associated with the active form of enlightenment mind. Following that, you should safeguard the discipline in such a way that you are willing to risk your life in order not to become tainted by a root transgression.[61] You should also strive not to become tainted by a lesser or middling form of outflow[62] or any of the misdeeds.[63] If you should become tainted by any of the latter forms of wrongdoing, you should purify yourself by carrying out the confession ritual that is a remedy for transgressions as it has been taught.

Next, you should train yourself in all of the six perfections taken as a group, and then following that, you should train yourself in particular in the method of achieving the essential nature of quiescence, which represents the perfection of meditative absorption, in order to gain the ability to apply your mind to a virtuous object in whatever manner you may desire. The statement that is made in this treatise that one should cultivate quiescence in order to develop supernatural knowledge[64] is meant only in the sense of being illustrative of one of its purposes, since Lord Atiśa himself also declared elsewhere that quiescence should be cultivated in order to be able to develop insight.[65] Therefore it should be understood that quiescence is pursued mainly for that latter purpose.

Following that, one should pursue the insight whose essential nature is wisdom. This is done by developing a certain understanding about the nature of ultimate truth on the basis of the view that perceives emptiness, in order to cut the bonds that consist of wrongly grasping at the two forms of self[66] and then cultivating unerringly the proper method of meditating on that view. Accordingly, the commentary[67] declares that all forms of spiritual practice that are cultivated following acceptance of the bodhisattva vow that relates to the active form of enlightenment mind, except for those that pertain to the pursuit of quiescence and insight, represent the Mahāyāna form of the Buddhist training that relates to morality, while those practices that pertain to the pursuit of quiescence {26} represent the Mahāyāna form of the Buddhist training that relates to the mind,[68] and those practices that pertain to the pursuit of insight represent the Mahāyāna form of Buddhist training that relates to wisdom.

In addition, all of the spiritual practices up to and including quiescence represent the aspect of means, the merit accumulation, the aspect of the path that is based upon relative truth, and stages of the extensive form of the path. In contrast with that, the effort to generate the three extraordinary kinds of wisdom[69] represents the aspect of wisdom, the wisdom accumulation, the [aspect of the path that is based upon] ultimate truth, and stages of the profound form of the path. Therefore, you should determine with great certainty about these forms of practice the proper order in which to cultivate them, that their number is fixed, and that supreme enlightenment cannot be achieved by practicing either wisdom without means or means without wisdom.

Having completed the process of training your mind in this manner in the common path,[70] you must enter the path of the Mantrayāna, because by entering that path you will be able to perfect the two accumulations much more quickly. On the other hand, if you are unable to pursue any practices other than just those of the common path, or if you do not wish to pursue the path of the Mantrayāna because the power of your spiritual lineage is too weak, then you should simply apply yourself to the further development of those very stages of the non-tantric Mahāyāna path.

If you should seek to enter the path of the Mantrayāna, you must cultivate the method of serving a spiritual teacher that is taught in all the Buddhist vehicles and especially the extraordinary method of doing so that is taught in the system of the Mantrayāna. Following that, after having ripened your mind by means of the consecration rituals that are found in the authentic scriptural collections of the tantra tradition, you must safeguard the commitments and vows that are received at that time, in such a way that you would risk your life [in order to avoid violating them]. In particular, although it is possible to receive the vows again[71] even if a root transgression is committed, you should strive to remain untainted by any of them because they will ruin your mind, making it extremely difficult for you to develop higher spiritual qualities.

You should also strive to avoid becoming tainted by the secondary transgressions. However, if you do become tainted by any of them, you should not remain indifferent to those infractions but rather purify yourself of them through engaging in the act of confession and making the firm conviction not to commit them again.

Next, you should receive instruction either in the spiritual practices that are accompanied by signs[72] as taught in any of the deity systems of the lower tantric traditions or the spiritual practices of the generation stage as taught in any of the deity systems of Highest Yoga Tantra. Having attained firmness in those initial forms of spiritual practice, train yourself either in the signless[73] spiritual practices as taught in any of the deity systems of the lower tantric traditions or the spiritual practices of the completion stage as taught in any of the deity systems of Highest Yoga Tantra.

The Buddha declared the need to develop the minds of disciples gradually in the *Sūtra on Questions of the King of the Lords of Dhāraṇī Spells* by explaining the analogy of the manner in which a skillful jeweler gradually refines gemstones to explain this point. Lord Nāgārjuna also declared in the following verse that disciples should be led gradually from the path to an elevated status to the path to the highest good:

> First are teachings about an {27} elevated status,
> later those that relate to the highest good,

> because one gradually reaches the highest good
> after having attained an elevated status.[74]

Likewise, Āryadeva also declared:

> In order for novice practitioners
> to gain entry to the highest truth,
> the perfect buddhas formulated this method
> in a manner that resembles a staircase.[75]

b. An Explanation of the Defining Attributes of the Paths for the Three Persons

This section of the text is made up of three parts: (1) a presentation of the defining attributes of a lesser person, (2) a presentation of the defining attributes of a middling person, and (3) a presentation of the defining attributes of a great person.

i. A Presentation of the Defining Attributes of a Lesser Person

> **One who by various means**
> **seeks only the happiness**
> **of samsara for him- or herself**
> **is known as a lesser person.** (3)

[The lesser person is] *one who* does not have attachment for this life and has the ability to pursue as a principal goal the aims that relate to the next life and beyond. He or she does so *by various means*, all of which are preceded by the faith that believes in the cause-and-effect nature of the doctrine of karma. They include such practices as the morality that abandons the ten unvirtuous deeds, the impure[76] meditative absorptions, and the states of composure that relate to the formless realm, and they are described collectively by such expressions as the Vehicle of the Worldly Gods and Brahmā's Vehicle. This type of person is one who *seeks only the happiness of samsara*, which in the case of human happiness has its highest form in that of a wheel-wielder[77] and in the case of worldly gods is the happiness that ranges from that of Śakra[78] to that of the gods of the formless realm. The one for whom the attainment of this happiness is intended is the lesser person *himself* or herself. This type of person is inferior to a middling person and a great person, respectively, because he or she seeks continued samsaric existence and because he or she has turned away from the welfare of others. Therefore, the individual whose is described here in this verse *is known as a lesser person*.

Speaking broadly, a lesser person can also be someone who merely seeks the aims of this life; however, in this context the meaning of the term requires that it refer to someone who has undertaken to practice the unerring means of obtaining an elevated status. Therefore, there is only one type of lesser person that is being described here and no other classifications are made.

The root practice in all of the paths that relate to the three types of person is the manner in which to serve a spiritual teacher. Once a practitioner has pleased that spiritual teacher, he or she should develop the desire to derive value from a life that possesses the qualities of leisure and fortune. Since you will not be able to initiate a program of spiritual practice that relates to any of {28} the paths associated with the three types of person until you have developed the desire to derive value from a life possessing the qualities of leisure or, put differently, until you have developed the desire to pursue some form of spiritual practice, the two topics of serving a spiritual teacher and reflecting on leisure and fortune are preliminary elements of the paths that relate to all three types of person. Therefore, when you are attempting to put into practice the body of instructions that have been received, you must do so in a way that follows their fixed order beginning with the manner in which to serve a spiritual teacher, and so on, with the remaining topics.

Moreover, in order to develop the spiritual attitudes that relate to a lesser person, you must reflect on the two topics of impermanence and the disadvantages of rebirth in the three lower realms. Following that, in order to carry out the two related forms of spiritual conduct, you must perform the act of going for refuge and, after reflecting on the doctrine of karma and its results, train yourself in the morality that abandons the ten unvirtuous deeds. Therefore, the main portion of the path that relates to a lesser person is made up of these four meditation topics.

ii. A Presentation of the Defining Attributes of a Middling Person

> **Turned away from the happiness of samsaric existence**
> **with a nature that avoids evil deeds,**
> **one who seeks only peace for him- or herself**
> **is said to be a middling person. (4)**

Having used many reasons to reflect on the suffering of all of samsara, which ranges from Avīci hell to the Peak of Existence, the middling person has no desire even for such great forms of ordinary happiness as that of a wheel-wielding monarch,[79] not even in his or her dreams. Therefore, as one who has *turned away from* all forms of *the happiness of samsaric existence*, the characteristic of a middling person's attitude is that he or she has overcome all attachment to samsara. Motivated by that attitude, the characteristic of a middling person's conduct is that of abiding correctly in any of the seven types of ascetic practice included within the moral code of the prātimokṣa[80] *with a nature that avoids* committing *evil*, unvirtuous *deeds* through any of the three doors. The characteristic pertaining to a result is the fact that the person endowed with these two qualities of attitude and conduct is one *who seeks for him- or herself only* the nirvana that is a state of *peace* in which the truths of suffering and origination have been completely terminated. An individual endowed with these three characteristics is described in this verse as a *person* because he or she has set out on a path in which the true dharma is being practiced unerringly, and *is* also *said to be* of a *middling* nature because he or she is superior to a lesser person by virtue of having developed aversion for all of samsaric existence and inferior to a great person by virtue of lacking the extraordinary attitude that takes responsibility for the welfare of the world.

The type of individual who is explicitly described here as a middling person can be classified in several ways. In terms of vehicles, there are two types: the middling person who has entered the Śrāvakayāna and the middling person who has entered the Pratyekabuddhayāna. In terms of the meditation object, there are also two types: the middling person who meditates on the four noble truths and the middling person who meditates upon the twelve limbs of dependent origination, both in their regular and their reverse orders. In terms of their categories, {29} there are three types: the individual who trains himself or herself in the morality of the ten virtuous deeds with an attitude that seeks liberation solely for his or her own benefit is the lesser form of a middling person; the individual who possesses that same attitude and meditates on the four noble truths is the middling form of a middling person; and the individual who possesses that attitude and meditates on the form of selflessness in which the two entities of external physical objects and the subjective mental states that perceive them are realized to be empty of the status of being distinct, real entities is the great form of a middling person.

Accordingly, since Atiśa was a follower of both the supreme Ārya Nāgārjuna and glorious Candrakīrti, it was also his position that a middling person can be classified as being of three types based upon the different meditation objects that are represented by the three forms of selflessness. This is because one must posit Hīnayāna persons as being of three types, in that they variously realize and meditate upon: the selflessness of the person, which is defined as the state in which the personal self is merely empty of being a separate and real substance; the selflessness of entities known as "grasped objects"[81]—which is to say, the state in which the entities that are thought of as aggregations of partless atoms are empty in the sense of not being real external physical objects; and the subtlest form of selflessness in which persons and entities are recognized as having natures that are merely conceptually ascribed and are therefore empty in the sense of lacking a real essence.[82]

Regarding the actual path that is practiced by middling persons, Sharawa[83] taught that the line "Turned away from the happiness of existence" indicates the truth of suffering. Similarly, he said that the second line, which includes the expression "evil deeds," indicates the truth of origination; the third line, which includes the phrase "one who seeks only peace for him- or herself," indicates the truth of cessation; and the phrase "with a nature that avoids," which also appears in the second line, indicates the truth of the path. Accordingly, the form of the path that relates to the four noble truths represents the principal object of meditation for those who seek liberation, and it is the mainstay of the path for middling persons because the doctrine of the twelve limbs of dependent origination is also included within that very doctrine.

Furthermore, that teaching on the four noble truths is defined by the fact that there are two topics that seekers of liberation must establish: the entities that relate to the process of mental affliction[84] and the entities that relate to the process of purification.[85] This is because the first of these topics is defined by two of the four truths (namely, the truth of origination that constitutes the cause that binds one to samsaric existence and the truth of suffering that constitutes the resultant state of being bound to samsaric existence) and the latter topic is defined by the remaining two truths (namely, the truth of cessation that constitutes the goal to be attained and the truth of the path that constitutes the means by which that goal is attained).

In addition, with regard to the order of the four noble truths, just as the truth of suffering was taught first, seekers of liberation must initially reflect on the general and specific disadvantages of samsara in order to develop a spiritual awareness that is characterized by an uncontrived desire to be liberated from that condition. After a sense of aversion has arisen through reflecting on the suffering of samsara, {30} the practitioner should undertake to reflect what the causes of samsara might be. By doing so, he or she should give rise to the desire to abandon the entities that make up the truth of origination, through gaining the realization that samsara is brought about by the mental afflictions and the forms of karma that are related to the outflows. Therefore, following that initial practice of reflecting on the truth of suffering, the practitioner should meditate on how the truth of origination constitutes the factor by which the process of samsara is set in motion. Ignorance, the principal element of the truth of origination, is a mental state that erroneously apprehends the nature of objects. Once the practitioner understands that it can be abandoned, he or she will also realize that the truth of cessation can be brought into being. That is why, following that second truth—that is, the truth of origination—the truth of cessation is taught third. And through realizing that the truth of cessation depends on the path, following the truth of cessation the truth of the path is taught last. This is a correct understanding of the order of the four truths because the most venerable Maitreya taught it in the following verse:

> An illness should be discerned, the cause of the illness removed,
> good health should be achieved, and the medicine should be taken.
> So, too, with suffering, its cause, cessation, and the path;
> they should be realized, abandoned, achieved, and pursued.[86]

iii. A Presentation of the Defining Attributes of a Great Person

This topic is made up of two parts: (1) a brief presentation and (2) an extensive explanation.

I) A Brief Presentation of the Defining Attributes of a Great Person

> **One who, through the suffering**
> **of his or her own continuum, truly desires**
> **to terminate completely all the suffering**
> **of others is a supreme person. (5)**

One who has trained his or her mind well and mastered the paths that relate to lesser and middling persons will perceive how he or she is tormented *by the suffering* of samsara that is present in *his or her own* mental *continuum*[87] at the beginning, middle, and end—that is, at all three stages of one's life. Once that point is reached, a practitioner should then reflect in a similar way on the *suffering of* those *others* who are wandering the ocean of samsaric existence—that is, he or she should reflect on the suffering of all mother sentient beings. Following that, motivated by the compassion that cannot bear that all of these sentient beings have to undergo being burned by the raging fire of all the manifold forms of suffering in the same manner as oneself, the practitioner should generate and abide in the precious enlightenment mind that seeks to attain the goal of supreme enlightenment and is accompanied by the aspiration that seeks that goal in order to accomplish the aims of others in a form that *truly desires to terminate completely all* of their suffering—as well as the entirety of the two obscurations and their traces, which represent the causes of that suffering—in such a way that those causes of suffering and the suffering itself cannot return again. Because the person who abides in any of the forms of conduct that are motivated by that enlightenment mind and that are cultivated by the offspring of the victors[88] has undertaken to cultivate the unerring method by which the Mahāyāna path is practiced, these are the defining attributes that are explicitly described in this verse {31} as those of *a supreme* or a great *person.*

This type of practitioner can be classified in several different ways. In terms of philosophical views, there are two kinds of great person: those who adhere to the Madhyamaka school and those who adhere to the Yogācāra school. In terms of vehicles, there are also two kinds: those who follow the sūtra form of the Mahāyāna tradition and those who follow the mantra form of the Mahāyāna tradition. In terms of the speed with which they are able to traverse the path, there are five types, which are the bodhisattva that travels by a cart drawn by an ox, and so forth.[89]

II) An Extensive Explanation of the Path of a Great Person

This topic is made up of two parts: (1) an extensive explanation of the nontantric path of the perfections and (2) a brief description of the manner in which the Mantrayāna path is entered.

A) An Extensive Explanation of the Path of the Perfections

The first part is further made up of two sections: (1) an explanation of the nature of the path and (2) an explanation of the nature of the result.

The first section also has two divisions: (1) a declaration of the intent to present the explanation and (2) the explanation of the correct path itself.

a) Declaration of the Intent to Present the Explanation

> **I shall explain to those excellent beings**
> **who seek supreme enlightenment**
> **the correct methods**
> **that the gurus have taught. (6)**

The phrase *I shall explain* sets forth the principal action of presenting an explanation. What is the subject matter that is to be explained? It is the *methods* that are indispensable for achieving unsurpassed enlightenment. To whom will these methods be explained? They will be explained *to those excellent beings* who have awakened their Mahayana spiritual lineage and possess the pure form of extraordinary attitude and *who* therefore *seek* to attain the state of *supreme enlightenment* in order to fulfill the aims that relate to others. What is the nature of these methods? They are not the author's own fabrication; rather, Lord Atiśa explained the methods that are *correct* because he follows the methods *that the* supreme *gurus*, such as Serlingpa[90] and the rest, *have taught* in their own words and that are also supported by authoritative scriptural citations and correct reasons.

Regarding the wording of this verse, the first two lines, which include the phrase "excellent beings," etc., identify the intended recipients for this teaching—that is, the individuals to whom it is meant to be explained. The two lines that end with the phrase "that the gurus have taught" identify the nectar-like teaching itself. Regarding the wording in these lines, the phrase "correct methods" indicates the element of the subject matter, the phrase "I shall explain" indicates the element of the purpose, and the phrase "that the gurus have taught" indicates the element of the means by which the subject matter is to be expressed, and the phrase "supreme enlightenment" corresponds to the ultimate purpose. The fact that these three aspects of the treatise are related to one another is the element known as the connection. The meaning of these four points is easily understood.

Now then, you might state the objection that the line in the first verse that declares "I shall explain *A Lamp for the Path to Enlightenment*," the lines in the second verse that declare "I shall write individual descriptions / that clarify their defining attributes," {32} and the words in this verse that declare "I shall explain . . . the correct methods" are all declarations of an intention to present an explanation, and therefore these multiple declarations are subject to the error of redundancy. However, they do not constitute such an error, because they indicate the intention to explain different topics. That is, the first statement is a declaration to compose the treatise as a whole, the second statement expresses the intention to explain the individual characteristics of the separate paths that relate to the three types of person, and the third statement expresses the intention to explain the unerring means by which individuals endowed with the Mahāyāna spiritual lineage can achieve unsurpassed enlightenment. Therefore, the words "excellent beings," and the rest, that appear in this verse should also be considered a brief statement of the subject matter that is to be presented in the subsequent portion of the treatise.

b) The Explanation of the Correct Methods

This section is made up of two parts: (1) the aspirational form of enlightenment mind, together with its precepts, and (2) the active form of enlightenment mind, together with its precepts.

i) The Aspirational Form of Enlightenment Mind, together with Its Precepts

The first of these has three subdivisions: (1) preliminary practices, (2) the main ritual, and (3) the concluding topic of how to cultivate the precepts.

The first topic is made up of three further sections: (1) collecting the merit accumulation, (2) carrying out the extraordinary form of taking refuge, and (3) training the mind in three attitudes.

(A) Collecting the Merit Accumulation

> **Facing a painting of the perfect Buddha, and the like,**
> **a caitya shrine, and a holy dharma scripture,**
> **perform acts of worship with flowers, incense,**
> **and other objects, according to your means. (7)**

Regarding this first point, if you ask, "What are the entities before which you should perform acts of worship, and what is the manner in which they should be performed?" The vessel[91] for the enlightened being's body can be *a painting of the perfect Buddha*—that is, Buddha Śākyamuni. The words *and the like* indicate that the body-vessel can also be a carved image of the Buddha or one that has been cast in metal. The vessel for the enlightened being's mind can be *a caitya shrine* that contains holy relics and the vessel for the enlightened being's speech can be a volume of *holy dharma scripture*[92] that contains some portion of the twelve divisions of the Buddha's word.[93] *Facing* them means that these objects should actually be present before you as you worship them. The Kadampa master Sharawa explained that the [Tibetan gerundive] particle *nas*, [associated with the participle "facing," should be understood] as also indicating the act of making prostration.

What are the objects that are used to make offerings? Offerings should be made *with flowers, incense,* lamps, perfume, and food—that is, with the first two that are mentioned in the verse, *and* the *other* three *objects* of respectful service.[94] Furthermore, should you offer whatever amount of these objects you like? You must *perform acts of worship according to your means*—which is to say, you should present all the forms of offerings, without leaving out any, and you should use as much of your wealth as you are able in order to obtain them. Lord Atiśa is reported to have said, "If you possess a bushel of white rice and you offer all of it, your enlightenment mind will be excellent. If you don't offer all of it, your enlightenment mind {33} won't be very excellent." These lines refer to offerings of objects that are arranged on an altar and actually presented. Master Potowa also said, "You must arrange offerings that are so astonishing to your companions that they become very upset with you."[95]

> **Also perform the sevenfold worship declared**
> **in the *Prayer for Excellent Spiritual Conduct.* (8ab)**

In addition, regarding the way in which to present offerings mentally, you should also present the *sevenfold* form of *worship* that is *declared in the* Prayer for Excellent Spiritual Conduct[96]—that is, prostrations, presenting offerings, confession, rejoicing, requesting, supplication, and dedication. Regarding these acts, which are called forms of "worship," the meaning of the term "worship"[97] is that of an act that pleases the entity that is being worshiped, because these seven activities cause the extraordinary entities to whom they are presented to become pleased.

(B) The Extraordinary Form of Taking Refuge

With an irreversible mind that is maintained
until you reach the seat of enlightenment (8cd)

and with devout faith in the Three Jewels,
and after placing your knees upon the ground
and joining your palms together,
first go for refuge three times. (9)

The extraordinary form of taking refuge is carried out for an extraordinary period of time[98]—which is to say, *until you reach the seat of enlightenment.* This expression means until you manifest a buddha's dharma body. As the omniscient Butön explained, there are two forms of the seat of enlightenment:[99] the seat of enlightenment that is a physical location and the seat of enlightenment that is a state of realization. The first of these also has two forms: the physical location that is the seat of enlightenment for a buddha's emanation body, such as the site known as Vajrāsana,[100] and the physical location that is the seat of enlightenment for a buddha's enjoyment body, such as the pure buddha field called Dense Array Below None.[101] The second meaning of "seat of enlightenment"—that is, the state of realization—is a buddha's unsurpassed wisdom body.

The extraordinary motivation for taking refuge is to do so with the great compassion that is directed toward all sentient beings and *with an irreversible mind that* is extremely firm and *is maintained* by never turning away from holding the Three Jewels as the true objects of refuge. The extraordinary entities in whom refuge is taken are the *Three* precious *Jewels*—that is, the buddha who has attained the ultimate forms of abandonment and realization; the scriptural and cognitional forms of the dharma; and the unique form of the sangha, the community of irreversible ārya bodhisattvas. The extraordinary attitude is to generate intensely *devout faith* in these Three Jewels by learning their individual attributes and to become filled with joyful enthusiasm. The physical conduct is to kneel by *placing the knees* of both *your* legs *upon the ground* or alternatively {34} to sit in a squatting position[102] *and*, after placing your upper garment[103] over one shoulder, *joining your* two hands' *palms together*. The occasion is the performance of the ritual for generating the aspirational form of enlightenment mind, the *first* step of which is for you to *go for refuge*. The main stage of this formal act is carried out *three times*—meaning that you repeat aloud three times the words that express the act of going for refuge to the Three Jewels—because the refuge vow is attained at the conclusion of the third recitation.

Regarding the Mahāyāna form of the refuge act, Sharawa declared, "You do not refrain from taking refuge in śrāvaka disciples because that would result in a lesser blessing; rather, you do so to avoid confusing your companions about an unfavorable path." This point is also made in the following verse from *The Ornament of Mahāyāna Sūtras*:

> Because it saves from all misfortunes,
> from the lower realms, from improper methods,
> from the perishable collection, and the Hīnayāna—
> therefore, buddhahood is the supreme refuge.[104]

This verse teaches that taking refuge because it saves you from misfortunes in this life, from the lower realms in your future lives, and from the improper methods of wrongful spiritual paths is the refuge act of a lesser person. Likewise, taking refuge because it will liberate you personally from all of samsara's suffering—that is, from the suffering that is the nature of the conditioned entities that make up the five impure heaps that are also known as the "perishable collection"—is the refuge act of a middling person. Lastly, taking refuge in the unique form of the Three Jewels out of fear that you might fall into the Hīnayāna and because you want to save all sentient beings from the perils of samsara represents the Mahāyāna form of taking refuge.

Well then, is there any difference between the extraordinary form of taking refuge and the aspirational form of enlightenment mind? Potowa declared, "The aspirational form of enlightenment mind is the desire to attain buddhahood for the sake of all sentient beings combined with the understanding that you will save sentient beings after attaining buddhahood. This is like a merchant chief[105] who intends to rely on his or her own abilities in order to act as a guide that will lead a group of merchants to their destination. The extraordinary form of taking refuge resembles an act in which a person who wants to liberate sentient beings from their suffering requests assistance from the Three Jewels, who possess the ability to bring about that result. Therefore, the latter act is like a merchant chief who relies on someone more capable[106] than him or her to act as a guide." This point is expressed in the line from *The Ornament of Mahāyāna Sūtras*, which states, "This one approaches with the desire to become that, and this should be known out of compassion."[107] This line indicates that a Mahāyānist approaches the Three Jewels for refuge with the desire to become a buddha. Regarding this topic, {35} instructions and explanations of the causes, objects, essential nature, precepts, and benefits of the act of taking refuge should be learned elsewhere.

(C) Training Yourself in the Three Attitudes

> **Following that, preceded by the attitude**
> **of loving-kindness toward all sentient beings,**
> **examine the entire world of beings who suffer**
> **in the three lower realms, through birth,[108] and so forth,**
> **and by falling downward when they die, and so forth. (10)**
>
> **Then, with the desire to liberate the world**
> **from the suffering of suffering,**
> **suffering, and the causes of suffering,**
> **generate the enlightenment mind**
> **that makes an irreversible pledge. (11)**

Following that means after you have completed the extraordinary form of the act of taking refuge, which itself was preceded by acts of worship that were performed to accumulate merit. [Meditation on compassion] must be *preceded by* cultivating *the attitude of loving-kindness* that is directed *toward all sentient beings*, who are recognized as being your mothers, because loving-kindness has been established as the cause for developing the compassion that is one of the elements in The Sevenfold Instruction of Cause and Effect.[109] Therefore, once you have developed an attitude that, in a very strong and vivid manner, cherishes all sentient beings and has great affection for them,[110] through having cultivated the meditation topics known as recognizing all sentient beings as your mothers, recalling your mothers' kindness, and developing a sense of gratitude toward them, you should meditate on compassion.

The objects that are meditated on to develop compassion are all the intense and long-lasting forms of suffering that are found *in the three lower realms*; the suffering of *birth*, old age, sickness, and death, *and so forth*, that is undergone by humans; and the suffering of *falling downward*[111] to a lower state of existence *when they die*, which is undergone by the six types of gods that are found in the desire realm. The suffering that is indicated by the second occurrence of *and so forth* is that of the two higher realms, which is described as having no thoughts about pursuing the dharma due to being intoxicated by the ease of one-pointed concentration and lacking the power to remain forever in those states of existence.

In short, *examine the entire world* with the eye of compassion in order to perceive the various ways that beings *suffer* from the three types of suffering—which is to say, reflect on how the suffering of the lower realms represents *the suffering of suffering*, how the suffering of humans and the desire-realm gods represents the *suffering* of change, how the suffering of the two higher realms represents the suffering of conditioned existence,[112] and how the root *causes* that generate those types *of suffering* are represented by the truth of origination in the form of the mental afflictions and karma. Following that, you must exert yourself in training your mind in the compassion that is characterized by the *wish to liberate* the entire world *from* those disadvantages and in the mind that aspires to attain the great enlightenment that is elicited by that compassion. This is because, as a sūtra declares, a bodhisattva should not train himself or herself in many dharma subjects—he or she should only train in one dharma subject. What is that single subject? It is great compassion.[113]

(II) The Main Ritual for Generating the Aspirational Form of Enlightenment Mind

After training yourself well in both the objects and the aspects of loving-kindness and compassion, you should *generate the* precious *enlightenment mind* in a way *that makes an irreversible pledge* never to give up the precious enlightenment mind. Furthermore, after accepting this {36} aspirational form of enlightenment mind, as this is done in a ritual ceremony and with an attitude that determines never to give it up for even an instant until enlightenment itself has been attained, you must train yourself in the five precepts that are described below. The specific ritual for accepting the aspirational form of enlightenment mind should be learned elsewhere.[114]

(III) The Conclusion of the Ritual, together with the Precepts

This topic is made up of five sections: (1) training yourself by recalling the benefits of the aspirational enlightenment mind, (2) training yourself by cultivating enlightenment mind, (3) training yourself by collecting the two accumulations, (4) training yourself not to mentally abandon sentient beings, and (5) training yourself in how to practice in relation to the eight white and black qualities.

(A) Training Yourself by Recalling the Benefits of Enlightenment Mind

> **The good qualities of having generated**
> **the aspirational mind in this way**
> **are declared by Maitreya**
> **in the *Gaṇḍavyūha Sūtra*. (12)**

The immeasurable *good qualities* or benefits *of having generated the aspirational* form of enlightenment *mind* in a ritual ceremony *in this way*—that is, as was described earlier—*are declared* extensively to the bodhisattva Sudhana *in the Gaṇḍavyūha Sūtra*[115] *by* the heir apparent[116] to the current buddha *Maitreya* in more than two hundred illustrative similes, such as the ones that state: "O son of good family, enlightenment mind is like a seed for all the spiritual qualities of a buddha. It is a fertile field, in that it causes all the world's virtuous qualities to grow," and so forth.

(B) Training Yourself by Cultivating the Aspirational Enlightenment Mind

> **That practitioner should read sūtras or hear them**
> **from a guru and learn the limitless good qualities**
> **of the mind directed toward complete enlightenment.**
> **To maintain that mind, it should be generated repeatedly. (13)**

That bodhisattva *practitioner* who has accepted the aspirational form of enlightenment mind in a ritual ceremony *should read sūtras* and commentarial treatises himself or herself, *or* he or she should *hear them from a guru*. After *learning* thoroughly and conclusively *the limitless* and immeasurable *good qualities* or benefits *of the* aspirational *mind* that is *directed toward complete enlightenment*, as they are taught in the scriptures of the Mahāyāna sūtra collection and other writings, for the purpose of, or as a causal factor, *to maintain that mind* in your own continuum—which is to say, to keep it from degenerating and to develop it further—*it should be generated repeatedly*, meaning at least three times during the day and three times at night. Furthermore, regarding this point, if you cannot accomplish this act by reciting an extensive version of the ritual for generating enlightenment mind, you should do so by reciting the verse that appears in Lord Atiśa's own treatises, which begins with the line "I go for refuge to the Buddha, dharma, and supreme assembly."[117]

Well then, where are those limitless good qualities of enlightenment mind described?

> **Among the descriptions of this mind's merit**
> **that are found in the *Sūtra on Vīradatta's Queries*,**
> **I shall write here just three verses**
> **as a summary. (14)**

Among the extensive descriptions of this enlightenment mind's merit and benefits, *which are found* {37} *in the Sūtra on the Householder Vīradatta's Queries*,[118] the author Atiśa declares, "*I shall write here*, in this treatise, *just three verses as a summary* statement."

Well, then, what is the nature of those verses?

> **If the merit of enlightenment mind**
> **were to become form,**
> **after completely filling the realm of space,**
> **there would be an excess of even more.**[119] **(15)**

Although *the merit* that is gained by having generated the *mind* that aspires to attain supreme *enlightenment* is not physical in nature, *if* it *were to become* a mass of physical *form*, even *after completely filling* to the brim—that is, occupying the whole of—*the* entire *realm of space* that lies in the ten directions, its benefit is that *there would be an excess of even more* than the amount that filled all of space, which is to say, it would not all fit into that area.

> **Between a person who would give**
> **to the guardians of the world**
> **buddha fields filled with excellent jewels**
> **equal in number to the sand grains of the Ganges (16)**
>
> **and a person who, having joined the palms together,**
> **would turn his or her mind to enlightenment,**
> **this latter act of worship is superior**
> **and one that has no limit.**[120] **(17)**

Moreover, *between a person who* is possessed of faith that *would give to* the extraordinary recipients who are *the guardians of the world* (that is, the lord buddhas) *excellent* divine *jewels* of the kind known as "the King of Rulers"[121] as a type of offering with which they *filled* as a type of container *buddha fields equal in number to the sand grains* on the banks *of the* River *Ganges*, or the number of particles of water that make up the river itself, *and a person who* possesses the Mahāyāna spiritual lineage and, while standing before the Three Jewels or his or her guru, *having joined* his or her *palms together* as an expression of faith, *would turn his or her mind to* unsurpassed and supreme *enlightenment* (that is, who would generate enlightenment mind), *this latter act of worship*, that of generating enlightenment mind, *is superior* (that is, it is much better) than the former one. Therefore, the merit of that act of generating enlightenment mind is *one that has no limit*.

(C) Training Yourself by Collecting the Two Accumulations

> **After having generated the aspirational enlightenment mind,**
> **you should cause it to develop through many exertions; (18ab)**

After having generated the aspirational enlightenment mind in combination with the two activities of recalling its benefits and cultivating it six times each day, *you should* (that is, you must) *cause it* (namely, that enlightenment mind) *to develop through many exertions* that seek to collect the two accumulations (that is, the merit accumulation, represented by such activities as worshiping the Three Jewels, honoring the sangha, presenting torma oblations[122] to the spirits, and charity to the poor, and the wisdom accumulation) because as a verse from the *Description of the Accumulations* states:

> A bodhisattva should reflect again and again,
> "What forms of the merit and wisdom {38}
> accumulations shall I perform today
> that would bring benefit to others?"[123]

The conjunction *and*[124] is meant to include the latter part of the verse.

(D) Training Yourself Not to Mentally Abandon Any Sentient Beings

> **and, in order to recall it even in other rebirths,**
> **you should also observe the precepts as they have been taught. (18cd)**

Zhang Rom[125] held the view that [training yourself not to mentally abandon any sentient beings] is indicated by the word *even* in the line "and, in order to recall it even in other rebirths." More specifically, the word *even* indicates that you should train yourself in the causes that will prevent you from losing the enlightenment mind that you generated in this life. Some sages[126] have asserted that Zhang Rom believed that abandoning even one sentient being mentally[127] will cause you to give up enlightenment mind that you generated, and they agreed that this understanding is most excellent.

(E) Training Yourself in How to Practice with Regard to the Eight White and Black Qualities

Is it sufficient for a person who has accepted the aspirational enlightenment mind in a formal ritual only to train him- or herself in the causes that will prevent enlightenment mind from being lost in this life, through observing the four precepts that have been explained above?

No, it is not sufficient. *In order to recall* (which is to say, to avoid forgetting) this enlightenment mind *even in other rebirths* (that is, even in future lives) *you should observe* and cultivate *the* two sets of four *precepts as they have been taught* in the sūtra titled *The Kāśyapa Chapter*.[128]

ii) The Active Form of Enlightenment Mind, together with Its Precepts

This topic is made up of three sections: (1) a transitional statement indicating that the vows associated with the active form of enlightenment mind must be adopted, (2) the manner in which to adopt the active form of enlightenment mind, and (3) indicating that you must train yourself in the practices after having received the vows.

(I) A Transitional Statement Indicating That the Vow Associated with the Active Form of Enlightenment Mind Must Be Adopted

> **Without the vow whose nature is active enlightenment mind,**
> **the correct aspiration will not become stronger.**
> **Therefore, one who desires to strengthen the vow to attain**
> **complete enlightenment must diligently adopt this vow. (19)**

Even though you generate the mind that aspires to attain enlightenment in the manner that was just described, it is not possible to become enlightened if you fail to train yourself in the conduct of a victor's offspring. Moreover, even though you may train yourself in generosity and the other perfections, if you fail to accept the bodhisattva vow, those activities will not constitute the genuine conduct of a victor's offspring. Therefore, the individual who has firmly accepted the aspirational form of enlightenment mind in a ritual ceremony must receive the bodhisattva vow that represent the foundation of the conduct of a victor's offspring, because *without* accepting *the vow whose nature is* the *active* form of *enlightenment mind*, the mind that is *the correct aspiration*[129] to attain the supreme state of enlightenment *will not become stronger* by developing to ever higher levels. Accordingly, *one who desires to strengthen* and bring to completion the aspirational form of enlightenment mind that is directed toward *complete enlightenment*—referred to here as *the vow*,[130] representing an instance in which the cause is referred to by the name for the result—must accept the bodhisattva vow. *Therefore*, for this reason, such a person *must* avoid all dejection and despondency and very *diligently adopt this vow.*

(II) {39} The Manner in Which to Adopt the Active Form of Enlightenment Mind

This topic is made up of three sections: (1) the type of person who can receive the vow, (2) the type of person from whom the vow should be received, and (3) the ritual that is the manner in which to receive the vow.

(A) The Type of Person Who Can Rceeive the Vow

> **The person who always maintains another vow—**
> **that is, one of the seven types of prātimokṣa discipline—**
> **has the good fortune to develop the vow**
> **of a bodhisattva; otherwise, he or she does not. (20)**

Only *the person who always maintains another* Buddhist *vow*, one which is observed for the duration of one's current lifetime—*that is, one of the seven* actual *types of* vow contained in the *prātimokṣa* system of *discipline*, which range from the male layperson's upāsaka vow to that of the fully ordained bhikṣu—or a person who maintains the form of restraint[131] whose nature is held in common with the restraint inherent in prātimokṣa vows—which is to say, the restraint that abandons naturally objectionable misdeeds[132]—*has the good fortune to develop the vow of a bodhisattva*; *otherwise, he or she*—that is, anyone other than such a person—*does not* have the ability to develop an excellent form of the bodhisattva vow. This is because the bodhisattva vow can only be generated by a person who is able to benefit others either directly or indirectly, and to accomplish that you must be someone who has abandoned harming others, together with the basis[133] of that harm.

You may think to yourself, "If the prātimokṣa vow is abandoned when the person who possesses it passes away, how could this requirement be appropriate?" The Great Yogi[134] declared, "An elderly person uses a staff as the basis for standing up. Later, that elderly person doesn't allow the staff to fall to the ground by keeping hold of its upper part. Similarly, the prātimokṣa vow serves as the basis for developing the bodhisattva vow. Following that, the bodhisattva vow is what prevents the person who has turned away from harming others, together with its basis, from losing that quality until he or she reaches the seat of enlightenment."

Among the seven types of prātimokṣa vow
that were taught by the Tathāgata,
the glory of chaste conduct[135] is the best,
which is understood to be the bhikṣu vow. (21)

Among persons who possess one of *the seven types of prātimokṣa vow*, are any of them considered better than the others? Yes, as a verse from the *Candrapradīpa Sūtra*[136] declares: "Because he fully knows the ten essential points, a bhikṣu is the best among the three types of vow-holders; / the one called śramaṇera is middling, while the householder is inferior to those two."

Well then, when a person who possesses one of the forms of the prātimokṣa vow receives the bodhisattva vow, does the prātimokṣa vow undergo a transformation or does that person possess two separate vows?[137] Naktso's[138] commentary also states:

> Does the combination of those two vows have a single nature or do they remain two distinct vows? The two vows have elements that are identical and elements that are distinct. That is to say, the bodhisattva morality of restraint[139] does not consist of any activity, and so on, that is different from that of the prātimokṣa system. Since whichever one of the seven forms of the prātimokṣa vow is being observed itself constitutes the bodhisattva morality of restraint, in that sense they are identical. Nevertheless, the prātimokṣa vow and the bodhisattva vow are also distinct in the following sense: The prātimokṣa vow is held to be made up of a substance,[140] and it is a vow {40} that constitutes the avoidance of harm in that the person who receives it has turned away from activities that cause harm to others, whereas the bodhisattva vow is not held to be made up of a substance, and it is a vow that accomplishes what is of benefit to others. Therefore, in that sense they are also said to be distinct.

(B) The Type of Person from Whom the Bodhisattva Vow Should Be Received

By means of the ritual that is explained
in the morality chapter[141] of *The Stage of a Bodhisattva*,

you should accept the vow from an excellent guru
who possesses the proper attributes. (22)

One who is skilled in the ritual for the vow,
who possesses a nature that abides in the vow,
who is able to confer the vow, and is compassionate
is understood to be an excellent guru. (23)

The second section in this part of the outline addresses the type of person from whom the vow can be received. First, the preceptor should be *one who* possesses the quality of excellent wisdom, in that he or she *is skilled in* the procedures associated with *the ritual for the vow*, including how to correctly receive the vow, how to preserve the vow in order to prevent it from becoming damaged, and how to remedy any transgressions if the vow should become damaged. Second, the preceptor should be endowed with the quality of excellent morality, in that he or she is one *who possesses a nature that abides in the* bodhisattva *vow*. Third, the preceptor should be endowed with the quality of excellent ability or confidence,[142] in that he or she is one *who is able to confer the* bodhisattva *vow*, and, fourth, the preceptor should possess the quality of an excellent attitude, in that he or she *is compassionate*. A person who possesses these four qualities *is understood to be an excellent guru*. Zhang Rom and other Kadampa masters[143] held that, among these four qualities, the first two are the most important.[144]

(C) The Ritual by Which to Receive the Vows

This third section on the ritual by which to receive the bodhisattva vow has two parts: (1) the ritual that is conferred by a guru and (2) the ritual that is carried out without a guru.

(1) The Ritual That Is Conferred by a Guru

By means of the ritual explained in the morality chapter that forms a section of *The Stage of a Bodhisattva*, a work that was composed by Ārya Asaṅga, *you should accept the vow* associated with the active form of enlightenment mind in a manner that includes the three elements of preliminary stage, main portion, and conclusion, *from an excellent guru who possesses* exceptional forms of *the proper attributes*.

Moreover, the preliminary stage of this ritual is made up of these seven elements: an entreaty,[145] generating enthusiasm,[146] accumulating merit,[147] a supplication,[148] developing an extraordinary attitude,[149] inquiry relating to common impediments,[150] and a summary statement of the precepts.[151]

The main stage of the ritual is made up of the affirmation that is voiced three times to accept all the precepts of the bodhisattva morality that have been, are, and will be observed by the victors and the spiritual offspring of the three times and the ten directions.

The concluding portion of the ritual is made up of these five elements: an announcement [to the buddhas and bodhisattvas that the disciple has accepted the discipline], a statement of the benefit that the knowledge-perception[152] of the buddhas and bodhisattvas will take effect, a statement that the recipient of the vow should not declare indiscriminately to others that he or she has received the vow, a brief statement of the training, and an offering of appreciation.[153]

(2) The Ritual That Is Carried Out without a Guru

This topic is made up of two sections: (1) a declaration of the intent to describe according to the scriptures, in a general and specific manner, {41} [the ritual that is carried out without a guru] and (2) the presentation of how to generate enlightenment mind and receive the bodhisattva vow as described in that sūtra.

(a) A Declaration of the Intent to Describe according to Scripture, in a General and Specific Manner, the Ritual That Is Carried Out without a Guru

> **If, after striving at this,**
> **you cannot find such a guru,**
> **I shall describe a different ritual**
> **for receiving the vow. (24)**

After striving at this—that is, even though you have sought with great diligence such a qualified guru from whom it is said that the bodhisattva vow should be received—what should you do *if,* because of inopportune circumstances relating to time or place, *you* absolutely *cannot find such a guru*? There is a special way in which an individual can accept the bodhisattva vow by himself or herself, a *different* ritual from that which is conferred by a lama, because the author states: "*I shall* also *describe* here *a ritual for receiving the vow* without a guru, as declared in a canonical scripture."

> **Regarding this, I shall write here clearly**
> **how Mañjuśrī generated enlightenment mind**
> **at a former time when he was Ambarāja, as declared**
> **in the *Mañjuśrībuddhakṣetrālaṃkāra Sūtra*. (25)**

Having made a declaration in the form of a general description of this other ritual, one might ask, "Well then, what is the canonical scripture in which it is mentioned?" The following is a specific declaration [of the intent to describe the ritual without a lama]. *Regarding this, at a former time*, which took place immeasurable eons ago, *when Mañjuśrī was* the wheel-wielding monarch *Ambarāja*, a name meaning King of the Sky, he *generated enlightenment mind* in the presence of the tathāgata named Meghasvaraghoṣarāja. [The author Atiśa then states:] "*I shall write here*—in this treatise—*clearly how* he did so, *as declared in the Mañjuśrībuddhakṣetraguṇavyūhālaṃkāra Sūtra*."[154]

(b) How to Generate Enlightenment Mind and Receive the Bodhisattva Vow as Described in That Sūtra

This topic is made up of two sections: (1) the way to generate enlightenment mind and (2) the way to receive the bodhisattva vow.

(i) The Way to Generate Enlightenment Mind

> **I generate the mind intent upon complete enlightenment**
> **in the presence of the lords.**
> **I invite the entire world of beings**
> **to liberate them from samsara. (26)**

In the presence of the buddhas and bodhisattvas, who are *the lords*[155] of all sentient beings, *I generate the mind intent upon* attaining unsurpassed true and *complete enlightenment*. To indicate the purpose for doing so, the verse states: *I invite*[156] *the entire world of* all sentient *beings* without exception, which reaches to the limits of space—which is to say, this act of generating enlightenment mind is done for their benefit. The verse concludes by saying: I summon them in order *to liberate them* (that is, those who have not been liberated) *from* the river of *samsara*'s suffering;[157] to set free those who have not been freed of the bonds of the truth of origination; to bring relief, by means of the truth of the path, to those who have not gained relief from the mistaken belief in a real self; {42} and to establish those who have not extinguished the misery created by dualistic conceptual thoughts in the state of complete satisfaction, by means of the truth of cessation.[158] Sharawa held that this [verse from the *Mañjuśrībuddhakṣetraguṇavyūhālaṃkāra Sūtra*] indicates the preliminary stage for generating the active form of enlightenment mind and the main stage for generating the aspirational form of enlightenment mind.

(ii) The Way to Receive the Bodhisattva Vow

This topic is made up of three sections: (1) accepting the morality of restraining oneself from misdeeds,[159] (2) accepting the morality that acts on behalf of beings[160] and (3) accepting the morality of acquiring virtuous qualities.[161]

Accepting the Morality of Restraining Oneself from Committing Misdeeds

> **I shall not develop malice,**
> **or a rancorous mind, or envy,**
> **or stinginess from this day forward**
> **until I achieve enlightenment. (27)**

Malice is an attitude that, due to a form of hatred that is based on any of the nine causes of animosity,[162] desires to kill another sentient being or commit other similar acts. *A rancorous mind* is one that becomes upset due to a contentious attitude that is held toward another person. *Stinginess* is the inability to give away one's possessions to others. *Envy* is an intolerance[163] that is felt toward another person's excellent qualities.[164] This verse states that *from this day forward* (that is, this day on which the bodhisattva vow is accepted) *until I achieve* unsurpassed *enlightenment*, *I shall not develop* any of these four mental states.

I shall practice chaste conduct,
I shall abandon sensory pleasures and evil deeds,
and I shall train myself as the buddhas did
by joyfully observing the vow of morality. (28)

[The first line of this verse states:] *I shall practice* the *chaste conduct* that eschews the act of sexual intercourse in which the two sexual organs are joined together. [The second line states:] *I shall abandon evil deeds and* their cause—namely, attachment for the objects of *sensory pleasure.*[165] [The second half of the verse states:] *I shall train myself* well, *as the buddhas did* in their supreme conduct, *by joyfully observing* a pure form of *the vow of morality.*[166]

Accepting the Morality That Acts on Behalf of Beings

I shall not strive here to attain
enlightenment in a swift manner.
I shall remain until the furthest end of time
for the sake of even a single sentient being. (29)

I shall not strive here[167] with an enthusiastic mind *to attain enlightenment in a swift manner. For the sake of* (—that is, for the benefit of)—*even a single sentient being, I shall remain until the furthest end of time*, that is, for as long as samsara continues to exist.

Accepting the Morality of Acquiring Virtuous Qualities

I shall purify a buddha field
that is immeasurable and inconceivable.
I shall cause my name to be celebrated
throughout the ten directions. (30)

You might wonder, "What is to be done while remaining in samsara in that manner?" The first half of the verse states: *I shall purify a buddha field that is immeasurable and inconceivable* in extent, by eliminating all faults, such as chasms, thorns, and the like. The second half of the verse states: *I shall cause my name* to be retained by others when it is heard, {43} and, with the desire to benefit beings even just by being seen, heard, recalled, or touched, I shall also purify and ripen the world of sentient beings through causing my name to abide and *to be celebrated*[168] *throughout the ten directions.*

Because a novice practitioner must especially value the morality of restraint, this form of practice is repeated and presented once again:

> **I shall cause my deeds of body and speech**
> **to become pure in every way.**
> **I shall also cause my mental deeds to become pure**
> **and I shall not perform any bad deeds. (31)**

I shall cause my deeds of body and speech to become pure in every way by ensuring that they are not tainted by any transgressions. *I shall also cause my mental deeds to become pure* by making them free of any transgressions. In short, *I shall not* ever *perform any bad deeds* of the three doors for as long as it takes me to attain enlightenment.

A Presentation of Undertaking the Trainings, after Having Accepted the Bodhisattva Vow

This topic is made up of three sections: (1) how to cultivate the training of morality, (2) how to cultivate the training of the mind, and (3) how to cultivate the training of wisdom.

How to Cultivate the Training of Morality

This topic is made up of two sections: (1) the actual description of the training of morality and (2) a description of its greatness.

The Actual Description of the Training of Morality

Well then, what is the cause by which the three doors become purified?

> **By abiding in the vow whose nature is active enlightenment**
> **mind—**
> **the cause that brings purity to your own body, speech, and mind—**
> **and training yourself well in the threefold training of morality,**
> **you will become one who greatly reveres the threefold training of**
> **morality. (32)**

The purpose for which a bodhisattva [cultivates the training of morality] is that, first, it serves as *the cause that brings purity to your own* three aspects of *body, speech, and mind* through preventing them from becoming tainted by transgressions, and, second, it serves as the cause by which you can benefit other sentient beings in the highest manner. Therefore, the person who possesses the Mahāyāna spiritual lineage *by abiding in the vow*[169] *whose nature is active enlightenment mind and* by *training* him- or herself *well* (that is, diligently and in the proper manner) *in* the object that is made up of *the threefold training of morality*,[170] on the strength of this repeated practice, *will become one who*, in the future, values and *greatly reveres the threefold training of morality* that was explained above.

Regarding this topic, it is said that the word *well* [in the phrase "by training yourself well"] refers to the three qualities of being pure, irreversible, and perfected. Therefore, by training yourself in the morality of restraint, your morality will become pure, like a person who has an excellent physical appearance. By training yourself in the morality that acts on behalf of beings, you will not turn away from the goal of complete enlightenment, like a person who has been cured of a fever.[171] By training yourself in the morality that accumulates virtuous qualities, {44} you will become like a vessel that has been filled completely. The meaning of the term "great bodhisattva" is based upon possessing these three attributes. That is to say, the morality of restraint brings the elimination of all faults, the morality that accumulates virtuous qualities brings the attainment or realization of all spiritual qualities, and the morality that acts on behalf of beings causes one to become a great being.[172]

The Greatness of the Training of Morality

> **Therefore, by striving for purity of the vow in the restraint**
> **of a being who seeks pure and complete enlightenment,**
> **the accumulations for complete enlightenment**
> **will be brought to fulfillment. (33)**

Therefore, since the three elements of body, speech, and mind will become pure by training oneself in the three forms of [Mahāyāna] morality, in order *for an* enlightenment *being* whose mind is directed toward, and *who seeks* to attain, the goal of unsurpassed *enlightenment* for the sake of others—a result that is *pure* through elimination of all the obstacles *and complete* through perfection of all the positive qualities—to safeguard and maintain *purity of the vow* associated with the threefold morality, of which the morality of *restraint*[173] is the principal element, they must *strive* diligently and with great devotion using recollection, vigilance, and mindfulness. *By* doing so, *the* two *accumulations* of merit and wisdom, which are the requisite causes *for* attaining *complete enlightenment, will be brought to fulfillment.*

How to Cultivate the Training of the Mind

This topic is made up of two sections: (1) cultivating quiescence because it is the cause for developing supernatural knowledge and (2) the actual method of cultivating quiescence.

Cultivating Quiescence Because It Is the Cause for Developing Supernatural Knowledge

> **All the buddhas agree that the cause**
> **for completing the accumulations,**
> **whose natures are merit and wisdom,**
> **is to develop supernatural knowledge. (34)**
>
> **Just as a bird that has not grown feathers**
> **cannot fly into the sky, one who lacks**
> **the power of supernatural knowledge**
> **cannot accomplish the welfare of beings. (35)**

All the buddhas of the three times *agree that the* special *cause* for *completing* and perfecting *the* two *accumulations, whose natures are merit and wisdom, is to develop* the six forms of *supernatural knowledge*. Moreover, the ability to accomplish the welfare of others flawlessly depends upon supernatural knowledge because, for example, *just as a bird* whose *feathers* are not fully developed *cannot fly into the sky*, similarly *one who lacks the power of supernatural knowledge cannot accomplish the welfare of* sentient *beings* extensively and in a manner that is best suited to their abilities. This point is declared in the *Mother*:[174] "O Subhūti, for example, just as a bird without feathers is unable to fly into the sky, {45} similarly a bodhisattva who does not rely upon supernatural knowledge is unable to teach the dharma to sentient beings," and ". . . he or she is unable to cause those sentient beings who are pursuing a wrong path to enter the genuine path."[175]

Furthermore, regarding those different forms of supernatural knowledge, by means of miraculous powers,[176] one is able to travel to buddha fields and wherever there are beings that need to be tamed spiritually.[177] By means of the knowledge of diverse states of mind,[178] one is able to realize the attitudes and constituent elements[179] that are possessed by sentient beings. By means of the divine ear,[180] one understands the languages of others. By means of the knowledge that recalls former existences,[181] one can realize the former karmic causes of one's own and others' current circumstances. By means of the divine eye,[182] one can perceive events that will occur in the future. By means of the realization that the outflows have been terminated, one can, through teaching the path that leads to purification and liberation, cause others to develop aspiration for whichever of the three vehicles is most suitable for them, as well as spiritually ripen them and liberate them.

The merit gained in a day and a night
by one who possesses supernatural knowledge
is not gained even in a hundred births
by one who lacks supernatural knowledge. (36)

In addition, with regard to individuals who are alike in that they are bodhisattvas, the amount of *the merit* accumulation that is *gained* through practicing during a full twenty-four-hour period of *a day and a night* by a bodhisattva *who possesses supernatural knowledge is not gained even in a hundred births by one who lacks supernatural knowledge.* This verse also serves to illustrate what is true for the wisdom accumulation.

One who desires to complete quickly
the accumulations that bring perfect enlightenment
will achieve supernatural knowledge
through exertion, not by idleness. (37)

For this reason, *one who desires to complete quickly the* two *accumulations* that serve as the causes for attaining *complete enlightenment* must develop the supernatural knowledge that serves as the means of acquiring that ability. Moreover, you *will achieve* the six types of *supernatural knowledge through* putting forth the great *exertion* of applying yourself with intense effort to its causes. Because you will *not* achieve supernatural knowledge *by* falling under the influence of *idleness*, you must generate effort.

> **One who has not attained quiescence**
> **will not develop supernatural knowledge;**
> **therefore, exert yourself repeatedly**
> **in order to achieve quiescence. (38)**

Well then, what are the causes of that supernatural knowledge that one must strive to generate? *One who has not attained* in the proper manner the *quiescence* that is supported by the genuine form of agility *will not develop* the extraordinary[183] forms of *supernatural knowledge* that arise on the strength of meditation. *Therefore*, for this reason, *exert yourself repeatedly* with regard to the nine ways of developing the states of mental stability *in order to achieve quiescence*.

The Actual Method of Training to Develop Quiescence

This topic is made up of three sections: (1) resorting to the requisites for attaining quiescence, (2) how to meditate in order to develop quiescence, {46} and (3) the benefits of having developed quiescence.

Resorting to the Requisites for Attaining Quiescence

Well then, can quiescence be achieved solely by generating effort?

> **One in whom the essential limbs for quiescence**
> **are absent may practice meditation zealously,**
> **but he or she will not achieve one-pointed concentration**
> **even after thousands of years. (39)**

> **Therefore, one who is well established in the essential limbs**
> **taught in *The Chapter on the Requisites for One-Pointed Concentration* (40ab)**

No, quiescence cannot be achieved solely by generating effort. *One in whom the essential limbs*[184] (that is, the collection of requisite causes) *for* pursuing *quiescence are absent may practice meditation zealously* with intense effort and for a long period of time, *but he or she will not achieve* the form of *one-pointed concentration* that constitutes quiescence *even after* a great many years (that is, even after *thousands of years*).

Therefore, since, in the manner that was just stated, quiescence will not be achieved if you lack the requisite expedient factors, you should develop one-pointed concentration by cultivating and becoming *well established in the essential limbs* as they are *taught in* such scriptural sources as the sūtra titled *The Chapter on the Requisites for One-Pointed Concentration* and *The Stage of a Śrāvaka*.[185]

How to Meditate in Order to Develop Quiescence

> **should fix the mind on any one**
> **of the many virtuous meditation objects. (40cd)**

The person who is established in the collection of requisite causes for pursuing quiescence in the manner that was just described *should fix* his or her *mind* one-pointedly and undistractedly *on any one of the many virtuous meditation objects* that are found in the authoritative sūtras and commentarial treatises.

The Benefits of Having Developed Quiescence

> **Once a meditator has attained quiescence,**
> **he or she will also achieve supernatural knowledge. (41ab)**

As explained above, *once a meditator* who has exerted him- or herself continually, like the current of a river, to develop one-pointed concentration *has* in fact *attained quiescence*, not only will *supernatural knowledge* be developed but *he or she will also achieve* nonconceptual wisdom. As the Lord himself declared, "To gain the power of supernatural knowledge / and to generate the uncontaminated path, / first one should develop quiescence."[186]

How to Cultivate the Training of Wisdom

This topic is made up of two sections: (1) indicating the need to cultivate insight, by presenting the justification for practicing wisdom and means jointly, and (2) the manner in which to cultivate insight.

Indicating the Need to Cultivate Insight, by Presenting the Justification for Practicing Wisdom and Means Jointly

The first section is further made up of three subsections: (1) the reason that wisdom in the form of insight must be cultivated, (2) the reason that wisdom and means must be cultivated jointly, and (3) an explanation of the path that combines wisdom and means jointly.

The Reason That Wisdom in the Form of Insight Must Be Cultivated

Well then, is it sufficient to develop quiescence and the supernatural knowledge that is elicited by it?

> **However, without the practice of perfection of wisdom,**
> **the obscurations cannot be destroyed. (41cd)**
>
> **Therefore, in order to abandon entirely the obscurations**
> **of the mental afflictions and to that which needs to be known,**
> **one should meditate continually on the practice of**
> **perfection of wisdom that is accompanied by means. (42)**

Even though you may succeed in abandoning the overt forms of the mental afflictions by means of the worldly form of meditative absorption,[187] {47} *without the practice of*, or meditation upon, the *perfection of wisdom* that realizes ultimate reality,[188] the seeds of both of *the* two types of *obscurations*[189] *cannot be destroyed*. As the great master Candragomī declared:

> Though many thickets of mental faults may be burned
> again and again by the forest fire of meditative absorption,
> without destroying the firm root of the view that perceives a self,
> they will arise before you, like a burnt forest moistened by rain.[190]

Therefore (which is to say, for this reason) *in order to abandon entirely the obscurations of the mental afflictions* (which are made up of desire, and the rest) *and* the obscurations *to that which needs to be known* (which include the mental traces that give rise to the error of dualistic appearances) it is necessary for *one* to *meditate continually* (that is, at all times) *on the practice of perfection of wisdom* in such a way *that* it *is accompanied by* the skillful *means* that is made up of generosity and the other perfections.[191] This is indicated in the following verse from *Entry into the Conduct That Leads to Enlightenment*:

> Emptiness is the antidote for the darkness of the obscurations
> of the mental afflictions and to that which needs to be known.
> How could one who desires to attain omniscience quickly
> not undertake to meditate on that?[192]

Regarding these six lines from the root text, the prior two lines[193] indicate that, since one cannot abandon any of the mental afflictions without the wisdom that realizes ultimate reality, even śrāvaka and pratyekabuddha disciples are able to realize the subtle object of emptiness. The latter four lines[194] indicate that since the Hīnayāna and the Mahāyāna paths are not differentiated on the basis of their view, those practitioners who wish to proceed by way of the Mahāyāna path must cultivate a form of wisdom that is supported by an extensive form of the type of spiritual practice known as means.

The Reason That Wisdom and Means Must Be Cultivated Jointly

> **Because both wisdom without means**
> **and means without wisdom**
> **were declared to be bondage,**
> **do not abandon either of them.** (43)

Accordingly, *because* buddhahood cannot be attained either through *wisdom* exclusively (that is, through wisdom *without means*) or by *means* alone (that is, through means *without wisdom*), a person who is desirous of attaining complete enlightenment must cultivate a path in which wisdom and means are developed jointly.

One might ask, "What is the reason for this?" It is because the Bhagavān[195] *declared* in the *Vimalakīrtinirdeśa Sūtra*: "Wisdom that is not supported by means is *bondage*," and "Means that is not supported by wisdom is bondage." Therefore, *do not abandon* or reject *either* one *of them*.

An Explanation of the Path That Combines Wisdom and Means Jointly

This topic is made up of {48} two sections: (1) a brief presentation and (2) an extensive explanation.

A Brief Presentation

> **In order to remove uncertainty about**
> **what wisdom and means are,**
> **I shall explain the distinguishing characteristics**
> **of means and wisdom. (44)**

Well then, what are the separate natures of these two qualities? *In order to remove* lack of understanding, mistaken understanding, and *uncertainty about what wisdom and means are*, the author Atiśa declared, "*I shall explain* unerringly and correctly[196] *the* individual *distinguishing characteristics* or special features *of means and wisdom*, whose defining attributes can appear to be intermingled, in such a way that they do not remain indistinguishable."

An Extensive Explanation

This topic is made up of three sections: (1) identifying means, (2) explaining the need to cultivate it, and (3) identifying wisdom.

Identifying Means

> **Excluding the perfection of wisdom,**
> **all the other virtuous qualities**[197]
> **of the perfection of generosity, and the rest,**
> **were declared by the victors to be means. (45)**

Excluding the perfection of wisdom (that is, setting it aside) *all the other* white,[198] *virtuous qualities* in their entirety (that is, those *of the perfection of generosity, and the rest,* which are supported by enlightenment mind,[199] *were declared by the victors to be* (that is, to make up the group of entities known as *means*).

Explaining the Need to Cultivate Means

> **One who meditates upon wisdom**
> **with a nature influenced by cultivation of means**
> **will attain enlightenment quickly,**
> **not by meditating on selflessness alone.** (46)

A bodhisattva *who meditates on wisdom* by taking hold of any suitable inner or outer entity and rejecting the notion of it as being a real object—and doing so *with a nature that is influenced by* a very firm *cultivation of means*, such as generosity or one of the other perfections, and that is also based on a foundation of impermanence and the doctrine of karma and its results—possesses great power to abandon the obscurations. Therefore, that *one will attain* unsurpassed *enlightenment quickly*. He or she will *not* achieve unsurpassed enlightenment *by meditating on selflessness alone*—that is, by disregarding the aspect of means.

Identifying Wisdom

> **Wisdom is explained to be the knowledge**
> **of emptiness regarding an essential nature,**
> **which realizes the nonorigination**
> **of the heaps, constituents, and bases.** (45)

The five *heaps*,[200] eighteen *constituents*,[201] and twelve *bases*[202]—these thirty-five entities—are the bearers of attributes[203] or mental objects.[204] The quality or aspect that must be ascertained in relation to them is that you must comprehend or realize that they do not originate in such a way that they come to possess a real essential nature. [This proposition is true for the following reasons.] The principal cause of our wandering in samsara is the mistaken adherence to the manner in which these entities appear {49} to be truly existent. Moreover, since among the various forms of adherence to truly existent nature of entities, the mistaken belief that entities arise by way of a real essential nature serves as the basis for other forms of mistaken belief in real entities, it is vital that it be overcome. And to accomplish that, one must realize that entities do not arise by way of a real essential nature. As such, *the knowledge of emptiness regarding a* real *essential nature* is one that *realizes* the *nonorigination* of all entities in that they do not arise by way of a real essential nature because they are primordially empty of such a nature, and it is not the case that they truly exist at an earlier time and then become nonexistent at a later time. Between the two elements of wisdom and means, *wisdom is explained to be* this knowledge, and it constitutes the principal aspect of the training in wisdom.

The Manner in Which to Cultivate Insight

This topic is made up of two sections: (1) an extensive explanation and (2) a conclusion.

An Extensive Explanation

This section is also made up of three subdivisions: (1) practicing the requisites for insight, (2) the way in which to meditate on insight, and (3) the result of that meditation.

Practicing the Requisites for Insight

This subdivision is made up of two parts: (1) the wisdom that derives from reflection and is based upon reasoning and (2) the wisdom that derives from listening and is based upon scripture.

The Wisdom That Derives from Reflection

This topic is made up of three sections: (1) the argument that examines the result and refutes that it either existed or did not exist prior to its origin, (2) the argument known as "diamond slivers" that examines the cause, and (3) the argument that examines the essential nature of entities in terms of not being a unity or a multiplicity.

The Argument That Refutes That the Result Existed or Did Not Exist Prior to Its Origin

> **It is not reasonable for an existent thing to arise;**
> **it is also not for a nonexistent one, like a sky-flower.**

> **Nor can that which is both come into existence**
> **because then both errors would follow. (48)**

Earlier it was indicated that wisdom is a mind that has determined through investigation that entities do not arise by way of a real essential nature. Regarding this point, realists assert that such a proposition is invalid because it is determined by direct observation that entities both arise and pass away by way of a real essential nature.

[In response to this claim, the realist can be asked:] "Well then, what is the case?" If a sprout arises by way of a real essential nature, did it exist at the time of its cause, or was it nonexistent at that time, or was it both existent and nonexistent at that time, or was it neither existent nor nonexistent at that time? If you claim the first alternative to be true, then consider a sprout as the subject of an argument. *It is not reasonable for* a sprout that is already *existent* at the time of its cause[205] *to arise* because since its existence has already occurred, there is no need for it to arise again. Or if you insist that a sprout whose existence is already established does arise again, then it would follow that the sprout would continue to arise endlessly.

Regarding the second alternative, *it is also not* reasonable *for a nonexistent one*—that is, one that does not exist at the time of its cause—to arise by way of a real essential nature because no matter how powerful the cause may be, {50} it could not cause a sprout to arise by way of a real essential nature, just *like*, for example, *a sky-flower* could not be made to arise. If something does not exist at the time of its cause, this does not necessarily mean that it could not come into existence in a general sense. However, if something that is claimed to be established by way of a real essential nature does not exist at the time of the cause, then it must be nonexistent in every respect. This point is established by the reasoning expressed in these lines:

> To say "It does not exist now, but it did
> exist previously" results in nihilism.[206]

Regarding the third alternative, *nor can* it be reasonable for *that which is both*—that is, for that which both exists and does not exist at the time of its cause—to *come into existence, because then both* of the *errors* that were just explained *would follow*. If you claim the fourth alternative to be true, that is also not valid because it is not possible for there to be a third mode of being such that an entity neither exists nor doesn't exist at the time of its cause.

Accordingly, the proof can be formulated as follows: Consider a sprout as the subject of the argument. It does not arise by way of a real essential nature because neither a sprout that is existent at the time of its cause, nor one that was nonexistent at the time of its cause, nor one that was both existent and nonexistent at the time of its cause, nor one that was neither existent nor nonexistent at the time of its cause can arise by way of a real essential nature. This unoriginated nature of entities that is the object of wisdom is proven by reasoning because a verse from the treatise *Seventy Verses on Emptiness* states:

> An existent entity does not arise, because it already exists;
> a nonexistent entity does not arise, because it does not exist.
> That which has both qualities cannot arise, because they are
> incompatible qualities.
> Since there is no arising, neither is there duration nor destruction.[207]

The Argument Known as "Diamond Slivers" That Examines the Cause

> **Entities do not arise from themselves;**
> **they also do not arise from something different than themselves,**
> **or from something that is both, or without a cause.**
> **Therefore, they lack an inherent essence. (49)**

Consider inner and outer *entities* as the subject of an argument. They *do not arise from themselves* because, in that case, it would follow erroneously that their arising would be meaningless or it would occur endlessly, and the objection that states, "If cause and result were one, / the generating entity and the entity being generated would be a unity"[208] would also apply.

Inner and outer entities *also do not arise from* causes that are *different* from them in an inherently real sense because if their causes were different in an inherently real sense, the relation between cause and effect of an assisting agent and an object being assisted would be lost, and in that case it would follow erroneously that everything could arise from everything, and the reasoning that states, "If cause and result were different, / causes would be the same as non-causes"[209] would also refute that position.

The crux of these two arguments is the proof known as "the absence of one and many,"[210] because the argument that refutes the position that entities arise from themselves refutes that causes and results have one and the same nature and the argument that refutes the position that entities arise from something other than themselves refutes that causes and results are distinct from one another in an inherently real sense.

Nor do inner and outer entities arise *from something that is both* identical with and different from themselves, {51} because each of the propositions of arising from themselves and arising from something other than themselves has been refuted individually. Nor do inner and outer entities arise *without a cause*, because, in that case, it would be meaningless for persons of the world[211] to exert themselves in cultivating fields for the sake of the result of harvesting a crop, and because this proposition becomes subject to the objection that states: "Because that which has no cause does not depend on something else, / either it always exists or it is always nonexistent."[212] It is unreasonable for entities to arise from any of the four extremes in the manner that was explained, so *therefore*, entities *lack an inherent essence.*

The Argument That Examines the Essential Nature of Entities in Terms of Not Being a Unity or a Multiplicity

> **Alternatively, when all entities are examined**
> **with regard to being a unity or a multiplicity,**
> **because no inherent nature can be perceived,**
> **it is determined that they lack a real essence.** (50)

Alternatively—that is, separately from the explanations that were given above—another argument is the following. Consider the subject of *all* inner and outer *entities. When* they *are examined with regard to being a unity* that exists by way of a real essence *or a multiplicity* that exists in that same way, *because no essential nature*—not even one the size of an atom—*can be perceived* as existing in relation to whatever object is examined, *it is determined that* all inner and outer entities *lack a real essence*, for example, just as reflections in a mirror lack a real essence.

The Wisdom That Derives from Listening and Is Based upon Scripture

> **The reasons in *The Seventy Verses on Emptiness*,**
> **as well as *The Root Verses on the Middle Way*, and the rest,**

explain how the emptiness of a real essence
is proven in relation to entities. (51)

In order for those individuals of discerning intellect to elicit correctly a determination of the profound meaning of emptiness, they should study extensively the works that *explain how* the true nature or mode of being *is proven in relation to* all *entities* to be *the emptiness of a real essence* and that it has been so primordially. This emptiness is established on the basis of scriptures of definitive meaning[213] in the *Compendium of Sūtras*,[214] and it is established on the basis of reasoning through *the reasoning* that is found *in* the treatise titled *The Seventy Verses on Emptiness, as well as* that of *The Root Verses on the Middle Way, and the rest* of the works that make up the collection of works on reasoning,[215] which determine the meaning of profound emptiness on the basis of limitless forms of reasoning, and especially through the works of Buddhapālita, Candrakīrti, and Śāntideva, which contain the most excellent explanations of the views of Ārya Nāgārjuna. [Having studied them extensively, those individuals of discerning intellect] should determine the meaning of this view with complete certainty.

Because the treatise would become too lengthy,
I have not expounded on this subject here.
Just the established tenets have been presented
so that they might be contemplated. (52)

Well then, what is the reason that those extensive scriptural passages and reasons were not set forth here? *Because* of concern that if those scriptural passages and reasons were set forth here, *the treatise would become* much *too lengthy*, the author states, *"I have not expounded on this subject* by presenting them *here."* Rather, *just* a brief presentation of *the tenets* that were *established* through scripture and reasoning {52} *have been presented* in a summary form *so that they might be contemplated.*

Moreover, according to the view that the line from verse 51, which states, "The reasons in *The Seventy Verses on Emptiness*," is meant as a reference to the great argument that is based upon the doctrine of dependent origination, the lines from the *Sūtra on Questions of Sāgaramati* [216] that declare, "Whatever entities are dependently arisen / do not exist by way of a real essence," clearly refute that entities are established by way of a real essential nature on the basis of the argument that entities are governed by dependent origination.

The following verse from the *Sūtra on Questions of the Nāga King Anavatapta*[217] also clearly declares this point:

> That which conditions have caused to arise has not arisen;
> its arising does not exist by way of an intrinsic nature.
> That which depends upon conditions is said to be empty;
> whoever knows emptiness has become mindful.[218]

Moreover, regarding this latter verse, the phrase "has not arisen" that occurs in the first line is explained by the second line as meaning that there is no arising by way of an intrinsic nature. Therefore, in refuting the arising of entities, the distinguishing characteristic of the object to be refuted must be applied. Likewise, the third line declares that emptiness means the condition of being subject to the dependent origination that is represented by a collection of conditions. Moreover, this explanation indicates that dependent origination means to be empty of the status of being established by way of a real essential nature; it does not mean to be empty of the causal efficacy that is limited to the level of ordinary appearances, such that the arising of entities is being rejected in an absolute sense.

The Root Treatise on Wisdom[219] also states, "Whatever comes into being dependently / that entity is tranquil[220] as relates to a real essence,"[221] which is to say, by virtue of being dependently originated, all entities are tranquil or empty of being established by way of an intrinsic nature.

This argument that is based on dependent origination is one that is highly praised. For instance, the *Sūtra on Questions of the Nāga King Anavatapta* declares, "A wise person comprehends dependent entities / and does not cling to an extreme view."[222] These lines indicate that by realizing dependent origination accurately, one avoids becoming attached to any form of extreme view. This is an unsurpassed quality of the system that was established by the great spiritual being and father Nāgārjuna and that is upheld by those followers who are his spiritual offspring.

Moreover, the following are the two principal obstacles and sources of error regarding the flawless correct view: first, the view that makes unwarranted imputations,[223] which is also known as the eternalistic view that holds entities to be truly existent and becomes fixed upon objects that are mistakenly regarded as self-existent, {53} and, second, the view that discredits what is valid, which is also known as the nihilistic view that cannot identify what is and is not the case regarding the nature of entities because its adherents are unable to explain correctly their own position regarding the doctrine of dependent origination as it relates to the fixed nature of the relation between causes and results.

Both of these mistaken views are abandoned in their entirety when you rely upon the reason that has elicited a certainty regarding the proposition that this or that specific result invariably arises from this or that set of causes and conditions in order to refute that entities are established by way of an intrinsic nature, because, by verifying the meaning of the argument's reason, you are able to completely eradicate the nihilistic view and by verifying the meaning that is asserted by the thesis, you are able to completely eradicate the eternalistic view.

Therefore, while outer entities, such as a sprout, and inner entities, such as formations,[224] do arise in dependence upon a seed, and the like, as well as ignorance, and the like, respectively, it is invalid to claim that if this is so, these entities must be established by way of a unique defining attribute,[225] because if something is established by way of an intrinsic nature, it must be established that it possesses its own independent and self-subsistent essential nature and that is incompatible with its being dependent upon causes and conditions.

This reasoning brings about the realization that entities such as a person and a pot, and so on, also lack a real essential nature because they are dependently ascribed in relation to their collections of parts. If an entity is something that either arises dependently or is ascribed dependently, it cannot be identical, in an intrinsically established sense, with that which it is dependent upon. If it were identical, then all producing agents[226] and produced objects[227] would become one and the same.

Nor are the elements that make up these two relations[228] distinct from one another in an intrinsically established sense because if they were distinct in that sense, you would be able to refute that any relation exists between them, and therefore it would be incompatible for a result or an entity to be dependent upon its cause, or causes, or its collection of parts. This point is made with regard to the causal relation in the verse from *The Root Treatise on Wisdom* that declares:

> Not only can that which comes into being
> in dependence on something not be that very thing,
> it also cannot be different from it. Therefore,
> the cause is neither destroyed nor eternal.[229]

Since eliciting an ascertainment of the emptiness that is free of all forms of objectification in which entities are conceived of as being real does not require you to give up your conviction about the certainty of the relation between causes and effects, this understanding is highly praised for the fact that it also promotes the observance of a form of practice that both avoids committing immoral acts and pursues the cultivation of virtuous acts. This point is described in the following verse from *The Commentary on Enlightenment Mind*:

> It is the most wondrous of wonders,
> as well as the most marvelous of marvels,
> for one to practice in accord with karma and its results
> after having realized that these entities are empty.[230] {54}

In order to elicit such an understanding, you must be able to differentiate between existing by way of a real essential nature and merely existing,[231] as well as between not existing by way of a real unique defining attribute and being nonexistent in an absolute sense, as is stated in the following passage from the *Commentary on "Entry into the Middle Way"*:

> What intelligent person, while understanding the cause-and-effect nature of unreal reflections, would make the determination that simply because entities such as the heaps of form and feeling, and so on—whose status conforms to the principles of cause and effect—are perceived to exist, this means that they possess real essential natures? Therefore, despite being perceived to exist, it is not the case that entities such as the heaps, and so on, arise by way of a real essential nature.[232]

It is said that by failing to make the distinctions that were described above, you will mistakenly conclude that if something exists, it must exist intrinsically and if it doesn't exist intrinsically, it must be completely nonexistent, which will not allow you to avoid becoming subject to the two extremes that make unwarranted imputations or discredit what is valid, respectively. Therefore, because entities do not exist intrinsically, you can escape all forms of the extreme of real existence, and because the cause-and-effect nature of entities that lack a real essential nature can be established in relation to that very absence of real existence, you can also escape all forms of the extreme of nonexistence. In short, holding that entities exist truly and holding that they do not exist in any way at all, or that they are nonexistent, constitute falling into one of the two extremes of eternalism and nihilism, which are the opposite of the correct mode of being. By contrast, holding that entities do not exist in an ultimate sense and holding that principles such as karma and its results, and so on, do exist conventionally are not forms of grasping an extreme, because an object that is held to exist merely as an appearance does in fact have such a mode of being. [Moreover, this formulation can be accepted as true] because it is described in the lines from *Seventy Verses on Emptiness* that declare: "Do not reject the worldly usage that states: / 'This comes into being in dependence on that.'"[233]

The Way in Which to Meditate on Insight

> **Therefore, this very meditation on the selflessness**
> **that is the nonapprehension of an essence**
> **in relation to the totality of entities**
> **is meditation upon wisdom. (53)**

The word *therefore* here means the following: because it has been ascertained that all the entities included within the formulations of the heaps, the constituents, and the bases[234] are characterized by *selflessness*.[235] That is to say, if it were true that *the totality of entities*—which includes both persons and entities, and so on—possessed *an essence*, one would have to be able to discover such an essence by searching for it on the basis of scripture[236] and reasoning. However, because this search results in *the nonapprehension*[237] of any such essence, not even one the size of an atom, *this very meditation on the selflessness* of persons and entities, which means on the awareness that they are not established by way of an intrinsic nature, and which is carried out after having examined those entities on the basis of reasoning in order to determine whether or not they possess a real essence, {55} constitutes *meditation upon* the perfection of *wisdom*. This description is correct, because the second *Stages of Meditation*[238] declares: "Because he or she meditates on the nonapprehension of any essence, after having employed wisdom to examine the totality of entities as to whether they possess a real essential nature, therefore such a person is called 'one who is absorbed in meditation on the superior form of wisdom.'"

Well then, how does that very wisdom in the mind of a person who has attained such a realization cause the mistaken form of grasping entities as real to be abandoned?

> **Just as with all entities, regarding which**
> **wisdom does not see an essence,**
> **meditate in a nonconceptual manner on that very wisdom**
> **that has been analyzed with discerning awareness. (54)**

Just as[239] *with all entities*, including persons, *regarding which*, upon examination, discriminative *wisdom does not see*[240] that any of them possesses a truly existent *essence*, when *that very wisdom* itself *has been analyzed with discerning awareness*,[241] it too is found not to be established by way of a truly existent essence because it is neither a truly existent unity nor a truly existent multiplicity. This realization that the mind[242] is unoriginated is the very state that one should *meditate* and remain fixed *on in a nonconceptual manner* because it has been determined to be the cause for attaining nondual transcendent awareness.

The Result of Meditating upon Insight

This topic is made up of two sections: (1) the actual result and (2) verifying that very result on the basis of scripture.

The Actual Result

> **This existence, which arises from conceptual thought,**
> **has the nature of conceptual thought.**
> **Therefore, the complete abandonment**
> **of conceptualization is supreme nirvana. (55)**

This entire samsaric *existence*, which is made up of the three realms[243] and *which arises from* and has as its root cause the form of *conceptual thought* that grasps entities as being truly existent, *has* a *nature* that has been falsely imputed and established by *conceptual thought. Therefore, the complete abandonment of* all *conceptualization* without remainder, including the mental imprints created by it, constitutes the attainment of *supreme* liberation, which is also known as nonabiding *nirvana*,[244] and is a state that accomplishes all one's own and others' spiritual aims.

Verifying That Result on the Basis of Scripture

Well then, what is the scriptural basis for the claim that samsara derives from conceptual thought and meditating on the insubstantiality of persons and entities enables one to abandon that very source of samsara?

> **Moreover, the Bhagavān declared this in the following manner:**
> **"Conceptual thought is the great ignorance**
> **that causes one to fall into the ocean of samsara.**
> **One who abides in the concentration that is free**
> **of conceptual thought shines like the stainless sky." (56)**

The Bhagavān declared in the *Sampuṭa Tantra* that this form of *conceptual thought*, which grasps entities as being truly existent, *is the great ignorance* that is the root cause of samsaric existence because it is the entity *that causes one to fall into the* bottomless and boundless *ocean of samsara*. As the antidote for this form of conceptual thought that grasps entities as being truly existent, one should use reasoning to investigate the meaning of the selflessness of persons and entities. At the conclusion of this analysis when a definite ascertainment of that meaning has been gained, {56} *one who abides in* and cultivates repeatedly *the concentration that is free of conceptual thought*, upon reaching the full perfection of that practice, *shines* forth—that is, he or she will directly perceive the clarity of the mind's true nature, a state that is free of conceptual thought—in a manner that is *like the stainless*[245] and cloudless autumn *sky*. The verse itself declares:

> Conceptual thought is the great ignorance
> that causes one to fall into the ocean of samsara.
> One who abides in the concentration that is free
> of conceptual thought shines like the stainless sky.[246]

> **The *Avikalpapraveśadhāraṇī Sūtra* also declares:**
> **"Once a victor's offspring has developed**
> **a nonconceptual attitude toward this true dharma**
> **and gone beyond concepts that are difficult to transcend,**
> **he or she will in due course attain freedom from conception."** (57)

Moreover, the *Avikalpapraveśadhāraṇī Sūtra* declares that *a victor's offspring* should develop *toward this* profound and *true* Mahāyāna *dharma* the nonconceptual one-pointed concentration that opposes and counteracts the form of attention[247] that habitually gives rise to the sign of an entity's identity.[248] Development of this one-pointed concentration is preceded by the two forms of wisdom that derive from learning and reflection, respectively. *Once* a victor's offspring *has developed* such *a nonconceptual attitude* and cultivated it repeatedly, he or she will *go beyond* the net of *concepts* that become fixed upon signs and *that are difficult to transcend*, and *he* or she *will, in due course, attain* the transcendent awareness that brings *freedom from conception*. The verse itself declares:

> Once a victor's offspring has developed
> a nonconceptual attitude toward this true dharma
> and gone beyond concepts that are difficult to transcend,
> he or she will in due course attain freedom from conception.[249]

These two scriptural verses, one from a tantra and the other from a sūtra, verify the result that is gained by meditating on insight.

Conclusion of the Discussion on the Practice of Insight

> **Having ascertained the unoriginated**
> **and insubstantial nature of all entities**
> **on the basis of scripture and reasoning,**
> **one should meditate free of conception.** (58)

Having ascertained and eliminated all mistaken imputations in this way, *on the basis of* passages found in *scriptures* of definitive meaning *and* on the basis of a collection of flawless forms of *reasoning*, that *all entities*, which include both persons and phenomena, are *unoriginated* in that they do not arise in a truly existent sense and are *insubstantial* in that they lack a form of arising that possesses a real essence, *one should meditate* one-pointedly in a manner that remains *free of conception*—which is to say, without giving rise to any signs of objective reality regarding the status of the ultimate mode of being. This assertion is true because of the lines of verse that declare: "Those who chiefly depend on a practice that accords with learning / become free of the fortress of birth without difficulty."[250]

Explaining the Result

> **After meditating on reality in this way**
> **and successively achieving Heat, and the rest,**
> **Joy, and the rest, will be attained**
> **and a buddha's enlightenment will not be far off. (59)**

Having cultivated *in this way* the process that consists of first training one's mind well in the paths for persons of lesser and middling ability, which begin with the common[251] form of taking refuge; {57} second, generating the two forms of enlightenment mind (that is, its aspirational and active forms); and third, *meditating on reality*[252] with the two practices of quiescence and insight in a manner that is supported by the great skillful means of generosity and the rest of the first five perfections, the practitioner will traverse the three levels of the accumulation path[253] (that is, its lesser, middling, and great levels). And after *successively achieving Heat,*[254] *and the rest* (that is, the four *levels of* the path that relates to penetrating insight)[255] the remaining levels of the overall path, beginning with the first ārya bodhisattva stage of *Joy,*[256] the second stage of Stainlessness,[257] *and the rest,* up to the penultimate result that is the stage known as the Diamond-Like Concentration[258] *will be attained. And,* after that, the final result of *a buddha's* great *enlightenment* (a state that is made up of three bodies and five forms of transcendent awareness) also *will not be far off,* meaning that it will be quickly attained. Following this attainment, there arises the ability to carry out the enlightened activities that ripen and liberate fortunate beings spontaneously and continuously, for as long as samsara exists, as indicated in the lines that declare: "Likewise, a buddha's deeds are also regarded / as occurring uninterruptedly, for as long as samsara exists."[259]

B) A Brief Description of the Manner in Which the Mantrayāna Path Is Entered

This topic is made up of three sections: (1) a presentation of the need to receive an initiation in order to enter the Vajrayāna path; (2) the manner in which it is, or is not, appropriate to confer the two higher initiations upon certain individuals; and (3) an investigation of whether or not it is appropriate to listen to or teach tantra, and engage in other activities, if one has not received the two higher initiations.

1) The Need to Receive an Initiation in Order to Enter the Vajrayāna Path

This topic is made up of three sections: a presentation of (1) the type of person who is suitable to practice tantra, (2) the manner in which the initiation that ripens should be conferred upon those individuals, and (3) the greatness of the initiation ceremony.

a) The Type of Person Who Is Suitable to Practice Tantra

> **Through the activities of pacifying and prospering, and the rest,**
> **which are gained through the power of mantra,**
> **as well as the power of achieving the vase of fortune, and so forth,**
> **and the eight great spiritual attainments, and the like, (60)**

As it was described above, it is possible to fully accomplish one's own and others' aims in the system of the Pāramitāyāna by practicing the six perfections and the four principles for gathering a following. What kind of spiritual qualities then does a person need in order to traverse the paths and levels of the Vajrayāna system of practice?

Some elements of the Vajrayāna path *are gained through the power of mantra* recitation. These include elements that are accomplished *through the* four types of *activities*, including those *of pacifying and prospering, and the rest,*[260] *as well as* elements that are accomplished by *the power of achieving the vase of fortune,* which fulfills all desires, *and so forth, and the eight great spiritual attainments,*[261] {58} *and the like.*

if you wish to complete with ease
the requisites for enlightenment,
and you wish to engage in the Secret Mantra practice
taught in the Kriyā, Caryā, and other tantras, (61)

If a person is one who *wishes to complete with ease* and swiftly *the requisites for* great *enlightenment* in order to fulfill his or her own aims, as well as to fulfill all the aims that relate to others, *and* he or she is one who also possesses the *wish* to carry out, in a proper manner, all the practices of the *Secret Mantra path*, as they are *taught in the Kriyā, Caryā, and other tantras,*[262] then that very person is understood to be a suitable candidate for the Secret Mantra path.

b) The Manner in Which the Initiation That Ripens Should be Conferred Upon Those Individuals

you should please a genuine lama in every way,
by honoring, giving jewels, and the like,
by following instructions, and so forth,
in order to receive the teacher's initiation. (62)

That very person who is a candidate for the Vajrayāna path and who wishes to enter the Secret Mantra path *should please a genuine*[263] *lama*—that is, one who possesses all the requisite qualifications. For what purpose should this be done? It should be done *in order to receive the teacher's initiation.*[264] This reference to the teacher's initiation is also meant to include the three higher initiations[265] that are regarded as supreme.

In what manner should such a lama be pleased? A genuine lama should be pleased *in every way*—that is, by making use of every form of object and activity that relates to the three doors of body, speech, and mind. These include *honoring* the lama through body and speech, *giving* him or her whatever objects may be desired, such as *jewels*, clothing, food and drink, servants, *and the like*, *and by* accepting and *following*, in a proper manner, whatever *instructions, and so forth,* you may be given. These activities should be carried out as described in the following lines: "One should serve a spiritual friend[266] with honor, material objects, / by waiting upon him or her, and through practice."[267]

By receiving the complete teacher's initiation
through having pleased the lama, (63ab)

Through having pleased the lama in this way and following the disciple's request to receive the consecration, *by receiving the complete teacher's initiation*, including the authorization that is received at the conclusion, the disciple him- or herself becomes a suitable vessel for the Secret Mantra path.

c) The Greatness of the Initiation Ceremony

you become one whose nature has been purified of all bad deeds
and one who is fit to pursue the spiritual attainments. (63cd)

Through having received all four Highest Yoga Tantra initiations in their entirety, as referenced above, the disciple him- or herself *becomes one whose nature has been purified of all bad deeds* that were previously committed through the three doors, together with their traces,[268] *and one who is fit to pursue* all *the* common and supreme *spiritual attainments*.

2) The Manner in Which It Is, or Is Not, Appropriate to Confer the Two Higher Initiations upon Certain Individuals

One who observes chaste conduct should not receive
the secret and wisdom consecrations,
because this is emphatically forbidden
in the *Ādibuddha Mahātantra*. (64)

Well then, is it acceptable for all persons who are desirous of gaining the spiritual attainments to receive[269] those two initiations? {59} *Because this is* strongly and *emphatically forbidden* by the Bhagavān *in the Kālacakra Root Tantra*, also known as the *Ādibuddha Mahātantra*, *one who observes chaste conduct* as part of his or her morality practice—that is, a celibate layperson[270] or any of the five types of individual who have gone forth[271]—*should not* confer either the *secret* consecration or the *wisdom*-knowledge consecration upon others nor should such a person him- or herself *receive* them in their actual form.

Well then, what fault is perceived in relation to those two initiations, such that they were forbidden for a celibate layperson, and so on?

If one who is observing the austerity
of chaste conduct were to receive those initiations,
the vow of austerity would be ruined
through having engaged in a forbidden act. (65)

If one is any of those persons *who is observing the austerity of chaste conduct* and the vows of a Buddhist ascetic who has gone forth, and he or she *were to receive* and accept *those* two *initiations*, then the *vow of* an ascetic who has gone forth and the *austerity* of chastity and *would be ruined through having engaged in an act* that was *forbidden* by the Master.[272]

That practitioner of austerity will incur
a transgression that is an extreme defeat
and, by falling into the lower realms,
will also not gain any spiritual attainments. (66)

That practitioner who is observing a form *of* moral *austerity* and who receives the secret and wisdom knowledge initiations will incur both a root *transgression that is an extreme defeat*[273] and a root transgression that resembles an extreme form of defeat.[274] Because those persons who have been ruined by those transgressions are certain to *fall into* the three *lower realms*, they will *also not* ever *gain any spiritual attainments*. Lord Atiśa himself declared:

> A teacher who practices chaste conduct and who has reached the path of liberation should not confer the secret and wisdom knowledge initiations, nor should a celibate disciple receive them. Because conferring or receiving those initiations will destroy their practice of chaste conduct, there is no doubt that such a teacher and disciple will both end up being reborn in the hells.[275]

3) Dispelling Uncertainty Regarding Whether It Is or Is Not Acceptable to Listen to or Teach Tantra and so Forth If the Two Higher Initiations Have Not Been Received

One who has been consecrated as a teacher
is permitted to hear and teach all the tantras
and to perform fire offerings, acts of worship, and the like.
There is also no offense for one who has knowledge of reality. (67)

You might think that, if it is unsuitable for an ordained person who practices celibacy to receive those two higher consecrations in their actual form, such an individual is not able to practice the Secret Mantra path. However, there is no such error {60} because *one who has been consecrated as a teacher,*[276] along with the other related elements of the initiation ritual, *is permitted*[277] as a disciple *to hear* of *all* four categories[278] of *the tantras*—including those of Kriyā Tantra, and the rest—and, as a preceptor, to *teach* them, and both together are permitted *to perform fire offerings* and *acts of worship, and the like.* This is also true because *there is also no offense*[279] *for* those persons *who have knowledge of* the ten forms of *reality.*[280]

3. The Cause That Led to the Composition of This Treatise

> **The elder Dīpaṃkara Śrī, who learned**
> **the teachings expressed in sūtras and other scriptures,**
> **composed this brief explanation of the path to enlightenment**
> **at the request of Jangchup Ö. (68)**

Dīpaṃkara Śrī—a crown jewel for all eighteen Indian Buddhist schools[281] and a great *elder*[282] in that he had received the bhikṣu vow of full ordination and maintained it continuously in a pure form for more than thirty years—is one who, having *learned*[283] in a truly correct manner the explanations of the dharma *teachings* that are *expressed in* the *sūtras and other scriptures*, which include the tantras and instructional commentaries, *composed this explanation of the* Mahāyāna *path* that starts from the stage of a novice and proceeds up *to* the final goal of supreme *enlightenment.* He did so in response to a *request* made by *Jangchup Ö*, a fully ordained Buddhist monk[284] from a royal family who had accepted the responsibility of fostering the Buddha's teaching in the land of Tibet, which was stated in these words: "We implore you to provide us with a treatise that will serve as a vehicle for the Mahāyāna doctrine in order to benefit the Buddha's teaching in its entirety."

Moreover, the aim of this work is indicated in the following verse:

> This life is short, the things to be learned are many,
> and since the precise duration of one's life is not known,
> it would be best to take up practice of one's own beliefs,
> like the goose that separates milk from water.[285]

That is to say, this work refrains from engaging in lengthy verbal elaborations that seek to refute others' views and prove one's own position and was *composed* in a form that is *brief* in its wording. As such, it is meant solely as an aid by means of which those who aspire to attain a buddha's omniscient state can pursue a form of spiritual practice that is complete in every respect.

Conclusion

This topic is made up of two points: (1) who the author was and (2) who the translators were.

The Author

> **This concludes *A Lamp for the Path to Enlightenment*, composed by the great teacher Dīpaṃkara Śrījñāna.**

The colophon states in part: *This concludes* the treatise titled *A Lamp for the Path to Enlightenment*, which is a crown jewel for beings living during a final five-hundred-year period. It was *composed* with great compassion *by the great* scholar and *teacher Dīpaṃkara Śrījñāna*, for the sake of countless fortunate disciples. {61}

The Translators

> **It was translated, edited, and established in its final form by the Indian master Dīpaṃkara Śrījñāna and the translator Gelong Gewe Lodrö.**

It was translated from Sanskrit into Tibetan *by the Indian master Dīpaṃkara Śrījñāna and the translator*, or "eye for the world,"[286] *Gelong Gewe Lodrö*. After having been *edited*, both for its words and meanings, it was put to use for both teaching and study.

May those individuals who seek liberation adopt this excellent treatise
that contains the entirety of the teaching as their most essential form of
practice.
It is the legacy of the ultimate state of well-being attained by the victors
of the ten directions and the sole pathway[287] of the bodhisattvas.

May such beings be looked after by spiritual teachers in all their
rebirths.
Having entered this excellent path of pure goodness,
may the supreme enlightenment mind they have engendered remain
firm and develop ever higher.
May they perfect an ocean of excellent spiritual conduct.

By the power of the glorious Dīpaṃkara's enlightenment mind
and aspirational prayers, may the stages of the path to enlightenment
be perfected in my own and others' minds without difficulty,
and may the two aims[288] be achieved spontaneously within this life.

As directed by the venerable lama, the omniscient one endowed with great compassion,[289] who declared, "It would be good if you could carry out the service of composing a commentary to this widely renowned and excellent treatise," I, Lodrö Taye—one who trains himself in the Muni's teaching in a nonsectarian manner and who merely wears the outer mark[290] of a victor's spiritual offspring—have composed this work by extracting essential elements from the writings of excellent spiritual teachers. May virtue and goodness abound!

5. {63} A Verse Compendium of the Spiritual Practices of the Stages of the Path to Enlightenment[1]

Tsongkhapa

{64} I bow my head to the chief of the Śākya clan,
whose body was created by ten million excellent acts of virtue,
whose speech fulfills the hopes of limitless beings,
and whose mind sees all objects of knowledge exactly as they are.

I make prostration to Ajita[2] and Mañjughoṣa,
supreme spiritual offspring of that unparalleled teacher
who, in accepting the duty to perform all of the Victor's enlightened deeds,
playfully appear through emanations in countless realms.

I make prostration to the feet of Nāgārjuna and Asaṅga,
whose names are renowned throughout the threefold world;[3]
they are the ornaments of the Rose Apple continent[4] who explained exactly
the meaning of the victors' *Mother*[5] that is so difficult to fathom.

I bow to Dīpaṃkara,[6] holder of the treasure of instruction
that contains, fully and unerringly, the essential points
of the paths of the profound view and the extensive conduct,
well-transmitted through the lineages of the two great champions.[7]

I make prostration reverently to the spiritual teachers
who, with skillful means prompted by compassion,

make clear the eye with which to view[8] all the myriad scriptures
and the supreme entry point for fortunate beings traveling to liberation.

The Stages of the Path to Enlightenment—
which has been well-transmitted successively from Nāgārjuna and
Asaṅga,
the two crown ornaments among all the learned scholars of the Rose
Apple continent,
whose banner of fame shines resplendently throughout the world—

is an instruction that resembles the jewel called the King of Rulers,[9]
in that it fulfills beings' every aim without exception. {65}
It is also an ocean of splendid eloquent speech
because it contains the rivers of a thousand excellent treatises.

It enables one to realize that the entire doctrine[10] is free of
contradiction,
to perceive all of the discourses as personal instruction,
and to comprehend easily the Victor's intent.
It also protects one from the abyss of great misconduct.

Therefore, what discerning person is there whose mind
would not be greatly captivated by the Stages of the Path
for the Three Types of Person, that supreme instruction taken up
by so many fortunate and learned scholars of India and Tibet?

Since teaching and hearing, for even a single period, this system
that condenses and summarizes the essence of all the discourses
is certain to collect the vast benefit and accumulation
of explaining and hearing the true dharma, contemplate this point.

Then, having seen that the root cause that correctly creates
the conditions for all the well-being in this and future lives
is to serve, properly and diligently, both in thought and action,
the genuine spiritual teacher who reveals the path;

never forsake him, even at the cost of your life; and please him
with the offering of a practice that follows his directions exactly.

I, a spiritual practitioner, have carried out such a practice,
and I urge those of you who seek liberation to do the same.

This human form possessed of leisure is more valuable than a wish-granting jewel;
to have found such an opportunity as this will only happen this one time.
Difficult to obtain and easily destroyed {66}, it is like a flash of lightning in the sky.
After reflecting on this subject, one must realize

that all worldly activities are like winnowing chaff
and then strive to derive value from this life throughout the day and night.
I, a spiritual practitioner, have carried out such a practice,
and I urge those of you who seek liberation to do the same.

There is no assurance that, after dying, you won't be born in the unhappy states;
yet it is certain that the Three Jewels can save you from that peril.
Therefore, practice going for refuge with great firmness
and avoid breaking the precepts that relate to this act.

Moreover, doing so depends on contemplating well black and white deeds and their results
and then properly undertaking to adopt good deeds and abandon wrongful ones.
I, a spiritual practitioner, have carried out such a practice,
and I urge those of you who seek liberation to do the same.

Since great progress cannot be made until you acquire a form
that possesses all the attributes for practicing the supreme path,
you should cultivate all of its causes, without exception.
As it is crucial to clear away the condition of having your three doors tainted

by the stains of evil deeds and transgressions, and especially karmic obscurations,
you should value a practice that continually applies all of the four powers.

I, a spiritual practitioner, have carried out such a practice,
and I urge those of you who seek liberation to do the same.

Since a true aspiration to achieve liberation cannot be developed
without diligently contemplating the disadvantages of the truth of
suffering,
and the method by which to cut samsara's root cannot be understood
without contemplating how the truth of origination gives rise to
samsara,

value cultivating the aversion that seeks deliverance from samsaric
existence,
along with developing the knowledge of what binds us to samsara.
I, a spiritual practitioner, have carried out such a practice,
and I urge those of you who seek liberation to do the same.

Generating enlightenment mind is the mainstay of the supreme
vehicle's path.
It is the foundation and support for the extensive bodhisattva activities.
It is like an alchemic elixir[11] for all forms of the two accumulations.
It is a treasure of merit that gathers myriad collections of virtue.

Having realized this, the heroic spiritual offspring of the victors
regard the jewel-like supreme mind as their most essential practice.
I, a spiritual practitioner, have carried out such a practice,
and I urge those of you who seek liberation to do the same.

Generosity is the wishing gem that fulfills the hopes of the world,
the supreme weapon that severs the knot of stinginess,
the conduct of the victors' offspring that generates dauntless
courage, {67}
and the basis for one's fame being proclaimed in the ten directions.

Having realized this, the wise practice the excellent path
of giving themselves, their wealth, and their virtue.
I, a spiritual practitioner, have carried out such a practice,
and I urge those of you who seek liberation to do the same.

Morality is the water that cleanses the stains of misconduct,
the moonlight that dispels the burning heat of the mental afflictions,
and, in the midst of beings, its majesty is like that of Mount Meru.
All beings bow to it, without having been threatened with force.

Having realized this, true spiritual beings[12] safeguard the morality
that they have accepted correctly, as if it were their eyes.
I, a spiritual practitioner, have carried out such a practice,
and I urge those of you who seek liberation to do the same.

Patience is the best of ornaments for those endowed with strength
and the foremost of austerities against the torment of the mental afflictions.
As a foe of the snake of hatred, it is the soaring garuḍa,[13]
and it is the strongest armor against the weapon of harsh speech.

Having realized this, one should cultivate the armor
of supreme patience in a multitude of different ways.
I, a spiritual practitioner, have carried out such a practice,
and I urge those of you who seek liberation to do the same.

When you don the armor of a resolute effort that is irreversible,
scriptural and cognitional knowledge will increase like the waxing moon.
All your conduct will become meaningful, and whatever spiritual activities
you undertake will be brought to completion as you intended.

Having realized this, the victors' offspring put forth
extensive forms of effort that dispel all laziness.
I, a spiritual practitioner, have carried out such a practice,
and I urge those of you who seek liberation to do the same.

Meditative absorption is the king that governs the mind—
when fixed on an object, it is as immovable as the lord of mountains;
and, when directed, it will engage every form of virtuous object.
It is a practice that elicits the great ease of physical and mental fitness.[14]

Have realized this, the lords of spiritual practice defeat the enemy
of distraction and continually develop one-pointed concentration.
I, a spiritual practitioner, have carried out such a practice,
and I urge those of you who seek liberation to do the same.

Wisdom is known as the eyes that see the most profound reality,
the path that extirpates the root of samsaric existence,
the treasure of good qualities extolled in all the discourses,
and the supreme lamp that dispels the darkness of ignorance. {68}

Having realized this, skillful seekers of liberation
put forth much effort to generate this path.
I, a spiritual practitioner, have carried out such a practice,
and I urge those of you who seek liberation to do the same.

Since one-pointed meditative absorption alone is not seen
to have the ability to cut the root of samsara
and no matter how much analysis is carried out, the wisdom that lacks
the path of quiescence cannot overcome the mental afflictions,

the wisdom that has fully ascertained the true mode of being
should ride the horse of unwavering quiescence
and destroy all the objects that are clung to by extremist beliefs
with the sharp weapon of Middle Way reasoning that is free of extremes.

Through extensive forms of wisdom that engage in proper analysis,
discernment of ultimate reality should be made to increase.
I, a spiritual practitioner, have carried out such a practice,
and I urge those of you who seek liberation to do the same.

What need is there to say that concentration can be achieved
through one-pointed meditation? But those who have seen
that an unwavering concentration that abides with extreme firmness
can also be developed through analysis that properly examines

the ultimate mode of being, and who then strive to attain
the union of the two, quiescence and insight, are truly marvelous.

I, a spiritual practitioner, have carried out such a practice,
and I urge those of you who seek liberation to do the same.

The conduct of the victors' offspring that combines wisdom and means
after meditating on the two forms of emptiness—the space-like state
of meditative composure and the post-meditative practice that likens
appearances to illusions—
is praised for taking one to the far shore of samsara's ocean.

After realizing this, the method for fortunate beings
is not to be satisfied with a path that is incomplete.
I, a spiritual practitioner, have carried out such a practice,
and I urge those of you who seek liberation to do the same.

Having developed correctly in this way the common paths
that are required in both the causal and resultant forms
of the supreme Mahāyāna path, one who relies upon a protector
that is a skillful guide and, having set out upon the ocean of tantra,

practices a complete set of instruction will have brought meaning
to the leisure and fortune that he or she has attained.
I, a spiritual practitioner, have carried out such a practice,
and I urge those of you who seek liberation to do the same.

A prayer of dedication: "Through the virtue of having explained,
in words that are easily understood, the complete path
that is pleasing to the victors, in order to instill its meaning
in my own mind and also to benefit other fortunate beings, {69}

may the entire world never be separated
from this excellent path that is completely pure."
I, a spiritual practitioner, have made such a prayer,
and I urge those of you who seek liberation to do the same.

This brief presentation of the spiritual practices of The Stages of the Path to Enlightenment, created as a memorandum to prevent me from forgetting its meaning, was composed by the well-read Buddhist monk and renunciate

Losang Drakpai Pel at the great mountain retreat named Genden Nampar Gyalwai Ling.[15]

(Note: It is an oral tradition that when this work is recited as a form a reflective meditation,[16] the final two lines of each section, which begin "I, a spiritual practitioner," and so on, should be revised to "My exalted and venerable[17] lama carried out such a practice / and he or she has urged me, a seeker of liberation, to do the same." May auspiciousness abound!)[18]

6. {71} The Flower Cluster of Spiritual Attainments

A Supplication Prayer to the Lineage Whose Blessings Are Near[1]

Tsongkhapa

I make supplication to the Victor Vajradhara,
whose wisdom terminates the bonds of samsaric existence
and whose compassion casts afar all desire for quiescent peace—
the lord of existence and peace who does not stand in the extremes of existence and peace.

I make supplication to Lord Mañjughoṣa,[2]
the wisdom body that incorporates within a single being
the limitless treasure of knowledge possessed by countless victors,
who are more numerous than the atoms in myriad divine realms.

I make supplication to the feet of Pawo Dorje,[3]
whose entire net of doubt was removed
by the direct presence of venerable Mañjughoṣa,
through the power of his great and long-standing prayers.

I make supplication to the feet of the glorious lama Tsongkhapa,
who, through reasoning, correctly realized the nature of the two truths
and who, by the power of having practiced the union of wisdom and means,
manifested the state of a buddha's three bodies.[4]

I make supplication to the lineage lamas,
those lords among teachers who appeared successively—

Gyaltsap Je,[5] Khedrup Gelek Pelsang,[6]
Sherap Senge,[7] Gendun Drupa,[8] and the rest.

I make supplication to the spiritual teachers
who with skillful means prompted by compassion,
make clear the eye with which to view all the myriad scriptures
and the supreme entry point for fortunate beings traveling to liberation.[9]

Please bless me to develop devotion and reverence effortlessly
and at all times, merely by bringing to mind
the benevolent lord who is the root of all excellent
and virtuous qualities, both mundane and transcendent.

Please bless me to have few wants,[10] to be satisfied with what I have,[11]
to remain calm and subdued,[12] to have a heartfelt desire for liberation,
to be one who speaks politely,[13] to associate with the best of companions
who cause me to observe mindfulness, and to develop pure, impartial perceptions.[14]

Please bless me to recall the certainty of death and the uncertainty of the time
of death in a way that is not mere words; through that, to realize
there is no time to spare; and having completely overcome attachment {72}
to gain and honor, to generate the awareness that they serve no purpose.

After realizing that all beings are my kind mothers
and recalling the suffering of all those who are tormented,
please bless me to reject pursuing my own happiness exclusively
and become one who develops compassion effortlessly.

Please bless me to understand in a truly correct manner
the sole medicine for curing all the illnesses of extreme views:
the profound meaning of dependent origination that is free of extremes,
as explained by the supreme Ārya and his spiritual progeny.

As exemplified by the virtue gained with this prayer,
may all my own and others' virtue roots of the three times,
however great they may be, never ripen for even an instant
in any subsequent rebirth in a manner contrary to supreme
enlightenment—

such as by serving as a cause for desiring to profit
from knowledge,[15] to obtain fame, a large retinue,
wealth, or gain and honor; instead may they serve
only as a cause for attaining unsurpassed enlightenment.

Through the marvelous blessings of the victors and their spiritual
offspring,
the infallible truth of dependent origination,
and the power of my own superior attitude,
may the aspirations of this pure prayer be achieved.

This work, titled *The Flower Cluster of Spiritual Attainments: A Supplication Prayer to the Lamas of the Lineage Whose Blessings Are Near*, was composed by the well-read Buddhist monk Losang Drakpai Pel at the base of the lord of snow mountains where the deity Ode Gung Gyal resides, which is situated among Tibet's range of snow mountains.[16]

7. {73} The Nectar That Is Like Highly Refined Gold

An Instruction Manual on the Stages of the Path to Enlightenment[1]

The Third Dalai Lama, Sönam Gyatso

{74} With great reverence, I make prostration and go for refuge to the feet of the venerable lama, the great being who is the complete embodiment of the threefold object of refuge. I beseech you to bestow your blessings upon me.

The Authoritative Source of the Teaching

The subject matter addressed herein is the spiritual practice that should be undertaken by those persons who wish to derive value from a human existence that is endowed with leisure and fortune.[2] These practices constitute the essence of the entirety of the Victor's[3] teachings, the sole pathway traversed by all the āryas of the three times, the system that incorporates the instruction formulated by the two great champions Nāgārjuna and Asaṅga, and the spiritual tradition for supreme individuals who are seeking to reach the state that is the knowledge of all modes.[4] They include, in their entirety, all the stages of spiritual practice that need to be cultivated by the three types of person. This teaching is none other than the one called The Stages of the Path to Enlightenment.

Regarding this system of instruction, the first point to be made is that the teaching that one intends to practice must have an extraordinary and authentic source. Moreover, this teaching that derives from an authentic source should not contain merely a portion of the path; it must contain all the elements of the entire body of the path, and it must do so in a manner that is unerring.

This graduated path that I am currently undertaking to practice is one that has an authentic source because it originated with the true and complete Buddha and it has been transmitted successively through separate lineages that were created by the two great beings Nāgārjuna and Asaṅga. This dharma system that has been transmitted by these authentic sources is like the jewel known as the King of Rulers[5] in that it easily fulfills beings' every aim without exception. {75} It is like the great ocean in that it contains the rivers of excellent sayings that are contained in all the excellent commentarial traditions of both the Hīnayāna and the Mahāyāna traditions. I am especially fortunate to have the opportunity to engage in the three activities of learning, reflecting, and meditating upon a teaching such as this one, because it contains the totality of all spiritual topics, in that it includes and teaches the key points of both the sūtra and tantra systems; it is easy to practice, in that it principally addresses the steps for taming the mind; and because it is adorned by the instruction of Vidyākokila,[6] who was extremely knowledgeable in the spiritual system established by Nāgārjuna, and that of Lama Serlingpa,[7] who was extremely knowledgeable in the spiritual system established by Asaṅga. These points are also expressed in the following verses from our lama's spiritual song:[8]

> The Stages of the Path to Enlightenment—
> which has been well-transmitted successively from Nāgārjuna and Asaṅga,
> the two crown ornaments among all the learned scholars of the Rose Apple continent,[9]
> whose banner of fame shines resplendently throughout the world—
>
> is an instruction like the jewel called the King of Rulers,
> in that it fulfills beings' every aim without exception.
> And it is also an ocean of splendid eloquent speech
> because it contains the rivers of a thousand excellent treatises.

Four Forms of Greatness

As such, this system of instruction is endowed with four forms of greatness that make it superior to others because it is endowed with the following four qualities:

(1) The greatness of enabling one to realize that all of the Buddha's teachings are free of contradiction means that, on the basis of this instruction, you will realize that, among all the forms of the Victor's excellent speech, some discourses are a means of teaching the principal elements of the path while others are a means of teaching subordinate elements of the path {76}. Thus, you will come to understand that every individual teaching constitutes an integral factor, either directly or indirectly, in the overall process by which any given individual, such as yourself, pursues the ultimate goal of enlightenment.

(2) The greatness of causing all discourses to be seen as personal instruction means that you will eliminate completely the mistaken conceptions that regard the sūtra and tantra discourses and the authoritative treatises that explain their meanings as merely explanatory teachings that serve to engender outer forms of extensive learning and incorrectly believe that the essential elements of spiritual practice are to be found elsewhere. In addition to that, you will come to recognize that this instruction subsumes all the subjects of the canonical discourses and their commentaries within the stages of the path that range from the manner in which to serve a spiritual teacher up to the meditation practices of quiescence and insight, and you will regard the explanations found in those canonical discourses and their commentaries as the most essential forms of instruction for those stages of spiritual practice. In this way, you will come to understand the meanings of the subjects [presented in those canonical discourses and the authoritative commentaries] as the instruction that teaches you how to practice analytic meditation in relation to those topics that require analytic meditation and how to practice fixed meditation in relation to those topics that require fixed meditation.[10]

(3) The greatness of enabling the Victor's intent to be comprehended easily means that, even though the great scriptures—that is, the canonical discourses, together with their commentaries—are the supreme forms of spiritual instruction, novice practitioners, such as myself, who have not trained themselves extensively in the meanings that are found in those extensive discourses, will not be able to gain a true understanding of the meanings contained in those great scriptures without relying on the personal instruction of a true spiritual teacher,

even if they were to study them and reflect upon their meanings. Or even if it is granted that they might gain such an understanding, it would take them a very long time to do so, and they would have to put forth an extremely great effort. However, by relying upon a teaching system like The Stages of the Path to Enlightenment—which is itself based upon *A Lamp for the Path*,[11] a work that contains the personal instruction of a genuine lama—it is possible [for novice practitioners like myself] to gain an understanding of the meanings found in the great scriptures without difficulty.

(4) The greatness of spontaneously terminating grave forms of misconduct[12] means that, when [an awareness of the Victor's intent] is gained in the manner that was described, you will recognize that all forms of the Buddha's word, either directly or indirectly, teach the methods of attaining enlightenment. In contrast with that, believing that only some of the Victor's discourses need to be practiced because they do teach a method of attaining enlightenment while others are rejected because they are considered to impede one's attainment of enlightenment {77} constitutes the misdeed of repudiating the dharma. Therefore, through relying on this instruction, merely by realizing with certainty, in the manner that was described earlier, that all of the teachings are free of contradiction, you will automatically give up the great misdeed of repudiating the dharma.

Accordingly, those who already possess or who desire to possess a discerning intellect should feel themselves irresistibly captivated by this supreme instruction on The Stages of the Path for the Three Types of Person that has been taken up and internalized by so many fortunate individuals and learned scholars in both India and Tibet, and they should apply themselves to it through carrying out the three activities of listening, reflection, and meditation, because this very instruction is endowed with the four forms of greatness that were described above. This is true, because Je Lama[13] has declared the following:

> It enables one to realize that the entire doctrine[14] is free of
> contradiction,
> to perceive all of the discourses as personal instruction,

and to comprehend easily the Victor's intent.
It also protects one from the abyss of great misconduct.

Therefore, what discerning person is there whose mind
would not be greatly captivated by the Stages of the Path
for the Three Types of Person, that supreme instruction taken up
by so many fortunate and learned scholars of India and Tibet?

The Proper Manner in Which to Teach and Hear the Teaching

Leaving aside the benefit that would be gained by teaching the entire system of practice known as The Stages of the Path for the Three Types of Person—an instruction that is endowed with these four qualities of greatness and that combines within a single work the essence of all the Victor's discourses—one should reflect on the benefit that is gained by teaching and explaining it in an unerring manner for just a single period of instruction. The correct manner in which to teach consists of generating reverence for the Master[15] and the dharma, followed by teaching the instruction unerringly to a person who is a qualified vessel, while exercising purity in thought and action. By doing so, it is certain that the collection of the vast benefit that derives from explaining the true dharma properly will occur. Likewise, by listening to this instruction in an unerring manner—meaning by avoiding the three defects of an inadequate vessel,[16] observing the six conceptions,[17] and so forth—{78} it is certain that the collection of the vast benefit that derives from hearing the true dharma will occur. For these reasons, you should strive to listen to and teach this instruction in a proper manner; indeed, you must do so, because Je Lama declared:

Since teaching and hearing, for even a single period, this system
that condenses and summarizes the essence of all the discourses
is certain to collect the vast benefit and accumulation
of explaining and hearing the true dharma, contemplate this
point.

You might then wonder, "If such a vast benefit is gained by properly listening to such an instruction, from what kind of person should one hear this extraordinary instruction?" Speaking generally about the spiritual teacher from whom it is appropriate to hear the true dharma, many different explanations of a spiritual teacher's defining attributes are described in the Mahāyāna and Hīnayāna traditions, as well as the sūtra and mantra systems. However, the spiritual teacher from whom the kindness of this precious instruction should be received is one who possesses the following ten qualities that are described in the *Ornament of Mahāyāna Sūtras.*[18]

He or she should be one who possesses the qualities of spiritual attainment,[19] which means to have brought his or her mental continuum under control by means of the three trainings. Thus, he or she should be one who has become (1) subdued on the basis of the morality training, (2) calm on the basis of the training of one-pointed concentration, and (3) tranquil on the basis of the wisdom training. He or she should also possess (4) the quality of scriptural learning,[20] which means to have extensive knowledge of the three baskets,[21] and so on. He or she should also be (5) one who possesses the wisdom that has cognized ultimate reality and (6) one whose good qualities are superior to those of his or her disciples. These six are the spiritual qualities that a dharma teacher should attain in relation to him- or herself.

He or she should also be (7) one who is both skilled at leading his or her disciples through the stages of the path and skilled in conveying meanings to them verbally. He or she should be (8) one who possesses the pure motivation of compassion, which means a person who teaches the dharma motivated by compassion while ignoring all concern for fame and honor, and the like. He or she should be (9) one who possesses the mental vigor that is energetic about accomplishing others' aims, through such activities as explaining the dharma, and the like. He or she should be (10) one who has abandoned all thoughts that dwell on the hardships associated with teaching, as well as all thoughts of vexation at the wrongful conduct of those who make up one's following. {79} These latter four represent the qualities that relate to supporting the welfare of others. One should rely on a teacher who possesses these ten qualities and receive Mahāyāna instruction[22] and counsel[23] from him or her.

Speaking generally, a person who listens to the dharma should also have the three qualities of (1) being impartial,[24] (2) possessing the intelligence[25] that can discern spurious ideas that might occur in relation to the true path, and (3) being diligent[26] about pursuing the path.[27] In addition to these, he or she should possess a fourth quality, which is (4) to be respectful of the dharma and the dharma teacher.[28]

In particular, the disciple who possesses the defining attributes that make him or her suitable to be led by a path such as this one should be considered to have six qualities. These include the four of: (1) having great diligence about pursuing the dharma, (2) having a mind that becomes well-fixed when listening to the instruction, (3) having great faith and respect for the dharma and the dharma teacher, and (4) having the ability to reject faulty explanations and embrace good explanations. In addition, he or she should (5) have a discerning intellect, which promotes those four qualities and (6) be impartial, which rejects what is unfavorable to them.

Therefore, if you wish to be a teacher of this path system, you should strive to develop the defining attributes of a spiritual teacher. And, as a disciple, you should train yourself so that you possess the defining attributes of a disciple when you are listening to the instruction.

How the Instruction Should Be Practiced

The Manner in Which to Serve One's Spiritual Teacher

The Six Preliminary Practices

Having properly listened to the instruction of The Stages of the Path for the Three Types of Person from a qualified spiritual teacher, the following explanation describes how to put the instruction into practice. First,[29] you should set up the "vessels"[30] for the Three Jewels in an agreeable place.[31] Next, arrange offerings that are free of deceit in an attractive manner on your altar. Following that, while sitting in a cross-legged position on a comfortable seat, imbue your mind with the heartfelt attitude of entrusting yourself to the Three Jewels and carry out the act of going for refuge many times. Then, meditate on the four immeasurables and generate enlightenment mind as you recite the verse that states in part, "I go for refuge until enlightenment to the Buddha, dharma, and supreme assembly . . ."[32]

Visualizing the Merit Field

As you recite the mantra that begins with *oṃ svabhāva*,[33] meditate that all ordinary entities dissolve into the emptiness that is the state of being empty of any real essential nature. From that emptiness, visualize that in the sky before you is the lama who is your teacher for this path system {80} and who is inseparable in nature from our Master,[34] seated upon a variegated lotus and a moon cushion atop a large, broad, bejeweled throne held up by eight great lions. Seated all around him is a vast host of spiritual beings that has also been invited. Adjacent to your root lama are the lamas of the Lineage of Extensive Conduct[35] and the Lineage of the Profound View.[36] Just beyond them are the buddhas and bodhisattvas of the ten directions, as well as śrāvaka and pratyekabuddha arhats, tantric heroes[37] and ḍākinīs,[38] and the pledge-bound protectors of the teaching.[39]

After visualizing the merit field, recite the following verses to invite the wisdom beings:

> Without wavering from the pure entity-source,
> you survey the ten directions' beings with immeasurable compassion
> and promote the furtherance of all the victors' enlightened deeds—
> O Lama of the three times, please draw near, together with your
> retinue.
>
> O Bhagavan, savior of all beings without exception, [40]

Next generate the bathhouse as you recite the verse that begins: "In exquisitely fragrant bathhouses . . . ."[41] Then carry out the acts of bathing all the beings in the merit field, drying their bodies and offering them clothing and ornaments as you recite the verses that appear in the work titled *Entry into the Conduct That Leads to Enlightenment*.[42] The bathing ritual concludes with the verse whose first line states, "In your compassion for me and all beings . . . ,"[43] which requests the figures that make up the merit field to return to their previous seats [so that you might worship them].

Following that, you should carry out the seven-limb devotional practice,[44] which includes the main elements for purifying yourself of misdeeds and accumulating merit. First, you should make prostrations as you recite a series of verses, which include the following lines: "[I make prostration to the lamas,] whose bodies contain the essence of the all buddhas . . . ," and so on,[45] [which is addressed to all the root and lineage lamas; "I make prostration to . . .] Vajradhara, the sugata possessed of great compassion . . . ," and so on,[46] which is addressed to the lamas of the Lineage of Divinely Inspired Practice; "[I make prostration to . . .] Maitreya, Asaṅga, Vasubandhu, and Vimuktisena . . . ," and so on,[47] which is addressed to the lamas of the Lineage of Extensive Conduct; "[I make prostration to . . .] Nāgārjuna, the Victor's son who destroyed the erring positions of being and nonbeing . . . ," and so on,[48] which is addressed to the lamas of the Lineage of the Profound View; "[I make prostration to the one who appeared] before the Victor [as Bhadrapāla] . . . ," and so on,[49] which is addressed to Lord Atiśa; "[I make prostration to . . .]" and so on,[50] which is addressed to Drom Tönpa; "[I make prostration to . . .]" Avalokiteśvara, the treasure of compassion that has no mental object . . ." and so on,[51] which is addressed to Lord Tsongkhapa; "[I make prostration to . . . the glorious lama, who accepted the duty of preserving] scripture and reasoning, / [possessed] the well-developed physical strength of powerful and profound wisdom . . ." and so on,[52] [which is addressed to Je Sherap Senge]; "[I make prostration to . . . the glorious lama, . . . who founded the gathering place for] the sangha, / who possess the excellent qualities of knowledge and liberation,"[53] [which is addressed to Gendun Drup]; [I make prostration to you, a wish-granting jewel] that fulfills all needs . . ." and so on,[54] [which is addressed to the lamas in general]; "[I make prostration to the ones] from whom we receive knowledge . . ." and so on,[55] [which is addressed to all the spiritual teachers from whom one has received dharma instruction directly]; {81} "[I make prostration to . . .] the unsurpassed teacher, the precious Buddha . . . "[56] and so on, [which is addressed to the Three Jewels]; and "[I make prostration to the one] who took birth in the Śakya clan, through skillful means and compassion . . . ,"[57] and so on, [which is addressed to Buddha Śākyamuni].

Then also recite the verses from the one that begins with the line "However many there are . . ." and continue up to the verse that ends "I make prostration and present offerings to all the victors."[58] Following that, present a mandala offering in either an extensive or abbreviated form followed by the verse that begins with the line "In addition to these, may diverse clouds of offering collections" and ends with "become situated throughout the sky above."[59] Next also recite the *General Confession*[60] three times, followed by the series of verses that begin with the line "Whatever evil I have committed, / influenced by desire, hatred, or ignorance" and end with "I dedicate it all to enlightenment."[61]

Following that, recite the Lamrim supplication prayer titled *Opening the Door to the Supreme Path*[62] in such a way that causes your mind to be affected by the words as you chant them. Then, request the divine figures that make up the merit field to return to their innate realms by reciting "May the objects of this devotional practice return to their innate realms." If you are practicing four or six meditation sessions each day, the act of requesting the merit field to return to their innate realms is carried out during the day's final meditation session. The above description represents the preliminary portion of the spiritual practice that relates to the topic of how to serve one's spiritual teacher.

The Main Meditation Practice for How to Serve One's Spiritual Teacher

The instructions that pertain to the main practice for how to serve one's spiritual teachers should be meditated upon using analytic meditation. Regarding that instruction, you should reflect to yourself in the following manner:

> My glorious lamas are the root cause for achieving the spiritual attainments;[63] they are the source through which I can obtain all forms of well-being that relate to both this life and all my future lives. Because lamas dispel the ultimate illness of samsaric suffering, just as an ordinary physician does with a sick person's temporary physical ailments, their kindness is inestimably great.[64] The fact that I have had to wander endlessly in samsara throughout beginningless time until now is due to my having failed to meet with such spiritual teachers as these, or, though I may have met with spiritual teachers, it is because I failed to carry out a spiritual practice that followed their directions. Therefore, now I must do everything possible to please my lamas. Their great kindness is not like that of someone who offers as many gold coins as one can physically carry to a person who is already enjoying an abundance of wealth and provisions; rather, it is like that of someone who provides a bowl of food to a person who is on the verge of starving to death. Therefore, it is an absolute certainty that my lamas' inestimably great kindness even surpasses that of the buddhas, as is expressed in the following verse from *The Five Stages*:
>
> > That being is the Self-Originated One, the Divine Lord,
> > the Unique One, the Supreme Deity.
> > However, the vajra teacher is superior to that being
> > because he or she bestows the personal instruction.[65]

{82} Previously,[66] in order to repay a lama's kindness, or to please a lama for having heard a teaching that consisted of just a half-verse from him, such as the one that states, "If there is birth, there will be death. / Their cessation is true happiness," or for having heard just a single verse of instruction, our Master[67] gave up his own body and all of his wealth. For instance, to repay a lama's kindness he offered such things as a hundred thousand gold coins, or such extremely dear beings as his son and queen, or he created a thousand lamps within his own body.[68] Since I, too, am a follower of this Master and I have heard countless dharma teachings from my current lamas, I should certainly recognize that their kindness is immeasurably great.

It might be thought that one only has an obligation to recognize one's current lama's kindness if he or she is someone that is considered to be very learned. If not, in addition to having no special regard for the teacher whatsoever, one might respond to his or her teaching by saying, "I have already heard that dharma teaching." However, this behavior indicates an extremely great misunderstanding of what is proper. For instance, one's parents may not possess any special good qualities, but we still have a responsibility to recognize their kindness. Just as a great benefit will be received by accepting that responsibility and a great detriment will be incurred by failing to accept it, this principle most definitely also applies to one's lamas.

If it is commonly said of someone who gives something of modest material value that he or she is very kind, we should recognize that a lama is someone who provides us with the happiness that relates to this life and all our future lives. If we examine this point carefully, it will become evident to us that the difference in well-being between the exalted buddhas and bodhisattvas on the one hand and ordinary householders on the other is due to the fact that the former beings pleased their lamas and the latter did not. Not only that, there have also been many instances in which a lama enabled his or her disciples to achieve buddhahood within a single lifetime. Therefore, by pleasing my lamas with the three methods of honoring[69] them, I too am certain to attain buddhahood swiftly.

Therefore, since the kindness of one's lamas is inconceivably great, it is important to please those kind lamas. Being able to meet with true spiritual teachers and be looked after by them in one's future lives depends entirely upon pleasing the current lamas with which we have developed a spiritual relationship. Therefore, I urge you to recognize that it is imperative for you to serve your spiritual teachers in an unerring manner. {83} All the sūtras and treatises repeatedly declare "You must practice in a way that pleases your lamas." This duty is not something we can choose not to do or something that we can argue about. There isn't anyone who doesn't want to gain merit. All the sūtras, tantras, and treatises declare that there is no higher field for accumulating merit than one's lamas. Moreover, the way to succeed in pleasing them is to cultivate a form of faith toward your lamas that is not mere words but rather is felt in the depth of your heart and the core of your bones in such a way that you never develop a thought that considers your lama as having any faults and you perceive everything that he or she does as being excellent. You should continue to meditate on this faith until you experience such reactions as the hairs on your body standing on end and tears streaming from your eyes at the mere hearing of your lama's name being uttered or whenever you bring him or her to mind.

Moreover, regarding this point, if the buddhas and bodhisattvas teach that it is wrong to have critical thoughts about any sentient beings at all, then needless to say we should not do so toward our lamas. If it should appear to us as though our lamas have some fault, we should reflect to ourselves as follows:

> My perceptions are erring. How could my lama have such a fault? Past examples of this include Ārya Asaṅga, who, after praying to Maitreya, perceived the deity as a female dog whose hindquarters were infested with maggots. Naropa also perceived his lama Telopa as frying live fish in a pan. The *Sūtra on the Meeting of Father and Son* and other scriptures also declare that buddhas even emanate themselves as Māra[70] in order to act on behalf of sentient beings. Therefore, how could my lama have any faults; it is absolutely certain that he or she is a genuine buddha.

If we fail to develop such a level of faith and disparage a lama through perceiving him or her as having faults, we should recall how scriptures such as the *Guhyasamāja Root Tantra* and the *Fifty Verses on the Guru* state that this is the greatest of all evil deeds. Therefore, reflect to yourself:

> I should follow the example of Drom Tönpa[71] and not seek out many lamas indiscriminately. I must ensure that I never allow myself to develop a disrespectful thought toward whomever I entrust myself to as a lama, even if this should require me to put my life at risk.

In his great compassion, Je Lama also instructed us about this topic as follows:

> Then, having seen that the root cause that correctly creates
> the conditions for all the well-being in this and future lives {84}
> is to serve, properly and diligently, both in thought and action,
> the genuine spiritual teacher who reveals the path;
>
> never forsake him, even at the cost of your life; and please him
> with the offering of a practice that follows his directions exactly.
> I, a spiritual practitioner, have carried out such a practice,
> and I urge those of you who seek liberation to do the same.

Developing the Aspiration to Derive Value from a Human Life of Leisure and Fortune

You might ask yourself, "Well then, if I must diligently serve a spiritual teacher who reveals the path to me in this way, and I must also please him or her by making an offering of my spiritual practice that follows his or her directions exactly, how should I carry out a practice that accords with my teacher's directions?" You should do so by putting into practice properly the true dharma, in the way that you were instructed by your spiritual teacher. And there is no other offering of spiritual practice in which you are following your teacher's directions exactly that is greater than that of deriving value from this human life that is endowed with leisure and fortune,[72] a life that is extremely difficult to obtain when considered both from the point of view of its causes and its nature of being a result, which can provide great value when it is obtained, and which should be regarded as more valuable than a wish-granting jewel. Therefore, you should reflect to yourself, "If I fail to put three fingers in my mouth[73] and strive to avoid wasting the human life that has been found this one time, then I am like one whose heart is rotten. I must forcefully put a stop to any of the white, black, or mottled forms of the eight worldly concerns,[74] such as pursuing this life's goal of defeating one's enemies and supporting one's allies in order to impress others or attending dharma teachings and accepting the vows of the morality training, and so forth, motivated by an attitude of desiring to obtain gain and honor. If I don't put a stop to them and fail to practice the dharma by meditating on the topics of impermanence, and the like, in such a way that my thoughts truly conform to my words, this does greater harm to the possibility of achieving my spiritual goals than any other form of wrongful conduct. Likewise, if I am able to practice a pure form of dharma in such a way that I don't have any reason to feel ashamed of myself, then I will have laid the foundation for attaining my spiritual goals and such a practice represents a form of good conduct that is greater than any others. Therefore, reflect to yourself:

> I shall turn away from these worldly activities that have little benefit and great potential for harm, and that are like the futile act of winnowing empty chaff in hopes of obtaining grain. Having done so, I shall make sure that I derive value from this human life, so that I have no need to feel any regret when I am facing my death. {85} Moreover, I shall undertake to accomplish this beginning right now.

You should meditate on this point in such a way that your desire to derive value from your current life that is endowed with leisure and fortune resembles the desire that a person who is tormented by thirst has for water. In addition, reflect to yourself, "I must remain mindful that Je Lama also declared the following about this topic":

> This human form possessed of leisure is more valuable than a wish-granting jewel;
> to have found such an opportunity as this will only happen this one time.
> Difficult to obtain and easily destroyed, it is like a flash of lightning in the sky.
> After reflecting on this subject, one must realize
>
> that all worldly activities are like winnowing chaff
> and then strive to derive value from this life throughout the day and night.

Generating a Conviction about the Path's Overall Structure

You may ask yourself, "Well then, if I must derive value from my human form that is endowed with leisure and fortune, how does one go about doing that?" Of the two topics[75] that are taught in response to this question, the first one is the manner in which to generate a conviction about the overall structure of the path. Since it is extremely important to develop an understanding of this topic, I shall explain it briefly by describing (1) the manner in which all the discourses are included in the paths for the three types of person and (2) the reason for leading disciples by means of the three types of person.

The Manner in Which All the Discourses Are Included in the Paths for the Three Types of Person

The Buddha's initial generating of enlightenment mind, his subsequent collecting of the two accumulations, and his final attainment of enlightenment were all done for the sake of sentient beings. It is also true that all of the Buddha's dharma teachings were made exclusively for the sake of sentient beings. [Those discourses can be understood in the following manner.] The aims to be achieved for sentient beings are twofold: (1) the temporary goal of an elevated status[76] and (2) the ultimate goal of the highest good.[77] Of these, everything that the Buddha taught in relation to the method of achieving the first goal can be included within the actual body of teachings for lesser persons or the body of teachings that are held in common with lesser persons. Regarding the characteristics of a lesser person, *A Lamp for the Path* declares:

> One who by various means
> seeks only the happiness
> of samsara for him- or herself
> is known as a lesser person.[78]

As this verse indicates, a lesser person is defined as one who is not predominantly attached to this life and who, desiring to obtain the happiness of the higher realms[79] in future lives, practices the causes for attaining that goal.

The goal of the highest good has two forms: the state of liberation that is merely deliverance from samsara {86} and the state of omniscience. Everything that the Buddha taught in relation to the first of these results can be included within the actual body of teachings for middling persons or the body of teachings that are held in common with middling persons. *A Lamp for the Path* describes this type of person as follows:

> Turned away from the happiness of samsaric existence
> with a nature that avoids evil deeds,
> one who seeks only peace for him- or herself
> is said to be a middling person.[80]

As this verse indicates, the spiritual practitioner who is just a middling person is defined as one who has turned away from desire for the well-being of samsara and considers merely the happiness of having abandoned samsara as the goal to be attained. In order to attain that goal, he or she takes up the practice of the three trainings.

Regarding the means of attaining the state of omniscience, there are two methods: the Secret Mantrayāna and the Pāramitāyāna. Both of these methods are included in the body of teachings for a great person. *A Lamp for the Path* describes a great person as follows:

> One who, through the suffering
> of his or her own continuum, truly desires
> to terminate completely all the suffering
> of others is a supreme person.[81]

As this verse indicates, a great person is defined as one who, through being under the influence of great compassion, has made buddhahood his or her goal in order to put an end to all the suffering that is experienced by others. To attain this goal, he or she trains him- or herself in the six perfections and the two stages of Highest Yoga Tantra.

The Reason for Leading Disciples By Means of the Three Types of Person

While this is how the nature of the three types of person is explained, at this point in the teaching it is necessary to understand how to utilize the practices that pertain to the lower two types of person as subsidiary elements of the process by which to lead disciples through the path for great persons. Moreover, regarding this topic, the disciple is not meant to be led either by the path for a mere lesser person who regards the prosperity of samsara as the goal to be attained or by the path for a mere middling person who regards liberating him- or herself from samsara as the goal to be attained. Rather, certain elements that are held in common with the paths for those two types of person are meant to be regarded as the preliminary stage in the process by which to lead disciples through the path for great persons. Following that preliminary exercise, disciples should be led by the main stage that consists of the path for great persons.

{87} The reason for doing so can be understood as follows. Since there is no other means of entering the system of the Mahāyāna than by generating the mind that aspires to attain supreme enlightenment, it is essential for one to generate that mind. In order to do that, one must first develop enthusiasm for the act of generating enlightenment mind by reflecting on its benefits. And the benefits of generating enlightenment mind are included within the two categories of temporary benefits and ultimate benefits. Of these, the temporary benefit, which is to attain the result of the happiness that is rebirth in the higher realms, is one that is easily achieved through generating enlightenment mind. The ultimate benefit of achieving omniscience is also one that comes about through generating enlightenment mind. Therefore, it is essential for one to generate the mind that aspires to attain supreme enlightenment.

Moreover, that act of generating enlightenment mind must be preceded by developing the great compassion that cannot bear to see that sentient beings are tormented by suffering. However, a necessary condition for developing that great compassion is to have a powerful form of the attitude that does not want to be tormented by suffering oneself. Therefore, one must first reflect, in relation to oneself, on the condition of being tormented by the suffering of the lower realms[82]—which represents the spiritual practice that pertains to a lesser person—in order to develop the mind that wishes to become free of that condition. In addition, one must also reflect on the fact that there is no genuine happiness in the higher realms—which represents the spiritual practice that pertains to a middling person—in order to develop the attitude of renunciation, which seeks to attain deliverance from all of samsara. Following that, using the understanding gained by reflecting on the suffering that you might have to experience yourself, you should generate the loving-kindness, compassion, and enlightenment mind that desires to liberate all sentient beings, who are to be regarded as our elderly mothers, from the suffering that torments them. Therefore, this is how to understand that training one's mind in the practices that are held in common with lesser and middling persons represents the supreme method for leading disciples through the path for great persons.

The Actual Method by Which to Derive Value from One's Life

This topic is made up of three sections,[83] of which the first is the method of training one's mind in the path that is held in common with lesser persons.

Training Your Mind in the Path That Is Held in Common with Lesser Persons

Reflecting on Impermanence

After drawing your full attention inward, reflect on the following points until you elicit a mental state in which your heart is overcome with terror and you feel so uncomfortable that you are unable to sit still.

> If a precious human life such as the one I have obtained—which is difficult to obtain and so valuable when it is obtained—does not remain in existence for very long and if death is certain but there is no certainty as to the time of death, then I must, this very moment, begin striving to derive value from it. Moreover, regarding this point, in the recent past, the Lord of Death has slain such a great number of good, bad, and middling persons, causing them to disappear like a crowd at a market that disperses in a sudden rush {88}. How very fortunate that I, too, have not died during this same period of time!

Then reflect further:

> Though I cannot bring any of my wealth, property, family, or friends with me when I go to my next life, I must carry all the evil deeds that I accumulated for their sake. How distressing this is!
>
> How many countless times I have indulged in this life's interests in the past, eating, enjoying myself, drinking, and having fun, or pursued the three aims of relationships with persons, accumulating wealth, and enjoying food, and the like. Now, with whatever remains of my current life, I must practice a genuine form of dharma and I must do so starting this very day.

Reflecting on the Suffering of the Lower Realms

You may ask yourself, "If nothing but the dharma can help me at the time of death, how does the dharma provide benefit? What is the way in which evil[84] causes me harm?" [In response to these questions, reflect in the following manner:]

> When I die, I do not cease to exist; I must take birth again, and that rebirth can only be in a happy migratory state or an unhappy migratory state.[85] Moreover, which of these two it will be is something that only karma can determine; I do not have the freedom to choose. Since I must take birth in whatever manner I am propelled by my white or black karma, if a virtuous state of mind is present at the time of my death, I will be reborn in a happy migratory state in my next life. If an unvirtuous state of mind is present at that time, I will be reborn in one of the three unhappy migratory states and will be forced to experience intense forms of suffering.

If you wonder what kind of suffering there is in the unhappy migratory states, Lord Nāgārjuna wrote:

> Each day the hells should be recalled,
> both the hot and the cold ones.
> Tormented spirits, which are tortured by hunger
> and thirst, should be recalled as well.
>
> Animals that walk bent over and are subject to the suffering
> of much ignorance should be considered and recalled.
> Abandon the causes of those unfortunate states and cultivate the causes of happiness.
> At a time when you have attained a human life
>
> in the Rose Apple continent, which is so difficult to obtain,
> strenuously avoid committing the causes of the lower realms.[86]

As these verses state, the various hells contain unbearable suffering caused by heat and cold; tormented spirits undergo the oppressive suffering of hunger and thirst; and animals experience such unbearable forms of suffering as being eaten by one another, {89} being unintelligent and unable to speak.

Using your current experiences as an example, meditate by reflecting on the following points until you elicit a mental state that is filled with extremely great fear and dread:

> If it would be difficult for me to endure inserting my hand into the *kukūla* firepit[87] and leaving it there for a brief moment, or have to remain naked outside for an entire day during the cold of winter, or have to go several days without any food whatsoever or be bitten by insects, and the like, how could I bear the suffering of being reborn in the hot and cold hells, or as a tormented spirit or an animal that is swallowed alive by another animal?

Then meditate as you reflect further:

> Therefore, at this time when I have obtained an excellent human form endowed with leisure, I must strive to accomplish the means of avoiding being reborn in the lower realms by abandoning the causes for being reborn in the lower realms and striving to create causes for being reborn in the happy migratory states.

Going for Refuge

If you ask yourself, "Well then, how should I strive to accomplish the means by which to avoid being reborn in the lower realms?" You should do so by generating fear at the prospect of having to undergo the suffering of the lower realms as described above, and then, after realizing that the Three Jewels have the ability to save you from that peril, going for refuge to the precious Three Jewels from the bottom of your heart.

The Three Jewels do have the ability to save you from the peril of the lower realms, because the jewel of the Buddha in particular is a worthy object to go to for refuge in that he is free of all fears, he is skilled in the ways of liberating others from all fears, he acts impartially and with great compassion toward everyone, and he acts on behalf of everyone, both those who have benefited him and those who have not.[88] These reasons also serve to illustrate why the jewel of the dharma and the jewel of the sangha are worthy objects to go to for refuge. In short, because these qualities are not present at all in non-Buddhist teachers, their teachings and their followers, they are not worthy objects to go to for refuge; however, because the Three Jewels do possess them, they are worthy objects to go to for refuge.

If you ask, "How do I go for refuge?" You go for refuge by entrusting yourself fully and from the depth of your heart to the Three Jewels, as you recite the following:

> I go for refuge to the Buddha, who is the supreme of all human beings.[89] {90} I beseech you to be the teacher who liberates me from the suffering of the lower realms and samsara. I go for refuge to the dharma, which is the supreme state of detachment. I beseech it to be the actual refuge that liberates me from the suffering of the lower realms and samsara. I go for refuge to the sangha, who is the supreme assemblage of spiritual beings. I beseech them to help me become liberated from the suffering of the lower realms and samsara.

If, after going for refuge to the Three Jewels in the manner that was just described, you fail to practice the related precepts, your refuge act will be ruined; therefore, you must keep the precepts. Moreover, regarding how to do that, you should reflect on the following precepts three times during the day and three times during the night:

> Having gone for refuge to the Buddha, I must not consider worldly deities, such as Rudra,[90] Viṣṇu, and the like, as a source of refuge. Moreover, I must conceive of even images of the Buddha as the actual Buddha, and act respectfully toward them.
>
> Having gone for refuge to the dharma, I must not harm any sentient being. I must also refrain from being disrespectful and always act respectfully toward even a single written letter.
>
> Having gone for refuge to the sangha, I must not associate with or befriend evil persons or followers of non-Buddhist religions. I must also refrain from being disrespectful and always act respectfully toward those who wear the yellow robes.[91]
>
> In addition, recognizing that all benefit, happiness, and virtue comes through the kindness of the Three Jewels, I must worship the Three Jewels in a variety of ways,[92] including offering them the first part of any food or drink that I am about to consume.

> I must pursue all temporary and ultimate aims only after beseeching the Three Jewels for their blessings. I should not rely on fortune-tellers or the deities of the Bön religion for support.
>
> To the best of my ability, I must encourage others to go for refuge to the Three Jewels.
>
> I must never forsake the Three Jewels, even to save my life, and I must never even let slip words that express the act of forsaking them.[93] {91}

In addition, I should go for refuge to the Three Jewels with deep sincerity three times during the day and three times during the night, and, while doing so, I should learn the individual spiritual qualities of each of the Three Jewels, learn their individual distinguishing characteristics, accept each of the Three Jewels in the appropriate way,[94] and disavow faith in other religions.

Developing a Practice That Accords with the Doctrine of Karma

You might ask yourself, "While it may be true that going to the Three Jewels for refuge can save me from being reborn in the lower states, how can I achieve rebirth in the world of the higher realms?"[95]

To accomplish this you must develop a practice in which you properly adopt virtuous deeds and abandon evil ones after reflecting on the different forms of white and black deeds and their results, as well as after reflecting on such principles as: (1) the separate and fixed nature[96] of virtuous and evil deeds; (2) the nature in which their results are greatly magnified;[97] (3) the manner in which a deed that has not been done will not yield any fruition;[98] and (4) the manner in which a deed that has been done will not perish.[99] Moreover, since this form of practice cannot be established through the type of reasoning that is based on the strength of observable objects,[100] you must develop a heartfelt conviction[101] about the truthfulness of the Buddha's word, as indicated in the following verse from the *King of Concentrations Sūtra*:

> The sky, along with the moon and the stars, may fall down;
> the earth, together with its cities and mountains, may disappear;
> the realm of space, too, may turn into something else;
> but you will never utter speech that is untrue.[102]

Following that, you should also reflect, in general, that all forms of unvirtuous deeds should be abandoned, and, in particular, that the maturation result[103] of having carried out any of the ten unvirtuous deeds in, a lesser, moderate, or great form, through the related form of the three doors,[104] will bring rebirth in the lower states, as well as that unvirtuous deeds also generate the additional unfavorable consequences of corresponding results,[105] governing results,[106] and the like. These points are indicated in verses such as the following:

> In that case, my proper concern,
> both day and night, should be this alone:
> suffering is certain to arise from wrongdoing;
> how can I free myself from that?[107]
>
> The sage declared that aspiration
> is the root of all virtuous deeds.
> The root of that aspiration, further, is to contemplate
> maturation results continually.[108]

A verse from *The Chapter on Truth*[109] states:

> O King, do not take another being's life;
> Life is most dear to all living beings.
> Thus, one who desires to remain alive for a long time
> should not consider taking a life, even in the depth of
> the mind.

As these lines indicate, you must cultivate extensively an attitude of restraint that stops you from forming the thought of committing such objectionable acts as taking another being's life, and so forth, even within some deep recess of your mind. {92} Make sure that you strive to practice every form of virtuous deed, such as that of refraining from taking a life, and the rest. Je Lama has also taught these points in the following lines:

> There is no assurance that, after dying, you won't be born in the
> unhappy states;[110]
> yet it is certain that the Three Jewels can save you from that peril.
> Therefore, practice going for refuge with great firmness
> and avoid breaking the precepts that relate to this act.

> Moreover, doing so depends on contemplating well black and
> white deeds and their results
> and then properly undertaking to adopt good deeds and abandon
> wrongful ones.

Moreover, regarding this topic, although you can obtain an excellent form of rebirth through observing the morality that abandons the ten unvirtuous deeds, in order to practice the supreme path that leads to the knowledge of all modes,[111] you must achieve a form that possesses the eight attributes of karmic maturation, which include being born into a family of high standing, having an excellent physical appearance, and the rest.[112] Therefore, you must cultivate the recollection[113] and vigilance[114] that will enable you to create the causes for achieving these qualities, which include practicing avoidance of harm toward other sentient beings, giving such things as sources of light and bright clothing to others, overcoming one's pride and showing respect toward others, and the like.

Nevertheless, if you should become tainted by evil deeds and moral transgressions due to such causes as having a strong tendency to develop the mental afflictions, you should not ignore having committed those misdeeds and practice the remedy[115] for the moral transgressions on suitable occasions and carry out the confession[116] of evil deeds in a way that includes all of the four powers. In addition to that, you should strive to avoid becoming tainted by evil deeds and moral transgressions. Je Lama also taught these points in the following lines:

> Since great progress cannot be made until you acquire a form
> that possesses all the attributes for practicing the supreme path,
> you should cultivate all of its causes, without exception.
> As it is crucial to clear away the condition of having your three
> doors tainted
>
> by the stains of evil deeds and transgressions, and especially
> karmic obscurations,[117]
> you should value a practice that continually applies all of the four
> powers.

Through practicing this way, when you develop an uncontrived[118] attitude that turns away from the attachments of this life and seeks to attain a future life endowed with excellence,[119] {93} you have achieved the sign[120] that indicates completion of the training associated with the path of a lesser person.

Training Your Mind in the Path That Is Held in Common with Middling Persons

Although you may obtain an extraordinary form of existence in the higher realms through having abandoned the ten unvirtuous deeds and cultivated the ten virtuous deeds, you still have not escaped the suffering of having to continue to be reborn in samsara. Therefore, you must attain the state of liberation in which suffering in its entirety has been abandoned. You might ask yourself, "Well then, how is it that samsara in its entirety possesses the nature of suffering?" The suffering of the three lower states should be understood as it was explained earlier. Moreover, regarding that instruction, you should reflect on it again here briefly, in order to elicit the related spiritual qualities—which is to say, you should reflect on the specific forms of suffering associated with each of the three lower states. Following that, reflect to yourself in the following manner:

> Since I cannot bear the thought of having to undergo these intense and long-lasting forms of suffering, it is an absolute necessity that I attain the liberation in which all the suffering of samsara—which is partially illustrated by these specific forms of existence—has been abandoned.

The Suffering of Human Beings

We also have not escaped from all the higher and lower forms of suffering that occur in the states of existence other than those of the lower states. For instance, a human being must undergo the suffering of birth, which includes the following events. Following conception, one experiences the suffering of having to reside in the mother's dark and fetid womb that contains an abundance of impure fluids, and the like. When the fetus is born at the end of the thirty-eighth week, it emerges from the womb as it is driven by karmic winds and must undergo extremely great suffering that is like being forced through the opening of an extrusion die or like sesame seeds that are squeezed to produce oil. After its birth, even if the infant is placed on a very soft cushion, it experiences unbearable suffering that feels like falling onto a bed of thorns.

After a human being has become fully grown following its birth, he or she must undergo the suffering of old age, which includes the following experiences. The back gradually becomes bent like a bow; the hair of the head turns white, like the flower of the hummingbird tree;[121] and the forehead becomes filled with wrinkles like the lines on a cutting board. When an old person sits down, it resembles the breaking of a rope that is used to hold up a heavy sack. When an old person stands up, it resembles someone trying to pull a bush out of the ground by its roots. When an old person speaks, the tongue cannot articulate words clearly. {94} When an old person walks, the gait is unsteady. The eyes and ears, and so on, of an old person don't perceive their objects clearly. The body loses its luster and resembles a corpse. The memory fades and one cannot remember things. Because it is difficult to digest food and drink, one cannot consume everything that might be desired. Because an old person's life span is almost exhausted, his or her demise is quickly approaching.

A human being must also undergo the suffering of illness. When there is an imbalance of the elements within the body and an illness is contracted, the skin becomes shriveled, the flesh atrophies, and attractive forms of food and drink must be avoided, out of fear that they will aggravate some form of disease. Against one's wishes, a sick person is forced to take unpleasant-tasting forms of food and drink, as well as medicines. A sick person must also endure harsh forms of medical treatment, such as bloodletting and moxibustion. Fearing that one will not recover, a sick person also experiences countless forms of mental distress.

A human being who becomes afflicted by a severe illness that is certain to cause his or her death comes to realize that he or she is going to die soon. One feels remorse for all the past misdeeds that were committed. There is a sense that one's life has been wasted and is empty of any meaning. One becomes aware of the inevitability of being separated from one's body, wealth, family, friends, retinue, and servants. The mouth becomes dry, the lips curl up, the nose flattens, the eyes sink into their sockets, and the breath becomes labored. Terrified by the thought of having to face the intense suffering of the lower states and with a feeling of great reluctance, one must submit to death itself.

A human also experiences various forms of the suffering of meeting with what is disagreeable. On some occasion, through meeting with a robber or a disagreeable enemy, and so on, all your wealth and means of sustenance may be destroyed, or you may be injured through being struck with such things as a weapon or a club. At another time, you may have to undergo the harm of being subjected to a variety of punishments imposed by the king or some other figure of authority. Or you may experience such unpleasantness as hearing disparaging things being said about you.

You may experience the suffering of being separated unwillingly from such desirable things as the wealth and means of sustenance that you overlooked pleasure, pain, and ill repute to obtain, or you may be separated from persons who are dear to you.

You may experience the suffering of seeking, but not being able to obtain, what is desired. In the case of a householder, an example of this would be for a farmer to work diligently at cultivating a crop, only to fail to obtain the harvest that was desired through such adversities as a drought, frost, {95} or hail. Or he might lose a crop that is being harvested by such things as excessive wind. For a merchant, this would mean such things as losing one's merchandise or failing to make a profit. In the case of those who have gone forth[122] into the homeless state of a Buddhist monk or nun, this would mean the suffering of failing to fulfill any of one's spiritual aims, such as being unable to observe the practice of morality properly.

In Short, the Five Heaps Have the Nature of Suffering

Merely through having taken on these five grasping heaps[123] at birth, they become the basis for undergoing such forms of suffering in this life as illness, old age, and death. They also produce the suffering that is experienced in future lives. They are the vessel in which two types of suffering are experienced—that is, the suffering of suffering[124] and the suffering of change.[125] In addition, because their nature is that of the suffering of conditioned existence,[126] their nature consists of nothing but suffering; not the slightest portion of their nature consists of genuine pleasure.

The Suffering of the Demigods and the Gods

Demigods are unable to escape such extremely severe forms of suffering as having their bodies slashed and split open. As for the gods of the desire realm, they also undergo countless forms of suffering. For instance, when the five signs[127] of their impending death appear, they experience a mental suffering that is much greater than that of the hells. Some lesser gods of the desire realm also experience the suffering of dejection and of being banished from their place of residence.

Among the gods of the higher realms,[128] while those that are ordinary beings[129] do not experience overt forms of the suffering of suffering, those that lie below the third state of meditative absorption are subject to the suffering of change. Those gods that reside in the fourth meditative absorption and in the formless realm have not escaped the suffering of conditioned existence, which is likened to the intense suffering of a boil.[130]

For these reasons, we must employ every means possible to attain the state of liberation in which all these general and specific forms of suffering have been abandoned. Regarding that goal, since it cannot be attained independently of the requisite causes and conditions, we must train ourselves properly in the three trainings that are the means of attaining liberation. Moreover, regarding those three trainings, we must train ourselves in the training of superior morality, as that is the indispensable foundation that enables us to cultivate the other two trainings. Regarding that training in superior morality, the first thing we must do is avoid committing any transgressions by examining ourselves carefully on the basis of recollection[131] and vigilance,[132] {96} in relation to the four causes that give rise to transgressions,[133] such as that of ignorance regarding what constitutes a transgression. If, despite this, a transgression is committed, we must not allow ourselves to remain tainted by it for a long period of time by carrying out, in a proper manner, the two elements of confession and restraint.[134]

In short, it is essential that you identify whichever mental affliction is the strongest within your mental continuum and then strive to meditate on its antidote so that you can avoid becoming tainted by any moral transgressions. I urge you to make certain that whatever activity or task you undertake, you will conduct yourself in such a way that you will not have any reason to be ashamed of yourself for having violated any of the Master's injunctions.

Je Lama has also expressed these points in the following lines:

> Since a true aspiration to achieve liberation cannot be developed
> without diligently contemplating the disadvantages of the truth of
> suffering,
> and the method by which to cut samsara's root cannot be understood
> without contemplating how the truth of origination gives rise to
> samsara,

value cultivating the aversion[135] that seeks deliverance from
samsaric existence,
along with developing the knowledge of what binds us to samsara.

Thus, when you have developed the attitude that turns away from samsara in the same way that a person who is trapped inside a burning house wishes to escape from it, you have achieved the sign[136] that indicates completion of the training associated with the path of a middling person.

Training Your Mind in the Path for Great Persons

Although you may be able to attain the limited goal that is represented by the state of liberation through practicing the path that consists of the three trainings in the manner that was described, this is not sufficient. While you will not have to continue wandering in samsara after achieving the limited goal of liberation, you still have not perfected your own spiritual aim because you have only abandoned a portion of the faults that need to be abandoned and developed a portion of the spiritual qualities that need to be developed. Due to this key point, you also have only achieved an incomplete form of the aims that relate to others. Therefore, it is necessary that you achieve the state of buddhahood in which the two aims have been perfected.

Moreover, buddhahood is not a goal that is pursued solely for one's own sake; it must be pursued for the sake of all sentient beings. This is because, just as you are immersed in the ocean of samsaric suffering, all sentient beings, without exception, are also oppressed by the condition of being tormented by suffering, and because there is not a single sentient being that has not been your father and mother in previous lives. {97} Moreover, without exception, they have done so countless times, and on those occasions they were the benevolent beings who nurtured us in their great kindness. Therefore, we should generate the mind that aspires to attain supreme enlightenment in order to liberate these kind mothers and fathers from their suffering and establish them in the unsurpassed state of nonabiding nirvana.[137]

The Seven-Point Instruction of Cause and Effect

Moreover, regarding the development of that attitude, you must generate enlightenment mind by means of the seven-point instruction of cause and effect. Further, regarding the seven points of cause and effect, they are made up of the following set of seven steps: (1) Through meditating on the topic of recognizing all sentient beings as our mothers, the recollection of all of their kindnesses will arise. (2) Through meditating on that recollection, the wish to repay their kindness will arise. (3) Through meditating on that wish, the attitude that regards all sentient beings in a favorable manner will arise. (4) Through meditating on that attitude, the loving-kindness and compassion that are able to bring forth the superior attitude will arise. (5) Through meditating on those two attitudes, the pure superior attitude will arise. (6) Through meditating on that superior attitude, enlightenment mind will arise. (7) Through having developed that enlightenment mind, the knowledge of all modes[138] will arise.

Developing Equanimity

In addition, before practicing these seven steps, you must meditate on the equanimity that views all sentient beings in an even-minded manner, because, if you fall into the partiality that discriminates among sentient beings through developing feelings of closeness toward those that you like, distance toward those that you dislike, and indifference toward neutral persons,[139] you will not be able to develop the genuine and complete form of the attitude that recognizes all sentient beings as your mothers and, though you may be able to develop a small degree of loving-kindness and compassion, they will be attitudes that are subject to partiality. For these reasons, you must start by meditating on equanimity.

Moreover, the way to carry out this practice is to begin by directing your attention to a number of neutral sentient beings from this life—that is, persons who have not benefited you or harmed you in any way. Then meditate by reflecting in the following manner:

> From their side, these beings are all the same in that they desire happiness and want to avoid suffering. From my side, they are all, without exception, my relatives in that they have been my parents in former lives. Therefore, I should avoid placing them into two groups in such a way that I feel close to some of them and want to benefit them, but I feel distant from others and want to do them harm. Rather, I should develop an attitude that views all of them with the same impartiality.

Following that, also develop the same equanimity toward your relatives and close friends from this life, as well as those sentient beings that have harmed you in this life. In this way, practice continually until you generate the immeasurable equanimity that feels a sense of even-mindedness toward all sentient beings.

Recognizing That All Sentient Beings Are Your Mothers

Once you have developed immeasurable equanimity, meditate in the following manner:

> Since samsara has no beginning, {98} my rebirths also have no beginning and they are, therefore, infinite in number. Based on that key point, I can conclude that there is not a single place in the universe about which it can be said, "I have never been born here," and there is not a single sentient being about which it can be said, "This sentient being has never been my mother." Moreover, each and every sentient being has been my mother innumerable times. Therefore, while I may not recognize all sentient beings as having been my parents due to the continuous fluctuations of birth and death, there is not a single one within the limitless sphere of sentient beings who has not been both my father and my mother many times.

Recalling the Kindness of All Sentient Beings

Each time that a sentient being was my father or my mother, he or she, without exception, acted as a benevolent parent who cared for me with great kindness, just as this life's mother has done. Then reflect in the following manner until your mind is overwhelmed with deep affection toward your mother of this life:

> How has this life's mother cared for me? My current mother cared for me while I was in her womb by doing such things as making a protective covering, out of concern that the heat of the sun might be harmful.[140] After I was born, she placed me on a cushion made of soft cloth. She lifted me up with the tips of her

> ten fingers, gazed at me with loving eyes, greeted me with a joyful smile, nursed me affectionately with milk from her breasts, held me against the warmth of her flesh, gave me food softened in her mouth with her own tongue, wiped away my snot by licking it away with the tongue of her own mouth, and wiped away my filth with her own bare hands.
>
> If I, her child, developed even a minor ailment, this would cause my mother greater suffering than if she were to find herself in a situation where her own life was in danger. Unable to use for her own benefit the wealth and property that she had obtained by ignoring all hardship and personal circumstances, she gave it all to me. In short, to the fullest extent of her abilities, she was an extremely kind parent who protected me from every harm and aided me in so many ways.

After that, direct your attention successively toward (1) your father of this life, as well as other close relatives and friends, followed by (2) neutral persons,[141] and then (3) beings who have harmed you in this life, each time reflecting on how they have all been your mother countless times. Moreover, they have all been your mother countless times in a human form of existence. And, each time that they were your mother, they were a beneficial parent who protected you from every harm and aided you in immeasurable ways, just as this life's mother did.

Cultivating the Wish to Repay the Kindness of All Mother Sentient Beings

Reflect to yourself in the following manner:

> Because the minds of all of these mother sentient beings who have taken care of me in their kindness countless times have been disturbed by the demon of the mental afflictions, they {99} have been helpless to stop themselves from being driven mad. Because their wisdom eyes have been blinded by ignorance, they lack the eyes with which to see the path that can lead them to the temporary goal of an elevated status[142] and the ultimate goal of the highest good.[143] They have no spiritual teacher who is like a guide

for the blind that can lead them to the city of liberation. Distracted uncontrollably by their attachment to wrongful conduct with each passing moment, they stumble unsteadily as they travel along the edge of the terrifying precipice that will cause them to fall into the lower states.

If these suffering, tormented beings do not place their hopes in me, their own child, in whom should they place their hopes? If it is not my responsibility to liberate these mothers from their suffering, whose responsibility is it? There could be no more inferior form of abashment[144] or shame[145] than for me to abandon these kind mothers in order to pursue my own liberation from samsara exclusively.

No matter how much samsaric happiness these mothers may achieve as the result of their own virtuous activities—such as being born as the deity Śakra, and the like—that happiness cannot be enjoyed forever. Therefore, now I shall ignore my own selfish interest and do whatever is necessary to free all sentient beings that are equal to space in their limitless nature from all of samsara's suffering permanently and establish them in the happiness of supreme liberation.[146]

Cultivating Loving-Kindness

Thus, I yearn deeply for all these elderly mothers,[147] who are bereft of genuine happiness, to obtain such happiness. I make the aspirational prayer that they obtain such happiness. I shall do whatever is necessary to bring it about that they obtain such happiness.

Cultivating Compassion and the Superior Attitude

I yearn deeply for all sentient beings, my elderly mothers who are oppressed by suffering, to become free of their suffering. I make the aspirational prayer that they become free of their suffering. Moreover, I, myself, shall bring it about that they become free of their suffering.

Cultivating the Aspirational Form of Enlightenment Mind

Then reflect to yourself in the following manner:

> If I ask myself, "Do you have that ability to free all sentient beings of their suffering and establish them in supreme happiness?" I will realize that, at present, I don't have the ability to free even one sentient being from samsara's suffering and establish him or her in the state of supreme happiness, let alone all sentient beings.
>
> Nevertheless, I have made such a vow to accomplish this aim. Therefore, since I will fall into the lower realms if I were now to ignore that vow and since no one except a buddha has the ability to free all sentient beings from their suffering {100} and establish them in the state of supreme happiness, I must attain the state of true and complete buddhahood, in order to save all sentient beings from every form of suffering and establish them in the state of supreme happiness.

How to Preserve and Maintain the Aspirational Form of Enlightenment Mind

It is not sufficient for you merely to develop this aspiration to attain supreme enlightenment; you must generate this attitude in the form of an enlightenment mind that is not allowed to diminish and become lost in this life, which is accomplished by cultivating these four spiritual exercises: (1) training yourself to reflect on the benefits of enlightenment mind, in order to strengthen your enthusiasm for it; (2) training yourself to generate enlightenment mind six times each day, in order to strengthen the actual mind itself; (3) training yourself not to mentally abandon the sentient beings for the sake of whom you generated enlightenment mind; and (4) training yourself in collecting the two accumulations.

(1) Reflect on the Benefits of Enlightenment Mind

Contemplate in the following manner:

> Just by generating the mind that aspires to attain enlightenment, I become worthy of veneration by all gods and human beings. I

will be superior to even the śrāvaka and pratyekabuddha arhats on the basis of my spiritual lineage. I will not be susceptible to contagious fevers and other illnesses nor to the harm inflicted by evil spirits, and I will be able to carry out successfully and effortlessly the collection of spiritual activities, such as those of pacification, and the like. I will not be born in the lower states and other unfavorable places. Even if I should be born there, I will be able to gain freedom quickly. I will quickly overcome even powerful evil deeds that are extremely terrifying.

Since the sūtras declare that, if the benefits of generating enlightenment mind were to take on the nature of form, they would not fit in the entire realm of space,[148] I must not lose this mind and I must continually develop it to ever higher levels.

(2) Generate Enlightenment Mind Six Times Each Day

Because I would experience a more grave karmic maturation if I were to abandon this enlightenment mind at some interval in the future than if I were to commit one of the "extreme forms of defeat,"[149] I must not relinquish it throughout the time during which I pursue buddhahood, and I should therefore generate enlightenment mind three times during the day and three times during the night by reciting the following verse three times during each of those two periods:

I go for refuge until enlightenment
to the Buddha, dharma, and supreme assembly.
Through this generosity, and so forth, done by me,
may I attain buddhahood in order to benefit the world. {101}

(3) Do Not Mentally Abandon Sentient Beings

Reflect to yourself:

Since I have generated enlightenment mind for the sake of sentient beings, no matter what sort of disagreeable circumstances I may encounter in relation to sentient beings, for my part I must never mentally abandon any sentient being.

(4) Collect Extensive Forms of the Two Accumulations

In order to prevent the enlightenment mind that you have generated this one time from becoming diminished or lost, as well as to develop it to ever higher levels, you must train yourself to collect extensive forms of the two accumulations through such activities as worshiping the Three Jewels.

Training Yourself in the Causes That Will Keep You from Losing Your Enlightenment Mind Even in Future Lives

You must train yourself in the causes that will keep you from losing your enlightenment mind even in future rebirths by abandoning the four black qualities and by cultivating the four white qualities.

Among the four black qualities, the first black quality is for you to lie to a preceptor, a lama, or any spiritual being worthy of being venerated, as a means of deceiving him or her; therefore, you must never commit such an act. As a remedy for that possibility, you must not utter falsehoods to any sentient being, whether to save your life or even only in jest.

The second black quality is to instill regret in the mind of another person who has performed a virtuous deed and who did not regret having done so. You should never commit such an act, and as a remedy for that possibility, if any disciple is a suitable vessel for you to ripen spiritually, you should refrain from establishing him or her in the Hīnayāna and instead establish that disciple in the Mahāyāna.

The third black quality is for you, having been prompted by hatred, to speak disparagingly to a person who has generated a mind that is devoted to the Mahāyāna. You must never commit such an act, and as a remedy for that possibility, you should develop the conception toward any Mahāyāna person that he or she is the Master.[150] And, if an appropriate situation arises, you should praise that person for the good qualities that he or she genuinely possesses. You should also cultivate pure appearances[151] toward all sentient beings.

The fourth black quality is to employ deceitfulness and guile toward sentient beings. You should never act in that manner, and instead you should maintain an honest attitude toward all sentient beings.

Je Lama also declared this about generating enlightenment mind:

Generating enlightenment mind is the mainstay of the
Mahāyāna[152] {102} path.
It is the foundation and support for the extensive bodhisattva
activities.
It is like an alchemic elixir[153] for all forms of the two
accumulations.
It is a treasure of merit that gathers myriad collections of virtue.

Having realized this, the heroic offspring of the victors
regard the jewel-like supreme mind as their most essential practice.

How to Train Yourself in the Six Perfections in Order to Ripen Your Own Mind Continuum

If you ask yourself, "Is it sufficient to train oneself in the aspirational form of enlightenment mind?" The answer is "It is not sufficient." In addition to that, you must accept the vow associated with the active form of enlightenment mind and train yourself in the extensive activities of a victor's offspring. Moreover, in order to train yourself in those activities, you must cultivate the six perfections[154] that serve to ripen your own mental continuum and the four principles for gathering a following[155] that serve to ripen the minds of others.

1. How to Train Yourself in Generosity

Among the six perfections that make up the first group of spiritual practices, the method of training yourself in the perfection of generosity is to teach an unerring form of the true dharma to all those beings who lack the true dharma, motivated by the attitude in which you reflect: "I shall attain buddhahood for the sake of all sentient beings." Generosity also means to protect those beings who are in fear of danger posed by the king or a war, and the like; those beings who are in fear of danger posed by such sentient beings as harmful spirits, wild animals, poisonous snakes, and the like; and those beings who are in fear of danger posed by such inanimate environmental conditions as fire and water, and so on. It also means to provide, unstintingly, food and drink, bedding and seats, medicine to cure ailments, and the like to those who lack such resources. In short, generosity consists of giving yourself, your wealth, and all the virtue that you accumulate during the three times, unstintingly.

Je Lama also described the practice of generosity in the following manner:

> Generosity is the wishing gem that fulfills the hopes of the world,
> the supreme weapon that severs the knot of stinginess,
> the conduct of the victors' offspring that generates dauntless courage,
> and the basis for one's fame being proclaimed in the ten directions.
>
> Having realized this, the wise practice the excellent path
> of giving themselves, their wealth, and their virtue.

2. How to Train Yourself in Morality

The method of training yourself in the perfection of morality is to generate the aspiration that reflects: "I seek to attain buddhahood for the sake of all sentient beings," and then, toward that aim, to reflect for a short while on each of the attitudes of recollection,[156] vigilance,[157] the moral sense of shame,[158] {103} and the moral sense of abashment.[159] In addition, you must cultivate a practice that avoids committing any kind of unvirtuous deeds, even if it places your life at risk to do so. On the basis of such a practice of the morality of restraining yourself from committing misdeeds,[160] you must also cause all six of the perfections to be developed to higher levels.[161] On the basis of these two types of morality, you should also accomplish the aims of sentient beings in a manner that remains free of objectionable acts,[162] thus training yourself in the three types of morality.

Je Lama gave this instruction on morality:

> Morality is the water that cleanses the stains of misconduct,
> the moonlight that dispels the burning heat of the mental afflictions,
> and, in the midst of beings, its majesty is like that of Mount Meru.
> All beings bow to it, without having been threatened with force.
>
> Having realized this, true spiritual beings[163] safeguard the morality
> that they have accepted correctly, as if it were their eyes.

3. How to Train Yourself in Patience

With regard to training yourself in the perfection of patience, you must carry out this practice from the depth of your heart as you cultivate the following three types of patience. The patience that forbears harm inflicted by others[164] is developed by reflecting in the following manner:

> It is improper for me to become angry with another person when he or she causes me some form of harm, because the blame for my being harmed by another person rests with the fact that I inflicted some harm upon him or her in the past. And, since the individual who harmed me was rendered powerless by his or her own hatred, it would be wrong for me to harm him or her in return. Moreover, each moment of hatred that I generate destroys virtue roots derived from three sources[165] that I accumulated over many kalpas. Therefore, I must make certain not to maintain a hateful thought even within some deep recess of my mind.

You must also practice the patience that tolerates suffering,[166] which is developed by generating an attitude that considers the practice of meditating upon the patience that tolerates harm done to you by others as a great benefactor that is like a lama who gives you personal instruction. [The meditation itself consists of contemplating such points as the following:]

> (1) Bad qualities such as pride and arrogance can be dispelled through experiencing the intense pain of being harmed by others. (2) Such disagreeable experiences also promote the development of the wish to gain deliverance from samsara. (3) When I give rise to a sense of aversion toward suffering, I should avoid forming the intention to engage in unvirtuous conduct by reflecting to myself: "Since this suffering was produced by unvirtuous conduct, if that cause is avoided, how could its result arise?" (4) Reflecting on the patience that tolerates harm done to me by others promotes the development of the remaining forms of the six perfections and ultimately leads to the attainment of enlightenment.

The patience gained by reflecting intently on a range of dharma topics[167] is developed through recognizing the virtuous qualities of the Three Jewels {104} and the inconceivably great powers of buddhas and bodhisattvas, and by fostering devotion toward the conduct of the victors' offspring as a means of generating the desire to train oneself in these qualities.

Je Lama described this practice in the following lines:

> Patience is the best of ornaments for those endowed with strength
> and the foremost of austerities against the torment of the mental afflictions.
> As a foe of the snake of hatred, it is the soaring garuḍa,[168]
> and it is the strongest armor against the weapon of harsh speech.
>
> Having realized this, one should cultivate the armor
> of supreme patience in a multitude of different ways.

4. How to Train Yourself in Effort

Laziness[169] arises due to both the indolence[170] associated with all three doors of action and an attachment to inferior forms of pleasure—such as sexual intercourse, the ease associated with overindulgence in sleep, and so on. The latter two qualities, themselves, are caused by the failure to meditate on aversion[171] toward the unsatisfactory nature of samsara. Therefore, you must abandon these causes of laziness and employ all three doors of body, speech, and mind in the exclusive pursuit of virtuous activities.

Moreover, regarding this practice, you must strive to carry out the three types of effort. When you generate a form of effort in which you reflect to yourself, "I will undertake any hardship to remove the suffering of even just a single sentient being, without consideration of any risk to my life or limb," this represents what is called "armor-like effort."[172] When you develop your practice of all six of the perfections to higher levels on the basis of this armor-like effort, this is called "the effort that collects virtuous qualities."[173] Striving to accomplish the aims of sentient beings while remaining free of objectionable acts is called "the effort that acts on behalf of sentient beings."[174]

Je Lama described the practice of effort in the following lines:

> When you don the armor of a resolute effort that is irreversible,
> scriptural and cognitional knowledge will increase like the waxing moon.

All your conduct will become meaningful, and whatever spiritual activities
you undertake will be brought to completion as you intended.

Having realized this, the victors' offspring put forth
extensive forms of effort that dispel all laziness.

5. How to Train Yourself in Meditative Absorption

Motivated by the mind that develops the aspiration to attain supreme enlightenment[175] you must cultivate the various forms of meditative absorption[176] in a manner that remains free of languor[177] and excitation.[178] There are two main types of meditative absorption: (1) mundane {105} meditative absorption;[179] and (2) transcendent meditative absorption.[180] In terms of its constituent elements, meditative absorption is made up of (1) quiescence,[181] (2) insight,[182] and (3) the union of quiescence and insight.[183] When classified according to specific functions, there are three types of meditative absorption: (1) the meditative absorption that enables you to abide in a state of ease during this life; (2) the meditative absorption that attains the higher spiritual qualities of supernatural wisdom, and the rest; and (3) the meditative absorption that accomplishes the aims of sentient beings.[184]

Je Lama described this topic in the following lines:

Meditative absorption is the king that governs the mind—
when fixed on an object, it is as immovable as the lord of mountains;
and, when directed, it will engage every form of virtuous object.
It is a practice that elicits the great ease of physical and mental fitness.[185]

Have realized this, the lords of spiritual practice defeat the enemy
of distraction and continually develop one-pointed concentration.

6. How to Train Yourself in Wisdom

Motivated by the mind that seeks to attain supreme enlightenment, you must cultivate (1) the wisdom that realizes the highest truth—which is to say, the wisdom that destroys the root of samsara by realizing the meaning of reality;[186] (2) the wisdom that realizes conventional objects; and (3) the wisdom that acts on behalf of sentient beings by means of those two just-mentioned forms of wisdom.

Je Lama has described this topic in the following lines:

> Wisdom is known as the eyes that see the most profound reality,
> the path that extirpates the root of samsaric existence,
> the treasure of good qualities extolled in all the discourses,
> and the supreme lamp that dispels the darkness of ignorance.
>
> Having realized this, skillful seekers of liberation
> put forth much effort to generate this path.

How to Train Yourself in the Four Principles for Gathering a Following as a Means of Ripening the Minds of Others

Motivated by the attitude that reflects, "I shall attain buddhahood for the sake of all sentient beings," first pursue the aim of gathering a following of beings by practicing material generosity.[187] Following that, {106} in order to please sentient beings, you should first present a smiling face and then put them at ease by speaking in a polite manner. Then engage in agreeable speech[188] by teaching the dharma through explaining the six perfections, and the like. After that, practice the beneficial conduct[189] that urges your followers to practice the dharma's meaning, in keeping with the way that you taught it to them. Then, also carry out the sameness of purpose[190] in which you also practice the six perfections in the same way that you urged others to do so. In this manner, train yourself in every way in these profound methods that accomplish the welfare of others.

To summarize, since the mistaken apprehension of a real self is the root cause of samsaric existence, you cannot cut this root cause merely by practicing one-pointed meditative absorption and without meditating on the path that directly opposes that erring mode of apprehension. You also cannot overcome the mental afflictions, no matter how much you engage in analysis, using a limited form of wisdom that simply recognizes that entities are not truly existent but is not accompanied by the state of quiescence that remains fixed one-pointedly on its object. This is because in order to attain the state of liberation in which all the mental afflictions have been abandoned, you must ride the horse of quiescence that does not waver from the object of the correct view that has gained complete certainty regarding the unerring mode of being that is the meaning of emptiness and expand your awareness of ultimate reality on the basis of the wisdom that correctly examines the meaning of that reality and eliminates all objects that are clung to by extreme forms of belief with the sharp weapon of the four great logical proofs[191] of the Middle Way school that are free of all eternalistic and nihilistic extremes.

Je Lama has described this in the following lines:

> Since one-pointed meditative absorption alone is not seen
> to have the ability to cut the root of samsara,
> and no matter how much analysis is carried out, the wisdom that lacks
> the path of quiescence cannot overcome the mental afflictions,
>
> the wisdom that has fully ascertained the true mode of being
> should ride the horse of unwavering quiescence
> and destroy all the objects that are clung to by extremist beliefs
> with the sharp weapon of Middle Way reasoning that is free of extremes. {107}
>
> Through extensive forms of wisdom that engage in proper analysis,
> discernment of ultimate reality should be made to increase.

Following that, you should reflect to yourself:

> Not only can the concentration known as quiescence be achieved through fixing the mind one-pointedly and unwaveringly upon a single object, what is truly marvelous is those practitioners who see that—while maintaining a state of one-pointed concentration—an extremely firm type of concentration that remains fixed on the meaning of emptiness can also be developed by properly examining the meaning of ultimate reality with an analytic form of wisdom, and who then strive to achieve this union of quiescence and insight.

Then, make this form of practice the object of an aspirational prayer and strive to establish the propensity for actually pursuing it.

Je Lama described this point in the following lines:

> What need is there to say that concentration can be achieved
> through one-pointed meditation? But those who have seen
> that an unwavering concentration that abides with extreme firmness
> can also be developed through analysis that properly examines
>
> the ultimate mode of being, and who then strive to attain
> the union of the two, quiescence and insight, are truly marvelous.

After having cultivated, in the manner just described, the space-like state of meditative composure that practices the union of quiescence and insight and remains fixed one-pointedly on the emptiness that is free of all extremist forms of conceptual elaborations, you will arise into the post-meditative state. During that period, even though the entities that you perceive do not exist by way of real essential natures, they will appear as if they do; therefore, you must meditate on the form of emptiness that regards these false appearances as resembling magically created illusions. In addition to cultivating these two ways of understanding emptiness, your practice should combine wisdom and means through being motivated by compassion and enlightenment mind. This form of practice constitutes the conduct of the victors' offspring that will take you to the far shore of the ocean of samsara,[192] making it worthy of the highest praise. Because fortunate beings have realized this, their system of spiritual practice is not to be satisfied with an incomplete path that lacks either wisdom or means, and to train themselves instead in the path that combines wisdom and means, we too should seek to strive in this way.

Je Lama said this in the following words:

> The conduct of the victors' offspring that combines wisdom and means
> after meditating on the two forms of emptiness—the space-like state
> of meditative composure {108} and the post-meditative practice that likens appearances to illusions—
> is praised for taking one to the far shore of samsara's ocean.

> After realizing this, the method for fortunate beings
> is not to be satisfied with a path that is incomplete.

Without question, after having trained yourself well in the practices that are common to both the sūtra and tantra paths, you should enter the Mantrayāna system of practice. The method of doing so is first to have your mental continuum ripened by a qualified vajra teacher through conferring a consecration ritual, in the manner that is explained in the tantric scriptures. You must also maintain the vows and commitments that were taken at the time of that ritual. Then, through cultivating both the spiritual practices that possess signs and the spiritual practices that are free of signs, as is taught in the three lower classes of tantra, or, through cultivating successively the two stages[193] of spiritual practice that are taught in Highest Yoga Tantra, you will have trained yourself in the entirety of the path's subject matter, which includes all the key elements of both the Sūtrayāna and Tantrayāna systems, ensuring that the human form of leisure and fortune you have attained in your current life has been rendered meaningful.

Then reflect to yourself:

> By proceeding in this manner, I must ensure that the Victor's precious teaching becomes fixed in my own mental continuum and that of others. This is how Je Lama carried out his own spiritual practice and how he also instructed both me and all of his followers by saying, "You should practice these teachings in the same way."

Following that, visualize that Je Lama is appearing before you and then reflect that he instructs you joyfully by reading the verses to you in a clear and distinct voice. Then recite all of the verses aloud to yourself in such a way that each one causes you to develop a genuine experiential awareness of its meaning in your mind.

Je Lama also described this in the following words:

> Having developed correctly in this way the common paths
> that are required in both the causal[194] and resultant[195] forms
> of the supreme Mahāyāna path, one who relies upon a protector
> that is a skillful guide and, having set out upon the ocean of
> tantra,

practices a complete set of instructions, will have brought
meaning {109}
to the leisure and fortune that he or she has attained.
I, a spiritual practitioner, have carried out such a practice,
and I urge those of you who seek liberation to do the same.

A prayer of dedication: "Through the virtue of having explained,
in words that are easily understood, the complete path
that is pleasing to the victors, in order to instill its meaning
in my own mind and also to benefit other fortunate beings,

may the entire world never be separated
from this excellent path that is completely pure."
I, a spiritual practitioner, have made such a prayer,
and I urge those of you who seek liberation to do the same.

As you reflect to yourself that this instruction has been imparted to you, make a heartfelt dedication prayer by reciting such verses as the following:

Please bless me so that, from today on and in all my future lives,
I will respectfully worship the lotus on which your feet rest,
I will heed your every word, and I will strive only to please you
in all the actions that I perform through my three doors.

Another verse states in part: "By the power of the Victor Tsongkhapa . . . in all my future lives."[196]

Through this unerring instruction that contains the key points
of The Stages of the Path to Enlightenment—the essence
of Lord Dīpaṃkara's and Tsongkhapa's instructions—
may the entire world traverse the path that pleases the victors.[197]

This instruction manual on The Stages of the Path for the Three Types of Person, which is titled *The Nectar That Is Like Highly Refined Gold*, has been arranged in a convenient length in conjunction with Je Lama's *Song of Realization*.[198] I, Sönam Gyatso, a Buddhist monk and dharma teacher who from an early age experienced signs of being blessed by Je Lama, have written it at the great and glorious Drepung Monastery in my private apartment at Tuṣita Palace, which is called Shining Rays of Sunlight, {110} in response to the fervent supplications of Dochö Chöje, an instructor of the Buddha's teaching who has great devotion to and interest in this Lamrim system, and who is an important figure at the monastic seat[199] founded by the Great Omniscient One, Sherap Pelsang. May this treatise have the ability to spread the essence of the Buddha's teaching throughout all the ten directions and for all time. May auspiciousness abound!

8. {111} The Easy Path That Leads to Omniscience

An Instruction Manual on the Stages of the Path to Enlightenment[1]

Losang Chökyi Gyaltsen

{112} I make obeisance at all times to the feet of the holy,[2] exalted, and venerable[3] lama who is inseparable from Munīndra[4] Vajradhara. I beseech you to look after me in your great compassion.

The subject matter presented here is an instruction manual on The Stages of the Path to Enlightenment, a profound method of spiritual practice that leads fortunate beings to the state of buddhahood. It is made up of two parts: (1) the proper manner in which to rely upon a spiritual teacher, which constitutes the foundation of the path, and (2) the stages in which to train your mind, once you have relied upon a spiritual teacher.

I. How to Rely upon a Spiritual Teacher

The first part is made up of two sections: (1) what to do during meditation sessions and (2) what to do during the time between meditation sessions.

A. What to Do during Meditation Sessions

The first section is made up of three divisions: (1) preliminaries, (2) main practice, and (3) conclusion.

1. The Preliminary Practices

With regard to the preliminaries,[5] in a place that is pleasing to the mind, sit on a comfortable seat while maintaining the eight attributes of posture[6] or while adopting whatever position is most suitable for you. Following that, examine your mental continuum carefully and then, while in a mental state of extraordinary virtue,[7] visualize the refuge object as you recite the following words:

> In the space directly before me, atop a tall, wide, and jewel-studded throne held up by eight majestic lions seated upon cushions of a variegated lotus, moon, and sun, is my kind root guru, appearing in the form of the Victor Buddha Śākyamuni. His or her body is the color of refined gold, and a crown protrusion marks the top of the head. He or she has one face and two arms, with the right in the earth-touching gesture and the left in the meditation gesture, holding an alms bowl {113} filled with divine nectar. His or her clear, bright, and radiant body, adorned with all the major and minor marks, is beautifully clothed in the three reddish-yellow monk's robes. He or she is sitting in the middle of an orb of light that radiates from his or her body with his or her legs in the vajra cross-legged position.
>
> Seated all around him or her is an assemblage of wisdom beings made up of direct and lineage lamas, tutelary deities, buddhas, bodhisattvas, heroes,[8] heroines,[9] and dharma protectors. Each of these beings has arranged before him or her an exquisite table on which there lies a radiant dharma scripture containing discourses that he or she has taught.

While you reflect that all the beings in this merit field are gazing at you with a pleased demeanor and as you also develop great faith toward all the beings in this merit field by recalling the virtuous qualities and compassion that are possessed by them, reflect further to yourself in the following manner:

> Throughout beginningless time until the present, I and all mother sentient beings have continually experienced the general suffering of samsara and especially the manifold forms of suffering that occur in the three lower realms. Even so, as long as we remain in our present state of ignorance, it is difficult to see how there could be any end or limit to this suffering in the future. Therefore, on this occasion when I have acquired this extraor-

> dinary human life that is so difficult to find and so meaningful when it is found, if I do not, from this very moment, seek to attain {114} the supreme liberation possessed by my lama who is an enlightened buddha, a state in which all the suffering of samsara has been abandoned, I will once again have to endure all the general forms of samsaric suffering and especially those that occur in the three lower realms.
>
> Because the lamas and the Three Jewels who are seated before me possess the ability to save all beings from this suffering, I must attain the precious state of a true and complete buddha for the sake of all mother sentient beings. In order to do so, I now go for refuge, from the bottom of my heart, to the lamas and the Three Jewels.

After initially carrying out the acts of going for refuge and generating enlightenment mind, as well as cultivating the four immeasurables,[10] perform the special exercise of generating the extraordinary form of enlightenment mind as you recite the following words seven or up to twenty-one times and reflect on their meaning:

> For the sake of all mother sentient beings, I must, swiftly, ever so swiftly, attain the precious state of a true and complete buddha. In order to do so, through the profound path of guru-deity yoga, I shall undertake to meditate on the instructions of the teaching system known as The Stages of the Path to Enlightenment.

Visualizing the Merit Field

Following that, visualize and reflect on the nature of the merit field as you recite the following words:

> In the space directly before me, atop a tall, wide, and jewel-studded throne held up by eight majestic lions upon cushions of a variegated lotus, moon, and sun, is my kind root guru, appearing in the form of the Victor Buddha Śākyamuni. His or her body is the color of refined gold, . . . (etc., up to) He or she is sitting . . . in the vajra cross-legged position.
>
> Seated in the area above and just behind him or her, upon

cushions of a variegated lotus, moon, and sun, is the Victor Vajradhara, surrounded by the lamas of the Lineage of Divinely Inspired Practice.[11] Seated on his or her right is Venerable Maitreya, surrounded by the lamas of the Lineage of Extensive Conduct.[12] Seated on his or her left is Venerable Mañjughoṣa, surrounded by the lamas of the Lineage of the Profound View.[13] Seated in front of him or her is my kind root lama, surrounded by the lamas with whom I have a direct spiritual relationship. {115}

Seated all around them is an assemblage of wisdom beings made up of tutelary deities, buddhas, bodhisattvas, heroes,[14] heroines,[15] and dharma protectors. Each of these beings has arranged before him or her an exquisite table on which there lies a radiant dharma scripture containing discourses that he or she has taught. These divine beings are also radiating out into the ten directions an inconceivably great array of emanations appearing in whatever form is appropriate to establish sentient beings in a state of spiritual self-discipline.

The principal figure and all of his or her retinue are emitting five-colored light rays from white *oṃ* syllables in the crowns of their heads, red *āḥ* syllables in their throats, blue *hūṃ* syllables in their hearts, yellow *svā* syllables in their navels, and green *hā* syllables in their secret regions. Lama Munīndra in particular emanates light rays from the *hūṃ* syllable in his or her heart into the ten directions, inviting countless sets of wisdom beings from the innate realms[16] that are identical in form to the entire merit field assemblage that is being visualized. Having dissolved into each assemblage being[17] within the divine assemblage, they all take on the nature of an all-encompassing object of refuge.[18]

The Seven-Limb Devotional Practice, together with a Mandala Offering, Followed by Supplication of the Lamas

Having developed this conviction regarding the presence of the merit field, carry out the devotional exercise known as the seven-limb practice, together with a mandala offering, followed by the act of imbuing your mental continuum with a strong attitude of supplication according to instruction.

After that, dissolve the merit field as you recite the following words:

> Light rays that emanate from the *hūṃ* syllable in Lama Munīndra's heart strike all the myriad peaceful and wrathful divine beings that are seated all around him or her, causing them to turn into light and dissolve into Lama Munīndra. Lama Munīndra then also dissolves into my root lama who is seated on the crown of my head. While retaining his or her essence, my kind root lama then takes on the outer form of the Victor Buddha Śākyamuni, who is seated on the crown of my head atop a lion throne upon lotus, sun, and moon cushions, . . . (etc., up to) He or she is sitting . . . in the vajra cross-legged position.

Following that visualization, direct your attention to your root lama and offer him or her an abbreviated form of the seven-limb devotional practice, together with a mandala offering. Then, as you recite the following verses of supplication, reflect that all mother sentient beings who are seated around you recite them with you, in one voice {116}:

> I make supplication to you, Munīndra Vajradhara,
> extraordinary guru-deity whose nature consists of the four bodies.
>
> I make supplication to you, Munīndra Vajradhara,
> guru-deity whose nature consists of the dharma body free of
> obscurations.
>
> I make supplication to you, Munīndra Vajradhara,
> guru-deity whose nature consists of the supremely blissful
> enjoyment body.
>
> I make supplication to you, Munīndra Vajradhara,
> guru-deity whose nature consists of multifarious emanation
> bodies.
>
> I make supplication to you, Munīndra Vajradhara,
> extraordinary guru-deity who embodies all the lamas.
>
> I make supplication to you, Munīndra Vajradhara,
> extraordinary guru-deity who embodies all the tutelary deities.

> I make supplication to you, Munīndra Vajradhara,
> extraordinary guru-deity who embodies all the buddhas.
>
> I make supplication to you, Munīndra Vajradhara,
> extraordinary guru-deity who embodies all of the dharma.
>
> I make supplication to you, Munīndra Vajradhara,
> extraordinary guru-deity who embodies all of the sangha.
>
> I make supplication to you, Munīndra Vajradhara,
> extraordinary guru-deity who embodies all the ḍākas and ḍākinīs.
>
> I make supplication to you, Munīndra Vajradhara,
> extraordinary guru-deity who embodies all the dharma protectors.

In particular, recite this supplication:

> I make supplication to you, Munīndra Vajradhara,
> extraordinary guru-deity who embodies the entire object of refuge.

Then recite this supplication:

> The manifold and intense forms of suffering that I and all mother sentient beings have experienced throughout the infinitely long time that we have been taking birth in samsara is due to our having failed to rely upon a spiritual teacher properly, both in thought and action. Therefore, O divine Root Lama, please bless me and all mother sentient beings so that we may now gain the ability to rely upon a spiritual teacher properly, both in thought and action.

Following that, visualize and reflect that, through having made this supplication, a stream of fivefold nectar, together with light rays, flows down from the body of your root lama who is seated on the crown of your head. Through entering the bodies and minds of you and all other sentient beings surrounding you, the nectar and light rays remove all the evil deeds and obscurations that you have accumulated since beginningless time, and especially the evil deeds and obscurations, together with the propensity to contract illnesses and be harmed by malevolent spirits, that hinder you from being able to rely upon a spiritual teacher properly, both in thought and action. {117} Having done so, your ordinary bodies are transformed into bodies that have the nature of transparent and radiant light. In addition, all the virtuous qualities, such as those associated with longevity and merit, etc., increase and become strengthened, both in your mental continuum and in the mental continua of all the other mother sentient beings that are surrounding you. In particular, both you and all sentient beings also gain the special realization that enables you to rely upon a spiritual teacher properly, both in thought and action.

2. The Main Practice

The main practice is made up of two sections: (1) how to rely upon a spiritual teacher in thought and (2) how to rely upon a spiritual teacher in action.

a. How to Rely upon a Spiritual Teacher in Thought

This first section is also made up of two parts: (1) cultivating the "root" quality of faith and (2) generating reverence toward your spiritual teachers through recalling their kindness.

i. Cultivating the Root Quality of Faith

Visualize that Lama Munīndra emanates all the lamas with whom you have a direct spiritual relationship from his or her heart and that they become seated in the space before you. Then, as you direct your attention to them, reflect in the following manner:

> These individuals who are my spiritual teachers are all actual buddhas because, just as the true and complete buddhas have declared in the precious tantra scriptures that Vajradhara reveals himself in the physical form of ordinary spiritual teachers during a degenerate age[19] and accomplishes the aims of sentient beings, my spiritual teachers only give the appearance of having the

> physical bodies of separate beings; in fact they are all Vajradhara appearing in the physical form of spiritual teachers in order to benefit those of us who do not have the fortune to directly perceive buddhas in their actual form. Therefore, O divine Root Lama, I beseech you to bless me and all sentient beings so that we recognize each of these spiritual teachers as being, in reality, Munīndra Vajradhara.

Then visualize and reflect that, through having made this supplication, a stream of fivefold nectar and light rays flows down from the body of your divine root lama seated on the crown of your head, entering the bodies and minds of you and all the other sentient beings surrounding you and removing all the various general and special obstacles. In addition, visualize that nectar and light rays also cause the various special forms of realization to arise in your mental continuum and in that of all the other sentient beings surrounding you. {118}

You may have the following thought: "Well, if a buddha is one who has terminated all faults and who possesses all spiritual qualities, then since my spiritual teachers possess this or that particular fault that is motivated by some form of the three poisons, it cannot be true that they are buddhas." In that case, you should reflect in the following manner:

> This mistaken belief is due to the impurity of my perceptions. For example, in the past, Sujyotiṣa,[20] due to the impurity of his perceptions, saw all the activities of the Master Buddha Śākyamuni, without exception, as false. Likewise, Asaṅga saw the exalted and venerable Maitreya as a female dog and Maitrīpa saw the lord of spiritual practice Śavaripa as someone who carried out such improper activities as killing pigs, and the like. In the same way, these individuals who are my spiritual teachers do not, in fact, possess the faults that I perceive them as having; these erring judgments are due to the impurity of my perceptions. Therefore, O divine Root Lama, I beseech you to bless me and all sentient beings so that we never develop, in our respective mental continua, any fault-finding thoughts toward these spiritual teachers for even an instant, and so that we develop, with ease, the great faith that sees whatever they do as virtuous.

Then visualize and reflect that, through having made this supplication, a stream of fivefold nectar and light rays flows down from the body of your divine root lama seated on the crown of your head, entering the bodies and minds of you and all other sentient beings surrounding you, and removing all the various general and special obstacles. In addition, visualize that nectar and light rays also cause the various special forms of realization to arise in your mental continuum and in those of all the other sentient beings surrounding you.

ii. Generating Reverence toward Your Spiritual Teachers through Recalling Their Kindness

After directing your attention to the spiritual teachers whom you are visualizing as seated before you, reflect in the following manner:

> These spiritual teachers have been exceedingly kind to me. The understanding that I have gained of the profound path that bestows, with ease, the supreme liberation in which all the suffering of samsara and the lower states has been abandoned—which is to say, the precious state of a true and complete buddha, {119}—is due to the kindness of these spiritual teachers. Therefore, O divine Root Lama, I beseech you to bless me and all the mother sentient beings surrounding me so that we develop, with ease, in our respective mental continua, the great reverence that recalls the kindness of these spiritual teachers.

Then visualize and reflect that through having made this supplication, a stream of fivefold nectar and light rays flows down from the body of your divine root lama seated on the crown of your head, entering the bodies and minds of you and all other sentient beings surrounding you, and removing all the various general and special obstacles. In addition, visualize that nectar and light rays also cause the various special forms of realization to arise in your mental continuum and in those of all the other sentient beings surrounding you.

b. How to Rely upon a Spiritual Teacher in Action

While visualizing your spiritual teachers who are seated before you, reflect in the following manner:

> For the benefit of these spiritual teachers who are, in fact, buddhas, I will sacrifice my body, life, and wealth, and so on, without hesitation. In particular, I shall strive to please them by making an offering to them of my spiritual practice in which I follow their directions exactly. O divine Root Lama, I beseech you to bless me and all the mother sentient beings to be able to fulfill this aim.

Then visualize and reflect that, through having made this supplication, a stream of fivefold nectar and light rays flows down from the body of your divine root lama seated on the crown of your head entering the bodies and minds of you and all other sentient beings surrounding you and removing all the various general and special obstacles. In addition, visualize that nectar and light rays also cause the various special forms of realization to arise in your mental continuum and in those of all the other sentient beings surrounding you.

3. What to Do at the Conclusion of the Meditation Session

While visualizing your divine root lama seated on the crown of your head, make supplication to him or her.[21] Then recite Buddha Śākyamuni's name mantra, and finally, with strong aspiration, dedicate the virtue roots that you have derived from this spiritual practice to the attainment of your own and all other sentient beings' temporary and ultimate goals.[22]

B. What to Do during the Time between Meditation Sessions

In addition, during the time between meditation sessions, you should read scripture texts and commentaries that explain the proper way to rely upon a spiritual teacher. Also, through maintaining recollection[23] and vigilance,[24] {120} you should restrain the doors of your faculties, exercise moderation with the amount of food that you eat, remain alert[25] as you strive to cultivate your spiritual practice, observe the instructions regarding what to do when you go to sleep, and strive to carry out the spiritual practices that relate to bathing and eating food.

II. Explanations of the Stages in Which to Train Your Mind

This topic is made up of two sections: (1) an admonition to derive value from a life possessing leisure and fortune and (2) the manner in which to derive value from your life.

A. An Admonition to Derive Value from a Life Possessing Leisure and Fortune

This topic is made up of two parts: (1) what to do during meditation sessions and (2) what to do during the time between meditation sessions.

1. What to Do during Meditation Sessions

This topic has three divisions: (1) preliminaries, (2) main practice, and (3) conclusion.

a. Preliminaries

Everything up to the lines, "I make supplication to you, Munīndra Vajradhara, / extraordinary guru-deity who embodies the entire object of refuge" is to be recited in the same manner that was described earlier. Following that, reflect in the following manner:

> The manifold and intense forms of suffering that I and all mother sentient beings have experienced throughout the infinitely long time that we have been taking birth in samsara is due to our having failed to develop in our mental continua the extraordinary realizations that relate to the great value of a human life possessing leisure and fortune and the difficulty of obtaining those qualities. Therefore, O divine Root Lama, please bless me and all mother sentient beings so that we may now gain the ability to develop in our mental continua the extraordinary realizations that relate to the great value of a human life possessing leisure and fortune, and the difficult of obtaining these qualities.

Then visualize and reflect that through having made this supplication, a stream of fivefold nectar and light rays flows down from the body of your root lama who is seated on the crown of your head, entering the bodies and minds of you and all other sentient beings surrounding you and removing all the evil deeds and obscurations that you have accumulated since beginningless time, and especially the evil deeds and obscurations that hinder you from being able to develop the extraordinary realizations that relate to the great value of a human life possessing leisure and fortune, and the difficulty of obtaining those qualities. Having done so, your ordinary bodies are transformed into bodies that have the nature of transparent and radiant light. In addition, all the virtuous qualities, such as those associated with longevity and merit, and so on, increase and become strengthened, both in your mental continuum and in the mental continua of all the other mother sentient beings surrounding you. In particular, both you and all sentient beings also develop the special realizations that relate to the great value of a human life possessing leisure and fortune and the difficulty of obtaining these qualities.

b. The Main Practice

This section is made up of two parts: (1) reflecting on the great value of a human life possessing leisure and fortune and (2) reflecting on the difficulty of obtaining these qualities.

i. Reflecting on the Great Value of Leisure and Fortune

While visualizing your divine root lama seated on the crown of your head, {121} reflect in the following manner:

> The term "leisure"[26] means to have the opportunity to practice the true dharma, and the term "fortune"[27] means to possess the inner and outer factors that are necessary to practice the dharma. In short, this human form we have obtained that possesses the qualities of leisure and fortune is extremely valuable because on the basis of it we are capable of accomplishing the generosity, morality, patience, and so on that are the causes for gaining an excellent form of existence that is endowed with abundance of wealth, which is referred to as an elevated status[28] and because, in particular, with this form of existence we are capable of generat-

> ing all three of the Buddhist vows, and we are capable of achieving, within the span of a short lifetime, in a degenerate age, and with ease, the state of a buddha. Therefore, I must derive value from, and not allow to go to waste, this form of existence that is currently endowed with all the qualities of leisure and fortune and that is so difficult to obtain and so meaningful if it should be obtained. O divine Root Lama, please bless me and all other sentient beings with the ability to do so.

Then visualize and reflect that through having made this supplication, a stream of fivefold nectar and light rays flows down from the body of your divine root lama seated on the crown of your head, entering the bodies and minds of you and all other sentient beings surrounding you and removing all your and their various general and special obstacles. In addition, visualize that nectar and light rays also cause the various special forms of realization to arise both in your mental continuum and that of all the other sentient beings surrounding you.

ii. Reflecting on the Difficulty of Obtaining the Qualities of Leisure and Fortune

While visualizing your divine root lama seated on the crown of your head, reflect in the following manner:

> Not only does this form of leisure and fortune that I have obtained possess great value, it is also a state that is extremely difficult to obtain. This is true for the following reasons: The majority of human beings, as well as those beings of the other migratory states,[29] engage in such misconduct as the ten unvirtuous deeds, and so on, to a great extent, and these acts become obstacles to the attainment of a human form possessing leisure and fortune. More particularly, if to obtain an excellent human form possessing all the qualities of leisure and fortune, one must establish a pure form of morality as the foundation for accomplishing this result, and if this foundation must further be accompanied by the factors of generosity, and so on, and if all of these conditions must be joined together with untainted aspirational prayers, it is evident that only a very few individuals are able to create all of

> these causes. It is also evident that compared to rebirth in one of the unhappy migratory states[30] as an animal, and the like, it is almost impossible even just to attain rebirth in any form of a happy migratory state.[31] Moreover, compared to being reborn in other forms of existence among the happy migratory states, it is as rare as a star that is visible during the daytime[32] {122} for someone to obtain a human form of existence with all the qualities of leisure and fortune such as this one that I currently possess. Therefore, I must derive something of value from this human form of existence that I have obtained this one time, a form that is so difficult to find and so meaningful if it is found, and I must not allow it to go to waste.
>
> Moreover, the proper method of deriving value from this special human form is to resort to my lama-buddha without allowing myself ever to become separated from him or her, and by putting into practice the spiritual essence that is the instruction of the supreme vehicle that he or she teaches me, to attain, with relative ease, the status of a buddha within just one lifetime. O divine Root Lama, please bless me and all other sentient beings with the ability to do so.

Then visualize and reflect that, through having made this supplication, a stream of fivefold nectar and light rays flows down from the body of your divine root lama seated on the crown of your head, entering the bodies and minds of you and all other sentient beings surrounding you, and removing all the various general and special obstacles. In addition, visualize that nectar and light rays also cause the various special forms of realization to arise both in your mental continuum and that of all the other sentient beings surrounding you.

c. What to Do at the Conclusion of the Meditation Session

The concluding activities are the same as the ones that were explained earlier.

2. What to Do during the Time between Meditation Sessions

During the time between meditation sessions, you should read scripture texts and commentaries that explain the teachings that relate to the topic of leisure and fortune, as well as carry out the other general practices that were described earlier.

B. The Manner in Which to Derive Value from Your Life

This portion of the instruction is made up of three parts: (1) training your mind in the stages of the path that are held in common with lesser persons, (2) training your mind in the stages of the path that are held in common with middling persons, and (3) training your mind in the stages of the path that pertain to great persons.

1. Training Your Mind in the Stages of the Path That Are Held in Common with Lesser Persons

This topic is made up of two parts: (1) what to do during meditation sessions and (2) what to do during the time between meditation sessions.

a. What to Do during Meditation Sessions

This topic has three divisions: (1) preliminaries, (2) main practice, and (3) conclusion.

i. Preliminaries

Everything up to the lines, "I make supplication to you, Munīndra Vajradhara, / extraordinary guru-deity who embodies the entire object of refuge" is to be recited in the same manner that was described earlier. Following that, reflect in the following manner:

> The manifold and intense forms of suffering that I and all mother sentient beings have experienced throughout the infinitely long time that we have been taking birth in samsara is due to our having failed to reflect on impermanence in the form of death, as well as our having failed to go to the Three Jewels for refuge {123} from the depth of our hearts, after becoming frightened by the suffering of the lower states, and also due to our having failed to carry a proper form of practice in relation to the white and black forms of karma and their results, after having developed

> the faith that believes in the doctrine of karma and its results. Therefore, O divine Root Lama, please bless me and all mother sentient beings so that we may now develop in our mental continua the ability to recall impermanence in the form of death, to go to the Three Jewels for refuge from the depth of our hearts, after becoming frightened by the suffering of the lower states, and to properly abandon evil deeds and cultivate virtuous ones, after having developed the faith that believes in the doctrine of karma and its results.

Then visualize and reflect that through having made this supplication, a stream of fivefold nectar and light rays flows down from the body of your divine root lama seated on the crown of your head, entering the bodies and minds of you and all other sentient beings surrounding you, and removing all the evil deeds and obscurations that you have accumulated since beginningless time and, in particular, removing the obstacles to developing the various special forms of realization both in your mental continuum and in the mental continua of all the other sentient beings surrounding you. Having done so, your ordinary bodies are transformed into bodies having the nature of transparent and radiant light. In addition, all the virtuous qualities, such as those associated with longevity and merit, and so on, increase and become strengthened, and all the various special realizations arise both in your mental continuum and in the mental continua of all the other mother sentient beings that are surrounding you.

ii. The Main Practice

This section is made up of four parts: (1) reflecting on impermanence in the form of death, (2) reflecting on the suffering of the lower states, (3) training yourself in the practice of going to the Three Jewels for refuge, and (4) generating the faith that believes in the doctrine of karma and its results.

I) Reflecting on Impermanence in the Form of Death

While visualizing your divine root lama seated on the crown of your head, reflect in the following manner:

> This human form possessing leisure and fortune, which is so difficult to obtain and so meaningful if it should be found, is one that perishes quickly. My death is certain in the sense that, first, the Lord of Death is certain to appear, and he cannot be turned back by resorting to any inner or outer factors; second, my life span cannot be extended, and it is being diminished continuously; and third, there is not much time to practice dharma, even during the time that I remain alive.
>
> Not only is it true that I will die, it is also the case that the time of my death is not certain because, first, the life spans of human beings in the Rose Apple continent[33] is not fixed;[34] second, there are a great many factors {124} that can cause one's death but only a few that sustain life; and third, my body is as fragile as a water bubble.
>
> At the time of my death, nothing can benefit me except for the dharma. No matter how great the affection of my family and friends that surround me on my deathbed, I cannot take a single one of them with me. No matter how large the heap of appealing wealth that I may possess, I cannot take even one atom of it with me. If I must be separated even from the body of flesh and bones that I was born with, what good is it for me to be attached to any form of prosperity that relates to this life?
>
> The enemy of death is certain to come, yet there is no certainty of the time that he will arrive. Because it is possible that I might die this very day, I must prepare for my death. Moreover, preparing for death means to forgo attachment for all the good fortune of this life and to practice a pure form of dharma starting right now. O divine Root Lama, please bless me and all other sentient beings with the ability to do so.

Then visualize and reflect that, through having made this supplication, fivefold nectar and light rays flow down from the body of your divine root lama seated on the crown of your head, entering the bodies and minds of you and all other sentient beings surrounding you and removing all the various general and special obstacles. In addition, visualize that nectar and light rays also cause the various special forms of realization to arise both in your mental continuum and in that of all the other sentient beings surrounding you.

II) Reflecting on the Suffering of the Lower States

While visualizing your divine root lama seated on the crown of your head, reflect in the following manner:

> This human form possessing all the qualities of leisure and fortune, which is so difficult to obtain and so meaningful if it should be found, is one that perishes quickly. However, following its destruction, I do not simply disappear and, therefore, must take on another rebirth. Moreover, the place of my rebirth can only be within the unhappy migratory states or the happy migratory states. If I should be reborn in the unhappy migratory states, I will have to undergo inconceivably great forms of suffering. Hell beings experience the suffering of the hot hells, the cold hells, and other related forms of great suffering; tormented spirits experience the suffering of hunger, thirst, and other related forms of great suffering; and animals experience the suffering of stupidity, ignorance, and the suffering of eating one another.
>
> Since I could not bear to undergo this suffering of the unhappy migratory states {125} during the time that I have obtained this human form that possesses all the qualities of leisure and fortune, a form that is so difficult to obtain and so meaningful if it should be obtained, I must attain the state of my lama-buddha in which all the suffering of the unhappy migratory states has been abandoned. O divine Root Lama, please bless me and all other sentient beings with the ability to do so.

Then visualize and reflect that through having made this supplication, a stream of fivefold nectar and light rays flows down from the body of your divine root lama seated on the crown of your head, entering the bodies and minds of you and all other sentient beings surrounding you and removing all the various general and special obstacles. In addition, visualize that nectar and light rays also cause the various special forms of realization to arise both in your mental continuum and that of all the other sentient beings surrounding you.

III) Training Yourself in the Practice of Going to the Three Jewels for Refuge

Visualize that your divine root lama seated on the crown of your head emanates from his or her body an assembly made up of lamas, tutelary deities, and the rest of the Three Jewels, including heroes, heroines, and dharma protectors that fills the space before you. Then visualize well this entire refuge object that is seated all around your divine root lama on the crown of your head. Following that, while recalling the good qualities of body, speech, mind, virtuous attributes, and spiritual activities that are possessed by these beings, and while you possess the aspiration in which you reflect, "I beseech you to save me and all mother sentient beings right now from the perils of samsara and the unhappy migratory states," perform the act of going for refuge a hundred, a thousand, ten thousand, a hundred thousand times, and so on by reciting the formula: "I go to the lamas, tutelary deities, and the Three Jewels for refuge." In addition, train yourself properly in the precepts[35] that relate to the practice of going for refuge with the knowledge of the temporary and ultimate benefits that are gained through this practice.

IV) Generating the Faith That Believes in the Doctrine of Karma and Its Results

While visualizing your divine root lama seated on the crown of your head, reflect in the following manner:

> The Victor's discourses declare the following: Through carrying out a virtuous cause, only a pleasant result will arise; a painful one will not arise. Through carrying out an unvirtuous cause, only a painful result will arise; a pleasant one will not arise.[36] Even though only a minor virtuous or unvirtuous cause {126} is committed, as long as they do not meet with an obstruction, a very great result will arise.[37] If a virtuous or an unvirtuous cause has not been committed, no pleasant or painful results will be experienced;[38] and as long as a virtuous or an unvirtuous cause that has been committed does not meet with an obstruction, a deed that has been performed will not perish; therefore, it will definitely give rise to a pleasant or unpleasant result as appropriate.[39] Moreover, karma is identified as being especially powerful

> on the basis of a particular field,[40] attitude, object, or agent. Having generated the faith that believes[41] in these principles, strive to develop a form of practice that carries out even minor forms of virtuous deeds, such as the ten virtuous karmic paths, and avoids having one's three doors become tainted by even minor forms of unvirtuous deeds, such as the ten unvirtuous karmic paths. O divine Root Lama, please bless me and all other sentient beings with the ability to do so.

Then visualize and reflect that through having made this supplication, a stream of fivefold nectar and light rays flows down from the body of your divine root lama seated on the crown of your head, entering the bodies and minds of you and all other sentient beings surrounding you and removing all the various general and special obstacles. In addition, visualize that nectar and light rays also cause the various special forms of realization to arise both in your mental continuum and that of all the other sentient beings surrounding you.

If, despite striving to develop such a practice, you should become tainted by unvirtuous deeds because your spiritual antidotes are too weak or your mental afflictions are too strong, then strive to cultivate the four powers[42] that relate to confession and restraint.

iii. What to Do at the Conclusion of the Meditation Session

The concluding activities are the same as the ones that were explained earlier.

b. What to Do during the Time between Meditation Sessions

During the time between meditation sessions, you should read scripture texts and commentaries that explain the teachings that are held in common with lesser persons, as well as carry out the other general practices that were described earlier. This completes the explanations on training your mind in the stages of the path that are held in common with lesser persons.

2. Training Your Mind in the Stages of the Path That Are Held in Common with Middling Persons

This topic is made up of two parts: (1) generating the mind that seeks to attain liberation and (2) establishing the nature of the path that leads to liberation.

a. Generating the Mind That Seeks to Attain Liberation

This section is made up of two parts: (1) what to do during meditation sessions and (2) what to do during the time between meditation sessions.

i. What to Do during Meditation Sessions

This topic has three divisions: (1) preliminaries, (2) main practice, and (3) conclusion.

I) Preliminaries

{127} Everything up to the lines "I make supplication to you, Munīndra Vajradhara, / extraordinary guru-deity who embodies the entire object of refuge" is to be recited in the same manner that was described earlier. Following that, reflect in the following manner:

> The manifold and intense forms of suffering that I and all mother sentient beings have experienced throughout the infinitely long time that we have been taking birth in samsara is due to our having failed to realize that the entirety of samsara consists of the nature of suffering and our having failed to generate an intense form of the mind that wishes to be freed from that suffering. Therefore, O divine Root Lama, please bless me and all mother sentient beings so that we may now develop in our mental continua the realization that the entirety of samsara consists of the nature of suffering and also generate an intense form of the mind that wishes to be freed from that suffering.

Then visualize and reflect that through having made this supplication, a stream of fivefold nectar and light rays flows down from the body of your divine root lama seated on the crown of your head, entering the bodies and minds of you and all other sentient beings surrounding you and removing all the evil deeds and obscurations that you have accumulated since beginningless time and, in particular, removing the obstacles to generating an intense form of the mind that wishes to attain liberation. Having done so, your ordinary bodies are transformed into bodies having the nature of transparent and radiant light. In addition, all the virtuous qualities, such as those associated with longevity and merit, and so on, increase and become strengthened, and, in particular, the realization that the entirety of samsara consists of the nature of suffering and an intense form of the mind that seeks to attain liberation arise, both in your mental continuum and in that of all the other mother sentient beings that are surrounding you.

II) The Main Practice

This section is made up of two parts: (1) reflecting on samsara's general forms of suffering and (2) reflecting on samsara's specific forms of suffering.

A) Reflecting on Samsara's General Forms of Suffering

While visualizing your divine root lama seated on the crown of your head, reflect in the following manner:

> Although I can attain the status of rebirth in the happy migratory states that transcends the suffering of the unhappy migratory states through training myself properly in the morality that abandons the ten unvirtuous deeds, unless I attain the liberation in which all of samsara's suffering has been abandoned from its roots, there is no time in which I experience genuine happiness for even an instant.
>
> For example, suppose a criminal {128} has been sentenced to die in a month, and each day until that time comes, he is also forced to experience severe forms of suffering, such as the punishments of having his body marked with lines of hot sealing wax and being beaten with clubs. Even if someone were to intervene on his behalf by appealing to a person of influence, and so on, and he did not have to experience the suffering of being beaten

with a club, he would not feel the slightest bit happy because with each passing day he would still be coming ever closer to undergoing the suffering of being executed. Similarly, as long as I have not attained the liberation in which all of samsara's suffering has been abandoned from its roots, no matter what form of happy migratory state I may attain, once the projecting force of the good karma that I accomplished previously is exhausted, I will fall into the three lower realms and have to experience many different kinds of intense suffering for a very long period of time.

Moreover, once I have taken birth in samsara by the power of karma and the mental afflictions, I will not be able to avoid being in a state that consists of the nature of suffering. Because an enemy can become a friend and a friend can also become an enemy, the status of being a person who benefits me or one who harms me is not reliable.[43] Since I have undergone the reentry of conception[44] again and again throughout beginningless time, the starting point of my rebirths cannot be perceived. Because no matter how much of samsara's prosperity I may obtain, in the end it must be abandoned, the attainment of prosperity is unreliable. Since I must go to the other world[45] alone, without any companions, companions are unreliable. Therefore, on this occasion when I have acquired an extraordinary human life that is so difficult to find and so meaningful when it is found, I must attain the precious status of my lama-buddha, a state in which all the suffering of samsara has been abandoned. O divine Root Lama, please bless me and all other sentient beings with the ability to do so.

Then visualize and reflect that, through having made this supplication, a stream of fivefold nectar and light rays flows down from the body of your divine root lama seated on the crown of your head, {129} entering the bodies and minds of you and all other sentient beings surrounding you and removing all the various general and special obstacles. In addition, visualize that nectar and light rays also cause the various special forms of realization to arise both in your mental continuum and in the mental continua of all the other sentient beings surrounding you.

B) Reflecting on Samsara's Specific Forms of Suffering

While visualizing your divine root lama seated on the crown of your head, reflect in the following manner:

> Once the grasping heaps[46] have been acquired, I will not be able to avoid being in a state that consists of the nature of suffering. There is no need to say that this is so for rebirth in the three lower realms. As for the happy migratory states, through having acquired the grasping heaps of a human being, I must experience the suffering of hunger and thirst, as well as those of having to seek a livelihood;[47] being separated from family relations and those things that are held dear; having to meet with enemies and those things that are disagreeable; seeking but failing to obtain those objects that are desired; having undesirable objects befall me; and birth, old age, sickness, and death, and so on.
>
> Through having acquired the grasping heaps of a demigod, I must experience the suffering that is the mental torment of the envy that cannot endure the prosperity of the gods. On the basis of that mental suffering, I will also have to experience the physical suffering that befalls me.[48]
>
> Through having acquired the grasping heaps of a desire-realm god, I must experience the suffering of having my limbs severed, my body slashed, or even being killed, and so on, while doing battle with the demigods. In addition, I will experience the suffering of being stricken by the five signs[49] of having to unwillingly undergo a natural death, and realizing that, after being separated from the prosperity of the gods, I will have to experience the suffering of being reborn in the lower states.
>
> Even if I were to acquire the grasping heaps of a being reborn in either of the two higher realms,[50] because I would not have the freedom to continue living indefinitely, once the projecting force of the good karma that I accomplished previously is exhausted, I will become subject to the immeasurably great suffering that arises from falling into the lower realms.
>
> In short, these grasping heaps that I currently possess are the basis for experiencing the suffering of birth, old age, sickness,

> and death, and so on, in this life. They also produce the suffering of suffering and the suffering of change both in this life and in my future lives. In addition, from the moment that the grasping heaps are acquired, {130} they take on the nature of heaps that are conditioned[51] in the sense of being under the control of karma and the mental afflictions. Therefore, I must attain the status of my lama-buddha, who has liberated himself or herself from the samsara whose nature consists of the grasping heaps. O divine Root Lama, please bless me and all other sentient beings with the ability to do so.

Then visualize and reflect that, through having made this supplication, a stream of fivefold nectar and light rays flows down from the body of your divine root lama seated on the crown of your head, entering the bodies and minds of you and all other sentient beings surrounding you, and removing all the various general and special obstacles. In addition, visualize that nectar and light rays also cause the various special forms of realization to arise both in your mental continuum and that of all the other sentient beings surrounding you.

III) What to Do at the Conclusion of the Meditation Session

The concluding activities are the same as the ones that were explained earlier.

ii. What to Do during the Time between Meditation Sessions

During the time between meditation sessions, you should read scripture texts and commentaries that explain how samsara in its entirety consists of the nature of suffering, and so on, as well as carry out the other general practices that were described earlier.

b. Establishing the Nature of the Path That Leads to Liberation

This topic is made up of two parts: (1) what to do during meditation sessions and (2) what to do during the time between meditation sessions.

i. What to Do during Meditation Sessions

This topic has three divisions: (1) preliminaries, (2) main practice, and (3) conclusion.

I) Preliminaries

Everything up to the lines, "I make supplication to you, Munīndra Vajradhara, / extraordinary guru-deity who embodies the entire object of refuge" is to be recited in the same manner that was described earlier. Following that, reflect in the following manner:

> The manifold and intense forms of suffering that I and all mother sentient beings have experienced throughout the infinitely long time that we have been taking birth in samsara is due to our having failed to generate the attitude that seeks to attain liberation and train ourselves properly in the path that consists of the three trainings.[52] Therefore, O divine Root Lama, please bless me and all mother sentient beings so that we gain the ability to generate the attitude that seeks to attain liberation and train ourselves properly in the path that consists of the three trainings.

Then visualize and reflect that through having made this supplication, a stream of fivefold nectar and light rays flows down from the body of your divine root lama seated on the crown of your head, entering the bodies and minds of you and all other sentient beings surrounding you, {131} removing all the evil deeds and obscurations that you and they have accumulated since beginningless time, and, in particular, removing the obstacles that hinder you and them from generating the attitude that seeks to attain liberation and training yourselves properly in the path that consists of the three trainings. Having done so, your and their ordinary bodies are transformed into bodies having the nature of transparent and radiant light. In addition, all the virtuous qualities, such as those associated with longevity and merit, and so on, increase and become strengthened, and, in particular, the extraordinary realization that generates the attitude that seeks to attain liberation and trains oneself properly in the path that consists of the three trainings arises, both in your mental continuum and that of all the other mother sentient beings that are surrounding you.

II) The Main Practice

While visualizing your divine root lama seated on the crown of your head, reflect in the following manner:

> While the mind's natural state is morally indeterminate,[53] after initially perceiving the subjective, personal self and the entities that pertain to that self, the mind erroneously gives rise to the belief that they exist by way of a real essential nature. Through that mind's having apprehended those entities as real,[54] the mind gives rise to attachment toward whomever is judged as belonging to one's own side and animosity toward whomever is judged as belonging to the side of others,[55] as well as other mistaken beliefs, such as the pride that holds oneself as superior to others. These errors, in turn, form the basis for the arising of both the wrong view that denies the existence of such things as the Master who revealed the doctrine of selflessness, the doctrines of karma and its results and the four truths that he also taught, or the Three Jewels, and the like, and the doubt that questions their existence. These mistaken views, taken as a whole, form the basis for the strengthening of all the other mental afflictions. After accumulating karma through the power of these mental afflictions, all of these manifold forms of suffering that I unwillingly experience in samsara have come about.[56]
>
> Therefore, since the ultimate root cause for all suffering is ignorance,[57] I must attain the status of my lama-buddha, who has abandoned all the suffering of samsara from its roots. In order to accomplish that, I shall train myself properly in the path of the three precious trainings. In particular, because a great benefit is gained by observing it and a very great disadvantage is suffered by failing to observe it, I will properly observe the form of morality that I have accepted and avoid forsaking it, {132} even to save my life.
>
> Furthermore, regarding this point, since lack of knowledge is a primary factor for incurring transgressions, as an antidote for that I should study and learn all the precepts. Since lack of respect is a primary factor for incurring transgressions, as an antidote for that I should develop respect for the Master, the

> trainings that were formulated by him, and those fellow spiritual practitioners who are training themselves properly in the trainings. Since lack of mindfulness[58] is a primary factor for incurring transgressions, as an antidote for that I should acquire mindfulness[59] through developing recollection,[60] vigilance,[61] and a sense of shame[62] and abashment.[63] Since having a strong propensity to generate the mental afflictions is a primary factor for incurring transgressions, as an antidote for that I should cultivate properly a pure form of morality that does not become tainted by offenses, through meditating on unattractiveness as an antidote for desire, on loving-kindness as an antidote for hatred, and on dependent origination as an antidote for ignorance, and so on.[64] O divine Root Lama, please bless me and all mother sentient beings with the ability to do so.

Then visualize and reflect that, through having made this supplication, a stream of fivefold nectar and light rays flows down from the body of your divine root lama seated on the crown of your head, entering the bodies and minds of you and all other sentient beings surrounding you and removing all the various general and special obstacles. In addition, visualize that nectar and light rays also cause the various special forms of realization to arise both in your mental continuum and that of all the other sentient beings surrounding you.

III) What to Do at the Conclusion of the Meditation Session

The concluding activities are the same as the ones that were explained earlier.

ii. What to Do during the Time between Meditation Sessions

During the time between meditation sessions, you should read about the precepts that relate to the prātimokṣa[65] system of moral discipline, as well as carry out the other general practices that were described earlier. This completes the explanations on training your mind in the stages of the path that are held in common with middling persons.

3. Training Your Mind in the Stages of the Path That Pertain to Great Persons

This topic is made up of two parts: (1) how to generate the mind that aspires to attain enlightenment and (2) how to train yourself in the conduct of a bodhisattva after having generated enlightenment mind.

a. How to Generate the Mind That Aspires to Attain Enlightenment

This section is made up of two parts: (1) the actual method of generating the mind that aspires to attain enlightenment and (2) the ritual for generating the aspirational form of enlightenment mind.

i. The Actual Method of Generating the Mind That Aspires to Attain Enlightenment

This topic has two divisions: (1) how to generate the mind that aspires to attain enlightenment on the basis of the seven-point instruction of cause and effect {133} and (2) how to generate the mind that aspires to attain enlightenment on the basis of the instruction called the Equality and Exchange between Oneself and Others.

I) The Seven-Point Instruction of Cause and Effect

Before practicing any of the seven points, you must develop an attitude of even-mindedness toward all sentient beings. Following that, the instruction consists of meditating on the topics that range from recognizing all sentient beings as your mothers up to enlightenment mind. This practice consists of two parts: (1) what to do during meditation sessions and (2) what to do during the time between meditation sessions.

A) What to Do during Meditation Sessions

This topic has three divisions: (1) preliminaries, (2) main practice, and (3) conclusion.

1) Preliminaries

Everything up to the lines, "I make supplication to you, Munīndra Vajradhara, / extraordinary guru-deity who embodies the entire object of refuge" is to be recited in the same manner that was described earlier. Following that, reflect in the following manner:

> O divine Root Lama, please bless me and all mother sentient beings so that we may develop in our mental continua the state of even-mindedness toward all sentient beings that is free of both the attachment that regards beings with a feeling of closeness and the hatred that regards beings with a feeling of distance, as well as the extraordinary realizations that recognize all sentient beings as our mothers, that recall their kindness, that wish to repay that kindness, and that engender loving-kindness, compassion, and enlightenment mind.

Then visualize and reflect that, through having made this supplication, a stream of fivefold nectar and light rays flows down from the body of your divine root lama seated on the crown of your head, entering the bodies and minds of you and all other sentient beings surrounding you, removing all the evil deeds and obscurations that you have accumulated since beginningless time, and, in particular, removing the obstacles that hinder you and them from developing the state of even-mindedness toward all sentient beings that is free of both the attachment that regards beings with a feeling of closeness and the hatred that regards beings with a feeling of distance, and so on. Having done so, your ordinary body and that of all the beings surrounding you are transformed into bodies having the nature of transparent and radiant light. In addition, all the virtuous qualities, such as those associated with longevity and merit, and so on, increase and become strengthened, and, in particular, the state of even-mindedness toward all sentient beings that is free of both attachment toward those regarded with a feeling of closeness and hatred toward those regarded with a feeling of distance, as well as the other subsequent extraordinary realizations, arise both in your mental continuum and that of all the other sentient beings surrounding you.

2. The Main Practice

Developing Immeasurable Equanimity

While visualizing your divine root lama seated on the crown of your head, clearly visualize in front of you a neutral person—that is, someone who has neither benefited nor harmed you in any way during this life—and then reflect in the following manner:

> Since this person is someone who, from his or her side, desires happiness and does not want to experience suffering, I should refrain from developing the two tendencies of wanting to benefit him or her on certain occasions through having developed a feeling of closeness[66] {134} and wanting to harm him or her on other occasions, through having developed a feeling of distance.[67] Instead, I should develop toward this neutral person the state of even-mindedness that is free of both the attachment that regards him or her with a feeling of closeness and the hatred that regards him or her with a feeling of distance. O divine Root Lama, please bless me and all mother sentient beings with the ability to do so.

Following this supplication, also carry out the additional related visualizations.[68]

When you develop even-mindedness toward that person, clearly visualize in front of you a sentient being that you consider to be attractive[69] and cultivate a state of even-mindedness toward him or her. Your lack of even-mindedness toward this person is due to your being under the influence of attachment. Therefore, as you also did previously,[70] meditate in such a way that you are able to overcome your attachment, by reflecting, "This very attachment toward persons and objects that are perceived as attractive is what causes me to take birth in samsara."

When you develop even-mindedness toward that person, clearly visualize in front of you a sentient being that you consider to be unattractive[71] and cultivate a state of even-mindedness toward him or her. Your lack of even-mindedness toward this person is an attitude that gives rise to hatred through regarding him or her with complete antipathy. You should meditate in such a way that you are able to overcome your hatred by reflecting,

"If I am unable to develop even-mindedness toward this person, it will not be possible for me to generate enlightenment mind."

When you develop even-mindedness toward that person, clearly visualize in front of you two individuals—one of whom is a sentient being that is extremely attractive, such as your mother, and the second of whom is a sentient being that is extremely unattractive, such as an enemy. Then reflect in the following manner and make the related supplication at the end:

> From their own side, these two individuals are the same in that they both desire happiness and do not want to experience suffering. From my side, the individual that I currently regard as a close relative[72] has also been my worst enemy countless times throughout beginningless samsara. Likewise, the individual that I currently regard as an enemy has also been a mother who lovingly cared for me countless times throughout beginningless samsara. Therefore, which is the one toward whom I should feel attachment, and which is the one toward whom I should feel animosity? What I should do is develop toward both of these individuals the even-mindedness that is free of the attachment that regards some persons with a feeling of closeness and the hatred that regards others with a feeling of distance. I also make the supplication prayer, "O divine Root Lama, please bless me and all mother sentient beings with the ability to do so."

[Following this supplication prayer, carry out the related visualizations.]

When you develop even-mindedness toward those two individuals, meditate on a state of even-mindedness toward all sentient beings. {135} The way to do so is as follows:

> From their side, all sentient beings are the same in that they desire happiness and do not want to experience suffering. From my side, since all sentient beings are properly viewed as being close relatives, I should refrain from developing the two tendencies of wanting to benefit certain individuals through having developed a feeling of closeness toward them and wanting to harm other individuals through having developed a feeling of distance

> toward them. Instead, I should develop the even-mindedness that is free of both the attachment that regards some individuals with a feeling of closeness and the hatred that regards others with a feeling of distance. I also make the supplication prayer, "O divine Root Lama, please bless me and all mother sentient beings with the ability to do so."

[Following this supplication prayer, carry out the related visualizations.]

Recognizing All Sentient Beings as My Mothers

The way to meditate on the topics that range from recognizing all sentient beings as your mother to generating enlightenment mind is, first, while visualizing your divine root lama seated on the crown of your head, to reflect in the following manner:

> Now then, I might ask myself, "What reason is there to justify the assertion that all sentient beings are my close relatives?" Since samsara has no beginning, my rebirths are also without beginning. In this limitless succession of rebirths that occur one after the other, there is not a single region or place about which it could be said, "I have never been born here." In fact, I have been born in every region and place countless times. There is also not a single type of sentient being about which it could be said, "I have never taken on the physical form of this type of sentient being." In fact, I have been born as every type of sentient being countless times. There is not a single sentient being about which it could be said, "This sentient being has never been my mother." In fact, every sentient being has been my mother countless times. With regard to each and every sentient being, there is not a single one about which it could be said, "This sentient being has never been my mother in the form of a human being." In fact, every sentient being has been my mother in the form of a human being countless times and will continue to do so in the future. Therefore, all sentient beings are definitely my mothers who have cared for me in their kindness.

Now then, you might think to yourself, "Since the number of sentient beings is limitless, it can't be true that all sentient beings are my mothers." In that case, you should reflect in the following manner:

> It doesn't necessarily follow that because the number of sentient beings is limitless, not all have been my mother. Just as the number of sentient beings is limitless, the number of my rebirths is also limitless; therefore, all sentient beings have been my mother.

You might think to yourself, "Not all sentient beings have been my mother, because I and all sentient beings do not recognize one another {136} as having had the relationship of mother and child." In that case, you should reflect in the following manner:

> It doesn't necessarily follow that because I and all sentient beings do not recognize one another as having had the relationship of mother and child, not all sentient beings have been my mother. There are many instances in which mothers and their offspring, in their current lives, do not recognize one another as having the relationship of mother and offspring.

Moreover, you might think to yourself, "Even though all sentient beings have been my mother in a former life, it is not valid to claim that they are still my mother, because all those individuals who were my mothers in past lives have since passed away." In that case, you should reflect in the following manner:

> Well then, since my mother of yesterday is "passed away" today,[73] according to that above-stated position it would follow that she is no longer my mother. Therefore, just as these two "individuals"—that is, my mother of yesterday and my mother of today—are no different, both as relates to being my mother and as relates to having cared for me in their kindness, both my mothers in my past lives and my mother in this life are also no different as relates to being my mother and as relates to having cared for me in their kindness. For these reasons, it is definitely true that all sentient beings are my mothers.

Recalling the Kindness of All Sentient Beings

When you have elicited an experiential awareness[74] regarding that topic of recognizing all sentient beings as your mothers, the topic of contemplating their kindness is done in the following manner. While visualizing your divine root lama seated on the crown of your head, visualize in front of you the image of your mother in this life at the stage when she had become elderly, not at the stage when she was still young, and then reflect in the following manner:

> This mother is someone who has not only been my mother in this life. Throughout my lives that are infinite because they have no beginning, she has been my mother countless times. In particular, during this life, initially she cared for me lovingly when I was in her womb. When I was born, she placed me on a soft cushion, gently rocked me as she held me with her ten fingertips, held me close against her warm flesh, greeted me with loving smiles, gazed at me with joyful eyes, wiped away my snot with her mouth, and wiped away my filth with her bare hands.
>
> It caused my mother greater suffering if I experienced a minor illness than if she were to encounter some form of suffering that posed a threat to her own life. Unconcerned about committing misdeeds, undergoing hardships, acquiring a bad reputation, or even putting her own life in danger, she lovingly gave me all the food and wealth that she drove herself to physical exhaustion to obtain. She was extremely kind to me in that, to the extent of her abilities, {137} she provided me with immeasurable forms of benefit and happiness and protected me from immeasurable forms of harm and suffering.

When you have elicited an experiential awareness regarding the kindness of this life's mother, you should meditate in the same way with regard to this life's father and other close relatives. The way in which to do so is to direct your attention to a clear image of such close relatives as your father and then reflect in the following manner:

> This father, and so on, is extremely kind, because he or she has been my mother countless times throughout my lives that are without

> beginning, and because each time that he or she was my mother, he or she took care of me in his or her kindness in the same way that my mother in this life took care of me in her kindness.

When you have elicited an experiential awareness regarding the kindness of this life's father, and so on, you should meditate in the same way in relation to all neutral[75] sentient beings. The way in which to do so is to direct your attention to the image of neutral sentient beings that are being visualized in front of you and reflect in the following manner:

> While, at present, it seems as though I have no particular kind of good or bad relationship with these sentient beings, in fact they all have been extremely kind to me, because they have all been my mother countless times throughout my lives that are without beginning, and because each time that they were my mother, they took care of me in their kindness in the same way that my mother in this life took care of me in her kindness.

When you have elicited an experiential awareness regarding the kindness of neutral sentient beings, you should meditate in the same way in relation toward enemies. The way in which to do so is to direct your attention to the image of an enemy that is being visualized in front of you and reflect to yourself in the following manner:

> What good does it do for me now to regard this individual as an enemy? He or she has been my mother countless times throughout my lives that are without beginning and each time that he or she was my mother, he or she provided me with immeasurable forms of benefit and happiness and protected me from immeasurable forms of harm and suffering. In particular, he or she and I, countless times, were so affectionate toward one another that I could not bear it when this individual was absent, and he or she too could not bear it when I was absent. The reason our relationship now has taken on this unfavorable nature is due to the power of bad karma; otherwise, he or she has been a mother who did nothing but care for me in his or her kindness.

Repaying the Kindness of All Mother Sentient Beings

After reflecting in this way on the kindness of all mother sentient beings, the way to meditate on the wish to repay their kindness is, first, while visualizing your divine root lama seated on the crown of your head, to reflect in the following manner:

> These mother sentient beings who have taken care of me in their kindness throughout beginningless time are deranged in that they have no control over their minds because their minds have been agitated by the demon of mental afflictions. They lack the eyes with which to see the path that leads to an elevated status and the highest good. They do not have a spiritual teacher who is like a guide for a blind person. With each passing moment, they stumble along impaired by their misdeeds. Because it would be extremely shameful if I were to abandon these beings who are traveling at the edge of the terrifying precipice of samsara's general suffering and especially that of the lower realms, in order to repay their kindness, I must free them from the suffering of samsara and establish them in the happiness of liberation. I also make the supplication prayer, "O divine Root Lama, please bless me and all mother sentient beings with the ability to do so."

[Following this supplication prayer, carry out the related visualizations.]

Loving-Kindness

Following that practice of meditating on the wish to repay all sentient beings' kindness, the way to meditate on loving-kindness is first to direct your attention to someone like your mother—that is, an individual whom you regard with the greatest affection and reflect in the following manner:

> How could this individual find any form of uncontaminated[76] happiness? She or he has not found even any form of contaminated happiness. These current experiences that this individual mistakenly thinks of as happiness change into forms of suffering.[77] Desiring happiness, she or he strives and strives with great

> fervor to obtain it; however, these efforts serve as a cause for her or him to experience the suffering of the lower realms in their future lives.[78] In this life as well, through undergoing hardship and fatigue, she or he causes herself or himself nothing but suffering and does not find any true form of happiness whatsoever. Therefore, I yearn deeply that this individual might find all forms of happiness and the causes of happiness. I make the aspirational prayer that she or he finds happiness and the causes of happiness. I pledge that I myself will cause her or him to find happiness and the causes of happiness. I also make the supplication prayer, "O divine Root Lama, please bless me and all mother sentient beings with the ability to do so."

[Following this supplication prayer, carry out the related visualizations.]

When you have elicited an experiential awareness of loving-kindness toward your mother, meditate in the same way that was just described, by directing your attention successively to your father and other close relatives, all neutral sentient beings, your enemies, and, finally, all sentient beings. {139}

Compassion

Following that practice of meditating on loving-kindness toward all sentient beings, the way to meditate on compassion is first, while visualizing your divine root lama seated on the crown of your head, to meditate upon beings that are overcome by suffering, such as a sheep that is in the midst of being slaughtered by a butcher. The way to do so is to visualize an image of such a being in front of you and reflect on how it is tormented by suffering:

> The sheep's legs are bound. The skin of its breast has been cut open. Because the butcher has inserted his hand into its chest cavity, the sheep is clearly aware that it is about to lose its life. It gazes with wide-open eyes at the butcher's face.

Then continue reflecting:

> Therefore, I yearn deeply that this sentient being might become free of all its suffering and the causes of its suffering. I make the

> aspirational prayer that it becomes free of all its suffering and the causes of its suffering. I pledge that I myself will cause it to become free of all its suffering and the causes of its suffering. I also make the supplication prayer, "O divine Root Lama, please bless me and all mother sentient beings with the ability to do so."

[Following this supplication prayer, carry out the related visualizations.]

When you have elicited an experiential awareness of compassion toward such a sentient being that is oppressed by suffering, direct your attention to and meditate in a similar way toward beings who are quite eagerly engaging in a variety of evil and unvirtuous deeds, such as heedlessly making personal use of property that belongs to a monastic community, or beings who are violating their moral practice, rejecting the dharma, adhering to wrong view, or harming other sentient beings. The way to do this is to direct your attention to an image of such beings that are visualized as being in front of you and reflect in the following manner:

> This sort of behavior that is being carried out now by these individuals will not bring them happiness in this life. There is also no doubt that, immediately following their death, they will be reborn in the lower realms. Having been reborn there, they will be forced to experience many different kinds of intense suffering for a very long period of time. Therefore, I yearn deeply that they might become free of all their suffering and the causes of their suffering. I make the aspirational prayer that they become free of all their suffering and the causes of their suffering. I pledge that I myself will cause them to become free of all their suffering and the causes of their suffering. I also make the supplication prayer, "O divine Root Lama, {140} please bless me and all mother sentient beings with the ability to do so."

[Following this supplication prayer, carry out the related visualizations.]

When you have elicited an experiential awareness of that compassion toward beings who are committing misdeeds, direct your attention to an image of close relatives, such as your mother, who are being visualized as present before you and reflect in the following manner:

> Having striven continually with great fervor to protect themselves from enemies and to assist their friends, these individuals have been tormented by two kinds of suffering—that is, the suffering of suffering and the suffering of change, but they have not found the slightest form of genuine happiness. Moreover, because they have been occupied with inferior activities during this life, they failed to cultivate any virtuous minds. For this reason, immediately following their death, they will be reborn in the lower realms and be forced to experience many different kinds of intense suffering for a very long period of time. Therefore, I yearn deeply that they might come to be free of all their suffering and the causes of their suffering. I make the aspirational prayer that they become free of all their suffering and the causes of their suffering. I pledge that I myself will cause them to become free of all their suffering and the causes of their suffering. I also make the supplication prayer, "O divine Root Lama, please bless me and all mother sentient beings with the ability to do so."

[Following this supplication prayer, also carry out the related visualizations.]

When you have elicited an experiential awareness of that compassion toward close relatives, such as your mother, meditate successively in the way that was just described with regard to neutral persons, enemies, and, finally, all sentient beings.

The Superior Attitude

When you have elicited the experiential awareness that is a mental transformation[79] in relation to loving-kindness and compassion, the way to meditate on the superior attitude[80] is, while visualizing your divine root lama seated on the crown of your head, to reflect as follows:

> I pledge that I myself will cause all sentient beings who are tormented by suffering and bereft of happiness to become free from their suffering and the causes of their suffering, and I pledge that I myself will cause them to find every form of happiness and all the causes of happiness. In particular, I pledge that I myself will

> cause all sentient beings to attain the status of a true and complete buddha who has abandoned the two obscurations together with their traces. O divine Root Lama, please bless me and all mother sentient beings with the ability to do so.

[Following this supplication prayer, carry out the related visualizations.]

Enlightenment Mind

Following that, the way to meditate on enlightenment mind is, while visualizing the divine root lama seated on the crown of your head, to reflect to yourself as follows:

> Well then, do you {141} possess the ability to establish all sentient beings in the status of a complete buddha? At present, I do not have the ability to establish even one sentient being in the status of a complete buddha. Not only that, even if I were to attain the status of either of the two types of arhat,[81] I could only accomplish the aims of sentient beings in a partial manner; I would not have the ability to establish all sentient beings in the status of a complete buddha.
>
> Who possesses such an ability? A true and complete buddha possesses it. A buddha's spiritual qualities include the following. His physical qualities include that his body is adorned in a clear and complete manner with all the thirty-two major marks and eighty secondary signs. His qualities of speech include that, with each moment of verbal utterance that possesses the sixty attributes, he is able to teach the dharma effortlessly to all sentient beings in such a way that it is heard by them in their own individual languages. His mental qualities include that he perceives directly all knowable entities, both in terms of their true mode of being[82] and in terms of their full range;[83] and, because a buddha's compassion takes effect impartially toward all sentient beings and in the same way that a mother feels compassion toward an only child, he never allows even a moment's opportunity to establish sentient beings in a state of spiritual self-discipline to slip by. His enlightened activities occur effortlessly and spontaneously. Even

> just a single ray of light emanated from his body, speech, or mind has the ability to establish countless sentient beings in the state of an omniscient buddha.
>
> In short, only a true and complete buddha possesses every kind of spiritual quality and is free of every kind of flaw. Therefore, since I must attain the status of such a buddha if I want to become one who has perfected both my own and others' aims, I must, swiftly, ever so swiftly, attain the precious status of a true and complete buddha for the sake of all mother sentient beings. O divine Root Lama, please bless me and all mother sentient beings with the ability to do so.

Then visualize and reflect that through having made this supplication, a duplicate of your divine root lama {142} that is seated on the crown of your head separates from his body like a candle that is lit by touching its wick to the flame of another candle that is already burning, and dissolves into you, causing you to take on the form of the Victor Śākyamuni seated atop a tall, wide, and jewel-studded throne held up by eight majestic lions upon cushions of a variegated lotus, moon, and sun. . . . (etc., up to) . . . sitting . . . in the vajra cross-legged position.[84]

Then visualize and reflect that, while appearing in the form of Munīndra, you give yourself, your wealth, and your virtue roots to all sentient beings by emanating them in the form of fivefold nectar and light rays, causing them to attain the excellent happiness of an elevated status and the highest good.

3) What to Do at the Conclusion of the Meditation Session

The concluding activities are the same as the ones that were explained earlier.

B) What to Do during the Time between Meditation Sessions

During the time between meditation sessions, you should also support the main practice by reading scripture texts and commentaries that present explanations of the topics of loving-kindness, compassion, and enlightenment mind. The rest of the instructions for what to do between meditation sessions are the same as were described earlier.

II) The Equality and Exchange between Oneself and Others

Begin by meditating on the three topics of (1) the equanimity that is a state of even-mindedness toward all sentient beings, (2) the recognition that all sentient beings are one's mothers, and (3) recalling the kindness of all mother sentient beings. Then, direct your attention clearly to all the sentient beings that are surrounding you and examine your mind in the following way, "When I consider myself and others as separate mental objects, which of the two do I cherish and which of the two do I abandon?" This exercise will reveal that the attitude of cherishing oneself and abandoning others is the one that arises naturally. At this point, you should reflect as follows:

> It is improper for me to cherish myself and abandon others, because I and others are the same in that we both desire happiness and do not want to experience suffering. Therefore, just as I cherish myself, I must also cherish others, because just as I would be pleased if others were to cherish me, others would also be pleased if I were to cherish them.
>
> Moreover, as I {143} sought to achieve a state of excellence throughout beginningless samsara, through maintaining a self-cherishing attitude, not only have I failed to achieve any of my own or others' aims whatsoever, I have continually experienced many different forms of suffering. Therefore, since the self-cherishing attitude is the source of every misfortune, such as the general suffering of samsara and especially that of the lower realms and so on, I should refrain from generating any forms of self-cherishing that I have not yet generated, and I should abandon those that I have generated previously. In addition, since the attitude that cherishes others is the source of all good qualities, I should generate the forms of the attitude that cherishes others that I have not yet generated, and I should develop more fully the forms that I have already generated. O divine Root Lama, please bless me and all mother sentient beings with the ability to do so.

[Following this supplication, also carry out the related visualizations.]

> In short, after having abandoned concern for himself and adopted the attitude that cherishes others, Munīndra[85] attained supreme

enlightenment through accomplishing the aims of others exclusively. If I had also done this, I would have attained enlightenment long ago. However, because I did not act in this way, I have continued to wander in samsara up to the present. Moreover, as long as I continue to keep the self-cherishing attitude within me, I will not be able to develop new forms of the attitude that cherishes others, and even though I may have developed it to some extent in the past, I will not be able to maintain it continually. Therefore, I must refrain from generating, for even an instant, the attitude that cherishes oneself and abandons concern for others, and instead I must develop the attitude that abandons concern for oneself and cherishes others. I pledge that, by taking onto myself all the suffering and evil deeds of others, and by giving to others all my happiness and virtue, I myself will free others—which is to say, all sentient beings—from their suffering and provide them with perfect happiness.

Moreover, regarding this aim, I recognize that I do not, at present, possess such an ability. So when I consider whether there is anyone who possesses this ability, I recognize that it is possessed by a true and complete buddha. Therefore, I {144} resolve to attain the status of a true and complete buddha for the sake of all sentient beings. O divine Root Lama, please bless me and all mother sentient beings with the ability to do so.

[Following this supplication prayer, carry out the related visualizations.]

ii. The Ritual for Adopting Enlightenment Mind

The topic of generating enlightenment mind in a ritual form is made up of two sections: (1) obtaining the vow that has not been obtained previously and (2) preserving the vow that has been obtained by preventing it from becoming damaged.

I) Obtaining the Vow That Has Not Been Obtained Previously

Although the point of view indicated in *The Stages of the Path* is the one in which the aspirational and active forms of enlightenment mind are adopted sequentially,[86] it is more expedient to adopt them simultaneously, in the manner of the tradition that was established by Śāntideva. Hence, the latter method is the one that is presented here.

After having performed the general activities of the preliminary stage[87] and, in particular, after having reflected on the main practices that range from how to serve one's spiritual teacher up to that of generating enlightenment mind,[88] in such a way that their meaning has been infused in your mind, visualize the divine root lama seated on the crown of your head and reflect to yourself:

> I must attain swiftly the state of a true and complete buddha for the sake of all mother sentient beings. To that end, from this moment on until I reach the seat of enlightenment,[89] after adopting the vow of a victor's spiritual offspring, I shall train myself in the extensive bodhisattva activities. And, until I achieve the state of a buddha, I shall always maintain this thought: "I shall attain buddhahood for the sake of all sentient beings."

Then reflect that you obtain the bodhisattva vow by repeating after Lama Munīndra the following lines three times:

> I beseech all the buddhas and bodhisattvas;
> may it please you to give heed to me.
>
> Just as the former sugatas
> adopted enlightenment mind
> and just as they practiced, in a regular way,
> the bodhisattva training,
>
> I, too, generate that enlightenment mind
> for the benefit of the world
> and I, too, shall practice
> those trainings in the proper order.[90]

After that, recite the following verses to rejoice at having generated the bodhisattva vow:

Now, my life has become fruitful;
this human {145} existence has been made worthwhile.
Today, I have been born into the family of the buddhas;
now I have become an offspring of the buddhas.

From now on my actions should accord however
is most fitting for my lineage,
so that that this flawless lineage
does not become stained.[91]

II) Preserving the Vow That Has Been Obtained by Preventing It from Becoming Damaged

While visualizing the divine root lama seated on the crown of your head, reflect to yourself in the following manner and perform the supplication described at the end:

> I must attain swiftly the state of a true and complete buddha for the sake of all mother sentient beings. To that end, after reflecting on the benefits of enlightenment mind, I shall reaffirm my enlightenment mind each day three times during the day and three times at night. From my side, I shall not mentally abandon a single sentient being, no matter what kind of behavior sentient beings, from their side, may carry out. In order to further develop the enlightenment mind that I have generated, I shall strive to collect the two accumulations through carrying out such practices as worshiping the Three Jewels. In addition, I shall train myself properly by abandoning such deeds as the four black qualities, which cause enlightenment mind to be damaged, as well as by practicing such deeds as the four white qualities, which cause enlightenment mind to develop further.[92] Among these, the four black qualities are to deceive such venerable beings as my lamas by uttering falsehoods to them, even in jest or to cause laughter; to instill regret in others about virtuous acts that they have performed; to defame, out of hatred, a bodhisattva who is established in the Mahāyāna; and to employ deceitfulness and guile toward others instead of a superior attitude. In short, I shall safe-

> guard a pure form of the bodhisattva vow through never becoming tainted by any of the eighteen root transgressions[93] or the forty-six secondary misdeeds[94]—even to save my life, and I shall do so until I reach the seat of enlightenment.[95] O divine Root Lama, please bless me and all mother sentient beings with the ability to safeguard the bodhisattva vow in this way.

b. Training Yourself in the Conduct after Having Generated Enlightenment Mind {146}

This topic is made up of two sections: (1) how to train yourself in the overall conduct for a victor's offspring and (2) how to train yourself, in particular, in the final two perfections.

i. How to Train Yourself in the Overall Conduct for a Victor's Offspring

This topic is also made up of two sections: (1) what to do during meditation sessions and (2) what to do in the time between meditation sessions.

I) What to Do during Meditation Sessions

This topic is made up of three parts: (1) preliminaries, (2) main practice, and (3) conclusion.

A) Preliminaries

Everything up to the lines, "I make supplication to you, Munīndra Vajradhara, / extraordinary guru-deity who embodies the entire object of refuge" is to be recited in the same manner that was described earlier. Following that, make the following special supplication, along with the appropriate visualizations, and reflect in the following manner:

> O divine Root Lama, please bless me and all mother sentient beings with the ability to train ourselves properly in both the profound and extensive forms of exalted activities for a victor's offspring.

B) Main Practice

This topic is made up of two parts: (1) practicing the six perfections that ripen one's own mental continuum and (2) practicing the four means of gathering a following that ripen the mental continua of others.

1) Practicing the Six Perfections

The Practice of Generosity

While visualizing the divine root lama seated on the crown of your head, and so on, reflect to yourself in the following manner and perform the supplication and related visualizations at the end:

> I must attain swiftly the state of a true and complete buddha for the sake of all mother sentient beings. To that end, I shall train myself properly in the practice of the three types of generosity: (1) giving the dharma, which means teaching the true dharma to the best of one's ability, to beings who are devoid of dharma, without regard to gain, honor, or fame, and so on; (2) giving protection, which means saving beings from the danger of being harmed by humans, nonhuman spirits and predatory animals, or the elements; and (3) giving material possessions, which means providing poor and destitute beings with whatever objects of material value are appropriate for them, without any expectation of repayment or karmic ripening, and having rejected any form of stinginess.
>
> In short, I must attain swiftly the state of a true and complete buddha for the sake of all mother sentient beings. To that end, I shall give my body, my wealth, together with my virtue roots, to all sentient beings, unstintingly. O divine Root Lama, please bless me and all mother sentient beings with the ability to do so. {147}

Following this supplication, also carry out the related visualizations. It should be understood that the practice of generosity consists of strengthening one's intention to give.[96]

The Practice of Morality

Following that, while visualizing the divine root lama seated on the crown of your head, and so on, reflect to yourself in the following manner:

> I must attain swiftly the state of a true and complete buddha for the sake of all mother sentient beings. To that end, I shall abandon the misdeeds that are antithetical to the vow that I have accepted, such as the promise to abandon the ten unvirtuous deeds, and so on. Having done so, I shall practice the six perfections of generosity, and so on, and develop in my mental continuum the pure virtuous acts of morality, and so on, that I have not yet developed, as well as augment those that I have developed. In addition, I shall cause all sentient beings to undertake the pure virtuous acts of morality, and so on, and establish them in the paths that ripen them spiritually and ultimately bring about their liberation. O divine Root Lama, please bless me and all mother sentient beings with the ability to do so.

[Following this supplication, carry out the related visualizations.]

The Practice of Patience

Following that, while visualizing the divine root lama seated on the crown of your head, and so on, reflect to yourself in the following manner:

> I must attain swiftly the state of a true and complete buddha for the sake of all mother sentient beings. To that end, even if all sentient beings were to rise up against me as enemies, I shall, without generating an angry mind for even an instant, strive to benefit them in response to their harm.[97] I shall perfect the qualities of a buddha, which consist of the perfection of patience, and so on, in my own continuum and in those of others. In addition, when I lack such things as food, wealth, a place for sleeping and sitting, and so on, or when I am stricken by such unwanted forms of suffering as an illness, and so on, these experiences are the results of bad deeds that were accumulated in the past. Since the negative

> effect of many bad deeds is eliminated on the basis of these experiences, I should not regard them as undesirable, and, in particular, since I am drawing nearer to the path that leads to omniscience by generating tolerance toward suffering that is incurred for the sake of the dharma, I should accept these forms of suffering[98] and terminate both my own and others' general suffering of samsara, as well as that of the three lower realms {148}. In addition to that, since generating devotion[99] with regard to the ripening of white and black deeds, the blessings of the Three Jewels, the inconceivably great powers of the buddhas and the bodhisattvas who are great beings, the nature of unsurpassed enlightenment, the twelve divisions of the Buddha's word, and all the elements of bodhisattva training[100] brings about an extremely great beneficial result, I shall generate devotion toward these topics, and in order to attain unsurpassed enlightenment, I shall train myself properly in the elements of the bodhisattva training that are the subject matter of the twelve divisions of the Buddha's word. O divine Root Lama, please bless me and all mother sentient beings with the ability to do so.

[Following this supplication, carry out the related visualizations.]

The Practice of Effort

Following that, while visualizing the divine root lama seated on the crown of your head, reflect to yourself in the following manner:

> I must attain swiftly the state of a true and complete buddha for the sake of all mother sentient beings. To that end, even if, in pursuit of buddhahood, I had to remain in Avīci hell[101] for a hundred thousand kalpas in order to achieve each of a buddha's spiritual qualities, such as the major and minor marks, and so on, as well as to achieve each of a bodhisattva's spiritual qualities, such as those of generosity, and so on, I would not abandon my effort and I would generate the mental exertion[102] to accomplish these aims.[103] Having done so, I shall attain unsurpassed enlightenment by gathering the profound and extensive spiritual quali-

> ties within my own mental continuum[104] and also by establishing others on the path of virtue.[105] O divine Root Lama, please bless me and all mother sentient beings with the ability to do so.

[Following this supplication, carry out the related visualizations.]

The Practice of Meditative Absorption

Following that, while visualizing the divine root lama seated on the crown of your head, reflect to yourself in the following manner:

> I must attain swiftly the state of a true and complete buddha for the sake of all mother sentient beings. To that end, I shall train myself in all the forms of meditative absorption that pertain to a victor's offspring. In terms of its essential nature, there is (1) worldly meditative absorption and (2) transcendent meditative absorption. In terms of its constituent elements, meditative absorption is made up three types: quiescence, insight, and the union of those latter two {149}—namely, quiescence and insight. In terms of its specific functions, there is the meditative absorption that enables you to abide in a state of ease during this life, the meditative absorption that is the basis for attaining extraordinary spiritual qualities, and the meditative absorption that accomplishes the aims of sentient beings.[106] O divine Root Lama, please bless me and all mother sentient beings with the ability to do so.

[Following this supplication, carry out the related visualizations.]

The Practice Wisdom

Following that, while visualizing the divine root lama seated on the crown of your head, reflect to yourself in the following manner:

> I must attain the state of a true and complete buddha for the sake of all mother sentient beings. To that end, I shall train myself in all the forms of wisdom that pertain to the Victor's offspring,

> which include knowledge of the true nature of entities (which is to say, the wisdom that realizes ultimate truth);[107] knowledge of the five branches of learning[108] (which is to say, the wisdom that realizes conventional objects); and the wisdom that realizes how to act on behalf of sentient beings. O divine Root Lama, please bless me and all mother sentient beings with the ability to do so.

[Following this supplication, carry out the related visualizations.]

Practicing the Four Means of Gathering a Following That Ripen the Mental Continua of Others

While visualizing the divine root lama seated on the crown of your head, reflect to yourself in the following manner:

> I must attain swiftly the state of a true and complete buddha for the sake of all mother sentient beings. To that end, I shall gather a retinue through practicing generosity[109] toward all sentient beings. Having done so, I will also practice the agreeable speech[110] that teaches dharma in the form of suppressing wrongful conduct and promoting proper conduct, the beneficial conduct[111] that prompts disciples to practice the meaning of the dharma that I taught them, and the sameness of purpose[112] in which I too carry out a form of spiritual practice that conforms with what I have taught others. On the basis of these excellent methods that accomplish the welfare of others, I shall establish all sentient beings in the paths that ripen them spiritually and ultimately bring about their liberation. I also make the supplication prayer, "O divine Root Lama, please bless me and all mother sentient beings with the ability to do so."

[Following this supplication prayer, carry out the related visualizations.]

C) What to Do at the Conclusion of the Meditation Session

The concluding activities are the same as the ones that were explained earlier.

II) What to Do during the Time between Meditation Sessions

During the time between meditation sessions, you should also support the main practice by reading scripture texts and commentaries that explain both the profound and extensive forms of exalted activities {150} for a victor's offspring. The rest of the instructions for what to do between meditation sessions are the same as were described earlier.

ii. How to Train Yourself in the Final Two Perfections

This topic is made up of two sections: (1) how to train yourself in the quiescence whose nature is meditative absorption and (2) how to train yourself in the insight whose nature is wisdom.

I) How to Train Yourself in Quiescence

This topic has two parts: (1) what to do during meditation sessions and (2) what to do in the time between meditation sessions.

A) What to do during Meditation Sessions

This topic is made up of three parts: (1) preliminaries, (2) main practice, and (3) conclusion.

1) Preliminaries

The activities to be done first are the general activities of the preliminary stage and, in particular, the mental training that relates to lesser and middling persons, as well as observing the collection of causal factors that promote the development of quiescence,[113] such as abiding in a state of pure morality in an isolated place that is pleasing to the mind and is a wholesome location where good companions are present,[114] avoiding excessive contact with many persons, giving up rough thoughts that constitute desire for sensory pleasures, and abiding in a state of both having few wants and being satisfied with what one has. Having done so, observe the favorable elements of posture, such as sitting on a comfortable seat with your body held erect, your legs in the vajra cross-legged position, your hands in the meditation gesture, and your breath brought under control, and so on.

2) Main Practice

Although many types of meditation object have been taught as the basis for cultivating quiescence, the best object to focus upon is that of a deity's physical form, as it accomplishes numerous purposes, among which the principal one is that of being the most excellent way to practice recollection of the Buddha. Other benefits include that of helping one to become a suitable vessel for meditating on the form of deity yoga that is practiced in the Mantrayāna.

The method of practice is as follows. Visualize that a light ray resembling a strand of spider silk emanates from the heart of the divine root lama seated on the crown of your head. On the tip of this light ray is the Victor Buddha Śākyamuni, whose body is the color of refined gold, seated atop a cushion consisting of a variegated lotus, moon, and sun, and so on, . . . (etc., up to) . . . He or she is sitting . . . with his or her legs in the vajra cross-legged position. Having emanated this figure that is about the size of the Indian *kulattha* bean,[115] visualize that he is seated in the sky in front of you at the same level as your navel and then meditate one-pointedly on this image.

Alternatively, visualize that a duplicate of your divine root lama seated on the crown of your head separates from him, in the manner of a candle that is lit by touching its wick to the flame of another candle that is already burning, {151} and that this figure dissolves into you, causing you to take on the form of the Victor Buddha Śākyamuni atop a tall, wide, and jewel-studded throne held up by eight majestic lions and seated upon cushions of a variegated lotus, moon, and sun, and so on. . . . (etc., up to) . . . you are sitting . . . with your legs in the vajra cross-legged position. Meditate by fixing your mind one-pointedly on this image that resembles a rainbow in the sky and that while it can be perceived, it lacks any real essential nature.

When you are attempting to visualize the meditation object, you may have such experiences as the following: Wanting to meditate on the color yellow, the object appears in a different color, such as red, and so on. Or, wanting to meditate on a seated form, the object appears in a form that is standing. Or, wanting to meditate on a single object, many objects appear. If such an experience occurs, do not allow it to continue; you should fix your mind one-pointedly on the intended form of the original object and meditate on that. While, at first, the meditation object may not appear with great clarity as a physical form whose nature is transparent and radiant light, you should fix your mind one-pointedly on the image of a physical body in which only about half of its features are evident[116] and meditate on that.

Furthermore, with regard to this exercise, begin by developing a strong aspiration in which you reflect to yourself, "During a meditation session that will last for such-and-such a period of time, I will do everything I can to make sure that no form of languor[117] or excitation[118] whatsoever arises. If either one should arise, I will become aware of that immediately and eliminate that flaw." Then cultivate continually that very mind that has been directed one-pointedly to the meditation object by recalling it repeatedly, in such a way that it is not lost from your field of awareness. This constitutes the most excellent means by which a novice practitioner cultivates mental stability.[119]

In short, one who attempts to cultivate a genuine form of one-pointed concentration must do so by practicing the eight factors that are the antidotes to the five faults, as stated in the lines:

> Abandonment of the five faults follows
> the practice of the eight factors.[120]

Moreover, regarding this topic, when you are practicing one-pointed concentration, laziness is a fault for which the antidote is fourfold: the faith that perceives the good qualities associated with one-pointed concentration; the aspiration that is desirous of attaining one-pointed concentration; the effort that puts forth exertion in order to attain one-pointed concentration; and the result of that exertion—which is to say, agility.[121]

When you are striving to cultivate one-pointed concentration, forgetting the instruction[122] is a fault for which {152} the antidote is recollection. Moreover, it is not sufficient for this recollection simply to keep you from losing the meditation object;[123] when your mind takes hold of the meditation object one-pointedly, recollection must cause it to take on the intensity of a strong definite understanding.

When you are trying to absorb yourself in a state of one-pointed concentration, the two mental states of languor and excitation together constitute a third fault for which the antidote is vigilance.[124] Moreover, regarding this mental factor, the role of vigilance is to examine effectively whether or not languor or excitation have arisen, which enables a person of highest mental acuity to abandon languor or excitation by recognizing either of them when they are just beginning to arise. A person of middling acuity will abandon either of them right after it has arisen, while a person of lesser acuity must abandon either of them after realizing that either of them has arisen, shortly after it has done so.

Well then, what are the defining characteristics of torpor,[125] as well as languor and excitation? Torpor is a mental factor that takes the form of a heaviness of body and mind in which the meditation object loses its clarity. It is a state in which the mind seems to be overcome by a state of darkness.

Rough languor is a state in which the mind has not strayed to some entity other than the meditation object; however, recollection, through having become weakened, has lost its clarity and brightness. In contrast to that, subtle languor is a state in which recollection retains its clarity and brightness; however, the firmness with which it cognizes the meditation object decisively has weakened slightly. The antidote for all of these states is to practice any of the following methods: reflect on the virtuous qualities of the Three Jewels to bring to mind an image of brightness,[126] or carry out the instruction in which the inseparable combination of your vital air and mind become mixed with space.[127]

If your mind does not remain fixed unwaveringly on the meditation object and begins to move slightly, this is subtle excitation. The antidote for this is to initiate recollection and vigilance as you continue to meditate. If, despite your effort to generate recollection and vigilance, your mind still does not remain fixed and it moves outward[128] to an object of attachment, this constitutes rough excitation, for which the antidote is to meditate on such topics as impermanence, the suffering of the three lower realms, and the general suffering of samsara, or to carry out a form of instruction that represents a forceful method of overcoming excitation.[129]

The failure to apply the corrective action[130] when either of the two flaws—that is, languor or excitation—occurs constitutes a fault, for which the antidote is to apply the proper corrective measure {153} that will cause languor or excitation to be abandoned as soon as you realize that either one has arisen.

Moreover, regarding this point, if you make a strong mental effort in order to bring intensity to your awareness, your meditation will have clarity; however, because this is likely to cause excitation, it will be difficult for you to develop stability. On the other hand, if you avoid making a strong exertion and allow your mind to relax, your meditation will have stability; however, this is likely to give rise to languor, and it will therefore be difficult for you to develop clarity. Therefore, you must examine your own mind in such a way that you can reflect to yourself, "If I increase the amount of effort that I apply to my awareness to this level, excitation will arise." Then you will arrive at a balanced state by easing up slightly before you reach that level. Likewise, if you can reflect to yourself, "When I let my mind relax to this level, languor will arise." Then you will arrive at a balanced state by initiating a slight amount of effort before you reach that level. Using these two points of reference, try to develop stability as you relax your mind in order to avoid distraction or excitation. Each time that you achieve stability, watch out for languor and try to elicit a clarity in which your awareness also possesses intensity. By practicing these two techniques alternately, you will be able to achieve a form of one-pointed concentration that is flawless. Do not, however, consider the state of mere lucidity that lacks the intense clarity of a definite understanding to be the requisite quality.

When you have eliminated even the subtle forms of languor and excitation as they were described above, it is a fault to make an unnecessary exertion when you are continually engaged in a state of one-pointed concentration. Therefore, the antidote is to let your mind remain at rest in a state of equanimity[131] and not make any further effort. Through practicing effectively in the manner that was described, after attaining successively the nine levels of mental stability, you will achieve the quiescence that is characterized by particular forms of physical and mental agility.

3) What to Do at the Conclusion of the Meditation Session

The concluding activities are the same as the ones that were explained earlier.

B) What to Do during the Time between Meditation Sessions

During the time between meditation sessions, you should also support the main practice by reading scripture texts and commentaries that explain the topic of quiescence. The rest of the instructions for what to do between meditation sessions are the same as were described earlier.

II) How to Train Yourself in Insight

This topic is made up of two sections: (1) what to do during meditation sessions and (2) what to do in the time between meditation sessions.

A) What to Do during Meditation Sessions

This section is made up of three parts: (1) preliminaries, (2) main practice, and (3) conclusion.

1) Preliminaries

The general preliminary activities that relate to insight are the same as the ones that were explained for quiescence. {154} In particular, the preliminaries that are indispensable for achieving realization of right view are to combine together these three factors: hearing instruction on the topic of insight through relying properly on a knowledgeable spiritual teacher, regarding your lama as inseparable in nature from your tutelary deity and making supplication to him or her with great fervor, and striving to carry out such practices as accumulation of merit and elimination of misdeeds and obstructions.

2) Main Practice

This section is made up of two parts: (1) how to establish the meaning of and then meditate on the insubstantiality of the person and (2) how to establish the meaning of and then meditate on the insubstantiality of entities.

a) The Insubstantiality of the Person

While limitless proofs that establish the meaning of selflessness have been taught in the Victor's discourses, since it is relatively easy for a novice practitioner to gain an understanding of selflessness by establishing it on the basis of the proof that consists of four key points, that method should be carried out in the following manner.

The First Key Point: Ascertaining the Manner in Which the Object to Be Negated Appears in the Mind

Even in a state of deep sleep, within the depth of our heart we have a very strong thought in which we think to ourselves, "Me, me." This thought is the innate belief in a real personal self. Moreover, regarding this thought, if we are wrongly accused by someone who says to us, "You committed this or that misdeed," we react by thinking, "Although I did not commit this misdeed, this accusation has been made against me," and we develop a very strong thought within the depth of the heart in which we think to ourselves, "Me, me." At this time, the way in which the innate belief in a personal self apprehends that self is particularly evident. Therefore, with another subtle aspect of your mind, you should examine where that mind holds the self is present and the manner in which it apprehends that self to exist. If that latter mind[132] is too strong, the former mind[133] will disappear, leaving nothing but a mental state that is empty of any content and making it impossible to carry out any sort of examination. Therefore, you must develop the main part of your consciousness—that is, the mind that is perceiving an "I"—in such a way that it maintains that nature continuously, and then examine it with another subtle part of your mind. When you are examining the mind that is perceiving an "I" in this way, you should recognize that the place where the self is perceived to be present by the innate belief in a real self {155} is neither one that is distinct from the five heaps or the mind-body complex nor is it one that exists within any of the five heaps individually or in either of the two separate elements that make up the mind-body complex.

Instead, this is the way that the innate belief in a real personal self apprehends the self: It holds that the "I" is not simply a conceptual ascription that is made in relation to the mere collection of the five heaps taken as a whole or the mere collection of the two elements that make up the mind-body complex; rather, it holds that, from the very outset, the "I" has been an entity that is able to stand on its own. The "I" that is the object of this mind's mode of apprehension[134] is the object that needs to be logically refuted. This object is not the object of an understanding that is gained from an explanation given to you by another person, nor is it a conceptual object that is gained merely through understanding the general meaning of words. Rather, it is an object whose nature must be ascertained nakedly,[135] within your own mental continuum. This exercise is the first key point—that is to say, the key point in which you ascertain the manner in which the object to be negated appears to your mind.

The Second Key Point: Ascertaining the Extent of Logical Possibilities

If the "I" that is grasped by the mind that apprehends a subjective self—very strongly and from deep within your heart—exists in relation to your five heaps, it must either be identical with the five heaps or it must be distinct from them; there is absolutely no possibility of a third mode of existence that is separate from those two. Therefore, you must reach the following logical decision in your mind: "Whatever entity there is, it must either exist in the form of a unity or it must exist in the form of a multiplicity. There is absolutely no possibility of a third mode of existence apart from those two."

The Third Key Point: Ascertaining the Absence of a Truly Existent Unity

If you think to yourself, "The 'I' that is apprehended in the manner that was described above is identical with the five heaps," this possibility leads to numerous errors, such as the following: Just as a single person has five heaps, the "I" would also have to consist of five distinct mental continua.[136] Alternatively, just as the "I" is a single entity, the five heaps would also have to constitute a partless unity. For reasons such as these, you should conclude to yourself, "Therefore, the 'I' that is apprehended in the manner that was described is not identical with the five heaps."

Moreover, this is another line of thought. If the "I" that is apprehended in the manner described were one with the five heaps, {156} just as the five heaps undergo arising and perishing, the "I" that the mind holds as being capable of standing on its own also would have to undergo arising and perishing. In that case, one would have to consider the following: Do the former and later moments of the "I" that arises and perishes exist as a unity or do they exist as distinct entities? If they exist as a unity, then all three selves consisting of the "I" of one's former life, the "I" of one's future life, and the "I" of this life would have to be a partless unity.[137] On the other hand, if the former and later moments of the "I" exist as distinct entities, while, in a general sense, it is unnecessary for entities that are distinct to be completely unrelated to one another, if they are distinct entities that exist by way of real essences, they do have to be distinct in such a way that they are completely unrelated. And since, in that case, all three selves consisting of the "I" of one's former life, the "I" of one's future life, and the "I" of this life would have to be distinct in such a way that they are completely unrelated, this would lead to numerous errors such as the following: A deed that has not been done will yield fruition or a deed that has been done will perish.[138] For reasons such as these, you should conclude to yourself, "Therefore, the 'I' that the mind apprehends in the manner that was described is not identical with the five heaps."

Moreover, this is a further line of thought. If the "I" that is apprehended in the manner described were one with the five heaps, the "I" and the heaps would have to be a truly existent unity and, therefore, a unity in every manner and respect. In that case, that would lead to numerous errors, such as the following: The "I" or the self could not be the agent that acquires[139] the five heaps, and the five heaps could not be the objects that are acquired by the "I" or the self. In this way, you should conclude to yourself, "Therefore, the 'I' that is apprehended in the manner that was described is not one with the five heaps."

4. The Fourth Key Point: Ascertaining the Absence of a Truly Existent Multiplicity

You may think to yourself, "The 'I' that is apprehended in the manner described cannot be established as possessing the nature of a unity in relation to the five heaps; however, it can be established as an entity that is distinct from the five heaps." If that were true, just as, after you have set apart each of the other four heaps of form and so on, you can still identify the fifth heap as a separate entity by asserting, "This is the consciousness heap," after having set apart each of the five heaps of form and so on, you would still have to be able to identify the personal self as an entity that is distinct from the five heaps by asserting, "This is the 'I' that is apprehended in the manner described." However, because this is not possible,[140] you should conclude to yourself, "Therefore, the 'I' that is apprehended in the manner that was described {157} cannot be established as an entity that is distinct from the five heaps."

Through having determined, on the basis of this analysis of four key points, that there is no self that exists in the manner that it is apprehended by the innate belief in a real self, you should meditate one-pointedly on the continuum of that definite understanding and do so while remaining free of languor and excitation. Moreover, regarding this practice, when the definite understanding of the nonexistence of a real self becomes weakened somewhat, novice practitioners should elicit a definite understanding of the self's lack of a truly existent nature once again by carrying out the four-point analysis in the same way that they did previously.

Those practitioners of greater acumen are able to elicit the same kind of definite understanding that the self does not truly exist simply by considering whether or not the "I" exists as it is perceived by the innate belief in a real self, as they can by carrying out the four-point analysis.[141] In either case, once that definite understanding has been elicited, the practitioner should combine together the following two elements of his or her awareness: a cognitive aspect, which is the very firm certainty that the "I" does not possess an independently real essence, and a perceptual aspect, which is the vivid discernment of a state of complete emptiness[142] that consists of the mere negation of the object to be refuted—which is to say, the negation of the self's truly existent nature. Having done so, this form of one-pointed meditation represents what is called "space-like meditative composure."

During the post-meditative period, you should meditate on the understanding that all entities perceived by ordinary dualistic thought, including the "I," resemble a manifestation of magically created illusions. Moreover, this latter form of practice means that, based upon having elicited a powerful form of the definite understanding that the "I" is not truly existent during a state of meditative composure, you should cultivate, during the post-meditative period, an understanding that recognizes that, while all entities that become evident to your ordinary, dualistic awareness appear to be truly existent, they are, in fact, false appearances because they are not truly existent and they therefore appear in a manner that resembles a manifestation of magically created illusions.

b) How to Establish the Meaning of and Then Meditate on the Insubstantiality of Entities

This section of the outline is made up of two parts: (1) how to establish the meaning of and then meditate on the insubstantiality of conditioned entities[143] and (2) how to establish the meaning of and then meditate on the insubstantiality of unconditioned entities.[144]

i) The Insubstantiality of Conditioned Entities

This topic is made up of three sections: (1) the insubstantiality of inanimate matter, (2) the insubstantiality of the mind, and (3) the insubstantiality of formations that do not accompany the mind.

The Insubstantiality of Inanimate Matter[145]

Take a sentient being's physical body as an illustration of this category of conditioned entity. The manner in which the object to be negated appears to the mind is that a sentient being's physical body is not simply a conceptual ascription that is made in relation to the solid body of flesh and bones that is a mere collection of five parts;[146] rather it undeniably has the appearance of being a distinct physical body {158} that from the very outset has existed as an entity that is able to stand on its own.

If such a truly existent physical body does exist in relation to the solid body of flesh and bones that is merely a collection of five parts, it either exists as a truly existent body that is one with the solid body of flesh and bones that is merely a collection of five parts or it exists as a truly existent body that is distinct from the solid body of flesh and bones that is merely a collection of five parts.

If the truly existent body were one with the solid body of flesh and bones that is merely a collection of five parts, this possibility leads to the following errors: Since the solid body of flesh and bones that is merely a collection of five parts is derived from the semen and egg of the related sentient being's parents, that combination of a drop of semen and an egg that is entered by the related sentient being's consciousness would have to be the solid body of flesh and bones that is merely a collection of five parts. In addition, just as the solid body possesses five parts, the truly existent body that is one with that solid body would have to be five separate bodies, each of which is made up of five parts.

On the other hand, if the truly existent body were distinct from the solid body of flesh and bones that is merely a collection of five parts, this possibility leads to the following error: After having set apart each of the five limbs of the head and so on, you would have to be able to point out the entity that corresponds to the truly existent body by asserting, "This is that body." However, since it is not possible to do so, you should elicit a definite understanding that concludes, "There is absolutely no such truly existent body" and meditate continuously on that understanding.

(II) The Insubstantiality of the Mind

Take today's mind as an illustration of this category of conditioned entity. If there were a self-existent form of today's mind that is not simply a conceptual ascription that is made in relation to the combination of the portion of today's mind that exists in the earlier part of the day and the portion of today's mind that exists in the later part of the day, that self-existent form of today's mind would either have to be one with those two portions of today's mind that exist in the earlier part of the day and in the later part of the day or it would have to be distinct from those two portions of today's mind.

If the self-existent form of today's mind were identical with the combination of those two portions of today's mind, it would follow erroneously that the later portion of today's mind would have to exist at the same time as the earlier portion of today's mind. On the other hand, if the self-existent form of today's mind were distinct from the combination of those two portions of today's mind, after having separated out individually the portion of today's mind that exists in the earlier part of the day and the portion of today's mind that exists in the later part of the day, you would have to be able to point out the entity that corresponds to the truly existent form of today's mind by asserting, "This is today's mind." However, since it is not possible to do so, you should elicit a definite understanding that concludes, "There is absolutely no such form of truly existent mind" and meditate on that understanding in the same way that was described above.

(III) The Insubstantiality of Formations That Do Not Accompany the Mind[147]

Take time[148] in the form of a year as an illustration of this category of conditioned entity. If there were such a thing as a self-existent year that is not merely a conceptual ascription {159} that is made in relation to the collection of twelve months that represent the basis of ascription for a year, that self-existent form of a year would either have to be identical with that collection of twelve months or it would have to be distinct from them.

If the self-existent year were identical with that collection of twelve months, just as there are twelve months in that collection, the self-existent year would have to be twelve in number. On the other hand, if the self-existent year were distinct from that collection of twelve months, after having separated out each of those twelve months individually, you would have to be able to point out the entity that corresponds to the truly existent year by asserting, "This is that year." However, since it is not possible to do so, you should elicit a definite understanding that concludes, "There is absolutely no truly existent year that exists in that way" and meditate on that understanding in the same way that was described above.

ii) How to Establish the Meaning of and Then Meditate on the Insubstantiality of Unconditioned Entities

Regarding this topic, take space[149] as an illustration of an unconditioned entity. Since space is made up of many parts, such as the regions that lie in the cardinal directions and those that lie in the intermediate directions, you should investigate whether a putative self-existent space could be identical with those parts or distinct from them, and after having elicited a definite understanding that space is not truly existent, meditate on that understanding in the same way that was described above.

By way of summary, on the basis of having properly cultivated these two forms of spiritual practice: The first is the space-like meditative composure in which you meditate one-pointedly on the definite understanding that has ascertained that not the slightest particle of any of the totality of entities that relate to both samsara and nirvana—including such things as the "I," the five heaps, mountains, houses, and the like—possesses a self-existent mode of existence such that it is not merely a nominally existent entity that has been ascribed by conceptual thought. The second is the cultivation of an understanding during the post-meditative period in which you recognize that all dualistic objects that appear in ordinary experience resemble magically created illusions in that, while they arise in dependence on a collection of causes and conditions, their nature is that of being false entities that are not truly existent,[150] the practitioner will be able to attain a second form of meditative composure that is imbued with the extraordinary ease of physical and mental agility. This very meditative composure in which physical and mental agility have been elicited on the strength of having applied an analytic form of awareness serves as the definition of authentic insight.[151]

3) What to Do at the Conclusion of the Meditation Session

The concluding activities are the same as the ones that were explained earlier.

B) What to Do during the Time between Meditation Sessions

During the time between meditation sessions, you should also support the main practice by reading scripture texts and commentaries that explain the topic of how to practice insight. The rest of the instructions for what to do between meditation sessions are the same as was described earlier.

After having trained your mental continuum in the Mahāyāna path that is common to both its sūtra and tantra traditions, you must enter the Vajrayāna path, because a practitioner is able to perfect the two accumulations easily on the basis of that path, without {160} having to do so over three vast periods of time, each one consisting of "countless" kalpas.[152] Moreover, training yourself in the topics ranging from how to rely upon a spiritual teacher up to those of quiescence and insight that have been presented in the form of an experiential instruction[153] and eliciting experiential forms of mental transformation in relation to these "stages of the path" by meditating on them each day for as many as four meditation sessions, or at least for one meditation session, represents the supreme method of deriving value from a human form possessing the qualities of leisure and fortune.

> The intent of the incomparable descendant of the Ikṣvāku clan,[154]
> clarified by Glorious Dīpaṃkara Śrī and his spiritual offspring,
> as well as by Losang Drakpa, who was a second victor,
> and arranged into this brief account on the stages of practice,
>
> has been formulated by the one called Chökyi Gyaltsen
> as an instrument to help the fortunate advance toward liberation.
> May this virtue enable myself and all other beings
> to complete the spiritual practice for the three types of person.

This explicit instruction[155] on the stages of the path to enlightenment, which is titled *The Easy Path That Leads to Omniscience*, was first delivered during a summer retreat[156] to an ocean-like assembly of the sangha community by the dharma teacher Losang Chökyi Gyaltsen as a way of reinforcing his own remembrance of this system of practice.[157] Having been transcribed by his disciples and presented to the master for his review, he edited the material into its current form. May this work serve as a victory banner ensuring that the precious Buddha's teaching will never decline.

9. {161} An Essential Summary of the Method of Practice in the System of the Stages of the Path to Enlightenment[1]

Jamyang Khyentse Wangpo

{162} *oṃ*[2] *svasti*[3] *siddhaṃ*[4]

The brief presentation set forth here of the traditional method for carrying out the recitations and so forth when practicing the instructions of *The Stages of the Path to Enlightenment* is made up of two parts: (1) what to do during meditation sessions and (2) what to do during the time between meditation sessions.

I. What to Do during Meditation Sessions

The first part is made up of three sections: (1) preliminaries, (2) main practice, and (3) conclusion.

A. Preliminaries

There are six preliminary practices:[5] (1) clean the practice area and set up vessels[6] of a buddha's body, speech, and mind; (2) arrange faultless offerings in an attractive manner; (3) sit on a comfortable seat while maintaining the posture for practicing meditative absorption and then imbue your mind with the spiritual attitudes that relate to taking refuge and generating enlightenment mind; (4) visualize the merit field; (5) purify your mental continuum by carrying out the seven-limb devotional practice, which contains the main elements for accumulating merit and eliminating obstructions; and (6) with a clear visualization of the entire merit field, present a mandala offering to the lamas and make supplication to them with regard to the three great aims.

The Third Preliminary Practice

Regarding this preliminary exercise, after having carried out the first two preliminary practices as they are taught in the instruction manuals and according to tradition, the third preliminary practice is carried out as follows: On a cushion that is suitable for practicing meditative absorption, observe the key bodily attribute of sitting upright in a cross-legged position and the key verbal attribute of developing a settled breath by focusing your mind and counting, unerringly, up to twenty-one breaths, as you allow the air to flow in and out in a natural manner.

Taking Refuge

In particular, you should also observe the key mental attribute of not allowing your mind to take on either an unvirtuous or an indeterminate[7] state, and with a mind of extraordinary virtue, which is developed by reflecting in numerous ways on renunciation[8] and {163} enlightenment mind, visualize the refuge object and then carry out the act of going for refuge by reciting the following as many times as you can:

> I and all sentient beings who are as limitless as space, from this moment on and until we reach the seat of enlightenment, go to the glorious and supreme lamas for refuge. We go to the buddha bhagavāns[9] for refuge. We go to the true dharma for refuge. We go to the ārya sangha[10] for refuge.

Following that, with palms joined and with intense faith and reverence, recite the following supplication seven, twenty-one, or some other suitable number of times:

> I go to the lamas and the precious Three Jewels for refuge. I beseech you to bless my mental continuum. In particular, I beseech you to bless me so that I may quickly develop in my mental continuum

the realizations that pertain to the stages of the path for the three types of person.

Generating Enlightenment Mind

While reflecting on the meaning of the following words, recite them three, seven, or some other suitable number of times:

> I seek to attain the status of a complete buddha for the sake of all sentient beings. To that end, I shall practice the stages of the path that relate to the three types of person.

As an abbreviated form of practice, it is also suitable to perform the acts of going for refuge and generating enlightenment mind jointly, by reciting the following verse:

> I go for refuge until enlightenment {164}
> to the Buddha, dharma, and supreme assembly.
> Through this generosity, and so forth, done by me,
> may I attain buddhahood in order to benefit the world.

The Fourth Preliminary Practice: Visualizing the Merit Field

Begin by directing your attention to the building you are in, as well as the offerings that have been arranged, and performing the extensive form of the four-part blessing[11] as it is performed in the rituals for the Medicine Buddha and Sixteen Elders. If you are unable to do so in such an extensive manner, you may recite the following more abbreviated version:

> By the truth of the Three Jewels, the blessings of all the buddhas and bodhisattvas, the great authority of the perfection of two accumulations, and the inconceivable power of the pure entity-source,[12] may this entire area now become a beautiful and appealing ground that is embellished with every form of excellent adornment and exquisite feature that is present in Lord Amitābha's pure realm. In this place is a dazzling palace made from the seven types of jewels whose beauty is enhanced by its

excellent design, a structure that is immensely wide and extensive. In its center is a throne made of various kinds of jewels held up by eight great lions, upon which is a seat consisting of a lotus and moon cushion. Surrounding this central seat on all sides are countless more lion thrones with seats consisting of a lotus and moon cushion. The space all around, both inside and outside this palace, is completely filled throughout with a vast ocean-like cloud of offerings made up of supreme forms of human and divine objects of enjoyment, such as exquisite varieties of food, clothing, musical instruments, and the like, as described in the *Three Heaps Sūtra*[13] and the *Aspirational Prayer for Excellent Spiritual Conduct*.[14]

May the ground everywhere
become free of gravel and the like,
as even as the palm of the hand,
smooth, and made of lapis lazuli.[15]

Recite the Offering Cloud dhāraṇī mantra three times:

oṃ namo bhagavate vajrasārapramardane tathāgatāya arhate saṃyak-saṃbuddhāya {165} *tadyathā oṃ vajre vajre mahāvajre mahātejavajre mahāvidyāvajre mahābodhicittavajre mahābodhimaṇḍopasaṃkramanavajre sarvakarmāvaraṇaviśodhanavajre svā hā*

Invoke the power of truth once again by reciting the following:

By the truth of the Three Jewels, the blessings of all the buddhas and bodhisattvas, the great authority of the perfection of two accumulations, and the inconceivable power of the pure entity-source, may everything come about in this way.

Following that, with single-minded aspiration and accompanied by billowing incense, make supplication to the merit field to appear before you by reciting the following verses in a melodious voice:

Without wavering from the pure entity-source,
you survey the ten directions' beings with immeasurable compassion

and promote the furtherance of all the victors' enlightened
deeds—
O Lama of the three times, please draw near, together with your
retinue.

O Bhagavan, savior of all beings without exception,
divine conqueror of the terrible Evil One's host,
you who know all entities, truly and completely,
please draw near, along with your retinue.

O Bhagavān, out of your love for beings
you refined your compassion and perfected the aims
of your vast aspirational prayers for many countless eons—
if this is a time to accomplish your aim of benefiting beings,

please draw near, together with your pure retinue,
from the spontaneous realm of your entity-source palace,
displaying your manifold miraculous powers and blessings
in order to liberate a limitless multitude of beings.

Then reflect and visualize that by having made this supplication, your benevolent root lama—who is inseparable in nature from the incomparable Master,[16] the king of the Śākya clan—surrounded by the lamas of both the Lineage of Extensive Conduct and the Lineage of the Profound {166} View, and also surrounded by the sangha of the three vehicles—both those who are still undergoing training and those who have completed the training—all of whom resemble a massive gathering of clouds, appear in the manner that is described in the *Sumaghadhā Avadāna*[17] and become seated on the thrones that have been prepared for them.

Generating Bathing Houses

In exquisitely fragrant bathing houses
with inlaid floors of brightly shining crystal,
dazzling columns aglitter with jewels,
and canopies festooned with shimmering pearls,[18]

Bathing

Just as all the tathāgatas are bathed
as soon as they have been born,
I, likewise, bathe and cleanse you
with water that is sanctified.[19]

Though the body, speech, and mind of the victors have no impurity,
in order to cleanse sentient beings of their obscurations of body, speech, and mind,
I offer this bathing water to the body, speech, and mind of the victors.
May sentient beings be cleansed of their obscurations of body, speech, and mind.

If you wish to, also recite the following verse together with the remaining similar ones that make reference to the six perfections:

This water has the nature of generosity,
it cleanses the stains of stinginess.
This water infused with the fragrance of giving
washes you well, and with it I offer this bath.[20]

Drying

I wipe their bodies with cloth beyond compare,
clean and scented with exquisite fragrances.[21]

Anointing

With the finest of perfumes, whose fragrance fills all the triple-thousand worlds,
I anoint the bodies of all these Lords of Sages,
which are ablaze with a splendor like gold
that has been fired, burnished, and washed.[22]

Offering Clothing

> By offering, with immutable faith,
> divine raiments that are fine, soft, and light
> to those who have attained the immutable vajra bodies,
> may I, too, achieve the vajra body.

I have written these preceding verses as they appear in the instruction manual *Mañjughoṣa's Oral Instruction.*[23] You can also offer clothing and ornaments {167} by reciting lines from *Entry into the Conduct That Leads to Enlightenment,* such as, "Then I offer them the most excellent forms of / beautifully dyed and well-perfumed garments," and so on.[24] Using these passages as illustrations, perform the bathing ritual in whatever extensive or abbreviated form is most suitable.

Following that, reflect and visualize that the figures of the merit field joyfully and securely return to their former thrones as you recite the following verse:

> In your compassion for me and all beings,
> by means of your miraculous powers,
> O Bhagavān, please remain present here
> as long as I continue to worship you.

The Fifth Preliminary Practice: The Seven-Limb Devotional Practice

Making Prostration

The first exercise of the seven-limb devotional practice that, taken collectively, includes the key elements for accumulating merit and removing obscurations, is the act of making prostration. This should be done in the following manner. While maintaining your visualization of the object of refuge, stand up and make prostrations repeatedly as you recite the series of supplication verses that appear below, after altering them slightly to express the act of prostration.[25] The modified version of the first of those verses states:

> The Master[26] and Bhagavān, who is the unparalleled leader;
> exalted Ajita,[27] protector and supreme dharma successor;

and the venerable Ārya Asaṅga, prophesied by the Victor—
I make prostration to these three, the Buddha and two
bodhisattvas.[28]

Then recite the verses from the *Aspirational Prayer for Excellent Spiritual Conduct* that begin with the words "However many there are . . ." and end with the words, "I praise all these sugatas."[29]

Presenting Offerings

Although the Fifth Dalai Lama's Lamrim treatise *Mañjughoṣa's Oral Instruction* states that you should present a mandala offering here at the beginning of the offering limb, I have followed the outline of the six preliminary practices that appears in Je Tsongkhapa's *Great Treatise on the Stages of the Path*, which references it at a different place in the ritual; thus, it appears below.[30]

To present the offerings of respectful service,[31] recite the following verse with your palms joined together:

Emitting light rays appearing as arrays of reception water,
garlands of reception water, canopies of reception water,
and manifold forms of reception water strewn about everywhere,
great beings make offerings to the victors and their offspring.[32]

Repeat this verse, each time replacing the words "reception water" with "foot water," "flowers," "incense," "lamps," "fragrant water," "food," and "instruments that play music," respectively.

Since the Fifth Dalai Lama's treatise states that you should also offer "the five sense objects, the seven symbols of royal authority, and the like," you may recite any additional series of extensive verses that give expression to such offerings or, as a more abbreviated version, offer them by reciting the following verses:

I present, with devotion, the excellent offerings of visible form,
sound, fragrance, taste, and touch in all the three times and ten
directions, {168}
to the victors and their offspring. Please accept them
and grant me the unsurpassed and supreme attainment.

Through offering these seven symbols of royal authority,
those which are actually arranged and those emanated by the
mind,
to all the buddhas and their spiritual offspring,
may all beings enjoy the inexhaustible treasure.

Just as the eight auspicious goddesses did to the chief of the gods[33]
after the demigods were defeated in battle,
I make offerings to the victors and their offspring
with the eight auspicious substances.[34]

You can also honor the merit field using any appropriate verses of offering, such as those found in *Entry into the Conduct That Leads to Enlightenment*.[35] As an abbreviated form of offering, it is sufficient to recite the verses that begin with the words "With the best flowers . . ." and end with "I honor and worship all the victors."[36]

The Remaining Five Limbs

Following that, perform the remaining limbs of the seven-limb devotional practice by reciting the verses of the *Aspirational Prayer for Excellent Spiritual Conduct* that begin with the lines, "Whatever evil deeds I have committed / due to the influence of desire, hatred, and ignorance, . . ." and end with the line, "I dedicate it all to enlightenment."[37]

The Sixth Preliminary Practice: Making Supplication to the Lineage Lamas

First prepare the base for making the mandala offering, the grain to be used for placing the heaps, and fragrant water. Begin by wiping the mandala base thoroughly and moistening it with fragrant water. Following that, the physical act is to place the heaps in the mandala, the verbal act is to recite the words of the mandala-offering ritual, and the mental act is to bring to mind the related visualizations. While performing these acts of the three doors simultaneously, present the mandala offering in any of the appropriate forms, which variously contain thirty-seven, twenty-three, or seven heaps, and so on, as you recite the wording of the ritual up to the phrase "this very offering, in which no element is missing, . . ." followed by the concluding statement "I offer this to the lamas and the precious Three Jewels. In your compassion, please accept it for the sake of all sentient beings. After receiving it, please bestow your blessings upon me." If you like, you can recite this final supplication using the following wording that explicitly addresses three great aims:

> After receiving it, please bestow your blessings so that I may quickly eliminate from my mental continuum all the erroneous thoughts that impede {169} my practice of the Mahāyāna path. Please bestow your blessings so that I may quickly develop all the extraordinary qualities of realization, such as the two forms of the precious enlightenment mind and so forth. Please also bestow your blessings so that I may terminate all the inner and outer obstacles.

Making Supplication to the Lamas of the Lineage of Extensive Conduct

Following that, once again generate intense devotion and reverence to the lineage lamas of this system of practice and then make supplication to them. Begin by reciting the following verses that are addressed to the lamas of the Lineage of Extensive Conduct:

> The Master and Bhagavān, who is the unparalleled leader;
> exalted Ajita, savior and supreme dharma successor;
> and the venerable Ārya Asaṅga, prophesied by the Victor—
> I make supplication to the feet of these three, the Buddha and two bodhisattvas.
>
> Vasubandhu, crown jewel of the Rose Apple continent's[38] paṇḍitas;
> Ārya Vimuktisena, founder of a middle path;
> and Bhadanta Vimuktisena, who attained the stage of faith—
> I make supplication to these three who open the eyes of the world.
>
> Paramasena, sublime object of wonder;
> Vinitasena, trained in the profound path;

and Vairocana,[39] a treasure of powerful activities—
I make supplication to these three kinsmen of all beings.

Haribhadra, who propagated the *Perfection of Wisdom*'s supreme path;
Kuśalī the Elder, holder of all the Conqueror's instructions;
and Kuśalī the Younger, who watches over all beings with loving-kindness—
I make supplication to these three guides of beings.

Suvarṇadvīpa Guru, master of enlightenment mind;
Dīpaṃkara,[40] who supported the great champions'[41] systems;
and precious Drom Tönpa, who elucidated the sublime path—
I make supplication to these three mainstays of the teaching.

Glorious Gönpawa, a lord of spiritual practice;
Neusurpa, who was firm in profound concentration;
and Takmapa, holder of the entire vinaya basket—
I make supplication to these three lamps {170} for an outlying country.

Namkha Senge, who strove arduously in his spiritual practice;
Namkha Gyalpo, who was blessed by the holy ones;
Senge Zangpo, who abandoned the eight worldly concerns;
and Gyalse Zangpo—I make supplication at your feet.

I make supplication to Namkha Gyaltsen,
who with his enlightenment mind perceives all beings as his children,
who was protected and blessed by the supreme deities,
and who is a supreme spiritual teacher to lead beings in this degenerate age.

Avalokiteśvara, the great treasure of nonapprehending compassion;
Mañjughoṣa, the lord of immaculate wisdom;
and Tsongkhapa, the crown ornament of the Snowy Land's learned ones—
O Losang Drakpa, I make supplication at your feet.[42]

Venerable Sherap Senge, the great realized scholar;
Gendun Drupa, the truly omniscient one;
and Norsang Gyatso, who attained the state of a buddha's three bodies—
I make supplication to these three glorious lamas.

Esteemed Gendun Gyatso, upon whom Sarasvatī smiled;
Gelek Pelsang, who was a sun among teachers;
and Lhatsun Sönam Pelsang, a realized scholar—
I make supplication to these three supreme spiritual teachers.

Venerable Sönam Gyatso, an emanation of Padmapāṇi;[43]
Chöphel Zangpo, lineage holder of the profound instruction;
Venerable Peljor Lhundrup, master of all the spiritual families—
I make supplication to these three realized scholars.

The one named Śrī Bhūti,[44] whose kindness was unequaled;
esteemed Losang Gyatso,[45] who was a lord of speech;
Ngawang Pelsang, a true embodiment of Mañjughoṣa;
I make supplication to these supreme spiritual guides.

Jampa Chöden, a supreme spiritual teacher;
esteemed Gelek Gyatso, my root lama;
glorious Ngawang Jampa, a mainstay of the teaching;
I make supplication to these guides for beings of a degenerate age.

Jampa Mönlam, a learned and righteous realized being;
Venerable Tenpa Rabgye, who perceived supreme knowledge;
and {171} Ngawang Chöpel, a supreme lord among teachers—
I make supplication to these three treasure-holders of scripture and knowledge.

I make supplication to the supreme spiritual teachers.
May I be watched over by the divine lamas who embody the four bodies of perfection;
holders of the glory of loving-kindness, treasures of nonapprehending compassion,
and the ones whose wisdom perceives the ultimate reality of all entities.

I make supplication reverently to the spiritual teachers
who, with skillful means prompted by compassion,
make clear the eye with which to view all the myriad scriptures
and the supreme entry point for fortunate beings traveling to
liberation.[46]

Making Supplication to the Lamas of the Lineage of the Profound View

Chief of the Śākya clan, unrivaled teacher and supreme leader;
Mañjughoṣa, embodiment of all the conquerors' wisdom;
and the supreme Ārya Nāgārjuna, who perceived the profound
meaning—
I make supplication to these three crown ornaments among teachers.

Candrakīrti, the one who elucidated the Ārya's[47] view;
Vidyākokila the Elder, his principal spiritual son;
and Vidyākokila the Younger, a spiritual son of the conquerors—
I make supplication to these three lords of reasoning.

Dīpaṃkara, who supported the great champions' systems
by accurately perceiving profound dependent origination,
and precious Drom Tönpa, who elucidated the sublime path—
I make supplication to these two ornaments of the Rose Apple
continent.

Glorious Gönpawa, a lord of spiritual practice;
Neusurpa, who was firm in profound concentration;
and Takmapa, holder of the entire vinaya basket—
I make supplication to these three lamps for an outlying country.

Namkha Senge, who strove arduously in his spiritual practice;
Namkha Gyalpo, who was blessed by the holy ones;
Senge Zangpo, who abandoned the eight worldly concerns;
and Gyalse Zangpo—I make supplication at your feet.

I make supplication to Namkha Gyaltsen,
who with his enlightenment mind perceives all beings as his
children,

who was protected and blessed by the supreme deities,
and who is the supreme spiritual teacher to lead beings in the
degenerate age.

Potowa, spiritual teacher and preserver of the conquerors' lineage;
Sharawa, who was unrivaled in his analytic powers;
and Chekawa, spiritual heir of instruction on enlightenment mind—
I make supplications to these three who fulfill beings' wishes.

Jilbuwa, a bodhisattva and master of the scriptural and cognitional
teaching;
Lungi Wangchuk, supreme paṇḍita and master of the immaculate
word;
and Drowe Gönpo, precious savior of all the three realms'
beings—
I make supplication to these three great elders.

Sangchenba, possessing the sweet fragrance of pure morality;
Tsonawa, master of the vinaya collection's hundred thousand
scriptures;
Möndrapa, who reached the far shore of the abhidharma's ocean
of teachings—
I make supplication to these three leaders {172} of all beings.

I make supplication to the feet of the glorious lama[48]
who mastered the profound and extensive *dharma*,
was a *savior* to all fortunate beings,
and propagated the teaching through his *sublime* activities.

I make supplication to the feet of Losang Drakpa—
he was a palace of wisdom filled with the wealth of the three trainings,
his excellent deeds are evident in the glory of his disciples,
and the light rays of his fame fill the Rose Apple continent's ten
directions.

The remaining supplication verses to the lamas of this lineage are the same as the ones that appear above, beginning with the line, "Venerable Sherap Senge, the great realized scholar."

Moreover, regarding these verses of supplication, among the lamas that make up this lineage, only those masters addressed in the first two verses, which end with Kokila the Younger, are lamas that are exclusively associated with the Lineage of the Profound View. All the remaining lamas are masters of a lineage in which both the Lineage of Extensive Conduct and the Lineage of the Profound View have merged together to form a single river of instruction; therefore, the latter group of lamas are not part of a lineage that is distinct from the Lineage of Extensive Conduct. Rather, they represent the lamas of a separate Kadam lineage, whose instructions Je Tsongkhapa received directly from his lama Drakor Khenchen Chökyap Zangpo. As Je Rinpoche[49] declares in his *Great Treatise on the Stages of the Path*:

> I heard the Kadampa lineage of instruction on the stages of the path that was transmitted from Gönpawa[50] to Neusurpa, as well as the Kadam lineage of instruction that was transmitted by Chengawa,[51] from the holy, exalted and venerable one named Namkha.[52] In addition, I heard both the Kadampa lineage of instruction on the stages of the path that was transmitted from Potowa through Sharawa and the Kadampa lineage of instruction that was transmitted from Potowa through Dölpa[53] from the holy, exalted and venerable one whose name ends with Zangpo.[54]

Alternatively, following Tönpa Rinpoche, you can recite the following verses of supplication to the lamas of a third Kadam Lamrim lineage:

> Tsultrim Bar, a great master of spiritual attainments;
> Zhönu Ö, who properly served his spiritual teachers;
> and Gyergompa, well trained in the path of the supreme vehicle—
> I make supplication to the feet of these three conquerors' sons.
>
> Sangye Ön, holder of a treasure of marvelous virtues;
> Namkha Gyalpo, who was blessed by the holy ones;
> Senge Zangpo, who abandoned the eight worldly concerns;
> And Gyalse Zangpo—I make supplication at your feet.
>
> I make supplication to Namkha Gyaltsen,
> who with his enlightenment mind perceives all beings as his children,

who was protected and blessed by the supreme deities,
and who is the supreme spiritual teacher to lead beings in the
degenerate age.[55]

The remaining supplication verses, beginning with the verse addressed to Je Tsongkhapa that contains the phrase "a palace of wisdom," are the same as the ones that are presented above.

After you finish reciting, with intense faith and devotion, the supplication verses that address the root and lineage lamas by name, you should recall the meaning of the words of the following verses as you carry out the stake-like supplication[56] for the purpose of requesting your lama's blessings so that you will be able to develop in your mental continuum {173} the realizations that relate to the principal topics of Lamrim practice.

Please bless me to see that properly serving the kind spiritual lord,
who is the source of all good qualities,
is the root of the path,
so that I might serve him or her with great effort and respect.

Please bless me to realize that this excellent human form
of leisure I have found this once is most difficult to acquire
and also has great value, so that I may develop an attitude
that pursues always, day and night, what is meaningful.

Please bless me to recall that body and spirit are as fragile
as a water bubble and that death's destruction comes quickly;
bless me also to acquire the firm conviction that white and black
karma
remain with me after my death, like a body and its shadow—

so that I may always maintain
the mindfulness that abandons
even the subtlest forms of wrongdoing
and pursues good deeds of every kind.

Enjoyment of pleasure never brings lasting satisfaction;
it is the source of all suffering and should not be viewed as reliable.

Please bless me to realize the defects of samsara's prosperity
and to develop great aspiration for the happiness of liberation.

Please bless me to develop, through this pure motivation,
great recollection, alertness, and mindfulness in adopting
the prātimokṣa vow,[57] which is the root of the teaching,
as the heart of my practice.

Please bless me to see that, just as I am immersed
in the ocean of samsara, so are all mother sentient beings.
Please bless me then to train myself in the supreme enlightenment
mind,
which instills in me the duty of liberating all beings.

Please bless me to see that merely generating this attitude
without practicing the three types of morality[58]
cannot bring about enlightenment, so that I will train myself
with great diligence in the vow of the victors' offspring.

Please bless me to overcome being distracted by improper objects
and to succeed in analyzing ultimate truth correctly;
so that I may quickly realize the path
that unites quiescence and insight.

Having become a vessel that is well trained in the common path,
please bless me to enter with ease the Adamantine Vehicle,[59]
that most excellent of all the spiritual vehicles
and the supreme gateway for {174} fortunate beings.

Please bless me to gain a genuine conviction about the assertion
that the purity of the vows and commitments received at that
time[60]
is the basis for achieving the two types of spiritual attainment,
and may I always safeguard them, even when my life is at risk.

Please bless me to learn correctly the two stages' key points,
which constitute the essence of all the tantras, and to cultivate

> diligently and unrelentingly the supreme four-session practice,
> according to the word of my holy lama.
>
> Please bless with long life those spiritual teachers
> who instruct us in this sublime path, as well as
> those dharma friends who carry out the practice properly.
> Please also quell the host of inner and outer obstacles.
>
> In all my future lives, may I never be separated from a true lama
> and may I always experience the glory of the dharma.
> After perfecting the virtuous qualities of the paths and their stages,
> may I quickly achieve the status of Vajradhara.

Following that, carry out the general supplication to achieve the three great aims as you did previously, or if you are going to meditate exclusively on the topic of properly serving a spiritual teacher, perform a supplication in conjunction with a mandala offering and then, at this point, also carry out a special form of supplication that addresses the particular meditation topic you are about to practice in such a way that you elicit a genuine experiential transformation of your mental attitude either by reciting the following words aloud or mentally reflecting on their meaning:

> Please bestow your blessings so that I may quickly eliminate all the erroneous thoughts that impede me from developing in my mental continuum the realizations that relate to the root of the path—which is to say, the practice of properly serving a spiritual teacher. Please bestow your blessings so that I may develop in my mental continuum the extraordinary realizations that relate to the practice of properly serving a spiritual teacher. Please also bestow your blessings so that I may terminate all the inner and outer obstacles.

When you have completed that exercise, visualize and reflect that a stream of fivefold nectar and light rays flows down upon you and all the sentient beings surrounding you[61] from the bodies of the divine spiritual beings that make up the merit field, and through entering the bodies and minds {175} of you and all other sentient beings surrounding you, the nectar and light rays remove, in general, all the evil deeds and obscurations that you have accumulated throughout all your lifetimes in beginningless samsara and especially all the evil deeds and obscurations that hinder you from being able to develop the spiritual realizations of the path that relate to the main practice. Having done so, your ordinary bodies are transformed into bodies that have the nature of transparent and radiant light. In addition, all the virtuous qualities, such as those associated with longevity, merit, and the scriptural and cognitional forms of the dharma, increase and become strengthened. In particular, for both you and all sentient beings this establishes the auspicious conditions, and it causes you to receive the blessings that will enable you to develop, effortlessly and spontaneously, the spiritual realizations of the path that relate to the main practice.

B. The Main Practice

This second topic is made up of two sections: (1) the root of the path, how to rely on a spiritual teacher, and (2) after relying on a spiritual teacher, how to train your mind.

Regarding the second section, it is made up of two parts: (1) an admonition to derive value from your human form and (2) the manner in which to derive value from your human form.

Regarding the latter part, it is made up of three topics: (1) training your mind in the stages of the path that are held in common with lesser persons, (2) training your mind in the stages of the path that are held in common with middling persons, and (3) training your mind in the stages of the path for great persons.

Regarding these methods of practice, when you are practicing, in the proper manner, the forms of analytic meditation[62] and fixed meditation[63] as they are described in the instruction manuals, you should also carry out the act of supplicating your lama who is inseparable in nature from the superior deity[64] for his or her blessings and the visualization known as Purification through the Downflow of Nectar.[65] Moreover, regarding the individual topics, analytic meditation is the principle method of practice for the topics that range from how to rely upon a spiritual teacher up through meditation on enlightenment mind and fixed meditation is the principal method of practice for the topics of quiescence, and the rest. For example, when you are practicing the topic of relying upon a spiritual teacher, practice analytic meditation when you are reflecting on your lama's spiritual qualities and so on. At the end of this process, practice fixed meditation by suspending all other conceptual thoughts and fixing your mind one-pointedly on the state of faith that you have generated toward your spiritual teacher. Moreover, scrutinizing repeatedly the key points that relate to the topics of quiescence and so on represents analytic meditation and then placing the mind one-pointedly on the meditation object represents fixed meditation. Therefore, after having gained an understanding of these key elements, carry out the practice until you develop the forms of experiential awareness[66] that relate to each of the topics. In addition, you should practice reflective meditation[67] by reciting on a regular basis {176} such verse texts as *A Compendium of the Stages of the Path* and reflecting on its meaning. You should strive in many different ways using these skillful methods that will enable you to derive value from a human form that is endowed with the qualities of leisure.[68]

C. Conclusion

Regarding the third topic, when you are preparing to end the meditation session, if you are willing and able to do so, perform the seven-limb devotional practice together with a mandala offering, and then make a fervent act of supplication to your root lama. In any case, if there is a physical vessel[69] for the spiritual beings that make up the merit field, visualize and reflect that your visualization of the merit field dissolves into that receptacle and, after merging inseparably with it, remains present there. Alternatively, it is also acceptable to reflect either that the merit field returns to the innate realms[70] or that it disappears by dissolving into the state of ultimate reality.

Using the virtue roots derived from the practice that you carried out during a single meditation period as an illustration, dedicate the entire collection of virtue of the three times that you have accumulated or will accumulate solely as a cause for attaining the omniscient state of a buddha. In addition, on the basis of having made such an act of dedication, using the topic of relying upon a spiritual teacher as an illustration, call forth your main practice and generate the wish that by the power of all sentient beings having developed in their mental continua uncontrived forms of the two types of precious enlightenment mind, may you and all sentient beings achieve every form of temporary and ultimate benefit, as well as every form of happiness, in whatever manner is desired.

Then recite an extensive aspirational prayer, such as the *Aspirational Prayer for Excellent Spiritual Conduct*, or if that is not possible, then such verses of dedication as the following:

> Just as the hero Mañjuśrī knows how to dedicate virtue,
> so, too, does Samantabhadra in the same way.
> Following their example with my own spiritual training,
> I dedicate all of this virtue.
>
> With the method of dedication that is supremely praised
> by the victors that appear in all of the three times,
> I dedicate all of this virtue
> to the highest form of excellent spiritual practice.[71]

Then, also recite the following verses:

> {177} By this virtue, may all beings
> perfect the accumulations of merit and wisdom
> and may they attain the two supreme bodies
> that arise from merit and wisdom.[72]
>
> May the precious enlightenment mind
> that has not yet arisen be caused to arise,
> and may that which has arisen not diminish
> and develop to ever higher levels.
>
> May I never be separated from enlightenment mind,
> may I always be devoted to the bodhisattva practice,
> may I be always be watched over by the buddhas,
> may I always abandon the deeds of Māra.[73]
>
> May the bodhisattvas bear in mind
> the aims of all sentient beings.
> May whatever the lords desire
> be achieved by all sentient beings.
>
> May all sentient beings obtain happiness,
> may all the unhappy migratory states always remain empty.

May the aspirational prayers of all those bodhisattvas
who abide in the ārya stages be fulfilled.

In addition, recite the following verses with single-minded aspiration:

However much of the two vast, space-like accumulations were collected
through my prolonged efforts in pursuit of this practice,
may it enable me to become a lord of victors who is a guide
for beings whose eyes of wisdom have been blinded by ignorance.

Until I reach that goal, may Mañjughoṣa, in his compassion, assist me
throughout all my future lives; and, having found the supreme path
that is complete in all the stages of the teaching,
may I please the victors through my practice of it.

Through having correctly realized the path's key points
and with skillful means brought forth by intense compassion,
may I clear away the darkness in beings' minds
and become one who long upholds the Victor's teaching.

May my mind be stirred by great compassion
to elucidate the treasure of well-being and happiness
wherever the supreme and precious teaching has not yet reached
or where it may have reached before but then declined.

May *The Stages of the Path to Enlightenment*,
produced by the marvelous deeds of the victors {178} and their sons,
bestow splendor on the minds of those who seek liberation
and long preserve the activities of the victors.

May all human and nonhuman beings who created favorable conditions
and eliminated adverse conditions for practicing[74] the sublime path

never be separated in all their future lives
from the completely pure path that is extolled by the victors.

When anyone strives to rightly practice the supreme vehicle
by carrying out the ten dharma activities,[75]
may the powerful ones always provide their assistance
and may an ocean of good fortune fill all the directions.[76]

After completing these recitations, you may then take up everyday activities.

II. What to Do during the Time between Meditation Sessions

Regarding this second topic, you should spend your time in such a way that all of your conduct does not lose the color[77] of the virtuous experiential states that you developed while carrying out the main practice of the meditation session and that, further motivated by vigilance[78] and mindfulness,[79] they avoid coming under the influence of unvirtuous or indeterminate mental states, and consist exclusively of behavior that is motivated by the roots of virtue.[80]

Using the topic of how to rely on a spiritual teacher as an example, the method of practice for the time between meditation sessions should be understood as follows. Repeatedly study the sūtras and treatises that explain this very subject, and, in particular, do the same with the sections of the longer and shorter versions of Je Tsongkhapa's *Treatise on the Stages of the Path* that address the topic of how to rely upon a spiritual teacher. You should also recite those passages aloud and develop a definite understanding of their meaning. The practice should further be carried out both by reflecting to yourself and saying out loud, "On this occasion when I have found a qualified Mahāyāna spiritual teacher, I shall serve my teacher properly, both in thought and action, and avoid coming under the influence of such faults as doubt, associating with him or her as an equal, and laziness, and so on."

The outline of the topics on how to practice the spiritual tradition known as The Stages of the Path for the Three Types of Person {179} is taken primarily from Je Tsongkhapa's *Great Treatise on the Stages of the Path*. The recitation material mostly follows the structure of the Fifth Dalai Lama, Ngawang Losang Gyatso's *Mañjughoṣa's Oral Instruction*.[81] Moreover, this essential summary of my holy lama's oral instruction was written by Mañjughoṣa,[82] one who had the good fortune to hear a brief amount of instruction on this Lamrim path system through the kindness of the exalted and venerable lama Ngaki Wangchuk Jampa Phuntsok Pel Zangpo,[83] whose knowledge and realizations are inseparable in nature from those of the great philosophical champions who are renowned throughout the Rose Apple continent. May the light of virtue and goodness cause the lotuses of benefit and happiness to flourish at all times throughout the three realms. May auspiciousness abound!

10. {181} The Essence of Nectar

A Manual of Instruction for the Three Types of Person on the Stages for Gaining Entry to the Victor's Teaching[1]

Tāranātha

{182} *namo buddhabodhisattvebhyaḥ*[2]

I make prostration to the Three Jewels.

> Having bowed to the lamas of the three lineages,[3]
> who are made radiant by the jewels of their many spiritual
> qualities,
> I shall explain here the essential meaning of the treatises on
> Dīpaṃkara Śrī's view,
> which constitutes the supreme path of the great champions.[4]

Regarding this subject matter, what is contained here is the very path that is meditated upon by the buddhas and bodhisattvas, together with the pratyekabuddhas and the śrāvakas—that is, all the āryas of the three vehicles—and the path by which they all achieve their respective goals of liberation and the supreme state of omniscience. This system of spiritual practice is variously known by such names as The Stages for Gaining Entry to the Teaching, The Stages of the Path for the Three Types of Person, The Stages of the Path to Enlightenment, and The Entry Point to the Instructions of Great Champions.[5]

The teaching on this system of spiritual practice is made up of three sections: (1) the root of all the paths, how to rely upon a spiritual teacher, (2) the actual stages of the path, how to train yourself in the attitudes that relate to the three types of person, and (3) how that training unites you with the result that is unsurpassed enlightenment.

I. The Root of All the Paths, How to Rely upon a Spiritual Teacher

After you have gained an understanding of the essential characteristics of a genuine spiritual teacher, as well as how to cultivate respect for him or her, you should practice in the following manner during the periods of meditative absorption that make up a session of spiritual practice. After taking up very pure forms of appropriate physical conduct, such as sitting in a cross-legged position, keeping your body erect, and so on, {183} you must direct your attention to the realm of space in front of you and visualize that it is filled with buddhas and bodhisattvas, and carry out a form of worship that includes the acts of making prostration and presenting offerings, in whatever length is suitable, as they appear in such exercises as the seven-limb[6] practice. Therefore, begin by performing the acts of making prostration and presenting offerings. Following that, while recalling the meaning of the verses, recite the verses that express the remaining elements of the seven-limb devotional practice that are found in the *Aspirational Prayer for Excellent Spiritual Conduct*[7] three times. Next, in a very elevated region of the sky in front of you, reflect and visualize that immeasurable numbers of buddhas and bodhisattvas are present. Likewise, visualize and reflect that the region of the sky directly in front of you is completely filled by a dense gathering made up of your root lama surrounded by all the various groups of lineage lamas. Then make this fervent supplication to all of these spiritual beings:

> All the buddhas and bodhisattvas who reside throughout the ten directions, as well as the true lamas who are the entire company of great spiritual teachers, please give heed to me. Please bestow your blessings upon me. Please enable me to terminate all the stains of erring forms of thought. Please enable me to generate all the unerring spiritual realizations. Please enable me to eliminate all the obstacles that prevent me from carrying out the Mahāyāna form of spiritual practice.[8]

After you have completed this act of supplication, you should also present to all these spiritual beings a mentally emanated offering.[9] Then visualize that the root lama and lineage lamas enter you through the crown of your head and become situated in your heart, enclosed within an orb of light. Then reflect that the buddhas and bodhisattvas disappear by dissolving into the state of ultimate reality in the very place where they were situated.

Then make the following dedication prayer:

> By means of these roots of virtue that I have created, {184} may I attain buddhahood for the sake of all sentient beings.

Also recite the following verse of dedication:

> By this virtue, may all beings
> perfect the accumulations of merit and wisdom
> and may they attain the twofold supreme excellence
> that arises from merit and wisdom.[10]

During the time between meditation sessions, you should also refrain from perceiving your lama as having any faults and you should only recall his or her virtuous qualities. You should also reflect to yourself:

> I do not possess the good fortune to meet with an actual buddha. Nevertheless, because the buddhas of the three times have revealed themselves to me in the form of a spiritual teacher who is a magical emanation created by their compassion, my lama is in actuality a true buddha. Due to the kindness that he or she has extended to me, my lama is much more beneficial than all the buddhas. Whichever of the three spiritual goals of rebirth in a higher realm, attainment of liberation, and attainment of buddhahood I may desire, he or she does not conceal from me and provides me with whatever method is needed to attain it. If I have developed even one virtuous quality in my mental continuum, or eliminated one flaw, it is due to the kindness of my lama. He or she is so exceedingly kind in that he or she has enabled me to obtain this profound form of spiritual practice that is so difficult to find.

In addition, reflect repeatedly in the following manner and ensure that these meanings are put into practice:

> I must sacrifice my body as well as all of my wealth for the sake of my lama. Physically, I must also carry out every form of honor, service, and assistance that meets with his or her approval. Verbally, I must praise my lama for his or her virtuous qualities of body, speech, and mind and speak about him or her only in ways that bring honor to him or her. In my conduct, I must do whatever pleases my lama's mind and carry out any verbal directives that I may receive from him or her.

Regarding this topic, the meaning of the supplication that is made at this juncture is as follows. There are five stains that are erring forms of thought: the stain of being entirely devoted to this life, the stain of not believing in the karmic doctrine of cause and effect, the stain of regarding samsara as a state of well-being, the stain of cherishing one's own aims, and the stain of regarding entities and their characteristics as truly existent. There are also five unerring realizations: the realization that future lives are more important than this life, {185} the realization that believes in karma and its results, the realization that samsara is a state of suffering, the realization that cherishes the aims of others more than one's own, and the realization that emptiness is ultimate truth and the entities that make up conventional truth are illusory. The obstacles that prevent you from carrying out your spiritual practice are the following. First, outer obstacles are the harm that is carried out by humans and nonhuman spirits. Second, intermediate obstacles are the illnesses that are caused by a disturbance of the elements in one's body. And third, inner obstacles are the mental afflictions and discursive thoughts that are contrary to the dharma. Therefore, one makes supplication to the lamas to help you eliminate these three types of obstacle.

This completes the explanation of the series of points that make up the first meditation topic.[11]

II. The Actual Stages of the Path: Training Yourself in the Attitudes That Relate to the Three Types of Person

This section is made up of three parts: (1) training yourself in the stages of the path that are held in common with lesser persons, (2) training yourself in the stages of the path that are held in common with middling persons, and (3) training yourself in the stages of the path that are unique to great persons.

A. Training Yourself in the Stages That Are Held in Common with Lesser Persons

Speaking in general terms, among the various Buddhist spiritual traditions, there are many different methods of instruction regarding this first section. Even within the instruction of our own system—that is, this Lamrim tradition that was established by the exalted and venerable Dīpaṃkara Śrī—there are a variety of different views. Some teachers hold that the starting point for the practice is to reflect on suffering, others hold that it should begin with the doctrine of karma and its results. Still others hold that it should begin with a human form that possesses leisure and fortune and the difficulty of obtaining it. However, the majority of teachers hold that the practice should begin with impermanence. Notwithstanding this diversity, all of these positions are based on one and the same key point, and thus there is no difference regarding the import of their views.

Nevertheless, even if it is held, in keeping with the most prevalent and well-known view that the starting point should be a human form that possesses leisure and fortune and the difficulty of obtaining it, since that very topic serves as the foundation for meditating on impermanence, the aim of that position is in no way different from that of the view that holds that the starting point of the practice should be to meditate on impermanence. Thus, it would appear that the topic of leisure and fortune is the most convenient way to begin for the present occasion. In order to explain the instruction based on this point of view, the first of the instruction's three main divisions is made up of these four topics: (1) reflecting on leisure and fortune, (2) reflecting on impermanence, (3) reflecting on the suffering of the lower realms, and (4) reflecting on the doctrine of karma and its results.

1. Reflecting on Leisure and Fortune

After having carried the preliminary exercises of making prostrations, presenting offerings, and carrying out the seven-limb devotional practice, as described earlier, you should also, in a somewhat brief manner, make the supplications that were explained above. Following that, {186} after scrutinizing all the circumstances that relate to your body, dwelling place, possessions, and regional domain, and so on, meditate in the following manner:

> The human form that I have obtained in this life would be

> extremely difficult to find again. I cannot allow it be empty of meaning. I must use it to pursue the dharma.

This basic point should be applied and meditated upon at the beginning of all your practice sessions. Regarding this topic of leisure and fortune, a summary verse states:

> A hell being, a hungry ghost, an animal, a barbarian,
> a long-lived god, someone who holds wrong view,
> one who is born at a time when a buddha has not appeared,
> and a mentally deficient person—these are the eight inopportune states.[12]

Regarding these eight inopportune states, you should reflect as follows:

> Someone who is born in any of the three lower states will have to experience intense suffering, and since those forms of existence are a most inferior basis for practicing the dharma, such beings lack the opportunity to do so. In addition, gods of the desire realm are distracted by their attachment to sensory pleasures, while most of the gods of the form and formless realms are intoxicated by the ease of one-pointed concentration. Therefore, none of these worldly gods possesses the good fortune of being able to hear the dharma. The demigods, too, are similar to the gods of the desire realm, yet their disadvantage is even greater; therefore, their form of existence is one whose inferiority resembles that of the three lower realms.
>
> In addition, if one is born as a human being (1) in a world sphere where a buddha has not appeared; (2) in a realm where a buddha has appeared but in a region where the dharma has not spread widely, or where the dharma is completely absent—that is, if one is born as a barbarian[13] in an outlying land; or, (3) if one is born as a human being in a land where the dharma is present, but as a person who holds wrong view[14] and is hostile to the dharma; or (4) as a dull-witted person who cannot speak and therefore as one who is unable to understand any of the elements that relate to spiritual practice—in all four of these latter cases he or she will not possess the good fortune of being able to practice dharma.

> However, in this life, I have obtained a physical form that is free of these eight inopportune states and that is capable of practicing the dharma.

Summary lines of verse:

> To be a human, to be born in central land, to have faculties that
> are not impaired,
> not to have lost the capacity to complete spiritual actions, and to
> have faith in the basis of spirituality.
> The appearance of the buddhas, the teaching of the dharma,
> the continuance of the teachings, its furtherance,
> and compassion from others.[15]

As expressed in these lines, recall the reasons that in your current circumstances, you must strive to practice dharma and reflect repeatedly on them:

> In general, (1) I possess the attribute of having attained birth in a human form. In particular, (2) I have been born in a central land where the dharma is flourishing. More specifically, (3) since I possess all five of the sense faculties, I am capable of knowing what wrongful acts to abandon and what virtuous ones to adopt. Most especially, (4) I have avoided developing wrong view and avoided committing any heinous deed prompted by wrong view, {187} such as any of the five immediate deeds.[16] (5) I also have the capacity to engender faith in the seat[17]—which is to say, the true spiritual system of dharma and vinaya.[18] Therefore, I possess the five fortunes that relate to oneself.
>
> In addition, it is the case (1) that the Buddha has appeared in this world; (2) that the true dharma has been taught; (3) that the Buddha's teaching has not disappeared and continues to exist; (4) that there are currently many individuals who are newly devoting themselves to the dharma; and (5) that it is currently possible to obtain a livelihood that accords with the dharma since, through the compassion of others toward dharma practitioners, there are many benefactors who provide dharma practitioners with food, clothing, and other necessary objects. Therefore, I also possess the five fortunes that relate to others.

> In this way, it should be understood that a form of existence such as this one, which is free of the eight inopportune states and is endowed with the ten fortunes, is extremely difficult to find. Therefore, on this occasion when I possess these qualities, I must strive to pursue the dharma.

At the conclusion of the meditation session, before you return to the period between sessions, dedicate the virtue that you just accumulated to the attainment of supreme enlightenment, as was described above.

This completes the explanation of the series of points that make up the second meditation topic.[19]

Once again, recognizing that the preliminaries and concluding activities are the same as before, for the main practice of the next topic[20] you should meditate on the following points:

> Among sentient beings, those who have been born in the lower realms are extremely great in number. For example, they are like the vast number of soil particles that make up the great earth. By contrast, the number of beings in the higher states is extremely small; for example, they are like the small number of soil particles that can fit on top of one's fingernail.[21]
>
> Another comparison is the following. The number of hell beings are like all the atoms that make up the great earth. The hungry ghosts are like snowflakes in a swirling blizzard. The majority of animals are found in the great oceans, and they are like the piles of fermented grain that are left over after beer has been brewed.[22] The animals that are scattered across the earth fill the surface of the land, the mountains, the rivers, and the sky. The number of worldly gods and humans is barely in the realm of possibility by comparison to those classes of beings.
>
> Furthermore, while the number of human beings in general is small, the number of humans that are born in the Rose Apple continent[23] in particular is smaller yet, and, even more specifically, the number of human beings that are dharma practitioners is barely within the realm of possibility.[24] Therefore, on this occasion when I am such a person, I definitely must strive to pursue the dharma.
>
> Moreover, the reason that the number of dharma practitioners

> is so rare is that among sentient beings, while the number that commits evil deeds is extremely large—which is to say, it is without limit—the number that carries out virtuous deeds in general is very {188} small. And, among those who carry out virtuous deeds, the number who observe the form of morality that has the ability to project a human existence in a future life is extremely rare, which is the reason that it is difficult to gain a human existence. In addition to that, since one must accumulate a great amount of merit to obtain a human existence that possesses all ten of the fortunes and also to have the opportunity to meet with the dharma, such a human existence is extremely difficult to gain. Nevertheless, by chance, I was able to accumulate a great amount of virtue in past lives, and therefore at present I have obtained this human form that is possessed of leisure and fortune. For this reason, I shall, on this occasion, strive to pursue the dharma.

This completes the explanation of the series of points that make up the third meditation topic.[25]

In relation to this topic, some teachers explain the point that is described as "the difficulty of obtaining an excellent human rebirth on the basis of similes." It is referred to in this manner simply because it consists of presenting similes that illustrate the rarity of finding such a rebirth. Therefore, it is not necessary to treat it as a separate meditation topic.

Furthermore, understanding that the preliminaries and concluding activities are the same as before, as the next form of main practice, recall the reasons that were just explained for the difficulty of obtaining a human form possessing leisure and fortune, and then meditate by reflecting in the following manner:

> On this occasion that I have obtained such a human form that is so difficult to find I must achieve something of great value. If I wish to attain excellent forms of happiness throughout numerous rebirths in samsara, I can achieve that goal effortlessly on the basis of this human form. If I want to pursue liberation from samsara, which is the form of enlightenment in the śrāvakas' and the pratyekabuddhas' vehicles, that is also currently not especially difficult to obtain. If I want to pursue unsurpassed enlightenment, even that goal is relatively easy to pursue and relatively

> easy to achieve. However, if I had failed to obtain a human form such as the one I presently have, I would not even know how to achieve a single form of samsaric happiness, let alone how to achieve liberation or buddhahood. Therefore, I must now derive something of genuine value from this human form.

Likewise, reflect again and again in the following manner:

> It would be an extremely great misfortune if the human form that I have obtained this once were allowed to go to waste. As a verse from *Entry into the Conduct That Leads to Enlightenment* declares:
>
> > If, after obtaining such leisure as this,
> > I should fail to cultivate virtuous deeds,
> > there could be no greater self-deception
> > and there could be no greater ignorance.[26]
>
> To allow this to happen would indeed be a grievous form of self-deception. It would be like traveling to a jewel island and returning empty-handed. When I have obtained, this one time, an exceptional human form that is capable of achieving any extraordinary goal {189} I might desire, it would be a great error for me to let it go to waste without carrying out any form of spiritual activities. I may have allowed this human form to go to waste during the earlier part of this life, but now, from today on, I must not let it remain empty of meaning, and I must strive to pursue the dharma.

Furthermore, if you think to yourself, "I cannot give up my desire for the happiness and the activities of this life," then reflect in the following manner:

> If this world contained an ultimate form of happiness that was long-lasting, I would not have any interest in the immediate happiness of remaining at ease for a few days or months. Instead, I would strive to attain that ultimate form of happiness. Similarly, in order to pursue the perpetual happiness that relates to all my future rebirths, I must not remain attached to the activities of this life. Instead, I must strive to carry out the activities that relate to the dharma.

The purpose of these points is to reflect on the difficulty of obtaining a human form and the necessity of deriving meaning from it when it has been found, as indicated in the following verse:

> This leisure and fortune so difficult to obtain
> that I have found accomplishes a human being's aims.
> If I fail to consider what will benefit it,
> how could this favorable encounter ever occur again?[27]

This completes the explanation of the series of points that make up the fourth meditation topic.

2. Reflecting on Impermanence in the Form of Death

a. The Certainty of Death

This section of the instruction is made up of three topics, the first of which is to reflect on the certainty and swiftness of death. This is done by contemplating in the following manner:

> A sūtra verse declares:
>
> > All those who have existed or will exist here,
> > will pass on after casting off their body.
> > A skillful person, realizing this universal disappearance,
> > abides in the dharma and practices spiritual conduct.[28]
>
> As indicated by this verse, no matter the place where I may choose to live, I cannot escape death. No matter the companions with whom I may choose to associate, I cannot escape death. All those beings who have existed in the past on this earth have died. All those who, from this point on, will appear in the future will also die. Among all these beings who are living right now, there is no one who is exempt from dying.
>
> From the time that we took birth in this life until today, how many of our close friends and relatives have died? How many neutral persons[29] and enemies, as well, have died? Not only have they all died, {190} there is no guarantee that I will continue living either.

> Speaking generally, I have no alternative but to die. More specifically, there is no one who can make an addition to the length of my life span. Since my life span does not stand still for even an instant and it is continually becoming shorter, with each passing moment I am coming ever closer to my death. With each passing day, I am coming even closer than that. With each month that goes by, I am coming especially closer to it. When each and every year goes by, I am coming exceptionally closer to it. For these reasons, death is coming swiftly.

If you think to yourself, "While it may be essential for me to practice dharma, since I still have not reached old age, I can do so at some later time," you must reflect in the following manner:

> I cannot think that this kind of spare time is available during this short life span. For example, in a lifetime of sixty years, my youth went by without my having practiced any dharma. After reaching old age, even if I have the desire to practice dharma, I will not be able to achieve any meaningful results because the vigor of both my mind and body will be depleted. Half of the remaining period of my life will be spent sleeping. Since I will also be occupied with a variety of spiritually meaningless activities that include doing what is necessary to obtain food and clothing, engaging in ordinary physical activities, such as walking and sitting, being distracted with other activities, and the like, even if I were someone who is able to develop great aspiration and effort, the amount of time that I can devote to dharma practice will not be very great.
>
> If I want to quickly achieve the dharma of realization[30] that the true spiritual beings[31] of the past attained through their extensive efforts, there is no way that it would be appropriate, during this short life span, to delay practicing the dharma, to engage in laziness, and to postpone undertaking spiritual practice for the time being.

It is important for you to reflect on these reasons and meditate on them again and again. This completes the explanation of the series of points that make up the fifth meditation topic.

b. The Uncertainty of the Time of Death

The second topic in this section, which is to reflect on the uncertainty of the time of death, consists of contemplating the following points:

> Not only do we human beings, in a general sense, have short life spans, it is also the case that the time of our death is unknown. While it is possible that, through our good fortune, our life span[32] that was projected by our former karma may have been projected to last for some sixty or seventy years, for most of us, it does not turn out to be that long. Even if you assume that it will last that long, this period of time is not measured using today as the starting point. Therefore, it's likely that half of our life span, or even most of it, has already been used up. On the other hand, it's also possible that our former karma only projected a life span of some thirty or forty years. {191} In that case, we may have already arrived at the door that will lead us before the Lord of Death.
>
> This life's enemies, close relatives, wealth, possessions, retinue, friends, and its three qualities of happiness, suffering, and reputation are all things that we don't get to spend time with for a very long time. Therefore, how can they be of any use?
>
> [Consider the following]:
>
> When not even[33] ashes will remain of physical bodies
> like the earth, Meru, and the oceans
> that are incinerated by seven blazing suns,
> what need to say of that most frail human body?[34]
>
> As this verse states, this body of mine is a fragile mass of flesh, blood, and pus. My breath is as unstable as the mist that arises in the fall, and I can never know when it will cease. Nor have I gained control of my mind. Since I have not achieved any guarantee of safety whatsoever over my physical or mental existence, the time of my death is uncertain.
>
> I should meditate on the following verse:
>
> It is wrong for me to remain at ease,
> thinking, "Death will not come today."

> The time will certainly come
> when I no longer exist.[35]

Nāgārjuna also declared:

> The factors that cause death are many;
> the ones that sustain life are few.
> The latter can also be causes of death;
> therefore, always practice dharma.[36]

As this verse states, among the outer factors that lead to death, some are caused by animate beings, such as humans, animals, harmful spirits, and the like. Inanimate factors include aspects of the physical environment, such as a precipice or circumstances that relate to the physical elements, such as fire or water. Inner factors include such things as any of the four hundred and four classes of illness that can afflict the body. In short, there is almost nothing about which it can be said, "This cannot be a factor that brings about death." Even all those things that are considered to be factors that prevent death and sustain life—such as food, clothing, a dwelling place, a bed, and medicine—can, in certain situations, become a factor that contributes to death, such as eating unsuitable food or taking the wrong kind of medicine. Therefore, if I am living in the middle of circumstances where the unfavorable factors that are hostile to my body and life are swirling around me like snow in a blizzard, the time of my death must be uncertain.

This completes the explanation of the series of points that make up the sixth meditation topic.

c. At the Time of Death, Nothing but the Dharma Can Benefit You

The third topic of this section, which is to reflect that, at the time of death, nothing but the dharma can benefit you, consists of contemplating the following points:

Śāntideva declared:

For someone seized by Yama's {192} messengers,
what good are relatives? What good are friends?[37]

As these lines indicate, at the time of my death, even though I may have a great quantity of wealth and possessions, I will not be able to take even a single sesame grain with me to my next life. Even though I may have a great many allies, such as relatives, friends, servants, followers, or persons of authority, I will not be able to take with me even the lowest of servants, a young child. Retainers cannot follow along with me in death. It is the nature of all these persons and things that I will have to part with them. None of them can benefit me in any way whatsoever. I should meditate on them in such a way that they cause strong feelings of aversion.

The same attitude should be developed toward all of these: enemies and friends or relatives, happiness and suffering, and favorable and unfavorable rumors.

If you ask yourself, "Well then, if none of these persons or possessions can follow me after my death, who or what does follow me?" reflect as follows:

The virtuous and evil deeds that I have accumulated are the two things that will follow me in death. Moreover, there is no way to leave behind those evil deeds that I have carried out; they will always be able to harm me. Also, whatever virtuous deeds I have accumulated will bring me benefit; they will not be left behind.

As Dharmika Subhūti[38] declared:

Except for good and evil deeds,
The entire world is left behind
And no one follows after you.
Realize this and conduct yourself well.[39]

Therefore, you should meditate in the following way:

Death is certain, it comes swiftly, and the time of death is uncertain. If nothing other than the true dharma can help me at the

> time of my death and following death, that is the only thing that will benefit me in limitless future lives, I must strive to pursue the dharma right now.

This completes the explanation of the series of points that make up the seventh meditation topic.

Concluding Points for the Practice of Impermanence

Now, you should meditate on the following concluding points that relate to the topic of impermanence in the form of death. Regarding this exercise, the following are called "the five root statements":

1. First reflect that you are not standing still and are always changing.
2. Reflect extensively on the death of others.
3. Reflect repeatedly on the many factors that can cause death.
4. Meditate on what will occur when you are on the verge of death.
5. Reflect on what will occur after you die.

1. Reflect on the following description in order to subdue your mind and place it in a state of intense aversion:[40]

> From the moment we take birth until the time of our death, the continuum of our five heaps is always changing into something different. It was that way at the beginning of this life when I was a small infant, it was that way when I was a child, and it was that way in my youth. It is that way now. {193} I am currently moving ever closer to death. Nothing whatsoever can help me avert this condition.

2. Having recalled this about yourself, count in detail the number of people who have died in each of the regions that surround you:

> During my lifetime until the present, this many people who used to be alive in this region are now dead. This many people who used to be alive in that neighboring region are now also dead. How many people older than me have died? How many have also died that were the same age as me or younger than me?

By reflecting in this way, you will realize that more people have died during this period than are currently alive. Moreover, not many of them died after living out the full measure of their life spans. Most of them experienced an untimely death sometime prior to their having lived out a full life. Then reflect in the following way:

> My own condition is the same as theirs. My own nature is no different from theirs. It is just my good fortune that I have not passed away prior to now along with them. Therefore, I must not fail to carry out a genuine form of dharma practice before I die.

Elicit a strong sense of impermanence as you reflect on these points. Have you not heard about or seen the death of beings other than yourself, both human beings and animals? Have you not seen how a person's youthfulness changes from childhood to old age? Even among those who have not died, how many arrogant persons have you seen or heard about that became helpless? How many helpless persons that became arrogant or wealthy persons that became beggars, and the like? Then reflect to yourself:

> I, all my associates and all my possessions, and so on, also possess the same nature as these beings and entities. We all have the same condition.

3. Following that, after considering the many factors that can cause your death as described above, reflect to yourself in the following manner:

> I have failed to realize how all these entities that are right in front of me could become factors that cause my death. I have not realized how they could do so even this very moment.

4. Reflect on the following consequences of dying in an unvirtuous state of mind:

> If I die while in an unvirtuous state of mind, I will experience terrifying forms of suffering, such as having to undergo a painful mortal injury.[41] My death will not occur in a willing or happy manner. Rather, it will occur against my will and in a sudden manner. I will not die joyfully and in a state of contentment.

> {194} I will die in a manner that is accompanied by intense suffering as my vital organs cease to function. I will not know what awaits me in the next world. I will have to wander unknowingly to some unfamiliar place.

5. Reflect to yourself in the following manner about the period following your death:

> Following my death, my mind will separate from my body. This body will either fall to the ground and turn into a mass of worms or, if cast into water, it will become food for fish and otters. If burned in a fire, it will become a handful of bone fragments. If carried to a mountaintop or some plain, it will be torn apart by the beaks of birds or the mouths of dogs, or eventually, after some days, no remnants of it will remain. Such is the final outcome of this body that I have cherished so greatly.
>
> As for my mind, carrying the burden of karma, it will have to go to some unknown place in order to be reborn. Therefore, is there any way that I can let myself fail to practice dharma? Is there any way I can let myself postpone doing so?

To sum up what should be accomplished by reflecting on these points, you should make the following determination as if you were donning armor, "Now I must carry out a genuine form of dharma," and then become one who completes that aim so that you will come to the end of your life with a sense of joy. You must pursue the aim of being one who aspires to come to the end of your life with everyone else saying about you, "He accomplished a genuine form of dharma practice."

In order to succeed in doing that, you must meditate on the teachings and attain a state of firmness about them. If you feel that you must still cultivate the practice and you still need to become self-sufficient, then you haven't attained a state of firmness.

If you encounter adversities, or your mind is not disposed to pursue the practice, if you are unable to bring the practice to a state of completion, if you act in a way that is contrary to the dharma and you also feel remorse for your actions, and if you face the danger of dying with everyone disparaging you emphatically, then you must make the following sincere vow to yourself repeatedly:

> There is no way that I can let myself be like this. Therefore, starting right now, I must apply myself to the aim of completing a genuine form of dharma practice for the rest of my life. I shall repudiate everything else, and I shall definitely not let myself remain at ease.

This very remedy is one that is vitally important to all current dharma practitioners. {195} This completes the instructions on the topic of impermanence. This final series of points make up the eighth meditation topic.

3. Reflecting on the Suffering of the Lower Realms

This section of the instruction is made up of three topics: (1) reflecting on the suffering of the hells, (2) reflecting on the suffering of hungry ghosts, and (3) reflecting on the suffering of animals.

a. Reflecting on the Suffering of the Hells

The Hot Hells

The preliminary and concluding practices as the same as before. Regarding the main practice, begin by reflecting as follows:

> I do not have the power to remain alive within the realm of human beings for a long period of time. The prospect of my death frightens me.
>
> If I examine this manner more carefully, death itself is not what I need to fear greatly. It's not my death that I should fear, but rather, more precisely, it is the fact that I must take birth in a manner over which I have no control. Since I have not accomplished much virtue, what will happen is that my evil deeds will cause me to be reborn in one or another form of the three lower states. What will I do if that should happen!

This basic point should be contemplated at the beginning of all meditations in which you reflect on the suffering of the lower realms. Following that, the next point is to reflect on the suffering of the hot hells. Several summary lines of verse state:

Revival, Black Lines, Compression,
Wailing, Great Wailing, Conflagration,
Great Conflagration, and Unrelenting Torment.[42]

Regarding this point, all the hot hells are regions that have no mountains or rivers and in which the ground is made of burning iron, with flames about a cubit in height that are continually burning. The ground is filled everywhere with ravines and crevices. It also contains what is variously described as molten copper or molten metal or molten lead. There are also springs filled with very hot and acrid caustic water, and swiftly flowing streams and lakes filled with similar kinds of liquid. The trees are also made of such material as burning iron and the like. These regions are filled with harmful birds, wild animals, as well as many karmically created demons and minions of Yama,[43] the Lord of Death.

It is explained that due to the power of their karma, the intermediate-state beings that are reborn in these hot hells first encounter intense experiences of cold, such as being driven by strong rain and wind. Following that, they see a region that is one of the hot hells. Thinking they will find warmth, their craving causes them to rush there, and when they arrive, they take birth as hell beings.

Moreover, regarding these hells, in general the fire of sandalwood is seven times hotter than ordinary fire, but the fire in Revival hell is seven times hotter than that. {196} It is understood that each lower hell is seven times hotter than the one that lies above it. All of the hell beings have minds whose awareness is precise, quick, and sharp. Their bodies are tender, soft, and sensitive. Both physically and mentally, they have little tolerance for pain. For these reasons, their suffering is also especially great. In those regions, all of the limbs and appendages of their bodies and all of their faculties are formed instantly. Their birth occurs suddenly as if you were waking up from sleep. That is, all hell beings undergo a spontaneously produced birth.[44] Most school systems hold that this is the way in which spontaneously produced birth occurs.

Here is a description of the different kinds of suffering in the various hot hells. In Revival,[45] the hell beings generate hatred toward one another, in the same way that people do when they see their worst enemy. Whatever objects they hold in their hands turn into sharp weapons, which they use to strike each other, causing their bodies to be chopped into many pieces. At first, this causes them to collapse and fall into a state of unconsciousness, as if they were dead. Then a cold wind arises in the sky, making a sound that states, "Revive yourselves." This causes them to be restored to life, after which they begin fighting again, as they did before. In this way, they are continually killed and revived, endlessly.

In Black Lines,[46] Yama's minions mark the bodies of the hell beings with many black lines and then cut them up with saws, chop them with axes, and split them apart with various other kinds of sharp weapons. Furthermore, regarding these experiences, when the upper part of the body is severed, the lower part is restored. When the lower part is severed, the upper part is restored. Their lives go by in this very manner endlessly.

In Compression,[47] the hell beings are crushed between large terrible animals such as rams and so on that fight with one another. Or they are crushed between mountains that resemble the heads of frightening animals, such sheep, goats, water buffaloes, or lions. Some are crushed beneath large mountains that press down on them from above. Also, many hell beings gather together upon an iron mortar[48] that is many leagues in breadth. Then they are crushed and pulverized by a mountain-sized pestle or a hammer. Then the face of the mountain opens up, or the pestle rises up, {197} after which the hell beings return to life as before. Following that, they are struck and crushed again and become pulverized.

In Wailing,[49] pursued by many frightening beings, the hell beings see a white house in the distance. Thinking "That is a safe place," they race there and enter inside, at which time the house turns into an iron building without any doors that bursts into flames throughout the inside and out. Because they are being burned and have no means of escape, the hell beings cry out loudly.

In Great Wailing,[50] the experiences are also similar to those that occur in Wailing. Some differences are that the iron building in this hell has two levels and the hell beings are also boiled in an iron pot or a large copper vessel, and so on.

In Conflagration,[51] hell beings are fully impaled with a sharp and blazing spear or pike from the crown of the head through their anus, or from the anus up to the crown of the head, causing their internal organs to be incinerated and fire and smoke to emerge continually from their nine orifices.

In Great Conflagration,[52] the experiences are also similar to those that occur in Conflagration. There are some differences, such as that the hell beings are pierced by a trident, and the like. All of the forms of suffering that occur in the various higher hell regions are found in the hell regions that lie below them. Those forms of sufferings that are described as being present in the successively lower hell regions are more severe than that of those in the regions above them.

In the hell region of Unrelenting Torment,[53] the suffering is immeasurably great and there is not the slightest opportunity for any ease. In that region, it is also explained that the hell beings undergo such experiences as having their entire bodies wrapped in sheets of burning iron. Then they are shaken back and forth in large iron winnowing baskets that contain burning embers and their tongues are plowed with five hundred plows. Because their entire bodies are burned inside and out by a blazing fire, like the flames that burn the wicks of a lamp, the hell beings cannot be distinguished from the flames that engulf them. It is only from the cries of anguish that one can infer the presence of sentient beings. This is the nature of the intense suffering that is found in the hot hells.

The great length of time that hell beings spend in those regions should be understood as follows. *The Treasury of Higher Learning* states:

> Fifty human years {198} are a day and a night
> for the lowest of the heavenly beings
> in the desire realm. In this way,
> their life span is five hundred years.
>
> Both are twice as much for the higher ones.[54]

The same text also states:

> Among the six hell regions of Revival and so on,
> a day and a night is equal to the life span
> of the corresponding desire-realm gods.[55]

Thus, fifty human years is equal to one full day in the realm of the deities that are related to the Four Great Kings.[56] This class of deities are able to live for five hundred such years. This entire period of time[57] is equal to one day in the Revival hell region. Five hundred such years is the life span of the hell beings in this region.[58] The number of years that make up a life span and the number of years that make up one full day in each of the five successively lower hell regions are both twice as long as in the region above it. In this way, it can be understood that the calculation of time in each successively lower hell region is four times greater than that of the region above it.[59]

The summary points about this meditation topic are as follows. This is how the severity and the duration of suffering in the hot hells should be understood. If, at present, we are unable to place even just one of our fingertips in a small flame for only a brief moment, there is absolutely no way that we could bear to undergo that kind of suffering in the hot hells at some time in the future and yet, once we have taken birth there, there is no way that it can be stopped. However, at the present time we do have a way of preventing that kind of suffering from occurring—that is, if we are able to purify ourselves of the evil deeds or bad karma that can cause us to be born in those hells, that is precisely the way to stop ourselves from having to experience that suffering. Therefore, you should reflect to yourself:

> I must strive to practice dharma in order to avoid being reborn in any of those hells.

This completes the explanation of the series of points that make up the ninth meditation topic. However, depending upon the level of development of the practitioner's mind, it would not be inappropriate to separate these explanations into several distinct topics.

The Cold Hells

Now, you should reflect on the suffering of the cold hells. Summary lines of verse declare:

> Blisters, Burst Blisters, and Aṭhaṭha,
> Hahava, Huhava, and split open like a Blue Lotus,
> a Red Lotus, and Great Red Lotus.

All the cold hells are similar in that the open ground, mountains, and valleys are covered in snow and ice, with few cavities or places of shelter. The region is filled everywhere with extremely cold wind accompanied by swirling snow blizzards. The cold winds pierce the skin and flesh and reach the marrow of one's bones. {199} Among these eight hells, each successively lower one is also said to be seven times colder than the one above it.

It is explained that, during the intermediate state, the beings that are to be born in these cold hells first undergo experiences in which they feel as though they are being burned in a fire. This causes them to generate a desire to find a cool place, after which they see a region that is one of the cold hells. They race there, and when they arrive, they take birth.

Among these regions, Blisters[60] is so cold that the hell beings develop blisters throughout the inside and outside of their bodies. Because Burst Blisters[61] is much colder than that, the hell beings' blisters burst open, causing their bodies to become covered in pus, which makes them feel even colder. The *Letter to a Disciple* also states that tiny creatures that are born from this pus pierce their bodies and eat their flesh.[62]

In Aṭhaṭha,[63] the hell beings emit wailing sounds in which syllables of speech are uttered in a faint voice. Because Hahava[64] is even colder than that, the hell beings aren't able to utter syllables of speech; they can only emit sounds of painful affliction. In Huhava,[65] which is even colder than that previous cold hell, the hell beings cannot emit any sounds, but their bodies shiver and their teeth make chattering sounds.

In Blue Lotus,[66] the hell beings' bodies split open into four, eight, or more segments. In Red Lotus,[67] the bodies split open into a hundred or more segments. Because Great Red Lotus[68] is the most extreme of the cold hells, each part of the hell beings' bodies splits into a hundred or even a thousand fragments.

The life span in Blisters is measured as follows. Consider the large Indian container for measuring grain called a *vāha*[69] that holds eighty *khel*[70] and is completely filled with sesame grains. If every hundred hears a single sesame grain were discarded, the length of time it would take to empty that container is said to be the life span of the hell beings in Blisters. The life spans in each successively lower cold hell is twenty times longer than the one above it.

Regarding this topic, the principal elements of the main meditation practice and the summary points to be considered at the end should be understood in a manner that is similar to the points that were described for the hot hells. This completes the explanation of the series of points that make up the tenth meditation topic.

The Adjacent Hells

Now, the practitioner should reflect on the suffering of the adjacent hells.[71] {200} *The Treasury of Higher Learning* states:

> All eight hells have sixteen additional regions.
>
> Firepit and also Putrid Swamp,
> Razor Path and so on, and the river
> are on the four sides of those eight hells.[72]

Firepit

Further, regarding this topic, each of the eight main hot hells have all four of these adjacent regions on their four sides. Regarding these, the Firepit[73] is a very expansive pit that is filled with burning embers. Whether a sentient being is born there initially or reaches there from the adjacent main hot hell, these hell beings solely undergo very intense forms of suffering; there is no place where they can be at rest. Moreover, in that situation, no matter where they try to flee, they end up in this pit of burning embers. Based on the severity of their karma, they may sink down to their knees or their waist or to some other depth. That is, the extent to which they sink down is not definite. Though they wish to escape, their confusion prevents them from doing so. Terrifying hell guards also watch over them from the edge of the pit and don't allow them to get out.

Putrid Swamp

When the hell beings are able to flee, they reach a filthy swamp filled with excrement that is called Putrid Swamp[74] The fetid smell causes the hell beings to feel as though their head will split apart and they fall into an unconscious state. Inside the swamp are many insect-like creatures that pierce the hell beings' bodies with iron and copper beaks and eat their flesh in the way that wood-boring insects eat the trunk of a tree.

Razor-Filled Path and the Other Regions

Regarding Razor-Filled Path[75] and the other regions, the hell beings see what appear to be attractive meadows in the distance. When they rush there, they reach a place where the ground is covered everywhere with razors that are four finger widths in length, which cut their feet and so on, causing them to experience great suffering.

Sword-Leaf Forest

The term "and the other regions" includes a place called Sword-Leaf Forest.[76] Feeling oppressed by heat, the hell beings see what appears to be a great forest in the distance. {201} Rushing there joyfully, when they arrive they find that all the leaves of the trees are weapons, such as swords and the like. When blown by the wind, these leaves fall like rain and cause the hell beings' bodies to be slashed apart into many pieces.

Iron Śālmalī Forest

The forest of iron *śālmalī* trees[77] is a place where the hell beings are chased by many vicious animals. When they see the *śālmalī* trees, the hell beings climb up their trunks, which have many iron thorns that are sixteen finger widths in length that are facing downward. As they do so, their bodies are pierced severely. Eventually, they reach the tops of the trees, where they undergo many terrible experiences, such as having their eyes plucked out and their flesh pecked apart by flocks of vicious birds. They also undergo additional experiences, such as when they climb down the trees, the iron thorns point upward and pierce their bodies again.

Because the hell beings experience the harm of weapons in all three of these regions, they are combined together as a single adjacent hell.

The River of No Ford

The fourth adjacent hell region is the River of No Ford[78] that contains corrosive water. Hell beings that are tormented by heat see a flowing river in the distance. When they reach there and jump into it without hesitation, they find that the water is extremely hot, as if it were mixed with fire, and the river itself is deep and wide. When their bodies sink into the water, they are boiled thoroughly, causing their flesh to separate from the bones. With their flesh removed and their life force still residing in their bones, their bare skeletons rise to the surface of the water, after which their flesh is immediately restored. Then they sink down again and so on.

Although the life spans of the hell beings in these regions is not fixed, since they must remain in each of these regions for many hundreds and thousands of years, the suffering is intense and long-lasting.

The principal elements of the main meditation practice and the summary points to be considered at the end are the same as before. This completes the explanation of the series of points that make up the eleventh meditation topic.

The Partial Hells

Now you should reflect on the suffering of the partial hells.[79] The location of these regions is not fixed; they are found below the earth, as well as in the mountains, in flatlands, and near waters, and so on, on the surface of the earth. The life spans of these hell beings also are indefinite. Some of these beings have life spans that are longer than the hell beings of the principal hell regions; some also have relatively short life spans. In addition, the manner in which these hell beings experience suffering is indefinite {202} and of different kinds. The sūtras declare such things as, during the daytime, beings in the partial hells experience pleasures that resembles that of worldly gods, while during the night they experience the suffering of the hells. They also describe these beings as having a variety of physical forms, such as bodies that resemble a seat, a wall, a mortar, a cauldron, a tree, and a broom, and so on.

The principal elements of this meditation topic and the summary points to be considered at the end should be understood in the same manner as before. This completes the explanation of the series of points that make up the twelfth meditation topic. For this topic, the practitioner should develop a certainty of understanding from such sources as the edifying narratives[80] of Saṃgharakṣita and Koṭikarṇa.

b. Reflecting on the Suffering of Hungry Ghosts

The preliminary practices and the principal elements of the main meditation practice should be carried out in the same manner as before. Moreover, the practitioner should reflect in the following manner:

> If I were to ask myself, "Though I may escape being reborn in any of the hells, should I be reborn as a hungry ghost, would I experience any form of happiness?" There is no happiness in that form of rebirth either. If one should become a hungry ghost, there are two classes: (1) those who have a fixed region and (2) those who live scattered about. The first type are found in a city called Kapila that lies five hundred *yojana*[81] below the surface of the earth. Rājadhānī, the palace of Yama Dharmarāja, who is the king of all the hungry ghosts, is found there. Countless hungry ghosts live in the area surrounding this palace.
>
> The hungry ghosts that are scattered about are also countless in number and they travel through the sky, on the surface of the earth, and below the earth. If a person who possesses supernatural knowledge[82] were to survey the surrounding area, he or she would be able to see that everywhere he or she goes is filled with the hungry ghost form of sentient being. They are so prevalent that one could not find a place to travel to or live in where there are no hungry ghosts.
>
> Among hungry ghosts, there are a few that possess great miraculous powers who experience some slight forms of well-being. All of the rest, however, undergo severe forms of suffering. The great *Sūtra on Closely Placed Recollection*[83] describes thirty-six types of hungry ghost. These can be subsumed within three categories: hungry ghosts that possess outer obstructions, hungry ghosts that possess inner obstructions, and hungry ghosts that are obstructed in relation to food and drink.
>
> {203} Hungry ghosts that possess outer obstructions include those who cannot find any kind of food or drink for a great many years. Others may see a heap of food in the distance, but when they go there it is perceived as a place that is empty and one where not even any traces of food are evident. There are also those who travel to the bank of a great river, but it turns into a ravine filled

with rubble and sand. Some arrive at the foot of a tree filled with fruit, but it becomes a dead tree. There are also some who are held captive by a great many demons and not allowed to escape.

Hungry ghosts that possess inner obstructions include those whose mouths have an opening that is no larger than the eye of a needle, which prevents them from initially placing any food or drink into their mouths. Or even if a small amount of food does enter their mouths, it disappears when it reaches the extremely large posterior region of their mouth cavity. Others have a great poison in their mouths that causes any drink that is imbibed to dry up. Some are such that even if they should swallow some form of food or drink, it cannot pass beyond their throats, which are as thin as a bowstring. Or if the food should pass through the throat, their stomachs can never be filled because they are the size of mountains.

Some hungry ghosts that are obstructed in relation to food and drink are burned by everything that they eat or drink because it bursts into flames when it enters their body. Others must eat only noxious things that cause them suffering, such as burning embers, feces, urine, pus, or blood; they can never find anything that is wholesome.

Speaking in general terms, all these hungry ghosts must endure the unbearable suffering of always being hungry and thirsty. Deprived of clothing, they also undergo immeasurable forms of suffering due to being tormented by both heat and cold. During the cold of winter, even the sunlight causes them to feel chilled, and in the heat of the summer, even the moonlight burns them. When it rains, they experience it as being burned by a deluge of fire.

Due to the suffering of weariness and exhaustion caused by having to constantly search for sustenance, and because they are unable to find any food or drink, their bodies become emaciated. When the three hundred and sixty joints that connect their bones rotate as they move, they give off flaming sparks, like hard stones that have been struck together. Because hungry ghosts view one another as enemies, {204} they also experience the fear of being seized, bound, beaten, and injured. Although they do not know where they might find a place of refuge, they run away

> in a state of extreme fear, as in the saying "A blind person who frightened himself."
>
> These are the kinds of intense suffering that hungry ghosts experience, and since those with the longest life spans live fifteen thousand human years, their suffering is long-lasting.

The summary points to be considered at the end of this meditation topic and the concluding activities are the same as before. This completes the explanation of the series of points that make up the thirteenth meditation topic.

Although it is not the case that the following point is not included among the series of reflections that relate to the current meditation topic of the suffering of hungry ghosts, there is a tradition that formulates a special point to be meditated upon in relation to those impoverished spirits that are classified among the hungry ghosts that are scattered throughout the world and that also travel through the sky. Accordingly, these particular hungry ghosts are variously said to be spirits that are reborn once again in the lower states because of the harm they commit against other sentient beings, or spirits that possess a powerful poison that causes harm to others, despite their not having the intention to do so, or spirits that use their great power to strike and beat others. In addition, it is said that there are spirits that experience great mental distress when they are blamed by others who say, "An evil spirit caused that misfortune," when they were not at fault or responsible. This reflection does not need to be made into a separate meditation topic; rather, it can simply be added to those that were explained above.

c. Reflecting on the Suffering of Animals

There are two classes of animals: those that are submerged in the great oceans and those that are scattered across the earth's surface. Animals that reside in a submerged place are the ones that are found in the great oceans. With no place of refuge, they move about driven by the waves and wander in an uncertain manner. They eat one another. Because they are always concerned about encountering an enemy, they live in fear and a state of distress. They undergo such unbearable forms of suffering as being eaten alive.

Animals that are scattered across the earth's surface are the ones that are found in the regions inhabited by humans and worldly gods. Those that are not kept by humans are always deprived of mental ease due to the fear of encountering an enemy. Those that are kept by humans have their hair shorn and the nose pierced, they are beaten and endure the hardship of having to carry a heavy load and so on. They undergo many kinds of suffering, such as being killed for the sake of their flesh, blood, skins, and bones. {205} They are also cut up and exploited. In addition, they also experience hunger and thirst, heat and cold, and weariness that is similar to those of hell beings and hungry ghosts. Their chief form of suffering is that of always living in fear of being eaten by one another, due to their extreme ignorance, like a person that has to watch out for an enemy that craves human flesh.

The principal elements of the main meditation practice and the summary points cultivated at the end of the main practice are the same as before. The preliminary and concluding practices are also the same as before. This completes the explanation of the series of points that make up the fourteenth meditation topic.

As the concluding points that summarize the key elements of the instruction that relates to the suffering of the lower states, reflect in the following manner:

> When I contemplate these forms of suffering that are experienced in the three lower states, I must recognize that there is no way that I could endure having to undergo them. Therefore, I need a source of refuge that can protect me from them. If I ask myself, "Who can protect me from that suffering?" And, if neither Brahmā, nor Śakra, nor a wheel-wielding monarch[84] can protect me, what other being of this world is there who could do so? If I further ask myself, "Well then, is there anyone else who can protect me?" then I should realize that the Three Jewels can protect me. Therefore, I shall go to the divine lords that make up the precious Three Jewels for refuge. I shall appeal to the Buddha as my teacher; I shall appeal to the dharma as that which embodies the spiritual practice; and I shall appeal to the sangha as the companions who will assist me in pursuing that spiritual practice.

Then further meditate continually in the following manner:

> Regarding their protection, although the Buddha is a source of refuge, the dharma is the entity that actually protects beings.

> Buddha is not someone who, when you are being swept away by water, can save you by taking hold of you by your hair. He saves you by teaching you the dharma and causing you to act in a manner that accords with the dharma.
>
> Buddha is the one toward whom I should cultivate faith; I should act in accordance with the explanations that are contained in the dharma that he taught; and I should also emulate the conduct that is carried out by the individuals who make up the ārya sangha.

It is also critically important, at the beginning and end of the meditation periods, to be diligent in carrying out all the virtuous activities expressed in the verbal recitation that accompanies the act of going for refuge.

The practitioner should be instructed here that the genuine form of the act of going for refuge that is developed at this stage is one that corresponds to a lesser person's system of spiritual practice. {206} This completes the explanation of the series of points that make up the fifteenth meditation topic.

At this stage, it is important for the disciple to be taught, in a general way, the meaning of the act of going for refuge. It is also important for the disciple to gain an understanding of that subject. In some of the early texts of this body of teachings known as The Stages of the Path, the instruction on the stages that relate to a lesser person are concluded at this point. However, there are also systems in which the topic of karma and its results are also included within this section of the teaching. In any case, as the majority of the systems associated with The Stages of the Path maintain, it is proper for a practitioner to meditate on karma and its results as a separate topic of instruction.

4. Reflecting on the Doctrine of Karma and Its Results

This topic is made up of two parts: (1) reflecting on general principles that relate to karma and its results and (2) reflecting on specific topics that relate to karma and its results.

a. The General Principles That Relate to Karma and Its Results

You should meditate on the following points:

White and black forms of karma and their results are fixed in nature in the sense that a white, or virtuous, deed can only give rise to an agreeable result and a black, or evil, deed can only give rise to a disagreeable result. For this reason, I must abandon unvirtuous deeds and take up virtuous ones.

Whether a deed is virtuous or evil, even though it may be small at the time that it constitutes a cause, it increases greatly at the time of its ripening when it becomes a result. Even in the smallest forms of augmentation, the results are magnified by a factor of a hundred or a thousand. In great forms of augmentation, the degree of magnification can be beyond measure. For this reason, it is important for me to abandon unvirtuous deeds and take up virtuous ones.

As long as the white or black deeds that I commit have not been destroyed by their respective counteragent,[85] it is not possible for them to perish before their corresponding results have ripened. If I have not performed the necessary white or black deed, it is also not possible for a corresponding result to arise in my mental continuum.[86] For these reasons, it is important for me to be careful in pursuing what ought to be adopted as well as turning away from what ought to be abandoned.

This completes the explanation of the series of points that make up the sixteenth meditation topic.

b. Reflecting on Specific Topics That Relate to Karma and Its Results

The second part of this section, reflecting on particular topics, is made up of two points: (1) reflecting on black causes and their results and (2) reflecting on white causes and their results.

i. Reflecting on Black Causes and Their Results

The preliminary and concluding practices for this topic are the same as before. However, in particular, after performing the seven-limb devotional practice, the practitioner must also carry out the act of going for refuge. In connection with the main practice, you should initially reflect on the following point:

> All the forms of suffering of the three lower states, as well as those of the higher-realm states, do not arise in the absence of causes and conditions; in fact they arise from causes that consist of unvirtuous deeds. {207}

While there are many forms of unvirtuous deeds, a summary listing of the more substantial or great instances of misconduct that are particularly important with regard to what should be adopted or abandoned in one's spiritual practice is the ten unvirtuous deeds.[87]

Taking a Life

Regarding the ten unvirtuous deeds, there are three forms of physical misdeeds, among which the first is the act of taking a life.[88] This act consists of killing another sentient being intentionally—that is, with the desire of depriving that sentient being of its life—and doing so unerringly, in the sense that the act is carried out in relation to the particular sentient being that was meant to be killed. Moreover, for the act to reach culmination, the intention to kill that sentient being should not be reversed before the object of the act has died.

Taking What Was Not Given

Taking what was not given occurs when you either seize by force or steal clandestinely something of value that belongs to another person and has not been given to you, and, after having done so, the act reaches culmination when you form the thought, "I have acquired that object of value."

Sexual Misconduct

Sexual misconduct is the performance of an unchaste act of sexual intercourse with a person that is not to be approached sexually. Examples of a person who is not to be approached sexually include a woman who has been taken in marriage by another man; one with whom you have a close family relation in any of the past seven generations; one who remains in the custody of another person, such as her parents, close relatives, the king, or a provincial leader; or one who has accepted a vow of chastity and is forbidden from having sexual relations by that vow. These are examples of persons that should not be approached sexually due to their unsuitability as a sexual partner.[89] Examples of persons who are not to be approached sexually due to it being an inappropriate time are a woman who is sick or grieving or one who is pregnant. Examples in which a person is not to be approached sexually due to the physical location are to have sexual relations with someone at such places as a temple, a religious park, a stupa, or a lama's residence. A situation in which a woman should not be approached sexually due to the unsuitability of the body part is for a male of insatiable sexual desire to resort to any aperture of the body other than that of the female sexual organ. These are the four categories that define the manner in which a person is not to be approached sexually. This description is made from the perspective of a layperson. A person who has accepted the religious austerity of celibacy will commit sexual misconduct whenever he or she engages in any form of sexual intercourse with another person, regardless of the circumstances.

Speaking a Falsehood

Among the four verbal misdeeds, speaking a falsehood is to alter one's conception of some fact and knowingly state what is not true. The act is completed when the object of the act, another human being, comprehends what was said.

Slander

Slander[90] is to speak words that are upsetting in order to create discord between at least two persons who are not in a state of conflict with one another.[91] {208} The act is completed when the intended parties comprehend what was said about them.[92]

Harsh Speech

Harsh speech is the utterance of words of criticism and the like that are meant to hurt the feelings of the person who directly hears them. The act is completed when the speech is understood by that person.

Idle Speech

Idle speech is all afflicted speech that is not any of the preceding three types, which includes such things as speech that constitutes flattery[93] or intimation,[94] as well as singing, acting, discussing topics like war, prostitutes, commercial activities, and spiritual traditions that propagate erroneous views.

Coveting

Among the three mental misdeeds, coveting is the deeply felt desire to obtain for oneself the property, wife, home, retainers, or land, and so on, that belongs to another person.

Malice

Malice is the desire to harm another person or persons or the deeply felt wish that they experience some form of suffering.

Wrong View

Wrong view is the strongly held belief that the doctrine of karma and its results is untrue, as well as the strongly held belief that such things as past and future lives, the Three Jewels, and so on do not exist.

These explanations of the ten unvirtuous deeds are based on the form of these acts that constitute "completed action-paths."[95] All those misdeeds that are incomplete but bear some similarity to these ten, such as mistakenly and/or unintentionally killing another sentient being, also represent forms of karma that must be abandoned. Therefore, you must meditate in such a way that you reflect to yourself repeatedly:

> These are the misdeeds that I must abandon at the very outset of my spiritual practice.

This completes the explanation of the series of points that make up the seventeenth meditation topic.

The Results of Black Deeds

Now the practitioner should reflect on the results of those unvirtuous deeds. He or she should meditate by reflecting again and again on the following points:

> If I carry out a powerful form of any one of these ten unvirtuous deeds, or if I carry it out repeatedly, I will be born in one of the hells. If I carry it out in a form that is of medium strength, I will be born as a hungry ghost. If I carry it out in a form that is of little strength, or if I only carry it out a few times, I will be born as an animal. To take birth in these forms of suffering migratory states[96] is the maturation result.
>
> Destroying another sentient being's life leads to a short life span; taking what was not given, to a shortage of wealth; sexual misconduct leads to having many enemies; lying leads to frequent disparagement; slander leads to conflict with one's associates; harsh speech leads to having to hear unpleasant words; idle speech leads to not having your speech heeded by others {209}; coveting leads to not being able to achieve your aims; malice leads to experiencing mental suffering and being frightened often and/or easily; and wrong view leads to being extremely dull-witted and ignorant. These are experiential corresponding results.[97] The behavioral corresponding result is for an individual to delight in carrying out the same misdeed in a future life as the one he or she committed in a former life.
>
> Governing results[98] are circumstances that occur in the outer physical world that is the vessel in which sentient beings reside. The governing result of destroying a life is for the crops and medicine in the region where one lives to have little salutary potency; that of taking what was not given is for the harvests to be poor; that of sexual misconduct is for the region where one lives to be dusty and foul smelling; that of lying is for the region where one lives to be uneven and difficult to traverse; that of slander is for the soil of the region where one lives to be salty and therefore unfertile; that of harsh speech is for the region where one lives to be filled with sand, rubble, and so on; that of idle speech is for the weather to be unseasonable—that is, a warmth that promotes

rotting in the winter, and freezing temperature in the spring, drought in the summer, and excessive rains in the fall; that of coveting is for grain to be small; that of malice is for food to have an unpleasant taste; and that of wrong view is for crops not to produce any fruit at all.

Of these results, corresponding results and governing results can arise in an indefinite manner and in a variety of ways, which is to say that they can occur in the very same rebirth that the deeds were carried out, as well as in a future life when one is reborn in a higher-realm existence.[99]

In this way, because all ten of the unvirtuous deeds are causes for many undesirable forms of suffering, I should refrain from committing any of them in the future, even if it puts my life at risk to do so. I should also strive to carry out the methods by which I can purify myself of those misdeeds that I committed in the past.

This completes the explanation of the series of points that make up the eighteenth meditation topic.

Reflecting on White Causes and Their Results

Now the practitioner should reflect on the nature of virtuous deeds. This should be done by contemplating the following points:

The happiness of attaining the physical form of a higher-realm existence, as well as all other forms of happiness in samsara, whatever they may be, arise from virtuous deeds. In addition, the three forms of transcendent enlightenment[100] {210} arise from virtuous deeds. Regarding the need to purify myself of all my evil deeds and to train myself as much as possible in all forms of virtuous deeds, while there are many kinds of virtuous deeds, the entry point for engaging in all virtuous deeds is what is referred to as "the pure spiritual practice of the ten virtuous deeds." Since this practice consists of the volition[101] that makes the determination to abandon the physical and verbal misdeeds, in particular, by refraining from committing them in body and speech, along

> with the conduct that supports this volition, after having mentally abandoned those ten unvirtuous deeds that were explained above, I must always abide in this form of practice.

The meaning of the phrase "after having mentally abandoned the ten unvirtuous deeds" is to realize that because those misdeeds are great faults that lead to misfortune, you never want to commit them. Likewise, the phrase "refraining from committing the physical and verbal misdeeds in body and speech" means that not only will you avoid committing any of those ten misdeeds continually, or just when you are in a relaxed state, if you ever commit any of them, then your practice will be a spurious form of spiritual benefit. While there are situations in which this aim can be accomplished without effort, through recalling that you have made the mental determination to abandon the ten unvirtuous deeds, you must become one who is absolutely incapable of committing any of those wrongful acts under any circumstances. With regard to the seven misdeeds that are physical or verbal, you must possess both of these attributes. As for the three mental misdeeds, it is sufficient that you make the determination to abandon them mentally. The volition that makes the determination to abandon the ten unvirtuous deeds is nothing other than the conviction that it is wrongful to commit unvirtuous deeds. Because this volition is an unerring conventional understanding that realizes the wrongfulness of an act that is wrongful, it is a form of the path in the sense of a spiritual quality that serves as an antidote to specific faults. Moreover, it is the very essence of morality.

Once you have been able to develop strong forms of this volition to abandon unvirtuous deeds a number of times, even when you are obstructed by drowsiness and torpor, or distraction, and so on, after bringing to mind that mental factor, you will realize that such misconduct is flawed and be able to restrain yourself from committing it. Because this ability is gained on the strength of that prior volition, and since that strength is also gained by the power of a seed, the volition that abandons the ten unvirtuous deeds, together with the seed created by it, are what constitute the ten virtuous deeds.

This completes the explanation of the series of points that make up the nineteenth meditation topic.

Now the practitioner should reflect on the benefits of the ten virtuous deeds {211}. This is done by meditating repeatedly on the following points:

> Moreover, regarding the benefits of the ten virtuous deeds, the sūtras declare that through practicing all ten of the virtuous deeds, you will experience the maturation result of taking birth as a worldly god; through practicing them in a lesser manner, you will obtain the maturation result of being reborn in the physical form of a human being; and by carrying out deeds that are virtuous, but that are also accompanied by mixed elements such as an impure intention, you will be reborn as a demigod. As for the corresponding and governing results, they are the opposite of the ones that were described previously in relation to the ten unvirtuous deeds, as described in the following lines:
>
> > A long life, wealth, absence of enemies,
> > praise, an abundance of friends, a favorable reputation,
> > speech that is accepted, achieving one's aims,
> > a happy disposition, and a high degree of intelligence—
> > these are the ten corresponding results of virtuous deeds.
> >
> > Potent food and medicine, good harvests, delightful
> > surroundings,
> > a domain with even contours, fields that are fertile,
> > abundant greenery and trees, seasonal weather,
> > large grain, delicious food, and abundant crops—
> > these are the governing results of the ten virtuous deeds.[102]
>
> Since the practice of abiding in the ten virtuous deeds is the cause for achieving happiness at all times both in this life and in future lives, I shall always abide in the ten virtuous deeds.

This completes the explanation of the series of points that make up the twentieth meditation topic. Since it is important to learn in detail the classifications that relate to karma and its results for this section of the practice, it is vital that lamas teach this instruction frequently and that disciples both contemplate it frequently and apply it to themselves rather than simply thinking of it in an impersonal manner.[103]

Now these are the essential points that represent the conclusions that the practitioner should reach after having reflected on the instruction that relates to the topic of karma and its results:

> I must reflect on the topic of black and white forms of karma and their results that were explained above. It is important for me to confess the unvirtuous evil deeds that I have done in the past in a manner that includes the four powers in their entirety. The power of the support[104] consists of the two acts of going for refuge and generating enlightenment mind. The power of engaging in an antidote[105] is whatever virtuous act is carried out for the purpose of purifying yourself of your past evil deeds. The power of self-censure[106] is the attitude of remorse that is felt toward the misdeeds that you committed in the past. The power of turning away from wrongdoing[107] is the determination to restrain yourself from committing misdeeds in the future. These are the four powers that must be present in their entirety.

Next, you should also perform such a confession exercise one time each, at the beginning and end of all meditation sessions. During the time between meditation sessions, you should frequently accomplish the act of making known and confessing[108] one's transgressions before your abbot, teacher, lama, the three vessels,[109] the sangha community, and so on. Even if such individuals have not gathered together, you can visualize the realm of space before you as filled with victors and their spiritual offspring {212} and offer an act of confession to them. Examples of the wording to use for such an act of confession are the *Three Heaps Sūtra* and the verses of confession that are found in the *Sūtra of Supreme Golden Light*.[110] A very important element of this exercise is for you not to hide or conceal whatever evil deed you may have committed and give expression to it by saying, "I have committed such-and-such an act."

You should further meditate by reflecting:

> Not only should I refrain from committing any of the ten unvirtuous deeds, I also should not commit any form of evil act, great or small, that constitutes an unvirtuous deed. Moreover, I should not induce others to commit evil deeds nor rejoice at the commission of evil deeds by anyone. I also should not praise or extol such acts.

As for white virtuous deeds, meditate by reflecting as follows:

> Not only should I cultivate the ten virtuous action-paths, I should cultivate as much as possible all forms of virtuous deeds, including such acts as saving the lives of other sentient beings, providing them with a means of livelihood, giving them objects that are needed to pursue a means of subsistence, observing morality, worshiping the Three Jewels, cultivating faith, and so on. I should also induce others to do so as well. In addition, I should cultivate the act of rejoicing in the virtuous deeds that I and others have carried out, as well as praise those who act in such a manner.

You should also meditate by reflecting as follows:

> While those many different kinds of indefinite activities that are neither virtuous nor evil and that are called "indeterminate,"[111] such as walking, standing, reclining, and sitting,[112] do not themselves have maturation results, I should not allow the time that I spend engaged in them to go by meaninglessly nor should I let them come under the influence of laziness[113] and distraction.[114] In addition, rather than permitting these deeds to be indeterminate in nature, I should alter my mind and my conduct so that they become exclusively virtuous in nature.

On an incidental basis during the time between meditation sessions, you should also reflect in the following manner:

> Because it is necessary for me to achieve a physical form of a higher-realm existence that possesses eight favorable spiritual qualities[115] as the causal means for collecting extraordinary amounts of the two accumulations[116] throughout the period of time spanning a series of lifetimes from one rebirth to the next, I should attain a long life by abandoning harmful intentions; an excellent physical appearance carrying out such acts as giving lamps and clothing to others; birth in an excellent family by avoiding the development of pride and maintaining respect toward my lama and fellow spiritual students; excellence of power[117]—that is, possessing abundant wealth—by practicing generosity toward such beings

as a field of benefit {213}, a field of suffering, and a field of virtue,[118] as well as giving a beggar whatever he or she is asking for; the quality of having one's speech accepted[119] by exclusively carrying out virtuous forms of speech; the quality of being regarded as eminent by honoring my lama, the Three Jewels, and my parents, as well as by making aspiration prayers to achieve a variety of spiritual qualities; the quality of being a person of the male gender by having admiration for male qualities and by protecting male sentient beings from being castrated; and excellence of strength by assisting others through helping them carry out morally upright activities without any expectation of receiving something in return. These eight qualities should be pursued in whatever manner is most appropriate.

This completes the explanation of the series of points that make up the twenty-first meditation topic. With everything that has been presented to this point, the instructions for the stages of the path that relate to a lesser person are now concluded.

B. Training Yourself in the Attitudes That Are Held in Common with Middling Persons

This section of the instruction is made of two parts: (1) reflecting on samsara in terms of its cause and its result and (2) reflecting on liberation in terms of its cause and its result.

1. Reflecting on Samsara in Terms of Its Cause and Its Result

The first section is made up of these two topics: (1) reflecting on the suffering that represents samsara's result and (2) reflecting on the classifications of the truth of origination, which represent samsara's cause.

The first of these topics is further made up of two parts: (1) reflecting on the suffering of the higher realms and (2) reflecting on the general suffering of samsara.

i. Reflecting on the Suffering of the Higher Realms

The Suffering of Humans

As preliminaries, carry out the three acts of prostration, making offerings, and confession in a somewhat extended form, followed by the remainder of the seven-limb devotional practice and the act of going for refuge. For the main practice, meditate by reflecting on the following points:

> I may think to myself, "Among the six classes of migratory states where I might take birth by the power of karma, if I were to be born in any of the three lower states, the suffering would be undesirable as it was described above. But, if I were born as a human, I would be happy." However, that is not a happy existence.
>
> Most human beings are born from a womb.[120] If you remain in the womb for a period of nine or ten months, you are continually subjected in that place of the womb to these three forms of suffering: the suffering of being in a constricted space, the suffering of being in a state of darkness, and the suffering of having to endure unpleasant odors.
>
> Some further examples of the suffering that you undergo in the womb are the following: When your mother is hungry, you experience a sensation that feels like being at the edge of a frightening precipice. When she is full, it feels like you are being crushed under a mountain. If she eats or {214} drinks hot food or drink, it feels like you are being boiled in a hot spring. If she eats or drinks something that is cold, it feels like you have been thrown onto an icy glacier.
>
> In addition, when you emerge from the womb at birth, it feels as if you are being squeezed between the boards of a sesame press and you experience a form of suffering that feels like all your joints are being separated and crushed. In the period immediately following your birth, whatever object you come in contact with feels rough and unpleasant. Even if you are wrapped in a smooth cloth, it feels like you have been tossed into a pit of thorns. When another person holds you, the sensation of suffering is similar to that of a baby bird that has been seized by a hawk.

It is only because we can no longer remember these birth experiences that we do not consider a human existence to be unsatisfactory. If we could recall them, we wouldn't need to reflect on any other points. If we reflected solely on the suffering of birth, we would not think that there is anything at all about the prospect of taking birth as a human being that is appealing, and we would conclude, "I must carry out a form of dharma practice that will enable me to avoid being reborn in samsara due to the power of karma."[121] These are the kinds of suffering that are experienced by a human being that is born from a womb.

Speaking more broadly, wherever you may be born throughout the three realms,[122] the experience of birth is characterized by suffering. No matter which of the five or six migratory states you are born into, the experience of birth is characterized by suffering. No matter in which of the four types of birth you take birth, the experience of birth is characterized by suffering. Indeed, birth is characterized by five types of suffering.[123]

Moreover, regarding those five types of suffering, the one that is described by the phrase "birth is accompanied by suffering"[124] means that you must take birth in a way that is accompanied by intensely painful physical experiences. The phrase "birth is accompanied by a state of indisposition"[125] means that you must take birth in such a way that your very being contains the seeds for generating and potentially also strengthening the mental afflictions. The phrase "birth is the source of suffering" means that the suffering of old age, sickness, and death, and so on, will inevitably occur after you have taken birth. The phrase "birth is the source of the mental afflictions" means that due to your having taken birth, whenever you encounter the various unfavorable conditions in the future, you will give rise to many forms of the mental afflictions and accumulate many forms of karma that are generated by them. The phrase "birth is powerless to stop its own destruction" means that every entity that arises undergoes destruction with each passing moment.[126] Having reflected on these points, you should conclude, "These are the ways in which birth is suffering."

This completes the explanation of the series of points that make up the twenty-second meditation topic.

Moreover, you should continue to meditate by reflecting on the following points:

> Human beings are subject to the suffering of old age. When they become old, they are subject to five types of suffering that are forms of deterioration. Of these five, the type described as "deterioration of color" means that the superiority of one's fleshy tissue, complexion, {215} and luster decline, resulting in a dark and unattractive complexion or one that becomes ashen. The hair of the head becomes as white as the flower of the hummingbird tree,[127] and the faculties lose their brightness. The phrase "deterioration of shape" means the teeth fall out, the body is bent over, the limbs become crooked, the flesh becomes shriveled, and the skin becomes loose. The face is also covered in wrinkles like an old leather cushion, making it unattractive to look at. The phrase "deterioration of strength" means such things as the following: You have to use both your hands, as well as your feet, to stand up; you wobble when you walk; you sit down like a load of salt that falls to the ground when the rope used to tie it onto a pack animal has snapped; and you stammer indistinctly when talking. The phrase "deterioration of faculties" means that your sight becomes clouded, you become deaf, and the like. To others, you appear to be pretending not to understand. The phrase "deterioration of enjoyments" means such things as you feel hungry because you can't eat enough food or you can't digest it when you eat too much. That is, you are unable to enjoy objects of sensory experience.
>
> In addition, you should reflect to yourself, "Since I have not abandoned the suffering of old age, if I have a long life and am able to reach an advanced age, in the end I will become someone who has to experience old age. The same is true for family relatives, close friends, enemies, and all these other beings as well."

This completes the explanation of the series of points that make up the twenty-third meditation topic.

In order to contemplate the suffering of illness, meditate by reflecting as follows:

> There are also other kinds of suffering. Due to my past karma and various incidental factors, I will experience many different kinds of illness. This same is true for my family relatives, close friends, enemies, and all other beings as well. Moreover, there are five aspects to the suffering of illness. The type that is described as "the increasing of physical suffering and mental distress" means that I will experience the suffering of overt pain. The phrase "a change in the nature of the body" means such things as one's flesh wastes away and one's skin becomes dried out. The two phrases "the freedom to enjoy attractive objects is lost" and "one is compelled to experience unattractive objects" mean, in the first instance, that I cannot partake of the food or engage in the behavior that I might desire to and, in the second instance, that I am forced to take harsh medicines and undergo medical treatments such as moxibustion and bloodletting. The phrase "one will be deprived of one's life force" means that I will die or that I will experience mental suffering because of the realization that I must die very soon. That is, illness itself is the harbinger of death. Since I am subject to illness, I am one who, {216} in the end, will become ill. All these other beings, such as my friends, enemies, and relatives, and so on, as well are identical to me in that they too will become ill.

This completes the explanation of the series of points that make up the twenty-fourth meditation topic.

The following is another form of suffering that you should contemplate:

> Five aspects of the suffering of death are that you will be deprived of the ability to experience excellent forms of enjoyment; you will be deprived of the ability to interact with like-minded supporters; you will be separated from an excellent retinue[128] and companions; you will be separated from your dearly cherished body; and the experience of death itself is accompanied by intense physical suffering and mental distress. These points indicate that we must die in such a way that we will become

separated from all the following entities toward which we feel both affection and attachment: land and region, home and family, wealth and possessions, persons of authority who are superior to us, servants who are beneath us in rank, and companions who are our equals. In addition, we must die in such a way that this experience is accompanied by intense forms of suffering as our vital organs cease to function.[129] A more extensive explanation of this topic was presented earlier in the section on impermanence in the form of death.

This completes the explanation of the series of points that make up the twenty-fifth meditation topic.

As before, meditate on the following points:

Another form of suffering is the suffering that is caused by not being able to acquire what is desired and sought after. Moreover, this can occur as we are even willing to engage in physical altercations, without regard for our life, in order to achieve a modest amount of wealth, verbal influence, and authority. This might require us to travel to a foreign land for many months or years. We may have to engage in work continuously throughout the four seasons for which we gain nothing in return. Our feet may bleed from walking on stones, our hands may bleed from grasping wooden objects, our legs may ache from riding a horse. Though I make a whip out of woolen thread and try to collect things from the south and send for things from the north, I may not succeed in achieving any of my aims. I must endure every form of hunger and thirst. I must ignore every form of cold and heat. There is no leisure throughout the entire day and night. Though I have shed even my flesh, blood, and hair repeatedly, I haven't even acquired enough wealth to provide for my food and clothing. Since my efforts have ended in failure, despair arises in my mind.

There is also a form of suffering that is called "the suffering of meeting with what is disagreeable." Examples of this are for you to experience such things as the following: to fall under the control of an enemy, to be stricken by a severe illness or an intense form of suffering, to encounter a creature that can take your life

> {217}, to fall over a precipice, to be swept away by water, to hear derogatory rumors spoken about you, to be imprisoned, and to experience some form of punishment.
>
> Another form of suffering is called "the suffering of being separated from what is agreeable." For example, if you are unable to avoid being separated from a parent, a close relative, a spouse, a friend, and the like, this causes you unbearable mental suffering and can even lead to physical decline. Likewise, this type of suffering can also occur when you experience a loss of wealth, when your power and influence declines, or when you lose a position of authority. In short, this type of suffering refers to the great mental distress that is experienced at the loss of any object, person, or circumstance that is cherished or longed for.

After meditating in this way on these additional topics, you should also reflect, as before, "I, too, am not exempt from these types of suffering," and the rest. While the beings of the other migratory states are also subject to these seven types of suffering, because humans are the main type of being that experience them, I have presented them here. Although there is a tradition that explains the eight types of suffering in this section of the instruction, I regard it as more convenient to do so at a later point. This completes the explanation of the series of points that make up the twenty-sixth meditation topic.

The Suffering of Demigods

Meditate by reflecting in the following manner:

> I might wonder to myself, "If I were to be reborn in the migratory state of demigods, would I be happy?" But, in fact, I would not be happy. Due to their natural jealousy toward the splendor of the worldly gods, demigods continually experience great mental unhappiness. Due to the weakness of their merit, when demigods do battle with the gods on various occasions, they experience a great many kinds of suffering, such as being killed, beaten, and having their limbs slashed or severed. Because the great majority of demigods are of the "black faction,"[130] they dislike the dharma. Even those few who are persuaded to gain devotion toward the

dharma lack the fortune to generate extraordinary realizations because they are subject to a maturation obscuration.[131]

I might think to myself, "Well then, I would attain happiness if I were reborn as a worldly god of the desire realm." However, I would not find happiness there either. For example, through heedlessly indulging in sensory pleasures, they do not realize that their lives will come to an end, and when it does, they experience great suffering. In addition, the worldly gods of lesser influence experience suffering when they are expelled from the place where they live. Some worldly gods of lesser merit {218} are also extremely impoverished and have no possessions whatsoever, except for such minor things as a lute. When they see other gods of great wealth, they experience immeasurably great mental suffering due to the anguish that is felt regarding their lack of merit.

In particular, the gods of the desire realm known as "the group of the Four Great Kings"[132] and those that reside in the Heaven of the Thirty-Three[133] experience the extremely great suffering that occurs through doing battle with the demigods. All the gods of the desire realm in general share the condition that is called "falling down to a lower state of existence when you die."[134] Regarding this condition, the gods experience the following five signs of their imminent death seven days before it occurs: the appearance of the body becomes unattractive, one becomes unhappy and displeased with one's seat, the flower garland that is one's physical adornment wilts, one's clothing becomes stained a dark color, and sweat forms on the body.[135] When these signs appear, even your male and female attendants and companions shun you and associate with other gods. While you still feel attachment for sensory pleasures, you realize that you have no control over being separated from them and there is no way to avert this result. You will experience suffering like that of a mother camel that has lost its baby, or a nāga[136] that has been seized by a garuḍa,[137] or a fish that is writhing in hot sand, or a person who has been shipwrecked in the middle of the ocean.

The duration of this experience is that of seven days of each type of god. This period is the shortest for the gods known as "the group of the Four Great Kings," which is equal to three hundred and fifty human years. Thus, this suffering that is called "falling down to a lower state of existence" is both severe and long-lasting, and following their death, it is almost impossible for these gods to be reborn once again as a god. It is only a very small number that is even reborn as a human; most of them are reborn in the lower states. This is described in the following verse:

> If after passing away from a divine realm,
> there is not any remainder of virtue,
> one is forced to arise in any one of the states
> of an animal, a hungry ghost, or a hell being.[138]

Because the supernormal knowledge[139] of the gods perceives what lies in the realms below them, when they are about to die, they realize where they will be reborn. And since even if they were to be reborn as a human, {219} the sensory pleasures of that realm do not appeal to them, they perceive that human existence as a place of much suffering. If they will be reborn within one of the three lower states, they recognize that they will have to experience the suffering of that state of existence, and this leads them to experience unbearably great mental torment. You should reflect to yourself, "That mental suffering of the desire-realm gods that are facing death is greater than the physical suffering that will have to be experienced in the three lower states."

This completes the explanation of the series of points that make up the twenty-seventh meditation topic.

[Reflect to yourself further in the following manner]:

I might think to myself, "Perhaps, I would attain happiness if I were to be reborn as a worldly god in one of the levels of either of the two higher realms."[140] However, there is no genuine happiness to be found there either. This can be understood as follows: When an ordinary being[141] examines the two higher realms, he or she only recognizes that no overt form of suffering is experienced there; however, an ārya is able to perceive that neither the form nor the formless realm is free from having a nature that is characterized by the suffering of conditioned existence.[142] Moreover, since the ordinary beings of these two realms behave as

> though they are intoxicated by the one-pointed concentration that they experience in these states of existence, they are unable to develop their good qualities to higher levels. Also, due to their attachment to the enjoyment of the bliss of one-pointed concentration, these ordinary beings are unable to separate themselves from those forms of one-pointed concentration. For these reasons, there are even some beings who die when their respective forms of one-pointed concentration are lost. In particular, when the projecting force of the karma that produced the rebirth of the ordinary beings who reside in these two higher realms comes to an end, they will once again be reborn in the desire realm.
>
> For these reasons, I should conclude that while the worldly forms of one-pointed concentration that were cultivated by such ordinary persons when they were previously in a human form of existence and the states of meditative absorption and formless states of composure that they enjoyed when they were reborn in those various levels of the two higher realms have the appearance of being very pleasurable and have the appearance of being states of great ease, they are not in the slightest way reliable, since they resulted in those beings having to fall back into a rebirth as a common, ordinary being who is subject both to developing intense forms of the mental afflictions and to experiencing great forms of suffering. Therefore, what genuine value is there in achieving such a rebirth in any of the levels of the two higher realms?

This completes the explanation of the series of points that make up the twenty-eighth meditation topic.

ii. Reflecting That the Entirety of Samsara Is Characterized by Suffering[143]

The preliminary practices and so on for this topic are the same as before. For the main practice, meditate by reflecting as follows:

> If the suffering in the hell regions is as it was just described and the suffering of those beings ranging from hungry ghosts, animals, humans, demigods, desire-realm gods, up to the gods of the form and formless realms is also as it was just described, {220} then the entirety of this samsara that is made up of three realms is

characterized by a nature of suffering in the sense of such classifications as the three forms of suffering, the six forms of suffering, and the eight forms of suffering, and so on. Moreover, samsara can also be described as having an interior that is densely packed with nothing but suffering and as being completely enveloped in suffering. Its suffering blazes like a fire, disturbs like swiftly flowing water, agitates like strongly blowing wind, and oppresses like a mountain. Any place that you may reside in is nothing but a place for suffering. Any form of physical body that you may take on is nothing but a body for experiencing suffering. Any companion that you may associate with is nothing but a companion in suffering. Any object of enjoyment that you might experience is nothing but a form of enjoyment that consists of suffering.

The Three Types of Suffering

Moreover, the suffering of samsara is of three types, of which the one called "the suffering of suffering"[144] refers to all painful feelings, such as those of heat, cold, and sickness, and so on. The type of suffering that is called "the suffering of change"[145] refers to all pleasurable sensations, ranging from such minor things as the experiencing of ordinary objects of enjoyment and so on up to the bliss associated with the states of meditative absorption. That which is called "the suffering of conditioned existence" is the foundation for both of those types of suffering—meaning that the formations[146] that make up the closely grasping heaps are the source and ground for all forms of samsaric suffering. Moreover, the circumstance in which only the name for this third type of suffering—that is, "the suffering of conditioned existence"—applies is when one's experience is accompanied exclusively by neutral feelings.[147]

[After reflecting on the above points, you should conclude to yourself:]

Because it is not possible for me to free myself from the other
two forms of suffering if I am unable to free myself from this
suffering of conditioned existence, I must do whatever is
necessary to free myself from all three types of suffering.

This completes the explanation of the series of points that make up the twenty-ninth meditation topic.

The Eight Types of Suffering

Seven forms of suffering—namely, the ones called "the suffering of birth," "the suffering of old age," "the suffering of sickness," "the suffering of death," "the suffering of meeting with what is disagreeable," "the suffering of being separated from what is agreeable," and "the suffering that is caused by not being able to acquire what is desired and sought after" were described earlier. Now, you should meditate by reflecting on the eighth form of suffering that makes up this group, which is described by the phrase "in short, the five grasping heaps are suffering." Moreover, this type of suffering is described in terms of the following five aspects:[148]

> (1) "The five grasping heaps constitute the vessel for the suffering that will be produced" means that they promote the arising of the suffering that will occur in the next life and beyond. (2) "They constitute the vessel for the suffering that is based upon their having been produced" means that on the basis of the five grasping heaps having been produced, it becomes possible for all the other forms of suffering such as birth, old age, sickness, death, and so on to arise. (3) "They constitute the vessel for the suffering of suffering" {221} and (4) "they constitute the vessel for the suffering of change" mean that each of those two forms of suffering arise on the basis of the existence of the five grasping heaps. (5) "Their nature consists of the suffering of conditioned existence" means to understand that the five grasping heaps themselves are made up of the suffering of conditioned existence. Therefore, the entirety of samsara's three realms has a nature that is made up of the eight forms of suffering.

This completes the explanation of how to reflect on the eight forms of suffering, which are the series of points that make up the thirtieth meditation topic.

The Six Types of Suffering

There is another formulation of the suffering of samsara, which you should contemplate repeatedly. The first in a group of six types of suffering is the suffering that is the fault of being uncertain. This means that the condition of being an enemy or a friend, a father or a son, as well as all such circumstances as one's dwelling place, physical form, and wealth, and so on, are not fixed in nature and will undergo change. This is described in the verse that begins with the following line:

> A father becomes a son, a mother becomes a wife, . . .[149]

The second type is the suffering that is the fault of providing no satisfaction. This means that no matter how much sensory pleasure we experience, it does not result in our becoming satisfied and no matter how much suffering we experience, it does not cause us to become dissatisfied with samsara. The verse that contains the following lines should be cited to illustrate this point:

> Each and every [samsaric being has drunk] more [milk]
> than the four oceans, . . . [150]

The third fault is that of having to discard one's body again and again. This means that you must experience death over and over again, as expressed in the verse that begins with the following line:

> The mountain of bones from each and every individual's past
> lives . . .[151]

The fourth fault is that of undergoing conception[152] again and again. This means that you must take on an endless number of rebirths, as expressed in the verse that contains the following line:

> Moreover, for counting the lineage of one's mothers with pellets
> of soil
> the size of jujube seeds, . . .[153]

The fifth fault is that of falling from a high position to a low one again and again. This means that even after having become Śakra,[154] one falls back to the earth, as well as even after having been a wheel-wielding monarch, one is reborn as the lowest of servants. It is also the case that even within the very same lifetime, you can never feel secure in the slightest way about the state of your well-being, position, or wealth, as expressed in the verse that contains the following line:

> Even after having been Indra, worthy of veneration by the
> world, . . .[155]

The sixth form of suffering is the fault of being alone, without any companion. This means that when you are born, you are born alone; when you die, you die alone; when you become old or undergo an illness, you experience these conditions alone; and when you enter the intermediate state, you must also do so alone. For these reasons, all companions {222} and friends are of no genuine value to you, as expressed in the verses that contains the following lines:

> Death being inevitable in this way, [seize the light]
> [of the lamp that is the threefold] merit; . . .[156]

This is the manner in which all of samsara is characterized by suffering in that its nature is made up of the six types of suffering. Even if you are born in the highest level of samsara, which is known as the Peak of Existence,[157] it is not at all difficult for you to land at the threshold of Avīci hell.[158] Suffering is always being prolonged again and again. It is like being in a house that is ablaze in fire. It is like merchants who have entered an island inhabited by female demons. It is like wandering in a roadless wilderness. Therefore, I must find a way to quickly liberate myself from this condition.

This completes the explanation of how to direct your attention to the six forms of suffering, which are the series of points that make up the thirty-first meditation topic.

b. Reflecting on the Cause of Samsara's Suffering, the Truth of Origination

You must meditate in the following manner:

> I should ask myself, "Well, if all of that great suffering that occurs in samsara does not arise without causes and conditions, and samsara must be ended by abandoning its causes, what then are its causes?"
>
> Those forms of suffering are produced by the accumulation of karma, and all karma must initially be caused to arise by the mental afflictions. Since no results of karma can arise subsequent to the elimination of the mental afflictions, the root cause of samsara rests in the mental afflictions.
>
> Moreover, there are six mental afflictions that are the root cause by which I and all sentient beings are forced to wander in samsara: desire, hatred, pride, ignorance, flawed views, and doubt. While there are also many other synonyms for the mental afflictions, such as the nine bonds,[159] and so on, they are all included within the three poisons of desire, hatred, and ignorance.
>
> While there are also a very large number of formulations that are made in relation to karma, all the karma that has the ability to project one into a samsaric rebirth can be included within three types. First, the type that is called "demeritorious"[160] karma refers to evil deeds, which have the ability to project one into a rebirth within the lower states. Second, the type that is called "meritorious"[161] karma refers to virtuous deeds of the desire realm that are not associated with any of the states of meditative absorption and includes such deeds as the generosity that is not part of the path to liberation and acts of morality within the desire realm and so on. These constitute causes for rebirth as a desire-realm god or a human being. Third, the type that is called "invariable"[162] karma {223} refers exclusively to the virtuous karma that is generated by one-pointed concentration associated with any of the four states of meditative absorption and the four formless states of composure. This type of karma has the ability to project one into a rebirth within the form and formless realms. All of these forms of karma are subject to the obscuration caused by the ignorance

that does not comprehend the nature of entities. Because they are motivated either by the mistaken apprehension of a real self[163] or the self-cherishing attitude,[164] both of which stem from attachment to the samsaric heaps, they constitute causes for continued samsaric existence.

Regarding the mental afflictions, ignorance or confusion[165] is a mental state that, when we examine our own mind, does not understand what the nature of samsara is or what constitutes the source from which it arises. Likewise, it also does not understand what the nature of liberation is or what constitutes the means by which liberation can be attained. In addition, it does not understand the manner in which those two[166] are brought into being by their respective causes. Although it is possible for you to develop a limited understanding of these subjects through engaging in the activities of learning and reflection, the manner in which ignorance manifests itself is just this: When you examine the way in which any aspect of these two subjects appears to your mind, no matter how you consider it, the thought that forms in your mind is a state of darkness and confusion that has no understanding whatsoever of the particular matter, like the mind of a person that is directed toward the region that lies on the far side of a mountain pass when that person has no knowledge of that place.

Because this ignorance does not comprehend the nature of these subjects, you develop doubt about what constitutes the truth regarding them. While there is no real, subjective self or "I," you mistakenly apprehend such a subjective self or "I" and then give rise to every wrongful mental state. Thus, all the afflicted views[167] are the retinue that follow ignorance. Further, due to their presence, first you develop attachment for your own body and mind. On the basis of that attachment, you similarly develop attachment for a woman/wife, relatives, a retinue, and so on—that is, all the sentient beings who are the "internal" entities [with which you have a close personal association]. You also develop attachment for food, clothing, possessions, a house, a field, wealth, objects of value, and your native land, and so on—that is, the "outer" entities that are objects of enjoyment. This very sense of pronounced joy that we currently feel toward our body and possessions is the mental affliction of desire.

It is on the basis of this desire that we give rise to every form of pride, stinginess, and jealousy. In addition, if any harm is shown toward you or any of your associates,[168] you develop anger. Thus, the very feeling of displeasure that you feel when you bring to mind an individual that has harmed you or a person or object that you embrace, or that you suspect of doing so, is the mental affliction of hatred or enmity. This mental affliction of hatred doesn't only arise in relation to such a person or persons {224}, it can also arise in relation to an inanimate object. This latter case can be illustrated by the displeasure that you feel when you bring to mind the land or house in which your enemy resides or even such circumstances as when you become upset by a stream of water that causes damage to your field. Powerful and extended forms of enmity can also give rise to a variety of other related forms of hatred, including overt feelings of malice, and such secondary mental afflictions[169] as anger,[170] spite,[171] and resentment.[172]

Therefore, I should form the conviction, "Because all three of these poisons are the principal causes that force me and all other sentient beings to continue to wander in samsara, now I must do whatever I can to develop the ability to abandon them." I must also meditate in such a way that enables me to recognize the mental afflictions that are a burden to my mental continuum and that continually arise in my mental continuum, as well as the forms of karma that are generated by them.

This completes the explanation of the series of points that make up the thirty-second meditation topic. If during this stage of the practice, you are able to develop an appropriate level of understanding of the formulations that relate to the topics of karma and the mental afflictions, your spiritual development will experience a great amount of progress.

2. Reflecting on the Causes of Liberation and the Liberation That Is Their Result

Reflect repeatedly on the following points:

If it is necessary for me to abandon samsara and attain liberation, I must investigate what the nature of that liberation is and if I do so, this is what I will discover. Liberation is not a physical location that I can flee to and arrive at by some method of travel. Rather, it involves bringing about the complete abandonment of the seeds of the mental afflictions that are present in my mind. In the case of some of the mental afflictions, this means causing them to be incapable of producing any results. Through abandoning karma and the mental afflictions, no new form of samsara can be generated and the remainder of the old form[173] will quickly come to an end. The term "liberation" refers to the state of stainlessness in which the mind abides following the termination of all the suffering of samsara's three realms. This is also referred to as a state of "abandonment that is irreversible," meaning that once liberation has been attained, it is impossible for that state to be lost.

The cause by which this liberation {225} is attained is the uncontaminated wisdom[174] that realizes the nature of such things as selflessness and the like. Liberation itself is attained through the abandonment of the obscurations that is accomplished by such realizations. To attain that wisdom, you must develop its cause, which is the form of concentration[175] that is a state of one-pointedness of the mind. In order to achieve one-pointedness of the mind, you must possess pure morality. Moreover, the form of morality that is supported by a pure attitude of renunciation[176] and the correct view that comprehends the meaning of selflessness also constitutes an efficacious cause for liberation.

Therefore, now I must cultivate morality in order to liberate myself from samsara, I must cultivate one-pointed concentration, and I must develop the wisdom that derives from meditation.[177] Following that, I shall develop a direct realization of the meanings of impermanence, suffering, emptiness, and selflessness.[178]

This completes the explanation of the series of points that make up the thirty-third meditation topic.

At this stage of the practice, it is recommended that a general overview of the common form of the peace of nirvana and each of the three trainings be presented. Although it is also permissible at this stage of the teaching to present an explanation on how to practice quiescence[179] and how to meditate on the selflessness of the person, because the actual path that relates to middling practitioners is not considered an essential part of this system of spiritual practice and because the main emphasis of this teaching on The Stages of the Path is on the attitudes that relate to a great person, I have followed here the customary practice of simply presenting those elements of the instruction that represent the topics to be contemplated in order to promote the desire to train oneself in the path that leads to liberation. [The instruction ranging from the twenty-second meditation topic down to this point completes the explanation of] the practices that relate to a middling person.

C. Training Yourself in the Stages of the Path That Are Unique to Great Persons

Now, with regard to training yourself in the attitude that is unique to a great person, there are two topics: (1) training yourself in the entry point for the attitude of a great person and (2) the forms of practice that complete the attainment of that very attitude.

1. The Entry Point for the Attitude of a Great Person

You should reflect repeatedly in such a way that you think to yourself:

> In connection with the preceding topics, when I reflect on the defects of samsara, I make the determination that I must attain the nirvana in which samsara has been abandoned. Moreover, if I must train myself in the three trainings in order to attain that goal, I should recognize that the nirvana that I seek to attain can be classified into three forms of enlightenment: the enlightenment of the śrāvakas, the enlightenment of pratyekabuddhas, and perfect enlightenment. {226} Of these three, the two forms of enlightenment that relate to śrāvakas and pratyekabuddhas do not represent the perfection of one's own aims in terms of the qualities of abandonment and realization. They also lack the quality that is the perfection of the aim that relates to others, which is represented by the ability to benefit sentient beings in an extensive manner.
>
> The incomplete form of abandonment means that only the obscurations of the mental afflictions[180] are abandoned; however,

the obscurations to that which needs to be known[181] are not abandoned. The incomplete form of realization means that only the insubstantiality of the person[182] and the partial form of dependent origination that relates to the stages of samsaric existence are realized; however, the insubstantiality of entities[183] and the ultimate form of dependent origination are not realized. Moreover, as relates to the characteristic of the spiritual qualities that are attained, only a limited number are attained and then only to a limited degree; they are not developed to an unlimited degree. In addition, since the śrāvaka and pratyekabuddha arhats pursue the methods for gaining their own deliverance exclusively, without seeking to free from their suffering those beings who have been kind to them, theirs is a liberation that has been sought in a shameless, inconsiderate, and ungrateful manner and one that abandons the welfare of others.

Because the āryas of those two forms of enlightenment do not return to samsara and their minds remain naturally in a state that is free of elaboration, and because they also possess many excellent spiritual qualities, in comparison to ordinary beings like ourselves, they are majestic beings whose nature cannot be fully comprehended by ordinary minds. Nevertheless, when compared with the inconceivable qualities of the buddhas and bodhisattvas, such as the manner in which buddhas and bodhisattvas abandon both types of obscurations, the manner in which they develop the transcendent knowledge of the true nature[184] of entities as well as the transcendent knowledge of the full range[185] of entities, the manner in which they possess limitless forms of spiritual qualities, the difficulty with which one can comprehend the manner in which they skillfully apply the power and strength of their compassion, and the manner in which they carry out activities on behalf of sentient beings throughout all the ten directions and the three times, the liberation of the śrāvaka and pratyekabuddha arhats is understood to be a state that is extremely meager. For example, the difference between them and fully enlightened buddhas is even greater than the difference between Mount Meru and a mustard seed. Therefore, I must attain the state of complete enlightenment that is the supreme form of liberation whose nature is such that by having perfected

> the abandonments and realizations that relate to the fulfillment of my own aim, I can accomplish the aims of others by carrying out inexhaustible forms of enlightened activities. In relation to this aim, I must do whatever is necessary for me to become a buddha.

This completes the explanation of the series of points that make up the thirty-fourth meditation topic.

2. The Forms of Practice That Complete {227} the Attainment of That Very Attitude

This topic is made up of two sections: (1) reflecting on the relation of cause and effect that exists between the elements of the instruction and (2) reflecting on the elements of the instruction that make up the relation of cause and effect.

a. Reflecting on the Relation of Cause and Effect

Moreover, regarding the first section, you should meditate in the following manner that is linked to the previous meditation topic:

> My purpose of wanting to attain buddhahood requires that I develop the enlightenment mind that represents a cause for attaining the status of a buddha. As a cause for developing that enlightenment mind, I must develop compassion. As a cause for developing that compassion, I must develop loving-kindness. As a cause for developing that loving-kindness, I must develop a sense of gratitude toward sentient beings for their kindness and the desire to repay that kindness. As a cause for developing that [sense of gratitude toward all sentient beings and the desire to repay their kindness], I must develop the recognition that all sentient beings have been my mother. Moreover, I must meditate on these topics in a sequential manner; that is, I must meditate by reflecting repeatedly on the following points: "All sentient beings have been and therefore are my parents and have treated me with great kindness. I deeply yearn for these sentient beings to become free of their suffering. I deeply yearn for them

> to experience happiness and be at ease. I shall attain buddhahood so that I can establish them in a state of happiness. Having attained buddhahood myself, I shall also place all sentient beings in the state of buddhahood."

This completes the explanation of the series of points that make up the thirty-fifth meditation topic.

At this point in the teaching, the system of instruction contained in this very text is the one that formulates the elements of cause and effect into five stages. This system has been transmitted through a lineage propagated by the spiritual teacher Tum Tönpa Lodrö Drak,[186] who was a disciple of the spiritual teacher Sharawa.[187] Another formulation is also expressed in a different Kadam lineage that was propagated by Tsangpa Rinpoche,[188] who was a disciple of Jayulwa.[189] The following statement appears in a work of the genre known as The Stages of the Teaching[190] that was composed by the spiritual teacher Mü Menpa[191] and is titled *The Stages of the Mahāyāna System of Mind Training*:[192]

> Atiśa's unique Mahāyāna teaching known as The Sevenfold Instruction of Cause and Effect teaches that you must train your mind in a sequential manner. Moreover, regarding these seven aspects of cause and effect, no effect can arise in the absence of the necessary causes and conditions. The relation between these seven elements is described as follows. The results of the Mahāyāna path, and ultimately supreme enlightenment, arise from the cause of enlightenment mind. That enlightenment mind arises from the pure form of the superior attitude.[193] That pure form of the superior attitude arises from great compassion. That great compassion arises from great loving-kindness. That great loving-kindness arises from the attitude that perceives all sentient beings favorably. That attitude that perceives all sentient beings favorably arises from the sense of gratitude toward all sentient beings for their kindness and the desire to repay that kindness. {228} That sense of gratitude toward all sentient beings for their kindness and the desire to repay that kindness arises from meditating on the understanding that all sentient beings are your mother. These are the seven elements of cause and effect.

Therefore, it should be understood that the expression describing the instruction on cultivating enlightenment mind as being made up of "seven elements of cause and effect" is also not a recent one that was devised at a later time.[194]

b. Reflecting on the Elements of the Instruction That Make Up the Relation of Cause and Effect

This section is made up of three divisions: (1) meditating on loving-kindness, (2) meditating on compassion, and (3) meditating on enlightenment mind.

i. Meditating on Loving-Kindness

Meditate by reflecting in the following manner:

> The expression "root mother" means the mother who gave birth to me in this life. She has been very kind to me. In the first period of my current life, she held me inside her body for between nine and ten months. During that time, she nurtured me with an affection that cherished me more than her own life. She gave me a human body, a life force, and a life span.
>
> Following my birth, she benefited me in a physical manner. For example, she lifted me up with the tips of her ten fingers, held me against the warmth of her flesh, nursed me with milk from her breasts, gave me food that she softened in her mouth with her own tongue, and wiped away my filth with her own hands. Indeed, our mothers take care of us from the time that we are like a helpless worm and unable to do anything for ourselves.
>
> She also benefited me in a verbal manner. That is, she always called out to me using a pleasing name. Though there was nothing to praise me for, she praised me nonetheless. Though I had no special good qualities, she recounted my good qualities nonetheless. She employed every kind of pretense in an effort to please me.
>
> She also benefited me in a mental manner. Her only thoughts were the following: "What can I do to ensure that my child has a long life span? What can I do to ensure that he or she remains free

> of illness? What can I do to ensure that people treat him or her with respect? I hope people will speak well of him or her. I hope he or she will be able to take care of himself or herself."
>
> When I first learned how to sit up, how to crawl, and how to speak my first words, this brought her immeasurable joy. After I grew up, not only did she not hesitate to give her child whatever she had, she did so happily. If she were able to give me the triple-thousand worlds[195] filled with jewels and servants, she would not think that was too much. That is the extent to which my mother has benefited me. How great is her love and kindness toward me! How deeply I yearn for my mother to be in a state of well-being at all times {229} and in all circumstances. How deeply I yearn for her always to be happy. I must establish my mother in an unsurpassed state of happiness and well-being.

This completes the explanation of the series of points that make up the thirty-sixth meditation topic. This practice of meditating on loving-kindness toward one's root mother is the basic form of meditating on the points that relate to loving-kindness. The lineage teachers declare that this form of the practice is one that will enable you to develop loving-kindness easily, and it is particularly important that you elicit this attitude in relation to your root mother.

Following that, in a manner that is similar to the previous topic, you should meditate by reflecting in the following manner:

> That is the way in which my mother has benefited me in this life. However, this mother has not done this in only one or two of my lives. She has been my mother in a great many lives, and she has benefited me countless times, just as she has as my mother in this life. In the same way, she has also been my father and benefited me an incalculable number of times. Likewise, she has also been a paternal relative, a maternal relative, a friend, an associate, and the like, limitless times. If you heaped together in one place all the clothes that she dressed me with and all the ornaments that she adorned me with, the pile would be higher than the supreme mountain Mount Meru. If you collected just the milk that she nursed me with, the amount would be greater than the water of the four great oceans. If you collected all the tears of grief that

> she cried in all those births in which she was either my father or mother, my child or a family relative, and I died before her, the water of a billion rivers would not equal their amount.
>
> She pursued my well-being single-mindedly, disregarding all concern for any evil deeds that she might commit, disregarding all concern for any suffering that she might have to endure, and disregarding all concern for any dishonor that she might incur. How great is the extent to which she has benefited me!

This completes the explanation of the series of points that make up the thirty-seventh meditation topic.

Following that, in addition to that previous meditation, add five or six individuals with whom you are familiar, such as your father, siblings, or other family relatives, and meditate by reflecting in the following manner:

> While some of these individuals have benefited me greatly in this life, others have done so to a middling degree, and still others only to a small degree, if I reflect on the manner in which samsara has no beginning, just as with my "root" mother, there is no difference in the amount of benefit that I have received from all of them. Since there is no difference in their kindness, I should meditate by reflecting as before: "How deeply I yearn for these individuals who have benefited me to such a great extent to find their own happiness. How deeply I yearn for them to enjoy well-being. I must establish them in the ultimate form of happiness and well-being." {230}

You must continue meditating in a similar way by progressively applying this form of reflection to more individuals. Regarding this effort, the systems of practice associated with the spiritual teacher Jayulwa[196] and the teacher from Narthang[197] contain an instruction that explains that you should meditate by progressively adding the beings that live in each of the directions. I regard this very system to be an especially effective method for the novice practitioner to use in meditating on this topic.

Following that previous topic, meditate on as many of the following types of beings as there are in each of these three categories within the region where you yourself reside: human beings who are either an enemy, a friend, or a neutral person;[198] animals that move about below the surface of the earth, upon the surface of the earth, or in the sky; and the hungry ghosts[199] that are spirits of high, middling, or inferior status. Meditate by applying the points that were described above to all of these beings in order to recognize them as having been your father and your mother in immeasurable numbers of your past rebirths in order to reflect on the ways in which they benefited you when they were your parents and in order to develop both the desire to repay the kindness they showed you and to cultivate loving-kindness toward them.

Following that, continue meditating in a similar way as you expand the size of the region in which these beings reside until, from the perspective of Tibetans, you meditate on all three classes of beings that reside within the entire country of Tibet. Following that, continue meditating in a similar way to include the three classes of beings that reside in the great neighboring countries, such as China that lies to the east of Tibet, India that lies to its south, Kashmir that lies to its west, and Mongolia and areas of Central Asia[200] that lie to its north. Following that, meditate on all three classes of beings that reside in the entirety of the Rose Apple continent.[201] Following that, meditate in the same way as before on those hungry ghosts and hell beings that reside in the regions that lie below the surface of the Rose Apple continent—that is, in the principal domain[202] of the hungry ghosts, as well as in the eight hot hells and the eight cold hells.

Likewise, also meditate in the same manner as described above for the three classes of beings[203] that fill the regions that lie above ground in the remaining three of the four continents—that is, the eastern continent Videha, the western continent Godānīya, and the northern continent Kuru, as well as the many different types of beings of the three lower realms[204] that lie below the surface of these continents.

The gods of the class of the Four Great Kings[205] are found mainly on the four terraces of Mount Meru; on its peak are the gods of the Heaven of the Thirty-Three.[206] The city where the principal demigods reside lies inside the portion of Mount Meru that lies beneath the surface of the oceans. Meditate in the same manner as described above for the beings that reside in these regions.

Following that, bring to mind the gods, yakṣas,[207] and animals that reside on the portions of the seven golden mountains[208] {231} and the outer circular iron mountain range[209] that rise above the surface of the oceans; the demigods, hungry ghosts, and great variety of animals that reside in crevices of the portions of the mountains that lie below the surface of the oceans; as well as the nāgas[210] and demigods that are found in the seven *śītā*[211] inner seas that are between those golden mountains and all the common sea animals that densely fill every portion of the great outer oceans.[212] Meditate in the same manner that was described earlier with regard to all of these sentient beings.

Among animals, there are three types that possess miraculous powers: the garuḍas[213] that travel in the sky, the kinnaras[214] that live on the surface of the earth, and the nāgas that dwell below the surface of the earth or in bodies of water. You should also devote a special meditation to these beings.

After you have meditated on all the individual reflections in this topic down to this point—which collectively address all the sentient beings that reside in the area that reaches from the golden ground[215] up to the Heaven of the Thirty-Three and extends outward as far as the circular iron mountain range—continue meditating in the same way as before by successively adding and directing your attention to the Yāma deities,[216] the Tuṣita deities,[217] Those Deities Who Delight in Magical Creations,[218] and Those Deities Who Control Others' Magical Creations.[219]

Following that, add to your meditation the following three divine regions that are found in the first level of meditative absorption, whose breadth is equal in size to that of a world system that is made up of the four continents, and so on:[220] the Brahma Group,[221] the Brahmapurohitas,[222] and the Mahābrahmāṇas.[223] At this juncture, the instruction states the following: "From this point on, throughout the entirety of this birth state that makes up the first level of the form realm,[224] all the beings are exclusively deities that are associated with the form realm; none of the sentient beings in any of the other five migratory states, or even gods of the desire realm, are found here. Only the deities identified with each of the three regions of the first level of the form realm are found here. By way of summary, speaking in general terms, the practitioner should meditate in the manner described above with regard to all of the sentient beings that reside in a single-world system that makes up Brahmā's realm and all of the desire realm's regions that lie below it in and around the four continents.

Now you should meditate in the same way as before on all the sentient beings of the six classes that reside in an area that extends out horizontally and encompasses in close proximity a thousand such single-world systems, all of which are surrounded at their outer edge by a single iron mountain range. It also rises upward to include the three regions of the form realm's second meditative absorption level, called Limited Light,[225] Immeasurable Light,[226] and Brilliant Light,[227] among which the great region of Brilliant

Light {232} serves as the uppermost covering for the entire region, which is known as "a realm comprised of a lesser-thousand-world systems."[228]

Next, you should meditate in the same way as before on all the sentient beings of the six classes that reside in an area that is arranged horizontally and extends out further than before to comprise a realm that consists of a thousand such lesser-thousand-world systems, which again is bounded by another single circular iron mountain range. This area also rises upward to include the three regions of the form realm's third meditative absorption level, called Limited Good Fortune,[229] Immeasurable Good Fortune,[230] and Complete Good Fortune,[231] respectively. Of these, the single region of Complete Good Fortune serves as the uppermost covering for this entire area, which is known as "a realm composed of a middling, second order of a thousand world systems."[232]

Once again, meditate in the same way as before on all the six classes of sentient beings throughout all three realms. This is done by visualizing the arrangement of the final thousand of those middling, second order of a thousand world systems, which continues to extend out horizontally and is again surrounded at its outer edge by another circular iron mountain range. This area is called "a great, third order of a thousand world systems."[233] Each of the triple-thousand individual world systems has its own golden ground as a foundation, beneath which lies its own disk of water. These billion water disks rest upon a single disk of air. This entire region extends upward from the disk of air that lies at the bottom and rises up as far as the first three ordinary[234] regions of the fourth meditative absorption, which are called Cloudless,[235] Born of Merit,[236] and Great Fruit,[237] respectively. In a similar manner, successively add the five regions known as Not More Exalted,[238] Free of Torment,[239] Excellent Vision,[240] Extremely Beautiful,[241] and Below None.[242] The single, latter region, Below None, serves as the uppermost covering for this great, third order of a thousand world systems. Following that, gradually also add the innumerable sentient beings that also reside in the formless realm.[243]

Following that, continue meditating by reflecting on the following points:

> Extending outward to the east of this realm that is made up of a triple-thousand world systems, there are countless, immeasurable numbers of such triple-thousand world systems. For example, imagine that I filled to the top an entire single triple-

> thousand world system with mustard seeds and I took out from that immense mass of mustard seeds just one and after placing it aside, reflected to myself that it represents a single triple-thousand world system that lies to the east of these triple-thousand world systems. If I were to continue placing aside mustard seeds in a similar way for each of the additional triple-thousand world systems that lie to the east of this one, eventually I would run out of mustard seeds, {233} but the number of triple-thousand world systems that lie to the east of this one would not be exhausted. And, if I were to repeat this entire process again and again, each time I would run out of mustard seeds, but the number of triple-thousand world systems that lie to the east of this one would not be exhausted. In fact, even if I were to continue doing this exercise for an endless number of kalpas, the number of triple-thousand world systems that lie to the east of this one would still not be exhausted. Following that, I should reflect to myself that each and every one of these world systems is filled with the six classes of sentient beings. Then, after cultivating the realization that they are all my mothers, I should meditate on loving-kindness toward them.

Now, meditate by reflecting to yourself in the following manner:

> All such limitless triple-thousands of world systems not only lie in an easterly direction, the entire myriad expanse of space that lies in all ten directions is just the same. There is no limit whatsoever to the expanse of space that extends into the ten directions, and however far space extends, those regions are all filled with the world systems that make up the inanimate physical world in which sentient beings reside. All the sentient beings that are found there without exception are my kind mothers and fathers. Each one has been both my father and my mother immeasurable times and each time has both benefited me in many different ways and eliminated many different forms of harm. May all these elderly mothers[244] obtain happiness. May they obtain well-being. I pledge to establish them in the ultimate form of happiness and well-being.

While this meditation topic contains a great many individual points, some flexibility should be used in teaching the instruction to students according to the type of mental acumen that they possess. Therefore, although it is difficult to assess their level of understanding, since they are all alike in that they must expand their experiential knowledge of loving-kindness, all these points have been combined into one large meditation topic that is designated as "the series of points that make up the thirty-eighth meditation topic." At this stage in the teaching, it is very important for the practitioner to develop an understanding of the nature of the animate and inanimate world. This completes the instructions on loving-kindness.

ii. Meditating on Compassion

The preliminary and concluding practices for this topic are the same as before. For the main practice, you should reflect to yourself in the following manner:

> While it is my duty to establish all these sentient beings in a state of ultimate happiness and well-being, when I examine the totality of the sphere of sentient beings, I recognize that the vast majority of them neither abide in states of happiness nor the causes of happiness;[245] instead they abide in states of suffering and the causes of suffering. While happiness is what they desire and suffering is what they wish to avoid, what actually befalls them is that they fail to obtain happiness and they experience nothing but suffering. Most sentient beings are abiding in overt states of suffering, {234} such as having to experience heat and cold in the hells, hunger and thirst among hungry ghosts, and the condition of eating one another that occurs among animals. Even in the higher realms, what is found there is that virtually no one can say that he or she has not experienced any of these kinds of suffering: shortened life spans, an abundance of illnesses, being powerless, being impoverished and destitute, being in a state of servitude, or being subjected to various kinds of punishment.
>
> Speaking generally, all living beings have performed immeasurable numbers of acts that constitute causes of their own future suffering. More specifically, even if it is acknowledged that some beings are not currently enduring the severe forms of suffering

that no one wants to experience, because they have accumulated terrible forms of evil deeds, as soon as their last, full breath is expelled, they will find themselves having been reborn suddenly in one of the hells. For this reason, such beings are even more deserving of my compassion than those who are presently experiencing overt forms of suffering. When someone's perceptions are so mistaken, what can be done for them?

For example, if my "root" mother of this life were blind, if her legs were disabled, if she had no one to guide her, if she had lost her walking stick, and if she were on the verge of falling over the edge of a steep precipice, what would I need to do? Without looking for anyone else to help, I would have to immediately rush there and pull her back from the edge of that precipice. As with this analogy, all these "elderly" mother sentient beings are blind in that they lack the eye of wisdom; their legs are broken in that they lack the means with which to benefit themselves spiritually; they have no spiritual teacher or virtuous friend to guide them; they lack the walking stick of merit; they repeatedly carry out every form of evil deed that should not even be contemplated much less actually performed; they stumble along the path of a higher-realm rebirth; and while they are on the verge of falling over the edge of the precipice into one of the three lower states, they continually engage in activities that constitute the terrible causes of their future suffering. How deserving they are of my compassion!

Now you should reflect to yourself in the following manner again and again:

I do not currently possess the means by which I can actually save all these sentient beings from their suffering. Therefore, the predominant form of overt suffering that they must continue to experience is that of the three lower realms, and the predominant form of conduct that they carry out in the three happy migratory states[246] is that which constitutes the cause of their own future suffering. I should recall the nature of their suffering as it was explained in the sections of the instruction that pertain to lesser and middling persons. If those forms of suffering were to befall me, I would not be able to endure even a portion of it. How

> could these sentient beings be expected to endure what I cannot endure? {235} Because they actually experience such suffering and they also continually engage in the causes of that suffering, as they do not know how to put an end to such conduct, they must successively undergo one form of suffering after another. How deserving they are of my compassion! May they be freed from all their suffering. May they be freed from all the karma and mental afflictions that are the causes of their suffering. I must save these six classes of sentient beings who are my "elderly" mothers from all their evil deeds and suffering. I must free them from the samsara that is the state in which that suffering is experienced.

This completes the explanation of the series of points that make up the thirty-ninth meditation topic.

Alternatively, regarding the above instruction, there is also a system that classifies them into three meditation topics: reflecting on the actual forms of suffering that sentient beings must experience, reflecting on the manner in which sentient beings carry out the conduct that is the cause of their suffering, and reflecting on both of these topics taken together. As I explained above in the section on loving-kindness,[247] practitioners will gain positive results if they meditate on compassion by generating a progressively expanding form of practice in which the points that were explained here are cultivated successively in relation to all the different classes of sentient beings that are found throughout the ten directions' limitless world systems. Moreover, since loving-kindness and compassion are two closely related spiritual attitudes, after having meditated one time on the instructions that relate to each of them separately, you can also meditate in such a way that each time that you reflect on a point that relates to loving-kindness, you combine with it the points that relate to compassion. It is also acceptable for loving-kindness and compassion not to be separated into two categories of meditation practice.

iii. Meditating on Enlightenment Mind

This topic has two sections: (1) meditating on the aspirational form of enlightenment and (2) meditating on the active form of enlightenment mind. These two headings are also described as training oneself in the attitude of enlightenment mind and training oneself in the practice of the perfections, respectively.

I) Meditating on the Aspirational Form of Enlightenment Mind

This section is also made up of three subsections: (1) training yourself in the actual form of enlightenment mind, (2) training yourself by recalling its benefits, and (3) promising to observe the precepts.

A) Training Yourself in the Actual Form of Enlightenment Mind

You should meditate in a manner that is linked with the practice of loving-kindness and compassion that was explained above, by reflecting to yourself repeatedly in the following manner:

> These mother sentient beings need to obtain happiness and they need to obtain well-being. How truly deserving they are of my compassion in that they lack happiness and well-being and they are experiencing suffering! It is imperative that I dispel their suffering. {236} It is imperative that I establish them in a state of happiness. However, I do not currently possess the ability to bring that about. Moreover, Brahmā, Indra, and a wheel-wielding monarch do not have that ability either. Well then, is there anyone who does have that ability? Only a complete buddha does. Nevertheless, because it is possible for me to attain buddhahood if I were to pursue that goal, I shall seek to attain the status of a buddha. And, after attaining it, I shall free all sentient beings from samsara. Therefore, I must attain buddhahood in order to benefit all sentient beings.

This completes the explanation of the series of points that make up the fortieth meditation topic.

Earlier, as part of the thirty-fourth meditation topic, which addressed the subject of training yourself in the entry point for the attitude [of a great person], you simply meditated on the wish to obtain complete buddhahood based on an understanding of the spiritual qualities that are possessed by a buddha as well as an understanding of the differences between the Hīnayāna and the Mahāyāna. However, that wish by itself and in that form is not sufficient for you to develop a complete and genuine form of enlightenment mind. However, at this point in the practice, you will develop a form of the aspirational form of enlightenment that possesses all of its defining qualities by meditating on the attitude that seeks complete enlightenment for the exclusive purpose of fulfilling the aims of others. While only a generalized form of the attitude that seeks the welfare of others is gained in the earlier form of practice, the practitioner does not at that time develop a mode of apprehension that is principally dedicated to the welfare of others through having cultivated complete forms of loving-kindness and compassion.

B) Training Yourself by Recalling the Benefits of Enlightenment Mind

Following that form of practice, the second section consists of training yourself by reflecting on the benefits of enlightenment mind, which include the following four:

1. The benefit of accomplishing one's own aims in their entirety. This is described in a sūtra passage that declares that enlightenment mind is like a seed in that it gives rise to all of the spiritual qualities of a buddha.[248]
2. The benefit of accomplishing the aims that relate to others. The sūtra states that enlightenment mind is like a field in that it causes the pure qualities of all beings to spring forth.
3. The benefit of eliminating all faults. The sūtra states that enlightenment mind is like a hole beneath the earth in that it causes all misdeeds to disappear.
4. The benefit of causing all virtuous qualities to be attained. The sūtra states that enlightenment mind is like the great ocean in that it is the gathering place into which all jewel-like good qualities flow.

Then, cultivate an attitude of intense joy toward your enlightenment mind by reflecting to yourself in the following manner:

> Now, through having meditated on enlightenment mind, the quality within my mental continuum that is the seed for attaining liberation has been awakened. All the traces of virtuous qualities that exist within my mental continuum also have been

> awakened. This auspicious attitude directly benefits sentient beings, and {237} it also enables me to acquire an extraordinary ability to carry out beneficial acts.
>
> Just by meditating on this enlightenment mind a great amount of evil deeds is eliminated, the intensity of such mental afflictions as desire, hatred, pride, and jealousy is diminished, and my mental continuum takes on a gentle nature, which enables all good qualities to arise. Moreover, after I make the pledge to pursue buddhahood, a recognition of the need to pursue many additional good qualities also follows naturally. From that point on until I reach the ultimate goal, this enlightenment mind will accomplish all such goals as the realization of my own aims, the ability to carry out the enlightened activities that fulfill the aims of others, the ability to abandon the obscurations that need to be abandoned, and the attainment of good qualities. In short, whatever good qualities omniscience possesses, enlightenment mind also possesses them. Whatever value buddhahood possesses, this enlightenment mind possesses it as well.

Following that, once again meditate on enlightenment mind in the same way that you did previously. Then do the very same thing once again. In addition, during the time between meditation sessions, reimagine yourself adopting enlightenment mind again and again by reviewing in your mind the formal ritual that you actually underwent to generate the mind that aspires to attain enlightenment.[249] Alternatively, if you have not yet engaged in the ritual act of generating enlightenment mind, since the final clause of the three verses known as the Daily Confession,[250] which states, "I shall . . . become a buddha to benefit all living beings," expresses the act of generating enlightenment mind, recite this seven-limb passage again and again.

This completes the explanation of the series of points that make up the forty-first meditation topic.

C) Promising to Observe the Precepts

1) The First Precept

The first precept is that you must train yourself in the attitude that refuses to abandon sentient beings. There are two ways in which sentient beings can be abandoned: (1) abandoning sentient beings in their entirety and (2) abandoning specific sentient beings.

a) Abandoning Sentient Beings in Their Entirety

The first type of abandonment is illustrated by various improper attitudes such as these: the wrongful attitude that refuses to take up the dharma in any form, by thinking, "I cannot develop any spiritual goal, such as the pursuit of my own aim or the aims of others, so therefore I shall pursue ordinary worldly aims"; and the wrongful attitude that rejects the aim of the Mahāyāna by thinking, "Because I am unable to pursue the aims of sentient beings, I must generate the attitude that aspires to follow the vehicles of the śrāvakas and the pratyekabuddhas."

b) Abandoning Specific Sentient Beings

The abandonment of specific sentient beings is the attitude in which you give up all compassion toward certain individuals with whom you are at odds by thinking, "Although there was a time when I sought to benefit you, now I shall not seek to benefit you in any temporary or ultimate way whatsoever."

{238} Whether you abandon sentient beings in their entirety or you abandon specific sentient beings, if you allow one period[251] of the day to go by without developing the antidote to that failing, your enlightenment mind will have been abandoned. Therefore, you must meditate by reflecting to yourself:

> I shall make certain that I never develop the mind that abandons sentient beings. If I should somehow become powerless to stop myself from developing such an attitude, I shall elicit the proper antidote to that failing and immediately confess my transgression. I pledge to benefit at some future time those sentient beings that I lack the ability to benefit in actuality right now.

This completes the explanation of the series of points that make up the forty-second meditation topic.

2) The Second Precept

The second precept is that you must strive to collect the accumulations. You must cultivate this precept by reflecting to yourself again and again:

> As I gradually develop my spiritual qualities to higher levels, I must train myself to cultivate ever greater forms of the two accumulations. In fact, I must train myself in the collection of the two accumulations starting this very day. I must do so by training myself in the activities that constitute forms of the merit accumulation, which are described in the sūtras and treatises as providing great benefits, such as worshiping the Three Jewels, serving the sangha, offering torma oblations to spirits, making prostrations and presenting offerings to spiritual teachers and the Three Jewels, circumambulating holy objects such as stupas and temples, reciting dhāraṇī mantras, cultivating faith, cultivating loving-kindness and compassion, and practicing patience.
>
> I must also train myself in the following practices, which constitute forms of the wisdom accumulation: hearing teachings on a range of dharma subjects, memorizing the words with which those teachings are expressed, and reflecting on the meaning of those words; eliminating all doubt through applying the reasoning that identifies what is contradictory and what possesses a valid logical relation to these topics; carrying out the exercise that is called "sealing a spiritual practice by not conceiving of its three spheres[252] as real"; and successively developing the three forms of wisdom[253] in relation to the teaching that the entirety of samsara and nirvana are not truly existent, by learning and gaining an understanding of this topic through hearing teachings on it, by ascertaining with certainty the nature of that meaning through reflecting on that understanding, and by meditating on that correct understanding because I must ultimately achieve a direct realization of the ultimate reality that the entirety of samsara and nirvana are not truly existent.
>
> I must also develop a practice in which the two accumulations are carried out jointly—meaning that the wisdom accumulation takes on the quality of merit and the merit accumulation takes on the quality of wisdom—by training myself in such a way that

> my practice of worshiping the Three Jewels, and so on, which constitutes the merit accumulation, is supported by the view that recognizes that these practices are not truly existent and my practice of the view regarding ultimate truth, which constitutes the wisdom accumulation, is informed by the altruistic nature of those virtuous practices.

This completes the explanation of the series of points that make up the forty-third meditation topic.

3) The Third Precept

The third precept is that you must train yourself by cultivating the four pairs of qualities that make up a total of eight.[254] {239} Of the eight, the four black qualities are, in a general sense, great misdeeds, and, in particular, they are causes that will lead you to forget the enlightenment mind you have generated after you have taken birth in a future life. Similarly, the four white qualities are, in a general sense, principles that will provide you with great benefits, and, in particular, they are causes that will enable you to recall your enlightenment mind in all your future rebirths. Therefore, you must abandon the four black qualities and cultivate the four white qualities.

Regarding the first pair of these qualities, it is a black quality for you to deceive your lama or someone who is worthy of receiving offerings or who is worthy of being venerated. The verb *to deceive*[255] here means to deceive such persons by lying to them. The antidote for this misdeed is for you to abandon all deliberate forms of lying. If you should avoid knowingly uttering even a small lie to an ordinary person, how could it be acceptable for you to deceive someone who is worthy of being venerated?

Regarding the second pair of qualities, it is said to be a black quality for you to instill regret in the mind of another person about something that does not need to be regretted. Although one should develop regret for having committed an evil deed, as that is a proper object of regret, if you engage in some method that is designed to instill regret in another person's mind for having carried out a virtuous act, which is not a proper object of regret, then you have committed a black quality regardless of whether that other person feels regret or not.

The wrongful manner in which to attempt to instill regret in another person can be illustrated by a variety of statements. For example, you might say to someone, "This gift is too great. If you give that much, then what will you eat?" Another example would be to say, "If you take monastic vows, all these women will become helpless." Or you might further say something like, "It was a mistake for you not to exact revenge on your enemy."

The antidote for such a misdeed is for you to cause sentient beings to aspire to engage in the virtuous acts associated with any of the three Buddhist vehicles. That is to say, you should train yourself in the corresponding white quality, which means to induce sentient beings to generate the spiritual attitude that is associated with whichever of the three vehicles they feel the strongest sense of devotion toward. In particular, you should, to the best of your abilities, cause others to pursue the Mahāyāna, and you should induce them to perform as many virtuous activities as they can. Moreover, you should encourage those persons to generate aspirational prayers to achieve enlightenment. If it is incumbent upon you to try as much as you can to induce those who are not engaging in virtuous activities to do so in the future, how could it be acceptable for you to cause someone to regret having performed a virtuous act in the past?

Now, you should also train yourself appropriately in relation to the third pair of qualities. Regarding this topic, it is said to be a black quality for you to express disparagement toward a person who has generated enlightenment mind. "Disparagement"[256] means voicing criticism toward someone, either directly {240} or in private. It doesn't matter whether the person has actually generated enlightenment mind or not, or whether he or she has lost their enlightenment mind or not; it is unacceptable to disparage anyone who affirms that he or she has generated enlightenment mind.

The antidote to this misdeed is the white quality in which you train yourself by cultivating the conception toward all sentient beings[257] that they are the Master.[258] The reason for doing so is that all sentient beings possess the embryo[259] of a buddha, and they are the same as a buddha in the sense that they also constitute objects in relation to which we accumulate merit and purify ourselves of obscurations. The latter point is expressed in the lines of verse that state "When a buddha's qualities are acquired / equally through sentient beings and victors, ..."[260] Therefore, after developing toward sentient beings the conception that they are the Master, you should always praise and voice your approval of them. And, if you should praise even ordinary sentient beings and avoid disparaging them, then what need is there to say that you should not disparage anyone who has generated enlightenment mind?

As for the fourth pair of qualities, engaging in deceitfulness[261] and guile[262] toward sentient beings is said to be a black quality. Thus, it is a black quality to employ false speech and deviousness toward others in order to achieve some personal aim. This also includes cheating others by means of fraudulent measuring boxes[263] and weighing devices. The antidote for this misdeed is the white quality in which you maintain a superior attitude[264] toward all sentient beings, as well as an attitude that seeks to benefit and bring happiness to them. The phrase "attitude that seeks to benefit and bring happiness to others" means to establish them in a state of happiness both in this life and in future lives. A "superior attitude" refers to the attitude that accepts the responsibility to achieve the aims that relate to others. It also is described as the attitude that refrains from engaging in the deviousness of deceitfulness and guile and that speaks to others politely[265] with an honest mind and without showing partiality, as parents do with their children. Therefore, you must train yourself in this way as well. If it is imperative for you to maintain the superior attitude that seeks to benefit all sentient beings, how could it be acceptable for you to allow yourself to engage in deceitfulness and guile toward others? You must make these four white qualities the essence of your spiritual practice and cultivate them with very great diligence. Regarding these eight qualities, reflect to yourself:

> I shall never engage in any of the four black qualities, and I shall train myself to develop the four white qualities as much as I can and to the best of my abilities.

This completes the explanation of the series of points that make up the forty-fourth meditation topic.

Regarding this {241} instruction on the four black and four white qualities, there is also a teaching system that classifies each of the four pairs of qualities into separate meditation topics. Those practitioners of lesser acumen will be able to develop the proper level of ascertainment regarding them more easily, and therefore achieve greater success by following this latter approach.

There is also a system that describes the precepts as being eight in number. This is done by adding the practice of recalling the benefits of generating enlightenment mind and the practice of formally generating enlightenment mind six times during each full day composed of both a day and a night to the precepts, and then counting the practice of not abandoning sentient beings and the practice of training oneself in the two accumulations, as well as each of the four pairs of qualities, as individual precepts.[266] The practitioner should carry out his or her practice in accordance with whichever of these systems is found to be most appropriate.

It seems to me that an effective way to proceed is for the practitioner to generate enlightenment mind after having received the above instructions on compassion. Following that, one can meditate on these latter instructions that explain the precepts relating to the aspirational form of enlightenment mind.

Another method is for you to first meditate on all of these topics.[267] Then you should generate enlightenment mind when you have reached this point in the teachings. If you proceed in this manner, you will be able to develop a strong and definite form of enlightenment mind at the time that you accept it within a formal ritual. For that reason, it can also be efficacious for you to generate enlightenment mind here.

Yet another approach that is also acceptable would be to wait until you have received all the instructions that make up this entire teaching. Then you can generate enlightenment mind just before you accept the bodhisattva vow.[268] Whichever of these methods is most suitable to the circumstances can be followed.

II) Meditating on the Active Form of Enlightenment Mind[269]

The importance of training oneself in the active form of enlightenment mind is that anyone who desires to achieve buddhahood must train himself or herself in the conduct that leads to enlightenment. If you wish to achieve buddhahood but fail to train yourself in the bodhisattva conduct, that is like saying that you desire to obtain a productive harvest, but you do not perform the agricultural work that is necessary to achieve that result. Speaking generally, simply aspiring to attain enlightenment does provide you with a great many benefits; however, because you will not be able to develop the necessary spiritual qualities to higher levels without carrying out the conduct that leads to enlightenment, it is necessary for you to train yourself in the bodhisattva conduct. Moreover, regarding this process, the bodhisattva conduct itself is made up of the six perfections and the four principles for attracting a following. In addition, the practice of the perfections and the four principles for attracting a following are not distinct from one another. The six perfections are what you yourself undertake to practice. What you teach others verbally and what you urge them to put into practice are these very same perfections. However, this latter form of the perfections also represents the four principles for attracting a following. Therefore, you should reflect repeatedly in the following manner:

> I shall make the ten perfections[270] the essence of my spiritual practice and cultivate them diligently. Moreover, I shall not put off doing so until a later time; {242} I shall undertake to cultivate them starting right now.

The general way in which to meditate on the active form of enlightenment mind is to make the promise that was just described and to say to yourself, "Starting this very day, I must ensure, as much as I can and to the best of my abilities, that my practice is carried out successfully and unerringly."

This completes the explanation of the series of points that make up the forty-fifth meditation topic.

If I must train myself in the conduct of a bodhisattva, I must begin by training myself in the perfection of generosity. Generosity can be classified into three types: giving material objects, giving protection, and giving the dharma.

Regarding the giving of material objects, train yourself by reflecting in the following manner:

> I shall satisfy all sentient beings by giving them material objects. While I do not currently have such an ability, in the future I must practice such a form of generosity by obtaining a form of wealth as great as that which is included in the dominion of a wheel-wielder.

For the present, you should practice generosity according to your current ability, which is to say that you should do so as much as you can and to the best of your ability, by giving such things as food and clothing, and so on, and limiting this generosity only to the extent that it would adversely affect your own dharma practice. You should think to yourself: "It is imperative that I practice generosity in such a way that I come just short of making myself into a destitute beggar." This should not be merely a form of mental practice; you must also ensure that you put this attitude into practice. That is to say, you must train yourself by performing such acts of generosity.

The giving of protection[271] means to cultivate the following attitude:

> I shall save all sentient beings from every kind of fear, such as the fear of illnesses, the fear caused by weapons, the fear posed by robbers, fear of poisons, the fear caused by such harmful living creatures as large predatory animals and poisonous snakes, the fear posed by precipices, the fear posed by narrow, perilous paths,[272] the fear of fire, the fear of water, the fear of punishment, and so on, up to and including the fear of being reborn in the lower realms.

You should also meditate in the following manner:

> For the present as well, I shall carry out actions directly, as much as I can and to the best of my ability, to protect beings from such fears as those caused by illnesses, harmful spirits, enemies, and the four elements, and so on.

Moreover, this latter meditation should not only be a mental practice, you must also train yourself by performing such actions, meaning that you should also put this mental attitude into practice as much as you can, but limiting yourself to activities that will not obstruct your morality {243} or other forms of spiritual practice, even if this just consists of giving verbal expression to your intent.

Giving protection is the name of an activity that is meant to alleviate the suffering of sentient beings. If the circumstances are not appropriate, or if your activity might serve to promote some form of evil action, there is a serious risk that the supposed gain achieved by taking some form of action will do nothing to eliminate the adversity. Therefore, these are situations in which you should cultivate the giving of protection mentally; however, you should forgo[273] actually carrying out some action to eliminate the danger.

You should practice giving the dharma mentally by reflecting to yourself:

> I shall satisfy all sentient beings spiritually by giving them the dharma. I shall teach them the dharma, ripening those sentient beings who are not spiritually ripened and liberating those who are ripened. I shall cause those who do not understand the dharma to gain an understanding of it, I shall cause those who

> have not achieved realizations of the dharma to gain such realizations, and I shall cause those who have not gained spiritual attainments to gain them.

Cultivate this practice mentally by reflecting in the following manner as well:

> For the present as well, if I possess the ability to teach the dharma, I must benefit others by teaching them, without harboring any desire for material gain and honor or profit and fame. Even if I am unable to benefit others in this way by actually teaching the dharma, I shall imagine myself teaching the dharma to human beings as well as nonhuman gods and spirits by devoting regular, daily sessions to the recitation of sūtras and the reading of scripture texts aloud.

You should not only carry out such a mental practice, you must also train yourself by putting these thoughts into practice and performing acts that constitute giving the dharma. In this way, there are two forms of practice for each of the three types of generosity—that is, they should be practiced both in thought and action—making a total of six spiritual exercises. Taken altogether, they make up the training that relates to the perfection of generosity.

This completes the explanation of the series of points that make up the forty-sixth meditation topic. This method of training oneself separately in thought and action should be applied to each of the remaining perfections.

Now, you should also train yourself in the perfection of morality. There are three types of morality: the morality of restraining yourself from committing misdeeds, the morality of gathering virtuous spiritual qualities, and the morality of acting on behalf of sentient beings.

Regarding the morality of restraining yourself from committing misdeeds, in general terms, it is a type of morality in which all forms of acts that are naturally objectionable,[274] such as the ten unvirtuous deeds, and so on, are abandoned. More specifically, {244} it is a type of morality in which you must refrain from violating any of the precepts associated with a form of Buddhist vow that you may have accepted, such as the precepts associated with the layperson's upāsaka vow, the fully ordained monk's bhikṣu vow, the novice monk's śramaṇerika vow, or any of the samaya commitments[275] associated with tantric morality. In short, it means a type of morality in which you avoid all forms of improper conduct that are described in the sūtras and related treatises on morality. Regarding this form of practice, you should meditate by reflecting:

> I shall train myself right away in relation to this form of practice.

The morality of gathering virtuous qualities means that you cannot allow yourself to pursue just a few forms of virtuous activity or to practice the six perfections in an incomplete manner. Rather, you must train yourself continually in all the practices that are included within the six perfections. Moreover, you must practice the six perfections as much as you can and to the best of your abilities starting right now.

The morality that acts on behalf of sentient beings refers to the practice of benefiting sentient beings by establishing them in many forms of happiness and causing them to take up many forms of virtuous activity. Moreover, you should meditate on this form of morality by reflecting in the following manner:

> Starting right now, as much as possible and to the best of my abilities, I shall do whatever I can to benefit sentient beings and establish them in states of happiness.

Restraining yourself from committing misdeeds is not something that can be put off until later. You must stop engaging in such behavior and turn away from it as soon as you hear the instruction that exhorts you to do so. Some forms of the latter two types of morality can be put off until later. That is, in keeping with your mental proficiency, you should practice whatever forms of them you currently have the capacity and the ability to carry out. However, with regard to those forms that you are not currently able to carry out, it is acceptable for you to treat them as objects of your aspirational prayers and defer carrying them out until sometime in the future.

Speaking generally, a bodhisattva's worst fault is to fail to act on behalf of others; therefore, it is necessary to practice the morality that acts on behalf of sentient beings. However, in order to be able to act on behalf of others, it is necessary for you to ripen your own mental continuum. Therefore, it is necessary to practice the morality that gathers virtuous qualities. And finally, although it is unacceptable for you solely to strive to keep yourself from becoming tainted by misdeeds, the morality of restraining yourself from committing misdeeds is the specific type that is important at the outset, as it serves as the foundation of your spiritual practice, because in its absence, you will not be able to develop correct forms of the other two types of morality.

This completes the explanation of the series of points that make up the forty-seventh meditation topic.

Now, the next practice is the perfection of patience, of which there are three types: the patience that forbears harm, the patience that tolerates suffering, and the patience that is gained by reflecting intently upon a range of dharma topics.

In order to cultivate the first of these, {245} the patience that forbears harm, meditate by reflecting in the following manner:

> When another person harms me by beating me or stealing my wealth, and so on, it is quite possible that I will react by losing my patience or giving rise to hatred. However, since I am someone who is striving to achieve buddhahood, what good could possibly come from my failing to tolerate such insignificant harm as that? I shall develop the patience that can even endure all the three realms' beings becoming my enemies and trying to harm me in every way possible. It is certainly a delusion for me to hope to attain buddhahood or to believe that I am a genuine dharma practitioner if I am unable to tolerate even such an insignificant form of harm.

Cultivate the patience that tolerates suffering by generating a strong antidote after reflecting in the following manner:

> What good could possibly come from my failing to tolerate such minor hardships[276] for the sake of the dharma as these: enduring heat, cold, hunger and thirst, undertaking a difficult journey, failing to obtain favorable outer conditions,[277] and having to endure such things as exhaustion, fatigue, and the discomfort caused by the three weather-related conditions of the sun, wind, and rain. Others do not hesitate to undertake every kind of suffering that is even a hundred or a thousand times greater than these for the sake of obtaining wealth or a woman. Therefore, if I must train myself in the liberating activities that were carried out by former

> bodhisattvas in order to attain buddhahood, it would be foolish of me to profess to be a Mahāyānist without being able to tolerate even such minor hardships as these for the sake of the dharma.

The patience that is gained by reflecting intently on a range of dharma topics refers to a form of practice in which one does not fail to comprehend fully such spiritual topics as any of the following:[278] the profound means, the qualities that relate to skillful means, wide-ranging spiritual activities, limitless spiritual qualities of buddhas and bodhisattvas, and the ultimate mode of being that is free of elaboration. It also is said to refer to the ability to keep one's mind fixed on emptiness for an extended period of time. Therefore, you should cultivate it by meditating in the following manner:

> Now, at this point in the practice, since all forms of harm and suffering resemble magically created illusions and are like experiences that occur in a dream, in that they are void of any true mode of existence and they appear to be real even though they are not, what form of harm and suffering is there that cannot be endured?

This completes the explanation of the series of points that make up the forty-eighth meditation topic.

Now, you must also practice the perfection of effort, {246} of which there are three types: armor-like effort, the effort of application, and irreversible effort. Regarding these, armor-like effort is the mental exertion[279] and the courage that does not become disheartened either by developing a sense of disdain toward all of the virtuous spiritual activities that must be carried out by thinking, "I don't need to carry out all of these virtuous activities," or by developing the despondency that thinks in relation to the virtuous activities that are especially difficult, "I am unable to perform such difficult activities as these." Rather, this mental exertion is illustrated by the thought "Not only is it necessary for me to carry out all of these virtuous activities, I am also capable of doing so. Moreover, I shall begin to carry them out right now and I shall perform them uninterruptedly." This attitude is one that you must instill in your mental continuum and cultivate repeatedly.

The effort of application[280] is, when you are directly carrying out the practice, to undertake virtuous activities immediately, with enthusiasm, and without coming under the influence of laziness or distraction, and to do so eagerly and for an extended period of time.

Irreversible effort is that which, even though neither the signs of warmth nor the benefits have developed immediately, does not lose its fervor until the goal associated with whatever activity is undertaken has been achieved, no matter how long it takes, and does not lose its fervor no matter how much hard work must be exerted.

There are also certain instruction systems associated with the tradition known as The Stages of the Teaching that describes effort in the following manner: the physical form of effort is the exertion and fortitude that is generated toward such activities as prostrations and circumambulations; the verbal form of effort is the exertion and fortitude that is generated toward such activities as mantra repetition and prayer recitation; and the mental form of effort is the mental exertion and fortitude that is generated toward virtuous activities in general and, in particular, toward this system of dharma teaching.

In any case, these descriptions all represent various aspects of effort. Therefore, you should meditate on this virtuous attitude by reflecting to yourself:

> I too shall develop effort and exert myself in the practice of virtuous activities, without allowing myself to come under the influence of laziness or procrastination.

This completes the explanation of the series of points that make up the forty-ninth meditation topic.

Now, another practice is the perfection of meditative absorption. Starting now, you must cultivate its requisite causal factors.[281] One quality that is a necessary cause for developing one-pointed concentration {247} is that of mental isolation. A necessary cause for that is physical isolation. A necessary cause for that is to have few concerns[282] and to have few activities.[283] A necessary cause for that is to have few wants[284] and to be satisfied with what you have.[285] A necessary cause for that is to be satisfied with food, clothing, and seats that are of inferior quality. Therefore, you should meditate repeatedly by reflecting in the following manner:

> If I should possess wealth, I shall cultivate one-pointed concentration without having any attachment to it. Even if I should lack wealth, that lack of wealth is a good thing; it allows me to remain

> free of obstacles with regard to the dharma. Therefore, I shall be satisfied with whatever material things I may receive.

This completes the topic of reflecting on the causal factors that promote one-pointed concentration, which constitutes the series of points that make up the fiftieth meditation topic.

Regarding the main practice, while there are many ways of classifying different types of meditative absorption, one type is called "the meditative absorption that enables you to abide in a state of ease during this life," which is meant to indicate that meditative absorption develops the ease associated with physical and mental agility.[286] A second type is called "the meditative absorption that achieves spiritual qualities," a distinction that is meant to indicate the forms of meditative absorption that produce such spiritual qualities as the various types of supernatural knowledge[287] and miraculous powers.[288] A third type is called "the meditative absorption that accomplishes the aims of sentient beings," which is meant to indicate either that one gains the ability to bless[289] other beings' minds on the strength of one-pointed concentration or that one can accomplish the aims of others on the basis of qualities related to miraculous powers. One must rely upon a form of quiescence that is flawless and possesses the full complement of defining attributes in order to develop all of these forms of meditative absorption. In relation to the pursuit of this goal, you should meditate by reflecting to yourself again and again:

> First, I shall absorb my mind in the state of composure that is quiescence. Following that, I shall pursue all the other qualities associated with states of one-pointed concentrations.

This completes the explanation of the series of points that make up the fifty-first meditation topic.

At this point in the teaching, it would be ideal to present a detailed explanation of the topic of quiescence so that practitioners will gain a sure understanding of it. And while it is warranted to present instructions on quiescence at this juncture, it is not necessary for a practitioner to possess a level of firmness in relation to quiescence in order to develop a sure understanding or gain an experiential understanding of the correct view regarding ultimate truth. Moreover, while it is the view of all the major treatises {248} that one can meditate on right view in order to pursue insight[290] only after having properly achieved a firm level of quiescence, and this does, indeed, constitute the great pathway that must be traversed, because it takes a long period of time for the individuals of today, whose faculties are relatively dull, to achieve flawless and firm states of mental stability,[291] out of concern that they will lose the opportunity to meditate on the perfection of wisdom, and because it is possible to achieve quiescence and insight simultaneously by cultivating mental stability after having gained an experiential understanding of correct view, it has clearly become customary not to give a detailed explanation of the topic of quiescence at this point in the teaching, based on the view that such an approach makes it easier for the teacher to present the instructions and for the disciples to gain experiential realizations of those instructions.

Therefore, now I shall present the perfection of wisdom, which is the foremost and most supreme among all the subjects to be learned, as well as the ultimate form of spiritual practice. Regarding this topic, there are three types of wisdom: wisdom regarding ultimate truth, wisdom regarding conventional truth, and the wisdom that knows how to accomplish the aims of others. The first of these is the wisdom that realizes the emptiness that is the ultimate nature of all entities. The second is the wisdom that knows unerringly the dependent origination that constitutes the nature, classifications, and cause-and-effect aspects of all entities that need to be known. The third is the wisdom that knows how to accomplish the aims of others on the basis of the four principles for gathering a following. Regarding those four principles, they consist of knowing how to please beings by giving them material objects in order to establish them in the dharma, knowing how to practice the agreeable speech that teaches the dharma in a way that conforms with others' minds, knowing how to practice the beneficial conduct that establishes others in the practice of the six perfections, and knowing how to practice the sameness of purpose in which you yourself do not stray from the practice of the six perfections. Among these four, establishing others in the practice of the six perfections is accomplished by knowing what methods will be most effective in causing specific followers to develop a state of spiritual self-discipline.

Alternatively, wisdom is made up of the wisdom that derives from learning, the wisdom that derives from reflection, and the wisdom that derives from meditation.[292] Through learning, one gains an understanding of the objects that need to be known; through reflection, one eliminates mistaken assumptions about the meaning of the instruction that has been learned; and through meditation, one develops the wisdom that gains a direct realization of the import of the most important elements of those instructions.

[You should reflect in the following way about these three types of wisdom:]

> I shall do everything necessary to generate all three of these forms of wisdom within my mental continuum.

This exercise consists of training oneself in the proper attitude to be developed toward the perfection of wisdom. This completes the explanation of the series of points that make up the fifty-second meditation topic.

Now, you must train yourself in the following three practices that relate to the perfection of wisdom: {249} (1) meditating on the insubstantiality of the person,[293] (2) meditating on the insubstantiality of entities,[294] and (3) training oneself in the emptiness that is filled with compassion.[295]

Meditating on the Insubstantiality of the Person

The preliminary and concluding practices, and so on, for this topic are the same as before. For the main practice, you should sit with your legs in a cross-legged position and place your hands in the meditation gesture. Hold your vertebrae erect, bend your neck forward slightly, extend your shoulders outward, allow your teeth and lips to remain in their natural position, place the tip of your tongue against the roof of your mouth, and focus your eyes on the tip of your nose. Following that, forcefully exhale a cleansing breath three times through your nose. Then allow your breath to return to its natural state.

Next, after meditating on renunciation[296] until you develop an intense form of aversion for samsara's suffering, meditate on loving-kindness and compassion until you elicit an experiential awareness in your mental continuum.[297] Next direct your attention to the three elements that make up your being—that is, your body, speech, and mind—and submit them to careful consideration, as you reflect in the following manner:

> Throughout samsara that has no beginning, because of my continuous habituation to the mistaken apprehension of a real, personal self, it does appear as though such a self really does exist.

> However, this is nothing more than a false impression, since what is referred to as the "I" or the "self" has no genuine mode of existence whatsoever.

These points constitute the foundation of this meditation exercise. Regarding this practice, if what is called the "I" or the "self" did have a genuine mode of existence, that would constitute a real personal self. However, since no such entity exists in reality at all, one cannot identify the existence of a real personal self in terms of what its essential nature might be. Nevertheless, according to the way in which the apprehension of a real self mistakenly believes in the existence of what does not in fact exist, the self is apprehended as being an entity that is permanent, independent, and a unity.

That mistaken belief either thinks, "Last year, I did such-and-such" or "Now, I am doing such-and-such." It also thinks, "The 'I' that existed last year is the same 'I' that exists now. This self will continue to exist in the future." These thoughts represent what is referred to as "apprehending the self as permanent." When the mistaken perception of a real self arises in the mind, it has the appearance of being a real entity whose existence is not combined together with that of any other inner objects and that possesses a nature that is able to stand on its own. This is what constitutes apprehending the self as a unity. Its appearance of being an entity that, according to circumstances, exercises control over such things as objects of enjoyment,[298] material possessions,[299] and a retinue[300] is what is referred to as "apprehending the self as an entity that is independent."[301]

While the self is apprehended in this manner by an erring mode of perception, it does not actually exist this way for the following reasons. If a permanent self were to experience happiness once, {250} it would have to undergo that happiness permanently. Or if a permanent self were to experience suffering once, it would have to undergo that suffering permanently. Similarly, if at some initial time, a permanent self were to become bound in samsara, it would not be possible for it to undergo liberation at some future time. Or if a permanent self did exist at some future time when it had undergone liberation, it would follow erroneously that it could not have experienced the samsaric condition in the past. However, since happiness and suffering are seen to occur alternately and the conditions of bondage and liberation are understood to occur on separate occasions, it can be established that there is no such thing as a permanent self.

Nor is it reasonable for the self to be a unity. Although the self appears to be present within the heaps that make up one's body and mind, the eye is not the self, nor are the ear, the nose, the tongue, the body,[302] and the mind. If each of these were identified with the self, then there would be multiple selves. On the other hand, if none of these, individually, is the self, then a self cannot be found.

Moreover, if the self were identified with the heaps, it would follow incorrectly that the self is impermanent. On the other hand, if the self were distinct from the heaps, when eye consciousness perceives something visible, it would be contradictory for one to give rise to the conception, "I see that object." [Likewise, the same would be true for the other sensory perceptions up to] when the body touches something, it would be contradictory for one to give rise to the conception, "I am touching that object." For these reasons, it cannot be established that the "I" or the "self" is a unity. Moreover, since the self is not a unity, it cannot be established that it is independent. And in particular, since it can be directly observed that all causes and effects are dependent upon conditions, it is not possible for there to be a self that is independent.

In addition, the self cannot be established as existing outside of the heaps. Nor does the self abide within the heaps. Nor is the self any one of the heaps individually. Nor can a self be found to exist in the wake of having eliminated the heaps. Nor can the self be identified with the universal of the heaps, since there is no universal that exists apart from the individual heaps. After reflecting on the reasoning presented in this instruction, you should meditate on the following conclusion:

> Therefore, what is called the "self" is merely an entity that is nominally ascribed by the mind. It is merely an object that is perceived by an erring mind. It is nothing but a false object. There is no self whatsoever that exists by way of a real essential nature.

This completes the explanation of the series of points that make up the fifty-third meditation topic. It should be understood that, depending upon the practitioner's mental capacity, the series of points that make up this topic of meditating on the insubstantiality of the person may be divided into several sections.

Meditating on the Insubstantiality of Entities

Now the insubstantiality of entities is to be taught. The term "entities" here refers to the heaps,[303] the constituents,[304] and the bases.[305] {251} Regarding these, if there were any entity whose existence was not merely nominally ascribed by the mind but that was something that is capable of standing on its own, that would constitute an entity that is substantially real. However, since nothing has ever existed in that manner, all entities are characterized by the ultimate nature known as the insubstantiality of entities. Nevertheless, in order to eliminate the dualistic concepts that, throughout beginningless samsara, have apprehended the heaps, constituents, and bases as entities that are capable of standing on their own, it is necessary to meditate on the insubstantiality of entities.

Regarding this spiritual exercise, you must begin by meditating on the fact that the five heaps of your own mental continuum lack any real essential nature. If you examine the first of the five heaps—which is to say, the entities within your own continuum that make up the form heap or your physical body—you will recognize that after the collective noun "body" has been assigned to the perception of a variety of different entities, you will think to yourself that there is a single entity that corresponds to this term. However, this supposed entity is one that has been apprehended by an erring mind; it does not exist in the way that it is believed to exist. This should be determined initially by reflecting in the following manner:

> The faculties[306] of the eye, ear, nose, tongue, and body that are present in this body are distinct from one another. There are also separate elements of the physical body that are distinct from the five sense faculties and that constitute the receptacles[307] in which each of these faculties reside. The body is also a composite that is made up of many different elements, such as the head, the neck, the chest, the back, the middle portion of the torso, the stomach, the belly, the two shoulders, the two upper arms, the two elbows, the two forearms, the upper parts of the two hands, the two hips, the two calves, the upper parts of the two feet, the internal elements of the five organs,[308] the six vessels[309] and so on, and the nine apertures[310] and so on. Therefore, what is called "the body" is just an entity that is nominally ascribed by the mind; it is not something that truly exists as an independent object. If each

> of those components were the body, I would possess multiple bodies. If each of them is determined not to be the body, then it cannot be found. If it is thought to be merely the collection of those parts, since there is no entity distinct from those components that constitutes a real collection, it becomes established that the body is nothing more than a nominally ascribed entity.

{252} This completes the explanation of the series of points that make up the fifty-fourth meditation topic.

Also, consider the following analysis: This body, which is made up of the form heap, is not truly existent, since it is understood to be composed of nine physical components: the (1–4) four limbs of the legs and arms, (5) the upper torso, (6) the lower torso, (7) the head, (8) the lower part of the chest, and (9) the internal organs. If you consider whether any of these nine physical components, individually, is truly existent, it can be determined that none of them is truly existent because it is understood that each of them is composed of three parts, and so on. If you consider whether any of those parts, individually, is truly existent, it can be determined that none of them is truly existent because it is understood that each one has a size that consists of multiple finger joints.[311] If you consider whether each portion of this body that is the size of a finger joint is truly existent, it can be determined that none of them is truly existent because it is understood that each finger-joint-sized portion has a size that measures seven barley grains.[312] It can be determined that none of those portions of the body, individually, that is the size of a barley grain, is truly existent because it is understood that each one measures seven lice.[313] Following that, the analysis can be continued with nits,[314] dust motes,[315] "cow particles,"[316] "sheep particles,"[317] "rabbit particles,"[318] "water particles,"[319] down to "iron particles,"[320] with the length of each successive unit of measurement being divisible into seven parts that make up the unit of measurement that follows it. If you consider whether any of these "iron particles," individually, is truly existent, it can be determined that none of them is truly existent because the length of an "iron particle" is equal to seven "minute particles."[321] Nor is a "minute particle" truly existent because it is equal in size to seven "atoms."[322]

If you combine the length, width, and height of these portions of physical matter, each of which is larger than the succeeding one by a factor of seven, then each preceding portion of physical matter is three hundred and forty-three times greater in volume than the succeeding one. This is because, as with the length, the width of each preceding portion of measurement is also seven times greater than that of the succeeding portion, making this two-dimensional area one that is greater in size by a factor of forty-nine, and because the height of each preceding portion of matter is also greater by the same sevenfold amount as the succeeding portion of physical matter.[323]

This completes the explanation of the series of points that make up the fifty-fifth meditation topic.

If you consider whether each atom, individually, is truly existent, it can be determined that none of them is truly existent, because each atom can be seen to have six spatial dimensions—that is, one for each of the four cardinal directions and an upper and a lower dimension—and it must also have a central portion, since without a center it would not be possible to recognize any of the eastern or southern portions, and so on. And since each of those seven elements can further be divided in the same way into another seven parts, none of them is truly existent either. Since there is no end to this analysis in that any physical object can be divided into its components in this way ad infinitum, that entity that is called the body is merely one that is nominally ascribed by the mind; it definitely is not one that has a real mode of existence. Therefore, while form is not rejected as being a mere appearance, {253} like a magical illusion, it has never existed by way of any kind of real essential nature. And, if none of these entities exists as a real unity, for that very reason, none of them can exist as a real multiplicity either because a real multiplicity can exist only by collecting numerous individual entities whose real unity has been established.

This completes the explanation of the series of points that make up the fifty-sixth meditation topic.

If you think to yourself, "Well then, the form heap may not be truly existent, but the mind does exist truly," you should meditate by reflecting in the following manner:

> Mind can be classified in the following manner: (1) The principal mental entity is consciousness,[324] which sees visible form, hears sounds, and so on. Since there are eight separate "collections"[325] of consciousness,[326] it follows that the consciousness heap is made up of multiple entities. (2) Since feelings[327] are made up of various types of experience,[328] such as those that are pleasurable, painful, and neutral, and so on, feelings are also not a single entity.

> (3) Since conceptions[329] apprehend the import of every kind of name, such as "high," "low," "good," "bad," and so on, they too cannot be identified as constituting a single entity. (4) All the remaining varied forms of dualistic conceptual states, such as desire, hatred, faith, and so on, are nothing more than a group of entities to which the mind collectively ascribes the term "formations."[330] Therefore, that which is called the "mind" is not a truly existent unity. Since it is not a real unity, it also cannot be a real multiplicity.

This completes the explanation of the series of points that make up the fifty-seventh meditation topic.

Now, you should meditate in the following manner:

> All of these varied and fleeting forms of awareness are nothing more than appearances; none of them is able to stand up to analysis in order to establish its reality. For example, they are like the reflection of a rocky mountain that appears on the surface of a body of water. If I examine these changing states of awareness, those mental states of the past have ceased and no longer exist, while those of the future also do not exist because they have not yet arisen. Even if I consider those states of awareness that exist in the present as momentary entities, they are not truly existent in the sense of having their own mode of being, since any single moment of awareness can also be separated into several components. One is the portion that constitutes its arising, which derives from its relation to the moment that preceded it; another is the portion that constitutes its cessation, which derives from its relation to the moment that follows it; and a third is the portion that occurs between those two and constitutes its duration.[331] If you examine the middle portion of a momentary state of awareness, it will be determined that since it can be analyzed endlessly by further separating it into three portions ad infinitum, {254} there is no momentary state of awareness that possesses a real essential nature consisting of a unity. As described earlier, since no real unity can be established, a real multiplicity cannot be established either.

This completes the explanation of the series of points that make up the fifty-eighth meditation topic. With these five topics, the process of ascertaining that the heaps within your own continuum are not truly existent is completed.

Just as it was ascertained that the five heaps that make up your own body and mind are not truly existent, now you should ascertain that the same is true for the five heaps that constitute the bodies and minds of all sentient beings. In particular, direct your attention to an individual toward whom you are inclined to develop strong mental afflictions, such as a hateful enemy or a beloved friend. Then examine his or her body in the same way that you examined your own body. Following that, examine his or her mind in the same way that you examined your own mind in terms of the heaps that constitute the "name"[332] aspect of your own being. Then you must meditate by training your mind in the following manner and applying the same reasoning to all sentient beings:

> Therefore, all these persons, such as the one named "so-and-so" or a different one named "this-or-that," are beings whose existence has been nominally ascribed by the mind and they are nothing more than entities that have been erringly ascribed by the mind as being this or that real sentient being. In reality, since they have no true mode of existence whatsoever, they are like magically created illusions.

This practice is called "meditating on the emptiness of all sentient beings who are the contents"[333] that inhabit the external physical world. This completes the explanation of the series of points that make up the fifty-ninth meditation topic.

Moreover, not only are the sentient beings who are the contents of the external physical world not truly existent, the outer world that is the "vessel"[334] in which they reside also is not truly existent. This exercise is carried out by cultivating the following series of determinations, which constitutes meditating on the emptiness of the external world that is the vessel in which sentient beings reside:

> A realm consisting of a triple-thousand world system can be divided into the thousand middling-thousand world systems of which it is composed. Similarly, each middling-thousand world

> system can be divided into a thousand lesser-thousand-world systems, each of which contains a single world made up of four continents, one of which is, for instance, the Rose Apple continent, which can be divided into individual kingdoms whose size is measured in units of distance called *yojana*,[335] which are made up eight *krośa*,[336] each of which, in turn, consists of five hundred *dhanu*,[337] each of which is made up four cubits,[338] which is defined as twenty-four individual finger widths,[339] and so on, which can be further divided into ever smaller units until you reach atoms, thereby establishing that each prior unit of space is not truly existent. And, since atoms, as described earlier, can also be divided into their own spatial components, ultimately, it can be determined that no single component of the external physical world is truly existent. And, as was also explained above, since no real unity can be established in relation to units of physical space, no real multiplicity can be established either.
>
> In short, the physical objects that are identified as being "this or that," or the objects described in such determinations as "This is a house," "This is a farmer's field," "This is grain," "These are forms of wealth and objects of material value," "This is a crop," as well as the objects that are perceived as being such things as a mountain, a plain, an expanse of land, or a country, and so on, {255} are all mere appearances that are formed by the mind in relation to collections of their respective components; none of them are entities that are truly existent. Having been ascribed by the mind in the form of distinct nominal designations, they are nothing more than objects that are erroneously apprehended as being truly existent. In reality, not the slightest portion of any of them can be established as being truly existent.

This completes the explanation of the series of points that make up the sixtieth meditation topic.

You should further carry out the practice known as "meditating on the emptiness of the entirety of the vessel and its contents." This is done by reflecting in the following manner:

> I and everything else—that is, the entirety of the vessel of the physical world and the sentient beings that are its contents—

are composed of all material entities that can be seen and heard and that possess resistance,[340] as well as all instances of mental activity. The former—that is, all material entities—can be subsumed within the five constituents of earth, water, fire, air, and space, and the latter—that is, all mental phenomena—can be subsumed within a sixth constituent of consciousness.

Regarding these, the four elements, in their subtlest form, cannot exist on their own independently, nor do atoms, which are the loci in which the elements reside in combination, exist as real entities. The first part of this proposition is true because each individual element only exists in combination with the other three elements. The second part of this proposition is also true because the elements only exist in such a way that they are mutually dependent on one another; no occasions are ever observed in which any of the elements is able to stand on its own independently.[341]

The constituent that is called "space" is nothing more than what is ascribed by the mind as a state that remains in the absence of material form; space lacks any efficacy and it is not a truly existent entity.

In addition, consciousness cannot be identified as anything more than a mere appearance[342] that arises on the basis of transient conditions. Therefore, I and everything else—that is, the entirety of the vessel of the physical world and the sentient beings that are its contents—do not possess any real mode of existence. While these objects that appear to the erring mind are not rejected in their entirety,[343] since they lack any real essence, they are like magically created illusions.[344]

This completes the explanation of the series of points that make up the sixty-first meditation topic.

Furthermore, you should reflect in the following manner, which is known as "the ultimate form of meditation that is free of elaboration." The term "unreality"[345] refers to a state that is merely ascribed on the basis of entities. Since it does not exist even as an object that pertains to spiritual practice in the sense of what should be adopted and what should be abandoned in a conventional sense, let alone as one that exists in an ultimate sense,[346] it is not something that exists in any sense whatsoever. Therefore, while all the entities described above that are well-known appearances[347] should be thought of as having never existed in reality,[348] the expression "entity that is empty" does not mean something that has never possessed any valid basis whatsoever. Since a barren woman's child[349] is not something that could ever have existed, it is not even possible to assert that "the barren woman's child does not exist." Moreover, since that kind of emptiness[350] is established by the mind in dependence upon its opposite, in other words that which is not an emptiness, you should place your mind in a nonconceptual state of great clarity where no determination whatsoever is made about that emptiness, such as that it exists or it does not exist or that anything can be either affirmed or denied about it, and therefore, the mind does not apprehend anything at all. If, after having placed your mind in that state, a dualistic concept should subsequently arise, you should analyze the nature of that {256} conceptualizing mind and, after determining that it lacks any identifiable nature, meditate upon that very state. It is of crucial importance to cultivate both the previous form of meditation[351] and this latter one[352] jointly, and they should be practiced repeatedly with clarity and for relatively short periods of time.

This completes the explanation of the series of points that make up the sixty-second meditation topic.

Following that, you should meditate in a manner that combines all of these methods of practice. After having reviewed in your mind the understandings that were explained above for a brief period of time, reflect in the following manner:

> Within myself and everything else—that is, the entirety of the vessel of the physical world and the sentient beings that are its contents—there is no "I" or "self," nor is there any agent that carries out actions. All entities that appear do so simply through the convergence of the conditions that make up the process of dependent origination. Because none of these entities exists at all as a real unity or a real multiplicity, they are nothing more than objects that appear to erring states of mind; they do not possess any true mode of existence whatsoever. If this point is examined correctly, it will be determined that what is referred to as being "unreal"[353] or "nonexistent" is nothing more than the ascribing of such a term to what has the appearance of being the contradictory of a construct that the mind has newly fabricated as the

> definition of "existent." When the mutually dependent nature of these two concepts is analyzed in this way, the tendency to perceive mental objects as real will disappear, and when it does, I should absorb my mind in this state where nothing at all is thought about. Moreover, I should keep my mind fixed in this nonconceptual state for as long as I do not lose the quality in which those former dualistic mental objects have been cleared away from my mind and it remains entirely free of any such identifications of false objects.

Moreover, if that state dissipates, the practitioner should not allow his or her mind to remain in what may be called a "nonconceptual" state[354] but in one that is merely one in which the quality of emptiness has disappeared. Since one must meditate continually on that former nondual awareness of emptiness, the spiritual teachers note that it is important for the practitioner to be able to differentiate between the point at which that proper awareness of emptiness has or has not begun to dissipate. In the initial stages of meditation practice, the practitioner will observe that he or she cannot maintain the proper aspect of the awareness of emptiness for any significant length of time; however, after the first elements of the proper experiential state have been achieved, the duration of this awareness will gradually become longer and longer.

Regarding this process, the stage in which you begin the process of fixing your mind on the meditation object is called "placement."[355] The stage in which you begin to keep the mind fixed on the meditation object continuously for longer periods of time is called "continued placement."[356] The stage in which you are able to put a stop to the occurrence of all conceptual states and return your mind to the meditation object is called "renewed placement."[357] The stage in which the duration in which you are able to keep your mind fixed on the meditation object becomes progressively longer is called "close placement."[358] The stage in which you develop an especially strong form of exertion toward the practice of meditation through having cultivated the joy that arises from recalling the good qualities of one-pointed concentration is called "subduing."[359] The stage in which such faults as distraction[360] {257} cease naturally, through having spent some time recalling the disadvantages of distraction and so on is called "pacification."[361] These latter two stages are defined in terms of generating enthusiasm for the good qualities that relate to one-pointed concentration and developing aversion for the faults that impede one-pointed concentration, respectively. The stage in which all occurrences of such conceptual states as expectation and apprehension or attachment and aversion are naturally quelled by examining their essential nature intently and then "sealing" those conceptual states with the understanding that you gained previously when you meditated on the point that all forms of awareness are not truly existent is called "heightened pacification."[362]

For a certain period of time, it is necessary to restore your mental continuum continually to a state of one-pointed concentration by means of these techniques, when it comes under the influence of flaws that are created by bad habits. Following that, through exerting effort in a variety of ways to keep the mind focused, it will become free of the faults of languor[363] and excitation,[364] and you will be able to keep your mind fixed for an extended period of time on the meditation object of emptiness that constitutes its cognitive aspect. This stage of the practice, during which effort must be exerted to keep the mind focused, is the one that is called "engendering one-pointedness" in the mental continuum. Ultimately, you will become able to fix your mind on that correct view just by recalling your prior experience of it, and by that method alone your mind will develop the ability to remain fixed for an extended period of time on that state of awareness whose cognitive aspect is emptiness. At that point, you must release all exertion and allow your mind to remain fixed naturally in that state. By doing so, you will have achieved the stage that is called "equipoise."[365]

This system of meditation is the one that is described in abhidharma literature as a method of cultivating quiescence that is carried out prior to practicing insight. It is similar to the system that is described in such works as Kamalaśīla's *Stages of Meditation*, and it is a method of meditation in which cultivation of a nonconceptual state of mind[366] is preceded by a form of analysis.[367] The *Udder*[368] of instructions taught by the great spiritual teacher Potowa declares that, according to the system of Glorious Atiśa, one-pointed meditation must always be preceded by analysis.[369] However, there are also a great many systems of instruction that teach a form of meditation in which analysis is eschewed, such as several of Atiśa's instructions on Mind Training, which represent the Sūtrayāna system, as well as many Mantrayāna instructions, such as those of the Great Seal tradition. Nevertheless, in the context of this treatise, which presents the instruction of the Kadam tradition known as The Stages of the Teaching, one should practice in the manner that was taught by the great spiritual teacher Potowa.

This completes the explanation of the series of points that make up the sixty-third meditation topic.

According to this type of system for meditating on the view regarding emptiness, when the state of mental stability[370] is achieved, insight will also be achieved; thus, its proponents maintain the position that the union of quiescence and insight exists from the outset. {258}

Training Oneself in the Emptiness That Is Filled with Compassion

Regarding the phrase "emptiness that is filled with compassion," it should be understood that because developing an awareness of emptiness by itself does not constitute the practice of the perfection of wisdom, you must cultivate a form of practice in which emptiness and compassion are united. Therefore, meditate by reflecting again and again in the following manner:

> In an ultimate sense, there are no entities whatsoever that are established as truly existent among those that appear and come into existence in ordinary experience. The concordant example is that they resemble space. When a practitioner directly perceives the nonexistence of those entities that are not truly existent, he or she realizes that there are no truly existent sentient beings that experience suffering and that there is no truly existent suffering that is experienced. Moreover, the process by which suffering is experienced—which is described as occurring repeatedly through the mutual interaction of the three factors of karma, mental afflictions, and suffering—is also one that has not ever been truly existent. However, when none of these points have been realized, the appearance of sentient beings who experience suffering will arise, the appearance of the suffering that is experienced will arise, and the appearance of the processes by which suffering is experienced and samsara occurs repeatedly will also arise. While all of these elements of ordinary experience appear despite their not being truly existent, how deserving of compassion are sentient beings who experience suffering in these varied ways in a manner that resembles sentient beings who have been deceived by magically created illusions. I shall clear away the errors of these beings and establish them in the state of buddhahood that realizes the ultimate nature of reality.

> I do not exist in an ultimate sense, these sentient beings do not exist in an ultimate sense, error does not exist in an ultimate sense, and the path that eliminates error also does not exist in an ultimate sense. Nevertheless, merely as conventional erring appearances, just as suffering and the obscurations appear to exist, so, too, does the path appear to exist. It is also the case that one becomes a buddha who eliminates error by meditating on the path and comes to abide naturally in the ultimate nature of reality. Thus, by teaching the dharma to sentient beings who resemble magically created illusions, I who resemble a magically created illusion shall cause this state of exhaustion caused by suffering that resembles a magically created illusion to disappear into the realm of ultimate truth.
>
> All relations of object or agent with regard to suffering are not truly existent. No entities that are appearances or that are commonly accepted to exist are truly existent. Nevertheless, even if one were to assume that there was such a thing as truly existent suffering, {259} there is no more extreme form of suffering that one could experience than this experience of suffering that is not truly existent. When suffering disappears of its own accord for one who realizes that it does not truly exist, how deserving of compassion are those who fail to realize it in this way.

This completes the explanation of the series of points that make up the sixty-fourth meditation topic.

Now, as a way of enhancing this form of practice, meditate exclusively on emptiness for one entire day. Then meditate exclusively on compassion for one entire day. Following that, meditate on the union of emptiness and compassion that was just explained for one entire day. By repeating this method of practice again and again, you will experience the occurrence of significant progress.

Alternatively, sometimes meditate exclusively on emptiness for one meditation session, then meditate exclusively on compassion for one meditation session, and then for either one or two sessions meditate on the union of emptiness and compassion. If you occasionally practice in this way repeatedly, you will experience the occurrence of significant progress. This represents a dose[371] of instruction.

Now, the following is referred to as the means of eliminating hindrances.

This practice in which emptiness and compassion are combined together is the most essential form of meditation. An obstacle that occurs in relation to it is attachment to the happiness of this life. This includes the desire to obtain great wealth and a favorable reputation, and to be a person whose speech is powerful in this life, as well as the wish that others regard you as an excellent dharma practitioner. It also includes the wish that you should become one who is superior to others. Having failed to completely[372] overcome desire and attachment, you act in any of the following ways: you profess to become a religious practitioner who has abandoned all ordinary activities, go into seclusion, seal yourself inside a meditation cell, engage in austerities, you beg for alms[373] but become a monk or nun out of a desire for food,[374] or you become a fully ordained monk who seeks fame or a monk or nun who proudly and arrogantly makes a pretense of being virtuous.[375] Because your ultimate wish is for everyone to develop faith toward you and for you to always be successful, you carry out actions that are meant to defeat others. While you profess to be acting in accord with the dharma, you are actually pursuing worldly self-aggrandizement. It is the very opposite of the spiritual practice that combines emptiness and compassion. Those actions are referred to as "eating food that has been mixed with poison." {260} While it is not surprising that, from the outset, both the thoughts and actions of a common, worldly person are extremely reprehensible in that they are entirely wicked,[376] these thoughts and actions should never even be considered by a person who makes a pretense of being virtuous, such that he or she would allow them to become mixed in with his or her ostensibly virtuous activities.[377] As the antidote to these corrupt thoughts and actions, you must recall again and again the spiritual attitudes that are meant to be cultivated by a lesser person.

The obstructive behavior that stems from attachment to the happiness of gods and humans in a future life should be understood as follows. Even though you may engage in certain acts of generosity, observe certain forms of morality, and engage in regular virtuous activities to some degree, if you do so with the aspiration of obtaining a state of well-being in a future life that is endowed with food, clothing, wealth, a house, a wife, a retinue, servants, and influence, because you have failed to overcome your attachment to the pleasures of samsaric existence, these activities will have taken on the quality of being inimical to the spiritual practice in which emptiness is filled with compassion. As the antidote to this form of attachment, you must meditate once again on the spiritual attitudes that relate to a middling person.

Even though your mind may have taken on a spiritual quality, if your attitude is one that is solely concerned about your own interests,[378] that is the very opposite of the spiritual practice that combines emptiness and compassion. Therefore, as its antidote, you must meditate on the system of instruction known as the Equality and Exchange between Oneself and Others. Moreover, in order to do so, it is important for you to know how to properly apply the points of the instruction in relation to your mind and body and not limit yourself merely to a general understanding of its meaning. The instruction for this teaching is set forth in the Mind Training tradition. It is also presented in an extensive form in *Entry into the Conduct That Leads to Enlightenment* and *The Compendium of Training*. The exalted heir apparent[379] Maitreya also declared:

> Having obtained toward others the state of mind in which they
> are equal to oneself,
> or the state that, in comparison to oneself, cherishes others as
> being more excellent,
> what then is the nature of one's own aims and what is the nature of
> the aims that relate to others
> for one who regards the welfare of others as more important than
> one's own?[380]

While emptiness is an object of understanding that is meditated upon again and again, it is not something that truly exists. Moreover, if the phrase "like a magically created illusion" is taken to mean some kind of object, then your practice is not being carried out correctly. If you continue to form the coarse concepts of "enemy," "friend," "wealth," "reputation," and so on, since they represent obstacles to the spiritual practice that combines emptiness and compassion, it is important to cultivate from the depth of your heart the knowledge of how to properly apply in relation to your body, mind, wealth, possessions, enemies, and friends the awareness that they resemble magically created illusions. {261} This also represents a dose of instruction.

In addition, you should meditate, each day or during each meditation session, on the topics of leisure and fortune and the difficulty of obtaining them; impermanence in the form of death; samsara's various forms of suffering; the cause and result aspects of the doctrine of karma; faith toward the dharma; loving-kindness, compassion, and enlightenment mind; and the two forms of selflessness.[381] Sometimes, you should meditate on them consecutively, in that regular order; at other times, you should do so in a reverse order. Sometimes, you should meditate on them until you elicit an experiential realization that extends to the marrow of your bones; at other times, you should meditate on them in an irregular or random manner. Sometimes, you should meditate on the particular topic that overcomes whatever obstacle that needs to be abandoned is harming your mind most strongly at that moment; at other times, you should meditate on whatever topic about which you think, "I feel most comfortable meditating on this topic." This represents a dose of instruction.

As your regular form of practice, you should meditate principally on these four topics: recalling impermanence until it is vividly experienced; reflecting on the meaning of karma and its results, which leads to a sense of embarrassment and care;[382] cultivating compassion toward all those sentient beings who are wandering in the three realms; and entering a state of meditative absorption upon the true nature of reality that is free of conceptual elaboration. The other topics mentioned above should be meditated on in a subordinate manner.

You should associate with holy lamas and excellent dharma companions who practice this dharma teaching. Reading sūtra scriptures or listening to discourses on them during the time between meditation sessions will also help to advance your meditation practice. Developing sure understandings about the dharma teachings will reinforce your faith. In particular, it is also crucially important for you to read and study the writings of former Kadam masters, such as the manuals that relate to the works of the class known as The Stages of the Teaching and to diligently instill their meanings into your mind. This is another dose of instruction.

These latter four sections of instruction address elements of your regular practice and methods of training yourself that will enhance your practice and eliminate obstacles. You do not need to make them into separate meditation topics; however, it would not be detrimental if you did treat them as separate meditation topics.

III. How the Training Enables You to Achieve the Result That Is Unsurpassed Enlightenment

This topic is one that can be understood in a detailed manner by listening to teachings on the great treatises. However, I shall not undertake to present such an explanation here. The Ārya Teacher[383] described the essence of this topic in the following manner:

> Others' aims are achieved by morality and generosity.
> One's own are achieved by effort {262} and patience.
> Meditative absorption and wisdom promote liberation.[384]
>
> Compassion achieves everyone's aims.[385]
>
> Through the simultaneous perfection
> of these seven qualities[386] in their entirety,
> the object of inconceivable knowledge,
> the state of the world's protector, is attained.[387]

Through cultivating the attitude of enlightenment mind and the conduct of the six perfections of generosity and so on, your mind will, of its own accord, avoid straying from the dharma, and your faith in the Three Jewels, your embarrassment and care[388] in relation to karma and its results, and your sense of aversion[389] toward the suffering of samsara will arise naturally.

Once you become free of any displeasure about meditating on the dharma and your willingness to practice grows stronger naturally, regardless of whether you have developed firm one-pointed concentration or not, you will have attained the initial stage of the path and developed in your mental continuum the lesser form of the path of accumulation.[390] Following that, while still on the path of accumulation, when a slight amount of clear vision regarding impermanence, suffering, emptiness, and selflessness has been gained, this is called "the meditative absorption that is practiced by immature beings."[391] Following that, through the combination of two strengths—that of one's meditation practice and that of having accumulated merit—when it is successively realized that the five heaps resemble magically created illusions, as in the canonical passage that states "form resembles a mass of foam," and so on,[392] and a clarity of vision regarding the insubstantiality of entities has been attained, this is called "the mental absorption that discerns objects."[393] Starting with the attainment of the path of seeing,[394] the arising of the transcendent awareness that directly realizes the absence of conceptual elaboration throughout the ten ārya bodhisattva stages is called "the meditative absorption whose object is suchness."[395] From the first to the seventh ārya bodhisattva stages there is only a slight approximation of what is called "the splendid meditative absorption of a tathāgata." On the eighth, ninth, and tenth stages, this meditative absorption is present in lesser, intermediate, and great forms, respectively. On the stage of a perfect buddha, it becomes what can be described as "the ultimate perfection of the splendid meditative absorption of a tathāgata." This fourth meditative absorption is the transcendent awareness that directly perceives the true essence of reality. This overall topic should be learned in detail from other sources. Although these four meditative absorptions {263} are not addressed in the writings of the former Kadampa masters, I have presented them here as they appear in a sūtra.[396]

Initially, during the period in which one has not yet gained the first stages of the path, the spiritual practice is somewhat more difficult to carry out. Therefore, it is important that you reject all other activities and strive exclusively to engage in spiritual practice. Following that, while you will still need to increase your effort, it will become somewhat easier [for you to carry out your spiritual practice]. When you give rise to the knowledge associated with the path of preparation,[397] through having developed your mental continuum by accumulating merit in a variety of different ways and by performing many different kinds of aspirational prayers, your spiritual practice will improve naturally, and it will become easier for you to pursue it. During the path of preparation, it is also necessary for you to exert yourself to a great extent in order to overcome subtle forms of the deeds of Māra,[398] eliminate obstacles, and achieve significant progress. Following that, eventually the direct realization of reality will arise, after which the practice will be carried out with progressively greater ease.

The state of buddhahood that is the Mahāyāna path's result includes the essence body,[399] which is characterized by the transcendent knowledge of the innate clear light that is free of elaboration; the enjoyment body,[400] which is the being that turns the ultimate form of the dharma wheel to the retinue of pure beings[401] in the buddha field known as Below None;[402] the emanation body,[403] which acts on behalf of beings in impure realms[404] in whatever form is best able to cause them to develop spiritual self-discipline; and enlightened activities that establish all sentient beings, in whatever way is most suitable to their spiritual status, in states of benefit and ultimate happiness by means of the three attributes of knowledge, compassion, and power.

There is no established position regarding how many "doses" of instruction are contained in this final topic. It should simply be explained in whatever manner is most appropriate to the circumstances. This marks the completion of the body of instructions that is known by the phrase "Gaining Entry to the Teaching."

Now I shall explain the ritual for generating the enlightenment mind and the ritual for accepting the bodhisattva vow, activities that may be performed as a result of having completed the teaching.[405] These topics are addressed in two sections: (1) the ritual for generating enlightenment mind and (2) the ritual for adopting the bodhisattva vows.

The Ritual for Generating the Aspirational Form of Enlightenment Mind

The sacred vessels[406] and offerings should be arranged on an altar. A mandala offering is presented to the spiritual teacher who is carrying out the ritual. Then the following words, which are recited by the officiating preceptor, should be repeated three times by his or her disciples:

> May all the buddhas and bodhisattvas who reside in the ten directions give heed to me. O Spiritual Teacher, please give heed to me. Just as all the former tathāgatas, {264} arhats, true and complete buddhas, and the bodhisattvas who reside on the great ārya stages first generated the mind that aspires to attain unsurpassed true and complete enlightenment, I, too, who am named so-and-so, request that you, O Spiritual Teacher, enable me to generate the mind that aspires to attain unsurpassed true and complete enlightenment.

Following that, after reciting once more the request to be given heed by the preceptor that was just described, the following words should be repeated three times:

> I, who am named so-and-so, from this moment on until I sit at the seat of enlightenment, go for refuge to the divine bud-

> dhas who are the supreme human beings among all two-footed human beings. I go for refuge to the dharma, the state of peace that is free of attachment and is the supreme doctrine among all spiritual doctrines. I go for refuge to the community of irreversible ārya bodhisattvas who make up the supreme assemblage among all assemblages of spiritual beings.

In the extensive form of this ritual, the initial request to be given heed is stated each time that the refuge formula is repeated. In a more abbreviated form, it is acceptable for it to be stated just once, as indicated here. When this point is reached, the verses from the *Aspirational Prayer for Excellent Spiritual Conduct*[407] that give expression to the seven-limb devotional practice should be recited three times as a means of accumulating merit.

For the main portion of the ritual, after the request to be heeded has been recited as described above, the officiating preceptor should direct his or her disciples to repeat the following words three times:

> By means of the roots of virtue whose natures are generosity, morality, and meditation that I, who am named so-and-so, have performed, both in this life and in other former lives, as well as those roots of virtue that I have caused others to perform and that I have rejoiced at when others have performed them, I, who am named so-and-so, from this moment on {265} until I sit at the seat of enlightenment, generate the mind that aspires to attain the unsurpassed true and complete state of great enlightenment, just as the former tathāgatas, arhats, true and complete buddhas, and the great bodhisattvas who reside on the great ārya stages generated this mind.
>
> I shall deliver those who have not been delivered;
> I shall liberate those who have not been liberated;
> I shall provide relief to those who are without relief;
> And I shall establish in supreme happiness those who have
> not attained supreme happiness.

Following that, the preceptor should explain, among those precepts pertaining to the aspirational form of enlightenment mind that were taught earlier, whichever ones are appropriate to the circumstances, or he or she should explain them in whatever other extensive or abbreviated manner is considered appropriate. The preceptor should also declare to the disciples that they should learn the precepts that appear in the *Sūtra on the Seven Spiritual Qualities Taught in Response to Ārya Avalokiteśvara's Inquiry*,[408] as well as the many benefits of enlightenment mind that are taught extensively in such scriptures as the *Gaṇḍavyūha Sūtra*.

Following that, suitable aspirational prayers should be made, or, as an abbreviated act, the verse that states "Through this virtue may all beings" and so on,[409] should be recited. Following that, the Three Jewels should be worshiped once again, and an offering should be presented to the spiritual teacher.

This constitutes the ritual for generating the aspirational form of enlightenment mind, which is widely known as "the ritual for generating enlightenment mind." Since there are no requirements such as that any potential candidate be examined as to whether he or she is a fit vessel, and it is not a prerequisite for someone to have taken any of the eight vows contained in the system of prātimokṣa,[410] it is permissible to perform it for all those who wish to undertake it.

This form of the ritual for generating enlightenment mind has been transmitted through a lineage that originates with Maitreya. It is believed that a separate ritual for generating enlightenment mind was composed by the master Ārya Asaṅga and that it exists in the Land of Āryas.[411] That version is said to have been based upon a ritual found in a sūtra titled *Bodhisattvapiṭaka* that is different from the one of the same name that is contained in the collection of sūtras known as the *Heap of Jewels*.[412] The viewpoint of that ritual is contained here, where it has been written in accordance with the wording expressed in the ritual for generating enlightenment mind that was composed by the Glorious Atiśa.[413]

The Ritual for Accepting the Bodhisattva Vow {266}

Since the Mahāyāna sūtras are the best source of extensive explanations on the precepts that must be observed by bodhisattvas, practitioners should attend numerous teachings on sūtra discourses. Alternatively, it is extremely beneficial for practitioners to listen to teachings on such works as *The Stage of a Bodhisattva*[414] and *The Compendium of Training*,[415] as they contain the essence of the entire Mahāyāna system of practice. At the very least, one should receive the oral transmission blessing gained through hearing the recitation of a Mahāyāna sūtra such as the *Jewel Cloud Sūtra*[416] or the *Ākāśagarbha Sūtra*.[417] While someone may have listened to the essence of the Mahāyāna teachings through having received a detailed explanation of the instructions from the system known as The Stages of the Teaching that were described above, it is imperative that he or she listen to the form of expression that is conveyed in the words of at least one Mahāyāna sūtra.

Following that introductory statement, the actual ritual for receiving the bodhisattva vow is carried out in the following manner. Offerings should be arranged in front of the three vessels.[418] Then, after making prostration to the preceptor[419] three times, with palms joined, you should also make the following request to him or her three times:

> O Spiritual Teacher, I wish to receive from you the acceptance of the discipline of bodhisattva morality. If it causes no trouble, may it please you, in your compassion, to hear me for a brief moment.

If the disciple has memorized these words, he or she may state the request by him- or herself. If not, they should be repeated after the preceptor or an associate.

Following that, the preceptor should state the following words:

> Hear me, O son or daughter of good family. Do you wish to lead across those who have not crossed over, liberate those who have not been liberated, provide relief to those who have not found relief, and establish in ultimate happiness those who have not attained ultimate happiness,[420] and do you also wish to preserve the lineage of the buddhas?

The disciples should reply:

> I do so wish.

Then the preceptor should declare:

> You should generate a firm attitude and a firm determination with regard to these aims.

Following this, the preceptor should ask the following two questions and the disciples should respond as indicated:

> Are you requesting the bodhisattva vow out of rivalry[421] with others?
>
> No, I am not.
>
> Are you requesting the bodhisattva vow at the instigation of others {267}?
>
> No, I am not.

Next, the devotional act of presenting offerings should be carried out by reciting the verses that begin with the phrase "Emitting light rays as arrays of reception water, / as garlands of reception water . . . ."[422] Following that, also recite verses of praise and prostration, such as the verse that contains the line "the Savior endowed with great compassion,"[423] in whatever manner is appropriate.

Following that, with great reverence toward the preceptor, the disciple(s) should recite the following words of request three times:

> May it please the preceptor to quickly bestow upon me the acceptance of the discipline of bodhisattva morality.

Then, the preceptor should ask the following:

> Are you, the one named so-and-so (or "Are you, O son or daughter of good family . . . "), a bodhisattva?

The disciples should reply:

> Yes, I am.

The preceptor should then further ask the following:

> Have you made the aspirational prayer to attain enlightenment?

The disciples should reply:

Yes, I have.

Following that, for the main portion of the ritual the preceptor begins by asking the following:

> Here me, O son or daughter of good family. Do you wish to accept from me all of the precepts and all of the forms of morality that are observed by all bodhisattvas?

The disciples should reply:

> I do so wish.

Following that, to carry out the main part of the ritual, the preceptor should state the following three times:

> O son of good family or daughter of good family who is named so-and-so, do you accept from me, a bodhisattva named so-and-so, all of the bodhisattva precepts and all of the bodhisattva morality—namely, the morality of restraint, the morality of acquiring virtuous qualities, and the morality of acting on behalf of sentient beings—those precepts and that morality that have been observed by all the bodhisattvas of the past, {268} those precepts and that morality that shall be observed by all the bodhisattvas of the future, and those precepts and that morality that currently are being observed by all the bodhisattvas of the present throughout the ten directions, those precepts and that morality with regard to which all the bodhisattvas of the past have trained themselves, with regard to which all the bodhisattvas of the future shall train themselves, and with regard to which all the bodhisattvas of the present are training themselves?

The disciple should reply:

> I do so accept them.[424]

By repeating these words three times, the bodhisattva vow will arise in the disciples. Following that, the preceptor should make the following announcement three times to the buddhas and bodhisattvas:

> The bodhisattva and son of good family or daughter of good family named so-and-so has acknowledged three times that he or she accepts the discipline of bodhisattva morality from me, the bodhisattva named so-and-so. I, the bodhisattva named so-and-so, am a witness to this acceptance of the bodhisattva discipline of morality by this bodhisattva named so-and-so, and I announce it to the supreme āryas in the endless and unlimited world spheres that lie in the ten directions who, though beyond our range of vision, possess an awareness whose range of vision perceives all entities everywhere.

The preceptor should indicate this act by rising and scattering flowers in each of the ten directions as he or she recites this declaration.

Following that, the disciples should stand up and make three prostrations to the preceptor and the Three Jewels. Then, after the disciple(s) have become seated again, the preceptor should declare the following to them:

> Now that you have accepted the bodhisattva vow, the buddhas and bodhisattvas will regard you as a spiritual son or daughter and a spiritual brother or sister, respectively, and they will always protect and safeguard you. All forms of the merit and wisdom accumulations that you possess {269} will be enhanced. It is important that you do not declare to individuals who lack faith and that you keep secret from them that you have accepted this bodhisattva vow. From today on, you must always avoid committing the four or eight acts that represent an extreme form of defeat,[425] as well as the forty-six secondary offenses,[426] and the like. You should also become knowledgeable about the means of safeguarding the bodhisattva form of morality, the differences between a transgression that is grave or light, and the confession ritual by which those transgressions can be remedied.

If the preceptor wishes to perform the ritual in an extensive manner, it would be beneficial at this point to describe all the precepts in a concise manner.

However, speaking in general terms, it is the position of this system regarding the acceptance of the bodhisattva vow that a candidate should ascertain the nature of the precepts prior to the acceptance of the vow; therefore, the failure of omitting an essential component of the ritual would not be incurred if the precepts are not described here.

After that, an offering should be presented to the officiating preceptor, followed by the act of dedicating the virtue gained during the ritual to enlightenment. When that has been carried out, the ritual for accepting the bodhisattva vow is completed.

This concludes the treatise that explains how to meditate on the instructions known as The Stages for Gaining Entry to the Teaching, also known as the instructions for the Three Types of Person, together with a description of how to carry out two rituals associated with generating enlightenment mind.

The dharma seeker who only wishes to pursue the Sūtrayāna path will find that all of its forms of spiritual practice are contained within this treatise. It also contains the blessings of an oral tradition that are not found in any other Sūtrayāna system of instruction that is current today. Therefore, you should consider this very dharma teaching as your principal form of spiritual practice. Moreover, those who desire to pursue the Mantrayāna path run the risk of developing an erring form of tantric practice if they do not first undertake this system of practice. For these reasons, all those who desire to attain their own spiritual betterment[427] should train themselves in this treatise that contains the authoritative views of all the victors and their spiritual offspring.

I make prostration, go for refuge, and make supplication to
the Lord of Compassion, the Victor, the Blessed One,
the heir apparent and exalted offspring of the Victor, the
  Protector Ajita,[428]
the master of the entire teaching, the Venerable Ārya Asaṅga,
and Vasubandhu, a second omniscient one and offspring of the
  victors.

I reverently make supplication to and pray to be blessed by
the supreme lamas of the Lineage of Extensive Conduct,
from Paramasena, {270} and the rest, up to King Survarṇadvīpī,[429]
the supreme masters of the Lineage of the Profound View,

who are the Victor's offspring Mañjuśrī, Ārya Nāgārjuna, and the
rest,
and the supreme masters of the Lineage of Divinely Inspired
Practice,
that is, the Lord of Secrets, the glorious Yoginī, Tilopa, and the
rest.

I make supplication to and pray for blessings from
all of these root and lineage lamas:
Atiśa, who possessed the mind that is a wish-granting jewel,
Gyalwai Jungne, the precious teacher from the Drom clan,[430]
Potowa, whose sphere of knowledge was highly developed,
Sharawa, who reached the far shore of the ocean-like scriptural
tradition,
Lodrö Drak,[431] the teacher from the Tum clan, who practiced
dharma properly,
the teacher from the Do clan,[432] a mainstay of the Kadam
teaching,
Glorious Dro,[433] whose transcendent wisdom shone with brilliant
light,
the teacher from the Kyo clan, Senge Kyap, whose practice of the
three trainings was pure,
the great Chim Namkha Drak,[434] a crown ornament among those
of the noble class,
Venerable Mönlam Tsultrim, lord of spiritual abilities and powers,
the one named Zeu Drakpa,[435] who benefited countless beings,
Losang[436] from the Chim clan, who reached the far shore of the
ocean of abhidharma,
the teacher from the Dro clan, Kun Gyalwa,[437] who possessed the
pure mind,
the teacher from the Pang clan, Drupa Sherap, a master of the
dharma,
Sönam Chokdrup, who possessed the most holy and supreme
mind,
Venerable and Glorious Döndrup,[438] who upheld the system on
the profound meaning,
the heart disciple[439] and elder Sönam Drakpa,[440]
Venerable Kunga Chokdrup, who possessed enlightenment mind,

Master Drölchok,[441] a heroic adept and a manifestation of Lord Mañjuśrī,[442]
and Venerable Lungrik Gyatso, who perceived the unoriginated ultimate reality.

Alternatively, for a different lineage, after reciting the first line expressing supplication, followed by the line that is addressed to Drom Tönpa Gyalwai Jungne, continue with the following lines that are for a separate lineage of Kadam masters:

I make supplication to and pray for blessings from
Chengawa,[443] in whom morality and wisdom shone brilliantly,
Jayulwa,[444] who was blessed by his supreme lama,
Tsangpa Rinpoche,[445] to whom the true state[446] {271} became evident,
The master from Mumen,[447] who reached the far shore of the ocean of instruction,

Following this last master, the lineage continues with the same ones listed above that range from Glorious Dro to great abbot Sönam Chokdrup. After that, the lineage continues with the following masters:

The great abbot Kun Gyalwa,[448] who attained supreme spiritual qualities,
Lha Chungwa Yeshe Rinchen, who possessed exceedingly pure wisdom
and put forth effort to practice in a one-pointed manner,[449]
and my root lama, whose name was Jampa.[450]

Moreover, as there are numerous other lineages, such as the one that proceeds through the master Neusurpa,[451] it is permissible to add whatever lines of supplication are appropriate. You should consider the lines of supplication that appear above for the two Kadam lineages known as the Treatise Followers[452] and the Instruction Followers[453] as the ones that are of foremost importance.

Following that, you should recite the following additional verses of supplication:

The path for lesser persons is a faith that is completely pure;
the path for middling persons is a renunciation that is completely pure;
the path for great persons is a superior attitude that is completely pure;
please bless me to achieve the three paths that are completely pure.

If I fail to develop an awareness of the impermanence of death,
no matter how much I strive, I will be one who adheres to this life.
Since my mind will not otherwise be able to take on the nature of the dharma,
please bless me to become free of the bonds of the eight worldly concerns.

If I fail to develop belief[454] in the infallibility of karma and its results,
all my dharma activities will become a pretense of virtue;
though my practice is said to be zealous, it is done to impress others
Therefore, please bless me to develop belief in the dharma.

If I fail to develop a mind that possesses loving-kindness and compassion,
though I may strive to practice, I will err by falling into the lesser vehicle.
Therefore, please bless me to accept the duty of eliminating the suffering of the entire world
and become one who has successfully cultivated the supreme enlightenment mind.

If I fail to realize the emptiness in which you become free of all conceptual elaboration naturally,
I will not understand that all entities resemble magically created illusions
and, being under the sway of grasping at signs, my mind cannot be liberated.
Therefore, please bless me to realize the ultimate state of reality.

The teachings that I have included in this text are based on explanations that I heard from the supreme scholar Jampa Lhundrup[455] on *A Lamp for the Path*,[456] {272} both the root-verse text and its commentary; *Entry into the Two Truths*,[457] both the root verses and its commentary;[458] the explanation of both the root verses and the commentary on *Instruction on the Middle Way*;[459] the instruction manual composed by the master from Mumen;[460] Lumpawa's[461] *Stages of the Path*; and Potowa's *Edifying Similes*,[462] both the root text and its commentary. I have also received oral transmissions from Khenchen Lungrik Gyatso[463] on Potowa's *Blue Udder*,[464] including both the root text and its commentary, the Narthang masters' root text and commentary on the Supreme Path,[465] and the instruction manuals associated with the tradition of the master from the Chim clan.[466] I have also received oral explanations [from Khenchen Lungrik Gyatso] in the form of a practical instruction[467] on the extensive methods of spiritual guidance associated with the system known as The Stages of the Teaching.[468] While I have also heard other miscellaneous teachings from several additional holy spiritual teachers, for this system of teachings the principal works are the ones that I have just mentioned.

> Through whatever virtue is derived from this brief account
> of the intent of all the victors and their spiritual offspring,
> may all sentient beings in their entirety, without exception,
> quickly attain the status of an omniscient victor.

This work, titled *The Essence of Nectar: A Manual of Instruction for the Three Types of Person on the Stages for Gaining Entry to the Teaching*, has been set forth by Tāranātha, one who wanders throughout the land.[469] It is an instruction manual that addresses how to meditate in the sense of the way in which to direct the mind as one reflects on the various individual topics. Explanations of the doctrinal meanings that one must understand in order to bring them to mind as the subject matter for reflection should be sought out from other writings composed by the former spiritual masters of this tradition. May this work also serve to promote the advancement and longevity of the Buddha's precious teaching.

The following addendum of lines of supplication to more recent lineage masters, as well as any others as appropriate, should also be included. Following the line addressed to Lungrik Gyatso, recite the following:

Drölwe Gönpo,[470] Lord of the Teaching, in both its sūtra and
tantra forms,
Rinchen Gyatsö De,[471] who was anointed as his spiritual heir,
Lodrö Namgyal, who was a Lord of the World,[472]
Venerable Ngawang Trinle, in whom the three trainings were
completely pure,
Kunsang Wangpo, a guide for the path to the highest good,[473]
the supreme knowledge holder,[474] Venerable Tsewang Norbu,
Chenresik Wangchuk,[475] the omniscient lord of the Drukpa
Kagyu lineage,
Gelek Pelbar, who brought happiness to the entire world,[476]
the one named Lhundrup, who bestowed the joy {273} of benefit
and happiness upon all,[477]
Venerable Kagyu Tenzin, who perfected all the stages of the path,
Lord Karma Lhaktong, who brought meaning to everyone he
met,
the supreme Shenpen Öser,[478] who was a lord of enlightenment
mind,
a true spiritual teacher who revealed the path to liberation.

This addendum was composed by Guṇa.[479]

11. {275} A Guidebook for the Path to Great Awakening

The Ritual for Generating Enlightenment Mind according to the System Followed in the Lineage of the Profound View[1]

Jamgön Kongtrul

{276} *namo gurubuddhabodhisattvāya*[2]
Homage to the gurus, the buddhas, and the bodhisattvas.

I pay homage respectfully to enlightenment mind
that is both meaningful and gives easy access to the pathway
that leads to the supreme city of the victors,
and to the one who taught it in many ways, along with his spiritual offspring.

I also bow with faith to all those who appeared in India and Tibet
and, without relying on others, conveyed the sun of the view and conduct
of the victors' offspring that are contained within this teaching
across the sky that is the minds of sentient beings.

Of the renowned systems of the two great champions, I shall set forth
the unerring procedure of the ritual for generating enlightenment mind
according to the tradition of the Lineage of the Profound View,
as found in the writings of the former spiritual offspring of the victors.

In order for a spiritual teacher who possesses in a proper manner the bodhisattva vow of this lineage to carry out the ritual for generating enlightenment mind according to the system of the Middle Way school, as it was established by the Victor's offspring Śāntideva, these are the three parts of the ritual: (1) preliminaries, (2) main activity, and (3) conclusion.

I. The Preliminary Activities

Inside a clean and attractive {277} physical space that has been well adorned with many decorative arrays, arrange on an altar extraordinary forms of the three holy vessels[3] according to your means,[4] such as an image of the Lord of Munis that contains relics of a tathāgata. In front of them, place, in an excellent manner, offerings as extensive as your resources will allow, such as a hundred rows of the two types of water offerings and a hundred rows of the five offerings of respectful service,[5] as well as a flower-filled mandala and a pure, four-part torma offering containing the three white substances[6] that is to be presented to the Three Jewels, the dharma protectors, the Glorious Lords,[7] and the regional spirits.

Following that, after bathing, the spiritual teacher should make prostrations while reciting the *Three Heaps Sūtra*[8] three times. Then, after first carrying out the seven-limb devotional practice by reciting the verses that begin: "However many man-lions whatsoever,"[9] he or she should accept the bodhisattva vow once again in order to renew the purity of the bodhisattva vow that is present in his or her mental continuum. This is done by kneeling with the palms joined together and reciting the following formula three times:

> I beseech all the buddhas and bodhisattvas who reside in the ten directions to give heed to me. I, {278} who am named so-and-so,[10] from this moment on until I reach the seat of enlightenment, / go for refuge to the buddhas; / (etc., up to) I, likewise, also go for refuge to the dharma/ and to the assemblage of bodhisattvas.[11]
>
> Just as the former sugatas, (etc., . . . up to)
> and so shall I practice the trainings in the proper order.[12]

Following that, the following verses up to the final one that is an aspirational prayer and a dedication should also be recited:

> Now my life has become fruitful, (etc.).[13]

and:

> May I generate those forms of the precious enlightenment mind, (etc.)[14]

Following that, the spiritual teacher should become seated on a high cushion atop a great dharma throne and then, after developing the wisdom that realizes the emptiness of all entities, the compassion that wishes to benefit all sentient beings and establish them in the state of ultimate happiness and, especially, the excellent attitude that wishes to enable his or her disciples to generate enlightenment mind, he or she should address the disciples who have bathed and are seated before him or her in rows with the following words:

> All of us carry the inconceivably great burden in our mental continuum that is the evil that we have accumulated throughout all our past lives that are without beginning. If we fail to confess this evil, whatever virtue we may carry out will be weak in its strength. Since it will also not be possible for our virtue to take on the nature of the path that is pleasing to the āryas, we must confess our past evil deeds. Moreover, since it is taught that, by confessing our evil on the basis of the four powers,[15] it can be eliminated no matter how great it may be, you should reflect in the following manner in order to accomplish that aim:
>
> > The power of the support consists of the following visualization. In the sky before you, the Lord of the Teaching, the King of the Śākyas, whose body is the color of purified gold, and whose two arms in the earth-touching and the meditation gestures, respectively, is seated atop a jewel-studded throne that is being held up by lions. Surrounding him, the sky is filled by an inconceivably great number of buddhas and bodhisattvas, among which the principal figures are the thirty-five buddhas who make up the object to whom you confess your transgressions.
> >
> > The power of engaging in self-censure is to emanate immeasurable duplicates of yourself and all sentient beings before these buddhas and bodhisattvas, {279} with each body having innumerable heads and tongues, and to develop a strong sense of regret for the evil deeds that

> you have carried out in the past. The power of engaging in an antidote is to reflect that you will not engage in such wrongful actions in the future, even if it puts your life at risk to do so.[16] The restorative power[17] is to reflect that this practice is certain to eliminate all your transgressions.

Having stated this, the spiritual teacher should then direct the disciples to perform prostrations as they recite the *Confession of Transgressions*[18] three times by saying:

> Now, while recalling the meaning of these four powers, I ask you to perform prostrations as you recite the *Confession of Transgressions* three times.

Following that, all the disciples should once again be seated in rows, after which the spiritual teacher should address them again with the following words:

> All of us have obtained an extraordinary human form that is difficult to obtain and that possesses the qualities of leisure and fortune. We have also met with the precious teaching of the Buddha that is difficult to meet with. Therefore, it is imperative that we strive to derive value from this human existence possessing leisure and fortune on this occasion in which we have gained the freedom to choose between samsara and nirvana. As Lord Nāgārjuna declared:
>
> > It is much more difficult for an animal to become
> > a human than for a turtle living in the vast ocean
> > to meet with the opening of a yoke. Therefore, O king,
> > make your life fruitful through practicing the true dharma.[19]
>
> Moreover, among the different forms of the true dharma, the principal cause that enables you to free everyone—that is, both yourself and others—from suffering and that also enables you to obtain for yourself and others both the temporary and ultimate form of supreme happiness is enlightenment mind. This is indicated in the following verse from *The Compendium of Training*, which declares:

With a desire to put an end to suffering
and the wish to reach ultimate happiness,
you should make firm the root of faith
and fix your mind firmly upon enlightenment.[20]

Therefore, in order to carry out the ritual for generating the enlightenment mind that is endowed with immeasurable good qualities, first I shall briefly describe the method by which to ascertain the nature of the bodhisattva vow, which includes the following topics: (1) the essential nature of the act of generating enlightenment mind, (2) the different types of enlightenment mind, (3) the boundaries that demarcate the two main forms of enlightenment mind, (4) {280} the causes that promote the arising of enlightenment mind, (5) the benefits and (6) disadvantages that relate to enlightenment mind, and (7) the different forms of the ritual.

[The spiritual teacher should present the following instruction.]

The Essential Nature of Enlightenment Mind

The essential nature of enlightenment mind is the desire to attain buddhahood for the sake of others, as described in *The Ornament of Clear Realization*, which states:

Generating enlightenment mind is the desire to attain
true and complete enlightenment for the sake of others.[21]

A line from *The Ornament of Mahāyāna Sūtras* also states:

The source of enlightenment mind is the volition
of the bodhisattvas that possesses a twofold aim.[22]

The Different Types of Enlightenment Mind

One type is the aspirational form of enlightenment mind, which is the desire to attain enlightenment for the sake of others, and a second type is the active form of enlightenment mind, which is the attitude that is maintained as one proceeds toward the enlightenment that is being sought for the sake of others. Of these, the former resembles the attitude of a person who desires to travel to some destination and the latter resembles the actions that a person undertakes as he or she travels to that destination. This is described in *Entry into the Conduct That Leads to Enlightenment*:

> In brief, enlightenment mind is known
> to be of these two types:
> the mind that aspires to enlightenment
> and the mind that is proceeding to enlightenment.
>
> As the difference is recognized between a person who desires
> to go somewhere and one who is actually going there,
> so too is the difference between those two minds understood
> by the wise, in the same order of enumeration.[23]

Enlightenment mind is also said to be of two types according to the distinction between the conventional and ultimate forms. As the *Nirvāṇa Sūtra*[24] declares:

> Distinguishing the conventional and the ultimate,
> there are two types of enlightenment mind.[25]

The act of generating conventional enlightenment mind is directed toward the outer object of sentient beings and represents a mental state that is primarily developed by ordinary persons. The act of generating ultimate enlightenment mind is directed toward the inner object of the mind and represents a mental state that is primarily developed within the mental continua of āryas.

Thus, the aspirational form of enlightenment mind can be developed merely through forming the aspiration to attain enlightenment. The act of generating the active form of enlightenment mind is characterized by the bodhisattva vow that arises on the basis of a ritual. Both of these are included within the category of generating the conventional form of enlightenment mind. The act of generating the ultimate form of enlightenment mind is gained on the strength of having meditated on the true nature of those two conventional forms of enlightenment mind.

The Boundaries That Demarcate the Two Main Forms of Enlightenment Mind

Aspirational enlightenment mind is present on the lesser stage of the path of accumulation,[26] as soon as one has generated that aspirational mind and prior to the acceptance of the bodhisattva vow. Active enlightenment mind {281} is present from the time that the bodhisattva vow associated with this active mind has been accepted and continues until the mental continuum's end-point.[27] This explanation is established by the verse that begins with "As the difference is recognized between a person who wants / to go and one who is actually going there, / . . ." If you ask whether active enlightenment mind is only present on an ārya level of the path, that is not necessarily the case, because it is established that an ordinary person is capable of possessing the bodhisattva vow and because otherwise[28] it would not be possible for someone to commit a root transgression after having accepted the bodhisattva vow.

The Causes That Promote the Arising to Enlightenment Mind

The three causes that promote the arising of enlightenment mind are (1) faith directed toward the Buddha, (2) compassion directed toward sentient beings, and (3) the desire to develop enlightenment mind through having learned its benefits. This is indicated in the following verse from *The Ornament of Mahāyāna Sūtras*:

> Developing enlightenment mind from another's speech
> is said to arise in either a stable or an unstable form
> through the power of a friend, a cause, a root,
> hearing instruction, and the cultivation of virtue.[29]

The cause from which enlightenment mind arises initially is one that is unstable. This is the act of generating the aspirational form of enlightenment mind through reliance upon a friend—that is, a spiritual teacher—from whom you hear instruction. The causes from which the active form of enlightenment mind arises—that is, through your own cultivation of virtue, through the material cause of awakening your spiritual lineage, and through the root cause of giving rise to compassion—are said to generate a stable form of enlightenment mind.

The Benefits of Generating Enlightenment Mind

One benefit of the act of generating aspirational enlightenment mind is that it surpasses all the merit of the spiritual attitudes and so on that have been generated by śrāvakas and pratyekabuddhas.[30] Active enlightenment mind is declared to have limitless benefits, such as the following. As long as you have not incurred a root transgression, active enlightenment mind will give rise to merit continuously, even if you are in a state of deep sleep or you have become inattentive.[31]

From then on,[32] even for one
who is asleep or in a heedless state,
continuous streams of merit as vast
as space will arise repeatedly.[33]

Among the limitless benefits that enlightenment mind has been declared to possess, I have described a mere portion of them at this preliminary stage.

The Disadvantages of Failing to Generate Enlightenment Mind

The disadvantages of failing to generate enlightenment mind are principally that you will fall into samsara and the lower realms {282} continuously and that no matter how much you strive to practice dharma, you will err by falling into the path of the śrāvakas and pratyekabuddhas. This is true because, even though falling into the hells is not a permanent obstacle to the pursuit of supreme enlightenment, if you fall into the state of a śrāvaka arhat or a pratyekabuddha arhat, that will prevent you from pursuing unsurpassed perfect enlightenment for countless eons.

Different Forms of the Ritual for Generating Enlightenment Mind

There are two systems that possess rituals for generating enlightenment mind. One, which is known as the system of the Middle Way school, follows the *Gaṇḍavyūha Sūtra*[34] and the *Ākāśagarbha Sūtra*,[35] and has been transmitted through a lineage that begins with Ārya Mañjuśrī and includes such masters as the spiritual father Lord Nāgārjuna and his spiritual offspring, as well as the victors' spiritual offspring Śāntideva. The other, which is known as the system of the Mind Only school, follows the great treatise titled *The Stage of a Bodhisattva*[36] and various other sūtras, and has been transmitted through a lineage that begins with Lord Maitreya and includes such masters as Asaṅga and his brother Vasubandhu, the great spiritual teacher Candragomī, and Lord Atiśa. The differences between these systems regarding (1) the spiritual being from whom to accept the bodhisattva vow, (2) the person who is qualified to accept the bodhisattva vow, (3) the ritual that is the means by which the vow is accepted, and (4) the method by which to safeguard the vow by not committing transgressions must be learned from the Mahāyāna sūtras and treatises. Here, I shall establish the ritual according to the system of the Middle Way school.

II. Main Activity

Establishing the Ritual according to the System of the Middle Way School

There are three stages to the bodhisattva vow: (1) the initial stage is the method of accepting the vow, (2) the intermediate stage is the method of safeguarding the vow by not committing transgressions, and (3) the final stage is the method of remedying any transgressions that may be committed.

A. The Method of Accepting the Vow

This section is made up of three explanations: (1) the spiritual being from whom to accept the bodhisattva vow, (2) the person who is able to accept the bodhisattva vow, and (3) the ritual that is the actual method of accepting the bodhisattva vow.

1. The Person from Whom to Accept the Bodhisattva Vow

The bodhisattva vow should be accepted from a person who is devoted to the Mahāyāna system of practice and is abiding in the bodhisattva vow. He or she should be knowledgeable about the bodhisattva collection of scriptures in general and, in particular, how to confer the bodhisattva vow and how to instruct disciples in the observance of the precepts. He or she should also be free of the negative mental qualities that oppose each of the six perfections—that is, stinginess[37] and the rest. As a verse from *Entry into the Conduct That Leads to Enlightenment* declares:

> Never, even to save your life,
> should you forsake a spiritual teacher {283}
> who is observing the bodhisattva discipline
> and is knowledgeable regarding the Mahāyāna.[38]

According to this system, it is explained that if you are unable to find a spiritual teacher who can confer the vow in order to newly generate enlightenment mind or before whom you can remedy transgressions of the bodhisattva vow, in both instances it is acceptable for you to perform these acts before a body-vessel.[39]

2. The Person Who Is Able to Accept the Bodhisattva Vow

It is explained that, except for the worldly deities of the formless realm and those worldly deities who lack conception,[40] all other sentient beings who can understand the verbal instructions that are conveyed to them during the ritual and who desire to accept the bodhisattva vow are capable of generating it. In particular, a candidate for the bodhisattva vow should possess the wisdom that properly realizes the nature of the extensive activities that are meant to be carried out by bodhisattvas, and even though it is understood that these activities are extremely difficult to carry out, because of his or her great compassion, he or she is desirous of liberating all sentient beings from their suffering. Moreover, realizing that one must attain buddhahood in order to accomplish this aim, he or she is willing to generate the mind that aspires to attain enlightenment in order to attain buddhahood and possesses the desire to cultivate the bodhisattvas' training. As *The Compendium of Training* declares:

> A great being, after having heard such explanations and after having realized with his or her wisdom the difficult nature of the bodhisattvas' activities, is resolute about taking up the obligation to liberate all beings from their suffering, after having made prostrations, presented offerings, confessed his or her evil deeds, rejoiced at his or her own and others' merit, requested the buddhas to turn the dharma wheel, beseeched them not to enter nirvana, and dedicated his or her virtue to enlightenment, should then, after beseeching a spiritual teacher to confer the bodhisattva vow, repeat the words of the ritual after that spiritual teacher or declare them by him- or herself.[41]

3. The Ritual That Is the Actual Method of Accepting the Bodhisattva Vow

The ritual for accepting the bodhisattva vow is made up of three parts: (1) preliminaries, (2) main activity, and (3) conclusion.

a. The Preliminaries

The preliminary portion of the ritual is also made up of four parts: (1) correcting one's attitude by means of an excellent instruction, (2) making supplication to an excellent being, (3) going for refuge to an excellent object {284}, and (4) accumulating merit and eliminating obscurations by means of an excellent method.

i. Correcting One's Attitude by Means of an Extraordinary Instruction

This topic is also made up of three sections: (1) generating aversion toward the suffering that is the extreme of samsara, (2) stopping attachment for the peace that is the extreme of nirvana, and (3) generating enthusiasm for the enlightenment mind that is the path that is free of the two extremes.

[The spiritual teacher should present the following instructions.]

1) Generating Aversion toward the Suffering That Is the Extreme of Samsara

This samsara has a nature that consists of suffering. Among the eighteen classes of regions that make up the hells, there are eight hot hells: Revival, Black Lines, Compression, Wailing, Great Wailing, Conflagration, Great Conflagration, and Unrelenting Torment. Within them are found inconceivably great forms of suffering, such as being struck by one another with weapons, being cut into pieces with saws and the like, being crushed by two mountains that converge, being pierced with blazing iron spears and then thrown upon a ground of blazing iron, being trapped in a blazing iron house with no doors, being boiled in a large cauldron filled with unbearably hot water, and being burned by fires that fill all the ten directions. All of these experiences are the results of great unvirtuous deeds. As a verse from *Entry into the Conduct That Leads to Enlightenment* declares:

> Crying out in pain from having had all one's skin removed by Yama's minions,
> with one's body bathed in copper liquefied by the oblation-bearer's heat,
> with pieces of one's flesh severed by hundreds of blows from blazing swords and spears,
> one falls onto a ground of extremely hot copper, all caused by a multitude of misdeeds.[42]

The eight cold hells are Blisters, Burst Blisters, Aṭhaṭha, Hahava, Huhava, split open like a Blue Lotus, a Red Lotus, and a Great Red Lotus {285}. Due to the extreme cold of these regions, masses of blisters form on the hell beings' bodies. They emit wailing sounds and they experience many forms of suffering such as having their flesh and bones split open. As a verse from the *Letter to a Disciple* declares:

> An incomparable cold that penetrates even the bones
> causes their decrepit bodies to tremble and curl into a ball.
> Hundreds of blisters that form and split open give rise to
> bugs
> that eat the pus, marrow, and fat flowing from their sores.[43]

There are many forms of suffering in the adjacent hells,[44] such as falling into the burning embers of the great Firepit or sinking into the Putrid Swamp, where insect-like creatures pierce the flesh and bones of the hell beings' bodies; traversing the Razor-Filled Plain,[45] where everything that your body touches is cut by razors, the Sword-Leaf Forest, where the wind causes swords to fall from trees that cut your body to pieces, or the forest of iron *śālmalī* trees, whose iron thorns that are sixteen finger widths in length pierce hell beings' bodies both when they climb up the trunks and when they descend again; and falling into the River of No Ford, whose extremely hot water reduces their bodies to bone skeletons. All of these regions of the adjacent hells are found on the four sides of each of the hot hells. As *The Treasury of Higher Learning* declares:

> Firepit and Putrid Swamp,
> Razor Path, and so on, and the river
> are on the four sides of those.[46]

There are also various kinds of partial hells[47] in such places as the edge of an ocean, where there are such forms of suffering as one's body being ablaze or being eaten by other creatures. These are the ways in which hell beings experience many different kinds of suffering. As a verse from the *Letter to a Friend* declares:

> The suffering of one who is forcefully stabbed here
> in a single day with three hundred spears
> does not amount to the total or {286} even a portion
> of a hell being's lighter suffering.[48]

Since hungry ghosts are unable to find even the slightest amount of food or drink for many months, they are tormented by hunger and thirst, and they also experience various other kinds of suffering, such as heat and cold. As a verse from the *Letter to a Friend* declares:

> Also, among hungry ghosts, unparalleled, incessant suffering
> produced by the failure to obtain what is desired
> as well as extremely severe suffering produced
> by hunger, thirst, cold, heat, fatigue, and fear is
> experienced.[49]

Animals undergo many forms of suffering, such as eating one another, being forced to work, and being killed for their flesh, fur, and the like.

> In animal births there are also many kinds of suffering,
> such as being killed, bound, or beaten, and so forth.
> For those deprived of the virtue for attaining peace,
> there is also the most horrible suffering of eating one
> another.
>
> Some die for the sake of pearls, wool,
> bones, flesh, or fur. Other helpless ones
> are struck with a kick, a hand, a whip,
> a hook, a goad, and the like, and forced to work.[50]

Human beings also undergo many kinds of suffering, such as those of birth, old age, sickness, death, failing to obtain what is desired, inability to preserve what one does possess, encountering hateful enemies, and being separated from loving friends, and so on. These are the experiences that we all can observe.

Demigods experience many kinds of suffering, such as having their bodies slashed in combat with the gods due to their jealousy of the gods' wealth. As a verse declares:

> Among demigods there is also great mental anguish
> because of their natural enmity toward the gods' prosperity.
> Despite their intelligence, they are incapable of seeing truth
> due to the obstruction of that migratory state.[51]

{287} The gods of the desire realm also develop attachment for the wealth of other gods when they experience signs of impending death and then also experience great suffering when they realize that they are going to die.

> While there is great pleasure in the celestial realms,
> the suffering of their falling down at death is even greater.[52]

Although the gods of the form and formless realms do not experience the suffering of suffering, when they fall down from those realms at their death, they are also reborn in the lower realms.

> Having obtained very great sensory pleasures in a heavenly realm
> or the blissful freedom from attachment of Brahmā's state,
> one undergoes again the incessant suffering
> of becoming fuel for the flames in Avīci hell.[53]

A verse from the *Sūtra on Closely Placed Recollection* declares:

> Hell beings are harmed by infernal fires,
> hungry ghosts are harmed by hunger and thirst,
> animals are harmed by eating one another,
> humans are harmed by insufficient subsistence,
> gods are harmed by heedlessness—
> there is no happiness at all in samsara,
> not even that which exists on the tip of a needle.

Lord Maitreya also declared:

> And in these five paths there is no happiness,
> just as excrement has no good smell at all;[54]

Therefore, you should generate aversion for samsara in its entirety and strive to free yourself from it, as there is no greater purpose whatsoever than that. As a verse from the *Letter to a Friend* declares:

> Even if your head or clothing should suddenly catch fire,
> you should forgo trying to extinguish it
> and strive to put an end to rebirth;
> there is no other greater aim than this.[55]

Therefore, I urge you to develop a heartfelt form of this thought: "I shall strive to practice the true dharma {288} in order to liberate myself from samsara."

2) Stopping Attachment for the Peace That Is the Extreme of Nirvana

You might think to yourself, "Since the nature of samsara is suffering, if I attain the nirvana without remainder[56] of the tradition of śrāvakas and pratyekabuddhas, I will have permanently removed my suffering; therefore, that is the goal that I should attain." However, this is not true. That goal cannot accomplish the aims of others, and since all sentient beings in samsara have extended to you the kindness of being your mother since beginningless time, to pursue the nirvana without remainder without accomplishing their aims is shameless conduct because it is a failure to recognize past benefits that were done for you. As two verses from the *Letter to a Disciple* declare:

> If one were to set out alone, abandoning those relatives who are in the ocean of samsara,
> while perceiving that they resemble beings who have fallen into a whirlpool,
> appearing and disappearing in the ever-turning cycle of birth and death,[57]
> no one could be more ungrateful than that.[58]
>
> Having drunk their breastmilk as a helpless infant
> while cradled in their arms, and having been cared for with affection
> as one engaged solely in many, useless acts of misconduct,
> what person indeed, even an inferior one, could abandon them here?[59]

Therefore, I urge you to reject the attitude that would abandon the welfare of others and seek to attain the happiness of Hīnayāna peace for yourself alone.

3) Generating Enthusiasm for the Enlightenment Mind That Is the Path Free of the Two Extremes

You may wonder to yourself, "If samsara in its entirety must be abandoned because its nature is suffering, and yet the nirvana in which all suffering has been abandoned is not a goal that should be attained, then what is the goal that I should attain?" Although a partial nirvana is not a goal that should be attained, Lord Maitreya declared the goal that should be sought:

> Having severed completely affection for himself through wisdom,
> a compassionate one does not go toward quiescence, out of affection for all beings.
> Relying thus on wisdom and compassion, the two methods for attaining enlightenment,
> the ārya does not turn toward either samsara or nirvana.[60] {289}

As this verse indicates, by means of wisdom, you can avoid abiding in the extreme of samsara, and by means of great compassion, you can avoid abiding in the extreme of nirvana; therefore, it is called "nonabiding nirvana,"[61] which is the very state of a true and complete buddha. By attaining that, all the forms of abandonment and realization that relate to your own aims will become perfected, and as relates to others' aims, you will be able to carry out innumerable forms of enlightened activities that reach to the ends of space throughout the ten directions, effortlessly and spontaneously, for as long as it takes to empty samsara of sentient beings. Since this constitutes the perfection of both one's own and others' aims, this is the goal that you should strive to attain. The principal cause that enables you to attain this goal is the act of generating the mind that aspires to attain enlightenment. As the *Mahāvairocanābhisambodhi Tantra* declares: "O Lord of Secrets, the transcendent knowledge of the Omniscient One . . . arises from the cause of enlightenment mind." Also, two lines from *The Collection of Verses on the Perfection of Wisdom* declare:

> Likewise, if there were no enlightenment mind here, how
> could the stream
> of the tathāgata's knowledge arise here throughout the world?[62]

As these lines indicate, buddhahood will not arise in the absence of enlightenment mind. Another verse declares:

> Water drops fill a pot little by little,
> gradually, from the first drip to the last.
> Likewise, the first thought is the cause of supreme enlightenment;
> gradually, beings become buddhas who are filled with pure
> qualities.[63]

Therefore, I urge you to generate great enthusiasm for developing the following thought: "In order to attain true and complete buddhahood for the sake of all sentient beings, I shall generate the mind that aspires to attain enlightenment."

ii. Making Supplication to an Excellent Being

Next, the preceptor directs the disciples to make a mandala offering that contains thirty-seven heaps:

Since you wish to request the preceptor to perform the ritual of generating enlightenment mind, you must make supplication to the spiritual teacher. Therefore, I direct you to conceive of the spiritual teacher as the Master[64] and present a mandala offering as part of your request that {290} he or she should perform the ritual for generating the mind that aspires to attain supreme enlightenment. You should also recite the statement of supplication that begins "From now until enlightenment . . ."[65] or some other suitable verse.

After the mandala offering has been presented, the preceptor should direct the disciples with the following words:

Now, after making prostrations, hold a flower between your joined palms, and while maintaining the strong aspiration that reflects, "Please confer upon me the act of generating enlightenment mind," repeat the following words of supplication three times:

"O son of good family, please bestow upon me the act of generating enlightenment mind that is the sole pathway of all the buddhas and that begins with the act of going for refuge to the Three Jewels."

iii. Going for Refuge to an Excellent Object

Next, the preceptor should declare:

The object to whom one goes for refuge is the Buddha, whose nature is made up of three bodies; the Mahāyāna dharma, with its aspects of scripture and realization; and the sangha, which is made up of irreversible ārya bodhisattvas. The length of time that one goes for refuge is until you reach the seat of enlightenment. The cause of going for refuge is to be motivated by the compassion that wishes to liberate all sentient beings from their suffering. Since you must attain buddhahood in order to liberate all sentient beings from their suffering and the attainment of buddhahood depends upon the Three Jewels, the essential nature of the act of going for refuge is for you to repeat the following formula that expresses the act of going for refuge three times, while maintaining the strong faith that reflects, "O Three Jewels, please be cognizant[66] that I aspire to attain buddhahood for the sake of all sentient beings."

I beseech all the buddhas and bodhisattvas who reside in the ten directions to give heed to me. I beseech the preceptor to give heed to me. Then state your name: "I, who am named so-and-so, from this moment on, / until I sit at the seat of enlightenment, / go for refuge to the buddhas; / I, likewise, also go for refuge to the dharma / and {291} to the assemblage of bodhisattvas."

As a precept for that act of going for refuge, form the following thought: "From now on, I shall hold the Buddha as my spiritual teacher, the Mahāyāna dharma as the path, and ārya bodhisattvas as companions who will assist me in practicing the path."

iv. Accumulating Merit and Eliminating Obscurations by Means of an Excellent Method

Making Prostration

To generate the object to whom the seven-limb devotional practice is presented, you should visualize that the Master of the teaching, the Lord who is the Great Sage is seated in the sky in front of you and he is surrounded by a retinue made up of an immeasurably great number of buddhas and bodhisattvas, among whom the principal figures include the eight preeminent spiritual sons.[67]

Then reflect that you emanate duplicates of your physical body that are equal in number to all the atoms in a buddha field and that you also lead all sentient beings in carrying out this devotional practice. As you reflect on the first act of making prostration, perform actual prostrations in which you bow down and touch the ground with the five parts[68] of your body as you simultaneously repeat the following verse three times. It is very important that you recite the verse slowly and distinctly.

> With prostrations equal in number to the atoms
> in all the buddha fields, I bow down to
> all the buddhas that appear in the three times,
> along with the dharma and the supreme assemblage.[69]

Presenting Offerings

Offerings That Are Actually Arranged

The act of presenting offerings has seven forms, of which the first is to present offerings that have actually been arranged. This is done in the following manner. Reflect that the offerings that have actually been arranged are flowers, incense, lamps, fragrant water, food, and music, all of which are made up of divine substances that are clean, translucent, and free of obstruction, and that fill the realm of space. Now I direct you to present these offerings as well as other flowers, and so on, that are found throughout immeasurable numbers of world systems, with one-pointed devotion and visualization, to the lamas and {292} to all the buddhas and bodhisattvas of the three times and ten directions, either by repeating the mantras and performing the mudras after me or by performing them simultaneously with me. Although the older texts do not state that the offerings need to be blessed before presenting them, in keeping with the more recent tradition, if you like, you can carry out the act of blessing the offerings in the manner that conforms to the system of the deity Sarvavid.[70] Alternatively, it is also acceptable to bless them by reciting the Offering Cloud dhāraṇī[71] mantra three times. The recitation for presenting the offerings is as follows:

However much reception water there is
in immeasurable myriad oceans,
as well as that which I have arranged here,
I offer to the victors and their spiritual offspring.
Please accept it in whatever manner pleases you.

oṃ sarvatathāgata arghaṃ pratīccha pūjameghasamudra-spharaṇa samaye hūṃ

In a similar manner, offer flowers, incense, lamps, fragrant water, food, and music by changing the words of the recitation verse appropriately and substituting for *arghaṃ* the words *puṣpe* and so on in the mantra. As a more abbreviated form of practice, you can also present the offerings by reciting just the mantras or by reciting just the offering verses.

Offerings That Are Not Owned by Anyone

Repeat after me the following words while reflecting that in order to accumulate merit, you are offering to the buddhas and bodhisattvas objects such as mountains made of jewels, wish-granting trees, grains, flowers, medicinal substances, and forests, all of which are not owned by anyone, and reflecting that you are requesting that they accept these offerings from you.

I shall make proper offerings to those tathāgatas,
to the true and immaculate dharma jewel,
and to the buddhas' offspring, who are oceans of virtue.[72]

As many flowers and fruits are there are,
whatever kinds of medicine there are,
as many jewels as there are in the world,
and waters that are clear and pleasing to the mind {293},[73]

mountains made of jewels, and, likewise,
forest regions that are secluded and delightful,
vines ablaze with the ornaments of beautiful flowers,
and trees whose limbs are bent down by excellent fruit,[74]

perfume, incense, wish-granting trees and trees
made of jewels in the worlds of gods and others,
ponds adorned with lotuses and filled with geese,
whose calls are exceedingly pleasant,[75]

various grains that grow without being cultivated,
and other beautiful objects worthy of being offered
that extend to the limits of the vast realm of space
and all of which are not owned by anyone.[76]

Having grasped these in my mind, I offer them
to those most eminent of sages and their spiritual offspring.
May these supreme ones among those who are worthy of receiving gifts,
who possess great compassion and regard me with pity, accept them from me.[77]

I who lack merit and who am extremely poor
have nothing else at all with which to make offerings.
Therefore, may those lords who are devoted to the welfare of others,
through their own power, accept this in order to benefit me.[78]

As an abbreviated version of this form of offering, just the final three verses—which begin with the line "Various grains that grow without being cultivated" and end with the line "Through their own power, accept this in order to benefit me"—may be recited.

Offering Oneself

> Repeat after me the following verses while reflecting to yourself, "Offering myself to the buddhas and bodhisattvas as their servant, I shall carry out exclusively their aims of acting on behalf of all sentient beings."
>
> I give myself completely to the victors
> and to those spiritual beings born from them.
> May these supreme beings accept me.
> With devotion, I enter into servitude to you.[79]
>
> Through the assistance provided by you, I am unafraid
> in worldly existence, and {294} I shall do what benefits beings.
> I shall rise above my former evil deeds
> and refrain from committing more evil deeds.[80]

Offerings That Are Emanated with the Mind

[The preceptor should then state:]

> When I recite the verse that begins "In exquisitely fragrant bathhouses . . . ," visualize in a vivid form that a bathhouse appears before you. Then, after I say, "I direct you to offer the following acts of devotion to all the buddhas and bodhisattvas," recite the following verses, slowly and distinctly.
>
> In exquisitely fragrant bathhouses
> with inlaid floors of brightly shining crystal,
> dazzling columns aglitter with jewels,
> and canopies festooned with shimmering pearls,[81]

with numerous pitchers made from fine jewels
filled with delightfully fragrant water and flowers,
I bathe the tathāgatas and the spiritual beings
begotten by them, accompanied by music and song.[82]

I wipe their bodies with unequaled cloths,
scented and washed free of any stains.
Then, I present to them superb monks' robes,
excellently dyed and well perfumed.[83]

I also adorn Samantabhadra, Ajita,
Mañjughoṣa, Lokeśvara, and the rest
with beautiful, divine, multicolored garments,
soft and smooth, as well as various superb ornaments.[84]

With the finest perfumes whose fragrance fills
all the triple-thousand worlds, I anoint
these lords of sages, whose radiant bodies shine like gold
that has been well-fired, well-burnished, and well-washed.[85]

I worship those lords of sages who are supremely worthy
of being worshiped with all flowers most fragrant and delightful,
such as māndārava, blue lotus, jasmine flowers, and the like,
as well as garlands whose shapes are pleasing to the mind.[86]

I perfume them with dense clouds of incense
whose pervasive fragrance is pleasing to the mind. {295}
I also present them an offering of various kinds
of edible enjoyments, and food and drink.[87]

I present jewel lamps arranged in rows
of five situated within golden lotuses.
I also scatter beautiful varieties of flowers
upon mosaic floors anointed with perfume.[88]

I also present to those who have a loving nature
a multitude of palaces that are made beautiful

with brilliant pendulous pearl garlands adorning
all regions and are filled with delightful songs of praise.[89]

I present to those great sages
exceedingly beautiful jewel umbrellas,
studded with pearls and raised up with shafts
made of gold that are pleasing in form.[90]

Dedication of Offerings

[Next, the preceptor should state:]

Repeat after me the following verses, and as you do so, make the aspirational prayer to please the buddhas and bodhisattvas with immeasurable numbers of additional varieties of offerings and the aspirational prayer that the realm of space should become filled with masses of offerings that alleviate the suffering of sentient beings.

Beyond these, may pleasing clouds
of offerings remain established for long,
as well as clouds of music and choral song
that bring delight to all sentient beings.[91]

May showers of flowers, jewels,
and the like rain down perpetually
upon all the jewels of the true dharma,
as well as caitya monuments and images.[92]

Unsurpassed Offerings

[Following that, the preceptor should state:]

Repeat after me the following verse, and as you do so, reflect to yourself, "Just as the great bodhisattvas, such as Lord Mañjughoṣa and the like, did not grasp the recipients of the offerings, the beings who present the offerings, or the offerings themselves as being truly existent when they presented immeasurably great offerings to all the victors of the ten directions, {296} I too make offerings to the victors and their spiritual offspring in the same way without grasping any of its elements as being truly existent."

Just as Mañjughoṣa and others[93]
make offerings to the victors,
I too make offerings to those lords,
the tathāgatas, and their spiritual offspring.[94]

An Offering of Praise

[The preceptor should then state:]

Repeat after me the following verse, and as you do so, reflect to yourself, "I praise the buddhas and bodhisattvas by intoning laudatory verses that express their spiritual qualities as they truly are."

I praise the oceans of virtue
with oceans of melodious hymns.
May clouds of laudatory songs
be made to them in the same way.[95]

Confession of Evil Deeds

[The preceptor should then state:]

The *Sūtra That Reveals the Four Spiritual Qualities*[96] declares that all one's evil deeds can be eliminated by relying on all of the four powers in combination: the power of engaging in self-censure, which is to regret the evil deeds that you committed in the past; the power of turning back from misdeeds, which is the conviction never to commit evil deeds in the future; the power of the support, which is to go for refuge to the Three Jewels and to have the aspiration to attain enlightenment for the sake of others; and the power of engaging in an antidote, which is those forms of practice that serve as an antidote for your evil deeds. Therefore, bring to mind the evil deeds you committed in the past and develop strong regret for having done so. Then make the strong resolve in which you reflect, "From now on, I will not commit any evil deeds, even when my life is at risk." Next, make the firm determination in which you think to yourself, "Now, in order to attain enlightenment for the sake of others, I shall rely on the support of the Three Jewels and carry out in a proper manner the spiritual practices that serve as antidotes for my evil deeds." As you do so, repeat after me three times the following words that are a confession of your evil deeds, {297} and then reflect to yourself, "I have been completely cleansed and purified of my evil deeds."

I beseech all the buddhas and bodhisattvas who reside in the ten directions to give heed to me. I beseech the preceptor to give heed to me.

Whatever evil deeds I, a confused fool,
have collected—either naturally objectionable
or those that are objectionable
through having been so prescribed[97]—

I confess all of them
standing before the lords
with palms joined and fearful of suffering,
having bowed down again and again.

May the lords recognize my transgressions
for their transgressive nature.
O Lords, these acts are deplorable,
I shall not commit them again.[98]

After reciting these verses three times, reflect that, because evil deeds are not truly existent, you have become fully cleansed and purified.

The Limb of Rejoicing

[The preceptor declares:]

Repeat after me the following verses, and as you do so, develop a heartfelt attitude of joy toward all the happiness and virtuous acts of āryas and ordinary beings.[99]

I rejoice with great joy at the virtue performed
by all sentient beings, which brings relief
from the suffering of the lower realms.
May those who suffer come to abide in happiness.[100]

I rejoice at the accumulated virtue
that is a cause for attaining enlightenment.[101]

I rejoice at the liberation of embodied beings
from the suffering of samsara.
I also rejoice at the states of a bodhisattva
and of a buddha that the saviors[102] achieve.[103]

I also rejoice at those teachers[104] whose development
of enlightenment mind is like an ocean,
who bring forth happiness for all sentient beings,
and who confer benefits upon all sentient beings.[105]

The Request to Turn the Dharma Wheel

[The preceptor should declare:]

Repeat after me the following verse of request, and as you do so, reflect that throughout the world systems of the ten directions, there are buddhas who have attained enlightenment but who have not yet turned the wheel of the dharma so that by requesting them to teach, petitioners may collect the two accumulations and so on. {298} Then reflect that you are making a heartfelt request to these buddhas that they turn the wheel of the dharma for the sake of their followers.

With joined palms I ask the complete buddhas
throughout all the directions: "Please light
the lamp of the dharma for those who have fallen
into suffering because of their ignorance."[106]

The Supplication Not to Enter Nirvana

[Next, the preceptor should declare:]

Repeat after me the following verse that makes a heartfelt supplication to certain buddhas that they not enter nirvana. As you do so, reflect that throughout the world systems that lie in the ten directions, certain buddhas have formed the intention to give the appearance of[107] entering nirvana in order to instill in beings thoughts such as that the appearance of a buddha is extremely rare. For the sake of the followers who live in those worlds, you are beseeching these buddhas to continue living for a very long time and not enter nirvana.

With joined palms I supplicate those victors
who are desirous of entering nirvana:
"Please continue living for limitless kalpas.
Please don't allow this world to become blind."[108]

Dedication

[The preceptor should declare:]

Repeat after me the following verses, and as you do so, reflect that all the virtue roots that you have created through making prostration and so on should serve as a cause both for dispelling every form of suffering that is experienced by all sentient beings and for bringing them every form of happiness.

Through whatever virtue I have obtained
by carrying out all these activities,
may I become the one who eliminates
all the suffering of all sentient beings.[109]

May I become medicine for the sick,
and may I also be a physician
as well as a caretaker for them,
until their illness no longer recurs.[110]

May I eliminate the pain of hunger and thirst
by raining down showers of food and drink.
May I become food and drink
during the intermediate kalpas of famine.[111]

May I become an inexhaustible treasure
for those beings who are impoverished {299}.
May I come into being before them
as many different kinds of useful objects.[112]

b. The Main Activity

This topic is made up of two sections: (1) the mental training and (2) the pledge.

i. The Mental Training

[The preceptor declares:]

> Repeat after me the following verses, and as you do so, reflect to yourselves: "Throughout beginningless time, all sentient beings who are as limitless as space have been my kind mothers over and over again. Since they are tormented by immeasurable forms of suffering in samsara, I shall offer myself to them, as well as all of my wealth and all my roots of virtue of the three times, so that these may serve as the causes that will produce whatever temporary or ultimate aims they may need. Moreover, I shall also take on every hardship or suffering that will help to bring about these goals."

Without expectation, I offer my bodies
and, likewise, my wealth and all my virtue

of the three times in order to accomplish
the aims of all sentient beings.[113]

Complete renunciation[114] is nirvana.
As one who desires nirvana, that is my intention.
If I am to give away everything,
better that it be given to sentient beings.[115]

I have made this body one that all beings
may do with as they please.
Let them strike it, revile it,
or always scatter dust upon it.[116]

Let them play with my body,
let them laugh at it or be amused by it.
As I have given my body to them,
why should I have this concern?[117]

Let them perform whatever acts
provide happiness to them.
May nothing unfortunate ever occur
through having relied upon me.[118]

In whomever an angry or an unsettled[119] mind
should arise through having relied upon me,
may that very attitude always be a cause
for them to achieve their every aim.[120]

Whoever accuses me falsely, {300}
whoever else harms me, ridicules me,
and, likewise, everyone else as well,
may they all partake of enlightenment.[121]

May I be a protector for those without a protector.
May I be a caravan leader for a group of travelers.
May I be a boat for those wishing to reach a far shore.
May I also be a causeway and a bridge.[122]

For all those embodied beings
who seek a place of refuge, may I be a refuge,
for those who seek a lamp, may I be a lamp,
for those who seek a bed, may I be a bed,
and for those who seek a servant, may I be a servant.[123]

May I be a wish-granting jewel,
a vase of fortune, an efficacious spell,
a great medicine, a wish-granting tree,
and a cow of plenty for embodied beings.[124]

Just as the elements of the earth and the rest
are objects of enjoyment in many ways
for immeasurable sentient beings that reside
throughout the entirety of space,[125]

likewise, may I be a source of livelihood
in many ways for the sphere of sentient beings
that reach to the ends of space
until they all become emancipated.[126]

Alternatively, it is also acceptable to recite just three of these verses—that is, the initial verse followed by the final two that begin with the line "Just as the elements of the earth and the rest."

ii. The Pledge

[Next, the preceptor states to the disciples,] "Reflect to yourself in the following manner":

> Even though all entities are free of all of the extremes that constitute elaborations regarding ultimately real forms of existence, in a conventional sense I and all others appear to undergo manifold forms of happiness and suffering. These appearances are described in the following verse from the *King of Concentrations Sūtra*:

Just as an illusionist creates variegated forms
such as elephant carriages and horse carriages,
but no carriages at all truly appear there,
realize that all entities are similar to that.[127]

Although everything lacks a true mode of existence, sentient beings mistakenly apprehend them as being truly existent because they lack this understanding. Therefore, they experience immeasurable forms of suffering in samsara. {301} Moreover, all these sentient beings who are experiencing suffering in this way have been my kind benefactors throughout beginningless time. Therefore, I must liberate them from their suffering. However, because I currently lack the ability to liberate them, I must attain buddhahood in order to gain the ability to liberate them. In order for me to attain unsurpassed enlightenment, I shall generate the mind that aspires to attain enlightenment, and I shall cultivate the bodhisattva training that consists of three types of morality—that is, the morality of restraint, the morality of acquiring virtuous qualities, and the morality that acts on behalf of sentient beings—in just the same way that the former buddhas and bodhisattvas have done.

[The preceptor should then state:]

When you state the words, "I beseech all the buddhas and bodhisattvas to give heed to me," reflect to yourself with a sense of conviction, "Because all the buddhas and bodhisattvas know in a precise manner what my thoughts and actions are, they are definitely cognizant of me now." Then, with a one-pointed state of mind that has faith in the lama and the Three Jewels and that develops the compassion that wants to liberate all sentient beings from their suffering, maintain the great aspiration in which you think to yourself, "For the sake of all sentient beings, I wish to attain buddhahood." Then repeat the following words after me:

I beseech all the buddhas and bodhisattvas who reside in the ten directions to give heed to me. I beseech the preceptor

> to give heed to me. I who am named so-and-so, from this moment on until I reach the seat of enlightenment, declare the following.
>
> Just as the previous sugatas
> took hold of enlightenment mind, {302}
> and just as they engaged successively
> in the trainings of the bodhisattvas,[128]
>
> so, too, do I generate enlightenment mind to benefit
> the world
> and so, too, shall I practice
> the trainings in due order.[129]

[Then the preceptor should introduce the second recitation by saying the following:]

> Now, while reflecting to yourself, "Just as the buddhas and bodhisattvas developed the aspirational form of enlightenment mind by forming the intention to attain buddhahood for the sake of all sentient beings and then practiced the active form of enlightenment mind by cultivating in a regular manner the bodhisattva training that includes the three types of morality, I too shall cultivate the aspirational and active forms of enlightenment mind in the same way," repeat the words of the ritual after me a second time.

[Following the second recitation, the preceptor should introduce the third recitation by stating the following:]

> Once again, as you maintain the three great qualities of great faith in the lama and the Three Jewels, great compassion for sentient beings, and the great aspiration that wishes to attain buddhahood, reflect to yourself, "Just as the former buddhas and bodhisattvas developed the two attitudes of the aspirational and active forms of enlightenment mind, likewise, I too shall generate the aspiration to attain buddhahood for the sake of all sentient beings and train myself in the three types of morality that make up the bodhisattva training and that are the cause that brings

> about the attainment of buddhahood. The lama, the buddhas, and the bodhisattvas who are present here are my witnesses for this act," and then repeat the words of the ritual after me a third time.

Because this third and final recitation is extremely important, the preceptor should provide a clear explanation of the ritual's meaning and recite the words that express the pledge that is being made in a slow and distinct manner. He or she should then also state the following:

> Because you participants will definitely give rise to the aspirational and active forms of enlightenment mind when the third repetition is completed, at that moment you should elicit a sense of great joy as you make the determination that the aspiration and the vow have been generated by reflecting to yourself, "Now I have given rise to the two forms of enlightenment mind."

iii. Conclusion

This section is made up of two parts: (1) cultivating joy and (2) making offerings of gratitude.

I) Cultivating Joy

This first topic {303} has two divisions: (1) cultivating joy yourself and (2) prompting others to cultivate joy.

A) Cultivating Joy Yourself

[The preceptor should state to the participants:]

> You should cultivate joy as you reflect to yourself, "Although I have taken birth in countless physical forms throughout the beginningless past, since I have not succeeded in achieving anything of great spiritual meaning, I still remain in samsara. However, because on this occasion I have developed in my mental continuum the precious enlightenment mind that is the cause that brings benefit and happiness to myself and all other sentient

beings, now I have achieved something that does have great spiritual meaning."

If you ask what benefits one gains from cultivating such a form of joy, there are a very great number of benefits, such as these seven: (1) your identity changes, (2) you abandon powerful evil deeds, (3) you acquire extensive merit, (4) you acquire limitless good qualities, (5) a presentation of benefits through similes, (6) it is an offering to the buddhas, and (7) benefits that are described in scriptural passages.

Your Identity Changes

A verse from *Entry into the Conduct That Leads to Enlightenment* states:

> As soon as enlightenment mind has been developed,
> a wretched being enchained in samsara's prison
> is immediately called an offspring of the sugatas
> and is worthy of being honored by the world of gods and
> humans.[130]

You Abandon Powerful Evil Deeds

> How could ignorant beings fail to rely upon
> that which instantly frees even one who has committed
> the most terrible of misdeeds, just as reliance
> on a hero allows one to escape great dangers?
>
> And which destroys great misdeeds in an instant,
> like the fire at the end of an eon.[131]

You Acquire Extensive Merit

A verse from the *Sūtra on Vīradatta's Queries* declares:

> If the merit of enlightenment mind {304}
> were to become form,
> after completely filling the realm of space,
> there would be an excess of even more.[132]

You Acquire Limitless Good Qualities

> Complete enlightenment mind, upholding the dharma,
> practicing the dharma, and compassion toward living beings—
> these four things possess limitless good qualities;
> the Victor did not declare that they have limits.[133]

A Description of Benefits through Similes

This topic has three sections, the first of which is a description of how enlightenment mind transforms what is inferior into something supreme through the simile of an alchemic elixir.

> A verse from *Entry into the Conduct That Leads to Enlightenment* states:
>
> > Firmly take hold of this elixir called enlightenment mind
> > that brings about the highest kind of transformation;
> > it turns this impure body that one has taken
> > into the priceless jewel of a victor's body.[134]
>
> The following verse is a description of how enlightenment mind is like a valuable jewel that is difficult to obtain:
>
> > Its great value has been well ascertained by those singular
> > caravan leaders of the world who possess immeasurable
> > wisdom;
> > those intent upon leaving the cities of the migratory states
> > should firmly take hold of the jewel of enlightenment
> > mind.[135]
>
> This verse is a description of how enlightenment mind is like a wishing tree whose fruit is inexhaustible and becomes increasingly more abundant:
>
> > All other forms of virtue are like the plantain tree
> > in that they simply perish after yielding their fruit;
> > but the tree of enlightenment mind thrives
> > and bears fruit continually without perishing.[136]

The Buddhas Will Be Honored

It is declared in the *Sūtra on Questions of Sāgaramati* that these three acts are an unsurpassed form of honoring the tathāgatas: {305} generating enlightenment mind, upholding the true dharma, and having compassion toward living beings.[137]

The *Sūtra on Skillful Means* also declares: "Whoever wishes to honor all the buddhas / should firmly generate enlightenment mind."

The *Sūtra on Vīradatta's Queries* also declares:

Between a person who would give
to the guardians of the world
buddha fields filled with excellent jewels
equal in number to the sand grains of the Ganges

and a person who, having joined the palms together,
would turn his or her mind to enlightenment,
this latter act of worship is superior
and one that has no limit.[138]

Benefits Described in Scriptural Passages

The *Buddha Avataṃsaka Sūtra*[139] describes how the youth Sudhana generated enlightenment mind in the presence of Ārya Mañjuśrī and then approached fifty-two lamas in order to gain extensive knowledge about the way in which to cultivate the bodhisattva training. Among these teachers, he came into the presence of Lord Maitreya in the southern region near the ocean at a time that the latter was teaching a large following. After making prostration, Sudhana said to Maitreya, "I am one who has generated enlightenment mind; however, because I do not know how to train myself in the trainings, please teach me at length about the way in which to train oneself in the bodhisattva trainings."

Then, Maitreya said to him, "O son of good family, you have been well favored by true spiritual teachers. Enlightenment mind is like a seed for all the spiritual qualities of a buddha. It is like a field, in that it causes virtuous qualities to grow in all the beings of the world. . . . It is like the fire that burns at the end of a kalpa, in that it incinerates all misdeeds. {306} It is like a hole beneath the earth, in that it causes all unvirtuous qualities to disappear. It is like the king of wish-granting jewels, in that it accomplishes all aims. It is like the vase of fortune, in that it fulfills all wishes. It is like a hook, in that it extracts those who move through the waters of samsara. It is like a caitya monument for the world of gods, humans, and demigods. In sum, as many as all the spiritual qualities of a buddha and all the good qualities of a buddha are, so many are the good qualities and benefits of enlightenment mind. Why is that? Because from it arises the sphere of bodhisattva conduct and from it come forth all the tathāgatas of the past, the future, and the present."[140]

[The preceptor should further declare to the participants:]

With joyful delight toward the enlightenment mind that you have engendered and that possesses the immeasurable good qualities that were described in this manner, now repeat the following verses after me, reflecting well on the meaning of the words contained in them and maintaining an attitude of joyful delight:

Now my life has become fruitful;
this human existence has been made worthwhile.
Today I have been born into the family of the buddhas;
now I have become an offspring of the buddhas.[141]

From now on my actions should accord however
is most fitting for my lineage,
so that this flawless lineage
does not become stained.[142]

As a blind man might obtain
a jewel from within refuse heaps,
thus has this enlightenment mind
somehow arisen in me.[143]

It is an elixir of life that was produced
to destroy the death of the world.
It is an inexhaustible treasure {307}
that eliminates the poverty of the world.[144]

It is the supreme medicine
that cures the illnesses of the world.
It is the tree that gives rest to the world made weary
from wandering on the road of samsaric existence.[145]

It is the universal causeway for all travelers
to cross over the unhappy migratory states.
It is a moon-like mind whose arising
extinguishes the world's mental afflictions.[146]

It is the great sun that dispels
the darkness of the world's ignorance.
It is the fresh butter that rises up
by churning the milk of the true dharma.[147]

For the caravan of beings traversing the road of samsaric existence
who wish to partake of the enjoyment of happiness,
it is the appearance of the munificent refuge of happiness
that satisfies all sentient beings who have arrived as guests.[148]

Alternatively, it is also acceptable simply to recite the first two of these verses.

B) Prompting Others to Cultivate Joy

The preceptor should then state to the participants:

> Repeat after me the following verse, and as you do so, maintain the thought in which you reflect to yourself: "Because, after generating enlightenment mind in the presence of all the buddhas, I have pledged to establish all sentient beings in temporary states of happiness, as well as in the state of ultimate happiness; everyone should rejoice at this."
>
> Indeed, before all the saviors,
> today I have invited the world to sugatahood
> and, in the interim, to states of happiness.
> May gods, demigods, and the like, rejoice.[149]

II) Making Offerings of Gratitude

[Next, the preceptor should tell the participants:]

> Because the act of generating enlightenment mind in this way is due to the kindness of the lama and the Three Jewels, the various forms of offering and a torma should be presented to them as an expression of gratitude. Therefore, I request that you repeat after me a recitation for presenting actual offerings or offerings that have been emanated with the mind.

To carry out this act, replenish the existing offerings and arrange new incense and lamps, and so on. Following these preparations, bless the offerings and then present them while chanting the same verses that were recited previously. In addition, offer yourself by reciting the verse that begins, "I give myself completely to the victors / and to those spiritual beings . . . ."[150] {308} Also present offerings by reciting the three verses from the *Aspirational Prayer for Excellent Spiritual Conduct* that begin, "With the best flowers" and so on.[151]

Dispel obstructive spirits from the tormas by sprinkling clean water on them as you recite the mantra *oṃ amṛte hūṃ phaṭ*. Then purify them by dissolving them into emptiness as you recite the mantra *oṃ svabhāva* and so on.[152] Following that, generate the sanctified tormas, which are excellent in color, odor, taste, and potency, by visualizing that they appear from that state of emptiness situated within large and spacious vessels made from jewels having a nature that consists of great oceans of the nectar of transcendent awareness. Complete the blessing by reciting the mantra syllables *oṃ āḥ hūṃ* three times.

Next visualize in the space before you the lama and the Three Jewels who were previously situated there, and then, while making the sky-treasure gesture, offer the torma by reciting three or five times the mantra *oṃ sarvaguru-buddhadharmasaṃgatebhyaḥ saparivāra* with the mantra *oṃ akāro* and so on[153] attached at the end. Also present the offerings that were made in the preliminary stage of the ritual by reciting this same name mantra followed by *arghaṃ* and so on, as before. Then make supplication to the lama and the Three Jewels by stating the following:

> O supreme lama and the precious Three Jewels, please accept this vast torma offering. I also implore you to bless the mental continua of our teachers and fellow disciples so that they may generate those forms of the precious enlightenment mind that they have not yet generated and so that they may develop to ever higher levels those forms of the precious enlightenment mind that they have generated.

Next, bless the second torma by reciting the three mantra syllables, and then emanate light rays from your heart to invite the glorious and great Black Vajra "brother and sister," together with their retinue. Then state the following supplication as you present a torma offering to them:

> O glorious and adamantine Mahākāla and consort, together with your retinue, please accept this vast torma offering. I also implore you to carry out extensive activities and forms of assistance that will cause the buddha's teaching to flourish, that will bring happiness and well-being to sentient beings, and that will enable our teachers and disciples to keep their precious enlightenment mind from declining and also enable them to develop it to ever higher levels.

Following that, bless the third torma by reciting the three mantra syllables,[154] and then invite the world guardians by reciting the mantra *oṃ lokapālasaparivāra ākarṣaya jaḥ*. After reciting the mantra *oṃ lokapālasaparivāra oṃ akā* {309} *ro* and so on, then state the supplication that begins, "O great world guardians, together with your retinue, please accept this vast torma offering . . ." (etc., up to) "I also implore you to carry out extensive activities and forms of assistance that will avert obstacles that keep our teachers and disciples from developing and strengthening their precious enlightenment mind."

After that, bless the fourth torma by reciting the three mantra syllables, and then summon the local spirits by reciting the mantra *oṃ bhūmipatisaparivāra ākarṣaya jaḥ*. Then dedicate the torma offering to them by reciting three times the first part of the same mantra,[155] followed by *oṃ akāro* and so on. Then recite the following:

> I present, offer, and provide this torma offering to the naturally abiding local spirits, regional spirits, village spirits, and spirits that are keepers of religious property. Please accept it and carry out excellent forms of assistance that will cause the buddha's teaching to flourish and will bring about every kind of happiness and well-being in this world realm. In addition, having developed joy and delight at the generating of precious enlightenment mind by our teachers and their disciples, please also assist them by protecting them from every form of obstacle.

Then invite them to return to their natural abodes by reciting their name mantra with the syllable *gaccha*[156] attached at the end.

B. The Method of Safeguarding the Vow by Not Committing Transgressions

The preceptor should explain the following topics to his or her disciples.

> This topic is made up of two sections: (1) identifying the precepts and (2) summarizing the practice by describing the manner in which to safeguard those precepts.

1. Identifying the Precepts

> This topic is made up two divisions: (1) the general precepts for both the aspirational and active forms of enlightenment mind and (2) the specific precepts for each form of enlightenment mind.

a. The General Precepts

> This first topic is made up of three qualities that are to be practiced and four qualities that are to be learned. The first group of three qualities are serving a spiritual teacher and maintaining devotion to him or her, not doing anything to terminate the lineage of the Three Jewels, and not mentally abandoning sentient beings. In addition, after having generated enlightenment mind,

you should safeguard it by not allowing it to decline, you should read the bodhisattva collection of canonical scriptures, and you should continually observe mindfulness.[157]

The second group of four qualities is to understand well what acts constitute transgressions, what acts do not constitute transgressions, what acts have the appearance of being transgressions {310} but are not transgressions, and what acts have the appearance of not being transgressions but are transgressions.

In sum, while the bodhisattva precepts that are to be practiced are inconceivably great in number, they can be classified into three types: those that serve to perfect that spiritual qualities of a buddha; those that serve to ripen sentient beings spiritually; and those that serve to purify one's own buddha field.

b. Specific Precepts

There are specific precepts for the aspirational form of enlightenment mind and specific precepts for the active form of enlightenment mind.

i. Specific Precepts for the Aspirational Form of Enlightenment Mind

The specific precepts for the aspirational form of enlightenment mind are to train oneself with regard to (1) the three aspirations of true spiritual beings, (2) the four black qualities that should be abandoned, and (3) the four white qualities that should be practiced.

The Three Aspirations of a True Spiritual Being

The three aspirations of a true spiritual being[158] are the aspiration regarding the result, in which one reflects, "I shall attain perfect enlightenment for the sake of sentient beings"; the aspiration regarding the method, in which one reflects, "I shall train myself in all the stages and paths"; and the aspiration regarding activities, in which one reflects, "I shall fulfill the wishes of all sentient beings."

The Four Black Qualities That Should Be Abandoned

You should strive to abandon these four black qualities: to deceive a guru or a person who is worthy of being venerated, to express words of blame about persons who are established in the Mahāyāna, to employ deceitfulness and guile toward sentient beings, and to instill regret in the minds of others about something that does not need to be regretted.[159]

The Four White Qualities That Should Be Practiced

The four white qualities that should be practiced are to avoid knowingly uttering falsehoods, even to save your life; to develop the conception toward all bodhisattvas that they are the Master and to praise them for their good spiritual qualities; having abandoned deceitfulness and guile, to maintain a superior attitude; and to induce all sentient beings that are capable of being ripened spiritually to pursue the virtuous deeds associated with the Mahāyāna tradition.[160] Through training yourself in these four white qualities, the four black qualities will be terminated in an incidental manner.

ii. The Precepts That Are Specific to the Active Form of Enlightenment Mind

This topic is made up of two sections: (1) that activities that are to be abandoned and (2) the activities that are to be practiced.

I) The Activities That Are to Be Abandoned

This topic is made up of (1) root transgressions and (2) secondary transgressions. {311}

A) Root Transgressions

The root transgressions are made up of five that are likely to occur for a bodhisattva who is a king, five that are likely to occur for a bodhisattva who is a minister, eight that are likely to occur for a bodhisattva who is a novice practitioner, and the transgression that is common to all bodhisattvas and that consists of abandoning the aspirational form of enlightenment mind.

The individual by whom root transgressions are committed is a person who possesses the bodhisattva vow. He or she must also be someone who is not insane, mentally agitated, or tormented by intense feelings,[161] and so on. This is because a person who is subject to any of these conditions cannot incur any of the root transgressions and because it is not necessary for a person to be motivated by a mental affliction to incur any of these root transgressions, since a transgression occurs either through failing to carry out actions that ought to be performed or failing to avoid actions that ought not to be performed.

Regarding these root transgressions, the first group of five that are likely to occur for a bodhisattva who is a king are to seize or steal the property of the Three Jewels; to reject the dharma or prohibit it from being practiced; to harm a bhikṣu who has gone forth into the homeless state by seizing their possessions or through other similar actions; to commit any of the five immediate misdeeds;[162] and through adherence to wrong view, to engage in the ten unvirtuous deeds oneself or to induce others to do so. The meaning of these five root transgressions that are mentioned in the *Ākāśagarbha Sūtra* are summarized in *The Compendium of Training* with these lines of verse:

> Confiscating the property of the Three Jewels is considered
> a transgression that is an extreme form of defeat.
> Rejecting the true dharma was declared
> by the sage to be a second root transgression.
> Taking the saffron robes of even an immoral monk,
> beating him, imprisoning him,
> forcing him to give up being a renunciate,
> or taking his life[163] is a third root transgression.
> Committing any of the five immediate sins;
> and adherence to wrong view;[164]

Since seizing the collective property of the sangha forms part of the first root transgression, the third root transgression specifies that it is an act committed in relation to a single bhikṣu.

Regarding the five root transgressions that are likely to occur for a bodhisattva who is a minister, the first four of the previous five are the same. {312} Instead of the misdeed of adherence to wrong view, the act of destroying a village or a town, and so on, is counted as one of the root transgressions, making a total of five. *The Compendium of Training* describes this last transgression with the lines:

> The destruction of a town, and so on, was also declared
> by the Victor to be a root transgression.[165]

Among the eight root transgressions that are likely to occur for a novice bodhisattva, the first is to cause another person's enlightenment mind to be lost through fear by teaching that person about emptiness without having trained him or her in the Mahāyāna instruction gradually. The second root transgression is to cause a person who is established in thought and action in the pursuit of perfect enlightenment to turn away from that goal. The third is to tell a person who possesses the śrāvaka's spiritual lineage that because there is no great purpose to train oneself in the discipline of prātimokṣa,[166] he or she should abandon that form of discipline and take up the Mahāyāna system of practice. The fourth is to believe yourself that the mental afflictions cannot be abandoned by means of the Śrāvakayāna and to cause others to adopt such a belief, thereby leading to the suppression of the teaching and hearing of that system of spiritual practice. The fifth is to praise yourself and disparage others for the sake of obtaining gain and honor and because of the envy that you develop toward those others who receive gain and honor. The sixth is to state the falsehood that you possess superhuman spiritual qualities[167] by declaring that you have attained realization of emptiness when you have not done so. The seventh is a transgression in which you create divisions between religious ascetics[168] and members of the kṣatriya caste[169] and then induce the latter to punish the religious ascetics by imposing fines on them and confiscating[170] their property. The eighth root transgression is to impose harmful rules on upright religious ascetics and to cause those ascetics to give up such forms of spiritual practice as the cultivation of quiescence, as well as to confiscate the property of bhikṣus engaged in the cultivation of meditative absorption and give it to monks who are devoted to the recitation of scriptures.

These eight root transgressions are described in the five and a half verses that begin with: "Describing emptiness to those beings whose minds have not been prepared . . ." and continue up to "These root transgressions are causes for being born in the great hells."[171] In this way, while the *Ākāśagarbha Sūtra* describes eighteen root transgressions in terms of the individuals by whom they are performed, their number is established as fourteen in terms of actual deeds. A root transgression that is common to all types of bodhisattva practitioners is the abandonment of the aspirational form of enlightenment mind {313}. Indeed, the gravest among all of the bodhisattva transgressions is for you to develop the attitude that desires to attain peace and happiness for yourself exclusively. It is declared in *The Collection of Verses on the Perfection of Wisdom* that

> Having practiced the ten virtuous karmic paths for ten million kalpas,
> if one should develop the desire to become a pratyekabuddha arhat,
> that person becomes one whose morality is defective and one whose morality is torn asunder;
> the production of this thought is graver than an extreme form of defeat.[172]

Thus, the inclusion of this transgression makes a total of nineteen root transgressions. In addition to those nineteen, it is also said that there are twenty root transgressions, since a sūtra in the collection known as the *Heap of Jewels* declares that failing to engage in virtuous deeds after having abandoned the active form of enlightenment mind constitutes a root transgression.

B) Secondary Transgressions

The secondary transgressions are those violations of the precepts done by body, speech, or mind that are not included in the root transgressions. The first is to violate precepts relating to physical behavior that should be observed, such as maintaining a gaze in which the eyes are cast downward, as well as to violate precepts relating to physical behavior that is prohibited, such as running or jumping without purpose. The second is to violate precepts relating to verbal behavior that should be observed, such as saying "welcome" when someone arrives, as well as to violate precepts relating to verbal behavior that is prohibited, such as engaging in idle talk. The third is to violate precepts relating to mental activities that should be observed, such as cultivating loving-kindness, compassion, recollection, vigilance, and mindfulness, and so on, as well as to violate precepts relating to mental activities that are prohibited, such as the failure to abandon attachment, hatred, and so on. It is explained that the secondary offenses associated with persons of middling and dull faculties are also included in these categories.

Regarding the root transgressions, although no distinctions are made in relation to such points as the strength or weakness of the mental afflictions that motivate them, the vow associated with the production of the active form of enlightenment mind is lost if any of the root transgressions are allowed to go unremedied for more than a four-hour period. The vow associated with the production of the aspirational form of enlightenment mind remains intact as long as you do not turn away from the aim of attaining complete enlightenment. Therefore, it is the position of the Middle Way school that abandoning the aspirational form of enlightenment mind is both a root transgression and a cause for losing the bodhisattva vow. If you develop regret for having incurred a root transgression before the passage of a four-hour period, the bodhisattva vow will not have been lost. A period[173] means one-sixth of a full twenty-four-hour day. With regard to secondary misdeeds, if a full twenty-four-hour day is allowed to go by without any remedy to the act {314}, then a secondary transgression is incurred.

II) Affirmative Precepts[174]

The affirmative precepts are to diligently train oneself in the three types of morality: the morality of restraining oneself from committing misdeeds, which consists of the volition that refrains from committing the transgressions that were just explained, together with the seeds of that volition; the morality of acquiring virtuous qualities, which consists of training oneself to carry out the multitude of virtuous activities that are included within the six perfections; and the morality that acts on behalf of sentient beings, which consists of the volition that desires to accomplish temporary and ultimate forms of benefit and happiness for all sentient beings, together with the seeds of that volition. Since the middling version of the *Mother*[175] declares that you should strive to generate these three minds—the mind that refrains from committing objectionable acts,[176] the mind that acquires virtuous qualities, and the mind that ripens sentient beings[177]—*The Stage of a Bodhisattva* also states that a bodhisattva's all-inclusive morality is limited to just these three types of morality,[178] which is to say that all the precepts to be observed by a bodhisattva are included within these three types of morality. Regarding those three forms of morality, you should abandon the activities that ought to be abandoned and you should train yourself with single-minded attention in relation to those acts that ought to be cultivated.

2. Safeguarding the Precepts

This topic is made up of two sections: (1) reflecting on the disadvantages of failing to safeguard the precepts and (2) the actual method by which to safeguard them.

a. The Disadvantages of Failing to Safeguard the Precepts

This topic is made up of three points. If you fail to safeguard the precepts, (1) you will have broken your pledge, (2) you will have lost your identity, and (3) you will fall into the lower realms.

i. You Will Have Broken Your Pledge

By having deceived the Buddha who is the supreme teacher, you will become an object of the Buddha's disapproval. By having deceived sentient beings who are the objects of your concern, sentient beings will be disappointed. By having deceived yourself, your own aim will be lost and you will be scorned by the world together with the gods. As the *Sāgaramati Sūtra* declares in part, a bodhisattva who has generated enlightenment mind but does not act in accord with what he or she has pledged to do will have deceived the world together with the gods.[179]

ii. You Will Have Lost Your Identity

The sūtras declare that like a king who has lost his kingdom, you will experience many forms of inauspiciousness in this life {315} and you will be tormented by grief at the time of your death.

iii. You Will Fall into the Lower Realms

The sūtras declare that you will go to the lower realms in your next life and it will be difficult for you to escape from there. They also declare that by having committed the offense of a root transgression, you will destroy all the roots of virtue that you previously gained through having generated enlightenment mind, and therefore, by having deceived the Three Jewels together with the gods, you will go to the lower realms in general, and, in particular, you will be reborn in the great hells. The latter point is indicated in the phrase "Because these root transgressions are causes for being reborn in the great hells . . . ."[180]

b. The Actual Method by Which to Safeguard the Precepts

The causes that give rise to the transgressions that possess the disadvantages that were just described are ignorance, lack of mindfulness, an abundance of mental afflictions, and disrespect.

Of these, ignorance means that despite your effort to pursue the training, you incur transgressions because you are not aware of their defining characteristics. The antidote for this shortcoming is to learn about the nature of the precepts through listening to teachings on them.

Lack of mindfulness[181] means that despite your knowing what constitutes the nature of the transgressions, you incur transgressions either by not recognizing what their disadvantages are or despite recognizing them, you fail to observe recollection and vigilance.[182] The antidote for this fault is to cultivate the recollection that keeps you from losing your hold on the mental objects and aspects that relate to the practice, the vigilance that examines your three doors with an understanding of what good qualities should be pursued and what faults should be avoided, the sense of shame[183] that feels embarrassment about wrongful actions for reasons relating either to yourself or the dharma, the abashment[184] that feels embarrassment about the prospect of being condemned by others, and the mindfulness that fears the karmic maturations of misdeeds.

An abundance of mental afflictions means that despite having some apprehension about committing transgressions, you incur transgressions because of the mental afflictions that you develop due to your strong tendency to give rise to any of the three poisons. The antidote to this condition is to examine your mental continuum and strive to cultivate the antidote to whatever mental affliction you have the strongest tendency to develop, as well as to avoid the lack of concern in which you think to yourself, "While this thought or action may be a violation of the bodhisattva morality, it is only a minor infraction."

Disrespect means that despite knowing what the transgressions are and so on, {316} you incur transgressions because you fail to apply yourself to the training due to being attracted to an inferior form of behavior. The antidote for this trait is to develop a sense of respect toward the Master and the rules of conduct that he established.

Moreover, regarding these four causes, ignorance and lack of mindfulness give rise to lesser forms of transgressions; an abundance of mental afflictions, to transgressions of middling severity; and disrespect, to great transgressions. The characteristics of the mental attitude that accompanies the transgressions also determine the nature of corresponding forms of transgressions. Therefore, you should strive to train yourself in all the elements that relate to the practice with a conviction that is willing to risk your life in order to avoid committing any moral offenses. As a verse from the *King of Concentrations Sūtra* declares:

> Whatever precepts I have taught
> to householders that wear white clothing,
> those precepts will not be found
> in the bhikṣus of that time.[185]

This means that at a time such as the present when the five precepts that are taught to lay practitioners are not even being observed by bhikṣus, striving to cultivate the morality training will bring especially great favorable results. Another verse from the same sūtra also declares:

> And one who practices the precept for a single day and
> night,
> when the true dharma is disappearing
> and the sugatas' teaching is being destroyed,
> this person gives rise to greater merit than that one.[186]

C. Remedying Transgressions

This topic is made up of two sections: (1) the method of confessing offenses and (2) the method of retaking the vow if it should be lost.

1. Confession of Offenses

The first section is also made up of two parts: (1) the general Mahāyāna system of confession and (2) the Middle Way school's own system of confession.

a. The General Mahāyāna System of Confession

The object before whom the confession is made is either a bodhisattva who has not been tainted by a root transgression or a consecrated body-vessel[187] of Buddha Śākyamuni. You should bow to either of these objects with an attitude of regret for the prior offense or offenses that you have committed and generate an attitude of resolve to restrain yourself from committing any such offense or offenses in the future.

After having beseeched the object to whom confession is being made to give heed, you should declare three times, "I, a bodhisattva named so-and-so,{317} have incurred such-and-such an offense or offenses. I, a bodhisattva named so-and-so, admit and confess my offense or offenses in the presence of all the buddhas and bodhisattvas of the ten directions. By admitting and confessing it or them, I will abide in happiness. If I fail to admit and confess it or them, I will not abide in happiness." Also, at the end make the declaration: "This is an excellent method."

b. The Middle Way School's Own System of Confession

If, out of fear of falling into the lower realms and while feeling great regret for having committed transgressions, you may confess your transgressions directly before Ārya Ākāśagarbha if you have the ability to perceive him.[188] If you lack that ability, you should awaken before dawn and while maintaining cleanliness and facing toward the east, present offerings[189] and make entreaty[190] to Aruṇa,[191] the god of dawn. Having done so, go back to sleep and in your dream make confession before Ākāśagarbha when he appears to you. Alternatively, you should practice confession through making prostrations and mantra recitation, until you directly perceive Ākāśagarbha or until you experience signs that your evil deeds have been eliminated. As *The Compendium of Training* declares, "The root transgressions should be confessed in a dream / while standing before Ārya Ākāśagarbha." A verse from *Entry into the Conduct That Leads to Enlightenment* also states:

> Three times at night and during the day
> you should recite the *Three Heaps Sūtra*.[192]
> By doing that, the remaining transgressions[193] are removed
> through relying on enlightenment mind and the victors.[194]

Since the *Sūtra That Reveals the Four Spiritual Qualities*[195] also teaches that all of the evil deeds of a bodhisattva can be eliminated by means of the four powers, these should be understood in the following manner: First, the power of the support is to prepare offerings before sacred images, as much as you can afford, and take refuge in the Three Jewels, as well as to refrain from giving up your enlightenment mind. Second, the power of self-censure[196] is to develop intense regret for the offenses you have committed in the past, as you might feel if you had ingested some deadly poison. Third, the power of engaging in an antidote is to strive to practice such virtuous acts as commissioning the construction of sacred images, {318} making prostrations, presenting offerings, performing circumambulations, carrying out mantra recitations, cultivating one-pointed concentration, and meditating on emptiness as antidotes for your transgressions. Fourth, the power of turning away from wrongdoing is gained by making the firm resolve, "In the future, I shall never commit any of these evil deeds even at the cost of my life."

2. The Method of Retaking the Vow If It Should Be Lost

If, after incurring a root transgression, you allow more than a four-hour period to go by without doing anything to remedy that offense, the bodhisattva vow will be lost and must therefore be retaken. If you cannot find a spiritual teacher from whom to retake the vow, it will arise if you take it once again before a body-vessel in the same way that was described earlier.

In short, according to the system of the Middle Way school, the bodhisattva precepts are for you to give yourself, your wealth, together with your collection of virtue, to all sentient beings; to protect these three things from being damaged; to purify them of any stains; and to increase their development to ever higher levels. This is described in the following lines from *The Compendium of Training*:

> You should learn here the key points
> by which to remain free of transgressions.[197]

If you ask what those key points are, the text continues:

> Giving your body,[198] wealth, and virtue
> of the three times to all sentient beings,
> as well as protecting, purifying,
> and increasing those three things.[199]

Moreover, the root element of all those key points can be identified as the act of protecting one's mind. This is affirmed in the lines from *Entry into the Conduct That Leads to Enlightenment* that state: "One who desires to safeguard the training / should guard the mind with great diligence."[200] As to the method of guarding the mind, the same text further states:

> To those who wish to guard their minds,
> I make this appeal with palms joined:
> even when your life is at risk, you must observe
> both recollection and vigilance.[201]

The Verses of the Nāga King Bherī also declares:

> I give my wealth to safeguard my body.
> I give both my wealth and parts of my body to safeguard
> {319} my life.
> But wealth, body, and so, too, one's life—
> all should be given here to safeguard the dharma.[202]

Therefore, you should strive in this way to safeguard the training.

III. Concluding Activities

[The preceptor should then state the following:]

> In the forgoing manner, I have properly conferred the ritual that is the great path and the sole way of conduct that is traversed by all the tathāgatas of the three times—that is, it is the great tradition that is renowned as the system of the Middle Way school for carrying out the ritual for generating the mind that is devoted to the attainment of unsurpassed, supreme enlightenment. Therefore, while reflecting to yourselves, "Through safeguarding the precepts as they have been explained and not allowing them to be damaged, I shall accomplish the welfare of sentient beings to

the best of my ability," repeat after me the following words three times:

> I shall do everything as the lord has instructed.

After that, the recipients should present a mandala offering, followed by recitation of the verse: "From today on,"[203] and so on.

[The preceptor should then add the following concluding remarks:]

> The immeasurable heap of merit that we have generated in this way, through properly conferring and receiving the vow associated with the act of generating the mind that seeks to attain supreme enlightenment, a spiritual exercise that represents the root of the entire Mahāyāna path, should be dedicated to the attainment of unsurpassed enlightenment. Therefore, I direct you participants now to perform the collective virtuous act of reciting dedication and aspirational prayers.

As an extensive form of this collective act, a dedication prayer and a Mahāyāna aspirational prayer, such as the *Aspirational Prayer for Excellent Spiritual Conduct*[204] or *Maitreya's Aspirational Prayer*,[205] along with verses of auspiciousness, should be recited. Or as an abbreviated version, whatever verses are considered appropriate, such as the one that begins "After achieving, by this merit, the All-Seeing One's state"[206] and so on and the one that begins "May I generate those forms of the precious enlightenment mind," and so on,[207] along with several verses of auspiciousness, may be recited.

At this juncture, Gyalse Tokme states in his work:[208]

> Although Śāntideva does not appear in the lineage for generating enlightenment mind that has been transmitted from one master to the next, Jetāri[209] identifies the ritual that he composed for generating enlightenment mind as being based on the system associated with Śāntideva's work *Entry into the Conduct That Leads to Enlightenment*. Since all the subsequent lineage holders were his disciples, while there may be some differences {320} in the wording of their works, the substance of all of these rituals represents the system of *Entry into the Conduct*. Moreover, the presentations of earlier lamas expressly state that theirs is the great master

> Śāntideva's system. In addition, while Jetāri separates the relevant sections of *Entry into the Conduct*, and indicates that the acts of accepting the aspirational form of enlightenment mind and the bodhisattva vow in conjunction with the active form of enlightenment mind are to be performed one after the other, Master Kṛṣṇapāda states in his *Pañjikā*[210] that if the aspirational enlightenment mind and the active enlightenment mind are to be adopted individually, the corresponding sections of Śāntideva's treatise should be separated from one another. However, if both minds are adopted jointly, this should be done by keeping both sections together just as they occur in the treatise. Therefore, the ritual that is presented in this work represents the form in which both forms of enlightenment mind are adopted jointly using the relevant sections just as they appear in Śāntideva's treatise.

It is also evident that, in this system of the Middle Way school, tradition has established three versions of the ritual—that is, an extensive, a middling, or an abbreviated form. The version that has been presented here is the extensive form, in which each portion of the ritual is explained continuously, one after the other. However, it is permissible to omit the section on how to carry out the elements of practice that represent the method of remedying transgressions.

To perform a middling version of the ritual, begin on p. 376 where the text states: "All of us have obtained an extraordinary human form that is difficult to obtain," and continue up to p. 381, at the section titled "Different Forms of the Ritual for Generating Enlightenment Mind" that begins with "There are two systems that possess rituals for generating enlightenment mind. One, which is known as the system of the Middle Way school, follows the *Gaṇḍavyūha Sūtra*" and ends with "Here I shall establish the ritual according to the system of the Middle Way school." Then, for the preliminary portion of the ritual, skip to the section that consists of making supplication to an excellent being [p. 390], followed by going for refuge. For the seven-limb devotional practice, it is acceptable to recite the appropriate verses from the *Aspirational Prayer for Excellent Spiritual Conduct*.[211] The main activity should be carried out as it is presented above [beginning on p. 402]. For the concluding portion of the ritual, after completing the section titled "Prompting Others to Cultivate Joy," perform the dedication prayers.

For an abbreviated form of the ritual, after performing the seven-limb devotional practice, carry out the act of going for refuge, by reciting the lines that begin "Until I sit at the seat of enlightenment" and so on. Then, following the recitation of the pair of verses that begin, "Just as the previous sugatas . . . ," as they appear above, complete the ceremony by carrying out the concluding portion that consists of generating joy in oneself and others. In addition, whichever of these forms of the ritual is performed, at the end recite in a proper manner the dedication and aspirational prayers.

Having planted well the genuine causes and conditions
for the seed of enlightenment mind, may the activities
that lead to great enlightenment increase and develop greatly,
far surpassing all the offspring of the victors that appear in the three
times.

Having awakened the jewel-like mind, effortlessly and all at once,
within their continua, may all beings that extend throughout space
cause their excellent spiritual conduct to reach the far side of the ocean,
enabling them to achieve Samantabhadra's state of inconceivable
liberation.

I, Lodrö Taye, one who merely holds the name of an offspring of the victors, have prepared this explanation of the ritual for generating enlightenment mind that follows the system of the great master Śāntideva {321} using the text composed by the offspring of the victors Tokme Zangpo Pel[212] as the basis for an outline that can be easily understood, as well as for several of the topics, such as the description of the precepts, to which I have added the authoritative and excellent explanations of a number of other true spiritual beings of the past. It was compiled with the aim of benefiting persons of limited understanding and I have done so in a manner that has avoided becoming tainted by the fault of creating a work that is my own fabrication at the great seat for spiritual practice known as Dzongshö, also known as the Place Where the Sugatas Gather, which is located in the Zabu region of Kham. May virtue and auspiciousness abound.

12. {323} The Excellent Path of the Bodhisattvas

A Ritual for Generating Enlightenment Mind and Accepting the Bodhisattva Vow according to the Mahāyāna System of Great Vastness[1]

Jamyang Khyentse Wangpo

{324} However much excellent benefit and happiness there is in samsara
and nirvana, it all derives from the power of the perfect buddhas,
and since buddhas are born from the victors' offspring, and they too
from enlightenment mind,
having bowed respectfully to the spiritual teachers who bestow the gift
of the priceless, supreme jewel,
in order to benefit others, I shall clearly explain the ritual for generating
enlightenment mind according to the System of Great Vastness.[2]

This topic should be understood in the following manner: Those who wish to attain the state that is the source of all worldly and transcendent goodness, the state that surpasses that of all the śrāvaka and pratyekabuddha arhats, the state of the spiritual father of all the bodhisattvas,[3] the state in which all those impurities that are, in all respects, defects, together with their traces, have been permanently abandoned and everlasting mastery of an ocean of inconceivably great spiritual qualities has been gained—that is to say, the state of a perfect buddha who is the unique friend toward all sentient beings, including those with whom he is not acquainted—must pursue the method of achieving that goal, which consists of generating the mind that seeks to attain supreme enlightenment and undertaking the spiritual conduct of the victors' offspring.[4] And since, in order to do so, such persons must first rely upon the ritual for accepting the bodhisattva vow, the purpose of this text is to enable those spiritual teachers who possess the genuine defining characteristics as they are described in various scriptural sources and who are desirous of performing the ritual for generating enlightenment mind and for accepting the bodhisattva vow according to the Mahāyāna System of Great Vastness, to do so so that they may establish those fortunate disciples who possess the Mahāyāna spiritual lineage in the path that leads to great enlightenment.

The ritual is made up of three parts: (1) preliminary activities, (2) main activity, and (3) concluding activities.

I. Preliminary Activities

In a clean and attractive physical space, before exceptional body-vessels,[5] of which the principal one should be an image of the Lord of Sages[6] who was the Lion of the Śākya clan, arrange in an attractive manner clean forms of the general offerings known as the five objects of respectful service,[7] and among them especially rows of incense, lamps, and food offerings, to the extent that your wealth will allow. If you wish to make torma offerings, also arrange two round, white tormas, as well as a torma for regional spirits.

The spiritual teacher should bathe and, if it is convenient, perform, for him- or herself, the act of generating enlightenment mind and accepting the bodhisattva vow. {325} Whether the latter act is performed or not, he or she should carry out, as appropriate, a series of devotional practices, such as reciting the *Confession of Transgressions*[8] and the like. Following that, after seating him- or herself on a high seat, the disciples, who are still outside the temple or dharma hall, should be instructed to perform a ritual cleansing,[9] after which they should enter the dharma hall and seat themselves in a respectful manner in a lower place, while holding a flower.

II. The Main Activity

The spiritual teacher—while possessing the wisdom that realizes the emptiness of all entities, the compassion that wishes to benefit all sentient beings and establish them in a state of genuine happiness, and especially the excellent attitude that wishes to cause his or her disciples to generate enlightenment mind—should state the following in a clear and pleasant voice:

All of us have obtained an extraordinary human form that is difficult to obtain and that possesses the qualities of leisure and fortune. We have also met with the precious teaching of the Buddha that is difficult to meet with. Therefore, it is imperative that we strive to derive value from this form possessing leisure and fortune on this occasion in which we have gained the freedom to choose between samsara and nirvana. As the great spiritual teacher Ārya Nāgārjuna declared:

> It is much more difficult for an animal to become
> a human than for a turtle living in the vast ocean
> to meet with the opening of a yoke. Therefore, O king,
> make your life fruitful through practicing the true
> dharma.[10]

Moreover, among the different forms of the true dharma, the unique cause that is a treasure of limitless merit and spiritual qualities; that enables you to free everyone—that is, both yourself and others—from suffering, together with its constituent elements; and that also enables you to obtain for yourself and others both the temporary and ultimate form of supreme happiness is enlightenment mind. This latter point is illustrated by the great spiritual teacher {326} Śāntideva, who declared in a verse:

> With a desire to put an end to suffering
> and the wish to reach ultimate happiness,
> you should make firm the root of faith
> and fix your mind firmly upon enlightenment.[11]

And, it is also illustrated by the following lines expressed by the great spiritual teacher Candragomī:

> [T]hat morality of the bodhisattvas who exist
> throughout all the directions and times,
>
> which is a treasure of all forms of merit, . . .[12]

Thus, the enlightenment mind that the victors and their spiritual offspring have lauded as the sole pathway to enlightenment has two forms: conventional enlightenment mind, which is developed on the basis of a ritual and ultimate enlightenment mind that arises through the power of meditation.

Regarding the first of these two minds, the defining characteristic of the conventional enlightenment mind that is to be generated is that it is the mind of a Mahāyānist who is still engaged in the process of spiritual training and a mind that, for the sake of the welfare of others, has taken hold of perfect enlightenment as its object, but that does not include the enlightenment mind of a bodhisattva ārya who is in a state of meditative composure.[13] Examples of conventional enlightenment mind are the forms of enlightenment mind that are present in the mental continuum of a bodhisattva during the accumulation and preparation levels of the Mahāyāna path, as well as the forms of enlightenment mind that occur during the post-meditative stage[14] of an ārya bodhisattva. It is classified into five types: that which is produced by the strength of a "friend"—that is, a spiritual teacher; that which is produced by the strength of having awakened the cause of one's spiritual lineage; that which is produced by the strength of the result—which is to say, through having developed one's virtue roots; that which is produced by the strength of having heard instruction on the path that is contained in the Mahāyāna collection of scriptures; and that which is produced by the strength of having cultivated extensively that very instruction that was heard. The first of these, which depends upon a spiritual friend, is an unstable[15] production of enlightenment mind. The latter four types are stable productions of enlightenment mind because it is difficult for them to be lost due to the influence of the negative qualities that oppose them.[16] This is described in the following verse from *The Ornament of Mahāyāna Sūtras*:

> Developing enlightenment mind from another's speech
> is said to arise in either a stable or an unstable form,
> through the power of a friend, a cause, a root,
> hearing instruction, and the cultivation of virtue.[17]

Regarding the principal subject to be discussed here—which is to say, the conventional enlightenment mind that is gained by the power of another person—its explanation is made up of these three categories: (1) the ritual by which one gains the enlightenment mind that has not yet been gained,

(2) the method of safeguarding the enlightenment mind once it has been gained, and (3) the method of remedying violations of the precepts.

I. The Ritual for Attaining the Enlightenment Mind and the Bodhisattva Vow That Have Not Yet Been Attained

Of these, the first topic to be considered {327} is the method of carrying out the ritual by which to attain the form of conventional enlightenment mind and the bodhisattva vow that have not yet been attained. The writings of the former learned scholars state that there are two systems for carrying out the act of generating enlightenment mind, that of the Middle Way school and that of the Mind Only school. The system of the Middle Way school follows such canonical works as the *Gaṇḍavyūha Sūtra* and the *Ākāśagarbha Sūtra*. It was taught by Ārya Mañjuśrī, transmitted through a lineage that begins with the great spiritual teacher Nāgārjuna, systematized by the great spiritual teacher Śāntideva, and promulgated by the great spiritual teacher Jetāri. This is the system that the great masters of the teaching within the glorious Ṣakyapa tradition have put into practice.

The system of the Mind Only school follows such canonical works as the *Bodhisattvapiṭaka*. It was taught by Ārya Maitreya, transmitted through a lineage that begins with Ārya Asaṅga, systematized by the great spiritual teacher Candragomī, and promulgated by the great Lord Atiśa. This is the system that the Kadampas have put into practice.

Some scholars have said that there are many differences between these two systems as relates to the person who performs the ritual, the persons who are its participants, the ritual by which the bodhisattva vow is accepted, the method of maintaining the vow after it has been accepted, and the method of remedying violations that may occur. Other learned scholars have said that it is incorrect to assert the differences in these various elements of the ritual, and so on. Here, I shall put aside any consideration of these controversies and present the tradition that has been transmitted in an unbroken lineage from the true and complete Buddha Śākyamuni down to our own great spiritual tutors,[18] as it is found in the writings of the great spiritual teacher Ārya Asaṅga and the great Lord Dīpaṃkara Śrījñāna, regarding which there are three points: (1) ascertaining the nature of the person who is able to generate enlightenment mind and accept the bodhisattva vow, (2) carrying out the ritual activities, and (3) establishing the nature of the ritual.

A. Ascertaining the Nature of the Participants

This first topic is made up of three sections: (1) generating aversion for the suffering that is present in the extreme of samsara, (2) overcoming attachment for the peace {328} that is represented by the extreme of Hīnayāna nirvana, and (3) generating enthusiasm for the enlightenment mind that is free of the two extremes.

1. Generating Aversion for the Suffering That Is Present in the Extreme of Samsara

The preceptor should establish this quality in the following manner:

> On this occasion in which we have obtained a human form that possesses the qualities of leisure and fortune, we must strive to cross over samsara's ocean of suffering and achieve unsurpassed enlightenment. Moreover, the reason that we must do so is that we are able to achieve these two aims with this human form and we are unable to do so with any other type of form. This is stated in the *Letter to a Disciple*:
>
> > Who here would ruin this human state,
> > which having been attained, enables beings to cross the ocean of existence
> > and plant the auspicious seed of highest enlightenment
> > and which by its multitude of virtues, greatly surpasses a wish-granting jewel.
> >
> > The path resorted to by the sugata and by which he became the leader of the world,
> > the path that humans can find with the great power of their minds,
> > cannot be found by gods or demigods, or by nāgas,
> > garuḍas, vidyādharas, kinnaras, or uragas.[19]
>
> It is difficult to obtain the qualities of leisure and fortune in a rebirth as a human being. The *Gaṇḍavyūha Sūtra* also declares "Sudhana thought to himself, . . . Attainment of the status of a

human is difficult to obtain, the virtuous purity of leisure and fortune are also difficult to obtain . . . ."[20]

The spiritual teacher Śāntideva also declared:

> Having found the human ship,
> cross over the great river of suffering.
> Fool, there is no time for sleep.
> This ship will be difficult to find again.[21]

A human existence that has been found also does not last very long. As Nāgārjuna declared:

> When this life, which is subject to many harms,
> is even more unstable than a wind-blown bubble of water,
> it is a wonder that one who has exhaled can inhale a breath
> or that one who has gone to sleep can awaken.[22]

Therefore, we must be swift in striving to carry out virtuous acts. If we fail to do so and engage in evil deeds, we will fall into the lower states. As Śāntideva declared:

> Without carrying out virtuous acts
> and while also accumulating evil deeds,
> not even the words "happy migratory state"
> will be heard for even a billion kalpas {329}.[23]

If you should take birth in the lower states, the various kinds of suffering, such as the heat and cold that occur in the hells, is incomprehensibly great. As Nāgārjuna declared:

> The suffering of one who is forcefully stabbed here
> in a single day with three hundred daggers
> does not amount to the total or even a portion
> of a hell being's lighter suffering.[24]

As a hungry ghost, there are many kinds of suffering such as hunger and thirst. As the same text declares:

> Also, among hungry ghosts, unparalleled, incessant suffering
> produced by the failure to obtain what is desired,
> as well as extremely severe suffering produced by hunger,
> thirst, cold, heat, fatigue, and fear, are experienced.[25]

Animals also experience such forms of suffering as eating one another:

> In animal births there are also many kinds of suffering,
> such as being killed, bound, or beaten, and so forth.
> For those deprived of the virtue for attaining peace
> there is also the most horrible suffering of eating one another.[26]

For these reasons, you must strive to abandon committing evil deeds. In addition, if you fail to perform the forms of virtue that constitute the path to liberation, meritorious and invariable deeds may cause you to take birth in the happy migratory states; however, in some forms of the happy migratory states, there is great suffering, and in others, even though there is no overt suffering, after passing away from those states, you will be reborn in such places as the hells, where you will have to experience great suffering once again. As *Letter to a Friend* declares,

> Having obtained very great sensory pleasures in a heavenly realm
> or the blissful freedom from attachment of Brahmā's state,
> one undergoes again the incessant suffering
> of becoming fuel for the flames in Avīci hell.[27]

In short, all of samsara has the nature of suffering. As Lord Maitreya declared:

> And in these five paths there is no happiness,
> just as excrement has no good smell at all;
> that suffering is constant, arising through contact
> with fire, weapons, cold, corrosive salt, and the like.[28] {330}

Therefore, you must strive to liberate yourself from that samsara. As Ārya Nāgārjuna declared:

> Even if your head or clothing should suddenly catch fire,
> you should forgo trying to extinguish it
> and strive to put an end to rebirth;
> there is no other greater aim than this.[29]

Therefore, I urge you to develop a heartfelt form of this thought,

"I shall strive to practice the true dharma in order to liberate myself from samsara."

2. Overcoming Attachment for the Peace That Is Represented by the Extreme of Hīnayāna Nirvana

[The preceptor should establish this quality in the following manner:]

> Although you may liberate yourself from samsara, seeking to obtain the nirvana in which there is no remainder of the heaps[30] and the ability to accomplish the welfare of others undergoes cessation is not a goal worthy of being sought by a Mahāyānist, because it is a form of extreme ignorance in that it resembles an individual who both sees that his mother is being swept away by a river and has the ability to extricate her from that plight but does not do so and chooses instead to remain in a state of ease on dry land. As the spiritual teacher Candragomī declared:
>
> > If one were to set out alone, abandoning those relatives who are in the ocean of samsara,
> > while perceiving that they resemble beings who have fallen into a whirlpool,
> > appearing and disappearing in the ever-turning cycle of birth and death,
> > no one could be more ungrateful than that.[31]
> >
> > Having drunk their breastmilk as a helpless infant
> > while cradled in their arms, and having been cared for with affection
> > as one engaged solely in many, useless acts of misconduct,
> > what person, indeed, even an inferior one, could abandon them here?[32]
>
> Therefore, I urge you to reject the attitude that abandons concern for the welfare of others and seeks to attain the ease of quiescent nirvana for oneself alone.

3. Generating Enthusiasm for the Enlightenment Mind That Is Free of the Two Extremes

As Lord Maitreya declared:

> Having severed completely affection for himself through wisdom,
> A compassionate one does not go toward quiescence, out of affection for all beings.
> Relying thus on wisdom and compassion, the two methods for attaining enlightenment,
> the ārya does not turn toward either samsara or nirvana.[33]

Thus, the goal that you should seek to achieve is the complete nirvana that does not abide in either of the two extremes of samsara and the quiescent form of nirvana, and that is called the state of "a true and complete buddha." This state is one in which all obscurations {331} together with their traces have been abandoned, in which the true nature and the complete range of those entities that need to be known are directly realized, and in which limitless forms of enlightened activity are carried out continuously and with effortless spontaneity. Moreover, the cause for achieving that goal is enlightenment mind. As a verse from *The Collection of Verses on the Perfection of Wisdom* declares:

> Water drops fill a pot little by little,
> gradually, from the first drip to the last.
> Likewise, the first thought is the cause of supreme enlightenment;
> gradually, beings become buddhas who are filled with pure qualities.[34]

Likewise, the *Mahāvairocanābhisambodhi Tantra* declares: "O Lord of Secrets, the root of the Omniscient One's transcendent knowledge is compassion, its cause is enlightenment mind, and it is brought to perfection by skillful means."[35]

The *Gaṇḍavyūha Sūtra* also declares: "O son of good family, enlightenment mind is like a seed in that it gives rise to all the spiritual qualities of a buddha." Therefore, I urge you to generate a sincere and intense aspiration in which you reflect, "I shall generate the mind that seeks enlightenment in order to attain buddhahood for the sake of all sentient beings."

B. Carrying Out the Ritual Activities

This topic is made up of two sections: (1) the ritual activities that relate to aspirational enlightenment mind and (2) the ritual activities that relate to active enlightenment mind.

1. The Ritual Activities That Relate to Aspirational Enlightenment Mind

This section has three parts: (1) preliminaries, (2) main activity, and (3) conclusion.

The preliminaries also include three elements: (1) making supplication to an excellent being, (2) going for refuge to an excellent object, and (3) accumulating merit by means of an excellent method.

i. Making Supplication to an Excellent Being

[The preceptor should state the following:]

> It is written that "After inviting all the buddhas and bodhisattvas of the ten directions, you should make prostrations and present offerings to them. Then you should generate the conception that the spiritual teacher is the Master,[36] and make prostrations to him or her and also present a mandala offering. Following that you should make the following supplication."[37] Therefore, with intense devotion and reverence, {332} you participants should first reflect that through having requested all the buddhas and bodhisattvas of the ten directions to appear before you, they are actually present in the sky before you. Then, with an attitude that wishes to make prostrations and present offerings to them, I direct you to recite the verses from the one that begins with "However many man-lions whatsoever" and continue up to the verse that ends, "I honor and worship all the victors,"[38] while making prostration by touching the ground with the five parts[39] of your body.

Following that, the preceptor should then direct the participants to make three additional prostrations by stating:

> Now, I direct you to make three additional prostrations to the spiritual teacher while forming the conception that he or she is the Master.

Next, the preceptor should instruct the participants to present a mandala offering by saying:

> Next, I direct you to present a mandala offering that should be regarded as a gift for conferring the act of generating the mind that aspires to attain supreme enlightenment.

Having said this, the preceptor should then direct the participants to present a mandala of seven heaps[40] using the usual recitation[41] to which the following words should be added: "This very mandala, which is not deficient in any way, is presented to the guru, as well as to the invited victors and their spiritual offspring, as an offering that accompanies the request to carry out the ritual for generating the mind that aspires to attain supreme enlightenment," and so on.

After having presented the mandala offering in this manner, the preceptor should state:

> With your palms joined, which are also holding flowers, repeat after me the following words three times:
>
> > Just as the former tathāgatas, arhats, true and complete buddhas, as well as the bodhisattvas who abide in the great ārya stages, first generated the mind that aspires to attain unsurpassed true and complete enlightenment, I too, who am named so-and-so,[42] beseech the spiritual teacher to confer the rite in which I shall generate the mind that aspires to attain unsurpassed true and complete enlightenment.

ii. Going for Refuge to an Excellent Object

[The preceptor should give the following explanation:]

> The act of going for refuge that is to be carried out here is that of the Mahāyāna tradition, which is superior to the ordinary act of going for refuge on the basis of three attributes. The attribute of time is that the act of going for refuge is carried out until you reach the seat of enlightenment. The attribute of the object to whom you go for refuge has three aspects: First, that of the buddha is the one whose nature is made of up the three bodies and, second, that of the dharma is that of its two aspects of the dharma of attainment and the dharma of canonical teachings. The dharma of attainment is the Mahāyāna truths of cessation and the path, and the dharma of canonical teachings is the Mahāyāna scriptures. Third, that of the sangha is the community of irreversible ārya bodhisattvas. The attribute of attitude is for you to reflect in the following manner: "All sentient beings {333} have been extremely kind to me in that they have benefited me innumerable times throughout beginningless time. These extremely kind beings truly are deserving of compassion because they have no means of liberating themselves from samsara as they have been afflicted by intense forms of suffering for an immeasurably long time and they are shackled by the bonds of karma and the mental afflictions." Following that, reflect to yourself further, "I must cause these sentient beings to gain all temporary and ultimate forms of happiness, and I must free them from their suffering. However, since I do not currently have the ability to bring this about, and buddhas alone possess this ability, I must attain the status of a buddha. Moreover, since the attainment of this goal depends upon the Three Jewels, I entrust myself to them as the true object of refuge." Finally, generate an intense aspiration that reflects, "May the Three Jewels be cognizant[43] that these are my thoughts."

As a line from *The Ornament of Mahāyāna Sūtras* declares: "That bodhisattva accepts[44] them with a desire for that state;[45] that act should also be known as arising from compassion."[46] Thus, it is said that, since you do not presently have the ability to

> liberate sentient beings from their suffering, you are carrying out the act of going for refuge in the manner of one who is calling out for help, saying, "These kind sentient beings are being swept away by the swift river of the truths of suffering and origination," just as a son or daughter with crippled arms would call out to others for help if his or her mother were being swept away by a river.

[At this point, the preceptor should state:]

> Therefore, I ask you to repeat after me three times, with a mind that is focused one-pointedly and is not distracted elsewhere, the following words that express the act of going for refuge, and that you do so while developing the extraordinary attitude that reflects, "May the Three Jewels please be cognizant that I currently wish to liberate all sentient beings from their suffering and that I wish, in the future, to gain the ability to liberate all sentient beings from their suffering." You should also maintain the awareness that reflects, "I am not a truly existent entity, like an object in a dream or a magically created illusion."

[The words to be repeated are as follows:]

> I beseech the preceptor to give heed to me. I, who am named so-and-so, from this moment on until I sit at the seat of enlightenment, go for refuge to the lord buddhas who are the supreme among all two-footed human beings {334}.
>
> I beseech the preceptor to give heed to me. I, who am named so-and-so, from this moment on until I sit at the seat of enlightenment, go for refuge to the dharma, the state of peace that is free of attachment and is the supreme among all spiritual doctrines.
>
> I beseech the preceptor to give heed to me. I, who am named so-and-so, from this moment on until I sit at the seat of enlightenment, go for refuge to the community of irreversible ārya bodhisattvas, who make up the supreme among all the assemblages of spiritual beings.

Following the repetition of the formula that expresses the act of going for refuge, the preceptor should state:

> After completing the act of going for refuge, the precepts to be observed in connection with this act are that you must generate a strong attitude and carry out actions in which, from today onward, you hold the buddha as the true spiritual teacher, the Mahāyāna dharma as the true path, and the ārya bodhisattvas as companions who will assist you in practicing the path.

iii. Accumulating Merit and Eliminating Obscurations by Means of an Excellent Method

Making Prostrations

[The preceptor should then state the following:]

> Although some scholars assert that only prostrations and offerings are to be performed, the great Lord Atiśa taught that the entire seven-limb devotional practice should be carried out. Therefore, the first act is to visualize the object toward whom the seven-limb practice is performed, which is done in the following manner. Visualize that immeasurable numbers of buddhas and bodhisattvas are present in the sky before you, with the principal figure being the lord who is the great sage[47] and the master of the teaching, who is surrounded by the eight preeminent spiritual sons[48] and the like. Following that, reflect that you and all other sentient beings emanate duplicates of yourselves equal in number to the atoms in a buddha field before this assemblage, including the spiritual preceptor, and that you express great respect with your three doors as you make prostrations to them. It is very important that you repeat the following recitation slowly and in a clear voice. Therefore, make prostrations by touching the ground with the five parts of your body as you repeat after me each of the following verses three times.

The preceptor should then direct the participants to make prostrations as they repeat the following verses {335}:

> I make prostrations to the lamas,
> embodiments of all the buddhas,

those whose natures are that of a vajra holder
and who are the root of the Three Jewels.

I make prostration to the tathāgatas,
lords who are endowed with great compassion,
teachers who are all-knowing,
and fields[49] who are oceans of merit and good qualities.

I make prostration to the tranquil dharma,
which is pure and the cause of freedom from desire;
its virtuous nature liberates beings from the lower realms
and it is the singular and supreme highest truth.

I also make prostration to the sangha,
those who have freed themselves and teach the path to freedom,
those who are highly respectful of the trainings,[50]
the best of fields who are endowed with good qualities.

Presenting Offerings

Offerings That Are Actually Arranged

After having made prostration to the lamas and the Three Jewels in this manner, the second limb, which is that of presenting offerings, is made up of five parts, the first of which is to present the offerings that have been actually arranged. First, the spiritual preceptor should introduce this practice by declaring, "The offerings are to be blessed with their respective vidyā mantras." Then he or she should cause the individual offerings of reception water, flowers, incense, lamps, perfumed water, food, and music, and so on, that have been actually arranged in excellent vessels made of precious gems and the like to be blessed into inconceivably great forms by reciting the mantras: *oṃ varja arghaṃ āḥ hūṃ*, *oṃ varja puṣpe āḥ hūṃ* (etc., up to) *oṃ varja śabda āḥ hūṃ*.

Having blessed the offerings in this manner, the spiritual preceptor should direct the participants to present offerings by stating:

> Reflect that the offerings of flowers, and so on, that are actually arranged on the altar serve as causes from which offering clouds

of divine substances that fills the entire sky are generated. Then reflect that these, as well as all the flowers and other offerings that exist throughout innumerable world systems, are being presented as you recite after me the following mantras:

> *oṃ sarvatathāgata* {336} *arghaṃ pratīccha pūjameghasamudraspharaṇasamaye hūṃ*

This mantra is repeated, as appropriate, substituting for *arghaṃ* the words *puṣpe* (etc., up to) *śabda*. If desired, it is also fitting to present these offerings in combination with the recitation of verses that state, as appropriate: "Emitting light rays as arrays of reception water" and so on.[51]

Offerings That Are Not Owned by Anyone

[The spiritual preceptor should declare:]

> Having taken hold of all the objects suitable to be offered that are not owned by anyone, such as the jewel mountains, wish-granting trees, grain, flowers, medicinal substances, and forests, that exist throughout all the ten directions' myriad, limitless world systems with a mind possessed of great clarity,[52] and having formed the thought "I offer these objects to the buddhas and the bodhisattvas, and I implore you to accept them so that I and all limitless sentient beings may be able to accumulate merit," repeat the following verses after me.
>
> As many flowers and fruits are there are,
> whatever kinds of medicine there are,
> as many jewels as there are in the world,
> and waters that are clear and pleasing to the mind,[53]
>
> mountains made of jewels, and, likewise,
> forest regions that are secluded and delightful,
> vines ablaze with the ornaments of beautiful flowers,
> and trees whose limbs are bent down by excellent fruit,[54]
>
> perfume, incense, wish-granting trees, and trees
> made of jewels in the worlds of gods and others,

ponds adorned with lotuses and filled with geese
whose calls are exceedingly pleasant,[55]

various grains that grow without being cultivated,
and other beautiful objects worthy of being offered
that extend to the limits of the vast realm of space
and all of which are not owned by anyone.[56]

Having grasped these in my mind, I offer them
to those most eminent of sages and their spiritual offspring.
May these supreme ones among those who are worthy of gifts, who possess
great compassion and regard me with pity, accept them from me.[57]

Offering Oneself

[The spiritual preceptor should declare:]

Repeat after me the following verse while reflecting to yourselves, "Offering myself to the buddhas and bodhisattvas {337} as their servant, I shall carry out exclusively their aims of acting on behalf of all sentient beings."

I give myself completely to the victors
and to those spiritual beings born from them.
May these supreme beings accept me.
With devotion, I enter into servitude to you.[58]

Offerings That Are Emanated with the Mind

[The spiritual preceptor should further state:]

As described in the verse that I shall now recite, which begins "In exquisitely fragrant bathhouses . . . ," visualize in a vivid form that a bathhouse appears. Then, after I prompt you by declaring, "I direct you to offer the following acts of devotion to all the buddhas and bodhisattvas," recite the following verses after me, slowly and distinctly.

In exquisitely fragrant bathhouses
with inlaid floors of brightly shining crystal,
dazzling columns aglitter with jewels,
and canopies festooned with shimmering pearls,[59]

with numerous pitchers made from fine jewels
filled with delightfully fragrant water and flowers,
I bathe the tathāgatas and the spiritual beings
begotten by them, accompanied by music and song.[60]

I wipe their bodies with unequaled cloths,
scented and washed free of any stains.
Then, I present to them superb monks' robes
excellently dyed and well perfumed.[61]

I also adorn Samantabhadra, Ajita,
Mañjughoṣa, Lokeśvara, and the rest,
with beautiful, divine, multicolored garments,
soft and smooth, as well as various superb ornaments.[62]

With the finest perfumes whose fragrance fills
all the triple-thousand worlds, I anoint
these lords of sages, whose radiant bodies shine like gold
that has been well-fired, well-burnished, and well-washed.[63]

I worship those lords of sages who are supremely worthy
of being worshiped, with all flowers most fragrant and
delightful,
such as māndārava, blue lotus, jasmine flowers, and the like,
as well as garlands whose shapes are pleasing to the mind.[64]

I perfume them with dense clouds of incense {338}
whose pervasive fragrance is pleasing to the mind.
I also present them an offering of various kinds
of edible enjoyments, and food and drink.[65]

I present jewel lamps arranged in rows
of five situated within golden lotuses.

I also scatter beautiful varieties of flowers
upon mosaic floors anointed with perfume.[66]

I also present to those who have a loving nature
a multitude of palaces that are made beautiful
with brilliant pendulous pearl garlands adorning
all regions and are filled with delightful songs of praise.[67]

I present to those great sages
exceedingly beautiful jewel umbrellas,
studded with pearls and raised up with shafts
made of gold that are pleasing in form.[68]

Dedication of Offerings

[The preceptor should then state the following to the disciples:]

> Repeat after me the following verse once, and as you do so, make the aspirational prayer to please countless buddhas and bodhisattvas with immeasurable numbers of additional varieties of offerings and the aspirational prayer that the realm of space should become filled with masses of offerings and that this cloud of offerings should descend in a great rainfall that alleviates the suffering of sentient beings.
>
> Beyond these, may pleasing clouds
> of offerings remain established for long,
> as well as clouds of music and choral song
> that bring delight to all sentient beings.[69]

Then the preceptor should direct the disciples to recite the Offering Cloud dhāraṇī mantra three times:

> *namo ratnatrayāya bhagavate vajrasārapramardane tathāgatāya arhate samyaksambuddhāya tadyathā oṃ vajre vajre mahāvajre mahātejavajre mahāvidyāvajra mahāvidyābodhicittavajre mahābodhimaṇḍopasaṃkramaṇavajre sarvakarmaviśodhanavajre svā hā*

At this point, if the preceptor desires to make torma offerings, he or she should state:

> This completes the main portion of the offering limb. Now, in conclusion, the spiritual teacher will make a series of torma offerings.

Then, after sprinkling the tormas {339} with holy water, the preceptor should state:

> May the tormas that are situated in vessels made of precious gems and the like and that possess a nature consisting of visible, audible, olfactory, gustatory, and tangible qualities become filled with inconceivably great forms of these sensory attributes.

Then, after blessing the tormas by reciting the mantra *oṃ akāro*[70] (etc.) three times, the first torma should be offered to the gurus and the Three Jewels, while reciting the mantra *oṃ sarva guru buddha dharma saṃgha saparivāra*, to which *oṃ akāro* (etc.) has been appended three or five times. Then the preceptor should recite the following statement of supplication:

> O gurus and the precious Three Jewels, please accept this vast torma offering and enable us, both the preceptor and disciples, to engender in our mental continua uncontrived forms of loving-kindness, compassion, and precious enlightenment mind that we have not previously engendered and to develop to ever higher levels those forms that we have previously engendered.

The second torma should be offered to the dharma protectors in general, by reciting the mantra *oṃ dharmapāla saparivāra*, to which *oṃ akāro* (etc.) has been appended, three times. Then the preceptor should recite the following request for assistance in achieving various desired aims:

> O glorious and adamantine Mahākāla and all the other dharma protectors, as well as the host of worldly gods, nāgas, yakṣas, and spirits who approve of those who are of the virtuous faction,[71] please accept this vast torma offering and carry out favorable activities and lend your assistance in propagating the Buddha's

> teaching, in bringing about extensive virtue and well-being in the world, in preventing the diminishment and promoting the augmentation of precious enlightenment mind in the mental continua of the spiritual preceptor and disciples, and in terminating obstacles.

The third torma should be offered to the ever-abiding local spirit-lords, whom the preceptor is regarding as directly present before him or her, by reciting the mantra *oṃ bhūmipati saparivāra*, to which *oṃ akāro* (etc.) has been appended three times. Then he or she should urge them to perform appropriate activities by reciting:

> I present, offer, and bestow this vast torma offering to all the ever-abiding local spirit-lords, regional spirit-lords, city spirit-lords, and property spirit-lords. Having accepted it, please help to propagate the Buddha's teaching and bring about every form of happiness and well-being through this world system. {340} Having felt joy at and rejoiced in the precious enlightenment mind that is being generated by the preceptor and disciples, please provide your excellent assistance in protecting us from all obstacles.

Confession of Evil Deeds

[The preceptor should state the following to the disciples:]

> Bring to mind and generate intense regret toward all the evil deeds and transgressions that you and all other sentient beings have accumulated in the past, misdeeds that were motivated and caused by the three poisons and that are associated with each of the perpetrators' three doors. Then generate the strong resolve in which you reflect to yourselves, "From now on, I will not commit any evil deeds, even if it puts my life at risk." Following that, reflect to yourselves with great sincerity, "Now, in order to attain buddhahood for the sake of all sentient beings, I shall rely upon the support of the Three Jewels and carry out in a proper manner the practices that serve as the antidotes to evil deeds," and as you repeat after me the following verse, form the conviction that reflects, "By reciting these words that constitute the act of

confessing evil deeds, I have purified myself completely of all my evil deeds."

Whatever evil there is that I have committed
due to the influence of desire, hatred, and ignorance,
and through body, speech, as well as mind,
I confess it all repeatedly.[72]

Rejoicing at Virtuous Deeds

[The preceptor should state the following to the disciples:]

With an attitude that rejoices in a heartfelt manner at all the happiness and virtue roots of āryas and ordinary beings,[73] repeat after me the following verse:

Whatever the merit of beings throughout the ten directions—
of those in training, those no longer training,
the solitary victors, the Buddha's offspring,
and all the victorious ones—I rejoice at it all.[74]

The Request to Turn the Dharma Wheel

[The preceptor should state the following to the disciples:]

Throughout all the world systems that lie in the ten directions, there are buddhas who have attained enlightenment but have not yet begun to turn the wheel of the dharma for such reasons as giving those who request them to do so the opportunity to accumulate merit. Therefore, with an attitude {341} that reflects in a heartfelt manner, "I request those buddhas to turn the wheel of the dharma for the sake of their disciples," repeat after me the following verse:

I beseech all those protectors throughout the ten directions—
who are lamps for the world and who successively awaken
to enlightenment and attain the unattached state—
to set in motion the unsurpassed wheel.[75]

The Supplication Not to Enter Nirvana

[The preceptor should declare to the disciples:]

> Throughout all the world systems that lie in the ten directions, there are some buddhas who, for such reasons as wanting to cause beings to form the conception toward a buddha that he is one of the Three Jewels, form the determination that they will give the appearance of entering nirvana. Therefore, with an attitude that reflects in a heartfelt manner, "I shall supplicate those buddhas not to enter nirvana and to remain for a very long time in order to benefit their disciples who live in that realm," repeat after me the following verse that is a supplication requesting buddhas not to enter nirvana:
>
> Those who wish to give the appearance of extinction
> I supplicate with palms joined to continue living
> for eons equal to the atoms in the buddha fields
> for the benefit and happiness of the entire world.[76]

Dedication

[The preceptor should declare to the disciples:]

> With a mind that reflects, "With the virtue gained in this way through the acts of making prostration, and so on, serving as an example, I dedicate all the virtue roots that I accumulate in the three times as a cause that dispels the suffering of all sentient beings and that also achieves for them every form of temporary and ultimate happiness," repeat after me the following verse:
>
> Whatever slight virtue I have collected
> through honoring, worship, and confession,
> and through rejoicing, beseeching, and supplication,
> I dedicate it all to enlightenment.[77]

With the completion of these forgoing activities, the preliminary stage of the ritual is concluded.

b. The Main Ritual for Generating the Aspirational Form of Enlightenment Mind

[The preceptor should express the following to the disciples:]

As declared in the following verse:

> Regarding this, after first awakening the seed
> of compassion through the efficacy of the lineage,
> the acceptance of enlightenment mind is accomplished
> through the excellence of thought and action.[78]

Therefore, the act of generating enlightenment mind {342} comes about through one's own strength, through the strength of others, and through the strength of spiritual practice. Of these, the first strength derives from the fact that one possesses the Mahāyāna form of spiritual lineage.[79] It can be determined that you disciples possess this lineage by the fact that you have developed the mind that wishes to carry out the act of generating enlightenment mind. The second strength is that the generating of enlightenment mind arises from such factors as hearing about a buddha's spiritual qualities and the benefits of developing enlightenment mind, as well as through carrying out the three activities of hearing, reflecting, and meditating on the Mahāyāna dharma teaching. You disciples also possess some form of these factors. The third strength is for you to form the attitude that the lama is a true buddha, the attitude that you are like an object perceived in a dream or a magically created illusion, and the attitudes of loving-kindness and compassion toward all sentient beings.

Regarding these attitudes, the first one is achieved by reflecting to yourselves, "This lama is the person who enables me to generate the enlightenment mind that is the principal cause for attaining buddhahood. Therefore, I should regard him or her as a true buddha." While it would be best for you to develop the attitude that the lama is a true buddha, if you are unable to do so, you must at least generate the thought "This lama is a bodhisattva who is qualified to serve as the spiritual preceptor for generating enlightenment mind."

The second attitude is achieved by reflecting to yourselves,

"The self is nothing more than an object that is nominally ascribed to the five heaps. The apprehension of a real self is caused by an erring cognition. Therefore, since the self is not a truly existent object, I am like a magically created illusion or an object perceived in a dream."

The following are scriptural citations that describe the third attitude. A verse from the *Essence of the Middle Way* declares:

> Because the enlightenment mind that is adorned
> by great loving-kindness, compassion, and knowledge
> is the seed of a buddha, the intelligent person
> should be fixed upon avoiding its abandonment.[80]

Likewise, *The Ornament of Mahāyāna Sūtras* states about enlightenment mind that "compassion is regarded as its root."[81] The sūtra titled *Bodhisattvapiṭaka* also declares: "Regarding this topic, great compassion is the predecessor[82] to a bodhisattva's conviction to seek enlightenment."[83]

Therefore, you disciples should ascertain the following points by reflecting carefully in this way: Throughout beginningless time, all sentient beings, who are limitless in number, have each been my mothers an incomprehensibly great number of times, at which time they protected me from harm and performed acts that benefited me. With an attitude that cherished me even more than they did themselves {343}, they benefited me in a multitude of ways, ignoring all concern that they might be committing evil acts and ignoring all suffering that they might have to endure. Countless times, they put forth great effort in which they experienced cold, heat, hunger, thirst, exhaustion, and fatigue, and so on, so that I might obtain, or not lose, some form of happiness. If someone were to collect all the tears that they shed because of not being able to bear the suffering of sickness or death, and so on, that I experienced, it would be a greater amount than all the water in the great ocean. Because they have kept me from harm and benefited me in these ways, all these sentient beings are extremely kind.

Following that, generate loving-kindness by reflecting to yourself, "How deeply I yearn for all these sentient beings to gain all temporary and ultimate forms of happiness," and "I shall establish them in those forms of happiness."

[Following that, the spiritual preceptor should instruct the disciples by saying:]

> Now reflect to yourselves how all these sentient beings, despite their desire for happiness, cannot avoid having to experience suffering. Throughout samsara, there is nothing but inconceivably great suffering. For instance, the beings in the hells undergo the suffering of hot and cold; hungry ghosts undergo the suffering of hunger and thirst; animals undergo such suffering as being eaten by one another; human beings also undergo such suffering as birth, old age, sickness, and death; demigods undergo such suffering as doing battle with the gods; and the gods of the desire-realm experience the signs of their imminent death.[84] Even in the two higher realms, those gods experience the suffering of falling from those states and being reborn in such places as the hells.[85]

As the *Sūtra on Closely Placed Recollection*[86] declares:

> Hell beings are harmed by infernal fires,
> hungry ghosts are harmed by hunger and thirst,
> animals are harmed by eating one another,
> humans are harmed by insufficient subsistence,
> gods are harmed by heedlessness—
> there is no happiness at all in samsara,
> not even just that which exists on the tip of a needle.

Another sūtra also declares:

> The desire realm is beset with faults,
> and the form realm is also beset with faults;
> likewise, the formless realm has many faults.

Verses from the vinaya scriptures[87] declare as well:

> On the earth, in divine cities, and in the pathways of the three lower realms,
> living beings are controlled by a desire for samsaric existence and ignorance;
> unaware as they circle among the five migratory states, {344}
> they are like the spinning wheel of a potter.[88]

The threefold existence is ablaze in the suffering of old age
and sickness;
burning with the fire of death, this samsaric realm has no
protector.
Continually bewildered about finding a place of refuge,
the world of beings is like a bee trapped in a jar.[89]

In sum, those sentient beings that perpetually experience nothing but some form of the suffering of suffering,[90] the suffering of change,[91] or the suffering of conditional existence,[92] no matter what form they make take birth as among the six classes of beings that are found throughout the three realms of existence, may wish to liberate themselves from that suffering; however, they are tightly bound by the shackles of karma and the mental afflictions. Moreover, because they are not under the care of spiritual teachers, because they lack virtuous companions who are proceeding toward liberation, and because they are not disciples of the āryas, they do not possess the means by which to become liberated from their suffering. Therefore, they truly are deserving of compassion.

As you reflect in this way, you should be moved to the extent that you feel that the responsibility for the suffering of all sentient beings has fallen upon you. Then cultivate a powerful form of compassion in which you think to yourselves, "How deeply I yearn for all these sentient beings to become free of all their suffering, together with its causes. I must bring it about that they become free of that suffering and its causes."

[The spiritual preceptor should further instruct the disciples:]

Now reflect to yourselves with heartfelt sincerity in the following manner. Although I accept responsibility for establishing all these sentient beings in every form of happiness and for liberating them from all of their suffering, and I do so willingly, not only do I currently lack that ability, even those beings who are superior to me, like Brahmā and Śakra, and those beings who are superior to them, like the śrāvaka and pratyekabuddha arhats, lack that ability.

Who, then, is there that has such an ability? Only a complete buddha who has perfected the two aims possesses this ability. Therefore, I must attain that state of enlightenment. Since the principal cause for doing so is the act of generating enlightenment mind, I shall accept that aspiration.

[The spiritual preceptor should again instruct the disciples:]

Now reflect to yourselves further. After having generated enlightenment mind, it is unquestionably certain that I shall attain buddhahood by training myself in the practices that relate to that goal. After having attained that buddhahood, I shall liberate all sentient beings from the torrents of suffering, I shall free them from the shackles of karma and the mental afflictions, I shall provide them with the relief that frees them from their suffering temporarily, and I shall place them in the ultimate state of nonabiding nirvana {345}.

[Following that, the spiritual preceptor should declare to the disciples:]

Now visualize and reflect to yourself that an immeasurably great assembly consisting of the Great Sage, along with other buddhas and bodhisattvas, are present in the sky before you. As you do so, when you recite the words, "Please give heed to me," generate an attitude of great firmness in which you think to yourselves, "I am certain that these supreme beings cognize me with their transcendent awareness and compassion." Then, while crouching[93] with your right knee upon the ground and with your palms joined together, you must fix your recollection one-pointedly in order to generate enlightenment mind by repeating the following ritual words after me three times.

The spiritual preceptor should prompt the disciples to repeat the ritual for the first time, by saying, "Repeat after me the words of ritual for the first time":

I beseech all the buddhas and bodhisattvas who reside in the ten directions to give heed to me. I beseech the preceptor to give heed to me.

Then, the spiritual preceptor should say, "Now, repeat after me, 'state your name' and the rest:

> By means of whatever roots of virtue having the nature of generosity, morality, or meditation that I, who am named so-and-so, have performed in any of my various past lives, that I induced others to perform, or that I have rejoiced at when they were performed by others, just as the former tathāgatas, arhats, and true and complete buddhas, as well as the bodhisattvas who are great beings that reside on the great ārya bodhisattva stages, generated the mind that aspires to attain unsurpassed true and complete enlightenment, I, too, who am named so-and-so, from this moment on until I reach the seat of enlightenment, generate the mind that aspires to attain unsurpassed true and complete great enlightenment.
>
> I shall deliver those who have not been delivered;
> I shall liberate those who have not been liberated;
> I shall provide relief to those who are without relief;
> and I shall establish all beings who have not attained complete nirvana in that state of complete nirvana.

After that first repetition {346} has been completed, the preceptor should then state:

> Because it is declared that an explanation of how to train one's mind should also be made for each of the second and third times that the ritual is repeated, you disciples should reflect in the following manner: Just as space is limitless, the realm of sentient beings is also limitless. Moreover, each of these limitless number of sentient beings has been my father and mother countless times, and each of these times, he or she has been nothing but a kind person who benefited me in immeasurable ways, just as my current father and mother have, and has protected me from harm to the best of his or her ability. Therefore, in order to repay their kindness, I shall benefit them and keep them from harm.
>
> What then is the means by which to benefit these beings? I

should begin by reflecting on three spiritual attitudes. First, because sentient beings are benefited directly by obtaining happiness and indirectly by performing virtue, I must develop the loving-kindness that reflects, "How deeply I yearn for these kind mothers to obtain happiness and the causes of happiness." Second, because sentient beings are harmed directly by experiencing suffering and indirectly by committing evil deeds, I must develop the compassion that reflects, "How deeply I yearn for these kind mothers to be freed from their suffering and the causes of their suffering." Third, I must also develop the thoroughly pure form of superior attitude[94] that accepts responsibility for achieving these two aims by reflecting, "I shall accomplish this myself."

The preceptor should further state, "After initially reflecting on these points, generate a strong conviction by reflecting in the following manner":

Because the ability to establish all sentient beings in every form of benefit and happiness depends entirely upon attaining the state of complete buddhahood, I absolutely must attain the state of complete buddhahood for the sake of all mother sentient beings. Moreover, since that will not occur without creating the necessary causes and conditions, I must generate the strong conviction that reflects, "The most important of all the causes and conditions is for me to generate the precious enlightenment mind by relying upon the strength of the entirety of whatever roots of virtue I have accumulated. Following that, I must achieve the result that is the omniscient state of a complete buddha by traversing the path of the victors' offspring. Having done so, I shall rescue all sentient beings from the ocean[95] of suffering and free them from the shackles of the truth of origination. I shall also give them relief from the realm of worldly existence and establish them in the great state of nonabiding nirvana.[96] {347}

[The preceptor should then state:]

After generating this conviction, repeat after me a second time the following words of the ritual, and as you do so, develop one-

> pointed faith and reverence as you reflect to yourself, "I am certain that the buddhas and bodhisattvas cognize me directly with their supreme transcendent knowledge."

Following that, the preceptor should recite the wording of the ritual, which begins with "I beseech all the buddhas and bodhisattvas who reside in the ten directions" and continues up to "I shall establish all beings who have not attained complete nirvana in that state of complete nirvana."

[The preceptor should then state:]

> Once again, after first developing immeasurable devotion and reverence toward the lamas and the precious Three Jewels, you disciples should ascertain the following points, by reflecting to yourselves in this way: "Although I and all sentient beings do not truly exist from the standpoint of ultimate reality, in accordance with conventional truth our present circumstances are such that due to our mistaken apprehension of an "I" and a "mine," we experience a great variety of suffering and happiness as entities that resemble magically created illusions and objects that appear in a dream. Further, since we are exactly alike in that we all desire happiness and wish to avoid suffering, I shall, in a temporary sense, give unstintingly all my happiness and whatever roots of virtue I possess to all kind mother sentient beings and I shall take upon myself all their suffering, together with its causes. In an ultimate sense, I shall attain the precious state of a complete buddha and then provide each and every sentient being with all forms of benefit and happiness. To that end, I shall now generate the precious enlightenment mind that is the sole pathway of all the victors and their spiritual offspring.

[The preceptor should further state:]

> In short, since it is very important for you disciples to perform the third repetition of the ritual while maintaining three great thoughts—great faith in the lamas and the Three Jewels, great compassion toward all sentient beings, and the great aspiration that desires to attain buddhahood—I have presented an explana-

> tion of them to you. Now, repeat after me the following words of affirmation slowly and clearly.

Following that, the preceptor should recite the wording of the ritual, which begins with "I beseech all the buddhas and bodhisattvas who reside in the ten directions" and continues up to "I shall establish all beings who have not attained complete nirvana in that state of complete nirvana."

[Then the preceptor should state:]

> With this final repetition, you disciples have developed in your mental continuum the extraordinary aspirational form of enlightenment mind. Therefore, I direct you now to generate the joy that arises from knowing that you have definitely achieved {348} the development of this mind.

c. Conclusion

This concluding portion of the ritual is made up of three parts: (1) generating enthusiasm, (2) explaining the precepts, and (3) presenting offerings of appreciation.

i. Generating Enthusiasm

[Then the preceptor should state:]

> Reflect to yourselves, "Although I have taken on immeasurable bodies in successive rebirths throughout beginningless time, I remain in samsara because I have not achieved anything of great spiritual value. Now, however, I have developed precious enlightenment mind in my mental continuum, an attitude that is the unique cause that will bring benefit and happiness to myself and all other sentient beings. Therefore, this human form possessed of life and endowed with leisure and fortune has found meaning. Because I have become an offspring of the victors, I have accomplished all my aims."

Then the preceptor should prompt the disciples to recite the following verse one time:

Now, reflect well on the words of the verse to follow and generate especially great joy as you repeat after me:

Now my life has become fruitful;
this human existence has been made worthwhile.
Today I have been born into the family of the buddhas;
now I have become an offspring of the buddhas.[97]

ii. Explaining the Precepts

Enlightenment Mind Should Be Generated Again and Again

[The preceptor should state:]

There are five aspects to the presentation of the precepts.[98] Listen to these words of instruction with your full attention. Regarding this topic, the first precept is the instruction to carry out the act of generating enlightenment again and again. A verse from the *King of Concentrations Sūtra* states:

I declare and make known to you
that however much a person reflects on some subject,
to that extent his or her mind will become inclined toward it
by virtue of those thoughts that are fixed upon it.[99]

The spiritual teacher Sharawa[100] also declared, "Develop one-pointed concentration regarding enlightenment mind as much as you can. Moreover, this is the very object to use for practicing meditative absorption in the Mahāyāna tradition."

Therefore, you should generate enlightenment mind again and again by performing the seven-limb devotional practice, the act of going for refuge, and whatever extensive or abbreviated form of the ritual for generating enlightenment mind is suitable to the circumstances. In order to further develop your enlightenment mind, you should at the very least generate enlightenment mind in a heartfelt manner as you recite the following verse three times each during the day and at night:

I go for refuge until enlightenment
to the Buddha, dharma, and supreme assembly.

Through this generosity, and so forth, done by me,
may I attain buddhahood in order to benefit the world.
{349}

Train Yourself in Collecting the Two Accumulations

You should immediately strive to carry out virtuous acts of generosity and the rest and do so with a mind in which the two qualities of emptiness and compassion have been joined together. It is reported that Lord Atiśa declared, "Strive in many ways to perform every form of virtuous act and then dedicate those acts right away to the attainment of omniscience. By acting in this way, your meritorious acts will take on the nature of the wisdom accumulation and your wisdom will take on the nature of the merit accumulation, thereby causing the two accumulations to be inseparably combined, and omniscience is a result that is produced by the two accumulations."

Train Yourself to Abandon Four Qualities and Adopt Four Qualities

You should abandon the four qualities that cause enlightenment mind to be lost and train yourself in the four qualities that prevent it from being lost.[101] The former lamas have held that these two sets of four qualities represent what is to be abandoned and their respective antidotes. Therefore, regarding them, the first quality to be abandoned is that of deceiving[102] one's lama or any person who is worthy of being venerated, which means deceiving such a person by lying to him or her. This occurs, for example, if you are asked about the commission of transgressions, and though you have incurred a transgression, you reply, "I did not commit any." It also occurs if you possess the ability to carry out some virtuous act but you say, "I am unable to do so." The antidote to this quality is to train yourself so that you will not knowingly utter a falsehood even to save your life.

The second quality to be abandoned is that of instilling regret in the minds of others about something that does not need to be regretted. This means either, in a general sense, to cause someone to regret that he or she engaged in some virtuous act, or, especially, to cause a person who has undertaken to pursue the Mahāyāna path to regret having done so. The antidote to this quality is to train yourself in such a manner that when you encourage certain individuals to engage in virtuous activities, you cause them to pursue unsurpassed complete enlightenment, not the stages of the śrāvakas' or pratyekabuddhas' paths.

The third quality to be abandoned is that of uttering words of blame about a bodhisattva in anger. The antidote to this quality is to develop the conception toward all those bodhisattvas who have generated enlightenment mind that they are the Master[103] and to fill the ten directions with statements that express their genuine good qualities, which means to act in the manner that is declared in the following verse from the *Sarvadharmāpravṛttinirdeśa Sūtra*:

> You should bow with your head to all the bodhisattvas
> three times during the day {350} and likewise at night.
> Do not look for the slightest faults in any of them.
> Always carry out the practice in the approved manner.[104]

The fourth quality to be abandoned is that of employing deceitfulness and guile toward any sentient being. The antidote to this black quality is for you to maintain the pure form of superior attitude toward all sentient beings and to train yourself to remain free of deceitfulness and guile. The term "superior attitude"[105] means the desire to provide all sentient beings with every form of benefit and happiness.

Train Yourself Not to Abandon Sentient Beings Mentally

The complete abandonment of the totality of sentient beings occurs when you abandon the mind that wishes to attain buddhahood for the sake of others[106] for such reasons as perceiving the faults of sentient beings[107] or when you make the determination that the Mahāyāna path is too difficult for you to pursue. If you should do so, you will have abandoned both the aspirational and the active forms of enlightenment mind, no matter whether you no longer wish to attain liberation for yourself at all or you maintain the wish to attain the liberation that is pursued by the followers of the śrāvakas' or the pratyekabuddhas' vehicles.

As a verse from *The Collection of Verses on the Perfection of Wisdom* declares:

> Having practiced the ten virtuous karmic paths for ten million kalpas,
> if one should develop the desire to become a pratyekabuddha arhat,
> that person becomes one whose morality is defective and one whose morality is torn asunder;
> the production of this thought is graver than an extreme form of defeat.[108]

A partial form of mental abandonment is for you to mentally reject a certain sentient being or beings by thinking to yourself, "I am obligated and have the ability to benefit this being or these beings, but I refuse to do so." Because this determination also results in the abandonment of the production of enlightenment mind that is directed toward all sentient beings, you should regain the mind that wishes to benefit whatever beings you may have mentally abandoned within a four-hour period,[109] for it is said that even if you do not directly benefit another person, you should make sure to avoid harming your own mind.[110] Therefore, generate the attitude that desires to benefit all sentient beings, as indicated in the following verse:

> Though one lacks the power to carry out acts that benefit others,
> an attitude dedicated to that purpose should always be maintained.
> In whomever such an attitude is present,
> that person is fixed upon that aim of benefiting others.[111]

Recalling the Benefits of Enlightenment Mind

It is declared in the *Gaṇḍavyūha Sūtra* that "enlightenment mind is like a seed for all the spiritual qualities of a buddha." {351} The same sūtra also declares, "In short, however many attributes and virtuous qualities make up all the attributes of a buddha and all the virtuous qualities of a buddha, it should be understood that just as many good qualities and benefits make up the good qualities of enlightenment mind and the benefits of enlightenment mind. Why is that? It is because the entire sphere of bodhisattva conduct arises from this enlightenment mind and because all the tathāgatas of the past, present, and future also arise from this enlightenment mind." These and all the other benefits mentioned there[112] should be recalled again and again.

The following statement is also made in a scripture:[113] "In particular, the person who wishes to attain supernatural knowledge[114] quickly should train him- or herself in the instructions that appear in the Mahāyāna sūtra titled *The Seven Spiritual Qualities Taught in Response to Ārya Avalokiteśvara's Inquiry*."[115] Therefore, you should train yourself in these seven qualities, which make up the subject matter taught in that sūtra: do not even have thoughts about sexual intercourse, much less actually engage in the union of the two sexual organs; do not approach an unvirtuous friend, even in your dreams, and do not assist an unvirtuous friend with a supportive attitude;[116] use wisdom and skillful means to avoid developing pride; abandon the mistaken apprehension of truly existent entities and develop a strong form of the door to liberation of emptiness; conduct yourself in samsara with a mind that regards entities as unreal, like magically created illusions and objects that appear in a dream; maintain a pure form of superior attitude toward all sentient beings; and do not discredit the principles of cause and effect that relate to the doctrine of karma.[117]

If you commit any of the four black qualities or the transgression of abandoning sentient beings mentally and you allow a period of time consisting of one-sixth of a twenty-four-hour day to go by without having corrected the offense, you will have abandoned the production of enlightenment mind. Therefore, after having carried out an act of confession and resolve not to commit the offenses again, adopt enlightenment mind once again by generating it in the same way that you did previously. If you develop the antidote to any of these offenses within the aforementioned period of time, when you carry out the act of confession, all the preliminary and subsequent elements of the act are done in the same way that was described earlier. In addition, it is said that the person to whom confession is made should be a bodhisattva, or if such a person is not available, confession should be made before a person who holds the prātimokṣa vow of a layperson or higher[118] by stating explicitly to him or her, "I committed such-and-such a transgression."

This body[119] of teachings on the act of generating the aspirational form of enlightenment mind {352} has been received exclusively in the system of instruction that has been transmitted orally in a lineage that extends from the Victor Maitreya down to the Lord.[120] Because this method of training the mind, the ritual for generating the aspirational form of enlightenment mind, along with the related precepts, are not found in the treatises of other Buddhist masters, Lord Atiśa has extended a great kindness to the Buddhist culture of Tibet in particular by transmitting this body of instruction, as well as his teachings on the act of going for refuge. Therefore, this teaching on the act of generating the aspirational form of enlightenment mind, together with the related explanations, is said to be the highest of Lord Atiśa's spiritual instructions. Moreover, because it is not limited to a particular type of disciple, it can be given to everyone.

iii. Presenting Offerings of Appreciation

The preceptor should make the following statement:

> Because it is due to the kindness of the lamas and the Three Jewels that you have been able to generate enlightenment mind in this manner, I now direct you, as an expression of your gratitude, to present, successively, the offerings that have actually been arranged, the act of offering oneself, together with the inconceivably great forms of offerings that are emanated with the mind, in the same manner that was done previously during the preliminary activities, while bringing to mind the visualizations of the buddhas and bodhisattvas that were also explained at that time.

After replenishing the offerings that have been actually arranged, the spiritual teacher should bless them, as was done earlier, during the preliminary activities. Then the spiritual teacher and the disciples should present these offerings together, while reciting the series of mantras that begin with *oṃ gurusarvatathāgata arghaṃ* and so on. Following that, they should perform the act of offering oneself by reciting the single verse that begins with the line, "I give myself completely to the victors / and to those spiritual beings born from them . . . ."[121] In addition, the preceptor should direct the disciples to recite once the three verses that begin with the line, "With the best flowers, the best garlands, . . ."[122] In this way, with these final recitations, the ritual for generating the aspirational form of enlightenment mind, together with the ancillary activities, is concluded.

2. Generating the Active Form of Enlightenment Mind

The act of generating the active form of enlightenment mind is described in *The Stage of a Bodhisattva* in connection with acceptance of the bodhisattva vow, and the ritual for accepting that vow is clearly described there as well. Just as the system that is formulated by the great Lord in his own treatise[123] on the ritual also follows *The Stage of a Bodhisattva*, the ritual for conferring the bodhisattva vow that is presented here is also made up of these three sections: (1) the person who accepts the vow, (2) the person from whom the vow is accepted, and (3) the ritual by which the vow is accepted.

a. The Person Who Accepts the Vow

Regarding the three sections of this topic, the first is a description of the person who accepts the bodhisattva vow. He or she should be someone who has already developed the aspirational form of enlightenment mind and who also possesses the firm aspiration {353} to train him- or herself in the bodhisattva training that is made up of the three types of morality. As *The Stage of a Bodhisattva*[124] states in part:

> Regarding this topic, whether he or she is a householder or one who has gone forth into the homeless state, a bodhisattva who wishes to train him- or herself in the bodhisattva training that relates to this threefold heap of morality and who has generated the aspiration to achieve unsurpassed true enlightenment . . . .[125]

The Lord also declared:

> A person who always maintains another vow—
> that is, one of the seven types of prātimokṣa discipline—
> has the good fortune to develop the vow
> of a bodhisattva; otherwise, he or she does not.[126]

b. The Person from Whom the Vow Is Accepted

The second section describes the person from whom the vow is accepted. The preceptor should be someone who possesses the bodhisattva vow him- or herself, who is knowledgeable about the nature of the ritual, and who is capable of conferring the vow with wording that the disciple is able to understand. *The Twenty Verses on the Bodhisattva Vow*[127] declares that the bodhisattva morality:

> Should be accepted . . .
> from a knowledgeable and capable guru
> who is maintaining the vow.[128]

c. The Manner in Which the Vow Is Accepted

The third section, which describes the ritual that represents the manner in which the vow is accepted, is made up of three parts: (1) preliminaries, (2) main activity, and (3) conclusion.

1. Preliminaries

The first part of the ritual has five sections: (1) making a supplication, (2) examining the recipient's attitude, (3) requesting that the vow be given soon, (4) asking about obstacles, and (5) after explaining the precepts, asking about the recipient's willingness to observe them.

1) Making a Supplication

The preceptor should instruct the disciples to make three prostrations by declaring:

> I direct you to make three prostrations to the spiritual teacher after forming the conception that he or she is the Master.[129]

Following that, the preceptor should instruct the disciples to present a mandala offering by declaring:

> I direct you to present a mandala offering as a gift that is made along with your request to receive the vow associated with the act of generating the active form of enlightenment mind.

After the mandala offering has been presented, the preceptor should declare:

> With your palms joined, which are also holding flowers, repeat after me the following supplication three times: "O Spiritual Teacher, I wish to receive from you the acceptance of the discipline of bodhisattva morality. If it causes no trouble, may it please you, in your compassion, to hear me for a brief moment."[130] {354}

2) Examining the Attitude of the Disciples

A) Examining the Strength of the Disciples' Intention

This exercise is made up of three parts, of which the first is for the preceptor to examine the disciples' intention, by making the following statement:

> You must possess the intention in which you think to yourself, "Nothing can forestall or prevent me from accepting the bodhisattva vow." Therefore, since it is said that candidates should be examined by addressing four qualities that qualify them as proper vessels for receiving the vow, I direct you to respond honestly to the following questions that I shall now ask.

The spiritual teacher should then ask this question:

> Since a bodhisattva must spiritually ripen all sentient beings, and he or she must train him- or herself in countless forms of spiritual training in order to do so, are you able to train yourself in all the forms of spiritual training that spiritually ripen all sentient beings?

The disciples should agree by answering affirmatively:

> Yes, I am able to do so.

In the same way, the spiritual teacher should then ask this question:

> Since a bodhisattva must purify countless pure realms and propitiate countless buddhas, are you able to train yourself in such a way that you are able to purify countless pure realms and propitiate countless buddhas?

The disciples should agree by answering affirmatively:

> Yes, I am able to do so.

Next, the spiritual teacher should declare the following, after which another question is asked:

> If you lose your bodhisattva vow, you will have betrayed all those sentient beings whom you promised to establish in a state of ultimate happiness. As a pair of verses from *Entry into the Conduct That Leads to Enlightenment* declare:
>
> It has been declared of even a minor object
> that if someone were to fail to give it
> after having mentally intended to do so,
> that person would become a hungry ghost.
>
> How much worse would it be if after proclaiming loudly and sincerely
> the intention to establish them in unsurpassed happiness,
> I were to betray the entire world of sentient beings?
> What migratory state would befall me then?[131]
>
> When asked, "If the karmic ripening of having broken your word to all sentient beings brings about the grave consequence of being reborn in such regions as the hells, are you not frightened by such a consequence?" you should respond after developing the understanding in which you reflect, "Although a grave consequence will occur if I lose my enlightenment mind, all will be satisfactory if I make certain not to lose it."

The disciples should then agree by answering:

> I am not frightened. {355}

Then, the spiritual teacher should declare the following, after which another question is asked:

> If you are able to observe the training without allowing it to become damaged, another pair of verses from *Entry into the Conduct That Leads to Enlightenment* declare:
>
> > From the moment that one adopts
> > the mind that seeks to liberate
> > an endless sphere of sentient beings
> > with unswerving determination,
> >
> > from that moment on, even while sleeping
> > or in an unmindful state, one will generate
> > many continuous streams of merit
> > that are as vast as space.[132]
>
> Therefore, since cultivating the training brings about such great benefits as producing merit continuously, are you eager to cultivate it with the desire to obtain that great benefit?

The disciples should agree by answering affirmatively:

> **Yes,** I am eager to do so.

B) Examining the Disciples' Level of Understanding

After addressing the disciples collectively with the expression "O sons and daughters of good family," the spiritual teacher should then refer to each of them by their personal names and ask them the following question:

> Have you, who are named so-and-so, heard teachings on the manual of the bodhisattva collection of scriptures?[133]

The disciples should answer:

> I have heard such teachings to a slight extent.

Similarly, the spiritual teacher should ask:

> Have you gained an understanding of the manual of the bodhisattva collection of scriptures?

The disciples should answer by saying:

> I have gained an understanding to a slight extent.

Next, the spiritual teacher should ask:

> Do you have faith in the bodhisattva collection of scriptures?

The disciples should answer this question by saying:

> I have great faith in it.

Lastly, the spiritual teacher should ask:

> Are you able to observe the precepts that are presented in the manual of the bodhisattva collection of scriptures?

The disciples should be prompted to answer affirmatively by saying:

> Yes, I am able to observe them.

C) Examining the Disciples' Aspiration

The spiritual teacher should inform the disciples in the following manner:

> First, you should develop the aspiration that is fixed with one-pointed attention on this determination: "I shall apply myself to the aim of attaining buddhahood, because it is a state in which one possesses spiritual qualities that are beyond measure, such as the ability to liberate all sentient beings from their suffering." Following that, you should respond to a series of questions that I shall ask you.

Then the spiritual teacher should ask the disciples:

> Hear me, O sons and daughters of good family. Do you {356} wish to lead across those who have not crossed over, set free those who have not been set free, comfort those who are in need of comfort, bring to nirvana those who have not reached nirvana, and preserve the lineage of the buddhas?[134]

The disciples should answer:

> Yes, I do so wish.

Following that, the spiritual teacher should instruct the disciples by saying:

> You should generate an enlightenment mind that is firm and make a firm determination regarding that aim.

The spiritual teacher should then ask:

> Are you accepting this discipline out of a sense of rivalry[135] with others?

The disciples should answer:

> No, I am not.

The spiritual teacher should further ask:

> Are you accepting this discipline at the instigation of others?

The disciples should answer:

> No, I am not.

3) Requesting That the Vow Be Given Soon

The spiritual teacher should state the following to the disciples:

> As it is said that the request to be given the vow should be preceded by a presentation of offerings and prostrations, first visualize that the Lord, the Great Sage, and all the ten directions' buddhas and bodhisattvas are actually present in the sky before you. Then, while recalling their immeasurably great qualities of wisdom, compassion, and power, and while having generated intense forms of the three types of faith—that is, clarity of mind,[136] aspirational faith,[137] and belief[138] toward the buddhas and bodhisattvas—I direct you to present to them the offerings that are actually arranged and to perform the act of offering yourselves to them, respectively.

The spiritual teacher should then bless newly arranged offerings in the same manner that was done previously. Following that, the spiritual teacher and the disciples should present the actually arranged offerings together either in an extensive form in which the mantras are accompanied by offering verses or in the more abbreviated manner of just reciting the series of mantras that begin with *oṃ sarvatathāgata arghaṃ pratīccha pūjameghasamudraspharaṇasamaye hūṃ*, followed by the same mantra that is repeated for each offering but that substitutes the words *puṣpe* (etc., up to) *śabda* for the word *arghaṃ*. Following that, the spiritual teacher then should also direct the disciples to recite the single verse that begins, "I give myself completely to the victors / and to those spiritual beings born from them . . ."[139]

Next, the spiritual teacher should say to the disciples:

> You should now make three prostrations to the spiritual teacher after forming the conception that he or she is the Master.

After the prostrations are completed, the disciples should situate themselves in their respective rows in a crouching position, joining their palms, which are also holding flowers {357}. Then the spiritual teacher should say to the disciples:

> Repeat after me the following supplication three times: "O spiritual teacher, please quickly bestow upon me the acceptance of the discipline of bodhisattva morality."

4) Inquiring about Obstacles

[The spiritual teacher should say to the disciples:]

> Since one must abide in the bodhisattvas' spiritual lineage[140] and also have developed the aspirational form of enlightenment mind as the basis for developing the bodhisattva vow, I direct you to answer this question regarding whether you are one who possesses such a spiritual lineage:

Following that, he or she should ask:

> O son or daughter of good family, who is named so-and-so, are you a bodhisattva?

The disciples should answer:

> Yes, I am.

Then, the spiritual teacher should ask:

> Have you generated the aspiration to attain enlightenment?

The disciples should answer:

> Yes, I have generated it.

5) Informing the Disciples about the Precepts and Inquiring about Their Willingness to Observe Them

First, the act of informing the disciples should be carried out. The spiritual teacher should inform the disciples in the following manner:

> While generating extraordinary joy as you reflect to yourselves, "Before long, I shall gain the bodhisattva vow, which is an inexhaustible, immeasurable, and unsurpassed treasure of merit, and the source of all the spiritual qualities possessed by a bud-

> dha," listen to the following words of instruction with your full attention.
>
> The morality of restraint is the volition,[141] together with its seeds, that abandons every form of unvirtuous deed. The morality of acquiring virtuous qualities is the volition, together with its seeds, that desires to accomplish the virtuous acts of the six perfections, and so on. The morality that acts on behalf of beings is the volition, together with its seeds, that desires to accomplish the welfare of all sentient beings. These three forms of spiritual practice are the precepts and the morality that are carried out by all the buddhas and bodhisattvas of the three times.

Following that, the spiritual teacher should state to the disciples:

> You should now answer the following question in which I shall ask you, "Do you wish to accept from me these bodhisattva precepts and these forms of morality?"

Then, he or she should formally ask the question:

> Do you wish to accept from me {358} these bodhisattva precepts and these forms of morality?

The disciples should answer:

> Yes, I do wish to accept them.

ii. The Main Ritual for Accepting the Bodhisattva Vow

The spiritual teacher should begin by stating the following:

> Although, in general terms, the bodhisattva vow is actually caused to arise through voicing your acceptance of the training three times, it is very important for you initially to reflect on and fix in your mind the following points: In an ultimate sense, all entities are completely free of any elaborations as to their being existent, nonexistent, and so forth. Regarding their

conventional nature, a verse from the *King of Concentrations Sūtra* declares:

> Just as an illusionist creates variegated forms
> such as elephant carriages and horse carriages
> but no carriages at all truly appear there,
> realize that all entities are similar to that.[142]

Thus, you should recognize that, while all phenomena appear to exist, they lack any true mode of existence. However, due to their failure to understand this point, all of the six classes of sentient beings that exist in all the regions that make up the three realms of samsara, by being under the control of their mistaken belief that outer grasped objects[143] and inner grasping mental states[144] are truly existent, though they desire happiness, they are unable to obtain it, and though they want to avoid suffering, they are forced to undergo inconceivably great forms of suffering. These beings who lack knowledge of the means by which to achieve happiness and to abandon suffering for themselves have been my father and mother again and again through beginningless time. On those occasions, they strove in many ways to benefit me and provide me with happiness, and they protected me from every form of harm to the best of their ability. In so doing, they thought about and brought to mind nothing other than me. Without exception, they are the kind beings who even gave up their own physical well-being and their own lives on my behalf countless times. Therefore, although it is my duty to free all of them from their suffering and to establish all of them in a state of ultimate happiness, in my current circumstances, I lack the ability to do so. Because only a buddha is able to free all sentient beings from their suffering and establish them in a state of ultimate happiness, I must attain that state myself. Moreover, since it cannot be attained without completing its causes and because the principal cause is for me to generate the bodhisattva vow, after having accepted it, I shall safeguard it everywhere, at all times, and in all my rebirths. {359}

Following that, the spiritual teacher should state:

> Having reflected in that manner, with an awareness that recognizes the lama as Buddha Śākyamuni and yourself as resembling a magically created illusion, fix your mind one-pointedly, and respond to the following question.

Then, the spiritual teacher should ask:

> O son or daughter of good family who is named so-and-so, do you accept from me, a spiritual teacher and bodhisattva who is named so-and-so, all of the bodhisattva precepts and all of the bodhisattva morality—namely, the morality of restraint, the morality of acquiring virtuous qualities, and the morality of acting on behalf of sentient beings—those precepts and that morality that have been observed by all the bodhisattvas of the past, those precepts and that morality that shall be observed by all the bodhisattvas of the future, and those precepts and that morality that currently are being observed by all the bodhisattvas of the present throughout the ten directions, those precepts and that morality with regard to which all the bodhisattvas of the past have trained themselves, with regard to which all the bodhisattvas of the future shall train themselves, and with regard to which all the bodhisattvas of the present are training themselves?[145]

The disciples should receive the vow by answering:

> I do accept all of them.

This exchange completes the first acceptance. Following that, the preceptor should then inform the disciples by stating:

> Because it is declared that a period of meditation on the Mind Training instruction should also be carried out before each of the second and third times that the vow is accepted, you disciples should now reflect in the following manner: "I absolutely must attain the precious status of a complete buddha in order to establish in a state of ultimate happiness and liberate from their suffering all those limitless sentient beings who are my mothers.

> Moreover, since that attainment will not occur without completing the necessary causes and conditions, the principal element among those causes and conditions {360} is for me to accept the precepts and the forms of morality that have been cultivated, are being cultivated, and shall be cultivated by the bodhisattvas and victors' offspring of the three times, and for me to safeguard that discipline in all places, times, and circumstances."
>
> After completing this reflection, you disciples should now listen to and then respond to my question for a second time with a mind that has the greatest enthusiasm for accepting the bodhisattva vow.

Following that, the question about the disciples' willingness to accept the vow and the disciples' acceptance of the discipline should be carried out in the same way as before.

Following that, the spiritual teacher should state the following:

> Once again, you disciples should generate the following understanding: Holding in your mind the three great thoughts—that is, first, the great faith that generates the conception that recognizes the spiritual teacher as the Master and has ascertained that the Three Jewels are the infallible object of refuge; second, the great compassion that desires to benefit and establish in a state of happiness all sentient beings, while recognizing that you and all sentient beings do not possess an essential nature that exists in an ultimate sense, but that, in a conventional sense, you resemble illusory beings and beings that appear in a dream who are experiencing nothing but illusory forms of suffering; and third, the great aspiration that for the sake of all those sentient beings desires to attain the precious state of an all-knowing and complete buddha who does not abide in either of the two extremes—develop the aspiration in which you reflect to yourselves with single-pointed attention, "I shall accept and train myself in every way in the principal cause for attaining buddhahood, which is none other than the bodhisattva vow that forms the foundation of the spiritual training undertaken by all the victors' offspring and that is a limitless treasure of merit and spiritual qualities."

> Having done so, you disciples should now listen to and then respond to my question for a third time.

Following that, the question about the disciples' willingness to accept the vow and the disciples' acceptance of the discipline should be carried out in the same way as before.

Finally, the spiritual teacher should state:

> In this way, through having carried out three times the act of asking a question about the willingness to receive the discipline and stating your acceptance of it, you disciples have definitely developed in your mental continua the actual bodhisattva vow. Therefore, I direct you now to generate the extraordinary joy that arises from knowing that you have definitely achieved the development of this vow.

iii. Concluding Activities

This section of the ritual is made up of five parts: (1) making an announcement,[146] (2) stating a benefit, (3) an instruction to observe secrecy, (4) explaining the precepts, and (5) presenting offerings of appreciation.

I) Making an Announcement {361}

After informing the disciples by saying, "The spiritual teacher shall now carry out a prescribed act," he or she should direct the disciples to remain situated in their crouching position. The spiritual teacher, him- or herself, should then descend from the throne and while standing before the image of Buddha Śākyamuni and facing toward the east, arrange a stick of incense or an incense censer in front of a flower-filled vase that has been placed in an eastern position. Then he or she should make prostration three times toward the east and, while making each prostration, declare, "I make prostration with great reverence to all the buddhas and bodhisattvas of the east." After each of these declarations, he or she should toss a handful of flowers into the eastern direction and make a gesture of offering incense toward the east. Mentally, the spiritual teacher should reflect that he or she has made prostrations before all the victors and their spiritual offspring that reside in the immeasurable number of world spheres that lie in an eastern direction and caused vast cloud-like masses of offerings to rain down upon them.

Following the same procedure, the spiritual teacher should then also make prostrations and present offerings, successively and in an unerring manner, to the three remaining cardinal directions of the south and so on, followed by the four intermediate directions. Then, in place of the downward direction, he or she should do so a second time toward the west, and, in place of the upward direction he or she should do so a second time toward the east.

Following this, the spiritual teacher should kneel by placing his or her right knee on the ground and place his joined palms, which are holding flowers, at his heart. Then, with the fragrance of incense wafting toward the Buddha image situated before him or her and while maintaining a one-pointed aspiration, he or she should toss flowers into the air while making the following announcement:

> The bodhisattva disciple who is named so-and-so has acknowledged three times that he or she accepts the discipline of bodhisattva morality from me, the bodhisattva named so-and-so. I, the bodhisattva named so-and-so, am a witness to this acceptance of the discipline of bodhisattva morality by this bodhisattva disciple named so-and-so, and I announce it to the supreme āryas in the endless and unlimited world spheres that lie in the ten directions who, though beyond our range of vision, possess an awareness whose range of vision perceives all entities[147] everywhere.

After the spiritual teacher has made this statement three times, the spiritual teacher and the disciples should reflect that all the ten directions' buddhas and bodhisattvas, {362} by means of their knowledge-perception,[148] become fully aware of this event[149] and view the disciples with compassion.

Following this, the spiritual teacher should declare to the disciples:

> Because the main portion of the announcement is now completed, I direct you disciples to accompany the spiritual teacher in making three prostrations and, while doing so, to visualize and reflect that you are paying respectful homage to all the ten direc-

tions' buddhas and bodhisattvas by touching your head to their immaculate, lotus feet.[150]

Then, the spiritual teacher should indicate that he or she will lead the recitation of the verses from the one that begins "However many man-lions whatsoever . . ." and continue up to the verse that ends "and extol all the ones who have attained ultimate well-being"[151] and that, while these verses are being recited, both teacher and disciples should make three prostrations to the image of Buddha Śākyamuni.

After the prostrations have been completed, the spiritual teacher should then give directions to the disciples by stating the following:

> I direct you to reflect to yourselves once again, "I shall raise myself and all sentient beings out from samsara," and then rise up quickly and stand with your palms joined and placed on the crown of your head.

While the spiritual teacher and the disciples remain standing, the spiritual teacher should make the gesture of giving protection[152] with his or her right hand and declare:

> This completes the act of making an announcement, together with its related elements.

II) Stating a Benefit

The spiritual teacher should state the following:

> Listen to this with your full attention.

Then he should address each of the disciples by name, {363} preceded by the epithet "bodhisattva":

> Hear this, O bodhisattva, you who are the one named so-and-so. A verse from *The Twenty Verses on the Bodhisattva Vow* declares:
>
> > Thenceforth, for the sake of his or her virtue,
> > he or she is always looked upon

> by the victors and their spiritual offspring
> with favorable thoughts, like a dear child.[153]

As this verse indicates, it is a fact of nature that immediately following completion of the rite of accepting the discipline of bodhisattva morality, a sign[154] will become evident to the buddhas and bodhisattvas of the ten directions' buddha fields, such that they will realize the following: "In this particular buddha realm, a bodhisattva disciple named so-and-so has taken up the acceptance of the discipline of bodhisattva morality from another bodhisattva named so-and-so." And those lord buddhas and bodhisattvas will then turn their attention toward that bodhisattva disciple and regard him or her with a form of spiritual affection in the way that one would a son or daughter or a brother or sister. Through being thought of in this way, it should be understood that this bodhisattva disciple's accumulations of merit and wisdom will increase greatly.

III) An Instruction to Observe Secrecy

Following that, while both the spiritual teacher and the disciples are seated, the spiritual teacher should instruct the disciples to observe secrecy by telling them not to divulge to any persons who lack faith that he or she has accepted this bodhisattva vow. He or she should do so by declaring the following:

> Hear this, O bodhisattva, you who are named so-and-so. You should not declare before any persons who lack faith that you have accepted this bodhisattva vow. This is because, if you were to reveal the nature of the bodhisattva vow to any persons who lack faith, those persons who lack faith would reject the bodhisattva vow due to their lack of faith. By doing so, however great might be the heap of meritorious karma that is possessed by the person who has become established in that bodhisattva vow, those persons who reject the bodhisattva vow would come to possess a heap of demeritorious karma that is equally great. Since a bodhisattva is one who wishes to protect all sentient beings from every kind of suffering, he or she should strive to turn them away from

evil deeds. Therefore, a supremely virtuous bodhisattva should maintain secrecy about having accepted the vow.

IV) Explaining the Precepts

[The spiritual teacher should present the following explanation.]

> It is not sufficient for you simply to accept the vow in this way; you must also abandon those unfavorable qualities that need to be avoided and cultivate those favorable qualities that need to be developed. Moreover, since the ability to do so depends upon knowing what are the actions that should be abandoned and what are the ones that should be adopted, you should learn this topic in detail as it is explained at length in the Mahāyāna sūtras and treatises. {364} However, I urge you here to listen with your full attention to the following abbreviated instruction that is the essence of those detailed explanations.
>
> Regarding the actions that should be abandoned, Master Candragomī declared the following in his *Twenty Verses on the Bodhisattva Vow*:
>
> > Praising oneself and discrediting others,
> > by one who is desirous of gain and honor.
> > Failing to give wealth and the dharma to those
> > who suffer and have no protector due to stinginess.
> >
> > Striking another out of anger and refusing
> > to accept an act of conciliation from another.
> > Rejecting the Mahāyāna and setting forth
> > a counterfeit form of the true dharma.[155]
>
> Regarding these four wrongful acts, they can be carried out on the basis of a lesser, middling, or a great perturbation.[156] Ārya Asaṅga states in *The Stage of a Bodhisattva*:
>
> > A bodhisattva does not lose the acceptance of the bodhisattva system of moral discipline by committing any of these four acts that represent an extreme form of defeat[157] if they are done on the basis of a lesser or middling perturbation.

> However, he or she does lose it if they are committed on the basis of a great perturbation. When the basis for committing any of these acts is such that a bodhisattva does not develop even a small amount of shame and abashment because he or she has engaged continually in these four acts that represent an extreme form of defeat, and due to that lack of shame or abashment, he or she is both pleased with and delights in that conduct, and he or she looks upon that very conduct as a good quality, this should be understood as constituting a great perturbation."[158]

Therefore, if all three of these elements are present when any of these four misdeeds is carried out, it is said to have been committed on the basis of a great perturbation.

The Stage of a Bodhisattva also states:

> In short, there are only two causes that can bring about the abandonment of the acceptance of the discipline of bodhisattva morality: (1) giving up the aspiration to attain unsurpassed true and complete enlightenment and (2) committing an act that represents an extreme form of defeat on the basis of a great perturbation.[159]

A passage from the *Collection of Determinations*[160] states:

> In short, there are four causes that can bring about the abandonment of that bodhisattva vow: first, if a bodhisattva generates a mind having a fixed resolve that is at odds with the mind that accepted the bodhisattva vow; second, if he or she expresses words that convey the intention to give up the bodhisattva practice before a person who has understood those words; {365} third, if he or she commits an offense that consists of all or any one of the four acts that represent an extreme form of defeat on the basis of a great perturbation; or fourth, if he or she causes another person to commit an offense that consists of all or any one of the four acts that represent an extreme form of defeat on the basis of a great perturbation, it is said that he or she has abandoned the bodhisattva vow.[161]

Therefore, the bodhisattva vow can be given up by any of these five causes: abandoning the mind that aspires to attain supreme enlightenment, carrying out any of the four acts that represent an extreme form of defeat on the basis of a great perturbation, carrying out all four of the acts that represent an extreme form of defeat on the basis of factors that are greater than a middling perturbation, developing a negative form of discipline[162] that turns away from the bodhisattva vow, and giving up the training.[163] As such, an individual who incurs any of these transgressions should carry out an act of confession and resolve not to commit the offense again, as well as activities that accumulate merit and purify him or her of prior misdeeds, and then accept the bodhisattva vow once again.[164] As *The Twenty Verses on the Bodhisattva Vow* declares: "The vow should be accepted once again."[165]

If any of the four acts that represent an extreme form of defeat should be carried out on the basis of a middling or a lesser form of perturbation, it is included among the secondary misdeeds. Therefore, if you generate even a small amount of shame[166] and abashment[167] for having committed that act that represents an extreme form of defeat and you turn away from it after having been requested to do so by another person, it constitutes a middling transgression and should be confessed before three or more persons. As the just-cited work states, acts created by "middling outflows should be confessed to three persons."[168] Those acts that represent an extreme form of defeat toward which you develop a strong form of shame and which you turn away from quickly, without needing to be urged to do so by another person, are lesser transgressions. Such offenses, as well as the forty-four secondary misdeeds that are described below, only need to be confessed before one or more persons. As the same work states: "The remaining offenses should also be confessed before one person."[169]

Likewise, *The Twenty Verses on the Bodhisattva Vow* lists forty-four secondary misdeeds[170] in the lines that begin with "failing to perform a threefold worship of the Three Jewels,"[171] which, depending on the nature of the motivation, can constitute either an afflicted offense,[172] an unafflicted offense,[173] or an act that is not an offense.[174] If there is no person available to whom one can make confession regarding these secondary misdeeds, you can become purified of an offense by confessing it in your own mind. This point is indicated in the same work by the line that declares "as afflicted and unafflicted offenses are [confessed] in your own mind."[175] {366} It is also true that in almost all cases, there will be no offense if you are able to greatly benefit other beings through committing any of these acts, and you do so while motivated by loving-kindness or great compassion. The same text also states: "There is no offense for one whose mind is virtuous to commit such acts / out of affection, as well as for one who possesses compassion."[176]

The complete range of the bodhisattva's spiritual training is contained within the three types of morality, as stated in the following passage from *The Stage of a Bodhisattva*:

> Moreover, this threefold morality accomplishes, in brief, three actions for a bodhisattva. The morality of restraint promotes the attainment of the levels of mental stability.[177] The morality of acquiring virtuous qualities promotes the ripening of a buddha's qualities in oneself. The morality of acting on behalf of sentient beings promotes the spiritual ripening of sentient beings other than oneself. These actions constitute the full extent of everything that a bodhisattva needs to accomplish. That is to say, mental stability is needed for one to abide in a state of ease in this life, and a person whose body and mind are not weary is able to ripen a buddha's qualities in him- or herself and is able to ripen other sentient beings. This is the full extent of a bodhisattva's morality.[178]

Therefore, since all the forms of training that are to be carried out by a bodhisattva are included in these three types of morality, you should strive diligently to train yourself in all three of them.

In addition, you should undertake to carry out those virtuous activities that will benefit both you and others in your future lives, even if doing so requires you or them to endure suffering in this life, and you should also prompt others to act in this same way. You should carry out those activities that bring both benefit and happiness in this and future lives. You should abandon those activities that bring happiness in this life but are causes for suffering in future lives, and you should cause others to abandon them as well. As *The Twenty Verses on the Bodhisattva Vow* states:

> That which both benefits and is pleasant should be done,
> as well as that which benefits though it is painful.
> What is harmful, even though pleasant, indeed should not
> be done,
> whether it is by others or oneself.[179]

All the activities and entities that ought to be abandoned and that ought to be pursued in keeping with this model should be learned properly from such works as *The Stage of a Bodhisattva* and then cultivated while maintaining recollection and vigilance in all circumstances. {367} As the great master Śāntideva declared:

> One who desires to safeguard the training
> should safeguard the mind diligently.[180]

He also states in another verse:

> To those who wish to guard their minds
> I make this appeal with palms joined:
> even when your life is at risk, you must observe
> both recollection and vigilance.[181]

Therefore, you should cultivate the training well while maintaining recollection[182] and vigilance.[183]

V) Presenting Offerings of Appreciation

[The spiritual teacher should say to the disciples:]

> Since the ability to gain the acceptance of the bodhisattva vow in this manner is due to the kindness of your lama and the Three Jewels, it is now time for you to express your appreciation by honoring them through making prostrations and presenting offerings. Therefore, I direct you to begin by performing prostrations

> in which you touch the ground with five parts of your body while reciting once the group of four verses that begin with the phrase "However many man-lions whatsoever . . ." and so forth.[184]

Following that, excellent fresh offerings should be arranged and blessed in the same manner as was done previously. Then the spiritual teacher should state the following to the disciples:

> I direct you to offer successively the actually arranged offerings, the act of offering oneself, and the other myriad mentally emanated cloud-like offerings and, as you do so, to bring to mind the visualizations that relate to each of these three offerings as they were explained earlier.

The actually arranged offerings should then be presented by reciting either just the series of mantras *oṃ guru sarvatathāgata arghaṃ* and so on[185] or the mantras accompanied by offering verses[186] in whichever form is appropriate.

Following that, the spiritual teacher should direct the disciples to perform the act of offering oneself by reciting the single verse that begins "I give myself completely to the victors / and to those spiritual beings born from them" and so on,[187] after which they should present the mentally emanated offerings by reciting the single verse that begins "With excellent flowers," and so on.[188]

[Next, the spiritual teacher should state:]

> After performing the acts of making prostrations and presenting offerings to both the lama and the Three Jewels jointly, I now direct you to make three prostrations to the spiritual teacher in particular, after recalling his or her great kindness and forming the desire to show respect.

After the disciples have been prompted to perform three prostrations, the spiritual teacher should direct them to stand up and, while bowing, state the following:

> Your kindness is indeed great.

C. Establishing the Nature of the Ritual

The spiritual teacher should state the following:

> The third principal section of this treatise, which is to establish the overall nature of the ritual, is made up of these divisions: (1) the causes that give rise to the aspirational and active forms of enlightenment mind; (2) the essential nature of these two minds {368}; (3) their divisions; and (4) their benefits that yield both temporary and ultimate results. However, as the first three divisions are taught extensively in such sources as the collection of extensive Mahāyāna discourses, the victors' offspring Ajita's[189] *Ornament of Mahāyāna Sūtras*, venerable Ārya Asaṅga's *Stage of a Bodhisattva*, and the great master Candragomī's *Twenty Verses on the Bodhisattva Vow*, these first three topics should all be learned by studying those writings. But since the benefits of generating these two forms of enlightenment mind should be explained during the ritual if it is performed in its most extensive form, I shall now explain this topic here to a limited extent.

4. The Benefits of the Aspirational and Active Forms of Enlightenment Mind That Yield Both Temporary and Ultimate Results

A verse from the aspirational prayer in the sūtra titled the *Chapter on Maitreya's Queries* states:

> I pay homage to the enlightenment mind
> that turns one away from all the lower realms,
> directs one toward the path to an elevated state,
> and leads one to freedom from old age and death.[190]

Several verses from the *Sūtra on the Householder Vīradatta's Queries*[191] also declare:

> If the merit of enlightenment mind
> were to become form,
> after completely filling the realm of space,
> there would be an excess of even more.

> Between a person who would give
> to the guardians of the world
> buddha fields filled with excellent jewels
> equal in number to the sand grains of the Ganges
>
> and a person who, having joined the palms together,
> would turn his or her mind to enlightenment,
> the latter form of worship is superior
> and one that has no limit.

A logical reason that proves that limitless merit derives from enlightenment mind is stated in these lines from the *Jewel Garland*:

> Since the realm of sentient beings is limitless,
> the wish to benefit them is also such.[192]

The *Sūtra on Sāgaramati's Queries* declares:

> The mind that seeks complete enlightenment, upholding the dharma,
> practicing the dharma, and compassion for sentient beings—
> these four entities possess unlimited good qualities;
> the Victor did not declare that they have a limit.

The *Sūtra on Siṃha's Queries* also declares:

> One should turn the mind toward enlightenment
> in order to liberate all sentient beings.
> This act causes the acquisition of spiritual qualities
> and through it {369} one will also come to be held dear.[193]

The Gaṇḍavyūha Sūtra also declares:

> O son of good family, ... Enlightenment mind is like a seed for all the spiritual qualities of a buddha. It is like a field in that it causes virtuous qualities to grow in all the beings of the world. It is like the earth in that it is relied upon by the entire world. . . . (etc., up to) It is like a father in that it protects all bodhisattvas. . . . It is like Vaiśravaṇa[194] in that it completely cuts off all poverty. . . . It is like the king of wish-granting gems in that it accomplishes all aims. It is like

> the auspicious vase in that it fulfills all wishes. . . . It is like a spear in that it defeats the enemies of the mental afflictions. It is like armor in that it protects you from improper forms of attention. It is like a scimitar in that it cuts off the heads of the mental afflictions. . . . It is like an axe that cuts down the tree of the mental afflictions.[195] It is like a weapon in that it protects you from all sudden attacks. It is like a hook in that it pulls out those who are immersed in the waters of samsara. It is like the sphere of wind in that it scatters all obscurations and hindrances. It is like a summary in that it includes all the conduct and aspirational prayers of a bodhisattva. It is like a caitya shrine[196] to be worshiped by all the world, which is made up of gods, humans, and demigods. O son of good family, such are the benefits of enlightenment mind, and it is possessed of immeasurable other special good qualities as well.

Another text also states:

> A wise person who cultivates enlightenment mind
> worships the victors and their spiritual offspring.
> This is a faultless flower that is
> extremely fragrant and beautiful.
> This method brings the buddhahood
> of a supreme victor before long;
> moreover, the desired results will also be attained.[197]

Ārya Nāgārjuna wrote:

> If you and the world desire {370}
> to attain unsurpassed enlightenment,
>
> its roots are an enlightenment mind
> as firm as the great king of mountains,
> compassion that reaches every quarter,
> and the wisdom that avoids the two extremes.[198]

In addition, you should develop an extraordinary form of sure understanding regarding the many points that have been taken from the sūtras and taught in such works as *Entry into the*

> *Conduct That Leads to Enlightenment.* Having done so, you must then strive to carry out the method that is a lotus flower of benefit and happiness for yourself and others, which is brought into supreme bloom by the sunlight of excellent activities that are accomplished by practicing properly the elements of the trainings that relate to abandoning wrongful activities and adopting virtuous ones, as they have been explained.

Some traditions explain that a mandala offering of appreciation should be presented at this point. While it would not be improper to do so if desired, it is also acceptable not to present it since extensive prostrations and offerings of appreciation were previously made.

Next, the spiritual teacher should make the following concluding statement:

> Having carried out all the activities in the forgoing manner, the sole pathway for all the tathāgatas of the three times and the entry point for the limitless spiritual offspring of the victors—that is, the ritual for generating the mind that aspires to attain supreme enlightenment according to the system that follows the Buddha's Exceedingly Vast Mahāyāna Discourses—a system that holds that the act of generating the aspirational form of enlightenment mind and that of accepting the bodhisattva vow in connection with the act of generating the active form of enlightenment mind are to be performed separately, has now been completed in accordance with the practices of the spiritual teachers and masters that make up this spiritual lineage.
>
> Since we must seal the immeasurable heap of merit that has been gained by explaining and listening to the dharma with an act of dedication in order to prevent it from being destroyed over time and to make it ripen in the form of a cause for bringing about a buddha's great awakening, I ask you to direct your thoughts to the collective virtuous act of performing prayers of dedication and aspiration.

Speaking in general terms, a dedication prayer of whatever length is appropriate should be carried out. Alternatively, the spiritual teacher should make the above statement from "Since we must seal . . . ," (etc., up to) "great awakening," followed by the words: "I ask you to make a prayer that combines the acts of dedication and aspiration." Then an extensive prayer of dedication and aspiration such as the esteemed *Aspirational Prayer for Excellent Spiritual Conduct* or the *Maitreya Aspirational Prayer* should be recited. In any case, at the very end, a recitation of verses of auspiciousness from a sūtra should be accompanied by the tossing of a shower of loose flowers into the air.

At this point, I would like to add some brief supplementary remarks. As explained above, when only the ritual for generating the aspirational form of enlightenment mind {371} is performed, it is not necessary for the participants to have previously taken any of the seven forms of the prātimokṣa vow or for them to be examined with regard to being suitable vessels. Since it is permissible to confer that portion of the ritual upon all those who wish to attend, when a ceremony for generating enlightenment mind is being given to a large gathering of persons, it should be limited to the act of generating the aspirational form of enlightenment mind.

In connection with that, where the text states above "the ritual for generating enlightenment mind and for accepting the bodhisattva vow," you should substitute just the words "the ritual for generating enlightenment mind," and where the text states "ascertaining the nature of the person who is able to generate enlightenment mind and accept the bodhisattva vow," you should substitute just the words "ascertaining the nature of the person who is able to generate enlightenment mind." Also, when you reach the section that is titled "Carrying Out the Preliminaries," you should perform all the sections as far as the section titled "Presenting Offerings of Appreciation" that relate to the act of generating the aspirational form of enlightenment mind. Following that, the concluding statement should be revised with the following words: "Having carried out all the activities in the forgoing manner, . . . the ritual for generating enlightenment mind, together with the subsidiary elements, according to the Mahāyāna System of Great Vastness has now been completed. Since we must seal the immeasurable heap of merit that has been gained by explaining and listening to the dharma . . . ," and so on. Then the event should be concluded with the recitation of a dedication prayer.

If the spiritual teacher is conferring the bodhisattva vow in conjunction with the act of generating the active form of enlightenment mind to a special group of spiritual aspirants, they should, in general, possess all the defining characteristics that were explained in the section titled "The Person Who

Accepts the Vow." In particular, it would be most excellent if the candidates have listened to and gained an understanding of a number of Mahāyāna sūtras or, if that is not possible, then that of *The Stage of a Bodhisattva* or *The Compendium of Training*. It is also essential and important that they receive the oral transmission blessing that is received by hearing the recitation of a sūtra such as the *Jewel Cloud Sūtra*[199] or *Akāśagarbha's Queries*.[200] Even if the disciples have previously listened to teachings such as the Stages of the Path or Mind Training, which address the meanings that are expressed in Mahāyāna doctrine, it is absolutely necessary for them to have received the oral transmission blessing gained through hearing the recitation of at least one Mahāyāna sūtra that contains the sacred wording by which that doctrine is expressed. Similarly, the preceptor should be heedful about following the traditional stages of the ritual just as they were explained above and not attempt to perform the ritual in some arbitrary manner, such as by adding tantric elements or carrying it out in a more simplified form, as that would cause him or her to incur the immeasurably grave offense of treating the dharma with contempt.

Since a person who is abiding in the spiritual system associated with the acts of generating enlightenment mind and accepting the bodhisattva vow must train him- or herself in the Mahāyāna path, he or she should learn the summary of the stages of the path that were described by Lord Maitreya in the following two verses from *The Ornament of Mahāyāna Sūtras*, in order to open the door to the wisdom that understands the elements of which it is composed:

> Spiritual lineage, devotion to the dharma,
> likewise, generation of enlightenment mind,
> practice of generosity and the rest,
> and entry into the state of flawlessness,
>
> the spiritual ripening of sentient beings,
> the purification of a buddha field,
> nonabiding nirvana {372}, supreme awakening,
> and the revealing of the path.[201]

Initially, the individual who possesses the fortunate person's support[202] of the Mahāyāna spiritual lineage,[203] as well as the signs of its having been awakened in him or her—namely, compassion, devotion, patience, and enthusiasm for carrying out virtuous activities, and the like—should apply him- or herself with inseparable devotion to this Buddhist spiritual tradition. Then, after having gone through both the door that provides entry to the teaching in general, which is the act of going for refuge, and the door that provides entry to the Mahāyāna path in particular, which is the act of generating the mind that aspires to attain supreme enlightenment, by practicing the six perfections of generosity and the rest, which serve to ripen oneself spiritually, and by striving, as much as possible both in states of meditative composure and in post-meditative states, to cultivate the four means of attracting a following that ripen other sentient beings spiritually, he or she will develop a mind that naturally avoids being led away from the dharma. Then, as his or her mental exertion[204] directed toward faith, renunciation,[205] meditation, and the like, increases naturally and without any sense of irritation, in the manner that a goose alights joyfully onto a lotus pond, such an individual will have given rise to the initial forms of the lesser stage of the accumulation path[206] in his or her mental continuum.

Following that, by striving to practice the path in order to develop such qualities of an ārya bodhisattva as flawless one-pointed concentration and the purification of a buddha field, the practitioner will initially attain a small degree of clear appearance[207] regarding the meaning of the four truths.[208] Through the combined strength of having meditated on the just-mentioned accumulation path and having collected the various forms of virtuous accumulations, the preparation path further consists of realizing that the five heaps are like magically created illusions and gaining progressively stronger forms of clear appearance regarding the selflessness of entities. The seeing path[209] arises when the true nature of the two types of selflessness[210] is directly perceived for the first time. The path of meditation[211] is characterized by the continuous cultivation of that extraordinary form of one-pointed concentration and entry point to the transcendent path, following its initial perception. Finally, the path beyond training[212] is the point at which the practitioner has reached a state of perfection regarding everything that needs to be known and everything that needs to be abandoned.

Moreover, regarding these paths, the realization of transcendent knowledge on the seeing path and the initial attainment of the first ārya bodhisattva stage occur at the same time. Following that, after having completed the ninth ārya bodhisattva stage, one enters the ocean-like tenth stage, called the Dharma Cloud,[213] in order to attain the path beyond learning. In short, regarding these stages and paths, a bodhisattva achieves the five paths on the basis of the ultimate form of enlightenment mind,[214] {373} which is to say that the wisdom aspect of meditating upon emptiness constitutes the material cause[215] and the means aspect of cultivating great compassion constitutes the cooperating condition.[216] Likewise, the ten stages are achieved on the basis of the conventional form of enlightenment mind,[217] which is to say that the means aspect of compassion is the material cause and the wisdom that realizes emptiness is the cooperating condition. Upon attaining buddhahood, the perfection of the path is represented by the dharma body and the perfection of the stages is represented by the form body. The result of having perfected the stages and paths in this manner is for one to avoid abiding in either of the two extremes—that is, a buddha's great wisdom prevents one from abiding in the extreme of samsara and great compassion prevents one from abiding in the extreme of quiescent nirvana. The expression "supreme awakening" refers to the fact that a buddha's spiritual qualities take effect spontaneously. Moreover, it is a certainty that a buddha's enlightened activity of teaching the path to the entire sphere of sentient beings will occur uninterruptedly for as long as space continues to exist.[218]

By the good deed of having clearly explained in this way the excellent path of the bodhisattvas that is the ritual method
for generating the mind and accepting the vow, according to the Mahāyāna System of Great Vastness,
may I quickly attain the omniscient state possessed of a marvelous body, mind, and activities
that through great wisdom transcends worldly existence yet through compassion does not fall into the extreme of peace.

Through writing this work, I have fulfilled the wishes of the master of the entire teaching, the dharma king of the three realms, the glorious Sakya spiritual teacher Jampel Zhönu Ngawang Dorje Rinchen Tashi Drakpei Gyaltsen Pel Zangpo. I have also composed it with the positive attitude of wanting to benefit other spiritual seekers. Through the kindness of the many spiritual activities carried out according to the dharma by my supreme spiritual mentor, I, Jamyang Khyentse Wangpo, an ignorant and dull-witted itinerant Buddhist monk who has listened to teachings on many Mahāyāna scriptural systems, have composed it at the lama's residence called Tharpa Tse Labrang,[219] located at the glorious Ewam Chöden Monastery, a place where many jewel-like spiritual qualities can be obtained, adorning it in a logically consistent manner with passages taken from the writing of that splendor of excellence, the Victor's offspring Asaṅga. May this work, by the power of giving rise to an uncontrived form of the precious enlightenment mind in my own mental continuum as well as those of other beings, serve as a cause that brings about extensive benefits both to the teaching and to all sentient beings.

The lineage for generating enlightenment mind and attaining the pure bodhisattva vow according to the tradition known as the Mahāyāna System of Great Vastness is as follows: The true and completely enlightened Buddha, Lord Maitreya, Ārya Asaṅga, Master Vasubandhu {374}, Ārya Vimuktisena, Bhadanta Vimuktisena, Paramasena, Vinitasena, Master Haribhadra, Kuśalī the Elder, Kuśalī the Younger, the master from Suvarṇadvīpa Dharmakīrti, the glorious Lord Atiśa Dīpaṃkara, the Victor Drom Tönpa, Chenga Tsultrim Bar, Geshe Jayulwa, Gyalse Charchenpa who is also known as Mumenpa, Dro Tön Dutsi Drak, Sangye Gompa Senge Kyap, Chim Namka Drak, Khenchen Senge Kyap, Khetsun Sönam Yeshe, the bodhisattva Sönam Drakpa, Gyalse Tokme Zangpo Pel, the great adept Buddhaśrī, Ngorchen Kunga Zangpo, Khedrup Pelden Dorje, Khenchen Könchok Tsultrim, Gorumpa Kunga Lekpa, Jamyang Khyentse Wangchuk, Je Wangchuk Rabten, Khenchen Ngawang Chödrak, Jamgön Kunga Sönam, the latter's son Sönam Wangchuk, Lhakang Khenchen Döndrup Leksang, Morchen Kunga Lhundrup, Nesarpa Lekpai Jungne, Sachen Kunga Lodrö, Muchen Sönam Pelsang, Muchen Chönyi Yeshe, Muchen Yeshe Gyaltsen, Yongzin Rinpoche Lodrö Gyatso, the glorious Sakya master Jamgön Lama Ngawang Dorje Rinchen, and the omniscient Jamyang Khyentse Wangpo, and the latter, in his great kindness, extended the teaching to me.[220]

Alternatively, a second lineage is the same as the previous one down to the bodhisattva Sönam Drakpa, then from him to Butön Rinchen Drup, Tukse Rinchen Namgyal, Khenchen Drupa Sherap, Paṇchen Gendun Drup, Duldzin Lodrö Beba, Paṇchen Lungrik Gyatso, Je Kyabchok Pel, Wensapa Losang Döndrup, Khedrup Sangye Yeshe, Paṇchen Losang Chögyen, Drungpa Tsöndru Gyatso, Tapukpa Damchö Gyaltsen, Drupkangpa Gelek Gyatso, Purbuchok Ngawang Jampa, Yongzin Yeshe Gyaltsen, Shenyen Losang Gyaltsen, Gyalse Sempa Chenpo Rinchen Losel Tenkyong, and the true Mañjughoṣa Khyentse Wangpo, and by him it was conferred upon me.

Or yet a third lineage is the same as the first one down to Gyalse Tokme Zangpo, then from him to Lochen Jangchup Tsemo, Depön Lochen Drakgyal, Bodong Paṇchen Chokle Namgyal, Jamling Paṇchen Sönam Namgyal, Serdok Paṇchen Shākya Chokden, Paṇchen Dönyö Drupa, {375} Jetsun Kunga Drölchok, Khenchen Lungrik Gyatso, Jetsun Kunga Nyingpo, Gyaltsap Yeshe Gyatso, Je Yönten Gönpo, the great adept Gönpo Peljor, the incomparable Gönpo Drak, lord of adepts Gönpo Namgyal, Rikzin Jamyang Gyatso, the all-seeing Trinle Shingta, Mokchokpa Kunga Gelek, Kunga Lhundrup Gyatso, Je Kagyu Tenzin, Lama Karma Lhaktong, and the lord of adepts Karma Norbu, and by him, in his great kindness, it was granted to me.

May auspiciousness prevail at all times!

13. {429} Opening the Door to the Dharma

The Initial Method of Training One's Mind in the Mind Training Tradition of the Stages of the Path to Enlightenment[1]

Chenga Lodrö Gyaltsen

{430} *namo gurubuddhabodhisattvasapārivarebhyaḥ*

(Homage to the gurus, buddhas, bodhisattvas, and their retinues.)

hitasukhaścākarabuddhadeśavardhani prasarahukuru maṃ

(I beseech them to cause the Buddha's teaching that is the source of all benefit and happiness to thrive and proliferate.)

sarvasattvaṃ ca mahāsukhasukhikarakuru maṃ

(I beseech them to cause all sentient beings to experience the happiness of great bliss.)

adhitiṣṭhatu māṃ

(I beseech them to bestow their blessings upon me.)

The title of this work is: *Opening the Door to the Dharma: The Initial Way to Train One's Mind in the Mind Training System of the Stages of the Path to Enlightenment*

I make prostration and go for refuge to the immaculate lotus feet of the supreme lama who is inseparable in nature from the ten directions' buddhas and bodhisattvas.

I bow respectfully to my lama along with the divine beings,[2]
who attained every form of excellence
while their lotus feet were respectfully venerated
by such preeminent beings of the three realms
as the World's Progenitor[3] and the Thousand-Eyed One.[4]
Prompted by affection for those who strive after the dharma
and those who practice the dharma wholeheartedly,
I shall present methods of practicing the true dharma
that are adorned by passages from sūtras and treatises,
and by the guidance of the lamas—instructions
that will captivate the attention of the wise.
Having bowed respectfully, listen with a one-pointed mind.

{431} (A verse from the *Garland of Birth Stories* states: "When one carriage has formed a path on the ground, / that enables the next one to proceed with greater assurance, and likewise with others. / My mind does not wish to reject this salutary earlier path / in order to establish a wrongful road."[5] Just as it is said that this initial way to train the mind is of indispensable importance because it will be impossible to achieve success in any other desired form of spiritual practice if one fails to develop this element of the Mahāyāna system for mind training—that is, the one that is to be explained below—all spiritual teachers have also declared this very point with a single voice. Therefore, I shall explain how it can be established using all the methods of scriptural authority, reasoning, and direct experience.)

My precious lama,[6] whose essence is that of all the three times' buddhas, said that on this occasion when a precious human form endowed with leisure[7] and fortune has been obtained, you must derive as much spiritual value[8] from it as you can. In order to do that, you should consider to yourself, "What difference is there between my own way of thinking and an animal's way of thinking? An animal is able to think to itself, 'I must obtain the happiness that is freedom from cold and hunger.' If my own way of thinking is no better than that, then I am no different from an animal." Therefore, it is important to derive true spiritual value from this life.

Regarding this aim of deriving value from one's human life, the first thing that must be done is to overcome attachment for this life. *The Secret General Tantra* declares:

A wise person enters the mandala
For the sake of the next world
and after having developed utmost faith {432}.
He or she does not long for this life's fruits.

("This life's fruits" means such forms of happiness as gain, honor, fame, and the like.)

One who longs for what is of this life cannot have
the same desire for what is of the next world.
However, a person who strives after the next world
gains abundant fruits of this life.[9]

As Jowo Je,[10] the great spiritual being and singular divine being, was about to pass away, the yogi Chaktri Chok[11] asked him, "Please tell me what I should meditate on after the Lord has passed away?"

(Jowo Je possessed spiritual qualities that in their totality are beyond description. He was a great paṇḍita who was proficient in the five branches of learning; he had attained one-pointed concentration, various forms of supernatural knowledge, and miraculous powers and was watched over by many tutelary deities and so on. He also founded many temples in India, Tibet, and Nepal, and he propagated the Buddha's teaching extensively during the seventeen years that he stayed in Tibet. He lived until the age of seventy-three. Atiśa's major Indian disciple was the paṇḍita Kṣitigarbha. He had many other disciples, including King Nayapāla. In Tibet, his major disciples were the trio of Khu, Ngok, and Drom,[12] with Gönpawa[13] making a fourth. There were also the Four Yogis: Jangchup Rinchen,[14] Sherap Dorje,[15] Chaktri Chok,[16] and Chakdar Tönpa.[17] The two disciples Gönpawa and Jangchup Rinchen also helped to found Radreng Monastery.[18] Among his many other disciples were the royal monk Jangchup Ö;[19] the great translator Rinchen Zangpo;[20] Gya Tsöndru Senge;[21] the one from the Naktso clan;[22] the translator from Ma, Gewe Lodrö;[23] Zhang Yerpawa;[24] and Rinchen Lama.[25] All the limitless spiritual qualities of these individuals can be learned from their respective biographies. Such texts as the account of Ramding Mawa's liberating deeds[26] state that Atiśa, Potowa,[27] and Ramding Mawa were all tulkus.[28] The sūtras declare that an inconceivably great number of emanations of buddhas and bodhisattvas have appeared in Tibet. They would have to be emanation bodies in order to have had such limitless extraordinary physical qualities. If they were not emanation bodies, it would not be possible to say that emanation bodies exist.)

The Lord replied, "Cast off and abandon all evil actions." Chaktri Chok then asked, "Well then, please tell me what I should teach," to which the

Lord gave the same answer. When Chaktri Chok further asked, "Should I teach some of the time and meditate some of the time?" the Lord still gave the same response. When Chaktri Chok asked, "What, then, should I do?" the Lord replied, "Mentally abandon this life."[29] It is said that Chaktri Chok {433} kept this instruction in his mind, and dwelt away from others like a wild animal among the juniper trees of Radreng, living out his life without so much as coming face to face with another human being.

(It is stated in the account of Götsangpa's[30] liberating deeds that Chaktri Chok was Milarepa's previous birth.)

Tönpa Rinpoche[31] said to a certain monk who was circumambulating a monastery, "Venerable one, it pleases me to see that you are making circumambulations, but it would please me even more if you were to practice dharma." This led the monk to think, "Perhaps it would please him if I were to make prostrations." But when he did that, Drom Tönpa again said the same thing to him. Likewise, Drom Tönpa also said it about the activities of scriptural recitation and meditation practice. So the monk asked, "What, then, should I do?" to which Drom Tönpa repeated three times, "Mentally abandon this life."

Since Tönpa Rinpoche had renounced all worldly activities, when he was invited to Rong to attend a "gold assembly,"[32] he summoned the disciple named Pelgyi Wangchuk[33] and told him, "This time you should go to this event. I can't go because I have renounced worldly activities." He usually wore an old torn garment. Sometimes, he would wear one that was tattered and patched. Since his two shoulders were exposed, he would drape an upper covering over his right and left shoulders. Then, sometimes as he walked into the juniper forest, or while leaning on a walking stick, he would recite:

> Knower of the world, be indifferent to and expel
> from your mind the eight worldly concerns—
> the ones called gain, loss, fame, dishonor,
> pleasure, pain, praise, and scorn.[34]

(This verse, composed by Master Nāgārjuna, is from *Letter to a Friend*.)

On some occasions, he would recite these lines:

The fetters of gain and honor are not fitting
for me, a person who yearns for liberation.[35]

At times, he would recite these passages in full; on other occasions, he would stand and nod his head[36] while reciting just the first few words or just the first half. {434} He said that he did not recite these lines for his own benefit; rather, he did it to instruct his followers.

Chengawa[37] also cultivated indifference to the eight worldly concerns while reciting these lines of verse. Therefore, you should abandon as if they were poison the reactions that are referred to in the formulation of the eight worldly qualities, which are to become pleased when you experience some form of happiness in this life and to become displeased when you experience some form of suffering and so on, as well as all the worldly activities and affairs of this life.

Moreover, the reason for this can be explained as follows: What makes deeds virtuous or unvirtuous is exclusively a function of the mind; ordinary physical and verbal deeds are morally indeterminate.[38] Therefore, since all the activities and conduct that are carried out on the basis of a desire for happiness, well-being, fame, and honor in this life or a desire to avoid suffering, disrepute, and the lack of honor are motivated by desire, hatred, or ignorance, the majority of such a worldly person's deeds are unvirtuous in nature. As such, all activities that are motivated by those mental afflictions, such as the livelihoods of farm work, the selling of merchandise, and money lending, as well as the behavior of engaging in physical conflicts and disputes, or seeking to defeat your enemies and support your allies, even the activities of hearing, reflection, and meditation upon the dharma, are nothing more than causes that bring continued rebirth in samsara and the lower states.

This is described in the following verses from the *Collection of Uplifting Sayings*:

Entities are preceded by the mind.
The mind is their preeminent factor;
they are impelled swiftly by the mind.
A person who speaks or acts with a wicked mind
will therefore be followed by suffering,
like the wheel that severed a head.

> Entities are preceded by the mind.
> The mind is their preeminent factor;
> they are impelled swiftly by the mind.
> A person who speaks or acts with a pure mind
> will therefore be followed by happiness,
> like the shadow that trails after you.[39]

Acts that are carried out with a wicked mind—that is, by any of the three poisons—will give rise to suffering, like one of two beggars who, in anger, said, "I wish I could cut off the heads of these members of the sangha." Not long after, he was decapitated by the wheel of a wagon while sleeping by the side of a road. The other beggar developed {435} faith toward the sangha and said, "I wish I could offer divine nectar to the sangha." Through the great amount of merit that he gained from having expressed this thought, the shadow of a tree under which he had gone to sleep in the morning still had not moved by the afternoon, which resulted in his being chosen as the successor to a wealthy merchant.[40]

Moreover, while the act of taking another being's life that is done intentionally is almost always an evil deed, because the leader of a group of merchants named Mahāsattva[41] was motivated by great compassion when he killed a certain wicked human being, not only was his act not an evil one, it was an extraordinary means by which he accumulated merit. This and other related points are addressed frequently in the *Teachings for the Sons*.[42] You can also understand this point if you observe what takes place in the world. For example, if you give food, drink, and the like, to others in a contemptuous manner, in addition to the absence of joy associated with the act itself, it can be seen that this will also lead to unhappiness in the future. On the other hand, if such objects are given with devotion and respect or with compassion and the like, it can be seen that such an act will generate extraordinarily great feelings of joy. Therefore, since it is evident that all such experiences are governed by characteristics of the mind, this is why it is important for you to keep yourself from giving rise to desire for the happiness of this life and, if it should arise inadvertently, for you to strive to abandon it.

The Lord Atiśa also declared, "If the root of a plant is poisonous, its branches and leaves will also be poisonous. If the root of a plant has medicinal properties, its branches and leaves will also be medicinal. In the same way, if the root cause of an act is desire, hatred, or ignorance, whatever is done will be an unvirtuous deed."

Geshe Tönpa asked Atiśa, "What are the results of acts that are carried out from a desire for happiness, honor, and the like in this life?"

(Drom Tönpa Rinpoche was born in the north in a region known as Tar or Tsakye. He served Lord Atiśa for eighteen years. Tārā prophesied that he was a great spiritual being who would uphold the teaching. He possessed limitless spiritual qualities of the scriptural and cognitional aspects of the dharma, one-pointed concentration, and visions of tutelary deities. Under the tutelage of Lama Setsun,[43] and other spiritual teachers, he trained his mind extensively in the three baskets of canonical scriptures. He founded Radreng Monastery. He had many great spiritual sons, such as the Three Brothers.[44] The entire body of the Kadam lineage descended from him. After founding Radreng Monastery, he lived there for seven years. He lived to the age of sixty-one.)

Atiśa replied, "The results will be to obtain those very things."

Drom Tönpa then asked, "What will the results be in future lives?" to which Atiśa declared, "They will be to be born in the hells {436}, as a hungry ghost, or an animal."

Geshe Gönpawa[45] said the following:

(Gönpawa was one of Drom Tönpa's four great spiritual sons; his ordination name was Wangchuk Gyaltsen. He was born in Kham into a family of the Dzeng clan. He lived almost to the age of seventy. He possessed limitless spiritual qualities of one-pointed concentration, miraculous powers, and supernatural knowledge, and the like. He helped to found the monastic seat of Radreng. The great spiritual son Gönpawa's four principal spiritual sons were Kamawa,[46] Neusurpa,[47] Dre Kode Lungpa,[48] and Nyen Namowa.[49] He had many other disciples, including Kharak Gomchung.[50])

> Regarding actions that are done with an attitude influenced by any of the eight worldly concerns, if you experience any of the four desired results, (that is, (1) gain and honor, (2) fame, (3) praise, and (4) happiness) those results will be limited to this life; they will not benefit you in future lives. If you experience any of the four results that are not desired (that is, the opposite of those previous four), they will not even benefit you in this life.

As Master Nāgārjuna declared:

> Attachment, hatred, and ignorance, and the deeds
> that arise from them are unvirtuous.
> Avoidance of attachment, ignorance, and hatred,
> and the separate deeds that arise from them are virtuous.[51]

A verse from a sūtra also declares:

> The world is brought forth by the mind,
> yet the mind does not see the mind.
> Deeds are accumulated by the mind,
> whether they are virtuous or unvirtuous.[52]

A pair of verses from *Entry into the Conduct That Leads to Enlightenment* state:

> Tigers, lions, elephants, and bears,
> snakes and all one's enemies,
> likewise, all the guards in the hells,
> female imps, and malignant demons—
>
> all of these become restrained
> by restraining one thing, the mind.
> By subduing one thing, the mind,
> all beings also become subdued.[53]

Several more lines also state:

> Those who have not cultivated this secret of the mind,
> which comprises the entirety of the dharma's value,
> seek to overcome suffering and attain happiness,
> yet they wander in vain throughout space.[54]
>
> Except for the austerity of guarding the mind,
> what use to me are many other austerities?[55]

Therefore {437}, whatever action you take, it is important to examine your motivation. An individual who undertakes any activities ranging from farming to practicing meditation with a desire to attain any of the three results of happiness, enjoyment, or fame in this life is called "a person devoted to this life" and he or she is no different from an animal. An individual who practices dharma or worldly activities with a desire to attain rebirth as a god or human being, and so on, in a future life is called "a lesser person."[56] Moreover, all the activities done by such a person serve only as causes for the continuation of samsara. An individual who desires to free him- or herself from samsara in its entirety and who practices the dharma after having developed aversion,[57] fear, and alarm regarding all samsaric activities carries out virtuous deeds that serve exclusively as causes for attaining liberation from samsara. Such an individual is called a "middling person."[58] All the actions that are not done merely to liberate oneself, but rather to liberate all sentient beings, serve as causes for attaining the status of a fully enlightened buddha. The person who acts is this manner is called a "great person" or a "supreme person.[59]"

Therefore, since all three types of lesser, middling, and great persons are defined solely on the basis of their respective minds, the spiritual activity of abandoning what is wrongful and adopting what is proper is carried out in relation to one's mind and, at the very outset, the very first activity that all dharma practitioners must accomplish is that of mentally abandoning attachment for one's current life by rejecting all desire for the well-being of this life. Without having rejected this desire, one does not deserve to be referred to as a dharma practitioner, since, as explained earlier, whatever one does from a desire for the well-being of this life is almost always conduct that is the very antithesis of dharma,[60] and thus it is not conduct that constitutes dharma practice. For example, since a horse lacks the defining attributes of a lion, one does not call it a lion. Therefore, this act of abandoning one's current life mentally is the starting point for the dharma. It is the first dharma practice and the first and earliest aim to be formed by a dharma practitioner.

As the Lord of Reasoning[61] stated:

(This epithet refers to Gyamawa, whose ordination name was Tashi Gyaltsen.[62] He was a descendant of the Gyer lineage. He took up residence at the monastic seats of the Lower Complex of Sangpu,[63] Lang Tang,[64] and Gyama Rinchen Gang.[65] He possessed the three qualities of learning, moral discipline, and kindheartedness[66] and was also renowned for limitless spiritual qualities of one-pointed concentration and supernatural knowledge. He had many great spiritual sons, such as Yakde Paṇchen[67] and others. He was also a dharma teacher in the Sakya tradition. He lived to the age of sixty-two.)

> Despite not having mastered a single form of dharma practice,
> you {438} vainly regard yourself a dharma practitioner. Oh, what a fool!
> Examine your mental continuum to see whether or not you possess
> the first dharma practice of having abandoned this life mentally.

Lama Yegönpa[68] also declared:

(This master founded Ölna Monastery[69] in the Tö region of central Tibet. He was a great spiritual son of Yakde Paṇchen.)

> Now I have lessened my long-standing attachment to homeland.
> I have shown the disinterest[70] of the back of my head to friends.
> I have developed satisfaction, the antidote to desire for wealth.
> This is the first advice for one who has renounced all worldly acts.[71]

Thus, whether or not you have practiced dharma in the past, to determine whether or not you will succeed in practicing the dharma now, examine whether or not you have mentally abandoned the qualities associated with this life's prosperity—which is to say, your homeland, family and friends, food and wealth, and so on. It is said that the translator Marpa gave the following parting advice to Jetsun Milarepa, who was leaving to visit his homeland:

> O spiritual son, if by having failed to abandon this life mentally,
> you mix together the affairs of this life and the true dharma, that
> very circumstance means the dharma has already been lost.
>
> O son, you must reflect on samsara's suffering.
> If I were to emanate a hundred tongues
> and explain for the unimaginable duration

of ten million kalpas, "Such is samsara's nature,"
I would not be able to describe it in full.
Don't waste the true dharma that I have taught you.

(Venerable Milarepa's limitless spiritual activities are elucidated in the account of his liberating deeds.[72] His actual names were Töpa Ga[73] and Dorje Gyaltsen.[74] He was from the region of Gungtang. He achieved the supreme spiritual attainment and lived to the age of eighty-four. His two spiritual heirs were Dakpo Lhaje[75] and Rechung Dorje Drak.[76] His great spiritual son who was the principal lineage holder of his teachings was Dakpo Lhaje. The five spiritual sons born of his breast[77] were Rechung Dorje Drak, Nyenchung Repa,[78] Ngendzong Tönpa from Chenlung,[79] Drigong Repa from Tamö,[80] and Seben Repa from Dotra.[81] His eight close spiritual sons were Repa Zhiwa Ö,[82] Repa Sangye Kyap,[83] Repa Tsapuwa,[84] Repa Dorje Wangchuk,[85] Zhengom Repa,[86] Rongchung Repa,[87] Kharchung Repa,[88] and Lengom Repa.[89] His six outer cotton-clad ones were Likor Charuwa,[90] {439} Wortön Gendun,[91] Kyotön Shākgu,[92] Dampa Gyakpuwa,[93] Seben Tönchung,[94] and Dreben Tashi.[95] The following spiritual song was sung as instruction to Repa Zhiwa Ö.)

Jetsun Milarepa also sang:

Son, if your desire to practice divine dharma[96] is heartfelt,
if you've developed a faith that is profound,
if you don't turn around and look back on this life,
and if it's true that you want to be my follower,
attachment to family is how Māra[97] pulls you back.
Don't regard them[98] as real; cut that entanglement.
Food and wealth are Māra's spies.
It is bad to associate with them; abandon that craving.
Sensory enjoyments are Māra's shackles.
They are certain to enchain you; give up that attachment.
Youthful companions are Māra's daughters.
They are certain to deceive you; exercise great caution.
Your homeland is Māra's prison.
It is difficult to escape from it; be quick to flee.
As you must one day leave all this behind and pass on,
it would be worthwhile for you to abandon them now.
If you listen to and practice the words this man has spoken,
you, son, will enjoy the good fortune of divine dharma.

Dakpo Lhaje declared the following:

(The ordination name of the dharma lord from Dakpo was Sönam Rinchen. He took vows within the Kadam tradition and studied extensively with the great lama Jayulwa,[99] as well as Chakri Gongkawa,[100] Nyukrumpa,[101] and others. He attained one-pointed concentration that could be maintained for more than ten days. Later, he met Milarepa and received consecration into the two stages of Highest Yoga Tantra. He possessed limitless miraculous powers and supernatural knowledge. He founded Gampo Monastery.[102] He had many great spiritual sons, including Je Pakmo Drupa,[103] the spiritual heir Dakpo Gomtsul,[104] the realized adept Use,[105] Je Barompa,[106] the realized adept and yogi Chöyung,[107] and others.)

> Appearances that seem benign cannot last permanently.
> The borrowed illusory body quickly disintegrates.
> Wealth and property are deceptive illusions that are a cause of suffering.
> Your homeland is Māra's prison and a source of confinement.
> Whoever remains attached to these things will wander about in samsara.
> Uproot samsara's innermost essence, the false apprehension of a self.

The Precious One Potowa[108] said:

(Potowa, Chengawa, {440} and Puchungwa were known as the Three Brothers.[109] Together with Khamlungpa,[110] these four were known as the Four Faces of the Kadam Tradition. Potowa, who was Geshe Tönpa's disciple, has limitless spiritual qualities. He gave expositions on major Indian treatises. He was considered to be an emanation of an ārya elder.[111] He lived to the age of seventy-nine and is credited with having caused nearly two thousand monks to abandon attachment for their current lives. He had ten great spiritual sons, two of which were like the sun and the moon and six of which were like the six stars in the Kṛttikā[112] constellation. The first two were Langri Tangpa[113] and Sharawa.[114] The six were the two of Tulku Ramding Mawa[115] and Nang Dreu Lhepa;[116] the two from Nyal, Nyalpa Chöbar[117] and Bünpa Lhaje;[118] and the two from Lo, Bande Tsenchungwa[119] and Rok Marzhurpa.[120] In addition, there were two who were skilled at compiling Potowa's oral discourses and who arranged the *Edifying Similes*[121] [that Potowa used when teaching]—namely, Po Drapa[122] and Drak Karwa.[123] Rok Marzhurpa is apparently the same individual who was also known as Jangsem Yangepa.[124] This latter individual, whose ordination name was Sherap Gyatso,[125] composed the *Blue Udder*.[126] That work and the *Edifying Similes* were widely disseminated.)

The fist of death, a hitching stake, overwhelmed by fear of water;
a yak's crupper, difficulty of *i*, wrapped in wet leather;
shooting an arrow a long distance with a bow, a hundred things
that are said with the mouth.[127]

The Fist of Death

If a person who is about to die is holding an object like a needle or thread in his or her clenched fist, it will not be possible to remove the object from that person's grasp after he or she has died.[128] Similarly, a person who clings to the happiness of this life with the clenched fist of death will not be able to free him- or herself from that attachment and will therefore not be able to develop a genuine dharma practice.

A Hitching Stake

Not seeing that it has been tethered to a stake driven into the ground, at first a calf that runs will travel as far as the length of the rope. But then, when the rope holds it back, the calf will move in a circle around the stake repeatedly until the entire rope gets wrapped around the stake leaving the calf's neck pressed against it and preventing the animal from being able to stand up. Similarly, a person who wants to practice dharma at first may be in a rush to do so, but then it will be seen that the hitching stake of attachment to the concerns of this life, such as food and clothing, will not allow him or her to make any progress, causing the person to return to a spiritually helpless state.

Geshe Selshe

A monk named Geshe Selshe died after having created discord within a monastic community.[129] Geshe Tönpa said of this: "If my disciple Geshe Selshe had died three years earlier, he would have died a master of the three baskets.[130] Unfortunately, he died three years too late." This act was carried out at his {441} Töpur[131] Monastery. If you are able to abandon any of the three— small, medium, or great—forms of the "hitching stake" of attachment, there is no reason for your dharma practice not to succeed.

Overwhelmed by Fear of Water

It is said that it will suffice to free a young goat whose teeth have become caught in its matted fur by making grunting sounds like a wild dzo.[132] It is also said that there is no need to tie up kid goats with a rope that is meant for cattle. However, when you are trying to get horses or cattle and the like to cross a river, if you don't send them into the water straight away without giving them an opportunity to hesitate, when the current begins to pull them, they will refuse to continue moving forward. If you try to push them, they will resist and try to come back toward the near shore. Also, if a young goat doesn't want to drink water and you try to force it to drink by pushing its face down into some water, this will only cause it to thrash about and try to keep the water from even touching its body.[133] Likewise, it is explained that if you don't forcefully put a stop to your attachment to this life in order to pursue the dharma, you won't be able to abandon your attachment, and then even if someone tries to encourage you to practice, you will react by voicing objections. Moreover, this attachment will even destroy whatever spiritual training you may have carried out in the past.

A Yak's Crupper

If the crupper under the tail of a yak is fastened too tightly, it will create a sore and the load the yak is carrying will become unstable. Similarly, it is explained that if you are unable to let go of your attachment to this life, you will create difficulties for everyone, both yourself and others. However, if you learn how to loosen your attachment to this life, your practice will be successful, and you will not be adversely affected by hardships.

The Difficulty of Voicing *i*

The simile "difficulty of *i*" means that when you start to sing a song and so on, at first it is difficult to voice the sound *i*. But if you are able to draw out the sound of the first part, after that it will be easy to go on with the rest of the song. Likewise, it is difficult to mentally abandon this life when you are first starting to practice dharma. But once you succeed in abandoning this form of attachment, your practice will become much easier.

Wrapped in Wet Leather

There is a saying, "The most difficult thing to give up attachment for is the sense objects. If you don't think that's true, then give them up! We Khampas[134] do not speak falsely to one another." True spiritual beings[135] declare with great emphasis, "If you mentally abandon this life, there is no reason for your dharma practice not to succeed. But this is very difficult to accomplish. So roll up all your effort into one and apply yourself to this aim." However, we keep a closed mouth about this teaching and look for some other "high" teaching. In the end, we fail to achieve anything of genuine spiritual value.

There is also the simile of a person who has been wrapped in wet leather. At first, that leather will appear to be loose, but after it dries out it will cause pain because the leather will bind the person so tightly that he or she cannot move. But if that leather is stripped away with a sharp knife, the person will become extremely happy. Likewise, the following lines from the *Collection of Uplifting Sayings* declare:

> Compared to regard for jewels, earrings, children, {442}
> or wives, by one whose mind is highly impassioned,
> āryas do not say that a fetter made of iron,
> wood, or *balbaja*[136] grass is one that is strong.
>
> But although the fetter of desire may seem loose,[137]
> āryas say it is difficult to free oneself from that.[138]

As these lines indicate, if you have attachment for the sensory objects of this life, this attachment may seem at first to be loose; however, it can become evident when a critical situation is encountered that you will be completely unable to overcome this attachment and may even be willing to abandon your vows. Therefore, in order to free yourself from attachment to this life, you must make yourself someone who possesses the sharp knife of wisdom and the strong nape[139] of faith.

It is said that freeing yourself from attachment to all five sense objects in general is difficult. But, among them, freeing yourself from the two objects of food and clothing are particularly difficult. Moreover, between those two, attachment to clothing is only one-fourth or one-fifth as strong as attachment to food. Therefore, attachment to food is the one that is especially difficult to free yourself from.

Shooting an Arrow a Long Distance with a Bow

An example of acting in an unsuitable manner is the following: When fighting in a war, it might be uncomfortable for an archer to wear a helmet if he is trying to shoot arrows with a bow. Since it wouldn't help for him to remove his leggings, it is the helmet that he must make every effort to remove. Then, after placing the target right in front of him, the archer shoots his arrow a long distance away. Similar examples are when, after a thief has run off into the woods, you go looking for him in a meadow or when a harmful spirit is staying in an eastern direction, but the ransom effigy[140] is cast toward the west.

While all the situations in which individuals do not succeed in their dharma practice are actually due to the failure to abandon this life, such persons typically and mistakenly claim that it is due to not having been able to carry out some high form of dharma practice. This explanation can be observed to be very accurate.

Nowadays, most scholars of Buddhist philosophy, persons who consider themselves great meditators, or other followers of the Kadam tradition want to know what the main obstacle is that prevents them from being able to dissolve the ordinary airs into the central channel or they want to learn about other similar highly advanced forms of spiritual practice. But the number of such individuals who are interested in investigating how success in these advanced practices depends upon "lower"—[that is, more fundamental]—elements of spiritual practice are, in fact, rarer than the daytime stars.[141] My own thought is that I would prefer to investigate those forms of spiritual practice that are indispensable for me right now rather than other high levels of realization and abandonment that I have not previously been able to practice more than one or two days. I consider these individuals to be like a person who is on the verge of starvation during a famine that goes to the home of a wealthy and generous individual, and instead of being brought food and drink that is essential to him or her right now, that needy person is brought such things as gold and silver {443} that could only be thought of as being of benefit at some later time.

A Hundred Things That Are Said with the Mouth

When persons from the Kham region tell a story, they say a hundred things with the mouth and stroke the "tail"[142] a thousand times, but then they tell the story in brief, saying, "This is the meaning of what I'm saying." Similarly, the master[143] said that whatever form of listening, reflection, or meditation you may carry out, if you fail to develop a genuine form of dharma practice, it is because you still have desire for the happiness of this life. O fellow practitioners, this spiritual teacher's statement is one that definitely has meaning for everyone.

For those of us who want to practice dharma during these current degenerate times, whatever we might say we want to learn—whether it is one of the Buddha's extensive discourses or we want to receive oral recitation blessings of many scriptural texts—all these statements can be summed up thus: "I don't currently have any particular spiritual goal that I am trying to achieve or any particular obstacle to my spiritual practice that I am trying to abandon. Therefore, what I actually think I need to apply myself to is some form of practice that will enable me to mentally abandon this life." All fellow practitioners, this is precisely the kind of teaching that we need. No other will be of any genuine benefit.

[Another group of similes includes the following:]

> A grouse, next to your threshold, a fox and a weasel.

A Grouse

The simile of a grouse[144] refers to a story in which a weasel[145] caught hold of a grouse by the neck in a ravine at the edge of a body of water. When the grouse flew to the far side of the water,[146] the weasel said, "I have killed a grouse that was like a *dri*[147] whose milk has dried up. I have permanently eliminated a dangerous resting place from the homeland." Similarly, it is said that when a person whose short-sightedness is limited to this life enjoys sensory pleasures, this causes him or her to completely eliminate the opportunity for achieving the higher states and liberation.

Next to Your Threshold

The simile "next to your threshold" means that when preparing to travel from here[148] to India, you shouldn't only take precautions about dangerous precipices that lie at a distance of more than a hundred *yojana*[149] from home because failing to exercise proper care about a precipice that lies "next to your threshold"[150] can cause you to fall into that one and die. Similarly, at the beginning of your spiritual path you shouldn't only investigate teachings about forms of realization and abandonment that pertain to high spiritual stages and paths, because failing to exercise proper care about the dangerous precipice of attachment to this life will cause you to fall into that precipice and have to experience the suffering of the three lower realms. Therefore, as it is said, "Though you may desire a deep thumb depression, you must be careful about the base of the depression."[151]

A Fox and a Weasel

The expression "a fox and a weasel" should be understood as follows. A fox is skillful at burying things; it can even bury a small stone behind itself. A weasel is skillful at covering things; it can even cover up a blade of grass. Because a lynx is skillful at hiding, it knows how to hide inside a crevice no larger than a horse's tail. Likewise, the quality of short-sightedness that focuses just on this life makes a person skillful at concealing things {444}, skillful at covering things, and skillful at hiding. It is taught that even someone who is said to possess all three attributes of learning, discipline, and kindheartedness, or the three attributes of listening, reflection, and meditation, or who is said to be a renunciate[152] that has given up all ordinary activities can become subject to the short-sightedness that focuses just on this life.

[Another group of similes includes the following:]

> The moon, livestock are superior, and the two can't exist together.

The Moon

"The moon" refers to a story in which the son of a person from the Zhok Lungpa region died. The father said that because his son's death was due to the moon's harmful astrological influence, he would exact revenge on the moon. So on the night of the fourteenth day of the lunar month, he made a plan to go to the top of a mountain at a place where the moon would appear. Then, on the night of the fifteenth day, he went to the mountaintop with a bow and arrow, but when he arrived there the moon had disappeared behind the far side one of the peaks, causing him to say, "Bah! This encircling wall of mountains sent the moon a message." Likewise, the Master said, "After thinking, 'I must practice dharma,' whatever activity you may carry out, such as the three of listening, reflection, and meditation, you will only end up being even farther away from the true dharma and never be able to meet with it."

Because mistakenly regarding this life as permanent will cause you to remain under the influence of a single fault, even if you possess a hundred good qualities, those efforts will not be of any benefit to your future lives. Therefore, if you remain attached to this life and don't think about your future lives, even an instruction that has been explained conclusively by a buddha or any other spiritual teacher will not benefit you. As Sharawa said, such behavior is no different from that of an animal. Potowa said, "If you only are concerned about being hungry but you never have any concern about dying . . ."

Livestock Are Superior

The expression "livestock are superior" can be understood as follows. If someone who is knowledgeable about this life is considered a clever and effective person, it should be recognized that both domesticated animals and other wild animals are superior to us humans at accomplishing the affairs of this life.

The master taught a variety of stories, including these: A lizard made a burrow that had an opening in the ceiling. When a snake followed him back to the burrow, the lizard went out through the hole in the ceiling and killed the snake by biting its middle. Also, behind a rocky crag in the Tre[153] region, a crow took revenge on an owl.

(The owl had killed and eaten a crow chick. So the crow took an owl chick to the same place where the owl had killed and eaten the crow chick and killed and ate the owl chick.)

In the Gyal[154] region, a hornless yak fought with a yak that had horns.

(The yak that had horns had previously battered the hornless yak, which caused the latter to feel resentment. So the hornless yak, after practicing how to fight, {445} clashed again with the horned yak and succeeded in killing it.) A magpie[155] assembled an army of magpies against the crows. (Because a magpie had been harmed by some crows, it summoned all the magpies from as far away as the Tölung[156] region, and they took revenge on the crows of Penyul.)

Animals are even more skilled than that at nurturing their relatives, offspring, and the like. For example, some animals can complete the development of their offspring so that they become the equal of their parents even within the span of a single month.[157] Observe how mice, swallows,[158] and bees are skilled at accumulating and collecting food and objects and building such things as nests. Therefore, the master said if someone is unable to achieve anything beyond this life's aims, it is astonishing to think that the meaning of the words "person" or "human being" would actually apply to him or her.

The Two Cannot Exist Together

The meaning of this phrase is that the two qualities of having failed to overcome attachment to this life and having developed a dharma practice that relates to future lives cannot be present together in one and the same person. As someone said, "You can't get from a single animal skin both one that remains covered in as much fur as one could carry by holding it against one's chest with one's arms and a second that has been stripped of its fur and made into a waterskin.

Sakya Paṇḍita also said:

> Since it is utter foolhardiness[159] (absence of deliberation and reflection) and ignorant, obsessive desire
> to hope for the ultimate benefit and happiness of liberation
> without giving up efforts to obtain the prosperity of this life,
> mentally abandon this life and pursue enlightenment strenuously.

Chöje Bu[160] also said:

> As it will be difficult to obtain this form of leisure and fortune in the future—
> a human body produced by a hundred virtuous deeds accumulated in the past—
> don't let this ship for crossing the great ocean of suffering
> go to waste meaninglessly, O Rinchen Drup.[161]

The Chöje Gyalsepa[162] said:

> No one at all can achieve at the same time
> both the true dharma and the aims of this life.
> There is no doubt that those who wish to pursue them both
> will only succeed in deceiving themselves.
> Since nothing but this can be said if the two should meet,
> in their separate domains apply body and speech to virtuous acts.

This passage implies that the proper remedial measure is to make a boundary that keeps them apart.

A verse from the *Heap of Jewels*[163] collection of sūtras also declares:

> All entities arise according to conditions; {446}
> they are dependent upon the root cause of aspiration.
> Whatever strong resolve a person may develop,
> such will be the result that is obtained.[164]

Several lines from *Entry into the Conduct That Leads to Enlightenment* state:

> The Sage declared that aspiration is
> the root cause of all virtuous acts.[165]

These last two passages do not state that you will attain the desired result of whatever aspiration, inclination, or intention you may generate after having developed a strong conviction in your heart. It certainly would not be taught that incidental to whatever various inferior aims you may achieve, you will also achieve additional results that are much greater than those inferior ones.

It is apparent that all the special characteristics of such spiritual traditions as those of the three persons and the three vehicles are determined entirely by the nature of a practitioner's aspiration and the mental attitude that he or she generates. Therefore, when the desires of this life become strongly fixed in our hearts, causing us to aspire to and become devoted to those aims and to generate a mental attitude that seeks to attain those aims, such that everything we do is meant to promote and benefit the attainment of those aims, if that will prevent us even from gaining the higher goal of a favorable rebirth in a future life, what need is there to say that it will preclude us from attaining supreme enlightenment?

Therefore, even being reborn in the hells in our next life is a result in which a prior misdeed and an intense aspirational desire to experience great warmth that arises in your heart as you are about to die cause you to arrive suddenly in the midst of the fires of one of the hot hells. Since it is apparent that every result that we experience is brought about by a particular desire that was created from our intense desires and aspirations and the multitude of deeds that we have accumulated in the past, it is certain that we have no alternative but to abandon the desires that relate to this life.

Venerable Mañjughoṣa also told Je Rinpoche:[166]

(Je Rinpoche—that is, Je Tsongkhapa—was a preeminent spiritual son of all the buddhas, who possessed inconceivably great power and ability and accomplished the well-being of the Buddhist teaching and sentient beings, who understood all of the Buddha's discourses on sūtra and tantra, and all entities that need to be known, whose love for sentient beings was like that of a mother for an only child, whose enlightened activities as vast as space were achieved spontaneously, and who, while having attained all the spiritual qualities of a buddha, will continue to act on behalf of all sentient beings in the form of an ordinary human, remaining free of any confusion for as long as samsara exists. His liberating deeds and limitless enlightened activities were directly evident to all. Scholars discussed among themselves that even in the past, there has rarely appeared a spiritual being who wrote such extraordinary treatises as he did or who benefited the teaching and sentient beings by means of activities as he did. The Lord himself founded Genden[167] Monastery and Sang Ngak Kar;[168] he restored Dzingchi[169] Temple, which had fallen into disrepair; and he gave instructions for the founding of such additional religious institutions as Tsunmo Tsel,[170] Drepung Monastery,[171] and Sera Monastery.[172] He lived to the age of sixty-three. Twelve of his direct disciples upheld religious seats: at Ganden Monastery, (1) Je Darma Rinchen,[173] (2) Je Khedrup [Gelek Pelsang],[174] (3) Je Shaluwa [Lekpai Gyaltsen],[175] (4) Je Lodrö [Chökyong],[176] and (5) Je Basowa [Chökyi Gyaltsen];[177] at Tsunmo Tsel Monastery, Je Duldzin [Drakpa Gyaltsen];[178] at Drepung Monastery, Je Jamyang Chöje;[179] at Sera Monastery, (1) Lama Dargye Zangpo[180] and (2) Je Gungru [Gyaltsen];[181] at Sang Ngak Kar, Lama Chok Chenpa;[182] at Dzingchi Monastery, Sang Kyongwa;[183] and, at Nyima Ling[184] Monastery, Lama Jangsempa.[185] In addition, he had limitless other disciples, such as Je Jamchen Chöje,[186] venerable Sherap Senge,[187] and Je Gendun Drupa,[188] whose spiritual activities were equal to space in their vastness. Seven[189] of his disciples attained the form of one-pointed concentration in which bliss and emptiness are combined inseparably. There were also such figures as the "heart disciple"[190] and bodhisattva from Demo Thang, [Lodrö Gyaltsen,][191] whose spiritual deeds were inconceivably great. The great spiritual being Kunsangwa[192] founded Do Ngak Ling[193] Monastery. Jangsem Radrengwa [Śākya Sönam][194] founded Gomo Tsokha[195] Monastery. The great bodhisattva Trel Zhingpa[196] founded Gönsar[197] Monastery, which is located in the Döl region, and the bodhisattva from Demo Thang served as its administrator. These and other disciples founded thirteen monasteries that were of varying size. For example, Khedrup Je founded Riwo Dangchen[198] Monastery; the bodhisattva from Maldro, Dulwa Gendun Rinchen,[199] founded Rinchen Ling[200] in the Tö area of Maldro; the priest-benefactor Lama Drakpa Rinchen,[201] founded Chakar[202] Monastery; and Je Gendun Drup founded Tashi Lhunpo Monastery.[203] All of these true spiritual teachers, without exception, were Je Tsongkhapa's direct disciples and spiritual sons born from his breast[204] who possessed limitless spiritual qualities. Limitless monastic institutions that were established by the spiritual activities of these great spiritual sons who received the direct blessings of that very Lord Tsongkhapa can be seen throughout the regions of Ü, Tsang, Dokham, China, Mongolia, and Ngari. The bodhisattva from Demo Thang propagated the lineage that was transmitted by Je Tsongkhapa's great direct disciple Ngok Chödor[205] and he offered {448} approximately a thousand silver *zho*[206] to this great bodhisattva who lived until the age of ninety. Je Tsongkhapa's direct disciple the great Lama Janglingba [Drakpa Rinchen],[207] in addition to being one of Tibet's great lamas, was apparently the Lord's disciple who had the longest life. Since all of Je Tsongkhapa's contemporaries who were spiritual teachers sought to meet him, Chöje Kunga Zangpo[208] and Chöje Rongpo[209] also heard teachings from him. These two individuals also founded the two monasteries Ngor Gönsar and Nalendra.)

> If you fail initially to develop the aversion that arises from dissatisfaction toward the entirety of samsara, whatever activities of listening, reflection, and meditation, and so on, you may undertake will all fail to rise above simply being causes that perpetuate samsara and bring rebirth in the lower realms. Therefore, for the time being, you must put aside trying to carry out such profound practices as those of the generation and completion stages[210] and direct all your efforts to the development of renunciation.

Tropu Lotsāwa also declared:

([Tropu Lotsāwa] Jampai Pel[211] established Jamchen[212] Monastery in the region of Tropu. His lama, Paṇchen Śākyaśrī,[213] performed its consecration. Tropuwa Sönam Senge[214] was his spiritual son and Butön Rinchen Drup[215] was the latter's disciple. The Tropuwa lineage of spiritual masters who resided in the Tsang region were followers of Je Pakmo Drupa's disciple Kunden [Repa].[216])

> If you fail to realize that your life force is like a water bubble
> and you fail to recall death in a heartfelt manner,

> though you may carry out many acts on the side of virtue,
> they will remain instruments that relate to this life.
>
> If you fail to realize that gain and fame are illusions
> and you fail to cast off a desire for status, profit, and fame,
> though you may be regarded as a wise spiritual being,
> you remain a slave to the eight worldly concerns.
>
> If you fail to cast aside concern for this life,
> no matter how much you strive after virtuous deeds,
> you will go to the next life naked and empty-handed.
> Alas! What will you take to your next life?
>
> If you fail to understand the faults of samsara
> and you have not had enough of sensory pleasures,
> though you may utter highly boastful speech,
> it will still remain deceitful and false.

Lord Atiśa also said:

> I said this to my disciple Gompa Rinchen Lama[217] about meditation: "If, while meditating, you think to yourself that your meditation practice will bring you great quantities of such things as bolts of silk cloth or boxes of tea, however much you meditate will be nothing but evil deeds. However, if, while meditating, you think to yourself that you want to put an end to the ocean of rebirth and to plant the seed for attaining supreme enlightenment, the merit of even just having had this thought {449} will not be able fit into the entire realm of space."

Chöje Bu[218] declared:

> In this life you may develop attachment and hatred toward friends and enemies,
> you may accumulate wealth and succeed in attracting a following,
> but your retinue and wealth will not follow you beyond this life,
> and you alone must experience the results of your deeds and suffering.

> Though you may attain such pleasurable results in samsara as being reborn as
> Brahmā, Śakra, or a wheel-wielder,[219] these are not permanent states of existence;
> nor is there any certainty that you will not be reborn in the lower states following your death.
> Therefore, Rinchen Drup, you must develop aversion for samsara.[220]

While this is advice that he gave to himself, it should be heeded by everyone.

Gyalwa Yangönpa[221] also said:

(Yangönpa studied with such teachers as Sakya Paṇḍita,[222] Kodrakpa,[223] and Götsangpa.[224] He possessed limitless virtuous qualities and is said to have been a tulku.[225])

> It is common for persons only to be attracted to high dharma teachings. Their minds are not satisfied with lower ones. They only like teachings that repeatedly mention the topics of emptiness and what does not exist and that are considered high teachings. These are persons in whom the ability to achieve a spiritual realization doesn't match the efficacy of the dharma teaching. It's not enough for the dharma teaching to be about the Great Completion;[226] the person must be someone who has taken on the spiritual qualities of the Great Completion. I have seen many instances where numerous explanations are given about a dharma teaching that has the value of a horse by a person who doesn't have the value of a dog. When the dharma becomes just words that are spoken but that are not put into practice, this is no different from the songs that are sung by a *pakshi*[227] or words that are recited by a parrot. When you receive one or two dharma teachings, they should be put into practice. When you gain one or two understandings, they must be applied to your mental continuum.
>
> There are many persons for whom the dharma teaching does not enter their mental continuum. Like failing to mix the tsampa[228] powder of the dharma with the water of their minds, they create an empty space between the dharma teaching and the

person who hears it that is large enough to hold a human being. Their understanding of the dharma remains on the surface, like sheep's lungs that are boiling in a pot of water. This means that they have not been able to accomplish the true purpose of the dharma. Nevertheless, remaining motionless[229] and assuming a haughty posture, they fail to heed the dharma's meaning. Though they have failed to achieve the purpose of the dharma, all such persons falsely declare, "I have made mentally giving up concern for this life my most essential form {450} of spiritual practice."

Gyalse Rinpoche said:

(Gyalse Tokme Zangpo Pel[230] had many lamas, including the lama Pang [Lotsāwa] Lodrö Tenpa,[231] the arhat [Rinchen] Sönam Drakpa,[232] and Butön [Rinchen Drup]. He possessed the three qualities of learning, discipline, and kindheartedness; he mastered the practice of cultivating enlightenment mind; his spiritual activities on behalf of disciples were extensive; and he attained visions of tutelary deities. He lived into his seventies and preserved the Buddhist teaching while residing at the dharma stronghold of Ngulchu[233] Hermitage. He had many great spiritual sons, including the three of Gya,[234] Jam,[235] and Pel.[236])

There is no greater obstacle for the true dharma
to become the path to liberation than the base thought
that pursues the excellence of this life one-pointedly.
Therefore, you must abandon it in every possible way.

Whatever virtue is performed in the three domains of listening,
reflection, and meditation,
if it becomes mixed with this base thought, there is no doubt
that it will turn what should be good into something bad,
as when food of a hundred flavors is mixed with putrid vomit.

Creating strife between teacher and student, spiritual companions,
and close friends,
this base thought makes you totally helpless to resist its prompting
to exert yourself greatly in the pursuit of wealth,
without trying to avoid any form of evil, suffering, or infamy.

With the demon of this base thought dwelling in your heart,
you fight and argue with intense physical and mental effort
in order to destroy the wealth and glory of others,
bringing ruin to yourself and others, in both this and future lives.

Though you carry the lamp of scripture in your hand
while you walk along the precipice of such evil deeds
as fighting and strife for the sake of gain, honor, or your associates,
your eyes remain wholly obscured by the impairment of this base thought.

Though you give much wealth, if it is for such reasons
as a desire for fame or to gain a large following, such great generosity
will be turned into the source of a small and inferior result.
This base thought is a cow[237] that will surely destroy you.

Though you safeguard morality strenuously, through being bound
by such fetters as desire for gain, you will be unable to traverse the path to liberation; {451} this is a shackle that confines you in the prison of samsara.
You are certain to remain in the grasp of this base thought.

Though you cultivate meditative absorption for a long time, attachment and hatred
cause you to praise yourself, criticize others, and engage in strife and controversy.
Practicing quiescence only gives rise to an unsettled mind.
These are due to the roots of this base thought's weeds.

Sickness, harmful spirits, robbers, enemies, and the like
are considered to be the obstacles to the true dharma.
But if your mind is capable, they can all become aids to your practice.
This base thought is the certain obstacle to the true dharma.

When you strive for this life's prosperity, it is difficult to obtain;
though you obtain it, it is not certain that you will have the freedom to enjoy it.

That which is sure to come to you is death,
at which time wealth, a retinue, and the like, will be of no use
and separation from them will bring you great suffering.
Having reflected in this way, abandon the arrogance of attachment
to this life.

This dharma practice that mentally abandons attachment to this life is one that is much more profound than other forms of profound spiritual practice. The term "profound" refers to something that is difficult for the mind to fathom and difficult to realize. It can also refer to an effective means of eliminating suffering and producing happiness and one that cannot be found elsewhere. This dharma practice that mentally abandons attachment to this life is difficult for the mind to fathom and difficult to realize. It was apparent in India itself that if someone were to assert before anyone who was a realist, from an adherent of the Mind Only school on down, that all entities lack the quality of being truly existent and that their ultimate nature is emptiness, that person would think to him- or herself, "How awful! Is this person who is speaking such meaningless words crazy?"

Similarly, someone may be a geshe[238] who holds the title of master of ten difficult subjects,[239] or a lama to whom a hundred or a thousand persons make prostrations, or a person who recites scriptures of the four classes of tantra and who has performed a hundred rituals for entering a deity's mandala, or a yogi who has spent a lengthy period of time carrying out a retreat practice in a meditation chamber whose entrance has been sealed with clay and meditating on a tutelary deity, the nāḍi channels, and the psychic airs, or a practitioner of the Great Seal[240] {452}, Pacification,[241] or the Great Completion whose exaggerated reputation has been proclaimed as far as the sound of thunder can travel, but if he or she remains attached to this life and has neither understood nor realized this dharma teaching, and if someone should say to him or her, "You must mentally abandon all the prosperity, happiness, and well-being of this life," this statement would be beyond this individual's comprehension, and he or she would think to him- or herself, "How awful! This is such a meaningless statement!" He or she would feel fear, alarm, and despondency toward this dharma practice.

Moreover, if others should see an individual that has mentally abandoned the prosperity of this life, they would say that he or she is a fool who didn't listen to his or her parents, relatives, friends, and the like, and had become a wandering beggar. They would consider him or her to be a stupid and incompetent person.

Most people think, "All the spiritual activities that you might carry out, such as the three of learning, reflection, and meditation, should keep you from having to undergo hardships and the like in this life. They should also allow you, after having entered the ranks of human beings in general, to enter the ranks of those human beings who enjoy happy lives. Such activities should enable you to be looked upon highly by other persons and be thought of as reliable. They should enable you to have an abundance of possessions and not have to depend on others for assistance. Without having to put out your hand or beg for assistance, you should be able to enjoy both butter tea and black tea,[242] as well as the three staples of meat, butter, and cheese, all of which are of good quality. Others should praise you and please you by saying that you are an excellent dharma practitioner or a learned scholar and the like. Such people strive to achieve this kind of life for themselves and also advise others to do the same. If it is thought that having such an understanding makes one stalwart and knowledgeable, then, needless to say, a different viewpoint, such as that of this profound dharma practice, will fall beyond the comprehension of ordinary householders and others, and, as is current nowadays, all such persons will be exuberant about such dharma practices as the nāḍi channels and the psychic airs, or emptiness. When two or three companions get together, they will have discussions that are exclusively about such topics as these. It is also evident that a great many individuals put forth effort and apply themselves to these types of spiritual practice. But it is quite rare to find someone who is exuberant about the dharma practice that mentally abandons this life. If you teach a dharma instruction that says you should mentally give up all the prosperity of this life, including friends, relatives, farmland, home, wealth, property, and the like, most persons take on a black facial expression, like a donkey whose head is being struck with a stick. They wrinkle their nose in obvious displeasure, suggesting that they do not wish to hear this instruction at all. This is a situation in which it is apparent that such persons have absolutely no desire to practice {453} such a teaching. However, this instruction is not false talk. If you wish to practice it, then come near. We Khampas do not have mouths that speak in a deceiving manner.

Drowe Gönpo[243] said:

(Drogön Rinpoche was the nephew of the Great Gyer.[244] He is said to have been an emanation of Avalokiteśvara. He possessed limitless forms of miraculous powers and supernatural knowledge. Among his fourteen great spiritual sons, there were two great nephews, Lopön Tönpa[245] and Lama Sangyön;[246] two were from the Dakpo region, Bangrimpa[247] and Sangmowa;[248] Umapa[249] was from the eastern part of Lhodrak and Geshongwa[250] was from its western part; Sewa Gangpa[251] was from the E region; Sa Jungwa[252] was from Nyal; Chewachenpa[253] was from Döl; Songönpa[254] was from Drap; Tang Tönpa[255] and Tsemawa[256] were from Shok; Lopön Lamowa[257] was from Jen; and two were from Tsang, Tsangtön Nyima[258] and Nyangtö Lagönpa.[259] Many of these disciples founded new monasteries and some presided over older existing monastic seats. They also upheld many teaching lineages and supported many monasteries.)

Great learned and disciplined meditators who are of this life[260]
want to be known as learned and righteous within this life.
They go into retreat and write admonitions on the door's lintel.
These great meditators who refuse to meet with anyone
want to be known in this life as great meditators who are virtuous.

Though they perform acts of generosity, they just want it to be known
in this life that they performed such acts and they were generous.
For example, this is like powdered tsampa that is thrown onto water;
it is hoped that every virtuous deed, including each offering
that is made to the Three Jewels, will be seen by other persons.

Because all these various kinds of improper thoughts
will be present in every act that is carried out,
whatever virtue is done will be lost to the desire for recognition.[261]
All such deeds will be stolen away by the horseman of vainglory.

Therefore, all practitioners must pierce with a spear
the thoughts that arise from attachment to this life.
If they fail to pierce them with their spear,
all learned and virtuous teachers and meditators
will fail to close the door to the three lower states.

What use is there {454} for learned and disciplined great meditators
who cannot turn away from the suffering of the lower states?

They have lost the meaning of the sūtras.
They reside their entire life in a monastery
and in their old age still have not abandoned this life.
Hence, they maintain attachment for their monastic residence,
and after carrying out such evil deeds as creating conflict
in the religious community, they leave behind their monastic residence
and proceed themselves into the fires of Avīci hell.
All of this is due to having failed to reflect on impermanence.

In short, if you fail to develop within your mental continuum
a realization of impermanence in the form of death,
the practice of Guhyasamāja will not be profound.
But when an awareness of death has arisen in the mental continuum,
the threefold statement of going for refuge will become profound.
All you practitioners, realize that by continually trying to reach
for lofty dharma teachings, you will end up falling into the abyss.
When that occurs, realize also that those profound instructions
are being used in a way that causes them to be turned inside out.

The former lamas have also taught that to accomplish the act of mentally abandoning this life you must resort to the four dedications, the three vajras, and the three acts of expelling, entering, and attaining.[262] The first four points are to dedicate your mind's ultimate aim to the dharma, to dedicate your ultimate form of dharma practice to living in a state of poverty, to dedicate your ultimate form of poverty to [remaining in a state of poverty even if it should result in] your death, and to dedicate your ultimate form of death to [a death that takes place in] an empty ravine. The three vajras are to send the vajra of invulnerability ahead of you, to place the vajra of unabashedness behind you, and to keep the vajra of transcendent awareness as your companion. The final three qualities are to expel yourself from the community of humans, to enter the ranks of dogs, and to attain the rank of a god.

If you understand that these principles illustrate the way in which the Bhagavān[263] left the householder state and went forth into the life of a homeless ascetic, how he engaged in extreme ascetic practices for six years, and how he taught his followers to go forth into the life of a homeless ascetic, and so on, these ten just-mentioned points will be recognized as extremely profound and they will be understood as representing the most essential form of dharma practice. These ten points are called the Ten Ultimate Jewels. Because by merely fixing them in the mind, you will destroy all worldly errors, you will dry up the ocean of desire and attachment, you will demolish the mountain of the eight worldly concerns, you will cause the fortress of the mental afflictions to collapse {455}, you will sink the ship of wrongful actions, and you will arrive at the favorable locale of spiritual antidotes, it is most evident that these are the highest form of ultimate riches. This can be realized when they are explained in detail among the instructions that are presented below.

Therefore, because this dharma practice that enables you to mentally abandon this life is difficult for the mind to fathom, and because it is both difficult for everyone to comprehend and can remain a "secret subject"[264] for them, it truly is a dharma practice that is both profound and an unsurpassed secret.

Moreover, because it contains methods of attaining benefits and happiness that are not found elsewhere, this dharma practice is both profound and superior to others, because it enables you, without difficulty, to achieve happiness in this life, happiness in future lives, and all spiritual qualities throughout the duration of time that any of the three forms of enlightenment[265] is being pursued.

You might think to yourself, "Isn't it true that mentally abandoning this life causes you to abandon the forms of happiness that are found in this life? How then does mentally abandoning this life enable you to achieve happiness in this life?" It may seem that your thought is true. However, as the saying goes, "Experience reveals what happens when you act however you like. By desiring a position of greatness, you will lose the opportunity to gain what is of genuine value. By desiring a high position, you will fall into an abyss." Therefore, a person who thinks to him- or herself "I will make myself as happy as I can and as comfortable as I can" doesn't find that happiness and comfort. That person him- or herself will ultimately realize that when they aren't achieved. As it is said, the person who thinks to him- or herself "I don't need to be happy" is the one who finds happiness. Is it not said that "although yogis do not seek logical reasons, logical reasons will not let go of them"? Did one who is called a buddha not utter the great saying, "The goal is in the place where desire has been abandoned"?

Tsangpa Gyare[266] said:

In the gatehouse of one who has achieved spiritual experience is a person who keeps watch over a state of happiness, but those who hanker after delicious food are not aware of his presence. In the gatehouse of one who has acquired spiritual antidotes is a person who keeps watch over the state of having mentally abandoned what is mundane, but those who are subject to desire and hatred are not aware of his presence. In the gatehouse of one who has investigated important subjects down to their roots is a person who keeps watch over contentedness of mind, but those who are subject to hopes and fears {456} are not aware of his presence. In the gatehouse of one who knows satisfaction is a person who keeps watch over an abundance of wealth, but those who have great desire are not aware of his presence.

Tokden Samten Pel[267] also said:

The desire for happiness in this life is suffering.
If you cast it to the wind, you will gain lasting happiness.

Shawo Gangpa[268] said:

(Shawopa's name was Pema Jangchup.[269] He was a disciple of the Three Brothers.[270] He nurtured disciples in the Gyal Shawo Gang[271] area of the Penpo region. He possessed extensive knowledge of the scriptural and cognitional forms of the dharma. It is said that when he died his entire corpse turned into holy relics.)

I think to myself, "If I had the ability to direct my mind, I would place it in a state of happiness." But when I think of how I might actually direct my mind, since I don't have any other method or any other instruction, I direct my mind to the act of mentally abandoning this life.

Shawo Gangpa also said:

Since the cause of all our suffering in this and future lives is our desires that relate to this life, we must cast off regarding this life's desires as objects that we wish to attain. If the objects that we want to attain in this life are great, our minds will not remain at ease. We will not know which way to turn. When that occurs, the three circumstances of evil deeds, hardships, and a bad reputation will all come to us at the same time. Therefore, we must turn back these many kinds of desires. When we are able to turn back our various desires, our happiness will have begun. Therefore, in order to achieve happiness in this and all our future lives, we must use as our ritual substance[272] not having any desires in our hearts and not accumulating any form of material wealth.

When we don't want to acquire any form of material gain, that constitutes the highest form of gain. When we don't want any fame,[273] that is the highest form of fame. When we don't want any renown,[274] that is the highest form of renown. When we don't want a large retinue,[275] that is the highest form of retinue. If we want to practice dharma from the heart, we must direct our minds to a willingness to live in a state of poverty. We must be willing to undertake the most extreme form of poverty, which is one that might even lead to our death.[276] When we are able to develop such a mind, it is a certainty that none of the three kinds of beings—that is, gods, spirits, and humans—will allow us to {457} undergo any such hardships. If we pursue the cravings that relate to the desires of this life, these are the circumstances that will come to us: We will create our own degradation. We will create our own hardships. We will become unhappy through being disparaged by others. In our future lives, we will go to the lower states.

Kyechokpa[277] also said:

(His ordination name was Samten Pel;[278] and he was a disciple of Gyadrak Chöje,[279] who was from the Penpo region. He possessed extensive knowledge of the scriptural and cognitional forms of the dharma and founded Gomo Yap[280] Monastery. He accomplished the welfare of others extensively and had many spiritual sons, including Yakde Paṇchen.[281] He was also known as Kyechok Chöje.[282])

If you are able to cast this life to the wind,
you will be designated "one who overcame attachment."
When you have no needs whatsoever,
your renown will pervade the surface of the earth.

When your body and life are dedicated to the dharma,
the breezes of fame will have been set in motion.

Master Nāgārjuna also gave the following advice:

While it is pleasurable to scratch an itch,
the absence of an itch is an even greater pleasure.
Likewise, one who longs for the world can find happiness,
but the absence of desires is an even greater happiness.[283]

The dharma alone is the highest mode of conduct.
Through the dharma the world becomes gratified.
One is not deceived either here or in another life
by a world that is gratified.[284]

Through the dharma, the kingdom will be happy,
a broad canopy of fame
will spread throughout all the directions,
and all ministers will bow to you.[285]

If your kingdom is governed in accord with the dharma
and not for the sake of fame or according to your desires,
that will bring results that are exceedingly fruitful;
otherwise, there will be unfortunate occurrences.[286]

In these verses, Nāgārjuna declared to a king: "If you act in accord with the dharma and abandon the desires of this life, you will obtain, even within this life, all forms that you may desire of such things as material gain and honor, or fame and renown. As you govern your kingdom, you should seek to benefit everyone—that is, both yourself and others {458}. But if you allow desire to become firmly fixed in the depth of your heart, your rule will result in misfortune."

Master Āryadeva states in his Middle Way treatise titled *Four Hundred Verses*:

Whoever wrongly sees this world
is a fool regarding the hereafter.
Those who follow such a person
will be led astray for a very long time.[287]

Since it's true that by practicing the dharma well, you will find greater happiness than others in this life, one who doesn't even realize this is a fool and a dolt, and he or she will bring ruin upon him- or herself, as well as others. Therefore, Āryadeva is saying that it is important to realize that practicing the dharma well allows you to reach a place where you will experience happiness.

Master Śāntideva states at the beginning of his *Compendium of Training*:

> Through hearing the dharma jewel, a humble-natured one[288]
> attains both a well-being that had not been attained before
> and never undergoes a loss of happiness.
> He attains a bodhisattva's supreme, imperishable happiness
> and a buddha's state of unequaled perfection.[289]

The Bhagavān also declared (in the *Collection of Uplifting Sayings*):

> If you desire every happiness,
> you should abandon all desires.
> One who abandons all desires
> increases happiness to perfection.
>
> As long as you pursue desires,
> the mind will not find satisfaction.
> Therefore, those who are perceiving the cessation of desires
> are the ones who are well satisfied, having become satisfied
> through wisdom.
>
> An excellent one finds satisfaction through wisdom;
> he does not become satisfied through desires.
> Craving does not gain control of the person
> who has become satisfied through wisdom.[290]

Ārya Asaṅga said that the happiness that arises from experiencing such sensory pleasures as food and drink, cohabiting with a man or a woman, and singing and dancing cannot compare to the happiness of those who live by means of wisdom[291] when they experience the enjoyment of the dharma. After raising the question as to how the two types of happiness differ, he states that the pleasure that arises from experiencing such things as food and drink is limited in that it does not pervade the entirety of your being; it cannot arise at any time because it depends on outer factors and it can therefore only occur at certain specific times;[292] it is not found throughout the three realms;[293] it cannot carry the ārya riches[294] into the future;[295] it can, through its enjoyment, become exhausted; it can be taken away by enemies and the like; it cannot be taken with you to a future life; it does not, through its enjoyment, culminate in satisfaction and contentment; it produces every kind of suffering in both this and future lives; it is a form of pleasure in name only, like the pleasure of scratching the itch of leprosy,[296] in that it refers to the temporary alleviation of suffering; it gives rise to the mental afflictions of desire and so on; and it gives rise to such misdeeds as the taking of life. By contrast, the happiness that arises from enjoying the dharma pervades your entire being; it can arise whenever you desire; it occurs throughout the three realms; it carries the ārya riches into the future; in addition to not becoming exhausted, it can be developed to higher levels; it cannot be taken away by enemies and the like; it can be taken with you to a future life; it can reach culmination and bring satisfaction; it does not generate any suffering either in this life or a future life; it is not a form of happiness in name only; and it destroys all the mental afflictions and all forms of misconduct. For these reasons, the latter kind of happiness is much more excellent than the former.[297]

When Geshe Ben's[298] patron said that he was coming to meet with him, he arranged the best offerings to the Three Jewels that he could. After examining his own motivation, it became apparent to Geshe Ben that his desire to arrange attractive offerings was because he wanted to make a favorable impression on his patron, so he threw a handful of dust on the offerings and said to himself, "Gelong,[299] refrain from being a fraud!" When Pa Dampa[300] heard this, he remarked, "Ben Gungyal's handful of dust was the best offering to the Three Jewels in all of Tibet."

Once, at a yogurt festival[301] that was being held at Gyal Temple,[302] as yogurt was being piled onto the servings being presented to the monks at the head of the row in which he was seated, Geshe Ben thought to himself, "The way the yogurt is being doled out, those of us here at the end of the row won't receive any." When he considered this thought, he said to himself, "You are worried about your mouth," and turned his bowl upside down. So when a portion was being held out for him, he refused it, saying, "It has already been consumed by my flawed mind."

After offering all of his meager possessions to Gyal Temple, Geshe Ben taught dharma there as an indigent beggar. At a certain time, in the Tö area of the Penpo region, there were many incidents of beatings carried out by robbers. Geshe Ben heard that this had prompted individuals to conceal and bury their riches and to stockpile supplies. Having no other possessions besides a dilapidated water pot and an extra set of monk's robes, after laying the monk's robes over his shoulder and while holding the water pot in his hand, he asked out loud, "Do I have any supplies other than these that I need to store away?" Pleased by this remark, Potowa said, "Ben's supplies are the right ones to have." Then Potowa sent Geshe Ben a long piece of cloth and said, "Because death is coming to him, he will need this to wrap up his corpse. Since it is not coming to us, we don't need one."[303] Potowa further said, "In order to practice dharma properly, we must be like him. You can't develop a genuine dharma practice by accumulating many provisions, including tea and other soup ingredients."[304]

Drak Karwa[305] is also reputed to have said: "I, a lowly one, have also sought to observe Gungyal's way of 'keeping supplies' {461} to a certain extent."

(Geshe Drak Karwa was a direct disciple of both Drapa[306] and Potowa, and the first compiler of the *Collection of Similes*.[307] Drak Karwa resided at Pabongkha and lived to the age of eighty. He had a following of three hundred monks. Drapa was from the Penpo region. He founded Drane Sar and Podrang Ding monasteries. His ordination name was Zhönu Ö and he lived to the age of sixty-five.)

Geshe Ben said:

> When I was a layperson, I fastened a bow and arrows to myself like thorns and carried two or three knives, yet I had many enemies and few friends. As an unmarried man, I grew crops that yielded forty [*khel*[308] of grain], so my neighbors gave me the nickname Forty Grower.[309] During the daytime, I was a bandit on mountain passes and at night I was a robber in the town. Yet I still didn't have sufficient food. Now, since I have abandoned weapons, I don't have a single enemy. Without having to do work that causes me to spit on rocks, I also have sufficient food. Whatever kind of famine might occur, I would have a quantity of food to eat such that my neck could be yoked to whoever was the richest of persons. In the past, food was so scarce that my mouth could not find food. Now, food is so abundant that it can-

> not find my mouth. Through eating, I will not run out of food. Through drinking, I will not run out of beverages. The thought has occurred to me two or three times repeatedly, "Dharma is the truth."

When Śākyaśrī,[310] the great paṇḍita from Kashmir, arrived in Tibet, Tibetan dharma teachers traveled to Ngari with horse-hoof-shaped silver ingots wrapped in iron seeking teachings on right view. Geshe Ben said of this:

> These individuals go [to hear teachings from Śākyaśrī] even though they have listened to dharma teachings their entire lives. I am someone who has not heard dharma teachings extensively, but when I consider whether I need to go and learn from this teacher, I ask myself, "If I listen to teachings from him, will my mental afflictions be reduced?" However, my mental afflictions have already become reduced. The fact that the mental afflictions of these individuals who have listened to dharma teachings in the past have not been reduced is due to the deterioration of their oral lineage.
>
> Now, it is apparent that this amount of learning I have is sufficient. So now I ask myself, "Have I acted as a dharma teacher? Or have I been a meditator, a leader of disciples, or an elder monk?"

It is said that when Geshe Ben was fighting with his mental afflictions, if a mental state of attachment should arise, he would take hold of his left arm with his right one and, referring to himself as Ben Gungyal, reproach himself with a hundred reprimands, thereby restraining himself. Similarly, when his mental afflictions would subside and become dormant, he would refer to himself as Gelong Tsultrim Gyalwa and, taking hold of his left arm with his right one, give himself encouragement.

(Having had a long life, it is said that Geshe Ben has not passed away and currently lives in a knowledge holder's[311] realm. He achieved the status of an excellent and happy dharma practitioner. His fame and renown are still being proclaimed. He achieved the status of being the most excellent among Potowa's disciples at developing antidotes to mental faults. {462} He was born in the Penpo region.)

Geshe Ben was a bandit-robber who somehow was able to exert himself in this way and by mentally abandoning this life, achieved such a state of happiness. Potowa also said:

> By practicing the dharma, you can gain an extraordinary result in this very life. When I was still a layperson, I went to mine for gold on three occasions, but was not able to acquire even a single *sho*[312] of gold. Now, I even receive many *sang*[313] each day. In the Yungwa region there is no one who enjoys greater happiness, well-being, and renown than Khamlungpa.[314] In Lungshö, there is no one that is happier than Chengawa.[315] These are circumstances that came about through practicing dharma properly.

At first, Chengawa would run out of tsampa, and so he had to limit the amount of food that he ate. Because he patched his skirt-like lower garment with pieces of leather, he was known as "The one who wears a leather lower garment." Later, he would say, "Now, I think to myself, 'If I tried to sustain all the inhabitants of the Rose Apple continent, I might be able to do so.'" Similar examples are Milarepa, Dakpo Lhaje, Götsangpa, and others, who at first underwent a variety of hardships while they were ordinary laypersons but, after entering the dharma and mentally abandoning this life, experienced greater happiness than young laypersons do.[316] {463} Likewise, if you examine the accounts of the spiritual lives of the former supreme lamas, without exception they all underwent similar experiences. Therefore, after reflecting on their lives, we too should think to ourselves, "O spiritual father, it is apparent that there are no descriptions of anyone having failed to find happiness by mentally abandoning this life, as well as no descriptions of anyone finding happiness by refraining from mentally abandoning this life. Therefore, why would I not mentally abandon this life?" Then you should cast away all your possessions, like a stone that you used to wipe your anus.

(Chengawa's ordination name was Tsultrim Bar. He had a dharma connection with Lord Atiśa but was mainly nurtured spiritually by Drom Tönpa. At Radreng Monastery, he and Kampa Yeshe Bar were two individuals who achieved excellent levels of one-pointed concentration. They were known as "the two named Bar." Chengawa founded Lo Monastery and possessed limitless spiritual qualities. He had many great spiritual sons, including the four who were said to be the equal of Chengawa himself—namely, Tölungpa Rinchen Nyingpo,[317] the tulku Jayulwa,[318] Tsöndru Bar[319] of Mangra Monastery, and Sarpa Pak Gom.[320] Chengawa lived to the age of seventy-one and attracted a following of some seven hundred disciples.)

Gyalwa Yangönpa[321] said:

> Resolve to have no regard for this life. Reduce your food and clothing to the bare necessity. Abandon concern for life and limb as if they were carrion. Reflect on the spiritual accomplishments of the tradition's lineage holders. Don the armor of fortitude and practice forbearance toward hardships. Remain in a secluded hermitage. Through a process of meditation in which you immerse yourself in the spiritual practice for an extended period, you will experience the arising of inner realizations.

Lama Yegönpa[322] said:

> Instead of the many forms of questionable advice that ordinary people offer, spread out before you as if they were a carpet the accounts of the spiritual lives of the buddhas and bodhisattvas and consider what kind of practice they carried out from the early period of their lives until the later stages. If you act in that way, you will definitely achieve an excellent and unfailing result.

Potowa said:

> By not understanding this instruction, you will engage in a "dance"[323] of an inferior nature. That is, you will exhibit many different kinds of debased conduct during this short lifetime.

He also said:

> If this instruction is understood, you will develop an awareness that avoids engaging in debased conduct and possesses the aim of being capable of fulfilling one's own spiritual needs.

When he was giving instructions to Geshe Dingpawa,[324] Potowa said, "I have no instructions. As I am a disciple[325] of my spiritual father, the elder master, I can only advise you about a spiritual aim."

(This individual, Geshe Dingpawa, was a disciple of Potowa who was from the Shangpa Tsap clan. His ordination name was Sherap Gyatso. He accomplished the welfare of others[326] in the Ding region and lived to the age of sixty-eight.)

Kyechokpa[327] said:

> There is no greater happiness {464} than maintaining a mind that is free of burdens. There is no greater ease than remaining free of ordinary activities. There is no greater purpose than keeping your mind free of ordinary responsibilities.

Sakya Paṇḍita said:

(Sakya Paṇḍita was an omniscient being. He experienced visions of Mañjughoṣa and other enlightened deities, propagated the Buddha's teaching throughout China and Tibet, and lived to the age of seventy. He had many disciples, among whom those who upheld his system of exposition were Uyukpa Rikpai Senge[328] and the rest, and the three who were renowned as the trio of Khang, Nyen, and Zhang.[329] The disciples who upheld his lineage of spiritual practice included Mar Chögyal,[330] Lhopa Künkyen Rinchen,[331] and the rest. Those who upheld his lineage of spiritual realization included Tsok Gompa Kunga Pel,[332] Druptop Yönten Taye,[333] and the rest.)

> Complete self-determination is happiness.
> Complete dependence upon others is suffering.[334]
>
> The supreme form of well-being is a happy mind.
> The supreme form of wealth is generosity.
> The supreme companion is one who does not deceive.[335]
>
> A wise person, even when pursuing matters of this life,
> will achieve them easily if he does so by means of the dharma.
> Consider the difference between the success
> of spiritual beings and that of robbers.[336]

Zhangtsun Yerpa[337] said:

(He was a bodhisattva who appeared as a direct disciple of Lord Atiśa and was a lama of the Three Brothers. When he passed away, everyone heard celestial music.)

> Having thought to myself, "Should I freeze to death, let that be how I die. Should I starve to death, let that be how I die," if I am able to practice a genuine form of dharma, it is neither certain that I will freeze to death nor that I will starve to death.

Zhang Nanam Dorje Wangchuk[338] said:

(He was the founder of Gyal Temple[339] and a figure who possessed limitless scriptural and cognitional knowledge of the dharma. He is included among the Tibetan teachers during the middle period of Buddhist transmission, such as Lu Me[340] and others. He was also a lama of Geshe Tönpa. Gyal Temple is included among the earliest and most excellent temples that currently exist in Tibet. He was an extraordinary individual who initially received especially great blessings from his lama.)

> After having been hungry for a few days when I was staying in the mountains, first a herdsman {465} gave me some of the food he carried when he traveled. After that, a villager was summoned, who came to give me some food.

The *Sūtra on Overcoming Wrongful Conduct*[341] declares:

> Śāriputra, my teaching will not become corrupted. My śrāvaka disciples will not be oppressed by their need for religious garments or having to beg for food. Therefore, Śāriputra, strive for buddhahood. Śāriputra, do not value worldly material things. Śāriputra, consider what I say to you: Billions of gods strive to provide those bhikṣus who are practitioners of meditation with every form of ease. Śāriputra, human beings are not able to perform such acts of veneration and honor.
>
> Śāriputra, whoever goes forth into the homeless state and strives to practice the dharma in order to become a tathāgata, those practitioners of meditation will receive religious garments and alms food from all the gods who have few desires, all humans who have few desires, and all sentient beings who have few desires.

The *Sūtra on the White Lotus of Great Compassion*[342] declares that in the past when the Bhagavān generated the intention to attain supreme enlightenment, he asserted that if a person who wears even just a four-finger-sized, saffron-colored strip of cloth as a religious garment should fail to acquire food or drink to the extent that he or she desires, he will have misled the buddhas, and he therefore made the vow that this should prevent him from achieving buddhahood.[343]

A verse also declares:

> Even though all those who are householders
> may plow on fields the size of fingernails,
> those renunciates who are my followers
> will not be without a means of livelihood.[344]

Chenga Rinpoche[345] said:

> Though we may lack the necessities of food and clothing that are a means of subsistence, through dedicating your ultimate aim to a life of poverty,[346] all those who possess faith will regard you as a person who is worthy of veneration. Therefore, the principal form of possession {466} is to be free of attachment. It is meaningless to collect and accumulate ordinary material property. Though people may disparage us, by making sure that there is no deceptiveness in our minds, we will come to be viewed favorably by everyone. Therefore, since the basis of fame and renown is to be faultless in our behavior, it is meaningless to engage in hypocrisy.[347]

Geshe Kharakpa[348] said:

(He was born in the Tö area of Tsang in a place called Dung Zhur[349] and devoted himself one-pointedly to spiritual practice in Dragyap, a place in the Tre area of the Penpo region. He was a great spiritual son of Gönpawa.[350] He was known as Kharak Gomchung[351] because he meditated in a cave named Black Hollow in Kharak. He was also a disciple of Bagom.[352] Kharakpa had a number of disciples, including Dultön,[353] Zangkar Dzökung,[354] and Lhopa Dharma Kyap.[355])

> Whatever food and clothing you may obtain in this life is
> adequate.
> After you die, you won't be able to seek the fruit of
> enlightenment.[356]

> Since you don't know if you will die tomorrow or the day after
> tomorrow,
> you should seek enlightenment with a sense of urgency.
> Though he may not have practiced farming or accumulation of
> possessions,
> has there ever been a great meditator who was seen or heard of
> that passed away due to cold or hunger?
> Nor will there ever be one who is seen or heard of in the future.

Potowa said:

> Though it may snow for nine days and nights, a sparrow will find its own shelter. Likewise, even when there are difficulties in the land and the dharma is experiencing unfavorable factors, if you practice dharma diligently, you will be able to find a place to hide, to reside in, and where it is safe to pursue the dharma.

Tsangpa Gyare[357] said:

(Tsangpa Gyare was a great spiritual son of the realized adept Lingrepa,[358] and he founded Druk[359] and Ralung[360] monasteries. He was considered to be an emanation[361] of Naropa. He had many disciples, such as Lo Repa[362] and Götsangpa,[363] the two of Pa[364] and Kyang,[365] and the two of Gya[366] and Dre.[367] He lived as a gelong.[368])

> The highest form of generosity is to remain unattached to this life through having abandoned it mentally. The highest form of accomplishing the aims of beings is for everything that you do to serve the welfare of sentient beings. The highest form of wealth {467} is to develop a sense of satisfaction toward every object. The highest form of homeland is to be content in whatever country you may be present. The highest form of a palace is to be comfortable in whatever place it is that you sleep. The highest form of companion is to be a person who consoles others effectively when they are experiencing misfortune. The highest form of a courageous person is one who brings to completion the activities that have been undertaken. The highest form of a person whose speech is influential and trustworthy is to be someone who has attained his or her own autonomy. The highest form of

> compassion is that of a person whose mind does not come under the influence of desire or hatred. The highest form of morality is for your mind not to form improper thoughts. The highest means of summoning celestial beings[369] is to have a mind that has gained spiritual realizations.

Gyalse Rinpoche[370] said that mentally abandoning this life is the most supreme method of eliminating mental obscurations.

A certain Geshe Kharakpa,[371] who was a disciple of Kunpang Drakgyal,[372] possessed great spiritual qualities and great virtue, yet he contracted leprosy. No matter what remedy he attempted, none was effective in alleviating this condition. One night, he thought to himself, "This illness has effectively caused me to be expelled from the company of humans. So now I shall become one who recognizes this expulsion. I shall give away all my possessions to individuals who are on the side of virtue. I will take up residence at the foot of a rocky mountain in Kyimo Dzatreng, beg for food from passersby, and recite the *maṇi* mantra." That night, he dreamt that while he was carrying water, a person of a light complexion took some of the water and, having placed it upon a rocky crag in Kyimo Dzatreng, the water dripped down upon his body. When he woke up the next morning, his bed was covered in water and his leprosy was cured.

This act of mentally abandoning one's life is a practice that is certain to cause you to generate spiritual realizations that you have not previously generated, as well as not only to keep from losing those that you have previously generated but also enable you to develop them to ever higher levels. The great spiritual adept Yumowa[373] said:

> The inability to develop your spiritual realizations
> is like the light of the moon being overwhelmed by that of the sun.
> This condition is due to having attachment for dualistic appearances.
> All you fortunate ones, cut this mental entanglement.

Tsangpa Gyare said:

> Meditative progress that lacks a caretaker[374]
> is like wealth that is swept away by wind,

a lion that becomes a companion to dogs,
or a jewel that sinks into a swamp.
Thus, the caretaker of detachment is needed.

If you succeed in overcoming every aspect of attachment to this life, improvement[375] in all your other dharma practices will come about without difficulty. However, if you lack this detachment, even though it may seem that you are developing every form of experiential realization, it is often seen and heard that those forms of realization are quickly lost. This result can also be established through reasoning.

Drogön[376] said:

If you don't cut through attachment to this life,
it may appear that the experiential awareness
of faith and higher concentrations have arisen,
but at a certain point they will be lost and disappear.
By gaining this one quality,[377] you will develop steadfastness.
Other spiritual qualities will arise in your mental continuum;
they will be maintained and developed to ever higher levels.
All forms of spiritual awareness will come into being,
as if they emerged from within the center of space.
For instance, like seeds that are planted downward into the earth,
this planting[378] will cause excellent forms of spiritual awareness to
arise.

Some individuals who have developed a faith that earnestly desires to practice dharma, and who have overcome their attachment and generated strong resolve, also seem to have gained the ability to adhere to their values but then become discouraged when they fail to develop genuine forms of one-pointed concentration. As a result, they think to themselves, "Though I tried to practice the dharma, it appears that I don't have the ability to elicit its powers" and give up their spiritual efforts. This plight is just what Tsangpa Gyare described when he said that "meditative progress that lacks a caretaker is like . . . a lion that becomes a companion to dogs." Therefore, if you fail to develop the attitude that has been described above at length, there is no way that you will be able to achieve any degree of genuine happiness or virtue. On the other hand, if you succeed in developing it, this state of mind in which attachment has been overcome and that enables you to gain every form of happiness and virtue according to your wishes is one that is extolled by all the buddhas and bodhisattvas. Therefore, each time that you elicit an instance of this awareness that is so difficult for all beings to develop, you should rejoice at having been able to do so.

The inability to sit down in a cross-legged position[379] is an indication of being someone who does not realize about him- or herself that he or she is a person of little merit. As Potowa said (in the *Blue Udder*):

> As the saying goes, "Even if you have no teeth, {469} mash your food with your gums." Likewise, although your mind may not be drawn to the dharma readily, if you can tell yourself, "I will try my best to practice the dharma," that is the way in which to improve your mind and develop a genuine form of the dharma.
>
> In this life, if you train your mind up to the aspiration[380]
> and merely plant seeds for the practices above that
> by continually generating prayers to cultivate them,
> that will be as meaningful as attaining the Great Seal.
>
> As this verse states, begin by training your mind in overcoming attachment to this life, which is also known as the practice of impermanence. Following that, fully absorb yourself in the subsequent forms of mind training up to and including the aspirational form of enlightenment mind. Although you may not be able to develop the practices above that, such as quiescence and insight, you should at least plant the seeds for doing so in the future. If you should die while making such aspirational prayers, that will be a spiritual accomplishment as meaningful as if you had attained the spiritual state of the Great Seal.
>
> The difference between great and small merit
> is not determined by having much or little wealth.
> It is determined by whether or not you develop
> erring attitudes in your mental continuum.
>
> Having an abundance of material possessions in this life is not what qualifies someone as being possessed of merit. Rather, a

meritorious person is someone who has developed such unerring attitudes as the overcoming of attachment.

Gyalse Rinpoche said:

> For your mental continuum to turn to the dharma is the ultimate way to collect the accumulations.
> For you to recall the uncertainty of the time of death is the ultimate form of a clever person.
> For you to abandon evil and cultivate virtue is the ultimate form of an intelligent person.
> For you to carry all beings on the crown of your head is the ultimate form of a noble person.
> For you to have a mind that knows satisfaction is the ultimate form of a rich person.
> For you not to have attachment toward anything is the ultimate form of a happy person.

Through reflecting in such a manner, you will be able to overcome attachment toward everything. If you succeed in overcoming attachment toward all of samsara by causing this attitude to develop further, then it can also be said that you have attained the first stages of the path. Without this quality, no matter what other attributes you may possess, you will not be someone who has attained the first stages of the path. But by having done so,[381] {470} you will have truly entered the company of genuine dharma practitioners.[382]

You might ask yourself, "If these are the benefits of mentally abandoning this life and the disadvantages of failing to abandon it, what then is the method by which to accomplish the act of mentally abandoning this life?" Regarding this point, Tsangpa Gyare[383] said that in order to mentally abandon this life, you must observe these eleven commitments:[384]

> (1) Dwell alone and do not conform to other's wishes; (2) abandon your homeland; (3) cultivate an attitude that exclusively feels dejection toward sensory objects; (4) adopt a lowly status but do not try to please anyone, no matter who they may be; (5) remain vigilant about cultivating antidotes that overcome adverse mental states; (6) do not give undue importance to what

> others say and remain undecided about what they say or claim to be true; (7) do not become unhappy if everything you cherish is swept away by the wind; (8) abandon your former ordinary life as a useless waste and live as if you were a beggar who is believed by others to have died; (9) continually count[385] the "forceful mantra" of having no needs;[386] (10) be one who keeps hold of his or her own nose-tether;[387] and (11) make your excellent spiritual practice resemble a multitude of clouds that have gathered in the sky.

Moreover, it is said that in order to mentally abandon this life, you must have a character possessed of a fortitude and strong decisiveness that can "break rocks." You must be easygoing about what is incidental but incapable of being swayed with regard to what is of profound importance like the neck of an old yak. You must be fearful of social interaction[388] like a deer that has caught the scent of a potential predator. You must be one who regards the failure to engage in forethought as being like a wrongdoer who has jumped over a precipice. You must be able to endure hardships like a widow who is raising her children.

Generally speaking, with regard to the term "desire" in the phrase "abandoning desire,"[389] Ārya Asaṅga said that there are two types of desire, the objects of desire and the desire that is a mental affliction.[390] He further said that both of these should be abandoned by those who have gone forth[391] into the homeless state. The objects of desire include a country, privately owned land, a house, one's father and mother and other relatives, and such property as material goods and grain, and the like. {471} The meaning of the term "one who has gone forth" and the individuals who are referred to by that term are those who have abandoned all of these things by leaving home and going forth into the homeless state.

Regarding the manner in which to mentally abandon this life, if all those renunciates who have gone forth into the teaching of the Bhagavān must act in that way, one should be able to understand how this is done through observation. However, since present-day persons of inferior intellect will not understand this subject unless it is explained to them in specific detail, in accord with the explanations that Tsangpa Gyare gave in the past, there are nineteen instructions that relate to the act of mentally abandoning this life.

1. Abandon Your Homeland

Among these, the first instruction, which is to abandon your homeland, is of great importance as it includes the objects that give rise to attachment—such as your relatives, and various forms of property and wealth, such as private land and a home, and so on—as well as the objects that give rise to anger, such as your enemies. And once your mind has come under the influence of attachment or hatred, you will not be able to carry out an effective form of dharma practice.

Even if you do not become subject to attachment or hatred, those individuals can develop attachment or hatred toward you. Family members will charge you with assisting them in carrying out their household duties that relate to this life. If you refuse to carry them out, this will prompt them to accumulate evil deeds. Your enemies will bring to mind prior experiences about which they possess resentment, and this will cause them to seek to harm you by means of their three doors.[392] In these ways, you will create evil deeds and suffering for both yourself and others. On the other hand, through abandoning your homeland, you will remain free of these faults. Potowa said about this:

> Abandon your birthplace and distance yourself from relatives.
> Abandon social interaction and practice proper attention.[393]
> Liberation is not far away for such a person.

The three principles of abandoning your birthplace, cutting off ties with your relatives, and abandoning all entities that have not been examined[394] are an instruction followed in the oral tradition of those monks who are from Radreng Monastery. All later individuals have found this to be an instruction that is difficult to carry out.

The *Sūtra Encouraging a Superior Attitude*[395] says:

> It is better for you to go farther than a hundred yojana[396] {472}
> from a place where elaborations[397] or disputes occur.
> Do not reside or dwell for the duration of an instant
> in a place where the mental afflictions occur.
> Those renunciates who seek meaning and spiritual qualities

should not engage in disputes with minds that are defiled.
You should not have fields or engage in agriculture or commerce,
for the sake of which[398] these elaborations occur.
You have no sons or daughters, and no wife,
no home and no group of family relatives,
no male or female servants, and no lordly status. . . .[399]

Tsangpa Gyare said:

Since mental afflictions arise from your native country,
it is through lack of courage that you don't abandon your homeland.
Since spiritual practice consists of developing antidotes,
it is through lack of courage that you don't cultivate the antidotes.
Since explaining the dharma is determined by proper conditions,
it is through lack of courage that you fail to meet with these conditions.
Though it is said you were taken by the wind after having abandoned
the homeland in which you were born, you should have no regret.
Though you may starve to death after having given all your possessions
to your lama's faction, you should have no regret.
Though you are said to be completely dried up while being in water
and that the time spent with your lama was too short, you should have no regret.
Leave behind the homeland where you were born and that will establish
the auspicious factors for developing spiritual antidotes.
If you perceive worldly happiness and success as unfavorable events,
that will establish auspicious factors for developing faith.
Mentally abandon worldliness, and that will establish
the auspicious factors for practicing generosity.

If you fail to abandon the homeland where you were born, you will give rise to attachment and hatred continuously; therefore, you must abandon the homeland where you were born. If you fail to give up worldly activities, you won't obtain the contentment of an ascetic's life; therefore, you must give up those activities. If you fail to cast wealth and possessions to the wind, your close relations will not be able to settle your estate; therefore, cast your wealth and possessions to the wind.

Gyalse Rinpoche said:

> It is the practice of a bodhisattva to leave behind your homeland,
> that place where attachment to family and friends {473}
> overwhelms you like a torrent,
> where aversion toward the faction of your enemies burns like a
> blazing fire,
> and where delusion's darkness makes you oblivious about what to
> adopt and reject.[400]

Je Rendawa[401] said:

(His ordination name was Zhönu Lodrö and he was an omniscient being who attained the one-pointed concentrations of both the generation and completion stages. He was a great spiritual son of such masters as the Lotsāwa Jangchup Tsemo,[402] and he fostered disciples such as the group known as the Seven Omniscient Ones,[403] which included Je Tsongkhapa and the like.)

> Do not remain for even an instant in a place
> where, by staying there, your attachments will grow stronger,
> your mental continuum will be bound by the fetters of gain and
> honor,
> and others' mental continua will be tormented by envy and
> competitiveness.

Barawa[404] wrote:

> Beings of an adverse time undergo many difficult experiences.
> Neighbors oppress and harm you as much as they can.
> Harsh taxes are relentless, excessive, and frequent.
> The distressed have no opportunity to find relief.
> It is difficult indeed to stay in one's homeland in adverse times.
> Develop aversion[405] in your mind and go to a hermitage.
> Though you know that your homeland gives rise to desire and hatred,

you may form a narrow, erring view that it offers abundant
resources.
When you realize what is right is for you to meditate in seclusion,
may that contented dharma practitioner be preserved by a lama's
compassion.

Gyalse Rinpoche wrote:

If after rejecting the honor of your own family, you desire
to be honored by others, develop an attitude of indifference.
If after completely abandoning your homeland, friends, and
wealth,
you become fettered by a mind that desires fame and renown,
that is like binding yourself with a cord after breaking free of
shackles.

As these lines indicate, even if the place where you live is not your homeland, you must abandon any region that causes your own or others' mental afflictions to grow stronger and become one who has no fixed place of residence.

Potowa {474} said:

Live your life by observing the conduct of begging for food.
Cultivate having few desires, and keep your mind free of anguish.
Be a wandering ascetic like the ever-moving sun and moon.
Don't reside in one region, and don't remain in a single place.
It is a failing to have a single long-term companion or patron.
Don't give the nape of your neck to anyone.[406]

Potowa also said:

If you sit, leave only the imprint of your buttocks, and if you walk, leave only the imprint of your feet. When a monk turns his shoe tips,[407] he must be done with all of his possessions. When you leave a certain place, carry out such actions as donating this and that object. It is not acceptable to say, "This or that must be taken on as a burden." It isn't acceptable to stay in a single place that is continually in conflict with the dharma. If a place causes you to accumulate evil deeds, you must leave. If it causes you to lose the dharma, it does you no good to avoid losing your native land.

The *Lamp of the Moon Sūtra*[408] (This sūtra is the same as the one that is called *The King of Samādhis*[409]) declares:

Those who have no conception of "mine"
and who have no objects at all to which they cling,
they live in this world like rhinoceroses,
moving about like the wind in the sky.[410]

The *Sūtra on Closely Placed Recollection*[411] also declares:

He accepts alms food at most once at midday,[412]
does not long for food of the following day,
and is satisfied with a full stomach;[413]
a proper bhikṣu is one who is like this.

It is also said that if you are such a person, you will also be one who can rise up and leave a particular region as soon as it causes harm to your dharma practice.

Khetsun Zhönu Drup[414] said:

(His birthplace was Yuwa Dong,[415] and he founded the Pelnam Samding[416] Monastery. His principal spiritual practices were the Six Teachings of Naropa and the Six Teachings of Niguma. He was an extraordinary being who was both a learned scholar and realized practitioner.)

Staying in a single place for a long time is a cause that gives rise to attachment and hatred.
Excessive familiarity with friends causes partiality and attachment to grow stronger.
Accumulating many possessions prevents the performance of physical and verbal virtuous practices.
{475} Search your heart to determine whether wandering through an unfamiliar land
will bring about a reputation of impropriety or affection.

He also said:

> Going about to visit many places will cause you to feel regret.
> Staying in your residence will bring increased virtuous activities.

He further said:

> Changing residences frequently will awaken virtuous activities.

Therefore, you should decide if it is correct to leave or remain in a particular place by examining whether doing so will increase your virtuous activities or not. As it is recorded in Potowa's sayings:

> Regarding what constitutes a suitable place and companions,
> the proper place is the one that, by residing there,
> will cause the three trainings prompted by enlightenment mind to develop.
> A proper companion is one whose association will also cause them to develop.
> The opposite of those is not a suitable place or companion.[417]

He also said:

> Like gathering kindling[418] as the forces to do battle with fire, if rather than harming your dharma practice, whatever suffering and adversity you experience only serves to enhance it, then you don't need to abandon that place.

(Since Fire and Kindling were not getting along with one another, Kindling gathered his forces. When Fire was told that Kindling was gathering his forces, Fire said, "No matter how great his forces may become, they will all be my allies.")

2. Abandon Your Close Relatives

No matter where you might be residing, it is important to sever your ties with close relatives. Tsangpa Gyare said:

> If you reflect with despair on the ways of ordinary persons, that is a sign you have severed your ties with worldly society. If you think of the ways of ordinary persons with a sense of gratitude, that is a sign you have sunk into the swamp of attachment and hatred. If you understand all worldly affairs to be mistaken, that is a sign you have overcome attachment for this life. If you understand everything to be truly existent, that is a sign you have become hardened[419] to virtuous activities.

Moreover, the act of abandoning close relatives must be such that you do not abandon concern for them as sentient beings and you maintain your compassion for them. Rather, what you must do to carry out this act properly is sever your physical and material ties with close relatives, because the failure to do so {476} will prevent you from practicing the dharma successfully. Thus, when you cut these ties, it is preferable that you ask for, and receive permission from, your parents to do so. However, no matter how much they may try to intimidate you, or how much sadness or complaining they may express, you must not become discouraged. Since the time of the Bhagavān, all dharma practitioners have had to enter a spiritual life after abandoning their close relatives while their eyes were filled with tears, as this circumstance is like a major causal factor for doing so.

Gyalse Rinpoche said:

> Out of affection, close relatives and others strive to obtain
> this life's prosperity and urge others to do the same.
> Those who seek this life's aims are actually foolish persons
> who, desiring to be helpful, bind you to what is harmful.
>
> Since, to become liberated, you must mentally abandon
> this life and exert yourself in cultivating the profound path,
> it is essential to abandon the former for the sake of the latter,
> and to strive at pursuing spiritual practice in solitude.

In wealth, others will pursue you even when you flee.
In poverty, others will flee when you approach them.
When even a son is capable of killing his father,
what person would place their trust in close relatives?

To your face, they display a pleasant demeanor;
in private, they spread many kinds of disrepute.
Companions that are fools[420] who harm you in return for your help
will deceive you even though they are supposed to be your friends.

When you are wealthy, they will smile and employ many kinds
of flattery[421] as a way of obtaining some of your wealth.
When you are poor, they scowl and oppose you. Indeed, it is a mistake
to nurture friends who do not benefit you in the slightest way.

When your many friends band together, they defeat adversaries;
should they split up, they develop attachment and hatred among themselves.
If certain circumstances arise, even fathers and sons will kill one another.
It is extremely rare for a friend to bring true benefit and happiness.

Geshe Kharakpa said:

Parents and children who are devoted to this life,
as well as the totality of all kinsmen and relatives,
are like visitors that have gathered in a common place.
You must bring to mind that you have no connection to them.

The Lord of Reasoning[422] wrote:

Sensory pleasures are like the worst of enemies;
close relatives are like shackles that bind;
desire for greatness is like a demon that has long possessed you;
O Gyamawa,[423] don't have many thoughts of attachment.

Kyechokpa said:

(His ordination name was Samten Pel[424] and he was a disciple of Gyadrak Chöje,[425] a practitioner of the Pacification tradition.[426] Kyechokpa himself cultivated Pacification instructions as his principal form of spiritual practice. He founded Gomo[427] and Yawa[428] Monasteries and was regarded to have attained one-pointed concentration.)

Attachment and hatred will arise toward the country of your
homeland;
if you're someone who possesses aversion, elicit a willingness to be
diligent.
A distressed mind will arise toward friends and close relatives;
if you're someone who wants to be a dharma practitioner, remain
disinterested.
Gathering and storing will arise toward wealth and possessions;
if you're someone who possesses detachment, remain inwardly
free.
Desire and craving will arise toward food that is delicious and
sweet;
if you're someone who possesses resolve, practice austerity.

Those close relatives who can never be pleased
only want more care when you do extend care to them.
It is better to sever the ties that bring mental distress.
These are heartfelt words of truth; hold them firmly in your mind.

Barawa said:

Though the closeness of one's relationship with friends and family
is the same,
a wealthy person's mouth, teeth, face, and hands[429] are held in high
regard.
However, those of a poor and destitute person are viewed as
inauspicious,
as having no influence, with disregard, and they are held in
contempt.
In adverse times, it is difficult to treat friends and associates fairly.

3. Abandon Servants and a Retinue[430]

Likewise, you should abandon attachment for your servants and retinue, as well as your disciples and so on. As several verses from *Entry into the Conduct That Leads to Enlightenment* declare:

> Out of desire for contact with those who are dear,
> you do not see things {478} as they truly are,
> you fall away from aversion for samsara,
> and you become consumed by sorrow.[431]
>
> Thinking about those persons, your life
> goes by in vain, swiftly and continuously.
> The eternal dharma is lost
> due to an impermanent entity.[432]
>
> Ordinary beings are difficult to please;
> instantly they become friends
> and instantly they become enemies.
> They become angered at an occasion for joy.[433]
>
> When told useful advice, they become angered.
> They prevent me from gaining what is beneficial.
> Moreover, if one does not listen to them,
> they become angry and proceed to the unhappy states.[434]
>
> In this way, when one person associates with another,
> this leads to meeting with what is harmful.
> Thus, I shall dwell alone happily
> with a mind that is free of agitation.
>
> One should flee far away from foolish persons.[435]

A verse from the *Collection of Uplifting Sayings* declares:

> It is suffering to associate with fools,
> who are like enemies in every way.

You should not look at or listen to fools,
nor should you associate with them.[436]

Chöje Bu said:

Many buddhas of the past could not spiritually tame them;
all the powerful bodhisattvas could not spiritually tame them.
When criticized, they become angry,
and when praised, they become haughty.
They hold the coarse attitudes of envy toward superiors,
rivalry toward equals, and pride toward inferiors.
Even when spoken to with words that conform to dharma, they develop attachment and hatred.
Therefore, you should reflect, "As I am presently unable to tame
such foolish persons, I should seek to tame my own mind."
Moreover, regarding the statement that "Others' aims are the dharma's chief form of practice,"
its meaning[437] is that, if you know the faculties, constituent elements, and disposition
of those to be tamed, as well as their accumulations and past and future lives,[438]
you should avoid being attached to your own aims and spiritually tame those that need to be tamed.
But if you try to act on behalf of others while desiring your own gain,
fame, happiness, and praise, and without having supernatural knowledge,
you will be like a person without wings who tries to fly up into the sky;
such acts will not accomplish others' aims and will only be a cause for your own aims to be lost.

Also, regarding the statement that "teaching and hearing the dharma serve to preserve the Buddha's doctrine,"
its meaning is that having relied upon renunciation[439] and pure morality,
a learned person should teach the canon's three baskets[440]

to a śrāvaka who is impartial, diligent, and intelligent.[441]
If you gather a following out of desire for this life's gain and renown
and teach dharma without faith, unwillingly and without having practiced it,
this will only serve as a cause for giving rise to attachment and desire,
and this act of teaching and hearing dharma will be a fetter that binds you to samsara.[442]

Tsangpa Gyare said:

> If you wish to be content, dwell alone. If you have a great quantity of food, let it be great; you don't need to share it with anyone else. If you have none, let it be so; you don't need to care for anyone else. Since you are free of worries, you will be content. Regardless of whether you are cold or hungry, you will be content by dwelling alone.

This point is quite true. It is evident that everyone's degree of contentment is determined by wealth and possessions. This can be illustrated by the fact that a monk almost never needs to take a loan from another person, while most ordinary individuals almost always need to do so.

Geshe Kharakpa said:

Nothing is rarer than a retinue that is faithful and respectful.
Nothing is worse that a leader of evil persons.
Don't take on the status of a leader of virtuous persons,
you must be one who adheres to a lowly position.

He also said:

Untrustworthy, unaccepting of advice, and selfish—
it is better not to have a retinue that causes the outflows[443] to grow stronger.
My attendants are effort and wisdom;
they accomplish all my goals and are tireless.

Barawa said:

> If someone is wealthy and has a sharp tongue,
> what such a person[444] {480} urges to be done will be heeded.
> But someone who lacks the power to benefit or harm
> will be scorned even after performing an act of kindness.
> In adverse times, it is difficult to be aided by a retinue.
> Anyone can know how to prepare food for oneself.
> The "indispensable attendant" is for you to have skillful hands.
> You don't need a person with a hypocritical virtuous manner;[445]
> you will be much more at ease with solitary conduct.
> The food of austerity does not become exhausted.
> A solitary person can obtain sustenance anywhere.
> The clothing of solitude will definitely keep you warm.
> The warmth of the caṇḍālī[446] fire is deep and strong.
> The practice of residing in solitude is supreme in every way.
> The meditation hut of selflessness is most pleasing.

4. Abandon Spurious Forms of Accomplishing Others' Aims, Such as Teaching and Learning, Giving Oral Transmissions of Scriptures, and Explaining Instructions

Drogön[447] said:

> Regarding those of us who are great meditators, in these times when we wear as clothing a cloak sewn of woolen cloth, hold prayer beads made of *arura*[448] seeds, and have the footprint of a bright meditation hut at Little Bird[449] in which to meditate, there are those of lesser effort who engage in the practice of teaching dharma when it will definitely not benefit others. The spiritual teacher known as the Great Gyer[450] did not advocate this. I also think to myself, "Is this not insane behavior?"

Tsangpa Gyare said:

> A person who hopes for a harvest when seeds have not been planted is a hungry demon.[451] A person who hopes to benefit beings at an inopportune time will experience fatigue.

As it is recorded in Potowa's sayings:

> In this way, ripening your own mental continuum
> should be the main practice of a novice.
> Don't make fulfilling others' aims your main goal.
> Mentally, have no concerns but that of others;
> however, don't take action directly in body and speech.[452]

Tropu Lotsāwa[453] said:

> If you don't know how to give yourself lasting advice,
> however much {481} others may treat you as a lord,
> in reality, you are just a slave who receives no wages.
> Alas, you are one whose name is empty and useless.[454]

Je Rendawa said:

> Until you gain a mind that possesses a firmness
> that is never influenced by the eight concerns,
> do nothing other than taming your mind in solitude;
> do not ruin your own aims by trying to fulfill those of others.

5. Abandon Desire for Gain and Honor

In order to mentally abandon this life, it is important to reject attachment to gain and honor. As the *Sūtra Encouraging a Superior Attitude* declares:

> Here, O Maitreya, a bodhisattva, a great spiritual being, should regard attachment to gain and honor as (having the disadvantage of) giving rise to desire. He or she should regard gain and honor as bringing ruin to one's recollection, (because seeking those flawed aims causes you to become inattentive to the spiritual learning that you developed previously). He or she should regard gain and honor as causing a sense of loftiness (due to pride) or dejection (due to despondency) through either obtaining or losing wealth, and so on.
>
> (Using the same predicate,) the sūtra also states that attachment to gain and honor should be regarded (that is, understood) as giving rise to delusion; as causing greed and attachment toward one's

family (of relatives and patrons) in order to accomplish one's own aims (that relate to this life);[455] as giving rise to guile[456] and deceitfulness,[457] (which is the deception of others and causes acts of hypocrisy); as engendering shamelessness,[458] (which occurs for reasons relating to oneself) and absence of abashment,[459] (which occurs for reasons relating to others) due to abandonment of the four attributes of the ārya lineage[460] (also known as the four qualities of a bhikṣu); as being forbidden by all buddhas (except when it accomplishes others' aims); as giving rise to pride,[461] (mental) conceit,[462] and (physical or verbal) arrogance;[463] as engendering disrespect toward those worthy of honor[464] (when material gain is obtained); as being the aspect of Māra's faction[465] (that consists of the {482} mental afflictions); as being in every respect the root of lack of mindfulness,[466] (which fails to cultivate virtuous acts and fails to abandon unvirtuous ones,) and the condition that steals one's roots of virtue[467] (that is, gain and honor steal the three roots of virtue because they generate attachment when they are obtained, hatred when they are not obtained, and ignorance when they are mistakenly believed to be real); as resembling lightning, a wheel, and a thunderbolt[468] (three similes of impermanence); as being tainted by many contaminants[469] (that is, mental afflictions); as causing one (out of attachment) to look for the homes of friends and the homes of those (benefactors) who are likely to give alms;[470] as engendering unhappiness (when you fail to obtain material gain); as bringing confusion to one's judgment (such as when a person of low standing is shown a position of high status and it is perceived as being like an unreal dream); as engendering sorrow (in the mind) when cherished (inner and outer) objects undergo change (that is, when they disappear); as causing inattentiveness of the four closely placed recollections[471] (of the body, feelings, the mind, and mental entities); as weakening your (cultivation of) pure spiritual practices; as causing the loss of the four forms of correct abandonment[472] (which consist of abandoning evil deeds that have arisen previously and developing virtuous acts that have not arisen previously, and so on); as causing the loss of (the four elements of) miraculous power[473] and (the five or six forms of) supernatural knowledge;[474] as causing one who previously (that is, before having obtained gain and honor oneself) showed honor to others later (that is, after having obtained gain and honor) to fail to show honor (to others); as causing one to associate with one's enemies (in a favorable manner) and to abandon one's friends (who do not offer gain and honor); as being like a prostitute in that it deceives others (through being a principal object that is longed for); as causing one to give up meditative absorption and the (four) immeasurables; and as causing one to fall in to the hells, the birth state of an animal, and Yama's realm.[475] One should regard attachment to gain and honor as being a form of behavior (that is, conduct) that is similar to that of {483} Devadatta and Udraka (who followed a different teacher and a different path). O Maitreya, these are the forms of disadvantages that a bodhisattva should regard as occurring in relation to gain and honor.[476]

(If you ask, "What is the benefit of regarding gain and honor in this way?") having regarded them in this way, a bodhisattva should rejoice in the virtuous quality of having few desires[477] (when gain and honor have not been obtained) and should not be tormented (by desire for gain and honor).

What is the reason for that (that is, not being tormented by desire for gain and honor)? O Maitreya, it is because a person who has few desires is not subject to any of those faults (that were just explained) as being of this form, and because that (person who has few desires) is not subject to any obstacles to a buddha's spiritual qualities (both those that relate to the cause of enlightenment and the result of enlightenment itself). He is not scorned by householders and renunciates who have gone forth (through having lost faith in him). As one who abides in a pure attitude, he or she is worthy of being protected (from adverse factors) by gods and humans. He or she is unafraid of falling into any of the unhappy migratory states. As one who is invulnerable to threats (such as that of not being offered objects of material value or having them confiscated), he or she cannot become overpowered by anyone. As one who is free of becoming an object of the influence of Māra, he or she is incapable of being be led astray (from virtue). He or she cannot be weakened by experiencing any kinds of distress (due to having failed to obtain material possessions). He or she is someone who is sought after by gods and humans (because he or she is viewed favorably by them). As one who is intent upon cultivation of (mundane and transcendent forms of) meditative absorption, he or she is one who (has a mind that) perceives (its object) clearly. Having abandoned guile[478] (a deviousness of mind and a form of dishonesty that arises through abandoning the cultivation of moral prescriptions) and deceitfulness[479] (an attitude that deceives others and that expresses something other than what is being thought), {484} he or she becomes mindful (a mental state that cultivates virtuous acts and abandons unvirtuous ones, develops spiritual self-discipline with regard to one's own mind, preserves the mental opinions of others, and restrains the doors of one's senses) through seeing the five sensory pleasures as having faults.[480] As one who (is disciplined) and abides in the four attributes of the ārya lineage,[481] he or she is one who acts in accord with what he or she states, (which means that he or she adheres firmly to his or her affirmations). He or she is sought after (that is, is viewed favorably and approached) by those who are learned (in the canonical scriptures) and by fellow spiritual practitioners (that is, those who are cultivating the three trainings that constitute the path to nirvana). O Maitreya, the wise bodhisattva who has learned the (twelve) benefits that have such forms should, by means of a superior attitude, rejoice in having few desires. This virtue of having few desires should be developed in order to abandon all forms of attachment to gain and honor.[482]

6. Abandon Collecting and Accumulating Material Possessions[483]

Gyalse Rinpoche said:

> Because it is a pitfall for dharma practitioners, abandon the
> haughtiness associated with attachment to this life.
> Because attachment to gain and honor is a fetter than binds you,
> cut the entanglement of desire for sensory pleasures.
> Because fame and renown are meaningless, abandon attachment
> for them.
> If you lack the awareness of being satisfied with whatever you
> have,
> that is a cause for increasing the suffering and evil deeds that
> derive from accumulating possessions.
> As it will naturally cause your happiness and virtuous acts to
> increase,
> my spiritual instruction is for you to cultivate the attitude of
> knowing satisfaction.[484]
> Therefore, having completely abandoned the thoughts and deeds
> that seek to acquire

gain and honor, and so on, which constitute this life's prosperity,
strive constantly and remain free of lassitude as you practice
the true dharma that is sure to benefit you at the time of death.

Kyechokpa said:

Because you lack satisfaction about wealth that is like a magically created illusion,
you accumulate it out of attachment; however, it will be left behind.
Thus, what you accumulated will be enjoyed by others.
This is heartfelt advice; hold it firmly in your mind.
Because you lack an aspiration that has an ultimate aim,
and a mind that has short-term needs is {485} not sufficient,
it will be difficult for you to overcome attachment.
May you be blessed to be able to give up acquisitiveness.
Though you did not attract a following of disciples with your fame,
you are unable to send away those who have faith in you.
Therefore, it will be difficult for you to become a renunciate.[485]
May you be blessed to be able to dwell alone without companions.

Je Rendawa said:

Except for the three spiritual garments, an alms bowl, and the like,
those material possessions that are needed to sustain oneself,
may I not keep for my own benefit even a sesame grain
of those excess objects, gold, or other objects of value.

Barawa said:

Though you see that no one can take anything that has been accumulated,
you still fail to develop a mind that will practice generosity;
when will you cut the entanglement of attachment to sensory objects?
Though you may control the wealth of the four continents,

except for the punishment of having to lose it,
the time will never come when it is sufficient or more than you need.
It will be seized by those more powerful or stolen by those less powerful.
It is difficult to keep wealth and property during adverse times.

7. Abandon Attachment to Food and Drink

Speaking generally, the activity of accumulating and storing riches and so on can be due to a variety of reasons, including craving food and drink, apprehension about starving or freezing to death, having the desire to perform such actions as making offerings to one's spiritual teacher, and not understanding the disadvantages of attachment to sensory pleasures. Among these, having attachment to food and drink is improper.

A disciple who was staying near Potowa was unable to succeed in his dharma practice because he was tormented by great concern about food. Potowa said to him, "One who would cause the sky to fall for the sake of food will not be able to gain the dharma."

Khetsun Zhönu Drup said:

A cause that gives rise to the wrong livelihood of hypocrisy in body and speech
is to indulge excessively in food that is offered in faith. As this is a factor that diminishes
your spiritual practice, would it not be proper to cut the root
of the entanglement of food that is delicious in taste
and reduce your food and clothing {486} to the bare necessity?

Tropuwa Sönam Senge[486] said:

Moreover, the hypocritical conduct shown to the faithful,
who, in their devotion, prepare and send excellent sustenance,
is done to preserve the opinion of others and thus is a cause that binds you.
My heartfelt advice is to practice the conduct of equal taste.[487]

At a former time, on an occasion when Geshe Drom Tönpa, the Four Yogis,[488] and others were traveling to Radreng Monastery, after they had finished eating "hot"[489] food, there was no warm food remaining for them to eat. As they were discussing what they should do, Gönpawa[490] said, "I shall eat what is coming to us from Pünadong." As soon as he made this statement that was based on his supernatural knowledge, a benefactor appeared who was carrying objects with which to serve them. Because Geshe Tönpa preferred that one's spiritual qualities should be kept hidden, he reprimanded him, saying "Gönpawa is outwardly great." All the former excellent Kadam spiritual beings made keeping their spiritual qualities hidden a fundamental principle, saying "By keeping spiritual qualities hidden, Māra cannot harm you."

They also said, "Spiritual beings should not strive to use their knowledge as a means of livelihood. They should delight in carrying out ascetic practices."

In the early part of their lives, all those disciples who are continually in the presence of their teacher[491] have to observe such austerities as limiting the amount of food that they eat and the like. They typically spend their lives enduring hunger. Chenga Tsultrim Bar didn't patch his religious garment with cloth; he used pieces of leather instead. For this reason, he came to be known as "Chenga, who wears a leather lower garment." He is reputed to have said, "Because I practiced meditation without engaging in any ordinary endeavors, I have even forgotten the names of the worldly concerns." Milarepa practiced austerities such as limiting the amount of food that he ate for nine years, and Mokchokpa[492] did so for twelve years. All the excellent spiritual teachers have done the same.

8. Do Not Even Accept Wealth That Is Obtained Effortlessly

In order to practice this kind of abandonment, it will not suffice to say, "I shall not stop the acquisition of material possessions if it should occur, nor shall I pursue it if it should not." As a verse from the sūtra (titled *The Questions Posed by Pūrṇa*[493]) declares:

> I do not seek the status of a lord.
> If it were obtained, I would abandon it.
> Now, I seek only the Buddha's profound teaching
> and a morality that is completely pure.

Also, as the saying goes, "It is better to abandon wrongful objects than to cultivate their antidotes." It has also been said frequently above that you should abandon those qualities that constitute the prosperity of this life, as they represent objects that give rise to the mental afflictions. It is also stated in the sayings of Potowa:

> The seeker of emancipation should choose
> the four worldly concerns that are unwanted.[494]
> If they are not experienced, your treasure will not be harmed.
> If they are experienced, (that very experience) will be taken by another.
> But even if the four of gain and the rest (that is, fame, praise, and pleasure)
> occur for another,
> that very person should be understood as having already died,
> like the lord from Dokham who caught a bee.

(It is said that the one in his hand attracted another, and then a second one, and then many, which, after biting him, were eliminated. Similarly, the four worldly qualities of gain and so on attract enemies and demons.)

> Therefore, the four qualities of gain and the rest should be
> regarded as enemies.
> Power and influence come to an end, but the ocean of suffering
> bursts forth.
> Understand that this also occurs when gain and so on are sought
> through a directive.

Nāgārjuna also wrote:

> Gentle sir, those who have few desires do not undergo suffering
> in the same way as those who possess extensive wealth.
> For as many heads as the foremost nāgas possess,
> such is the misery that is brought about by them.[495]

It is also stated in the sayings of Potowa:

> It's improper to follow the saying, "If the food is chewed for them, even a small child will eat it. If something is offered, even

an ārya will accept it." You must be like an ārya who will not accept anything, even if it has been offered.

9. Abandon Being Conciliatory and Obsequious[496]

Geshe Puchungwa said:

(Puchungwa was one of the Three Brothers.[497] He did not nurture disciples and kept himself in isolation. His decision not to teach others is described as "eating the meat of a quarter carcass[498] by oneself." It seems that he was the rebirth of a great realized adept and that a great many individuals were able to establish a modicum of a spiritual connection with him. He was from the Zurtsang clan. His ordination name was Zhönu Gyaltsen. Having served Drom Tönpa for eleven years, he was the one who, among the Three Brothers, spent the longest time in close proximity with this teacher. Chengawa served Drom Tönpa for nine years, and Potowa did so for seven. Puchungwa passed away at the age of seventy-six at Dowo Monastery. Adding Khamlungpa to the Three Brothers as a fourth, they were called the Four Kadampas.)

> If you practice dharma assiduously, you must not allow persons devoted to this life to interact with you, just as an *ölwa* hawk is not able to penetrate the rings in a coat of mail. If you are too conciliatory or a person is overly pleased with you, Māra will lead you astray. A person's dissatisfaction will accomplish your desire. If someone is dissatisfied with you, he will not approach you. If that person criticizes you, others will not approach you. In that situation, even if you have no other provisions except for some yogurt, at least your mind will be at ease during that time, and you will be able to pursue virtuous activities. If you are able to strengthen your virtuous activities, your ability to accomplish others' aims will improve spontaneously.

Tsangpa Gyare said:

> Abandon your homeland, which is the root of attachment and hatred.
> Abandon the householder's life, which is the root of suffering.
> Abandon wealth and possessions, which are the root of avarice.
> Abandon obsequiousness, which is the root of distraction.

Tropuwa Sönam Senge said:

In a town, a monastery, a hermitage, or the like,
wherever you stay, don't seek out friends as requisite companions.
Whomever you associate with, don't argue or make enemies.
My heartfelt advice is for you to remain self-reliant.

Moreover, as you sit inside a dwelling, striving after spiritual excellence
within a state of solitude {489}, being concerned about meaningless activities,
such as the arrangement of the room and so on, is a cause that wastes your life.
My heartfelt advice is for you to give up all nonessential activities.[499]

Khetsunpa[500] said:

Thinking about tea, beer, and cooking food, and the like,
is a cause that distracts you from pure and virtuous spiritual activities.
Don't pursue companionship with persons of high station in this life.
O Zhönu Drup, knock down the wall of conciliatoriness.

Barawa said:

As your authority increases, your suffering becomes greater.
The object of thought for persons of higher standing is how to support those of lower standing.
What presses down on the neck of average persons is a treasure of wealth.
There is no relief from this involvement with suffering.
Even in prosperity it is difficult to be happy.
Generate a sense of aversion and proceed to a hermitage.

Kyechokpa said:

It is said that by not placing your attention on the difference between
a higher and a lower state, you won't mentally abandon this life.
It is said that by not making whatever you encounter into an element of the path,
you will become deceived by the occurrence of favorable circumstances.
It is said that whether your meditation and realizations are good or bad
will become evident when you encounter conditions that challenge you.

These lines are, in fact, a repetition of the sayings of Gyadrak Chöje.[501]

The Lama from Ölna[502] said:

If you listen to a gossip's tales, you will not attain a level of spirituality.
It is easy to make a person who has many thoughts give up his aim.
One who procrastinates about practicing dharma will never reach the goal.
If your life ends up being wasted, what will you do then?

Whatever the place in which you reside, forgo accumulating possessions.
Whatever the country to which you travel, limit those with whom you become well-acquainted.
Though you may have many compatible friends, don't give up your independence.
This is the way that a renunciate remains self-reliant.

No matter who the person or what they may say, do not consider it essential.
Anything proper that you are asked to do, do it tirelessly.
However far {490} you may have progressed, generate a willingness to endure hardships.
This is the way that a renunciate remains resolute.

Gyalwa Yangönpa said:

One, the courage to cast this current life to the wind.[503]
Two, an urgency that doesn't have time to conform to others' wishes.
Three, a satisfaction with the present that abandons making needless plans for the future.
Four, the aversion that cuts through the entanglement of sensory pleasures.
These are what is truly needed in order to mentally abandon this life.

Barawa also said:

When favorable conditions are prevalent, pursue virtuous activities.
When they are not prevalent, solicit them from someone you don't depend upon.
When you are able to make the best of whatever circumstances arise,
let conciliatory persons[504] be held in the lama's compassion.

10. Abandon the Merit and Turmoil of This Life

You should not delight in the turmoil of many activities that occurs when it is said of you: "He is one whose merit[505] has developed greatly." Instead, you should reject it as if it were poison. As Geshe Kharakpa said:

Fame and renown are Māra's tossing of tsampa powder.[506]
Gain and honor are shackles that bind you.
Merit is an obstacle to virtuous activities.
You must not regard poison as medicine.

The Lord of Reasoning[507] said:

Merit[508] is like a deceitful old man.
Your mind is like an empty-headed child.
Everyday affairs are like a game of disproving and proving.
O Gyamawa, don't have many attachments.

One of the "ornaments" among the disciples of Dampa Gyagar[509] was Dampa Kunga,[510] who received five forms of spiritual attainment from his teacher Pa Dampa Sangye. He said:

> Please bless me to have no fixed country or hearth.
> Please bless me to have no food or drink.
> Please bless me to have no acquaintances and friends.
> Please bless me to not be seen by any other human being {491}.
> Please bless me to not develop even a sesame grain of merit.[511]

It is recognized that after having expressed these words of apprehension, he pursued ascetic practices and meditation, which enabled him to attain excellent forms of one-pointed concentration.

It is also declared in the *Sūtra Encouraging a Superior Attitude*:

> Excitation,[512] regret,[513] and, likewise, wrongful deliberation[514]—
> all of these faults arise from social interaction.
> One who engages in meaningless social interaction
> carries out impure activities and becomes undisciplined.
>
> Foolish persons delight is worldly conversation.
> Foolish persons also avoid here the best forms of discourse.
> They increase their anger and elevate wrongful deliberation.
> One should not be attracted to this conduct due to these faults.[515]

Gyalse Tokme Zangpo is reported to have said:

> In the early part of last year, I was having regular dreams about virtuous activities that I had performed in the past. Since then, those dreams have been obscured by the turmoil of excessive activities. I have fully recovered from the illness that I had incurred in recent days. Moreover, I wish there had not been all this talk about my being someone who has developed merit.

Likewise, in order to mentally give up attachment to this life, you should abandon all those useless affairs, activities, and deeds, such as performing dog mantras[516] and the like. As Kyechokpa said:

Engaging in many beneficial activities is a stick that obscures.[517]
If you want to be self-reliant, devote yourself to only one thing.
Having much knowledge about the trainings is like rituals that are done for food.
It is imprudent to understand this but fail to act accordingly.

A verse from the *Sūtra Encouraging a Superior Attitude* says:

That one develops intense desire. He is absorbed
and filled with desire for all manner of tastes.
He is not satisfied with whatever is obtained.
These are the faults of being attached to worldly activities.[518]

A verse from the *Sky-Treasure Sūtra*[519] declares:

Having abandoned the householder's existence
and living freely in remote borderlands,
we shall become like wild forest animals,
with few affairs and few distracting activities.[520]

11. Recall the Disadvantages of Sensory Pleasures

The ability to recall these disadvantages depends on whether or not you realize what the disadvantages of sensory pleasures are. Ārya Asaṅga commented on the following verses that are found in the *Main Treatise on the Stages*:[521]

Sentient beings who conceive of objects of expression
become established in these objects of expression.
Having failed to fully realize objects of expression,
they come to be united with death.

But having fully realized objects of expression,
a wise person does not recognize any being that utters expressions.
That entity by which others speak of a being that utters expressions
certainly does not exist for him or her.[522]

The meaning of these verses is as follows. Bhikṣus, brahmans, and householders are given instructions by means of words and they must seek material necessities by means of verbal expressions. Because of their need for objects of enjoyment,[523] the five objects of sensory experience are also referred to in these verses as "objects of expression."[524] In addition, sensory pleasures are also referred to as "objects of expression" because the buddhas and bodhisattvas express the disadvantages of sensory pleasures to immature beings who are ignorant of their disadvantages and who indulge in them as much as they wish. Even though these objects of expression, or sensory pleasures, have limitless disadvantages, ordinary sentient beings are not aware of them. As they enjoy sensory pleasures, they accumulate karma and repeatedly undergo birth and death. On the other hand, having correctly realized the disadvantages of sensory pleasures, wise persons abandon all their close relatives and wealth, no matter how many they have or how much they possess, and having gone forth into the homeless state, they strive to attain nirvana.

Another person might ask, "My good man, have you abandoned the pleasures of this life against the wishes of your close relatives {493} in order to strive for the pleasures of a future life?" However, a wise person is not subject to such a fault.[525] This question never even arises in his or her mind such that he or she might think, "Is there such a fault?" because he or she does not seek either the pleasurable experiences of this life or those of future lives.

> Having severed here craving for name and form,
> and having also abandoned pride, he or she does not become attached.
> Throughout the world of gods and humans, sentient beings do not perceive this one
> who has quelled the smoke, remains uninjured, and is free of expectations.[526]

The meaning of this verse is as follows. The expression "name and form" refers to the five closely grasping heaps.[527] When the four noble truths are perceived by realizing that the five closely grasping heaps possess the nature of suffering, craving for them is completely severed. When this understanding develops further and one becomes an arhat, the latency[528] of craving also disappears.

The term "smoke" here refers to craving[529] because craving is preceded by the fire of the three poisons. The smoke of craving is also a harmful irritant to the eye of wisdom because craving causes you to develop inferior forms of deliberation,[530] which in turn do not allow you to remain in a state of equanimity and therefore cause you to be become agitated.

After such craving has been quelled—which is to say, abandoned—when an arhat seeks a livelihood, he or she does not become attached to benefactors even if they offer food and other material necessities of good quality, in large amounts, and quickly; therefore, he or she remains uninjured by desire. When an arhat experiences the opposite[531] of that from those benefactors, he or she does not become discouraged or angered; therefore, he or she remains uninjured by hatred. Through perceiving the disadvantages of material acquisitions, an arhat makes use of them while maintaining a proper state of recollection; therefore, he or she remains uninjured by ignorance. An arhat does not approach a benefactor expectantly, such that he or she thinks, "This benefactor is likely to give me the material acquisitions that I desire." Rather, an arhat maintains an awareness of death such that he or she reflects at all times of the day and night, "There are a great many causal factors that can bring about my death. I am sure to die very soon." {494} Since an arhat who possesses these qualities will not be reborn following his or her death, the verse states that "throughout the world of gods and humans, beings do not perceive him or her." Thus, it is important to understand what the disadvantages of sensory pleasures are. A great many descriptions of them can be found in the sūtras and treatises. I have explained them extensively in *Becoming Well Restrained*[532] and other works.

12. Explaining Abandonment of the Eight Worldly Concerns

In general, it is important to remain untainted by the eight worldly concerns. Drigung Chöje said:

(He was also known as Jikten Gönpo[533] from the Kyura clan. His religious name was Rinchen Pel.[534] Based on the testimony of Paṇchen Śākyaśrī, he was considered to be an emanation of Nāgārjuna. A direct disciple of Je Pakmo Drupa,[535] he possessed limitless spiritual qualities, including supernatural knowledge and miraculous powers. He had many disciples who were realized adepts, such as Nyö Gyalwa Lhanangpa,[536] also known as Gyere.[537] He founded Drigung Thil Monastery[538] and established eighteen great communities of practitioners.)

Indeed, they[539] are completely useless. At death
all worldly activities, as well, are untrue and false.
Indeed, examine whether or not you have fixed your mind
on the rainbow-like shapes of the eight worldly concerns.

The Lord of Reasoning said:

As long as you are one who pursues
the eight worldly concerns with thoughts
of delight or discontent toward
praise and blame, fame and disrepute,
gain and loss, and pleasure and pain,
do not think, "I am a dharma practitioner."
Ask your mind whether or not the motivation
of the eight concerns is or will be present
in your past, current, or future actions.

13. Abandon the Desire to Obtain Pleasure

The spiritual teacher Sangmowa[540] said:

(He was born into the ministerial lineage of Je Sangmowa Dakpo Lhapa,[541] {495} which ruled an area of more than ten districts and which was also a lineage that included several great realized adepts. He possessed knowledge of many canonical scriptures and had trained himself in the teachings of the four classes of Buddhist tantra. Having cultivated the Six Teachings of Naropa, he became skilled in the caṇḍālī[542] practice. At a later time, he served Gyama Drogön[543] as a disciple for twelve years. He perceived Drogön as a true buddha and even after the latter's passing, was able to meet with him whenever he desired and was able to see all of Drogön's continued activities, such as those in which he acted on behalf of his followers. Once, when Sangmowa was receiving an initiation and the ritual act for generating enlightenment mind from Drogön, the latter directly revealed in his heart the hundreds of spiritual deeds carried out by the Norsang Lamas. It is said that this act was first revealed by the Great Gyer to Drogön and then Drogön revealed it to Sangmowa. This trio of masters and disciples carried out limitless such deeds that illustrated their respective paths to enlightenment. Sangmowa later established a monastic seat for Drogön at Sangmo Monastery in the upland above the valley at Samye. He lived to the age of seventy-eight. He achieved many forms of miraculous powers and supernatural knowledge. Among his major disciples were the ones named Lha Gendun Gangpa,[544] Lha Samkhawa,[545] Lhapu Gönsarwa,[546] and Lha Trasowa,[547] and, in the Balam region, Ge Marwa,[548] all of whom founded monasteries. He also had many other great disciples.)

> These qualities, known as the eight worldly concerns, are something that affect us and all sentient beings. The worldly concern that affects us the most is the joy that we feel when some form of pleasure is experienced. All of the sentient beings that are traveling here and there across this great earth are wandering about in search of this or that form of pleasure. However, because a form of pain lies at the root of every pleasurable experience, you should neither delight in pleasurable experiences nor feel dejection toward painful ones. If you strive to obtain the greatest amount of pleasure for yourself in this life, your future lives will at the same time become lost.
>
> Therefore, reflect to yourself in the following manner: "If I pursue either what is meant to be a form of dharma practice or some worldly enterprise after thinking to myself, 'Through acting in this way, I will be able to obtain some form of pleasure or happiness,' alas, I will have become a person who is dedicated to this life and someone who is subject to the eight worldly concerns." Reflect in the same way with regard to the remaining forms of the eight worldly concerns. {496}

If you fail to obtain whatever pleasurable experience you may have desired, then, after thinking to yourself, "I would very much have liked to obtain that pleasurable experience," you will give rise to the craving that desires to meet with that experience. If it appears certain that you will obtain that pleasurable experience, then, after thinking to yourself, "How delightful it will be to obtain that pleasurable experience," you will give rise to the craving that anticipates a delightful experience. When that pleasurable experience occurs, you will think to yourself, "I must not be separated from this pleasurable experience," and then give rise to the craving that desires not to be separated from that favorable experience. When you reflect about a happy experience that was experienced previously but is no longer present and think to yourself, "How nice was the joy and happiness that I experienced at that time!" the craving with regard to past pleasurable experiences that is called "craving about the past" will arise.

If you undergo a painful or unwanted experience, after thinking to yourself, "I wish I didn't have to experience this," you will give rise to the craving that desires to be separated from such an experience. If you are able to avoid such an experience, after thinking to yourself, "Wasn't it good that I didn't have to experience that," you will give rise to the craving that desires not to meet with such an experience. If you undergo an experience that is neither pleasurable nor painful, then you will give rise to the craving that desires that experience not to come to an end. Whenever any of these reactions occur, you have come under the influence of craving and attachment, which means that you are a person who is subject to the eight worldly concerns and a person who is attached to this life.

If you ask, "Well then, how can I avoid having any of these reactions?" the Lord of Reasoning[549] said:

> Those for whom an axe and sandalwood are the same
> are said to have attained freedom from desires.[550]

These lines mean that an arhat would not become delighted if another person, with great respect, should anoint one side of his or her body with sandalwood oil, nor would he or she become upset if that same person should chop the other side of his or her body with an axe. Similarly, when a practitioner has the same indifference toward all the experiences of this life that most other individuals either desire or wish to avoid, he or she has developed equanimity toward the eight worldly concerns. Although we novice practitioners are unable currently to develop an uncontrived and heartfelt form of such equanimity, it is important that we undertake to cultivate the contrived mind that abandons those thoughts of delight and discontent that arise in reaction to favorable and unfavorable experiences.

Moreover, you will remain free of corruption by doing the following: As you seek and experience objects of desire[551] for the sake of the dharma, or when you fail to obtain them and so on, you should avoid developing thoughts of delight and {497} discontent and maintain an understanding of their disadvantages as you make use of them and so on. You should continually reflect on the disadvantages of these objects of desire as they have been explained above and as they will also be explained further below. You should generate intense aversion for objects of desire and strive to abandon them as much as possible. As for those that you are unable to abandon, you should perform the appropriate act of recollection for a specific occasion[552] beforehand and reflect to yourself, "I was unable to avoid making use of these objects of desire for the sake of the dharma," as well as ensure that enlightenment mind is the motivation under whose influence you make use of them by reflecting, "Since the Master Buddha Śākyamuni also permitted this behavior, I had to make use of these objects of desire for the sake of sentient beings."

The Great Gyer[553] said:

(The ordination name of the Great Gyer was Zhönu Drakpa.[554] He mainly served Neusurpa[555] as a disciple, and achieved limitless forms of scriptural knowledge and spiritual realization. He also attained limitless other spiritual qualities, such as acquiring many forms of supernatural knowledge and miraculous powers and achieving visions of many tutelary deities. He founded Rinchen Gang[556] Monastery and organized the construction of Nyingpa[557] Temple. He attracted a following of eight hundred monks and lived to the age of eighty-two. He had eight great spiritual sons, two of which were spiritual sons born of his breast[558]—namely, [1] Drogön[559] and [2] the meditator Sherap Drak.[560] The others were [3] Lhopa Jangom,[561] [4] Trisorwa Geshe,[562] [5] Dingpowa,[563] and the three known as Ba Ja Suk.[564] Among the latter three, [6] Ba nurtured disciples in Yardrok and founded a monastery there, [7] Ja was the first individual known as Japa Anak Chenpo[565] from the ruling family of Japa Tripön Tsang,[566] and [8] Suk founded monasteries in the Lhodrak and Ro regions. The Great Gyer also had many other great disciples, all of whom worked to preserve the Buddhist teaching.)

> As was formerly the practice of Geshe Tönpa, we too must cultivate the antidote to the eight worldly concerns and abandon them, at least by reciting the words of that verse.[567]

Je Rinpoche said:

> As exemplified by the virtue gained with this prayer,
> may all my own and others' virtue roots of the three times,
> however great they may be, never ripen for even an instant
> in subsequent rebirths in a manner contrary to supreme
> enlightenment {498}—
>
> such as by serving as a cause for desiring to profit
> from knowledge, to obtain fame, a large retinue,
> wealth, or gain and honor; instead may they serve
> only as a cause for attaining unsurpassed enlightenment.

> Just by recalling the excellence of samsara as being devoid
> of happiness and causing the torment of a hundred forms of
> suffering,
> may my mind remain free of even a sesame seed of desire,
> as if I were trapped in a burning house made of iron.[568]

These verses state that we must generate the aspirational prayer to become a practitioner who avoids having any attachment to pleasures and is able to accept suffering as one pursues the dharma.

A verse from the *Collection of Uplifting Sayings* declares:

> Those bound to happiness who are seekers of pleasure
> are certainly persons that will undergo birth and old age.
> Those creatures who are fraught with cravings
> are like rabbits that run straight into a net.[569]

Khetsunpa[570] said:

> If you fail to free yourself from having ultimate desires,
> this life's activities and needs will be like the ocean's waves.
> After one is finished, many more will arise after that.
> Would few physical and verbal activities not be more fitting?

Sakya Paṇḍita said:

> An excessively enterprising mind is distracted by social
> interaction.
> It is made busy by endless activities that follow one after the other.
> You are continually deceived by desires that need this and that.
> Do you not realize that your life will be consumed by such
> behavior?

Kyechokpa said:

> Cast this life's happiness and well-being to the wind.
> Take on suffering's burden to support your spiritual practice.
> Sacrifice your body and life to support an ascetic life.

The Precious Je Tsongkhapa said:

> There is absolutely no genuine form of happiness in samsara. Even those pleasures such as eating food and the like that we mistakenly believe to be forms of pleasure are merely experiences in which the disappearance of the suffering of hunger and thirst is nominally designated as pleasure.
>
> How is this to be understood? If the suffering of hunger is prolonged, that suffering will become progressively greater. Similarly, if you eat food too energetically, instead of experiencing further pleasure, your suffering will become greater. This is a sign that there was no pleasure at the outset and that even then it was a form of suffering. Moreover, the act of eating simply causes the suffering of hunger to cease. When the suffering of eating begins, we mistakenly believe that to constitute a genuine form of pleasure. Similarly, every form of pleasure in samsara is actually a form of suffering that is only nominally designated to be pleasure. Despite this, we mistakenly take it to be genuine pleasure, develop attachment for it, and generate aversion toward its opposite. Our failure to understand the characteristic of suffering that pertains to these experiences leads us to accumulate karma on the basis of ignorance and to therefore continue to wander in samsara. For these reasons, you should reflect to yourself, "Now then, what reasonable person would develop attachment for the pleasures of samsara?"[571]

14. Train Yourself to Regard Suffering as an Ornament

Not only should you avoid becoming attached to pleasure, you should even regard suffering as an ornament and tolerate it as if it were medicine. Potowa said:

> Drom Lodengpa had three neighbors, Ngachokpa,[572] Yuchokpa,[573] and Tongrawa.[574] Ngachokpa, who was called Mangtsen,[575] had a wife, who said to him, "Would you rather drink hot water for three years and after that always eat regular food, or would you rather eat regular food for three years and after that always

drink boiled water?" He replied, "I already have a full tea churn[576] affixed with turquoises such as the ones called Infinite {500} Light, Great Star, and Lion Shoulders that I obtained by drinking hot water for three years." When practicing dharma, you must be willing to accept hardships and difficulties in a similar manner.

Without practicing dharma in a way that involves experiencing hardships, your mind will not experience the root of things, and you will not become filled with knowledge. Launderers who think to themselves, "I shall perform the work effectively," as they scrub their clothing will not be able to clean them well. But if they think to themselves as they scrub, "If this clothing were my mother, my effort would cause her to die," they will be able to clean them well. Similarly, when you practice dharma, you will be successful only if you do so unfalteringly. A person who comes with all his weapons of a spear and a sword is not a courageous person, but someone who approaches without all those weapons is a courageous person. Therefore, you must be able to say of yourself, "I carried out a dharma practice without all the beneficial forms of support."

Keep in the depth of your heart the attitude that you have dedicated yourself to a life of poverty. Also commit the final stage of poverty to your death,[577] and then think to yourself, "I must adjust myself to the notion that tomorrow, or the day after that, dogs will be scratching at the feet of my lifeless body and infants will be grasping at my head." If you don't want to be reborn in samsara in general, in the three lower realms in particular, and especially in Avīci hell, you must be able to think to yourself, "If all there is to put in my stomach is for me to drink the rinse water from washed dinner plates, I will drink that. If all I have to wear as clothing is the cloth mat that I use for a cushion, I will wear that."

Je Tsongkhapa said:

No prosperity of worldly existence is free of deception.
That which is wholly beneficial is the true dharma.
To meet with the teaching happens only rarely.
For these reasons, reflect on its meaning.[578]

Geshe Shawopa[579] said:

> If you fail to remain seated on your cushion in the morning, you will become one who makes a false promise each evening. Therefore, since all those who are young have the ability to develop potent antidotes at a time when their bodies and minds are still strong, you must do battle with the mental afflictions in your youth. {501} Once you have become old, when your body is bent over and wrinkles have formed on your forehead, you will have done everything that is inappropriate—that is, the mental afflictions you should have caused to weaken with age will not have become weakened, and the antidotes you should have prevented from being weakened with age will have become weakened. Then you will have made yourself into an example of what is bad for others to see.

The Bhagavān taught three types of patience in many sūtras—the patience that tolerates suffering,[580] the patience that forbears the harm inflicted by others,[581] and the patience that arises from attentive reflection upon entities.[582] They are explained extensively as well in the commentarial treatises. The former lamas taught the three types of patience and the like and, in particular, the suffering that tolerates suffering, which can also be described as the practice that regards suffering as an ornament in such instructions as the four dedications[583] that form part of the teaching known as the Ten Ultimate Jewels.[584] The patience that arises through attentive reflection upon entities is synonymous with the aphorism "Keep the vajra of wisdom as your companion,"[585] which means that you should train your mind in those eight topics[586] using analytic meditation.

When Geshe Yönlungpa[587] was doing a retreat, someone took hold of his robe and requested to be given an instruction, to which the Geshe said:

> You became a homeless ascetic in your youth. Make certain that you have no regrets when you reach the moment of your death. In order to accomplish that, you must eat just enough tsampa to keep yourself alive, wear poor clothing that is sufficient to keep your back warm, make yourself unfamiliar even to your neighbors, maintain a lowly status, wear tattered clothing, abandon your homeland, drink your spiritual teacher's advice as if it were

> water, and be someone who forcefully scorns this life. If you are able to cope with trees falling in the upland above a valley or floods occurring in the lowland at the bottom of a valley, then you will be someone who has no regrets.

Potowa's writings state:

> Others may view you as an object of compassion,[588]
> but if you always remain in a joyful state of mind, {502}
> such a person possesses the dharma; otherwise, not.[589]

He also said:

> At a time when the Buddha's teaching is in decline,
> those who delight in the side of darkness[590] are more powerful,
> and those who delight in the side of virtue are weaker.
> Therefore, those who are dedicated to wickedness
> receive much assistance, live long lives, and remain free of illness,
> while those dedicated to the dharma experience the opposite.
> Because this is the nature of things, those dedicated to the dharma
> should not become despondent.
> This is what Geshe Tönpa said to me.
> Therefore, you should reflect on this as an antidote.[591]

Thus, since it is virtually impossible for you to be free of suffering during degenerate times, you must not be afraid of suffering. Sakya Paṇḍita said:

> In this age of strife it is rare among a hundred persons
> for someone to possess an abundance of merit.
>
> When a faulty reservoir becomes full of water,
> it is inevitable that one side should collapse;
> likewise, it is very rare that one who is wealthy
> should be succeeded by a family lineage.
>
> If one has a son, it is rare to possess great wealth.
> If one possesses that,[592] enemies will come forward.[593]

If someone possesses excellence in everything,
many such persons die too soon.[594]

Geshe Kharakpa said:

Misfortune is a spiritual teacher.
Obstacles are an incitement to perform virtuous activities.
Suffering is a broom for sweeping away evil.
You mustn't regard an unhappy mind as inauspicious.

Several verses from *Entry into the Conduct That Leads to Enlightenment* declare:

Having gained the food of discontent,
an inflamed anger destroys me.[595]

I shall not allow my joy to be disturbed
even by a very undesirable experience.[596]

If, indeed, there is a remedy,
what good is discontentment {503} about that?
And if there should be no remedy,
what good is discontentment about that?[597]

Additional benefits of suffering are that
through distress, arrogance is dispelled;
compassion arises toward the beings of samsara;
and there is fear of evil and elation toward the Victor.[598]

If you become one who understands how to think in this way, you can turn a disadvantage into a favorable quality and suffering can appear as a form of well-being. Thus, you will become someone for whom nothing can become a hindrance or an obstacle that impedes your dharma practice. As Potowa said:

Among merchants, some will say when it snows, "This is good for the horses' hooves." When it rains at night, they will say, "This will keep enemies from coming for us." Similarly, by turning illnesses, poverty, verbal abuse, even down to suffering experienced in a dream into elements of the path, you can gain many favorable qualities, such as purification of your evil deeds, etc. For these reasons, finding yourself on a dangerous path or experiencing hindrances can be turned into something favorable. Such a person can turn misfortune into something that is an aid to his or her dharma practice.

If you ask yourself, "Well then, what is the way to turn suffering into an element of the path?" to accomplish that, as expressed in the earlier quotations from *Entry into the Conduct That Leads to Enlightenment* and in the statements made by former lamas, an important element of spiritual instruction is for you to elicit intense joy by reflecting on the reasons why it is inappropriate to become discontented no matter what undesirable experience you may encounter and to reflect on the reasons why it is appropriate to be joyful about such experiences. In addition, generate a motivation that is imbued with enlightenment mind and dedicate the suffering to the welfare of sentient beings, as described in the story of Maitrakanyaka,[599] and also carry out the practice of giving and taking. While this is how you should practice, in the case of an illness, since that is a condition that can be cured, it is the view of wise persons that you should seek appropriate medical treatment, and so on. Therefore, it is not improper for you to do so.

The bodhisattva Chekawa[600] said:

(His ordination name was {504} Yeshe Dorje[601] and he was from the Ja[602] clan. His birthplace was Loro.[603] Initially, he studied the canonical scriptures; later, after serving Sharawa as a disciple, he attained mastery of enlightenment mind. The place called Shara[604] is in the Tre[605] region. The place known as Shar Bumpa[606] is in the lowland valley in Daryul.[607] Chekawa founded Cheka Monastery and attracted a following of about nine hundred monks. He passed away at the age of seventy-five in the upland region called Tapu.[608] Chekawa possessed limitless spiritual qualities. His major disciple, Se Jilbuwa,[609] founded a monastery at Jilbu. Genpa Dare[610] founded a monastery at Kharu. Naljorpa Jangsem[611] is said to have been a disciple of both Chekawa and Sangye Ön.[612] He founded Dropa[613] Monastery, where a system for teaching and study of the vinaya flourished. Naljorpa Jangsem lived to the age of seventy-six and is regarded as having attained limitless spiritual qualities.)

Always maintain solely a happy mind.
Use what is encountered suddenly in your meditation practice.

> Place all the blame on one.
> Meditate on the great kindness of all beings.
> The fourfold practice is the supreme method.[614]

Former lamas also taught that no matter what kind of unwanted experience you may undergo, you should let go of the thought that it is something disagreeable and not continue to hold it that way, and they described this practice as the method of turning an unfavorable circumstance into an element of the path. As Tsangpa Gyare said:

> A person who is bound up by the cord of worldly thoughts will naturally become inundated by suffering as well as feelings of attachment and hatred. A person who knows how to keep his or her mind relaxed will never become separated from a state of great ease.

Gyalwa Yangönpa also said the same thing frequently. If, in the manner just described, you learn how to turn an unfavorable circumstance into an element of the path, you will be able to maintain a continuous state of happiness and well-being. The former spiritual teachers have said:

> These occurrences of happiness and suffering are false experiences. They are caused by knowing or not knowing how to correct one's mind. These mental afflictions of varying strength {505} are false entities. They are due to the varying strength of antidotes.

Geshe Kharakpa said:

> If you don't know how thoughts arise and cease,
> no matter what you do, your mind will never be at ease.
> But for the wise who know how they arise and cease,
> unfavorable circumstances can truly be advantageous.

Tsangpa Gyare said:

> If you are able to perceive suffering as an ornament, that is the measure of having developed the practice. If you are able to cast away behind you all that is cherished by worldly persons, that is

> the measure of being an intelligent person. If you remain unwavering no matter what kind of unfavorable circumstance or obstacle you may encounter, that is the measure of having attained steadfastness.
>
> In the gatehouse of one who possesses devotion and reverence is a person who keeps watch over his or her lama, but those who possess wrong view are unaware of this. In the gatehouse of one who possesses faith is a person who keeps watch over the true dharma, but those who do not perceive suffering as an ornament are unaware of this.

Kyechokpa said:

> If you don't remove attachment from the deepest part of your mind, though you may drink the water of austerities, you will not be able to bring them to completion. If you don't realize samsara's suffering nature, you will not be able to develop the aversion that leads to renunciation. If you don't realize how thoughts arise and cease, even trivial forms of reasoning will not come to mind when you are experiencing pleasure.

Therefore, you must realize that pleasure and suffering do not exist within the objective nature of an experience; rather, they are characteristics that are governed by the manner in which you train your mind. As such, you should mentally abandon all worldly activities.

Tropu Lotsāwa said:

> Though you display the arrogance of this life,
> you will achieve nothing, and your mind will be miserable.
> Though you strive to create a favorable image of yourself, your deception will cause you to go wrong.
> Now you must abandon all your deeply held desires.

Je Rinpoche said:

> This human form possessed of leisure is more valuable than a wish-granting jewel;

to have found such an opportunity as this will only happen this
one time.
Difficult to obtain {506} and easily destroyed, it is like a flash of
lightning in the sky.
After reflecting on this subject, one must realize

that all worldly activities are like winnowing chaff[615]
and then strive to derive value from this life throughout the day
and night.
I, a spiritual practitioner, have carried out such a practice;
and I urge those of you who seek liberation to do the same.[616]

15. Abandon the Desire to Pursue Wealth Even for the Sake of Your Lama or for Any Other Reason

Langri Tangpa[617] said:

(Langri Tangpa's ordination name was Dorje Senge.[618] He was from the Shuk Cham[619] clan. He was a major disciple of Potowa. He founded Langtang Monastery and attracted a following of two thousand monks. He lived to the age of seventy and possessed limitless spiritual qualities. He was said to have been an emanation of Vairocana and was also considered to be an emanation of Amitābha.)

It is enough to live in solitude with little food and clothing;
stop the torment of striving to accumulate merit.
Spend all day and night performing virtuous activities;
stop the torment of seeking persons to associate with.
Remain seated on your cushion without thinking about it;
stop the torment of carrying out conciliatory actions.
You will please your lama through spiritual practice;
stop the torment of offering gain and honor.
It is enough to entrust yourself to spirits for protection;
stop the torment of reciting forceful mantras.

Because a certain excellent spiritual teacher known as Lopön Jetsun[620] failed to attend a memorial service for his lama, a chief from Tsalpa named Gade[621] said to one of Lopön Jetsun's disciples: "The geshes from Ü who are here now are morally upright. Is it not improper that some have failed to attend the lama's memorial service?" The disciple then went before Lopön and reported what everyone had being saying, to which the latter replied:

> I am neither one who lacks devotion and reverence for my lama, nor one who is devoid of material resources. I did not attend the memorial service for these reasons: It is definitely the case that many who have assembled there have done so with the aim of obtaining material resources. Attending the service distracts the sangha and causes them to interrupt their virtuous activities, and it is unproductive for those venerable monks whose antidotes are weak. What I am trying to do is ensure that I do not allow any of my three vows to become tainted by offenses or transgressions. Acting in this way will serve to fulfill my lama's wishes.

Gyalse Rinpoche remarked about this statement: "Those comments have truly identified the meaning of a memorial service. They are a very great marvel!"

Je Rendawa said:

> There is no other honor that is more pleasing to the victors and their spiritual offspring than pursuing the act of learning until the deepest level of understanding has been reached and then making the act of mentally abandoning this life the essence of one's spiritual practice. Compared to that, the way that the process of teaching and learning is carried out nowadays is a spurious attempt to act on behalf of others. Those activities such as conferring initiations, giving oral transmissions of scriptures, and explaining instructions that are done as a means of fulfilling the desire for honor and material gain, as well as those efforts to attract a following that is a spurious way of acting on behalf of others, are all meaningless.

Therefore, since all of these activities are meaningless, no matter how you consider them, it is important to avoid having any attachment for this short life and mentally abandon it as much as you can.

16. Reflecting on Impermanence in the Form of Death

This topic describes the practice of the unique and direct cause for mentally abandoning this life. While it is indispensable for you to become one who has mentally abandoned this life, if you lack the practice that is the principal cause for accomplishing this aim, there is no way that you will be able to succeed in mentally abandoning this life. Therefore, you must learn this principal form of spiritual practice. If you wonder what this practice is, it is the act of reflecting properly on impermanence in the form of death.

Regarding the disadvantages {508} of failing to meditate on the recollection of death, Je Rinpoche said:

> Although everyone thinks to themselves, "At some point in the future, death will ultimately come to me," with each passing day until the very moment of their death, their minds also give rise to and cling to the position that they are not going to die anytime soon,[622] which leads them to think to themselves, "I will not die today, I will not die today." Unless they bring to mind the antidote to this tendency, they will be obscured by such an attitude, and through having developed the thought that they will remain alive in this life for a considerable period of time, they reflect continuously to themselves, "I need this or that," and seek only to obtain the pleasures and eliminate the sufferings that are limited to this life. As a result, through failing to develop the attitude of wanting to pursue such great spiritual aims as future lives, liberation, and omniscience, this tendency prevents them from applying themselves to the dharma. Even if, by chance, they should happen to pursue such activities as learning, reflecting, and meditating upon the dharma, since these activities are being carried out merely for the sake of one who is devoted to this life, whatever virtuous activities such individuals may perform will be weak in strength, and since they have been carried out in connection with misconduct, evil deeds, and moral transgressions, it will rarely be the case that they are not commingled with causes for being reborn in the lower states.
>
> Even if it is allowed that such individuals are carrying out spiritual activities with an aim that is directed toward future lives, they will not be able to put a stop to the laziness of procrastination in

which they think to themselves, "I shall practice these activities at a later time." And since they will allow time to go by without engaging in spiritual practice, due to such forms of distraction as sleep and torpor,[623] idle talk, consuming food and drink, and so on, they will not engage in spiritual practice properly and with great effort.

Moreover, not only will they simply fail to engage in spiritual practice properly, due to their eager pursuit of the prosperity associated with this life, their mental afflictions and the misconduct brought forth by those mental afflictions will become stronger, causing them to turn their backs on the nectar of the dharma and be led to rebirth in the lower states. What is there that could be more ruinous than this?

A verse from *Four Hundred Verses* states:

For one subject to the ruler of the triple world—
that Death who himself is controlled by no other—
what could be more ruinous than to remain at rest,
like a person that is secure?[624]

{509} A verse from *Entry into the Conduct That Leads to Enlightenment* also states:

Many kinds of evil deeds have been committed
for the sake of those who are dear and those who are not,
without having realized this: "Everyone must be left behind
when one passes on."[625]

With regard to the benefits gained by having meditated on the recollection of death, the same text also states:

If a genuine form of realization arises from meditation on the recollection of death, such that, for example, you develop the conviction that you might very well die even today or tomorrow, those individuals who possess even a slight understanding of the dharma will recognize that their relatives and so on will not accompany them following their death, and they will overturn their attachment for such individuals, and, as almost everyone will naturally develop the desire to derive genuine value from their lives through carrying out such practices as generosity and so on, they will turn away from misdeeds through recognizing that all efforts to achieve the worldly aims of gain and honor, and so on, are meaningless. In addition, since they will raise themselves to an excellent spiritual state by accumulating virtuous deeds such as the act of taking refuge and the cultivation of morality and also lead other beings to that same state, what is there that could have greater meaning than this?

For these reasons, this practice is praised with many similes. For example, the *Mahāparinirvāṇa Sūtra*[626] declares that, among all the forms of agricultural activity, gathering the autumn harvest is the best; among all footprints, that of the elephant is the best; and among all conceptions, those of impermanence and death are the best, as those two latter topics dispel all forms of desire for the three realms, as well as ignorance and pride. Similarly, meditating on the recollection of death is also praised by such phrases as: it is a hammer that immediately destroys all the mental afflictions, and it is the door that immediately leads to practicing all forms of virtuous activities.

In short, the time for pursuing a true human aim {510} is on this very occasion when we have achieved an extraordinary existence. We sentient beings reside for the vast majority of time in the unhappy migratory states and only reach a happy migratory state on very rare occasions. However, because even then it is usually in an inopportune form of existence,[627] in such circumstances there is no opportunity to practice dharma. Therefore, if we should obtain a form of existence in which it is possible to practice dharma but we fail to do so in a proper manner, it is because of the thought in which we reflect to ourselves, "I will not die anytime soon." Therefore, the attitude that clings to the position that you are not going to die anytime soon is the door that leads to all misfortune, and the recollection of death is the door that leads to all spiritual excellence.

For these reasons, you should neither hold the thought "This topic is a spiritual practice for those who have no other more profound dharma teaching to meditate upon" nor the thought "Although this topic should be meditated upon, it should only be meditated upon for a short time at the outset of one's spiritual career; it does not need to become a practice that is cultivated

> continually." Rather, you should meditate on it after having developed the certain conviction from the depth of your heart as to its necessity at the beginning, middle, and end—that is, at all three stages—of one's spiritual career.[628]

Chöje Bu said:

> This life has no time to spare; death comes quickly.
> With each passing moment we come nearer to death,
> like an animal being led to its place of slaughter.
> Reflect on the certainty of death, Rinchen Drup.
>
> Don't think of a hundred tasks, never completing those you want
> to accomplish today and tomorrow; instead, master a single goal.
> After being summoned before the terrifying Lord of Death,
> when you are on your final bed and your breath stops and your life ends,
> nothing but the dharma will benefit you, Rinchen Drup.[629]

My precious lama[630] said that a person who fails to develop a powerful awareness of impermanence in the form of death will be overcome by any one of such things as wanting to achieve observable results, wanting to have attractive things, or wanting fame and renown, causing any and all forms of the three virtuous acts of learning, reflection, and meditation that he or she may carry out to become virtuous acts that are spurious in nature and therefore not bring any benefit {511} to one's future lives. While it will seem that you are not engaging in such forms of procrastination as sleep and torpor, idle talk, and consuming food and drink, and so on, you will in fact have come under their influence. But if you succeed in developing a powerful awareness of impermanence, since you will not only avoid having any regret when you are about to die but also be able to feel joy and happiness about your impending death, it is important to reflect about death.[631]

Potowa is recorded to have said:

> Teachers desire a dharma instruction for teachers. The elderly desire a dharma instruction for the elderly. Those who have been detached from their mothers (Just as a lamb that is rejected by its mother in order to wean it is said to have been "detached from its mother," a monk[632] or

> nun who is sent forth by his or her preceptor and instructor is said to have been "detached from his or her mother.") desire a dharma instruction for one who has been detached from his or her mother. I have no instruction to recite except for impermanence.

He also said:

> A person who regards impermanence as nothing more than a dharma practice for children and women and who considers this dharma practice to be insignificant will not achieve any form of dharma.

At a former time, when Tibetan dharma teachers were investigating whether appearances are to be logically eliminated or not and whether a buddha possesses transcendent awareness or not, Potowa said:

> The means of eliminating appearances[633] is this practice of impermanence; that is, all the appearances of this life are eliminated by this practice of impermanence.

He further said:

> In the north, when *shöbu*[634] offerings were being presented as food in a healing ritual for a sick person, someone was chided for taking one of the offerings, to which that individual replied, "If it's a bad thing, so be it. Find your own northern gold mine of *shöbu* offerings." Similarly, a person who meditates on impermanence is also carrying out a very bad[635] practice. You must generate a realization of this in your mental continuum. That would be sufficient.

When a disciple asked Potowa about changing his meditation object, the master replied:

> You should not change it. Keep meditating on this very topic.[636] There is none that is more profound.

He further said:

> If your understanding is higher than mine, then it will not benefit you to remain here. {512} If it is equal to mine, since this practice that is a great means of eliminating appearances has benefited me, it will also be one that benefits you.
>
> The story is told that a tantric practitioner's daughter said to her father, "My mirror is too small." Her father replied, "First use this one to look at your face. If you decide that it is too small, you can set up my gong and use that." Similarly, to those who say that impermanence is a dharma practice that is too small, generate a realization of it in your mental continuum. After that, you can consider other topics.

Potowa further said:

> Moreover, all the dharma practices of a person who has not cultivated recollection of impermanence are like building a fortress upon ice. When you are in a state of ease, such topics as emptiness and so on will seem to come to mind readily; however, when you meet with a critical situation, it will become evident that they crumble from their foundation. If you develop a realization of this topic of impermanence, your meditation will not be subject to reversal. If you fail to develop a realization of this impermanence, every other form of spiritual practice will undergo reversal. If you develop a realization of this impermanence, your understanding of all spiritual practices such as enlightenment mind, emptiness, and so on will arise as if they have been gathered together into a heap.

Shawopa also said:

> Everything I have offered here as an explanation about the realizations that I have gained from meditating on impermanence stems from my understanding having reached the deepest levels of the dharma. The realizations to be gained by meditating on emptiness do not lie very far beyond that.

A young monk who was Shawopa's disciple reported that he told his teacher, "My feet hurt from doing circumambulations because I have not been able to comprehend impermanence." He further reported that Shawopa replied that his statement was indeed a truthful one.

Gönpawa said:

> To believe that the topics of impermanence and karma and its results need not be listened to by students or taught by teachers, and to treat them as dharma teachings that are only appropriate for female disciples, are not the view of a wise person nor that of a disciplined and virtuous monk.

Shangtsun Yerpa said:

> If you fail to develop an awareness of impermanence in the morning, then by midday you will have become a person who is dedicated to this life. If you fail to develop it at midday, the evening will have become dedicated to this life. If you become a person who is dedicated to this life, {513} whatever you do will fail to become a genuine form of dharma.

Chenga Rinpoche said:

> If you fail to cultivate impermanence for a meditation period during the morning, it is evident that all your activities of that day will become those of a person who is attached to this life.

It is said that when Drom Tönpa Rinpoche was asked by a person named Lotik Yeshe Jung[637] to give him spiritual instruction, he took on the demeanor of a lord who was displeased with an impudent subject and said:

> O follower of Lord Atiśa, the dharma is something that is needed when you meet with a crucial situation. If you lack any form of spiritual practice that you can apply when you encounter such a situation, the faith that you possess when you are at ease is nothing more than the recitation of a parrot. The person who is able to bring to mind the dharma when he or she encounters a crucial situation is likely to be someone who has reflected extensively on impermanence and the doctrine of karma and its results. Therefore, the following verse was taught:

> All suffering arises from unvirtuous actions;
> the same is true for all the unhappy migratory states.
> All the happy migratory states arise from virtuous actions,
> as does as all the happiness in one's rebirths.[638]

This must always be understood!

When Chengawa repeated this incident to Potowa, the latter said, "O my, Geshe Tönpa has taught an instruction that he alone, and no one else, possesses and that resembles a hidden object."[639]

Mangra Gompa[640] said:

(This master was also called Nyukrumpa;[641] his ordination name was Tsöndru Bar.[642] His spiritual qualities were limitless. He founded the two monasteries of Nyukrum and Tangkya[643] and attracted a following of eight hundred monks. While he had a spiritual connection with all of the Three Brothers, he was principally a great spiritual son of Chengawa.[644] He passed away at the age of sixty-eight at Tangkya Monastery.)

> I have never taught the dharma without first having reflected on impermanence for an entire meditation session.

He taught this dharma topic as personal instruction to everyone. He also said:

> We mistakenly consider everything about this dharma topic to be of little importance.

A certain Dortsul[645] from the Kyangchi region of Gyal[646] said to Potowa, "As I am boiling water up there[647] to make tea, I would like to request a quick dharma teaching." Potowa {514} responded to him, saying:

> Meditate extensively on impermanence. If you do, it will not be difficult for you to abandon this life, and it will be easy for you to pursue the aims of future lives. At present, it is easy for you to drink tea, but it is difficult for you not to drink tea.[648]

He gave similar, somewhat brief explanations of the topics of karma and its results, the disadvantages of samsara, enlightenment mind, and emptiness. When Shawo Gangpa related this incident to Puchungwa, the latter is reported to have immediately taken off his hat and said repeatedly: "O my! This is indeed the very teaching of Atiśa that is my practice."

Khampa Lungpa[649] said:

(Khamlungpa was from the Yungwa[650] region of Penyul. He observed the layperson's vow[651] and was a great spiritual son of Geshe Tönpa. He possessed limitless spiritual qualities and attracted a following of eight hundred disciples. His religious name was Śākya Yönten[652] and he lived to the age of ninety-one.)

> My wish is to practice dharma after having meditated on impermanence. Otherwise, what can I expect to experience except unhappiness of mind. If you recall impermanence, you will develop an attitude that sees no value in pursuing anything that is contrary to the dharma. When it is likely that we shall die as soon as the day after tomorrow, even if all the water in the world were to turn into ghee, all the mountains were to turn into gold, and all human beings were to become my sons and daughters, what would I be able to do with that?

Puchungwa said:

> Meditate on these topics: impermanence and karma and its results. Regarding them, I have become someone who resembles an object in which they can be perceived directly. I have lost my hair and my teeth have fallen out; therefore, I am what is called an old person. If you meditate on these topics, even though you may have committed the four extreme forms of defeat,[653] you will be able to purify yourself of your evil deeds. This is my final testament.

Neusurpa[654] said:

(He was from the Tre[655] area in the Neusur region of Penyul. His ordination name was Yeshe Bar.[656] From his childhood, he possessed firm one-pointed concentration. He served Geshe Gönpawa as a disciple. He was a great scholar and realized adept who possessed supernatural knowledge and miraculous powers. He possessed limitless spiritual qualities, {515} such as having achieved visions of tutelary deities and heard the dharma from them, and so on. In the Neusur region, he attracted a following of a thousand disciples. He lived to the age of seventy-six years. When he first met Gönpawa, the latter placed his hands on his head to bless him, and this left an impression on the top of his head that remained visible for the rest of his life. At the time of Neusurpa's passing, his great spiritual son Döntengpa[657] received the crown of his teacher's head as a relic, and after founding Dönteng Monastery in Ngam Shö,[658] he enshrined the crown of Neusurpa's head in a great reliquary stupa that was placed there as the principal religious icon in the main temple. One of Neusurpa's hands was enshrined in the stupa known as Gold Dust,[659] which is located in the Nyal region. It is said that limitless numbers of disciples still gather there to perform acts of religious service. When Lha Drigangpa[660] of Ön met Döntengpa, the latter had a vision in which he saw the thirty-five buddhas seated on Lha Drigangpa's *namjar*.[661] By prostrating to them, a relationship of teacher and disciple was established between them. Lha Drigangpa founded Drigang Monastery and caused the dharma to flourish greatly. Potowa's great spiritual son, Dölpa Rok Marzhurpa,[662] was also known as Yangepa.[663] He was a bodhisattva possessed of limitless spiritual qualities who was also born as a human being in seven consecutive lives. He compiled the *Blue Udder*, and his great spiritual son Lha Drigangpa composed an extensive commentary to it. Among Neusurpa's great spiritual sons, the two from Tsang were Chiwo Lhepa[664] and Tsangpa Rinpoche;[665] the ones from Ü were Gyamawa, who was also known as the Great Gyer, and Döntengpa; the one from Samye was Geshe Draktokpa.[666] There were also many other disciples who appeared.)

> These three spiritual activities have the same level of importance: to develop recollection of death in your mind, to mentally abandon this life, and to practice the dharma. Likewise, these three activities have the same level of harmfulness: to avoid thinking that you are going to die anytime soon, to cling to this life with the clenched fist of death, and to commit evil deeds.

He also taught the following points extensively:

> Meditation on impermanence saves you from attachment to this life. Meditation on the doctrine of karma and its results saves you from the eight inopportune occasions.[667] Meditation on the disadvantages of samsara saves you from all of samsara's three realms.[668] Meditation on loving-kindness and compassion saves you from the Hīnayāna.[669] Meditation on emptiness saves you from giving rise to signs.[670] {516}

In former times, reflection upon impermanence was also used as a supreme form of instruction. It is declared in the vinaya scriptures[671] that King Rudrāyaṇa had a queen named Candraprabhā who was certain to die within seven days. She was entrusted to Bhikṣuṇī Śailā, a female arhat, for spiritual training. Having been ordained as a nun, Candraprabhā was instructed to meditate on impermanence. After seven days, she passed away and was reborn as a goddess. Following that, after hearing the dharma from the Bhagavān, she achieved a vision of the truths.[672]

Therefore, this topic of reflecting on impermanence is a main form of spiritual practice. It is a great misunderstanding for you to think to yourself, "This topic of impermanence is not a main practice; there is a different one that is a main practice. This one is merely a preliminary form of spiritual practice that constitutes a means of gaining entry to the dharma." If that were true, then it would be acceptable to say that such topics as enlightenment mind, emptiness, and the like are not actually main forms of dharma practice. However, you won't find any difference between these two points.[673] It can also be realized by that just-mentioned story that meditation upon impermanence is a profound form of dharma practice to carry out when passing away[674] or when you are on the verge of death.

That notion is also a correct one. Among the three doors to liberation[675] that the Bhagavān taught, the one called the door to liberation of wishlessness[676] means that the practitioner does not wish for any portion of the entirety of the world through having meditated on the fact that the entirety of the world consists of impermanence and suffering.

In this treatise, the practitioner is meant to properly learn and then meditate on the nature of impermanence that is both the momentary disintegration of all composite entities and the disintegration of a continuum.[677] Although the Bhagavān had previously achieved limitless forms of one-pointed concentration that represented the practices of quiescence and insight, he still had not attained the state of liberation. Later, he gained an understanding of the transcendent path, which is made up of the sixteen aspects[678] of the four noble truths that consist of impermanence and the rest and which are not found in any of the mundane forms of the path. Through meditating on this understanding, he is said to have achieved the deathless {517} state.[679]

The impermanence that is to be meditated on here is this very same one that is one of the four aspects of the noble truth of suffering. Therefore, the fortunate and wise person who meditates on this impermanence should do so with the knowledge that it constitutes the most essential form of the Buddha Bhagavān's dharma teachings.

The *Sūtra on Closely Placed Recollection* also declares:

> The coming of death is praised
> as the supreme object of recollection.
> Its cultivation leads to the highest peace
> that is free of contamination.
>
> Through recalling fear of the Lord of Death,
> how could the mind rush after wicked deeds?
> Moreover, by remaining free of offenses,
> all impurities will become forever stilled.
>
> The tathāgatas declared mindfulness
> to be the highest state of well-being.
> At all times, recall the Lord of Death
> and also abandon unvirtuous deeds.

Gyalse Rinpoche said:

> It is declared in the sūtras that frequent meditation upon impermanence is an act by which you honor all the buddhas. It will cause you to be encouraged by all the buddhas. It will cause you to be prophesied by all the buddhas. It will cause you to receive the blessings of all the buddhas.

Although it is declared hundreds of times in all the spiritual sources—that is, the sūtras, the treatises, and oral instructions—that this practice of meditating on impermanence is the supreme path, that it causes you to abandon all attachment to the world, and that, especially at the present time, there is no practice anywhere that is more important or more eminent than that of meditating on impermanence, those persons of little merit still do not believe it.

Drogön said:

> Because this practice of recalling impermanence is profound, it is very difficult to develop an awareness of it in your mental con-

> tinuum. The Master Buddha Śākyamuni and all the great meditation masters feel disappointment about this.

Gyalse Rinpoche said:

> If you develop an uncontrived awareness of impermanence, you will become someone who never brings to mind anything that is contrary to the dharma. There are only a few dharma practitioners who have developed a pure form of this experiential awareness.

Puchungwa said to Shawo Gangpa:

> Today I must listen to a dharma teaching from you. Tell me about the corpses that are to be burned at Lemo Tang.[680]

When Shawo Gangpa replied that the body of the person named "so-and-so" is being burned at this or that place, Puchungwa remarked:

> Pema Jangchup,[681] I cannot believe the way that all noblemen fail to recognize the significance of these overt acts of continually carrying to agricultural fields the fertilizer created by burning human corpses, and yet they say that their minds are drawn to the topic of emptiness. They are persons who claim to know how to practice dharma while they swing the jagged horns and rashly stamp the hooves of their mental afflictions.

Shawopa said:

> There are also more scholars than there are wise persons.

In former times when the Bhagavān was alive, among the sangha of bhikṣuṇīs, the arhatī Mahāprajāpatī Gautamī, who was Buddha Śākyamuni's maternal aunt, together with her retinue, primarily cultivated states of meditative absorption, while the arhatī Yajñā and her retinue principally engaged in the activity of teaching and listening to the dharma. In order to preserve each other's opinion by observing compatible conduct, on those occasions when the two groups were together, those nuns who were practitioners of meditative absorption would recite sūtras that contained teachings on the topic of impermanence rather than engage in meditation on impermanence, and those nuns who were followers of Yajñā would teach passages from the vinaya scriptures that described meditating on impermanence.

As discussed earlier[682] in the section that addressed Ārya Asaṅga's interpretation of several sūtra verses, it was explained that even arhats meditate on impermanence in the form of death at all times.

Potowa said:

> If even a bodhisattva who has attained the second ārya stage meditates on this great means of eliminating appearances[683] that is a practice I follow, I do not think it is an instruction that is too small for practitioners such as Gutön.[684]

Drogön said:

> Because this practice of meditating on impermanence is very important, it is taught in all the scriptural sources—sūtras, tantras, and treatises. In the vinaya scriptures, it is even declared that depictions of skeletons should be drawn in the halls that monks or nuns use for walking about as a way of promoting recollection of impermanence.

He also would say that until Lord Atiśa came to Tibet, impermanence was not known to be a topic of instruction. He also wrote the following verses:

> By not reflecting on the uncertainty of the time of death
> you will commit a variety of evil deeds in this life
> in order to benefit your friends
> and bring harm to your enemies.
>
> Yet, after having left behind all those
> who appear to be friends and enemies,
> you will go to the endless lower realms.
> What other loss is there greater than this?

With the uncertainty of the time of death,
one who, facing death, shortsightedly thinks,
"There is no need for any further wickedness,"
is like an insect whose nose detected a twig.[685]

You definitely need to gain the complete detachment
that is repulsed by all the recurrent activities
of this life and develops intense aversion for them.

Through having meditated thus upon the impermanence
of death, if the spear of understanding pierces the thoughts
of this life, every activity that you carry out
will take on a nature that conforms to the dharma.

Samsara's disadvantages, karma and its results,
enlightenment mind, and the absence of any real essence—
all these will be realized on the basis of this impermanence.
Meditating on it also engenders various positive attitudes.

Je Milarepa also sang about a system of practice that is identical with Lord Atiśa's Stages of the Path:

Having feared continually {520} the eight inopportune states,
I meditated on impermanence and the faults of samsara,
I entrusted my deepest thought to the refuge of the Three Jewels,
and I developed earnest conviction about the teachings of karma
and their results.

Having trained my continuum in the means aspect of
enlightenment mind,
I stopped the continuous stream of the obscurations' traces
and realized that whatever appearances may arise are illusions.
Now I have no trepidation regarding the three lower realms.

Having feared continually this temporary life force,
I created the conditions for the path of the channels and the vital
airs.[686]

Pa Dampa said:

(It is also stated in the account of Pa Dampa's spiritual life that he was a great tulku[687] of a buddha. He possessed limitless forms of supernatural knowledge and miraculous powers. It is also said that, once, while Sakya Paṇḍita was experiencing a vision of Mañjughoṣa, Pa Dampa appeared there after having taken hold of the bridle of the lion that Mañjughoṣa was riding, and so on. He founded Dingri Langkor[688] Monastery. The account of his spiritual activities states that he had very many great spiritual sons, such as Dampa Kunga.[689] It is also said that he had many disciples who were yogis and yoginīs, such as So Chungwa,[690] the Great Meditator Patsap,[691] and Kamshila,[692] and so on)

> If you reflect on death, you will have no ordinary needs.
> People of Dingri, bear in mind your impending death.[693]

Moreover, some teachers taught a system of practice that introduces disciples to the dharma through the doctrine of the four noble truths.[694] Others introduce them through the doctrine of dependent origination.[695] While there are many different systems, this method of introducing disciples to the dharma through reflecting on death is one whose key points are profound.

This practice of meditating upon impermanence in the form of death is very important. It is indispensable in the beginning, middle, and end—that is, in all three stages of one's dharma practice. If you develop an understanding of impermanence, in the beginning it will serve as a cause that prompts you to take up the dharma. In the middle period, it will serve as a goad that prompts you to generate effort. In the final period, it will cause you {521} to attain the clear-light state of a buddha's dharma body.[696]

Götsangpa[697] said:

(Götsangpa is renowned to have been a reincarnation of Milarepa, a claim that is asserted in the sealed account of his liberating deeds.[698] He possessed limitless forms of supernatural knowledge and miraculous activities. It is said that he displayed the buddha activity known as "The dispelling of suffering by the tathāgata." It is said that, among his many great spiritual sons—such as Ogyenba,[699] Neringpa,[700] and Yangönpa[701]—disciples such as Jang Lingpa[702] and Bariwa,[703] who are included among the ones known as "the thirteen that attained the ultimate goal," were spread throughout the Rose Apple continent. Götsangpa, himself, was a disciple of Tsangpa Gyare. He was from the region of Lhodrak, and his ordination name was Gönpo Dorje.)

> Ending your ties to your homeland,
> dissolving the glue of clinging to your family,

and severing the entanglements of food and wealth—
these three are achieved by meditating on the impermanence of death.

Refraining from engaging in meaningless activities,
striving day and night to carry out spiritual deeds,
and abandoning evil companions—
these three are achieved by meditating on the difficulty of
obtaining leisure and fortune.[704]

Regarding sensory pleasures as a source of misfortune,
entrusting yourself to the Three Jewels,
and overcoming attachment for the worldly concerns—
these are achieved by meditating on samsara's faults.

Kyechokpa said:

Do not think about the goals that are longed for in this life;
reflect continually on death and the lack of time to spare.
This life that is just a brief moment and a fleeting instant
does not last, and there is no time to spare;
you must reflect on a death that comes swiftly.
These are heartfelt words of truth; hold them firmly in your mind.
Your life will be wasted on the path of distraction.
If you don't recall death, you will be swept away by distractions.
You must reflect on the uncertainty of the time of death.

Yangönpa said:

You must increase your faith by reflecting on the topics of impermanence in the form of death, karma and its results {522}, and the disadvantages of samsara. You must strengthen your detachment[705] by perceiving sensory pleasures as detrimental and by reducing your desirous thoughts through developing a sense of satisfaction.[706] You must strengthen your devotion and reverence toward your lama by purifying yourself of any erroneous thoughts that perceive him or her to have faults, which is accomplished by regarding whatever your lama does as excellent, and by performing the stake-like supplication[707] to him or her.

Pakmo Drupa said:

> Always reflect upon death, and count the deeds you have accumulated.

Karmapa Rölpai Dorje[708] said:

(The Karmapas are emanations of Mahākaruṇika,[709] and it is held that they make up a reincarnation lineage that consists of eleven individuals. Among Dakpo's[710] great spiritual sons were the Three Men from Kham—namely, Use,[711] Pakmo Drupa, and Seltong Shore.[712] Of these, the first Karmapa was the one known as Use. He served Chapa Chökyi Senge[713] as a disciple, at which time he studied the three baskets of Buddhist canonical literature. He also served Dakpo Lhaje as a disciple and became renowned as a great realized adept. Pakmo Drupa had many great spiritual sons, such as the two of Dri[714] and Tak,[715] Ya Kelden,[716] Tropuwa,[717] Tsangpa Kunden,[718] Je Chengawa[719] and others. Düsum Kyenpa[720] founded Tsurpu Monastery. His reincarnation, Karma Pakshi,[721] was born in Kham, and the latter's reincarnation, Rangjung Dorje,[722] was born in Shurmo. Rangjung Dorje's reincarnation was Karmapa Rölpai Dorje. The reincarnations that followed them were Deshin Shekpa,[723] Tongwa Dönden,[724] Chödrak Gyatso,[725] Mikyö Dorje,[726] and the rest.[727])

> At the time that Yamarāja,[728] the Lord of Death, appears,
> it will be difficult for your mind to remain at ease;
> and, as there's no way to know where you will go in your next life,
> now is the time that you must reflect with great care.
>
> Continue to engage in proper acts of reflection.
> If your mind should develop conviction,[729] that is wonderful.
> If not, from now on generate a courageous fortitude.[730]

Tropu Lotsāwa said:

> To ensure that whatever you do is genuine dharma,
> you must cherish recollection of impermanence and suffering.
> They are like prodding a good horse with a whip.
> It would be a great wonder if attachment and aversion were to
> disappear on their own.

Gyalse Rinpoche said:

If you cannot discipline your own mind in a place of seclusion
where there are no enemies to tame, no friends to support,
no lord that you must obey, no servant that must obey you,
what other activity[731] is there, O reciter of the *maṇi* mantra?

Since it is not certain that what is gathered in the fall can be enjoyed next spring,
it is said, "Fool, don't gather your provisions for the spring in the fall."
Since death is certain, and the dharma is certain to benefit you at the time of death,
it is very foolish of you not to start practicing right now.

It will be difficult to achieve even rebirth as a human or worldly god, let alone enlightenment,
with a mind that strives after the prosperity of this life.
Therefore, strive to meditate on the recollection of death
with a mind that abandons attachment for this life.

If you fail to recall the uncertainty of the time of death,
though you may strive after learning, reflection, and meditation,
the mind that wants to achieve the prosperity of this life
will cause those efforts to become like food of a hundred flavors
that have had vomit and poison mixed into them.

He also said:

Though there's no assurance of not dying this very day,
the complacent person who prepares to live forever
risks having to beat his or her breast when facing death.
Please bless me to practice recollection of death.

A person from Kham offered a bolt of cloth to the realized adept and yogi named Chöyung,[732] who was an ornament within Je Dakpo's[733] company of disciples, and then asked him for a dharma teaching. When he wasn't given any instruction, the person asked again in a more insistent manner. After grasping him by the arm, Chöyung repeated three times, "I am going to die. You are also going to die." Then he said, "My lama doesn't teach anything other than that. I also have no practice other than that. You, too, should meditate on that." Then he swore an oath that there could be no greater practice than this. It is said that the person from Kham became a realized adept through meditating on this instruction.

A verse from *Entry into the Conduct That Leads to Enlightenment* states:

> When shall I go to the final resting place for bodies
> so that I might compare my own body,
> which is subject to disintegration,
> with the skeletons of other persons?[734]

Therefore, if it is apparent that all the sūtras and treatises, as well as all the individual Tibetan dharma lineages—despite having disagreements about certain philosophical tenets—are in agreement about the necessity to meditate on impermanence in the form of death, about performing aspirational prayers and supplication prayers to develop this realization in one's mental continuum, and about fostering the hope "When will the time come that, through meditating on this impermanence, I am able to develop a realization of it in my mental continuum?" who is there that would refrain from striving to meditate on the recollection of death, that supreme path about which all doubt has been eliminated?

Therefore, this very topic is the one that must be meditated upon first. This can also be understood from the earlier explanations that the act of mentally abandoning this life is the indispensable and first spiritual practice to be undertaken. Potowa said:

> Meditating on impermanence is the starting point of the dharma. The phrase "In the language of India"[735] and such acts as making prostration and so on are not its starting point.

He also said:

> Individuals who illustrated the proper method of recalling impermanence are those like Shangtsun Yerpa, Nyantön Śākjung,[736] and Ben Gungyal.[737]

Yerpawa[738] would always seem concerned about having to leave. If he developed even a slight illness, he would use that as a reason and say, "Now I must go, I must go." Then he would give away all his possessions to others and say about certain objects that were indispensable, "I am lending this to you for as long as I remain alive." Then, as he left, everyone {525} would hear clear sounds of divine music.

Puchungwa would say about having surplus provisions of less than six *kel*[739] when no one is present to whom they might be given, "Make offerings to the Three Jewels," whereas it is reported that Potowa would say, "Distribute it to the sangha."[740]

At first, Nyantön was proud of his scriptural knowledge and also very tightfisted[741] about sharing it with others. Later, influenced by the death of a younger brother, he carried out the act of mentally abandoning this life, and because of his anguish, he meditated exclusively on impermanence. Even when he had recovered from his sadness, he would always repeat this verse, among others:

> It is an established principle of the world,
> a process that brings very painful sorrow,
> that even after having lived together for a long time,
> one is separated from others by their death.[742]

A teacher from Tropu Monastery named Zhönu Tsul[743] is said to have asked disdainfully, "It is said that Nyantön is a great teacher and that he meditates on impermanence. Is that true?" Naljorpa Chenpo[744] replied:

> If there is anything that is true, that fact[745] about him is one that is true.

One of Nyantön's attendants asked the master about preparing the rainy-season sticks.[746] Nyantön replied, "There's no certainty that we shall live through the rainy season. What do you hope to accomplish by preparing sticks?" After further saying, "If you know that you will remain alive, show me how that is so," the master made no plans for remaining until the end of the rainy season. Potowa said about him, "Nyantön seems to have been one who perceived truth.[747]"

It is said that, because Potowa himself had also gained a realization of impermanence, his face would darken with disapproval in a manner that corresponded to the amount of gain and honor, and so on, he received. He states a little way into his *Extended Monologue*:[748]

> By thinking to myself, "If I were to die tonight, what would I do?" I have often stopped myself from considering goals that pertain to the time period that lies beyond tomorrow."[749]

On a certain occasion, Tönpa Dorje[750] offered about one hundred and seventy scripture volumes, the foremost of which was a copy of the Extensive Version[751] of the *Perfection of Wisdom Sūtra*. After the cloth covers for these scriptures had been sewn, Potowa said that cloth covers should also {526} be made for the scriptures that had been offered by Betön.[752] Geshe Drak Karwa[753] asked the master for permission to make the additional cloth covers at a later time because there was not sufficient brocade, felt cloth, and other materials to do so then. Potowa replied:

> I don't have any time to spare. If you have enough for one cloth cover, make one. If you have enough for two, make two.

Following that, about three hundred cloth covers were made for the scripture volumes at Poto Monastery. Three days after that, the master became ill and then passed away in seven days. It is said that he must have possessed the supernormal knowledge that perceived the exact time of his own death.

Potowa observed the practice of never staying in a fixed place. Whenever he came to a particular location, he would attract more than two thousand monks. Among these, as many as five hundred were individuals who had mentally abandoned this life and who knew how to practice recollection of impermanence.

Gyalse Rinpoche said about this: "How very wonderful! Nowadays, it is difficult to find even one or two such individuals." He also said: "Those like Kharak Gomchung are the ones who know how to practice recollection of impermanence."

(Kharak is the name of a cave near Dragyap in the Tre area of Penyul.)

Kharak Gomchung stayed in a rocky cave known as Black Hollow[754] near Kharak. Next to the opening was a rose brier, which he first thought to remove when he tore his clothing by brushing up against it. But right after that, he thought to himself, "What good will it do to cut down this brier? It would be better to let it remain there as I come and go." It is said that the bush was not cut down for the remainder of his life.

Gyalse Rinpoche also recounted incidents about the lives of Geshe Sangpuwa,[755] Shentön Yungdrung Gyatso,[756] and others.

(When he heard that Ngok Lekshe[757] had not died, Atiśa[758] remarked, "O follower of Jowo,[759] you must give up ordinary activities." The Geshe replied, "I am watching over the forest in Sangpu." Atiśa further said, "O spiritual son, though you may not have abandoned the erroneous apprehension of a real 'self'[760] in relation to inner entities, are you still grasping at the 'self' of outer entities?")

(When it was heard that Shentön had not died, Atiśa said, "The primordial dharma is profound!" and then he further said, "The most profound forms of explicit instruction[761] are all the instances in which one sees and hears {527} for oneself that someone has died." It is also said that someone spoke about Shentön behind his back, to which he said, "I am right here." Gyalse Rinpoche would say that these incidents relate to the practice of recalling death. Both of these individuals were disciples of Jowo Atiśa. Ngok Lekshe founded Sangpu Monastery and became a great scholar and realized adept. Shentön nurtured disciples in the Samye region and gave rise to many great spiritual sons).

If you ask, "Well then, if the practice of meditating on impermanence is of great importance and possesses great benefits in the manner that has been described, do you meditate on this topic by organizing it into a great many sections?" Generally speaking, the Kadampa spiritual teachers did not create detailed outlines that organized the topic into separate sections. Nevertheless, there are many descriptions that follow outlines made by several former wise scholars. There are no differences among all of them regarding the subjects that are to be reflected and meditated upon. The complete range of points can be found in Drolungpa's[762] treatise on *The Stages of the Path*.[763] Recently, Je Rinpoche, the spiritual father created an outline, propagated by his spiritual sons, that identifies three roots[764] and nine reasons.[765] Nowadays, this system is one that is widely known.

The former lineage of wise scholars that descends from Chaksorwa[766] developed a system of reflection on three types of impermanence: rough impermanence, subtle impermanence, and sudden impermanence. The first has two aspects: reflecting that because, in a general sense, individuals are made up of conditioned entities,[767] we are certain to perish, and reflecting that we die because we are powerless to stop it. Subtle impermanence means to reflect upon our condition of undergoing momentary impermanence by means of such similes as water flowing over a precipice and livestock that are driven by a herdsman {528}. There are four kinds of sudden impermanence, which are to reflect that we die suddenly because of an imbalance of the four elements, having disturbed the gods, both an imbalance of the elements and having disturbed the gods, and unfavorable factors related to such things as food, clothing, and dwelling, and so on.

(Chaksorwa met and received teachings from Naktso Lotsāwa[768] and many of Jowo Atiśa's direct disciples and close disciples. He achieved siddhis and developed many great spiritual sons, including Ja Duldzin[769] and others.)

Many other spiritual teachers have taught two types of impermanence: outer impermanence and inner impermanence. The first is made up of the impermanence of the "vessel"[770] and the impermanence of its "contents."[771] There are three types of inner impermanence: the disintegration of conditioned entities that occurs with each passing moment; the impermanence of a continuum,[772] which is that your life span has a definite limit that goes by more quickly than an arrow that has been shot into the air or a powerful river whose water flows by swiftly; and sudden impermanence, which is a death that occurs suddenly in four ways: when a life span comes to an end, when the karma that produced a life span is exhausted, when the merit that sustains a life span is exhausted, and due to lack of mindfulness.[773]

My lama said that when you meditate on the points that relate to impermanence and other topics, you should sit with your body maintaining Vairocana's seven qualities[774] of posture. Having thoroughly ascertained the nature of the points for each topic to be meditated upon, as well as the fixed nature of their number and the order in which to cultivate them, you should develop a strong aspiration in which you think to yourself, "I shall not allow myself to proceed in a manner that is different from this." From the outset, you must meditate in a manner that accords with the aspiration that you made and without allowing your mind to develop bad habits.[775] Therefore, having recognized the importance of ascertaining the number and order {529} of the points to be cultivated when meditating on the topic of impermanence in the form of death, I have written my explanation in the manner that appears above.

(My lama Je Khedrupa's[776] ordination name was Gelek Pel Zangpo.[777] He was from a region in the northern part of Latö known as Dedak.[778] He mastered myriad forms of the Buddha's speech and was an incomparable spiritual heir of Je Tsongkhapa. He founded Riwo Dangchen[779] Monastery and also established Pelkor Chöde,[780] located in the Nyangtö area of Changra,[781] as a monastic seat for the followers of the Genden[782] tradition. He developed many disciples and passed away at Genden[783] Monastery at the age of fifty-seven.)

As Drogön said, "There are two methods: to reflect on the topics just as they are presented in this text, without mixing up the order of their presentation and to reflect on them in whatever order you may choose to follow." Thus, first you should meditate on the points without mixing up the order of their presentation for as long as it takes to familiarize yourself with them. However, once you have become familiar with them, you may reflect on the topics in whatever manner you please. Therefore, at that point, the order in which to reflect on them no longer needs to remain fixed.

As for the larger or smaller number of points to reflect on in relation to each topic, you must consider this to be an issue of great significance. Regarding this issue, as Ārya Asaṅga explains in *The Stage of a Śrāvaka*,[784] Je Tsongkhapa also states that your practice will become more powerful through reflecting on a large number of individual points.[785] I have also determined this to be so for myself:

> When you perceive many reasons that show
> how friends have done harm to you,
> it becomes easy to abandon attachment to friends.
> Just as when you perceive many reasons
> that show how enemies have helped you
> this quells your hatred toward enemies,
> and enables you to develop loving-kindness quickly,
> consider how powerful hatred also will arise
> when you perceive many reasons that show
> how enemies have done harm to you.

If you ask, "Well then, if it is granted that those are the topics that should be meditated upon, what is the manner or form in which to meditate on them?" that can be understood in the following manner: A person who possesses wisdom should distinguish each of the objects to be held in the mind separately and without mixing them together, clearly bring each of them to mind in order to cause him- or herself to become familiar with them. If you habituate yourself to them in this way, your mind will clearly ascertain their meaning and be able grasp them clearly, causing you to become one who clearly perceives them. When you clearly bring to mind a particular point, if your mind remains fixed on just that meaning, without having its clarity become diminished and without losing its hold of that object,[786] then your mind will remain fixed in that very state in such a way that it flows naturally to its object, without the need to make a renewed effort to meditate on it. For example, if someone describes to you the physical attributes of the Chinese king {530} and you are able to bring them to mind without forgetting them, you will be able to recall them vividly at any time, without needing to have them described to you again. On the other hand, if the meditation object or the physical features of the Chinese king should be forgotten,[787] it will be necessary to repeat the entire process of bringing the object to mind and fixing your attention on it once again. This latter point is equally true for both the analogy and the main subject that is being explained.

The teacher Setön[788] said:

(Setön was a Kadam spiritual teacher.)

> I have put aside all the other good qualities of the wise persons, principal figures, and teachings that relate to the system of this teaching lineage and laid open just the method of carrying out reflection.

Drogön said:

> Jowo Je[789] praised deliberative analysis more than one-pointed concentration.

Chenga Rinpoche[790] once took Geshe Yönlungpa[791] by the arm and said:

> At the time of my death, I would prefer that it be caused by a spirit[792] and not be due to an illness caused by an imbalance of the elements. If you ask why, it is because although it is possible to practice the patience that tolerates suffering[793] in relation to an illness caused by the elements, you cannot practice the patience that forbears the harm inflicted by others[794] in that situation. But with a death caused by a spirit, it is possible to practice both. Even better than that, if someone that you have not harmed in any way should stab you with a knife, while it would be best if you did not die, you still would undergo suffering. If you are able to develop a sincere attitude that this person has been very kind to you, you would engender the patience that arises from attentive reflection

upon entities and thus could develop all three types of patience. However, this cannot be accomplished simply on the basis of a theoretical understanding, as indicated in the following lines:

> The process of meditation consists of thought,[795]
> examination,[796]
> and attentive contemplation[797] that are done
> repetitively. . . .[798]

The precious Neusurpa said:

> You cannot succeed in your practice simply by thinking to yourself, "When I die, when I die." You must meditate in a manner that deliberates and reflects on the basis of a lama's instruction.

This assertion, a spiritual statement that no one else possesses {531}, is a truly extraordinary declaration that was embraced by the holy lama Khedrup. It is virtually impossible to find a person who understands a point like this one.

Neusurpa further said:

> Through developing in this present life a conviction about impermanence that is based upon words, you will gain an awareness that resembles a direct realization of impermanence in your next life. This dharma teaching of Atiśa has not existed before now. It has appeared now, but it will not do so again.

17. Carry Out Your Spiritual Practice Continuously

Precious Sharawa said:

> You may have reflected at length on all the disadvantages of the three lower realms, but if you fail to do so continuously,[799] hearing about the turmoil[800] of worldly events may prompt you to engage in such worldly activities. The initial belief[801] in the dharma that a novice practitioner possesses will become weakened if he or she is distracted[802] even just to a small extent. When the eagerness that all young monks have diminishes with each passing year, the dharma and the antidotes[803] that they developed previously will become like a conch shell that has been polished.[804]

Precious Potowa stated:

> Therefore, you should also reflect diligently and in a variety of ways on each of the ancillary subjects that pertain to these statements (about such topics as the difficulty of finding leisure and fortune, and so on). You should not do so simply once or twice, and so on. If you reflect on this very point until you develop an understanding of its import, you will, in due course, achieve success in relation to all the other dharma subjects as well. Furthermore, with regard to this topic, the three items of companions, spiritual teachers, and residence should be reflected on only if they possess elements that are favorable to your spiritual practice, and not otherwise.

Je Rinpoche said:

> Just as a leper whose arms and legs have been amputated will gain nothing at all by taking just one or two doses of medicine, it is not sufficient that we who have been afflicted with the severe illness of the mental afflictions throughout beginningless time should only practice the meaning of an instruction once or twice. Therefore, it is necessary to strive continuously, like the current of a river, to fully investigate all the elements of the path, using analytical wisdom. As a verse from *In Praise of Confession* states:
>
> Having contracted the illness over a long period of time
> and having also been continually unaware of that,
> what does a leper who has no arms or legs
> gain by taking medicine only a few times?[805]

Candragomī also stated:

> As the tree of the mind that has existed throughout beginningless time
> has been saturated by the bitter liquid of the mental afflictions,
> this has made it incapable of taking on the nature of a sweet taste.
> What is accomplished by a mere drop of water having good qualities?[806]

As this verse indicates, it is said that if these instructions are practiced in a regular and continuous manner, they will become effective when your mind has become habituated to them. Therefore, while it is rather difficult to train your mind at the beginning, later you will gain the ability to undertake the practice more naturally.

At present, when you set about trying to meditate on impermanence or any other topic, you may become discouraged and say, "Last year, even though I had not meditated on this topic, I would experience a very intense sense of apprehension when I contemplated the prospect of my death. Now, though, no matter what I meditate on, I find that my mind becomes confused and I cannot make any progress." But how could you expect that as soon as you try to meditate according to your holy lama's instruction, you will develop a continuous and intense attitude of renunciation. If that were so, because you would also be able to develop a realization of emptiness, as well as other subjects, as soon as you started to meditate on them, you would be able to perfect all the elements of the path in just a few days. As Gyalwa Yangönpa said:

> The latent propensities of bad mental habits are like a rolled-up scroll;
> though new experiences may arise, they are destroyed by incidental factors.
> Since you cannot eliminate errors within a short span of time,
> all you great meditators, pursue your meditation for an extended period.

Yangönpa also said:

> Lama Zhang[807] wanted to have an immediate sign of heat. That is {533} an omen that the practice will be given up right away. If the duration must be extended, what else is there to be done?

And he said further:

> Don't be impatient about practicing for an extended period;
> do not consume tsampa powder too quickly.[808]

These statements have great significance. I received very great benefit from them. Spiritual teachers declare that you must carry out a meditation practice for an extended period because it is necessary to abandon unfavorable qualities to which you have become greatly habituated over lifetimes that are without beginning and because it is necessary to generate favorable qualities to which you are not habituated.

18. Cultivate the Causes That Will Enable the Practice to Be Developed in Your Mind

Spiritual teachers have said that by meditating in this way, in the case of impermanence, for example, you should reflect on it for as long as your mind is favorably disposed to do so. If your mind resists engaging in the practice, arrange offerings to the Three Jewels according to your means and perform the seven-limb devotional practice.[809] Then return to reflecting on impermanence once again. If that proves unsuccessful, don't try to force yourself to meditate on the main topic. Instead, reflect on such subjects as karma and its results. If that does not appeal to you, then purify yourself of your past evil deeds. If that proves unsuccessful, reflect on any subject that appeals to you and that you are able to carry out effectively. That is, pursue this or some other method that brings the desired result. When you regain a favorable state of mind, suspend those measures and reapply yourself intently to that very earlier main topic.

When you are training your mind in relation to impermanence, for instance, associate with a lama or a companion who is also cultivating the practice of impermanence. Moreover, as relates to dharma texts to review, read those that are available on the topic of impermanence. All your efforts to accumulate merit and purify yourself of obscurations should also be done to improve your understanding of impermanence. As Je Rinpoche wrote:

> Initially, your inner attitude will gain strength
> through relying upon the power of the field.[810]
> So I urge you to carry out, uninterruptedly, acts of worship
> toward your spiritual teachers and the Three Jewels.[811]

Therefore, having performed acts of worship and presented torma offerings to your tutelary deity, lama, and dharma protector, you should beseech them to bless you so that you will develop that strong inner attitude. Moreover, in conjunction with reflecting properly on the benefits of meditating on these points and the disadvantages of failing to meditate on them, you should also generate a powerful aspiration {534} to train your mind in this topic of impermanence.

You should not only meditate on the meaning of the two root categories of the uncertainty of the time of death and the complete worthlessness of friends, wealth, and so on at the time of death during the actual meditation sessions; you should also repeatedly cultivate recollection[812] and vigilance[813] in relation to these points at all times during the intervals between meditation sessions. Moreover, you should remind yourself about them by reciting aloud passages whose wording conveys their meaning in the most incisive and clear manner. In addition, you should carry out, as little as possible, even other activities that relate to the dharma but that are not part of this practice of impermanence, let alone engage in activities of a worldly nature. You should dispel, as much as possible, whatever hindrances and unwanted obstacles may arise by means of whatever meditation practice you may carry out. More generally, having abandoned whatever adverse factors may arise and collected those favorable conditions that are indispensable, you should think to yourself, "Now, I should not carry out any activities other than these."

In addition, you should, as much as possible, carry out such activities as prompting others to meditate on this dharma practice, praising this practice to others, and helping others to obtain favorable conditions. It is said that if these qualities are acquired in this life, you should definitely give rise to the appropriate realizations in this life. Or even if you fail to give rise to them, you will be able to give rise to them without difficulty in your next life.

In the distant past, a certain man saw a woman's corpse whose stomach was torn open and thought to himself, "All women are like this, and my body is also like this." After having brought this thought to mind repeatedly, upon his death he was reborn in India as the son of a great merchant chief whose wealth rivaled that of Vaiśravaṇa.[814] After this son of a noble family, who was named Yaśa, had become an adult, he lived surrounded by a retinue of courtesans and would fall asleep after enjoying all the forms of sensual pleasure. One night, when he awoke and saw the women asleep, he thought to himself, "I am in a charnel ground," and formed the conceptions that the place was unattractive, disgusting, repulsive, and frightening. He rose up from his bed and fled from his house, after which he met the Bhagavān. After hearing the dharma, it is said that he perceived the truth {535} and became an arhat.

(This is how the great arhat named Yaśa appeared. After the Bhagavān began to teach the dharma in the world, the scriptures refer to early disciples with such expressions as "the first group of five[815] disciples" and "the lesser group of five disciples,[816] made up of Yaśa and the rest, came into being." This individual was that early disciple Yaśa).[817]

In the same way, if you now intently cultivate an awareness of impermanence, even though you may not develop any other spiritual quality, wherever you are reborn in the future you will recall impermanence, and remaining free of attachment for any worldly object, you will consider whatever is unrelated to the dharma as worthless and thereby become one who is able to proceed unimpeded toward buddhahood. Therefore, I urge you to strive to meditate upon impermanence.

19. Train Yourself in the Higher Paths and Believe in Your Lama's Instruction

If in addition to that practice of impermanence, you add meditation on other topics, your spiritual development will become even more excellent. Two brothers named Diri[818] and Drakpo[819] had approached Geshe Tönpa in order to hear instructions on Buddhist philosophical doctrine.[820] Tönpa Rinpoche said to them:

> In India there is one "inner" Buddhist system and seven "outer" non-Buddhist systems. We Tibetans meditate on a lama's instruction. What is that instruction? It is that meditating extensively on death and the doctrine of karma and its results will cause your morality to become pure. You should meditate steadfastly on loving-kindness, compassion, and enlightenment mind. By the force of these practices, you will accumulate merit and purify yourself of your obscurations in many ways. This is my instruction.

In addition, when someone named Tönpa Öser Gyatso[821] requested teachings, Geshe Tönpa said the same thing to him.

Also, when Khampa Pelbar[822] requested a dharma teaching for his departure,[823] Tönpa Rinpoche said:

> There is a teaching that enables all physical behavior of walking, standing, reclining, and sitting[824] to become forms of one-pointed concentration. This can be achieved by {536} an individual who cultivates the instruction mentally as well as physically during his or her youth. We meditate on a lama's instruction. What is that instruction? It is that meditating extensively on death and the doctrine of karma and its results will cause your morality to become pure. You should meditate steadfastly on loving-kindness, compassion, and enlightenment mind. By the force of these practices, you will accumulate merit in a variety of ways and purify yourself of your obscurations in a variety of ways. This is the instruction.

Potowa said:

> Through correct reflection on the Master's[825] spiritual qualities,
> a disciple is prompted to take refuge and thereby becomes a
> Buddhist.
> Then, after being introduced to the difficulty of obtaining leisure
> and fortune,
> he or she is directed to practice recollection of death.
>
> Then, through continual reflection on the four truths,
> a disciple should realize that all of samsara is flawed.
> Having realized that the nature of others is the same as one's own,
> he or she should develop loving-kindness and compassion toward
> all beings.
> The disciple will come to possess the enlightenment mind
> generated by them.
> All of the dharma in its entirety is contained in this system.
> If a final testament were cast to the wind,[826] this is what it would be.[827]

Drogön said:

> As for the pure dharma that is to be practiced
> by those of us who have gone forth,[828]

> there is nothing beyond that of the three baskets
> and the various classes of tantra. All you spiritual persons[829]
> should train your mind in this teaching on the stages of the path
> that ranges from impermanence to ultimate reality.

Neusurpa Rinpoche said:

> Members of a group of tantric practitioners were uneasy about sprinkling the first portion of some beer into the air as an offering, so a tantric practitioner name Lha Mebar[830] made the offering and recited, "May the Three Jewels accept this. May the dharma protectors accept this. May the fathers and mothers of the three times accept this. May the six classes of sentient beings accept this." Similarly, there are no meanings from the four classes of tantra and {537} the three baskets that are not included in this teaching of Glorious Atiśa on the stages of the path to enlightenment. Because this spiritual medicine of the Lord is such a well-prepared form of treatment, I urge you to take some of it. I request you not to vomit it up after you have consumed it. If you feel like you are going to vomit, I urge you to expel saliva and exhale your breath, and even to do such things as place a cold rock on your chest as a moist compress and pull your hair. Then, even if you don't take this spiritual medicine right now, I urge you to place it in your left breast pocket so that you can take it later. If you are concerned that it might fall out of your pocket, I urge you to place it in the deepest part of that pocket.[831]

Shawopa said:

> This system of training the mind that relates to the three types of person—that is, those that are best, middling, and lesser—promotes both the conferring of vows and the pursuit of spiritual studies. If your mind becomes proficient in this practice, you will not give rise to an attitude that is desirous of seeking wealth, which will cause everyone to develop faith toward you. Therefore, this teaching system also promotes both efforts to accumulate merit and to maintain congenial relations.

Je Rinpoche wrote:

> Leisure and fortune have great meaning and are very difficult to
> obtain;
> they also undergo destruction swiftly, like a water bubble.
> Reflect as well for a long period of time on this teaching
> of dependent origination, in which nothing accompanies you after
> death
> and even minor forms of white and black deeds have unfailing results.[832]

With regard to these two topics of the great meaning of a human life that possesses the qualities of leisure and fortune and the difficulty of obtaining such a life, as well as those of impermanence and the doctrine of karma and its results, he also wrote:

> If the roots of these four teachings become firmly established,
> the remaining virtuous practices will arise with ease.[833]

(Two of the four teachings are the great meaning of leisure and fortune and the difficulty of obtaining them; the other two are impermanence and karma together with its results.)

And further:

> Those who pride themselves as scholars and meditators
> but who have not established the roots of benefit and happiness
> through these practices
> are like merchants who return empty-handed from a voyage to an
> island of gold.[834]

He also wrote:

> The Stages of the Path to Enlightenment—
> which has been well-transmitted successively from Nāgārjuna and
> Asaṅga, {538}
> the two crown ornaments among all the learned scholars of Rose
> Apple continent,
> whose banner of fame shines resplendently throughout the world—

is an instruction like the jewel called the King of Rulers,
in that it fulfills beings' every aim without exception.
It is also an ocean of splendid eloquent speech
because it contains the rivers of a thousand excellent treatises.

It enables one to realize that the entire doctrine is free of
contradiction,
to perceive all of the discourses as personal instruction,
and to comprehend easily the Victor's intent.
It also protects one from the abyss of great misconduct.

Therefore, what discerning person is there whose mind
would not be greatly captivated by the Stages of the Path
for the Three Types of Person, that supreme instruction taken up
by so many fortunate and learned scholars of India and Tibet?

Since teaching and hearing, for even a single period, this system
that condenses and summarizes the essence of all the discourses
is certain to collect the vast benefit and accumulation
of explaining and hearing the true dharma, contemplate this
point.[835]

He further declared:

If you strive mainly to firmly establish the roots in this way,
among all the holy dharma teachings that the Victor proclaimed,
some of them can be practiced right now;
others should be made objects of aspirational prayers.

Do not discard even one, for all are a means of achieving
buddhahood.
If you know how to retain within the path the complete teaching
of the Victor in this way, you are a person of preeminent
learning.[836]

If you have a heartfelt desire to pursue the dharma in this way, the very activity that is most important to accomplish at the outset is to mentally abandon the three types of this life's activities—those that are white, black, and mottled. Moreover, regarding them, black activities are the very worst forms of human behavior—that is, killing, stealing, and the like—which are not only wrongful, but also easily recognized. It is also evident that many persons are able to abandon them. However, the white or mottled types are such restless activities as these that are carried out by persons who have not abandoned attachment to this life: conferring initiations, teaching dharma, constructing images of deities, carrying out acts of generosity, performing religious rituals in laypersons' homes, making *tsa tsa*[837] images, writing protection diagrams, reciting mantras to subdue demons, reciting scriptures throughout the day, and so on. It is quite evident that there are few individuals who are able to abandon these activities.[838] Was it not said that no matter how good an activity may seem, it is quite worthless if it is carried out with a mind that has not become free of attachment toward this life? In general, it is a function of the mind that determines the virtuous and unvirtuous nature of all activities. Therefore, although you must ensure that neither gods nor demons nor humans have any reason to find fault with your state of mind, *The Fulfillment of Knowledge*, (which was composed by King Indrabhūti,) also states:

> Whatever deed may be performed
> is an act of body, speech, or mind.
> There is no other fourth kind;
> they alone should be examined thus.
>
> In the absence of the mind,
> the body is unable to do anything.
> Speech, too, without that mind
> is never able to do anything.
>
> Therefore, the deeds of body and mind
> can only occur when the mind is present.
> Whatever good or bad the world creates,
> all of it is due solely to the mind.
>
> The supreme victors proclaim that
> whatever deeds have a beneficial use,
> all are good conduct and the opposite
> of that are demeritorious.

But the guru for the world said that
whatever is good or bad,
all is created by the mind alone,
and by the mind alone it is destroyed.[839]

The Kaśyapa Chapter also declares:

Just as a person may be swept away
by the ocean's water and then die of thirst,
so, too, {540} readers[840] situated in the ocean of dharma
with craving for much dharma may go to the lower realms.

Just as a physician carrying a quantity of medicine
might wander throughout the world,
if he cannot cure his own illnesses,
that medicine is of no use to him.

So, too, a bhikṣu might possess morality's qualities
and be endowed with learning, but if he cannot cure the illness
of wrongly generating mental afflictions,
his effort at gaining learning is useless exertion.[841]

Reflect carefully on everything that is expressed in this sūtra passage. As it indicates, someone may spend his or her entire life practicing the dharma in such a way that others think, "He or she is a true follower of the dharma," and that person him- or herself may also think, "I am a true follower of the dharma." But then, who is it that these lines refer to, when they declare that, after having been immersed in the ocean of the dharma, one might die of thirst and end up having to go to the lower realms?

When someone confers initiations, gives dharma teachings, or even recites scriptures aloud throughout the day,[842] while being unable to bear this life's suffering, having failed to abandon attachment to this life's happiness, and always seeking to enjoy abundant ease, comfort, and a very good reputation, the fault for all of this lies with this person having dedicated him- or herself to the activities of this life. However, since all the suffering that is experienced here in samsara is due to the eight worldly concerns, all these activities that only serve to strengthen and augment the white, black, and mottled forms of the eight worldly concerns are meaningless.

This behavior is described as resembling the act of running around with a bag of medicine that does not benefit one's illness. Therefore, have you not now understood the reason that you must avoid thinking about any of this life's pleasures and comforts and mentally abandon them in their entirety?

You might wonder, "Well then, do all forms of the eight worldly concerns and all activities that are generated by the mental afflictions constitute evil deeds that are causes for being reborn in the lower realms {541}?" Speaking in general terms, all of those white, black, and mottled activities that are motivated by any of the eight worldly concerns can only serve as causes for experiencing samsara's suffering, unless they are also carried out under the influence of an extraordinary form of renunciation.[843] This is why it is said that every form of dharma activity that is motivated by the mental afflictions is meaningless.

Whether or not such purported dharma activities constitute evil deeds that serve as causes for being reborn in the lower realms depends on additional factors. Such activities can be of two types.[844] Among the virtuous deeds of lesser, intermediate, and great persons, all the virtuous deeds that are accumulated by lesser persons are performed with the desire to obtain a samsaric form of happiness. Therefore, they are performed and accumulated[845] under the influence of the eight worldly concerns and the mental afflictions. Moreover, among the mental afflictions, since they are virtuous activities that are accumulated on the strength of desire, they are virtuous activities and not evil deeds. In addition, those lesser persons who wish to achieve the prosperity of gods and human beings of the desire realm accumulate such forms of merit[846] as acts of generosity, morality, and the like. Those lesser persons who wish to achieve the prosperity of the form and formless realms carry out such activities as meditating on forms of one-pointed concentration that constitute quiescence, insight, and the union of quiescence and insight. While both of these types of activities are performed under the influence of mental afflictions and the eight worldly concerns, they are virtuous deeds, not evil ones. The major treatises refer to these kinds of virtuous deeds as "virtuous deeds that are related to merit."[847]

Likewise, all the mental afflictions that are included within the two higher realms and the deeds that are accumulated under their influence are not unvirtuous in nature. In addition, activities such as the morality that protects one from peril and that is associated with proper aspirations, as well as the generosity that is associated with proper aspirations, are not unvirtuous deeds. Therefore, although such acts are performed {542} and accumulated under the influence of the eight worldly concerns and such mental afflictions as desire and so on, there are indeed many examples of acts that are neither evil deeds nor unvirtuous activities. Ārya Asaṅga has said that all the mental afflictions of the two higher realms, such as deceitfulness and guile,[848] and so on, are not unvirtuous in nature, due to the firmness of quiescence and the fact that they are influenced by many virtuous qualities.

You might think to yourself, "Well then, what deeds are virtuous in nature and what deeds are unvirtuous in nature?" Those deeds that the buddhas and bodhisattvas disparaged and never extolled, as well as the mental afflictions that give rise to them, are the ones that are said to be unvirtuous in nature. All the deeds that are their opposites, as well as the mental states that give rise to them, are the ones that are said to be virtuous in nature. The three types of deeds—that is, those that are physical, verbal, and mental—that are neither virtuous nor unvirtuous in nature are the ones that are said to be indeterminate.[849]

Accordingly, while there are many activities generated by mental afflictions that are not evil deeds, such activities as conferring initiations, explaining dharma teachings, reciting sūtras, and reciting mantras, and so on, that are carried out for the sake of obtaining gain and honor or fame in this life, or to obtain pleasure and comfort, are evil deeds and do represent great heaps of obstruction. Because all the evil deeds and obstructions, such as selling profound dharma scriptures, covetousness, malice, guile and deceitfulness, hypocrisy, flattery, intimation, oppression, acquiring gain through gifts,[850] and idle speech, occur continuously like a great rainfall, the former lamas, based on this understanding, have often said that if you fail to free yourself from attachment to this life, everything that you do will constitute an evil deed.

It is also possible that you will think to yourself, "I doubt that everything done with attachment to this life is a meaningless and evil deed {543}, such that the former lamas, based on this understanding, have declared all these deeds to be evil." However, the key point relating to the practice of mentally abandoning this life can be summarized as follows: Except for those situations in which it is indispensable to pursue this life's pleasures and the causes of those pleasures, as well as to avoid this life's forms of suffering and the causes of that suffering, in order to benefit others in an unselfish manner or to enable you to pursue enlightenment, for those individuals who have developed an intense aspiration to adopt virtuous qualities and reject unvirtuous ones,[851] all such efforts are instances in which one has come under the influence of the mental afflictions, attachment, craving, the eight worldly concerns, and avid clinging to this life. Therefore, those efforts should be terminated forcefully by means of an appropriate antidote. Regarding essential forms of food and clothing, and so on, the Bhagavān has taught many ways to reflect so that you can avoid coming under the influence of craving and also develop extraordinary forms of merit. These methods of reasoning should also be made known to others in order to ensure that they do not come under the sway of craving. Speaking generally, causing all your activities to be motivated by renunciation and enlightenment mind is the king of methods for ensuring that they do not fall under the influence of desire or hatred. Therefore, you should recall this method and avoid seeking to pursue any form of pleasure or reject any form of suffering.[852] In those situations where such actions must be pursued, causing them to be motivated by those two attitudes[853] will ensure that you quickly achieve either the status of an arhat who is free of attachment for adopting or rejecting any aspect of the three realms or that of a fully enlightened buddha.

Whatever virtue I may achieve
by having composed this spiritual advice,[854]
may it cause the entire world to become free
of attachment toward all of the three realms
and quickly attain the state of omniscience.

With a desire to honor and revere all the victors,
I shall venerate the bodhisattvas.
May this cause all the victors to be pleased.
May I set free the ten directions' beings that are imprisoned
and establish them in the state of a wheel-wielding monarch.
It is said that whoever wishes to see, has faith in,
or praises a bodhisattva will gain countless merit from that.

Having read and heard teachings on a great ocean of scriptures,
I have proclaimed here the liberating deeds of wise spiritual beings
and the profound true doctrine that is the essence of their
  knowledge,
thereby gaining extensive value from my human form of leisure.

In all my future lives may I never be separated from all wise
spiritual beings
and, having pleased them and been fostered by them,
may I view their instruction as essential and follow it in my
practice,
and may I quickly attain the state of unsurpassed enlightenment.

The dharma teacher and monk, Lodrö Gyaltsen Pel Zangpo, who takes the dust under the feet of the omniscient Je Rinpoche, the spiritual father Shar Tsongkhapa,[855] as well as that of his spiritual sons, onto the crown of his head, composed this treatise, titled *Opening the Door to the Dharma: The Initial Method of Training One's Mind in the Mind Training Tradition of the Stages of the Path to Enlightenment*, at the great monastic center Gyama Rinchen Gang.[856] May it bring extensive benefit to the Buddhist teaching and to all sentient beings. May virtue abound!

PART THREE

The Instruction Lineage

14. {377} A Listing of the Mahāyāna Works on Mind Training[1]

Jamgön Kongtrul Lodrö Taye

The great learned scholar and teacher, Zhönu Gyalchok, and his disciple, Könchok Gyaltsen, also known as the Great One from Mü,[2] compiled the most precious collection of Mahāyāna Mind Training works[3] that were created by both Indian and Tibetan masters. The listing of works from that volume that are included here are: (1) *How Atiśa Relinquished His Kingdom and Sought Liberation*, which was composed by Drom Tönpa; (2) *The Story of Atiśa's Voyage to Sumatra*; (3) Annotated *Root Lines of Mahāyāna Mind Training*; (4) *Root Lines of Mahāyāna Mind Training* without annotations; (5) *A Commentary on the "Seven-Point Mind Training"*; (6) *The Wheel of Sharp Weapons*; (7) *The Peacock's Neutralizing of Poison*; (8) *Melodies of an Adamantine Song: A Chanting Meditation on Mind Training*; (9) a Mind Training text composed by Maitrī Yogi,[4] titled *Stages of the Heroic Mind*,[5] which is made up of four sections: (a) "Teaching on the Presentation of the Grounds, the Afflictions," (b) "Teaching on the Contrary Forces, the Antidotes," (c) "Teaching on Humiliating One's Own Negative Mental Continuum," and (d) "Teaching Cultivating the Power of Tainted Virtues"; (10) *A Mind Training Teaching That Serlingpa Taught to Jowo [Atiśa] for the Purpose of Taming Inhabitants of a Borderland*;[6] (11) *A Teaching on Taking Afflictions onto the Path*; (12) *Guru Yoga Mind Training*; (13) *Mahāyāna Purification of Grudges*; (14) *Two Yoginīs' Admonition to Atiśa to Train His Mind*; (15) *Kusulu's Accumulation Mind Training*; (16) *Mind Training Taking Joys and Pains onto the Path*; (17) *Mind Training Instruction That Two Yoginīs Gave to Sumpa Lotsāwa*;[7] (18) *Bodhisattva Samantabhadra's Mind Training*; (19) *Eight-Sessions Mind Training*, which contains these eight sections: (a) "Mind training pertaining to food," (b) "Mind training pertaining to breathing," (c) "Training the mind by multiplying your body into the number of grains of sand in the Ganges and taking upon yourself the sufferings of beings of the six realms," (d) "Mind training pertaining to flesh and blood," (e) "Mind training pertaining to torma offerings," (f) "Mind training pertaining to the natural elements," (g) "Training the mind by transforming your body into a wish-fulfilling jewel," and (h) "Mind training as an instruction for the moment or death"; (20) *Mind Training Removing Obstacles* {378}; (21) *Mahāyāna Mind Training Removing Future Adversities*; (22) *Atiśa's Seven-Point Mind Training*; (23) *Chim's Mind Training*;[8] (24) *Mind Training Instruction That Atiśa Gave to Namdak Tsuknor*;[9] (25) *Virwapa's Mind Training*; (26) *A Commentary on Langri Tangpa's Mind Training in Eight Verses, together with a Story [of Its Origin]*; (27) *The Story of the Repulsive Mendicant*;[10] (28) *A Mind Training Teaching That Serlingpa Taught to Jowo [Atiśa] for the Purpose of Taming Inhabitants of a Borderland*;[11] (29) *A Mahāyāna Mind Training Treatise in a Single Chapter*; (30) *Zhang Ratnaguru's Great Public Teaching*; (31) *Yangönpa's Instruction on Training the Mind*; (32) *Guide to the Heart of Dependent Origination.*

sarvamangalam![12]

15. {379} How Atiśa Relinquished His Kingdom and Sought Liberation[1]

Drom Tönpa

Translated by Thupten Jinpa

{380} Sanskrit title: *Guruguṇadharmākaranāma*
Tibetan title: *bLa ma'i yon tan chos kyi 'byung gnas*
English title: *The Qualities of My Teacher, Which Are the Source of Dharma*
Homage to the excellent masters, friends of the doctrine.

For beings tormented by heat waves of the afflictions,
you send forth clouds of love in the space of ultimate expanse
and dispel grief through a rain of great compassion—
to you, O dharma king, I bow with reverence.

From the stainless ocean of his life's events,
as I respectfully extract here mere drops,
uncluttered by words of exaggeration and denigration,
and relate them with the skills of my intelligence, please listen.

In the supreme land of Zahor[2] in eastern India
is a town called Bangala.[3]
Its sovereign is the dharma king Kalyāṇaśrī,
in whose dominion prosperity showers like rain.

His palace is adorned with golden victory banners
and encircled by a hundred thousand households.
It has twenty-five thousand bathing pools
enclosed within seven hundred and twenty gardens.

He has more than fifty-six thousand banyan trees
and thirty-five thousand subjects.
This town has seven perimeter fences
and three hundred and sixty-seven bridges.

There golden victory banners number twenty-five thousand.
The central palace sports thirteen gilded roofs.
His wealth and power {381} rival that of the Eastern emperor.[4]
His majesty resembles that of the celestial Indra himself.

The population rivals the city of Gandhava's;[5]
the flourishing of dharma wealth resembles Dharmodgata's.[6]
The queen of this dharma king is
the glorious Śrīprabhā, who is like a goddess.

Shy, conscientious, and glowing with beauty,
she propitiates the Three Jewels and is a mother to all.
To this goddess was born three sons:
Śrīgarbha, Candragarbha, and Padmagarbha.

Their numbering three is mentioned as an aside.[7]
The middle one, Candragarbha,[8]
is today my sublime spiritual teacher.

When the fortunate one was born to his mother,
showers of blossoms rained upon the kingdom;
the center of the sky was filled with rainbow tents;
heavenly songs and melodies were heard by all.

Everyone was joyful and experienced a sense of purity.
For eighteen months he stayed in the palace,
nurtured and cared for by eight wet nurses.
To the north of this kingdom
lay the monastery of Vikramalapūri.[9]

To make offerings at this religious site,
the parents, ministers, and subjects set forth in fifty carriages,

with young men and women adorned in beautiful clothes.
All were encircled by hundreds of skilled musicians.

{382} The entourage carried countless precious offerings.
As they ventured forth with dancing and song,
our teacher looked three years of age, with an attractive physique
and a beautiful face, which even constant gazing upon could not sate.

Adorned with celestial clothes and jewelry
and dressed in *pāñcālika* silk, he was carried in the king's lap.
As people saw this celestial being,
they gasped with joy and glowed with happiness.

It's said they gazed upon him with affection and could not pull
themselves away.
Thus those who saw him uttered these words:
"When you were born, flowers rained down,
the sun shone like a tent, and enchanting tunes were heard.

"Thinking 'When will we see your face?' our hearts felt pangs;
today we have seen you, and it is truly a miracle."
Then the excellent prince uttered the following:
"O my parents, who are these people?"

Both his parents replied thus:
"O prince, these are your loyal subjects."
To this the prince responded:
"May they have perfect parents like me;
and possessing kingdom, power, and blazing merit,
may they be born as the chief sons of kings;
may they all be sustained by the sublime dharma."

Then, as they arrived with their entire retinue
at the monastery of Kamala,[10]
the prince paid homage to the Three Jewels
and, in a melodious tune, uttered the following praise:

"I've obtained the human life of leisure and opportunity,
free from any deficiencies; I follow you, the Three Jewels.
Always I take you to my crown;
from this very day, pray be my refuge."

When he uttered these words,
everyone, his parents, ministers, and subjects,
as well as many monks, heard them.
Utterly delighted, they felt a sense of wonder.
Unanimously, all agreed he was a sublime being.

Then {383} his parents, together with their retinues,[11]
gathered merit by making offerings, service, and reverence.
And they prayed: "May we throughout this and all other lives
make offerings to the Three Jewels,
serve the spiritual community, and reveal the sublime dharma.
May we dispel the pain of afflictions and enjoy freedom."

As he heard these words of aspiration,
while looking at his parents, the prince uttered:
"May I never be chained by the lifestyle of a householder
but attain dharma wealth in the midst of ordained monks;
free of conceit, may I make offerings to the Three Jewels
and look on all beings with the eyes of compassion."

When they heard the prince's words,
his parents and all the others felt deeply awed.
Those words were the first lesson of my teacher.

When the prince reached the age of three,
he became versed in arithmetic, letters, and Sanskrit.
When he reached the age of six,
he could differentiate Buddhist and non-Buddhist tenets.

From this point till he reached the age of ten,
he went for refuge to the Three Jewels,
observed day-long precepts, and gave charity;
he read scriptures and committed them to recitation.

He made supplications and sought the sublime dharma,
served his parents and honored them.
All his songs and dances were rooted in dharma;
upon seeing spiritual practitioners, he would receive them from afar.

He looked after his subjects and nurtured them with compassion.
He protected those who were bereft of refuge.
Thus he engaged in countless deeds of a sublime being.

When the prince reached the age of eleven,
the ministers and his subjects offered as his bride
twenty-two girls of noble patronage;[12]
the prince's parents showered them with gifts.

One day the king summoned all his ministers and ordered:
"At dawn, {384} prepare well thirteen horse-drawn carriages;
adorn them with various ornaments of beauty.
Atop the center, on an especially beautiful and compliant carriage,
pitch an umbrella of peacock feathers with cooling screens.
In the center below, on a beautiful throne made of precious jewels,
you should place Candragarbha, attired in rich silks.

"On thirteen horse-drawn carriages bedecked with ornaments,
the ministers should be seated beautifully clothed;
singing joyful songs, they should play all kinds of music.
Three horse-drawn white carriages should take the lead,
three red carriages should bring up the rear,
three yellow carriages should flank on the right,
while three green carriages should flank on the left.

"Within these carriages should sit five hundred youths,
with celestial ornaments matching their direction's color.
The prince's carriage should be of five different colors,
with its four corners adorned with carved arching peacock heads.

"These should be encircled by offering goddesses,
and surrounded too by subjects who rob people's hearts

by playing lutes, flutes, drums, and cymbals,[13]
all of which creates a symphony of most melodious tunes.

"At the outskirts of the great city,
in the great parks, which are places of utter joy,
people should be captivated with spectacles and games.
For the duration, a half a month or so,
make everyone happy and keep them entertained.

"Then everywhere, in all directions,
you should seek out girls who might please the prince.
When the ministers see the girls,
they should summon them and extract firm pledges."

Once the king had issued these firm orders,
the ministers made all the preparations in seven days—
thirteen carriages bedecked with ornaments,
three thousand five hundred youths adorned with jewels.

The prince was at the center of a carriage adorned with jewels.
Twelve carriages were filled with skilled musicians,
who played varieties of musical instruments.
Then {385} at the outskirts of the great city,
at the crossroads and in the spacious town squares,
games were staged that captured the minds of the people.

Candragarbha and his retinue of two thousand five hundred
were seated in the carriages.
At that time, in all directions and in all the towns,
at the outskirts and in the lotus groves,
and at all the wide crossroads here and there,
crowds gathered as if he were a universal monarch.
All went there to see the emanation body.

The assembly of celestial girls such as Kiraṇdevī,[14]
those of noble lineage and their close friends,
all of them said, "Let's go watch."

As the throngs of people gathered there,
there arrived, too, the daughters of King Sönamzin,[15]
the daughters of King Mukhyüzin,
the daughters of King Chudakzin,
the daughters of King Tumbula,
twenty-two girls excelling in nobility, physique, wealth, and power,
who had all been broached as prospective brides.[16]

In each carriage sat seven girls,
and each girl was accompanied by seven maids.
Thus there were twenty-two stunning carriages,
all adorned with diverse ornaments.

With melodious tunes and ecstatic hearts they arrived.
None could take their eyes off the prince,
for, like the celestial maidens, they too were attached.
Thoroughly amorous, the hairs stood up from their pores.

At that point an emanation of a ḍākinī,
assuming the form of a girl with dark bluish skin,
exhorted the prince thus in a melodious singing voice:

"Do not be attached, O sole lord, fortunate one.
If, like elephants enamored with muddy waters,
you should become entrapped in the mires of desire,
will this not veil the one enrobed with ethical discipline?

"Through five hundred and fifty-two lives,
you have led the life of a pure, learned monk;
so, {386} like swans plunging into a lotus lake,
you'll become a renunciant in this life.

"In the city are girls devoted to cleanliness;
they are but messengers of Māra stealing away morality's glow.
With seeming love, they will seduce and deceive you.
Know this, O prince of beguiling appearance.

"Like the clear reflection of the moon in a lake,
O exalted body, clear, transparent, and unblemished,
who wears his hair in five locks and is adorned with heavenly jewels,
O beautiful one, you've robbed the minds of all people.

"At this time when you've obtained the precious human life so rare,
since you must expend your life in study, reflection, and meditation,
thoroughly seek a spiritual guide, which is their principal condition,
so that all knots of lingering doubts can be cut."

As the ḍākinī uttered these words,
the prince brightened with a smile and responded:
"Well said, well said! Extremely well said!
The prince of wisdom is happier in the forests;[17]
peacocks' well-being lies in the forest of poisonous trees;
due to the force of habit, swans are happier in lakes.

"How can crows plunge into a lotus lake
as they would into a mire of filth?
How can persons with the noble lineage
immerse themselves in towns like mere ordinaries?

"In the past the prince Siddhārtha[18]
felt revulsion toward the kingdom and wealth
of King Śuddhodana[19] as if it were a mire of filth;
forsaking sixty thousand queens, he sought liberation.

"Acclaimed and revered as 'the Able One,'
he was hailed by the entire world, including the gods.
This dharma king endowed with major and minor noble marks
attained awakening through the twelve great deeds.[20]

"So if I do not renounce my kingdom,
attachment will proliferate in this mire of desire.
All friends are but Māra's tricksters;
I'll recognize all sense objects as salt water.[21]

{387} "Now I shall search for many learned teachers;
and throughout this life I'll seek supreme awakening.
No matter how joyfully one indulges in the sense objects,
like the moon's reflection in water, they are devoid of essence.

"Like echoes, they have no content;
like emanations, they lack identifiable nature;
like reflections, they are devoid of self-subsistence.

"In this vast ocean of afflicted foundational consciousness,
the rivers of birth, aging, sickness, and death flow perpetually;
if, in the past, I lacked power over the lower realms due to karma,
why don't I search today when all the conditions are perfect?

"Reflecting deeply upon cyclic existence in general,
I will seek a teacher and strive in the sublime dharma."
As the prince uttered these words of teachings,
the people of the kingdom all felt, "With such manner of speech,
will he ever reign over the kingdom?

"If he does, doubtless he will be a dharma king;
otherwise he will seek the learned and realized teachers
and will reign over the kingdom like the king of the Śākyas.[22]
Amazing indeed is this!" Such shouts were echoed.

Feeling attached, circumambulating, they gazed at him over and over;
the girls of noble lineage who came to strengthen familial standing,
though delighted to see him, were saddened by his words.
Approaching their parents, they exclaimed:

"The great prince says that he is disenchanted by samsara;
he says he will forsake the kingdom and become a renunciate monk;
he says that Prince Siddhārtha left behind his queens;
he says he is not attached to his retinue and subjects.

"So, O parents together with your retinues,
pray venture forth to the royal palace;

engage in various activities to attract the prince's mind;
with wealth and various resources, captivate him."

Thus the girls exhorted their parents.
So the parents, ministers, and subjects
strove hard with songs, dances, and {388} clusters of girls.
As the caravans approached the kingdom,[23]
the prince, taking with him one hundred and fifty horsemen,
dressed in battle costume and roamed the hills.

On one cliff sat the mendicant Jetāri.
In the manner of a mendicant, he was reciting verses of poetry;
Jetāri was honoring sages of pure conduct with his crown,
and the prince saw him as someone utterly victorious over the afflictions.

Without dismounting from his horse,[24]
the prince offered the following words to the sage:
"You practice the ascetic life and what is taught in the scriptures in solitude;
as pure conduct you consume food borne of untainted livelihood;
apart from renouncing sense objects and venerating the sages,[25]
what other higher qualities have you attained?"[26]

As he asked this,
the prince felt that the mendicant, without even looking,
responded in the following manner:
"Even if the king prohibits the mendicant's provisions,
other than casting me by karma's power to the lower realms,
like a flower in a garden at season's end,
I see no long-term result, so I shall remain here in the wilderness.

"Fearing that, like cattle, dogs, and pigs,
I may be reborn as a worm living in mires of filth,
I strive in the ascetic life and practice pure conduct.
Failing to see any essence in illusory material possessions,
I contemplate the other shore[27] and honor sages with my crown."

When the prince heard the mendicant's words,
he uttered the following response to test the mendicant:
"Monks are even more conceited than others.[28]
Why did you not rise when the lord of the land arrived?"

The great mendicant responded:
"O lord of the land, who are you? And from where do you hail?
As I've neither friends nor enemies, I failed to recognize you;
as I've no possessions, I am happier in the forest;
the sole foe of this body and mind is the Lord of Death;
as I've no conceit, I have forsaken all distracting pursuits."

Hearing the mendicant's words, the prince replied:
"I have come from the palace with golden victory banners;
{389} I am a scion of the king Kalyāṇaśrī.
Who can rival me in this forest today?
Not recognizing the lord of the land, you've transgressed the law."

To this the great mendicant replied:
"I am an outcast to human ranks, and I am outside the law;
I have no ruler, no servants, nor anyone to act with deference toward.
O lord of the land, when one departs to the other shore,
one does so alone on foot, with no horses and no companions.

"With no food, no clothes, naked, one will roam in the intermediate state;
with no place, no country, none familiar, the journey will be long.
Even a prince has no guarantee on how long he may live.
Because of this I prefer to live in the forest."

As the prince heard the mendicant's words,
dismounting his horse, he offered him the three spheres.[29]
With deep reverence and palms folded, he made the following plea:
"To test your higher qualities, O learned one,
as if with arrogance I uttered these insolent words.[30]

"However, six times throughout day and night
I contemplate samsara's defects and feel disenchanted by it.

So since I wish to renounce my kingdom and achieve true liberation,
O great mendicant, sustain me under your care."

To this the great mendicant replied:
"Come here, come here! I'll bless you so that,
unassailed by conceit, you'll become a master of the doctrine."

Stating thus:

He conferred the blessing of the Three Jewels and the awakening mind.
Rising up, the prince once again offered the master
his horse-drawn carriages[31] as gifts for granting refuge and the
awakening mind;
to perfect the prince's merit, he accepted the gifts for a while,
and he gave the following instruction:

"O prince, even ghosts can pursue for a while
the mundane ambitions of those who are unreflective;
the pursuit of self-interest is done even by falcons and wolves.
Even self-realized ones seek a partial awakening.

"Even serfs consume food adequate to fill their stomachs;
how can anyone, even a king, have a full stomach in all lives?
O prince, devote your mental continuum to dharma practice.
Relinquish your kingdom and {390} seek true liberation."

Again, the excellent prince made further supplication:
"Teacher, I am a prisoner under house arrest,
as if tied with silk scarves inside a royal palace.
First, caught tightly in a marriage of addictions and karma,

"I fear being deceived by everyone under the guise of love,
leading me further into the mires of cyclic existence.[32]
Bless me, teacher, O bless me,
so that I cannot be harmed by my king."

To this the great mendicant stated:
"Family lineage is samsara's strong chain;

kingdom is the great mire of filth and refuse;
'kinghood' is the great, endearing title of Māra;
ministers are the great family members of Māra.

"Certainly and swiftly you must remain vigilant;
do not remain here, but depart to Nālandā.
There resides the teacher Bodhibhadra,
with whom you've had close connections since beginningless time;
receive mind generation teaching and create karmic connections.
This learned master will benefit you greatly."

Thereupon the great mendicant returned all the offerings
and offered the prince the following advice:
"Leave home, and come forth to me;
I will nourish you with various instructions."

Then the prince returned to his palace.
He gathered various articles, such as gold and silver,
and together with his retinue, ventured forth to Nālandā.

Frightened, the king of Nālandā welcomed from afar
the prince and his retinue of soldiers.
When they met, the king offered these words:
"O lord of the land, from where do you hail?
Where do you venture forth, you who resemble a universal monarch?
Wearing battle attire, to where are you off to crush your enemy?
Since I saw you from afar, I've come to meet you."

To this the prince replied:
"I hail from the east, the land of Zahor;
I have come from the palace with golden victory banners;
{391} I am journeying to conquer the foe of cyclic existence;
I am traveling to destroy the Māra foe, the Lord of Death."

The king of Nālandā responded:
"You are the son of the Zahor king in the east,
the lord of the land, the dharma king Kalyāṇaśrī.

The universal monarch is victorious over the forces of evil;
fortunate it is that his son has visited our region.

"In your Vikramaśīla, the palaces of the Three Jewels are
like the gods' celestial mansions;
inconceivable numbers of ordained monks reside there,
as well as a great many learned paṇḍitas resembling the sun and moon.
O lord of the land, which learned master do you seek?"

To this the excellent prince replied:
"The great learning center of Nālandā is,
like an ocean, a source of precious jewels;

in it is found a multitude of starlike mahāpaṇḍitas.
Bodhibhadra, most highly acclaimed, is my teacher,
as prophesied by the mendicant Jetāri.
O lord of the land, pray help remove my obstacles."

To this the great king replied:
"The great hero Bodhibhadra is unwavering,
like the king of mountains clad in snow.
He abides resplendent, brilliant, and at ease.

"Affluent like Vaiśravaṇa,[33]
he has found the fortune of the noble ones' riches.[34]
O come, come near the environs of my palace.
With pleasant tales and material gifts I'll entertain you."

The prince said "Wonderful" to this invitation, and, led by the king's welcoming procession and amid an offering of music, they ventured forth to Nālandā.

To its south, in the region of lotuses,
was the palace called Samantabhadra,
surrounded by a hundred thousand homes;
it was to this the noble prince was invited.
Seated on an expansive throne adorned with precious jewels,
he was accorded the honor befitting a royal prince.

Then they departed to the monastery of Nālandā,
{392} to the presence of the teacher Bodhibhadra.
Upon entering the monastic complex,
the prince saw the teacher and felt immeasurable joy,
a joy that was most extraordinary.

Upon hearing of the excellent prince's arrival,
Bodhibhadra, too, felt great joy and rose from his seat.
He uttered the following teaching in eloquent words:
"You have arrived, O son of a dharma king.
Is the dharma jewel flourishing in the land of Zahor?
Are you not tired from the long journey?"

At this point the excellent prince replied:
"Yes, my father is well, and he lives in accord with dharma;
Though the road was long, I have now met you.
O learned master, are you not exhausted due to
study, reflection, and meditation on the Buddha's teaching?"

To this the teacher replied, "I too am happy
through day and night thanks to the sublime dharma.
O prince, be seated and tell me what you seek."

Then, with deep reverence, the prince prostrated
and pleased the teacher with offerings of precious jewels;
he also respectfully made the following plea:
"O teacher of sentient beings, listen to this tale with compassion.

"Afraid of being harmed by great kingdom, the Trickster,
in the bottomless mire of filth that is samsara,
I fled to the forest with my soldiers.
There I found residing a teacher totally victorious over foes.

"When I appealed to him to confer the awakening mind,
with his vision of compassion the great learned master advised:
'Go to Nālandā, the great center of learning;
there resides the excellent teacher Bodhibhadra,

who has sustained you with compassion in past lives.
Receive from him the instructions on awakening mind.'

"Immediately I gathered offering articles from my palace
and have arrived here today;
so, with compassion, {393} kindly grant me now
the various instructions on the awakening mind."

Instantly, as he sat down on the cushion,
the teacher entered into deep meditative absorption
and blessed the three doors[35] to make them serviceable;
he then gave many instructions on awakening mind.

Such were the instructions conferred:
"O prince, to achieve meaning in this life,
renounce your kingdom and seek liberation. If you do not,
when you fall to lower realms due to the power of karma,
you will regret it intensely; but then it will be too late.

"At this point while you are laying the foundation of your ultimate welfare,
if you fail to persevere with great hardships,
then, when you have definitely squandered your chance for liberation,
O son of good family, there is no hope to regain it in the future.

"Even if you are courageous, firm, and well-armored,
when you are led through the narrow gorges of the afterlife by Yama,[36]
simply feeling the remorse of a powerless desperate person
will be of no benefit and purpose at all.
Contemplate this sublime teaching, O prince.

"Over there, to the north of Nālandā
lives the one known as the bodhisattva Vidyākaukila,
who has been your father since beginningless time.
Transcending life and abiding in solitude,
he is untainted by elaborations of the eight mundane concerns.[37]

Wearing the attire of ethical discipline, he possesses unobstructed
clairvoyance.
Go to him and receive instructions of dharma."

When he heard these words of the master Bodhibhadra,
while reluctant to part from him,
he ventured forth to meet the noble Vidyākaukila.
Prostrating and making offerings, he uttered the following plea:

"I live in the east in the land of Zahor;
I am a son of the king of Bangala;
I come from the palace with golden victory banners;
I have been to the monastery of Nālandā
and have received the awakening mind from Bodhibhadra.

"Having granted the instruction, he advised me thus:
{394} 'Do not remain here but go to the north;
for there resides a bodhisattva called Vidyākaukila,
who has been your father since beginningless time;
go forth to him and request the awakening mind.
He will benefit you.'

"Immediately, though reluctant to part from the master,
I came here to you with joy rising in my heart.
O teacher, take me within your fold
so that I may not be harmed by my father."

The sublime teacher was thoroughly pleased.
"Wonderful indeed that the lord of the land has come!
Come here, I shall bless you within nonduality;
I'll expound the truthful words of reality's unchanging nature;
with compassionate heart, I will teach you the sublime dharma."

Then respectfully the prince made offerings of articles.
He prostrated at the teacher's presence and folded his palms.
Forsaking pride, he sat down on a cushion.
The excellent Kaukila revealed the instructions of the awakening mind.

The key instruction, hailed to be supreme, was this:
"O prince, even if you enjoy all the prosperities in this life,
if you fail to plant the seed for life's ultimate welfare,
obtaining a human life of leisure and opportunity has little meaning.
To lose this jewel would be an immense loss for the future.

"O prince, the conqueror Nāgārjunagarbha stated the following:
'The nature of all, dream-like, illusion-like, is devoid of elaborations.
The mind itself is uncontrived and abides in the innate nature.
He who fails to contemplate these two in his thoughts
will remain entrapped in the mires of cyclic existence.'[38]

"O prince, abide in meditative equipoise on the space-like ultimate.
In the illusion-like subsequent periods, reflect on karma and its fruits."
When the teacher revealed this profound teaching, the prince attained
the path of preparation[39] and realized the "heroic" meditative
absorption.

He then recounted his realization to the teacher thus:
"When I remain in equipoise, one-pointed in meditative absorption,[40]
like the sky that is totally free of clouds,
everything is clear, translucent, and devoid of obscurations.
O teacher, is this reality's true mode of being?

{395} "Then as I rise from this meditative absorption,
without clinging to appearances, thoughts of sentient beings arise;
though appearances are false, I find respect for the minute facets of
karma.
O teacher, are these experiences of mine deluded?"

In response, the teacher stated:
"Well done, prince, you are indeed a fortunate son;
I am an ordained monk free of exaggeration and denigration.
Though being cleansed in the space-like meditative equipoise,
out of compassion I lead sentient beings in subsequent periods.
Yes, this is indeed the mode of being of the two truths.
This, then, is my excellent instruction.

"So if you wish to be free from your kingdom,
then to the south of the dark rocky mountain called Summit;
there resides my teacher, Avadhūti.
He was your teacher too in the past.

"Go to him and receive the instructions of the awakening mind.
Receive from him the instructions for renouncing your kingdom."
When the prince heard the teacher's words,
though saddened to depart from the master, he felt deep joy.

Together with his retinue, he paid his farewell homage,
and entered the road with the demeanor of a hero.
The great king of Nālandā as well
gathered together manifold provisions.

And, followed by his retinue, he accompanied them up to three
yojana.[41]
As the king turned his back to return home,
The prince, reluctant to part, uttered the following words:

"O king, though you've found the joys of higher rebirth,
if you fail to vanquish the enemy of cyclic existence,
when you are later led away chained by Yama,
remorse will be too late, so seek the wealth of dharma.

"With warmth in our hearts we have bonded for a few days,
yet, like merchants gathered at a market, this is all transient.
Though I may be leaving, do not cast me from your affection.
I shall meet you soon, in full accord with the dharma."

The king, too, responded in the following manner:
"By my good fortune I have met you today.
My heart has been moved by meeting you, O prince of a dharma king.
I feel saddened since you, my son, are leaving today.
But I pray that we will meet again in the near future."

Then the prince went forth to find the teacher Avadhūti,
venturing toward the south of Summit Mountain.

At that {396} time the sublime teacher, the excellent being,
was living in a cave on a dark rocky cliff.

Draped over his body was a black woolen shawl;
he was seated on a *kṛṣṇasāra*[42] pelt;
and around his chest hung a large meditator's belt;
his body stout, he had an extremely large, round belly.

His eyes red and his skin a slight blue,
with a sense of abandon, he sat in half-lotus posture,
and the entire world and its contents were distilled in a single skull cup.[43]
The prince saw the teacher living thus, free of attachment.

Dismounting his horse, the prince prostrated from a distance.
Together with his retinue, he sat down in the teacher's presence.
Suddenly the teacher looked at them and uttered:
"Has the bubble of your pride not yet burst?

"Have you not been afflicted by the forces of darkness?
Are you not sunk in the mires of a household?
Have you not been seduced by Māra's daughters?
Have you not wasted the perfect human existence?
Where do you hail from, you who resemble a prince?"

With folded palms, the prince replied:
"I hail from the palace with golden victory banners;
I come here disenchanted with the life of royalty;
I come seeking refuge from the ways of cyclic existence.

"I have been to the great monastery of Nālandā
and have sought refuge in Vidyākaukila.
That elder sent me here to your presence.
So, master, please grant me your protection now."

Avadhūti uttered the following response:
"Though I was born in the royal lineage,
as I feared greatly the army of afflictions and karma,

I shunned my kingdom as if it were a drop of spit.
Can you follow Avadhūti's lifestyle?

"The riches of royalty are like a poisonous sea:
the instant you drink from it, the life of freedom is threatened.
The riches of royalty are like a barrier of fire:
the instant you cross it, suffering is engendered.

{397} "Go! Go back to your palace today;
Observe the defects of a householder's life and return soon."
When the prince heard the teacher's words,
he made offerings, paid his respects, and swiftly returned home.

When the subjects saw the prince,
they shouted his praise, offering songs, dance, and music.
As the prince reached his home,
his parents, the king and queen, were utterly overjoyed.

"O Candragarbha, where did you go?
Are you not exhausted after such a journey?
Seeing the problems, were you not saddened?
Wonderful it is that you're back," they exclaimed joyfully.

The prince answered them in great detail:
"I went to different places to pursue my aspirations;
I went to vanquish with skill the enemy of doctrine;
I went seeking an able teacher for my refuge.

"I went searching for solitude in mountains and in cliffs.
Wherever I went I saw the defects of cyclic existence;
whoever I met spoke of samsara's flaws;
no matter what I did, my mind remained restless.

"So open the way, for I shall go forth to dharma practice."
In response his parents said:
"O prince, if you are saddened by the samsaric realm,
uphold the kingdom and make offerings to the Three Jewels.

"With compassion make the poor and the destitute content;
create sacred books and always support the monastic community;
cultivate love and compassion free of discrimination.
If you conduct yourself in this manner, you will always be happy."

To this, the prince replied:
"If you love me, my sole father, listen to me.
In this palace of precious gems and gold,
I'll be bound tightly with unyielding silk knots;
I will be afflicted in this palace indeed.

"As I observe well the nature of this cyclic existence
and reflect on the sufferings of all sentient beings,
{398} I feel no sense of attachment to this kingdom,
not even the size of a saliva drop.

"Six times during day and night,
I reflect on the extensive defects of a householder's life.
Toward the seductive daughters of Māra, though enchanting,
I feel not even a fleeting instant of attraction.

"When I view all of this false appearance of the world,
I see no distinction, not even the slightest,
between the three sweets—sugar, molasses, and honey—
and impurities like a leper's brain, dog's meat, pus, and blood.[44]

"If there is not even the slightest difference
between being richly adorned—with beautiful silk clothes
and heavenly ornaments of turquoise and coral—
and wearing a woolen cloak found in the midst of filth,

"I shall go, I shall go to the forest to engage in meditative absorptions;
I shall go to the eight cemeteries to play all kinds of sports.
I shall go, I shall go to the land of the ḍākinīs;
I shall go to secret places to generate bliss;
I shall go to seek a fortress in the realm of nonattachment.

"I shall go, I shall go to Summit Mountain;
I shall go to the presence of the most holy Avadhūti.
I shall go, I shall go to the lands of the ḍākinīs;
I shall go savor the supreme taste of Vajrayāna.

"I shall go, I shall go to the land of Udhyāna;[45]
I shall go attract the wisdom ḍākinīs as my partners.
I shall go, I shall go to the realm of Akaniṣṭha;[46]
I shall go touch the feet of Vairocana with my crown.

"I shall go, I shall go to the land of Tuṣita;[47]
I shall go seek supreme Maitreya as my teacher.
I shall go, I shall go to all the buddha fields;
I shall go celebrate the joyful feast of dharma.

"I shall go, I shall go to the land of the noble ones;
I shall go to Sukhāvatī[48] to nurture ecstatic experience.
Do not chain me, do not chain me, O Kalyāṇaśrī.
If you love your son, my sole father, take me to a secure place.

"Do not bind me, do not bind me, O Śrīprabhā.
Mother, if you love your son, connect me to the dharma.
With affection prepare for me this day
a few provisions—some rice beer and {399} meat,
some milk, sugar, and honey as well.

"I shall go to the presence of most holy Avadhūti;
I shall go to serve him and to discipline my mind."
Thus sang the excellent prince these words in a song;
he offered these words to his parents' ears.

Just as the king of the gandharvas'[49] singing
stirs the hearts of many,
the parents' hearts were deeply stirred.
Unable to reply, they gave the prince all he desired.

Then with various provisions, such as rice beer,
he left for the forest along with a thousand riders.

Satisfying Avadhūti with all the offerings,
with palms folded, the prince touched the feet of the teacher.
The teacher initiated him into the Mahāyāna awakening mind.

At that instant, like a universal monarch
protected from all threats by his surrounding retinue,
the prince was encircled by his riders, none dismounting,
and they shouted merrily *ha! ha!* and *ku! ku!*

Setting torches aflame, they offered melodious songs.
After such merriment the teacher said:
"Go to the temple of the dark mountain;
go to the yogi of glorious {400} Hevajra.[50]

"Go to the yogi of the oath-bound guardian Yama;
enter the presence of glorious Rāhula;
take from him initiations and awakening-mind instructions.
He, too, was your sublime teacher in the past.
Depart with joy; linger not, but leave straight away."

When the prince heard the teacher's words,
he set forth like a great hero embarking on a campaign.

Surrounded by a thousand horsemen wearing full armor,
wielding axes, hatchets, hammers, and spears,
shooting arrows into the sky while shouting battle cries and
singing songs of joy, he and his retinue all charged toward the temple.

At the temple of the dark mountain
lived the yogi of glorious Hevajra
teaching an assembly of countless yogis and yoginīs
classes of tantra from the Secret Mantrayāna.
He saw the arrival of youthful Prince Candra.

Though psychically he knew the prince had come for dharma,
out of great compassion he issued a threatening gesture,
sending forth a lightning bolt upon the prince.
The lightning, reluctant to descend, hovered momentarily in the sky

and instead crashed upon the mountain of the tīrthikas'[51] black
reliquary.
Deeply surprised by this, the yogis asked the prince:
"Against whom is the royal prince waging battle?"

To this the teacher immediately responded:
"For five hundred and fifty-two lives,
he lived the life of a pure learned monk;
today in Bangala he has been born
as the son of the dharma king Kalyāṇaśrī.

"Not being attached to his retinue and great kingdom,
he desires to endure the hardships of an ascetic.
From Summit Mountain the master Avadhūti
prophesied my name, and today he has come here.
Is this not amazing, O fortunate men and women?"

When he spoke thus,
all exclaimed "*A la la!* Amazing this is indeed;
Wonderful indeed that this great hero has come today!"
From everywhere, near and far, they welcomed him.

The great prince dismounted from his horse;
the thousand riders did the same.
Approaching the abode of the teacher,
the prince respectfully pleaded:

"O sublime teacher, most excellent one, pray listen to me.
Though I wish to renounce home and seek true liberation,
I find myself today in a renowned high family,
and there is a danger I may be trapped in Bangala.

"Although I have sought teachers realized in higher attainments,
such as Jetāri and Bodhibhadra,
Vidyākaukila and Avadhūti,
still I am not free from the realm of kingship.
I have now been sent to your presence, O teacher.

Initiate me into the Mahāyāna awakening mind;
release me decisively from this bondage."

{401} Then the teacher, the excellent hero,
led the prince alone into the mandala palace[52]
and conferred the Hevajra empowerment,
giving him the secret name Jñānaguhyavajra.
Day and night showers of instruction rained;
for thirteen days empowerments were performed;
all concluding rites were fully performed as well.

Throughout this time all the members of the retinue
did not sleep; they strolled around, played sports,
sang songs, danced, and played various musical instruments.
Apart from the wish "When will the prince come out?"
no other thoughts entered their minds.

On the thirteenth day,
the prince appeared wearing the apparel of Heruka.[53]
Gazing on his subjects, he sang a song of impermanence;[54]
observing the three spheres, he saw their lack of essence.

Then he sang this melodious song:
"In the sky of ultimate expanse utterly free of elaborations
resound empty words echoing reality's unborn nature.
My kingdom, which resembles a dream object, is devoid of essence.
Subjects are mere deceptions, illusions.

"If I fail to renounce all this and seek enlightenment,
then I am not a fortunate one who has amassed great merit.
Day and night I shall contemplate the meaning of ultimate nature;
I shall always seek vast and extensive learning."

Then the yogis of glorious Hevajra,
the activity yoginīs who represent impermanence,
and the heroes, the yogis who have gained higher attainments—
eight such terrifying naked male and female adepts—

holding trumpets of human thigh bones in their right hands,
their left hands grasp a human hand, whose flesh they tear with their teeth,
shouting aloud from their throats the sounds of *hūṃ* and *phat*,
and sprinting fast, they circled around the prince.

"Go to Bangala and transform the king's mind;
change his mind so that the prince is spared from statecraft;
take the prince to the presence of excellent Avadhūti;
dress him in a woolen cloak, and {402} send him with the few provisions of a commoner;
free him from rich silk cushions and give him instead a *kṛṣṇasāra* pelt;
free him from retinues and horses and let him learn to journey alone.

"Lose no heart, lose no heart, this is the time to seek liberation;
definitely, this is the time to vanquish afflictions with antidotes;
go this moment," ordered the excellent teacher.
Then the prince, in the guise of a realized adept,
and surrounded by a thousand horsemen, mounted his horse.
As he entered the road, he sang the following vajra song:

"In the unborn vajra[55] mind
I have found the immutable Vajra Vehicle;
in the extremely blissful vajra of experience,
visions of vajra experience dawn vividly.

"In the vajra of meditation deities, clear and lucid,
reflections of action free of defects appear;
in the precious vajra mandala of body,
manifestations of fearlessness, the vajra of no-self, arise.
This secret vajra, the nonconceptual wisdom,
has certainly won the battle against samsara."

When the prince sang his vajra song,
the great internal minister Vīryavajra,
the great minister Pegöl Rapjom,
the great minister Karmarāja,

and the great minister Abhaya—
these four sang the following lament:

"*Emaho!* The domain of karma is most powerful indeed;
in the excellent land of Zahor praised by all,[56]
in the town of Bangala, affluent with riches,
is the palace of golden banners striking to behold.

"Abandoning the extraordinary king Kalyāṇaśrī,
the goddess Śrīprabhā, a mother to all,
and ministers and subjects that are as apparitions,
the excellent prince hastens to the forest.

"Forsaking his horses, elephants, and carriages,
he hastens to journey on foot like a lowly person.
Forsaking heavenly ornaments and silk garments,
he hastens to wear a woolen cloak, a garment of the poor.

"Forsaking his peacock-supported throne and cushions,
he hastens to spread out a *kṛṣṇasāra* pelt inside a hut.
Instead of taking a beautiful goddess for his wife,
{403} he hastens to roam in cemeteries and live on the food of the dead.
O you who shone with light the moment you were born,
can you part from your loved ones who've gathered here?"

Singing songs of lament, they approached the vicinity.
Everyone, on arriving near the palace,
sensed this resolve as they looked upon the prince.
Like the ten directions' guardians embarking on a campaign,
dressed in solid armor, the prince inspired awe by his heroism.
Attractive, breathtaking, he was a spectacle of wonder.

Sounds like cymbals and drums resounded.
The ministers felt awed by their own prince,
and for three months even they attired themselves
in combat gear and kept their horses saddled.

Some competed in horsemanship while others sang and danced;
yet others stood on guard as if engaged in battle;
male and female yogis jumped and sprinted about;
the prince displayed acts of insanity in the midst of town.

Everyone concluded that the prince would renounce his kingdom;
saddened to lose him, they all shed tears wherever they lived.
Like a flock of deer fawns chased by animals of prey,
the prince's parents erupted in cries of grief for their son.

In particular, the father uttered the following words:
"*Ema!* O son, when you were born amid auspiciousness,
we observed wondrous signs and felt you would rule the kingdom.
With this thought our hearts were filled with joy and hope.
How is it that now you wish to seek the forests?"

To this the prince replied thus:
"O dharma king, pray listen.
If I were to rule the kingdom as you advise,
I may live close to you in this brief life, my father,
but in all future lives we would not recognize each other as father and son.
With no benefit, it will be a source of grave consequences.
"If, in contrast, I thoroughly renounce the great kingdom
and seek the path of enlightenment that holds definite freedom,
through all lives we'll join each other with joy and happiness;
so grant me today such an opportunity."

{404} Then his mother uttered the following words:
"What can we do? Though it's most difficult to part from my son,
for all beings the power of karma is the most important force.
O supreme master, permit him to go to dharma where he is happy;
let's pray that we will be together perpetually in the future."

Early at dawn the next day, together with the yogis,
the prince ventured forth to the forest;
in Avadhūti's presence he embraced the life of an ascetic.
Free of desire, he studied the Middle Way teachings;

from the age of twelve till he reached eighteen,
while adopting the lifestyle of Avadhūti,
he accomplished study, reflection, and meditation on one seat.

In this way, our most venerable teacher, great compassionate one,
through persevering despite hundreds of hardships,
thoroughly renounced his unimaginably great kingdom
as if expelling gobs of spit.
He sought true liberation, the unmistaken freedom.

Therefore, as none can rival him,
he is the master of doctrine who has realized all the aims.
To him, I, Drom Tönpa, bow my head extremely low
and pay respectful homage until samsara is emptied.
For any stains of exaggeration and omission herein,
O most compassionate one, I seek your forbearance.

From the ocean-like events of the teacher's liberating life, Drom Tönpa presented here a broad sketch of the teacher's excellent qualities of how he renounced his kingdom and sought true liberation.[57]

16. {405} The Story of Atiśa's Voyage to Sumatra[1]

Attributed to Atiśa

Translated by Thupten Jinpa

Part One

{406} Homage to the most holy Maitreya and Avalokiteśvara!

I, the monk Dīpaṃkara Śrījñāna, was aboard a ship for thirteen months when I went to the see the teacher Serlingpa. About five months into the journey, to create obstacles for my awakening mind, Maheśvara, the son of the gods, sent hostile storms, and assuming the form of a large sea monster *makara*,[2] he obstructed the boat's bow and sent thunderbolts down upon me from above. At that point, I meditated on loving-kindness and extraordinary compassion, and the hostile storms subsided. I even saw six powerful lightning bolts freeze in the sky. Still the large sea monster makara blocked our passage forward, and because of the storm, the sea had become turbulent. Like a flag fluttering violently in the wind, the large ship tossed about—bouncing, at times lifted high in the air and at others feeling as though thrown into the ocean's depths. Even though the sails in each of the four directions were lowered and four cast-iron balls dropped to the ocean depths to anchor, gales of wind blew and rattled thunderously, like massive drums being pounded in the four cardinal directions. Powerful and massive lightning bolts continued to strike. Because of this, the members of the retinue grew extremely frightened and trembled with fear.

As I remained balanced in meditative absorption on {407} loving-kindness and compassion, the learned monk Kṣitigarbha supplicated his teacher:[3]

Rise, rise, O teacher of great compassion!
As you have no rival on this earth, I beseech you;
pray pacify with your great compassion
these terrors and threats posed today by dark forces.

As I strive to free all beings from the ocean of existence,
the forces of darkness today defy me.
Alas! They send turbulent storms and blazing lightning bolts;
a monstrous makara threatens us from the front.
Most holy teacher, protect us from this grave danger.

The sea is racked by storms, and waves jump high in the air;
disturbing noises blare, red lightning bolts dance around.
Violently tossed, the ship too is turbulent and unstable;
it jumps high in the air and is thrown down into the water's depths.
O most holy teacher, protect us now from this danger.

In the space-like expanse of your excellent qualities,
oath-bound guardians hover like garuḍa birds;[4]
circling about, they dispel all obstacles.
Not protecting us today when we are facing obstacles,
but abiding instead in solitary expanse, how can your compassion be so meager?

Now, ḍākinīs, dharma protectors of inner and outer mantra,
{408} arhats, and the assembly of heroes and heroines, wisdom deities—
all of you who delight in the forces of light,
from all directions come encircle us here on this great ocean.
Teacher, avert this danger with your power of compassion.

The lord Red Yamāntaka,[5] undefeated by anyone,
who is surrounded by a retinue of terrifying yamas,
the guardian Acala[6] together with the ten wrathful deities,
and the goddess of blazing auspiciousness who guards from eight dangers,[7]
O teacher, dharma king, help avert this danger through your might.

Most holy blessed Buddha, the master of doctrine,
most venerable Avalokiteśvara of the stainless mandala circles,
dharma king father and son,[8] who dispel the sufferings of sentient beings,
the time has come now to exert the power of your great compassion.
Pray help long perpetuate the river of untainted blessings.

I heard clearly and very well this supplication being delivered. I too saw Lord Yamāntaka, who was red[9] with a large round belly. His dark brown hair stood upward, and his bloodshot eyes, open wide, peered in all ten directions. The instant I saw him, it was as if all the hand implements of other wrathful deities had fallen into his hands, and he wielded his vajra-cudgel in the sky. With his left hand in a threatening gesture, and circling a lasso over his head, he swung his vajra-cudgel, which struck Mount Meru, splitting it down to its base and up to the golden ground beneath. This shook the great ocean, causing it to boil violently and turning the makara into a mere skeleton. The makara then assumed the form of a young boy with a bluish face but with no flesh at all on his body. He entered the ship and made prostrations and, with his palms folded, made the following plea:

O king of wrathful deities, most mighty one,
O great compassionate one, {409} the sole refuge of all beings,
I have wronged you by causing grave danger.
Protect me today through your great compassion.

As he pleaded in this manner, I too picked up a cudgel in my hand and exclaimed:

Hūṃ! I'm the grand master of the life of all beings.
Due to the power of my great compassion,
I have mercifully not annihilated you.
From now on, never teach my students
the false paths of the heretics
or false practices such as divination and animism,[10]
for I now own your very being and life force.

After I uttered these words, he offered this penitent reply:

O great compassion, pray attend to me.
I shall never show your students
any of the false teachings.
Bear me in your thoughts with compassion.
You are now the master of my life force.

Then from the furnace arose a white man who was heard to utter this:

You've not traveled across the land of snows
confined in this Nepalese ship;[11]
you've not traveled to the small islands,
such as the island of copper mines,
for they all are barred by water.
bhrūm hrī yakṣa

Thereupon the entire storm calmed down; the violent waves, the lightning, and the noises disappeared, and the ship regained its course. Everyone sighed with relief and began joyfully conversing with each other.

Still, without dismantling my generation-stage visualization of wrathful Yamāntaka, I stood by, leaving rainbow beams around the ship's deck, and swung down my vajra-cudgel as if it were a staff. The ship became as stable as a vast landmass with no turbulence. As I looked about, wondering what was happening, I heard the laughter of youthful maidens. When I looked, there in the ocean was the king of wrathful deities Acala standing with his two legs submerged up to his knees. Like a strong young man holding a container in his arms, {410} he held the ship from its two ends and lifted it to his crown, which was up in the clouds. On the edge of the ship were twenty-one young maidens with their faces turned outward. They were exclaiming, "O brothers and sisters, had it not been for us, there could have been a great crisis today."

Then I made the following supplication:

Homage to the lady who protects from the eight dangers.
Homage to the lady who sets ablaze the glory of auspiciousness.
Homage to the lady who closes the doors to the lower realms.
Homage to the lady who leads us on the path to the higher realms.
You have always sustained me in your care.
Guard me still with your great compassion.

As I appealed thus, the maidens replied, "If it were not for your son Kṣitigarbha, we would have not known. Just as we were entertaining the thought 'Let us reduce the heretic city Svabhāvanātha[12] to ashes,' we heard your prayer."

They continued: "Alas! Supreme among all beings is this great bodhisattva. We have come here to help him. If, in the future, this youth with a blue face recovers, strike him."

"Youth, from this day, do not attack this Nepalese ship," they commanded.

Then they exhorted Kṣitigarbha: "O most venerable one, shoot this bolt of the sky[13] and strike Svabhāvanātha with it. We, the ladies, shall bear responsibility for any possible transgression of the precepts of refuge and the generation of the awakening mind."[14]

By holding one thunderbolt with a threatening gesture, the most learned Kṣitigarbha wielded it and shot it to the north of the heretic city Svabhāvanātha, where the goddess Cacika resides. The heretics' temple and the goddess were both annihilated. He shot forth another bolt of lightning and struck the image of Maheśvara, splitting it in two from the head down. A fragment from this hit the tīrthika king, causing the right part of his body to become paralyzed. Another fragment struck the palace of the Turukas[15] in the hinterlands, and it is said that for thirteen years the incursions of Mongol hordes {411} to Bodhgaya ceased. One fragment struck the Black Tent palace of the Shangshung king, causing the destruction of the teachings of Bön.[16] The one or two that were left were chased away and escaped, it is said, into the Kailash mountain range. With another fragment the palace of Dark Poison Sea in the south was demolished, which, it is said, brought an end to the disease of leprosy.[17] One fragment struck Laṅka, the land of rākṣasas,[18] reducing to ashes the palace of the rākṣasa king Laṅkapuri, and the lineage of the man-eating rākṣasas was brought to an end. Kṣitigarbha was then heard to exclaim the following words of pride:

I am the master of this mandala of earth;
run, run, forces of evil, for I shall reduce you to ashes.
I, a great hero, am the lord of the land;[19]
in Udhyāna the neighing of the Hayagrīva horse head resounds
aloud:
Annihilate! Annihilate! Annihilate Maheśvara to mere dust.
Steal away the powers of the gods of animism.

oṃ padmantakrita śvata hayaṃgrīva hulu hulu hūṃ phat[20]

Then the king of wrathful deities Acala and the Blessed Yamāntaka both suddenly disappeared. I too found myself seated on my cushion in my normal form as a monk. All the members of my retinue felt deep admiration and exclaimed the following:

> Spontaneously arising and uncontrived,
> O dharma king, you resemble Mount Meru.
> You, who bear the name of Jñāna,[21]
> have today made us all content.
>
> *Emaho!* O mighty and glorious protector;
> O tathāgata, as we are threatened
> with terror here in the ocean,
> without fail pray protect us
> within the fold of your great compassion.

They had been unable to move anywhere for twenty-one days, but the moment the retinue was freed from the terror, the sails were hoisted in all four directions, and the massive cast-iron anchors were pulled up. Assisted by favorable winds, the ship sailed for a month and {412} a half both day and night without interruption.

Seven months into the journey, another storm arose, pushing them back to a distance of a day's voyage. However, as we prayed to the teachers, the Three Jewels, the ḍākinīs, and the protectors, the storm calmed down. However, the winds that could blow us in the right direction were not strong. Due to the inadequate merit among the sentient beings on the ship, we were thus stranded for about half a month. Then, by cultivating loving-kindness and compassion, we sailed in accord with a favorable wind. So in two months and twenty-six days, we went from shore to shore across the ocean.

Thus ends the story of how Atiśa conquered Maheśvara in the ocean and coped with adversities, which is part of the tale of how Atiśa endured hardships for the sake of finding his teacher. This is indeed a source of wonder.

Part Two

Homage to the most venerable Maitreya and Avalokiteśvara!

Immediately after crossing the great ocean, I, Atiśa, went to the site of the golden reliquary of the tathāgata built by a Tibetan king,[22] where there lived six meditator monks,[23] students of the teacher Serlingpa. This reliquary was located to the west of the forests of Sumatra, to the south of the joyful lotuses, to the north of the dangerous mires, and to the east of the sea monster Kekeru.[24] I spent fourteen days there inquiring after the liberating life story of the teacher Serlingpa. I found out what spiritual practices the teacher undertook as his heart practice, what scriptures he accepted as authoritative, what treatises and systems of thought he had mastered, what scriptural knowledge and reasoning methods he embodied, what levels of realization he had attained, and to what degree he had trained his mind. On all these points I questioned the meditators, and they explained these things to me without exaggeration or omission. {413} Because of this, I experienced such joy as if I had attained a bodhisattva ground.

The meditators in turn asked the learned Kṣitigarbha and others the biographical details of the teacher. He explained how I, Atiśa, had renounced my kingdom and sought the life of a renunciate, how I had relied on countless teachers, how I had overseen countless monasteries, and how I had mastered great knowledge. To this the meditators responded, "Is it possible that this great paṇḍita is the Indian master known as Dīpaṃkara Śrījñāna?" Kṣitigarbha replied:

> He is hailed in the entire world as the second Buddha.
> He is venerated by all fifty-two learned paṇḍitas.
> He is praised by the followers of both Great and Lesser Vehicles.
> He is known universally as the great Indian master.

All the meditators responded:

> O lord of the land, welcome to our abode.
> Though saddened before by only hearing your fame,
> today we have become fortunate indeed.
> Welcome, O great scholar; you have arrived by ship.

Were you disturbed by māras in your course?
Did the sea monster and storms throw up obstacles?
Did you long suffer any lack of provisions?

Kṣitigarbha replied:

For thirteen months we sailed aboard the ship.
Maheśvara harassed us with makara and violent storms.
In an instant, through love and compassion,
Māra was defeated, and we found the good fortune of safety.

Again as our sea voyage continued,
since the most holy teacher has mastery over the sky treasury,[25]
the hundred and twenty-five passengers did not suffer from hunger. [30]
Adversities were pacified with words of truth.

When Kṣitigarbha uttered these words, the meditators were delighted, and with great joy they approached where I was sitting and respectfully uttered the following plea:

When we heard your fame from afar,
with joy in our hearts {414} we yearned to see you.
When the great scholar came here today,
we erred due to our veil of ignorance.[26]
Now with our body, speech, and mind,
with deepest respect, we pay you homage.

With this they prostrated in front of me; and abandoning pride, I also prostrated before them with respect. Again all the meditators exclaimed:

Please explain to us, O most excellent being,
what the purpose is of your visit here.
With reverence we shall help you to pursue your goal;
do tell us what you seek.

I responded:

I've come here to be in the presence of the teacher of Serling;
I've come here to seek the essence of human existence.
Please go to the teacher and convey my request,
thus opening the way for the fulfillment of my wish.

Then the meditators went to the teacher Serlingpa and pleaded:

> O sublime teacher, pray listen to us. The Indian master known as Dīpaṃkara Śrījñāna is currently here in our region with his retinue of a hundred and twenty-five students. For thirteen months in the ocean, he chained Māra and the tīrthika god Maheśvara with loving-kindness and compassion. Now without loss of any majesty of his body, speech, and mind, he has arrived here. For fourteen days we engaged with him in conversations pertaining to dharma; we developed deep admiration for him and feel content. Now to convey the main point, the great scholar has come to see you. He wishes to listen primarily to the *Mother* [that is, the Perfection of Wisdom scriptures] that gives birth to all the conquerors of the three times, to generate the aspiring and engaging aspects of the mind of supreme awakening, to train his mind in the Mahāyāna, and to immerse himself both day and night in the teacher's ocean-like treatises. So out of great compassion, please open the way for him.

Hearing these words, {415} the teacher Serlingpa said:

Welcome, O lord of the land.
Welcome, O royal prince.
Welcome, O great scholar.
Welcome, O master of beings.

Welcome, O great hero,
welcome! You've come with your retinue.
Wonderful indeed that you've endured great hardships.
Wonderful indeed that you've defeated Maheśvara.
Wonderful indeed that you were victorious over the adverse
forces.

Wonderful indeed that the banner of your fame is fluttering.
Wonderful indeed that you've arrived unharmed.
O monks, put on your ceremonial robes
and welcome this most excellent being.

In this way, standing at the head of five hundred and thirty-five monks all clad in the three robes of similar colors, holding small water bottles and staffs[27] and possessing the extremely peaceful demeanor of arhats, the teacher Serlingpa extended his welcome. He was joined also by sixty-two novices. In brief, in single file, five hundred and ninety-seven monastics welcomed me from a distance.

Instantly, I felt deeply moved and experienced a profound joy, thinking how the blessed Buddha must have been surrounded by arhats in this way when he was alive. At this point, I loaded two elephants with various articles and had four lay practitioners take charge of all the possessions. To put on a display for the teacher, I had all the paṇḍitas learned in the five fields of knowledge and all the monks versed in the three scriptural collections—not excluding a single one—dressed in sandals and clad in the three robes excellently dyed with the Kashmiri saffron praised by the Mahāsāṃghika tradition. Due to the auspiciousness of the occasion, all of them held metal alms bowls of perfect size and free of cracks and holes, as well as copper water containers capable of carrying one *dre*,[28] according to the Magadha measurement system. They also carried the monk staffs praised by the master of doctrine {416} and that contained all the required features intact with their corresponding symbolism. All the paṇḍitas wore hats symbolizing their absence of pride and held white tail-fans.

The congregation of great paṇḍitas included Drowa Sangpo, Dharmamitra, Puṇyākara, Vīryavajra, Devamati, Sūryagupta, Kṣitigarbha, Jñānagarbha, Vāgīśvara, Dhānaśrīmitra, Prajñābhadra, Candrabhadra, Samantabhadra, Guhyagarbha, Matinanta, Gyatso Balap, Rirap Gyalpo, and Pawo Rölpa.[29] There were also one hundred and eight monks, such as Jñānabhadra, who were versed in the three scriptural collections. There were thirteen novice monks and four great fully ordained monks. Thus, one hundred and twenty-five monks followed behind me, all in a close line, not touching but leaving a space of one person in between. Neither too close nor too far apart and resembling a five-colored rainbow, we all went to where teacher Serlingpa was residing. Since all the conditions were perfectly gathered, the gods let descend a rain of flowers.

Although I had close connections with the teacher in lives since beginningless time, I had not yet received instructions from him in this life. Behind me were many great learned paṇḍitas, and together we paid our homage. Since I had made sure that we all possessed complete higher qualities, beginning with the ethical discipline of prātimokṣa, it was as if all our hearts were one and the same. We shared the same view and conduct, and everyone was a student following in my footsteps. Unable to bear the majesty of my highly learned students and myself, the teacher and his retinue all made reciprocal prostrations as if falling to the ground.

Serlingpa then performed a consecration that caused me later to become revered by all, Indians and Tibetans. {417} At that time, I filled a precious jewel vase—one with a large body, a firm flat base, a long neck, and a spout protruding from its mouth—with gold, silver, pearls, coral, and lapis lazuli, and offered the vase to the teacher. Everyone else each offered a gold coin. The teacher Serlingpa then queried in verse to determine if there were any obstacles on the path:

Welcome, O upholder of monastic ethics.
Welcome, the one clad in discipline.
Welcome, O great compassionate one.
O dharma king, you have come here.

Your fame is great even from afar.
Welcome, it is indeed good to see you.
In the dharma palace of India,
performing vast deeds for sentient beings,
pith compassion free of prejudice,
have you been a refuge, an ally, and a friend?

Learned one, have you been industrious from your depths?
Have you been nurtured by many spiritual teachers?
Have you been honored by many learned scholars?
Wonderful it is indeed that you have come here today.

O master of beings, I have heard that
for thirteen months you've sailed the ocean;
amazing is your endurance of hardship.
I have heard that you defeated the black Īśvara.

Amazing indeed is the extent of your renown;
amazing is your surmounting of dangers.
O learned one, were your mind and body
not exhausted by this long journey?

With compassion, were you not saddened
by the jealousy of the dark forces?
Welcome, O most excellent being.
Here we are but a few scattered residents.

Most of us are engaged in learning and reflection;
others have come here to see you.
Fortunate it is indeed that we meet today.
Now let us enter the monastery.

Let's go to the courtyard where congregations gather;
we can share tales of your journey in due course.
{418} Let us converse in accord with the dharma.

I then offered the following response:

Yes, I've come; I come from central India.
I come with freedom from obstructive factors.
I've flourished due to the glory of the Three Jewels' kindness.
Through powerful rites, black Īśvara was defeated.

Our three doors triumphed over the dark forces.
Unharmed, we have arrived in good health.
O conqueror, are you living splendidly,
undeterred from the welfare of beings?

By perfectly elucidating the ocean of treatises,
are you immersed in its brilliance?
By vanquishing the entire host of māras,
are you residing in the ocean of wisdom?

You are the most learned in Sumatra.
With love and compassion you look after

the welfare of all beings both day and night
and reside as a master of doctrine, I've heard.

So, all-knowing one,
as I appeal to you to be my teacher,
please expand my understanding
in the vast sphere of knowledge.

As I made this request, all the monks joined in unison:

Welcome, O most excellent one.
Together with you we too shall
become sated by the bliss of sublime dharma.

The residents and visitors together went to the courtyard of the monastic community. An elder was in the midst of teaching a group of monks. I prostrated to him, but he did not prostrate in return. Then, with a golden parasol hoisted above, we entered the teacher's residence, and as we were seated, the elder completed his teaching session and prostrated to me in full accordance with the teachings, saying, "I did not welcome you when you arrived here, O most excellent one. However, I have no conceit, {419} for I believe that to please a sublime being is to act according to the dharma."[30]

When I heard these words, I admired him. I felt that it was an amazing expression of the greatness of the teacher Serlingpa and his teachings. Then, as the groundwork had been well laid, indicating the immensity of the interdependent factors that led to this auspicious occasion, the teacher gave a clear elucidation in fifteen sessions of *The Ornament of Clear Realization*.[31] He thus perfectly conferred this teaching upon me. Following this, I set up residence in the palace of silver parasols and spent my time pursuing study, reflection, and meditation.

All of this relates the account of Atiśa's journey to Sumatra and his meeting with great joy the peerless great Serlingpa Dharmakīrti, the lord of all beings.[32]

Most excellent is this glorious ocean of wonders![33]
Bless me so that I may train in the awakening mind for all.
Bless me so that I may free the numberless beings from samsara.

Bless me so that renunciation and revulsion toward samsara arise in me.
Born of royal lineage, he was learned in all five fields of knowledge.
As prophesied by Tārā, he came to the glorious land of snows.
Trained in cherishing others more than self, he engaged in others' welfare—
To you, O unrivaled Atiśa, I make supplications.
Confer blessings upon me this very instant.

Instantly remove the sufferings of beings.
Eliminate all the miseries of cyclic existence.
Clear away the obstacles to dharma practice.
Bless me so that I may have nothing to do but practice dharma.

Due to making such fervent supplications without interruption, may the uncontrived precious awakening mind exchanging self and others, which is the pure altruistic thought that cherishes others more than one's own self, arise in all sentient beings, both self and others, equal to the expanse of space. {420} May I thus be born soon as a great navigator who will liberate all beings.

17. {421} Annotated Root Lines of Mahāyāna Mind Training[1]

Attributed to Atiśa

Translated by Thupten Jinpa

{422} Homage to the sovereign who has accomplished all purposes and who is the glorious auspicious jewel swiftly granting all happiness.

I

1

First, a trainee whose mind is trained in the three scopes and who, having taken the aspiring and engaging [aspects of the awakening mind], is cognizant of the precepts should[2] *train in the preliminaries* by reflecting on the human existence of leisure and opportunity, on karma and its fruits, and on the defects of cyclic existence.

Contemplate all phenomena—encompassed by self and others, the outer environment, and the inner sentient beings—*as dream-like,* nonexistent but appearing to exist due to the force of the deluded mind.[3]

Experience, free of identification, is *the* thoroughly *unborn nature of awareness,* which cognizes in such manner.

The remedy, which cuts across both body and mind, *is itself freed in its natural place,* free of grasping at existence and nonexistence.

During the interval between sessions, that is, afterward, *create the illusion-like person* as it arises on the basis of the above two.

2
Train alternately in the two—giving (to others of your body, resources, and roots of virtue) *and taking.*

Place the two (giving and taking) *astride your breath* as it exits.

There are three objects (the desirable, the undesirable, and the neutral), *three poisons* (attachment, anger, and delusion), and (their exterminations) *three roots of virtue.*

In all your actions (such as when gathering [merit] and so on) *train* by directing the focus of your mind *by means of the words.*

3
The negativities (and their fruit) *of the world* (the external) *and beings* (the inner) *within cyclic existence* and the afflictions[4]—

Transform the adverse conditions (derived from either sentient beings or the natural elements) *into* aids on the *path of enlightenment.*

How is this so? Whatever undesirable events befall, *banish all blames to the single source,* which is not others {423} but rather self-grasping.

Toward all beings (humans, nonhumans, enemies, friends, and in particular the perpetrators of harm), *contemplate their great kindness.*

4
Contemplating the illusions arising from your mind as the four (as presented in your palms) *buddha bodies,* that is, the adverse forces and their antidotes[5]—

Emptiness (all in the nature of mind) is among *protection unsurpassed.*
The fourfold practice (making offerings to meditation deities and teachers, purifying negative karma, giving offerings to the harmful forces, and propitiating the dharma protectors) *is the most excellent method.*
Relate whatever you can (adverse conditions such as the arising of intense suffering or afflictions) *to your meditation right now.*[6]

5
In brief, to present the points of the practice of a lifetime, *the essence of instruction is this:*[7]

Apply yourself to the five powers[8]—intention, familiarity, positive seed, eradication, and aspiration.

As the Pāramitāyāna, *Mahāyāna's transference instruction is* the five powers (noted above) *alone, their practice* in particular *is vital,* that is, treat this with critical importance.[9]

The intent of all teachings converges on a single point: whether or not it can help subdue you.

6
Of the two witnesses (between others' speech and your own mind, train your mind by ensuring that you do not disgrace yourself, but train in accordance with your aspiration) uphold the principal one.

Cultivate constantly the joyful mind alone.

If this can be done even when distracted, you (your mind) *are trained* in the remedies.
Train constantly in the three general points[10] to ensure that your mind training does not violate your precepts and that it does not become sarcastic.

7
Transform your attitudes (the aspirations of self-grasping) *but remain as you are* with respect to the objectives that have not been assigned.

{424} *Do not speak of the defects [of others]* in conduct of body and speech.

Do not dwell on others' (those who have entered the spiritual order, in particular) shortcomings.

Discard all expectations of reward as a fruit of practicing Mind Training, in either this life or the future life, including even the attainment of buddhahood.

i. *Discard poisonous food* (the virtues mixed with the false views and self-grasping).
ii. *Do not maintain* [inappropriate] loyalty that retaliates against harms caused by others.
iii. *Do not torment with malicious banter* that hurts others in the heart.
iv. *Do not lie in ambush* to take revenge.
v. *Do not strike at the heart* anyone, whether human or nonhuman.
vi. *Do not place the load of a dzo* (the undesirable accusations and their burden) *onto an ox.*[11]
vii. *Do not sprint* (by giving an advantage to yourself when what you desire is owned communally) *to win the race* but instead accept the defeat.
viii. *Do not abuse the practice,* seeking victory for yourself.
ix. *Do not turn gods* (the Mind Training) *into demons.*
x. *Do not seek misery* for others *as a means to happiness* for yourself.

8
Accomplish all yogas (the yoga of eating and so on) *through* not others but *a single means.*

There are two tasks to pursue—*one at the start* (in the morning) *and one at the end* (in the evening).

Whichever of the two (benefit and so on) *arises, bear them both* without conceit or dejection.

Guard the two (the precepts revealed in the teachings in general and the precepts presented in this [Mind Training teaching] in particular) *even at the cost of your life.*[12]

9
Train (on the basis of a qualified teacher, the ability to channel your mind, and the coming together of the external and internal conditions) *in the three difficult challenges:* the difficulty of recalling the antidotes of the afflictions [at the beginning], the difficulty of averting them in the middle, and the difficulty of exterminating their continuum.

Adopt the three principal conditions.

Contemplate the three ([undiminished] reverence for your teacher [and so on]) *that are free of degeneration.*

Be endowed with the three inseparable factors, as if your body, speech, and mind were competing [among themselves in their accumulation of] the three virtuous activities.[13]

10

Train constantly toward the chosen objects: those living together [with you], those hostile toward you, and those unappealing to you.

Those who have the good fortune to practice this Mind Training should adopt a standpoint such that they *do not depend on other conditions.*

If relapsed, take this inability to realize when practicing Mind Training as your very basis, and *meditate on it as the remedy itself.*

Engage in the principal practices right now—especially bodhisattvas on the beginner's level—now that you have obtained the human life of leisure and opportunity and encountered the sublime spiritual teacher. {425}[14]

xi. *Do not apply misplaced understanding.*[15] Learn to cultivate joy in the virtuous activities and do not engage in the six [distorted understandings], such as [misplaced] heedfulness.
xii. *Do not be sporadic*, sometimes training and sometimes not.
xiii. *Train with decisiveness* the task of measuring whether you can do this.
xiv. *Be released*, whether or not your mindstream has attained familiarity with the examples, *through the two: investigation and close analysis* (when self-grasping arises).
xv. *Do not boast* to anyone, ever, when you engage in the practice *of your good deeds.*
xvi. *Do not be ill-tempered*, regardless of how others treat you.
xvii. *Do not be fickle*, fluctuating in your expressions of likes and dislikes.
xviii. *Do not be boisterous*, [even] in words of thanks.

11
Like a diamond, like the sun, and like a tree in full blossom, including even medicines[16]—

Understand (such as the purpose of practice and so on) *the words, their meanings* (the words and their contents), *and so on.*

Through this proliferation of the five degenerations due to the abundance of conditions for practicing Mind Training
[Everything] is transformed into aids to *the path of enlightenment.*
The heart practice of Atiśa, the instruction that has stemmed from Maitreya (The Blessed One transmitted it to Maitreya; he, to Asaṅga; he, to Vasubandhu; he, to Kuśāli the Elder; he, to Kuśāli the Younger; and he transmitted it to the teacher Serlingpa) *is concluded.*

II

12
Relinquish all biases (those negative acts—done out of attraction to the gods' realms, or related to wealth or loss—that are the causes [of suffering] of yourself and others).[17]
Transform everything (the degenerate era and the afflictions, which are the underlying motives) *into the Mahāyāna path.*
Cherish your training toward the entire human race (all yogas, and all conduct), *all its breadth and depth,* for as each moment of consciousness arises, this training sees it as in the nature of suffering and so on.
Train in both the main (the two—giving and taking—and the precepts; [Combat] not the gods, demons, and so on, but rather the self-grasping) *and the secondary practices.*

13
Apply abstention and adoption forcefully with regard to the fierce one.[18]
Transform the adverse factors into aids of practice.
Destroy all rationalizations, for example, losing your enthusiasm for giving and taking because of thoughts like "Others are harming me."
Purify first whichever affliction is strongest by examining your mind and applying the antidotes against whatever is strongest. [Purify also] discriminatory thoughts, such as "near and distant," "love and hate," "high and low." {426}

14
Train without partiality toward [any] object, for if you settle your mind in this training, everything turns into an aid.[19]

This greatly surpasses all other virtues; even merely hearing about it as news again and again [enhances] its potency.
When both are present, since you have discarded sufferings, you can *take them all* (those of others).
Learn to ensure ease in your practice. Although this is advice pertaining to an achieved objective, you must integrate it right from the start.

15
Begin the sequence of taking from your own self such as those [sufferings] you are likely to experience toward the latter part of your life, [the sufferings of] your actual mother, [and so on].
The defining characteristic of the act (the practice of exchanging self and others) *is that of letting go* of attachment and clinging to all—to this life and future lives, to cyclic existence and its transcendence [nirvana].[20]
The sign that you are trained is when you are endowed with the five [marks of] greatness, the foremost of which is the practice of a fully ordained monk, an upholder of monastic ethics.
Do not be a stranger, but instead relate to others affectionately with the awakening mind.[21]
Do not give "clarifications" of others' negative acts and shortcomings, for this prevents your realization.
Do not harbor expectations (of others).
This is the end.

III

Take many, for you are aware of the discarding of others' sufferings.
In the future, always put on the armor with the thought "I shall not allow myself to fall prey to all the conditions that preoccupy me in my life."
When stability is attained, reveal the secret: the two (giving and taking), the profound meaning (the experience of the exchanging of self and others) [the relation between] negative karma and suffering, and so on.

This concludes the treatise on Mind Training. This was composed by Master Atiśa. May goodness prevail!

18. {427} Root Lines of Mahāyāna Mind Training without Annotations[1]

Attributed to Atiśa

Translated by Thupten Jinpa

[35] Homage to the sovereign who has accomplished all purposes and who is the glorious auspicious jewel swiftly endowing others with great happiness.

First, train in the preliminaries.
For the main practice, train alternately in giving and taking.
There are three objects, three poisons, and three roots of virtue—
this, in brief, is the instruction for subsequent practice. (1)

Begin the sequence of taking from your own self.
Place the two astride your breath.
In brief, this is the distilled essence of instruction:
in all actions, train by means of the words. (2)

Relate whatever you can to meditation right now.
When both are present, take them all.
Train constantly toward the chosen objects. (3)

Banish all blames to the single source.
Toward all beings, contemplate their great kindness.
Train in the three difficult challenges.
There are two tasks—one at the start and one at the end. (4)

Contemplate the three that are free of degeneration.
Train constantly in the three general points.

Transform your attitudes but remain as you are.
Adopt the three principal conditions.
Train in the five powers. (5)

The intent of all teachings converges on a single point.
Of the two witnesses uphold the principal one.[2]
Cultivate constantly the joyful mind alone;
if this can be done even when distracted, you are trained.

Do not torment with malicious banter.
Do not boast of your good deeds.
Do not be ill-tempered.
Do not be boisterous.
Do not be fickle.
Do not lie in ambush.
Do not place the load of a dzo onto an ox.
Do not sprint to win a race.
Do not maintain inappropriate loyalty.
Do not be sporadic.
Do not abuse this practice.
Be released through the two: investigation and close analysis.
Train with decisiveness.
Be endowed with the three inseparable factors. (6)

Accomplish all yogas through a single means.
If relapsed, meditate on it as the very remedy.
Whichever of the two arises, bear them both;
do not speak of the defects of others. (7)

{428} Do not dwell on others' shortcomings.
Do not turn the gods into demons.
Do not seek misery as a means to happiness.
Do not depend on other conditions.
Recognize what is primary.
Forsake all expectations of reward.
Discard poisonous food.
Do not strike at the heart. (8)

This proliferation of the five degenerations
is transformed into the path of enlightenment.
When stability is attained, reveal the secret. (9)

This distilled essence of pith instructions
stems from the lineage of most sublime masters. (10)

These are the root lines. This was composed by Atiśa.

Abbreviations

AA Maitreya Nātha. *The Ornament of Realization.* English translation: *Abhisamayālaṃkāra with Vṛtti and Āloka.* Translated by Gareth Sparham. 4 vols. Fremont, CA: Jain Publishing, 2006–2012. Sanskrit text: *Abhisamayālaṃkāra.* Edited by T. Stcherbatsky and E. E. Obermiller. Leningrad: Bibliotheca Buddhica, 1929. Tibetan text: Dg.T. shes phyin, vol. 1 (*ka*), ff. 1b–13a. (Toh. 3786)

AAA Haribhadra. *Illuminating the Ornament of Realization.* English translation: *Abhisamayālaṃkāra with Vṛtti and Āloka.* Translated by Gareth Sparham. 4 vols. Fremont, CA: Jain Publishing, 2006–2012. Sanskrit text: *Abhisamayālaṃkārāloka.* In *Aṣṭasāhasrikā Prajñāpāramitā*, pp. 267–558. Buddhist Sanskrit Texts, no. 4. Darbhanga, India: Mithila Institute, 1960. Tibetan text: *'Phags pa shes rab kyi pha rol tu phyin pa brgyad stong pa'i bshad pa mNgon par rtogs pa'i rgyan gyi snang ba.* Dg.T. shes phyin, vol. 6 (*cha*), ff. 1b–341a. (Toh. 3791)

AK Vasubandhu. *Root Verses of the Treasury of Higher Learning.* English translation in *Abhidharmakośabhāṣyam.* 4 vols. Translated by Leo M. Pruden. Berkeley: Asian Humanities Press, 1988. Sanskrit text: *Abhidharmakośakārikā.* Edited by G. V. Gokhale. *Journal of the Royal Asiatic Society*, vol. 22. Bombay: Royal Asiatic Society, 1946. Tibetan text: *Chos mngon pa mdzod kyi tshig le'ur byas pa.* Dg.T. mngon pa, vol. 61 (*ku*), ff. 1–25a. (Toh. 4089)

AKBh Vasubandhu. *A Commentary on the Treasury of Higher Learning.* English translation: *Abhidharmakośabhāṣyam.* 4 vols. Translated by Leo M. Pruden. Sanskrit text: *Abhidharmakośabhāṣyam.* Edited by Prahlad Pradhan. Patna: K. P. Jayaswal Research Institute, 1975. Tibetan text: *Chos mngon pa'i mdzod kyi bshad pa.* Dg.T. mngon pa, vol. 61 (*ku*), f. 25a–vol. 62 (*khu*), f. 97b. (Toh. 4090)

AKV Yaśomitra. *Clarification of the Meaning: A Subcommentary to "The Treasury of Higher Learning."* Sanskrit text: *Sphuṭārthābhidharmakośavyākhyā.* 4 vols. Edited by Swami Dwarikadas Shastri. Varanasi: Bauddha Bharati, 1970. Tibetan text: *Chos mngon pa'i mdzod kyi 'grel bshad.* Dg.T. mngon pa, vols. 63–64 (*gu–ngu*). (Toh. 4092)

AM Abhayākaragupta. *The Flower Cluster of Instruction. Āmnāyamañjarī. dPal yang dag par sbyor ba'i rgyud kyi rgyal po'i rgya cher 'grel pa man ngag gi snye ma.* Dg.T. rgyud, vol. 6 (*cha*), ff. 1b–316a.

AS Asaṅga. *The Compendium of Higher Learning.* English translation in *The Compendium of the Higher Teaching.* Translated from French by Sara Boin-Webb. Berkeley: Asian Humanities Press, 2001. Sanskrit text: *Abhidharmasamuccaya.* Edited by Prahlad Pradhan. Shantiniketan, India: Visva-Bharati, 1950. Tibetan text: *Chos mngon pa kun las btus pa.* Dg.T. sems tsam, vol. 55 (*ri*), ff. 44a–120a. (Toh. 4049)

ASBh Jinaputra. *A Commentary on the Compendium of Higher Learning.* Sanskrit text: *Abhidharmasamuccayabhāṣyam.* Edited by Nathmal Tatia. Patna, India: K. P. Jayaswal Research Institute, 1976. Tibetan text: *mNgon pa chos kun las btus pa'i rnam par bshad pa.* Dg.T. sems tsam, vol. 56 (*li*), ff. 119a–296a. (Toh. 4054)

BBh Asaṅga. *The Bodhisattva Stage.* English translation: *The Bodhisattva Path to Unsurpassed Enlightenment.* Translated by Artemus B. Engle. Boulder: Snow Lion, 2016. Sanskrit text: *Bodhisattvabhūmi.* Edited by Nalinaksha Dutt. Patna: K. P. Jayaswal Research Institute, 1978. Tibetan text: (*rNal 'byor spyod pa'i sa las*) *Byang chub sems dpa'i sa.* Dg.T. sems tsam, vol. 50 (*wi*), ff. 1b–213a. (Toh. 4037)

BBhVy *Samudramegha (rGya mtsho sprin). *A Commentary on the Bodhisattva Stage, a Section from "The Stages of Spiritual Practice." Bodhisattvabhūmivyākhā.* Tibetan text: *Byang chub sems dpa'i sa'i rnam par bshad pa.* Dg.T. sems tsam, vol. 54 (*yi*), ff. 1b–338a.

BCA *Śāntideva. Entry into the Conduct That Leads to Enlightenment.* English translation: *A Guide to the Bodhisattva Way of Life.* Translated by Vesna A. Wallace and B. Alan Wallace. Ithaca, NY: Snow Lion, 1997. Sanskrit text: *Bodhicaryāvatāra.* Edited by Vidushekhara Bhattacharya. Calcutta: The Asiatic Society, 1960. Tibetan text: *Byang chub sems dpa'i spyod pa la 'jug pa.* Dg.T. dbu ma, vol. 26 (*la*), ff. 1–40a. (Toh. 3871)

BCAP Prajñākaramati. *A Commentary on the Difficult Points of "Entry into the Conduct That Leads to Enlightenment."* Sanskrit text: *Bodhicaryāvatārapañjikā.* Buddhist Sanskrit Texts, no. 12. Darbhanga, India: Mithila Institute, 1960. Tibetan text: *Byang chub kyi spyod pa la 'jug pa'i dka' 'grel.* Dg.T dbu ma, vol. 26 (*la*), ff. 41b–288a. (Toh. 3872)

BCP *The Aspirational Prayer for Excellent Spiritual Conduct.* In *The Flower Ornament Scripture*, translated by Thomas Cleary, pp. 1511–18. Boston: Shambhala, 1993. Sanskrit text: *Bhadracaryapraṇidhānam.* In *Gaṇḍvyūhasūtram*, pp. 428–36. Buddhist Sanskrit Texts, no. 5. Darbanga, India: Mithila Institute, 1960. Tibetan text: *bZang po spyod pa'i smon lam gyi rgyal po.* Dg.K. phal chen, vol. 6 (*cha*), ff. 336b–341a. (Toh. 1105)

BHSD *Buddhist Hybrid Sanskrit Dictionary.* 2 vols. Edited by Franklin Edgerton. New Haven, CT: Yale University Press, 1953. Reprint, Delhi: Motilal Banarsidass, 1970.

BŚPBh Guṇaprabha. *A Commentary to the Chapter on Bodhisattva Morality. Bodhisattvaśīlaparivartabhāṣya.* Tibetan text: *Byang chub sems dpa'i tshul khrims kyi leu'i bshad pa.* Dg.T. sems tsam, vol. 53 (*'i*), ff. 182a–191a. (Toh. 4045)

BŚPṬ Jinaputra. *An Extensive Commentary to the Chapter on Bodhisattva Morality. Bodhisattvaśīlaparivartaṭīkā.* Tibetan text: *Byang chub sems dpa'i tshul khrims kyi leu'i rgya cher 'grel pa.* Dg.T. sems tsam, vol. 53 (*'i*), ff. 191a–221a. (Toh. 4046)

BSV Candragomī. *Twenty Verses on the Bodhisattva Vow.* Translated by Mark Tatz. In *Candragomin's Twenty Verses on the Bodhisattva Vow and Its Commentary.* Dharamsala: Library of Tibetan Works and Archives, 1982. Sanskrit text: *Bodhisattvasaṃvaraviṃśikā.* Sanskrit text (vv. 1–9a, 11c, and 20cd): Kano Kazuo, Li Xueshu, and Ye Shaoyong, ed. "Sanskrit fragments of Candragomin's *Bodhisattvasaṃvaraviṃśikā.*" *Mikkyō Gakkaihō, The Annual Bulletin of the Esoteric Buddhist Society* 53 (March 2015): pp. 480–95. Tibetan text: *Byang chub sems dpa'i sdom pa nyi shu pa.* Dg.T. sems tsam, vol. 59 (*hi*), ff. 166b–167a. (Toh. 4081)

CŚ Āryadeva. *Four Hundred Verses.* English translation: *Aryadeva's Four Hundred Stanzas on the Middle Way with Commentary by Gyel-tsap.* Translated by Ruth Sonam with Geshe Sonam Rinchen. Ithaca, NY: Snow Lion, 2008. *Catuḥśatakam.* Sanskrit text: *Catuḥśatakam.* Edited by P. L. Vaidya. Nagpur, India: Alok Prakashan, 1971. Tibetan text: *bsTan bcos bzhi brgya pa zhes bya ba'i tshig le'ur byas pa.* Dg.T. dbu ma, vol. 18 (*tsha*), ff. 1b–18a. (Toh. 3846)

CŚṬ Candrakīrti. *A Commentary on the Four Hundred Verses on a Bodhisattva's Spiritual Conduct.* English translation (chs. 1–4): *Four Illusions: Candrakīrti's Advice to Travelers on the Bodhisattva Path.* Translated by Karen C. Lang. Oxford: Oxford University Press, 2003. Sanskrit (incomplete): Haraprasad Shastri, ed. "*Catuḥśatakaṭīkā.*" In *Memoirs of the Asiatic Society of Bengal* 3, no. 8 (1914): pp. 449–514. Sanskrit text (portions of chs. 7–16): *Catuḥśatakam.* Edited by P. L. Vaidya. Nagpur, India: Alok Prakashan, 1971. Tibetan text: *Byang chub sems dpa'i rnal 'byor spyod pa bzhi brgya pa'i rgya cher 'grel pa.* Dg.T. dbu ma, vol. 24 (*ya*), ff. 30b–239a. (Toh. 3865)

GB2 *sGra sbyor bam po gnyis pa.* Dg.T. sna tshogs, vol. 126 (*cho*), ff. 131b–160a. (Toh. 4347)

JM Āryaśūra. *Garland of Birth Stories.* English translation: *Garland of the Buddha's Past Lives.* 2 vols. Translated by Justin Meiland. New York: New York University Press and JJC Foundation, 2009. Sanskrit text: *Jātakamālā.* In *Garland of the Buddha's Past Lives.* 2 vols. New York: New York University Press and JJC Foundation, 2009.

KCS Lechen Kunga Gyaltsen (Las chen Kun dga' rgyal mtshan). *A Lamp That Illuminates the History of the Kadam Spiritual Tradition. bKa' gdams kyi rnam par thar pa bka' gdams chos 'byung gsal ba'i sgron me.* BDRC MW23748.

LRCh Tsong kha pa (bLo bzang grags pa'i dpal). English translation: *The Great Treatise on the Stages of the Path to Enlightenment.* 3 vols. Ithaca, NY: Snow Lion, 2000–2004. Tibetan text: *Byang chub lam gyi rim pa chen mo.* In Collected Works, vol. 13 (*pa*). New Delhi: Mongolian Lama Guru Deva, 1978–1983. (Toh. 5392)

MA Candrakīrti. *Entry into the Middle Way.* English translation (root text verses): *Illuminating the Intent: An Exposition of Candrakīrti's Entering the Middle Way.* Translated by Thupten Jinpa. Somerville, MA: Wisdom, 2021. Sanskrit text (chs. 1–5): *Candradrakīrti's Madhyamakāvatārabhāṣya.* Edited by Horst Lasic, Xueshu Li, and Anne MacDonald. Beijing and Vienna: China Tibetology Publishing House and Austrian Academy of Sciences Press, 2015. Sanskrit text (ch. 6): Li Xuezhu, ed. "*Madhyamakāvatāra-kārikā* Chapter 6." *Journal of Indian Philosophy* 43 (2015): pp. 1–30. Tibetan text: *dBu ma la 'jug pa.* Dg.T. dbu ma, vol. 23 (*'a*), ff. 201a–219a. (Toh. 3861)

MMK Nāgārjuna. *Root Verses on the Middle Way.* English translation: *The Fundamental Wisdom of the Middle Way: Nagarjuna's Mulamadhyamakakarika.* Translated by Jay L. Garfield. New York: Oxford University Press, 1995. Sanskrit text: *Mūlamadhyamakakārikā.* In *Mūlamadhyamakaśāstra of Nāgārjuna.* Buddhist Sanskrit Texts, no. 10. Darbhanga, India: Mithila Institute, 1960. Tibetan text: *dBu ma rtsa ba'i tshig le'ur byas pa shes rab ces bya ba.* Dg.T. dbu ma, vol. 17 (*tsa*), ff. 1b–19a (Toh. 3824)

MSA Maitreya Nātha. *The Ornament of Mahāyāna Sūtras.* English translation in *A Feast of the Nectar of the Supreme Vehicle.* Translated by Stephen Gethin and the Padmakara Translation Group. Boulder: Shambhala, 2018. Sanskrit text: *Mahāyānasūtrālaṃkāra.* Sanskrit verses in Buddhist Sanskrit Texts, no. 13. Darbhanga, India: Mithila Institute, 1970. Tibetan text: Dg.T. shes phyin, vol. 1 (*ka*), ff. 1b–13a. (Toh. 3786)

MSAVṛBh Sthiramati. *A Subcommentary on the Commentary on "The Ornament of Mahāyāna Sūtras." Mahāyānasūtrālaṃkāravṛttibhāṣyam.* Tibetan text: *mDo sde rgyan gyi 'grel bshad.* Dg.T. sems tsam, vols. 46 (*mi*) and 47 (*tsi*).

MSAVy Vasubandhu. *A Commentary on "The Ornament of Mahāyāna Sūtras."* English translation: *The Universal Vehicle Discourse Literature.* Translated by L. Jamspal et al. New York: American Institute of Buddhist Studies, 2004. Sanskrit text: *Mahāyānasūtrālaṃkāravyākhyā.* Buddhist Sanskrit Texts, no. 13. Darbhanga, India: Mithila Institute, 1970. Tibetan text: *mDo sde'i rgyan gyi bshad pa.* Dg.T. sems tsam, vol. 44 (*phi*), ff. 129b–260a. (Toh. 4026)

MVBh Vasubandhu. *A Commentary on "Distinguishing the Middle Way from the Extremes."* English translation in *Seven Works of Vasubandhu*. Translated by Stefan Anacker. Delhi: Motilal Banarsidass, 1984. *Madhyānta-vibhāgabhāṣyam*. Sanskrit text in *Madhyānta-Vibhāga-Śāstra*. Edited by Ramchandra Pandeya. Delhi: Motilal Banarsidass, 1971. Tibetan text: *dBu dang mtha' rnam par 'byed pa'i 'grel pa*. Dg.T. sems tsam, vol. 45 (*bi*), ff. 1b–27a. (Toh. 4027)

MVK Maitreya Nātha. *Root Verses on Distinguishing the Middle Way from Extremes*. English translation: *Seven Works of Vasubandhu*. Translated by Stefan Anacker. Delhi: Motilal Banarsidass, 1973. *Madhyāntavibhāga-kārikā*. Sanskrit verses in *Madhyānta-Vibhāga-Śāstra*. Edited by Ramchandra Pandeya. Delhi: Motilal Banarsidass, 1971. Tibetan text: *dBus dang mtha' rnam par 'byed pa'i tshig le'ur byas pa*. Dg.T. sems tsam, vol. 44 (*phi*), ff. 40b–45a. (Toh. 4021)

MVṬ Sthiramati. *A Subcommentary to "Distinguishing the Middle Way from Extremes"* (not translated into English). *Madhyāntavibhāgaṭīkā*. Sanskrit text in *Madhyānta-Vibhāga-Śāstra*. Edited by Ramchandra Pandeya. Delhi: Motilal Banarsidass, 1971. Tibetan text: *dBu dang mtha' rnam par 'byed pa'i 'grel bshad*. Dg.T. sems tsam, vol. 45 (*bi*), ff. 189b–318a. (Toh. 4032)

MVy *Mahāvyutpatti*. *Bye brag tu rtogs pa chen po*. Dg.T. sna tshogs, vol. 126 (*cho*), ff. 1b–131a. (Toh. 4346)

MW Sir Monier Monier-Williams, ed. *Sanskrit-English Dictionary*. London: Oxford University Press, 1899. Reprint, Delhi: Motilal Banarsidass, 1963.

NgG Chim Jampai Yang (mChims 'Jam pa'i dbyangs). *Ornament of Abhidharma: A Commentary on Vasubandhu's Abhidharmakośa*. Translated by Ian Coghlan. Library of Tibetan Classics, vol. 23. Somerville, MA: Wisdom, 2018. Tibetan text: *Chos mngon mdzod kyi tshig le'ur byas pa'i 'grel pa mngon pa'i rgyan*. Lhasa: Khun grub zil gnon rje 'bum lha khang, n.d. BDRC: MW2CZ8096.

PK Nāgārjuna. *Five Stages*. *Pañcakrama*. Sanskrit text: *Pañcakrama: Sanskrit and Tibetan Texts Critically Edited with Verse Index and Facsimile Edition of the Sanskrit Manscripts*. Edited by K. Mimaki and T. Tomabechi. Tokyo: Center for East Asian Cultural Studies for UNESCO, 1994. Tibetan text: *Rim pa lnga pa*. Dg.T. rgyud. vol. 34 (*ngi*), ff. 45a–57a. (Toh. 1802)

PP Candrakīrti. *In Clear Words*. English translation (ch. 1): *In Clear Words: The Prasannapadā Chapter One*, vol 2. Translated by Anne MacDonald. Vienna: Austrian Academy of Sciences Press, 2015. Sanskrit text: *Prasannapadā*. In *Madhyamakaśāstra of Nāgārjuna*, pp. 1–259. Buddhist Sanskrit Texts, no. 10. Darbhanga, India: Mithila Institute, 1960.

Tibetan text: *dBu ma rtsa ba'i 'grel pa tshig gsal ba zhes bya ba*. Dg.T. dbu ma, vol. 23 (*'a*), ff. 1a–197a. (Toh. 3860)

PS Vasubandhu. *Five Heaps*. English translation: *The Inner Science of Buddhist Practice*, pp. 229–44. Ithaca, NY: Snow Lion, 2009. Sanskrit text: *Pañcaskandhaka*. In *Vasubandhu's Pañcaskandhaka*. Edited by Li Xueshu and Ernst Steinkellner. Beijing and Vienna: China Tibetology Publishing House and Austrian Academy of Sciences Press, 2008. Tibetan text: *Phung po lnga'i rab tu byed pa*. Dg.T. sems tsam, vol. 57 (*shi*), ff. 11b–17a. (Toh. 4059)

PSB Sai Tsalak (Sa'i rtsa lag). *A Commentary on "The Summary of the Five Heaps." Pañcaskandhaprakaraṇabhāṣyam*. Translation: *Phung po lnga'i rab tu byed pa bye brag tu bshad pa*). Dg.T. sems tsam, vol. 58 (*si*), ff. 32a–139a. (Toh. 4068)

PSV Sthiramati. *A Commentary on "The Five Heaps."* English translation in *The Inner Science of Buddhist Practice*, pp. 245–369. Ithaca, NY: Snow Lion, 2009. *Pañcaskandhakavibhāṣā*. Sanskrit text edited by Jowita Kramer. Vienna: Austrian Academy of Sciences Press, 2013. *Phung po lnga'i rab tu byed pa bye brag tu bshad pa*. Dg.T. sems tsam, vol. 57 (*shi*), ff. 195b–250a. (Toh. 4066)

PV Dharmakīrti. *Extensive Treatise on Knowledge* (no complete English translation; selected chapters and portions of chapters translated by various scholars). *Pramāṇavārttikakārikā*. Sanskrit text in *Pramāṇavārttika: The Kārikās with Manorathanandi's Vṛtti*. Varanasi: Bauddha Bharati, 1968. Tibetan text: *Tshad ma rnam 'grel gyi tshig le'ur byas pa*. Dg.T. tshad ma, vol. 95 (*ce*), ff. 94b–151a. (Toh. 4210)

PVS *The Perfection of Wisdom in Twenty-Five Thousand Lines* (recast version). Extensive portions of English translation: In *The Large Sūtra on Perfect Wisdom*. Translated by Edward Conze. Berkeley: University of California Press, 1975. Sanskrit text: *Pañcaviṃśatisāhasrikāprajñāpāramitāsūtram*. (Recast version of the original sūtra that conforms to the sections of the *Abhisamayālaṃkāra*) 3 vols. Bibliotheca Indo-Tibetica Series, 61. Edited by Dr. Vijay Raj Vajracharya. Sarnath, India: Central Institute of Higher Tibetan Studies, 2006–2008. Tibetan text: *Shes rab kyi pha rol tu phyin pa stong phrag nyi shu lnga pa*. Dg.K. sher phyin stong phrag nyi shu lnga pa, vols. 1–3 (*ka–ga*). (Toh. 9)

PVṬ Karṇakagomī. *A Subcommentary on "Commentary on Pramāṇavārttikavṛttiṭīkā*. Sanskrit text: *Pramāṇavārttikavṛttiṭīkā*. In *Karṇakagomin's Commentary on the Pramāṇavārttikavṛtti of Dharmakīrti*. Edited by Rahula Samkrtyayana. Kyoto: Rinsen, 1982. First printed in 1843 in Allahabad.

RA Nāgārjuna. *The Jewel Garland*. English translation: *The Precious Garland and the Precious Song of the Four Mindfulnesses*. Translated by Jeffrey Hopkins and Lati Rinpoche with Anne Klein. New York: Harper and Row, 1975. Incomplete Sanskrit text: *Nāgārjuna's Ratnāvalī*, edited by Michael Hahn. Bonn: Indica et Tibetica Verlag, 1982. Tibetan text: *rGyal po la gtam bya ba rin po che'i phreng ba*. Dg.T. spring yig, vol. 93 (*ge*), ff. 116a–135a. (Toh. 4158)

RGSG *The Verses That Summarize the Perfection of Wisdom*. Incomplete English translation: In *The Perfection of Wisdom in Eight Thousand Lines and Its Verse Summary*, pp. 1–73. Translated by Edward Conze. Bolinas: Four Seasons Foundation, 1973. Sanskrit text: *Ratnaguṇasaṃcayagāthā*. In *Mahāyāna Sūtra Saṃgraha*, pp. 352–98. Buddhist Sanskrit Texts, no. 17. Darbanga, India: Mithila Institute, 1960. Tibetan text: (*'Phags pa*) *Shes rab kyi pha rol tu phyin pa sdud pa tsigs su bcad pa*. Dg.K. sher phyin sna tsogs, vol. 1 (*ka*), ff. 189–215a. (Toh. 13)

RGV Maitreya Nātha. *Distinguishing the Three Jewels and the Mahāyāna Spiritual Lineage*. English translation: In *When the Clouds Part*. Translated by Karl Brunnhölzl. Boston: Snow Lion, 2014. Sanskrit text: *Ratnagotravibhāga* (a.k.a., *Uttaratantraśāstra*). Root verses in *Ratnagotravibhāga Mahāyānottaratantraśāstra*. Edited by E. H. Johnston. Patna: Bihar Research Society, 1950. Tibetan text: *Theg pa chen po rgyud bla ma'i bstan bcos*. Dg.T. sems tzam, vol. 44 (*phi*), ff. 51a–69a. (Toh. 4024)

ŚBh Asaṅga. *The Śrāvaka Stage*. Sanskrit text: *Śrāvakabhūmi*. Tibetan Sanskrit Works Series vol. 14. Edited Karunesha Shukla. Patna: K. P. Jayaswal Research Institute, 1973. Tibetan text: (*rNal 'byor spyod pa'i sa las*) *Nyan thos kyi sa*. Dg.T. sems tsam, vol. 49 (*dzi*), ff. 1b–195a. (Toh. 4036)

SL Nāgārjuna. *Letter to a Friend. Suhṛllekha*. English translation: *Nāgārjuna's Letter*. Translated by Geshe Lobsang Tharchin and Artemus B. Engle. Dharamsala, India: Library of Tibetan Works and Archives, 1979. Sanskrit text: In *Ta la'i lo mar bris pa'i rGya dpe bris ma bshes springs skor gyi dpe bsdur zhib 'jug*, edited by dNgos grub tshe ring, pp. 133–84. Lhasa: bod ljongs bod yig dpe rnying dpe sprun khang, 2020. Tibetan text: *bShes pa'i spring yig*. Dg.T. spring yig, vol. 94 (*nge*), ff. 40b–46b. (Toh. 4182)

ŚL Candragomī. *Letter to a Disciple*. English translation: In *Invitation to Enlightenment*, translated by Michael Hahn, pp. 51–131. Berkeley: Dharma Publishing, 1999. Sanskrit text: *Śiṣyalekha*. In *Invitation to Enlightenment*, translated by Michael Hahn, pp. 51–131. Berkeley: Dharma Publishing, 1999. Tibetan text: *Slob ma la springs pa'i spring yig*. Dg.T. spring yig section of Tg., vol. 94 (*nge*), ff. 46b–53a. (Toh. 4183)

SR *The King of Samādhis Sūtra*. English text: 84000: Translating the Words of the Buddha, 2018. Translated by Peter Alan Roberts. Sanskrit text: *Samādhirājasūtram*. Buddhist Sanskrit Texts, no. 2. Darbanga, India: Mithila Institute, 1961. Tibetan text: *'Phags pa chos thams cad kyi rang bzhin mnyam pa nyid rnam par spros pa ting nge 'dzin gyi rgyal po zhes bya ba theg pa chen po'i mdo.* Dg.K. mdo mang, vol. 9 (*ta*), ff. 1–269b. (Toh. 127)

ŚS — *Śāntideva. Compendium of Training.* English translation: *The Training Anthology of Śāntideva.* Translated by Charles Goodman. New York: Oxford University Press, 2015. Sanskrit text: *Śikṣāsamuccaya.* Buddhist Sanskrit Texts, no. 11. Darbhanga, India: Mithila Institute, 1960. Tibetan text: *bsLab pa kun las btus pa.* Dg.T. dbu ma, vol. 111 (*khi*), ff. 3a–194b. (Toh. 3940)

TB — Sthiramati. *A Commentary on "Thirty Verses."* English translation: *Vasubandhu's Vijñapti Mātratā Siddhi with Sthiramati's Commentary.* Edited and translated by K. N. Chatterjee. Varanasi: Kishor Vidya Niketan, 1980. Sanskrit text: *Sthiramati's Triṃśikāvijñaptibhāṣya.* Edited by Hartmut Buescher. Vienna: Österreichische Akademie der Wissenschaften, 2007. Tibetan text: *Sum cu pa'i bshad pa.* Dg.T. sems tsam, vol. 57 (*shi*), ff. 146b–171b. (Toh. 4064)

TK — Vasubandhu. *Thirty Verses.* English translation: *Seven Works of Vasubandhu,* translated by Stefan Anacker, pp. 181–90. Delhi: Motilal Banarsidass, 1998. Sanskrit text: *Triṃśikākarikā.* In *Sthiramati's Triṃśikāvijñaptibhāṣya.* Edited by Hartmut Buescher. Vienna: Österreichische Akademie der Wissenschaften, 2007. Tibetan text: *Sum cu pa'i tshig le'ur byas pa.* Dg.T. sems tsam, vol. 57 (*shi*), ff. 1b–3a. (Toh. 4055)

TshCh — *The Great Tibetan-Chinese Dictionary. Bod rgya tshig mdzod chen mo.* Beijing: Mi rigs dpe skrun khang, 1985.

UV — *Collection of Uplifting Sayings.* Translated by W. Woodville Rockhill. Amsterdam: Oriental Press, 1975. First printed in 1884. Sanskrit text: *Udānavarga.* Edited by Franz Bernhard. Gottingen: Vandehoeck and Ruprecht, 1965. Tibetan text: *Ched du brjod pa'i tsoms.* Dg.K. mdo mang, vol. 26 (*la*), ff. 320b–387b. (Toh. 326)

VS — Asaṅga. *Collection of Determinations. Viniścayasaṃgrahaṇī.* Tibetan text: *rNam par gtan la dbab pa bsdu ba.* Dg.T. sems tsam, vol. 57 (*zhi*), ff. 1b–289a. (Toh. 4038)

YBh — Asaṅga. *The Stages of Spiritual Practice. Yogācārabhūmi.* Sanskrit text: Parts 1–5 in *The Yogācārabhūmi of Ācārya Asaṅga,* edited by Vidhushekhara Bhattacharya, pp. 1–232. Calcutta: University of Calcutta, 1957. Parts 8, 9, 11, and 14 in *Buddhist Insight,* pp. 327–31 and pp. 333–52. Delhi: Motilal Banarsidass, 1984. (See separate listings for *Śrāvakabhūmi* [part 13] and *Bodhisattvabhūmi* [part 15].) Tibetan text: Parts 1–12, 14, 16–17 (referred to as *Sa mang po pa*) in Dg.T. sems tsam, vol. 48 (*tshi*), ff. 1–283a.

Notes

Series Introduction

1. 'Jam dbyangs mkhyen brtse dbang po (1820–1892), mChog 'gyur bDe chen gling pa (1829–1870), Mi pham rgya mtsho (1846–1912), and many more masters were involved in this movement, including Kongtrul's guru Si tu Pad ma nyin byed (1774–1853). See Smith, *Among Tibetan Texts*, 247–50; Jamgön Kongtrul, *Treasury of Knowledge, Book 8, Part 4: Esoteric Instructions*, 25–48; Ringu Tulku, *The Ri-me Philosophy of Jamgön Kongtrul the Great*; etc.
2. The specific text by Shes rab 'od zer that expounds the eight chariots is *Meditation's Ambrosia of Immortality* (*sGom pa 'chi med kyi bdud rtsi*). A study of this has been done by Marc-Henri Deroche: "'Phreng po gter ston Shes rab 'od zer (1518–1584) on the Eight Lineages of Attainment." According to Deroche, "This text may be considered as an (if not the) original source of the '*ris med* paradigm' of the eight lineages of attainment" (17). It is interesting to note that the eight lineages are arranged in a different sequence in that text—Nyingma, Kadampa, Shangpa Kagyu, Lamdre, Marpa Kagyu, Zhije, Jordruk, Dorje Sumgyi Nyendrup—which may have been more chronological than Kongtrul's preferred order.
3. One finds this idea developed in the volume on esoteric instructions in *The Treasury of Knowledge*, where Kongtrul describes in incredibly condensed detail the basic principles and sources of these eight lineages. It is expounded in the catalog of *The Treasury of Precious Instructions* (*DNZ*, vol. 18), published in English as *The Catalog of The Treasury of Precious Instructions*, trans. Richard Barron (Chökyi Nyima). Also see Stearns, *Luminous Lives*, 3–8.
4. Jamgön Kongtrul Lodrö Taye, *Catalog*, 21.
5. *The Treasury of Precious Instructions. gDams ngag rin po che'i mdzod* (*DNZ*), 12 vols. (Delhi: N. Lungtok and N. Gyaltsan, 1971–1972). Known as the Kundeling printing.
6. *The Treasury of Precious Instructions. gDams ngag rin po che'i mdzod* (*DNZ*), 18 vols. (Delhi: Shechen Publications, 1998). Known as the Shechen printing.

Translator's Introduction

1. Lha bla ma Ye shes 'od, 947–1019/1024. Lha Lama, literally "divine lama," is an epithet that means "royal monk" and indicates a figure from a ruling family who has received ordination as a Buddhist monk.
2. Lha bla ma Byang chub 'od, d.u.
3. mTho lding. The name is also pronounced Toding.
4. Nag tsho lo tsā ba, 1011–1064. This epithet means "the translator from the Naktso clan." His ordination name was Tsultrim Gyalwa (Tshul khrims rgyal ba). He was sent to India with the goal of inviting Atiśa to Tibet and remained an important disciple for an extended period.
5. *Byang chub lam gyi sgron ma.*
6. 'Brom ston pa rGyal ba'i 'byung gnas, 1004/5–1064.
7. The name of the source text is identified as *The Shorter Treatise on the Sevenfold Tradition of Deities and Teachings* (*Lha chos bdun ldan chung ba*); however, no exemplar has been located. *ngo mtshar bka' ni sde snod gsum po ste / gdams pa skyes bu gsum gyis phyug pa yin / bka' gdams rin chen gser gyi phreng ba la / 'gro ba gang gis bgrangs kyang don yod 'gyur.*
8. *dge lugs*. This is the most familiar among the various names for this tradition.
9. Titled *An Ocean of Auspicious Renown* (*bKra shis grags pa'i rgya mtsho*), this catalog addresses the entire eighteen-volume collection of *The Treasury of Precious Instructions*. As such, it provides insight into the compilers' perspective regarding the organization and makeup of the two Kadam volumes. An English translation by Richard Barron is available as a separate work. See *The Catalog of "The Treasury of Precious Instructions"* (New York: Tsadra Foundation, 2013).
10. *gzhung*. In this context, this term should be taken to mean an authoritative text.
11. **avavāda, gdams ngag*. This term should be understood as referring to teachings that are received orally from a spiritual teacher. *BBhVy* (ff. 130b–131a) gives two classic Indian interpretations of the term: "Instruction is the enjoyment of spoken discourse because it generates correct understanding (**samyag avabodhatvād vādāsvāda ity avavāda, yang dag par rtogs pa'i phyir smra ba'i tshig gi ro myong ba ni gdams ngag ces bya'o*)." Also: "Instruction is the speaking of suitable words to someone after having understood the nature of his or her mind" (**cittam avagamyānukūlavādanam ity avavāda, sems shes nas mthun pa'i tshig smra ba ni gdams ngag*).
12. *āmnāya, man ngag.* While this term is not significantly different in meaning from the previous one that is translated as "instruction," it is meant here in the sense of oral instruction that is of a more restricted or "secret" nature.
13. *zhar byung.*
14. *rjes su 'brel ba.*
15. Po to ba Rin chen gsal, 1027–1105.
16. sPyan snga ba Tshul khrims 'bar, 1038–1103.
17. Phu chung ba gZhon nu rgyal mtsan, 1031–1106.

18. *Thig le bcu drug.*
19. *Byang chub lam gyi rim pa chen mo.*
20. *Byang chub lam gyi rim pa chung ba.*
21. Zhwa dmar rTogs ldan mKha' spyod dbang po, 1350–1405.
22. Bya yul ba gZhon nu 'od, 1075–1138.
23. *Lam rim bsdus don.*
24. *Nyams mgur.*
25. *dben sa snyan brgyud.* Wensa, literally "isolated place," is the name of a hermitage founded by Sönam Chökyi Langpo (bSod nams phyogs kyi glang po, 1439–1504), a figure who was identified as the reincarnation of Khedrup Gelek Pelsang (mKhas grub dGe legs dpal bzang, 1385–1438), one of Je Tsongkhapa's foremost direct disciples. The name of this lineage stems from the next reincarnation of Khedrup Gelek Pelsang—namely, Wensapa Losang Döndrup (dBen sa pa bLo bzang don grub, 1505–1566). Paṇchen Losang Chökyi Gyaltsen is considered to be the reincarnation of this latter figure. This lineage traces its origins to Khedrup Gelek Pelsang and his younger brother Baso Chökyi Gyaltsen (Ba so ba Chos kyi rgyal mtshan, 1402–1473) and is regarded as preserving some of the most esoteric instructions of the Geluk tradition.
26. *adhyeṣaṇa, gsol 'debs.*
27. **ṣaṭ prayogadharma, sbyor ba'i chos drug.* This is the name of a devotional exercise that is meant to be carried out at the beginning of each meditation session on the Lamrim instruction.
28. *Bodhicaryāvatāra, Byang chub sems dpa'i spyod pa la 'jug pa.*
29. *shin tu rgyas pa'i lugs.*
30. *rgya chen spyod brgyud.*
31. Sha ra ba Yon tan grags, 1070–1141. Sharawa was an early Kadampa master who propagated the system of instruction taught by Potowa Rinchen Sel (Po to ba Rin chen gsal, 1027–1105).
32. *A Lamrim Text Composed by the Spiritual Teacher Zhang Sharwapa Yönten Drak* (*dGe ba'i bshes gnyen zhang shar ba pa yon tan grags kyis mdzad pa'i lam rim*). Lhasa: Ser gtsug nang bstan dpe rnying 'tshol bsdu phyogs bsgrigs khang, 2019. See pages 161–68 of this edition.
33. *Byang chub gzhung lam.*
34. *tshe 'di blos gtong ba.*
35. *hīnapuruṣa, skyes bu chung ngu.* Verse 3 of Atiśa's *Lamp for the Path* defines this type of individual as follows: "One who by various means / seeks only the happiness / of samsara for him- or herself / is known as a lesser person." The phrase "happiness of samsara" here refers to the temporary Buddhist goal of an "elevated status," which means a favorable future rebirth as a human being or a worldly god. See also ch. 4, "The Brilliant Illumination of the Path to Enlightenment," note 19.
36. *A Lamp for the Eyes That Requires Little Difficulty: A Treatise for Those Who Mentally Abandon the World* (*'Jig rten blos btang rnams kyi bstan bcos tshegs

chung mig gi sgron me), in Collected Works (Kathmandu: Ven. Khenpo Shedup Tenzin and Lama Thinley Namgyal, 1998), pp. 259–69.

37. gTsang pa rgya ras Ye shes rdo rje, 1161–1211.
38. *lakṣaṇa, mtshan nyid.*
39. *samaya, dam tshig.* The sense of the original Sanskrit term is that of a spiritual "agreement" or an "obligatory observance." The Tibetan equivalent is typically translated as "pledge" or "commitment." Commentaries interpret it to mean a precept that is not to be violated or transgressed (*alaṅghya, 'da' bar mi bya ba*). While the term is often associated with a formal system of Buddhist vows, these are meant to be understood as principles that an ascetic should pledge him- or herself to observe as a committed practitioner.
40. *Adhyāśayasaṃcodanasūtra, Lhag pa'i bsam pa bskul ba'i mdo.* All of the citations from this sūtra can also be found in Śāntideva's *Compendium of Training* (*Śikṣāsamuccaya, bsLab pa kun las btus pa*).
41. *lābhasatkāra, rnyed pa dang bkur sti.*
42. *blo sbyong.* The term "mind" refers to the altruistic attitude of a bodhisattva. This form of practice is made up of special techniques for cultivating such a mind.
43. *bLo sbyong don bdun ma.*
44. 'Chad ka ba Ye shes rdo rje, 1101–1175.
45. rGyal sras Thogs med bzang po, 1295–1369. The root text is the second item in vol. 3, and the commentary from which it was extracted appears in vol. 4.
46. *mdzad pa.* This verb, literally "to do" or "to make," can be understood to mean that Chekawa is considered to have been the individual who first compiled the instruction into its seven sections.
47. *bLo sbyong brgya rtsa.* This collection was compiled in the fifteenth century by the Sakya figures Zhönu Gyalchok (gZhon nu rgyal mchog, d.u.) and his disciple Könchok Gyaltsen (dKon mchog rgyal mtshan, 1300–1469). The most readily accessible edition of this collection is a wood-block edition that was published in Lhasa in the early twentieth century by the Zhide (bZhi sde) printing house.
48. For reasons that are not known, the final three items enumerated in this listing do not actually appear in the published wood-block edition.
49. Se sPyil bu ba Chos kyi rgyal mtshan, 1121–1189. He spent twenty-four years as a disciple of Chekawa Yeshe Dorje. Se is a clan name; he is known as Jilbuwa in recognition of the eponymous Jilbu Monastery that he founded.
50. This catalog (*dkar chag*) has its own title, *The Heat-Dispelling Moon* (*gDung sel zla ba*). The word *moon* in this title is a metaphor for such virtuous qualities as those of the Mind Training practice and is meant to indicate that the instruction has the ability to dispel the "heat," or torment, of the mental afflictions.
51. Since the wording of this title appears explicitly in the poem listed as item eleven, Thupten Jinpa's English translation assigned this title exclusively to item eleven.

52. This is item eight in ch. 14, "A Listing of the Mahāyāna Works on Mind Training."
53. *gyer sgom rdo rje'i glu dbyangs.*
54. *bdag gzhan mnyam brje.* This expression refers to a two-step practice that is taught in ch. 8 of Śāntideva's *Entry into the Conduct That Leads to Enlightenment* (*Bodhicaryāvatāra, Byang chub sems dpa'i spyod pa la 'jug pa*). The first stage, meditating on the equality between oneself and others, seeks to develop an attitude in which the welfare of others is recognized as being as important as one's own. The second stage, exchanging oneself and others, is not pursued until the first stage has been mastered. It consists of developing an altruistic attitude in which the practitioner exchanges concern for his or her welfare with concern for others.
55. *gtong len.* Giving is cultivated by reflecting intently on beings toward whom we generate compassion, and Taking is cultivated by doing the same for beings toward whom we generate loving-kindness. In the former exercise, the practitioner visualizes giving his or her body, wealth, and virtue to others in order to provide them with various kinds of happiness. For Taking, the practitioner cultivates compassion by visualizing that he or she removes the suffering of others and dissolves it into their own heart.
56. This section title doesn't appear in ch. 14, "A Listing of the Mahāyāna Works on Mind Training"; however, vol. 4 does include this heading just as it appears in the catalog *The Heat-Dispelling Moon.* This section begins with a short instruction that is not identified by name; nevertheless, Thupten Jinpa's translation assigns the title to this unnamed instruction, which he translates as *An Instruction on Purifying Negative Karma.* We have placed the instruction at the beginning of item thirteen, which is titled *A Mahāyāna System of Practice for Eliminating Grudges.*
57. That is, *An Instruction on Purifying Negative Karma.*
58. *sde dkrug.* This act occurs when a state of dissension is created within a group of monks or nuns through divisive speech that results in the formation of two opposing factions, with each one being comprised of at least four individuals.
59. *karṇaparaṃparā, snyan brgyud.* This expression refers to a teaching that is only transmitted orally. In some cases, such teachings eventually find their way into written form.
60. *rlabs po che'i sems.*
61. *mi bsgul ba'i sems.*
62. *rdo rje lta bu'i sems.*
63. The wording of this section heading does appear right after the end of item nineteen, *Eight-Sessions Mind Training,* on the same folio page. Immediately following that, the separate title of item twenty—called *A Mahāyāna Mind Training Instruction That Dispels Obstacles*—is stated.
64. gLang ri thang pa rDo rje seng ge, 1054–1123.
65. That is, after explaining the six preliminary practices in some detail, the seven

topics of the teaching are simply listed followed by a few brief statements about the practice itself.

66. That is, the work titled *An Essential Summary of the Method of Practice in the System of the Stages of the Path to Enlightenment.*
67. Jamgön Kongtrul's catalog (see note 16, this chapter) lists an aspirational prayer that is referred to as *The Seeds of Eternal Happiness* (*gTan bde'i sa bon*). Either the title that appears here in vol. 4 is an alternate name or it is a replacement for the work mentioned in the catalog.
68. *Zhus lan nor bu'i phreng ba.* An English translation is contained in Thupten Jinpa's translation, *The Book of Kadam*, 65–393. Since Drom Tönpa is regarded as the patriarch of the Kadam tradition, this longer work is also known as the *Father's Teaching* (*Pha chos*).
69. rGyal ba rgya mtsho.
70. *Za ma tog gi bkod pa.* (Toh. 116)
71. *Dvikramatattvabhāvanā, Rim gnyis kyi de ko na nyid bsgom pa zhes bya ba'i zhal gyi lung.* The original Sanskrit is not extant.
72. *abhiṣeka, dbang.* The term "consecration" is related to the Sanskrit term, which literally means "sprinkling" to indicate the anointing of a disciple with sacred water as a form of purification. The term "empowerment" derives from the Tibetan equivalent, which suggests that the ceremony is a necessary prerequisite that empowers or authorizes the disciple to engage in the esoteric practice.
73. Gung thang dKon mchog bstan pa'i sgron me, 1762–1823. He is the third figure in this reincarnation lineage.
74. *zin bris.* This term is used to describe notes taken by disciples of a spiritual teacher's oral discourse. Many such compilations are edited into texts that are included in the teacher's Collected Works. In this instance, a recitation text together with related explanatory instructions has been created on the basis of an oral teaching that was given on the practice.
75. Brak dgon dKon mchog bstan pa rab rgyas, 1801–1866. The forty-ninth abbot of Labrang Tashi Kyil Monastery, located in the Amdo region of Tibet.
76. *Yi dam rgya mtsho'i sgrub thabs rin chen 'bung gnas*, in Collected Works, vol. 15.
77. *anujñā, rjes su gnang ba.* The term is meant to indicate that by having received the ritual's blessing, a disciple obtains permission to meditate on a particular deity, recite its mantra, and so on. In a true permission ritual, the officiating lama must invoke the particular deity several times in order to confer specific blessings associated with its body, speech, and mind.
78. *lung 'bogs tshul.* This usage of the expression suggests that the lama is merely providing the disciples with a blessing that will authorize them to carry out the sādhana ritual themselves.
79. *sgrub thabs.* In the present context, this term—which literally translates as a "means of accomplishment"—refers to a means of accomplishing any form of a range of spiritual practices. Often, it is a ritual for invoking a particular deity, identifying with it, and engaging in the spiritual practices that will enable the

practitioner to gain the forms of realization that promote attainment of the ultimate goal.

80. See note 74 (this chapter).
81. dPal spungs thub bstan chos 'khor gling. Palpung is a major Karma Kagyu monastery in the Derge region of Kham. It was established in 1727 by the Eighth Tai Situ, Chökyi Jungne, on the site of an earlier Drigung Kagyu monastery. It was the seat of Jamgön Kongtrul Lodrö Taye.
82. sNyug la paṇ chen Ngag dbang grags pa, 1458–1515.
83. 'Jam mgon Kun dga' bsod nams, 1597–1659/1660.
84. Kun dga' grol mchog, 1507–1566.
85. *Lam gyi gtso ba rnam gsum.*
86. Tsha kho Ngag dbang grags pa, b. 1365. Tsakho is a region in the area of Gyalrong. Records indicate the letter was sent in 1398.
87. *niḥsaraṇa, nges par 'byung ba.* The Sanskrit and Tibetan equivalents of this term literally mean "deliverance," a synonym for liberation, or nirvana. In traditional exegesis, this type of usage is described as one in which the cause is figuratively referred to by a term that stands for the result. In other words, the attitude is called "renunciation" or "deliverance" because it is a mind that seeks to achieve the goal of deliverance from samsara.
88. *bodhicitta, byang chub kyi sems.* This attitude, which is described as the aspiration to attain supreme enlightenment for the sake of all sentient beings, marks the entry point to the Mahāyāna path.
89. *samyagdṛṣṭi, yang dag pa'i lta ba.* In this context, the term "right view" refers to the wisdom that correctly understands the ultimate nature of all entities to be that they are empty of any self-existent, or real, essence.
90. *tshig 'grel.*
91. dNgul chu Dharmabhadra, 1772–1851. His commentary is titled *The Lamp That Illuminates the Meaning of the Words: A Commentary on the Three Principal Elements of the Path* (*Lam gyi gtso bo rnam gsum gyi ṭīka tshig don gsal bar byed pa'i sgron me*).
92. Paṇ chen bLo bzang chos kyi rgyal mtshan, 1570–1662.
93. **mahāsukhaprabhāsvara, bde chen gyi 'od gsal.*
94. *marmaccheda, gnad du bsnun pa.* The practitioner "pierces" the vital points of the adamantine body by applying force to them with his or her mind during meditation.
95. *grub pa sde bdun.* The seven texts are Mahāsukha Nātha's (a.k.a., Saroruha Vajra) *Guhyasiddhi* (*gSang ba grub pa*); Anaṅga Vajra's *Prajñāviniścayasiddhi* (*Thabs dang shes rab rnam par gtan la dbab pa grub pa*); Indrabhūti's *Jñānasiddhi* (*Ye shes grub pa*); Lakṣmiṅkarā's *Advayasiddhi* (*gNyis med grub pa*); Ḍombi Heruka's *Sahajasiddhi* (*Lhan cig skyes pa'i grub pa*); Dārikapa's *Mahāguhyatatattvopadeśasiddhi* (*Gsang ba chen po'i de kho na nyid grub pa*) and Yoginī Cintā's *Vyaktabhāvānugatatattvasiddhi* (*dNgos po gsal ba'i rjes su 'gro ba'i de kho na nyid grub pa*).
96. *snying po skor gsum.* This expression is a reference to Saraha's three poems

written in doha couplets: *The King's Couplets* (*rGyal po'i do ha*); *The Queen's Couplets* (*bTsun mo'i do ha*); and *The People's Couplets* (*dMangs kyi do ha*).

97. *śamatha, zhi gnas*. See ch. 7, "The Nectar That Is Like Highly Refined Gold," note 181, for a general description of this form of one-pointed concentration.
98. *vipaśyanā, lhag mthong*. This is a form of wisdom practice that can only be developed after first attaining quiescence. See ch. 4, "The Brilliant Illumination of the Path to Enlightenment," note 65 and ch. 10, "The Essence of Nectar," note 290.
99. *śamathavipaśyanāyuganaddha, zhi gnas dang lhag mthog zung du 'brel ba*. This is a form of practice in which quiescence and insight are practiced alternately, as appropriate, as the means of ultimately attaining a transcendent realization.
100. Mang thos kLu sgrub rgya mtsho. Mangtö is an epithet that means simply "learned one." This individual was a disciple of Tsarchen Losal Gyatso (Tshar chen bLo bsal rgya mtsho, 1502–1566) and an important master in the Sakya Lamdre Lopshe transmission lineage.
101. The term "great champion" (*mahāratha, shing rta chen po*) is used most often to refer to the two Indian Mahāyāna masters Nāgārjuna and Asaṅga, who are credited with having established the Buddhist Madhyamaka and Yogācāra schools, respectively. See also ch. 4, "The Brilliant Illumination of the Path to Enlightenment," note 10, and ch. 5, "Verse Compendium of the Spiritual Practices of the Stages of the Path," note 7.
102. *Guidance Manual of the Three Appearances. gSung ngag slob bshad snang gsum gyi khrid yig zla ba bdud rtsi'i thigs phreng skal bzang ku mud gsar pa'i kha 'byed*, in *Sa-skya Lam-'bras Literature Series*, vol. 15 (*ba*), 31–151 (ff. 1b–61a) (Dehra Dun: Sakya Centre, 1983).
103. Jamyang Khyentse Wangpo created the title, inserted the opening verses, and added a statement following the verses. At the end of the text, he also summarized a few lines after the directly quoted material has ended and added the colophon.
104. *gZhan stong dbu ma chen po'i lta khrid rdo rje'i zla ba dri ma med pa'i 'od zer*.
105. *mGon po a ti sha gtsI bor gyur pa'i bka' gdams bla ma rnams mchod cing gsol ba 'debs pa'i cho ga bkra shis grags pa'i rgya mtsho*.
106. See note 76 (this chapter).
107. *sGrub thabs rin 'byung las khol du phyungs pa dzam dkar lha lnga'i sgrub thabs rjes gnang dang bcas pa*.
108. Gri gug ma.
109. See note 78 (this chapter).

1. A Lamp for the Path to Enlightenment: A Mahāyāna Scripture on the Stages of the Path

1. *Theg pa chen po lam gyi rim pa'i gzhung / bKa' gdams gzhung gdams ngag gi rtsa ba*, *DNZ*, vol. 3 (*ga*), pp. 1–8. Second source: In T.PD., vol. 64, pp. 1641–48 (Beijing: Krung go'i bod rig pa'i dpe skrun khang, 1994–2008).

2. Tengyur editions of the root text have a slightly different reading of the second line: "Or facing a holy caitya shrine." This extracanonical version includes the word *chos,* or dharma scripture, and makes the adjective *dam pa* modify that word. Compare this to *BBh*, book 1, ch. 16, which describes the first two of ten types of worship as body worship (*śarīrapūja, sku la mchod pa*) and shrine worship (*caityapūja, mchod rten la mchod pa*). The third type of worship, "face-to-face worship" (*sammukhapūja, mngon sum du mchod pa*), is that which is done in the presence of either of the first two types, as described in this verse.
3. The original Sanskrit of vv. 15–17 is cited in *BCAP*, pp. 25, 26.
4. A fully ordained Buddhist monk; gelong (*dge slong*) in Tibetan.
5. The original Sanskrit of vv. 26–31 is cited in *ŚS*, p. 11.
6. The canonical edition of this verse has "virtuous accumulations" (**śuklasambharād, ge ba'i tshogs rnams*) in place of "virtuous qualities" (**śukladharma, dge ba'i chos rnams*).
7. The canonical edition has the transitive form of this verb (*bsgoms*) instead of the intransitive form (*goms pa*).
8. *Sampuṭa Tantra*, ch. 10, section 4, vv. 7cd–8ab. The original Sanskrit version of these lines are extant.
9. The original Sanskrit of this verse is cited in unpublished digital version of Ratnarakṣita's *Padminī*, ch. 13. Tibetan text: *dPal sdom pa 'byung ba'i rgyud kyi rgyal po chen po'i dka' 'grel pad ma can*, ch. 13. Dg.T. rgyud, vol. 18 (*tsha*), ff. 1b–101b. (Toh. 1420)

2. The Root Text of the Mahāyāna Instruction Known as "The Seven-Point Mind Training"

1. *Theg pa chen po'i gdams ngag blo sbyong don bdun ma'i rtsa ba, DNZ*, vol. 3 (*ga*), pp. 8–11.
2. Changkya Ngawang Losang Chöden's (lCang skya Ngag dbang blo bzang chos ldan, 1672–1714) *Great Secret of the Swift Path* (*gSang chen myur lam*, f. 4a), a commentary on the generation-stage practice of the Ārya Nāgārjuna lineage of the Guhyasamāja system, gives the following description of the meaning of the mantra syllable *oṃ*: "As *oṃ* contains the three syllables *a*, *u*, and *ma*, it symbolizes the three vajras of body, speech, and mind. Because these three syllables combine to form a single syllable, *oṃ* represents the state of Vajradhara in which the three vajras are united inseparably. By reciting the mantra *oṃ* while recalling this meaning, one makes (1) an affirmation to achieve Vajradhara's state and obtains the benefits of (2) auspiciousness, through undertaking to learn and reflect upon the practice in order to achieve that goal; (3) good fortune, by putting into practice the meaning that has been learned; and (4) prosperity, by gaining the power to obtain everything that is desired through carrying out the practice. [Reciting *oṃ* also includes the benefits of] (5) bestowing the wealth of manifold forms of dharma and enabling one to both (6) possess the splendor of

the ultimate state of the inseparable United Pair and (7) achieve the supreme spiritual attainment." The canonical source for these seven qualities is the following passage from the *Vajraśekhara Tantra* (*rDo rje rtse mo*, Dg.K. rgyud, *tha*, f. 156a): "How is the meaning of *oṃ* explained? It is called the mantra that is a holder of riches (**vasuṃdhara, nor bu 'dzin pa*) in that / it bestows (1) the most excellent reward (*vara, mchog*) and (2) wealth (*dhana, nor*). / It possesses the qualities of / (3) splendor (*śrī, dpal*), (4) prosperity (**lakṣmī, g.yang*), and (5) good fortune (*subhaga, skal ba bzang ba*). / It is (6) an affirmation (*pratijñā, dam bca' ba*) to achieve success, and it (7) signifies auspiciousness (*maṅgalam, bkra shis*)." A number of Tibetan commentaries, including *NgG* (f. 26b), interpret the phrase "holder of riches" to mean that the practitioner who recites the mantra *oṃ* while understanding how it represents the inseparable union of a buddha's three vajras will gain an incalculable amount of merit.

3. An expression invoking auspiciousness that literally means "Let there be goodness!"
4. 'Chad ka ba, 1101–1175. He was also known as Yeshe Dorje (Ye shes rdo rje), a name he was given when he took ordination as a novice Buddhist monk (*śrāmanera, dge tshul*). As his family was from the Ja (*bya*) clan, he was also referred to as Ja Chekawa.
5. That is, the main practice of meditating on the ultimate form of enlightenment mind.
6. That is, the post-meditative practice.
7. In Buddhist literature, the external physical world is referred to as a "receptacle" or a "vessel" (*bhājana, snod*).
8. The sentient beings that inhabit the external world are referred to as its "contents" or "essence" (*bcud*).
9. That is, transforming adversity through thought on the basis of ultimate enlightenment mind.
10. gSer ling pa. This is an epithet that means "the one from the Isle of Gold," which may tentatively be reconstructed as Suvarṇadvīpī in Sanskrit. His ordination name was Dharmakīrti, and he is said to have been born into a royal family of the Śrīvijaya kingdom, whose capital was located on the island of present-day Sumatra. Atiśa traveled to the Isle of Gold, accompanied by a contingent of Buddhist monks, to study with this teacher, and it is reported that he remained there for twelve years. See ch. 16, "The Story of Atiśa's Voyage to Sumatra." Atiśa considered Lama Serlingpa to be his most revered teacher because it was under his tutelage that Atiśa was able to develop genuine enlightenment mind. Several texts attributed to this teacher are contained in the Tibetan Tengyur collection.
11. rGyal sras Thogs med bzang po dpal, 1295–1369. Gyalse is an epithet that literally means spiritual "offspring of the Victor" and is understood to be a synonym for a bodhisattva. Its use here is meant to indicate that Tokme Zangpo Pel had achieved that status. The root text presented here was extracted from this mas-

ter's commentary on this teaching system that appears in vol. 4 of *The Treasury of Precious Instructions*.

3. Bodhisattva's Jewel Garland: A Root Text of Mahāyāna Instruction from the Precious Kadam Scripture

1. *Theg pa chen po'i man ngag bka' gdams glegs bam rin po che'i rtsa tshig byang chub sems dpa'i nor bu'i phreng ba*, *DNZ*, vol. 3 (*ga*), pp. 11–14.
2. "Faith" here refers to a profound faith in the law of karma.
3. The Tibetan term *khenpo* (*mkhan po*), which is translated here as "preceptor," can also mean an abbot of a monastery. Here the term refers to spiritual masters who have conferred vows and precepts upon you.
4. The Dg.T. edition reads: "Dispel the ground of hostility and unpleasantness."
5. "Both" here refers to the two ends of the spectrum of one's fluctuating state, namely, self-importance (which arises when one's state of mind is overly excited) and discouragement (which arises when one's state of mind becomes too deflated). The Dg.T. edition reads: "always meditate on emptiness."
6. The Dg.T. edition reads: "strive diligently, with no distinction of day and night."
7. The two defilements are the obscuration of afflictions and the subtle obscurations to omniscience.
8. The Dg.T. edition reads: "are the seven inexhaustible treasures."

4. The Brilliant Illumination of the Path to Enlightenment: A Commentary That Summarizes the Essence of *A Lamp for the Path to Enlightenment*

1. *Byang chub lam gyi sgron ma'i 'grel pa snying por bsdus pa byang chub lam gyi snang ba rab tu gsal ba*, *DNZ*, vol. 3 (*ga*), pp. 15–61.
2. That is, Buddha Śākyamuni.
3. *śāstā*, *ston pa*. This epithet, which literally means "teacher," is a reference to Buddha Śākyamuni.
4. *rgyun mtha'*. Dungkar Losang Trinle's *Great Tibetan Dictionary* (*Dun dkar tshig mdzod chen mo*, s.v. "rgyun mtha'") states: "It is called 'the mental continuum's endpoint' because it is the final state of a being's mind prior to the attainment of buddhahood" (*sangs rgyas ma zin pa'i shes pa'i mtha' yin pas na / rgyun mtha' zhes btags pa yin*).
5. *abhisaṃpratyayākārā śraddhā*, *yid ches kyi dad pa*. Asaṅga's *AS* (p. 6) describes this type of faith as one that is developed in relation to entities that exist as opposed to virtuous entities or entities that are capable of being attained. While this faith is often described as the type that believes in the doctrine of karma, in the Lamrim tradition this type of faith is also meant to be developed toward one's spiritual teacher, and it consists of the confidence and conviction that such an individual is a genuine source from whom to receive the Buddha's teaching.

6. That is, the Tibetan Kadam lineage established by Atiśa.
7. The Old Kadam (*bka' gdams rnying ma*) tradition refers to the lineage of teachers from the time of Drom Tönpa to Je Tsongkhapa; New Kadam (*bka' gdams gsar ma*) is another name for the Geluk tradition, which has preserved the Kadam instructions in several Lamrim lineages.
8. These two lines are a reference to the Kadam tradition. The syllable *ka* (*bka'*) refers to the word of the Buddha, and *dam* (*gdams*) is short for personal instruction. The name is interpreted as meaning that the followers of Atiśa viewed the Buddha's word as the supreme form of personal instruction.
9. That is, Atiśa's root text, *A Lamp for the Path to Enlightenment*.
10. *mahāratha, shing rta chen po*. This term is used most often to refer to the two great Indian Mahāyāna masters Nāgārjuna and Asaṅga, who are credited with having established the Buddhist Madhyamaka and Yogācāra schools, respectively. See also ch. 5, "A Verse Compendium of the Spiritual Practices of the Stages of the Path," note 7. The Sanskrit term *ratha* (*shing rta*), which literally means "chariot," is also used to designate a person as a "warrior," a "champion," or a "hero." In this spiritual context, it is used metaphorically to refer to a great Buddhist philosophical innovator.
11. Vikramaśīla was an important Buddhist monastic university founded by the Pāla king Dharmapāla in the late eighth or early ninth century. Its ruins are located near the city of Bhagalpur district in India's Bihar State. Atiśa was in residence there prior to his coming to Tibet in 1040.
12. The author's formal ordination name was Dīpaṃkara Śrījñāna (dPal Mar me mdzad ye shes, 982–1055).
13. *mahāpaṇḍita, mkhas pa chen po*. A traditional Indian title denoting a scholar who has mastered five major and five minor branches of learning (*vidyāsthāna, rig pa'i gnas*). The five major sciences are the "inner science" of religion and philosophy (*adhyātmavidyā, nang don rig pa*); the science of logic (*hetuvidyā, gtan tshigs rig pa*); the science of grammar (*śabdavidyā, sgra rig pa*); the science of medicine (*cikitsāvidyā, gso ba rig pa*); and the science of crafts and mechanical skills, such as carpentry, architecture, making jewelry, metalworking, and so on. (*śilpavidyā, bzo rig pa*). The five minor sciences are poetry (*kāvya, snyan ngag*); word meaning and usage (*abhidhāna, mngon brjod*); prosody (*chanda, sdeb sbyor*); performing arts (*nāṭaka, zlos gar*); and astronomy/astrology (*jyoti, dkar rtsis*).
14. *jo bo rje*. Literally "the Great Lord," this is another epithet for Atiśa.
15. dPal ldan A ti sha. One interpretation of the Indian name Atiśa is explained in Tibetan texts as meaning "preeminent one" (*phul du byung ba*). See reference in the translator's introduction.
16. *rgyal po'i rigs*. One of the four principal Indian castes, it is the ruling or military caste.
17. The exact nature of this place name remains the subject of speculation. The prevalent view today is that Atiśa was born in Vikramapura, a major city in the kingdom of the Pāla dynasty.

18. rDo rje gdan. Literally "Adamantine Seat," this is the Buddhist name for Bodhgaya, the site of Buddha Śākyamuni's enlightenment in the current Indian state of Bihar.
19. *abhyudaya, mngon par mtho ba*. This term refers to the temporary goal of a favorable rebirth that will permit one to continue to practice the Buddhist path to either of the two ultimate goals of nirvana and supreme enlightenment. *MSAVṛBh* (vol. 126, f. 5a) states: "An elevated status means a samsaric existence that is possessed of wealth and happiness."
20. *niḥśreyasa, nges par legs pa*. This term literally means "the state that has no better," of which there are two forms. The first is the state of nirvana that consists of deliverance or liberation from samsara and is achieved through the Hīnayāna path. The second is the supreme enlightenment of buddhahood, also known as the state of "nonabiding nirvana" (*apratiṣṭhitanirvāṇa, mi gnas pa'i mya ngan las 'das pa*), which is the goal of the Mahāyāna path.
21. Nag tsho lo tsā ba, 1011–1064. This epithet means "the translator from the Naktso clan." His ordination name was Tsultrim Gyalwa (Tshul khrims rgyal ba). He was sent to India with the goal of inviting Atiśa to Tibet. He served as his translator in Tibet and was also a disciple for an extended period.
22. *bsTod pa brgyad cu pa*. The most readily accessible complete version of this text is found in *The Anthology of Precious Kadampa Writings*, *Legs par bshad pa bka' gdams rin po che'i gsung gi gces btus nor bu'i bang mdzod* (Delhi: D. Tsondu Senghe, 1985), pp. 30–39.
23. See note 10 (this chapter).
24. *chu bo gsum 'dres kyi man ngag*. The three systems of instruction are the ones known as the Lineage of Extensive Conduct (*rgya chen spyod brgyud*), the Lineage of the Profound View (*zab mo lta brgyud*), and the Lineage of Powerful Conduct (*rlabs chen spyod brgyud*). The first lineage was transmitted by Buddha Śākyamuni to Maitreya, who taught it to Asaṅga; the second was transmitted to Mañjuśrī, who taught it to Nāgārjuna; and the third was also transmitted by Mañjuśrī, who then taught it to Śāntideva.
25. The two Indian teachers are identified as Vidyākokila the Younger (Rig pa'i khu byug chung ba; also known as Avadhūtipa), from whom Atiśa learned Madhyamaka doctrine, and Lama Serlingpa, from whom he learned Yogācāra doctrine.
26. These three reasons are known as the three great attributes (*khyad chos chen po gsum*) of this teaching system.
27. While the outline identifies four sections, the Tibetan text here only mentions the first three. Since the outline of Jamgön Kongtrul's work is clearly based on the structure of the Paṇchen Lama, Losang Chökyi Gyaltsen's commentary on Atiśa's root text, we have added the fourth section as it is indicated in that latter text.
28. *byang chub*. Like the Sanskrit *buddha*, the noun *bodhi* also derives from the verbal root *budh*, which includes such meanings as "to awaken" and "to perceive." As with the Tibetan translation for the word *buddha*—*sang gye* (*sangs*

rgyas)—the Tibetan translation for *bodhi* is also made up of two syllables, *jang chup*. In both cases, the first syllable indicates the "elimination" of all faults, and the second syllable represents the attainment of complete "realization."

29. *byang*. This is the translation of the first syllable in the Tibetan word for enlightenment—that is, *jang*.
30. *chub*. This is the translation of the second syllable in the Tibetan word for enlightenment—that is, *chup*.
31. *yathāvadbhāvikatā, ji lta ba yod pa nyid.*
32. *yāvadbhāvikatā, ji snyed ba yod pa nyid.*
33. *mngon pa'i chos* also *chos mngon pa*. This refers to the collection of Buddhist canonical writings that primarily address doctrinal matters and thus are related to, among the three Buddhist trainings, the training of wisdom. In the Indian Sarvāstivāda tradition, this collection was said to be made up of seven treatises. Only a portion of this literature was translated into Tibetan.
34. *UV* (ch. 21, v. 5cd) states: "I have conquered all evil qualities; therefore, Upagā, I am a victor (*jina, rgyal ba*)." The same text (ch. 21, v. 4cd) states: "And, throughout the worlds, including those of the gods, I am the victor who has defeated Māra."
35. *Lalitavistara* (ch. 25, v. 17a) states: "Arise, you who have been victorious in your battle. . . ."
36. *āgama, lung. AK* (ch. 8, v. 39ab) states: "The true dharma of the Master is twofold; its nature is that of doctrine and attainment." *AKBh* (Sanskrit edition, p. 429) states: "'Doctrine' means the collections of sūtra, vinaya, and abhidharma teachings." *AKBh* (p. 429) also states: "The dharma of realization is represented by the spiritual qualities conducive to enlightenment" (*bodhipakṣyā, byang chub kyi phyogs dang mthun pa rnams*).
37. *AKV* (vol. 4, p. 1102) states: "In the case of the passage 'What is the dharma? It is the eightfold noble path,' this is a reference to the dharma as represented by spiritual practice (*pratipattidharma, sgrub pa'i chos*). This aspect of the dharma is also often described as the "dharma of realization" (*adhigamadharma, rtogs pa'i chos*).
38. *rtogs pa*. This term usually is translated as "realization" and is identified with the "dharma of realization" (*adhigamadharma, rtogs pa'i chos*). However, the text here seems to be addressing a different form of the dharma, which more properly refers to the results that are attained through spiritual practice. For example, *AKV* (vol. 4, p. 1102) describes a third meaning of dharma as "the dharma that is the fruit of spiritual practice" (*phaladharma, 'bras bu'i chos*): "Similarly, in the phrase 'I go for refuge to the dharma,' this is a reference to the dharma that is the fruit of spiritual practice—that is, it refers to nirvana." This seems to more closely match the sense of the phrase "dharma of attainment" in this instance.
39. *avetyaprasāda, shes nas dad pa thob pa*. In the strictest sense, "faith born of insight" does not arise until after one has achieved a direct realization of ultimate truth during the seeing path. Canonical sources describe this type of faith

as being of four kinds: faith born of insight regarding the Buddha, faith born of insight regarding dharma, faith born of insight regarding the sangha, and the pure forms of conduct that are dear to āryas (*āryakāntāni śīlāni*, *'phags pa dgyes pa'i tshul khrims rnams*).

40. *skyabs gnas.* That is, the lamas and the Three Jewels.

41. *Triśaraṇasaptati* (*gSum la skyabs su 'gro ba bdun cu pa*, v. 33) states: "Because the Buddha, the dharma, and, likewise, the sangha / cannot be divided, by even a billion / of Māra's minions, therefore the community is called the sangha." *AKBh* (Sanskrit edition, p. 216) states: "Whoever goes for refuge to the sangha, goes for refuge to the spiritual qualities that qualify those who are still undergoing training [*śaikṣa*, *slob pa*; that is, āryas who have not yet attained the status of an arhat] and those who have no need for further training [*aśaikṣa*, *mi slob pa*; that is, arhats] as the individuals who make up the sangha community. Those spiritual qualities are the ones that, through having been achieved, cause the eight types of āryas to remain united as a community, in the sense that they cannot be separated from their devotion to the path."

42. The four fruits of the path are stream-enterer, once-returner, nonreturner, and arhat. The eight types of spiritual persons are differentiated on the basis of either being an individual who is seeking one of these four fruits or an individual who has already achieved it.

43. *adhyaśaya*, *lhag pa'i bsam pa.* Je Tsongkhapa's *Great Treatise on the Stages of the Path to Enlightenment* (*Lam rim chen mo*, f. 193a) describes this attitude as a deeply felt form of courage that accepts the duty to provide all beings with every form of happiness and free them from every form of suffering. Asaṅga devotes an entire chapter of the *BBh* (book 2, ch. 3) to this topic. He defines the term (English translation, p. 513) as "the conviction (*adhimokṣa*, *mos pa*), understanding (*pratyavagama*, *so sor rtog pa*), and determination (*niścaya*, *nges par 'byed pa*) regarding a buddha's qualities, which are preceded by faith and the discernment of entities."

44. *lha bla ma.* Literally "divine lama," this epithet indicates a royal figure who has received ordination as a Buddhist monk.

45. *skyes bu.*

46. These lines are from the verse text known as the *Blue Udder* (*Be'u bum sngon po*), which was composed by Geshe Dölpa Marshurpa Sherap Gyatso (dGe bshes Dol pa dmar zhur pa shes rab rgya mtsho, 1059–1131). The work is considered a record of the manner in which the Kadampa master Potowa Rinchen Sel (Po to ba Rin chen gsal, 1027–1105) taught the Lamrim instruction.

47. See note 19 (this chapter).

48. *svarga*, *mtho ris.* In native Tibetan literature this term is usually understood to mean "the status of being reborn as a worldly god or a human being." However, the literal meaning of the original Sanskrit term is that of "an abode of light" or a "celestial realm" and thus typically meant rebirth in the region of a worldly class of gods and therefore not rebirth as a human being.

49. *pha rol tu phyin pa.* A number of interpretations of this term are found in Buddhist literature. Perhaps the most familiar one is that it means to have "gone to the far shore," which is understood to mean attainment of the ultimate enlightenment of a buddha. The six practices of generosity, morality, patience, effort, meditative absorption, and wisdom are also referred to as "perfections" in that they are the means by which to reach that enlightenment. Sometimes, the list is expanded to ten perfections, which adds those of skillful means, aspirational prayer, power, and knowledge.
50. They are the generation stage (*utpattikrama, bskyed rim*) and the completion stage (*sampannakrama, rdzogs rim*).
51. *Viniścayasaṃgrahaṇī, rNam par gtan la dbab pa bsdu ba* (Toh. 4038). This is one of the works that make up the collection of Indian Yogācāra literature known as The Five Sections on the Stages (*sa sde lnga*). In his *Great Treatise on the Stages of the Path* (*Lam rim chen mo*, f. 59a), Je Tsongkhapa identifies the *Collection of Determinations* (Dg.T., vol. 52, ff. 161b–165a) as the principal source for this formulation of three types of person. *The Anthology of Precious Kadampa Writings* (*Legs par bshad pa bka' gdams rin po che'i gsung gi bces btus nor bu'i bang mdzod*, pp. 12–24) quotes this material extensively and provides some analysis in the form of interlinear notes.
52. Vasubandhu presents a description of the three types of person in the following verses from his *AKBh* (Sanskrit edition, p. 182): "A lesser person, by various means, seeks happiness within his own continuum. / A middling person seeks only an end to suffering and not happiness, for that is a seat of suffering. // The highest person seeks the happiness of others through the suffering of his or her own continuum, / as well as a complete end to suffering, because the suffering of others is a cause of suffering for him or her."
53. *LRCh* (f. 59b; English translation, vol. 1, p. 132) cites several verses from the opening portion of *A Collection of Words of Praise That Constitute Instruction for Meditating on the Conventional Form of Enlightenment Mind* (*Kun rdzob byang chub kyi sems bsgom pa'i man ngag yi ger bris pa*). The passage identifies "conduct that brings about happy migratory states" (i.e., practices for a lesser person) and "conduct that leads to peace" (i.e., the practices for a middling person) as subordinate elements (*aṅga, yan lag*) of the path to the highest good (i.e., the Mahāyāna). See listing in bibliography under the author Aśvaghoṣa.
54. That is, in the system that is taught in Atiśa's root text.
55. This is an epithet for a buddha. Asaṅga states in his *Stage of a Bodhisattva* (English translation, p. 165): "[Buddha] is the Sugata because he has attained [the state of] supreme excellence and because he has attained it irreversibly." He also states in his *Commentary on Recollection of the Buddha* (f. 13b): "The term 'sugata' (*bde bar gshegs pa*) indicates one who has reached that place that ought to be reached. Thus, the Sugata is one who has fared well, like a fever that has been properly dispelled in the sense that it will not return. The Sugata is [also] one who has attained a realization that is complete. [That is,] he is like a

pitcher that is completely full because he has realized everything that needs to be known without remainder."

56. *BCA*, ch. 1, v. 9.
57. *bodhisattva, byang chub sems dpa'.*
58. *Śikṣāsamuccaya, bsLab pa kun las btus pa.*
59. *BCA*, ch. 1, v. 24.
60. *catvāri saṃgrahavastūni, bsdu ba'i dngos po bzhi.* The four principles are generosity (*dāna, sbyin pa*); agreeable speech (*priyavaditā, snyan par smra ba*); beneficial conduct (*arthacaryā, don spyod pa*); and sameness of purpose (*arthasamānatā, don mthun pa*).
61. *mūlāpatti, rtsa ba'i ltung ba.* Committing a root transgression causes one to destroy the system of vows. In the system established by Je Tsongkhapa and adhered to by his followers, the four root transgressions described in the morality chapter of *BBh* are combined with fourteen that are based on the passages from the *Ākāśagarbha Sūtra* that Śāntideva cites in his *Compendium of Training* (*Śikṣāsamuccaya, bsLab pa kun las btus pa*), to make a total of eighteen.
62. *āsrava, zag pa.* "Outflow" is a synonym for the more common term "mental affliction" (*kleśa, nyon mongs*). *AKBh* (p. 308) states: "They are the outflows because they cause beings to sit [that is, abide or remain] in samsara and because they flow out through the wounds of the six bases [that is, the five sense faculties and the mind] into the three realms that range from the peak of existence to Avīci hell." Asaṅga gives the following description of the term (*AS*, p. 49): "There are three types of outflows: the desire outflows [*kāmāsrava, 'dod pa'i zag pa*; that is, all the mental afflictions of the desire realm with the exception of ignorance]; the existence outflows [*bhāvāsrava, srid pa'i zag pa*; that is, all the mental afflictions of the form and formless realms with the exception of ignorance]; and the ignorance outflows [*mohāsrava, ma rig pa'i zag pa*; that is, the ignorance that is associated with all three realms]. They are called 'outflows' because they cause the mind to be sent forth in a stream-like manner. How, then, do they do this? The desire outflows cause it to be sent forth in a manner that is directed outwardly; the existence outflows cause it to be sent forth in a manner that is directed inwardly; and the ignorance outflows constitute the basis for causing it to be sent forth in both of these ways." In the morality chapter of *The Stage of a Bodhisattva*, Asaṅga uses the term "perturbation" (*paryavasthāna, kun nas dkris pa*) to describe a lesser, middling, and great form of mental affliction in relation to the root transgressions of the bodhisattva vows. Asaṅga glosses the noun several times. *AS* (p. 47) states: "They are perturbations because they overpower the mind by disturbing it repeatedly." Also, *YBh* (p. 167) states: "They are perturbations because they occur repeatedly." Although use of this term is not limited to them, abhidharma literature identifies the following eight secondary mental afflictions as being specifically associated with this term: torpor, sleep, excitation, regret, envy, stinginess, shamelessness, and absence of abashment. The relevant passage in *The Stage of a Bodhisattva* that uses this term in

relation to the bodhisattva vows states: "Moreover, a bodhisattva does not lose the acceptance of the bodhisattva system of moral discipline by committing any of these four acts that represent an extreme form of defeat if they are done on the basis of a lesser or middling perturbation. However, he or she does lose it if they are committed on the basis of a great perturbation. When [the basis for committing any of these acts is such that] a bodhisattva does not develop even a small amount of shame and abashment because he or she has engaged continually in these four acts that represent an extreme form of defeat, and due to that lack of shame or abashment, he or she is both pleased with and delights in that conduct, and he or she looks upon that very conduct as a good quality, this should be understood as constituting a great perturbation."

63. *duścarita, nyes byas*. In his commentary on bodhisattva morality (*Byang chub gzhung lam*), Je Tsongkhapa enumerates forty-six secondary offenses or misdeeds based on the descriptions that are presented in the morality chapter of *BBh* (see English translation, pp. 269–300). These offenses are further defined as being either afflicted or free of affliction, depending on the circumstances in which they are committed and the attitude of the practitioner.

64. *abhijñā, mngon par shes pa*. See *A Lamp for the Path to Enlightenment*, v. 38. Asaṅga's *BBh* (part 1, ch. 5) discusses six forms of supernatural knowledge. They are miraculous powers (*ṛddhi, rdzu 'phrul*); the divine ear (*divyaṃ śrotra, lha'i rna ba*); knowledge of diverse states of mind (*cetaḥparyāyajñāna, sems kyi rnam grangs shes pa*); recollection of former existences (*pūrvanivāsānusmṛti, sngon gyi gnas rjes su dran pa*), the divine eye (*divyaṃ cakṣu, lha'i mig*) that perceives the circumstances of sentient beings' death and rebirth, as well as remote objects and very subtle objects; and the realization that the outflows have been terminated (*āsravakṣayajñāna, zag pa zad pa shes pa*).

65. *vipaśyanā, lhag mthong*. A monastic text of Sera Me College states: "The definition of insight is the form of wisdom that rests upon quiescence as its foundation and that, on the strength of analyzing its object, is supported by the extraordinary ease of the mental factor called agility." Regarding the mental factor called agility (*prasrabdhi, shin tu sbyangs pa*), *AS* (p. 6) states: "What is agility? It is a fitness (*karmaṇyatā, las su rung ba nyid*) of the body and mind that is attained through having quelled the indisposition of the body and mind." *PSV* (p. 288) states: "Indisposition (*dauṣṭhulya, gnas ngan len*) is a condition of the body and mind. [Indisposition] of the body is a state of unfitness while [indisposition] of the mind is the seeds of afflicted entities. . . . Fitness of the body is that condition of the body that enables it to engage in activities readily. Fitness of the mind is a distinct mental factor that engenders both joy and a quality of swiftness in the mind of a person who has attained right attention. It is called 'fitness of the mind' because the mind that possesses this mental factor is able to engage a meditation object in an unhindered manner."

66. *ātma, bdag*. Mahāyāna doctrine posits two forms of erring belief: the mistaken apprehension of a real personal self (*gang zag gi bdag*) and the mistaken appre-

hension of real essences (*svabhāva, rang bzhin*). The latter error is principally associated with the mistaken belief that the entities that make up the five heaps are real.

67. This is a reference to Atiśa's *Commentary on the Difficult Points in "A Lamp for the Path to Enlightenment"* (*Byang chub lam gyi sgron ma'i dka' 'grel*).
68. *adhicittaśikṣā, lhag pa sems kyi bslab pa*. This is the second of the three Buddhist trainings, which is also referred to as "the training that relates to one-pointed concentration" (*adhisamādhiśikṣā, lhag pa ting nge 'dzin gyi bslab pa*).
69. The three types of wisdom are described in Asaṅga's *BBh* (part 1, ch. 14). They are the wisdom that realizes ultimate truth, the wisdom that realizes relative truth, and the wisdom that realizes how to act on behalf of sentient beings. The second form of wisdom is understood to mean the wisdom that develops knowledge in the five major branches of learning (see note 13, this chapter).
70. *thun mong ba'i lam*. The non-tantric form of the Mahāyāna path is known as the "common path" because it is also included in the tantric form of the Mahāyāna path.
71. While this is true of both the non-tantric bodhisattva vows and the tantric Mahāyāna vows, if an ordained person commits any of the four offenses that lead to expulsion as prescribed in the prātimokṣa moral code, the prātimokṣa vow cannot be restored. See also note 273 (this chapter).
72. *sanimitta, mtshan bcas*.
73. *animitta, mtshan med*.
74. *RA*, ch. 1, v. 3.
75. The original Sanskrit of this verse is cited at the end of ch. 1 in Āryadeva's *Caryāmelāpakapradīpa*. Despite this attribution, its authorship is generally regarded as uncertain.
76. The terms "impure" and "pure" are somewhat loose translations of a pair of technical Buddhist expressions that literally mean "related to the outflows" (*sāsrava, zag bcas*) and "unrelated to the outflows" (*anāsrava, zag pa med pa*). *AK* (ch. 1, v. 8ab) states: "Those entities that are related to the outflows are the grasping heaps" (*upādānaskandha, nye bar len pa'i phung po*). The term applies to all conditioned entities (*saṃskṛtadharma, 'dus byas kyi chos rnams*), with the exception of the truth of the path, because of their capacity to cause the outflows (see note 62, this chapter)—that is, the mental afflictions—to become stronger. Thus, they are identified with the first two of the four noble truths. In this instance, the four meditative absorptions of the form realm are said to be impure because they are not informed by the wisdom that is the antidote for the mental afflictions, and they therefore do not contribute to the attainment of liberation.
77. *cakravartī, 'khor los sgyur ba*. This is a mythical figure that is described in various traditions of Indian culture, including Buddhism, as a universal monarch who rules in an ethical and benevolent manner. *AKBh* (p. 433): "The wheel-wielders are those [monarchs] whose nature it is to exercise sovereignty by means of a

[magical] wheel." The text further notes that, according to the *Prajñaptiśāstra* (see ch. 10, note 42), there are four kinds: a wheel ruler who possesses a golden wheel and has dominion over all four continents; one who possesses a silver wheel and governs three continents; one who possesses a copper wheel and governs two continents; and one who possesses an iron wheel and governs only one continent. As described in *AK* (ch. 3, vv. 95–96), they do not appear at times when human life spans are shorter than eighty thousand years.

78. This epithet, which literally means "powerful one," is an alternate name for the god Indra, who reigns over the Heaven of the Thirty-Three at the top of Mount Meru. The Tibetan translation (brGya byin) is a reference to the name Śatakratu, another Sanskrit epithet for Indra, which came to be interpreted as meaning the One Who Performed a Hundred Offerings.

79. *'khor lo sgyur ba'i rgyal po*. Here the Tibetan includes the noun "monarch." See note 77 (this chapter) for an explanation of the term "wheel-wielder."

80. *so sor thar pa*. This term refers to the Hīnayāna system of moral discipline that includes seven types of vows that are meant to be observed for the duration of one's life. These are the vows of a fully ordained monk, a fully ordained nun, a probationary nun, a novice monk, a novice nun, a layman, and a laywoman. See also ch. 8, "The Easy Path," note 65 for an explanation of the meaning of the term.

81. *grāhya, gzung ba*. That is, the objects of sensory perception that are erroneously perceived as real external physical objects.

82. This formulation is typically described as "three forms of selflessness that have different degrees of subtlety" (*bdag med phra rags gsum*). The first of the three views is considered the least subtle and can be described as the conventional understanding of the selflessness of the person (*pudgalanairātmya, gang zag gi bdag med*) that is common to most Buddhist philosophical schools, Hīnayāna and Mahāyāna alike. It is a view that is associated mainly with the Hīnayāna followers of the Śrāvakayāna, who develop it on the basis of the doctrine of the four noble truths. The second view is the realization of the rough form of the selflessness of entities (*dharmanairātmya, chos kyi bdag med*), which is associated with the doctrine that there is no real external or physical world. This is often described as the "emptiness" in which grasped objects (i.e., the external world; see note 66, this chapter) and the "grasping" mental states that perceive them (*grāhaka, 'dzin pa*; i.e., the "internal," or subjective, mental aspect of dualistic thought) are recognized as lacking the status of separate real substances. This meditation object is associated with the Hīnayāna followers of the Pratyekabuddhayāna, who develop it on the basis of the doctrine of the twelve limbs of dependent origination. The third view is referred to as the subtle form of the selflessness of entities and is typically recognized to be the object of meditation for the followers of the Madhyamaka, or Middle Way, school. This threefold interpretation is most often identified with the so-called Yogācāra Madhyamaka Svatantrika school (*rnal 'byor spyod pa'i dbu ma rang rgyud pa*).

According to this school, the third view is the exclusive meditation object for Mahāyāna follows of the Middle Way school. However, the commentary here identifies the third view with the unique interpretation of Candrakīrti's so-called Madhyamaka Prasaṅgika school, according to which Hīnayāna followers not only can but actually must meditate on this subtlest form of right view in order to attain their goal of liberation from samsaric existence. This position maintains that the selflessness of the person and the selflessness of entities are both equivalent to the subtlest form of emptiness. Atiśa's Tibetan biographies suggest that he regarded Candrakīrti's interpretation as his own ultimate view, one that he learned from an Indian teacher named Avadhūtipa, and also known as Vidyākokila the Younger (Rig pa'i khu byug chung ba).

83. Sha ra ba Yon tan grags (1070–1141), an important early Kadampa master and lineage holder who was a direct disciple of Potowa Rinchen Sel (see note 46, this chapter).
84. *saṃkleśikapakṣa, kun nas nyon mongs pa'i phyogs.*
85. *vyavadānapakṣa, rnam par sbyang ba'i phyogs.*
86. *Ratnagotravibhāga*, ch. 4, v. 52. See listing in bibliography under Maitreya Nātha.
87. *saṃtati, rgyud.* The basic meaning of this term is a "continuity" or an "unbroken series." In Buddhist literature, it refers to the continuous series of a person's collection of mental states. The interpretation of the second line that is made in the commentary is that a practitioner must first reflect on his or her own samsaric suffering before being able to generate the proper degree of compassion toward the suffering of others. Another interpretation of the line might be that bodhisattvas, due to their compassionate nature, feel mental pain when they recognize others' suffering, and this is what prompts them to strive to remove all sentient beings' suffering. This notion is suggested by Atiśa's autocommentary to *A Lamp for the Path*, which cites the following line from Vasubandhu's *AKBh* (Sanskrit edition, p. 182): "A separate spiritual lineage [that is, of the bodhisattva] comes forth, which is made up of that type of person, such that the individual feels suffering at the suffering of others and feels happiness at their happiness but does not feel the same way about his or her own suffering and happiness." Similarly, Vasubandhu's verse that describes the three types of person (see note 52, this chapter) states that the reason a great person seeks to benefit others is "because the suffering of others is a cause of suffering for him or her." In a larger sense, these two interpretations can be seen as entirely compatible with one another.
88. *jinasuta, rgyal ba'i sras.* This expression is a synonym for a bodhisattva.
89. These five types of bodhisattva are referred to as the bodhisattva that travels in an ox cart (*paśurathagatika, phyugs kyi shing rta lta bus 'gro ba*); the bodhisattva that travels in a cart drawn by an elephant (**hastirathagatika, glang po che'i shin rta lta bus 'gro ba*); the bodhisattva that travels by the sun and the moon (**candrasūryagatika, zla ba dang nyi ma lta bus 'gro ba*); the bodhisattva that travels

by the miraculous powers of a śrāvaka disciple (*śrāvakarddhigatika, nyan thos kyi rdzu 'phrul lta bus 'gro ba*); and the bodhisattva that travels by the miraculous powers of a Tathāgata (**tathāgatarddhigatika, de bzhin gshegs pa'i rdzu 'grul lta bus 'gro ba*). Reference to these five types of bodhisattvas can be found in a number of Mahāyāna sūtras. The *Niyatāniyatāvataramūdrā Sūtra* (Tibetan translation, Toh. 202), in particular, explains how the descriptive phrases are to be understood. The initial distinction that is made regarding them is that the first two types of bodhisattva are at risk of falling away from the Mahāyāna path, while the latter three are not.

90. See ch. 2, "The Root Text of the Mahāyāna Instruction Known as 'The Seven-Point Mind Training,'" note 10.

91. *rten*. This term applies to the consecrated religious objects that are placed on an altar and regarded as the actual body, speech, or mind of enlightened spiritual beings.

92. The reading of the second line that is found in all Tengyur editions only makes reference to a "holy *caitya* shrine"; it does not include the expression "holy *dharma* scripture" (*dam pa'i chos*). However, the version of this line found in Atiśa's autocommentary does include the reference to the holy *dharma*, as in the verse presented here, which seems to have become the standard that is found in later, "extracanonical," editions. *BBh* (book 1, ch. 16) describes the first two of ten types of worship of a buddha as body worship (*śarīrapūjā, sku la mchod pa*) and shrine worship (*caityapūjā, mchod rten la mchod pa*). The third type of worship, "face-to-face worship" (*sammukhapūjā, mngon sum du mchod pa*) is that which is done in the presence of either of the first two types. Regarding the methods of worshiping the dharma and the sangha, *BBh* states simply: "Just as with the description of worship of the tathāgatas, the descriptions of worship of the dharma and worship of the sangha should be understood in a similar way, according to the particular circumstances of those topics."

93. *dvādaśāṅgapravacana, gsung rab yan lag bcu gnyis*. They are discourses (*sūtra, mdo'i sde*); mixed prose and verse (*geya, dbyangs kyis bsnyad pa'i sde*); explanatory responses (*vyākaraṇa, lung du bstan pa'i sde*); verses (*gāthā, tshigs su bcad pa'i sde*); uplifting sayings (*udāna, ched du brjod pa'i sde*); statements of theme or subject matter (*nidāna, gleng gzhi'i sde*); narratives of spiritual lives (*avadāna, rtogs par brjod pa'i sde*); accounts of past events (*itivṛttaka, de lta bu byung ba'i sde*); stories of the Buddha's past lives (*jātaka, skyes pa'i rabs kyi sde*); extensive discourses (*vaipulya, shin tu rgyas pa'i sde*); marvels (*adbhūtadharma, rmad du byung ba'i chos kyi sde*); and instruction (*upadeśa, gtan la phab pa'i sde*).

94. *upacāra, nye bar spyod pa*. While these five objects are often translated as "enjoyment offerings," the original Sanskrit term derives from a verbal root whose meanings include "to serve" and "to attend" and thus the noun indicates forms of religious "service."

95. This saying apparently means that your offerings should be so great as to cause others to think you have been too extravagant.

96. *Bhadracaryapraṇidhāna*, *bZang po spyod pa'i smon lan*. This aspirational prayer appears at the very end of the *Stem Array Sūtra* (*Gaṇḍvyūhasūtra*, *sDong po bkod pa'i mdo*). The sevenfold form of worship is presented in the first twelve verses.
97. *pūjā*, *mchod pa*.
98. *The Preeminent One's Joyful Feast* states: "The ordinary form of taking refuge is an act that is carried out only for the duration of one's current life." (Losang Chökyi Gyaltsen, *Phul byung bzhad pa'i dga' ston*, f. 19b)
99. *bodhimaṇḍa*, *byang chub kyi snying po*.
100. *rdo rje gdan*. See note 18 (this chapter).
101. **akaniṣṭhaghanavyūya*, *'og min stug po bkod pa*.
102. *utkuṭikasthita*, *tsog pur 'dug pa*. The Pali Text Society's Pali-English Dictionary (s.v. "utkuṭikasthita") describes this position as follows: "soles of the feet are firmly on the ground, the man sinks down, the heels slightly rising as he does so, until the thighs rest on the calves and the hams are about six inches or more from the ground. Then, with elbows on knees, he balances himself. . . . When the palms of the hands are also held together upward, it indicates submission."
103. *uttarasaṃga*, *bla gos*. A shawl-like garment worn by ordained Buddhist monks and nuns over the shoulders and upper body.
104. *MSA*, ch. 9, v. 8 *upadravebhyaḥ sarvebhyo apāyād anupāyataḥ | satkāyād dhīnayānāc ca tasmāc charaṇam uttamam*. This verse is actually meant to describe the various ways in which the supreme enlightenment of buddhahood is the highest form of refuge. Vasubandhu's gloss of the last point is that buddhahood can save those practitioners whose spiritual lineage is not fixed (*aniyatagotra*, *ma nges pa'i rigs*) from falling into the Hīnayāna path by ensuring that they fulfill their spiritual potential through pursuing the Mahāyāna path. This point seems to be the one that Sharawa was making in his explanation of why a Mahāyānist should not take refuge in śrāvaka disciples.
105. *śreṣthī*, *tshong dpon*. The head or chief of an association made up of individuals who follow the same trade or industry.
106. *drag po*. This spelling more typically means someone who is "strong" or "powerful," hence the translation "capable"; however, it could also have the same meaning as the more common spelling *drag pa*, which means "better" or "superior."
107. *MSA*, ch. 1, v. 11a. The original Sanskrit of this verse is not extant.
108. Birth is the first element in a standard Buddhist canonical description of the Truth of Suffering: "Further, O mendicants (*bhikṣus*), this verily is the Noble Truth of Suffering. Birth is suffering; old age is suffering; disease is suffering; death is suffering; meeting with disagreeable things is suffering; separation from agreeable things is suffering; not acquiring what is desired and sought after is also suffering. In short, the five closely grasping heaps are suffering." Regarding the suffering of birth, the *Collection of Determinations* (*rNam par gtan la dbab pa bsdu ba*) states: "How is birth suffering? [Birth is suffering] in five ways: (1) it is accompanied by suffering; (2) it is accompanied by a state of indisposition;

(3) it is a source of suffering; (4) it is a source of the mental afflictions; and (5) it possesses the quality of causing us to undergo an unwanted separation." Je Tsongkhapa discusses this passage in *LRCh* (see English translation, vol. 1, pp. 272, 273).

109. *The Preeminent One's Joyful Feast* (f. 21b) states this point somewhat more distinctly: "The *Sayings of Sharawa* (*Sha ra ba'i gsung bgros*) declares: 'The attitude of loving-kindness that is to be meditated upon in this instruction is a unique spiritual awareness that holds all sentient beings as its object (*ālambana, dmigs pa*), and using as a reason the exercise of recalling their kindness, its aspect (*ākāra, rnam pa*) is to cherish them with great affection.' It is apparent that this is the loving-kindness that regards all sentient beings as dear (*yid 'ong gi byams pa*), and it is absolutely necessary that it serve as the cause for, and therefore that it must precede, meditation upon the form of compassion that is one of the elements in The Sevenfold Instruction on Cause and Effect. Although meditation on the generic form of great loving-kindness, which is defined simply as the desire that all sentient beings meet with happiness, does not necessarily need to precede meditation on compassion and serve as its cause, it must be acknowledged that this portion of the treatise does teach that in this instruction system, loving-kindness must be cultivated prior to compassion, and therefore it must also be meditated upon at this stage in the practice."

110. This clause should be understood as describing the loving-kindness that regards all sentient beings as dear (see note 109). This type of loving-kindness can only be developed through cultivating the first three steps of the instruction that are also mentioned here: recognizing or "knowing" all sentient beings as your mothers (*mātṛjña, mar shes*); recalling their kindness (**prasādānusmṛti, drin dran pa*); and acknowledging their past benefits or developing a sense of gratitude for their past benefits (**kṛtavedī, drin du gzo ba*).

111. *cyuti, 'chi 'pho ltung ba.*

112. See *Inner Science of Buddhist Practice*, pp. 105–38, for an overview of the topic titled "The Three States of Suffering."

113. This is an abbreviated paraphrase of a well-known passage that is found in the *Dharmasaṃgīti Sūtra*. A more literal translation of the passage states: "The bodhisattva, the great spiritual being Avalokiteśvara then said the following to the Lord Buddha: 'O Lord, a bodhisattva should not train himself or herself in a great many dharma subjects. O Lord, a bodhisattva should undertake to revere well and penetrate well a single dharma subject. By doing so, all of the spiritual qualities of a buddha will come to be possessed in the palm of his or her hand. What is that single dharma subject? It is, to be specific, great compassion.'"

114. *The Preeminent One's Joyful Feast* (f. 22b) states that detailed explanations of this ritual can be found in the "extensive Lamrim" (i.e., Je Tsongkhapa's *Great Treatise on the Stages of the Path*; cf. English translation, vol. 2, pp. 61–68) and in the "root text and commentary of the *Supreme Path*" (*Lam mchog rtsa 'grel*). The root text of this latter reference is a verse text titled *The Precious Supreme*

Path That Is the Oral Commentary of the True Spiritual Teacher (*Yang dag pa'i dge ba'i bshes gnyen gyi zhal gyi gdams pa lam mchog rin po che*), written by the fourth abbot of Narthang Monastery, Drotön Dutsi Drak (Gro ston bdud rtsi grags, 1153–1232). Dutsi Drak's verse text is embedded in, and forms the framework for, a commentary by Chim Namkha Drak (mChims nam mkha' grags, 1210–1285), the seventh abbot of Narthang, which is titled *The Supreme Mahāyāna Path* (*Theg chen lam mchog*).

115. *sDong po bkod pa'i mdo*. While this text is often described as a distinct sūtra, it makes up the last chapter of the *Avataṃsaka Sūtra* (*Sangs rgyas phal po che*). The final section of this sūtra, where these benefits of enlightenment mind are described, is referred to as the "Liberating Deeds of Maitreya" (*Maitreyavimokṣa, Byams pa'i rnam par thar pa*).

116. *yuvarāja, rgyal tshab*. Literally "young king," this term refers to the fact that Maitreya is the next buddha to appear in this eon.

117. The full verse states: "I go for refuge until enlightenment / to the Buddha, dharma, and supreme assembly. / Through this generosity, and so forth, done by me, / may I attain buddhahood in order to benefit the world." This well-known verse is cited in several of Atiśa's works, including *Instructing a Novice Bodhisattva on Entering the Path* (*Byang chub sems dpa'i las dang po pa'i lam la 'jug pa bstan pa*) and *The Ritual Method for Generating Enlightenment Mind and Receiving the Bodhisattva Vow* (*Sems bskyed pa dang sdom pa'i cho ga'i rim pa*).

118. *Vīradattagṛhapatiparipṛcchāsūtra, Khyim bdag dpas byin gyis zhus pa'i mdo*. This sūtra is found in the *Ratnakūṭa* (*dkon brtsegs*) section of the Tibetan Kangyur.

119. *bodhicittād dhi yat puṇyaṃ tac ca rūpi bhaved yadi | ākāśadhātuṃ saṃpūrya bhūyaś cottari tad bhavet.*

120. *gaṅgāvālikasaṃkhyāni buddhakṣetrāṇi yo naraḥ | dadyāt sadratnapūrṇāni lokanāthebhya eva hi || yaś caikaḥ prāñjalir bhūtvā cittaṃ bodhāya nāmayet | iyaṃ viśiṣyate pūjā yasyānto 'pi na vidyate.*

121. *vaśirāja, dbang gi rgyal po.* A type of extraordinary jewel referenced several times in the *Gaṇḍavyūha Sūtra.*

122. *bali, gtor ma.* This is the name of a cake-like offering whose shape and appearance varies according to customs established within individual lineages. The offering is presented to deities, dharma protectors, and spirits to request their blessings and/or assistance. The original Sanskrit term, *bali,* or variations of it, typically appear in the mantra that is recited as part of the offering.

123. *Sambhāraparikathā* (*Tshogs kyi gtam*; Toh. 4166), v. 1. This is a work written by Vasubandhu.

124. *zhing*. Because the Tibetan conjunction occurs at the end of the first half of this verse, it is included in this part of the commentary. In the English translation, it appears as the first word in the second half of verse 18.

125. Zhang rom. This is another name for Sharawa Yönten Drak (see note 83, this chapter).

126. *sat, dam pa.* This term is meant to refer to earlier spiritual masters of this tradition.
127. *LRCh* (f. 215a) states: "The measure by which to determine that you have mentally abandoned someone is to give rise to the thought 'Now, I will not do anything to help this individual' based on circumstances such as having been treated improperly by that person."
128. *Kāśyapaparivarta, 'Od srungs kyi le'u.* The four black qualities, which will prevent a bodhisattva from remembering his or her enlightenment mind in a future life, are described in the following statement: "O Kāśyapa, the bodhisattva who acquires four qualities will lose his or her enlightenment mind. What are the four? They are to break one's word to a teacher, a guru, or one who is worthy of being venerated; to instill regret in the minds of others about something that does not need to be regretted; to voice words of blame, infamy, and disrepute about beings who are established in the Mahāyāna; and to employ deceitfulness and guile toward others, instead of a superior attitude." The four white qualities are described in these words: "O Kāśyapa, the bodhisattva who acquires four qualities will manifest enlightenment mind in all his or her future rebirths as soon as he or she has taken birth and will not lose it in the interim until he or she is seated at the seat of enlightenment. What are the four? They are not to utter falsehoods even to save your life, or only in jest; to maintain a superior attitude in the presence of all sentient beings, and to remain free of deceitfulness and guile; to develop the conception toward all bodhisattvas that they are the Master, and to fill the four directions with their praises; and to induce all those sentient beings that you have ripened to adopt the goal of unsurpassed true enlightenment by causing them not to be eager to pursue the limited vehicle." The expression "limited vehicle" (*prādeśikayāna, nyi tshe ba'i theg pa*) refers to what is more commonly describes as the Hīnayāna, the "lesser" or "inferior" vehicle (*theg dman*).
129. The opening statement for *BBh* (ch. 2) is as follows: "A bodhisattva's initial development of enlightenment mind is the first correct aspirational prayer (*samyakpraṇidhāna, yang dag pa'i smon lam*) among all the correct aspirational prayers of a bodhisattva and the one that causes all the other correct aspirational prayers to be undertaken." In *BBh* (book 1, ch. 17; English translation, pp. 450–51), Asaṅga identifies five types of aspirational prayers, of which correct aspirational prayer is the fourth. It is described there as "the brief or extensive form of aspirational prayer to obtain in the future all the spiritual qualities and all the virtuous qualities of a bodhisattva."
130. This reading of "vow" (*saṃvara, sdom pa*) instead of "aspiration" (*praṇidhi, smon pa*) appears in the extracanonical editions of the root text. The Tengyur versions of the root text all have "aspiration" here, which obviates any need for this interpretation described as "an instance in which the cause (i.e., the aspiration) is referred to by the name of the result (i.e., the vow)." Nevertheless, the reading "vow" does also appear in Atiśa's autocommentary.

131. *saṃvara, sdom pa.* The Buddhist term that is usually translated as "vow" in English actually more literally means "restraint" in the sense of refraining from committing forms of misconduct such as taking another sentient being's life, and so on. *AKBh* (Sanskrit edition, p. 205) states: "Restraint means the act of putting a stop to, and the complete cessation of, the immorality that has been occurring continuously." The same text continues: "There are three kinds of restraint: the restraint of the system of discipline known as prātimokṣa, which is the morality that occurs in the desire realm and pertains to those human beings who are of this world; the restraint that arises from the meditative absorptions, which is the morality that occurs in the form realm; and the restraint that is pure, which is the morality that is free of the outflows." It is a Buddhist doctrine that only humans can receive the vows, or "restraint," of prātimokṣa. However, it is also a Mahāyāna doctrine that worldly gods and even certain animals, such as nāgas, can generate the bodhisattva vow. Since these nonhumans cannot receive the prātimokṣa vow, they observe the Mahāyāna ethics of restraint in the form of abandoning naturally objectionable misdeeds (see note 132, this chapter).

132. *PSV* (English translation, p. 284) states: "An objectionable act (*sāvadya, kha na ma tho ba*) is one that is evil because it is reproached by those who are wise and because it has an undesirable maturation" A naturally objectionable misdeed (*prakṛtisāvadya, rang bzhin gyi kha na ma tho ba*) is one that is wrongful regardless of whether one has accepted any system of moral discipline. Examples of such naturally objectionable misdeeds are any of the ten unvirtuous karmic paths.

133. The "basis" for harming others is the mental afflictions that motivate you to commit such acts.

134. This is a reference to Ame Jangchup Rinchen (A mes byang chub rin chen; 1015–1077), a close disciple and personal attendant of Atiśa.

135. *brahmacarya, tshangs par spyod pa.* This term generally applies to the celibate life of any Buddhist monk or nun.

136. *Zla ba sgron ma'i mdo*, Toh. 127. This is an alternate name for the *Samādhirāja Sūtra* (*Ting nge 'dzin gyi rgyal po*); however, the source of this quotation is misidentified. This line of verse is actually from the *Vimalaprabhā* (*Dri ma med pa'i 'od*, Toh. 1347), a commentary to the *Kālacakra Tantra* (vol. 2, p. 4): *daśatattva-parijñānāt trayāṇāṃ bhikṣur uttamaḥ | madyama śramanerākhyo gṛhasthas tv adhamas tayoḥ*. It appears that the error stems from the fact that in the Paṇchen Lama's *Preeminent One's Joyful Feast* (f. 29a), this line is preceded by a different quotation that is identified as being from the *Candrapradīpa Sūtra*. The lines from this latter source declare (ch. 20, v. 10cd): "With the state of a bhikṣu that is the highest form of austerity, / generate the mind that aspires to attain the most excellent and supreme enlightenment." Apparently, Jamgön Kongtrul assumed both passages were from the same text.

137. Jamgön Kongtrul's commentary here leaves out the answer to this first question that appears in the Paṇchen Lama's work (f. 29a): "Neusurpa's *Stages of*

the Teaching explains that Lord Atiśa held that the lower vow of prātimokṣa is incorporated into the higher bodhisattva vow, resulting in a vow that 'possesses' [i.e., carries out] two actions" (*yar ldan bya ba gnyis ldan du bzhed*).

138. Naktso Lotsāwa Tsultrim Gyalwa (Nag tsho lo tsā ba Tshul khrims rgyal ba, 1011–1064). Source text not identified.

139. *saṃvaraśīla, sdom pa'i tshul khrims*. This is the first of the three types of bodhisattva morality. It is largely identified with whatever form of the prātimokṣa vow (*so sor thar pa'i sdom pa*) an individual may have taken. *BBh* (English translation, p. 240) states: "The morality of restraint is the acceptance of the discipline of Individual Liberation." "Individual Liberation" is an English translation of *prātimokṣa*, the term for the Hīnayāna system of morality. See Paṇchen Lama's *Easy Path* (chapter 8, this volume), note 65 for several interpretations.

140. *dravya, rdzas*; i.e., it has a physical quality, referred to as "noninformative form" (*avijñaptirūpa, rnam par rig byed ma yin pa'i gzugs*). Not all Indian Buddhist philosophical traditions adhere to this view.

141. This reading matches the version that appears in the Narthang edition of the Tengyur. The Derge edition of the Tengyur has the modifier "well" (*legs*) instead of the word "chapter" (*le'u*).

142. *pratibhāna, spobs pa*. This term refers to a form of intelligence that includes such qualities as confidence, clarity of understanding, quick-wittedness, and eloquence. The primary sense in this context seems to be that of confidence in one's ability to perform the ritual. Atiśa's *Commentary on the Difficult Points* (*dKa' 'grel*, f. 264b) states: "The expression 'able to confer' (*'bogs bzod*) means to be capable of bestowing the vow to the recipient, by saying with a joyful mind 'this is the correct way to apply yourself' and by reflecting to oneself, 'I shall bestow the vow without hesitation.'"

143. The Paṇchen Lama's commentary specifically mentions Geshe Laksorwa (dGe bshes Lag sor ba, d.u.) as another early Kadampa master who held this view. He was a disciple of Naktso Lotsāwa Tsultrim Gyalwa (Nag 'tsho lo tsā ba Tshul khrims rgyal ba, 1011–1064).

144. See also Asaṅga's *Stage of a Bodhisattva* (English translation, p. 260) for a brief description of the qualifications of the preceptor. Another authoritative source is Candragomī's *Twenty Verses on the Bodhisattva Vow* (vv. 1cd–2), which states "That morality of the bodhisattvas who reside / in all of the ten directions and three times, // which is a treasure for all forms of merit, / should be accepted with a supreme attitude / from a guru who abides in the discipline / and who is knowledgeable and capable."

145. *adhyeṣaṇā, gsol ba gtab pa*. *BBh* (English translation, pp. 260–61) states: "Regarding this topic, whether he or she is a householder or one who has gone forth into the homeless state, a bodhisattva who wishes to train him- or herself in the bodhisattva training that relates to this threefold heap of morality and who has generated the aspiration to achieve unsurpassed true enlightenment should initially throw him- or herself at the feet of a bodhisattva who is

an exemplary dharma follower and who has also made the aspiration to attain enlightenment, is wise and is able to convey the meaning of the verbal informative form, and make the following entreaty: 'O son of good family' or, 'O daughter of good family,' 'I wish to receive from you the acceptance of the discipline of bodhisattva morality. If it causes no trouble, may it please you, in your compassion, to hear me for a brief moment.'"

146. *spro ba bskyed pa. BBh* (English translation, p. 261) states: "Following this, the bodhisattva who is capable of conducting the ritual should describe at length the benefits of the bodhisattva system of discipline to the bodhisattva who is desirous of receiving it. He or she should also describe the heavy and light precepts to the individual who is desirous of receiving the discipline and cause him or her to develop enthusiasm by saying the following: 'Hear me, O son of good family' or 'Hear me, O daughter of good family.' 'Do you wish to lead across those who have not crossed over, set free those who have not been set free, comfort those who are in need of comfort, bring to nirvana those who have not reached nirvana, and preserve the lineage of the buddhas? You should generate a firm attitude and a firm determination regarding this.' This should be said to those who are recognized to be unaware of these points in order to cause them to develop enthusiasm."

147. *tshogs bsags*. After making salutation (*samīcīṃ kṛtvā, mchod pa byas nas*) to the buddhas and arya bodhisattvas of the three times and the ten directions, the individual desirous of receiving the vow should reflect on the spiritual qualities of the buddhas and bodhisattvas and generate deep reverence (*prasādaṃ cetasa, dang ba'i sems*) toward them. Following that, he or she should also perform acts of worship (*saṃpūraskṛtya, legs par mchod par byas*) before an image of the Buddha. Atiśa's *Ritual Method for Generating Enlightenment Mind and Receiving the Bodhisattva Vow* (*Sems bskyed pa dang sdom pa'i cho ga'i rim pa*, f. 49b) states more specifically that one should "present the five types of outer offerings to the best of one's ability and make prostration."

148. *bskul ma gdab pa. BBh* (English translation, p. 261) states: "The candidate should place his or her right knee on the ground or sit in a squatting position and humbly address the knowledgeable bodhisattva with the following words: . . . 'please bestow upon me the acceptance of the discipline of bodhisattva morality.'"

149. *bsam pa khyad par can bskyed pa. BBh* (Ibid.) states: "Having spoken these words, the candidate should fix his or her recollection one-pointedly and, with a state of mind that steadily becomes ever more reverential, remain silent while reflecting on the following thought: 'Before long now, I shall gain an inexhaustible, immeasurable, and unsurpassed treasure of great merit.'"

150. *bar chad thun mong ba dri ba. BBh* (Ibid.) states: "Then, while standing or sitting and with an undistracted mind, the knowledgeable bodhisattva should address the candidate bodhisattva who has spoken in this way as follows: 'Hear me, O son of good family' or 'Hear me, O dharma brother, who is named so-and-so.' Or 'Hear me, O daughter of good family' or 'Hear me, O dharma sister, who is

named so-and-so.' 'Are you a bodhisattva and have you made the aspiration to attain enlightenment?' The bodhisattva candidate should then affirm, 'Yes, it is so.'" Je Tsongkhapa's *Commentary on the Morality Chapter* (*Byang chub sems dpa'i tshul khrims kyi rnam bshad byang chub gzhung lam*, f. 36b) states: "The purpose of these two questions is to awaken the potential of the candidate's spiritual lineage and to strengthen his or her aspirational enlightenment mind."

151. *bslab pa mdor bsdus brjod pa.* Atiśa's *Ritual Method for Generating Enlightenment Mind and Receiving the Bodhisattva Vow* (*Sems bskyed pa dang sdom pa'i cho ga'i rim pa*, f. 47a) states: "Then the spiritual teacher should instill in the disciple an understanding of a summary of all the precepts and all the aspects of the morality that relate to all the bodhisattvas of the three times—that is, the morality of restraint, the morality of acquiring virtuous qualities, and the morality that acts on behalf of beings. Then the spiritual teacher should ask the disciple, 'Do you wish to receive from me these precepts that pertain to all the bodhisattvas and this morality that pertains to all the bodhisattvas?'"

152. *BBh* (English translation, pp. 263–64) states: "It is also a fact of nature that immediately following the rite of accepting the discipline of bodhisattva morality, a particular type of sign (i.e., that the seats of the buddhas and bodhisattvas will tremble) will become evident to the tathāgatas and the bodhisattvas who have achieved the great ārya stages and who exist, remain, and live in the endless and unlimited world spheres that lie in the ten directions. Because of this sign, those tathāgatas and bodhisattvas will realize the following: 'A bodhisattva has taken up the acceptance of the discipline of bodhisattva morality.' And immediately thereafter, their attention will turn toward that bodhisattva. And with that attention, their knowledge-perception (*jñānadarśana*, *ye shes kyi gzigs pa*) will take effect. By means of this knowledge-perception, those buddhas and great bodhisattvas become fully aware, in accordance with reality, that a bodhisattva named so-and-so in this particular world sphere has received the acceptance of the discipline of bodhisattva morality from another bodhisattva named so-and-so. And, with favorable minds, they will all react compassionately toward him or her, as one would a son or daughter or a brother or sister. It should be expected that the virtuous qualities of the bodhisattva who is looked upon in this way with a favorable mind and sympathy will increase greatly and they will not decline. It should be understood that the buddhas and great bodhisattvas thus recognize this announcement regarding the acceptance of the discipline of bodhisattva morality."

153. The Paṇchen Lama's commentary (f. 30b) states: "A detailed explanation of these points should be learned from Atiśa's *Ritual for Accepting the Vow* (see note 147, this chapter) and Je Tsongkhapa's *Commentary on the Morality Chapter* (see reference to this text in note 150, this chapter). The outline for the seven points of the preliminary stage and the five points of the concluding stage appear to have been taken from Chim Namkha Drak's *Mahāyāna Supreme Path*, ff. 99b–103a.

154. *'Jam dpal gyi sangs rgyas kyi zhing gi yon tan bkod pa* (Dg.K. *dkon brtsegs*, vol. 3 (*ga*) ff. 248b–297a). The original Sanskrit of the five verses cited here in *A Lamp for the Path to Enlightenment* can be found in Śāntideva's *ŚS*, p. 11.

155. In the Sanskrit original of this verse, the word *lord* (*nātha*, *mgon po*) is in the genitive singular, presumably a reference to the tathāgata Meghasvaraghoṣarāja, before whom Ambarāja recites these verses. In the Tibetan verse of Atiśa's root text, the plural particle *rnams* is added to the noun *lord*. Since it is customary to invite the buddhas and bodhisattvas of the ten directions to witness the act of receiving the bodhisattva vow, it is appropriate to understand the term in the plural, as the commentary has done here.

156. *nimantraye*, *mgron du gnyer*. This verb, which literally means to "invite" or "summon," is meant in the sense that a bodhisattva willingly announces his or her intention to secure the ultimate well-being of all sentient beings.

157. The original Sanskrit reads "to liberate them from poverty" (*dāridryān mocitāsmi tat*), a metaphorical reference to samsara's suffering.

158. The following fourfold declaration is found in many rituals associated with Mahāyāna vows: "I shall deliver those who have not been delivered, I shall liberate those who have not been liberated, I shall provide relief to those who are without relief, and I shall establish all beings in supreme happiness" (*atīrṇān tārayiṣyāmi amuktān mocayāmy ahaṃ | anāśvastān āśvāsayiṣyāmi sarvasattvān sthāpayiṣyāmi nirvṛttau*). *The Preeminent One's Joyful Feast* (f. 24a–24b) makes reference to two scholars' interpretations of these statements, one by the Kadampa master Sharawa and a second by The Omniscient Chim (mChims thams cad mkhyen pa)—which is to say, Chim Namkha Drak (see note 89, this chapter). The latter scholar's explanation, which associates each statement with one of the four noble truths, is the one that appears here.

159. *saṃvaraśīla*, *sdom pa'i tshul khrims*. See note 139 (this chapter).

160. *sattvārthakriyāśīla*, *sems can la phan 'dogs pa'i tshul khrims*. *BBh* (English translation, pp. 242–43) states: "What is a bodhisattva's morality that acts on behalf of beings? In brief, it should be understood as having eleven forms." For a description of the eleven forms, see *BBh*, English translation, pp. 243–44 and pp. 249–60.

161. *kuśaladharmasaṃgrāhakaśīla*, *dge ba'i chos sdud pa'i tshul khrims*. *BBh* (English translation, p. 240) states: "The morality of acquiring virtuous qualities is whatever virtue a bodhisattva accumulates by body and speech for the sake of achieving enlightenment, following acceptance of the morality discipline."

162. The nine causes of animosity (*āghāta*, *kun nas mnar gsems pa*) are the following judgments: this person harmed me in the past, this person is harming me now, this person will harm me in the future, this person harmed my friend in the past, this person is harming my friend now, this person will harm my friend in the future, this person benefited my enemy in the past, this person is benefiting my enemy now, and this person will benefit my enemy in the future.

163. *amarṣa*, *mi bzod pa*. *AS* (p. 8) states: "What is envy (*īrṣyā*, *phrag dog*)? It is a

form of anger created by a feeling of intolerance toward the excellent qualities of others and a complete vexation of the mind that is possessed by a person who is highly attached to gain and honor. Its action is to cause one to become dejected and to remain in a discontented state."

164. *PSV* (p. 305) states: "Excellent qualities, such those of gain, honor, fame, family lineage, morality, learning, and the like."

165. The original Sanskrit of this line could be read simply as "I shall abandon evil desires," with the word "evil" being an adjective that modifies "desires." The Tibetan translation of the sūtra reflects this reading (*sdig pa'i 'dod pa yongs su gtang*). However, the Tibetan translation of the line that appears in *A Lamp for the Path to Enlightenment* (*sdig dang 'dod pa spang bar bya*) has rendered the two as separate nouns and the commentary reflects this interpretation.

166. The English translation of the second half of the verse adheres to the Tibetan version. However, a more literal translation of the original Sanskrit states: "I shall train myself as the buddhas did, / in relation to the morality of the vow and self-control" (*buddhānām anuśikṣiṣye śīlasaṃvarasaṃyame*). Ratnākaraśānti glosses these lines in his commentary to Nāgārjuna's *Anthology of Sūtra Passages* (*Sūtrasamuccaya, mDo kun las btus pa*; Dg.T. vol. 109, f. 242a) as follows: "With reference to the morality of a monk or nun who has gone forth into the homeless state, the verse declares, 'I shall train myself as the buddhas did, / in relation to the morality of the vow and self-control,' because the principal forms of the morality of collecting virtue are preservation of the bodhisattva vow (*saṃvara, sdom pa*) and carrying out acts of self-control (*saṃyama, nges pa*). Alternatively, all of the six perfections are the practices for collecting virtue, and they are indicated by the phrase 'the vow and self-control.' Or the word 'vow' refers to the acceptance of the bodhisattva system of morality and the word 'self-control' refers to the avoidance of harm to others. Hence, this phrase indicates that the morality of collecting virtue and the rest can be accomplished when a practitioner develops an excellent physical form."

167. *iha*. This Sanskrit word is not rendered in the Tibetan translation. *Iha*, or "here," typically means "in this world" (which is to say, "now" and "in this life").

168. *viśruta*. The Sanskrit past participle conveys such meanings as "to be heard far and wide" and "to be celebrated" (*MW*, s.v. "viśruta"). The English translation follows the simplicity of this single term. The Tibetan translation renders it with two modifiers: "I shall cause my name *to be retained* (*gzung ba*) and *to abide* (*rnam par gnas*) throughout the ten directions. These interpretations are preserved in the commentary. The Tibetan translation of this verse as it appears in the Kangyur version of the sūtra states: "I shall cause my name to be heard throughout the ten directions" (*phyogs rnams bcu po thams cad du / bdag gi ming ni thos par bya*).

169. *saṃvara, sdom pa*. See note 131 (this chapter). Here the translation "vow" seems more appropriate than "restraint."

170. They are the morality of restraint, the morality of accumulating virtuous quali-

ties, and the morality of acting on behalf of beings. See also notes 131 (regarding the term "vow" and "restraint"), 139 (regarding "the morality of restraint"), 160 (regarding "the morality of acting on behalf of beings"), and 161 (regarding "the morality of accumulating virtuous qualities") (all in this chapter).

171. *jvara, rims nad.* The Sanskrit term refers principally to fevers, but the Tibetan translation is often taken to mean an illness that is contagious (*'go ba 'i nad*).

172. This explanation is based on the syllables of the Tibetan of the epithet *mahābodhisattva,* literally "great enlightenment being," which is *jangchup sempa chenpo* (*byang chub sems dpa' chen po*). *Jangchup* is Tibetan for *bodhi*—that is, enlightenment; *sempa chenpo* is Tibetan for *mahāsattva* or "great being." The Tibetan word *jangchub* combines words for the *elimination* of all obstacles (*jang*) and the *attainment* of all spiritual qualities (*chup*).

173. Note 131 (this chapter) explains how the Tibetan term *sdom pa* (*saṃvara*) literally means "restraint" when it refers to the vow. However, the Tibetan verse here contains the term *sdom pa* twice (*sdom pa'i sdom dag ni*). Therefore, I have translated the phrase containing these two instances of *sdom pa* as "[by striving for] purity of the vow in the restraint [of a bodhisattva]." Atiśa's *Commentary on the Difficult Points* (*dKa' 'grel,* f. 268a) provides this explanation: "The phrase '[by striving for] purity of the vow in the restraint [of a bodhisattva]' means the bodhisattva vow of one who is observing Ārya Asaṅga's system [of Mahāyāna morality] and the bodhisattva vow of one who is observing Master Śāntideva's system [of Mahāyāna morality]. The lineage gurus have declared that if, after taking up the two paths established by such great champions (i.e., Asaṅga and Śāntideva), [an individual] makes effort and strives [to practice them], he or she shall, after having fulfilled the two accumulations of merit and wisdom, become fully awakened in true and complete enlightenment." It is also possible to interpret the syllable *dag* in the phrase *sdom pa'i sdom dag* as the dual ending of the second instance of the noun *sdom*—i.e., "vow" or "restraint"—and thus read the phrase as "[by striving to observe] the two [systems of] restraint pertaining to [a bodhisattva's] vow." While this passage from the *Commentary on the Difficult Points* might seem to support such a reading, Jamgön Kongtrul's commentary clearly takes *dag* to mean the noun "purity" and so our translation supports that interpretation.

174. *mātā, yum.* This epithet of the Perfection of Wisdom occurs numerous times in various sūtras that are titled *Prajñāpāramitā,* or *Perfection of Wisdom.* It is meant in the sense that buddhas are generated by this knowledge.

175. This statement is found in chapter 14 of the *Eighteen-Thousand-Line Perfection of Wisdom Sūtra.*

176. *ṛddhi, rdzu 'phrul.*

177. *vineya, gdul bya.* This noun is formed from the future participle of a Sanskrit verbal root, *vinī,* which has a range of meanings, including "to lead," "to take away," "to chastise," as well as "to train," "to tame," "to guide," and "to instruct." The Tibetan translation centers on the sense of "taming" (*'dul ba*), which we

qualify as taming spiritually. Therefore, this particular noun generally means "someone to be trained" or "someone to be tamed spiritually." However, in certain specific contexts, it can simply be understood to mean "a disciple."

178. *cetaḥparyāyajñāna, sems kyi rnam grangs shes pa.*

179. *dhātu, khams.* In this context, the term means the positive or negative propensities of a sentient being based on his or her spiritual lineage (*gotra, rigs*) and his or her unfavorable mental traits (*carita, spyod pa*).

180. *divyaṃ śrotra, lha'i rna ba.*

181. *pūrvanivāsānusmṛti, sngon gyi gnas rjes su dran pa.*

182. *divyaṃ cakṣu, lha'i mig.*

183. *The Preeminent One's Joyful Feast* (*Phul byung bzhad pa'i dga' ston*, f. 36a) acknowledges that quiescence does not need to be attained for certain lesser forms of supernatural knowledge that can be acquired naturally (i.e., by birth), or that are achieved on the basis of ritually consecrated substances and mantra recitation, or that merely consist of recalling details relating to experiences in a prior life.

184. **aṅga, yan lag.* This term literally means a "limb," as of the body, or a "subordinate division," for instance of some subject of inquiry. However, it can also mean an "expedient" in the sense of a condition or factor that promotes some purpose or desired result, and that is how it is meant here. It is a synonym for the more common term that means "requisite" (*sambhāra, tshogs*) when it is used in this context (cf. *MW*, s.v. "sambhāra": "a collection of things required for any purpose").

185. This citation of scriptural references that relate to the requisites for quiescence is an abbreviated description of three views that are referenced in *The Preeminent One's Joyful Feast* (f. 37a–37b): (1) Atiśa's *Commentary on the Difficult Points*, which cites the nine requisite factors discussed in Bodhibhadra's work *The Chapter on the Requisites for One-Pointed Concentration* (*Ting nge 'dzin gyi tshogs kyi le'u*, Toh. 3924); (2) an unidentified source in which the Kadampa master Sharawa indicates that Ma Lotsāwa Gewe Lodrö (dGe ba'i blo gros, fl. eleventh century), the original translator of Atiśa's *Lamp for the Path*, regarded the sources to be a collection of works, including *The Stage of a Śrāvaka*, an unidentified Lokeśvara sādhana, Bodhibhadra's just-mentioned work, and a sūtra titled *The Chapter on the Requisites for One-Pointed Concentration* (no sūtra with this title was found in the Tibetan Kangyur collection); and (3) Je Tsongkhapa's reference to the thirteen "requisites" that are found in *The Stage of a Śrāvaka*.

186. These lines appear in Atiśa's work titled *A Brief Arrangement of the Means by Which to Achieve the Mahāyāna Path* (*Theg pa chen po'i lam gyi sgrub thabs yi ger bsdus pa*, Toh. 3954).

187. The four meditative absorptions (*dhyāna, bsam gtan*) and the four formless states of mental composure (*samāpatti, snyoms par 'jug pa*) can bring about a temporary suspension of various elements of the mental afflictions, in that their

overt form is prevented from arising through the power of one-pointed concentration. Asaṅga (*AS*, Sanskrit edition, p. 63) describes this as a "suppression" (*nigraha, nyams smad pa*) of the mental afflictions: "What is cessation in the conventional sense? It is a cessation that is achieved through suppressing the seeds [of the mental afflictions] by means of the mundane paths."

188. *tattva, de kho na nyid.* This term is one of a number of synonyms for emptiness (*śūnyatā, stong pa nyid*), including "suchness" (*tathatā, de bzhin nyid*); "ultimate truth" (*paramārthasatya, don dam pa'i bden pa*); the "summit of being" (*bhūtakoṭi, yang dag pa'i mtha'*); and the "sphere of reality" (*dharmadhātu, chos kyi dbyings*), to mention a few.

189. *āvaraṇa, sgrib pa.* Verse 42 identifies the two principal forms of obscuration: the obscurations of the mental afflictions (*kleśāvaraṇa, nyon mongs pa'i sgrib pa*) and the obscurations to that which needs to be known (*jñeyāvaraṇa, shes bya'i sgrib pa*). However, Atiśa's *Commentary on the Difficult Points* also makes reference to karmic obscurations (*karmāvaraṇa, las kyi sgrib pa*) and maturation obscurations (*vipākāvaraṇa, rnam par smin pa'i sgrib pa*). A karmic obscuration is to have committed any of the five immediate deeds (*pañcānantaryāni, mtshams med pa lnga*)—that is, (1) killing one's mother, (2) one's father, or (3) an arhat, (4) causing a division in the sangha wheel, and (5) through malice, doing physical injury to a tathāgata that causes him to shed blood. These five deeds are obscurations because a person who has committed any of them has very little opportunity of attaining the transcendent path in his or her current life. They are called "immediate deeds" because a person who commits any of them will typically be reborn in the hells in his or her very next life. A maturation obscuration is to be reborn in any of the three lower realms, as a human being of the northern continent Kuru, or as a worldly long-lived deity, such as those that lack conception. Birth in any of these forms of existence is an obscuration because such beings are incapable of developing spiritually or attaining the transcendent realizations. A worldly god that lacks conception (*asaṃjñisattva, 'du shes med pa'i sems can*) is one who, as a result of having generated the state of composure without conception (*asaṃjñisamāpatti, 'du shes med pa'i snyoms par 'jug pa*), is reborn in a level of the form realm associated with the fourth meditative absorption (*dhyāna, bsam gtan*) where the worldly gods are called Those of Great Fruit (*mahatphalā, 'bras bu che ba*). These beings manifest a conception only at the time of their birth and their death. As a sūtra declares: "And after having lived for a very extensive period of time, in conjunction with the arising of a conception, those beings fall away (i.e., die) from that place." Without exception, they are reborn in the desire realm, like an arrow that falls to the earth after its momentum has been exhausted.

190. *In Praise of Confession*, v. 34 (*bShags pa'i bstod pa*, Dg.T. bstod tshogs, vol. 1 [ka], ff. 204a–206b).

191. The commentary here interprets the word *rnal 'byor* in the second half of the verse to be the abstract noun "spiritual practice" (*yoga*); however, it could also

be an abbreviation of *rnal 'byor pa*, or "practitioner" (*yogī*), in which case the latter half of the verse could be translated "The practitioner should meditate continually on / perfection of wisdom that is accompanied by means."

192. *BCA*, ch. 9, v. 55.
193. *The Lamp for the Path*, v. 41cd.
194. Ibid., v. 42.
195. *bcom ldan 'das*. This is a respectful epithet of the Buddha that is often translated as "Blessed One" or "Lord." In classical Buddhist literature, it is interpreted in two ways, one of which identifies the word *bhaga* as being derived from the verbal root *bhañj*, which means "to break" or "to defeat" (*bcom pa*). This sense is indicated in the following statement from Asaṅga's *BBh* (English translation, p. 167): "Buddha is the Bhagavān because he defeated the great assemblage of Māra's army in its entirety." Another interpretation is that the word *bhaga* means "good fortune," "prosperity," and "excellence," in which case *bhagavān* should be taken to mean "one who possesses fortune." A frequently cited verse that appears in the *Saṃpuṭa Tantra* (*Yang dag par sbyor ba'i rgyud*; also known as *Kha sbyor gyi rgyud*) describes a buddha's fortune as follows: "Fortune refers to these six: / complete power, knowledge, / renown, glory, beauty / and activity that fulfills aims." According to *GB2*, the final syllable *'das* in the Tibetan equivalent *bcom ldan 'das* was added by the Tibetan translators to indicate that a buddha's qualities are "transcendent" and therefore superior to those of all other beings.
196. The commentary construes the Tibetan syllables *yang dag* in the root text as the adverb "correctly" (**samyak, yang dag par*), which should be associated with the verb "explain," resulting in the reading "explain correctly." It is also possible that these syllables are a prefix attached to the noun "characteristic" (**bheda, dbye ba*), forming the noun *sambheda* (*yang dag dbye ba*). In that case, the noun could remain translated simply as "characteristic" or the prefix could be read as "complete" characteristics or "correct" characteristics.
197. The canonical edition of this verse reads "virtuous accumulations" (**śuklasambharā, dge ba'i tshogs rnams*) in place of "virtuous qualities" (**śukladharmā, dge ba'i chos rnams*).
198. *śukla, dkar po*. In addition to "white," this adjective also means "pure" or "unsullied," and thus is also a synonym for "virtuous."
199. "Supported by enlightenment mind" (*byang chub kyi sems kyis zin pa*) is a Tibetan idiom that literally means an act is "held by the color" (*rtsis zin pa*) of enlightenment mind. More loosely, it means that an act is controlled by, or is under the influence of, that motivation.
200. The original Sanskrit term translated here as *heap* (*phung po*) is *skandha*. While several interpretations are recorded in Buddhist abhidharma literature, the principal one is *rāśi* (*AKBh*, ch. 1, v. 20a), which literally means a "heap," as does the Tibetan equivalent. The classic sūtra passage in support of this interpretation declares: "Whatever form there is of the past, future, or present, outer or

inner, coarse or subtle, inferior or excellent, whatever is far or near, all of that collected together as one is considered the form heap."

201. *AKBh* gives two interpretations of the term "constituent" (*dhātu, khams*): "multitude" (*gotra, rigs*) and "class" (*jāti, rigs*). Both are found in the *Mahāvibhāṣaśāstra*. Regarding the first, *AKBh* (p. 13) states: "The meaning of constituent is that of a multitude (*gotra, rigs*; *MW*, s.v. "gotra"). Just as the many multitudes (*gotrāṇi, rigs*) of ore, such as iron, copper, silver, gold, and the like, that are found on a single mountain are called "constituents" (*dhātavaḥ, khams*), the eighteen multitudes of entities that exist within a single support or continuum are called the 'eighteen constituents.' Here, the word 'multitudes' (*gotrāṇi*) refers to 'abundant sources' (*ākarā, 'bung gnas*) of various types of entities. In what way are those entities of the eye, and the rest, abundant sources of something? They are abundant sources of the entities that are of the same class as themselves because they are their 'like causes' (*sabhāgahetu, skal ba mnyam pa'i rgyu*)." While the Sanskrit term *gotra* does include the meaning of "class" or "species" (*MW*, s.v. "gotra") and the Tibetan translation of *rigs* conforms to that sense, the just-mentioned explanation seems to indicate that the more appropriate sense of *gotra* here is that of a "multitude" of a particular class or type of entities.

AKBh (Ibid.) presents a second interpretation of *dhātu* as follows: "According to others, *dhātu* is a word that expresses the meaning of a 'class' (*jāti, rigs*) of entities. Thus, the nature of the eighteen constituents is that of the classes of the eighteen types of entities."

AS (p. 15) states: "What is the meaning of the term 'constituent'? Its meanings are that of being the seeds for all entities, that of possessing unique defining attributes, that of possessing a nature that demonstrates the relation of cause and effect, and that of possessing the nature of being a collection for all the various types of entities."

202. *AKBh* (p. 13) states: "The meaning of the term 'basis' is that of being the 'door'—that is, the source for the arising of mind and the mental factors." There are six inner bases, which are the six faculties of eye, ear, nose, tongue, body, and mind. There are six outer bases, which are the objects of the six forms of consciousness—that is, visible forms, sounds, smells, tastes, tangible objects, and mental entities. See *Inner Science of Buddhist Practice*, pp. 347–53.

203. *dharmin, chos can*. *MW* (s.v. "dharmin") defines this as "the bearer of any characteristic mark or attribute, object, thing."

204. *ālambana, dmigs pa*. This term literally means "that which the mind rests upon" or a "mental support." *AKBh* (p. 19) states: "A mental support is that entity that is grasped by the mind and its associated mental factors."

205. That is, at the time of the seed's existence.

206. *MMK*, ch. 15, v. 11.

207. *Śūnyatāsaptati*, v. 4.

208. *MMK*, ch. 20, v. 20ab.

209. Ibid., v. 20cd.
210. **ekānekarahitayukti, gcig du bral gyi rigs pa*. The phrase *ekāneka* can also be understood to mean "identity and distinctness."
211. *laukika, 'jig rten pa*. Here this term refers to ordinary working persons, like farmers. It is not meant in the pejorative sense of persons who have no interest in spiritual matters.
212. *PV*, ch. 3, v. 35ab.
213. *nītārthasūtra, nges don gyi mdo*. Khedrup Tenpa Dargye's *Overview of the Perfection of Wisdom* (*Phar phyin spyi don*, f. 113b): "The definition of a sūtra of definitive meaning is a sūtra that explicitly teaches ultimate truth as its principal subject."
214. *Sūtrasamuccaya, mDo kun las btus pa*. An anthology of sūtra passages compiled by Nāgārjuna. Although the original Sanskrit version is not extant, the Tibetan translation is available in the Tengyur collection (Toh. 3934).
215. *rigs pa'i tshogs*. This phrase is generally associated with the following six works of Nāgārjuna: (1) *Root Verses on the Middle Way* (*Mūlamadhyamaka, dBu ma rtsa ba*), (2) *Aphorisms That Split Asunder* (*Vaidalyasūtra, Zhib mo rnam par thag pa*), (3) *Seventy Verses on Emptiness* (*Śūnyatāsaptati, sTong pa nyid bdun cu pa*), (4) *The Elimination of Discord* (*Vigrahavyāvartanī, rTsod pa bzlog pa*), (5) *Sixty Verses on Reasoning* (*Yuktiśaṣṭikā, Rigs pa drug cu pa*), and (6) *The Jewel Garland* (*Ratnāvalī, Rin chen phreng ba*).
216. Sanskrit original not extant; Tibetan translation in Kangyur collection, Toh. 152.
217. Sanskrit original not extant; Tibetan translation in Kangyur collection, Toh. 156.
218. The original Sanskrit is cited in *PP*, p. 219, and *BCAP*, p. 172.
219. *rTsa ba shes rab*. This is an alternate Tibetan name for Nāgārjuna's *Root Verses on the Middle Way*. See also note 215 (this chapter).
220. *śānta, zhi ba*. Literally "tranquil," "pacified," "calm," "extinguished," "destroyed." Hence the line might also be rendered as: "That entity is free of a real essence" or "That entity is naturally tranquil." Candrakīrti glosses "tranquil" (*sānta, zhi ba*) as "lacking a real essential nature" (*svabhāvavirahita, rang bzhin bral ba*) in his commentary *In Clear Words* (*Prasannapadā, Tshig gsal*).
221. *MMK*, ch. 6, v. 16ab.
222. The original Sanskrit is cited in *PP*, p. 220.
223. *samāropa, sgro 'dogs*.
224. *saṃskāra, 'du byed*. This is a reference to the second of the twelve limbs in the doctrine of dependent origination. *PP* (Sanskrit edition, p. 238) states: "A person who is obstructed and obscured by ignorance forms—that is, gives rise to—various types of volition that are virtuous, and the like, for the sake of, and for the purpose of, a rebirth—that is, in order to give rise to a rebirth. These [volitions, i.e., karma] are [called] 'formations' because they cause the formation of a rebirth."

225. *svalakṣaṇa, rang gi mtshan nyid.* This term is understood to be roughly equivalent to "essential nature" (*svabhāva, rang bzhin*).
226. *janaka, bskyed byed.* That is, causes.
227. *janya, bskyed bya.* That is, results.
228. That is, the relation between a result that arises in dependence upon its causes and the relation between an entity and the collection of its parts, which is the basis upon which its existence is ascribed.
229. *MMK*, ch. 18, v. 10. In his *Ocean of Reasoning* (*Rigs pa'i rgya mtsho*, f. 192a), Je Tsongkhapa makes the additional point as part of his commentary on this verse: "This verse should be understood as also being a means of abandoning the two extremes of nihilism and eternalism, and the erring propositions of being identical or distinct in an intrinsically established sense, with regard to all instances of entities that are dependently ascribed, not just with regard to the relation of cause and effect."
230. *Bodhicittavivaraṇa*, v. 88. While the complete Sanskrit original of this work is not extant, this verse is available (see bibliography).
231. That is, existing in a conventional sense.
232. *dBu ma la 'jug pa'i bshad pa* (Toh. 3862). See bibliography under Candrakīrti. This passage makes up most of the explanation to ch. 6, vv. 37–38ab of the root text. These lines state: "It is not the case that it is not well-known that empty phenomena, / such as reflections and the like, are dependent on a collection of conditions. / Moreover, just as, from an empty thing such as a reflection and the like / a mind comes into existence having such an aspect, // likewise, all entities that are empty, as well, / undergo their origin from conditions that are empty."
233. *Śūnyatāsaptati*, v. 71ab.
234. The entities contained in the five heaps are limited to those that are conditioned (*saṃskṛta, 'dus byas pa*) and do not include those that are unconditioned (*asaṃskṛta, 'dus ma byas pa*); however, the eighteen constituents and the twelve bases do include all entities—that is, both the conditioned and the unconditioned.
235. *nairātmya, bdag med.* This term should be understood in the sense of the "selflessness" or insubstantiality of entities (*dharmanairātmya, chos kyi bdag med*) and not just the "selflessness" of the person (*pudgalanairātmya, gang zag gi bdag med*), a form of selflessness that is identified with emptiness (*śūnyatā, stong pa nyid*). Parenthetically, it should also be noted that, according to the position of Candrakīrti's so-called Prāsangika branch of the Middle Way school (*madhyamaka, dbu ma*), the selflessness or insubstantiality of the person is equivalent to the insubstantiality of entities, in that both have the same ultimate-truth nature of emptiness.
236. Jamgön Kongtrul adds the word "scripture" (*lung*) here and almost certainly intends the meaning to be "searching for an essence on the basis of scripture and reasoning" (*lung dang rigs pa*), which is a common expression. However,

the Paṇchen Lama's text actually reads "searching for an essence on the basis of discriminating awareness (*rig pa*) and Jamgön Kongtrul's commentary also preserves this spelling. While this could be interpreted as a misspelling of the word "reasoning" (*rigs pa*), this spelling could also be meant to suggest that the ascertainment of ultimate truth can only be accomplished by a special type of analysis that is carried out on the strength of a form of discriminative awareness that seeks to determine the ultimate nature of entities (*mthar thug dpyod byed kyi rigs shes*). This description is one that features prominently in Gelukpa philosophical writings on the nature of the two truths.

237. **anupalambha, mi dmigs pa.*

238. *Dvitīyabhāvanākrama, bsGom rim bar ba.* This is the second of Kamalaśīla's three treatises that are all known by the same title *Stages of Meditation.* It is generally understood that these works were written specifically for a Tibetan readership.

239. In the canonical or Tengyur editions of this verse, the first half does not contain the relative adverb of comparison "just as" (*bzhin*). Rather, it ends with the simple conjunction "and" (*zhing*). In that reading, the verse can be understood to assert that one should meditate in a nonconceptual manner on two objects: (1) all entities that wisdom has determined to lack a real essence (lines one and two) and (2) that very wisdom itself (the end of line three and all of line four), after it too has been analyzed and determined to be unreal.

240. *adarśana, ma mthong ba.* The first of Kamalaśīla's three *Stages of Meditation* (*Bhāvanākramaḥ prathamaḥ, bsGom pa'i rim pa dang po*) includes this passage: "The seeing of ultimate reality is that mental state of non-seeing in which the perception of correct knowledge occurs through having examined all entities with the eye of wisdom. This is also declared in a sūtra in the following manner: 'What is the seeing of the highest truth? It is the non-seeing of all entities.'"

241. Instead of the phrase "that has been analyzed with discerning awareness" (*rig dpyad pa*), the canonical editions have the reading "that has been explained with discerning awareness" (*rig bshad pa*). Atiśa's *Commentary on the Difficult Points* (f. 281b) has yet a third reading, "that has been explained with correct reasoning" (*rigs bshad pa*). Atiśa's *Commentary* further glosses this latter version: "Moreover, when that very wisdom has been explained and refuted with the four great forms of correct reasoning, it cannot be established that it truly exists."

242. The Paṇchen Lama's text states, "This very realization in which it has been perceived in this way that both mental objects and subjective mental states (*yul yul can*) are unoriginated . . . ."

243. That is, the desire realm, the form realm, and the formless realm.

244. *apratisthitanirvāṇa, mi gnas pa'i mya ngan las 'das pa.* The state of supreme enlightenment or buddhahood is referred to by this term because it does not abide in either of the two extremes of samsaric existence or Hīnayāna nirvana.

245. *nirmala, dri med.* The adjective "stainless" appears in the original Sanskrit of

this verse; the Tibetan translation does not, presumably for reasons relating to meter.

246. Ch. 10, section 4, vv. 7cd–8ab. Sanskrit is found in unpublished digital version.

247. *manaskāra, yid la byed pa*. This is one of the basic mental factors that is identified in Buddhist literature. Asaṅga (*AS*, p. 6) defines it as follows: "What is attention? It is the bending of the mind. Its action is to cause the mind to keep hold of an object." Sthiramati (*PSV*) glosses "bending of the mind" (*cetasa ābhoga, sems kyi 'jug pa*) as "the condition by which the mind is caused to turn toward an object." An important distinction is made between "proper" (*yoniśa, tshul bzhin du*) and "improper" (*ayoniśa, tshul bzhin ma yin par*) forms of attention. Candrakīrti (*PP*, p. 196) cites the following unidentified canonical passage to describe how ignorance arises from improper forms of attention: "O bhikṣus, ignorance too has a cause, a conditioning factor, a motivating factor. O bhikṣus, what is the cause of ignorance? O bhikṣus, improper attention is the cause of ignorance. O bhikṣus, a clouded form of attention, a form of attention that arises from confusion, is the cause of ignorance."

248. The expression "giving rise to a sign" (*nimittodgrahaṇa, mtshan mar 'dzin pa*) occurs in early abhidharma literature as the principal characteristic of conceptions or judgments (*saṃjñā, 'du shes*), the mental factor that makes up the third of the five heaps. Yaśomitra's subcommentary (vol. 1, p. 48) glosses this phrase as follows: "a 'sign' (*nimitta, mtshan ma*) means the particular condition (*avasthā, gnas skabs*) of an entity, such as that of being 'blue,' etc. 'Giving rise' (*udgrahaṇa, 'dzin pa*) to that means to make such a determination (*pariccheda, yongs su gcod pa*)." However, the use of the expression here corresponds to the view of the Madhyamaka school that making such a determination about an entity's "sign" or "mark" is tantamount to forming the conceptual thought that it exists by way of an intrinsic essence.

249. The original Sanskrit of this verse is cited in an unpublished digital version of Ratnarakṣita's *Padminī*, ch. 13.

250. *Jātakamālā*, ch. 31 (*Sutasoma Jātaka*, v. 38cd). I follow the Tibetan in translating the Sanskrit noun *durga* as "fortress." Literally it means a place "that is difficult of access" or "that is impassable." The compound term "fortress of birth" (*janmadurga, skye ba'i rdzong*) is a reference to samsara.

251. *thun mong ba*. That is, the form of the act that is not unique to the Mahāyāna path.

252. *tattva, de nyid* or *de ko na nyid*. See note 188 (this chapter). Atiśa's *Commentary on the Difficult Points* (f. 285b) cites this line of the root text as "Through meditating on emptiness in this way, . . ." (*de ltar stong nyid bsgom byas nas*). In connection with this verse, the text also identifies the Indian commentarial tradition associated with the *Abhisamayālaṃkāra* as the ideal source for learning the overall Mahāyāna path system.

253. *sambhāramāraga, tshogs lam*. This is the first of five stages that make up the overall Buddhist path. Its three levels are described as lesser, intermediate, and great.

254. *ūṣmagata, dro bar gyur pa. ASBh*, Sanskrit edition, p. 343: "It is called Heat because it resembles the arrival of the hot season; [it occurs] because it is a portent of the fire of the [transcendent] *ārya* path that incinerates the fuel of the mental afflictions."
255. *nirvedhabhāgīya, nges par 'byed pa'i cha dang mthun pa.* This is a synonym for what is known more commonly as the "path of preparation" (*prayogamārga, sbyor lam*), the second of the five Buddhist paths. The four stages of this path are called: heat, summits, forbearance, and the foremost of worldly entities. "Penetrating insight" is another name for the "path of seeing" (*darśanamārga, mthong lam*). Thus, the path of preparation is that which leads to the attainment of penetrating insight, or the path of seeing.
256. *pramuditā, rab tu dga' ba.* This is the first of the ten ārya bodhisattva stages.
257. *vimalā, dri ma med pa.*
258. *vajropamasamādhi, rdo rje lta bu'i ting nge 'dzin.*
259. *AA*, ch 8, v. 34ab.
260. The remaining two are controlling activities and forceful activities.
261. *aṣṭamahāsiddhi, dngos grub chen po brgyad.* The eight powers alluded to in this expression are described variously. The *Caturdevīparipṛcchā Tantra* (*Lha mo bzhis yongs su zhus pa*) lists the eight forms of spiritual attainment as those of the pill, eye ointment, traveling beneath the earth's surface, the sword, flying into the sky, becoming invisible, avoiding death, and destroying illnesses. Another list of eight that is often cited appears in the *Vajrapañjara Tantra*. These are also sometimes referred to as the middling forms of spiritual attainment.
262. Buddhist literature contains a number of classification schemes that identify the different categories of Buddhist tantra. Atiśa's autocommentary (f. 287a–287b) lists seven categories and cites as the source for this classification the *Jñānavajrasamuccaya Tantra* (*Ye shes rdo rje kun las btus pa*). The seven categories are Action Tantra (*kriyātantra, bya ba'i rgyud*); Conduct Tantra (*caryātantra, spyod pa'i rgyud*); Practice Tantra (*kalpatantra, rtog pa'i rgyud*); *Tantra That Contains Both Elements* (*ubhayatantra, gnyis ka'i rgyud*); Yoga Tantra (*yogatantra, rnal 'byor gyi rgyud*); Great Yoga Tantra (*mahāyogatantra, rnal 'byor chen po'i rgyud*); and Unsurpassed Yoga Tantra (*niruttarayogatantra, rnal 'byor bla na med pa'i rgyud*). Atiśa's text further cites the titles of several tantras that relate to each category.
263. *sat, dam pa.* This adjective, whose most basic sense is that of "existing" and being "present," also has a wide range of connotations, especially when it is used to describe a person. These include "real," "true," "good," "right," "wise," "venerable," and "honest" (*MW*, s.v. "sat"). I have chosen to render it as "genuine" in that this term supports the idea of being a lama who is fully qualified and therefore not spurious. While the Tibetan equivalent *dam pa* is often understood to mean "most excellent" or "supreme," or even "holy," in this context I believe the more accurate sense is that of the original Sanskrit, as described.
264. *ācāryābhiṣekha, slob dpon gyi dbang.* This element of the initiation ritual is

meant to authorize the recipient to impart the esoteric teachings to other disciples. In a Highest Yoga Tantra initiation, this part of the consecration is performed during the latter portion of the first of four main stages of the ceremony, which is most commonly described in Tibetan literature as the "pitcher initiation" (*kalaśābhiṣeka, bum pa'i dbang*).

265. A complete Highest Yoga Tantra initiation is made up of four parts: pitcher initiation, secret initiation, wisdom knowledge initiation, and word initiation. Subsequent verses of the root text only address explicitly the second and third of these four initiations.

266. The word "friend" (*mitra, bshes gnyen*) here is meant in the sense of a spiritual teacher (*kalyānamitra, dge ba'i bshes gnyen*) or, in this case, a tantric teacher.

267. *MSA*, ch. 18, v. 11ab.

268. Even arhats, who have completely eliminated the "seeds" of the mental afflictions, are still affected by the subtler traces (*vāsanā, bag chags*) or imprints of their mental afflictions and prior misdeeds. Only a completely enlightened Buddha is free of these deeply ingrained imperfections. *BBh* (English translation, pp. 655–56) states: "Regarding this topic, a tathāgata's quality of not displaying any physical actions pertaining to bodily movement, gaze, speech, or comportment that correspond to the existence of a mental affliction is called a tathāgata's 'complete destruction of the traces' (*vāsanāsamudghāta, bag chags yang dag par bcom pa*). By contrast, even though arhats have terminated the mental afflictions, they still display actions that correspond to the existence of mental afflictions in their bodily movements, manner of gazing, speech, or comportment." Various commentaries give as examples of an arhat's behavior that is caused by the traces of the mental afflictions that he or she may at times still jump like a monkey because of having previously been born as a monkey, or may refer to a woman as a "female servant" (*dāsī, dmangs mo*). The latter example represents use of a derogatory term that relates to the caste system because of having previously been born as a brahmin, even though the Buddha condemned the use of such terms.

269. Paṇchen Lama Losang Chökyi Gyaltsen's *Preeminent One's Joyful Feast* (f. 50a) includes the qualification that it is not acceptable to receive the two higher initiations "in their actual form" (*dngos dbang du*). The "actual form" would be for both the teacher who confers those initiations and the individual who receives them to actually engage in sexual union with a tantric partner. The unstated implication of this distinction is that ordained persons who observe celibacy can confer and receive these initiations in a form in which a consort is mentally visualized.

270. *tshangs spyod dge bsnyen*. The principal form of the Buddhist layperson's vow is associated with the observance of five precepts in which the practitioner abandons all forms of the acts of killing, stealing, sexual misconduct, lying, and consuming alcohol. This does not typically include the precept of observing celibacy. In other less austere forms of the layperson vow, less than all five of

these precepts are observed. However, in the most austere form of the Buddhist layperson vow, for which there are also five precepts, the practitioner remains celibate instead of merely abandoning sexual misconduct.

271. There are five forms of celibate vows that are observed by individuals who have left the householder state and "gone forth" (*pravrajita, rab tu byung ba*) into the homeless state of a Buddhist religious ascetic. They are novice monk (*śramaṇera, dge tshul*), novice nun (*śramaṇerikā, dge tshul ma*), probationary nun (*śikṣamānā, dge slob ma*), fully ordained monk (*bhikṣu, dge slong*) and fully ordained nun (*bhikṣuṇī, dge slong ma*).

272. This epithet, which literally means "teacher," is understood to mean Buddha Śākyamuni, not one's personal teacher. See note 3 (this chapter).

273. *pārājika, phas pham pa*. In the prātimokṣa system of morality, this term refers to four misdeeds: killing a human being, stealing an object of even modest value, engaging in sexual intercourse, and professing superhuman powers. Such an offense results in the loss of the celibate vow and requires permanent expulsion from the community of ordained monks and nuns.

274. *parājikasthāniya, pham pa'i gnas lta bu*. This term appears in the morality chapter of *BBh* and refers to root transgressions of the non-tantric Mahāyāna system of vows. Such misdeeds cause the bodhisattva vow to be lost. In that sense they are similar to the prātimokṣa system's four forms of "extreme defeat" (see note 273, this chapter). However, Mahāyāna root transgressions do not prevent one from retaking the bodhisattva vows again.

275. *Instruction on the Middle Way: A Chest of Jewels That Has Been Laid Open* (*dBu ma'i man ngag rin po che'i za ma tog kha phye ba*), Dg.T. dbu ma, vol. 31 (*ki*), f. 116a. (Toh. 3930)

276. I take the words *slob dpon dbang bskur* to be the compound *acāryasikta*, which means "one who has been consecrated as a teacher" or "one who has received the teacher's initiation."

277. I take the verb *brnyes 'gyur* (also rendered as *rnyed 'gyur* in some editions) that occurs in the third line to mean "to be permitted" or "to be allowed."

278. A well-known Tibetan classification of tantra identifies these four main categories: Action Tantra (*kriyātantra, bya ba'i rgyud*), Conduct Tantra (*caryātantra, spyod pa'i rgyud*), Yoga Tantra (*yogatantra, rnal 'byor gyi rgyud*) and Highest Yoga Tantra (*niruttarayogatantra, rnal 'byor bla na med pa'i rgyud*).

279. **āpatti, nyes pa*. The term "offense" is meant in the sense of a violation of the tantric system of morality. See last paragraph of note 280 (this chapter).

280. The commentary here interprets the phrase "one who has knowledge of reality" (**tattvavid, de nyid rig pa*) to mean "one who has knowledge of the ten essential principles" (*daśatattvavid, de kho na nyid bcu rig pa*). In this latter usage the Sanskrit term *tattva*, or "reality," means an "essential principle" rather than being a synonym for ultimate truth or emptiness. The phrase "ten essential principles" refers to a series of tantric practices that identify the essential qualifications for being a tantric teacher. The term appears in verse 9a of Aśvaghoṣa's *Fifty Verses*

on the Guru (*Gurupañcāśikā, bLa ma lnga bcu pa*) in the expression "thorough knowledge of the ten essential principles (*daśatattvaparijñātā, de nyid bcu yongs su shes pa*). In his commentary *The Fulfillment of All Hopes* (*bLa ma lnga bcu pa'i rnam bshad slob ma'i re ba kun skong*), Je Tsongkhapa cites several canonical sources where this phrase appears and focuses the main portion of his discussion on a passage from the final chapter of the *Vajrahṛdayālaṃkāra Tantra* (*rDo rje snying po'i rgyan gyi rgyud*, Toh. 451), which lists two sets of ten principles, one an outer set and the other a secret, or inner, set (see English translation, pp. 41–44).

By contrast, Atiśa's *Commentary on the Difficult Points* interprets the phrase "one who has knowledge of reality" to mean a tantric practitioner who has attained a certain level of knowledge regarding ultimate reality (*tattva, de kho na nyid*), or emptiness. In this sense, the phrase does not necessarily refer to a tantric teacher. Atiśa's text describes five distinct interpretations of various Indian teachers regarding what that level of knowledge was held to be. The sense of the final line is that such a person will no longer commit moral transgressions.

281. *sde pa bco brgyad.* Atiśa's biographies record that he received the bhikṣu vow of full ordination in the lineage of the Mahāsāṃghika school. The purpose of this reference to "eighteen schools" (*sde pa bco brgyad*) is to indicate that Atiśa was knowledgeable in all the tenets held by these separate Indian traditions and viewed them all with respect. It is not likely that all eighteen were still thriving at this period in Indian history. According to tradition, the eighteen Hīnayāna schools of Indian Buddhism arose at different times and were based in different geographic regions of the subcontinent. These schools had their own canonical collections and held specific tenets that differentiated them from one another. Some accounts suggest that the eighteen schools arose from these four early traditions: Sthavira (*gnas brtan pa*), Sarvāstivāda (*thams cad yod par smra ba*), Sammatīya (*mang po skur ba pa*), and Mahāsāṃghika (*dge 'dun phal chen gyi sde*). One list of the names of the eighteen schools appears in the Tibetan *Mahāvyutpatti* (s.v. "bye brag tu rtogs pa chen po," entries 9077–9098). Tāranātha's *History of Buddhism in India* (ch. 42) and *History of Buddhism by Butön* (pp. 97–100) provide brief overviews of this topic. André Bareau's *Les Sectes Bouddhiques du Petit Véhicule* discusses a wide range of primary historical sources and also presents specific tenets held by each of the schools. Traditional Indian accounts that are followed by Tibetan scholars are found in Bhavya's *Tarkajvāla* (*rTog ge 'bar ba*, ff. 148a–156a; Toh. 3856), Vinītadeva's *Nikāyabhedopadeśanasaṃgraha* (*sDe pa tha dad pa bstan pa bsdus pa*, Toh. 4140) and Vasumitra's *Samayabhedavyūhacakra* (*gZhung lugs kyi bye brag bkod pa'i 'khor lo*, Toh. 4138).

282. *sthavira, gnas brtan.* An honorific for a senior monk. The traditional explanation is that it refers to a fully ordained monk who has been observing the vows properly for at least ten years.

283. While the Tibetan literally means "seen" (*mthong ba*), the presumed Sanskrit

equivalent, *dṛṣṭa*, can also mean "learned" or "understood," which fits well in the present context.

284. *bhikṣu*, *dge slong*.
285. This verse is from Atiśa's *Introduction to the Two Truths* (*bDen pa gnyis la 'jug pa*).
286. *'jig rten mig*. This term is a translation of the Sanskrit term *lokacakṣu*, which is recognized as the source for the Tibetan term *lotsāwa* that is taken to mean, more simply, "translator."
287. *ekāyana*, *bgrod pa gcig pa'i lam*. While this expression can mean "a narrow way or path that is accessible for only one person," it can also mean "the only way or manner of conduct" (*MW*, s.v. "ekāyana"). The latter sense is the one that is meant here, and it is the one that is typically understood in the Tibetan tradition.
288. *don gnyis*. The two aims are one's own and that of others, which are fulfilled by achieving a buddha's wisdom body (*dharmakāya*, *chos sku*) and physical body (*rūpakāya*, *gzugs sku*), respectively.
289. *kun mkyen brtse ba chen po*. This descriptive phrase includes the syllables *kyen* and *tse*, which are abbreviations of "knowledge" and "compassion," respectively, and are clearly meant as a reference to Jamgön Kongtrul's teacher/collaborator Jamyang Khyentse Wangpo ('Jam dbyang mkhyen brtse dbang po, 1820–1892).
290. That is, the robes of a Buddhist monk. This is meant as a statement of modesty in the sense that the author makes no claim as to being a great spiritual practitioner.

5. A Verse Compendium of the Spiritual Practices of the Stages of the Path to Enlightenment

1. *Byang chub lam gyi rim pa'i nyams len bsdus don gyi tshigs su bcad pa*, *DNZ*, vol. 3 (*ga*), pp. 63–69. Second source: *Byang chub lam gyi rim pa'i nyams len gyi rnam gzhag mdor bsdus te brjed byang du bya ba* (also known as *Lam rim bsdus don* and as *Nyams mgur*), in Collected Works, vol. 2 (*kha*), pp. 308–13 (New Delhi: Mongolian Lama Guru Deva, 1978–1983). (Toh. 5275)
2. Mi pham. This term, which means literally "Invincible One," is another name for Maitreya.
3. *bhuvanatraya* or *tribhuvana*, *sa gsum*. That is, heaven, earth, and the regions beneath the earth.
4. *jambudvīpa*, *'dzam bu'i gling*. Buddhist cosmology describes our world—which can be interpreted as corresponding roughly to planet Earth—as being made up of four major continents and eight minor ones. Of the four major continents, the Rose Apple continent is the name of the southern continent, which corresponds roughly to the area of greater South Asia. (Despite this fact, most modern Tibetans use the Tibetan word for this continent to refer to the entire planet Earth.) It is described in the *AKBh* as being shaped like a chariot—that

is, roughly triangular. In its center lies the Adamantine Seat (*vajrāsana*, *rdo rje gdan*), where the buddhas attain enlightenment. The name of this continent is said to derive from a great rose apple (*jambu*) tree that lies near Lake Anavatapta at the northern edge of the continent. This lake is sometimes associated with Lake Manasarovar.

5. See ch. 4, "The Brilliant Illumination of the Path to Enlightenment," note 174.
6. Mar me mdzad. This is a shortened form of Atiśa's ordination name. His full name is Dīpaṃkara Śrījñāna (dPal mar me mdzad ye shes).
7. *ratha*, *shing rta*. This term, which literally means "chariot," is also used to designate a person as a "warrior," a "champion," or a "hero" (*MW*, s.v. "ratha"). In this spiritual context, it is used metaphorically to describe great Buddhist philosophical innovators, in this case Nāgārjuna and Asaṅga.
8. Chone Drakpa Shedrup (Co nas grags pa bshad sgrub, 1675–1748) writes in his *Brief Word Commentary That Clarifies the Lamrim Compendium* (*Lam rim bsdus don gyi tshig 'grel mdor bsdus gsal ba*: "It is apparent that some scholars interpret the phrase 'the eye with which to view' (*lta ba'i mig*) as referring to one's spiritual teachers; however, Je Tsongkhapa indicates clearly at the end of his *Great Treatise on the Stages of the Path* that he intended for it to refer to the Lamrim teaching itself." This statement appears to be a reference to the first verse in the *Great Treatise*'s closing series of verses, where Je Tsongkhapa describes the Lamrim system of instruction as "the singular eye with which to examine all the Muni's myriad discourses, even just one of which is able to comprehend well and accurately all the scriptural systems." The verse here uses the single verb *gsal mdzad*, or "to make clear," to indicate that the Lamrim teaching both "makes clear the eye with which to view all the myriad scriptures" and "makes clear the supreme entry point for fortunate beings traveling to liberation."
9. *vaśirājaṃ nāma maṇiratnaṃ*, *nor bu rin po che dbang gi rgyal po zhes bya ba*. This is the name of a special jewel that is cited in the Maitreya section of the *Gaṇḍavyūha Sūtra* as a metaphor for enlightenment mind. It is described as being such that even while situated in the Rose Apple continent, it causes the arrays of appearances in the palaces of the sun and moon, which are situated at a distance of forty thousand yojanas, to be seen. Enlightenment mind is said to resemble this jewel in that it causes all spiritual qualities to become cleansed of any impurities and because, even while it remains in samsara, it causes the great sun and moon of the tathāgatas' knowledge, which travels in the sky of the reality-sphere to be seen, as well as the arrays of appearances that are present in all the buddha realms.
10. *bstan pa thams cad*. Citing a passage from an Indian treatise, Je Tsongkhapa glosses this term in his *Great Treatise on the Stages of the Path* to mean the entirety of the Buddha's well-spoken discourses.
11. That is, it transforms ordinary virtuous deeds into causes that will bring the attainment of supreme enlightenment.
12. *sat*, *dam pa*. Literally a "good person" or a "wise person," the related Sanskrit

term *satpuruṣa* (*skyes bu dam pa*) is often understood to mean a "holy person" or a "great spiritual being." I translate the term *dam pa* here as "true spiritual being" to indicate a person who is both virtuous and wise. *MSA*, ch. 13, v. 8, states: "A bodhisattva with extensive learning / who has perceived the truths, / and who is eloquent, compassionate, and tireless / should be recognized as a great spiritual being."

13. *nam mkha' lding* or *khyung*. A mythical bird that is the king of the feathered race and the enemy that devours all members of the serpent race.
14. *PSV* (English translation, p. 288) states: "Fitness of the body is that condition of the body that enables it to engage in activities readily. Fitness of the mind is a distinct mental factor that serves as a cause for bringing delight and facility to a mind that is accompanied by right attention."
15. This is an alternate name of Ganden Monastery, the first major Gelukpa religious seat, founded by Je Tsongkhapa in 1409.
16. *shar sgom* or *bshar sgom*. The following description of this form of practice appears in Pabongkha Rinpoche's *Downpour of Auspicious Virtue* (an instruction manual on the six preliminary practices), pp. 160–61): "Reflective meditation is analogous to looking down from atop a high mountain and reciting the names of the various regions below as you point to them with your finger. That is, you merely review in your mind, one by one, the various stages of the path without actually generating experiential realizations of them." Its value derives from its ability to generate in a practitioner's mind a propensity for a complete system of practice.
17. *rje btsun*. The original Sanskrit term (*bhaṭṭāraka*) is a respectful title used for learned Buddhist teachers that means both a "great lord" and a "person who is worthy of veneration" (*MW*, s.v. "bhaṭṭāraka"). Akhu Ching Sherap Gyatso's (A khu ching Shes rab rgya mtsho, 1803–1875) commentary *Opening the Door to the Realm of Nectar* (*bDud rtsi'i dbyings kyi sgo 'byed*, f. 33b) states: "An easily understood explanation of this term is that the word *rje* means a 'lord.' Just as an ordinary lord has authority over his subjects, a spiritual lord wields authority over the spiritual domain of the three realms by means of the dharma wheel. *Tsun pa* means one who has turned away from the respective bad qualities that pertain to body, speech, and mind." Based on this explanation, I have rendered this honorific as "exalted and venerable."
18. These final sentences have been added by the editors of *The Treasury of Precious Instructions*.

6. The Flower Cluster of Spiritual Attainments: A Supplication Prayer to the Lineage Whose Blessings Are Near

1. *Byin rlabs nye brgyud kyi gsol 'debs dngos grub kyi snye ma*, *DNZ*, vol. 3 (*ga*), pp. 71–72. Second source: *Byin rlabs nye brgyud kyi bla ma rnams la gsol ba*

'debs pa / dNgos grub kyi snye ma, in Collected Works, vol. 2 (*kha*) (New Delhi: Mongolian Lama Guru Deva, 1978–1983), pp. 206–8. (Toh. 5275)

2. An alternate name of Mañjuśrī, the deity who is recognized as the embodiment of all buddhas' wisdom.
3. The Sanskrit equivalent of this name is Vīravajra, which translates as "Adamantine Hero." This is a reference to the teacher known more popularly as Lama Umapa (bLa ma dBu ma pa, "lama of the middle way"). His personal name was Tsöndru Senge (brTson 'grus seng ge). Je Tsongkhapa met him in the spring of 1390 and had close spiritual interactions with him until the fall of 1392, when the Lama returned to his native region in Kham. This lama was a visionary who first served as a medium between Je Tsongkhapa and Mañjuśrī, until Je Rinpoche began having visions of the deity himself, which first took place at a time when Je Rinpoche and Lama Umapa were in retreat together at Gadong Monastery (*dga' gdong*).
4. This and the next two verses do not appear in Je Tsongkhapa's original composition.
5. rGyal tshab Dar ma rin chen, 1364–1432. He was recognized as Je Tsongkhapa's successor as the official head of the Gelukpa tradition with the title "Holder of the Ganden Throne" (*dga' ldan khri pa*).
6. mKhas grub dGe legs dpal bzang, 1385–1438. He was one of Je Tsongkhapa's closest personal disciples.
7. Shes rab seng ge, 1383–1445. This disciple formally accepted in Je Tsongkhapa's presence the responsibility for persevering his master's system of tantric teachings.
8. dGe 'dun grub pa, 1391–1474. An important direct disciple of Je Tsongkhapa who retroactively was recognized as the first in the line of Dalai Lamas. He founded Tashi Lhunpo Monastery in 1447.
9. This is a slightly revised version of a verse that appears in ch. 5, "A Verse Compendium of the Spiritual Practices of the Stages of the Path."
10. *alpeccha, 'dod pa chung ba*. This is the antidote for the fault of having great desire (*mahecchatā, 'dod pa che ba*), which Vasubandhu (*AKBh* Sanskrit edition, p. 335) defines as "the craving to acquire, in an excellent or an abundant form, something that one has not obtained."
11. *saṃtuṣṭi, chog shes pa*. This attitude is the antidote for the fault of not being satisfied with what one does possess (*asaṃtuṣṭi, chog mi shes pa*), which again Vasubandhu (*AKBh*, p. 335) defines as "a state of discontent caused by the feeling that what one has obtained is not of sufficiently good quality or is not sufficiently great in quantity."
12. *zhi zhing dul ba*. When cited together, this pair of qualities is often described as referring to the proper type of composed demeanor to observe in the presence of one's spiritual teacher; or it can simply describe the mark of a well-disciplined monk or spiritual practitioner. It is also characterized as a state that is free of the agitation caused by anger and pride.

13. *pūrvābhilāpī, gsong por smra ba.* The Tibetan equivalent of this term is usually described as meaning "to be honest and truthful in one's speech." However, the Sanskrit original literally means "one who speaks first," a trait that is considered a mark of graciousness or respect (cf. *BHSD*, p. 352). *BBhVy* (f. 198b) states: "In order to show oneself as being amicably disposed, a bodhisattva is the first to speak to those who have arrived in his or her presence and addresses them with such greetings as 'Welcome.'"
14. "Pure perceptions" (*dag snang*) is a term that can be interpreted a number of ways. One important explanation is that, as a Mahāyānist practitioner, one should avoid judging other beings critically by perceiving them as having faults. To be "impartial" (*phyogs med*) would typically mean to develop the equanimity (*upekṣā, btang snyongs*) that does not feel attachment and favoritism toward those persons regarded as close friends or animosity and disfavor toward those considered to be adversaries.
15. **jñātrakāma, shes kyi khe 'dod pa.* The Sanskrit original is uncertain. This fault is described as a form of desire and pride in which a person carries out activities such as teaching the dharma because he or she wants to receive something in return. For example, by becoming recognized as a knowledgeable person, he or she hopes to achieve fame, honor, and offerings of material value.
16. This prayer was composed sometime during a period of retreat practice from late 1392 to 1395 that was carried out in the vicinity of Ölka Valley (*'ol kha*), located in the Lhoka (*lho kha*) region of central Tibet. During this time, Je Tsongkhapa was accompanied by a chosen group of eight disciples.

7. The Nectar That Is Like Highly Refined Gold: An Instruction Manual on the Stages of the Path to Enlightenment

1. *Byang chub lam gyi rim pa'i 'khrid gser gyi yang zhun*, *DNZ*, vol. 3 (*ga*), pp. 73–110. Second source: *Byang chub lam gyi rim pa'i khrid gser gyi yang zhun*, in Collected Works (Dharamsala: Library of Tibetan Works and Archives, 2000).
2. *kṣaṇasampad, dal 'byor.* This noun compound refers to a human life that is endowed with eighteen qualities that are ideal for pursuing a meaningful spiritual life. "Leisure" (*kṣaṇa, dal ba*) refers to eight opportune states. In Tibetan Buddhism, the classic source for these eight states is the canonical passage from the *Ekottarāgama* (*gCig las 'phros pa'i lung*) that Nāgārjuna cites in his *Sūtrasamuccaya* (*mDo kun las btus pa*). The eight qualities are not to have been born in the hells, as a tormented spirit, as an animal, as a long-lived deity, as a human being in an outlying region who is a foreigner/barbarian (*mleccha, kla klo*), as a human being who adheres to a form of wrong view, as a human being who is dull-witted and unable to differentiate between what has been well taught and what has been badly taught, and as a human being who has

been born at a time when a buddha has not appeared in the world. While the complete sūtra is not available in either Sanskrit or Tibetan, a Pali version can be found in the *Aṅguttara Nikāya*, the Book of Eights, sutta 29, titled "Inopportune Moments" (*Akkhaṇasutta*). The eight qualities are also addressed in Nāgārjuna's *SL*, vv. 63, 64. "Fortune" (*sampad, 'byor ba*) refers to the combination of five fortunes that relate to oneself and five fortunes that relate to others. These ten qualities are described in the opening portion of Asaṅga's *Stage of a Śrāvaka* (*Śrāvakabhūmi, Nyan thos kyi sa*). The five fortunes that relate to oneself are to be born as a human, in a central land, to possess all of one's faculties intact, not to have lost the capacity to bring religious endeavors to completion, and to have faith in the "seat" (*āyatanagata, gnas*)—that is, the Buddhist system of dharma and vinaya. The five fortunes that relate to others are the appearance of the buddhas, the teaching of the dharma by the buddhas and their śrāvaka disciples, the continuance of the teaching that has been taught, the furtherance of the teaching, and compassion that is felt by others.

3. *jina, rgyal ba.* This is an epithet that Buddha Śākyamuni used in reference to himself. See ch. 4, "The Brilliant Illumination of the Path to Enlightenment," note 34.
4. *sarvākārajñatā, rnam pa thams cad mkhyen pa nyid.* This is a term from the Prajnāpāramitā sūtras and related literature that refers to a Buddha's supreme omniscience.
5. *vaśirājaṃ nāma maṇiratnaṃ, nor bu rin po che dbang gi rgyal po zhes bya ba.* See ch. 5 "A Verse Compendium of the Spiritual Practices of the Stages of the Path," note 9.
6. Rig pa'i khu byug. There were two Indian gurus who were known by this epithet; this master was the younger of the two. He was also known as Avadhūtipa and was Atiśa's principal teacher of Madhyamaka philosophy. Biographical accounts record that Atiśa studied with him for seven years.
7. bLa ma gSer gling pa. See ch. 2, "The Root Text of the Mahāyāna Instruction Known as the Seven-Point Mind Training," note 10.
8. *gsung mgur.* This term, as well as the expression "song of realization" (*nyams mgur*), is commonly used to refer to Je Tsongkapa's *Compendium of the Stages of the Path* (*lam rim bsdus don*). In addition to describing what is addressed in the two verses from Je Tsongkhapa's *Spiritual Song* that follow, this paragraph also identifies what are known as the Lamrim instruction's "three great attributes" (*khyad chos chen po gsum*). The source for this point is a passage from Je Tsongkhapa's *Great Treatise* (f. 8b), where he refers to Atiśa's *Lamp for the Path to Enlightenment* (*Byang chub lam gyi sgron ma*) as the root text for the instruction known as the Stages of the Path and describes it as superior to other teaching systems in that it is endowed with these three attributes.
9. *jambudvīpa, 'dzam bu'i gling.* See ch. 5, "A Verse Compendium of the Spiritual Practices of the Stages of the Path," note 4.
10. Je Tsongkhapa's system of the Lamrim practice addresses two principal forms

of meditation: "analytic meditation" (*dpyad sgom*) and "fixed meditation" (*'jog sgom*). Analytic meditation is the exercise of eliciting experiential realizations of each element of instruction by applying discriminative wisdom as the means of reflecting on relevant scriptural citations and forms of reasoning. Fixed meditation is the exercise of fixing the mind one-pointedly on any given object of meditation.

11. That is, Atiśa's *Lamp for the Path to Enlightenment*, which is regarded as the root text of the system of instruction known as the Stages of the Path (*lam rim*).
12. **mahāduścarita, nyes spyod chen po*. While this general term can apply to any number of serious offenses, Je Tsongkhapa's *Great Treatise* singles out the misdeed of repudiating the true dharma (*saddharmapratikṣepa, dam pa'i chos spong ba*) as the most important one that will be avoided through learning the instruction on the Stages of the Path.
13. *rJe bla ma*. An epithet of Je Tsongkhapa which means "the Lama who is the lord."
14. *bstan pa thams cad*. See ch. 5, "A Verse Compendium of the Spiritual Practices of the Stages of the Path," note 10.
15. *śāstā, ston pa*. Literally "teacher," this term is a reference to Buddha Śākyamuni, who first taught the true dharma in this world.
16. *snod kyi skyon gsum*. The canonical statement that is interpreted as embodying this point declares: "Listen both well and intently to the following instruction, and bear it in mind." (*śṛṇu sadhu ca suṣṭhu ca manasi kuru*). The three defects are a downward-facing pot, a dirty pot, and a leaky pot. A pot that is upside down is a metaphor for a disciple who doesn't even try to understand to what is being taught (*apratipattyā*). A dirty pot is a metaphor for a disciple who listens with a wrongful motivation (*viparītapratipattyā*). A leaky pot is a metaphor for a disciple who does not listen with a mind that is firmly attentive (*asthirapratipattyā*). In his *Abhisamayālaṃkārāloka* (p. 333), Haribhadra identifies this as Ācārya Vasubandhu's interpretation of the three-part metaphor.
17. *'du shes drug*. The six conceptions are to think of yourself as a sick person, to think of the dharma as medicine, to think of your spiritual teacher as a skilled physician, to think that practicing the dharma intently will cure your illness, to think of the tathāgata as a holy being, and to wish that the dharma might remain for a long time.
18. *Mahāyānasūtrālaṃkāra, Theg pa chen po mdo sde'i rgyan*. These ten qualities are described in *MSA* (ch. 17, v. 10), which states: "Rely upon a friend who is subdued, calm, and tranquil, / has superior qualities, is energetic and rich in scriptural learning, / has cognized reality, is endowed with eloquence, / has a compassionate nature, and is tireless."
19. *adhigama, rtogs pa. AK* (ch. 8, v. 39ab) states: "The Master's true dharma is twofold, as its nature consists of scripture (*āgama, lung*) and realization" (*adhigama, rtogs*). The commentary identifies "scripture" as the three collections of sūtra, vinaya, and abhidharma and "realization" as the thirty-seven spiritual

qualities that are conducive to enlightenment (*bodhipakṣyā, byang chub kyi phyogs dang mthun pa rnams*).

20. *āgama, lung.* See note 19 (this chapter).

21. *tripiṭaka, sde snod gsum.* Literally, the Sanskrit term *piṭaka* means a "basket" or "container," such as for grain. It is also used to refer to the collections of Buddhist canonical literature, such as the three "baskets" of sūtra (discourses), vinaya (the Buddhist code of moral discipline), and abhidharma (systematic formulations of essential doctrine).

22. *avavāda, gdams ngag. BBh* (pp. 199–201) describes instruction as being eightfold in nature. For the first four, a teacher first examines and realizes (1) the mind, (2) faculties, (3) attitude, and (4) latent propensities of an individual and then "causes him or her to undertake any of a variety of means of practice, in whatever manner is suitable and in whatever manner is appropriate to that person." The next two are (5) to teach the Middle Way "as the antidote to wrongly grasping at the eternalistic extreme" and (6) to teach it "as the antidote to wrongly grasping at the nihilistic extreme." The final two are (7) to provide instruction that "causes that person to abandon the exaggerated pride in which he or she mistakenly thinks that he or she has accomplished something that has not been accomplished" and (8) to provide instruction that "causes that person to abandon the exaggerated pride in which he or she mistakenly thinks that he or she has attained some result that has not been attained, reached, or realized." Sāgaramegha's commentary to *BBh* (ff. 130b–131a) gives two interpretations of the term: "Instruction is the enjoyment of spoken discourse because it generates correct understanding." Also, "Instruction is the speaking of suitable words to someone after having understood the nature of his or her mind."

23. *anuśāsana, rjes su bstan pa. BBh* (pp. 201–2) describes counsel as being "fivefold in its nature: forbidding conduct that engages in what is objectionable, approving of conduct that engages in what is free of objection, admonishing a person who has engaged in erroneous conduct that relates to actions that are forbidden and approved, prompting those who continually develop disregard for proper conduct and behave erroneously to observe recollection by censuring them with an attitude that is not impure and that is unaltered and friendly, and giving encouragement to those who are engaged in correct practice regarding those things that are forbidden and approved by making an agreeable statement about their genuine good qualities."

24. *madhyastha, gzu bor gnas pa.*

25. **vicāraka, blo ldan.*

26. *arthī, don gnyer can.*

27. Āryadeva's *Four Hundred Verses* (ch. 12, v. 1ab) states: "The śrāvaka who is impartial, discerning, and diligent is said to be a fit vessel."

28. Candrakīrti adds this quality in his commentary (f. 184a) to Āryadeva's *Four Hundred Verses*.

29. What follows is a brief overview of the manner in which to carry out a formal

meditation session on the instruction itself in relation to the initial topic of serving a spiritual teacher. The session is divided into three parts: preliminary exercises, main meditation practice, and concluding prayers. The first part is made up of a devotional exercise known as the six preliminary practices (**ṣaṭ prayogadharma, sbyor ba'i chos drug*), a form of practice that Je Tsongkhapa identifies as having been followed by Atiśa's teacher Serlingpa. Commentaries describe the six preliminary activities as follows: clean the practice area and set up vessels of a buddha's body, speech, and mind; arrange faultless offerings in an attractive manner; sit on a comfortable seat while maintaining Vairocana's seven attributes of posture and then, with a mind of extraordinary virtue, take refuge, generate enlightenment mind, and meditate on the four immeasurables; visualize the merit field; perform the seven-limb devotional practice—which contains the main elements for accumulating merit and purifying oneself of obstructions—together with a mandala offering; and imbue your mental continuum with an attitude of supplication according to instruction.

30. *rten*. See note 29 (this chapter) and ch. 4, "The Brilliant Illumination of the Path to Enlightenment," note 91, for an explanation of this term.
31. *anukuladeśa, mthun pa'i yul.* An agreeable place is the first of the six requisites for cultivating quiescence and insight that are described in Je Tsongkhapa's *Great Treatise on the Stages of the Path*. The text cites the second of Kamalaśīla's three works entitled *Stages of Meditation* (*Bhāvanākrama, bsGom pa'i rim pa*) as the source for this topic. *MSA* (ch. 17, v. 7) states: "An intelligent person practices in a place having these qualities: material needs are easily obtained, it is safe to reside there, the ground is healthy, good companions are present, and it is conducive to spiritual practice."
32. The full verse states: "I go for refuge until enlightenment / to the Buddha, dharma, and supreme assembly. / Through this generosity, and so forth, done by me, / may I attain buddhahood in order to benefit the world."
33. The complete mantra is *oṃ svabhāvaśūddhāḥ sarvadharmāḥ svabhāvaśuddho 'ham*. It can be translated as: "*oṃ*. All entities are pure in that they are free of any real essential nature, and I am one with that purity of being free of any real essential nature."
34. See note 15 (this chapter). In this visualization, one's spiritual teacher is visualized as appearing in Buddha Śākyamuni's form. Further details regarding this visualization can be found in commentaries.
35. *rgya chen spyod brgyud*. This is the name of the lineage of teachings that has been transmitted from Buddha to Maitreya, and from the latter to Asaṅga, and so forth. It is recognized as being the main source of instructions on the bodhisattva activities. See also note 47 (this chapter) for the names of additional Indian masters who make up this lineage.
36. *zab mo lta brgyud*. This is the name of the lineage of teachings that has been transmitted from Buddha to Mañjughoṣa, and from the latter to Nāgārjuna,

and so forth. It is recognized as being the main source of instructions on the profound view that realizes emptiness. See also note 46 (this chapter).

37. *vīra, dpa' bo*. This is a name for male tantric deities, such as the twenty-four that are associated with the Cakrasaṃvara system. Another term for these deities is *ḍāka* (*mkha' 'gro*), which literally translates as "sky-goer."

38. *mkha' 'gro ma*. The feminine form of *ḍāka* (see note 37, this chapter).

39. The visualization of this assemblage of beings is referred to as the "merit field" (*tshogs zhing*). It is a field in the sense that one can reap the benefit of accumulating an abundance of merit or virtue by worshiping the beings who are present before you. The word *tshogs* in this term literally means "accumulation," of which there are two types, merit and wisdom. Because it is primarily the merit accumulation that is generated by worshiping this assembly of spiritual beings, the term is translated as "merit field."

40. The full second verse states: "You who are the protector of all beings without exception, / the divine conqueror of the terrible evil one with his host, / you who know the totality of entities as they truly are, / O Bhagavān, please draw near, together with your retinue."

41. The full verse (*BCA*, ch. 2, v. 10) states: "In exquisitely fragrant bathhouses / with inlaid floors of brightly shining crystal, / dazzling columns aglitter with jewels, / and canopies festooned with shimmering pearls—"

42. *BCA*, ch. 2, vv. 10–14. Liturgy for the bathing ritual can be very extensive and would typically include recitations that include many more than just these five verses.

43. The full final verse states: "In your compassion for me and all beings / and by means of your miraculous powers, / O Lords, please remain seated here / as long as I continue to worship you."

44. **saptāṅgakā, yan lag bdun pa*. The seven elements that make up this practice are prostration (*vandanā, phyag 'tshal ba*), presenting offerings (*pūjanā, mchod pa*), confession (*deśanā, bshags pa*), rejoicing (*anumodanā, rjes su yi rang ba*); requesting that the dharma wheel be turned (*adhyeṣaṇā, bskul ba*), a supplication not to enter nirvana (*yācanā, gsol ba 'debs pa*), and dedication (*pariṇāmanā, yongs su bsngo ba*).

45. The full verse states: "I make prostration to the lamas, whose bodies contain all buddhas, / whose natures are that of the vajra holder, / and who are the root sources of the Three Jewels."

46. The full verse states: "I make prostration to the Lineage of Divinely Inspired Practice— / which includes Vajradhara, the sugata possessed of great compassion, / Telopa and Naropa, seers of the supreme reality, / and the glorious Ḍombīpa and Atiśa." This is a third lineage of tantric instruction that was also transmitted in Tibet through Atiśa.

47. The full verse states: "I make prostration to the Lineage of Extensive Conduct, / which includes Maitreya, Asaṅga, Vasubandhu, and Vimuktisena, / Paramasena, Vinitasena, and the glorious Kīrti, / Haribhadra, the two Kuśalīs, and Suvarṇadvīpī."

48. The full verse states: "I make prostration to the Lineage of the Profound View, / which includes Ārya Nāgārjuna, the victor's son who destroyed the erring positions of being and nonbeing, / Candrakīrti, Vidyākokila the Elder, and the rest, / the spiritual father and sons who preserved the Buddha's true intent.
49. The full verse states: "I make prostration to the glorious Atiśa, / who appeared before the Victor as Bhadrapāla, / in the Snowy Land was the glorious Dīpaṃkara, / and is currently in Tuṣita as *Vimalāmbara."
50. The full verse states: "I make prostration to the feet of the Teacher Drom, / a spiritual teacher for all, a protector for all, / a victor's offspring and patriarch of the Victor's spiritual lineage, / and the precious source through which to achieve one's own and others' aims."
51. The full verse states: "I make prostration to the feet of the Losang Drakpa, / the crown ornament of the Snowy Land's scholars / who embodies Avalokiteśvara, the great treasure of compassion that has no mental object / and Mañjughoṣa, the lord of immaculate wisdom."
52. The full verse states: "I make prostration to the feet of the glorious lama, / made resplendent by the locks of having accepted the duty of preserving scripture and reasoning, / whose physical strength of powerful and profound wisdom was greatly developed, / a majestic lion of teachers for the snow mountain of the Muni's teaching."
53. The full verse states: "I make prostration to the feet of the glorious lama whose virtuous deeds furthered the teaching, / the most glorious of all scholars and the lord / of spiritual attainments who founded the principal gathering place for the sangha / who possess the excellent qualities of knowledge and liberation."
54. The full verse states: "I make prostration to you, a wish-granting jewel that fulfills all needs, / who achieved all spiritual qualities without needing to study, / you perfected learning, reflection, and contemplation, / achieved the attainments and perform spiritual deeds uninterruptedly."
55. The full verse states: "I make prostration to the direct lamas / from whom we receive knowledge, / who teach us sūtras, tantras, treatises, and personal instruction, / and confer the morality training, initiations, and blessings."
56. The full verse states: "I make prostration to the object of refuge, the Three Jewels: / the unsurpassed teacher, the precious Buddha, / the unsurpassed protector, the true dharma, / and the unsurpassed guides, the precious sangha."
57. The full verse states: "I make prostration to the King of the Śākyas, / who took birth in the Śākya clan through skillful means and compassion, / who conquered the 'invincible' Evil One's host, / and whose resplendent body is like a golden mountain."
58. This is a reference to the first seven verses of *The Aspirational Prayer for Excellent Spiritual Conduct* (*Bhadracaryapraṇidhāna*, *bZang po spyod pa'i smon lam*).
59. The full verse states: "In addition to these, may diverse clouds of offering collections, / accompanied by music delightful and melodious / that dispels the suffering of sentient beings, / also become situated throughout the sky above."

60. *spyi bshags*. This is the name of a recitation that expresses the act of confessing transgressions of all general misdeeds, as well as transgressions of the three systems of Buddhist morality—that is, the prātimokṣa vow, the non-tantric Mahāyāna vow, and the tantric vow.
61. *The Aspirational Prayer for Excellent Spiritual Conduct*, vv. 8–12.
62. *lam mchog sgo 'byed*. This supplication prayer (*gsol 'debs*) to receive the lamas' blessings represents the last of the six preliminary practices. The verses were composed by Je Tsongkhapa and are addressed to the Indian masters of the two Indian lineages associated with the Lamrim tradition, the Lineage of Extensive Conduct (*rgya chen spyod brgyud*) and the Lineage of the Profound View (*zab mo lta brgyud*), as well as three Tibetan Kadam lineages, namely the Lamrim Followers (*lam rim pa*), the Treatise Followers (*gzhung pa ba*), and the Instruction Followers (*gdams ngag ba*). This prayer is the first item in the collection of Je Tsongkhapa's miscellaneous works (*bKa' 'bum thor bu*, Toh. 5275).
63. *siddhi*, *dngos grub*. There are two types: common spiritual attainments (*sāmānyasiddi*, *thun mong gi dngos grub*) and the supreme spiritual attainment (*paramasiddi*, *mchog gi dngos grub*). Common spiritual attainments include such spiritual powers as the ability to carry out any of the four main types of tantric activities or any of various extraordinary powers such as, for example, the "eye ointment," which enables one to see treasures and other precious objects that lie below the surface of the earth, or the "sword," which enables one to travel in the sky or travel instantly to any particular location that is desired. The supreme spiritual attainment is a buddha's ultimate enlightenment.
64. The Tibetan description of a spiritual teacher as *sku drin che*, or *bka' drin che*, translates literally as one who is "great in kindness"; however, the term carries a unique sense that is much more profound than other forms of kindness and is used exclusively to describe one's lama. Its sense is likely related to the Sanskrit term *prasāda*, which refers to the grace or spiritual favor and blessings that a lama confers upon his or her disciples.
65. *PK*, ch. 4, v. 2. The pronoun "that" in the first line is a reference to Vajrasattva, who is mentioned in the preceding verse. Muniśrībhadra glosses the epithet "Self-Originated One" (*svayaṃbhūr*) as follows: "Vajrasattva is the Self-Originated One because He became Himself (*svayaṃ bhavatīti*) through having realized the insubstantiality of all entities" (*niḥsvabhāvasarvavastuparijñānāt*). The first half of this verse appears in the *Sarvabuddhasamāyoga Tantra* (ch. 1, v. 2ab).
66. This adverb is meant in the sense of the lives prior to Buddha Śākyamuni's attainment of enlightenment—that is, while he was still a bodhisattva. Descriptions of the incidents alluded to here can be found in such works as the sūtra titled *The Great Skillful Means in Which the Buddha [Teaches about] Repaying Kindness* (*Thabs mkhas pa chen po sangs rgyas drin lan bsab pa'i mdo*, Toh. 353) and the *Sutasoma Jātaka* in Āryaśūra's *Garland of Birth Stories* (*Jātakamālā*, *sKyes pa'i rabs kyi phreng ba*).

67. See note 15 (this chapter).
68. A Brahmin tells a wheel-wielding monarch (*cakravartī rāja, 'khor los sgyur ba'i rgyal po*) who was a bodhisattva in a former life of Buddha Śākyamuni that he will teach him dharma only if the king cuts a thousand gashes in his own body, pours oil into the cavities, inserts wicks, and then lights the wicks to honor him with a thousand such lighted lamps. This story appears in chapter 3 of the *Sūtra on Repaying Kindness* (*Drin lan bsab pa'i mdo*; see note 66, this chapter).
69. *mchod pa gsum. MSA* (ch. 17, v. 11ab) states: "One should serve a spiritual friend with honor, material objects, / by waiting upon him or her, and through practice."
70. *bdud*. This term, which literally means "destructive force," is also translated as the Evil One when it refers to a particular worldly god that seeks to lead spiritual practitioners astray. *ŚBh* (pp. 344–45) describes four forms of māra. Three are impersonal conditions that exist within a samsaric being's own nature—namely, the five impure heaps, the mental afflictions, and the condition of being mortal. The fourth is identified as a worldly god of the desire realm who obstructs the efforts of spiritual practitioners to transcend samsaric existence. This latter form is the one that is meant here.
71. 'Brom ston pa. Literally "the teacher from the Drom clan," this is a reference to Atiśa's principal Tibetan disciple. He was also known by the name Gyalwai Jungne (rGyal ba'i 'byung gnas, 1004/5–1064).
72. *kṣaṇasampad, dal 'byor*. See note 2 (this chapter) for a description of the eight leisures and ten fortunes.
73. *sor mo gsum khar bcug*. This colloquial expression is meant to suggest a willingness to put forth great effort to complete some task.
74. *aṣṭau lokadharma, 'jig rten gyi chos brgyad*. The eight worldly concerns are to react with delight toward acquisition of material wealth (*lābha, rnyed pa*), pleasure (*sukha, bde ba*), praise (*praśaṃsā, bstod pa*), and a good reputation (*yaśa, snyan pa*), as well as to feel displeasure in response to the loss of material wealth (*alābha, ma rnyed pa*), pain (*duḥkha, sdug bsngal*), blame (*nindā, smad pa*) and ill repute (*ayaśa, mi snyan pa*). The "black" form of these eight worldly concerns is the most familiar one. It is unvirtuous in nature and caused by attachment to this life. The mottled form (*khra bo*) is one in which a spiritual practitioner is indifferent to the occurrence of any of these eight circumstances; however, he or she still possesses the self-cherishing attitude that stems from the desire to attain liberation for oneself alone and therefore lacks the altruistic attitude of a bodhisattva. The white form is one that is possessed by a bodhisattva who is free of the self-cherishing attitude but who has not yet developed a proper understanding of emptiness and is therefore still subject to the mistaken notion that these eight circumstances possess real, self-existent natures.
75. The second topic is the actual method through which to derive value from one's human life, which is made of these three sections: training oneself in the stages of the path that is held in common with lesser persons, training oneself in the

stages of the path that is held in common with middling persons, and training oneself in the stages of the path for great persons.

76. *abhyudaya, mngon par mtho ba*. See ch. 4, "The Brilliant Illumination of the Path to Enlightenment," note 19.
77. *niḥśreyasa, nges par legs pa*. This term literally means "the state that has no better," of which there are two forms. The first is the state of nirvana that consists of deliverance, or liberation from samsara, and is achieved through the Hīnayāna path. The second is the supreme enlightenment of buddhahood, also known as the state of "nonabiding nirvana" (*apratiṣṭhitanirvāṇa, mi gnas pa'i mya ngan las 'das pa*), which is the goal of the Mahāyāna path.
78. v. 3.
79. *svarga, mtho ris*. The literal meaning of the original Sanskrit term is that of "an abode of light" or a "celestial realm," and thus typically means rebirth in the region of a worldly class of gods and not rebirth as a human being. However, in native Tibetan literature this term is usually understood to mean "the status of being reborn as a worldly god or a human being."
80. v. 4.
81. v. 5.
82. *apāya, ngan song*. They are generally recognized as being of three kinds: rebirth in the hells, as a tormented spirit (*preta, yi dags*), or as an animal. The term is synonymous with "unhappy migratory state" (*durgati, ngan 'gro*, see note 85, this chapter). The reader should be aware that throughout this volume "three lower realms" and "three lower states" have been used interchangeably.
83. See note 75 (this chapter).
84. *adharma, chos min*. Addition of the negative prefix to the term *dharma* does not mean simply the "absence of virtue" or the "absence of spirituality"; rather, it means that which opposes virtue or that which is the antithesis of virtue—hence, "evil" or "wickedness."
85. Buddhist literature (cf. *AK*, ch. v. 4) generally recognizes five migratory states (*pañca gataya, 'gro ba lnga*): hell beings, animals, spirits, humans, and gods. Tibetan literature often adds a sixth class of being: demigods (*asura, lha ma yin*). The happy migratory states (*sugati, bde 'gro*) are made up of gods and humans. The unhappy migratory states (*durgati, ngan 'gro*) are represented by hell beings, animals, and spirits. *AKBh* (p. 115) gives the following literal explanation of a migratory state: "A migratory state (S: *gati, 'gro ba*) is that state to which sentient beings go."
86. *A Drop of Nourishment for Beings: A Treatise on Political Ethics* (*Lugs kyi bstan bcos skye bo gso ba'i thigs pa*), Dg.T. thun mong ba lugs kyi bstan bcos, vol. 94 (*ngo*), ff. 113a–116b. (Toh. 4330)
87. Me ma mur. This is the first of four "additional regions" (*utsada, lhag pa*) that lie adjacent to and just beyond each of the eight hot hells. These regions are described both in the *Abhidharmakoṣabhāṣya* and the *Yogācārabhūmi*. Vasubandhu's text (Sanskrit edition, p. 163) states: "The knee-deep firepit is a place

where the skin, flesh, and blood of sentient beings disintegrate when their feet are placed down and their skin, flesh, and blood are restored when their feet are raised."

88. This description of the four reasons that the Buddha jewel is a worthy object of refuge is a direct quote from Je Tsongkhapa's *Great Stages on the Path to Enlightenment*. That passage itself is a paraphrase of the following excerpt from the *Collection of Determinations* (*rNam par gtan la dbab pa bsdu ba*, Dg.T. sems tsam, vol. 51, f. 185a): "There are four reasons that one should go for refuge to those Three Jewels: the tathāgata is one who has removed his own faults absolutely, he is skilled in every respect at the means of removing the faults of his followers, he is possessed of great compassion, and one does not please him by presenting material offerings but rather does so by making an offering of one's spiritual practice."
89. *dvipad, rkang gnyis*. Literally "biped," this is a classical Sanskrit term that means a human being.
90. Rudra is a deity mentioned in the Rigveda. It is also recognized as being another name for Śiva.
91. That is, those who wear the robes of a Buddhist monk and nun.
92. The classic source for the ways in which to worship the Three Jewels is Asaṅga's *Stage of a Bodhisattva* (book 1, ch. 17) which describes ten forms of worship and six types of superior attitude (*adhyāśaya, lhag pa'i bsam pa*) to employ when worshiping the Three Jewels.
93. This last clause is often expressed as "not forsaking the Three Jewels, even merely in jest."
94. That is, you should accept the Buddha jewel as the teacher who reveals to you how to achieve the state of refuge, the dharma jewel as the actual state of refuge, and the sangha jewel as the body of companions who can assist you in pursuing that state of refuge.
95. See note 79 (this chapter).
96. That is, a virtuous deed will always yield a favorable result, never an unfavorable one, and an unvirtuous deed will always yield an unfavorable result, never a favorable one.
97. That is, even relatively minor good and bad deeds yield results that are much greater in their scope and duration.
98. *akṛtānabhyāgama, ma byas pa dang mi phrad pa*. This principle means that a specific result cannot arise without the prior occurrence of an appropriate cause. Thus, the failure to carry out the appropriate cause or the commission of an inappropriate cause cannot yield a particular desired result. This principle can also be interpreted to mean that an undesirable result can be avoided by not committing its cause.
99. *kṛtāvipranāśa, byas pa chud mi za ba*. That is, good and bad deeds do not lose their power to bear fruit. Thus, if spiritual practice is carried out properly, it is certain to bring about the intended results. Likewise, if wrongful actions are

committed, it is inevitable that undesirable consequences will be experienced at some appropriate time in the future.

100. *vastubalapravṛttānumāṇa, dngos po stobs zhugs kyi rjes dpag.* Ordinary inferences are based on two types of logical relation: the relation that exists among elements that are part of an entity's essential nature and the relationship of cause and effect. In contrast with this, the validity of the doctrine of karma is based upon faith in the infallibility of the word of the Buddha. See note 101 (this chapter).

101. *sampratyaya, yid ches pa.* This quality is identified as the nature of one type of faith. In this context, it refers to a sense of conviction about the truthfulness of the doctrine of karma, and it is considered a special form of inference that is based upon scriptural authority (*āgamānumāna, lung gi rjes su dpag pa*). This type of inference is described in an aphorism formulated by Dignāga that appears in his *Compendium of Knowledge* (*Pramāṇasamuccaya*, ch. 2, v. 5), which states: "An authoritative person's speech possesses the nature of inference because of its universal noncontradictoriness." Dharmakīrti explains this assertion in a series of verses of his *Extensive Treatise on Knowledge* (*Pramāṇavarttika*, ch. 1, vv. 213–17), along with the related portions of his autocommentary. I have addressed this topic in *Inner Science of Buddhist Practice*, pp. 70–89.

102. *Samādhirājasūtra*, ch. 14, v. 9. The pronoun "you" is referring to the Buddha.

103. *vipākaphala, rnam smin gyi 'bras bu.* This term indicates the type of rebirth that a particular deed will produce. For example, the maturation result of a great unvirtuous deed is to be reborn in one of the hells, that of a moderate unvirtuous deed is to be reborn as a tormented spirit, and that of a lesser unvirtuous deed is to be reborn as an animal.

104. *sgo gsum.* The expression "three doors" refers to one's body, speech, and mind, which constitute the means by which virtuous and unvirtuous acts are committed. Among the ten unvirtuous deeds, the first three—killing, stealing, and sexual misconduct—are carried out with the body. The next four—lying, slander, harsh speech, and idle speech—are carried out with speech. And the final three—coveting, malice, and wrong view—are carried out with the mind.

105. *niṣyandaphala, rgyu mthun gyi 'bras bu.* The original Sanskrit of the term translated as "corresponding" literally means that which "flows down." The corresponding result of taking a life is to have a short life and to undergo many illnesses, that of stealing is to be destitute, and so on.

106. *adhipatiphala, bdag po'i 'bras bu.* Governing results relate to qualities of the external environment in which one lives. The governing result of taking a life is to live in a place where one's food, medicine, and the like, have little power to maintain one's good health. That of stealing is to live in a place where the harvests are meager and where bad weather, such as frost, hail, draughts, and the like, are frequent.

107. *BCA*, ch. 2, v. 63.

108. *BCA*, ch. 7, v. 40.

109. *Satyakaparivarta, bDen pa po'i le'u.* This is another name for the *Sūtra Teaching the Miracles in the Domain of Skillful Means That the Bodhisattvas Have at Their Disposition* (*Byang chub sems dpa'i spyod yul gyi thabs kyi yul la rnam par 'phrul ba bstan pa zhes bya ba theg pa chen po'i mdo*).
110. See note 85 (this chapter).
111. See note 4 (this chapter).
112. The remaining six maturation qualities are having a long life span, possessing the power (*aiśvarya, dbang phyug*) gained by having much property and a large retinue, being a person whose speech is accepted, being regarded as eminent (*maheśākhyatā, dbang che bar grags pa*), being a person of the male gender, and possessing strength. The source for this topic is a section from Asaṅga's *Bodhisattvabhūmi*, book 1, ch. 3 (English translation, pp. 48–55).
113. *AS* (p. 6) states: "What is recollection (*smṛti, dran pa*)? It is the avoidance of inattentiveness toward a familiar object. Its action is to prevent distraction." In other words, the main purpose of recollection is to retain in the forefront of one's mind whatever understanding or meditation object a practitioner is attempting to cultivate. Recollection is a key mental factor in many forms of spiritual practice, including the four forms of closely placed recollection (*catvāri smṛtyupasthānāni, dran pa nye bar bzhag pa bzhi*; see *Inner Science of Buddhist Practice*, pp. 138–92).
114. *samprajanya, shes bzhin.* Vigilance is a form of wisdom that is meant to be exercised both in a range of ordinary activities and while practicing meditation. Its role is to observe both your mind and the physical surroundings in order to avert potential obstacles. *BCA* (ch. 5, v. 108) states: "In short, the essential nature / of vigilance is simply this: / to examine again and again / the state of your body and mind." Another verse from the same text (*BCA*, ch. 5 v. 33) further notes that the ability to develop a proper degree of vigilance is dependent on the cultivation of recollection: "The time at which vigilance arrives / and, once come, does not depart again / is when recollection, in order to guard / the mind, remains fixed at its door." For a comprehensive treatment of the practice called "observance of vigilance" (*saṃprajānadvihāritā, shes bzhin tu spyod pa nyid*), see Asaṅga's discussion in the *The Stage of a Śrāvaka* (Sanskrit text, pp. 121–27, a portion at the end is missing; Tibetan text, ff. 44a–52a). An abbreviated account of that presentation also appears in Je Tsongkhapa's *Great Treatise on the Stages of the Path to Enlightenment.*
115. *pratikriyā, phyir bcos.* This term refers to the confession ritual of atonement for moral transgressions.
116. *deśanā, bshags pa.* This is a more general term for a form of practice that is meant to purify oneself of bad deeds. A classic source for this topic is ch. 8 of Śāntideva's *Compendium of Training* (*Śikṣāsamuccaya, bsLab btus*). This chapter also identifies and gives examples of the four powers (*catvāri balāni, stobs bzhi*).
117. *karmāvaraṇa, las kyi sgrib pa.* See ch. 4, "The Brilliant Illumination of the Path to Enlightenment," note 189.

118. *bcos ma ma yin pa.* This adjective is meant to indicate that a practitioner has reached a level in which he or she can elicit a particular spiritual attitude naturally and without further need of reflecting on the instruction.
119. *sampad, phun tshogs.* The qualities of "excellence" that are meant here can be understood to mean the eight maturation qualities referenced earlier (see note 112, this chapter, and related text). *BBh*, ch. 3 (English translation, pp. 49, 50) identifies the specific acts that serve as the causes for achieving these eight qualities. *MSA* (ch. 16, v. 2) also describes how generosity, morality, patience, and effort serve as causes for the attaining the excellence of a human rebirth endowed with wealth, a large following, and the ability to bring one's activities to completion.
120. *lag rjes.* This term, which literally means "handprint," often carries the sense of a result. Here it represents the measure (*tshad*) by which one can determine that this portion of the practice has been completed.
121. See ch. 10, "The Essence of Nectar," note 127.
122. *pravrajita, rab tu byung ba.* This term, which is also translated as "renunciate," refers to a Buddhist monk or nun. See also ch. 4, "The Brilliant Illumination of the Path to Enlightenment," note 271, for a list of the five types of vow that relate to the act of going forth into the homeless state.
123. *pañca skandhā, phung po lnga.* In Buddhist doctrine, an individual is made up of these five constituent elements or "heaps": form, feeling, conception, formations, and consciousness. For an extensive description of this topic, see *Inner Science of Buddhist Practice*, pp. 227–369. Regarding the adjective "grasping" (*upādāna, nye bar len pa*), *AKBh* (p. 5) states: "'Grasping' refers to the mental afflictions. The impure heaps are called 'grasping heaps' because they originate from grasping, as in the expression 'grass fire' and 'straw fire.' Or they are so designated because they are governed by grasping, as (a person who is subject to a king's rule) is called a 'king's man.' Or they are so designated because grasping arises from the impure heaps, as in the expressions 'flower tree' and 'fruit tree.'"
124. *duḥkhaduḥkhatā, sdug bsngal gyi sdug bsngal. AKBh* (p. 328) states: "Those impure conditioned entities that are unattractive are characterized by suffering in terms of the suffering of suffering.... An unpleasant feeling is a state of suffering by the very nature of its unpleasantness. Again, the sūtras declare, 'An unpleasant feeling is unpleasant when it arises and unpleasant while it lasts.'" *ŚBh* (p. 256) states: "That which is described as suffering in such scriptural expressions as: 'birth is suffering' up to 'the failure to acquire what is desired is suffering'—that is, what is referred to as 'unpleasant feelings, together with their seats' are the experiences that make up the suffering of suffering. This constitutes a presentation of the suffering of suffering." The expression "together with their seats" (*sādhiṣṭhānā, rten dang bcas pa*) here refers to all the other aspects of the five heaps that accompany these unpleasant feelings. See also *Inner Science of Buddhist Practice*, pp. 105–11.
125. *pariṇāmaduḥkhatā, 'gyur ba'i sdug bsngal.* The suffering of change is mainly

identified with impure, pleasant physical and mental feelings, along with the impure conditioned entities that accompany those feelings. Cf. *Inner Science of Buddhist Practice*, pp. 111–20.

126. *saṃskāraduḥkhatā, 'du byed kyi sdug bsngal.* This type of suffering is difficult for ordinary beings to comprehend. The following verses are cited to convey this notion: "Just as an eyelash is unrecognized by humans / when situated in the palm of the hand, / but that very object causes displeasure and pain / if it should become lodged in the eye, // the immature, like the palm of the hand, / do not perceive the eyelash of the suffering / of conditioned existence; but for the wise, / who resemble the eye, it causes deep agitation." These verses, whose authorship is unknown, appear in both Vasubandhu's *AKBh* (p. 329) and Candrakīrti's *PP* (p. 209). *AKBh* (pp. 328–29) states: "Those impure conditioned entities that are neither attractive nor unattractive are also characterized as suffering in terms of the suffering of conditioned existence. . . . A feeling that is neither pleasant nor unpleasant is a state of suffering by virtue of being a conditioned entity. The sūtras further declare, 'That which is impermanent is suffering, because it is produced by cooperating causes.'" *ŚB* (p. 257) states: "As for the suffering of conditioned existence, it is present in every form of the five closely grasping heaps. Briefly, this is what the suffering of conditioned existence refers to: Excluding those forms of the heaps that represent the suffering of suffering and the suffering of change—with the latter including mental afflictions and pleasant feelings together with their seats—it is all those remaining forms of the heaps that are accompanied by feelings that are neither unpleasant nor pleasant, those that arise from the heaps that were just described, those that constitute the conditions that cause the just-mentioned heaps to arise, and those that constitute the vessel in which the heaps that have arisen continue to exist. Those heaps that are impermanent, in that they arise and pass away, that are accompanied by grasping (*sopādānā, nye bar len pa dang bcas pa*), that are closely connected with the three types of feeling (*trivedanābhir anuṣaktā, tshor bag sum dang rjes su 'brel ba*), that are accompanied by a state of indisposition (*dauṣṭhulyopagatā, gnas ngan len dang ldan pa*), that constitute a state in which one's welfare is not secure (*ayogakṣemapatitā, grub pa dang bde bar gtogs pa ma yin pa*), that are not free from the suffering of suffering and the suffering of change, and that are not under one's control (*asvavaśavartina, rang gis dbang sgyur ba med pa*) are referred to as a state of suffering in the sense of the suffering of conditioned existence. This constitutes a presentation of the suffering of conditioned existence." See also *Inner Science of Buddhist Practice*, pp. 120–24.

127. *AKBh* (p. 157) presents two sets of five signs. The following five are said to always occur: one's clothing becomes stained, one's flower garlands wilt, sweat forms in one's armpits, one's body emits an unpleasant odor, and one becomes displeased with one's seat. A second set of five signs is said to be uncertain, which is to say that they occur occasionally but not always: a disagreeable sound arises from

one's clothing and ornaments; the luster of one's body becomes diminished; droplets of water remain on one's body after having bathed; despite having a mind that normally moves quickly, one's mind remains now fixed on a single object; and the eyes open and shut [unlike before, when they always remained open].

128. Here the term "higher realms" means the two realms that lie above the desire realm—that is, the form realm and the formless realm.

129. *pṛthagjana, so so skye bo.* This term is meant in the technical sense of a sentient being that has not attained the status of an ārya (*'phags pa*). While the general sense of ārya is that of a person who is "worthy of honor or respect," a classic interpretation (*nirukti, nges tshig*) states: "Āryas are those beings who have reached a state that is far removed from evil, unvirtuous entities." The precise doctrinal meaning is that of a being who has attained a direct realization of ultimate reality.

130. *YB* (p. 99) states: "How, then, should the embodied form of all beings that occupy the three realms be viewed? It should be viewed like a painful boil because it is accompanied by a state of indisposition (*dauṣṭhulyānugata, gnas ngan len dang ldan pa*).... How should the occurrence of a feeling that is neither pleasant nor unpleasant in an embodied form be viewed? Like the condition of pain that is naturally present in a painful boil itself, apart from any cool or caustic sensation that might be applied to it. Therefore, the Lord declared that ... those feelings that are neither pleasant nor unpleasant are suffering in that they represent the suffering of conditioned existence."

131. See note 113 (this chapter).

132. See note 114 (this chapter).

133. *ltung ba 'byung ba'i rgyu bzhi.* The four are ignorance regarding what constitutes a transgression, having a strong propensity to develop the mental afflictions, lack of mindfulness, and disrespect for observance of the precepts.

134. *sdom sems.* "Restraint" here means specifically to form the resolve not to commit such transgressions again in the future.

135. The term "aversion" (*udvega, skyo ba,* also *skyo shas*) refers to a state of mind that is central to the process of developing the attitude often referred to as "renunciation" (*niḥsaraṇa, nges par 'byung ba*), which, in fact, literally means "deliverance" and is a synonym for liberation, or nirvana, itself. In traditional exegesis, this type of usage is one in which the cause is figuratively referred to by a term that stands for the result. In other words, the attitude is called "deliverance" (i.e., renunciation) because it is a mind that seeks to achieve the goal of deliverance from samsara. Aversion for samsara is developed by reflecting on its faults (*ādīnava, nyes dmigs*)—which is to say, all the various forms of suffering. The Tibetan equivalent of "aversion" is *skyo ba,* which can be misleading, as its meaning in ordinary usage is that of "sadness," which is too passive for this particular context. The original Sanskrit, *udvega,* suggests more a sense of intense agitation, distress, anxiety, and fear. Thus, properly understood, it represents the

antithesis of desire for and attachment to samsaric existence. It also acts as the antidote for complacency and lack of concern about our everyday condition.

136. See note 120 (this chapter).

137. *apratisthitanirvāṇa, mi gnas pa'i mya ngan las 'das pa*. See ch. 4, "The Brilliant Illumination of the Path to Enlightenment," note 244.

138. That is, the omniscience of a buddha's supreme enlightenment. See note 4 (this chapter).

139. *bar ma*. Literally one who is "in the middle," this is generally described as a person who has neither harmed nor benefited you in any significant way. It can also refer to someone who is neither an ally nor an adversary and is indifferent to your well-being.

140. *gnod kyi dogs g.yor bzo ba sogs kyis skyangs*. The translation of this line is somewhat conjectural.

141. See note 139 (this chapter).

142. See note 76 (this chapter).

143. See note 77 (this chapter).

144. *AS* (p. 6) states: "What is abashment (*apatrāpya, khrel yod pa*)? It is embarrassment about objectionable acts because of one's relationships with others. Its action is the very same as that of shame." Abashment and shame (see note 145, this chapter) are two virtuous mental factors that are central to the cultivation of Buddhist morality in that they constitute a moral impetus or strength to restrain oneself from engaging in unvirtuous behavior.

145. *AS* (p. 6) states: "What is shame (*hrī, ngo tsha shes pa*)? It is embarrassment about objectionable acts that is felt of one's own accord. Its action is to provide the support that enables you to restrain yourself from committing misdeeds."

146. That is, in the enlightenment of a true and complete buddha.

147. The adjective "elderly" in the expression "elderly mothers" (*ma rgan rnams*) is meant to suggest that most ordinary sentient beings lack the ability to help themselves in an ultimate spiritual sense.

148. See ch. 1, "A Lamp for the Path to Enlightenment," v. 15, which cites a verse from the *Sūtra on Vīradatta's Queries*.

149. *catvāraḥ pārājikā dharmāḥ, phas pham par 'gyur ba'i chos bzhi*. This expression is the name for the four transgressions that cause a Buddhist monk or nun to lose their vows and undergo expulsion from the sangha community. The four offenses are to engage in sexual intercourse, to steal something of material value, to kill a human being, and to profess falsely that you possess supernormal powers.

150. That is, you should develop the conception that he or she is Buddha Śākyamuni. See note 15 (this chapter).

151. *dag pa'i snang ba*. The meaning of this term can vary depending on the context in which it is being used. Here it means to view another person solely in terms of having positive qualities and to forgo considering any faults he or she may have.

152. Though the sense is the same, Je Tsongkhapa's verse reads "the supreme vehicle's path" instead of "the Mahāyāna path."
153. That is, just as an alchemic elixir is said to transmute iron into gold, enlightenment mind transforms ordinary virtuous deeds into causes that will bring the attainment of supreme enlightenment.
154. They are generosity, morality, patience, effort, meditative absorption, and wisdom. See the descriptions that follow.
155. *catvāri saṃgrahavastūni, bsdu ba'i dngos po bzhi*. They are generosity, agreeable speech, beneficial conduct, and sameness of purpose. See *BBh*, book 1, chs. 9 and 15.
156. See note 113 (this chapter).
157. See note 114 (this chapter).
158. See note 145 (this chapter).
159. See note 144 (this chapter).
160. The opening clause of this sentence is describing the first of the three types of Mahāyāna morality, which is known as "the morality of restraint" (*saṃvaraśīla, sdom pa'i tshul khrims*). See *BBh*, English translation, pp. 240–42 and pp. 248–49.
161. The latter half of this sentence is referring to the second of the three types of Mahāyāna morality, which is called "the morality of acquiring virtuous qualities" (*kuśaladharmasaṃgrāhakaṃ śīlam, dge ba'i chos sdud pa'i tshul khrims*). *BBh* (English translation, p. 240) provides this brief description: "The morality of acquiring virtuous qualities is whatever virtue a bodhisattva accumulates by body and speech for the sake of achieving enlightenment, following acceptance of the morality discipline." For a comprehensive description, see *BBh*, English translation, pp. 240–42 and pp. 248–49.
162. This sentence is a reference to the third type of Mahāyāna morality, which is called "the morality that acts on behalf of beings" (*sattvārthakriyāśīla, sems can gyi don bya ba'i tshul khrims*). *BBh* (English translation, pp. 242–44 and pp. 249–60) describes eleven types of activity that are the means of benefiting others. Regarding the term "objectionable act" (*avadya, kha na ma tho ba*), *PSV* (English translation, p. 283) states: "An objectionable act is one that is evil (*pāpa, sdig pa*) because it is reproached by those who are wise and because it has an undesirable maturation."
163. *sat, dam pa*. See ch. 5, "A Verse Compendium of the Spiritual Practices of the Stages of the Path," note 12.
164. *parāpakāramarpaṇākṣānti, gzhan gnod pa byed pa la ji mi snyam pa'i bzod pa*. See *BBh*, English translation, pp. 315–18.
165. The three sources of virtue roots (*gzhi gsum gyi dge rtsa*) are the virtue derived from generosity, the virtue derived from morality, and the virtue derived from meditation.
166. *duḥkhādhivāsanākṣānti, sdug bsngal dang du len pa'i bzod pa*. Cf. *BBh*, pp. 319–23.

167. *dharmanidhyānādhimuktikṣānti, chos la nges par sems pa la mos pa'i bzod pa*. Cf. *BBh*, English translation, pp. 323–24, which lists eight topics that relate to this form of patience. See also *BBh*, notes 840 and 859, which identify this type of patience as having the nature of wisdom.
168. *nam mkha' lding* or *khyung*. A mythical bird that is the king of the feathered race and the enemy that devours all members of the serpent race.
169. "Laziness" (*ālasya, le lo*) includes both indolence (see note 170, this chapter) and attachment to or a readiness to carry out unvirtuous activity. The latter form of laziness is often described specifically as "the laziness that is attachment to inferior activities" (*kutsitāsakti, ngan pa la zhen pa*). Additional forms of "laziness"—or, more properly, obstacles to effort—are dejection (*viṣāda, sgyid lug pa*) and a low opinion of oneself (*ātmāvamanyanā, bdag nyid la brnyas pa*). The author's opening statement about laziness is largely based on *BCA*, ch. 7, vv. 2 and 3.
170. *kausīdya, snyoms las*. While this term is synonymous with laziness (*ālasya, le lo*), it is also used to describe a generalized indisposition to engage in any sort of activity (*kāyamanasor akarmaṇyatā*).
171. *udvega, skyo ba*. See note 135 (this chapter).
172. *saṃnāhavīrya, go cha'i brtson 'grus*. Cf. *BBh*, pp. 332–33.
173. *kuśaladharmasaṃgrāhakaṃ vīryam, dge ba'i chos sdud pa'i brtson 'grus*. Cf. *BBh*, pp. 333–34.
174. *sattvārthakriyāvīrya, sems can gyi don bya ba'i brtson 'grus*. Cf. *BBh*, p. 334.
175. The phrase "the mind that develops the aspiration to attain supreme enlightenment" is an expanded description of the Sanskrit compound that literally means "development of the mind" (*cittotpāda, sems bskyed*), where the word "mind" refers to the conventional form of enlightenment mind (*bodhicitta, byang chub kyi sems*).
176. *ŚBh* (p. 450) states: "The term 'meditative absorption' (*dhyāna, bsam gtan*) refers to a state in which the mind meditates correctly on an object and recollection holds fast to an object one-pointedly."
177. *LRCh* (ff. 334b–335a) states: "Languor (*laya, bying ba*) is a condition in which the mind does not grasp the meditation object firmly or with great clarity due to its having relaxed its hold on that object. Therefore, the mind has come under the influence of languor when, despite the presence of some lucidity (*dwangs cha yod kyang*), it does not keep hold of the meditation object with exceptionally great clarity (*'dzin stangs shin tu gsal ba med pa*). [This explanation is correct] because Kamalaśīla's second *Bhāvanākrama* [Sanskrit edition, p. 240] declares that 'when the mind does not perceive the meditation object with exceptionally great clarity, like someone who is blind from birth or a person who has entered a dark place or someone whose eyes are closed, it should be understood that the mind has become languid.'" Oral instruction further distinguishes two kinds of languor: coarse and subtle. Coarse languor occurs when the mental factor of recollection (*smṛti, dran pa*) is able to keep the mind fixed on the meditation

object, but the quality of clarity is lacking. Subtle languor occurs when both stability and clarity are being maintained, but the clarity lacks intensity because the mind's hold on the object has become weakened.

178. *AS* (p. 6) states: "What is excitation (*auddhatya, rgod pa*)? It is an unsettled state of mind that is a form of desire, and it occurs because the mind is following after an attractive image. Its action is to obstruct quiescence." Regarding the expression "attractive image" (*śubhanimitta, sdug pa'i mtshan ma*), Pabongkhapa states: "An example of forming an 'attractive image' in the mind is when you watch a performance of the Lhamo folk opera during the daytime and then find yourself recalling vivid images of those scenes later that night. Thus, it is the image that arises in the mind when you recall an attractive object that you feel desire for." *Liberation in Our Hands, Part 3* (Howell, NJ: Mahayana Sutra and Tantra Press, 1990–2001), p. 247. Oral instruction also distinguishes a rough and a subtle form of excitation. Coarse excitation is when we lose the meditation object completely and it is no longer present in the mind. Subtle excitation is when an extraneous thought begins to stir from a different part of the mind while the meditation object is still present in the mind. This latter type of excitation is described as being like water flowing beneath a layer of ice.

179. See *Inner Science of Buddhist Practice*, pp. 169–78, for a description of the four meditative absorptions of the form realm that make up the mundane path. *AS* (p. 19) states: "'Mundane' refers to that which is included in the three samsaric realms." The mundane path is a form of insight meditation (*vipaśyanā, lhag mthong*; see book 1, ch. 8, the section titled "Meditation") in which a lower level of consciousness is regarded as coarse (*audārika, rags pa*) and a higher level as tranquil (*śānta, zhi ba*). This type of practice is described as resulting in "freedom from attachment" (*vairāgya, 'dod chags dang bral ba*) toward eight different levels of samsaric existence—that is, the desire realm, the four levels of the form realm, and the first three of the four levels that make up the formless realm.

180. *lokottara, 'jig rten las 'das pa. AS* (p. 19) states: "'Transcendent' refers to the nonconceptual states of mind (*nirvikalpa, rnam par mi rtog pa*) that are antidotes for all of the three realms in that they do not conceive of any of the four errors (*viparyāsa, phyin ci log*) and they are free of conceptual elaboration" (*niṣprapañca, spros pa*). The principal form of transcendent meditative absorption in the Mahāyāna path does not occur until after the seeing path (*darśanamārga, mthong lam*) has been attained. This requires cultivating quiescence (see note 181, this chapter), insight (see ch. 4, note 65), and the union of quiescence and insight, in relation to the meditation object of ultimate truth until the practitioner achieves a direct realization of ultimate truth.

181. A monastic text of Sera Me College states: "The definition of quiescence (*śamatha, zhi gnas*) is the form of mental concentration that, on the strength of being fixed one-pointedly on its object, is supported by the extraordinary ease of the mental factor called agility." On agility, see ch. 4, "The Brilliant Illumination of the Path to Enlightenment," note 65.

182. For the definition of *insight*, see ch. 4, "The Brilliant Illumination of the Path to Enlightenment," note 65.
183. *śamathavipaśyanāyuganaddha, zhi gnas dang lhag mthong zung du 'brel ba*. Quiescence must be achieved initially, before insight can be developed for the first time. However, once insight has been attained, both forms of practice can be practiced jointly—which is to say, by developing them alternately, as needed.
184. The source for this description of meditative absorption is the opening passage of the chapter on meditative absorption in Asaṅga's *Bodhisattvabhūmi* (see English translation, pp. 343–44).
185. *karmaṇyatā, las su rung ba nyid*. See ch. 4, "The Brilliant Illumination of the Path to Enlightenment," note 65.
186. *tattva, de kho na nyid*. This term is a synonym for emptiness (*śūnyatā, stong pa nyid*) or ultimate truth (*paramārthasatya, don dam pa'i bden pa*).
187. *āmiṣadāna, zang zing gi sbyin pa*. In addition to being one aspect of the first of the six perfections, when this type of generosity is used to support potential followers, it represents the first of the four principles for gathering a following (*catvāri saṃgrahavastūni, bsdu ba'i dngos po bzhi*). The Sanskrit term *āmiṣa* (*zang zing*) that is translated here as the adjective "material" can mean variously "flesh," "an object of enjoyment," "desire," or a "gift" (*MW*, s.v. "āmiṣa"). When used in relation to the practice of generosity, it generally means a physical object of material value that can serve as a means of subsistence. *ASBh* (p. 109) states: "Material generosity is a means of support for the body, because it benefits the physical form of the person who is its recipient, through food, drink, and other objects that represent a means of subsistence."
188. This sentence and the one that precedes it both represent elements of agreeable speech (*priyavāditā, snyan par smra ba*). *BBh* (book 1, ch. 17, pp. 365–66) describes this second principle for gathering a following as being made up of three types: speech that is friendly, speech that is pleasing, and speech that contains dharma teachings endowed with every type of spiritual good quality.
189. *arthacaryā, don spyod pa*. This is the third principle for gathering a following. See *BBh*, book 1, ch. 17, pp. 371–79.
190. *samānārthatā, don mthun pa*. This is the fourth principle for gathering a following. See *BBh*, book 1, ch. 17, pp. 379–81.
191. *gtan tshigs chen po bzhi*. These four proofs are known as: the absence of a unity and a multiplicity (*ekānekarahitayukti, gcig du bral gyi rigs pa*), diamond slivers (*rdo rje gzegs ma'i rigs pa*), refutation of the arising of a truly existent or a nonexistent entity (*yod med skye 'gog gi rigs pa*), and dependent origination, the king of proofs (*pratītyasamutpādayukti, rten 'brel gyi rigs pa*).
192. The phrase "transport you to the far shore" is a reference to the Sanskrit term *pāramitā* (*pha rol tu phyin pa*), often translated as "perfection." Among the several literal interpretations of the term, Je Tsongkhapa follows Candrakīrti's description in ch. 1, v. 16 of his *Madhyamakāvatāra*. In the autocommentary to this verse, Candrakīrti states: "Regarding this point, *pāram* means the far shore

or bank of the ocean of samsara—which is to say, the state of buddhahood, whose nature is that of having abandoned in their entirety the obscurations of the mental afflictions and the obscurations to that which needs to be known. Hence, the term *pāramitā* means the state in which one has *gone* to (i.e., arrived at) that far shore." Je Tsongkhapa notes that when the term refers to the object (i.e., the goal) of the practice, it refers to buddhahood, and when it refers to the action by which the practice leads to that goal, it can also mean the path itself.

193. That is, the generation stage (*utpattikrama, bskyed pa'i rim pa*) and the completion stage (*sampannakrama, rdzogs pa'i rim pa*).

194. *rgyu yi theg pa.* "Causal vehicle" is an expression that refers to the non-tantric form of Mahāyāna practice, which is also described as the Pāramitāyāna, or "vehicle of the perfections" (*phar phyin gyi theg pa*).

195. *'bras bu'i theg pa.* "Resultant vehicle" is an expression that refers to the tantric form of Mahāyāna. This means that in tantric practice the practitioner adopts an attitude in which "the result of the path is taken as the very form of the path itself" (*'bras bu lam byed*).

196. The full verse states: "By the power of the Victor Tsongkhapa having acted / as my direct spiritual teacher for the supreme vehicle, / may I never waver, for even an instant, in all my future lives / from the excellent path that is extolled by the victors." Both this verse and the previous one are from a devotional poem of supplication to Je Tsongkhapa that was composed by his disciple Khedrup Gelek Pelsang. It is known by the popular name Glorious Master of the Threefold World (*dpal ldan sa gsum ma*).

197. This verse is Sönam Gyatso's concluding aspirational prayer for his composition.

198. *nyams mgur.* This is a common expression used to refer to Je Tsongkhapa's short verse text on the Stages of the Path. Although Je Tsongkhapa did not give this Lamrim poem a formal title, the edition that appears in his Collected Works contains the following descriptive phrase: "This brief presentation of the spiritual practices of the Stages of the Path to Enlightenment, created as a memorandum to prevent me from forgetting its meaning, . . ." Another common descriptive title is *A Compendium of the Stages of the Path* (*Lam rim bsdus don*). The translation that appears in ch. 5 of this volume is titled *A Verse Compendium of the Spiritual Practices of the Stages of the Path to Enlightenment.*

199. This monastery, named Mountain of Increasing Virtue (*ri bo dge 'phel*), was founded in the fourteenth century by the Omniscient One from Shang, Sherap Pelsang (Shangs pa kun mkhyen Shes rab dpal bzang). Shang is a district in the Tsang region of central Tibet.

8. The Easy Path That Leads to Omniscience: An Instruction Manual on the Stages of the Path to Enlightenment

1. *Byang chub lam gyi rim pa'i khrid yig thams cad mkhyen par bgrod pa'i bde lam*, *DNZ*, vol. 3 (*ga*), pp. 111–60. Second Source: *Byang chub lam gyi rim pa'i*

dmar khrid thams cad mkhyen par bgrod pa'i bde lam, in Collected Works, vol. 4 (*nga*), pp. 367–431 (New Delhi: Mongolian Lama Guru Deva, 1973). (Toh. 5944)

2. *dam pa.* Here the term is adjectival and, when being used in relation to a person, typically means such things as "true," "good," "wise," "venerable," and "honest." I translate it here as "holy" as it is referring to one's root lama, the spiritual teacher with whom one has the closest relationship.
3. *rje btsun.* See ch. 5, "A Verse Compendium of the Spiritual Practices of the Stages of the Path," note 17.
4. *thub pa'i dbang po.* An epithet of Buddha Śākyamuni, which means literally "Lord of Sages."
5. This preliminary exercise consists of a devotional ritual referred to as the "six preliminary practices" (**ṣaṭ prayogadharmā, sbyor ba'i chos drug*). See ch. 7, "The Nectar That Is Like Highly Refined Gold," note 29, for a listing of the six activities.
6. *lus 'dug lugs brgyad.* Wensapa Losang Döndrup (dBen sa pa blo bzang don grub, 1505–1566) wrote in a verse text: "Legs, arms, and midriff are three. / Teeth, lips, and tongue combined are a fourth. / Head, eyes, shoulders, and breath make four more. / These are the eight attributes of Vairocana." The poem is titled "The Stages of the Path Arranged as Supplication Prayers" (*Lam rim gsol 'debs su sgrigs ba*). See *Liberation in Our Hands, Part 1,* pp. 134–37, for an explanation of the eight qualities.
7. The purpose for "examining your mental continuum" is to determine what your current motivation (*samuttāna, kun slong*) is. After doing so, you should engage in a reflective exercise known as "correcting your motivation" (*kun slong bcos tshul*) in order to develop "the mental state of extraordinary virtue," which means an experiential awareness of the aspiration to attain supreme enlightenment.
8. *vīra, dpa' bo.* This is a synonym for a *ḍāka* (*mkha 'gro*), which is a class of male tantric deities. See ch. 7, "The Nectar That Is Like Highly Refined Gold," note 37.
9. *virā, dpa' mo.* This is the female consort of a "hero." Another name for this class of female tantric deity is *ḍākinī* (*mkha' 'gro ma*). See also ch. 7, "The Nectar That Is Like Highly Refined Gold," note 38.
10. *catvāry apramāṇāni, tshad med bzhi.* They are immeasurable equanimity (*upekṣā, btang snyoms*), immeasurable loving-kindness (*maitrī, byams pa*), immeasurable compassion (*karuṇā, snying rje*), and immeasurable joy (*muditā, dga' ba*). In the context of the six preliminary practices, the four immeasurables are cultivated as a supplementary exercise to strengthen the enlightenment mind that was just generated.
11. See ch. 7, "The Nectar That Is Like Highly Refined Gold," note 46.
12. Ibid., note 35.
13. Ibid., note 36.
14. See note 8 (this chapter).

15. See note 9 (this chapter).
16. *rang bzhin gyi gnas*. Khedrup Gelek Pelsang (mKhas grub dge legs dpal bzang) writes in his *Ocean of Spiritual Attainments* (*bsKyed rim dngos grub rgya mtsho*), f. 18a: "Regarding the place from which the lama/merit field is invited that is referred to as the 'innate realm' (*rang bzhin gyi gnas*), as a phrase from the *Abhidhānottara Tantra* [ch. 4] states, 'And having urged the ones who previously attained the ultimate goal,' this should be identified as the region where buddhahood is first attained—which is to say, the mandala of transcendent awareness that is associated with a buddha's enjoyment body (*saṃbhogakāya, longs spyod rdzogs sku*). Moreover, recognizing the term 'innate' (*svabhāva, rang bzhin*) to mean a buddha's dharma body (*dharmakāya, chos kyi sku*), which is inseparable from the innate nature that is the emptiness of all entities, it is beings who have arisen from this state of the wisdom body into a form body (*rūpakāya, gzugs sku*) who are being invited when it is said that the lama/merit field is 'invited from the innate realm.'"
17. *samayasattva, dam tshig sems dpa'*. Abhayākaragupta's *AM* (f. 122a) provides an authoritative explanation of the term "assemblage being." His description turns on two interpretations of the Sanskrit term *samaya*—first, "coming together," in the sense of the entity that the wisdom being or beings enter and, second, a "conventional meaning" for a divine being. The term *sattva* is also interpreted both in the sense of, first, the "strength of character" that acts on behalf of sentient beings and, second, a "being" that is completely pure. The complete passage states: "Regarding the entry of the wisdom being into the assemblage being, an assemblage being is a divine figure that appears in a form having arms and so on and one whose essence is that of a mental image that was generated after having abandoned all consideration of oneself as being ordinary [i.e., nondivine]. Sometimes the term also refers to a 'seed' syllable in addition to the divine figure, and in some cases, it refers to a seed syllable alone. Because the divine figure that has become evident in this form takes on the essential nature of nondual transcendent wisdom, *samaya* means that entity with which the wisdom being (*jñānasattva, ye shes sems dpa'*) 'comes together'—that is, it is that entity with which the wisdom being unites. It is also a *sattva* [i.e., an entity that possesses strength of character] because it acts on behalf of sentient beings and because it is the object of a conventional form of usage that refers to a being that is completely pure. A seed syllable can also be referred to as a sentient being in the same way that [a newly conceived sentient being that develops through the stages of fetal development known as *kalala* and so on can be referred to as a sentient being]."
18. *skyabs gnas kun 'dus pa'i bdag nyid*. That is, each figure in the merit field embodies all three aspects of the Three Jewels.
19. *AKBh* (p. 183) states: "The life spans and so on that are inferior following their decay are called degeneracies because they have become deteriorated." Vasubandhu's *AKBh* (p. 183) interprets the five factors of degeneracy (*pañca kaṣāyā,*

snyigs ma lnga) as follows: degeneracy of life span means an era during which the life spans of human beings is relatively short—that is, a hundred years or less; degeneracy of sentient beings means an era during which sentient beings have diminished physical size, beauty, health, strength, intelligence, recollection, effort, and firmness; degeneracy of mental afflictions means that householders, in particular, are highly prone to desire and the other emotional forms of the mental afflictions; degeneracy of views means that religious ascetics, in particular, are very susceptible to erring views and flawed forms of religious conduct; and degeneracy of a kalpa or eon means an era during which food and medicine have diminished nutritive and curative benefits. The description of the five degeneracies that appears in Asaṅga's *BBh* (book 1, ch. 18, pp. 419–21) differs somewhat in relation to several of these five factors.

20. *Legs pa'i skar ma*. A disciple of the Buddha who, despite being a master of the three baskets of canonical teachings, was unable to develop faith in the Master.
21. Commentarial literature states that the following words of supplication should be recited repeatedly: "I make prostration, present offerings, and go for refuge to my root lama, who is inseparable from the Victor Buddha Śākyamuni." Paṇchen Losang Yeshe's (bLo bzang ye shes) *Swift Path* (*Myur lam*, f. 33a–33b) adds that the following visualization should then be carried out: "Through having made this supplication, a duplicate of Lama Munīndra separates from him or her and dissolves into you, causing you also to instantly take on the physical form of Lama Munīndra. Then reflect that you, appearing as Lama Munīndra, emanate light rays from the *hūṃ* syllable in your heart, which strike all the sentient beings that are surrounding you and establishes them in Munīndra's enlightened state. Following that, with you and all sentient beings appearing as Munīndra, visualize and direct your attention to the mantra *oṃ mune mune mahāmunaye svā hā* that is surrounding a white *a* syllable marked by a yellow *hūṃ* syllable standing atop a moon cushion in all of your hearts and then recite the mantra as often as time permits."
22. Paṇchen Losang Yeshe's *Swift Path* mentions that you should recite the verse: "By this virtue may I quickly attain / the status of my Buddha lama, / and then establish in that state / all beings without exception," followed by such recitations as *The Aspirational Prayer for Excellent Spiritual Conduct* (*Bhadhracaryapraṇidhāna, bzang po spyod pa'i smon lam*), if possible. It has also become a traditional practice to recite the seven verses that appear at the end of Je Tsongkhapa's *Great Treatise on the Stages of the Path to Enlightenment* as an aspirational prayer (*smon lam*).
23. See ch. 7, "The Nectar That Is Like Highly Refined Gold," note 113.
24. Ibid., note 114.
25. Tibetan text reads "avoid sleeping" (*mi nyal bar*); however, this is a translation of the Sanskrit *jāgarika*, which literally means to remain "wakeful"—which is to say, alert and attentive to one's spiritual practice. The remaining activities of restraining the senses (*indriyasamvara, dbang po'i sdom pa*), exercising moder-

ation in food (*bhojane mātrajñatā, zad kyi tshod rig pa*), how to sleep, and so on are all described in detail in the first chapter of Asaṅga's *Stage of a Śrāvaka* (*Śrāvakabhūmi, Nyan thos kyi sa*).

26. *kṣaṇa, dal ba*. See ch. 7, "The Nectar That Is Like Highly Refined Gold," note 2.
27. *sampad, 'byor pa*. Ibid.
28. *abhyudaya, mngon par mtho ba*. See ch. 4, "The Brilliant Illumination of the Path to Enlightenment," note 19.
29. *gati, 'gro ba*. See ch. 7, "The Nectar That Is Like Highly Refined Gold," note 85.
30. The unhappy migratory states (*durgati, ngan 'gro*) are represented by hell beings, animals, and tormented spirits.
31. The happy migratory states (*sugati, bde 'gro*) are made up of worldly gods and human beings.
32. Among the rare "stars" that can be seen in the daytime, the most common is the planet Venus. Apparently, it is also possible, but extremely rare, to see Jupiter and Mars in the daytime sky.
33. *jambudvīpa, 'dzam bu gling*. See ch. 5, "A Verse Compendium of the Spiritual Practices of the Stages of the Path," note 4.
34. *AK* (ch. 3, v. 78) states: "A life for the Kurus lasts a thousand years; / for two others, it reduces twice by half. / Here, it is not fixed—ten years at the end, / while beyond measure at the beginning." The word "here" refers to the Rose Apple continent. Again, Buddhist cosmology states that in the Rose Apple continent human beings live for an immeasurably great number of years at the beginning of a kalpa or eon. Gradually, their life spans reduce to a period of only ten years. Following that, their life spans gradually increase again to a period of eighty thousand years and then fluctuate between these two extremes eighteen times, with each cycle representing what is called an "intermediate kalpa" (*antarakalpa, bar gyi bskal pa*). The end of each "intermediate kalpa" is marked variously by outbreaks of widespread murder, pestilence, or famine. *AK* (ch. 3, v. 99ab) states: "The end of an intermediate kalpa is accompanied by weapons, illness, and famine." This is the general sense in which the life span of a human being in the Rose Apple continent is described as being "not fixed" (*aniyata, ma nges pa*).
35. One of the most comprehensive sources on the precepts that relate to the act of going for refuge is Je Tsongkhapa's *Great Treatise on the Stages of the Path* (English translation, vol. 1, pp. 191–207). See also ch. 7, "The Nectar That Is Like Highly Refined Gold," pp. 129 and 130, for a brief discussion.
36. These two statements express the principle that karma is fixed or invariable in the sense that a virtuous deed only generates a favorable result and an unvirtuous one only generates an undesirable result.
37. This statement expresses the principle that even a minor karmic deed has the capacity to produce very great results.
38. This principle is expressed formally as "what has not been done will not yield any fruition." See *BBh* (English translation, note 533) and ch. 7, "The Nectar That Is Like Highly Refined Gold," note 98.

39. This principle is expressed formally as "what has been done will not perish." See *BBh* (English translation, note 533) and ch. 7, "The Nectar That Is Like Highly Refined Gold," note 99.
40. *kṣetra, zhing.* Vasubandhu's *AK* (ch. 4, v. 117) enumerates several types of "field": "Fields are distinguished by class of sentient being, benefit, suffering, and virtue." The first of these fields (class of sentient being) is based on the principle that more merit is gained through performing virtuous acts relative to a higher class of sentient being (for instance, a human being) than to a lower one (such as an animal). The "field of benefit" (*upakārakṣetra, phan btags pa'i zhing*) is one's father and mother, teachers, and other individuals who have provided extraordinary benefit during one's life. The "field of suffering" (*duḥkhakṣetra, sdug bsngal gyi zhing*) is any person who is ill, poor, exposed to extreme weather conditions, or experiencing some other form of painful circumstances. The "field of virtue" (*guṇakṣetra, yon tan gyi zhing*) is identified as the Three Jewels and other exceptionally virtuous persons, such as individuals who have just arisen from a deep meditative state. See also *Great Treatise on the Stages of the Path* (English translation, vol. 1, pp. 231–33).
41. *abhisampratyaya, yid ches pa.* This is one of three types of faith addressed in Buddhist abhidharma literature. It is understood to represent a form of belief that is justified and rises to the level of firm conviction. Buddhist scholars formulated instructions for how to develop this type of faith in relation to the doctrine of karma. See *Inner Science of Buddhist Practice*, pp. 70–89, for the version that is presented in Dharmakīrti's *Extensive Treatise on Knowledge* (*Pramāṇavārttikakārikā*).
42. *catvāri balāni, stobs bzhi.* The scriptural sources for this instruction are the *Sūtra That Reveals the Four Spiritual Qualities* (*Caturdharmanirdeśasūtra, Chos bzhi bstan pa'i mdo*) and the commentary presented in chapter 8 of Śāntideva's *Compendium of Training* (*Śikṣāsamuccaya, bsLab pa kun las btus pa*). See also *Great Treatise on the Stages of the Path to Enlightenment* (English translation, vol. 1, pp. 251–59). The four powers are the power of the support (*āśrayabala, rten gyi stobs*), which is to go for refuge to the Three Jewels, the Buddha, dharma, and sangha, as well as to never forsake enlightenment mind; the power of engaging in self-censure (*vidūṣanāsamudācāra, rnam par sun 'byin pa kun tu spyod pa*), which is to develop deep regret repeatedly for all one's past misdeeds; the power of turning away from wrongdoing (*pratyāpattibala, nyes pa las slar ldog pa'i stobs*), which is to develop the resolute conviction that refrains from committing evil deeds and transgressions in the future; and the power of engaging in an antidote (*pratipakṣasamudācāra, gnyen po kun tu spyod pa*), which is to put forth great effort in carrying out virtuous deeds. Śāntideva's *Compendium of Training* presents a range of specific activities that represent this form of antidote.
43. *yid brtan med pa.* That is, relations with others, both favorable and unfavorable, are not fixed (**aniyata, nges pa med pa*) and can undergo change, both within our present lifetime as well as in future lives.

44. *pratisaṃdhi, nying mtshams sbyar ba*. This term, which literally means "reunion" or "reentry" into the womb, is the technical term for the first moment of conception that marks the beginning of a rebirth.
45. *paraloka, 'jig rten pha rol*. That is, the next rebirth that follows death in this life.
46. *upādānaskandhā, nyer len gyi phung po*. Sthiramati (*PSV*, English translation, p. 293; slightly revised here) describes the term *grasping* (*upādāna, nye bar len pa*) in his discussion of "egoistic pride" (*asmimāna, nga'o snyam pa'i nga rgyal*), one of seven forms of pride mentioned in Buddhist abhidharma literature: "The term *grasping* refers to aspiration (*chanda, 'dun pa*) and desire (*rāga, 'dod chags*). Aspiration means longing for a future existence. Desire is attachment for the present existence. Thus, as a future existence is grasped at in the sense of having aspiration for it, and as your present heaps are grasped at in the sense that your desire for them makes you not want to give them up, these two attitudes are called 'grasping.' The heaps that are associated with them are the grasping heaps." See also ch. 7, "The Nectar That Is Like Highly Refined Gold," note 123. The expression "impure heaps" here means the heaps that are associated with, or related to, the outflows (*sāsravaskandhā, zag pa dang bcas pa'i phung po*). For this latter expression, see also ch. 4, "The Brilliant Illumination of the Path to Enlightenment," note 62.
47. *tshol 'gro*, also variously spelled *tshol gro* and *tshol khro*. Paṇchen Lama Losang Yeshe explains this term in his *Swift Path* (*Myur lam*), f. 55a: "The suffering of having to seek a livelihood means having to experience the following type of suffering. Without shying away from any form of evil deed, hardship, or disrepute as you strive to obtain material wealth through any of a variety of methods, when you do obtain even a small amount of prosperity, everyone else forces you to give up that wealth, even though you are 'unable' [i.e., unwilling] to do so, through imposing undeservedly heavy taxes, or through borrowing or stealing your property and so on."
48. That is, the envy that is felt toward the gods prompts the demigods to do battle with the gods in order to seize their wealth. In the course of this strife, the demigods experience many forms of physical injury and even death.
49. See ch. 7, "The Nectar That Is Like Highly Refined Gold," note 127.
50. *khams gong ma gnyis*. That is, the two realms that lie above the desire realm (*kāmadhātu, 'dod pa'i khams*). They are the form realm (*rūpadhātu, gzugs kyi khams*) and the formless realm (*arūpyadhātu, gzugs med pa'i khams*). The form realm is associated with four states of meditative absorption (*catvāri dhyānāni, bsam gtan bzhi*) and the formless realm with four formless states of composure (*catasraḥ samāpattaya, snyoms par 'jug pa bzhi*).
51. The term "conditioned" (*saṃskāra, 'du byed*) here is a reference to the suffering of conditioned existence (*saṃskāraduḥkhatā, khyab pa 'du byed kyi sdug bsngal*). This state of suffering is the most difficult for ordinary individuals to comprehend because to appreciate its meaning properly, one must gain an understanding of subtle impermanence. As indicated here, it is a state of helplessness that

is due to being under the control of one's karma and the mental afflictions. See also ch. 7, "The Nectar That Is Like Highly Refined Gold," note 126.

52. *tisra śikṣā, bslab pa gsum*. The three Buddhas trainings are morality, meditative absorption, and wisdom.

53. *avyākṛta, lung ma bstan*. The Buddha declared (*vyākṛ, lung bstan pa*) that acts motivated by a virtuous mind have attractive or favorable karmic results and those motivated by an unvirtuous mind have unfavorable results. Acts that were not specified as having either a favorable or an unfavorable result are understood to be morally neutral and are therefore called "indeterminate."

54. The Tibetan text contains the past tense form of the phrase "apprehension of a self" (*ātmagraha, bdag tu 'dzin pa*). The term "self" here is not restricted to the sense of a personal subjective self and should be taken as synonymous with the broader sense of mistakenly grasping any entity as being self-existent or real.

55. *parapakṣa, gzhan phyogs*. "Other" here can mean that which contrasts with what is judged as belonging to oneself. But it can also mean more narrowly someone who is considered to be a foe or an adversary. "Side" means a "faction" or "class" of beings.

56. This paragraph is essentially a rewording of the section from Je Tsongkhapa's *Great Treatise* titled "The stages in which the mental afflictions arise" (*ji ltar skye ba'i rim pa*). At the end of that section, the following verse (*PV*, ch. 2, v. 221) is cited: "The notion of 'other' occurs when that of a self exists. / From the conception of self and other, attachment and hatred arise. / Those who are bound by these two mental afflictions, / give rise to all the other mental faults" (*ātmani sati parasaṃjñā svaparavibhāgāt parigrahadveṣau / anayoḥ sampratibaddhāḥ sarva doṣāḥ prajāyante*).

57. Ignorance, as it is to be understood here, is synonymous with the phrase "apprehension of a self" that is addressed in note 54 (this chapter).

58. *pramāda, bag med*. *AS* (p. 9) states: "What is lack of mindfulness? It is the failure to cultivate virtuous qualities and the failure to guard the mind against those qualities that are related to the outflows, based upon forms of desire, hatred, and ignorance that are accompanied by laziness. Its action is to support the strengthening of unvirtuous qualities and the decrease of virtuous ones."

59. *apramāda, bag yod*. *AS* (p. 6) states: "What is mindfulness? It is the cultivation of virtuous entities and the guarding of the mind from entities that are related to the outflows, on the basis of avoidance of desire, avoidance of hatred, and avoidance of ignorance that are accompanied by effort. Its action is to develop and perfect all mundane and transcendent forms of excellence." *PSV* (p. 289) states: "'Mundane excellence' means to attain a superior state in samsaric existence and superior forms of those qualities that sustain samsaric existence. 'Transcendent excellence' means to attain the enlightenment of the Śrāvakayāna or that of any of the other yānas."

60. *smṛti, dran pa*. See ch. 7, "The Nectar That Is Like Highly Refined Gold," note 113.

61. *samprajanya, shes bzhin*. Ibid., note 114.
62. *hrī, ngo tsha shes pa*. Ibid., note 145.
63. *apatrāpya, khrel yod pa*. Ibid., note 144.
64. At various places in *The Stage of a Śrāvaka* (*Śrāvakabhūmi, Nyan thos kyi sa*), Asaṅga discusses a range of issues that relate to different kinds of personality types. One classification of seven types is based on the degree to which an individual may be susceptible to any of five mental afflictions. They are described as one who has a strong tendency to develop desire, one who has a strong tendency to develop hatred, one who has a strong tendency to develop ignorance, one who has a strong tendency to develop pride, one who has a strong tendency to develop discursive thoughts, one who is equally but only moderately disposed to all the mental afflictions, and one whose mental afflictions are weak. The first five types are said to be individuals who, because they indulged in one of the five named mental afflictions extensively and habitually in past lives, will develop that fault in an intense and long-lasting form whenever they encounter objects that have the potential to evoke it. Among four categories of meditation object that are discussed in *The Stage of a Śrāvaka*, one is called "the object that purifies an unfavorable mental trait" (*caritaviśodhanālambana, spyad pa rnam par sbyong ba'i dmigs pa*). This category identifies the meditation object that is essential for each of the five types of person who are particularly susceptible to developing one of the five mental afflictions just mentioned. The meditation object for those who are highly prone to develop desire is unattractiveness (*aśubha, mi sdug pa*); the one for those who are highly prone to develop anger is loving-kindness; the one for those who are highly prone to develop ignorance is dependent origination; the one for those who are highly prone to develop pride is the diversity of the constituents (*dhātuprabheda, khams kyi rab tu dbye ba*; see *Inner Science of Buddhist Practice*, note 582); and the one for those who are highly prone to develop discursive thoughts is to cultivate mindfulness of one's breath (*ānāpānasmṛti, dbugs 'byung rngub dran pa*; see *Inner Science of Buddhist Practice*, pp. 156–57).
65. *prātimokṣa, so sor thar pa*. The Kadampa vinaya master Tsonawa Sherap Zangpo (mTsho sna ba Shes rab bzang po, fl. late thirteenth to fourteenth centuries) presents three explanations of the term *prātimokṣa*, often translated as "individual liberation," in his commentary *Light Rays of the Sun* (*Nyi ma'i 'od zer*). All three are based on different interpretations of the prefix *prāti*. The first takes it to mean "individual" (*so sor*) and thus prātimokṣa discipline is a "discipline of individual liberation" in the sense that each individual person who observes morality is able to gain his or her own liberation from the lower realms and samsara, but no one can gain liberation through someone else's observance of morality. According to a second interpretation, *prāti* means "first" (*dang por*), and hence prātimokṣa discipline is a "discipline of first liberation" because in the first moment that the prātimokṣa discipline is achieved, one is liberated from whatever form of negative discipline one may have possessed before. A

third interpretation uses Sanskrit grammatical theory to derive the sense of being a "means" (*thabs*), and thus prātimokṣa discipline is a "discipline that provides a means of attaining liberation."

66. "Closeness" (*nye ba*) here should be understood as attachment—that is, a form of the root mental affliction of desire (*rāga, 'dod chags*), not the virtuous affection of loving-kindness (*maitrī, byams pa*).
67. "Distance" (*ring ba*) is meant in the sense of aversion or animosity—which is to say, a form of the root mental affliction of hatred (*pratigha, zhe sdang*).
68. The text here abbreviates by simply saying "and so on" (*sogs*), which is meant to indicate that you should carry out the exercise of visualizing that a stream of fivefold nectar and light rays flows down from the body of your root lama, and so on, as described several times above. In this case, you should reflect that the blessings enable you and all the sentient beings that surround you to develop immeasurable equanimity.
69. *yid du 'ong ba ngos shes pa'i sems can*. This descriptive phrase is interpreted in several commentaries as referring to an "extremely dear family relative, such as one's mother." The adjective "attractive" (*yid du 'ong ba*) means someone that you view favorably and toward whom you feel attachment.
70. Ngulchu Dharmabhadra's commentary (*Rin chen bang mdzod*, f. 79a) interprets "previously" (*sngar*) as a reference to the earlier practice of overcoming attachment by recognizing it as a source of continued samsaric existence, which formed part of the instruction that relates to middling persons. This conforms to a similar passage in Je Tsongkhapa's *Great Treatise* (f. 95a), which states: "Reflect on the manner in which all friends and enemies can quickly undergo change and become their opposites, as explained previously in the section on the fault of samsara's uncertainty" (e.g., see note 43, this chapter).
71. *yid du mi 'ong ba ngos shes pa'i sems can*. This simply means someone who is regarded as an adversary or enemy. The adjective "unattractive" (*yid du mi 'ong ba*) means someone that you view unfavorably and toward whom you feel animosity.
72. **bandhu, gnyen*. The general sense of this term is someone with whom you have a close personal connection, including a close family relative or a friend.
73. That is, the person who existed yesterday does not exist today.
74. *myong ba thon pa*. Distinct spiritual realizations (*rtogs pa*) are associated with most of the topics in the Lamrim teaching, especially those that range from how to develop a relationship with a spiritual teacher up to that of developing enlightenment mind. These realizations are developed by means of "analytic meditation" (*dpyad sgom*), a form of contemplative practice that is emphasized in the Gelukpa tradition. See appendix F of *Liberation in Our Hands, Part 2*, pp. 323–44, for a verse text describing the nature of this type of meditation and how to cultivate it in relation to a number of the early Lamrim topics. The spiritual realizations generated through this type of meditation contain a particular affective quality or feeling, referred to by the expression "experiential

awareness" (*myong ba*). The above-mentioned text that is found in *Liberation in Our Hands* describes three stages to analytic meditation: developing a proficient understanding of the practice (*nyams 'og tu tshud pa*), eliciting contrived forms of experiential awareness (*rtsol bcas kyi myong ba 'don pa*), and eliciting uncontrived forms of experiential awareness (*rtsol med kyi myong ba 'don pa*). The third and final stage of developing "uncontrived forms of experiential awareness"—which is to say, forms of spiritual realization that arise naturally and effortlessly, without further need to reflect on the instructions—is what is meant here by the phrase "eliciting an experiential awareness."

75. That is, all those sentient beings who have neither benefited you nor harmed you in this life.

76. *anāsrava, zag pa med pa*. On the outflows, see ch. 4, "The Brilliant Illumination of the Path to Enlightenment," note 62. The terms "uncontaminated" and "contaminated," also often rendered as "pure" and "impure," are somewhat loose translations of a pair of technical Buddhist expressions that literally mean "unrelated to the outflows" (*anāsrava, zag pa med pa*) and "related to the outflows" (*sāsrava, zag bcas*), respectively. *AK*, ch. 1, v. 8ab, states: "Those entities that are related to the outflows are the grasping heaps." The term applies to all conditioned entities (*saṃskṛtadharmā, 'dus byas kyi chos rnams*), with the exception of the Truth of the Path, because of their capacity to cause the outflows—that is, the mental afflictions—to become stronger. Thus, they are identified with the first two of the four noble truths. "Contaminated happiness" refers to pleasurable experiences that are be identified with the Truth of Suffering and "uncontaminated happiness" to pleasurable experiences associated with the Truth of the Path. "Uncontaminated happiness" is achieved only after a practitioner has attained a direct realization of selflessness and achieved the path of seeing (*darśanamārga, mthong lam*) related to one of the three Buddhist vehicles—that is, the Śrāvakayāna, Pratyekabuddhayāna, and the Mahāyāna.

77. This is a reference to the suffering of change (*pariṇāmaduḥkhatā, 'gyur ba'i sdug bsngal*). *AKBh* (p. 329) states: "Those impure conditioned entities that are attractive (*manāpa, yid du 'ong ba*) are characterized by suffering in terms of the suffering of change. As the sūtras declare, 'A pleasant feeling is pleasant when it arises and pleasant while it lasts but unpleasant when it undergoes change.'" That is to say, ordinary sense pleasures, material prosperity, and other samsaric forms of well-being represent the suffering of change (*pariṇamaduḥkhatā, 'gyur ba'i sdug bsngal*) in that they are transitory and our attachment to them generates suffering when they come to an end.

78. That is, in their pursuit of happiness they accumulate unvirtuous karma. Cf. *BCA* (ch. 1, v. 28), which states: "Wishing to escape suffering, ordinary beings rush toward nothing but suffering. Though desiring only happiness, in ignorance, they destroy their own suffering, as if it were an enemy."

79. *yid 'gyur*. "Mental transformation" here is more or less synonymous with the expression "experiential awareness" (*myong ba*) that has occurred repeatedly

above. The mental transformation that is meant here is that of an "uncontrived experiential awareness" or spiritual realization (*rtogs pa*), as described in note 74 (this chapter).

80. See ch. 4, "The Brilliant Illumination of the Path to Enlightenment," note 43.
81. That is, the arhat of the Śrāvakayāna or the arhat of the Pratyekabuddhayāna.
82. *yathāvadbhāvikatā, ji lta ba yod pa nyid.* The expression "true mode of being" refers to the emptiness (*śūnyatā, stong pa nyid*) of all entities.
83. *yāvadbhāvikatā, ji snyed ba yod pa nyid.* This expression refers to the conventional aspect of all entities.
84. The complete description of this visualization appears above at the beginning of the explanation of the preliminary practices.
85. See note 4 (this chapter).
86. Ngulchu Dharmabhadra's *Treasury of Jewels* (*Rin chen bang mdzod*, f. 90b) interprets this statement as follows: "[Panchen Losang Chökyi Gyaltsen] suggests implicitly here that after having taught the ritual method for adopting the aspirational form of enlightenment mind in the *Great Treatise on the Stages of the Path*, Je Tsongkhapa taught the ritual method for adopting the active form of enlightenment mind in his *Guidebook for the Path to Enlightenment*" (*Byang chub gzhung lam*). Adopting the two forms of enlightenment mind sequentially can also be understood to mean that it is possible to perform the rituals on separate occasions.
87. This is a reference to the six preliminary practices that are to be carried out at the beginning of each meditation session.
88. Ngulchu Dharmabhadra's *Treasury of Jewels* (*Rin chen bang mdzod*, f. 91a) states: "Regarding the statement '[After having reflected on the main practices that range] from how to serve one's spiritual teacher' and so on, this means that the person to whom either the aspirational or the active form of the vow is to be given should have previously trained his or her mind in the instruction on the stages of the path. If the individual is going to adopt the vow associated with the act of generating enlightenment mind by him- or herself, it is sufficient for one to reflect intently on the topics addressed in the prayer known as "The Source of All Good Qualities" (*Yong tan gzhir gyur ma*) when the six preliminary practices are carried out; it is not necessary to recite the entire text of *The Easy Path*, beginning with the topic of serving a spiritual teacher and so on."
89. See ch. 4, "The Brilliant Illumination of the Path to Enlightenment," note 99, and the commentary to verse 8 for an explanation of the phrase "until I reach the seat of enlightenment."
90. *BCA*, ch. 3, vv. 22, 23.
91. Ibid., ch. 3, vv. 25, 26.
92. See ch. 4, "The Brilliant Illumination of the Path to Enlightenment," note 128, for the canonical source on the four white and four black qualities.
93. *mūlāpatti, rtsa ba'i ltung ba.* See ch. 4, "The Brilliant Illumination of the Path to Enlightenment," notes 61 and 62.

94. *duścarita, nyes byas.* These offenses are also considered transgressions of the bodhisattva vow, albeit of lesser gravity than the root transgressions. See ch. 4, "The Brilliant Illumination of the Path to Enlightenment," note 63.
95. *ābodhimaṇḍa, byang chub snying po la mchis kyi bar du.* See ch. 4, "The Brilliant Illumination of the Path to Enlightenment," p. 50, for an explanation of this expression.
96. That is, the practice of generosity is principally the act of cultivating this attitude in one's own mind; its perfection is not measured by how much poverty one is able to eliminate. Cf. *BCA* (ch. 5, vv. 9, 10), which states: "If the perfection of generosity / were achieved through causing the world to become free of poverty, / since there is still poverty in the world today, / how could the former saviors have achieved it? // The perfection of generosity was explained / as being the mind that is willing to give all one's possessions, / along with the result of that giving, to all beings without remainder. / Therefore, to be precise, it is a state of mind."
97. This is known as "the patience that forbears the harm inflicted by others" (*parāpakāramarṣaṇā kṣānti, gzhan gyis gnod pa byed pa la ji mi snyam pa'i bzod pa*). See *BBh*, English translation, pp. 315–18.
98. This is known as "the patience that tolerates suffering" (*duḥkhādhivāsanā kṣāntiḥ, sdug bsngal dang du len pa'i bzod pa*). See *BBh*, English translation, pp. 319–23.
99. *adhimukti, mos pa.* The literal sense of this term is that of a mind that is directed with firmness toward an object. Asaṅga's *BBh* (ch. 8, p. 95) defines it as "a sense of certainty (*niścaya, nges pa*) and eagerness (*ruci, 'dod pa*) that is preceded by the faith that is a clarity of mind toward the eight objects of devotion." The text here makes reference to seven of the eight topics. The final object is the nature of reality (*tattvārtha, de kho na nyid kyi don*). The devotion that arises through reflecting attentively on these eight topics results in a third type of patience, called "the patience of the devotion that is gained by reflecting on entities" (*dharmanidhyānādhimuktikṣānti, chos la nges par sems pa la mos pa'i bzod pa*). See *BBh*, English translation, pp. 323–24.
100. *byang chub sems dpa'i bslab pa'i gnas rnams.* While the expression *bslab pa'i gnas* can mean the precepts that are associated with the Buddhist vows, the term here should be taken more broadly to mean all the elements of Mahāyāna spiritual training. In *BBh* (p. 95) this topic of devotion is described as "all of the paths that make up the bodhisattva training" (*sarve bodhisattvaśikāmārgāḥ, byang chub sems dpa'i bslab pa'i lam thams cad*).
101. mNar med. This is the most severe of the eight hot hells. *AKBh* (p. 163) states: "It is called Avīci because its suffering is uninterrupted."
102. *utsāha, spro ba.* This is the essential quality of the virtuous mental factor known as "effort" (*vīrya, brtson 'grus*). *AS* (p. 7) states: "What is effort? It is the exertion of the mind toward virtuous activities, which can be applied in an armor-like, endeavoring, dauntless, unrelenting, or unquenchable manner. Its action is to accomplish and complete all practices that are virtuous in nature."

103. The effort described in this statement is called "armor-like effort" (*saṃnāhavīrya, go cha'i brtson 'grus*).
104. This is called "the effort that collects virtuous qualities" (*kuśaladharma-saṃgrāhakaṃ vīrya, dge ba'i chos sdud pa'i brtson 'grus*).
105. This is called "the effort that acts on behalf of sentient beings" (*sattvārthakriyāvīrya, sems can gyi don bya ba'i brtson 'grus*).
106. For clarification of these classifications, see ch. 7, "The Nectar That Is Like Highly Refined Gold," notes 176–83.
107. *paramārtha, don dam pa*. This term is a synonym for emptiness (*śūnyatā, stong pa nyid*).
108. *pañca vidyāsthānāni, rig pa'i gnas lnga*. They are the inner science (*adhyātma-vidyā, nang don gyi rig pa*); the science of logic (*hetuvidyā, gtan tshigs kyi rig pa*); the science of grammar (*śabdavidyā, sgra'i rig pa*); the science of treating disease (*vyadhicikitsāvidyā, nad gso ba'i rig pa*); and the science of the categories of crafts and occupations (*śilpakarmasthānavidyā, bzo dang las kyi gnas kyi rig pa*).
109. This form of material generosity (*āmiṣadāna, zang zing gi sbyin pa*) is the first of the four principles for gathering a following.
110. *priyavāditā, snyan par smra ba*. This is the second of the four principles. See *BBh*, English translation, pp. 365–66, for further explanation.
111. *arthacaryā, don spyod pa*. This is the third principle for gathering a following. See *BBh*, English translation, pp. 371–79.
112. *samānārthatā, don mthun pa*. This is the fourth principle for gathering a following. See *BBh*, English translation, pp. 379–81.
113. Je Tsongkhapa's *Great Treatise* (ff. 314a–315a) describes six requisite qualities (*śamathasaṃbhāra, zhi gnas kyi tshogs*) for developing quiescence that are mentioned in the second of Kamalaśīla's three *Stages of Meditation* treatises: staying in a favorable place, having few wants, being satisfied with what one has, avoiding involvement in many activities, having a pure moral practice, and giving up thoughts about sense objects and the like.
114. A favorable place (*anukūladeśa, mthun pa'i yul*) for carrying out meditation is described in a verse from *MSA* (ch. 13, v. 7) as having five qualities. Two of the five are mentioned here: first, a "wholesome location" (*subhūmi, sa bzang ba*) means one that is conducive to good health; and, second, one where there are "good companions" (*susahāyaka, grogs bzang pa*) means a place where there are individuals whose conduct and views are compatible with your own. The other three qualities are a place where material necessities can be acquired easily; an area that is safe in that robbers and other malicious persons do not reside there; and a place that is conducive to meditation in that it is free of disturbances caused by crowds, people talking, and other noises. The verse states: "The place where a wise person practices / should allow material needs to be easily gained, / be a safe area and a wholesome location, / have good companions present, and be conducive to meditation."

115. *rgya sran*. Commonly known as "horse gram," this is a legume that is mainly used as horse feed but is also used for human consumption. It can be green, brown, or reddish brown in color, it is kidney shaped, and its size is about 5 mm. in length.

116. *cha phyed tsam gsal ba*. *Swift Path* (*Myur lam*, f. 76b) states: "Moreover, regarding this point, initially you should be satisfied with meditating on an image in which only about half of the physical form's features are evident, such as the head, two arms, two legs, and the abdomen." *Treasury of Jewels* (f. 110b) states: "Visualize successively the body's head, two arms, torso, and two legs several times. When the image of a physical body with only about half of its features arises, you should be satisfied with that object and meditate by fixing your mind on it one-pointedly."

117. *laya, bying ba*. See ch. 7, "The Nectar That Is Like Highly Refined Gold," note 177.

118. *auddhatya, rgod pa*. See ch. 7, "The Nectar That Is Like Highly Refined Gold," note 178.

119. *cittasthiti, sems gnas pa*. This term literally means "a state in which the mind remains stationary or fixed." It is a reference to the nine stages of mental stability that culminate in the attainment of quiescence.

120. *MVK*, ch. 4, v. 3cd. The five faults are laziness, forgetfulness, languor and excitation, the failure to apply the necessary corrective action, the applying of some form of exertion when none is necessary. In this context, "laziness" (*kausīdya, le lo*) is more precisely the disinclination to engage in meditation practice.

121. *prasrabdhi, shin tu sbyangs pa*. See ch. 4, "The Brilliant Illumination of the Path to Enlightenment," note 65.

122. *avavādasya sammoṣaḥ, gdams nga brjed pa*. This fault means the inattentiveness that does not keep hold of the meditation object.

123. *asampramoṣa, ma brjed pa*. The Tibetan literally means "not to forget" the meditation object; however, Sthiramati explains the Sanskrit original to mean "the quality that enables you to keep from losing hold of a mental object."

124. *samprajanya, shes bzhin*. See ch. 7, "The Nectar That Is Like Highly Refined Gold," note 114.

125. *styāna, rmugs pa*. *AS* (p. 6) states: "What is torpor? It is an unfitness of the mind that is a form of ignorance. Its action is to support the arising of all the root mental afflictions and secondary mental afflictions."

126. *ālokanimitta, snang ba'i mtsan ma*. To explain this expression, Je Tsongkhapa quotes the following line from Asanga's *Stage of a Śrāvaka*: "Visualize the image of the brightness of either a lamp, the light of a fire, or the sun."

127. *Treasury of Jewels* (*Rin chen bang mdzod*, f. 113b) explains this instruction as follows: "Dampa Sangye wrote, 'When languor occurs, dispel it with the syllable *phaṭ*.' As this line indicates, recognize your body as having a nature that resembles the light of a rainbow. Then visualize the inseparable combination of your subtlest vital air and mind as a red and white drop the size of a sparrow's

egg in the center of your navel. As you vocalize the syllable *phaṭ*, visualize that the mind-air drop reaches your heart. As you vocalize the syllable *phaṭ* a second time, visualize that the mind-air drop reaches your throat. As you vocalize the syllable *phaṭ* a third time, visualize that the mind-air drop separates from your body through the crown of your head, and after traveling upward a great distance, it merges inseparably with the realm of space. When your languor has disappeared, you should apply yourself once again to the previous meditation practice." The above line of verse is from a text identified as *The True Dharma That Quells Suffering* (*Dam chos sdug bsngal zhi byed*) in Paṇchen Losang Chökyi Gyaltsen's autocommentary to his root text on the Great Seal (*mahāmudrā, phyag rgya chen po*).

128. This "outward movement" (*visāra, 'phro ba*) of the mind is the defining characteristic of distraction. *AS* (p. 6) states: "What is distraction (*vikṣepa, rnam par g.yeng ba*)? It is a form of desire, hatred, or ignorance that is an outward movement of the mind."

129. *Treasury of Jewels* (*Rin chen bang mdzod*, f. 114a) states: "Dampa Sangye wrote, 'When the mind flows outward, the root should be cut.' As this line indicates, draw in the upper, white life-sustaining air (*prāṇa, srog 'dzin*) through the nostrils and push it down to the navel region. Then contract the lower, yellow evacuative air (*apāna, thur sel*), and after fixing your mind on a drop the size of a sparrow's egg, continually hold the upper and lower airs that have been joined together at the navel as long as you can. When you are unable to hold the airs any longer, release your breath through your nostrils. Then repeat this process and hold the two airs at the navel once again. You can also carry out the form of prāṇāyāma (*srog rtsol*) practice that is taught in Kriyā Tantra, which is to repeatedly hold the upper air while visualizing yourself appearing in the deity's physical form and maintaining that as your meditation object. After the excitation has stopped, you should apply yourself once again to the previous meditation practice."

130. *asaṃskāra, 'du mi byed pa.*

131. *upekṣā, btang snyoms. AS* (p. 6) states: "What is equanimity? It is the evenness of mind, inactivity of mind, and the state of effortlessness of mind that opposes abiding in an afflicted state of mind and that is gained on the basis of avoidance of attachment, avoidance of hatred, avoidance of ignorance, together with effort. Its action is to provide support for keeping the mental afflictions from having an opportunity to arise." This equanimity is distinct from the equanimity that avoids attachment toward those that are held dear and hatred toward those that are considered an adversary.

132. That is, that subtle aspect of the mind that engages in the examination.

133. That is, the main aspect of the mind that is perceiving a personal self.

134. *'dzin stangs kyi yul.* This is an epistemological expression that refers to the manner in which a particular mental state holds its object. In this case it is an erring mode of apprehension (*'dzin stangs*). Thus, the nominal self, which does exist

conventionally, is not what needs to be refuted; rather, what needs to be refuted is a self that is erroneously believed to exist independently by way of its own objectively real, essential nature.

135. *rjen cher gyis.* That is, the object to be refuted must be identified as it occurs naturally within your own mind through introspection.

136. *MA* (ch. 6, v. 126ab) states: "If the self were the heaps, because of that, since they are many, there would similarly be numerous selves."

137. That is, the distinct and separate beings of those three lives would have to be completely identical and consist of one and the same undifferentiable individual.

138. These errors are the opposites of the following two fundamental axioms of the doctrine of karma: what has been done will not perish and what has not been done will not yield any fruition.

139. *upādātṛ, nye bar len pa po.* The five samsaric heaps are often referred to as the five "grasping heaps" (*upādānaskandhā, nye bar len pa'i phung po*). One basic notion of "grasping" or "acquiring" often is identified with the mental affliction of desire or attachment. In a different context, the action of "acquiring" is meant to refer to the act of taking birth in the sense of taking on or "acquiring" a new set of five heaps. The nominally existent agent that carries out that act is the self, and therefore, it is referred to as the "acquirer" or the "acquiring agent." Likewise, the five heaps are referred to as the "acquisitions" or the "objects that are acquired."

140. *MMK* (ch. 27, v. 7) states: "Nor is it reasonable for the self to be distinct from the acquisitions; / for, if they were distinct, it should be apprehended without the acquisitions, but it cannot be apprehended in that way." *MA* (ch. 6, v. 124ab) states: "Therefore, there is no self that is distinct from the heaps because it is not established that it can be apprehended after separating out the heaps."

141. In other words, these practitioners of higher acumen do not need to carry out the entire four-point analysis once again in order to develop once again a vivid definite understanding of the self's lack of inherently real existence.

142. *stong sang nge ba.* That is, a state in which one's mind is free of all appearances or any form of objective content.

143. *saṃskṛta, 'dus byas.* Buddhist philosophical doctrine identifies two fundamental types of entities: conditioned and unconditioned. Conditioned entities (*saṃskṛta, 'dus byas*) are those that are produced by causes, and they are impermanent in that they only exist for an instant. *AKBh* (p. 4) states: "They are conditioned entities in that they are produced by the convergence and combination of conditional factors." There are three types: form, mind, and formations that do not accompany consciousness (see discussion below in the main body of the text).

144. *asaṃskṛta, 'dus ma byas.* Unconditioned entities are those that are not produced by causes and that are therefore designated as being permanent. They include such entities as space (see discussion in the main body of the text), analytic ces-

sations (*pratisaṃkhyanirodha, so sor brtags pa'i 'gog pa*), and emptiness (*śūnyatā, stong pa nyid*). "Analytic cessation" is a technical expression for the Truth of Cessation.

145. *jaḍa, bem po*. This term, which literally means "lifeless" or "inanimate" matter, is synonymous with the more common Buddhist term that is usually translated as "form" (*rūpa, gzugs*).

146. *yan lag lnga*. That is, two arms, two legs, and a head.

147. The term "formation" (*saṃskāra, 'du byed*) is the name for the fourth of the five heaps. It is made up of two types of entities: mental factors (*caitta, sems byung*) and formations that do not accompany consciousness (*cittaviprayuktasaṃskāra, sems and mtshungs par ldan pa ma yin pa'i 'du byed*). The latter category is the one that is being discussed here. Buddhist philosophical literature identifies a variety of entities that are of this type, including such things as life force (*jīvita, srog*), impermanence (*anitya, mi rtag pa*), the stage of an ordinary being (*pṛthagjanatva, so so skye bo nyid*), and time (*kāla, dus*). These entities are typically identified as nominally existent relations. See *Inner Science of Buddhist Practice*, pp. 312–26, for a fuller discussion.

148. *AS* (p. 11) states: "What is time? Time is the nominally existent entity that is ascribed to the continuous occurrence of causes and results."

149. *ākāśa, nam mkha'*. *AS* (p. 13) states: What is space? It is the absence of form in the sense of that which affords the opportunity for the occurrence of all physical action."

150. This lengthy introductory description of the two forms of spiritual practice should be understood to be describing the process by which quiescence (*śamatha, zhi gnas*) is developed. Paṇchen Losang Chökyi Gyaltsen here addresses quiescence implicitly with the phrase "on the basis of having properly cultivated" a form of spiritual practice that meditates one-pointedly. Quiescence is essentially a form of one-pointed concentration that is imbued with the extraordinary ease of agility. See ch. 7, "The Nectar That Is Like Highly Refined Gold," note 181.

151. *vipaśyanā, lhag mthong*. Ch. 4, "The Brilliant Illumination of the Path to Enlightenment," note 65, also describes how the same two forms of agility are also developed during the practice of insight meditation. The principal difference between quiescence and insight is that the former elicits this agility on the strength of one-pointed concentration, while the latter does so by cultivating a form of wisdom that continues to analyze the meditation object further.

152. This is the traditional description of the length of time that is required to attain supreme enlightenment through the non-tantric form of the Mahāyāna path. In Buddhist cosmology, a single "great kalpa" is the vast period of time during which a region of the universe that encompasses a "great triple-thousand"—that is, a billion—world systems passes through four phases of equal duration: voidness, formation, stability, and destruction. In his *Commentary on "The Treasury of Higher Learning"* (*AKBh*, pp. 178–82), Vasubandhu explains the

term "countless" (*asaṃkhya, grangs med*) to mean one times ten raised to the power of fifty-nine. Thus, three such spans of time constitute the length of time encompassed by "three periods of countless kalpas" (*bskal pa grangs med gsum*).

153. *myong khrid.* This term can refer either to a particular form of oral teaching or to a particular type of written instruction manual. Here the term is being used in the latter sense. The author also refers to this treatise in the colophon as an "explicit instruction" (*dmar khrid*) or, more literally, a "red" instruction. The word "red" metaphorically alludes to the blood of a freshly opened cadaver. See note 155 (this chapter). Pabongkha Rinpoche describes an experiential form of oral teaching in his *Liberation in Our Hands* as follows: "In an experiential instruction, the teachings are presented one topic at a time. After the students have received each set of instructions, they are directed to meditate on them until they generate true spiritual realizations. Only then are subsequent topics taught."

154. The *Vinayavastu* contains an account of the how the Śākyas were descended from the Ikṣvāku clan and came to settle in Kapilavastu. The expression "incomparable descendant of Ikṣvāku" is a reference to Buddha Śākyamuni.

155. *Liberation in Our Hands, Part 1* (p. 25) states: "In an explicit instruction (*dmar khrid*), the wording of a particular text is not explained in detail. Rather, a teacher presents the essential instructions in a plain and open manner, just as a skilled physician cuts open a fresh corpse and directly introduces the five major organs, six hollow organs, and so forth to his students."

156. *varṣā, dbyar gnas.* This period begins on the sixteenth of the sixth month and continues until the twenty-ninth of the seventh month of the lunar calendar. The Paṇchen Lama makes a statement in his autobiography that suggests this teaching took place during that period in the year 1652. He writes (ff. 145b–146a): "During the rainy-season retreat, in the main assembly hall of Tashi Lhunpo Monastery, I gave teachings from [several texts contained in Wensapa] Losang Döndrup's Collected Works, including an extensive explanation of his instructions on *The Stages of the Path*, as well as a reading transmission (*lung*) of several texts and several *anujñā* (*rjes gnang*) or 'permission' rituals, including that of the goddess Vijayā" (rNam par rgyal ma). The specific year is indicated by the author's statement that it occurred several months after the Fifth Dalai Lama's departure for China, when the Paṇchen Lama was eighty-two years old.

157. *zin thun du stsal ba.* Paṇchen Losang Chökyi Gyaltsen's observation that he gave the teaching "as a way of reinforcing his own remembrance of this system of practice" should be taken as an act of self-effacement. Compare this with the colophon of Je Tsongkhapa's Lamrim poem *A Compendium of the Stages of the Path* (*Lam rim bsdus don*), where he describes his work as having been "created to avoid forgetting its meaning." I understand the Paṇchen Lama's remark to mean that his original intent was simply to deliver an oral discourse on the Lamrim instructions, as he had learned them from his own teacher Sangye Yeshe (Sangs rgyas ye shes, 1525–1591). This Lamrim tradition is heavily

influenced by elements of the larger body of esoteric teachings known as the Wensa Oral Transmission Lineage (*dben sa snyan brgyud*) that was propagated by the Paṇchen Lama's prior incarnation, Wensapa Losang Döndrup (dBen sa pa bLo bzang don grub, 1505—1566). Several of the latter figure's Lamrim works include *Guru-Deity Yoga within the Lamrim Tradition* (*Lam rim bla ma lha'i rnal 'byor*) and *The Method of Practicing the Essence of the Stages of the Path to Enlightenment* (*Byang chub lam gyi rim pa'i snying po nyams su len tshul*).

9. An Essential Summary of the Method of Practice in the System of the Stages of the Path to Enlightenment

1. *Byang chub lam gyi rim pa nyams su len tshul gyi phyag bzhes snying por dril ba*, *DNZ*, vol. 3 (*ga*), pp. 161–79.
2. See ch. 2, "The Root Text of the Mahāyāna Instruction Known as the Seven-Point Mind Training," note 2.
3. Ibid., note 3.
4. An expression that is meant as an invocation for success.
5. See also ch. 7, "The Nectar That Is Like Highly Refined Gold," note 29, and the descriptions that appear in the main text.
6. See ch. 4, "The Brilliant Illumination of the Path to Enlightenment, note 91.
7. See ch. 8, "The Easy Path," note 53.
8. See ch. 7, "The Nectar That Is Like Highly Refined Gold," note 135.
9. See ch. 4, "The Brilliant Illumination of the Path to Enlightenment," note 195, for an explanation of this epithet.
10. *'phags pa'i dge 'dun*. An ārya is someone who has achieved a direct realization of either the insubstantiality of the person or the insubstantiality of entities, and thereby achieved the transcendent path of any of the three vehicles. (See also ch. 7, "The Nectar That Is Like Highly Refined Gold," note 129.) While the conventional meaning of the term sangha is any group of at least four fully ordained Buddhist bhikṣu monks, the ultimate form of the Mahāyāna sangha jewel that is one aspect of the refuge object is any individual Mahāyāna ārya who possesses any of the eight qualities of knowledge and liberation. The eight qualities are as follows: knowledge of ultimate reality (*yathāvatbhāvikatājñāna, ji lta ba yod pa nyid rig pa*) is the direct realization that all beings and their heaps are void of any self-existent essence; knowledge of far-ranging reality (*yāvat-bhāvikatājñāna, ji snyed pa yod pa nyid rig pa*) is the realization that the minds of all sentient beings, including animals, possess the purity that is represented by the absence of any self-existent essence; introspective knowledge (*pratyāt-majñāna, so so rang gis rig pa*) is the realization that only a Mahāyāna ārya, by his own personal experience, can perceive such knowledge; liberation from the obstruction of attachment (*saṅgāvaraṇātvimukta, chags pa'i sgrib pa las grol ba*) is the state of being free of any attachment to the belief in the self-existence of sentient beings, a quality that results from the knowledge of the innate purity

of all beings; liberation from the obstruction of being impeded mentally (*pratihatāvaraṇātvimukta, thogs pa'i sgrib pa las grol ba*) is a state that is brought about by the ability of the ārya's far-reaching knowledge to engage all knowable entities; liberation from the obstruction of being inferior (no equivalent in text, *dman pa'i sgrib pa las grol ba*) is the state of being near to supreme buddhahood by virtue of possessing the three just-mentioned knowledges; a general quality of knowledge represented by the three knowledges; and a general quality of liberation represented by the three liberations. The principal source for this explanation is the *Treatise on the Higher Science of the Mahāyāna* (*Mahāyānottaratantraśāstra, Theg pa chen po rgyud bla ma'i bstan bcos*, ch. 1, vv. 13–22).

11. *byin rlabs bzhi skor*. This phrase refers to a liturgical exercise in which the following four elements are blessed: the area, the temple, the seats, and the offerings.
12. *dharmadhātu, chos kyi dbyings*. *MVK* (ch. 1, vv. 15, 16) identifies this term as one of a number of synonyms for ultimate truth. *MVBh* (p. 39) interprets it as follows: "Emptiness is called the 'entity-source' because it is the cause of an ārya's spiritual qualities in the sense that the spiritual qualities of an ārya arise from the mind that holds that emptiness as its object. Here the meaning of the word 'source' (*dhātu, dbyings*) is that of a cause." Sthiramati's commentary (*MVṬ*, p. 39) adds: "Here the word 'entity' (*dharma, chos*) means all the spiritual qualities of an ārya, such as the eight of right view and so on, and the remaining ones that end with right knowledge of the attainment of liberation" (*samyagvimuktijñāna, yang dag pa'i grol ba'i ye shes*).
13. *Triskandhaka Sūtra, Phung po gsum pa'i mdo*. This scripture is usually understood to mean the confessional recitation that appears in the *Vinayaviniścaya Upāliparipṛcchā Sūtra* (*'Dul ba rnam par gtan la dbab pa nye bar 'khor gyis zhus pa'i mdo*, Toh. 68). This recitation is also cited in Śāntideva's *Compendium of Training*, ch. 8.
14. *Bhadracaryapraṇidhāna, bZang po spyod pa'i smon lam*. This well-known Buddhist aspirational prayer appears at the very end of the *Gaṇḍavyūha Sūtra* (*sDong pos bskod pa'i mdo*), a canonical text that makes up the last section of the *Avataṃsaka Sūtra* (*mDo sde phal po che*).
15. *BCA*, ch. 10, v. 35.
16. That is, Buddha Śākyamuni.
17. Sumagadhā was a daughter of the wealthy merchant Anāthapiṇḍada from Śrāvasti, a major benefactor of the Buddha who donated the Jetavana Grove. The *Sumagadhā Avadāna* (Tibetan translation, Toh. 346) tells how Sumagadhā, after marrying the son of a Jain family, went to live with him in a place far from the Buddha. Through the power of her faith and strong prayers, she was able to summon the Buddha, who flew through the air accompanied by many elder disciples to deliver a teaching. Marvelous spectacles were displayed as each disciple, and finally the Buddha, arrived.
18. *BCA*, ch. 2, v. 10.
19. This is an often-cited verse for the act of bathing the buddhas.

20. That is, the water of morality cleanses the stains of bad conduct, the water of patience cleanses the stains of hatred, the water of effort cleanses the stains of laziness, the water of meditative absorption cleanses the stains of distraction, and the water of wisdom cleanses the stains of deficient understanding (*kuprajñā, shes rab 'chal ba*). The mantra that accompanies the act of bathing is *oṃ sarvatathāgata abhiṣekata samaya śrīye āḥ hūṃ*.
21. *BCA*, ch. 2, v. 12ab.
22. *BCA*, ch. 2, v. 14.
23. *'Jam pa'i dbyangs kyi zhal lung*. This is a work written by the Fifth Dalai Lama, Ngawang Losang Gyatso (Ngag dbang blo bzang rgya mtsho, 1617–1682).
24. *BCA*, ch. 2, vv. 12cd. The next verse (*BCA*, ch. 2, v. 13) continues: "I also adorn Samantabhadra, Ajita, Mañjughoṣa, / Lokeśvara, and the rest, with fine, soft, / and beautiful divine multicolored raiments, / as well as various kinds of the most excellent of ornaments."
25. In other words, recite here all the verses of supplication that appear below, but substitute "I make prostration" for the words "I make supplication" in each verse.
26. See ch. 4, "The Brilliant Illumination of the Path to Enlightenment," note 3.
27. *mi pham*. An alternate name for Maitreya.
28. The language for the verses that address the Lamrim lineage lamas from the Buddha down to Lhodrak Drupchen Namkha Drak and Drakor Khenchen Chökyap Zangpo were composed by Je Tsongkhapa. They appear in his supplication prayer titled *Opening the Door to the Supreme Path* (*Lam mchog sgo 'byed*), which is the first work in the collection of his miscellaneous compositions (*bka' 'bum thor bu*, Toh. 5275).
29. This is a reference to the first four verses of this aspirational prayer. See note 14 (this chapter).
30. That is, at the beginning of the sixth preliminary practice.
31. *upacāra, nye bar spyod pa*. This term is primarily associated with the devotional act of offering these five objects: flowers, incense, lamps, scented water, and food. As indicated here, these five offerings are often also combined with two types of water offering at the beginning—that is, "reception water" (*argham, mchod yon*) and water for washing the feet (*pādyam, zhabs sil*)—as well as a final offering of music. This group of eight offerings are collectively known as the "outer offerings," to differentiate them from other more specialized forms of tantric offerings. While this term is often translated by Tibetan scholars as "enjoyment offerings," the original Sanskrit term derives from a verbal root whose meanings include "to serve" and "to attend," and thus the noun indicates a form of religious "service."
32. This is a codified version of one of a series of verses that appears in the *Ratnolkādhāraṇī Sūtra* (also ch. 12 of the *Avataṃsaka Sūtra*). They describe acts by which great bodhisattvas emanate light rays from themselves that appear as a variety of elaborate forms of offerings in the sky. The sūtra passages do

not include the terms "reception water" or "foot water," but they do mention a range of objects such as flowers, incense, perfumes, clothing, jewels, victory banners, and parasols.

33. *devendra, lha yi dbang po*. This is the principal deity in the Heaven of the Thirty-Three, known by the epithets Indra and Śakra.
34. They are a mirror; yogurt; *dūrvā* grass (*cynodon dactylon*); *bilva*, or bael fruit (of the wood-apple tree); white, right-turning conch shell; bovine bile concretion (*gorocanā*, *gi wang*; a medicinal substance); *sindhūra*, or vermilion powder; and white mustard seeds.
35. Cf. *BCA*, ch. 2, vv. 15–25.
36. *The Aspirational Prayer for Excellent Spiritual Conduct*, vv. 5–7.
37. Ibid., vv. 8–12.
38. See ch. 5, "A Verse Compendium of the Spiritual Practices of the Stages of the Path," note 4.
39. rNam par snang mdzad. Various Tibetan works identify him as an upadhyāya (*mkhan po*), which means a senior teacher or preceptor. Both Tāranātha's and Butön's historical works identify him as the master from whom Haribhadra received instruction on the Perfection of Wisdom doctrine. His place in this lineage is described in biographical literature on Lord Atiśa.
40. That is, Lord Atiśa, whose ordination name was Dīpaṃkara Śrījñāna.
41. This expression most often refers to Nāgārjuna and Asaṅga. See the translator's introduction, note 101.
42. This verse, which was composed by Je Tsongkhapa, was originally addressed to his spiritual teacher Rendawa Zhönu Lodrö (Re mda' ba gzhon nu blo gros, 1349–1412). Rendawa replied that the wording applied more fittingly to his student, Je Tsongkhapa. Since then, the verse was revised so as to refer to Je Tsongkhapa. The first two lines are meant to describe Tsongkhapa as being the embodiment of both Avalokiteśvara and Mañjughoṣa.
43. Phyag na padma. This is an alternate name for Avalokiteśvara.
44. This is a Sanskritized reference to the Fifth Dalai Lama's teacher Khöntön Peljor Lhundrup ('Khon ston dPal 'byor lhun grub, 1561–1637). Khöntön is an epithet that means "teacher from the Khon clan."
45. That is, the Fifth Dalai Lama, Ngawang Losang Gyatso, author of the Lamrim treatise *Mañjughoṣa's Oral Instruction*, the source text for this work by Jamyang Khyentse Wangpo. See note 23 (this chapter).
46. This verse appears in ch. 5, "A Verse Compendium of the Spiritual Practices of the Stages of the Path to Enlightenment," with the verb "prostration" in the first line instead of "supplication," as written here. See also that work's note 8.
47. That is, Ārya Nāgārjuna.
48. Chökyap Zangpo (Chos skyabs bzang po, d.u.). Italicized words of the verse are elements of his name: Chö (dharma) kyap (savior) Zangpo (sublime). He was known as Drakor Khenchen (Grwa skor mkhan chen), or "the great abbot from the monastery for itinerant monk-scholars." The proper name for

his monastery was Rinchen Ling (*rin chen gling*). The monastery is referred to as Drakor because it served as one of a series of monastic centers of the day that on a rotating basis hosted formal gatherings of monk-scholars. At these events, newer scholars would undergo oral examinations on topics relating to major areas of Buddhist doctrinal study, such as the perfection of wisdom (*prajñāpāramitā*), epistemology (*pramāṇa*), higher learning (*abhidharma*), and monastic discipline (*vinaya*).

49. rJe Rin po che. This is a well-known epithet of Je Tsongkhapa, which literally means "precious lord."
50. Gönpawa Wangchuk Gyaltsen (dGon pa ba dBang phyug rgyal mtshan, 1016–1083). The Lamrim lineage transmitted by this master is known as the Kadam tradition of Lamrim Followers (*lam rim pa*).
51. Chengawa Tsultrim Bar (sPyan snga ba Tshul khrims 'bar, 1038–1103). The Lamrim lineage transmitted by this master is known as the Kadam tradition of Those Who Follow a Master's Personal Instruction (*man ngag pa*).
52. That is, Lhodrak Drupchen Namkha Gyaltsen (Lho brag grub chen Nam mkha' rgyal mtshan, 1324–1401). Je Tsongkhapa met this lama in 1395 and studied with him at his Drowa Monastery (*sgro ba dgon*) for approximately seven months.
53. That is, Geshe Dölpa Marshurpa Sherap Gyatso (dGe bshes Dol pa dmar zhur pa shes rab rgya mtsho, 1059–1131), the author of the *Blue Udder*. See ch. 4, "The Brilliant Illumination of the Path to Enlightenment," note 46.
54. Drakor Khenchen Chökyap Zangpo. See note 48 (this chapter). Of the two Kadampa lineages of instruction that Je Tsongkhapa received from Chökyap Zangpo, the one that was transmitted from Potowa Rinchen Sel (Po to ba rin chen gsal, 1027–1105) through his disciple Sharawa Yönten Drak (Sha ra ba Yon tan grags, 1070–1141) is known as the Kadam tradition of Treatise Followers (*gzhung pa ba*) in recognition of the fact that this tradition relied heavily on the following six Indian Buddhist treatises (*bka' gdams gzhung drug*): (1) *Śikṣāsamuccaya*, (2) *Bodhicaryāvatāra*, (3) *Jātakamālā*, (4) *Udānavarga*, (5) *Mahāyānasutrālaṃkāra*, and (6) *Bodhisattvabhūmi*.
55. These verses are addressed to the Kadam lineage known as the Those Who Follow the Master's Personal Instruction (*man ngag pa*). See note 51 (this chapter).
56. *phur tshugs gsol 'debs*. *Liberation in Our Hands, Part 1*, p. 231, states: "As if you were forcefully planting a stake into one spot of ground, make the 'stake-like supplication' to the lone figure of your Root Lama."
57. *prātimokṣa*, *so sor thar pa*. This is the name of the Hīnayāna system of moral discipline. See ch. 8, "The Easy Path," note 65. While there are seven types of male and female prātimokṣa vows, this reference should be taken to mean that the ideal form of spiritual life is to adopt the celibate vows of a monk or nun that are observed by those who have left the householder state and "gone forth" (*pravrajita*, *rab tu byung ba*) into the homeless state.
58. The major divisions of Mahāyāna ethical practice are restraint from wrongdo-

ing, accumulating virtue, and accomplishing the welfare of sentient beings. A primary source for explaining Mahāyāna ethics is the morality chapter of Asaṅga's *Stage of a Bodhisattva*.

59. *vajrayāna, rdo rje'i theg pa*. That is, the tantric form of Mahāyāna practice.
60. That is, at the time of the initiation ritual of one of the Yoga Tantra or Highest Yoga systems. Only these two classes of tantra include the conferring of tantric vows and commitments.
61. Although the text does not state this point explicitly, from the beginning of the third preliminary practice when you carry out the act of going for refuge, you should visualize that all sentient beings are surrounding you and performing the spiritual practices along with you.
62. *dpyad sgom*. See ch. 8, "The Easy Path," note 74. Several lines from a poem in appendix F of *Liberation in Our Hands, Part 2*, give this brief description: "Analytic meditation is the exercise of eliciting experiential realizations / by contemplating a particular meditation topic from every standpoint / and in every way, using scriptural citations and sharp reasoning."
63. *'jog sgom*. Fixed meditation is a form of practice that culminates in the attainment of quiescence (see ch. 7, "The Nectar That Is Like Highly Refined Gold," note 10).
64. *atideva, lhag pa'i lha*. In the Lamrim tradition, the principal figure in the merit field is visualized as one's root lama appearing in the form of Buddha Śākyamuni.
65. Both the act of supplication and the visualization exercise are described at the end of the previous section.
66. *myong ba*. See ch. 8, "The Easy Path," note 74.
67. *bshar sgom*. See ch. 5, "A Verse Compendium of the Spiritual Practices of the Stages of the Path to Enlightenment," note 16.
68. *dal ba'i rten*. See ch. 7, "The Nectar That Is Like Highly Refined Gold," note 2.
69. *rten*. This term, which might also be rendered as "receptacle," in this context refers to a consecrated religious icon that is meant to be regarded as the actual being or object that it represents. In the case of the merit field, the physical "vessel" for the merit field would typically be a tangka painting.
70. See ch. 8, "The Easy Path," note 16.
71. *The Aspirational Prayer for Excellent Spiritual Conduct*, vv. 55. 56.
72. This well-known verse is a slightly revised version of verse 60 from Nāgārjuna's *Sixty Verses on Reasoning* (*Yuktiṣaṣṭikā*).
73. *mārakarma, bdud kyi las*. The phrase "Māra's deeds" refers to any circumstances that a spiritual practitioner may encounter in which he or she might be vulnerable to being led astray. See also ch. 7, "The Nectar That Is Like Highly Refined Gold," note 70.
74. The original version of this verse reads "for composing (*bsgrig pa*) the sublime path," which is meant to refer to Je Tsongkhapa as the author of *The Great Treatise on the Stages of the Path*. However, according to oral tradition, this wording

should be altered to read "for practicing (*sgrub pa*) the sublime path" in order to identify oneself as a practitioner who is reciting this verse of the aspirational prayer on behalf of the benefactors and others who have supported one's spiritual activities.

75. They are to copy scriptures, to present offerings, to practice generosity, to hear dharma, to read dharma, to take up dharma, to teach dharma, to recite dharma, to reflect on the dharma's meaning, and to meditate on the dharma's meaning. See *Differentiating the Middle View from Extremes* (*Madhyāntavibhāga, dBus mtha' rnam 'byed*), ch. 5, vv. 9cd–10.
76. These seven verses appear at the end of Je Tsongkhapa's *Great Treatise on the Stages of the Path*. They are popularly referred to as the "Lamrim aspirational prayer" (*Lam rim smon lam*).
77. *rtsi*. This term is meant in the sense of being influenced by the positive spiritual mental states that were developed during the meditation sessions.
78. See ch. 7, "The Nectar That Is Like Highly Refined Gold," note 114.
79. See ch. 8, "The Easy Path," note 59.
80. Buddhist abhidharma literature describes three mental states as constituting "roots of virtue": (1) avoidance of attachment (*alobha, 'dod chags med pa*); (2) avoidance of hatred (*adveṣa, zhe sdang med pa*); and (3) avoidance of ignorance (*'moha, gti mug med pa*). *AS* (p. 6) states: "What is avoidance of attachment? It is the antidote to attachment to samsaric existence and the objects that sustain samsaric existence. . . . What is avoidance of hatred? It is the antidote to animosity toward sentient beings, suffering, and the objects that cause suffering. . . . What is the avoidance of ignorance? It is the knowledge and firm consideration that can be developed on the basis of karmic maturation [i.e., knowledge obtained from birth], scriptural learning, or realization that is gained through spiritual practice." All three roots of virtue are described as having the same action, which is "to provide support for the avoidance of misdeeds." Because these states are not the mere absence of desire and so on, I translate them as "avoidance" of attachment and so on. See *Inner Science of Buddhist Practice*, pp. 285–87 for further explanations.
81. For the sake of consistency, I have cited the title of this work here as it was referenced earlier. This is, in fact, the name that is used in the Fifth Dalai Lama's Collected Works—that is, *'Jam pa'i dbyangs kyi zhal lung*. However, as Jamyang Khyentse Wangpo does here, it is also frequently cited as *Mañjuśrī's Oral Instruction* (*'Jam dpal zhal lung*).
82. This is the Sanskrit original form of the Tibetan Jampai Yang ('Jam pa'i dbyangs) or Jamyang in its shorter form, which is the author's reference to himself.
83. Ngag gi dbang phyug byams pa phun tshogs dpal bzang po. This is the name of the teacher from whom the author received instruction on the Lamrim system of practice.

10. The Essence of Nectar: A Manual of Instruction for the Three Types of Person on the Stages for Gaining Entry to the Victor's Teaching

1. *rGyal ba'i bstan pa la 'jug pa'i rim pa skyes bu gsum gyi man ngag gi khrid yig bdud rtsi'i nying khu*, *DNZ*, vol. 3 (*ga*), pp. 181–273. Second source: In *Jo nang mdo sngags rig pa'i dpe tshogs*, vol. 5 (Chengdu: Si khron mi rigs dpe skrun khang, 2009).
2. "Homage to the buddhas and bodhisattvas."
3. *brgyud pa gsum*. Atiśa's teaching system was known as "the merging of three rivers" (*chu bo gsum 'dres*. See ch. 4, "The Brilliant Illumination of the Path to Enlightenment," note 24, for a reference to the bodies of literature and instruction associated with the three traditions known as the Lineage of Extensive Conduct (*rgya chen spyod brgyud*), the Lineage of the Profound View (*zab mol ta brgyud*), and the Lineage of Powerful Conduct (*rlabs chen spyod brgyud*). The principal Indian masters associated with these lineages are Nāgārjuna, Asaṅga, and Śāntideva, respectively.
4. *mahāratha, shing rta chen po*. This term is a reference to great Buddhist philosophical innovators, such as Nāgārjuna and Asaṅga. If we add the third Lineage of Powerful Conduct (see previous note), this term would also refer to Śāntideva. See also ch. 5, "A Verse Compendium of the Spiritual Practices of the Stages of the Path," note 7, and ch. 4, "The Brilliant Illumination of the Path to Enlightenment," note 10.
5. *shing rta chen po'i 'jug ngogs*. This phrase should be understood to mean that the teaching system of the Stages of the Path provides a practitioner with the means of gaining an understanding of the profound and vast instructions of the traditions established by Nāgārjuna and Asaṅga—which is to say, the philosophical views and forms of spiritual practice contained in the literature of the two Mahāyāna schools known as the Madhyamaka and Yogācāra.
6. **saptāṅgakā, yan lag bdun pa*. See ch. 7, "The Nectar That Is Like Highly Refined Gold," note 44.
7. *Bhadracaryapraṇidhāna, bZang po spyod pa'i smon lam*. See ch. 9, "An Essential Summary of the Method of Practice," note 14. The remaining elements of the seven-limb devotional practice are confession, rejoicing, requesting that the dharma wheel be turned, a supplication not to enter nirvana, and dedication. These five practices are addressed in verses 8 through 12 of the prayer.
8. This is known as "the supplication that relates to the three great aims" (*don chen po gsum gyi sgo nas gsol ba gtab pa*), which are to terminate all erroneous thoughts, to develop with ease all correct thoughts, and to quell all inner and outer obstacles. See the final paragraph of this section where the author enumerates multiple examples of these three aims.
9. *yid kyis sprul pa'i mchod pa*. This phrase refers to an act in which great bodhisattvas, by the power of their one-pointed concentration, are able to emanate

light rays from themselves that appear as a variety of elaborate forms of offerings in the sky. Even if one does not possess this ability, a practitioner can imagine and visualize that he or she is performing this act. See also ch. 9, "An Essential Summary of the Method of Practice," note 32.

10. See ch. 9, "An Essential Summary of the Method of Practice," note 72, and the related verse of dedication in his text, which is a slightly different version of the one that appears here. "Twofold supreme excellence" refers to a buddha's supreme mental and physical aspects—that is, the dharmakāya and the rūpakāya.
11. That is, the topic of how to serve a spiritual teacher.
12. This is a root verse from chapter 2 of the important and early Lamrim work known popularly as *The Great Treatise on the Stages of the Teaching* (*bsTan rim chen mo*), a work by Drolungpa Lodrö Jungne (Gro lung pa bLo gros 'byung gnas; fl. eleventh century). The full title is *A Detailed Explanation of the Stages for Entering the Sugata's Teaching* (*bDe bar gshegs pa'i bstan pa la 'jug pa'i rim pa rnam par bshad pa*). See also ch. 7, "The Nectar That Is Like Highly Refined Gold," note 2, for canonical source texts regarding this topic.
13. *mleccha, kla klo*. The original Sanskrit term is based on a verbal root that means "to speak indistinctly," which refers to a person who does not speak an Indic language and who therefore is considered a foreigner. More loosely, the term is also understood to mean a "barbarian" in the sense of someone who does not observe the customs of Indian society and culture.
14. *mithyādṛṣṭi, log lta*. Wrong view, one of the root mental afflictions. *AS* (p. 6) states: "What is wrong view? It is the sense of acceptance, the sense of approval, the erring determination, the reflection, and the view that develops wrongful thoughts about and disavows causes, results, and religious acts, and denies the existence of entities that actually do exist. Its action is variously described as to cut the roots of virtue, to give support to the strengthening of the roots of nonvirtue, to cause one to engage in unvirtuous deeds, and to prevent one from engaging in virtuous deeds."
15. These lines, written in verse form in the Tibetan, are often cited and are typically identified as being from Asaṅga's *Stage of a Śrāvaka*. While this work is certainly the source for this formulation of the ten fortunes (*sampat, 'byor pa*)—five of which relate to oneself and five of which relate to others—this versified listing of them is not a direct quote from that text. It is possible that they were formulated based on the discussion of this topic that appears in the *Great Treatise on the Stages of the Teaching* (*bsTan rim chen mo*). See note 10 (this chapter). See also ch. 7, "The Nectar That Is Like Highly Refined Gold," note 2, for another listing of the ten fortunes.
16. *pañca ānantaryakarmāṇi, mtshams med pa'i las lnga*. They are matricide, patricide, killing an arhat, causing a schism in the sangha wheel, and maliciously shedding the tathāgata's blood. These evil deeds are called "immediate" because a person who performs any of them will be reborn in the hells "immediately"—that is, in his or her very next birth.

17. *āyatanagataḥ prasāda, gnas la dad.* The term *āyatana* (*gnas*), literally a "support" or a "seat," is also used in a spiritual context as a basis or source. *ŚBh* explains the term *āyatana* (*gnas*) in this context to mean "the spiritual system of dharma and vinaya that has been taught by the Tathāgata."

18 18. *dharmavinaya, chos 'dul ba.* While the common understanding of the terms *dharma* and *vinaya* are "teaching" and "discipline," respectively, when the two occur in this Sanskrit compound, the term *dharma* represents the means of attaining transcendent knowledge (i.e, the truth of the path) and *vinaya* represents the "removal" or "expulsion" of the mental afflictions and the obstructions to omniscience (i.e., the truth of cessation) (cf. *MW*, s.v. "dharmavinaya"). For this reason, I have left the terms untranslated. *BBhVy* (f. 68b) states: "With regard to the phrase 'this system of dharma and vinaya,' it should be understood that 'this' means the spiritual system 'of the tathāgata.' Regarding the compound *dharmavinaya*, the term 'dharma' means that this spiritual system brings about the attainment of right knowledge and the term 'vinaya' means that it brings about the abandonment of the two types of obstruction. That is, this phrase is a clear indication that the attainments gained in the tathāgata's teaching are characterized by knowledge and abandonment—which is to say, they are characterized by the path and its result."

19. This is the topic of identifying the nature of a human form that possesses the eighteen attributes of leisure and fortune.

20. The next topic is still part of the section on leisure and fortune—which is to say, the difficulty of obtaining those qualities.

21. This analogy is recorded as having been taught by Buddha Śākyamuni in the *Articles of Discipline* (*Vinayavastu, 'Dul ba lung gzhi*), 'dul ba, vol. 1 (*ka*), ff. 121b–125a (section 8).

22. This image is meant to convey masses of sentient beings stacked atop one another at the bottom of the ocean.

23. See ch. 5, "A Verse Compendium of the Spiritual Practices of the Stages of the Path," note 4.

24. *srid mtha' tsam.* That is, they are so rare as to be almost nonexistent.

25. This is the topic of recognizing the difficulty of obtaining a human form that possesses the qualities of leisure and fortune.

26. *BCA*, ch. 4, v. 23.

27. Ibid., ch. 1, v. 4.

28. *UV*, ch. 1, v. 26.

29. *bar ma.* See ch. 7, "The Nectar That Is Like Highly Refined Gold," note 139.

30. See ch. 7, "The Nectar That Is Like Highly Refined Gold," note 19.

31. See ch. 5, "A Verse Compendium of the Spiritual Practices of the Stages of the Path," note 12.

32. *āyu, tshe.* In Buddhist abhidharma doctrine, a life span is a nominal entity that is classified as a "conditioning formation that does not accompany consciousness" (*cittaviprayuktasaṃskāra, sems dang ldan pa ma yin pa'i 'du byed*). *PSV* (English

translation, pp. 237–38) states: "What are the formations that do not accompany consciousness? They are entities that are nominally ascribed to a particular state of form, consciousness, or the mental factors. They are not entities that are ascribed to form, consciousness, or the mental factors themselves or to something distinct from them." This means it constitutes a conditioned entity (*saṃskṛtadharma, 'dus byas kyi chos*)—that is, an impermanent entity produced by causes and conditions but one that is neither exclusively mental nor physical in nature. Thus, it is more strictly a condition or state that is nominally ascribed to a number of entities. See also ch. 8, "The Easy Path," note 147. Regarding the definition of a life span, in particular, *AS* (p. 6) states: "What is the faculty of a life force (*jīvitendriya, srog gi dbang po*)? It is the fixed period of time for the continued existence of a particular class affiliate that is projected by past karma, and it is the nominally ascribed entity that is called a life span." *PSV* (English translation, p. 319) states: "The term 'class affiliate' (*nikāyasabhāga, ris mthun pa*) refers to the continuum of heaps that occurs within a particular sentient being's single birth."

33. Manuscript incorrectly reads "all" (*kun*); correct reading is "even" (*kyang*).
34. *SL*, v. 57. The reference to "seven suns" is explained in the *Sutta of Seven Suns*, which describes the destruction of the physical world at the end of a great kalpa. Cf. *Anguttara Nikāya*, Book of Sevens, sutta 66.
35. *BCA*, ch. 2, v. 59.
36. *RA*, ch. 3, v. 78.
37. *BCA*, ch. 2, v. 42ab.
38. Chos ldan rab 'byor. This is another name for the Indian Buddhist poet Mātṛceta.
39. *Letter to the Great King Kaniṣka*, v. 63.
40. *udvega, skyo ba*. In the context of the instruction for lesser persons, this form of aversion should be understood as an antidote to attachment toward the pleasures of this life. See also ch. 7, "The Nectar That Is Like Highly Refined Gold," note 135.
41. *marmaccheda, gnad gcod pa*. This term, which literally means "the cutting of a vital point," can indicate to experience a mortal injury, such as by a weapon, or, more figuratively, to undergo intense pain.
42. These lines are found in *The Great Treatise on the Stages of the Teaching* (*bsTan rim chen mo*). They form part of a passage that Drolungpa Lodrö Jungne cites from the Tibetan translation of the *Lokaprajñapti* (*'Jig rten gzhag pa*). This text forms one of the three sections that make up the *Prajñaptiśāstra* (*gDags pa'i bstan bcos*), which is identified as one of the seven texts that made up the abhidharma canon of the Sarvāstivāda school. Its compilation is attributed to Maudgalyāyana and its three sections are the only portion of the overall corpus that was translated into Tibetan.
43. gShin rje.
44. *upapāduka, rdzus te skye ba*. *AKBh* (pp. 118–19) states: "What is the sponta-

neously produced form of birth? It is the form of birth undergone by those beings who are born all at once, with their faculties complete and unimpaired and possessing all their limbs and appendages. Therefore, because they act in an exceptional manner with regard to their own birth, they are called 'those whose are spontaneously produced.'"

45. *saṃjīva, yang sos. AKV* states: "Revival is where winds restore to life sentient beings who are dying."
46. *kālasūtra, thig nag. AKV* states: "Black Lines is where black lines are made on sentient beings' bodies and then they are chopped up."
47. *saṃghāta, bsdus 'joms. AKV* states: "Compression is where mountains and other objects that have the shape of rams and so on rush toward each other from two directions and crush sentient beings."
48. *gtan pa.* This reading is uncertain. All editions that were consulted have this spelling, which dictionaries gloss as a bolt for securing a door; however, this meaning does not seem to fit this context. I have speculated that this could be a corruption of the spelling for a mortar (*gtun po*, also *gtun khung*). *Lokaprajñapti* (f. 81a) describes a scene in which many hell beings gather on an area of ground made of iron (**ayasī bhūmi, lcags kyi sa gzhi*) that is many leagues in breadth, where they are crushed from above by an immense iron hammer.
49. *raurava, ngu 'bod. AKV* states: "Wailing is a hell region where the beings who are being tortured cry out in extreme distress."
50. *mahāraurava, ngu 'bod chen po. AKV* states: "Great Wailing is where the experiences of Wailing occur to a greater degree."
51. *tāpana, tsha ba. AKV* states: "Conflagration is where sentient beings are burned by fire and other similar means."
52. *pratāpana, rab tu tsha ba. AKV* states: "Great Conflagration is where the experiences that occur in Conflagration do so to a greater degree."
53. *avīci, mnar med. AKV*: "Unrelenting Torment is where there is no interval of time during which there is a respite that brings ease to the beings who are engulfed in the flames of an exceedingly great fire."
54. *AK*, ch. 3, v. 79–80a. The line "Both are twice as much for the higher ones" means that both the number of human years that make a day is doubled in the region of each successively higher desire realm god and the number of such "divine years" that make up the life spans of each successively higher desire realm god is double the number of divine years in the life span of the desire-realm gods that lie below it.
55. *AK*, ch. 3, v. 82abc. Regarding the life span of the beings in the lowest two hot hells, *AK* (ch. 3, v. 83ab) declares: "In Great Conflagration it is one-half; in Unrelenting Torment it is an intermediate kalpa." Thus, the life span of beings in Great Conflagration is one-half of an intermediate kalpa, and that of the beings in Unrelenting Torment is an entire intermediate kalpa. A great kalpa is a span of time measured in terms of four phases: the period during which a region of the universe remains completely empty of any world spheres, the

period during which the physical realms of a great triple-thousand world spheres are formed within that region, the period during which those physical realms remain populated by sentient beings, and the period during which those particular triple-thousand world spheres undergo destruction. Each of these phases lasts for a period of twenty intermediate kalpas. The length of an intermediate kalpa is defined by recurring cycles of fluctuating human life spans that take place during the third phase. During the first cycle, human life spans gradually decrease from a maximum number of years to a minimum of ten years. This marks the end of the first intermediate kalpa. This is followed by eighteen cycles during which life spans increase to a maximum and then return to the minimum of ten years. The twentieth and final intermediate kalpa ends when human life spans increase from a minimum of ten years and reach a maximum. Each time human life spans reach the shortest period of ten years, this event is marked variously by outbreaks of widespread murder, pestilence, or famine. Cf. *AK*, ch. 3, vv. 89–93, and v. 99.

56. *cāturmahārājakāyikā, rgyal chen bzhi'i ris.* The Four Great Kings are the deities Virūḍaka ('Phags skye bo), Virūpākṣa (Mig mi bzang), Dhṛtarāṣṭra (Yul 'khor srung), and Vaiśravaṇa (rNam thos kyi bu). Their principal domain is the uppermost of four level areas or terraces that lie along the side of Mount Sumeru. The immediate retinue for each of the Four Kings is also found there. In addition, the three levels below that one and the seven golden mountains that ring Mount Sumeru are the abodes for the rest of this lowest class of the desire realm's gods.
57. That is, nine million years.
58. That is, one quadrillion six hundred and twenty trillion (1,620,000,000,000) human years.
59. This does not mean that the life span of the hell beings in Black Lines is four times greater than the life span of the hell beings in Revival, and that the life span of the hell beings in Compression is four times greater than that of the hell beings in Black Lines, and so on. The calculation is understood as follows. A hundred human years is equal to one day in the deities of the Heaven of the Thirty-Three (*trayastriṃśā, sum cu rtsa gsum*) and the deities of this region live for a thousand such years, which is equal to 12,960,000,000,000 human years. This period of time is equal to one day in the Black Lines hell region and the life span of the hell beings there is one thousand such hell years, or four hundred sixty-six quadrillion five hundred sixty trillion human years (466,560,000,000,000), which is actually two hundred and eighty-eight times longer than the number of human years that make up the life span of the beings in Revival (i.e., 1,620,000,000,000 human years).
60. *arbuda, chu bur can.*
61. *nirbuda, chu bur brdol.*
62. *ŚL*, v. 52, states: "An incomparable cold that penetrates even the bones / causes their decrepit bodies to tremble and curl into a ball. / Hundreds of blisters that

form and split open give rise to bugs / that eat the pus, marrow, and fat flowing from their sores."

63. *a chu zer ba.*
64. *kyi hud zer ba*
65. *so tham tham pa.*
66. *utpala, utpal ltar gas pa.*
67. *padma, padma ltar gas pa.*
68. *mahāpadma, padma ltar cher gas pa.*
69. *sbyang. AKBh* describes a *vāha* as equivalent to twenty *khārīka*, which is said to be about three bushels in size, making a *vāha* a container that can hold some sixty bushels of grain.
70. *khal.* The Tibetan *khel* is a unit of measure that is slightly less than a bushel.
71. The most commonly used Tibetan word for these regions literally means a "neighboring" or "adjacent" (*nye 'khor*) hell. The proper Sanskrit term for these regions is *utsada* (*lhag pa*), which, as the glosses below indicate, can be rendered either as an "additional region" or a "subsequent region." *AKBh* (p. 134) states: "They are called 'additional regions' because they are places of additional torture. . . . According to others, they are called 'subsequent regions' because sentient beings sink into distress in these places after having been confined in the main hot hells."
72. *AK*, ch. 3, vv. 59d–60abc.
73. *kukūla, me ma mur gyi 'obs.*
74. *kuṇapa, myags kyi 'dam.*
75. *kṣuradhārācito patha, spu gri'i sos gtams pa'i lam.*
76. *asipatravana, ral gri lo ma can gyi tshal.*
77. *ayaḥśālmalīvana, lcags kyi shal ma li'i tshal.* Śālmalī is the name of the Seemul or silk-cotton tree, a tall and thorny tree with red flowers.
78. *nadī vaitaraṇī, chu bo rab med.*
79. *pratyekanaraka, nyi tshe ba'i dmyal ba.* In contrast with the sixteen principal hells, which are physical realms that are produced by the common karma of sentient beings, *AKBh* (p. 165) states: "The partial hells are produced by the karma of the specific individuals themselves who are born there, which can be many in number or even just one or two. The regions where these hell beings reside have many different forms and are not found in a fixed location, since they exist in different places, such as near rivers, on mountains, and in deserts, or even below the surface of the earth."
80. *avadāna, rtogs pa brjod pa.* This term refers to a genre of Buddhist literature that recounts incidents surrounding religious figures, a number of whom were contemporaries and disciples of Buddha Śākyamuni. They often contain descriptions of persons and their actions that are meant to illustrate the doctrine of karma. The scriptures that make up the Tibetan vinaya collection contains numerous such accounts, including those of Saṃgharakṣita and Koṭikarṇa. The Tibetan version of the Saṃgharakṣita avadāna appears in *The Articles of*

Discipline (*'Dul ba lung gzhi*, Dg.K.'dul ba, vol. 1 (*ka*), section 9, ff. 140b–164a). The Koṭikarṇa avadāna appears in the same volume and section, ff. 352a–373b). English versions can be found in chapters 1 and 23 of the translation of the *Divyāvadāna*, *Divine Stories* (Somerville, MA: Wisdom, 2008).

81. *yojana, dpag tshad.* The original Indian term is an ancient unit of distance that literally means the distance that animals can travel without having to be unyoked or unharnessed. *AK* (ch. 3, v. 88a) defines a *yojana* as eight *krośa* (*rgyang grags*), itself a term that literally means the distance that the sound of a shout can carry. A *krośa*, in turn, is defined as five hundred lengths of a bow (*dhanu, gzhu 'dom*), each of which is four cubits (*hasta, khru*) or the equivalent of the span of a person's two outstretched arms. If a "bow-length" is taken to be five and a half feet, then a *yojana* is four and one-sixth miles.
82. *abhijñā, mngon par shes pa.* Buddhist literature identifies six types of supernatural knowledge. Among the spiritual powers that can be attained are several types of clairvoyance known as the five eyes. Of these qualities, the most basic is the "corporeal eye" (*māṃsacakṣu sha'i spyan*), which is able to perceive visible objects both large and small that lie at vast distances.
83. *Saddharmasmṛtyupasthānasūtra, Dam pa'i chos dran pa nye bar bzhag pa'i mdo.* See listing in bibliography titled *The Application of Mindfulness of the Sacred Dharma.* This is an extensive sūtra that takes up some three and a half volumes of the Tibetan Kangyur collection. The original Sanskrit version is not extant in its entirety; however, a Sanskrit palm-leaf manuscript of 236 folios has been discovered in Tibet that represents about half of the sūtra. An edition of the Sanskrit text of the second of the sūtra's ten chapters, with an English translation, has been published. The chapter on hungry ghosts is chapter 4.
84. See ch. 4 "The Brilliant Illumination of the Path to Enlightenment," note 79.
85. *pratipakṣa, gnyen po.* The Sanskrit version of this term, which literally means the "opposing side," fits this context as it can refer to an entity that opposes and, in effect, neutralizes the karmic force of either a good or a bad deed. The Tibetan equivalent term, however, typically is used to describe only the positive "antidote," or "remedy," for some negative quality. Since that is not the intended sense here, I have translated the term in a neutral sense as a "counteragent."
86. The principles addressed in these first two sentences are described formally as "what has been done will not perish" and "what has not been done will not yield any fruition," respectively. See also ch. 7, "The Nectar That Is Like Highly Refined Gold," notes 98 and 99, as well as ch. 8, "The Easy Path," notes 38 and 39.
87. *AK* (ch. 4, v. 66bcd) states: "Collecting the greatest among them, / ten were declared to be good and bad / karmic paths, according to circumstances."
88. *prāṇātipāta, srog gcod pa.* This expression literally means "destruction of a life."
89. *yul gyi sgo nas.* Literally "in terms of being an unsuitable object"—i.e., person—with whom to have sexual relations.
90. *paiśunya, phra ma.* The original Sanskrit term derives from a noun that has the

more generic literal sense of a "wicked," "malicious," or "treacherous" person (*piśuna*). Thus, this verbal misdeed might be rendered as "malicious speech." *AK* (ch. 4, v. 76ab) defines *paiśunya* in the Buddhist sense as "the speech of a person whose mind is afflicted in order to cause discord between others." In this sense, the alternate translation of "divisive speech" conveys a more precise, if not literal, description of the act.

91. *AKBh* (p. 64) and other commentaries indicate that this act can be committed both in relation to persons who are in accord with one another, as well as persons who are at odds with one another. In the latter case, the slander is intended to maintain the state of conflict or discord.

92. In other words, the intention of wanting to create or maintain discord does not have to be achieved in order for the misdeed to have been committed.

93. *lapanā, kha gsag*. Flattery is one of five principal forms of wrong livelihood (see ch. 13, "Opening the Door to the Dharma," notes 421 and 850). It occurs when a Buddhist monk or nun speaks favorably or shows deference to a potential benefactor in order to obtain something of value from that person.

94. *naimittikatva, gshog slong*. Intimation is another form of wrong livelihood by which Buddhist monks and nuns seek to obtain objects of material value by subterfuge or some indirect means.

95. *karmapatha, las kyi lam*. This term, which appears in the sūtras, is explained several ways. Regarding the word "path," one explanation is that physical movement and verbal sound are paths in that they provide the means by which the volition to carry out the "action" is set in motion. Another is that the ten virtuous and unvirtuous actions are paths in that they lead to happy or unhappy migratory states, respectively. To say that these action-paths are "completed" means that all the elements of object, attitude, method of execution, and culmination take place unerringly.

96. Buddhist abhidharma literature refers to these three types of rebirth as the "unhappy migratory states" (*durgati, ngan 'gro*). Together with the two "happy migratory states" (*sugati, bde 'gro*) of humans and worldly gods, these are the five migratory states (*pañca gata, 'gro ba lnga*) that occur in samsara (cf. *AK*, ch. 3, v. 4ab). Tibetan literature often adds a sixth class of being—that is, demigods (*asura, lha ma yin*).

97. *myong ba rgyu mthun gyi 'bras bu*. The expression "corresponding result" (*nisyandaphala, rgyu mthun gyi 'bras bu*) literally means one that "flows" (*nisyanda*) naturally from the cause. The Tibetan equivalent suggests that it is a result that is "similar in nature to the cause." The qualifier "experiential" here identifies one of two types of corresponding result. For this type of corresponding result, the person who committed the original misdeed *experiences* a result that is similar to that act.

98. *adhipatiphala, bdag po'i 'bras bu*.

99. *svarga, mtho ris*. In native Tibetan literature this term is usually understood to mean "the status of being reborn as a god or a human being." However, the

original Sanskrit term carries the sense of a "celestial" or "heavenly" realm and thus refers more specifically to the abode of worldly gods.

100. That is, the enlightenment of the Śrāvakayāna, that of the Pratyekabuddhayāna, and the supreme enlightenment of buddhahood.

101. *cetanā, sems pa. AS* (pp. 5–6) states: "What is volition? It is the shaping of consciousness and the activity of the mind. Its function is to direct the mind toward virtuous, unvirtuous, and indeterminate entities."

102. The source of these verses was not identified.

103. *kha phyir ltas su ma song bar.* While this adverbial phrase literally means "without allowing the mind to be directed outwardly," the intended sense is that one should internalize the instruction by applying it to oneself.

104. The primary sources for the instruction on the four powers are the *Caturdharmanirdeśa Sūtra* (see listing in bibliography titled *Sūtra Teaching the Four Factors*) and the commentary presented in chapter 8 of Śāntideva's *ŚS*. The first of the four, called the "power of the support" (*āśrayabala, rten gyi stobs*), is described in the *Caturdharmanirdeśa Sūtra* as follows: "Regarding this topic, the support force is to go for refuge to the Buddha, dharma, and sangha, as well as to avoid abandoning enlightenment mind."

105. *Caturdharmanirdeśa Sūtra* states: "Regarding this topic, 'engaging in an antidote' (*pratipakṣasamudācāra, gnyen po kun tu spyod pa*) is for one, even after having engaged in unvirtuous deeds, to put forth great effort in carrying out virtuous deeds." *ŚS* describes six types of activities that represent antidotes.

106. *Caturdharmanirdeśa Sūtra* states: "Regarding this topic, 'engaging in self-censure' (*vidūṣaṇāsamudācāra, rnam par sun 'byin pa kun tu spyod pa*) is for one who engages in unvirtuous deeds to develop deep regret repeatedly toward all those very actions." The Sanskrit edition of *BCAP* (p. 75) contains an interpretation of how the noun *vidūṣaṇā* (*rnam par sun 'byin pa*) should be understood here. "Regarding this topic, 'engaging in self-censure' (*vidūṣaṇāsamudācāra*) means that, having committed an unvirtuous deed, one engages in the act of confessing that evil in a manner that is a form of self-reproach characterized by regret. Carrying out that practice is engaging in that (i.e., self-censure)" (*tatra vidūṣaṇāsamudācāraḥ akuśalaṃ karma kṛtvā vipratisārarūpātmavigarhaṇā* [my emendation] *pāpadeśanā tadanuṣṭhānaṃ tatsamudācāraḥ*). This passage does not appear in the Tibetan translation of *BCAP*.

107. *Caturdharmanirdeśa Sūtra* states: "'The power of turning away from wrongdoing' (*pratyāpattibala, nyes pa las lar ldog pa'i stobs*) is to develop the restraint that does not commit further misdeeds through having accepted a system of morality training that consists of restraint" (*pratyāpattibalaṃ saṃvarasamādānād akaraṇasaṃvaralābhaḥ*). *AKBh* (p. 205) states: "'Restraint' (*saṃvara, sdom pa*) means the act of putting a stop to, and the complete cessation of, the immorality that has been occurring continuously."

108. *mthol bshags.* This statement seems to be alluding to a formal confession ceremony that is usually carried out in an assembly of ordained monks and nuns.

Buddhist monks and nuns are expected to carry out the bimonthly *poṣadha* (*gso sbyong*) confession ritual that is prescribed in the prātimokṣa system of the vinaya code. There are also confession rituals that can be performed for the non-tantric Mahāyāna vow, as well as the tantric Vajrayāna vow. The latter ceremonies can be attended and participated in by laypersons, as well as monks and nuns.

109. *rten gsum*. This term refers to the religious icons and objects that are placed on an altar and regarded as the actual body, speech, and mind of the spiritual beings that make up the merit field of this teaching system. Ideal forms of the body-vessel are an image of Buddha Śākyamuni, along with any other lamas and divine beings associated with this teaching system. The ideal form of speech vessel is a copy of the versions of the Perfection of Wisdom sūtras, and that of the mind vessel is a stupa reliquary.

110. *Suvarṇaprabhāsottamasūtra, gSer 'od dam pa*. This is a reference to the verses that appear in chapter 2 of this sūtra.

111. See ch. 8, "The Easy Path," note 53. *AK* (ch. 4, v. 9d) and *AS* (p. 24) both identify two unconditioned entities—space and the nonanalytic cessation (*apratisaṃkhyānirodha, so sor brtags pa ma yin pas 'gog pa*)—as indeterminate in an absolute sense. Four paradigmatic examples of indeterminate conditioned entities are the following: the maturations of virtuous and unvirtuous deeds; the four types of physical activity (i.e., walking, standing, sitting, and reclining) when carried out in a state of mind that is neither virtuous nor under the influence of any of the mental afflictions; the activity of practicing any of the various physical or manual arts (*śilpasthāna, bzo yi gnas*); and the mind that produces emanations (*nirmāṇacitta, sprul pa'i sems*) (i.e., a mental power that can manifest physical objects and that stems from having attained one-pointed concentration).

112. These are known as "the four modes of physical behavior" (*īryāpatha, spyod lam rnam bzhi*). *BBhVy* (f. 182b) states: "Both that which causes one to walk and so on and the actions of walking and so on are established as the forms of physical behavior. The mind that causes the actions of walking and so on to occur is 'physical behavior' because it is the force that incites them (**īraṇa, skul bar byed pa*). That is, the mind sets the body's four elements in motion and drives them and causes them to reach a different place. Its path (*patha, lam*) is the actions of walking and so on. That is, by means of the actions of walking and so on one arrives at a particular place."

113. *AS* (p. 6) states: "What is laziness? It is a form of ignorance that is the mind's lack of exertion, which is due to indulgence in such comforts as sleep, resting on one's side, and reclining. Its action is to obstruct the pursuit of entities that are virtuous in nature." See also ch. 7, "The Nectar That Is Like Highly Refined Gold," note 169, for additional descriptions.

114. *AS* (p. 6) states: "What is distraction (*vikṣepa, rnam g.yeng*)? It is a form of desire, hatred, or ignorance that is an outward movement of the mind. . . . Its

action is to obstruct the attainment of freedom from attachment." Asaṅga's work further identifies six distinct types of distraction.

115. Cf. the discussion of the eight maturation qualities (*vipāka, rnam par smin pa*) and their role in the aim of collecting the two accumulations in *BBh*, book 1, ch. 3.

116. *sambhāra, tshogs*. That is, the two accumulations of merit and wisdom. Commenting on *MSA* (ch. 18, v. 40), Vasubandhu explains the term "accumulation" as follows (*MSAVy*, p. 134): "The syllable *sam* means 'continually.' The syllable *bhā* means 'having attained proficiency at meditation.' The syllable *ra* means the 'acquisition of merit and wisdom to a greater and greater degree.'" *MSAVṛBh* (Dg.T., vol. 126, f. 102b) augments this interpretation: "In short, 'accumulation' means those activities that bring about the *acquisition* of a buddha's three bodies through *continually meditating* upon the perfections of generosity and the rest and by meditating upon the virtues of the six perfections *to a greater and greater degree*." *MW* (s.v. "sambhāra") describes this term as meaning "a collection of things required for any purpose."

117. *BBh* (English translation, pp. 48–49) states: "Excellence of power (*aiśvarya-saṃpat, dbang phyug phun sum tshogs pa*) is the quality of possessing much property and the condition of having a large number of supporters as well as having a large retinue."

118. *AK* (ch. 4, v. 117ab) enumerates several types of "field" (see ch. 8, "The Easy Path," note 40). The "field of virtue" (*guṇakṣetra, yon tan gyi zhing*) is identified as the Three Jewels and other exceptionally virtuous persons, such as individuals who have just arisen from a state of meditative absorption.

119. *BBh* (English translation, p. 49) states: "To be trustworthy and credible, to be considered an authoritative arbiter for persons who are involved in every manner of legal dispute, to be someone who does not cause any loss to property that has been entrusted to him or her because he or she is free of deceit and guile and would not commit fraud by misrepresenting brass as something more valuable than it actually is or commit theft by using false weights, and the like, to be someone who does not break his or her word—and for these reasons to be someone whose word is well-received by others—is called "the quality of having one's speech accepted" (*ādeyavākyatā, tshig btsun pa*).

120. *jarāyuja, mngal nas skyes pa*. The Sanskrit term *jarāyu* more precisely means the "covering," or amniotic sac, that surrounds the embryo or fetus in the womb; however, following accepted usage, I translate this term as "born from a womb." *AK* (ch. 3, v. 9a) states: "Humans and animals are born in the four ways" (*caturdhā naratiryañca*). *AKBh* (p. 119) states: "Examples of human beings that were born from an egg (*aṇḍaja, sgo nga las skyes pa*) are the elders Śaila and Upaśaila, who were born from a curlew (*kroñcī*, also *kruñcā, khrung khrung mo*), the thirty-two children of Mṛgāra's mother, and the five hundred children of a king of Pañcāla. Examples of human beings that were born from a womb are the humans of today. Examples of human beings that were born from moisture and

heat (*saṃsvedaja, drod gsher las skyes pa*) are King Māndhātar, Cāru and Upacāru, Kapotamalinī, and Āmrapālī. Examples of human beings that were born spontaneously (*upapāduka, rdzus te skye ba*) are human beings that are born at the beginning of a kalpa."

121. Presumably, the phrase "due to the power of karma" is meant to leave open the fact that a bodhisattva is willing to be reborn in samsara by the power of his or her aspirational prayer in order to help sentient beings and pursue the ultimate goal of buddhahood.

122. That is, the desire realm, the form realm, and the formless realm. Taken collectively, they represent the entirety of samsara.

123. This paragraph is meant to indicate that the remainder of this discussion on the suffering of birth addresses that of any and all samsaric beings, not just that of a human being that is born from the womb. The principal source for the five types of each of eight forms of suffering discussed here is Asaṅga's *Collection of Determinations* (*rNam par gtan la dbab pa bsdu ba*, Dg.T., vol. 130, f. 160a–161b; Toh. 4038; Sanskrit original, *Viniścayasaṃgrahaṇī*, not extant). However, Tāranātha does not always present the five types exactly as they are outlined in Asaṅga's work. See also ch. 4, "Brilliant Illumination of the Path to Enlightenment," note 108.

124. Asaṅga's *Collection of Determinations* explains this point as meaning that the spontaneous birth of hell beings and rebirth as tormented hungry ghosts are subject to intense suffering throughout the entire existence of these beings, not just the birth event itself. For humans, which are primarily born from a womb, and for animals, which are primarily born either from a womb or an egg, the phrase is understood to refer more specifically to the painful experiences that occur during the period ranging from the moment of conception in the mother's womb or egg, as well as throughout the time that the embryo or fetus develops in the womb and even in the period immediately following emergence from the womb or egg, as described above.

125. The general meaning of the term "indisposition" (*dauṣṭhulya, gnas ngan len*) is that of an unfitness of the body and/or mind that is caused by the dormant state (*anuśaya, bag la nyal*) or "seeds" of the mental afflictions. This condition is not abandoned until all the mental afflictions are destroyed and the status of an arhat is attained.

126. Tāranātha's description of this fifth point differs from the final point in Asaṅga's *Collection of Determinations* (f. 160a–160b). In that latter work, the last of the five descriptions is worded "birth is suffering because it is endowed with the quality of leading to an unwanted separation" (**aniṣṭaviyogadharmitvāt, mi 'dod bzhin du 'bral ba'i chos can nyid yin pa'i phyir ro*). The expression "unwanted separation" is explained to mean death rather than the quality of subtle impermanence that is described here.

127. *bakapuṣpa, spra ba'i me tog*. Botanical name: *Sesbania grandiflora*. The flower of a small ornamental tree that produces large white flowers resembling small birds.

128. *parivāra, 'khor. BBhVṛ* (f. 52b) states: "A retinue is made up of children, wife (or spouse), male and female servants, workers, and the like."
129. *marmacchedaduḥkha, gnad gcod kyi sdug bsngal.* See note 41 (this chapter).
130. The "black faction" (*kṛṣṇapākṣika, nag phyogs pa*) means those who "are on the side of evil," or who are harmful beings in that they obstruct practitioners that pursue virtuous spiritual activities.
131. A maturation obscuration (*vipākāvaraṇa, rnam par smin pa'i sgrib pa*) is the condition of being reborn as a being who is either incapable of developing spiritually to any significant degree or one who is incapable of attaining the transcendent realizations. These include rebirth in any of the three lower realms, as a human being of the northern continent Kuru, and as certain worldly long-lived deities, such as those that lack conception (*asaṃjñisattva, 'du shes med pa'i sems can*). See also ch. 4, "The Brilliant Illumination of the Path to Enlightenment," note 189.
132. *cāturmahārājakāyikā, rgyal chen bzhi'i ris.* See note 56 (this chapter).
133. *trayastriṃśā, sum cu rtsa gsum. AKV* (vol. 2, p. 380) states: "They are called the group of Thirty-Three deities because they were born in that place [i.e., Indra's heaven that lies atop Mount Sumeru] through having done good deeds together. That is to say, [they were born there] through their common merit. According to others, it is the general view of the world that these very deities are called the group of Thirty-Three because the following beings are held to be the foremost ones: the eight Vasu deities (*nor lha*), the two Aśvins (*tha skar gyi bu gzhon nu*), the eleven Rudras (*drag po*), and the twelve Ādityas (*nyi ma*). They are also designated with the same names in Buddhist scripture to conform to this belief."
134. *cyuti, 'chi 'pho ltung ba.* The original Sanskrit term can mean both "to fall down from a divine existence" and "to die," which is precisely how the Tibetan translates the term.
135. This description of the five signs corresponds to Nāgārjuna's *Letter to a Friend* (*Suhṛllekha, bShes pa'i spring yig*, v. 99). See also ch. 7, "The Nectar That Is Like Highly Refined Gold," note 127, for a description of the signs that are detailed in *AKBh*, p. 157.
136. A nāga (*klu*) can refer to a semi-divine, serpent-like animal that lives in nether regions or in bodies of water; it can also refer to an ordinary snake. Canonical scriptures state that some nāgas used magic powers to transform themselves into a human form so that they could attend discourses of the Buddha.
137. A garuḍa (*nam mkha' lding*) is a mythical bird that is the king of the feathered race and the enemy of the nāga, or serpent, race.
138. *SL*, v. 101.
139. One form of supernatural knowledge (*abhijñā, mngon par shes pa*; see also note 70, this chapter) is known as the "divine eye." *BBh* (English translation, p. 635) states that gods of the desire realm possess a limited form of this quality: "There is also a divine eye that the gods who live in the desire realm obtain at birth and

that resembles the tathāgata's eye only to the extent that it has the same name." This form of clairvoyance is the means by which it can be seen where someone will die and be reborn. *BBh* (English translation, p. 125) states: "In this world, a tathāgata or a bodhisattva, by means of the pure divine eye that surpasses that of humans, sees beings at the time of their death and also sees the good or bad appearance of those who have died and the inferior or excellent circumstances into which they are reborn in the future." This form of supernatural knowledge is called "perceiving death and rebirth" (*cyutyupapādadarśana, 'chi 'pho ba dang skye ba mthong ba*). Presumably it is by means of their own limited form of the divine eye that the gods of the desire realm can perceive where they will be reborn in the future, as long as it will be in a realm that lies below the one they presently inhabit.

140. The two higher realms are the form realm and the formless realm. The form realm is made up of four levels associated with the four states of meditative composure (*catvāri dhyānāni, bsam gtan bzhi*). These are further distinguished into seventeen divisions, the first twelve of which can include both ordinary beings and āryas. The last five are inhabited exclusively by āryas. The formless realm is likewise divided into four main levels known as: the sphere of unlimited space (*ākāśānantyāyatana, nam mkha' mtha' yas skye mched*); the sphere of unlimited consciousness (*vijñānānantyāyatana, rnam shes mtha' yas skye mched*); the sphere of nothingness (*ākiṃcanyāyatana, ci yang med pa'i skye mched*); the sphere in which there is neither conception nor absence of conception (*naiva saṃjñā nāsaṃjñāyatana, 'du shes med 'du shes med min gyi skye mched*).

141. *pṛthagjana, so so skye bo*. This Buddhist term has the technical sense of a sentient being that has not attained the status of an ārya (*'phags pa*). An ārya is someone who has achieved a direct realization of either the insubstantiality of the person or the insubstantiality of entities, and thereby achieved the transcendent path of any of the three vehicles.

142. See ch. 7, "The Nectar That Is Like Highly Refined Gold," note 126.

143. This heading corresponds to the earlier phrase: "reflecting on the general suffering of samsara."

144. *duḥkhaduḥkhatā, sdug bsngal gyi sdug bsngal*. See ch. 7, "The Nectar That Is Like Highly Refined Gold," note 124.

145. *vipariṇāmaduḥkhatā, 'gyur ba'i sdug bsngal*. *ŚBh* (p. 256) states: "A pleasant feeling together with its seat, by virtue of its transience, is subject to transformation. Thus, it is classified as suffering on the strength of its changing into something different." See also *Inner Science of Buddhist Practice*, pp. 111–20, for a comprehensive discussion.

146. *saṃskārā, 'du byed rnams*. This is the active form of a noun that is sometimes used to refer only to the fourth of the five heaps, which I usually translate as "the formations heap" (*saṃskāraskandha, 'du byed kyi phung po*). That form of the noun is meant to suggest that impermanent entities exert a causal efficacy,

and hence the term might also be translated "conditioning entities." A similar term, "conditioned entities" (*saṃskṛtā, 'dus byas rnams*), which is formed from the past participle of the same verb (*saṃskṛ, 'du byed pa*), is meant to indicate that all impermanent entities are the products of causes. However, in some instances, such as the present context, the two terms are interchangeable. For example, *PSV* (p. 273) states: "All the entities that are included in the five heaps of form and the rest are formations (*saṃskārā, 'du byed rnams*) in the sense that they are produced by the convergence and combination of conditional factors."

147. *upekṣā, btang snyoms.* This type of feeling is also described as one that is "neither pleasant nor unpleasant." It refers to those feelings (*vedanā, tshor ba*) about which you are indifferent—that is to say, you neither wish for them to continue nor wish for them to end. See ch. 7, "The Nectar That is Like Highly Refined Gold," note 126, for further remarks about the suffering of conditioned existence.

148. The source for this fivefold interpretation of the canonical statement "In short, the five grasping heaps are suffering" is Asaṅga's *Collection of Determinations* (f. 161b).

149. *SL*, v. 66. The full verse states: "A father becomes a son, a mother becomes a wife, / and one who was an enemy becomes a friend. / Because the opposite of this can occur as well, / there is no certainty whatsoever in samsara."

150. Ibid., v. 67. The full verse states: "Each and every samsaric being has drunk / more milk than the four oceans, / and much more suffering is still to be drunk / by those who follow the nature of an ordinary being."

151. Ibid., v. 68ab, states: "The mountains of bones from each and every individual's past lives / would be equal in size to that of Mount Meru."

152. *pratisaṃdhi, nying mtshams sbyor ba.* See ch. 8, "The Easy Path," note 44.

153. *SL*, v. 68cd: "Moreover, for counting the succession of one's mothers with pellets of soil / the size of jujube seeds, the entire earth would not suffice." The Tibetan translation of Mahāmati's Indian commentary to Nāgārjuna's text cites the following sūtra passage in explanation of these lines: "O bhikṣus, for example, suppose a certain person were to take a pellet of soil the size of a jujube seed and cast it aside saying, 'This represents my mother,' and then he or she were to take another and cast it aside again saying, 'This represents my mother's mother.' O bhikṣus, the soil of this great earth would be exhausted very soon, but the entirety of a person's maternal lineage would not."

154. brGya byin. This is an alternate name for Indra, the chief deity of the Heaven of the Thirty-Three that lies at the top of Mount Meru.

155. *SL*, v. 69. The full verse states: "Even after having been Indra, worthy of veneration by the world, / one falls again to the earth, through the force of karma; / or, even after having been a wheel-wielding monarch / in samsara, one arrives again into a state of servitude."

156. *SL*, v. 76. The full verse states: "Death being inevitable in this way, seize the light / of the lamp that is the threefold merit; / for you must enter alone the unlimited darkness / that cannot be overcome by the sun or the moon."

157. *bhavāgra, srid pa'i rtse mo.* This is another name for the fourth level of the formless realm, also known as "the sphere in which there is neither conception nor absence of conception." See notes 140 and 243 (this chapter).

158. Literally "Unrelenting Torment." See note 53 (this chapter).

159. *saṃyojana, kun tu sbyor ba. AS* (pp. 44–46) identifies the nine bonds as: attachment (*anunaya, rjes su chags pa*), hatred, pride, ignorance, views, supreme considerations (*parāmarśa, mchog tu 'dzin pa*), doubt, jealousy (*īrṣyā, phrag dog*), and stinginess (*mātsarya, ser sna*), and describes each of them as "binding one to suffering in the sense of producing worldly, [i.e., samsaric,] suffering in the future."

160. *apuṇya, bsod nams ma yin pa.*

161. *puṇya, bsod nams.*

162. *āneñja, mi g.yo ba. AKBh* (pp. 277–78) states: "The deeds that occur in the form and formless realms are never able to ripen from one level into a different level. Therefore, because the ripening of this type of deed is of a fixed nature, it is called 'invariable.'"

163. *ātmagraha, bdag tu 'dzin pa.* This term can be limited to the mistaken belief in a real personal self, for which the Buddhist technical term is "the view of the perishable collection" (*satkāyadṛṣṭi, 'jig tshogs la lta ba*). *AS* (p. 7) states: "What is the view of the perishable collection? It is the acceptance, approval, judgment, consideration, and view that mistakenly regards the five grasping heaps as 'I' and 'mine.'" However, in certain contexts, the term "self" is not restricted to the sense of a personal self and should be taken as synonymous with the broader sense of mistakenly grasping any entity as being self-existent or real.

164. *bdag gces 'dzin.* This attitude or motivating impulse is one in which a person places his or her own interests above the needs and concerns of others. At its worst, this is a crude form of selfishness that can lead to every form of immoral conduct. Even at its most refined, it is represented by the self-interest of a Hīnayāna follower who finds it morally acceptable to pursue his or her own liberation exclusively.

165. *moha, gti mug.* This is a synonym for ignorance (*avdiyā, ma rig pa*).

166. That is, samsara and liberation.

167. There are five afflicted views: the view of the perishable collection (*satkāyadṛṣṭi, 'jig tshogs la lta ba*; see note 163, this chapter); the view that grasps an extreme (*antagrāhadṛṣṭi, mthar 'dzin par lta ba*); wrong view (*mithyādṛṣṭi, log par lta ba*); the consideration that views are supreme (*dṛṣṭiparāmarśa, lta ba mchog tu 'dzin pa*); and the consideration that morality and asceticism are supreme (*śīlavataparāmarśa, tshul khrims dang brtul zhugs mchog tu 'dzin pa*). For a description of these flawed views, see *Inner Science of Buddhist Practice*, pp. 296–302.

168. *svapakṣa, rang phyogs.* Literally "your faction," meaning the class of beings that is made up of your family, friends, supporters, and other like-minded individuals toward whom you feel a sense of affinity.

169. *upakleśa, nye ba'i nyon mongs pa. PSV* (revised English translation, p. 275) states:

"They are called 'secondary mental afflictions' because they are secondary forms of the root mental afflictions, because, like the root mental afflictions, they too cause the mind to become agitated, and because they occur at a time that is near to that of the root mental afflictions."

170. *krodha, khro ba. AS* (p. 8) states: "What is anger? It is the mental animosity that is a form of hatred and that occurs when a cause of harm is present. Its action is to give support to the ardent desire for such actions as taking up a club or taking up a weapon, and so on."

171. *pradāśa, 'tshig pa. AS* (p. 8) states: "What is spite? It is the mental animosity that is a form of hatred and that is preceded by anger and resentment. Its actions are to give support to intense and strong forms of harsh speech, to engender demeritorious deeds, and to prevent one from remaining in a contented state."

172. *upanāha, khon du 'dzin pa. AS* (p. 8) states: "What is resentment? It is a form of hatred that following the occurrence of hatred is unwilling to let go of an attitude of enmity. Its action is to give support to remaining in a state of impatience.

173. The "old" form of samsara is a reference to the remainder of one's current life, which was produced by previous elements of karma and the mental afflictions. After abandoning karma and the mental afflictions, once this current samsaric life comes to an end, then samsara will cease to exist.

174. *anāsravaprajñā, zag pa med pa'i shes rab.* This form of wisdom is the essence of the Truth of the Path. The terms "contaminated" and "uncontaminated" are somewhat loose translations of a pair of technical Buddhist expressions that literally mean "related to the outflows" (*sāsrava, zag bcas*) and "unrelated to the outflows" or "free of the outflows" (*anāsrava, zag pa med pa*), respectively. "Outflow" (*āsrava, zag pa*) is a synonym for mental affliction (*kleśa, nyon mongs*). The Vaibhāṣika description that appears in *AKBh* (in the explanation of ch. 5, v. 40, of the root text) is that the mental afflictions are outflows in the sense that they flow out through the "wounds" of the six inner bases (*āyatana, skye mched*; i.e., the faculties) of the eye and so on, reaching everywhere from the Peak of Existence down to the Hell of Unrelenting Torment. Vasubandhu then presents an alternative explanation that he considers preferable: "The mental afflictions are called 'outflows' because they cause the mental continuum to flow along—that is, go forth (*gaccanti, 'gro ba*)—toward objects." He also explains that the expression "related to the outflows" applies to all conditioned entities (*saṃskṛtadharmā, 'dus byas kyi chos rnams*), with the exception of the Truth of the Path, because of their capacity to cause the mental afflictions to become stronger (*AK*, ch. 1, v. 4).

175. *samādhi, ting nge 'dzin. AS* (p. 6) states: "What is concentration? It is the one-pointedness of mind toward a familiar object that is being closely examined. Its action is to provide support for transcendent knowledge."

176. *niḥsaraṇa, nges par 'byung ba.* This term refers to the attitude that wishes to attain complete liberation from samsara. Literally, it means "departure" in the sense of leaving samsara. Thus, it is actually a synonym for liberation and this

usage is a case in which the name of the result (i.e., liberation) is ascribed to the attitude that is its cause (i.e., the wish to attain that result).

177. *bhāvanāmayī prajñā, bsgom byung gi shes rab*. This is the third of three levels of wisdom; the other two are the wisdom derived from hearing (*śrutamayī prajjñā, thos byung gi shes rab*) and the wisdom derived from reflection (*cintāmayī prajñā, bsam pa la byung ba'i shes rab*). The wisdom derived from meditation is first achieved when a practitioner develops the ability to practice quiescence and insight jointly (*śamathavipaśyanāyuganaddha, zhi gnas dang lhag mthong zung du 'brel ba*).
178. These four objects are the four aspects of the Noble Truth of Suffering. Attainment of direct realization of the four noble truths marks the attainment of the path of seeing (*darśanamārga, mthong lam*), which represents the attainment of the transcendent path and the abandonment of the first elements of the mental afflictions' seeds.
179. *śamatha, zhi gnas*. See ch. 7, "The Nectar That Is Like Highly Refined Gold," note 181.
180. *kleśāvaraṇa, nyong mongs pa'i sgrib pa*.
181. *jñeyāvaraṇa, shes bya'i sgrib pa*.
182. *pudgalanairātmya, gang zag gi bdag med*.
183. *dharmanairātmya, chos kyi bdag med*.
184. *yathāvadbhāvikatā, ji lta ba yod pa nyid*. The abbreviated Tibetan equivalent *ji lta ba*, which literally means "as it truly is," functions as a noun that is a synonym for ultimate truth or emptiness.
185. *yāvadbhāvikatā, ji snyed pa yod pa nyid*. The abbreviated Tibetan equivalent *ji snyed pa*, which literally means "as much as" or "as many as" there are of any particular group of entities, functions as a noun that refers to the full range of relative truth entities. This knowledge can encompass a vast range of things besides merely the existence of these entities. In the case of buddhas and bodhisattvas, this knowledge is principally applied to the aim of benefiting all sentient beings.
186. gTum ston pa bLo gros grags (1106–1166). Tum (*gtum*) is the clan with which he was affiliated, hence the epithet Tum Tönpa, which means "teacher from the Tum clan." He founded the influential Kadam monastery of Narthang (*snar thang*) in 1156 near Shigatse and served as its first abbot. The monastery was completely destroyed in 1966 by Chinese extremists.
187. Sha ra ba yon tan grags (1070–1141). Sharawa was one of the principal disciples of Potowa Rinchen Sel (Po to ba Rin chen gsal, 1027–1105), who is regarded as the patriarch of the Kadam lineage known as the Scripture Followers (*gzhung pa ba*), a tradition that placed great importance on these six Indian treatises: *Śikṣāsamuccaya, Bodhicaryāvatāra, Jātakamālā, Udānavarga, Mahāyānasutrālaṃkāra*, and *Bodhisattvabhūmi*.
188. gTsang pa Rin po che. This epithet, which means "the precious one from Tsang province," refers to Rinchen Namkha Dorje (Rin chen nam mkha' rdo rje, 1077–1161). He lived most of his life as a celibate lay practitioner (*tshangs spyod*

dge bsnyen); however, *KCS* (f. 182a–182b) states that he took full ordination as a bhikṣu in the final year of his life.

189. Bya yul ba gZhon nu 'od (1075–1138). This teacher is associated with a lineage known as the Instruction Followers (*gdams ngag pa*), which indicates that they taught the Lamrim teachings on the basis of a lama's personal instruction. The patriarch of this lineage was Jayulwa's teacher, Chengawa Tsultrim Bar (sPyan snga ba tshul khrims 'bar, 1038–1103).

190. *bstan rim*. This is an expression that was commonly used by early Kadam teachers to describe the Lamrim system of instruction.

191. Mus man pa bDud rtsi char chen, fl. eleventh century. He was a disciple of Jayulwa Zhönu Ö. See note 189 (this chapter).

192. *Theg pa chen po blo sbyong gi rim pa*. I have not been able to locate a version of this text.

193. *adhyāśaya, lhag pa'i bsam pa*. See ch. 4, "The Brilliant Illumination of the Path to Enlightenment," note 43.

194. That is, at a time long after that of the early Kadam teachers.

195. *stong gsum*. This is an abbreviated version of the expression "world sphere made up of a great triple-thousand systems" (*trisāhasromahāsāhasraḥ lokadhātuḥ, stong gsum gyi stong chen po'i 'jig rten gyi khams*). See also *AK*, ch. 3, v. 74c. A "triple thousand"—that is, a billion—is the number of world systems that are created and undergo destruction at the same time during the cosmic period of a great kalpa. See the explanation of this expression that appears below in the thirty-eighth meditation topic.

196. See note 189 (this chapter).

197. This is presumably Tum Tönpa Lodrö Drak. See note 186 (this chapter).

198. See note 29 (this chapter).

199. *preta, yi dwags*. While the translation "hungry ghost" has become the commonly used expression for this class of sentient being, the original Sanskrit term means literally "one who has departed" and is meant to refer to the spirit of a dead person. Some of these spirits are considered to be powerful; others are miserable and suffer from being deprived of food and drink. The latter type is the one that is most often associated with this class of samsaric being. The three categories listed here are meant to include those of varying status.

200. *stag gzig*. This term is associated with areas of Central Asia that were formerly part of the Persian empire; it is considered a corruption of the word Tajik.

201. See ch. 5, "A Verse Compendium of the Spiritual Practices of the Stages of the Path," note 4.

202. The principal locale of hungry ghosts is said to be a city named Kapila, which is described as lying five hundred yojana (see note 81, this chapter) below the earth's surface and is referred to in *AKBh* (p. 165) as the King's Palace (*rājadhānī, rgyal po'i khab*), which is presided over by Yama, the Lord of Death. See the description above in the section on the suffering of hungry ghosts.

203. See the first paragraph above that describes the following three classes of beings

that reside in the same region as you do—that is, human beings, animals, and hungry ghosts.

204. That is, the animals, hungry ghosts, and hell beings that reside below the surface of these three continents.

205. See note 56 (this chapter).

206. See note 133 (this chapter).

207. *gnod sbyin.* A class of powerful spirits that is said to be ruled over by Kubera (a.k.a., Vaiśravaṇa), one of the Four Great Kings (see note 56, this chapter) who is considered a god of wealth. Many of these spirits are benevolent, but some are also harmful.

208. Seven golden mountains encircle Mount Meru, with inner seas in between them (see note 212, this chapter). The first golden mountain rises up to half the height of Mount Meru—that is, forty thousand yojana (see note 81, this chapter). Each successive golden mountain is half the height of the preceding one.

209. *cakravāḍa, khor yug.* This term, which literally means "circular enclosure," refers to a circular iron mountain range that lies at the outer edge of the outer oceans and rises to a height of three hundred and twelve yojana.

210. See note 136 (this chapter).

211. *rol mtsho.* The meaning of the Sanskrit term is uncertain. The Tibetan translation literally means "sea of play," an expression that native Tibetan texts suggest stems from the notion that these are bodies of water in which the nāga kings enjoy themselves. These inner seas (*ābhyantaraḥ samudraḥ, nang gi mtsho*) are said to be the principal domain of the *nāgas*. The second section of Asaṅga's *Yogācārabhūmi* lists these eight as the nāga kings that reside there and live for a kalpa: Nanda (dGa' bo), Upananda (Nyer dga' bo), Aśvatara (rTa'i gzhi), Mucilinda (bTang bzung), Manasvī (gZi can), Dhṛtarāṣṭra (Yul 'khor srung), Mahākāla (Nag po chen po), Elapatra (Ela'i gdab). Their names often appear in canonical literature. The inner seas are said to be filled with fresh water having these eight qualities: (1) cool, (2) sweet, (3) light, (4) soft, (5) clear, (6) fragrant, and, when drunk, harmful to neither (7) the throat or (8) the stomach. The first inner sea lies between Mount Meru and the first golden mountain that encircles it. The width of the first of the seven *śītās* is eighty thousand yojana (see note 81, this chapter), with each successive *śītā* half as wide as the preceding one.

212. The great outer oceans (*bāhyaḥ mahāsamudraḥ, phyi'i rgya mtsho chen po*), which lie between the last of the seven golden mountains and the circular iron mountain range, are filled with salt water. The distance between the last golden mountain and the outer iron mountain range is said to be three hundred and twenty thousand yojana.

213. *bya khyung,* also *nam mkha' lding.* See note 137 (this chapter).

214. *mi'am ci.* A benevolent mythological creature that is said to be half-human and half-bird. They appear in both a male and a female form.

215. When a new physical realm begins to form in a portion of the universe that has remained empty space for a period of twenty intermediate kalpas, a very

gentle wind begins to move, which gradually becomes stronger and eventually forms the disk of wind (*vāyumaṇḍala, rlung gi dkyil 'khor*) that supports the lower physical regions of the desire realm. Next, due to the shared karma of sentient beings, gold-filled clouds (*kāñcanagarbhā meghā, gser gyi snying po'i sprin*) form above the disk of wind that release immense quantities of rain for a vast period of time, eventually forming the disk of water (*apmaṇḍala, chu'i dkyil 'khor*). Then, karmically produced wind agitates the disk of water, causing a solid layer to form on its upper surface that becomes the golden ground (*kāñcanamayī pṛthvī, gser gyi rang bzhin gyi sa gzhi*). After that, karmically produced clouds that are filled with a variety of minerals (*nānādhātugarbhā meghā, khams sna tshogs kyi snying po'i sprin*) release another vast quantity of rain that forms a layer of water on top of the golden ground. Through the agitation of this second deluge of water, Mount Sumeru, the seven golden mountains, the four continents, the eight subcontinents, the inner and outer oceans, and the rest of this aspect of the physical world becomes formed. The length of time that it takes for these physical components to be created is one intermediate kalpa.

216. *'thab bral. AKV* (vol. 2, p. 380) states: "They are called Yāma deities because they have escaped suffering and reached their celestial realm through merit. Or they are called Yāma deities because they have put a stop to suffering."

217. *dga' ldan. AKV* (vol. 2, p. 380) states: "They are called Tuṣita deities because they are content and have gone to their celestial realm happily. Or they are called Tuṣita deities because they experience contentment."

218. *nirmāṇaratayā, 'phrul dga'. AKV* (vol. 2, p. 380) states: "These deities are called Those Who Delight in Magical Creations because they enjoy the magical creations that they have created themselves."

219. *paranirmitavaśavarttina, gzhan 'phrul dbang byed. AKV* (vol. 2, p. 380) states: "These deities are called Those Who Control Others' Magical Creations because it is their nature to take control of enjoyments that have been magically created by others." These are the remaining four classes of deities of the desire realm. Their heavens are celestial regions that lie above the surface of the previously described regions.

220. As relates to the desire realm, the phrase "a single world system that encompasses the four continents" should be understood to include all of the regions in the desire realm in which all six classes of sentient beings reside—that is, the eight hot and the eight cold hells, as well as all the regions where hungry ghosts, animals, human beings, and the six classes of desire-realm gods are found.

221. *brahmakāyika, tshangs ris pa rnams. AKV* (vol. 2, p. 382) states: "Brahmā is the deity who has come into being through great roots of virtue. Who is he? He is the one called the Great Brahmā. He is great because, through having attained the superior level of the first meditative absorption, he is born before and dies after all the other deities of his realm and because he is greater in size and other characteristics. The deities known as the Brahma Group are those who form

his group in that they are found in his abode (i.e., the first dhyāna of the form realm)."

222. *tshangs pa'i mdun na 'don. AKV* (vol. 2, p. 382) states: "They are called Brahmapurohitas because they place Brahmā foremost."
223. *tshangs chen pa. AKV* (vol. 2, p. 382) states: "They are called Mahābrahmāṇas because Brahmā exceeds them in life span, physical appearance, and other characteristics."
224. *rūpadhātu, gzugs khams.* That is, throughout the three just-named sections of Brahmā's realm that are identified with the first meditative absorption.
225. *parīttābha, 'od chung. AKV* (vol. 2, p. 382): "The deities of this region are called Those of Limited Light because their light is limited in relation to the other deities of their level."
226. *apramāṇābha, tshad med 'od. AKV* (vol. 2, p. 382) states: "The deities of this region are called Those of Immeasurable Light because it is not possible to measure their light."
227. *ābhāsvara, 'od gsal ba. AKV* (vol. 2, p. 382) states: "The deities of this region are called Those of Brilliant Light because they illuminate entirely other heavenly regions."
228. *sāhasrikaś cūḍiko lokadhātuḥ, stong spyi phud kyi 'jig rten gyi khams,* also *stong chung ngu'i 'jig rten gyi khams.*
229. *parīttaśubha, dge chung. AKV* (vol. 2, p. 382) states: "The well-being that relates to a mental level of existence is called 'good fortune' (*śubha, dge ba*). The deities of this region are called Those of Limited Good Fortune because their good fortune is limited in relation to the other deities of their level."
230. *apramāṇaśubha, tshad med dge. AKV* (vol. 2, p. 382) states: "The deities of this region are called Those of Immeasurable Good Fortune because their good fortune is immeasurable."
231. *śubhakṛtsna, dge rgyas. AKV* (vol. 2, p. 382) states: "The deities of this region are called Those of Complete Good Fortune because their good fortune is complete. The meaning of the name is that no more excellent form of ease than this exists anywhere else."
232. *dvisāhasro madhyamo lokadhātuḥ, stong gnyis pa bar ma'i 'jig rten kyi khams.*
233. *trisāhasramahāsāhasro lokadhātuḥ, stong gsum gyi stong chen po'i 'jig rten gyi khams.*
234. They are "ordinary" because they are regions where non-āryas reside.
235. *anabhraka, sprin med. AKV* (vol. 2, p. 382): "The deities of this region are called the Cloudless Ones because, unlike clouds, they have no connection with any ground. That is to say, the celestial mansions that belong to each of these divine beings arise and disintegrate at the same time that they do."
236. *puṇyaprasava, bsod nams skyes. AKV* (vol. 2, p. 382) states: "The deities of this region are called Those Born of Merit because they are born of merit in the sense that their rebirth is produced by unvarying karma (*āniñjyakarma, mi g.yo ba'i las*)." Unvarying karma is that which is generated by attaining any of the

four meditative absorptions of the form realm or the four states of mental composure associated with the formless realm. It is called "unvarying" in the sense that it can only ripen in a manner that causes a being to be reborn in the very same level of the form or formless realms. Thus, the karma that is generated by achieving the fourth meditative absorption of the form realm will only ripen as a rebirth in the fourth level of the form realm.

237. *bṛhatphala, 'bras bu che ba. AKV* (vol. 2, p. 382) states: "The deities of this region are called Those of Great Fruit because the fruit that is experienced by these deities is much greater than those associated with any other region inhabited by ordinary beings." Implicit in this explanation is the understanding that the next five levels of the form realm, which are referred to as the pure abodes, are inhabited exclusively by nonreturner āryas.

238. *abṛha, mi che ba. AKV* (vol. 2, p. 382) states: "The deities of this region are called Those Who Are Not More Exalted because they are not more exalted than those deities of the other four pure abodes."

239. *atapa, mi gdung ba. AKV* (vol. 2, p. 382) states: "The deities of this region are called Those Free of Torment because, through having attained extraordinary one-pointed concentration, the mental afflictions do not torment anyone here. Alternatively, they are called Those Free of Torment because, due to their virtuous attitudes, they do not torment any other beings."

240. *sudṛśa, shin tu mthong ba. AKV* (vol. 2, p. 382) states: "The deities of this region are called Those of Excellent Vision because, due to their completely pure vision, they see things in an excellent manner."

241. *sudarśana, gya nom snang ba. AKV* (vol. 2, p. 382) states: "The deities of this region are called Those Who Are Extremely Beautiful because their appearance is very beautiful."

242. *akaniṣṭha, 'og min*. This is the highest of the seventeen levels that make up the form realm. It is also the uppermost of the last five, which are called pure abodes (*śuddhāvāsa, gnas gtsang ma*) because only āryas are reborn there. This region should not be identified with the buddha field of the same name. *AKBh* (p. 170) explains this term as follows: "Moreover, there is no physical place higher than this one. Therefore, because it is the uppermost region of the form realm, the deities who reside there are called Those Who Are Below None.

243. The formless realm is made up of these four states of mental composure (*samāpatti, snyoms par 'jug pa*): the sphere of unlimited space (*ākāśānantyāyatana, nam mkha' mtha' yas skye mched*); the sphere of unlimited consciousness (*vijñānānantyāyatana, rnam shes mtha' yas skye mched*); the sphere of nothingness (*ākiṃcanyāyatanam, nas ci yang med pa'i skye mched*); and the sphere in which there is neither conception nor absence of conception (*naiva saṃjñā nāsaṃjñāyatanam, 'du shes med 'du shes med min gyi skye mched*).

244. *ma rgan*. The adjective "elderly" is meant in a metaphorical sense in order to suggest that most sentient beings are unable to help themselves in an ultimate spiritual sense.

245. The phrase "causes of happiness" should be understood to mean the virtuous acts that will ripen in the future as various forms of well-being.

246. *sugati, bde 'gro.* Indian Buddhist literature (cf. *AK,* ch. v. 4) generally recognizes five migratory states: hell beings, animals, spirits, humans, and gods. Tibetan literature typically adds a sixth class of being: demigods (*asura, lha ma yin*). In that formulation, the three happy migratory states are worldly gods, demigods, and human beings. See also ch. 7, "The Nectar That Is Like Highly Refined Gold," note 85.

247. See the explanations presented in the thirty-eighth meditation topic.

248. This is the first in an extensive list of similes and analogies that are presented in the penultimate section of the *Gaṇḍavyūha Sūtra,* which is titled the "The Liberating Activities of Maitreya" (*maitreyavimokṣa, byams pa'i rnam par thar pa*; see also ch. 4, "The Brilliant Illumination of the Path to Enlightenment," note 96). The statement is not placed in quotes here because it does not represent the exact language that appears in the passage. After praising the pilgrim Sudhana for having developed enlightenment mind, Maitreya says to him, "You are watched over by all the buddhas and you are well cared for by all spiritual teachers due to the superior attitude by means of which you have generated the mind that aspires to attain unsurpassed perfect enlightenment. Why is that?" Following this rhetorical question, he lists all the similes and analogies as the reasons. The first simile states: "O son of good family, it is because enlightenment mind is the seed of all the spiritual qualities possessed by a buddha." The descriptions of the next three benefits also paraphrase the wording that appears in the sūtra.

249. This is a reference to the ritual for generating the aspirational form of enlightenment mind (**praṇidhicittotpādavidhi, smon pa sems bskyed kyi cho ga*) rather than the ritual for generating the active form of enlightenment mind (**prasthānacittotpādavidhi, 'jug pa sems bskyed kyi cho ga*).

250. Literally "The Seven Limbs of Regular Confession" (*rGyun bshags yan lag bdun pa*). The full three verses of this recitation state: "I confess all my misdeeds to the Three Jewels who are my refuge. / I rejoice at the merit of the world and fix my mind upon a buddha's enlightenment. // I go for refuge until enlightenment to the Buddha, dharma, and supreme assembly. / I create the mind that aspires to enlightenment mind to achieve my own and others' aims. // I generate the most excellent and supreme enlightenment mind and invite as my guests the multitude of all sentient beings. / I shall practice the revered and excellent bodhisattva activities and become a buddha to benefit all living beings."

251. *prahara,* also *yāma, thun tshod.* A duration of four hours.

252. *'khor gsum.* The three spheres of a spiritual practice are its object, agent, and action. In the case of generosity, these would be the giver, the recipient, and the act of giving. For the act of generosity, sometimes the object that is given is also identified as one of the three spheres or elements.

253. While the phrase "three forms of wisdom" does not appear here, the description clearly makes reference to the process by which they arise. They are the wisdom

derived from hearing; the wisdom derived from reflection; and the wisdom derived from meditation. See also note 177 (this chapter).

254. These eight qualities are presented in a section of the *Kāśyapaparivarta Sūtra*. See ch. 4, "The Brilliant Illumination of the Path to Enlightenment," note 128, for a translation of the relevant passages.

255. *visaṃvad, bslu ba*. While the Tibetan translation of this term typically means explicitly "to deceive," the primary meaning of the original Sanskrit verb is "to break one's word," which can, but does not necessarily, imply a conscious intention to mislead.

256. *aśloka, tshigs su bcad pa ma yin pa*.

257. The *Kāśyapaparivarta Sūtra* itself states that one should "develop the conception toward all bodhisattvas that they are the Master," not all sentient beings. It seems that Tāranātha has revised that text to express a more expanded view.

258. That is, Buddha Śākyamuni.

259. *garbha, snying po*. This term is a reference to the doctrine known popularly as Buddha nature, which asserts that all sentient beings have the potential to become a buddha and, in fact, are destined to become enlightened.

260. *BCA*, ch. 6, v. 113ab. The full verse states: "When a buddha's qualities are acquired / equally through sentient beings and victors, / what sort of manner is it that one's respect for beings / is not the same as it is for victors?"

261. *māyā, sgyu*. *AS* (p. 8) states: "What is deceitfulness? It is a form of desire and ignorance in which a person who is attached to gain and honor gives the appearance of possessing qualities that he or she does not possess. Its action is to give support to wrong livelihood."

262. *śāṭhya, g.yo*. *AS* (pp. 8–9) states: "What is guile? It is a form of desire and ignorance in which a person who is attached to gain and honor conceals faults that he or she possesses. Its action serves to obstruct the obtaining of correct spiritual instruction."

263. The text reads *dre* (*bre*), which is the name of a square wooden container typically used for measuring grain. It is defined as being equivalent to six "handfuls" (*phul*) and thus is roughly equal to about two pints.

264. See note 193 (this chapter) and ch. 8, "The Easy Path," note 43.

265. See ch. 6, "The Flower Cluster of Spiritual Attainments," note 13.

266. The first system only identifies three precepts. This second system adds the act of recalling the benefits of enlightenment mind and the act of generating enlightenment mind six times each day to the first two precepts of the first system, and then dividing each of the four pairs of qualities that make up the third precept of the first system into four separate precepts, making a total of eight.

267. That is, meditation topics thirty-four through forty-four.

268. This approach is one in which the aspirational and active forms of enlightenment mind are developed within a single ritual event.

269. Earlier the author noted that this topic can also be described as "training oneself in the practice of the perfections."

270. This is another way of referring to the six perfections and the four principles for attracting a following.
271. *abhaya, mi 'jigs pa.* This term literally means "to provide freedom from fear," which means to protect beings from any of a wide range of possible dangers.
272. *lam 'phrang.* This term typically refers to a hazardous footpath along a narrow ledge that protrudes from the side of a steep precipice.
273. *upekṣā, btan snyongs su bzhag.* One sense of this verb is literally "to disregard" something, which in this context would mean not to take any action.
274. Sthiramati (*TB*, p. 76) provides the following explanation of the term "objectionable act" (*avadya, kha na ma tho ba*): "An objectionable act is one that is evil, because it is condemned by those who are wise and because it has an undesirable maturation." There are two types of objectionable act: a misdeed that is "naturally objectionable" (*prakṛtisāvadya, rang bzhin gyi kha na ma tho ba*) and one that is "objectionable by having been so prescribed (*prajñaptisāvadya*). A naturally objectionable act is one that is wrongful regardless of whether one has taken any form of vow, such as any of the ten unvirtuous karmic paths. An act that is "objectionable by having been so prescribed" means one that was prescribed by Buddha Śākyamuni as a transgression that violates a precept included in one of the various forms of Buddhist vows. For instance, a person who has taken a form of Buddhist vow that includes the precept not to take another being's life commits such a misdeed by taking another being's life. Some transgressions contain aspects of both types of misdeed, such as the one just described. These are designated "an offense that contains elements of both types of misdeed" (*gnyis ka'i cha dang ldan pa'i ltung ba*). Others are misdeeds only on the strength of having been so designated by the Buddha, such as the precept for ordained monks and nuns not to eat food after midday. This latter type is described as "an offense that is wrongful only by having been so prescribed by the Blessed One" (*bcas rkyang gi ltung ba*).
275. *samaya, dam tshig.* The sense of the original Sanskrit term is that of a spiritual "agreement" or an "obligatory observance." The Tibetan equivalent is typically translated as "pledge" or "commitment." Commentaries interpret it to mean a principle that is not to be violated or transgressed (*alaṅghya, 'da' bar mi bya ba*). Tantric vows and commitments are associated with the two higher classes of Tantra—that is, Yoga Tantra and Highest Yoga Tantra.
276. *duṣkara, dka' spyad.* Literally a "difficult act," this term can also be rendered as an "austerity."
277. *mthun pa'i rkyen.* This term can refer to spiritual practices that serve to accumulate merit in order to promote the success of the main spiritual practice. However, in this context, it refers to outer material necessities. Cf. *BBh* (English translation, p. 320), which refers to these four "supports" (*saṃniśraya, rten*): monastic robes, alms food, beds and seats, and medicine for curing the ill and other permitted personal belongings.
278. *BBh* (book 1, ch. 11, English translation, pp. 323–24) describes eight topics in

relation to which this form of patience is cultivated. They are the virtuous qualities of the Three Jewels, the nature of reality, the great powers of the buddhas and the bodhisattvas, the ten kinds of causes, the five kinds of results, the goal of buddhahood that is to be achieved for oneself, the means [i.e., the path] of achieving that goal, and the field of that which needs to be known. Regarding the last category, *BBhVy* (f. 184a) states: "The phrase 'field of that which needs to be known' means to gain an accurate determination of the four noble truths' aspects of impermanence and so on in such a manner that one recognizes 'its nature is thus and not otherwise.'" Another list of the eight objects of devotion appears in *BBh*, book 1, ch. 8, in the section titled "Abundance of Devotion." Since the eighth topic is identified there as the twelve categories of the Buddha's word, the "field of that which needs to be known" should be understood to refer to all of the Buddha's teachings, not just the four noble truths.

279. *cittotsāha, spro sems.* This is the essential attribute of effort. The basic sense of this term is a "power" or "strength of will" (*MW*, s.v. "cittotsāha") that possesses the willingness or enthusiasm to engage in virtuous activities.

280. *prayoga, sbyor ba.*

281. *sambhāra, tshogs.* This is the same term that is translated as "accumulations" when referring to the two elements of merit and wisdom. However, in this context, it refers to causal factors that are necessary for an individual to possess in order for the practice of meditative absorption to be successful.

282. *alpārthatā, don nyung ba.* That is, few matters that are thought about mentally.

283. *alpakṛtyatā, bya ba nyung ba.* That is, few physical and verbal activities.

284. *alpeccha, 'dod pa chung ba.* See ch. 6, "Flower Cluster of Spiritual Attainments," note 10.

285. *saṃtuṣṭi, chog shes pa.* See ch. 6, "Flower Cluster of Spiritual Attainments," note 11.

286. *prasrabdhi, shin tu sbyangs pa.* See ch. 4, "The Brilliant Illumination of the Path to Enlightenment," note 65. While I translate the term as "agility," I don't believe this is literally accurate. The original Sanskrit term suggests a physical and mental condition that "quells" or "stills" the corresponding forms of indisposition of body and mind.

287. *abhijñā, mngon par shes pa. BBh* (book 1, ch. 5) lists these six types: miraculous powers (*ṛddhi, rdzu 'phrul*); the divine ear (*divyaṃ śrotra, lha'i rna ba*); knowledge of diverse states of mind (*cetaḥparyāyajñāna, sems kyi rnam grangs mkhyen pa*); recollection of former existences (*pūrvanivāsānusmṛti, sngon gyi gnas rjes su dran pa*); perceiving death and rebirth (*cyutyupapattijñāna, 'chi 'pho ba dang skye ba mkhyen pa*); knowledge that the outflows have been terminated (*āsravakṣayajñāna, zag pa zad pa mkhyen pa*).

288. *ṛddhi, rdzu 'phrul. BBh* (book 1, ch. 5, English translation, pp. 106–21) identifies two main types: transformational miraculous powers (*nairmāṇikī ṛddhi, yongs su bsgyur ba'i rdzu 'phrul*) and creative miraculous powers (*nairmāṇikī ṛddhi, sprul pa'i rdzu 'phrul*), and describes numerous examples of each.

289. *adhiṣṭhā, byin gyis rlob pa*. Here is an oral description of the meaning of the term "blessing": "The term for 'blessing' in Tibetan is *byin rlabs*, which is understood to mean a 'transformation of one's luster.' The first syllable, *byin*, is understood to mean 'luster,' and the second syllable, *rlabs*, 'transformation.' Thus, a blessing has the power to transform you from a prior state, in which you lack the luster of some spiritual quality, into a subsequent state, in which you take on the luster or majesty of a more favorable spiritual quality."

290. *vipaśyanā, lhag mthong*. *AS* (p. 75) states: "What is insight? It is the form of meditation that examines, investigates, fully considers, and accomplishes a thoroughly profound contemplation of entities, with regard to the nature of sensory objects, antidotes, indisposition, signs, and the fetters, with regard to the erroneous views of those who are overcome by desire, and with regard to causing the unerring mind to remain fixed in that unerring state." Because of the discrepancy between the Sanskrit and Tibetan versions of the first two of the final three clauses, each of which begins with the phrase "with regard to," their translation should be considered tentative.

291. *cittasthiti, sems gnas pa*. This term literally means "a state in which the mind remains stationary or fixed." It is a reference to the nine stages of mental stability that culminate with the attainment of quiescence.

292. See note 177 (this chapter).

293. See note 182 (this chapter).

294. See note 183 (this chapter).

295. *śūnyatākaruṇāgarbha, stong pa nyid snying rje'i snying po can*.

296. See note 176 (this chapter).

297. *rgyud 'gyur*. Literally "a transformation of your mental continuum," this expression refers to vivid states of experiential awareness in which immeasurable loving-kindness and compassion have been generated in one's mental continuum.

298. *bhoga, longs spyod*. This noun is formed from a verbal root that means "to enjoy" and "to experience." Hence it refers to objects of sensory experience and pleasure.

299. *dravya, rdzas*. This is a general term for substances, objects, and things. It often refers to possessions, wealth, material objects of value.

300. *parivāra, 'khor*. The term "retinue" typically refers to one's children, wife (or wives), male and female servants, workers, and the like. In the case of a spiritual teacher, it can also refer to one's followers.

301. *svatantra, rang dbang can*. The Sanskrit original literally means "self-dependent," in the sense of not being subject to another's control; in this context, it can be understood more specifically as the ability of the putative self to exercise control over other things.

302. "The body" does not appear in the manuscript.

303. *skandha, phung po*. That is, the five heaps of form, feeling, conception, formations, and consciousness. The heaps are coextensive with all impermanent

conditioned entities. There are both pure (*anāsrava, zag pa med pa*) and impure (*sāsrava, zag pa dang bcas pa*) forms of the heaps. The pure heaps are identified with the Noble Truth of the Path (cf., *AK*, ch. 1, v. 4).

304. *dhātu, khams*. There are a number of contexts in which this term is used. The most comprehensive sense is that of the eighteen constituents that encompass all entities, both permanent and impermanent. These eighteen can be classified into the six objects of consciousness, the six types of consciousness, and the six faculties. See ch. 4, "The Brilliant Illumination of the Path to Enlightenment," note 201, for a description of two interpretations of the term that are presented in Vasubandhu's *AKBh* (p. 13), as well as four interpretations found in Asaṅga's *AS* (p. 15).

305. The term *basis* (*āyatana, skye mched*) refers to the entities that are the "sources for the arising of consciousness" (*vijñānāyadvāra, rnam par shes pa skye ba'i sgo*). There are six inner bases and six outer bases. The six inner bases are the faculties of the eye, ear, nose, tongue, body and mind, and the six outer bases are visible objects, sounds, smells, tastes, tangible objects, and the entities that are the objects of mind consciousness. This latter category (that is, the entity basis; *dharmāyatāna, chos kyi skye mched*) includes the three heaps of feelings, conceptions, and formations, and the four types of unconditioned entities—namely, space, the nonanalytic cessation, the analytic cessation, and emptiness. The nonanalytic cessation is a permanent state that is due to the insufficiency of conditions—which is to say, a state in which certain types of future are permanently obstructed from arising. The analytic cessation is a state in which the seeds of the mental afflictions and the seeds of the subtle obstructions to omniscience have been permanently eliminated through the attainment of transcendent wisdom.

306. Abhidharma literature describes the five sense faculties of the eye and so on as being made up of "clear form" (*rūpaprasāda, gzugs dwang ba*), which is not perceptible to the senses. *AK* (ch. 1, v. 9cd) states: "The supports for those five sensory forms of consciousness are the eye and so on, which are made up of clear form." *PSV* (English translation, p. 253) states: "The meaning of the term 'clear' here is as follows. Just as the reflection of a visible form appears on the surface of a clear mirror or a container of clear water in dependence on that visible form, the various sense perceptions of visible form, sound, and so forth arise in dependence on those visible forms, sounds and so on, and through the medium of the five faculties of the eye and the rest that have the nature of clear form."

307. *dbang rten khog pa*. That is, the rear portion of the eyeball is the anatomical region where the eye faculty resides; likewise, the interior of the ear is where the ear faculty resides, the interior of the nostrils is where the nose faculty resides, the surface of the tongue is where the tongue faculty is situated, and the entirety of the physical body is the locus of the body faculty.

308. *don lnga*. They are the heart, the lungs, the liver, the kidneys, and the spleen.

309. *snod drug*. They are the stomach, the large intestine, small intestine, the gall

bladder, the urinary bladder, and the prostate gland (the female homologue is the Skene's glands).

310. *bu ga dgu*. They are the two eyes, the two ears, the two nostrils, the mouth, the urethra, and the anus.

311. *aṅgulīparvan*, *sor tshigs*. A classic unit of measurement. Cf. *AK*, ch. 3, vv. 85d–86.

312. *yava*, *nas*. *AK*, ch. 3, vv. 85d–86 lists a series of units of measurements, each one of which is seven times greater than the previous one. Seven barley grains are said to equal one finger joint.

313. *yūkā*, *shig*.

314. *likṣā*, *sro ma*. That is, a unit of measure that is the size of a louse egg.

315. *vātāyanacchidrarajas*, *nyi zer gyi rdul*. The original Sanskrit term for this unit of measure is tentatively translated as "a particle that can be perceived in a window opening"; the Tibetan equivalent suggests "a particle that is visible in rays of sunlight."

316. *gorajas*, *glang rdul*. *MW* (s.v. "gorajas") describes as "a particle of dust that collects on a cow-hair." Chim Jampai Yang (mChims 'jam pa'i dbyangs; dates uncertain) states in his *Ornament of Higher Learning* (*mNgon pa'i rgyan*) that the terms "cow particle," "sheep particle," and "rabbit particle" are not to be taken to mean the width of the tips of their respective hairs because they are terms that describe various kinds of "particles" (*rajas*, *rdul*); however, he does not give a precise interpretation of their meaning.

317. *eḍakarajas*, *lug rdul*. Following note 316 (this chapter), this term could tentatively be translated as "a particle of dust that collects on a sheep-hair." The term suggests that since a sheep's hair is finer than a cow's hair, the particle that collects on it would be finer than the particle that collects on a cow's hair.

318. *śaśarajas*, *ri bong rdul*. Per note 316 (this chapter), "a particle of dust that collects on a sheep-hair." This term suggests that this particle is smaller because a rabbit's hair is finer than a sheep's hair. See note 317 (this chapter).

319. *abrajas*, *chu rdul*. Exact meaning is uncertain, perhaps fine particles of "mist."

320. *loharajas*, *lcags rdul*. It isn't clear how this could be seven times smaller than a "water particle."

321. *aṇu*, *rdul phran*.

322. *paramāṇu*, *rdul phra rab*. This term is understood to mean the smallest particle of matter.

323. That is, because the length, width, and height of each preceding portion of physical matter is seven times greater than that of the succeeding portion, in a three-dimensional sense, each one is 343 times larger than the succeeding portion.

324. *AS* (pp. 2–3) states: "What is the defining attribute of consciousness? Its defining attribute is awareness. Consciousness is that entity that, by a particular form of consciousness, apprehends visible forms, as well as sounds, odors, tastes, tangible objects, and mental entities."

325. *kāya, tshogs*. Each of the eight types of consciousness is made up of a collection of momentary entities.

326. One branch of the Buddhist Yogācāra school identifies eight types of consciousness. Six are referred to as the "active forms of consciousness" (*pravṛttivijñānāni, 'jug pa'i rnam par shes pa*), which are eye, ear, nose, tongue, body, and mind consciousness. A seventh is called the "storehouse consciousness" (*ālayavivijñāna, kun gzhi'i rnam par shes pa*), because it is the place where the seeds of all afflicted entities are stored. The eighth form of consciousness is called the "afflicted mind" (*kliṣṭamanas, nyon mongs pa'i yid*) because it mistakenly apprehends the storehouse consciousness as a real self.

327. *vedanā, tshor ba*. This is the name of the second of the five heaps, whose entities have the defining attribute of being an experience. See next note.

328. *anubhava, myong ba*. This term represents the defining attribute of feelings. *PSV* (English translation, p. 267) states: "Experience is experiential awareness. Its nature is to make directly evident the qualitative essence of an object that is either pleasurable, painful, or neither of those two. Alternatively, an experience is that which experiences the qualitative essence of an object that is either pleasurable, painful, or neither of those two."

329. *saṃjñā, 'du shes*. This is the name of the third heap. *AS* (p. 2) states: "What is the defining attribute of conception? Its defining attribute is identification. It is that entity that by apprehending signs and making distinctions assigns names to objects in the manner that they were seen, heard, thought about, and ascertained."

330. *saṃskāra, 'du byed*. This is the name of the fourth heap, which contains all the mental states (*caitta, sems byung*) other than feelings and conceptions, as well as the formations that do not accompany consciousness (*cittaviprayuktasaṃskāra, sems dang mtshungs par ldan pa ma yin pa'i 'du byed*). For a description of this latter type of formation, see ch. 8, "The Easy Path," note 147.

331. *sthiti, gnas pa*. This term represents the period of time during which the entity remains in existence, albeit for only a moment.

332. The word "name" (*nāma, ming gzhi*) here should be understood as the first element of the compound "name and form" (*nāmarūpa, ming dang gzugs*). This compound noun is synonymous with the psycho-physical complex that is described by the term "five heaps." The word "form" in this compound is the same as the name of the first of the five heaps and corresponds to the physical body. The word "name" is identified with the remaining four heaps of feelings, conceptions, formations, and consciousness, which are for the most part mental in nature. *AKBh* (p. 142) states: "Now, what is the meaning of the compound 'name and form'? Form has been described extensively in the first chapter of *AKBh*. *AK*, ch. 3, v. 30a: 'Name is the heaps that do not possess form.'"

333. *bcud*. The term "world" (*loka, 'jig rten*) has two senses, which are described by the words "vessel" (*bhājana, snod*) and "contents" (*bcud*). The first of these, "vessel," refers to the external, inanimate physical world, and the second term,

"contents," refers to the sentient beings that inhabit the physical world. I have not encountered the original Sanskrit term that corresponds to this Tibetan term, if there is one. Typically, the term that is found in Sanskrit texts is the compound *sattvaloka* (*sems can gyi 'jig rten*), which means the "world of sentient beings."

334. See note 333 (this chapter).
335. *dpag tshad*. See note 81 (this chapter).
336. *rgyang grags*. Literally a "shout," meaning the distance that the sound of a shout can carry. See also note 81 (this chapter).
337. *'dom*. A "bow-length," which is equated with the space between a person's two outstretched arms.
338. *hasta, khru gang*. A cubit is the distance from the tip of the middle finger to the elbow.
339. A cubit is twenty-four finger widths.
340. *sapratigha, thogs bcas*. Abhidharma literature describes three types of resistance, of which the principal form and the one that is meant here is identified as "obstruction-opposition" (*āvaraṇapratighāta, sgrib pa'i thogs pa*). *PSV* (English translation, p. 360) states: "Obstruction-opposition is the quality by which one entity opposes the arising of another object in the space that it occupies. Thus, both the entity that prevents something else from arising in the space that it occupies and the location where that obstruction occurs indicate the meaning of possessing resistance."
341. This entire sentence is missing from the text. It has been restored on the basis of a critical edition of the author's works.
342. *snang cha*. This noun can be taken to mean an object that is observed to occur within ordinary experience.
343. That is, it is not maintained that they are nonexistent.
344. The text seems to have a corrupt reading (*rang bzhin med pas sam lta bu'o*) that cannot be easily construed. I have emended it to read "like magically created illusions" (*sgyu ma lta bu'o*) on the basis of a critical edition of the author's works.
345. *abhāva, dngos med*. The affirmative form of this term, *bhāva* (*dngos po*), has several senses, among which the two most salient would be "entity" or "mode of being." The latter is the sense that is meant here, and more specifically, a *real* mode of being. Hence the negative of the term can be understood to mean the absence of a real mode of being, or more succinctly, "unreality."
346. *paramārthatas, don dam par*. This is an adverbial word that is formed from a noun that means literally "the highest meaning." It is also understood to mean "in reality" (*MW*, s.v. "paramārthata").
347. See note 342 (this chapter) for a description of the term "appearance." The term "well-known" (*prasiddha, grags pa*) also refers to the objects of ordinary experience that are referred to in everyday discourse. This term also occurs in an expression that can be rendered as "recognized in the world" (*lokaprasiddha, 'jig

rten gyi grags pa). *BBh* (English translation, pp. 64–65) states: "The expression 'recognized in the world' refers to that substance (*vastu, dngos po*) toward which all worldly beings (*laukika, 'jig rten pa*; i.e., a non-ārya) share the same view based on judgments that operate through gaining familiarity with convention and accepted usage, such as when one says about the earth element: 'This is earth; it is not fire.' Just as with the earth element, such shared views also occur in relation to fire, water, air, visible form, sounds, smells, tastes, tangible objects, food, drink, vehicles, clothing, objects that are applied as ornaments, implements and household utensils, incense, garlands, scented oils, objects that relate to dance, song, music, objects that are used to create light, objects that relate to sensual pleasures enjoyed by men and women, and objects that relate to the cultivation of fields, the operation of commercial shops, and the maintenance of private dwellings. Such shared views also occur in relation to the nature of pleasure and suffering, such as when worldly beings agree: 'This experience is a form of suffering; it is not a form of pleasure' or 'This experience is a form of pleasure; it is not a form of suffering.' In short, it is anything that is an object of settled and firm belief for all worldly persons, such that it is held: 'The nature of this object is this; it is not that' or, 'This object exists or is used in this manner; it does not exist nor is it used in some other manner.' Likewise, the existence of these objects is recognized by such persons with their own conceptual thought simply on the basis of familiarity with the traditional usage of terms; it is not a belief that is held through having engaged in reflection, contemplation, and investigation. This is called 'the form of reality that is recognized as true in the world.'"

348. The translation of this sentence is based on the wording of a critical edition of the author's works. The version in vol. 3 reads *gang du* instead of *gong du*, which suggests the following possible alternative translation: "All these entities should be thought of as having never existed in the manner that they appear to exist and in the manner that they are commonly believed to exist."
349. *vandhyāputra, mo gsham gyi bu*. This contradictory expression is an example of what is meant by the phrase "something that has never possessed any valid basis whatsoever." Another well-known example of an impossible entity is described by the expression "sky-flower" (*khapuṣpa, nam mkha'i me tog*).
350. That is, emptiness as properly understood.
351. That is, the form of reflection in which the mind is initially placed in a nonconceptual state.
352. That is, the method of reversing any dualistic thought that may arise after you have placed your mind in a nonconceptual state.
353. *asiddha, ma grub pa*. This adjective is the negative of the past participle of a verbal root that in a philosophical sense means such things as "to be valid," "to be proved," or "to be demonstrated." However, in the present context, "to be unproved" actually means that something has been proven *not to exist* as a real entity; hence I have translated it here as "unreal."

354. *mi rtog pa*. This Tibetan term is ambiguous in that it can refer to a cognitive state that perceives emptiness and is free of dualistic thought, as in the phrase nonconceptual wisdom (*avikalpajñāna, rnam par mi rtog pa'i ye shes*). However, it can also refer to a mental state that simply remains fixed on its object without engaging in any discursive thought. One form of a discursive mental state is called "deliberation" (*vitarka, rtog pa*). *AS* (p. 6) states: "What is deliberation? It is an investigative form of mental discourse that is based upon either volition or wisdom. Moreover, it is a coarseness of mind." Thus, a nonconceptual or, more correctly, a nondiscursive mental state is one that is free of deliberation and thus remains still. While this quality can promote one-pointedness of mind, the absence of such discursive thought should not be mistaken for the nondual state that perceives emptiness.
355. *sthāpanā, 'jog pa*.
356. *saṃsthāpanā, rgyun du 'jog pa*.
357. *avasthāpanā, glan te 'jog pa*.
358. *upasthāpanā, nye bar 'jog pa*.
359. *damana, dul bar byed pa*.
360. See note 114 (this chapter).
361. *śamana, zhi bar byed pa*.
362. *vyupaśamana, rnam par zhi bar byed pa*.
363. *laya, bying ba*. See ch. 7, "The Nectar That Is Like Highly Refined Gold," note 177.
364. *auddhatya, rgod pa*. See ch. 7, "The Nectar That Is Like Highly Refined Gold," note 178.
365. *samādhāna, mnyam par 'jog pa*.
366. *mi rtog pa*. This use of the term *nonconceptual* is meant in the sense of a nondiscursive state of one-pointed concentration. See note 354 (this chapter) and the related portion of the main text.
367. *dpyad pa*. The analysis that is meant here is that process by which one develops a proper understanding of emptiness, which then becomes the object of one-pointed meditation that culminates in the attainment of quiescence.
368. *Be'u bum*. This term is used to refer to "a small treatise that is a compilation of a large number of oral instructions" (*TshCh*, 1842). It is sometimes translated as "calf's nipple," as appears in Sarat Chandra Das's *Tibetan English Dictionary* (p. 876). This particular reference is to the *Blue Udder* (*Be'u bum sngon po*), which was composed by the Kadampa Geshe Dölpa Marshurpa Sherap Gyatso (Dol pa dmar shur pa Shes rab rgya mtsho, 1059–1131), a direct disciple of Potowa Rinchen Sel (Po to ba Rin chen gsal, 1027–1105). Written in verse, an English translation appears in *Stages of the Buddhas' Teachings* (pp. 37–117) under the title *Blue Compendium*.
369. This particular phrase does not appear in the *Blue Udder*. However, there are several places where analysis (*sor sor rtog pa*) is described as being of great importance and should be pursued prior to one-pointed meditation.

370. See note 291 (this chapter) for an explanation of this term.
371. *thun*. This term, which often means a period of time or session that is devoted to meditation, can also mean a "dose" or an appropriate amount of medicine that is used to treat a particular ailment. In a spiritual context, this latter sense can indicate an explanation or series of instructions that relate to a particular aspect of one's practice.
372. Literally "having failed to overcome desire and attachment from the heart," suggesting an inability to the uproot it in its entirety.
373. *ldum bu*. This is one meaning of this term.
374. *ldo 'dod*. That is, enter the sangha as a means of obtaining subsistence.
375. *kuhanā, tshul 'chos*. The original Sanskrit of this term is derived from a verbal root that literally means "to cheat by trickery." It is the name for one of five principal forms of wrong livelihood (*mithyājīva, log par 'tsho ba*) that are to be avoided by monks and nuns in particular. Often translated as "hypocrisy," it is derived from a verbal root that literally means "to cheat by trickery." *ŚBh* (p. 48) describes this type of wrong livelihood as follows: "Further, in a manner that is not proper, this monk or nun who is greedy, not easily satisfied, difficult to nourish, and difficult to maintain fabricates an unnatural and altered mode of physical behavior that is meant to be an indication that he or she has developed spiritual qualities and presents to others a false show that he or she possesses faculties that are free of excitation, faculties that are unwavering, and faculties that are tranquil, in order to obtain robes, a begging bowl, bedding, a seat, medicine that is required to treat illnesses, and other permissible forms of personal belongings. He or she does this in such a way that is designed to make others think, 'This monk or nun is one who has developed spiritual qualities, and therefore offerings ought to be given and ought to be made to him or her—that is to say, offerings of robes, a begging bowl, bedding, a seat, medicine that is required to treat illnesses, and other permissible forms of personal belongings.'"
376. *nag rkyang*. Literally "nothing but black."
377. The translation of this sentence is somewhat tentative. There appears to be some corruption in the original Tibetan as well. The sentiment being expressed seems to be that the thoughts and actions that arise from attachment to this life are expected for an ordinary worldly person but are absolutely unacceptable for someone aspiring to be a spiritual practitioner.
378. *svārthamanaskāra, rang don yid byed*. The term *manaskāra* is often translated as "attention"; however, its meaning can vary depending upon the context in which it is being used. As it can also refer to a habitual mode of thought, I translate it here as "attitude." *AS* (p. 6) states: "What is attention? It is the bending of the mind. Its action is to cause the mind to keep hold of an object."
379. *yuvarāja, rgyal tshab*. In a secular sense, this term is applied to the crown prince of a reigning sovereign. In the dharma, it applies to Maitreya in the sense that he is the next buddha to appear in the world and, therefore, the successor to Buddha Śākyamuni.

380. *MSA*, ch. 5, v. 2.
381. That is, the selflessness of the person and the selflessness of entities. Earlier, selflessness was translated as "insubstantiality."
382. *'dzem bag*. This expression, translated as "embarrassment and care," is an abbreviation of two terms. The first syllable, "embarrassment" (*'dzem*), refers to the essential quality of both shame (*hrī, ngo tsha shes pa*) and abashment (*apatrāpya, khrel yod pa*). *AS* (p. 6) states: "What is shame? It is embarrassment (*'dzem pa, lajjā*) about objectional acts for reasons relating to oneself. Its action is to provide the support that allows you to restrain yourself from committing misdeeds. What is abashment? It is embarrassment about objectional acts for reasons relating to others. Its action is the very same as that of shame." The second syllable, "care" (*bag*), is an abbreviation of the term for mindfulness (*apramāda, bag yod*). *AS* (p. 6) states: "What is mindfulness? It is the cultivation of virtuous qualities and the guarding of the mind against contaminated qualities on the basis of avoidance of desire, avoidance of hatred, and the avoidance of ignorance, in conjunction with effort. Its action is to bring to culmination all mundane and transcendent excellence."
383. *āryācārya, slob dpon 'phags pa*. That is, Nāgārjuna.
384. *RA*, ch. 4, v. 81abc.
385. Ibid., ch. 5, v. 38d.
386. That is, the six perfections and compassion.
387. *RA*, ch. 5, v. 39.
388. *'dzem bag*. See note 382 (this chapter).
389. *udvega, skyo ba*. See this chapter, note 40 and ch. 7, "The Nectar That Is Like Highly Refined Gold," note 135.
390. *sambhāramārga, tshogs lam*. This is the name of the first of five levels in the overall Buddhist path. This path is described as having lesser, intermediate, and great forms. In the case of the Mahāyāna path, the path of accumulation is entered when a practitioner develops a genuine form of enlightenment mind. *AS* (p. 65) describes the principal forms of spiritual practice that are cultivated during this stage: "What is the path of accumulation? It consists of the following practices that are engaged in by ordinary persons: morality, restraining the doors of the senses, knowing moderation in relation to food, striving to remain alert throughout the day and during the first and last periods of the night, and abiding in a state of vigilance. It also consists of other virtuous factors, as well as the forms of wisdom that are derived from listening, reflection, and meditation, and through their cultivation one becomes a fit vessel for achieving the clear realization of ultimate reality and attaining the state of liberation."
391. *bālopacārikaṃ dhyāna, byis pa nye bar spyod pa'i bsam gtan*. This term appears in the *Laṅkāvatāra Sūtra*. There it is described as a form of spiritual practice cultivated by followers of the śrāvakas' and pratyekabuddhas' vehicles. The term "immature being" (*bāla, byis pa*) generally refers to an individual who has not achieved the status of an *ārya*.

392. This is the first line of the first of two verses that Candrakīrti cites in his *In Clear Words* (*Prasannapadā, Tshig gsal*). The complete first verse states: "Form resembles a mass of foam, feelings resemble a water bubble, / conceptions are like a mirage, formations are similar to the plantain trunk, / and consciousness resembles illusions—so declared the Kinsman of the Sun." Candrakīrti also refers to these verses in his *Commentary on "Entry into the Middle Way"* (*Madhyamakāvatārabhaṣya, dBu ma la 'jug pa'i bshad pa*) and his commentary to Āryadeva's *Four Hundred Verses* (*Catuḥśataka, bZhi brgya pa*). He identifies the verses as being from a sūtra of the Śrāvakayāna. See *Samyutta Nikāya*, part 3, section 22, *Connected Discourses on the Heaps* (*Khandhasaṃyutta*), sutta 95, titled "A Lump of Foam." Seven verses appear at the end of the discourse.

393. *arthapravicayadhyāna, don rab 'byed pa'i bsam gtan*. This expression also appears in the *Laṅkāvatāra Sūtra*, where it is described as a form of meditative absorption upon the insubstantiality of entities.

394. *darśanamārga, mthong lam*. *AS* (p. 66) states: "What is the path of seeing? In brief, it is a nonapprehending form of one-pointed concentration that is combined with wisdom and that follows the stage of the path of preparation known as the supreme worldly entity. It is also a form of knowledge that perceives apprehended objects and apprehending mental states precisely and in the same manner. In addition, it is a form of knowledge in which one experiences for oneself the true state of being in which the mental object associated with a conventionally designated personal self, the mental objects associated with conventionally designated entities have been eliminated, and the true state of being in which the mental objects associated with both forms of conventional designation have been entirely eliminated."

395. *tathatālambanadhyāna, de bzhin nyid la dmigs pa'i bsam gtan*.

396. All four of the meditative absorptions mentioned here, along with brief descriptions, appear in the second chapter of the *Laṅkāvatāra Sūtra*.

397. *prayogamārga, sbyor lam*. *AS* (p. 65) states: "What is the path of preparation? Those virtuous qualities that are present on the path of accumulation are also present on the path of preparation. There are also virtuous qualities on the path of preparation that are not present on the path of accumulation. They are the roots of virtue that are produced by a practitioner who has collected the accumulations and that are conducive to the attainment of complete discernment. Its four stages are the attainment of heat, the uppermost state, the forbearance that conforms to the truths, and the supreme worldly entity." "Complete discernment" (*nirvedha, nges par 'byed pa*) is a synonym for the path of seeing (see note 255, this chapter). Each of this path's four stages is described in terms of the one-pointed concentration and wisdom that possess progressively deeper forms of awareness regarding the nature of the truths and ultimate reality. This awareness culminates in the direct realization that marks the attainment of the path of seeing.

398. *mārakarma, bdud kyi las*. This phrase is used to describe an extensive range

of circumstances and reactions that constitute obstacles to the pursuit of the Mahāyāna path in the sense that they can confuse the practitioner or lead him or her astray. The entire eleventh chapter of the *Eight-Thousand-Line Perfection of Wisdom Sūtra* is devoted to this topic and numerous examples are presented there. See also ch. 7, "The Nectar That Is Like Highly Refined Gold," note 70.

399. *svabhāvakāya, ngo bo nyid sku.* Two principal Indian commentarial sources that describe a buddha's essence body are *The Ornament of Realization* (*Abhisamayālaṃkāra, mNgon par rtogs pa'i rgyan*) and *The Sublime Science of the Mahāyāna* (*Mahāyānottaratantraśāstra, Theg pa chen po'i rgyud bla ma'i bstan bcos*). Both describe it in terms of being a state that is unconditioned (*asaṃskṛta, 'dus ma byas*) and pure. Its unconditioned nature refers both to the ultimate nature of a buddha's transcendent awareness, which is its emptiness, and the quality of having attained the cessation of all the obscurations. Its purity also refers to these two unconditioned qualities. That is, the innate purity of the buddha's essence body is that the emptiness of a buddha's ultimate awareness is a quality that has existed primordially. The adventitious purity refers to the condition that is achieved through having abandoned all the obscurations. Tāranātha's description of the essence body includes the quality of a buddha's supreme transcendent knowledge. This knowledge is also associated with a separate aspect of buddhahood known as the "dharma body" (*dharmakāya, chos kyi sku*).

400. *sambhogakāya, longs spyod kyi sku.* The enjoyment body is described as possessing five fixed or certain attributes: certainty of location, which means it always remains in a buddha field known by the term Below None; certainty of retinue, which means that it is surrounded only by ārya bodhisattvas; certainty of physical attributes, which means that it is adorned with the thirty-two major marks and eighty minor marks of a great being; certainty of dharma teaching, which means that it teaches Mahāyāna dharma exclusively; and certainty of duration, which means that it will not give the appearance of entering nirvana until samsara has been emptied of all sentient beings.

401. This term refers to Mahāyāna āryas, who are the only beings besides other fully enlightened buddhas that are capable of coming to this realm in order to hear the Mahāyāna dharma directly from a buddha's enjoyment body.

402. *akaniṣṭha, 'og min.*

403. *nirmāṇakāya, sprul pa'i sku.* A buddha's emanation body can appear in many forms, including animals and even inanimate objects. Buddha Śākyamuni is an example of a "supreme" emanation body (*mchog gi sprul sku*) who appears in the world as a being who possesses all one hundred and twelve major and minor marks, gives the appearance of attaining enlightenment, and performs the twelve major deeds that begin with his descent from Tuṣita Paradise and end with his entering into nirvana.

404. That is, in ordinary samsaric realms.

405. *grub 'bras.* This term literally means "a result that is achieved" through having

successfully accomplished some task. In this case, it means that at the conclusion of a teaching within this tradition called the Stages for Entering the Teaching, it is often customary for either of these two rituals to be performed.

406. *rten*. See note 109 (this chapter) and ch. 4, "The Brilliant Illumination of the Path to Enlightenment," note 91. After having been consecrated, these objects are meant to be regarded as the actual entities of a buddha's body, speech, or mind, and not just their symbols.

407. *Bhadracaryapraṇidhāna, bZang spyod smon lam*. This devotional exercise is expressed in the first twelve verses of the prayer.

408. *'Phags pa spyan ras gzigs kyi dbyang phyug gis zhus pa'i chos bdun pa*. The colophon of the Tibetan version of this sūtra identifies Atiśa as the Indian paṇḍita under whose guidance it was translated. In his work on the rituals for generating enlightenment mind and receiving the bodhisattva vow (see note 413, this chapter), Atiśa notes that the seven spiritual qualities (*saptadharmā, chos bdun*), or precepts, that are taught in this sūtra promote the swift attainment of supernatural knowledge (*abhijñā, mngon par shes pa*). The seven spiritual qualities are as follows: do not even have thoughts about sexual intercourse, much less actually engage in the union of the two sexual organs; do not approach an unvirtuous friend, even in your dreams; do not assist an unvirtuous friend with a supportive attitude; use wisdom and skillful means to avoid developing pride and selfishness; abandon the mistaken concepts of being and nonbeing and develop a strong form of the door to liberation of emptiness; with a mind that conceives of it as being false and untrue, avoid taking pleasure in the illusory and dream-like samsara; and do not discredit the principles of cause and effect that relate to the doctrine of karma.

409. By this virtue may all beings / complete the accumulations of merit and wisdom / and attain the two forms of highest excellence / that arise from wisdom and merit." This is the final verse of Nāgārjuna's *Sixty Verses on Correct Reasoning* (*Yuktiśaṣṭikā, Rigs pa drug cu pa*).

410. This term is the name for the Hīnayāna system of moral discipline and vows. See ch. 8, "The Easy Path," note 65, for an explanation of the term. There are seven forms of prātimokṣa vows that can be taken by men and women as a lifelong form of discipline. These are the vows of (1) a fully ordained monk, (2) a fully ordained nun, (3) a probationary nun, (4) a novice monk, (5) a novice nun, (6) a layman, and (7) a laywoman. The eighth form of discipline is a one-day vow of fasting and abstinence from sensory pleasures (*upavāsasaṃvara, bsnyen gnas kyi sdom pa*).

411. *āryadeśa, 'phags pa'i yul*. An honorific name for the Indian subcontinent.

412. *Ratnakūṭa, dKon mchog brtsegs pa*. This is the name of a collection of forty-nine Mahāyāna sūtras that are grouped together in a distinct section of the Tibetan Kangyur.

413. This work is titled *The Ritual Method for Generating Enlightenment Mind and Receiving the Bodhisattva Vow* (*Sems bskyed pa dang sdom pa'i cho ga'i rim pa*).

It addresses rituals for generating both the aspirational and active forms of enlightenment mind.

414. *Bodhisattvabhūmi, Byang chub sems dpa'i sa.* This work, whose authorship is attributed to Ārya Asaṅga, forms section fifteen of a major work titled *The Stages of Spiritual Practice* (*Yogācārabhūmi, rNal 'byor spyod pa sa*).
415. *Śikṣāsamuccaya, bsLab pa kun las btus pa.* This is an anthology of passages taken mostly from Mahāyāna sūtras that were arranged by the compiler Śāntideva according to his own system of spiritual practice.
416. *Ratnameghasūtra, dKon mchog sprin gyi mdo.*
417. *Nam mkha'i snying po'i mdo.*
418. See note 109 (this chapter).
419. *ācārya, slob dpon.* While this term typically is understood to mean a spiritual "guide" or "teacher," it literally means one who is knowledgeable in the rules of conduct (*ācāra, spyod pa*). Here it refers to the individual who leads the ritual for receiving the bodhisattva vow. Asaṅga (*BBh*, English translation, p. 260) gives a brief description of the attributes that the preceptor should possess. They are generally considered to be threefold: the preceptor should be one who possesses and is observing the vow, one who is knowledgeable about the entire range of bodhisattva practice, and one who is capable of performing the ritual for conferring the vow. Later in the chapter (English translation, pp. 265–56), Asaṅga also identifies a series of bad qualities that the preceptor should not possess.
420. According to the traditional interpretation, "those who have not crossed over" (*atīrṇā, ma brgal ba rnams*) refers to arhats of the Hīnayāna who have not abandoned the obscurations to that which needs to be known; "those who have not been liberated" (*amuktā, ma grol ba rnams*) refers to beings like the worldly god Brahmā who are bound by both types of obscurations; "those who have not found relief" (*anāśvastā, dbugs ma phyin pa rnams*) refers to hell beings and the like who are suffering in the lower realms; and "those who have not attained ultimate happiness" (*anirvṛtā, mya nga las ma 'das pa rnams*) refers to all beings generally who have not yet achieved the "nonabiding nirvana" that is supreme enlightenment. Cf. the Tibetan translation of Abhayākaragupta's *Āmnāyamañjarī* (*Man ngag gi snye ma*), Dg.T. rgyud, vol. 6 (*cha*), f. 109b.
421. *spardhayā, 'gran pa'i phyir.* The original Sanskrit term can mean either "out of rivalry" or "out of emulation." I have used the former term to comply with the Tibetan translation; however, the notion of accepting the discipline out of a desire to emulate others or "follow the crowd" may be just as apt.
422. The first full verse states: "Emitting light rays as arrays of reception water, / as garlands of reception water and canopies of reception water; / scattering many kinds of reception water everywhere, / the great beings make offerings to the victors and their spiritual offspring." Additional verses can be recited by replacing the word "reception water" with the names of other forms of offerings, such as foot water, flowers, incense, lamps, scented water, food, and musical

instruments. See also ch. 12, "The Excellent Path of the Bodhisattvas," note 51, regarding the scriptural source of this verse.

423. The full verse states: "I make prostration to the tathāgata, / the savior endowed with great compassion, / the omniscient one and the supreme teacher, / and the field who is the ocean of merit and virtue" (*mgon po thugs rje che ldan pa / thams cad mkhyen pa ston pa po / bsod nams yon tan rgya mtsho'i zhing / de bzhin gshegs la phyag 'tshal lo*). There are also verses of homage to the dharma and the sangha that are often recited together with this verse that is addressed to Buddha Śākyamuni.

424. That is, all the bodhisattva precepts and all the bodhisattva morality.

425. *catvāri pārājayikasthānīyadharmāḥ, pham pa'i gnas lta bu'i chos bzhi*. While these four acts are not the same as the four expulsory offenses (*pārājikaḥ dharmaḥ, phas pham pa'i chos*) of the Śrāvakayāna moral code, they are meant to correspond to or resemble them in the sense that they cause the bodhisattva discipline to be destroyed. The four are (1) praising oneself and disparaging others by one due to being attached to gain and honor; (2) even though you possess wealth, refusing to give material objects to petitioners who are suffering and who have approached you in a correct manner, because of a greedy nature, as well as refusing to share dharma teachings with those who seek them and who have approached you in a proper manner because of your stinginess about the dharma; (3) due to having been overcome by anger, striking, harming, or causing injury to sentient beings, as well as, through harboring anger, refusing to accept an acknowledgment of wrongdoing made by others; and (4) because of being firmly devoted to counterfeit form of dharma, disparaging the bodhisattva collection of scriptures and taking pleasure in teaching a counterfeit form of dharma. Although Asaṅga's *BBh* describes them as numbering four acts, other scholars have interpreted them as being eight acts because each of the four is described in terms of two aspects.

426. These secondary offenses (*duścarita, nyes byas*) are presented in the morality chapter of Asaṅga's *BBh* (English translation, pp. 269–300) and are also listed in Candragomī's *Twenty Verses on the Bodhisattva Vow* (verses 9–20ab).

427. *śreyor 'rthin, legs par 'dod pa*. According to *MW* (s.v. "śreyor 'rthin"), this somewhat idiomatic Sanskrit term, which literally means "one who desires a better condition," can also be understood to mean "one who desires ultimate bliss"—i.e., the supreme goal. It is my impression that in Tibetan usage the term is meant in the more general sense of "betterment."

428. This epithet is another name for Maitreya (Mi pham).

429. This is a reference to Lama Serlingpa's royal heritage.

430. This patriarch of the Kadampa lineage is widely known by this epithet, that is, Drom Tönpa ('Brom ston pa).

431. See note 186 (this chapter).

432. The manuscript inserts his personal name, Sherap Drak (Shes rab grags), as an annotation.

433. Dro (*gro*) is the name of this master's clan; hence he is known by the epithet Dro Tönpa. His personal name, Dutsi Drak (bDud rtsi grags) is also included as an annotation.
434. mChims nam mkha' grags. Chim is a clan name.
435. The full personal name Drakpa Tsöndru (Grags pa brtson 'grus) is inserted as an annotation.
436. Full personal name is Losang Drakpa (bLo bzang grags pa).
437. This is an abbreviated version of the personal name Kunga Gyaltsen (Kun dga' rgyal mtshan, 1338–1440/01). He served as the thirteenth abbot of Narthang Monastery.
438. This lineage holder may be the individual listed on the BDRC website as Söpa Peldrup (bSod pa dpal grub; 1401–1470), who was the seventeenth abbot of Narthang Monastery.
439. *aurasaḥ putraḥ, thugs kyi sras.* In Tibetan usage, this term refers to a master's close and principal disciple. In a secular context, the Sanskrit term, which literally means "a son or daughter born from one's breast," is understood to mean a "legitimate son or daughter," that is, one born by a wife of the same caste married according to the rules (*MW,* s.v. "aurasa"). In the following passage from the sūtra titled *The Lion's Roar of Śrīmaladevī* ([*'Phags pa*] *Lha mo dpal phreng gi seng ge'i sgra*, f. 274a), the term is used to refer to an ārya bodhisattva: "Whatever beings see correctly, they are the sons or daughters of the Blessed One who are born from his breast."
440. This is possibly the Sakya master listed on the BDRC website as Drakpa Sönam (Grags pa bsod nams, fl. fifteenth century).
441. Full personal name is Kunga Drölchok (Kun dga' grol mchog).
442. The Tibetan epithet Jamgön (*'jam mgon*) is an honorific term meant to indicate that the teacher is considered to be an emanation of Mañjuśrī. The first syllable *jam* (*'jam*), usually translated as "gentle," is the Tibetan equivalent of the Sanskrit word *mañju*, which is the first part of Mañjuśrī's name. The second syllable *gön* (*mgon*), which means "lord" or "protector, is the Tibetan equivalent of the Sanskrit word *nātha*. Thus, the Sanskrit version of the title can be reconstructed as Mañjunātha.
443. *spyan snga ba.* This epithet, which literally means "one who is before the eyes," is given to a close disciple who is always in the presence of, and attending to, a spiritual master. This Kadampa master's personal name, Tsultrim Bar (Tshul khrims 'bar), which means "one whose morality shines brilliantly," forms part of the description of his spiritual qualities.
444. Bya yul ba. This descriptive name literally means "the one from the region of Ja." His personal name was Zhönu Ö (gZhon nu 'od).
445. gTsang pa Rin po che. See also note 188 (this chapter).
446. **stithi, gnas lugs.* This term is a synonym for the ultimate nature of emptiness.
447. Mus sman pa. It is assumed that Mumen is a place name. His personal name was Dutsi Charchen (bDud rtsi char chen).

448. This master also appears in the previous lineage. See note 437 (this chapter).
449. This master's name, Lha Chungwa Yeshe Rinchen, is separated into two parts with Yeshe Rinchen (Ye shes rin chen) addressed in one line and Lha Chungwa (Lha chung ba) in a second line.
450. His full personal name was Jampa Lhundrup (Byams pa lhun grub).
451. sNe'u zur pa. This epithet means "the one from Neusur," the name of a region in Tibet. His personal name was Yeshe Bar (Ye shes 'bar). This third Kadam lineage is generally identified as having been established by Gönpawa Wangchuk Gyaltsen (dGon pa ba dBang phyug rgyal mtshan), who was Neusurpa's teacher.
452. *gzhung pa ba*. This lineage proceeds from Potowa Rinchen Sel (Po to ba rin chen gsal, 1027–1105) through his disciple Sharawa Yönten Drak (Sha ra ba Yon tan grags, 1070–1141). The name derives from the six Indian treatises that were taught as the principal sources for the instruction. See also ch. 9, "An Essential Summary of the Method of Practice in the System of the Stages of the Path to Enlightenment," note 54.
453. *gdams ngag pa*. This Kadam lineage was propagated by Chengawa Tsultrim Bar (sPyan snga ba Tshul khrims 'bar). This lineage derives its name from the fact that the teachings were largely given on the basis of the lamas' personal instructions.
454. *abhisaṃpratyaya, yid ches pa*. This term refers to the type of faith that one should develop toward the doctrine of karma. The ideal form of this "belief" is a form of conviction that derives from having conducted a proper investigation of the Buddha's doctrine. Dharmakīrti describes a threefold method of investigation in his *Extensive Treatise on Knowledge* (*Pramāṇavarttika*), ch. 2, vv. 215–17. This view is presented in support of Dignāga's aphorism (*Pramāṇasamuccaya*, ch. 2, v. 5): "An authoritative person's speech possesses the nature of inference because of its universal noncontradictoriness." I have discussed this analysis in *The Inner Science of Buddhist Practice*, pp. 70–89.
455. See note 450 (this chapter).
456. *Bodhipathapradīpa, Byang chub lam gyi sgron ma*. See translation of the root text in chapter 1 of this volume. The commentary could be any of a number of commentaries on the verses, not all of which have survived.
457. *Satyadvayāvatāra, bDen pa gnyis la 'jug pa*.
458. There are no Indian commentaries to this text listed in the Tengyur. Assuming this is a reference to a native Tibetan work, I am uncertain of its identity.
459. *Madhyamakopadeśa, dBu ma'i man ngag*. While it is not certain that Tāranātha is referring to this commentary, there is a *vṛtti* or explanatory commentary to Atiśa's root text in the Tengyur that was written by an Indian scholar named Prajñāmokṣa (Shes rab thar pa).
460. See note 447 (this chapter) for this master's name. I have not located any instruction manual (*khrid yig*) by this individual.
461. Lum pa ba. His personal name was Yeshe Wangchuk (Ye shes dbang phyug). He

is identified as having being a disciple of both Potowa Rinchen Sel and Kamapa Rinchen Gyaltsen. I have not located this text.

462. *dPe chos,* pp. 57–59. Potowa Rinchen Sel developed many similes to explain different points in the Lamrim teachings. Historical records indicate that three editions of these similes were compiled by his disciples. The collection most widely available today is called *The Jewel Heap of Edifying Similes* (*dPe chos rin chen spungs pa*), compiled by Chegompa Sherap Dorje (lCe sgom pa Shes rab rdo rje, fl. early twelfth century). This scholar also wrote a commentary on the similes known as *An Extensive Commentary on "The Jewel Heap of Edifying Similes"* (*dPe chos rin chen spungs pa'i 'bum 'grel*).

463. mKhan chen Lung rigs rgya mtsho. A Sakya master of the sixteenth century. This figure recognized Tāranātha as the reincarnation of his own teacher Kunga Drölchok (Kun dga' grol mchog, 1507–1566).

464. See note 368 (this chapter) for description of the root text. The best-known commentary is a work by Lhadri Gangpa (Lha 'bri gang pa) titled *A Commentary on the Kadam Instruction Manual Titled "Blue Udder"* (*bKa' gdams kyi man ngag be'u bum sngon po'i 'grel pa*).

465. I believe this reference should be understood as follows. The "root text" is a verse text titled *The Precious Supreme Path That Is the Oral Commentary of the True Spiritual Teacher* (*Yang dag pa'i dge ba'i bshes gnyen gyi zhal gyi gdams pa lam mchog rin po che*), written by the fourth abbot of Narthang Monastery, Drotön Dutsi Drak (Gro ston bdud rtsi grags, 1153–1232). Dutsi Drak's verse text is embedded in, and forms the framework for, a commentary by Chim Namkha Drak (mChims nam mkha' grags, 1210–1285), the seventh abbot of Narthang, which is titled *The Mahāyāna Supreme Path* (*Theg chen lam mchog*). These two works constitute the "root text and commentary on the Supreme Path."

466. I assume this "Chim" to be Chim Namkha Drak (mChims nam mkha' grags). See also note 434 (this chapter). I do not know what specific "instruction manuals" (*khrid yig*) are being referenced in this statement.

467. *nyams khrid.* This is a form of oral teaching in which a lama explains instructions in a manner that his or her own personal experience has determined to be most beneficial to the development of the disciples. While this type of instruction is also translated as "experiential instruction," I use the term "practical" here to differentiate this system from a different form of instruction, for which I reserve the term "experiential instruction" (*myong khrid*). According to that system, disciples are taught instructions for each individual topic, one at a time, and then directed to meditate on those instructions until they generate genuine spiritual realizations. Following that, the instructions that pertain to subsequent topics are presented in a similar manner until the entire body of teachings have been presented.

468. The expression "Stages of the Teaching" (*bsTan rim*) is also a generic term for Kadam works on this genre of teachings.

469. *rgyal khams pa.* This expression is meant to indicate an individual does not

reside in any fixed location and prefers to move about frequently to different places.

470. sGrol ba'i mgon po, also written as sGrol ma'i mgon po. This is the Tibetan form of the epithet Tāranātha, which literally means "the lord who liberates." His personal name was Kunga Nyingpo (Kun dga' snying po).
471. Rin chen r gya mtsho'i sde. The last syllable of the name as it appears here, De (*sde*), is the Tibetan equivalent of the Sanskrit honorific *sena*, which is affixed to the names of persons as a kind of title (*MW*, s.v. "sena"). Otherwise, this master's personal name can be written simply as Rinchen Gyatso.
472. *jagannātha, 'gro ba'i mgon po*. An honorific title that means "savior of the world."
473. *niḥśreyasa, nges par legs pa*. See ch. 4, "The Brilliant Illumination of the Path to Enlightenment," note 20, for an explanation of this term.
474. *vidyādhara, rig 'dzin*. A title that is used generally to refer to a tantric teacher. It also is understood to describe a person who has attained transcendent awareness and possesses extraordinary spiritual powers. The Sanskrit *vidyā* (*rig pa*) can refer variously to such things as "knowledge," "spells," or "magical skills."
475. sPyan ras gzigs dbang phyug. This honorific, which is the Tibetan form of Avalokiteśvara, is presumably meant to suggest that this master was regarded as an emanation of this deity. This line is a reference to Trinle Shingta ('Phrin las shing rta), the seventh hierarch of the Drukpa Kagyu lineage.
476. This descriptive phrase includes the word *kunga* (*ānanda, kun dga'*) or "happiness," which is part of this master's name: Kunga Gelek Pelbar (Kun dga' dge legs dpal 'bar).
477. This descriptive phrase also includes the word *kunga* that forms part of the master's full name—Kunga Lhundrup Gyatso (Kun dga' lhun grub rgya mtsho).
478. This master from the Karma Kagyu lineage was one of Jamgön Kongtrul direct teachers and his inclusion here suggests that the latter received teachings from him on this body of instruction.
479. This name refers to Jamgön Kongtrul, identifying him as the author of this addendum. *Guṇa* is Sanskrit for the Tibetan "yönten" (*yon tan*), which is part of his ordination name, Ngawang Yönten Gyatso (Ngag dbang yon tan rgya mtsho).

11. A Guidebook for the Path to Great Awakening: The Ritual for Generating Enlightenment Mind according to the System Followed in the Lineage of the Profound View

1. *Zab mo lta brgyud lugs kyi sems bskyed pa'i cho ga byang chub chen po'i gzhung lam*, *DNZ*, vol. 3 (*ga*), pp. 275–321.
2. "Homage to the gurus, buddhas, and bodhisattvas." This Sanskrit statement of homage is written with a dative singular ending. The more standard spelling would show the dative plural ending: *namo gurubuddhabodhisattvebhyaḥ*.
3. *rten*. This term refers to the religious objects that are to be placed on an altar and

regarded as the actual body, speech, and mind of an enlightened being or beings. The vessel for speech would be a scripture volume, such as a sūtra on the Perfection of Wisdom. The vessel for an enlightened being's mind is typically a stupa reliquary. See also ch. 7, "The Nectar That Is Like Highly Refined Gold," note 29.

4. *ci 'byor pa*. That is, in the most excellent manner that your resources will permit.
5. *upacāra, nye bar spyod pa*. See ch. 9, "An Essential Summary of the Method of Practice," note 31.
6. That is, milk, butter, and yogurt.
7. *dPal mgon*. This term is often a reference to a group of seventy-five protector deities.
8. *Triskandhaka Sūtra*. *Phung po gsum pa'i mdo*. This "sūtra" is, in fact, an excerpt from the *Vinayaviniścaya Upālipariprcchā Sūtra* (*'Dul ba rnam par gtan la dbab pa nye bar 'khor gyis zhus pa'i mdo*) that is also known by the title *A Bodhisattva's Confession of Transgressions* (*Byang chub sems dpa'i ltung ba bshags pa*). The "three heaps" are the spiritual acts of confessing one's misdeeds, rejoicing at the virtue carried out by oneself and others, and dedicating one's virtue. The recitation begins with statements of homage to thirty-five buddhas who are said to have special powers to purify a practitioner of his or her bad deeds.
9. This is a reference to the first twelve verses of *The Aspirational Prayer for Excellent Spiritual Conduct* (*Bhadracaryapraṇidhāna, bZang po spyod pa'i smon lam*).
10. That is, as these words are being repeated, each disciple should state his or her name in place of the phrase "so-and-so."
11. "Until I reach the seat of enlightenment, / I go for refuge to the buddhas; / I likewise also go for refuge to the dharma / and to the assemblage of bodhisattvas."
12. *BCA*, ch. 3, vv. 22, 23. "Just as the previous sugatas took hold of enlightenment mind, / and just as they engaged successively in the trainings of the bodhisattvas, // so, too, do I generate enlightenment mind to benefit the world / and so, too, shall I practice the trainings in due order."
13. *BCA*, ch. 3, vv. 25, 26. "Now my life has become fruitful; / this human existence has been made worthwhile. / Today I have been born into the family of the buddhas; / now I have become an offspring of the buddhas. // From now on my actions should accord however / is most fitting for my lineage, / so that this flawless lineage / does not become stained."
14. May I generate those forms of the precious enlightenment mind / that I have not yet generated; / and may those forms that I have generated never diminish / and develop further to ever higher levels."
15. *catvāri balāni, stobs bzhi*. See ch. 8, "The Easy Path," note 42.
16. This power is usually explained to mean carrying out virtuous deeds for the purpose of purifying yourself of your past evil deeds. Śāntideva's *Compendium of Training* presents a range of specific activities that represent this form of antidote.
17. *sor chud pa'i stobs*. This is not the traditional name for any of the four powers. Nevertheless, it is part of the Mahāyāna doctrine relating to the practice

of confession that it has the ability to eliminate the negative force that one's former misdeeds would otherwise retain.

18. See note 8 (this chapter).
19. *SL*, v. 59. In his *Sūtra Anthology* (*Sūtrasamuccaya, mDo kun las btus pa*), Nāgārjuna identifies the canonical source for this simile as a sūtra from the *Saṃyuktāgama* collection. While the Sanskrit original of this discourse does not survive, a Pali version, which is titled the *Chigalla Sutta*, can be found in the *Saṃyutta Nikāya* (56.48).
20. *ŚS*, v. 2.
21. *Abhisamayālaṃkāra, mNgon par rtogs pa'i rgyan*, ch. 1, v 19ab.
22. *Mahāyānasūtrālaṃkāra, Theg pa chen po mdo sde'i rgyan*, ch. 4, v. 1d. Vasubandhu's commentary to these lines identifies the twofold aim as the mind being fixed upon (1) attaining "great"—that is, supreme—enlightenment and (2) acting on behalf sentient beings.
23. *BCA*, ch. 1, vv. 15, 16.
24. *Myang 'das*. This appears to be a reference to the *Mahāparinirvāṇa Sūtra* (*Mya ngan las 'das pa chen po*); however, these lines do not appear in that scriptural source.
25. I have not identified this source text.
26. *sambhāramārga, tshogs lam*. This is the name of the first of five paths. It is entered at the point that one succeeds in generating enlightenment mind. See ch. 10, "The Essence of Nectar," note 390, for a listing of the spiritual practices that are cultivated during this stage of the path.
27. *rgyun mtha'*. See ch. 4, "The Brilliant Illumination of the Path to Enlightenment," note 4.
28. That is, this unwanted consequence would be true, if only an ārya can generate active enlightenment mind.
29. *MSA*, ch. 4, v. 7.
30. The *Gaṇḍavyūha Sūtra* states: "O son of good family, just as even a cracked diamond, which is the best of all precious gems, surpasses a gold ornament, in the same way the diamond that is the act of having generated the intention to attain omniscience, even though it may be cracked in that it is an attitude that has fallen short of action, still surpasses all the gold ornaments of the spiritual qualities that are possessed by śrāvakas and pratyekabuddhas."
31. *pramatta, bag med gyur*. This is the noun formed from the past participle of the verb "to be heedless" (*pramad, bag mi bya*). It means "one who has become heedless" or "one who has become inattentive."
32. That is, from the point that you have generated the active form of enlightenment mind.
33. *BCA*, ch. 1, v. 19.
34. *sDong po bkod pa'i mdo*. This sūtra is not listed as a separate entry in the Tibetan Kangyur; rather it forms the final section of the *Avataṃsaka Sūtra* (*mDo sde phal po che*).

35. *Nam mkha'i snying po'i mdo.*
36. Book 1, ch. 10 (English translation, pp. 237–311) contains an extensive explanation of the topic of Mahāyāna morality. This presentation also includes a description of the ritual for conferring the bodhisattva vows (see pp. 260–65).
37. *mātsarya, ser sna. AS* (p. 8) states: "What is stinginess? It is the acquisitiveness of mind toward personal possessions that is a form of desire possessed by persons who are attached to gain and honor. Its action is to provide support for the avoidance of simplicity." "Simplicity" (*saṃlekha, yo byad bsnyungs pa*) is the virtuous principle by which an individual seeks to keep desire in check by avoiding the accumulation of possessions that are not necessary for the pursuit of a spiritual life.
38. *BCA*, ch. 5, v. 102.
39. See ch. 4, "The Brilliant Illumination of the Path to Enlightenment," note 91, and ch. 10, "The Essence of Nectar," note 109.
40. *PSV* (English translation, p. 318) states: "Regarding this description, the beings referred to here as 'deities' are the ones called Those of Great Fruit (*bṛhatphala, 'bras bu che*). They inhabit a region that lies within the third level of the fourth meditative absorption." They are born in this region as a result of having generated the state of composure without conception (*asaṃjñisamāpatti, 'du shes med pa'i snyoms par 'jug pa*). These beings manifest a conception only at the time of their birth and their death. The state of composure without conception is not meant to be cultivated because it leads to rebirth among those long-lived deities who have no opportunity for further spiritual development and who are destined to fall back to the desire realm in their next life. It is only developed by those who mistakenly consider it a means of attaining liberation.
41. *ŚS*, p. 11.
42. *BCA*, ch. 7, v. 45.
43. *ŚL*, v. 52.
44. *nye 'khor ba'i dmyal ba*. See ch. 10, "The Essence of Nectar," note 71.
45. sPu gri brdal ba'i thang. This is another name for a region that is also called the "Razor-Filled Path." See ch. 10, "The Essence of Nectar," note 75, and the related description in the main body of the text.
46. *AK*, ch. 3, v. 60abc. The pronoun "those" is a reference to the eight hot hells.
47. *pratyekanaraka, nyi tshe ba'i dmyal ba*. See ch. 10, "The Essence of Nectar," note 79.
48. *SL*, v. 86.
49. Ibid., v. 91.
50. Ibid., vv. 89, 90.
51. Ibid., v. 102.
52. Ibid., v. 98ab. See ch. 10, "The Essence of Nectar," note 134, regarding the phrase "falling down at death" (*cyavanam* also *cyuti, 'chi pho ltung ba*).
53. Ibid., v. 74.
54. *RGV*, ch. 4, v. 50b.

55. *SL*, v. 104.
56. *nirupadhinirvāṇa*, *lhag med kyi mya ngan las 'das pa*. This refers to the state that is entered when a Hīnayāna arhat dies.
57. *ājavaṃjavavivartanadṛṣṭanaṣṭa*, *skye shi 'phos pa ngo ma shes pa*. The Sanskrit expression *ājavaṃjava* literally means "coming and going swiftly," but it is understood to mean the condition of being born and dying in samsara continuously. The Tibetan translation adds that beings are not "recognized" (*ngo ma shes pa*) as being one's relatives, but this is only implied by the Sanskrit phrase that they are "appearing and disappearing" (*dṛṣṭanaṣṭa*).
58. *ŚL*, v. 96.
59. Ibid., v. 97.
60. *RGV*, ch. 1, v. 39.
61. *apratisthitanirvāṇa*, *mi gnas pa'i mya ngan las 'das pa*.
62. *RGSG*, ch. 5, v. 8ab.
63. Ibid., ch. 19, v.5.
64. *śāstā*, *ston pa*. Literally "the teacher," in this context the epithet refers to Buddha Śākyamuni.
65. This is presumed to be the beginning of a statement of supplication addressed to the spiritual master in which the disciple requests to be watched over from now until the attainment of enlightenment.
66. This phrase "please be cognizant" is expressed in Tibetan by the single word *kyen* (*mkhyen*), which is the imperative of the verb "to know." It means that you believe the Three Jewels' protection will occur through their awareness of your faith in them.
67. These eight spiritual beings are recognized as having attained the tenth ārya stage of the Mahāyāna path: Maitreya, Mañjuśrī, Vajrapāṇi, Avalokiteśvara, Samantabhadra, Kṣitigarbha, Ākāśagarbha, and Sarvanivaraṇaviṣkambhī.
68. That is, your forehead, two hands, and two knees.
69. *BCA*, ch. 2, v. 24.
70. *Kun rig*. This is a deity of the Yoga Tantra class.
71. This mantra is *oṃ namo bhagavate vajrasārapramardane tathāgatāya arhate samyaksambuddhāya tadyathā oṃ vajre vajre mahāvajre mahātejavajre mahāvidyāvajra mahābodhicittavajre mahābodhimaṇḍopasaṃkramaṇavajre sarvakarmaviśodhanavajre svā hā*.
72. *BCA*, ch. 2, v. 1.
73. Ibid., ch. 2, v. 2.
74. Ibid., ch. 2, v. 3.
75. Ibid., ch. 2, v. 4.
76. Ibid., ch. 2, v. 5.
77. Ibid., ch. 2, v. 6.
78. Ibid., ch. 2, v. 7.
79. Ibid., ch. 2, v. 8.
80. Ibid., ch. 2, v. 9.

81. Ibid., ch. 2, v. 10.
82. Ibid., ch. 2, v. 11.
83. Ibid., ch. 2, v. 12.
84. Ibid., ch. 2, v. 13.
85. Ibid., ch. 2, v. 14.
86. Ibid., ch. 2, v. 15.
87. Ibid., ch. 2, v. 16.
88. Ibid., ch. 2, v. 17.
89. Ibid., ch. 2, v. 18.
90. Ibid., ch. 2, v. 19.
91. Ibid., ch. 2, v. 20.
92. *BCA*, ch. 2, v. 21b.
93. That is, other great ārya bodhisattvas.
94. Ibid., ch. 2, v. 22.
95. Ibid., ch. 2, v. 23.
96. *Caturdharmanirdeśasūtra*, *Chos bzhi bstan pa' mdo*. See ch. 8, "The Easy Path," note 42.
97. See ch. 10, "The Essence of Nectar," note 274, for an explanation of these two types of "objectionable act" (*avadya*, *kha na ma tho ba*).
98. *BCA*, ch. 2, vv. 64–66.
99. See ch. 10, "The Essence of Nectar," note 141.
100. *BCA*, ch. 3, v. 1.
101. These two lines only appear in the Tibetan translation of *BCA*, not in the extant Sanskrit editions.
102. *tāyin*, *skyobs pa*. *BCAP* (p. 37) gives two glosses of this term. One is that the term literally indicates that a buddha is a "speaker" in the sense that he reveals the path that he himself experienced. In support of this gloss Prajñākaramati cites a line from Dharmakīrti's *Pramāṇavarttikā* (ch. 2, v. 147a), which states: "The Buddha is a savior in that he proclaimed the path that he himself experienced" (*tāyaḥ svadṛṣṭamārgokti*). The second interpretation is that the term literally means that a buddha is a "continued succession" (*saṃtāna*, *rgyud*) in the sense that that he remains in the state of nonabiding nirvana for as long as samsara exists.
103. Ibid., ch. 3, v. 2.
104. *śāsin*, *ston pa*. The Tibetan translation does not explicitly include this term; however, it does occur in the Sanskrit original. *BCAP* (p. 37) interprets the term as referring to bodhisattvas. Prajñākaramati also glosses it two ways. One interpretation is that bodhisattvas are "teachers" in a figurative sense because they will become buddhas through cultivating the methods that bring about the attainment of enlightenment. In support of this explanation, he again cites a line from Dharmakīrti's *Pramāṇavarttikā* (ch. 2, v. 140cd), which states: "Prior to his or her enlightenment, the bodhisattva is one who cultivates the spiritual methods; in keeping with this sense, this is understood to be the act of

teaching" (*upāyābhyāsa evāyaṃ tādarthyāc chāsanaṃ matam*). A second gloss is that bodhisattvas are "teachers" in that they possess the discipline of morality, which they employ to draw sentient beings to the dharma by practicing generosity and the rest of the four means of gathering a spiritual following. In this way, they cause sentient beings to enter the true path.

105. *BCA*, ch. 3, v. 3.
106. Ibid., ch. 3, v. 4.
107. The phrase "give the appearance of" (*nidarśana, tshul bstan pa*) is meant to signify that, in reality, buddhas are immortal and never truly enter nirvana. The following verse is found in the *Suvarṇaprabhāsottamasūtra* (ch. 2, v. 30): "The buddha does not enter nirvana. / The dharma does not disappear. / A buddha gives the appearance of entering nirvana / in order to ripen sentient beings."
108. *BCA*, ch. 3, v. 5.
109. Ibid., ch. 3, v. 6.
110. Ibid., ch. 3, v. 7.
111. Ibid., ch. 3, v. 8. The end of an intermediate kalpa is marked variously by outbreaks of widespread murder, pestilence, or famine. See ch. 8, "The Easy Path," note 33, and ch. 10, "The Essence of Nectar," note 54, for further descriptions of the term "intermediate kalpa."
112. *BCA*, ch. 3, v. 9. The Sanskrit term *upakaraṇa* (*yo byad*), which is translated here as "useful objects," has a range of meanings, including "the act of assisting," "implement," and "a means of subsistence." *BCAP* (p. 39) glosses the term as "whatever objects sentient beings desire, beginning with beds, seats, clothing, food, jewelry, and unguents."
113. *BCA*, ch. 3, v. 10.
114. *sarvatyāga, thams cad btang ba*. "Complete renunciation" is an expression that is a synonym for nirvana itself. It is different from the attitude that aspires to achieve liberation, which is also often rendered as "renunciation." See ch. 7, "The Nectar That Is Like Highly Refined Gold," note 135.
115. *BCA*, ch. 3, v. 11.
116. Ibid., ch. 3, v. 12.
117. Ibid., ch. 3, v. 13.
118. Ibid., ch. 3, v. 14.
119. The Tibetan translation reads the Sanskrit *kruddhāprasannā* as "angry" or "tranquil"—that is, *kruddhā* or *prasannā* (*dad pa*); however, Sanskrit rules of orthography allow the words to be interpreted as "angry" or "unsettled"—which is to say, *kruddhā* or *aprasannā* (*ma dad pa*). Both Prajñākaramati and Vibhūticandra read the two terms in the latter manner in their commentaries, which would seem to be the preferred meaning for this context.
120. *BCA*, ch. 3, v. 15.
121. Ibid., ch. 3, v. 16.
122. Ibid., ch. 3, v. 17.
123. Ibid., ch. 3, v. 18. The Tibetan translation adds a line to this verse, apparently

because the first word *dīpa* (*mar me*), or "lamp," in some editions is read as *dvīpa* (*gling*), or "island," which can also figuratively mean "a place of refuge" or "shelter," as it is understood here. Prajñākaramati and Vibhūticandra both read the word as *dīpa*; Kalyāṇadeva's (*dge ba lha*) commentary reads it as *dvīpa*. None of these Indian commentaries give both interpretations.

124. *BCA*, ch. 3, v. 19.
125. Ibid., ch. 3, v. 20.
126. Ibid., ch. 3, v. 21.
127. *SR*, ch. 9, v. 16.
128. *BCA*, ch. 3, v. 22.
129. Ibid., ch. 3, v. 23.
130. Ibid., ch. 1, v. 9.
131. Ibid., ch. 1, vv. 13–14ab.
132. This verse is cited in *A Lamp for the Path to Enlightenment*, v. 15.
133. I am not aware of an extant Sanskrit version of this verse. The verse that appears in the Tibetan translation of the sūtra is slightly different. It has "merit" (*puṇya*, *bsod nams*) for "good qualities" (*guṇa*, *yon tan*) and "sugata" (*bde gzhegs*) for "victor" (*jina*, *rgyal ba*).
134. *BCA*, ch. 1, v. 10.
135. Ibid., ch. 1, v. 11.
136. Ibid., ch. 1, v. 12.
137. This does not appear to be a quote from the sūtra. However, the following passage from Drolungpa's *Great Treatise on the Stages of the Teaching* (*bsTan rim chen mo*) may well be the source for this statement: "It is declared in the *Sūtra on Questions of Sāgaramati* that these three acts are an unsurpassed form of reverence and honor to the tathāgatas: generating enlightenment mind, upholding the true dharma, and having compassion toward living beings."
138. These verses are also cited in *A Lamp for the Path to Enlightenment*, vv. 16, 17.
139. *Sangs rgyas phal po che*. The account of Sudhana's pilgrimage to meet spiritual teachers makes up the subject matter of the *Gaṇḍavyūha Sūtra*, which forms the final section of the *Avataṃsaka Sūtra*. See also note 34 (this chapter).
140. While this passage is cast as though it were a direct quote from the *Maitreyavimokṣa* section of the *Gaṇḍavyūha Sūtra*, it is actually a close paraphrase of the corresponding passage; moreover, the similes cited here are only a small selection of the ones that are presented in the sūtra.
141. *BCA*, ch. 3, v. 25.
142. Ibid., ch. 3, v 26.
143. Ibid., ch. 3, v 27.
144. Ibid., ch. 3, v 28.
145. Ibid., ch. 3, v 29.
146. Ibid., ch. 3, v 30.
147. Ibid., ch. 3, v 31.
148. Ibid., ch. 3, v 32.

149. Ibid., ch. 3, v 33.
150. See above, p. 395.
151. *BCP*, vv. 5–7. "With the best flowers, the best garlands, / the best music, unguents, and parasols, / the best lamps, and the best incense, I make offerings to these victors. // With the best clothing and the best fragrances, / with packets of aromatic powder equal in size to Mount Meru, / with all the best forms of superior arrangements, /I make offerings to these victors. // I also emanate before all the victors / the extensive offerings that are unsurpassed. / By the power of this devotion to excellent spiritual conduct, / I honor and worship all the victors."
152. The complete mantra is *oṃ svabhāvaśūddhāḥ sarvadharmāḥ svabhāvaśuddho 'ham.*
153. *oṃ akāro mukhaṃ sarvadharmāṇām ādyanutpannatvāt.*
154. That is, the three syllables *oṃ āḥ hūṃ.*
155. That is, *oṃ bhūmipatisaparivāra.*
156. This is the second person imperative of the verb "to go."
157. *apramāda, bag yod.* See ch. 8, "The Easy Path," note 59, for a definition of this virtuous mental factor.
158. *satpuruṣa, skyes bu dam pa.* Literally a "good person" or a "wise person," I translate the term as "true spiritual being" to indicate a person who is both virtuous and wise. See also ch. 5, "A Verse Compendium of the Spiritual Practices of the Stages of the Path," note 12.
159. See ch. 4, "The Brilliant Illumination of the Path to Enlightenment," note 128, for the canonical source of this topic.
160. Ibid.
161. The term "feeling" (*vedanā, tshor ba*) refers to the second of the five heaps, which can be either painful, pleasurable, or neither pleasurable nor painful. It would seem that in this context the term refers to intense forms of physical or mental pain.
162. *pañcānantaryāṇi karmāṇi, mtshams med pa lnga'i las.* They are to kill one's father; to kill one's mother; to kill an *arhat*; through an act of malice, causing the tathāgata to shed blood; and to create a schism in the wheel of the sangha. They are called "immediate" because a person who commits any of them will be reborn in the hells in his or her very next life.
163. While taking the life of a bhikṣu is mentioned in the *Ākāśagarbha Sūtra* as part of the description of this third root transgression, this line does not appear in Śāntideva's summary verses. The line does, however, appear in the summary verses in Ngulchu Tokme Zangpo's treatise (f. 90b), which is the principal source used by Jamgön Kongtrul for his own work (see colophon).
164. *ŚS*, p. 41.
165. Ibid.
166. Meaning "individual liberation" (*prātimokṣa, so sor thar pa*), this is the name for the Hīnayāna system of moral discipline. See ch. 8, "The Easy Path," note 65, and ch. 10, "The Essence of Nectar," note 410.

167. *uttarīmanuṣyadharmamṛṣāvāda, mi'i chos bla ma rdzun du smra ba.* This form of falsehood constitutes one of the four transgressions that are called "extreme forms of defeat" (*pārājika, phas pham pa*) in that they lead to expulsion from the sangha if committed by a fully ordained monk or nun. While this exact expression does not occur in either the *Ākāśagarbha Sūtra* or Śāntideva's *Compendium of Training*, this root transgression does address the false claim of having attained a realization of emptiness. See ch. 4, "The Brilliant Illumination of the Path to Enlightenment," note 273, ch. 7, "The Nectar That Is Like Highly Refined Gold," note 149, and ch. 13, "Opening the Door to the Dharma," note 653, for comments about the four "extreme forms of defeat."
168. *śramaṇa, dge sbyong.* A generic term that can be used to refer to followers of any spiritual tradition; here it is meant to refer to Buddhist monks and nuns.
169. *rgyal rigs.* This is the name of the second of the four major Indian castes. It is made up of those who carried out military and governing duties, as opposed to Brahmins, who represented the religious class.
170. The Tibetan text reads *'bril ba*, which is not a familiar term. The *Ākāśagarbha Sūtra* describes how members of the ruling class collect the fines by forcing the religious ascetics to turn over their property to corrupt ministers, who then dole it out to members of the ruling class.
171. *ŚS*, p. 41. The complete passage states: "Describing emptiness to those whose minds have not been prepared; / diverting from enlightenment those who have set out for buddhahood; / joining others to the Mahāyāna after having induced them to give up the moral code of prātimokṣa; / holding that the Śrāvakayāna does not abandon desire and the rest; / causing others to hold that view; proclaiming one's own virtuous qualities; / disparaging others for the sake of gain, honor, or praise; / falsely claiming 'I have attained forbearance of the profound'; / causing ascetics to be punished; giving away the property of the Three Jewels; / appropriating what has been donated; causing the practice of quiescence to be given up; / and causing the property of meditators to be given to those who recite scriptures— / these root transgressions are causes for being born in the great hells."
172. *RGSG*, ch. 31, v. 5. For a description of the expression "extreme form of defeat" (*pārājika, phas pham pa*), see ch. 4, "The Brilliant Illumination of the Path to Enlightenment," note 273.
173. See ch. 10, "The Essence of Nectar," note 251 and ch. 12, "The Excellent Path of the Bodhisattvas," note 109.
174. *sgrub pa'i bslab bya.* Earlier this heading was expressed as "The activities that are to be practiced" (*sādhya* or *sādhanīya, sgrub bya*).
175. See ch. 4, "The Brilliant Illumination of the Path to Enlightenment," note 174. The middling version of this discourse is the *Perfection of Wisdom Sūtra* in twenty-five thousand lines.
176. See ch. 10, "The Essence of Nectar," note 274, for an explanation of these two types of "objectionable act" (*avadya, kha na ma tho ba*).

177. This statement does not appear to be a direct quote.

178. The morality chapter of the *Stage of a Bodhisattva* is made up of nine sections, of which all-inclusive morality (*sarvaśīla, tshul khrims thams cad*) forms the second. This opening portion of this topic makes these two assertions: (1) all-inclusive morality is made up of the morality that pertains to householder bodhisattvas and the morality that pertains to bodhisattvas who have gone forth into the homeless state; and (2) the morality that is observed by both of these factions consists of these three types: the morality of restraint, the morality of acquiring virtuous qualities, and the morality that acts on behalf of beings.

179. This statement is a paraphrase of a passage from this sūtra that is cited in *ŚS*, p. 10.

180. *ŚS*, p. 41. This phrase appears in a line from Śāntideva's summary verses on the root transgressions of the bodhisattva vow, some of which were quoted earlier.

181. See ch. 8, "The Easy Path," note 58. This mental factor is counted as one of twenty secondary mental afflictions (*upakleśa, nye ba'i nyon mongs pa*). For a description of its antidote, mindfulness, see ch. 8, "The Easy Path," note 59.

182. In addition to the four virtuous mental factors that represent the essence of mindfulness—that is, avoidance of desire, avoidance of hatred, avoidance of ignorance, and effort—cultivation of recollection and vigilance is also considered essential. *BCA*, ch. 5, v. 23: "To those who wish to guard their minds, / I make this appeal with palms joined: / You must use every effort to observe / both recollection and vigilance." Asaṅga describes the generic form of recollection as follows (*AS*, p. 6): "What is recollection (*smṛti, dran pa*)? It is the avoidance of inattentiveness toward a familiar object. Its action is to prevent distraction." Śāntideva describes vigilance (*samprajanya, shes bzhin*), which is a form of wisdom, as follows (*BCA*, ch. 5, v. 108): "In short, the essential nature / of vigilance is simply this: / to examine again and again / the state of your body and mind." The role of vigilance is to observe both one's body in its physical surroundings and one's mind in order to avert potential obstacles and to recognize any improper motivations or mental attitudes that might arise. Moreover, the ability to develop a proper degree of vigilance is dependent on the cultivation of recollection. Again, Śāntideva (*BCA*, ch. 5, v. 33) states: "The time at which vigilance arrives / and, once come, does not depart again / is when recollection, in order to guard / the mind, remains fixed at its door."

183. *hrī, ngo tsha shes pa*. See ch. 7, "The Nectar That Is Like Highly Refined Gold," note 145.

184. *apatrāpya, khrel yod pa*. See ch. 7, "The Nectar That Is Like Highly Refined Gold," note 144.

185. *SR*, ch. 24, v. 28.

186. *SR*, ch. 35, v. 4. The verse immediately before this describes a person who, with a pure mind, would honor ten million trillions of buddhas with food, drink, parasols, banners, and lamp offerings, for tens of millions of kalpas that equal

the number of the sands of grain in the Ganges River. This verse then compares that person to one who observes the precepts for one day and a night during a time of degeneration and states that the latter person would obtain greater virtue.

187. See ch. 4, "The Brilliant Illumination of the Path to Enlightenment," note 91 and ch. 10, "The Essence of Nectar," note 109.
188. This method of confession is presented in *The Compendium of Training* (ch. 4, p. 40), based on a passage from the *Ākāśagarbha Sūtra*, which declares in part: "If those bodhisattvas who have heard the name of the bodhisattva Ākāśagarbha wish to see him and, out fear of falling into the lower realms, wish to confess their root transgressions to him, and if they make salutation to bodhisattva Ākāśagarbha and they call out his name, that son of good family (*kulaputra, rigs kyi bu*—i.e., Ākāśagarbha) will appear before them according to the nature of their fortune, either in his very own form or as a Brahmin, up to he will stand before them as a young girl. Then he will prompt that novice bodhisattva to confess his or her transgressions, however they may have arisen." The passage goes on to describe that, following the confession, Ākāśagarbha will instruct the novice bodhisattva in such a way that he or she will become established in a state of irreversibility.
189. The *Ākāśagarbha Sūtra* describes perfuming the area with incense.
190. The entreaty is worded as follows: "O Aruṇa, Aruṇa, Highly Compassionate One, Highly Fortunate One, Highly Ascendant One, please cover me here in the Rose Apple continent with compassion. Please make my words known quickly to Ākāśagarbha, the highly compassionate one. Please ask him to reveal to me in a dream, the means by which I may confess my transgression and regain the qualities of wisdom and means within the esteemed Mahāyāna."
191. Literally "reddish-colored one," meaning the color of the early morning at dawn.
192. See note 8 (this chapter).
193. *śeṣāpattī, ltung ba lhag ma. BCAP* (p. 75) states: "The expression 'remaining transgressions' means those transgressions other than the root transgressions. Or it means those transgressions other than the ones that were committed knowingly and then remedied. Or it means those transgressions that were committed due to loss of recollection and lack of vigilance."
194. *BCA*, ch. 5, v. 98.
195. *Caturdharmanirdeśasūtra, Chos bzhi bstan pa'i mdo*. This is a short discourse that is the canonical source for the four powers described here. The original Sanskrit of the central presentation from this discourse is found in Śāntideva's *Compendium of Training*, ch. 8.
196. See ch. 10, "The Essence of Nectar," note 106.
197. *ŚS*, vv. 3cd. "Here" means in this treatise, *The Compendium of Training*.
198. *ātmabhava, bdag gi lus*. The Sanskrit term *ātmabhāva* is almost universally translated into Tibetan as *lus*, which has the unambiguous meaning of the

"physical body." However, the Sanskrit term literally means "existence of the self" and thus can also refer to a "soul" or "self." Given the Buddhist doctrine of selflessness, the latter would never be its intended meaning, except in a nominal sense. As evidence that even for Buddhists the term's meaning is not limited to the physical body, *PSV* (English translation, p. 270) glosses the Sanskrit *amiṣa* as "craving for one's individual existence" (*ātmabhāvatṛṣṇā*, *lus la sred pa*) and then further glosses "individual existence" (*ātmabhāva*) in this context as referring to the "inner grasping heaps" (*ādhyatmikā upādhānaskandhā*, *nang gi nye bar len pa'i phung po rnams*), clearly indicating that the term is not limited to the physical body. At another place in the same text (*PSV*, p. 342), the term *ātmabhāva* is glossed as "name and form" (*nāmarūpa*, *ming dang gzugs*), a term that in Buddhist usage is identified with all of the five heaps, and thus represents the totality of an individual's being—both mental and physical—not just the body. Therefore, in those cases, I translated the term as "individual existence." Here, I have left it translated as "body," with the understanding that it can also be taken to refer to one's entire being.

199. *ŚS*, v. 4.
200. *BCA*, ch. 5, v. 1ab.
201. *BCA*, ch. 5, v. 23. The wording of the original verse has been altered here. The original text states: "You must use every effort to observe / both recollection and vigilance." See note 182 (this chapter). The phrase "even when your life is at risk" also does not appear in the original verse.
202. The Sanskrit original of this verse does not appear to be extant. It is likely that the Sanskrit word translated here as "body" is *aṅga*, which can mean both a "limb" of the body and the "body" itself. The Tibetan version of this verse that appears in the Kangyur collection (Toh. 325) is worded slightly differently: "Wealth is given for the sake of human limbs. / Limbs are given for the sake of one's life. / But, wealth, limbs, and so, too, one's life— / All should be given here to safeguard the dharma."
203. The full verse states: "From today on, I offer myself / To you as a servant. / Please accept me as a disciple / And enjoy my share-offerings."
204. See ch. 9, "An Essential Summary of the Method of Practice in the System of the Stages of the Path to Enlightenment," note 14.
205. *Maitreyapraṇidhāna*, *Byams pa'i smon lam*. This prayer appears in the first of the two sūtras entitled *Maitreya Paripṛcchā Sūtra* (Toh. 85) that is included in the *Ratnakūṭa* (*dKon brtsegs*), or *Heap of Jewels*, section of the Tibetan Kangyur.
206. The full verse states: "After achieving, by this merit, the All-Seeing One's state / and defeating the enemy of wickedness, / may I rescue the world from the ocean of existence / that is convulsed by the great waves of old age, sickness, and death." The Sanskrit original of this verse is found in Haribhadra's commentary *Abhisamayālaṃkārāloka*, where it is described as an aspirational prayer that was performed by the Bhagavān while still a bodhisattva.
207. The full verse states: "May I generate those forms of the precious enlightenment

mind, / that I have not yet generated; / and may those forms that I have generated never diminish / and develop further to ever higher levels."

208. This work doesn't have a formal title and is simply described at the end as *The Ritual for Generating the Aspirational and Active Forms of Enlightenment Mind according to the System of the Great Master Śāntideva* (*sLob dpon chen po zhi ba lha'i lugs kyi smon 'jug sems bskyed kyi cho ga*). The passage cited here appears at the very end of the work.
209. dGra las rnam par rgyal ba. This Indian master was one of Lord Atiśa's spiritual teachers. See listing in bibliography under author's name.
210. This is a reference to his commentary on Śāntideva's *Entry into the Conduct That Leads to Enlightenment (Bodhicaryāvatāra)*. See listing in bibliography under author's name.
211. That is, the first twelve verses of this aspirational prayer.
212. Thogs med bzang po dpal, 1295–1369. The second work in this volume, a root text for the Seven-Point Mind Training, was extracted from this master's commentary on this teaching that appears in vol. 4 of *The Treasury of Precious Instructions*. See note 208 (this chapter) for Tokme Zangpo Pel's work on the ritual for conferring the two forms of enlightenment mind.

12. The Excellent Path of the Bodhisattvas: A Ritual for Generating Enlightenment Mind and Accepting the Bodhisattva Vow according to the Mahāyāna System of Great Vastness

1. *Theg chen shin tu rgyas pa'i sems bskyed dang sdom pa'i cho ga byang chub sems dpa'i lam bzang*, *DNZ*, vol. 3 (*ga*), pp. 323–75.
2. *shin tu rgyas pa'i lugs*. This is a Mahāyāna lineage of instruction that was transmitted by Maitreya to Asaṅga. It is generally thought of as the lineage whose instruction is the principal source on the topic of extensive bodhisattva activities. The principal source for the ritual described in this treatise is the morality chapter of Asaṅga's *Stage of a Bodhisattva*.
3. *pitā bodhisattvānām*, *byang chub sems dpa' rnams kyi yab*. This phrase appears in a list of the Buddha's qualities presented in *SR*, ch. 3.
4. *jinaputra* also *jinasuta*, *rgyal ba'i sras*. "Victors' offspring" is a synonym for a bodhisattva. "Victor" (*jina*, *rgyal ba*) is a synonym for a buddha. See ch. 4, "The Brilliant Illumination of the Path to Enlightenment," note 34, for an explanation of this latter epithet.
5. See ch. 4, "The Brilliant Illumination of the Path to Enlightenment," note 91, and ch. 11, "A Guidebook for the Path to Great Awakening," note 3.
6. Munīndra, Thub pa'i dbang po. This is an epithet of Buddha Śākyamuni.
7. See ch. 9, "An Essential Summary of the Method of Practice in the System of the Stages of the Path to Enlightenment," note 31.
8. *lTung gshags*, *Āpattideśanā*. This is a shortened form of the title *A Bodhisattva's*

Confession of Transgressions, which is an alternate name for what is also referred to as the *Three Heaps Sūtra* (*Phung po gsum pa'i mdo*). See ch. 11, "A Guidebook for the Path to Great Awakening," note 8.

9. This is typically done by rinsing the mouth with consecrated water and reflecting that this cleanses you of impurities.
10. *SL*, v. 59. For additional details on scriptural sources for this simile, see ch. 11, "A Guidebook for the Path to Great Awakening," note 19.
11. *ŚS*, v. 2.
12. *BSV*, v. 1cd–2a. The first two verses of this treatise, in their entirety, state the following: "Having bowed with devotion to the buddhas and their spiritual offspring, / and having worshiped them to the best of your ability, / that morality of the bodhisattvas who exist / throughout all the directions and times, // which is a treasure of all forms of merit, / should be accepted with a supreme attitude / from a knowledgeable and capable guru / who is maintaining the vow." This text is a summary of the bodhisattva vow as it is taught in the morality chapter of Asaṅga's *Stage of a Bodhisattva*.
13. The final subordinate clause of this description is meant to indicate that the enlightenment mind of such a bodhisattva ārya is the ultimate form of enlightenment mind, whose object, emptiness, is being realized in a nondual manner and therefore could not conform to the defining characteristic of the conventional enlightenment mind that is defined by the main clause.
14. *pṛṣṭalabdhajñāna*, *rjes thob ye shes*. This type of awareness occurs after a practitioner has arisen from a state of mental composure in which he or she has experienced a direct realization of ultimate truth. It is referred to as a "mundane" form of knowledge because it does not directly perceive the true nature of entities; nevertheless, it is considered an element of the truth of the path in that the practitioner's mind is still informed by his or her prior transcendent realization.
15. *MSAVṛBh* (vol. 154, f. 54b): "Regarding the five types of generating enlightenment mind that are referred to as the form of enlightenment mind that is accepted through a verbal agreement (*samādānasāṃketika*, *yang dang par blang ba brda' las byung ba*), the conventional enlightenment mind that is generated by the power of a spiritual friend is said to arise in a form that has the quality of being unstable because it is capable of being given up at a later time."
16. *vipakṣa*, *mi mthun phyogs*. This term refers to a negative quality that opposes or is the opposite of a specific virtuous quality. For example, stinginess is the negative quality that opposes generosity.
17. *MSA*, ch. 4, v. 7.
18. *samparigraha*, *yongs 'dzin*. This term literally means "complete assistance." Here it refers to the "outer" assistance that is received in the form of one's spiritual teachers. The term is found in the *Perfection of Wisdom Sūtra* literature and the related *Abhisamayālaṃkāra* treatise, which describe both an inner and an outer form of "complete assistance." *AA* (ch. 1, v. 37) states: "The qualities of mental

fearlessness and so on, and the person who instructs about insubstantiality and so on, / and the abandonment of their opposing factors are in every way the qualities of complete assistance." Thus, inner complete assistance is the practitioner's own skillful means that remains fearless regarding the implications of profound emptiness and that avoids developing such opposing qualities as the selfish attitude of a śrāvaka or pratyekabuddha. Outer complete assistance is the spiritual teacher who gives instruction in such subjects as the insubstantiality of all entities, as well as the need to reject the opposing factors of Māra's deeds and evil companions.

19. *ŚL*, vv. 63, 64. All the beings other than humans mentioned in the second verse are either worldly gods or different classes of celestial spirits. No Sanskrit version of verse 64 is extant.
20. *durlabho mānuṣyapratilābhaḥ | durlabhā kṣaṇasaṃpadviśuddhiḥ*. These statements appear in the section of the sūtra in which the young pilgrim Sudhana approaches the teacher Jayoṣmāyatana (rGyal ba'i drod kyi skye mched). When Sudhana is told by the teacher to jump over a precipice into a pit of fire, he hesitates, reflecting to himself about the rare and favorable human existence he would be giving up in order to comply with what he was told to do. As he reflects in this manner, he experiences a series of visions that encourage him to go forward with the act. When he jumps off the cliff, he develops a form of one-pointed concentration called "well established" (*supratiṣṭhita, shin tu brtan pa*) as he is falling and another concentration called "supernormal knowledge of the bliss of tranquility" (*praśamasukhābhijña, rab tu zhi ba'i bde ba mngon par shes pa*) when his body touches the fire.
21. *BCA*, ch. 7, v. 14.
22. *SL*, v. 55.
23. *BCA*, ch. 4, v. 19.
24. *SL*, v. 86.
25. Ibid., v. 91.
26. Ibid., v. 89.
27. Ibid., v. 74.
28. *RGV*, ch. 4, v. 50bc.
29. *SL*, v. 104.
30. *nirupadhiśeṣanirvāṇa, lhag ma med pa'i myang ngan las 'das pa*. This is the nirvana that occurs when a Hīnayāna arhat's life comes to an end.
31. *ŚL*, v. 96.
32. Ibid., v. 97.
33. *RGV*, ch. 1, v. 39.
34. Ibid., ch. 19, v.5.
35. The original Sanskrit of this passage is cited in the first *Bhāvanākrama*.
36. Śāstā, sTon pa. This is an epithet of Buddha Śākyamuni. This instruction means that you should regard the preceptor as appearing in the form of Buddha Śākyamuni.

37. I have not identified the source of this citation.
38. This is a reference to the first seven verses of the *BCP.*
39. Two hands, two knees, and forehead.
40. These seven heaps represent Mount Meru, the four continents, and the sun and moon.
41. This appears to be a reference to the well-known verse: "Having been visualized as a buddha field, I offer this ground—anointed with incense and upon which flowers are strewn, / adorned by Mount Meru, the four continents, and the sun and moon. / May all beings partake of a supremely pure buddha field."
42. That is, as these words are being repeated, each disciple should state his or her name.
43. See ch. 11, "A Guidebook for the Path to Great Awakening," note 66.
44. That is, he or she accepts the Three Jewels as an object of refuge.
45. **tadbhāva, de dngos*. That is, he or she takes refuge as one who desires to attain the state of buddhahood.
46. *MSA*, ch. 3, v. 11a. The Sanskrit original of this verse is not extant.
47. *mahāmuni, thub pa chen po*. That is, Buddha Śākyamuni.
48. This group of spiritual beings, who are all tenth-stage ārya bodhisattvas, is made up of Kṣitigarbha, Ākāśagarbha, Avalokiteśvara, Vajrapāṇi, Maitreya, Sarvanirvaraṇaviṣkambhin, Samantabhadra, and Mañjuśrī.
49. *kṣetra, zhing*. See ch. 8, "The Easy Path," note 40, for a description of this term. In this context, the term should be understood to mean a "field of virtue" (*guṇakṣetra, yon tan gyi zhing*).
50. An alternate version of this line states: "Those who are firmly established in the trainings."
51. That is, the verse would be recited first, followed by the mantra. These verses are an adaptation of a series of verses that appear both in chapter 12 of the *Flower Garland Sūtra* (*Avataṃsakasūtra, Sangs rgyas phal po che*) and a separate sūtra titled *The Jewel Lamp Dhāraṇī Sūtra* (*Ratnolkādhāraṇīsūtra, dKon mchog ta la la'i gzungs*, Toh. 145). These verses are also cited in chapter 18 of Śāntideva's *Compendium of Training*. The first verse in the latter work states: "Emitting light rays as flower arrays, / as flower garlands, and as flower canopies; / scattering many kinds of flowers everywhere, / the great beings make offerings to the victors." This verse would be recited here, inserting "reception water," "flowers," "incense," "lamps," "perfumed water," "food," and "musical instruments" for each of the respective offerings. The last line is also usually revised to as follows: "The great beings make offerings to the victors and their spiritual offspring." See also ch. 9, "An Essential Summary of the Method of Practice," note 32, for a reference to these verses.
52. *suprasannacitta, rab tu dang ba'i sems*. The term "clarity" (*prasāda, dang ba*) refers to the type of faith that is developed toward the Three Jewels. Besides this sense of purity of mind, the term also includes the qualities of tranquility and

reverential joy. *PSV* (English translation, pp. 283, 284) states: "Faith in the Lord Buddha is the clarity of mind that is demonstrated by a bristling of the body hair or the flowing of tears and is felt toward that object that has perfected all virtuous qualities and completely removed all faults. Faith in the dharma is clarity of mind toward that state which is the termination of suffering and its cause [i.e., the Truth of Cessation and especially nirvana itself], as well as that which directly brings the attainment [of that state; i.e., the Truth of the Path] or that which elucidates [either of those two; i.e., the scriptural form of the dharma]. Faith in the sangha is clarity of mind toward those who have escaped from the mire of samsara and those who are traversing the path that will free them from the mire of samsara."

53. *BCA*, ch. 2, v. 2.
54. Ibid., ch. 2, v. 3.
55. Ibid., ch. 2, v. 4.
56. Ibid., ch. 2, v. 5.
57. Ibid., ch. 2, v. 6.
58. Ibid., ch. 2, v. 8.
59. Ibid., ch. 2, v. 10.
60. Ibid., ch. 2, v. 11.
61. Ibid., ch. 2, v. 12.
62. Ibid., ch. 2, v. 13.
63. Ibid., ch. 2, v. 14.
64. Ibid., ch. 2, v. 15.
65. Ibid., ch. 2, v. 16.
66. Ibid., ch. 2, v. 17.
67. Ibid., ch. 2, v. 18.
68. Ibid., ch. 2, v. 19.
69. Ibid., ch. 2, v. 20.
70. *oṃ akāro mukhaṃ sarvadharmānāṃ ādyanutpannatvāt.*
71. *śuklapakṣa, dkar phyogs.* The "white" or virtuous faction refers to dharma practitioners and other individuals who are aligned with the dharma.
72. *BCP*, v. 8.
73. *pṛthagjana, so so skye bo.* See ch. 7 "The Nectar That Is Like Highly Refined Gold," note 129, and ch. 10, "The Essence of Nectar," note 141.
74. *BCP*, v. 9.
75. Ibid., v. 10.
76. Ibid., v. 11.
77. Ibid., v. 12.
78. This verse is cited in *AAA* (p. 283); the source text was not identified.
79. *gotra, rigs.* In explanation of *MSA*, ch. 3, v. 4d, Vasubandhu (*MSAVy*, p. 11) writes: "It should be understood that the term *gotra* means that which causes good qualities to come out. Thus, it means 'that from which all good qualities

arise and come forth.'" The Mahāyāna form of the spiritual lineage is the quality by means of which a bodhisattva becomes fit for and capable of attaining unsurpassed true and complete enlightenment.

80. *Madhyamakahṛdaya*, ch. 1, v. 6.
81. *MSA*, ch. 4, v. 3a.
82. *pūrvaṃgamā, sngon du 'gro ba.* That is, it is the mental state that necessarily precedes the generating of enlightenment mind.
83. *Theg pa chen po'i sde snod* (Toh. 56). While there is a very similar passage (Dg.K. dkon rtsegs, vol. *ga*, f. 144a) in the sūtra of this name that is contained in the *Ratnakūṭa* section of the Kangyur collection, it does not have the exact same wording as the passage that is cited here. The identical wording, however, is found in in Nāgārjuna's *Sūtrasamuccaya*, and this seems to be the source for this citation. The original Sanskrit does not appear to be extant; however, the very next statement in the *Bodhisattvapiṭaka* also appears in a quotation from the *Akṣayamatinirdeśa Sūtra* that is cited in Śāntideva's *Compendium of Training* (ch. 16, p. 151).
84. See ch. 7, "The Nectar That Is Like Highly Refined Gold," note 127.
85. See citation of Nāgārjuna's *Letter to a Friend*, v. 74, p. 440.
86. *mDo dran pa nye bar bzhag pa.* See ch. 10, "The Essence of Nectar," note 83 for a description of this canonical source.
87. These two verses are actually found in the *Lalitavistara Sūtra.*
88. *LV*, ch. 13 v. 71.
89. Ibid., ch. 13 v. 69.
90. *duḥkhaduḥkhatā, sdug bsngal gyi sdug bsngal.* See ch. 7, "The Nectar That Is Like Highly Refined Gold," note 124.
91. *vipariṇāmaduḥkhatā, 'gyur ba'i sdug bsngal.* See ch. 8, "The Easy Path," note 77. See also *Inner Science of Buddhist Practice* (pp. 111–20) for a comprehensive discussion of various Buddhist scholars' views on this type of suffering.
92. See ch. 7, "The Nectar That Is Like Highly Refined Gold," note 126.
93. The text here describes a body position that is a form of kneeling. However, *BBh* (Sanskrit edition, p. 105; English translation, p. 262) describes either of two positions that may be assumed. The relevant passage states that "the candidate should place his or her right knee on the ground or sit in a squatting position." There, the Tibetan phrase *tsog pur 'dug pa* (*utkuṭikasthita*) refers to a position different from kneeling that can best be described as a crouching or squatting position. For a physical description of this position, see ch. 4, "The Brilliant Illumination of the Path to Enlightenment," note 102.
94. *adhyāśaya, lhag pa'i bsam pa.* See ch. 4, "The Brilliant Illumination of the Path to Enlightenment," note 43.
95. *ambhonidhi, chu gter.* Literally "treasury of waters," this is a poetic term for the ocean.
96. *apratiṣṭhitanirvāṇa, mi gnas pa'i mya ngan las 'das pa.* The supreme enlighten-

ment of a buddha is referred to by this term because it does not abide in either of the extremes of samsaric existence or Hīnayāna nirvana.

97. *BCA*, ch. 3, v. 25.

98. These precepts (*śikṣāpada, bslab bya*) are the ones associated with the acceptance of the aspirational form of enlightenment mind. The precepts associated with the bodhisattva vow are discussed below.

99. *SR*, ch. 4, v. 16.

100. Sha ra ba Yon tan grags, (1070–1141). An early Kadampa master who propagated the system of instruction taught by Potowa Rinchen Sel (Po to ba Rin chen gsal, 1027–1105).

101. This topic is also known as abandoning the four black qualities and cultivating the four white qualities. See ch. 4, "The Brilliant Illumination of the Path to Enlightenment," note 128, for the canonical source of this instruction.

102. *visaṃvādanatā, slu ba*. This original Sanskrit of this term typically means "to break one's word," but it can also mean to make a false assertion (cf. *MW*, s.v. "visaṃvādanatā"). However, because the Tibetan equivalent is usually understood to mean "to deceive," that is how we have translated the term here. The source for this topic is the *Kāsyapaparivarta Sūtra*. See ch. 4, "The Brilliant Illumination of the Path to Enlightenment," note 128.

103. Śāstā, sTon pa. This is an epithet of Buddha Śākyamuni. This means that you should regard all bodhisattvas as if they were the Buddha himself.

104. v. 31. Sanskrit original is extant. See online version at University of Oslo's Bibliotheca Polyglotta: https://www2.hf.uio.no/polyglotta/index.php.

105. See ch. 4, "The Brilliant Illumination of the Path to Enlightenment," note 43.

106. "Others" should be understood to mean "all sentient beings."

107. That is, due to seeing the extent to which sentient beings are subject to faults, you make the decision that you are no longer willing to pursue the welfare of all sentient beings.

108. *RGSG*, ch. 31, v. 5. The term "extreme form of defeat" (*pārājika, phas pham pa*) refers to any of four offenses that lead to expulsion from the sangha. See ch. 4, "The Brilliant Illumination of the Path to Enlightenment," note 273.

109. *yāma*, also *prahāra, thun tshod*. This term is understood to constitute one-sixth of a day—which is to say, a timespan of four hours. It is regarded as the span of time during which a mental lapse can be corrected without destroying one's production of enlightenment mind.

110. The phrase "harming your own mind" should be understood here to mean the act of mentally abandoning some particular sentient being or beings.

111. This verse appears in *Asvabhāva's (Ngo bo nyid med pa) *Upanibandhana* commentary (Dg.T., sems tsam, vol. 12 (*ri*), f. 253b) to Asaṅga's *Mahāyānasaṃgraha.*

112. See *The Flower Ornament Scripture* (English translation of the *Avataṃsaka Sūtra*) (Boston: Shambhala, 1993), pp. 1476–8.

113. This passage appears in Atiśa's *Ritual Method for Generating Enlightenment*

Mind and Receiving the Bodhisattva Vow (*Sems bskyed pa dang sdom pa'i cho ga'i rim pa*).

114. See *Bbh*, part 1, ch. 5 (English translation, pp. 106–29) for a discussion of six forms of supernatural knowledge (*abhijñā*, *mngon par shes pa*).
115. See also ch. 10, "The Essence of Nectar," note 408, for a description of this scripture.
116. *bya dang 'dra ba'i sems kyis*. The Tibetan phrase literally reads "with a bird-like mind," which would seem to be an odd expression. I take it to be a translation of the Sanskrit *sapakṣacittena*, which means literally "with the mind of a partisan or friend" (*sapakṣa*, *phyogs dang bcas pa*), and, thus, "with the mind of one who is supportive."
117. In the sūtra, Avalokiteśvara asks Buddha Śākyamuni what qualities should be cultivated by a bodhisattva who has just developed enlightenment mind. The Buddha responds by identifying these seven. The listing of the qualities that is given here differs somewhat from the version that appears in the sūtra. In addition to slightly different wording for the individual qualities, what has been identified here as the sixth quality does not appear at all in the Tibetan translation of the sūtra. See also ch. 10, "The Essence of Nectar," note 408, for the version of the seven qualities as they are described in the sūtra.
118. There are seven forms of the prātimokṣa vow that are meant to be observed for one's lifetime. See ch. 4, "The Brilliant Illumination of the Path to Enlightenment," note 80.
119. *skor*. This term is translated variously as a particular "cycle," "set," or "body" of teachings. It can also mean simply explanations "about" or "concerning" some particular subject.
120. That is, Lord Atiśa, Dīpaṃkara Śrījñāna.
121. See note 58 (this chapter) and the complete verse that is cited in the main text.
122. This is a reference to *BCP*, vv. 5–7. See note 36 (this chapter) for an earlier reference to the first seven verses from this prayer. These three verses state: "With the best flowers, the best garlands, / the best music, unguents, and parasols, / the best lamps, and the best incense, / I make offerings to these victors. // With the best clothing and the best fragrances, / with packets of aromatic powder equal in size to Mount Meru, / with all the best forms of superior arrays/ arrangements, / I make offerings to these victors. // I also emanate before all the victors/ the extensive offerings that are unsurpassed. / By the power of this devotion to excellent spiritual conduct, / I honor and worship all the victors."
123. See note 113 (this chapter). See also Atiśa's *Lamp for the Path to Enlightenment*, v. 23, where he makes explicit reference to *The Stage of a Bodhisattva* as the authoritative source for this ritual.
124. *Bodhisattvabhūmi*, *Byang chub sems dpa'i sa*.
125. English translation, p. 260.
126. *A Lamp for the Path to Enlightenment*, v. 21.
127. *Bodhisattvasaṃvaraviṃśikā*, *Byang chub sems dpa'i sdom pa nyi shu pa*.

128. *BSV*, v. 2cd. These two lines are the continuation of a statement that begins in verse 1cd. The complete statement declares: "That morality of the bodhisattvas who exist / throughout all of the directions and times, // which is a treasure of all forms of merit, / should be accepted with a supreme attitude / from a knowledgeable and capable guru / who is maintaining the vow."
129. See note 36 (this chapter).
130. English translation, pp. 260–61.
131. *BCA*, ch. 5, vv. 5, 6.
132. Ibid., ch. 1, vv. 18, 19.
133. *bodhisattvapiṭakamātṛkā, byang chub sems dpa'i sde snod kyi ma mo*. Within *The Stage of a Bodhisattva*, Asaṅga makes reference to his treatise with this expression a number of times. The Sanskrit term being translated here as "manual," *mātṛkā* (*ma mo*), is an expression that was also used to refer to the early Buddhist tabular compilations of abhidharma terminology and their defining characteristics. As such, *The Stage of a Bodhisattva* can be described as a guidebook for all of the vast and profound subjects taught throughout the canonical literature of the Mahāyāna tradition.
134. English translation, p. 261.
135. *spardhayā, 'gran pa'i phyir*. The original Sanskrit term can mean either "out of rivalry" or "out of emulation." I have used the former term to comply with the Tibetan translation; however, the notion of accepting the discipline out of a desire to emulate others or "follow the crowd" may be just as apt.
136. *cetasaḥ prasādaḥ, sems kyi dang ba*. *PSV* (English translation, pp. 283, 284): "Faith in the Lord Buddha is the clarity of mind that is demonstrated by a bristling of the body hair or the flowing of tears and is felt toward that object that has perfected all virtuous qualities and completely removed all faults." Also (*PSV*, English translation, p. 284): "The type of faith that is called 'clarity of mind' is a quality that opposes turbidity of mind. Therefore, if the mind is accompanied by it, the turbidity of the root mental afflictions and the secondary mental afflictions will not arise. It is called 'clarity of mind' because the presence of faith causes the mind to become clear and bright. This clarity of mind is a mental factor that resembles the special jewel that can cause water to become clear. It is described as clarity of mind to indicate that it does not have the nature of clear form (*rūpa*, *gzugs*), since it is not form. Its action is to serve as a support for aspiration."
137. *abhilāṣa, mngon par 'dod pa*. *PSV* (English translation, p. 284): This type of faith "desires to achieve or develop those entities possessed of good qualities that are capable of being achieved or developed. Since this is a form of desire, would it not then be either craving (*tṛṣṇā, sred pa*) or aspiration (*chanda, 'dun pa*)? It is not either one. It is not craving, because it has a virtuous entity as its object. Nor is it aspiration, because aspiration must be preceded by faith."
138. *abhisaṃpratyaya, yid ches pa*. *PSV* (English translation, p. 284): This type of faith "believes in entities that do exist and are either possessed of good qualities

or bad qualities." Here, it is the faith that believes with justification and conviction that the buddhas and bodhisattvas do, in fact, possess the spiritual qualities that they are said to possess.

139. This verse is recited to carry out the act of offering oneself to the buddhas and bodhisattvas. See p. 450, the text that accompanies note 58 (this chapter), for the complete verse.

140. See note 79 (this chapter).

141. *cetanā, sems pa*. See ch. 10, "The Essence of Nectar," note 101.

142. *SR*, ch. 9, v. 16.

143. *grāhya, gzung ba*. See ch. 4, "The Brilliant Illumination of the Path to Enlightenment," note 81.

144. *grāhaka, 'dzin pa*. Ibid., note 82.

145. English translation, pp. 262–63.

146. *ārocana, mkhyen par gsol ba*. The original Sanskrit term simply means a "declaration" or "announcement" (cf. *BHSD*, p. 104); however, the Tibetan equivalent translates literally as "a request that asks the buddhas and bodhisattvas to be cognizant" that the disciples have accepted the bodhisattva vow.

147. *Bbh* (English translation, p. 263) has "perceives all sentient beings" rather than "perceives all entities."

148. *jñānadarśana, ye shes kyi gzigs pa*. *BŚPBh* (f. 173b) states: "Knowledge grasps what is not visible; perception grasps an object that is directly present." *BŚPṬ* (f. 202b) states: "The perception that arises by the knowledge that is preceded by a buddha's or a great bodhisattva's attention is 'knowledge-perception.' Alternatively, a buddha's and a great bodhisattva's knowledge itself is perception because it engages objects in a direct manner."

149. *Bbh* (English translation, p. 264) states: "Those buddhas and great bodhisattvas become fully aware, in accordance with reality, that a bodhisattva named so-and-so in this particular world sphere has received the acceptance of the discipline of bodhisattva morality from another bodhisattva named so-and-so."

150. *pādapadma, zhabs kyi pad ma*. *MW* (s.v. "pādapadma") defines this as "'foot-lotus,' a foot beautiful as a lotus."

151. This is a reference to the first four verses of the *BCP*: "However many man-lions whatsoever that appear / in all the three times and the ten directions, / I honor them all without exception, / pure in body, speech, and mind. // With bodies equal in number to the atoms in the fields / and a mind that is present before all the Victorious Ones, / I make obeisance to all the victorious ones / by the power of the prayer for excellent spiritual conduct. // In each atom there are buddhas equal to all the atoms, / each one seated in the midst of the buddhas' spiritual progeny— / I conceive of the entire entity-source thus, / as filled in its entirety with victorious ones. // Expressing their inexhaustible oceans of praiseworthy qualities / with oceans of sound arising from all the limbs of voice, / I recite the spiritual qualities of all the victorious ones / and extol all the ones who have attained ultimate well-being."

152. *Abhayamudrā, skyabs sbyin gyi phyag rgya.* Literally the "gesture that conveys freedom from fear," it is made by holding the right hand next to the chest with the palm facing outward and the fingers pointing upward.
153. *BSV*, v. 3.
154. *BŚPṬ* (f. 202b) states: "'A particular type of sign' refers to the trembling of the buddhas' and bodhisattvas' seats."
155. *BSV*, vv. 5, 6.
156. *paryavasthāna, kun nas kris pa.* This is a synonym for the mental afflictions. Asaṅga glosses the noun several times. *AS* (p. 47) states: "They are perturbations because they overpower the mind by disturbing it repeatedly." Also, *YBh* (p. 167) states: "They are perturbations because they occur repeatedly."
157. *catvāri pārājayikasthānīyadharmā, pham pa'i gnas lta bu'i chos bzhi.* While these four acts are not the same as the four extreme forms of defeat (*pārājikaḥ dharma, phas pham pa'i chos*; see note 99, this chapter) of the Śrāvakayāna moral code, they are meant to correspond to or resemble them in the sense that they cause the bodhisattva discipline to be destroyed. A principal difference between the two systems is that the discipline of a monk or nun who follows the Śrāvakayāna cannot be restored, but the bodhisattva system of discipline can be restored by accepting it again. Bodhibhadra's *Commentary on "The Twenty Verses on the Bodhisattva Vow"* (*Byang chub sems dpa'i sdom pa nyi shu pa'i dka' 'grel*, f. 199a) states: "The term 'extreme defeat' literally means 'having defeated the practitioner who commits them, they cause his or her discipline to be lost.'" The term *sthāniya* (*lta bu*), which is only used in the Mahāyāna system of morality, functions as a suffix in a compound and means (*MW*, s.v. "sthāniya") "occupying the place of" or "representing." The Tibetan translation suggests the sense of "resembling."
158. English translation, p. 268.
159. Ibid., p. 269.
160. *Viniścayasaṃgrahaṇī, rNam par gtan la dbab pa bsdu ba.* The original Sanskrit has not survived. The Tibetan translation spans one entire volume and 127 folios of a second volume in the Derge Tengyur. This work is one of the five treatises that make up the principal corpus of Indian Yogācāra philosophical literature. Butön Rinchen Drup describes them as the "five sections on the stages" (*sa sde lnga*). See *BBh*, English translation, translator's preface, xvii–xviii, for a brief description of these texts.
161. Dg.T. sems tsam, vol. 131 (*zi*), ff. 38b–39a.
162. *asaṃvara, sdom pa ma yin pa.* This term is found in Buddhist abhidharma literature. It is the antithesis of the term that is usually translated as "vow" (*saṃvara, sdom pa*) but which can also be rendered as "discipline." Vasubandhu describes its literal meaning as follows (*AKBh*, p. 205): discipline is "that which restrains or stops ongoing immorality." Vasubandhu glosses "negative discipline" in the following way (*AKBh*, Sanskrit edition, p. 211): "It is negative discipline because it fails to restrain one in body and speech." In a general sense, it is possible for a

person to "acquire" negative discipline by adopting a form of livelihood that is harmful to other beings—for example, the lifestyle of those who slaughter animals for a living, fishermen, hunters, thieves, and the like. Here, the term means simply a resolve that is contrary to, and the antithesis of, the determination and aspiration to seek enlightenment.

163. *śikṣānikṣepa, bslab pa 'bul ba*. This expression usually refers to an act in which a monk or nun had been observing such a vow formally communicates to a member of the sangha that he or she no longer is able to maintain that vow. Here the expression describes the second example cited in the passage from the *Collection of Determinations*.

164. *BBh* (English translation, p. 269) states: "Moreover, even if a bodhisattva has lost the acceptance of the system of moral discipline, he or she is still capable of once again receiving the acceptance of the discipline of bodhisattva morality in that same life. He or she is not incapable of receiving it again, as, for example, a bhikṣu or bhikṣuṇī who has accepted the discipline of individual liberation is incapable when he or she has incurred any of the extreme forms of defeat."

165. *BSV*, v. 8a.

166. *hrī, ngo tsha shes pa*. See ch. 7, "Nectar That Is Like Highly Refined Gold," note 145.

167. *apatrāpya, khrel yod pa*. Ibid., note 144.

168. *BSV*, v. 8b. Bodhibhadra's commentary to the *Twenty Verses on the Bodhisattva Vow* states (f. 202a): "The term 'act created by a middling outflow' (*madhyāsrava, zag pa 'bring*) refers to the mental affliction that is the cause for committing any of the four acts of praising oneself and so on. That is, it is any of those acts that are produced by a middling level of mental perturbation." On the outflows, see ch. 4, "The Brilliant Illumination of the Path to Enlightenment," note 62.

169. *BSV*, v. 8c.

170. *duṣkṛta, nyes byas*. This is the term that is typically used in Tibetan literature to refer to secondary transgressions of the bodhisattva vow. The term that appears in Asaṅga's *Stage of a Bodhisattva* for these secondary misdeeds is "offense" or "transgression" (*āpatti, ltung ba*).

171. *BSV*, v. 9a. A person who has accepted the bodhisattva vow is obligated to worship the Three Jewels on a daily basis. The threefold worship is through body, speech, and mind. Bodily worship is done by making prostrations to the Three Jewels, verbal worship by reciting praises of the Three Jewels, and mental worship by generating reverential faith or "clarity of mind" (*prasāda, dang ba*; see notes 52 and 136, this chapter) toward the Three Jewels after recalling their virtuous qualities.

172. *kliṣṭāpatti, nyong mongs pa can gyi nyes pa*. For the offense of failing to worship the Three Jewels on a daily basis, *BBh* (English translation), p. 270, describes disrespect (*agaurava, ma gus pa*), idleness (*ālasya, snyom las*), or laziness (*kausīdya, le lo*) as possible motivations for an afflicted offense.

173. *akliṣṭāpatti, nyong mongs pa can ma yin pa'i nyes pa*. *BBh* describes lapse of recol-

lection (*smṛtisampramoṣa, brjed pa*) as a possible cause of an unafflicted offense. The sense is that an "unafflicted offense," while still a moral infraction, is less severe than an "afflicted offense."

174. *anāpatti, ltung ba med pa*. It is not an offense for a person who is mentally disturbed (*kṣiptacetasa, sems 'khrugs pa*) to fail to perform daily worship of the Three Jewels. The same is true for a bodhisattva who has attained any of the ten ārya bodhisattva states.
175. *BSV*, v. 8d. *BBh* (English translation, p. 302) states: "If there is no suitable person before whom one can make confession, one should earnestly generate the conviction not to commit such forms of wrongdoing again. In the future, one should also observe such restraint. In this way, a bodhisattva is said to be raised up from those offenses."
176. *BSV*, v. 20cd.
177. *cittasthiti, sems gnas*. This term literally means "a state in which the mind remains stationary or fixed." *ŚBh* (pp. 363–64) describes nine levels of mental stability that culminate in the attainment of the form of one-pointed concentration known as "quiescence" (*śamatha, zhi gnas*).
178. English translation, p. 311.
179. *BSV*, v. 4. See also *BBh* (English translation), pp. 40–41 and pp. 626–27 for descriptions of "the four ways of taking up what is right" (*dharmasamādāna, chos yang dag par blang ba*).
180. *BCA*, ch. 5, v. 1ab.
181. Ibid., ch. 5, v. 23. The wording of the Tibetan version of this verse that appears here differs from the one that appears in the Tengyur edition. See also ch. 11, "A Guidebook for the Path of Great Awakening," note 194, and the citation of the verse in the main body of the text.
182. *smṛti, dran pa*. See ch. 11, "A Guidebook for the Path to Great Awakening," note 182.
183. *samprajanya, shes bzhin*. Ibid.
184. See note 151 (this chapter) for a complete version of the four verses.
185. See p. 449 for the complete mantra.
186. See note 51 (this chapter).
187. See above p. 450 for the full verse.
188. See above, p. 471 where the text states that three verses should be recited once. If the text is accurate here, the direction is presumably to recite only the first of the three verses. Alternatively, the text should be understood as before, which is that all three verses should be recited once. See also note 122 (this chapter) for the complete text of the three verses.
189. *ma pham pa*, also *mi pham*. This term, which means literally "the invincible one," is another name for Maitreya.
190. This is the second verse of the prayer, which appears as the first (*Byams pas zhus pa'i le'u*, Toh. 85) of two sūtras with similar titles in the *dkon brtsegs* section of the Kangyur.

191. *Vīradattagṛhapatiparipṛcchāsūtra, Khyim bdag dpas byin gyis zhus pa'i mdo.* While the original Sanskrit of these verses is extant, the entire discourse is not. The Tibetan translation (Toh. 72) is contained in the *dkon brtsegs* section of the Kangyur.
192. *RA*, ch. 5, v. 87cd. That is, the merit of that wish must also be limitless. This statement is preceded by the line: "Here also is the logical proof." That is, if the wish to benefit a single benefit is meritorious, then the merit of the wish to benefit limitless beings must also be limitless.
193. This verse is the Buddha's answer to the following question posed by Prince Siṃha: "What act causes the acquisition of all spiritual qualities to arise and causes one to become dear to sentient beings wherever one is born?"
194. rNam thos kyi sras. A god of wealth and the guardian of the northern quarter.
195. This simile in the sūtra actually states: "It is like an axe in that it cuts down the tree of *suffering*" (*duḥkhavṛkṣa, sdug bsngal gyi shing*).
196. *mchod rten*. Any of various dome-shaped monuments symbolizing a buddha's enlightenment that contain relics of the Buddha or some great spiritual being and are regarded as objects toward which to direct worship. Here, a bodhisattva's enlightenment mind is being compared to such an object.
197. The source of these lines was not identified.
198. *RA*, ch. 2, vv. 73cd–74. The "you" in this verse is understood to be a king of the Sātavāhana dynasty, the individual to whom Nāgārjuna addressed the poem. The two extremes that should be avoided are those of realism and nihilism. The original Sanskrit of these lines is not extant.
199. *Ratnameghasūtra, dKon mchog sprin gyi mdo.*
200. The title is simply *Ākāśagarbha Sūtra* (*Nam mkha'i snying po'i mdo*, Toh. 260); the word "queries" (*paripṛcchā, zhus pa*) does not appear in the name of the sūtra.
201. *MSA*, ch. 19, vv. 62, 63. Vasubandhu's commentary states that the ten elements indicated in these two verses represent a summary of the entire Mahāyāna spiritual tradition. The original Sanskrit does not identify the last element as "revealing the path" (*lam ston pa*), as rendered in the text here; rather, the term is simply an unspecified act of "revealing" or "manifesting" (*darśanā, ston pa*), which Sthiramati describes in his commentary as the act of revealing all twelve of a supreme emanation body's deeds, beginning with descending from Tuṣita Paradise and ending with passing into parinirvana.
202. *ādhara, gzhi. BBh* (English translation, p. 4) states: "In this context, through depending upon and relying upon the Mahāyāna spiritual lineage, a bodhisattva becomes fit for and capable of attaining unsurpassed true and complete enlightenment. Therefore, the Mahāyāna spiritual lineage is called a support in that it is a capability."
203. *gotra, rigs.* See note 79 (this chapter).
204. *utsāha, spro ba.* This is the essential quality of effort (*vīrya, brtson 'grus*). *AS* (p. 7) states: "What is effort? It is the exertion of the mind toward virtuous activi-

ties, which can be applied in an armor-like, endeavoring, dauntless, unrelenting, or unquenchable manner. Its action is to accomplish and complete all practices that are virtuous in nature."

205. *niḥsaraṇa, nges par 'byung ba.* The Sanskrit and Tibetan equivalents of this term literally mean "deliverance," a synonym for liberation or nirvana. In traditional exegesis, this type of usage is described as one in which the cause is figuratively referred to by a term that stands for the result. In other words, the attitude is called "renunciation" or "deliverance" because it is a mind that seeks to achieve the goal of deliverance from samsara. In fact, this is precisely how renunciation is defined in Buddhist literature. A key element in the process of developing renunciation is cultivating "aversion" (*udvega, skyo ba*) for samsara by reflecting on its the faults.

206. *sambhāramārga, tshogs lam.* The Mahāyāna path of accumulation is entered when a genuine form of enlightenment mind has been generated. The following description is general in that it applies equally to the path systems of all three Buddhist vehicles. *AS* (p. 65) states: "What is the path of accumulation? It is made up of morality, the practice of guarding the doors to the six inner faculties, knowing moderation in relation to eating food, the continual avoidance of sleep during the first and last periods of the night, coupled with the cultivation of effort, the practice of quiescence and insight, and the observance of vigilance, all of which are practiced by ordinary persons. Alternatively, it is any additional causal virtuous qualities, as well as the wisdom that arises from learning, the wisdom that arises from reflection, and the wisdom that arises from meditation. Through the cultivation of these spiritual qualities, one gains the status of becoming a proper vessel for attaining realization and liberation."

207. *sphuṭapratibhāsa, gsal bar snang ba.* This term describes a unique quality of wisdom born of meditation (*bhāvanāmayī prajñā, bsgom byung gi shes rab*) as it occurs on the path of preparation, when a practitioner first gains the ability to practice quiescence (*śamatha, zhi gnas*) and insight (*vipaśyanā, lhag mthong*) jointly.

208. This marks the beginning of the path of preparation (*prayogamārga, sbyor lam*).

209. *darśanamārga, mthong lam.*

210. These are the selflessness of the person (*pudgalanairātmya, gang zag gi bdag med*) and the selflessness of entities (*dharmanairātmya, chos kyi bdag med*).

211. *bhāvanāmārga, sgom lam.*

212. *aśaikṣamārga, mi slob lam.* In the case of the Mahāyāna path, this path marks the attainment of buddhahood. Another name for this state is "the path of perfection" (*niṣṭhāmārga, mthar phyin pa'i lam*).

213. *dharmameghā, chos kyi sprin.*

214. *pāramārthikacittotpāda, don dam sems bskyed.* This is a Mahāyāna ārya's mind that perceives the ultimate nature of supreme enlightenment in a nondual manner.

215. *upādānahetu, nyer len gyi rgyu.*

216. *sahakāripratyaya, lhan cig byed rkyen.* This condition is similar to the Aristotelian notion of an "efficient cause."
217. *saṃvṛticittotpāda, kun rdzob sems bskyed.* This form of enlightenment mind is the attitude that seeks to attain supreme enlightenment for the sake of all sentient beings, as described in the *AA* (ch. 1, v. 17ab): "Generating the mind is the desire to attain true and complete enlightenment for the sake of others." It has two principal aspects: the aspirational and the active forms of enlightenment mind.
218. These four paragraphs serve as an explanation of the ten elements mentioned in the just-cited two verses from *MSA.*
219. *thar pa rtse bla brang.*
220. This last reference to Jamyang Khyentse Wangpo's successor is no doubt to Jamgön Kongtrul. The same is true for the next two lineages. Note that Jamyang Khyentse Wangpo does not form part of the third and final lineage.

13. Opening the Door to the Dharma: The Initial Method of Training One's Mind in the Mind Training Tradition of the Stages of the Path to Enlightenment

1. *Byang chub lam kyi rim pa la blo sbyong ba la thog mar blo sbyong ba chos kyi sgo 'byed, DNZ,* vol. 3 (*ga*), pp. 429–544. Second source: *Byang chub lam kyi rim pa la blo sbyong ba la thog mar blo sbyong ba chos kyi sgo 'byed,* in Collected Works, vol. 1. BDRC W1KG2144. Although this work appears as the last item in the Tibetan Shechen Publications edition of vol. 3 of *The Treasury of Precious Instructions* and it is placed after several Mind Training works that are associated with the second category of Kadam writings, referred to as "The Scripture Lineage," it is actually meant to form part of the group of works that make up the first category of Kadam writings, referred to by Jamgön Kongtrul as "The Treatise Lineage."
2. *lha bcas.* The phrase "along with the divine beings" here refers to the tutelary deities, buddhas and bodhisattvas, and so on, who, together with one's root lama, make up the merit field (*tshogs zhing*) of the Three Jewels.
3. Lokapitāmaha, 'Jig rten mes po. An epithet of Brahmā.
4. Sahasracakṣu, Mig stong ldan. An epithet of Indra.
5. *JM,* ch. 5, v. 26. This verse appears in "The Birth Story of the Merchant Aviṣahya." This chapter of *JM* addresses the practice of generosity, the theme of which is that a spiritual practitioner should not give up this practice out of concern that his or her wealth will be depleted or because of a desire to maintain abundant wealth. The lines are cited here by the author to indicate that the practice of abandoning attachment for this life is a salutary path that must be pursued from the outset and must not be given up at a later time.
6. The author refers to his personal lama three times in this text. Only one of these times does he specifically identify him as Khedrup Gelek Pelsang (mKhas grub

dge legs dpal bzang, 1385–1438). See annotation on p. 662. As this passage does not appear to be a direct quote from any of Khedrup Je's writings, it should be taken as instruction that was received orally.

7. See ch. 7, "The Nectar That Is Like Highly Refined Gold," note 2.
8. *sāragraha, snying po len pa*. Literally "gaining an essence"—that is, true spiritual meaning and value.
9. The full title of the tantra in the Kangyur is *The Secret Tantra on the General Rules for All Mandala Rites* (*dKyil 'khor thams cad kyi spyi'i cho ga gsang ba'i rgyud*). The original Sanskrit of these verses also appear in Dīpaṃkarabhadra's *Guhyasamāja Mandala Ritual* (*Guhyasamājamaṇḍalavidhi, dPal gsang ba 'dus pa'i dkyil 'khor gyi cho ga*).
10. *jo bo rje*. This is a well-known epithet of the Indian master Atiśa Dīpaṃkara Śrījñāna (982–1054) that means Foremost Lord.
11. Phyag khri mchog, d.u. An early Kadam figure who was one of the group of disciples referred to as one of the "Four Yogis."
12. *khu ngok 'brom gsum*. Khu was Khutön Tsöndru Yungdrung (Khu ston brTson 'grus g.yung drung, 1011–1075); Ngok was Ngok Lekpai Sherap (rNgog Legs pa'i shes rab, 1018–1115); and Drom was Drom Tönpa Gyalwai Jungne ('Brom ston pa rGyal ba'i 'bung gnas, 1004/5–1064).
13. Gönpawa Wangchuk Gyaltsen (dGon pa ba dBang phyug rgyal mtshan, 1016–1082). "Gönpawa" is an epithet that means "one who dwells in an isolated place." He is regarded as the patriarch of the Kadam lineage known as the Lamrim Followers (*lam rim pa*).
14. Ame Jangchup Rinchen (A me Byang chub rin chen, 1015–1077). He was also known by the epithet Naljorpa Chenpo (rNal 'byor pa chen po), or "the Great Yogi."
15. Naljorpa Sherap Dorje (rNal 'byor pa Shes rab rdo je, d.u.).
16. See note 11 (this chapter).
17. Phyag dar Ston pa.
18. *rwa sgreng*. This was the first Kadampa monastery established in Tibet. Its founding, a year or more after Atiśa's passing, is most often associated with Drom Tönpa, who was Atiśa's principal Tibetan disciple.
19. The epithet "royal monk" (*lha bla ma*), which literally translates as "divine lama," indicates a royal figure who has received ordination as a Buddhist monk. Jangchup Ö (Byang chub 'od, d.u.) was a royal patron from the western Tibetan region of Guge and was responsible for inviting Atiśa to come to Tibet.
20. Rin chen bzang po, 958–1055.
21. rGya brTson 'grus seng ge, 1186–1247.
22. Naktso Lotsāwa Tsultrim Gyalwa (Nag tsho lo tsā ba Tshul khrims rgyal ba, b. 1011). This monk traveled to Vikramaśīla monastery in 1037 with the express purpose of inviting Atiśa to Tibet, a mission that proved successful. After traveling back to Tibet with Atiśa, he served as his translator during the early period of his time in Tibet. He also was instrumental in helping to compile an early

biography of Atiśa at the urging of one of his own disciples, Rongpa Chaksorwa (Rong pa Phyag sor ba; see note 766, this chapter).

23. Ma Lotsāwa Gewe Lodrö (rMa lo tsā ba dGe ba'i blo gros, d.u.) He was also a disciple of Lotsāwa Rinchen Zangpo and was the official translator of Atiśa's seminal work titled *A Lamp for the Path to Enlightenment* (*Byang chub lam gyi sgron ma*).
24. This is an alternate way of referring to a figure also described as referred as Zhangtsun Yeshe Bar from Yerpa (Yer pa'i Zhang btsun Ye she 'bar). Zhangtsun, which means "the monk from Zhang," identifies him as being from an area in the region of Yerpa. His ordination name was Yeshe Bar.
25. Gompa Rinchen Lama (sGom pa rin chen bla ma).
26. Ramding Mawa's (Ram sding ma ba) ordination name was Jungne Dorje ('Byung gnas rdo rje); he was a disciple of Potowa Rinchen Sel (see note 27, this chapter). The term translated here as "liberating deeds" literally means simply "liberation" (*vimokṣa, rnam par thar pa*). It is a general term for the account of a holy being's spiritual deeds that describe the process by which he or she attained enlightenment. While often translated as "biography," it more closely resembles the classic meaning of the term "hagiography." As a genre of literature, its main purpose is to engender faith and reverence in the minds of disciples and ideally to inspire them to emulate the activities of the subject that the work describes. Other sources report that there were three separate such spiritual biographies of this figure, one of which was titled *The Account of [Ramding Mawa's] Liberating Deeds throughout Sixteen Lifetimes* (*sKye ba bcu drug pa'i rnam thar*).
27. Po to ba Rin chen gsal, 1027–1105. See below for numerous references to this figure who was an important disciple of Drom Tönpa.
28. *nirmāṇakāya, sprul pa'i sku*. This Tibetan term, which literally means "emanation body," refers to the physical form of a buddha that ordinary beings are able to perceive. Buddha Śākyamuni is considered a supreme emanation body (*mchog gi sprul sku*) in that he possessed the one hundred and twelve physical marks of a great being and carried out the twelve major spiritual deeds of a buddha. In the present context, the term refers to the widespread Tibetan custom of identifying rebirths of spiritual masters as emanation bodies of their predecessors, who were considered enlightened beings.
29. *tshe 'di blos thong*. Literally, this phrase means "With your mind, abandon this life." Akya Yongdzin's *Mirror That Answers Questions and Reveals the Meaning of Terms from [the Work Titled] "The Initial Method of Training One's Mind"* (*Thog mar blo sbyong gi dris lan brda don gsal ba'i me long*, f. 1a) states: "The starting point of the Lamrim practice is established as being recollection of impermanence in the form of death. Thus, since this [work], *The Initial Method of Training One's Mind*, makes teaching about impermanence in the form of death its central concern, the effect of having properly contemplated impermanence is for [the practitioner] to develop [the quality in which] his or her mind does not engage in [thoughts about] the prosperity or affairs, and so on, of this

life and gives up any craving or attachment for them. That is what is meant by the expression to 'mentally abandon this life.'"

30. Götsangpa Gönpo Dorje (rGod tshang pa mGon po rdo rje, 1189–1258) was an important religious figure who was a disciple of Tsangpa Gyare (gTsang pa rgya ras), the founder of the Drukpa branch of the Kagyu tradition.
31. sTon pa Rin po che. This epithet, which means "Precious Teacher," is a reference to Drom Tönpa Gyalwai Jungne ('Brom ston pa rGyal ba'i 'byung gnas, 1004/5–1064), who was Atiśa's foremost Tibetan disciple.
32. *gser mdun*. Chahar Geshe Losang Tsultrim's (Cha har dge bshes bLo bzang tshul khrims, 1740–1810) *Answers to Questions Relating to [the Work Titled] "The Initial Way to Train One's Mind"* (*Thog ma'i blo sbyong las brtsams pa'i dris lan*, f. 8b) states: "The expression 'gold assembly' means a gathering of monks at which gold is distributed to those in attendance."
33. dPal gyi dbang phyug.
34. *SL*, v. 29.
35. *BCA*, ch. 6, v. 100ab.
36. Chahar Geshe's *Collected List [of Explanations] of Various Phrases from "The Initial Way to Train One's Mind"* (*Thog mar blo sbyong gi gzhung 'ga'i tho yig btus te bkod*, f. 2b) states: "This facial gesture was meant to indicate to others the appropriateness [of adhering to the meaning conveyed by these words]."
37. sPyan snga ba Tshul khrims 'bar (1038–1102). The epithet Chengawa, which literally means "one who was before the eyes," refers to a disciple who spent much time in the presence of his teacher. This Kadam master was one of Drom Tönpa's main disciples and he is regarded as the patriarch of the lineage known as the Instruction Followers (*Gdams ngag pa*).
38. *avyākṛta, lung ma bstan*. This adjective, which literally means "undeclared," indicates that the Buddha didn't declare or specify whether the act in question was virtuous or unvirtuous in nature; hence, it is deemed indeterminate.
39. *UV*, ch. 31, vv. 23, 24.
40. The stories that are briefly described here to illustrate the meaning of these verses can be found in the Tibetan translation of Prajñāvarman's commentary to the *Collection of Uplifting Sayings*. The commentary relates that two youthful beggars—one a brahmin and the other a member of the kṣatriya, or warrior, caste (*rgyal rigs*)—were both hungry and approached a group of Buddhist monks to ask for food. Because the brahmin did so at an inopportune time, which was before the monks had finished eating themselves, he was not given anything to eat. His anger at this refusal caused him to utter the wish to decapitate the monks. The warrior youth came later, after the monks had finished eating, and received an abundant amount of their leftover food. Each youth made a statement based on the nature of his experience and underwent correspondingly favorable and unfavorable results.
41. sNying stobs chen po. The name literally means "Great Courage." This story appears in the *Sūtra on Questions of the Bodhisattva Jñānottara* (Dg.K. dkon

brtsegs, vol. 6 [*cha*], ff. 79a–139b). In the sūtra, Buddha Śākyamuni tells the bodhisattva Jñānottara that he—that is, Buddha Śākyamuni—was this leader of the merchants in a former life during the time of Buddha Dīpaṃkara.

42. *Bu chos*. This is the portion of *The Book of Kadam* in which Atiśa relates the birth stories of his principal disciple Drom Tönpa to Ngok Lekpe Sherap and Khutön Tsöndru Yungdrung, who are the figures referred to as "sons."
43. Se btsun dBang phyug gzhon nu, d.u. Drom Tönpa was his disciple for some nineteen years, from the age of nineteen to thirty-eight, prior to his meeting of Atiśa.
44. *sku mched gsum*. They were Potowa Rinchen Sel (Po to ba Rin chen gsal, 1027–1105), Chengawa Tsultrim Bar (sPyan snga ba Tshul khrims 'bar, 1038–1103), and Puchungwa Zhönu Gyaltsen (Phu chung ba gZhon nu rgyal mtshan, 1031–1106).
45. See note 13 (this chapter).
46. Ka ma ba Shes rab 'od, 1057–1131. He founded Kama Monastery.
47. See ch. 10, "The Essence of Nectar," note 451, and notes 555 and 654 (this chapter), along with related annotation.
48. 'Bre ko de lung pa, d.u. The name Kode Lungpa is an epithet that means literally the "one from the Kode area." This is another name for a well-known Kadampa figure Geshe Ben Gungyal (dGe bshes 'Ban gung rgyal), whose ordination name was Tsultrim Gyalwa (Tshul khrims rgyal ba). See also pp. 541–44 for spiritual sayings attributed to him.
49. gNyan sna mo ba, d.u.
50. Kha rag sgom chung, fl. eleventh century. His ordination name was Wangchuk Lodrö (dBang phyug blo gros). See also the annotation on p. 548, where the origin of this epithet is described. He was also referred to as Geshe Kharakpa (dGe bshes Kha rag pa).
51. *RA*, ch. 1, v. 20. The three mental factors of avoidance of attachment (*alobha, 'dod chags med pa*), avoidance of hatred (*adveṣa, zhe sdang med pa*), and avoidance of ignorance (*amoha, gti mug med pa*) are known as the three roots of virtue (*kuśalamūlāni, dge ba'i rtsa ba*). See also ch. 9, "Essential Summary of the Method of Practice in the System of the Stages of the Path to Enlightenment," note 80.
52. This verse is from the *Jewel Cloud Sūtra* (*Ratnameghasūtra, dKon mchog sprin*).
53. *BCA*, ch. 5, vv. 4, 5.
54. Ibid., v. 17.
55. Ibid., v. 18cd.
56. *hīnapuruṣa, skyes bu chung ngu*. See ch. 4, "The Brilliant Illumination of the Path to Enlightenment," verse 3 and related commentary.
57. *udvega, yid 'byung ba*, also *skyo ba*. This term refers to a state of mind that is central to the process of developing renunciation (*niḥsaraṇa, nges par 'byung ba*). It represents the antithesis of desire for and attachment to samsaric existence. See ch. 7, "The Nectar That Is Like Highly Refined Gold," note 135.

58. *madhyapuruṣa, skyes bu 'bring*. See ch. 4, "The Brilliant Illumination of the Path to Enlightenment," verse 4 and related commentary.
59. *śreṣṭhapuruṣa, skyes bu mchog*.
60. *adharma, chos min*. The term *dharma*, which is not exclusive to Buddhism, literally means "that which holds" or "that which is steadfast," and by extension, "that which is right" or more broadly "virtue," "morality," and even "religion." By adding the privative particle *a*, the term comes to mean the opposite of *dharma*, which can be translated variously as "unrighteousness," "injustice," "wickedness," or, as rendered here, "antithesis of dharma."
61. *nyāyeśvara, rigs pa'i dbang phyug*. This epithet indicates that the person is a master of Buddhist logic and epistemology. His ordination name, Tashi Gyaltsen, is given in the annotation.
62. bKra shis rgyal mtshan, fl. first half of the fourteenth century. According to Sönam Lhayi Wangpo's *Thousand Rays of Sunlight* (*Nyin mor byed pa'i 'od stong*), he came to Rinchen Gang Monastery at age forty-three, which I estimate to have been the year 1333, and served as abbot for nineteen years. He also presided over the ordination of one of Je Tsongkhapa's teachers, Lhodrak Drupchen Namkha Gyaltsen (Lho brag grub chen Nam mkha' rgyal mtshan).
63. *gsang phu'i gling smad*.
64. *glang thang*.
65. *rgya ma rin chen sgang*. Founded in 1159 by the Great Gyer Zhönu Drakpa (see notes 244, 553, and annotation, p. 587, this chapter).
66. *mkhas btsun bzang gsum*.
67. g.Yag sde Paṇ chen, 1299–1378.
68. Ye dgon pa. This is an epithet, literally "the one from Ye Monastery," of the master known as "the hermit Gönpo Yeshe" (ri khrod pa mGn po ye shes).
69. *'ol sna*.
70. *gdong chung*. Literally "small face," this expression can also mean such things as "conscientiousness" or "disregard." Here it seems to refer to the attitude of turning away from and giving up interest in associating with ordinary worldly friends.
71. This verse appears in a work titled *A Spiritual Song of the Realized One Gönpo Yeshe* (*rTogs ldan mgon po ye shes kyi gsung mgur*).
72. *vimokṣa, rnam thar*. See note 26 (this chapter).
73. Thos pa dga'. Literally "Joy upon Hearing," which tradition says stems from the fact that when his father learned of his birth, he exclaimed, "I am overjoyed to hear the news that the child has been born a son."
74. rDo rje rgyal mtshan. This was one of Milarepa's tantric names given to him by his root lama Marpa Chökyi Lodrö. He was also given the tantric name Zhepe Dorje (bZhad pa'i rdo rje).
75. Dwags po lha rje, 1079–1153. Dakpo is a reference to his clan; Lhaje is an epithet that means "physician." This figure was also known as Gampopa Sönam Rinchen (sGam po pa bSod nams rin chen).

76. Ras chung rDo rje grags, 1085–1161. See *Hundred Thousand Songs* (*mGur 'bum*), chapter 10.
77. *aurasa putra, thugs kyi sras*. See ch. 10, "Essence of Nectar," note 439.
78. gNyan chung ras pa. The term *repa* (*ras pa*) that appears in many disciples' names means "cotton-clad one" and indicates that the individual was an ascetic meditator.
79. gCan lung gi Ngan rdzong ston pa. This individual's name is also written Ngamdzong Tönpa (Ngam rdzong ston pa). The place name is also variously written as Chamlung (*lcam lung*) or Chenlung (*gcen lung*) in other source texts.
80. rTa mo'i 'Bri sgom ras pa. See *Hundred Thousand Songs*, ch.16.
81. mDo bkra'i Se ban ras pa. See *Hundred Thousand Songs*, ch. 15.
82. Ras pa Zhi ba 'od. See *Hundred Thousand Songs*, ch. 17.
83. Ras pa Sangs rgyas skyabs.
84. Ras pa rTsa phu ba. Also referred to as Tsapu Repa (rTsa phu ras pa). See *Hundred Thousand Songs*, ch. 11.
85. Ras pa rDo rje dbang phyug. See *Hundred Thousand Songs*, ch. 32.
86. gShen sgom ras pa. See *Hundred Thousand Songs*, ch. 24.
87. Rong chung ras pa. He is mentioned at the very end of chapter 27 in *Hundred Thousand Songs*.
88. mKhar chung ras pa. See *Hundred Thousand Songs*, ch. 20.
89. gLan sgom ras pa. See *Hundred Thousand Songs*, ch.40.
90. Li kor cha ru ba. See *Hundred Thousand Songs*, ch. 44.
91. 'Or ston dge 'dun. This is either an alternate spelling or a misspelling of the name Lotön Gendun (Lo ston dge 'dun). See *Hundred Thousand Songs*, ch. 42.
92. sKyo ston Shākya guṇa. The Tibetan text gives the name in the condensed form of Shākgu. See *Hundred Thousand Songs*, ch. 13.
93. Dam pa rGyags phu ba. See *Hundred Thousand Songs*, ch. 19, where the name is rendered Dampa Gyakpupa (Dam pa rgyag pu pa).
94. Se ben ston chung. This is apparently the same person referred to earlier as Seben Repa. See note 78 (this chapter).
95. 'Bre ban bkra shis. Various editions give different spellings of this name, most likely the disciple known as Dretön Tashi Bar ('Bre ston bKra shis 'bar) and also Dretön Repa ('Bre ston ras pa). See *Hundred Thousand Songs*, chapter 43.
96. *lha chos*. *The Great Tibetan Dictionary* (s.v. "lha chos") states: "[The expression] 'divine dharma' can mean [either] the Buddha's teaching or supramundane virtuous practice."
97. *māra, bdud*. See ch. 7, "The Nectar That Is Like Highly Refined Gold," note 70, for a classic description of four forms of māra, or "destructive force." The form that is meant here is identified as a worldly god of the desire realm who is sometimes referred to in translation as the Evil One in that he obstructs the efforts of spiritual practitioners to transcend samsaric existence. Other texts identify his being as the chief deity of the class of desire-realm gods known as Those Who Control Others' Magical Creations (*paranirmitavaśavarttina, gzhan 'phrul dbang*

byed). Tibetan literature also refers to him as Māra, the Lord of Pleasure (bDud dGa' rab dbang phyug), possibly a reference to Kāmadeva, who is also known by the names Rativara and Ratikānta, both of which mean Rati's Husband.

98. That is, family members.
99. See ch. 10, "The Essence of Nectar," note 189.
100. rGya lCags ri gong kha wa. The name is an epithet that means "the one who resided a Chakri Gongka Monastery." His ordination name was Jangchup Pel (Byang chub dpal) and he was a principal disciple of Langri Tangpa Dorje Senge (gLang ri thang pa rDo rje seng ge, 1054–1153).
101. sNyug rum pa, also written sMyug rum pa, 1042–1109. The name means "the one from Nyukrum" as he founded the monastery of that name.
102. This monastery, also known as Dakpo Gampo (*dwags po sgam po*), was founded in 1121.
103. Phag mo gru pa rDo rje rgyal po, 1110–1170.
104. Dwags po sGom tshul Tshul khrims snying po, 1116–1169. He was a nephew of Gampopa.
105. dBu se. This is an epithet of the first Karmapa, also known as Düsum Kyenpa (Dus gsum mkhyen pa, 1110–1193), which means "the one who knows the three times," suggesting his omniscience.
106. rJe 'Ba' rom pa Dar ma dbang phyug, 1127–1199/1200.
107. The text gives an abbreviation of the name Chökyi Yungdrung (Chos kyi g.yung drung). See also note 732.
108. See note 27 (this chapter).
109. See note 44 (this chapter).
110. Khams lung pa, 1025–1115. Literally "the one from the Kham region." He was a lay disciple; his personal name was Śākya Yönten (Shākya yon tan). See also note 649 (this chapter), where he is referred to as Khampa Lungpa.
111. *sthavira*, *gnas brtan*. The name of a group of sixteen arhats who were disciples of Buddha Śākyamuni who are immortal and continually serve to preserve the Buddhist teaching. Potowa is said to have been an emanation of the arhat Angaja (Yan lag 'byung).
112. *smin drug.*
113. See annotation on p. 597.
114. Sha ra ba, 1070–1141. His ordination name was Yönten Drak (Yon tan grags). He was also referred to as Sharwapa (Shar ba pa).
115. sprul sku Ram sdings ma ba. See notes 26 and 28 (this chapter) for an explanation of the word *tulku*.
116. sNang bre'u lhas pa. His ordination name was Yeshe Gyaltsen (Ye shes rgyal mtshan).
117. gNyal pa chos 'bar. He was also known as Nyö Dragorwa (gNyos Bra gor ba); Nyö is a clan name and Dragor is the name of a monastery that he founded.
118. Bun pa lha rje. This disciple may be the disciple also known as Lang Jarapa (gLang bya rab pa) from Nyal.

119. Bande Tsan chung ba. The term Bande is an epithet that means a Buddhist monk. This person may also have been referred to as Bemön Buchungwa ('Be mon bu chung ba).
120. Rog dMar zhur pa, 1059–1131. Rok is a place name. He was also known as Dölpa Marshurpa (Dol pa dmar zhur pa). As stated here, his ordination name was Sherap Gyatso (Shes rab rgya mtsho).
121. *dPe chos*. As suggested here, Podrang Dingpa Zhönu Ö (see note 122, this chapter) and Geshe Drak Karwa are the two earliest names associated with compiling Potowa Rinchen Sel's similes. Chegomba Sherap Dorje (lCe sgom pa Shes rab rdo rje) is a third figure who prepared a later version that is most widely available today and includes a commentary titled *An Extensive Commentary on "The Jewel Heap of Edifying Similes"* (*dPe chos rin chen spungs pa'i 'bum 'grel*).
122. Po grab pa. He was also known as Podrang Dingpa (Pho brang sdings pa); his ordination name was Zhönu Ö (gZhon nu 'od, d.u.). He was a long-time disciple of Potowa Rinchen Sel.
123. dGe bshes Brag dkar ba, 1032–1111.
124. Byang sems Yang gad pa. Jangsem is an abbreviation of the Tibetan word for bodhisattva. Yangepa is an epithet that means "the one from Yange," the name of a monastery that he founded.
125. Shes rab rgya mtsho.
126. *Be'u bum sngon po*. Written in verse, an English translation appears in *Stages of the Buddhas' Teachings* (pp. 37–117), under the title *Blue Compendium*. The twelfth-century Kadam scholar Lha Drigangpa (Lha 'Bri sgang pa) also wrote a commentary to the verse text, titled *A Commentary on the Kadam Instruction Manual Titled "Blue Udder"* (*bKa' gdams kyi man ngag be'u bum sngon po'i 'grel pa*).
127. These lines mention a series of similes formulated by Potowa Rinchen Sel to illustrate points related to the Lamrim instruction. While some of the similes are the same, the lines do not match the more widely known edition compiled by Chegomba Sherap Dorje with a commentary that is titled *An Extensive Commentary on "The Jewel Heap of Edifying Similes"* (*dPe chos rin chen spungs pa'i 'bum 'grel*).
128. Because the fist is clenched so tightly.
129. *sde 'khrugs*. This act is defined as fomenting dissension in an ordained community of monks or nuns that results in the formation of two opposing factions, each of which is made up of at least four monks or nuns. It approximates, but is not identical with or as severe as, the act of causing a schism in the sangha wheel, one of the five most grave misdeeds that are called "immediate deeds" (*ānantaryakarma, mtshams med pa'i las*) in the sense that the person who commits any of them will be reborn in the hells in his or her very next life. The act referred to as a schism in the sangha wheel can only occur when a buddha is still living. For example, such an act was perpetrated by Buddha Śākyamuni's cousin Devadatta.

130. *tripiṭaka, sde snod gsum.* This expression refers to a monk who is knowledgeable in all three collections of Buddhist canonical literature: sūtra (discourses), vinaya (code of moral discipline), and abhidharma (systematic formulations of essential doctrine).
131. *rtod phur.* The name of this monastery is the same term that means "hitching stake." This incident presumably is mentioned here as an alternate explanation of this simile.
132. *mdzo.* A hybrid bovine that is a cross between a yak and a cow.
133. These remarks are interpretations of the simile described as "overwhelmed by fear of water" (*chu rdugs 'khyer*).
134. That is, persons from the Kham region of eastern Tibet.
135. See ch. 5, "Verse Compendium of the Stages of the Path," note 12.
136. *balbaja.* A species of coarse grass, which presumably can be used to make rope.
137. *śithila, lhod pa.* This term does not appear in the extant Sanskrit edition of this verse; however, it does occur in the Prakrit and Pali versions. Prajñāvarman's commentary explains it as an adjective that modifies desire and notes that persons are unconcerned by this fetter because they mistakenly regard it to be one that is loose—that is, one that can be overcome easily. This interpretation fits the explanation of the simile that is being explained here by Chenga Lodrö Gyaltsen. However, in the Pali version, the term is taken to mean a "lax person" who is brought down by this fetter.
138. *UV*, ch. 2, vv. 5, 6ab. The Tibetan translation of these lines does not mirror exactly any of the available Sanskrit, Prakrit, or Pali versions that were consulted. However, it does conform well to the explanation that is found in Prajñāvarman's commentary. The final half of the second verse states: "Having cut that bond, the steadfast, / who have no regard for sensory pleasures, go forth swiftly."
139. *ltag tshan.* The term *ltag* or *ltag pa* can mean the back of the head and, in that sense, is used to indicate the act of turning away from something. However, it can also mean the neck or the nape of the neck and combined with the modifier *tshan*, appears to mean literally a "strong nape." I have found several instances of its use. One is in combination with the word "antidote" (*ltag tshan gyi gnyen po*), suggesting a powerful or effective antidote; another uses it to describe a dharma protector that is particularly strong or powerful in its ability to provide wealth swiftly (*nor sgrub mthu myur ltag tshan che ba'i chos skyong*). The term also appears in one of Milarepa's songs where it describes a person who possesses strong resolve to overcome bad deeds (*las ngan ltag tshan ches pa*).
140. *glud.* This is an object usually made of dough that is offered to a malicious spirit in a ritual as an inducement to stop it from causing harm to someone.
141. *nyin mo'i skar ma.* This expression refers to the quite rare phenomenon in which it is possible to perceive such planets as Venus, Jupiter, and Mars in the daytime sky.
142. *rnga ma.* The term "tail" here means the hairs of a long chin beard.

143. The word master does not occur in the Tibetan text. However, given that Potowa Rinchen Sel was the source of these similes, it is likely that he is the person who gave this instruction.
144. *gong mo*. Also known as the Tibetan snowcock (*Tetraogallus tibetanus*).
145. *sre mo*. Also known as mountain weasel (*Mustela altaica*).
146. Chegompa Sherap Dorje's explanation of this simile in his commentary to Potowa's *Collection of Similes* (see notes 121 and 307, this chapter) provides additional details (book edition, p. 81). He states that after the weasel bit the grouse on the top of its head, the grouse flew off with the weasel still attached to it. Once it landed on the far side of the water, the grouse died, at which point the weasel made the statement that is recorded here.
147. *'bri*. Female of the yak species.
148. That is, from Tibet.
149. *yojana, dpag tshad*. See ch. 10, "The Essence of Nectar," note 81, for an explanation of this unit of distance, which is approximately four miles.
150. In other words, a precipice that is close to home.
151. Akya Yongdzin (in *Thog mar blo sbyong gi dris lan*) interprets the wording of the analogy/simile and then refers the reader to the *Commentary on the "Blue Udder"* (*Be'u bum sngon po'i 'grel pa*) by Lhadri Gangpa (Lha 'bri sgang pa, b. twelfth century) for a more complete explanation. The text here reads *skyu rtsa*, which means "the base of the depression." However, the commentary to the *Blue Udder* has *ske rtsa*, which means "the base of the neck" and appears to be more idiomatic. I think it is reasonable to understand both expressions are referring to the same thing—that is, the thickness of the food that lies below the depression made with the thumb and that forms a supporting base. The *Commentary on the "Blue Udder"* (f. 55a–55b) describes how two persons from the Dokham region were sharing a portion of ghee. The greedier of the two pressed his thumb down into his food to make a deep depression, so that he could fill it with a large amount of ghee. But because he pushed his thumb down too far, when he raised the food to his mouth, the bottom fell apart and he lost both the food and the ghee. His companion, who was embarrassed and thought it was important to be skillful when trying to obtain a large amount of ghee, said, "You must be careful about the base of the neck." The commentary then provides this interpretation: "Likewise, while deep subjects like emptiness that enable one to attain buddhahood instantly are also important, at this early stage of spiritual practice, you must exercise care with more fundamental topics, such as recollection of the Buddha, the difficulty of gaining a human form possessed of leisure, recollection of death, and the doctrine of karma and its results, which are like the base of the neck-like depression made in the food. If you fail to exercise care about these topics, you will not even attain the food-like temporary goals of rebirth as a human or a worldly god, much less the ghee-like ultimate goal of buddhahood. Therefore, if you want to experience the meaning of profound topics, be meticulous about practicing these topics that relate to a

lesser person and that resemble the base of the neck-like depression. [Master Potowa] taught that it is important to reflect again and again with great diligence on these topics until you have developed a realization of them in your mental continuum."

152. *bya btang*. Literally "one who has given up activities," this expression means a spiritual practitioner who has abandoned all ordinary activities in order to take up the life of a spiritual recluse.
153. *spras*. A region in Penpo, which lies northeast of Lhasa.
154. *rgyal*.
155. *ke ka*. A black and white bird known as the "black-rumped magpie" (*Pica bottanensis*).
156. *stod lung*. A region that lies to the west of Lhasa.
157. Dragyap Losang Norbu (Brag rgyab rJe btsun bLo bzang nor bu, 1913–1968) elaborates in his *Treasury of Jewel-Like Instructions* (*Man ngag rin chen bang mdzod*, book 2, p. 13): "Birds large and small begin by building a nest, during the interim period they incubate their eggs with the warmth of their body, and finally they nurture their offspring with food after the eggs hatch, such that even within the span of a month they can raise their offspring to become the equal of their parents.
158. Losang Norbu describes how swallows (*khug rta*) skillfully build their nests on the sides of cliffs.
159. *zu lums*. This note "absence of deliberation and reflection" is meant to gloss this Tibetan term with which the reader may be unfamiliar.
160. Chos rje Bu. That is, Butön Rinchen Drup (Bu ston Rin chen grub, 1290–1364). The epithet Chöje (*dharmasvāmī*, *chos rje*) means "dharma lord" or "dharma master."
161. These lines appear among the closing verses to Butön Rinchen Drup's work known popularly as *Butön's History of Buddhism* (*Bu ston chos 'byung*).
162. Chos rje rGyal sras pa. This is an epithet of Gyalse Tokme Zangpo (rGyal sras Thogs med bzang po dpal, 1295–1369). The epithet Gyalse (*jinasuta*, *rgyal sras*) literally means "[spiritual] offspring of the Victor" and is understood to be a synonym for a bodhisattva. Its use here is meant to indicate that Tokme Zangpo Pel had achieved that status. His important commentary to the Seven-Point Mind Training instruction appears in the second volume of Kadam literature.
163. *Ratnakūṭa*, *dKon mchog brtsegs pa*. This is the name of a collection of forty-nine Mahāyāna sūtras that are grouped together in a distinct section of the Tibetan Kangyur. See next note for the specific sūtra in which this verse appears.
164. This verse appears in the *Mañjuśrībuddhakṣetraguṇavyūha Sūtra* (*'Jam dpal gyi sangs rgyas kyi zhing gi yon tan bkod pa'i mdo*).
165. *BCA*, ch. 7, v. 40ab.
166. This epithet, which means "precious lord," refers to Je Tsongkhapa, who is considered to have had visions of Mañjughoṣa that enabled him to communicate with this enlightened being.

167. *dge ldan*. This is an alternate spelling for Ganden Monastery (*dga' ldan*), the first major monastery that Je Tsongkhapa established in 1409.
168. *gsang sngags mkhar*. Literally "Fort of Secret Mantra," this is the name of one of the earliest Geluk monasteries dedicated to the teaching and study of the Guhyasamāja system of Buddhist tantra.
169. *rdzing phyi*. A well-known temple founded in the tenth century in the Ölka Valley that housed a Maitreya image. Je Tsongkhapa's restoration in 1394 is considered one of his four most important spiritual deeds.
170. *btsun mo tshal*. Founded in 1420 by Duldzin Drakpa Gyaltsen ('Dul 'dzin Grags pa rgyal mtshan, 1374–1434).
171. *'bras spungs*. Founded in 1416 by Jamyang Chöje Tashi Palden ('Jam dbyangs chos rje bKra shis dpal ldan, 1379–1449).
172. *se ra theg chen gling*. Founded in 1419 by Jamchen Chöje Śākya Yeshe (Byams chen chos rje Shākya ye shes, 1354–1435).
173. rJe Darma rin chen, 1364–1432. As he was Je Tsongkhapa's spiritual heir, he is known by the epithet Gyaltsap Je (rGyal tshab rje).
174. mKhas grub rje, 1385–1438. His ordination name was Gelek Pelsang (dGe legs dpal bzang).
175. rJe Zha lu ba Legs pa'i rgyal mtshan, 1375–1450.
176. rJe bLo gros chos skyong, 1389–1463.
177. rJe Ba so ba Chos kyi rgyal mtshan, 1402–1473. He was the younger brother of Khedrup Je. The epithet Basowa stems from his association with Baso Lhundrup Dechen Monastery.
178. See note 170 (this chapter).
179. See note 175 (this chapter).
180. Dar rgyas bzang po, d.u. In accordance with Je Tsongkhapa's instruction, after founding Sera Monastery, Jamchen Chöje appointed him as the monastery's first *lopön*, or spiritual teacher. He served as abbot for fourteen years.
181. Gung ru rgyal mtshan bzang po, 1384–1450.
182. bLa ma Cog chen pa. I believe this epithet indicates the region that this lama was from, and it refers to Tashi Gyatso (bKra shis rgya mtsho), a disciple who was renowned for being a great ascetic.
183. This disciple, known as Neten Sang Kyongwa (gNas brtan bZang skyong ba), was one of Je Tsongkhapa's eight disciples with whom he stayed in extensive retreats in the Ölka region. The group were known as "the retinue of eight pure ones" (*'khor dag pa rnam brgyad*).
184. *nyi ma gling*.
185. bLa ma Byang sems pa. The name is an epithet that means "Bodhisattva Lama." Also known as Tokden (*rtogs ldan*) Jangsempa, or "the realized bodhisattva," he was another member of the retinue of eight pure ones (see note 183, this chapter).
186. See note 172 (this chapter). Besides founding Sera Monastery, Je Tsongkhapa

directed this disciple to go in his stead to serve as a religious advisor to the Yongle emperor in China.

187. Shes rab seng ge, 1383–1445. He founded the first Gelukpa tantric monastery.
188. rJe dGe 'dun grub pa, 1391–1474. He founded Tashi Lhunpo (*bkra shis lhun po*) Monastery in 1447 and was retroactively identified as the first Dalai Lama.
189. Biographical sources identify the seven as: Gyaltsap Darma Rinchen, Duldzin Drakpa Gyaltsen, Khedrup Gelek Pelsang, Jangtse Chöje Namkha Pel, Shartse Chöje Rinchen Gyaltsen, Tokden Jampel Gyatso, and Tokden Namkha Shokrel.
190. This expression translates literally as "spiritual son born from the breast." See ch. 10, "The Essence of Nectar," note 439.
191. Byang sems bde mo ba thang pa bLo gros rgyal mtshan. The Tibetan text gives an abbreviated version of this epithet.
192. Sems dpa' chen po Kun bzang ba.
193. *mdo sngags gling.*
194. Byang sems Rwa sgreng ba. This epithet means "the bodhisattva from Radreng." His ordination name was Śākya Sönam (Shākya bsod nams).
195. *sgo mo mtsho kha.*
196. Byang sems sPrel zhing pa chen po.
197. *dgon gsar.*
198. *ri bo gdangs can.*
199. 'Dul ba dge 'dun rin chen.
200. *rin chen gling.*
201. bLa ma Grags pa rin chen.
202. *cha dkar.*
203. See note 188 (this chapter).
204. *aurasa putra, thugs kyi sras.* See ch. 10, "The Essence of Nectar," note 439.
205. rNgog Chos rdor. The name rendered as Chödor is an abbreviated form of the name Chöku Dorje (Chos sku rdo rje).
206. *zho.* A monetary unit that is equal to about one-tenth of any ounce.
207. bLa ma Byang gling pa Grags pa rin chen.
208. Chos rje Kun dga' bzang po.
209. Chos rje Rong po. This name means "the dharma lord from Rong." Je Tsongkhapa's biographies mention that he had several disciples from this region. One, in particular, was known as Jaknakpa (lJags nag pa), or Black-Tongued One. His ordination name was Gendun Gyaltsen (dGe 'dun rgyal mtshan).
210. The generation stage (*utpattikrama, bskyed rim*) and the completion stage (*niṣpannakrama, rdzogs rim*) are the two main levels of the Buddhist Highest Yoga Tantra system of practice.
211. Khro phu lo tsā ba Byams pa'i dpal, also Byams pa dpal, 1173–1236.
212. *byams chen chos sde.* The original monastery, also known as Tropu Monastery (*khro phu dgon pa*), was founded in 1212 by Gyaltsa Rinchen Gönpo (rGyal tsha Rin chen mgon po, 1118–1195), the uncle of Tropu Lotsāwa.

213. Shākya shrī bha dra, 1127–1225. Tropu Lotsāwa was able to invite this Indian teacher to Tibet in 1204.
214. Khro phu ba bSod nams Seng ge.
215. See note 160 (this chapter).
216. Kun ldan ras pa, 1148–1217.
217. sGom pa Rin chen bla ma, d.u.
218. See note 160 (this chapter).
219. *cakravartī, 'khor los sgyur ba*. This is a mythical figure that is described in various traditions of Indian culture, including Buddhism, as a universal monarch who rules in an ethical and benevolent manner. See also ch. 4, "The Brilliant Illumination of the Path to Enlightenment," note 79.
220. These verses appear at the end of *Butön's History of Buddhism* (*Bu ston chos 'byung*).
221. rGyal ba Yang dgon pa (1213–1258). His ordination name was Gyaltsen Pel (rGyal mtshan dpal). The term *gyalwa* (*jina, rgyal ba*), which literally means "Victor," is an epithet that is used to refer to Buddha Śākyamuni. It is interpreted to mean that he was victorious in defeating Māra and eliminating all his mental faults. As in this instance, the epithet is also used with other historical figures to indicate that they are regarded as enlightened beings. See ch. 4, "The Brilliant Illumination of the Path to Enlightenment," note 34.
222. Sa skya Paṇḍi ta. This is an epithet of the Sakya patriarch Kunga Gyaltsen (Kun dga' rgyal mtshan).
223. Ko brag pa, 1182–1261. His ordination name was Sönam Gyaltsen (bSod nams rgyal mtshan).
224. rGod tshang pa, 1189–1258. His ordination name was Gönpo Dorje (mGon po rdo rje).
225. See note 28 (this chapter).
226. *rdzogs pa chen po*. A form of meditation associated with the Nyingma tradition of Tibetan Buddhism.
227. *pak shi*. This term refers to performers who traveled in groups that toured the countryside of Tibet performing instrumental music, songs, and dances in the open areas of villages and towns.
228. *tsam pa*. The Tibetan staple of barley grain that is roasted and then ground into a powder form.
229. *cha 'bal le*. Akya Yongdzin (*Thog mar blo sbyong gi dris lan*, f. 4a) states: "to sit completely still like a rabbit that has fallen asleep."
230. See note 162 (this chapter).
231. dPang lo tsā ba bLo gros brtan pa, 1276–1342.
232. Rin chen bsod nams grags, 1273–1345.
233. *dngul chu*.
234. rGya. Identity uncertain, Tokme Zangpo's biographies refer to a Lama Gyamapa (bLa ma rGya ma pa).

235. Dakchen Jamyang Dönyö Gyaltsen (bDag chen 'Jam dbyangs don yod rgyal mtshan, 1310–1344).
236. Drupchen Sangye Pel (Grub chen sangs rgyas dpal, 1339–1420).
237. *ba mo.* This metaphor is presumably meant ironically as something that will bring ruin instead of abundant results.
238. *dge bshes.* This epithet is an abbreviation of *gewe shenyen* (*dge ba'i bshes gnyen*), which is the Tibetan equivalent of the Sanskrit term *kalyāṇamitra.* The original Sanskrit literally means "virtuous" or "wholesome" friend but more accurately refers to a spiritual teacher. In Tibet, the shortened form is used as a title for a monk-scholar.
239. *dka' bcu.* This is a traditional title that is conferred upon a scholar who has completed study of five major Buddhist philosophical treatises, along with related commentaries.
240. *mahāmudrā, phyag rgya chen po.* A meditation system that employs techniques for meditating on the ultimate nature of the mind.
241. *zhi byed.* A lineage and system of teachings introduced into Tibet by Pa Dampa Sangye. See Sarah Harding, trans., *Zhije: The Pacification of Suffering,* The Treasury of Precious Instructions, vol. 13 (Boulder: Snow Lion, 2019).
242. *ja dkar nag.* Literally "white and black tea." "White tea" is the traditional Tibetan drink of tea mixed with the butter of a *dri* (female of the yak species).
243. *jagannātha, 'gro ba'i mgon po.* This epithet, often shortened to Drogön, literally means "world protector," and is considered a synonym for an enlightened being. Known as Sangye Öntön (Sangs rgyas dbon ston, 1138–1210), he was a Kadam master of a Lamrim lineage that descended from Chengawa Tsultrim Bar (sPyan snga ba Tshul khrim 'bar, 1038–1102).
244. dGyer chen po. See note 553 (this chapter) and description in related annotation.
245. sLob dpon ston pa. Lopön is an epithet that means "teacher" or "instructor." He was the oldest son of Sangye Öntön's elder brother.
246. bLa ma Sangs yon, 1180–1241. Sangyön is an abbreviation of the name Sangye Yönten (Sangs srgyas yon tan), who was a younger brother of Lopön Tönpa.
247. Bang rim pa.
248. bZang mo ba, 1158–1234. Sangmowa means "the one from Sangmo," a reference to his residence at a monastery of that name. He was referred to as Tokden (rTogs ldan), an epithet that means "one who is possessed of spiritual realization." His ordination name was Zhönu Senge (gZhon nu seng ge). See below where he is cited again with a quotation.
249. dBu ma pa. His ordination name was Namkha Sherap (Nam mkha' shes rab).
250. dGe shong ba. *KCS* gives a different spelling for his epithet—that is, Geworpa (dGe 'or pa)—and identifies him further as Sumtön Rinchen Senge (Sum ston Rin chen seng ge).
251. Se ba sgang pa. *KCS* gives the name as Sewo Gangpa (Se bo sgang pa) and provides a brief description about him.

252. Sa 'byung ba. *KCS* gives the name as Seng Jungwa (Seng 'byung ba).
253. mChe ba can pa.
254. Zong dgon pa. *KCS* gives the name as Zangpo Gönpa (bZang po dgon pa).
255. Zhogs Thang ston pa. Zhok is a place name.
256. mTshe ma ba. *KCS* gives a slightly different spelling and refers to him as Tönpa Tsema (sTon pa Tshe ma ba) and provides a brief description. Tsema is an area of the Shok region where he was born.
257. sLob dpon La mo ba. The spelling of this person's name is corrected based on *KCS*, which provides a brief description of him. The text here associates him with the Jen (*byen*) region, where he established a Nakmo monastery. For this reason, he was also known as Nakmowa (Nags mo ba), which is to say, "the one from Nakmo [Monastery]."
258. gTsang ston Nyi ma.
259. Nyang stod La dgon pa. Nyangtö is an area in Tsang. *KCS* gives this person's name as Lok Gönpa (Logs dgon pa).
260. That is, they have not given up attachment to this life.
261. *lo lor 'chor*. I take the particle *lo* here to be a reference to the earlier usage in which it is attached at the end to indicate a person who has the vain desire to be known as "learned" (*mkhas lo*), "morally upright" (*btsun lo*), "kindhearted" (*bzang lo*), "generous" (*gtong lo*), and the like.
262. These ten points collectively make up the Kadam instruction known as the Ten Ultimate Jewels (*phugs nor bcu*).
263. *bcom ldan 'das*. This is a respectful epithet of Buddha Śākyamuni that is often translated as "Blessed One" or "Lord." See ch. 4, "The Brilliant Illumination of the Path to Enlightenment," note 195, for an explanation of its meaning.
264. *guhyasthāna*, *gsang ba'i gnas*. That is, "secret" in the sense of not being fully understood.
265. These three are the enlightenment of the Śrāvakayāna, the enlightenment of the Pratyekabuddhayāna, and the enlightenment of the Mahāyāna.
266. gTsang pa rGya ras, 1161–1211. An important disciple of the Kagyu master Lingrepa Pema Dorje (gLing ras pa Padma rdo rje). He was referred to by the epithet Drogön ('Gro mgon), or World Protector (see note 232, this chapter). He was also known by the name Yeshe Dorje (Ye shes rdo rje).
267. rTogs ldan bSam gtan dpal, 1291–1366. See below where he is also referred to both as Kyechok (sKyes mchog) and Kyechokpa (sKyes mchog pa). "Tokden" is an epithet that means "one who possesses spiritual realizations."
268. Shwa bo sgang pa, 1067–1131. As indicated here, he was also referred to as Shawopa (Shwa bo pa).
269. Padma byang chub.
270. See note 44 (this chapter).
271. rGyal sha bo sgang.
272. *yas rtags* or *yas stags*. This term refers to substances that are offered to deities and

spirits in various kinds of rituals that are designed to remove obstacles or obtain favorable circumstances that relate to this life.

273. *yaśas, snyan pa.* This is the term that appears in the list of the eight worldly concerns.
274. *kīrti, grags pa.* This term is not substantially different from the previous one.
275. *parivāra, 'khor.* This term can refer to family members, dependents, disciples, followers, assistants, attendants, retainers, and so on.
276. This statement describes the third of the four "dedications" that form part of the Kadam instruction known as the Ten Ultimate Jewels. See above, p. 535 and also note 577 (this chapter).
277. sKyes mchog. This spiritual master came to be known by this general epithet that literally means "best of men." This is the same individual referred to above as Tokden Samten Pel (see note 267, this chapter).
278. bSam gtan 'phel. See note 267 (this chapter).
279. rGya brag chos rje. This epithet means "the dharma lord from Gyadrak"; his ordination name was Yeshe Zhönu (Ye shes gzhon nu).
280. *sgo mo yab.* The text here appears to be referring to a single monastery. In a later annotation (see below, notes 427 and 428), two separate monasteries are referenced. It's not clear if the text here is corrupt and also intended to refer to the second monastery named Yawa.
281. gYag sde Paṇ chen, 1299–1378. His ordination name was Tsöndru Dargye (brTson 'grus dar rgyas).
282. sKyes mchog chos rje.
283. *RA*, ch. 2, v. 68. The original Sanskrit is not extant.
284. Ibid., ch. 2, v. 28.
285. Ibid., ch. 3, v. 77. The original Sanskrit version is not extant.
286. Ibid., ch. 4, 27.
287. *CŚ*, ch. 12, v. 4.
288. *anuddhatātmā, g.yeng ba med pa'i tshul can.* The Tibetan translation interprets *anuddhata* as "undistracted"; however, the standard meaning is that of being "not arrogant," hence "humble."
289. *ŚS*, opening vv. 2, 3ab. These lines are not from the root text verses of *ŚS* but rather the author's opening verses to the treatise. The Tibetan lines quoted here differ from the version found in the Tengyur. In particular, these lines leave out the two predicates of the singular subject "humble-natured one," which make up most of the first half of verse 2. The Sanskrit original of the first half of verse 2 states: "Through the hearing of which, a humble-natured one gives up committing evil deeds and destroys entirely extensive amounts that were committed in the past." The noun "dharma jewel," which appears in the Tibetan passage here, does not occur in the original Sanskrit until the second half of verse 3. All three verbs in the passage that appears here are in the third-person plural in the Sanskrit original. The subject of the verbs, which is not mentioned in

this Tibetan quote and which appears near the end of verse 3, is "those who have obtained leisure." It is they who "attain both a well-being that had not been attained before / and never undergo a loss of happiness." They are also the ones who "attain a bodhisattva's supreme, imperishable happiness and a buddha's state of unequaled perfection" rather than the "humble-natured one," as indicated here. (*labdhakṣaṇā, dal ba thob pa rnams*).

290. *UV*, ch. 2, vv.12–14.

291. *prajñājīvin, shes rab kyis 'tsho ba*. The word "live" can also mean "to nourish" or "to sustain" oneself; hence the expression could also be rendered "one who sustains him- or herself by means of wisdom."

292. As opposed to the happiness that arises from the ārya riches, which can occur at any and all times (*sārvakālika, dus thams cad pa*).

293. Because sensory pleasures only occur within the desire realm.

294. There are seven ārya riches: faith, morality, shame, abashment, spiritual learning, generosity, and wisdom. The action of the virtuous mental factors of shame (*hrī, ngo tsha shes pa*) and abashment (*apatrāpya, khrel yod pa*) is to "provide the support that allows you to restrain yourself from committing misdeeds." See *Inner Science of Buddhist Practice*, pp. 284, 285.

295. Ordinary sensory pleasures cannot carry ordinary riches into the future either; however, the happiness that arises from the ārya riches can convey the ārya riches into the future.

296. Cf. Nāgārjuna's *Jewel Garland* (*Ratnāvalī, Rin chen phreng ba*, ch. 2 v. 69), which states: "Though there is pleasure in scratching an itch; / being free of an itch is a greater pleasure. / Similarly, though worldly desires can bring pleasure; / being free of desire is a greater pleasure."

297. This statement, which is not a direct quote, is based on a passage that appears in the *Yogācārabhūmi* (Sanskrit edition, pp. 95–99; Tibetan edition, ff. 49a–51a). It begins by stating that there are two types of happiness: that which arises from what is unrelated to the ārya riches (*anāryadhanaja, 'phags pa ma yin pa'i nor las byung ba*) and that which arises from the ārya riches (*āryadhanaja, 'phags pa'i nor las byung ba*). The former category refers mainly, but not exclusively, to ordinary sensory pleasures.

298. dGe bshes 'Ban, fl. eleventh century. Ben Gungyal Tsultrim Gyalwa was a disciple of the Kadam master Gönpawa Wangchuk Gyaltsen. See note 48 (this chapter) where he is referred to as Dre Kode Lungpa.

299. *dge slong*. The Tibetan for *bhikṣu*, or fully ordained Buddhist monk.

300. Pha Dam pa. This is a reference to Pa Dampa Sangye (Pha Dam pa Sangs rgyas, d. 1117). He is also referred to below as Dampa Gyagar (Dam pa rGya gar, see note 509, this chapter).

301. *zho ston*. Name of a yearly traditional festival held in the summer.

302. *rgyal lha khang*. An early Kadam temple founded by Zhang Nanam Dorje Wangchuk (see below) in the Penpo region in 1012.

303. The first sentence is meant to show that Potowa understood that Geshe Ben

had developed an awareness of his own mortality through meditating on impermanence in the form of death. The second sentence is meant in the sense that others have failed to cultivate this practice.

304. Akya Yongdzin (*Thog mar blo sbyong gi dris lan*, f. 4b) states: "'Soup ingredients' (*chu sdor*) is the name for food staples that are added to soup stock, such as salt, meat, butter, cheese, and the like."
305. See note 123 (this chapter).
306. See note 122 (this chapter).
307. *dPe chos*. See note 121 (this chapter). Geshe Drak Karwa consulted with Podrang Dingpa to compile the first version of the *Collection of Similes*.
308. *khal*. This term does not appear in the original text. It does appear in the interpretation that is given in *KCS*. A *khal*, which literally means a "load," is a unit of measure that is typically used for grain. It is defined as being made of twenty *dre* (*bre*). A *dre* is equivalent to about a quart and is the name of a square measuring box.
309. A different interpretation of this statement is that Geshe Ben was given this name because he stole the grain of forty neighboring farmers.
310. See note 213 (this chapter).
311. *vidyādhara*, *rig pa 'dzin pa*. *MW* (s.v. "vidyādhara") defines this as "a kind of supernatural being possessed of magical power."
312. *zho*. A unit of weight roughly equivalent to several grams.
313. *srang*. Ten *zho* equal one *sang*.
314. See note 110 (this chapter).
315. This is a reference to Drom Tönpa's disciple Tsultrim Bar. See notes 37 and 44 (this chapter). Chengawa is an epithet that indicates someone as a close attendant of a master—in this case, Drom Tönpa, whom he served for eight years.
316. *mgo nag gi mi*. Literally "black-headed person," the term suggests healthy, young laypersons who have long, black hair.
317. sTod lung pa Rin chen snying po, 1032–1116.
318. Bya yul ba gZhon nu 'od, 1075–1138.
319. Mang ra dgon pa brTson 'grus 'bar, d.u.
320. Zar pa phag sgom rDo rje ye shes, d.u.
321. See note 221 (this chapter).
322. See note 68 (this chapter).
323. *gar*. In the sense of a lifetime of useless conduct.
324. dGe bshes sDings pa ba. As the annotation here indicates, his ordination name was Sherap Gyatso (*Shes rab rgya mtsho*). *KCS* refers to him as Zhang Dingpa (Zhang sDings pa). This individual is different from Dölpa Sherap Gyatso (see note 120, this chapter), also a disciple of Potowa.
325. *bu*. Literally "son." That is, he was referring to himself as a spiritual son of Drom Tönpa.
326. This expression should be taken to mean that he taught disciples.
327. sKyes mchog pa. See notes 267 and 277 (this chapter), along with the related

annotation in the main text. See also below where an annotation identifies his ordination name, the name of his principal spiritual teacher, and several additional details.

328. 'U yug pa Rig pa'i seng ge.
329. *khang gnyan zhang gsum*. That is, the teacher from Khang, Öser Gyaltsen ('Od zer rgyal mtshan); Nyan Darma Senge (gNyan Dar ma seng ge); and Zhang Dode Pel (Zhang mDo sde dpal).
330. dMar Chos rgyal.
331. Lho pa Kun mkhyen Rin chen dpal.
332. Tshogs sgom pa Kun dga' dpal, 1210–1307.
333. Grub thob Yon tan mtha' yas.
334. *Treasury of Jewel-Like Excellent Sayings* (*Legs par bshad pa rin po che'i gter*), ch. 6, v. 24ab.
335. Ibid., ch. 6, v. 60, abd. The order of these lines is different in the original verse.
336. Ibid., ch. 9, v. 32.
337. Zhang btsun yer pa, d.u. His ordination name was Yeshe Bar (Ye shes 'bar). The epithet Shangtsun means "the monk from the Shang region." See also note 24 (this chapter).
338. Zhang sna nam rDo rje dbang phyug, 976–1060.
339. *rgyal lha khang*. Founded in 1012.
340. kLu mes Shes rab tshul khrims. A lineage holder of the first system of vinaya that was introduced to Tibet by Śāntarakṣita and is known as the Lower Vinaya (*smad 'dul*). He was a teacher of Zhang Nanam Dorje Wangchuk.
341. *Buddhapiṭakaduḥśīlanigraha*, *Sangs rgyas kyi sde snod tshul khrims 'chal ba tshar gcod pa*.
342. *karuṇāpuṇḍarikasūtra*, *sNying rje padma dkar po'i mdo*.
343. This statement is a paraphrase of a passage that appears in the Tibetan translation of the sūtra.
344. Panchen lamas Losang Chökyi Gyaltsen and Pelden Yeshe both cite essentially the same verse and attribute it to the Buddha; however, I have not identified its canonical source.
345. sPyan snga Rin po che. "Chenga" is an epithet that literally means "before the eyes" (see note 35, this chapter). "Rinpoche" is also an epithet that means "precious one" and is a term of reverence. This is likely a reference to the Kadam master who was one of Drom Tönpa's principal disciples and whose ordination name was Tsultrim Bar (sPyan snga Tshul khrims 'bar, 1038–1102).
346. This is a reference to the second of the four dedications that form part of the Kadam instruction known as the Ten Ultimate Jewels. The aphorism states, "Dedicate your ultimate form of dharma practice to living in a state of poverty."
347. *kuhanā*, *tshul 'chos*. See ch. 10, "The Essence of Nectar," note 375.
348. dGe bshes Kha rag pa. See note 50 (this chapter).
349. Text reads *zhur ba*, as though it were a verb. However, *KCS* (f. 118a) reads "in a

placed called Dungshur" (*dung zhur*), indicating that it is the name of the place where he was born.

350. dGon pa ba. See note 13 (this chapter).
351. See note 50 (this chapter).
352. *sBa sgom bSod nams rgyal mtshan*. *KCS* identifies this teacher as a household priest (*mchod gnas*) who was supported by Potowa Rinchen Sel's father and who possessed a lineage of instruction that was originated by a master referred to as Aro (A ro). *The Blue Annals* identifies the latter as Aro Yeshe Jungne (A ro Ye shes 'byung gnas) and his instruction as a system of Great Completion practice.
353. rDul ston rDo rje rin chen.
354. Cog ro Zangs dkar mdzod khung. *The Blue Annals* lists this person as a disciple of Bagom.
355. Lho pa Dhar ma skyabs.
356. That is, you will not regain the ability to pursue enlightenment in a future life if you squander the opportunity you have to do so in this life.
357. See note 266 (this chapter).
358. gLing ras pa Padma rdo rje, 1128–1188. He was a principal disciple of Pakmo Drupa Dorje Gyalpo (Phag mo gru pa rDo rje rgyal po, 1110–1170).
359. *'brug*. Founded in 1205.
360. *ra lung*. Founded in 1180.
361. *sprul pa*. That is, an emanation body (*nirmāṇakāya, sprul sku*), or reincarnation, of Naropa.
362. Lo ras pa, 1187–1250. His personal name was Wangchuk Tsöndru (dBang phyug brtson 'grus).
363. See note 30 and annotation on p. 614 (this chapter).
364. sPa. The text reads *Sa*, not *sPa*, but this is probably a corruption, and the reference is to a disciple known as Pariwa (sPa ri ba).
365. rKyang. An abbreviated reference to the disciple known as Kyangmokhawa (rKyang mo kha ba).
366. rGya. An abbreviated reference to the disciple known as Gya Yakpa (rGya yags pa).
367. 'Bras. An abbreviated reference to the disciple known as Dremowa Sangye Bum ('Bras mo ba Sangs rgyas 'bum).
368. *dge slong*. That is, a fully ordained Buddhist monk, or bhikṣu.
369. The male form is called a *ḍāka* (*mkha' 'gro*) and the female form a *ḍākinī* (*mkha' 'gro ma*).
370. See note 162 and the annotation at p. 530 (this chapter).
371. dGe bshes Kha rag pa. This individual does not appear to be the same one as Kharak Gomchung (see note 50, this chapter).
372. Kun spangs Grags rgyal. Kunpang is an epithet that means "one who has abandoned everything" and indicates that all material possessions and ordinary

activities have been given up. Drakgyal is probably a shortened form of the name Drakpa Gyaltsen (Grags pa rgyal mtshan).

373. Yu mo ba. This was the popular name of an eleventh-century Kālacakra master. His ordination name was Depa Gyalpo (Dad pa rgyal po) and his tantric name was Mikyö Dorje (Mi bskyod rdo rje).

374. *bdag po med pa.* The adjectival phrase that literally translates as "lacking a caretaker" or even "lacking an owner" typically is used to indicate that a person is failing to carry out some activity that needs to be done or accomplished. In this context, this first line should be taken to mean that "meditative progress" (*sgom skyes*) is not occurring because of some shortcoming or failure in one's practice. The noun "caretaker" in the last line means that the spiritual quality of detachment is what will correct the inability to achieve progress in one's meditation.

375. *kha spos pa.* Literally a "shift in position," which here means a change for the better; hence, "improvement."

376. See note 266 (this chapter). Drogön is a shortened form of the epithet Drowe Gönpo.

377. That is, by having successfully abandoned attachment to this life.

378. Again, the quality of having mentally abandoned this life.

379. *sgyid pa bgrad pa.* Literally "with the knees spread apart."

380. *smon pa.* That is, the aspirational form of enlightenment mind. This is the first of two levels of the conventional form of enlightenment mind. The second is the active form of enlightenment mind.

381. That is, by having overcome attachment for all of samsara and attained the first stages of the path. This point is identified as the entry point of the "accumulation path" (*sambhāramārga, tshogs lam*), the first of the five stages of the Buddhist path to liberation.

382. *dharmin, chos pa.* While this term literally means "one who possesses dharma," it could be understood more loosely to mean simply "a virtuous person" or "a religious person."

383. See note 266 (this chapter) and annotation, p. 549.

384. See ch. 10, "The Essence of Nectar," note 275, for an explanation of this term. The commitments referred to here are found in a work by Tsangpa Gyare titled *A Lamp for the Eyes That Requires Little Difficulty: A Treatise for Those Who Mentally Abandon the World* (*'Jig rten blos btang rnams kyi bstan bcos tshegs chung mig gi sgron me*).

385. This verb is used with the act of reciting mantras as a practitioner typically keeps count of their number with a string of prayer beads.

386. *dgos med kyi drag sngags.* The phrase "having no needs" should be taken to mean that you give up any interest in a meaningless, worldly life. To "count" a mantra means to recite it continually; thus, this commitment means to cultivate continually the attitude that abandons attachment to this life.

387. *sna thag.* This term refers to the rope that is tied to a cow's nose ring in order to

control its movement. This commitment is an admonition to maintain spiritual self-control and discipline.

388. *saṃsarga, 'du rdzi.* This term is meant to indicate that associating with corrupt or immoral persons (*asatpuruṣa, skyes bu dam pa ma yin pa*) carries the risk of unfavorable consequences.

389. *kāmaprahāṇa, 'dod pa spong ba.*

390. The referenced passage appears in the ninth section of the *Yogacārabhūmi*, as commentary to the first in the series of verses called *The Verses on the Meaning of the Body* (*Śarīrārthagāthā, 'Dus pa'i don gyi tshigs su bcad pa*).

391. *pravrajita, rab tu byung ba.* That is, a Buddhist monk or nun. See ch. 4, "Brilliant Illumination of the Path to Enlightenment," note 271. This term is also translated here as "renunciate." See notes 152 and 485 (this chapter) for a different Tibetan term that is also translated as "renunciate."

392. That is, the three doors that are the means of carrying out deeds—namely, one's body, speech, and mind.

393. *manaskāra, yid la byed pa. AS* (p. 6) states: "What is attention? It is the bending of the mind. Its action is to cause the mind to keep hold of an object." Sthiramati explains the phrase "bending of the mind" as "the condition by which the mind is directed toward an object." "Proper attention" (*yoniśo manaskāra, tshul bzhin du yid la byed pa*) means the form of attention that accords with the dharma.

394. Akya Yongdzin (*Thog mar blo sbyong gi dris lan*, f. 5b) states: "'Entities that have not been examined' means those objects that have not been examined and investigated as to whether they are favorable to the practice of dharma or not."

395. *Adhyāśayasaṃcodanasūtra, Lhag pa'i bsam pa bskul ba'i mdo.* Several passages from this sūtra, including the verses cited here, appear in Śāntideva's *Compendium of Training* (*Śikṣāsamuccaya, bsLab pa kun las btus pa*).

396. *dpag tshad.* See note 149 (this chapter). This unit of distance is understood to be slightly more than four miles.

397. *prapañca, spros pa.* Candrakīrti (*PP*, p. 159) states: "Elaboration is speech, since that is what causes entities to be elaborated upon." Also, *BBhVy* (f. 60a) states: "Elaborations are the objects that are formed in the mind on the basis of such conventional expressions as 'permanent' and the like, and they are the conventional expressions that derive from conceptual thought." In this context, the term appears to be understood as conceptual thought and verbal expression about secular topics that only serve to distract you from the pursuit of genuine spiritual endeavors.

398. *yasyārthāya.* The Tibetan translation of this phrase is "for the sake of whose wealth," which, though a possible reading, seems less plausible than the more straightforward "for the sake of which."

399. For original Sanskrit of these verses, see *ŚS*, p. 65.

400. *Thirty-Seven Verses on the Practices of the Victors' Spiritual Offspring* (*rGyal ba'i sras kyi lag len sum cu so bdun ma*), v. 2.

401. Re mda' ba gZhon nu blo gros, 1348/49–1412.
402. Lo tsā ba Byang chub rtse mo, 1303–1380.
403. *KCS* (f. 311b–312a) gives the following list of seven disciples who were spiritual teachers: Kunkhyen Sherap Ö (Kun mkhyen Shes rab 'od), Losang Drakpai Pel (bLo bzang grags pa'i dpal), Kunga Pel Zangpo (Kun dga' dpal bzang po), Nyima Gyaltsen (Nyi ma rgyal mtshan), Peljor Sherap (dPal 'byor shes rab), Sönam Sherap (bSod nams shes rab), Darma Rinchen (Dar ma rin chen).
404. 'Ba' ra ba. This figure is Barawa Gyaltsen Pelsang ('Ba' ra ba rGyal mtshan dpal bzang, 1310–1391).
405. See note 57 (this chapter).
406. *Blue Udder* (*Be'u bum sngon po*). Akya Yongdzin (*Thog mar blo sbyong gi dris lan*, f. 6a) states: "Regarding the line 'Don't give the nape of your neck to anyone,' for example, if someone takes hold of you by the flesh on the back or nape of your neck, you will not be able to move and you will come under that person's control. Likewise, the meaning of this phrase is 'Don't relinquish your freedom to another person.'"
407. *lham sna bsgyur ba*. This idiom means to depart from some place. Regarding the full statement, Akya Yongdzin (*Thog mar blo sbyong gi dris lan*, f. 6a) states: "A monk must not accumulate and hoard any objects. Whenever he desires to go somewhere else, . . . he must be able to depart after having disposed of all his possessions and without leaving anything behind."
408. *Candrapradīpasūtra, Zla ba sgron me'i mdo*.
409. *Samādhirājāsūtra, Ting nge 'dzin gyi rgyal po'i mdo*.
410. ch. 19, v. 14.
411. *Saddharmasmṛtyupasthānasūtra, Dam pa'i chos dran pa nye bar gzhag pa'i mdo*.
412. The text here states "alms food at most at midday" (*nyi ma phyed nas bsod snyoms mchog*). The Kangyur edition states "alms food at most once a day" (*nyi ma gcig la bsod snyoms mchog*). The extant Sanskrit verse confirms this latter version (*ekāhaparamaṃ piṇḍam ādattte śvo na kāṅkṣate | dvibhāgakukṣisantuṣṭo bhikṣur bhavati tādṛśa*).
413. In place of the phrase "one who is satisfied with a full stomach" (*lto 'grangs tsam gyis chog byed pa*) in the Tibetan of this verse, the Sanskrit original states "one who is satisfied with a stomach two-thirds full" (*dvibhāgakukṣisantuṣṭo*), suggesting the principle of knowing moderation in food (*bhojane mātrajñatā, zas kyi tshod rig pa*).
414. mKhas btsun gZhon nu grub (b. mid-thirteenth century, d. 1319). An important master of the Shangpa Kagyu lineage. The first two-syllable word of this name is an epithet that describes a monk as "wise and a morally upright." He received ordination at Narthang Monastery and studied with Sakya teachers. Later, he became a disciple of Sangye Tönpa Tsöndru Senge (Sangs rgyas ston pa brTson 'grus seng ge). He was a lineage holder for a particular system of the chöd (*gcod*), or severance, practice.
415. *yu ba gdong*.

416. *dpal rnam bsam sdings.*
417. *Blue Udder* (*Be'u bum sngon po*).
418. *rtswa shing.* Literally "grass and twigs."
419. *dred po.* This meaning of "hardness" is that of insensitivity and loss of appreciation for what is spiritual.
420. *bāla, byis pa.* In ordinary usage this term can mean a "child"; in a religious context, it refers to a spiritually immature and foolish person. In a more technical sense, it is synonymous with the term "ordinary person" (*pṛthagjana, so so skye bo*), which applies to anyone that has not achieved the status of an ārya.
421. *lapanā, kha gsag.* The original Sanskrit of this term and its Tibetan translation are the names for one of five forms of wrong livelihood that are described in Buddhist literature. It occurs when an individual, typically a monk or nun, speaks favorably or shows deference to someone as a means of obtaining something of value from him or her. See also note 850 (this chapter).
422. See note 61 (this chapter).
423. This is a self-reference to the author himself, who was known by this epithet because he resided at Gyama Rinchen Gang Monastery (see note 65, this chapter).
424. See note 267 (this chapter).
425. See note 279 (this chapter).
426. *zhi byed.* A lineage and system of teachings introduced into Tibet by Pa Dampa Sangye. Cf. Sarah Harding, trans., *Zhije: The Pacification of Suffering*, The Treasury of Precious Instructions, vol. 13 (Boulder: Snow Lion, 2019).
427. *sgo mo dgon.*
428. *ya ba dgon.*
429. Akya Yongdzin (*Thog mar blo sbyong gi dris lan*, f. 6a) states: "The meaning of this line is that the approving or disapproving nature of the words from a rich person's mouth, his or her pleased or displeased [literally "white or black"] teeth and facial expressions, and the generosity and so on carried out by his or her hands are what are held in high regard and hoped for."
430. *g.yog 'khor.* Here "servants and a retinue" means any form of companions or attendants while in seclusion.
431. *BCA*, ch. 8, v. 7.
432. Ibid., ch. 8, v. 8.
433. Ibid., ch. 8, v. 10
434. Ibid., ch. 8, v. 11
435. Ibid., ch. 8, vv. 14–15a. The Tibetan of these lines states: "If, in this way, my association with other persons / leads only to ruin, / that person does not accomplish my aims, / nor do I accomplish his. / Therefore, one should flee far away from foolish persons."
436. *UV*, ch. 25, v. 24. This citation does not state the complete verse. The final line states: "However, it is pleasant to associate with / those who are steadfast, as when meeting with close relatives."

437. *abhiprāya, dgongs pa.* This term is used to indicate that certain canonical statements in particular, and even just important spiritual principles, sometimes need to be interpreted as to how they should be properly understood.
438. Literally "past and future ends" (*pūrvāparānta, sngon dang phyi ma'i mtha'*); this phrase here means past and future lives, and thus knowledge of them is a reference to the forms of supernatural knowledge that can perceive other persons' past and future lives, which are known as "recollection of previous existences" (*pūrvanivāsānusmṛti, sngon gyi gnas rjes su dran pa*) and "perceiving death and rebirth" (*cyutyupapādadarśana, 'chi pho ba dang skye ba mthong ba*) respectively.
439. **niḥsaraṇa, nges par 'byung ba.* This term is understood to mean the aspiration to attain liberation (*thar pa don gnyer gyi blo*).
440. *piṭaka, sde snod.* Literally this term means a "basket" or container, such as for grain. It is also used to refer to the collections of Buddhist canonical literature, such as the three "baskets" of sūtra (discourses), vinaya (code of moral discipline), and abhidharma (systematic formulations of essential doctrine) literature.
441. These three attributes that should be possessed by a person who wants to listen to the dharma are found in Āryadeva's *Four Hundred Verses* (*Catuḥśatikā, bZhi brgya pa*), ch. 12, v. 1.
442. These lines appear among the closing verses to Butön's work known popularly as *Butön's History of Buddhism* (*Bu ston chos 'byung*).
443. On the outflows, see ch. 4, "The Brilliant Illumination of the Path to Enlightenment," note 62. For the Vaibhāṣika description that appears in *AKBh* (in explanation of ch. 5, v. 40 of the root text), see ch. 10, "The Essence of Nectar," note 174.
444. *mgo nag gi mi.* Literally "black-headed person," this is an idiomatic general term for any individual, especially a layperson, who does not have a shaved head, like a monk or nun.
445. *tshul 'chos kyi bzang tshul.* The original text uses the term that is usually translated as "hypocrisy"; see ch. 10, "The Essence of Nectar," note 375.
446. *gtum mo.* This term refers to a form of spiritual exercise practiced in Highest Yoga Tantra that generates heat within the central channel (*rtsa dbu ma*) of the body.
447. Two individuals are referred to in this text as Drogön, or "world protector": Tsangpa Gyare (see note 266, this chapter) and Sangye Öntön. This reference appears to be to the latter figure. See note 243 (this chapter) and annotation on p. 534.
448. This is the Tibetan name of the myrobalan tree, whose fruit is used in Ayurvedic medicine. The seeds can also be used to make prayer beads.
449. *byi'u.* The seems to be a reference to the name of one of eight monasteries that existed in the vicinity of Lake Manasarovar. "Footprint" thus can be taken as a metaphor for the meditation hut itself.
450. See notes 244 and 553 (this chapter).

451. *ltogs 'gong. The Great Tibetan Dictionary* (s.v. "ltogs 'gong") describes this expression as "a disdainful term for a harmful spirit."

452. This passage appears near the end of the *Blue Udder*. A line before the last two that is left out here states: "Conduct yourself as taught in the *Sūtra Encouraging a Superior Attitude*." This is a reference to the advice that is presented in several passages from this sūtra that are cited in Śāntideva's *Compendium of Training*, ch. 5. The lines that follow the last one cited here state: "Acting on behalf of sentient beings while lacking supernormal knowledge / is like a blind person who shoots an arrow upon hearing the word 'deer.' / Therefore, mainly strive to avoid being too hasty."

453. Khro phu lo tsā ba Byams pa dpal, 1173–1236. His name is abbreviated here as Trolo.

454. *skam po*. Literally "dry" or "shriveled" but with the sense of having no value.

455. The Sanskrit edition of this passage can be read as associating the phrase "in order to accomplish one's own aims" with the quality of "giving rise to guile" rather than the phrase "causing greed and attachment toward one's family."

456. The Tibetan text here reads "guile and deceitfulness" (*g.yo sgyu*); however, the original sūtra passage, both in the Tibetan and the Sanskrit versions, only mentions "guile" (*śāṭhya, g.yo*). *AS* (pp. 8–9) states: "What is guile? It is a form of desire and ignorance in which a person who is attached to gain and honor conceals faults that he or she possesses. Its action serves to obstruct the obtaining of correct spiritual instruction."

457. *māyā, sgyu*. While this term appears here, it does not appear in the sūtra passage. *AS* (p. 8) states: "What is deceitfulness? It is a form of desire and ignorance in which a person who is attached to gain and honor gives the appearance of possessing qualities that he or she does not possess. Its action is to give support to wrong livelihood."

458. *āhrīkya, ngo tsha med pa*. *AS* (p. 9) states: "What is shamelessness? It is a form of desire, hatred, or ignorance that is the lack of embarrassment about objectionable acts for reasons relating to oneself. Its action is to facilitate all the root and secondary mental afflictions."

459. *AS* (p. 9) states: "What is absence of abashment? It is a form of desire, hatred, or ignorance that is the lack of embarrassment about objectionable acts for reasons relating to others. Its action is to facilitate all the root and secondary mental afflictions."

460. *catvāra āryavaṃśā, 'phags pa'i rigs bzhi*. The four attributes are to be satisfied with dharma robes, alms food, and a bed and seat, no matter what their quality might be, and to delight in abandoning the mental afflictions and practicing meditation.

461. *AS* (p. 7) states: "What is pride? It is the swelling up of the mind that occurs on the basis of the view of the perishable collection (*satkāyadṛṣṭi, 'jig tshogs la lta ba*; see ch. 10, "The Essence of Nectar," note 163). Its action is to give support to the arising of disrespect and suffering."

462. *mada, rgyags pa. AS* (p. 9) states: "What is conceit? It is a form of desire that is accompanied by joy and gladness, and it arises from possessing such qualities as health or youth, or from having perceived an indication that one will have a long life or having perceived oneself as having some other form of samsaric good fortune. Its action is to give support to all the root and secondary mental afflictions." *ASBh* (p. 7) states: "The phrase 'some other form of samsaric good fortune' should be understood to mean an eminent family, strength, beauty, intelligence, knowledge, wealth, power, and so on."
463. *darpa*, also *garva, dregs pa*. This term does not appear in the sūtra passage.
464. *guru, bla ma*. Use of this term is not restricted to a spiritual teacher, as it is commonly understood in everyday language. *BBhVy* (f. 9a) states: "For laypersons, 'those worthy of honor' means one's father and mother; for homeless ascetics i.e., monks and nuns, it means one's preceptor (*upādhyāya, mkhan po*) and one's instructor (*ācārya, slob dpon*)."
465. *mārapakṣa, bdud kyi phyogs. ŚBh* (pp. 344–45) describes four forms of Māra. See note 97 (this chapter).
466. See ch. 8, "The Easy Path," note 58.
467. There are three roots of virtue (*kuśalamūla, dge ba'i rtsa ba*). See ch. 9, "Essential Summary of the Method of Practice in the System of the Stages of the Path to Enlightenment," note 80.
468. *aśani, lce 'bab*. The Tibetan translation, which literally means "tongue descent," is glossed as *thog*, the more familiar term for "lightning" as well as "thunder."
469. *bahupaligodhapaliguddha, sbags pa mang pos sbags pa*. The Tibetan translation suggests a general sense of "taint or "contaminant" for the Sanskrit *paligoddha*; hence, the term is glossed as being synonymous with the mental afflictions generally. However, *BHS* suggests that the original term is more narrowly associated with "greed" and "attachment"; thus, the phrase might be rendered "gain and honor are craved after with much greed."
470. This phrase addresses the principle that Buddhist monks should not single out the homes of those who are disposed to give food when seeking alms.
471. *catvāri smṛtyupasthānāni, dran pa nye bar bzhag pa bzhi*. See *Inner Science of Buddhist Practice*, pp. 138–92 and pp. 216–23 for a comprehensive description.
472. *catvāri samyakprahāṇāni, yang dag spong ba bzhi*. This fourfold practice is identified as essentially a form of effort (*vīrya, brtson 'grus*). Canonical scriptures give this description: "The practitioner develops aspiration, strives, initiates effort, takes hold of his or her mind, and places it in order to keep from developing those evil and unvirtuous entities that have not arisen previously; in order to abandon those evil and unvirtuous entities that have arisen previously; in order to develop those virtuous entities that have not arisen previously; and in order to maintain possession of, avoid indistinctness about, complete meditation on, as well as increase, strengthen, and augment those virtuous entities that have arisen previously." *ŚBh* (pp. 307–14) gives a detailed analysis of every expression that appears in this passage. Buddhist Sanskrit literature also refers to this prac-

tice by another term that means "correct placement" (*samyakpradhāna, yang dag par rab tu 'jog pa*). For example, *AKBh* (p. 384) states: "Why is effort called 'correct placement'? Effort is called that because it causes the body, speech, and mind to be correctly placed." Yaśomitra's subcommentary (*AKV*, vol. 3, p. 1019) glosses the verb "to be placed" (*pradhīyante, rab tu 'jog pa*) as "to be kept steady" (*dhāryante, 'dzin pa*) and "to be controlled" (*niyamyante, nges par byed pa*).

473. *catvāra ṛddhipadā, rdzu 'phrul gyi rkang pa bzhi*. The four elements of miraculous power are forms of one-pointed concentration that serve as the basis for achieving various kinds of magical powers, such as the ability to transform one object into many and many objects into one. They are differentiated into four types because of the manner in which the practitioner enters a state of one-pointed concentration: through a strong aspiration to perform virtue, through maintaining constant effort, through prior cultivation of one-pointed concentration, and through applying discriminative awareness gained by receiving instruction from others. See *BBh*, book 1, ch. 5, English translation, pp. 106–22, for a description of various kinds of miraculous power.

474. See *BBh*, book 1, ch. 5, English translation, pp. 106–29.

475. That is, rebirth as a preta spirit (*yi dwags*), a term that is often translated as "hungry ghost."

476. The original Sanskrit of this passage appears in Śāntideva's *ŚS*, ch. 5, pp. 61–62.

477. *alpecchatā, 'dod pa chung ba*. This virtue is the form of avoidance of desire (*alobha, 'dod chags med pa*) that is the antidote for the unvirtuous quality of "having great desires" (*mahecchatā, 'dod pa che ba*), which Vasubandhu (*AKBh*, p. 335) defines as "the desire for excellent and large amounts of material possessions that one has not obtained" (*alabdhapraṇītaprabhūtecchā mahecchatā*).

478. See note 456 (this chapter).

479. See note 457 (this chapter).

480. The formatting of the published Sanskrit edition of this statement and two previous ones suggests a slightly different reading: "As one who is intent upon cultivation of meditative absorption, he or she is longed for by gods and humans. As one who has abandoned deceitfulness and guile, he or she perceives clearly. As one who sees the five sensory pleasures as having faults, he or she becomes mindful."

481. See note 438 (this chapter).

482. *ŚS*, ch. 5, p. 62.

483. *upakaraṇa, yo byad*. The Sanskrit term can mean (*MW*, s.v. "upakaraṇa") "instrument" or "implement" (that is used for accomplishing some particular activity) or, more generally, a "means of subsistence" and "anything that supports life"; hence, in the present context, "material possessions."

484. *saṃtuṣṭi, chog shes pa*. "Knowing satisfaction," which is to say, being satisfied with what one has, is the opposite of lack of satisfaction. *AKBh* (p. 335) states: "Lack of satisfaction (*asaṃtuṣṭi, chog mi shes pa*) is the distress that is caused by obtaining material possessions that are not excellent or not in large amounts."

485. *bya btang byed pa.* Literally "to be one who gives up all ordinary activities." See also note 152 (this chapter).

486. See note 214 (this chapter) and the annotation on p. 527.

487. *samarāsa, ro snyoms.* This term refers to a range of practices, all of which share the general quality of developing an attitude of equanimity. The most basic form would be to develop the equanimity of indifference to the eight worldly concerns. A middling form of this practice is to recognize all forms of samsaric pleasure and pain as having the same "taste" or nature of suffering. A more advanced form is to view all diverse conceptual distinctions of good, bad, and so on, with an equanimity that perceives them all to have the "taste" of the same ultimate nature. Here it is meant in the context of not developing attachment by discriminating between excellent and poor food.

488. Four early Kadam disciples of Drom Tönpa. They are identified in notes 11, 14, 15, and 17 (this chapter). They were Naljorpa Jangchup Rinchen, Chaktri Chok from Lhodrak, Chakdar Tönpa, and Naljorpa Sherap Dorje.

489. Probably "hot" in the sense of being cooked over a fire.

490. Gönpawa Wangchuk Gyaltsen. See note 13 (this chapter).

491. *spyan snga.* Literally "one who is before the eyes," this epithet is given to disciples who are always in the presence of their spiritual teacher (see note 37, this chapter).

492. rMog cog pa (also written rMog lcog pa). While there were several individuals who were known by this epithet, this is likely a reference to Rinchen Tsöndru (Rin chen brtson 'grus, 1110–1170), who was a principal disciple of Khyungpo Naljor (Khyung po rnal 'byor).

493. *Pūrṇaparipṛcchā, Gang pos zhus pa.* The Tibetan translation of this sūtra is contained in the *Ratnakūṭa* collection.

494. That is, loss, disrepute, blame, and suffering.

495. *SL*, v. 35.

496. *ngo bsrung.* Literally "preserving the face," the sense here is that of acting in a conciliatory manner in order to maintain another person's favorable opinion of you. A similar phrase is "preserving the mind" of another person (*sems bsrung ba*).

497. See note 44 (this chapter).

498. *sha gzug. The Great Tibetan-Chinese Dictionary* states: "*sha gzug* means one portion of a carcass that has been separated into four quarters."

499. *bya ba gtong ba.* This idiomatic phrase means to adopt the lifestyle of a renunciate who gives up all needless activities or concerns. See also notes 152 and 485 (this chapter).

500. This is a reference to Khetsun Zhönu Drup. See note 414 (this chapter).

501. See note 279 (this chapter).

502. bLa ma dBol sna ba. Possibly a reference to Yegönpa Gönpo Yeshe (see notes 68 and 322, this chapter).

503. *rlung la bskur ba*. The phrase "to cast something to the wind" means to abandon it completely.

504. *ngo bsrungs mkhan*. Since this quality is expressly addressed in this section as one to be avoided, this last line seems to be meant in a somewhat ironic sense. The point of the verse appears to be that it is best to be resourceful and resilient.

505. Generally speaking, it is desirable for a dharma practitioner to generate merit (*puṇya, bsod nams*). Merit is a synonym for virtue. *AK* (ch. 4, v. 46ab) states: "Merit is a virtuous deed of the desire realm." The sense here seems to be that a person who gains a reputation for being religious can see his or her worldly fortunes improve and that notoriety can become an obstacle to further spiritual progress and, in particular, to the solitude that is necessary for the life of a meditation practitioner.

506. *phye gtor*. It is a Tibetan custom to toss *tsampa* powder into the air as an auspicious offering, typically to the gods, in order to invoke success and victory. The reference here is that if Māra does so, it is an indication of his ability to impede your spiritual progress. See the description of "the Māra that is a [worldly] god" (*devapūtramāra, lha'i bu'i bdud*) in note 97 (this chapter).

507. This epithet refers to Gyamawa Tashi Gyaltsen. See note 61 (this chapter).

508. *sku bsod*. This is an honorific form of the word for "merit," but it also includes the connotation of a person whose merit enables him or her to be fortunate and successful.

509. Dam pa rGya gar, d. 1117. This epithet, which literally means "the holy one from India," is another name for Pa Dampa Sangye (*Pha Dam pa sangs rgyas*). See note 300 (this chapter).

510. Dam pa Kun dga', 1062–1164. This individual was Pa Dampa Sangye's foremost Tibetan disciple.

511. The desire not to develop merit, an aim that is seemingly contrary to the dharma, is meant in a specific sense. See note 505 (this chapter).

512. *AS* (p. 9) states: "What is excitation (*auddhatya, rgod pa*)? It is the lack of calmness in the mind that follows attractive images and is a form of desire. Its action is to obstruct the attainment of quiescence." *PSV* (p. 308) describes the cause of excitation to be "recalling previous experiences that are consistent with desire, such as occasions of laughter, amusement, and the like."

513. The verse cited in *ŚS* (p. 62) has "laughter" (*hāsya*) in place of regret. However, the Tibetan translations of both the verses that appear in *ŚS* and the Kangyur version of the sūtra itself have "regret" (*kaukṛtrya, 'gyod pa*), which is considered a mental factor that can be virtuous or unvirtuous in nature, depending on the circumstances. *AS* (p. 9) states: "What is regret? It is a form of ignorance that is the mind's sense of remorse, and it is a mental factor that occurs in relation to an action that was done willingly or unwillingly, as well as an action that was done with or without a reason. Regret can be virtuous, unvirtuous, or indeterminate in nature, and it can occur in relation to acts done at an oppor-

tune or an inopportune time or acts that are proper or improper. Its action is to obstruct mental stability." In the verse passage cited here, regret is meant in the sense of an unvirtuous mental factor that is a secondary mental affliction. For example, regret is identified as an aspect of one of the "five hindrances to mental absorption" (*snyoms 'jug gi sgrib pa*; see note 623, this chapter). The term "mental stability" (*cittasthiti, sems gnas pa*) that appears in the description of the action or regret means "a state in which the mind remains stationary or fixed." *ŚBh* (pp. 363–64) describes nine levels of mental stability that culminate in the attainment of the form of one-pointed concentration known as "quiescence" (*śamatha, zhi gnas*).

514. *AS* (p. 9) states: "What is deliberation (*vitarka, rnam par rtog pa*)? It is a form of mental discourse that investigates an object or a topic on the basis of volition or discrimination. It is also a relatively coarse mental state." This mental factor also can be virtuous or unvirtuous in nature, depending on the circumstances. Here it is understood to be an unvirtuous form of mental activity, such as deliberation about one's relatives (*jñātivitarka, nye du'i rnam par rtog pa*), deliberation about one's homeland (*janapadavitarka, yul gyi rtam par rtog pa*), or deliberation that one is not at risk of dying" (*amaravitarka, mi 'chi ba'i rnam par rtog pa*). The word translated as "discrimination" in Asaṅga's description of deliberation is *prajñā* (*shes rab*), which usually is understood to mean "wisdom." However, as this mental activity can be incorrect, I render it here with a neutral term. For example, the view of the perishable collection (*satkāyadṛṣṭi, 'jig tshogs la lta ba*) is a mental affliction that Vasubandhu (*Inner Science of Buddhist Practice*, p. 235) describes as "afflicted wisdom" (*kliṣṭaprajñā, shes rab nyon mongs pa can*). Sthiramati (*Inner Science of Buddhist Practice*, p. 300) interprets this term as follows: "The phrase 'afflicted wisdom' suggests that, if this view were not a confused state, it would not conceive of something that is not a self as being a self. Thus, the term 'afflicted' means that this form of discriminating awareness is accompanied by ignorance and is erroneous."

515. Cited in *ŚS*, p. 62.

516. Ngawang Tsering Kyap (f. 13b) states: "'Performing dog mantras' (*khyi sngags byed pa*) means treating wounds caused by dog bites with saliva infused with mantra blessings." While there might be demand for a monk to carry out this kind of spiritual assistance, it is a distraction and an obstacle for a meditation practitioner.

517. *sgrib shing*. This expression is usually interpreted as a "stick that hides," in which case it refers to a charm that can make you invisible. Here I take the expression in a pejorative sense, which means that undertaking many activities, even to benefit others, can result in behavior that "obscures"—that is, deters—your ultimate spiritual practice.

518. Cited in *ŚS*, p. 64.

519. *Gaganagañjaparipṛcchāsūtra, Nam mkha' mdzod kyis zhus pa'i mdo*.

520. Cited in *ŚS*, p. 29. This verse does not appear to be from the sūtra of a similar name that appears in the Kangyur.

521. *Sa'i dngos gzhi.* This is the Tibetan descriptive name for the principal work in the Yogācāra collection of treatises. The complete work is made up of seventeen "stages," or bhūmis, and its Tibetan translation is contained in three volumes of the Tengyur collection.

522. These are the first two verses from the second topic of the third and final section of the eleventh bhūmi of the *Main Treatise on the Stages*, which is titled "The Stage That Consists of Reflection" (*cintāmayī bhūmi, bsams pa las byung ba'i sa*). The verses in this section are referred to collectively as *The Verses on the Meaning of the Body* (*Śarīrārthagāthā, 'Dus pa'i don gyi tshigs su bcad pa*).

523. *bhoga, longs spyod.* Literally "object of enjoyment," this term can refer to such things as "food," "possessions," "property," "wealth," and "revenue" (*MW*, s.v. "bhoga"). In this case, the term can refer both to alms food and other necessities of a spiritual practitioner's life, as well as ordinary sensory pleasures. The former are the objects that a spiritual practitioner needs on a limited basis for his or her sustenance, while the latter is something that should be avoided.

524. *ākhyeya, brjod bya.* Asaṅga states that while this term generally applies to all conditioned entities (*sarvasaṃskṛtā, 'dus byas thams cad*), here it refers to the five objects of sensory enjoyment (*pañca kāmaguṇā, 'dod pa'i yon tan lnga*).

525. That is, one should not seek the dharma merely to obtain the temporary result of obtaining a favorable rebirth in samsara, such as that of a worldly god.

526. This is the fourth and final verse of the group of four that make up the second topic of "The Verses on the Meaning of the Body" (see note 522, this chapter).

527. *pañcopādānaskandhā, nye bar len pa'i phung po lnga.* "Heap" (*skandha, phung po*) is the expression that Buddha Śākyamuni used to describe the collection of momentary physical and mental phenomena that make up the totality of a sentient being. As the often-quoted sūtra passage states, "O monks, whatever ascetics or brahmins perceive a self, they all perceive nothing but these five grasping heaps." Regarding the term "grasping" (*upādāna, nye bar len pa*), Buddhist treatises give varying interpretations. Vasubandhu's *Treasury of Higher Learning* identifies it with all the mental afflictions. Sthiramati (*Inner Science of Buddhist Practice*, p. 293) states: "The term "grasping" refers to aspiration (*chanda, 'dun pa*) and desire (*rāga, 'dod chags*). Aspiration means desire for a future existence. Desire is attachment. Thus, you grasp at a future existence in the sense of having aspiration for it, and you grasp at your present heaps in the sense that your desire for them makes you not want to give them up. Therefore, these two attitudes are called 'grasping.' The heaps that are associated with them are the grasping heaps."

528. *anuśaya, bag la nyal.* This term refers to the dormant or potential state of any of the mental afflictions. *YBh* (p. 167) states: "They are latencies because they possess the character of seeds that strengthen all things that are worldly."

529. *tṛṣṇā, sred pa.*
530. *anarthopasaṃhito vitarka, rtog pa ngan pa.* Yaśomitra's subcommentary to *The Commentary on the Treasury of Higher Learning* lists eight examples: deliberation about sensory pleasures, malice toward another person, harming another person, close relatives, homeland, not being at risk of dying, treating another person with contempt, and the loftiness of one's family.
531. That is, when benefactors offer material necessities of poor quality, in small amounts, and in a tardy manner.
532. *Legs bsdams.* This is the abbreviated title of the author's work whose full title is *Becoming Well Restrained: Nectar from the Mouths of Holy Lamas* (*bLa ma dam pa'i zhal gyi bdud rtsi legs bsdams*).
533. *lokanātha, 'jig rten mgon po.* Literally "Lord of the World," the original Sanskrit of this epithet is variously used as a reference to Brahmā, worldly gods generally, Buddha Śākyamuni or any buddha, and Avalokiteśvara in particular (*MW*, s.v. "lokanātha"). In the Buddhist context, it suggests that the person is an enlightened being.
534. Rin chen dpal, 1143–1217.
535. See note 103 (this chapter).
536. gNyos rGyal ba Lha nang pa. His religious name was Sangye Rinchen (Sang rgyas rin chen, 1164–1224).
537. Gye re.
538. Founded in 1179, it is also known as Drigung Thil Jangchup Ling (*'bri gung mthil byang chub gling*).
539. The pronoun "they" here does not appear in the Tibetan; however, it is implied and references worldly activities or the eight worldly concerns.
540. bZang mo ba gZhon nu seng ge, 1158–1234. See also note 238 (this chapter), where he is identified as a disciple of Sangye Öntön.
541. rJe bZang mo ba Dwags po lha pa.
542. *gtum mo.* See note 446 (this chapter).
543. This is a reference to Sangye Öntön. See note 243 (this chapter).
544. Lha dge 'dun sgang pa.
545. Lha bsam kha ba. Possibly a corrupt spelling. *KCS* gives his name as Lha Sekhangpa (Lha Sas khang pa).
546. Lha phu dGon gsar ba. *KCS* gives his name as Sangye Joten (Sangs rgyas jo stan) and notes that he founded Lhepu Gönsar Monastery (*lhas phu dgon gsar*).
547. Lha Phra so ba. Possibly a corrupt spelling. *KCS* gives his name as Lha Trangpowa (Lha 'phrang po ba).
548. Gad dmar ba.
549. This epithet previously referred to the Tibetan lama Gyamawa Tashi Gyaltsen (see note 62, this chapter). Here it refers to the Indian master of Buddhist epistemology Dharmakīrti (Chos kyi grags pa).
550. *PV*, ch. 2, v. 254ab. Here "freedom from desires" (*vairāgya, chags bral*) means

the state of an arhat who has permanently eradicated all the mental afflictions and attained liberation.

551. "Objects of desire" here refers to the material objects of food, clothing, medicine, and so on that represent a spiritual practitioner's means of subsistence.

552. *dus dran*. The general sense of this term refers to a range of acts of recollection that fully ordained bhikṣus and bhikṣuṇīs are meant to carry out in a variety of circumstances. In the present context, the expression refers more specifically to precepts that relate to prohibited acts, such as touching fire, which are permitted in certain circumstances provided a series of conditions are met beforehand. In this instance, the act is that of making use of objects of desire that cannot be avoided. The central elements that need to be recalled are that the act is being carried out for a particular legitimate purpose, with the understanding that the Bhagavān permitted it in such circumstances, and with the recognition that the monk or nun will remain cognizant of the training during the time that the act is being carried out.

553. dGyer chen po, 1090–1171. This figure was also referred to as the Great Gyergom (dGyer sgom chen po), or "the great meditator from the Gyer clan."

554. gZhon nu grags pa.

555. sNe'u zur pa, 1042–1118. See note 654, this chapter, and annotation, pp. 607–8. See also ch. 10, "The Essence of Nectar," note 451. His ordination name was Yeshe Bar (Ye shes 'bar; see note 656).

556. *rin chen sgang.*

557. *rnying pa.*

558. See ch. 10, "The Essence of Nectar," note 439.

559. See note 243 (this chapter). He was the Great Gyer's nephew, Sangye Öntön.

560. sGom pa Shes rab grags.

561. Lho pa Byang sgom.

562. dKri sor ba dge bshes. *KCS* (f. 134b) gives the name as Tripsor Geshe (Kribs sor dge bshes).

563. sDings po ba.

564. rBa Bya Zug. Regarding these three individuals, *KCS* (f. 134b) speculates that Ja may have been the person known as Lhopa Jagom (Lho pa Bya sgom). Cf. the name in note 560 (this chapter). This may be a variant spelling of that person's name.

565. Bya pa A nag chen po.

566. Bya pa Khri dpon tshang.

567. This is apparently a reference to the *SL*, v. 29 that is cited above. See p. 508.

568. The first two of these three verses are from *The Flower Cluster of Spiritual Attainments*. The third is from a poem in praise of Maitreya titled *The Jewel-Illuminating Lamp* (*Rin po che gsal ba'i sgron me*).

569. *UV*, ch. 3. In the Tibetan edition of this text, these lines form verse 5; in the Sanskrit edition they make up vv. 5cd–6ab.

570. See note 414 (this chapter).

571. This passage does not seem to appear in any of Je Tsongkhapa's published writings. It may be a paraphrase of an oral teaching heard by the author. This is an explanation that relates to the topic of the suffering of change. See *Inner Science of Buddhist Practice*, pp. 111–20.
572. sNga phyogs pa.
573. g.Yu phyogs pa.
574. sTong ra ba.
575. Mang btsan.
576. Akya Yongdzin (*Thog mar blo sbyong gi dris lan*, f. 7a) states: "A full *dung* (*mdung*) means a full tea churn."
577. The previous sentence and the first clause of this one both allude to two of the aphorisms from the instruction known as the Ten Ultimate Jewels (*phugs nor bcu*). They are to dedicate your ultimate form of dharma practice to living in a state of poverty and to dedicate your ultimate form of poverty to your death. That is, you should be committed to remaining in a state of poverty even if it results in your death. See note 262 (this chapter) and the related paragraph in the main text. See also note 583 (this chapter).
578. This single verse makes up item 108 in Je Tsongkhapa's collection of miscellaneous writings (*bka' 'bum thor bu*) and is identified as an instruction for a minister of the dharma king of the Mangyul (*mang yul*) region of Kyidrong (*skyid grong*).
579. See note 268 (this chapter).
580. *duḥkhādhivāsanākṣānti, sdug bsngal dang du len pa'i bzod pa*. See *BBh* (English translation), pp. 319–23.
581. *parāpakāramarṣaṇā kṣānti, gzhan gyis gnod pa byed pa la ji mi snyam pa'i bzod pa*. See *BBh* (English translation), pp. 315–18.
582. *dharmanidhyānādhimuktikṣāntiḥ, chos la nges par sems pa la mos pa'i bzod pa*. See *BBh* (English translation), pp. 323–24.
583. *gtad pa bzhi*. These are the first four aphorisms of the instruction known as the Ten Ultimate Jewels (see note 262 and related text, as well as note 577, this chapter). The four dedications are as your ultimate aim, dedicate yourself to the dharma; as your ultimate form of dharma, dedicate yourself to a life of poverty; as your ultimate form of poverty, dedicate yourself to remaining in poverty even if it leads to your death; and as your ultimate form of death, dedicate yourself to dying in a barren ravine.
584. *phugs nor bcu*. This instruction is made up of the four dedications, the three vajras, and the three qualities of banishing, entering, and attaining.
585. *ye shes rdo rje rang dang 'grogs*. This is the third of the three vajras. See note 584 (this chapter).
586. The patience that arises through attentive reflection upon entities is gained through contemplation of eight topics: the virtuous qualities of the Three Jewels; the nature of ultimate reality; the great spiritual powers of the buddhas and bodhisattvas (see *BBh*, book 1, ch. 5); the ten causes (see *BBh*, book 1, ch. 8,

pp. 175–85); the five results (see *BBh*, book 1, ch. 8, pp. 185–87); the unerring aim of unsurpassed enlightenment; the bodhisattva training that is the means of attaining unsurpassed enlightenment; and the twelve divisions of the well-spoken dharma (see *BBh*, note 529).

587. dGe bshes Yon lung pa. Not identified.
588. That is, others may pity you for your lack of material possessions, but the ascetic who maintains a joyful mind in his or her spiritual practice is the one who is truly successful.
589. *Blue Udder*.
590. *kālapakṣa, nag po'i phyogs*. That is, wickedness.
591. *Blue Udder*. That is, reflect on this point as an antidote to becoming despondent.
592. That is, not only a son, but also wealth.
593. The final two words of this line in the standard edition of Sakya Paṇḍita's text are different: "it will be destroyed by enemies" (*dgra bos 'joms*), not "enemies will come forward" (*dgra bo 'ong*).
594. *Treasury of Jewel-Like Excellent Sayings* (*Legs par bshad pa rin po che'i gter*), ch. 6, vv. 36cd–38.
595. *BCA*, ch. 6, v. 7cd.
596. Ibid., ch. 6, v. 9ab.
597. Ibid., ch. 6, v. 10
598. Ibid., ch. 6, v. 21. The Tibetan translation has "delight in virtue" (*dge la dga'*) instead of "elation toward the Victor" (*jine spṛhā*). *BCAP* glosses "elation" (*spṛhā, dga' ba*) here as "devotion" (*bhakti, gus pa*), "faith" (*śraddhā, dad pa*), and "clarity of mind" (*cittaprasāda, sems kyi dang ba*). The latter phrase is a particular kind of faith. *PSV* (English translation, pp. 283–84) states: "Faith in the Lord Buddha is the clarity of mind that is demonstrated by a bristling of the body hair or the flowing of tears and is felt toward that object that has perfected all virtuous qualities and completely removed all faults."
599. *mDza' bo'i bu mo*. Sanskrit versions can be found in the *Avadānaśataka* (ch. 36) and the *Divyāvadāna* (ch. 38). There are also several Tibetan versions in the Kangyur collection. One appears in vol. 13 (*pa*) of the *'dul ba* section of the Lhasa edition of the Kangyur; another can be found in vol. 29 (*ha*) of the *mdo sde* section.
600. 'Chad ka ba, 1101–1175. This epithet reflects that he founded Cheka Monastery in the Maldro (*mal gro*) region in 1141 or 1142.
601. Ye shes rdo rje.
602. *bya*.
603. *lo ro*.
604. *sha ra*.
605. *spras*. A section of the Penpo region.
606. *shar 'bum pa*.
607. dar yul. This is also a place located in the Penpo region.
608. *mtha' phu*.

609. Se sPyil bu ba, 1121–1189. Se is a clan name. His epithet reflects that he founded Jilbu (*spyil bu*) Monastery. His ordination name was Chökyi Gyaltsen (Chos kyi rgyal mtshan).
610. Gan pa da re.
611. rNal 'byor pa Byang sems.
612. See note 243 (this chapter).
613. *gro pa.*
614. These lines are aphorisms from the widely renowned Seven-Point Mind Training Instruction (*bLo sbyong don bdun ma*). See translation of the entire root text above in chapter 3.
615. This simile refers to a meaningless act. The act of winnowing is to *remove* chaff from grain; to winnow chaff itself, which contains no grain, is an exertion that will yield no meaningful result.
616. *Verse Compendium of the Stages of the Path* (*Lam rim bsdus don*), vv. 13, 14.
617. gLang ri thang pa, 1054–1123. This epithet means "the one from Langri Tang,"
618. rDo rje seng ge.
619. *bzhugs 'chams.*
620. sLob dpon rje btsun. This is an epithet that means "venerable teacher."
621. dGa' bde.
622. *mi 'chi ba'i phyogs 'dzin pa.* Literally "adhering to the proposition that one is not going to die anytime soon." This attitude is referred to in Buddhist literature as "the deliberation that avoids death" or "the deliberation that one is not at risk of dying" (*amaravitarka, mi 'chi ba'i rnam par rtog pa*). See also note 514 (this chapter). Nāgārjuna describes it in *RA* (ch. 5, v. 25): "Likewise, the deliberation that avoids death is / a state that is not concerned by fear of death."
623. These two mental factors make up one of the five "hindrances to meditative composure" (**samāpattinivaraṇa, snyoms 'jug gi sgrib pa*). *AS* (p. 48) states: "There are five hindrances: the hindrance of desire for sense pleasures (*kāmacchanda, 'dod pa la 'dun pa*); the hindrance of malice (*vyāpāda, gnod sems*); the hindrance of torpor and sleep (*styānamiddha, rmugs pa dang gnyid*); the hindrance of excitation and regret (*auddhatyakaukṛtya, rgod pa dang 'gyod pa*); and the hindrance of doubt (*vicikitsā, the tshom*). A hindrance should be understood as an entity that constitutes a lack of clarity regarding all things that are of a virtuous nature."
624. *CŚ*, ch. 1, v. 1. The original Sanskrit of this verse is not extant.
625. *BCA*, ch. 2, v. 35. This passage is from *The Great Treatise on the Stages of the Path to Enlightenment.* A portion of the explanation near the end of this discussion has been left out here.
626. *Mya ngan las 'das pa chen po'i mdo.*
627. *akṣaṇa, mi khom pa.* Among the eight inopportune occasions, three are to be born in the three lower states, one is to be born among long-lived gods, and four occur in rebirths as a human being. The reference here is to the latter five inopportune states, among which the four human ones are a human being who

is born among barbarians in a borderland where the fourfold retinue of Buddhist followers does not travel, a human being who is dull-witted and incapable of understanding the dharma, a human being who holds a form of wrong view, and a human being who is born at a time when the tathāgata has not appeared in the world and the well-spoken dharma has not been taught.

628. Except for the excision of two verses from the *Collection of Uplifting Sayings* (*Udānavarga, Ched du brjod pa'i tshoms*) and a few minor expressions, this is the entirety of Je Tsongkhapa's discussion on the benefits of practicing recollection of death that is presented in his *Great Treatise.*

629. These verses appear at the end of *Butön's History of Buddhism.*

630. As noted above (see note 6, this chapter) this should be understood as a reference to Khedrup Gelek Pelsang (see note 777, this chapter).

631. This does not appear to be a quote from any of Khedrup Je's published works.

632. Literally "one who has gone forth" (*pravrajita, rab tu byung ba*). See ch. 4, "Brilliant Illumination of the Path to Enlightenment," note 271.

633. *snang sel.* Potowa's use of the expression "eliminating appearances" here involves a play on words. The context for his assertion is provided by Baso Chökyi Gyaltsen's (Ba so chos kyi rgyal mtshan, 1402–1473) annotation to a similar passage that occurs in Je Tsongkhapa's *Great Treatise on the Stages of the Path to Enlightenment.* The annotation states: "A certain scholar who wanted to disparage Potowa asked him a question about logical validation (*sādhana, sgrub pa*) and negation (*pratiṣedha, 'gog pa*). He asked, 'According your philosophical system, what explanation is there that validates appearances (*pratibhāsa, snang ba*) and what explanation is there that negates exclusions (*apoha, sel ba*)?' Understanding the intent of his questioner, Potowa gave an indirect response that addresses the dharma practice of impermanence in the form of death." The related passage in Je Tsongkhapa's *Great Treatise* states: "Potowa said, 'My means of eliminating appearances is this very practice of meditating on impermanence. After you eliminate all the appearances of this life, such as attachment to relatives and possessions, and so on, and realize that you shall pass on suddenly to the next life, alone and unaccompanied, such that you think to yourself, "I definitely must not engage in any activity that is contrary to the dharma," at that point, you will have become free of attachment for this life. Until this realization has been developed in your mind, the path to all forms of dharma practice will remain blocked.'" While the questioner was asking Potowa to explain the epistemological topic of validating "appearances" in the sense of perceptual objects and negating "exclusions" (*apohana, sel ba*) as understood in the Buddhist theory of language, Potowa changed the sense of the two nouns into the phrase "means of eliminating appearances" (*snang sel*). At the end of the passage, he also changes the noun "negation" (*'gog pa*) into the verb form "blocked" (*'gags*).

634. *bshos bu.* This term is the name for a small torma offering.

635. The adjective "bad" here is meant in the sense of a forceful and effective practice.

636. That is, the topic of impermanence.
637. Lo tig ye shes 'byung.
638. *RA*, ch. 1, v. 21.
639. *lkog na mo 'dra ba zhig*. Ngawang Tsering Kyap's commentary glosses this phrase as the more straightforward epistemological term "hidden object" (*rahogata* or *parokṣa*, *lkog gyur*), which means one that is not evident to the senses and can only be realized through correct inference, such as subtle impermanence, selflessness of the person, and emptiness.
640. Mang ra sgom pa, 1042–1109.
641. sNyug rum pa, also spelled sMyug rum pa. See also note 101 (this chapter).
642. brTson 'grus 'bar.
643. *thang skya*.
644. See notes 37, 44 (this chapter) and various references to this spiritual teacher in the main text.
645. rDor tshul. This is the contraction of a name, probably Dorje Tsultrim (rDo rje tshul khrims).
646. *rgyal gyi skyang ci*.
647. *ya gi na*. This is a vague reference to a physical location, perhaps the private residence of the speaker.
648. By saying, "At present, it is easy for you to drink tea, but it is difficult for you not to drink tea," Potowa was implying that Dortsul was attached to that form of pleasure and therefore had not yet mentally abandoned this life.
649. Khams pa lung pa, 1025–1115. See also note 110, where he is referred to as Khamlungpa.
650. *yung ba*.
651. *upāsaka*, *dge bsnyen*.
652. Śākya yon tan.
653. *pārājika*, *phas pham pa*. This is the name for the four most serious transgressions in the Buddhist system of morality known as prātimokṣa (*so sor thar pa*; see ch. 8, "The Easy Path," note 65, for an explanation of this term). Commission of any of these four acts results in the loss of the celibate vow and requires permanent expulsion from the community of ordained monks and nuns. The four acts are killing a human being, stealing an object of even modest value, engaging in sexual intercourse, and professing superhuman powers.
654. See note 555 (this chapter).
655. *spras*.
656. Ye shes 'bar.
657. Don stengs pa. Literally "the one from Dönteng," in recognition of his having founded the eponymous monastery. Sönam Lhayi Wangpo's (bSod nams Lha'i dbang po) *Thousand Rays of Sunlight* (*Nyin mor byed pai 'od stong*) gives his ordination name as Chökyap Zangpo (*Chos skyabs bzang po*).
658. *ngam shod*.
659. *gser phye*.

660. Lha 'bri sgang pa, d.u.
661. *saṃghāti, snam sbyar.* One of the three prescribed articles of clothing to be worn by a bhikṣu. It is a long shawl-like cloth with strips of material sewn to it in a patchwork pattern that is worn over the shoulders and upper body.
662. gDol pa Rog dmar zhur pa. See notes 121–24 (this chapter) for additional references to this individual.
663. Yang gad pa.
664. sPyi bo lhas pa, b. 1144. His ordination name was Jangchup Ö (Byang chub 'od).
665. gTsang pa Rin po che.
666. dGe bshes Brag thog pa.
667. See note 627 (this chapter).
668. That is, the desire realm, the form realm, and the formless realm.
669. *theg dman.*
670. *nimittodgrahaṇa, mtshan mar 'dzin pa.* See ch. 4, "The Brilliant Illumination of the Path to Enlightenment," note 248, for an explanation of this expression.
671. The Tibetan version of this narrative appears in the vinaya text entitled *Differentiation of the Discipline* (*Vinayavibhaṅga,'Dul ba rnam par 'byed pa*; Dg.K. 'dul ba, vol. 8 (*nya*), ff. 147a–189b, section 70). A Sanskrit version is found in chapter 37 of the *Divyāvadāna*. An English translation of the latter can be found in *Divine Stories*, part 2, pp. 287–344.
672. *dṛṣṭasatya, bden pa mthong.* This phrase indicates that she attained a direct realization of the four noble truths and therefore became an ārya.
673. That is, between the topic of impermanence on the one hand and those of enlightenment mind and emptiness, and the like, on the other.
674. The Tibetan term for this type of practice is *powa* (*'pho ba*), often translated as "transference" and for which there are numerous esoteric tantric instructions. The original Sanskrit term is *utkrānti*, a noun formed from a verbal root that means literally "to step up" or "to ascend" but which also is used in the straightforward sense of "to pass away" or "to die." A principal aim of such practices is to ensure a favorable rebirth following one's death.
675. *trīṇi vimokṣamukhāni, rnam par thar pa'i sgo gsum.* The three doors of liberation are those of signlessness (*animitta, mtshan ma med pa*), emptiness (*śūnyatā, stong pa nyid*), and wishlessness (*apraṇihita, smon ma med pa*).
676. *apraṇihitaṃ vimokṣamukha, rnam par thar pa'i sgo smon pa med pa.*
677. *rgyun 'jig pa.* The phrase "disintegration of a continuum" should be understood to mean a sentient being's death. The term "continuum" refers to that of a particular sentient being's five heaps.
678. Each of the four noble truths is made up of four aspects. The four aspects of the Noble Truth of Suffering are impermanence (*anitya, mi rtag pa*), suffering (*duḥkha, sdug bsngal ba*), emptiness (*śūnyam, stong pa*), and selflessness (*anātmam, bdag med pa*). The four aspects of the Noble Truth of Origination are cause (*hetu, rgyu*), origination (*samudaya, kun 'byung ba*), source (*prabhava, rab

skyes), and contributing factor (*pratyaya, rkyen*). The four aspects of the noble truth of cessation are cessation (*nirodha, 'gog pa*), peace (*śānta, zhi ba*), goodness (*pranīta, gya nom pa*), and deliverance (*niḥsaraṇa, nges par 'byung ba*). The four aspects of the Noble Truth of the Path are path (*mārga, lam*), rightness (*yukti, rigs pa*), means of attainment (*pratipad, sgrub pa*), and factor that leads to deliverance (*nairyāṇika, nges par 'byin pa*).

679. *amṛtapada, bdud rtsi'i go 'phang*. While the Tibetan *dutsi* (*bdud rtsi*) means "nectar," the Sanskrit equivalent literally means "deathlessness" or "immortality," and also final emancipation (*MW*, s.v. "amṛta"). In Indian mythology, the gods possessed the "nectar" (*amṛta*, *bdud rtsi*) that confers immortality.

680. *sle mo thang*.

681. Pema Jangchup is the ordination name of Shawo Gangpa. See notes 258 and 259 (this chapter).

682. See topic 11, titled "Recall the Disadvantages of Sensory Pleasures."

683. *snang sel*. The phrase "eliminating appearances" means the kinds of thoughts that are forms of attachment to this life. See note 633 (this chapter).

684. mGu ston. This is said to be the name of one of Potowa's disciples.

685. *'bu snar shing bu gsur ba 'dra*. Akya Yongdzin's commentary (*Thog mar blo sbyong gi dris lan*, f. 7b) states: "When an insect's nose comes in contact with or detects a twig, it curls up and makes its body smaller." This simile is meant to indicate that a foolish person, when faced with his or her imminent death, will react by thinking "I should not perform any more evil actions." However, one should recognize the importance of ceasing wrongful behavior long before that time.

686. These lines appear in a song from Milarepa's *Hundred Thousand Songs*, which is titled "Gaining a Fearless Understanding and Achieving Assurance with Regard to Realizations" (*Mi 'jigs pa khong du chud cing rtogs pa gdeng du gyur pa'i mgur*). See English translation, ch. 28.

687. See note 28 (this chapter).

688. *ding ri glang 'khor*.

689. See note 510 (this chapter).

690. So chung ba, 1062–1128. He was also known by the name Gendun Bar (dGe 'dun 'bar).

691. Pa tshab sgom chen, also spelled elsewhere as sPa tshab.

692. sKam shi la. This reference is difficult to decipher with certainty. *sKam* is probably an abbreviated reference to Kamgom Yeshe Gyaltsen (sKam sgom Ye shes rgyal mtshan). However, it is unclear how to identify *shi la*; it could be a corruption.

693. *Hundred Verses of Advice to the People of Dingri*, v. 29.

694. *KCS* (f. 6b) identifies this as a system that was propagated by Chengawa Tsultrim Bar.

695. Per *KCS* (f. 6b), this is a method of instruction that was employed by Puchungwa Zhönu Gyaltsen.

696. *dharmakāya, chos kyi sku.* Buddhist scriptures define a buddha's dharma body in a variety of ways. In the philosophical system of the *Abhisamayālaṃkāra*, the resultant dharma body (*'bras bu chos sku*) is understood to mean the state of enlightenment as a whole, which is made up of four elements: essence body (*svabhāvakāya, ngo bo nyid sku*); dharma body of [ultimate] knowledge (*jñāna-dharmakāya, ye shes chos sku*); enjoyment body (*saṃbhogakāya, longs sku*); and emanation body (*nirmāṇakāya, sprul sku*). According to this formulation, the dharma body of [ultimate] knowledge is made up of twenty-one categories of transcendent realization. By identifying the dharma body here with the clear-light state, it is understood to mean a buddha's pure, ultimate awareness that directly realizes the actual clear-light state (*don gyi 'od gsal*).
697. See note 30 (this chapter).
698. See note 26 (this chapter) for a general explanation of the Tibetan term *namtar* (*vimokṣa, rnam thar*). A "sealed" *namtar* is one that describes a holy person's spiritual activities and realizations that are considered to be esoteric in nature, and therefore such accounts should be restricted to especially devoted followers. It is sometimes called a "secret namtar" (*gsang ba'i rnam thar*).
699. O rgyan pa, 1229–1309. His ordination name was Rinchen Pel (Rin chen dpal).
700. Ne rings pa, 1225–1281. His ordination name was Delek Gyaltsen (bDe legs rgyal mtshan).
701. Yang dgon pa. See note 221 (this chapter). The writings of this figure are cited several times in this text.
702. Byang gling pa.
703. Ba ri ba.
704. *kṣaṇasampat, dal 'byor.* This noun compound combines the terms "leisure" and "fortune." It refers to a human life that is endowed with eighteen qualities that are ideal for pursuing a meaningful spiritual life. "Leisure" refers to eight opportune states, and "fortune" refers to the combination of five fortunes that relate to oneself and five fortunes that relate to others. See ch. 7, "The Nectar That Is Like Highly Refined Gold," note 2, for a description of all eighteen qualities.
705. *zhen pa log pa.* Literally "reversal of attachment," this expression is often translated by such terms as "revulsion," "aversion," and "disgust."
706. See note 484 (this chapter).
707. *phur tshugs gsol 'debs.* This is a supplication prayer in which you earnestly beseech the lone figure of your lama to confer his or her blessings upon you. It is called "stake-like" because it is made with a resolve that resembles striking a stake repeatedly in order to fix it firmly into the ground.
708. Karma pa Rol pa'i rdo rje, 1340–1383. This spiritual figure was the fourth in the line of Karmapa reincarnations.
709. Thugs rje chen po. Literally "the one who is the embodiment of great compassion," this is an epithet of Avalokiteśvara.
710. That is, Dakpo Lhaje or Gampopa Sönam Rinchen. See note 75 (this chapter).

711. See note 105 (this chapter).
712. gSal stong sho re. He was also referred to as Seltong Shogom (gSal stong shwo sgom).
713. Cha pa Chos kyi seng ge, 1109–1169. The first part of this individual's name is also spelled *phywa pa*.
714. 'Bri. This is an abbreviation of Drigung Jikten Gönpo Rinchen Pel ('Bri gung 'Jig rten mgon Rin chen dpal, 1143–1217). He founded Drigung Jangchup Ling Monastery in 1177, which became the seat of the Drigung branch of the Kagyu school. See also notes 533 and 534 (this chapter).
715. sTag. This is an abbreviation of Taklung Tangpa Tashi Pel (sTag lung thang pa bKra shis dpal, 1149–1209/1210).
716. g.Ya' skal ldan. This figure is also known as Zarawa Kalden Yeshe Senge (Zwa ra ba sKal ldan ye shes seng ge, birth year uncertain, death 1207).
717. Khro phu ba. This figure is Gyaltsa Rinchen Gön (Khro phu rGyal tsha rin chen mgon, 1118–1195). The epithet Tropuwa is a reference to the Tropu Monastery, which he founded. He is not to be confused with Tropu Lotsāwa, who was his nephew (see notes 211 and 453, this chapter).
718. gTsang pa Kun ldan. This individual, known as Kunden Repa (Kun ldan ras pa, 1148–1217), was a relative of Gyaltsa Rinchen Gön (see previous note). Some sources say that he was the latter's brother, others that he was his nephew.
719. rJe sPyan snga ba. While Chengawa is a frequently used epithet that indicates someone as a close attendant of a master, this is likely a reference to Drakpa Jungne (sPyan snga Grags pa 'byung gnas, 1175–1255), who was given the title for his service to Jikten Gönpo Rinchen Pel (see annotation, p. 583).
720. This is an alternate epithet of Use. See also note 105 (this chapter).
721. Karma Pakshi, 1204–1283. The term *pakshi* is a Mongolian word for "religious teacher."
722. Rang 'byung rdo rje, 1284–1339.
723. De bzhin gshegs pa, 1384–1415.
724. mThong ba don ldan, 1416–1453.
725. Chos grags rgya mtsho, 1454–1506.
726. Mi bskyod rdo rje, 1507–1554.
727. Since the author of this work died before the birth of this last individual, he could not have written the entirety of this annotation.
728. 'Chi bdag rgyal po. This is the name of the Lord of Death, also known in Tibetan as Shinje (gShin rje).
729. *abhisampratyaya, yid ches pa*. While the Tibetan equivalent often means simply to believe something, it also carries a more technical sense of "conviction" or "confidence" about some subject. It is distinguished from states of mind that constitute genuine knowledge (*pramāṇa, tshad ma*) in the epistemological sense. Nevertheless, the term is also used to describe a type of faith in the doctrine of karma and its results, for instance, that represents a special kind of

inference gained on the recognition of the "overall uncontradictoriness of an authoritative person's [i.e., the Buddha's] speech." (*āptvādāvisaṃvādasāmānyād anumānatā, yid che'i tshig mi slu ba'i spyi las . . . rjes su dpag pa nyid*). This faith is considered to be reasonable in that it is derived from a threefold examination that determines the buddha's speech to be free of error (*dpyad pa gsum gyis dag pa'i lung*). Here the conviction seems to be that of a being sure that your future life will be a favorable one.

730. *snying rus.* Literally "a bone in the heart." This would be a fortitude that pursues the dharma in order to avoid having to experience an unfavorable rebirth.
731. That is, what other activity is there that is preventing you from the main goal of disciplining your mind?
732. Chos g.yung. This figure was known as Ölkawa Drölgom Chöyung ('Ol kha ba Grol sgom Chos g.yung, 1103–1199).
733. rJe dwags po. That is, Gampopa Sönam Rinchen.
734. *BCA*, ch. 8, v. 30.
735. *rgya gar skad du.* This phrase is used to identify the original Sanskrit title of virtually every scriptural work that is contained in the Tibetan Kangyur and Tengyur collections.
736. gNyan ston Śāk 'byung. He was a disciple of Drom Tönpa.
737. See note 298 (this chapter).
738. This is another name for Zhangtsun Yerpa. See note 24 (this chapter).
739. *khal.* A unit of measure for dry goods, roughly equivalent to a bushel.
740. The translation of this statement is somewhat speculative. The point seems to be that any surplus material possessions should be disposed of before leaving the place where one has been staying. A commentary of memorial notes (*zin bris*) to a four-day discourse by Yeshe Thupten Gyatso (Ye shes thub bstan rgya mtsho) on this text titled *The Great Ascetic's Oral Instruction* (*Drang song chen po'i zhal lung*, f. 17a) states: "Regarding the statement about 'Having surplus provisions of less than six *kel*,' the master said that we monks who have gone forth into the homeless state should not leave behind any possessions at all in the wake of our death, like a young bird when it flies away from its nest."
741. *muṣṭi, dpe mkhyud.* Literally "clenched fist," this term is used to indicate that a person who possesses a certain dharma teaching or teachings does not want to share it with others out of concern that it might serve to diminish his or her own reputation as a spiritually learned person.
742. *JM*, ch. 19, v. 1. The Tibetan translation is a somewhat free rendering of the original version of this verse. The English translation follows the Sanskrit more closely.
743. gZhon nu tshul.
744. rNal 'byor pa chen po. This is an epithet of Ame Jangchup Rinchen (see note 14, this chapter).
745. That is, the fact that he meditates on impermanence.

746. *dbyar shing*. These are small sticks that are used in a ritual carried out at the beginning of the rainy-season residence to determine which monks will be in attendance.
747. *satyadarśī, bden pa mthong ba*. The expression "one who has perceived truth" is understood to mean someone who has attained a direct realization of ultimate reality and achieved the status of an ārya (*'phags pa*).
748. *Chig lab ring mo*.
749. The wording of this passage that appears in separate editions of Potowa's work is slightly different: "By thinking to myself, 'What would I do if I were to die tonight,' I do not even consider any goals for tomorrow or the future thereafter" (*nga la do nub shi na ji tsug byed snyam nas sang phan chad kyi 'dun ma dran pa yang ma byung*).
750. sTon pa rdo rje. Ngawang Tsering Kyap's (Ngag dbang tshe ring skyabs) commentary, titled *A Collection of Various Notes on the Treatise Titled "The First Way of Training the Mind"* (*Thog mar blo sbyong gi gzhung 'ga'i tho yig btus te bkod pa*), states that this is the name of a certain benefactor.
751. *rGyas pa*. This is the hundred-thousand-line version of the *Perfection of Wisdom Sūtra*, which typically is contained in twelve volumes of the Kangyur collection.
752. 'Be ston.
753. See notes 121 and 307 (this chapter).
754. *phug nag*.
755. dGe bshes gSang phu ba, b. tenth century, also known as Ngok Lekpai Sherap (rNgog Legs pa'i shes rab), he served Atiśa as a disciple for ten years. The epithet Sangpuwa is a reference to Sangpu Neutok Monastery, which he founded in 1072 at the urging of Atiśa.
756. gShen ston g.Yung drung rgya mtsho.
757. rNgog Legs shes. Lekshe is an abbreviation of Lekpai Sherap. See note 12 (this chapter).
758. The text does not identify who made this statement. The fact that one of the statements refers to Geshe Sangpuwa as "son," suggests that it was made by his teacher, Atiśa.
759. *jo bo pa*. This epithet means "follower of the Lord"—that is, Lord Atiśa—who was referred to as Jowo, or "lord."
760. The term "self" (*ātman, bdag*) here does not refer to a personal self but rather to the mistaken apprehension of real essences (*svabhāva, rang bzhin*) in relation to the entities that make up the five heaps. The correct view of these entities is known as realization of "the insubstantiality of entities" (*dharmanairātmya, chos kyi bdag med*). As this statement suggests, realization of the insubstantiality of outer entities is considered to be less difficult than that of inner entities.
761. *dmar khrid*. Literally "red instruction," this expression is suggestive of a freshly opened cadaver in the sense a teaching that is presented in a plain and straightforward manner, without referring to the wording of a text, just as a physician

cuts open a fresh corpse and identifies the five major organs, six hollow organs, and so on, to teach human anatomy to his students.

762. Gro lung pa bLo gros 'byung gnas, b. eleventh century.

763. *Lam rim*. This is likely a reference to Drolungpa's work, known by the popular title *The Great Stages of the Teaching* (*bsTan rim chen mo*), which is an exhaustive commentary on his own root text that is written in verse. The third chapter of this work's ten chapters is devoted to the topic of impermanence. The full title is *A Commentary on "The Stages of the Path for Entering the Sugata's Precious Teaching"* (*dBe bar gshegs pa'i bstan pa rin po che la 'jug pa'i lam gyi rim pa rnam par bshad pa*).

764. *rtsa ba gsum*. The three roots are the certainty of death, the uncertainty of the time of death, and at the time of death, nothing but the dharma can benefit us.

765. *rgyu mtshan dgu*. Each of the three roots is made up of three supporting reasons. The three that relate to the certainty of death are the Lord of Death is certain to appear and cannot be turned back by any means, our life span cannot be increased and the portion that remains is constantly growing shorter, and during the time that we remain alive, there is little time to practice the dharma. The three for the uncertainty of the time of death are the life spans of humans in the Rose Apple continent are not fixed, there are a great many factors that contribute to death but only a few that sustain life, and the body is very fragile. The three for the point that nothing except the dharma can benefit us at the time of death are our wealth is of no help, our family and friends are of no help, and even our body is of no help.

766. Rong pa Phyag sor ba, d.u. He was also known as Geshe Laksorwa (dGe bshes Lag sor ba). He sought out and became a principal disciple of Naktso Lotsāwa and established a distinct teaching lineage.

767. *saṃskṛta, 'dus byas*. Vasubandhu's *AKBh* (p. 4) states: "Conditioned entities are those that are created by the convergence and combination of conditional factors" (*sametya sambhūya pratyayai kṛtā iti saṃskṛtā*). Conditioned entities—which are represented by the five heaps (*skandha, phung po*)—are, by their very nature, impermanent.

768. Naktso Lotsāwa Tsultrim Gyalwa (Nag 'tsho lo tsā ba Tshul khrims rgyal ba, 1011–1064).

769. Bya 'Dul 'dzin, 1100–1174. Duldzin is an abbreviation of the epithet Dulwa Dzinpa ('Dul ba 'dzin pa), which means "upholder of the vinaya." His ordination name was Tsöndru Bar (brTson 'grus 'bar). *History of the Kadam Spiritual Tradition* (ff. 337b) lists him as one of Chaksorwa's "four spiritual sons from Rong."

770. The external physical world is the "vessel" (*bhājanaloka, snod kyi 'jig rten*) in which sentient beings reside.

771. The Tibetan term *bcud* literally means "essence" or "contents" that are present inside a vessel, which in this context refers to the sentient beings that inhabit the physical world.

772. See note 677 (this chapter).
773. *AS* (p. 9) states: "What is lack of mindfulness (*pramāda, bag med pa*)? It is the failure to cultivate virtuous qualities and to guard the mind from impure qualities that occurs on the basis of forms of desire, hatred, and ignorance that are accompanied by laziness. Its action is to support the strengthening of unvirtuous actions and the decrease of virtuous actions." Death that is due to lack of mindfulness means an accidental death caused by rash or careless behavior.
774. *rnam snang gi chos bdun*. They are called the "qualities of Vairocana" because he is the embodiment of a buddha's form heap. The seven qualities are legs in the vajra cross-legged position, eyes focused on the tip of the nose, torso held in an upright position, shoulders held at the same level, hands in the meditation gesture, neck bent forward slightly, and teeth and lips in a natural position with the tip of the tongue touching the roof of the mouth.
775. This does not appear to be a direct quote from any of Khedrup Je's writings. It paraphrases a brief passage that appears in Je Tsongkhapa's *Great Treatise on the Stages of the Path to Enlightenment* on general principles relating to meditation on the instruction. See English translation, vol. 1, pp. 99–100.
776. rJe mKhas grub pa. He is more commonly referred to as Khedrup Je.
777. dGe legs dpal bzang po, 1385–1438.
778. *sde bdag.*
779. *ri bo gdangs can.*
780. *dpal 'khor chos sde.*
781. *nyang stod lcang ra.*
782. *dge ldan*. This term is one of the names used for the tradition established by Je Tsongkhapa, most commonly known as Geluk (*dge lugs*).
783. This is another name for Ganden Monastery (*dga' ldan*), one of the main seats of the Geluk school, which was founded in 1409 by Je Tsongkhapa.
784. *Śrāvakabhūmi, Nyan thos kyi sa*. In the relevant passage (Sanskrit edition, pp. 410–11), Asaṅga likens the practitioner to a metal worker who removes impurities from gold and silver by inserting them in fire and washing them in water, thereby rendering them suitable to be fashioned into ornaments. Similarly, by turning the mind away from mental stains and afflicted states, a meditation practitioner becomes fit to apply his or her mind in whatever manner is appropriate to develop either quiescence or insight.
785. Je Tsongkhapa explains the general principles of his views on meditation in *The Great Treatise on the Stages of the Path to Enlightenment* in a section titled "A Brief Presentation on How to Meditate" (*sKyong tshul mdor bsdus te bstan pa*).
786. *asaṃpramoṣa, mi brjed pa*. This Tibetan term, which is used to describe the essential nature of the mental factor recollection (*smṛti, dran pa*), literally means "not forgetting." I don't believe that this English phrase captures the intended meaning of the original Sanskrit. Sthiramati glosses *asaṃpramoṣa* as "the quality that prevents the continued grasping of a mental object from being lost" (*ālambanagrahaṇāvipranāśakāraṇa*). This led me to render the term as

"avoidance of inattentiveness." *AS* (p. 6) states: "What is recollection? It is the avoidance of inattentiveness toward a familiar object. Its action is to prevent distraction." However, in the present context, I use the language of Sthiramati's gloss as a substitute for "avoidance of inattentiveness."

787. Here the word "forget" (*brjed pa*) is appropriate for the example of a person's physical features. To "forget" the meditation object means for you to lose your grasp of it (see note 786, this chapter), which is to say, it is no longer present in your conscious awareness.
788. Se ston.
789. See note 10 (this chapter).
790. sPyan snga Rin po che.
791. See note 587 (this chapter).
792. *amanuṣya, mi ma yin*. While the term literally means "a nonhuman," it typically means a demon or harmful spirit.
793. See note 580 (this chapter) and related discussion in the main text.
794. See note 581 (this chapter).
795. *cintā, sems pa*.
796. *tulana, 'jal ba*.
797. *nidhyāna, nges par rtog pa*.
798. *AA*, ch. 4, v. 53ab. The second half of the verse states that this process occurs "on the limbs to penetrating insight, the path of seeing, and the path of meditation itself." The phrase "limbs to penetrating insight" is a reference to the stages that make up the path of preparation (*prayogamārga, sbyor ba'i lam*).
799. Literally "at all times" (*rtag tu*).
800. *'du long*. This spelling of the Tibetan means the "turmoil" of worldly activities. However, several commentaries note that some editions of the text have the variant reading *mdo long* and state that while some scholars consider this a corruption, this is the correct spelling of an archaic term that means "an easygoing attitude that is free of apprehension" (*'tsher snang med pa'i gu yangs kyi blo*). This interpretation would suggest an "easygoing, unconcerned person" who does not hesitate to undertake worldly activities.
801. *yid ches pa*. This term refers to a particular type of faith. In this context, it seems to indicate a generalized faith that believes in the validity of the dharma. See also note 729 (this chapter) for a discussion of the term.
802. That is, distracted by secular events that are antithetical to the dharma.
803. *gnyen po*. This term refers to the practices that serve as antidotes for mental flaws or wrongful conduct.
804. *dung phyis pa bzhin du 'gro*. This is a shortened form of the simile. Longer versions state that virtue, blessings, the dharma itself, and so on will disappear "like the dust that is removed from a conch shell when it is polished." Thus, the statement means that improper attitudes or behavior will destroy whatever prior virtuous qualities an individual may have achieved previously.
805. *Deśanāstava, bShags pa'i bstod pa*, v. 41.

806. Ibid., v. 42.
807. Lama Zhang Tsöndru Drakpa (bLa ma Zhang brTson 'grus grags pa, 1123–1193) was a disciple of Gampopa.
808. Ngawang Tsering Kyap's gloss of these lines (f. 17b) states: "Just as consuming tsampa too hastily can result in the error of its getting caught in your throat, being impatient about the spiritual practice can result in the error of failing to bring it to completion."
809. See ch. 7 "The Nectar That Is Like Highly Refined Gold," note 44. A frequently used recitation for carrying out this practice is the first twelve verses of *The Aspirational Prayer for Excellent Spiritual Conduct.*
810. The term "field" here refers to a "field of virtue" (*guṇakṣetra, yon tan gyi zhing*). As the second half of the verse notes, this should be understood to mean your spiritual teachers and the Three Jewels. See also ch. 8, "The Easy Path," note 40.
811. This verse appears in a missive written in verse by Je Rinpoche in response to a letter received from an official named Namkha Pelsang (Nam mkha' dpal bzang). The poem is titled "A Letter Establishing the Basis of Benefit and Happiness" (*'Phrin yig phan bde'i gzhi 'dzin*). This poem is found among the collection of Je Tsongkhapa's miscellaneous works found in vol. 2 (*kha*) of his Collected Works (item 78, *bKa' 'bum thor bu*; Toh. 5275), f. 178b–179b.
812. *smṛti, dran pa*. See ch. 7, "The Nectar That Is Like Highly Refined Gold," note 113. See also ch. 11, "A Guidebook for the Path to Great Awakening," note 182, for additional comments that relate to both recollection and vigilance.
813. *samprajanya, shes bzhin*. See ch. 7, "The Nectar That Is Like Highly Refined Gold," note 114. See also ch. 11, "A Guidebook for the Path to Great Awakening," note 182, for additional comments that relate to both recollection and vigilance.
814. rNam thos kyi sras. This is the name of a being that is regarded as a god of wealth. His name means "the son of Viśravas." He is also known by the name Kubera or Kuvera and is considered to be a powerful yakṣa spirit.
815. *pañcavargīya, lnga sde*. This was the group of five ascetics to whom the Buddha taught the dharma for the first time at Deer Park on the outskirts of Varanasi. They were Kauṇḍinya, Bhadrika, Vaśpa, Mahānaman, and Aśvajit.
816. *nye ba'i lnga sde*. They are identified as Yaśa, Vimala, Pūrṇa, Gavampati, and Subāhu. Yaśa was the Buddha's sixth disciple, a young layperson whom he taught soon after the first discourse and who became the sixth individual to become an arhat. See *Inner Science of Buddhist Practice*, p. 2–3, for a brief account of Yaśa's conversion.
817. Yaśa was the Buddha's first disciple who received teachings as a layperson. See the description of this individual that appears in Dg.K. 'dul ba, vol. 4. ff. 45b–48a. A brief account of this disciple is presented in *Inner Science of Buddhist Practice*, pp. 2–3.
818. lDi ri.
819. Drag po.

820. *siddhānta, grub mtha'.* This term literally means "established end" or "settled doctrine." It can refer either to the individual doctrinal points that make up a philosophical school's established views or it can refer to the entire system of a philosophical school.
821. sTon pa 'od zer rgya mtsho.
822. Khams pa dPal 'bar.
823. *'gro chos.* This term usually means a teaching that is given upon a disciple's departure from his teacher or when a disciple is about to go on a journey.
824. These are known as the four modes of physical behavior (*īryāpathāni, spyod lam*).
825. Śāstā, sTon pa. This term is a reference to Buddha Śākyamuni.
826. *kha chems rlung la bskur.* The commentary to this line states that Geshe Tönpa declared that this teaching on the stages of the path was meant to be revealed in a restricted manner. However, he taught it in a public assembly because the overall Buddhist teaching was in decline. He described this act as casting his final testament to the wind for the benefit of those who possess good fortune and have a karmic propensity for it.
827. These lines are from the *Blue Udder* (*Be'u bum sngon po*).
828. *pravrajita, rab tu byung ba.* That is, those who have gone forth into the homeless state of a Buddhist monk or nun. See also note 391 (this chapter) and related comments in the main text.
829. *puruṣa, skyes bu.* This term, which literally means a "man," "person," or "human being," is used in this teaching system to describe three levels of practitioner. The teaching on the Stages of the Path to Enlightenment is a system that relates to three types of person, referred to as being of lesser, intermediate, or great capacity. See *Lamp for the Path*, vv. 3–5.
830. Lha me 'bar.
831. Akya Yongdzin (*Thog mar blo sbyong gi dris lan*, f. 8a–8b) interprets all the descriptions in this extended metaphor as ways to ensure that the teaching is practiced and that all activities that would cause it to be forsaken are avoided.
832. *A Letter Establishing the Basis of Benefit and Happiness* (*'Phrin yig phan bde'i gzhi 'dzin*). See note 811 (this chapter).
833. Ibid.
834. Ibid.
835. *Verse Compendium of the Stages of the Path* (*Lam rim bsdus don*), vv. 6–10.
836. *A Letter Establishing the Basis of Benefit and Happiness.*
837. A religious activity in which images of deities and stupas are created by pressing clay into a mold.
838. See ch. 7, "The Nectar That Is Like Highly Refined Gold," note 74, for a somewhat different explanation of the black, mottled, and white forms of the eight worldly concerns.
839. *Jñānasiddhi, Ye shes grub pa*, ch. 9, vv. 5–9.
840. *paṭhaṃtā.* This term indicates a person or persons who merely read (perhaps

also recite aloud) spiritual texts but do not internalize their meanings. The Tibetan equivalent, "heedless persons" (*bag med pa*), suggests either a different Sanskrit original or an inexact rendering.

841. *Kāśyapaparivarta*, *'Od srung gi le'u.*

842. *nyin klog 'don pa.* This phrase describes a dharma activity in which monks, individually or in groups, are requested to recite scriptural texts throughout the day, or even for several days, often on behalf of a householder, in order to create virtue for the individual who makes the request.

843. *nges par 'byung ba khyad par can.* See note 439 (this chapter).

844. As described in this paragraph and the following, some activities that are performed under the influence of the eight worldly concerns can be virtuous in nature. Following that, successive paragraphs identify examples of deeds that are unvirtuous and indeterminate in nature, and, in particular, activities that appear to be virtuous in nature but in fact constitute evil deeds.

845. One of the formulations relating to karma is the distinction between deeds that are "performed" (*kṛta, byas pa*) and those that are "accumulated." Asanga's *Levels of Yoga Practice* (*Yogācārabhūmi*) states: "What is performed karma? It is that which is thought in the mind or that which, after having been thought in the mind, is then carried out in body or speech. . . . Accumulated karma is any deed with the exception of these ten types: that which is done in a dream; that which is done unknowingly; that which is not done deliberately; that which is neither done with intensity nor continually; that which is done erroneously; that which is done because of a lapse of memory; that which is done unwillingly; that which has an indeterminate (see note 849, this chapter) nature; that which has been eliminated through regret; and that which has been eliminated by an antidote. Hence, accumulated karma is any deed other than these ten types. . . . An act of taking life that is accumulated but not performed occurs when the possibility of taking a particular being's life has been considered and reflected on for a long time but that being's life is not taken." A deed that is both performed and accumulated is said to be one that is "certain to be experienced" (*niyatavedanīya, nges par myong bar 'gyur ba*), which means that unless it has been expiated, it will retain the power to produce a result at some point in the future. See also the discussion in *AKBh* explaining ch. 4, v. 120 of the root text.

846. See note 505 (this chapter).

847. See *AK* (ch. 4, v. 125cd), which identifies three types of virtue: that which relates to merit (*puṇyabhāgīyaṃ kuśala, bsod nams cha mthun gyi dge ba*); that which relates to liberation (*mokṣabhāgīyam, thar pa cha mthun*); and that which relates to penetrating insight (*nirvedhabhāgīyam, nges 'byed cha mthun*). The first of these three does not constitute an element of the path because it is not accompanied by renunciation. The second is synonymous with the path of accumulation (*sambhāramārga, tshogs lam*) and the third with the path of preparation (*prayogamārga, sbyor lam*).

848. See ch. 10, "The Essence of Nectar," notes 261 and 262.

849. *avyākṛta, lung ma bstan.* Abhidharma texts define two types of indeterminate entities: obstructive indeterminate ones (*nivṛtāvyākṛta, sgrib lung ma bstan*) and nonobstructive indeterminate ones (*anivṛtāvyākṛta, ma sgrib lung ma bstan*). Examples of obstructive indeterminate entities are the mental afflictions of the two higher realms, which is to say that no unvirtuous entities exist there. There are four kinds of nonobstructive indeterminate entities, of which three can be described as activities: the four kinds of physical behavior (*īryāpathāni, spyod lam*)—that is, walking, standing, sitting, and reclining; activities relating to physical crafts and other manual arts (*śilpasthāna, bzo'i gnas*); and the state of mind that creates magical emanations (*nirmāṇacitta, sprul pa'i sems*). The fourth type of nonobstructive indeterminate entities is the maturation results of virtuous and unvirtuous entities.

850. The five terms from "hypocrisy" through "acquiring gain through gifts" are the names of five kinds of wrong livelihood (*mithyājīvita, log 'tsho*) that monks and nuns must avoid. For a description of hypocrisy (*kuhanā, tshul 'chos*), see ch. 10, "The Essence of Nectar," note 375. Flattery (*lapanā, kha gsag*) is when an individual speaks favorably or shows deference to someone as a means of obtaining something of value from him or her. Intimation (*naimittikatvam, gshog slong*) is to obtain material gain by subterfuge or some indirect means. Oppression (*naiṣpeṣikatva, thob kyis 'jal ba*) is when an individual tries to coerce someone into making a gift. An example of acquiring gain through gifts (*labhena lābhaniṣpādanā, rnyed pas rnyed pa sgrub pa*) is when reference to a previous gift is made as a means of obtaining some object that is desired. *ŚBh* (Sanskrit edition, p. 48) describes all of these four acts in one detailed passage.

851. *blang dor.* This term is a combination of the participial nouns "adopting" (*blang ba*) and "rejecting" (*dor ba*) and thus addresses the effort to both adopt virtuous qualities and reject unvirtuous ones. It can be rendered loosely as "spiritual practice."

852. This statement should be understood in relation to these two forms of the eight worldly concerns.

853. That is, renunciation and enlightenment mind.

854. *subhāṣita, legs bshad.* The original Sanskrit of this term is often understood to mean "eloquent speech"; however, it does not sound appropriate for someone to describe his or her own composition with such a lofty expression. Hence, I have rendered it with this more neutral language.

855. Shar Tsong kha pa. Tsongkhapa's epithet is often written with this additional syllable, describing the Tsongka region of Amdo as one that lies to the east, or *shar* (*shar*), of the Machu River (*rma chu*).

856. See notes 65 and 423 (this chapter). Gyama is the region where the monastery is located; it was founded by Gyergom Zhönu Drakpa (See annotation on p. 587).

14. A Listing of the Mahāyāna Works on Mind Training

1. *Theg pa chen po'i blo sbyong gi dkar chag*, *DNZ*, vol. 3 (*ga*), pp. 377–78.
2. Mu (*mus*) is a place name for a valley and a village in the region of Tsang. The epithet used here, "the great one from Mü," (*mus pa chen po*), is often rendered in an abbreviated form as Muchen (*mus chen*). In this instance, the epithet likely also is meant as a reference to the fact that Könchok Gyaltsen founded Müsu Yama Monastery in this region in 1459.
3. This is a reference to the important collection known as *A Hundredfold Collection of Mind Training Works* (*bLo sbyong brgya rtsa*), the source text from which this selection of works has been extracted. The collection has been translated into English by Thupten Jinpa under the title *Mind Training: The Great Collection* (Boston: Wisdom, 2006).
4. *Byams pa'i rnal 'byor pa*. This individual, who was one of Atiśa's many Indian gurus, is also known as Kuśalī the Younger (dGe ba can). He is considered one of Atiśa's three principal teachers on the Mind Training instruction.
5. The Tibetan reference to this work describes it as *A Mind Training Work by Maitrī Yogi*, as it is considered by many to have been authored by that master. However, the title that appears in the collection is as described here (*bLo sbyong sems dpa'i rim pa*).
6. *Mind Training: The Great Collection* identifies this work by the title *Leveling Out All Conceptions.*
7. *Mind Training: The Great Collection* identifies this work by the title *Sumpa Lotsāwa's Ear-Whispered Mind Training.*
8. *Mind Training: The Great Collection* identifies this work by the title *Mind Training in a Single Session.*
9. *Mind Training: The Great Collection* identifies this work by the title *Advice to Namdak Tsuknor.*
10. This very short piece is not named in the above listing as a separate work; however, it is included in *DNZ*, vol. 4 (*nga*), pp. 169–70.
11. This work is a commentary to item 10. *Mind Training: The Great Collection* identifies it by the title *A Commentary on "Leveling Out All Conceptions."*
12. This Sanskrit phrase is a benedictory utterance calling for spiritual success. It means "May all auspiciousness come to pass!"

15. How Atiśa Relinquished His Kingdom and Sought Liberation

1. *Jo bo rjes rgyal srid spangs nas thar pa sgrub pa'i rnam par thar pa*, *DNZ*, vol. 3 (*ga*), pp. 379–404.
2. Alaka Chattopadhaya provides a brief survey of the various attempts by modern writers at understanding the meaning of this word and concludes that the Tibetan term *zahor* is Persian in origin and is a corrupt form of the word *śahor*,

which literally means "city." See *Atiśa and Tibet: Life and Works of Dipamkara Srijnana in Relation to the History and Religion of Tibet* (Delhi, Motilal Banarsidass, 1999), pp. 63–66. *The Great Tibetan-Chinese Dictionary* (s.v. "za hor"), on the other hand, provides a somewhat straightforward meaning for the term when it states that *zahor (za hor)* is a degeneration of an Indian word and refers to what is the modern state of Bengal.

3. Although "Bangala" is the old Indian way of writing "Bengal," the two terms do not refer to exactly the same thing. "Bengal" is the name of a state in modern India that borders Bangladesh in the east, Orissa in the south, Madhya Pradesh in the west, and Bihar in the west and northwest. In contrast, "Bangala" in its old usage seems to have covered a larger area, which included large parts of what today comprises the central Indian state of Bihar. In this text, however, the author appears to be using the term as the name of a city where the royal palace of Atiśa's parents was said to be located.
4. The Derge edition states: "His wealth and power resemble that of China's Tongkhün." The Tibetan term *tongkhün* (spelled *stong khun),* which I have translated here as "Eastern," is, as suggested by Stein, probably a degeneration of the Chinese term *T'ang kiun* ("sovereign of T'ang"). See Rolf Alfred Stein, *Les tribus anciennes des marches sino-tibétaines: légendes, classifications et histoire* (Paris: Presses universitaires de France, 1961). For an alternative meaning of this term, see Tsongkhapa, *The Great Treatise on the Stages of the Path to Enlightenment, vol. 1* (Ithaca, NY: Snow Lion, 2000), ch. 1, note 8.
5. This is probably a reference to the legendary city of Gandhara, which is mentioned in various Buddhist sources and thought to have been "located in an arc reaching from the western Punjab through the northwest frontier to Kabul and perhaps into southern Afghanistan." John Keay, *India: A History*, (Oxford: Oxford University Press, 2000), p. 58.
6. Dharmodgata (Chos 'phags) is often cited as an example of a bodhisattva who possesses enormous resources to make offerings to the spiritual teachers.
7. The Derge edition states: "Stories of the three are found in brief elsewhere."
8. The Derge edition states: "The youngest, who is known as Candragarbha . . . ."
9. This probably refers to Vikramaśīla, which later became the monastic university where Atiśa became a prominent master. To date, although no conclusive archeological site of this famous Buddhist monastery has been found, it is widely believed that it existed somewhere on the shores of the Ganges River in modern Bihar. See Keay, *India: A History*, p. 193.
10. This is an abbreviation of Vikramaśīla.
11. This follows the Derge edition.
12. The Derge edition states: "Twenty-one girls of noble patronage."
13. This follows the Derge edition.
14. Since the events being described are supposed to have taken place in India, wherever possible, I have attempted to give the names referred to in the text written in Sanskrit. Those that I have failed to reconstruct in Sanskrit, I have

left as they are in the Tibetan original. I would like to thank Acharya Lobsang Dorje Rabling of the Central Institute of Higher Tibetan Studies, Sarnath, for helping with the reconstruction of many of the Sanskrit names.

15. The names of the ministers have been left as they appear in the Tibetan text.
16. The Derge edition states: "Who were all at the threshold of betrothal age."
17. This follows the Derge edition.
18. Siddhārtha is the name of the historical Buddha before he attained full enlightenment under the Bodhi tree.
19. The father of the historical Buddha Śākyamuni.
20. The "twelve great deeds" refer to the key events of the historical Buddha's life as recounted in the Buddhist texts. These are often the subject of mural paintings in the Buddhist temples in India, Tibet, Sri Laṅka, China, and other traditionally Buddhist countries in Asia.
21. The more one drinks salt water, the more one feels thirsty; in the same manner, the more one indulges in the sense objects, the more one craves them.
22. "The king of the Śākyas" is an epithet for Śākyamuni, the historical Buddha.
23. This follows the Derge edition.
24. This follows the Derge edition.
25. This follows the Derge edition.
26. This follows the Derge edition.
27. "Other shore" refers to existence beyond this present life, such as future lives. This expression is also often used to refer to liberation, the "other shore" (*pha rol*), as opposed to cyclic existence, which is "this side of the shore" (*tshu rol*).
28. This follows the Derge edition.
29. The term *three spheres* (*'khor gsum*) normally refers to the three key elements of a given act—the object of the act, the doer, and the act itself—but this does not make much sense here. Most probably it is a typographical error, and the Tibetan expression should read *khornam* (*'khor rnams*), which refers to the prince's retinue. So here the text probably states that the prince offered his entire retinue to the master.
30. This follows the Derge edition.
31. This follows the Derge edition.
32. This follows the Derge edition.
33. Vaiśravaṇa is a god of wealth in the classical Indian Buddhist pantheon and also the guardian of the western direction. He is depicted holding in his right hand a mongoose that is spewing out wish-fulfilling jewels.
34. This is a reference to what are known as the "seven riches of a noble one." The seven riches are listed by Atiśa at the end of his *Bodhisattva's Jewel Garland*: faith, morality, giving, learning, conscience, a sense of shame, and wisdom. See ch. 3, v. 25, pp. 22–23.
35. Body, speech, and mind—the three "doors" through which beings perform actions.
36. Yama is the lord of death in ancient Indian mythology, in both the Buddhist

and non-Buddhist traditions. His abode is thought to be in the southern direction, and he is often depicted, especially in the Tibetan tradition, with a buffalo head.

37. "The eight mundane concerns" are the four pairs of contrasting reactions that reflect a deep-seated attachment to the concerns of this life. They are being elated when one finds resources and dejected when one does not, being elated when hearing pleasant words and dejected when hearing unpleasant words, being elated when praised and dejected when belittled, and being elated when enjoying happiness and dejected when undergoing unhappiness.
38. This appears to be a paraphrase rather than a direct quote. Most probably, "Nāgārjunagarbha" refers to the famous second-century Buddhist thinker Nāgārjuna, the author of the highly influential *Fundamental Wisdom of the Middle Way.*
39. This is the second in the fivefold topology of the path to enlightenment. The other paths are the path of accumulation, the path of seeing, the path of meditation, and the path of no more learning.
40. This follows the Derge edition.
41. A unit of measurement for distance in the classical Indian system, the value of which varies according to the particular source consulted. In the standard *Abhidharmakośa* system, it is roughly equivalent to five standard miles. For a discussion of the conflicting values of this unit of measurement, including a general discussion of the classical Indian methods of computation, see William McGovern, *A Manual of Buddhist Philosophy* (Lucknow, India: Oriental Reprinters, 1976), pp. 39–48.
42. *MW* (s.v. "kṛṣṇasāra") identifies *kṛṣṇasāra* as the spotted antelope.
43. This expression alludes to the yogi's profound meditative realization, in which his entire perspective is free of duality between dichotomous categories like subject and object, the external environment and the beings within, and so on.
44. This follows the Derge edition.
45. A major center of Vajrayāna Buddhism in ancient times that modern writers identify as the Swat Valley of modern Pakistan.
46. This is the realm where, according to Mahāyāna Buddhism, all the buddhas attain their full enlightenment in the form of the saṃbhogakāya, the buddha body of perfect resource.
47. The celestial realm where Maitreya, the future Buddha, is believed to reside at present.
48. The pure land of Buddha Amitābha.
49. In classical Indian and Buddhist mythology, the king of Gandharva is identified to be the most skilled musician.
50. An important meditation deity belonging to the class of "mother tantras" of Vajrayāna Buddhist teachings. An English translation of this deity's root text can be found in *The Hevajra Tantra*, a two-volume study of the tantra by D. L. Snellgrove (London: Oxford University Press, 1959).

51. The Sanskrit term *tīrthika*, when found in Buddhist texts, usually refers to the non-Buddhist schools of ancient India. In this usage, the term refers to the "upholders of extreme views," such as those of absolutism or nihilism.
52. This follows the Derge edition.
53. Known also as Cakrasaṃvara, Heruka is an important meditation deity belonging to the category of "mother tantras" in Highest Yoga Tantra.
54. This follows the Derge edition.
55. The term *vajra*, which can be translated as "diamond" or "adamantine," connotes indivisibility and indestructibility.
56. This follows the Derge edition.
57. This prose "colophon" appears in the Derge edition of *The Book of Kadam* (*bKa' gdam legs 'bam*) in verse with three lines. It was most probably added by a subsequent editor.

16. The Story of Atiśa's Voyage to Sumatra

1. *Jo bo mnyam med gser gling pa dang mjal ba'i rnam thar*, *DNZ*, vol. 3 (*ga*), pp. 405–20. The full title of this work is *The Liberating Story of Master Atiśa's Meeting with the Peerless Serlingpa Dharmakīrti* (*Jo bo rjes mnyam med gser gling pa chos kyi 'grags pa dang mjal ba'i rnam thar*). "Serlingpa" literally means "the one from Serling," the Sanskrit for which is Suvarṇadvīpa, which in turn literally means a "land of gold" or an "island of gold." Modern scholars identify Suvarṇadvīpa as the Indonesian island of Sumatra.
2. *MW* (s.v. "makara") identifies *makara* as "a kind of sea monster (sometimes confounded with the crocodile, shark, and dolphin, etc. . . .)." In the context of the story, it could refer to some kind of whale.
3. This is probably a reference to Atiśa himself, who was a teacher of the learned Kṣitigarbha.
4. The garuḍa is the mythological king of birds in the classical Indian mythology and also the mount of the scepter-wielding Vedic god Indra. It is often depicted devouring serpents and is considered to be the counterforce of nāgas, the serpentine spirits.
5. Yamāntaka, literally meaning "the enemy of Yama," refers to a class of meditation deities regarded as the counterforce of Yama, the Lord of Death. Vajrabhairava is the most well-known Yamāntaka in the Highest Yoga class of the Vajrayāna.
6. Acala is one of the four principal meditation deities of the Kadam school and is the guardian protector. The other three divinities are Buddha Śākyamuni as the master of the teachings, Avalokiteśvara as the buddha of compassion, and Ārya Tārā as the buddha of enlightened activity.
7. This is a reference to the Buddhist goddess Tārā, whose key feature is her protection against "eight dangers": lions and the associated emotion of conceit, elephants and the associated emotion of delusion or bewilderment, fire and the associated emotion of anger, poisonous snakes and the associated emotion

of jealousy, robbers and the associated mental states of destructive views, the chains of bondage and the associated emotion of miserliness, water and the associated emotion of attachment, and ghosts and the associated emotion of wavering doubts. The close association of the name of Tārā with protection against these dangers seems to have been part of the myth of Tārā from the earliest stages of the evolution of her rites. For a contemporary analysis of Tārā, including translations of some liturgical texts connecting with her meditative practice, see Stephen Beyer, *The Cult of Tārā: Magic and Ritual in Tibet* (Berkeley: University of California Press, 1973).

8. This expression "father and son" is probably a reference to Atiśa and his spiritual teacher Serlingpa. If this is correct, then it is interesting to note that even though, at this point in the narrative, Atiśa and Serlingpa haven't met yet, the learned Kṣitigarbha refers to Serlingpa and Atiśa as "father and son."
9. This follows the Derge edition.
10. I have translated the Tibetan expression *mo bön*, which is an abbreviation of the two terms *mo* and *bön*, as "divination and animism." Although the second term, *bön*, can also refer to Tibet's pre-Buddhist religion of Bön, I believe that it refers more broadly here to some kind of animistic or shamanistic rites. Interestingly, the expression "divination and animism" (*mo bön*) appears quite frequently in many early Kadam writings.
11. It is difficult to speculate on the meaning of the rather intriguing expression "Nepalese ship" (*bal po'i zings*). Given that Nepal is a landlocked country, it is highly unlikely that it had any history of maritime activity. It is conceivable that the Tibetan word *belpo* (*bal po*), which is an adjectival form of the noun *belyul* (*bal yul*, Nepal), once had a wider meaning that encompassed other ethnic groups. However, given the geographical proximity of Bengal and Nepal, we cannot rule out the possibility that there may have been a tradition of Nepalese craftsmen skilled in shipbuilding at some point in the past.
12. It is difficult to speculate about the identity of this city or whether there even was such a historical place. In the Derge edition, the name of the city is "Svabhāvanātha."
13. In the Lhasa Shol edition of this text in *Mind Training: The Great Collection* and the Lhasa Shol and Derge editions in *The Book of Kadam*, this line reads, "Throw this sky-flower and strike . . ." (*nam mkha'i me tog 'di . . .*). This, I think, is a typographical error.
14. The act of striking the heretics' city with a lightning bolt might entail transgression of the Buddhist precepts of going for refuge and generating the awakening mind. When generating the mind of awakening, one vows never to abandon the well-being of other sentient beings even at the cost of one's life.
15. This is a reference to the central Asian Turks, who had, by the eleventh century, already begun their frequent raids into the vast Indian subcontinent, especially in the northern and central parts of India.
16. This allusion to Bön and its principal center of activity, the land of Shangshung,

is most intriguing given that at the supposed time of the events narrated in this story, Atiśa had not yet made his journey to Tibet. It is, however, conceivable that Atiśa and his student Kṣitigarbha are familiar with Bön as being the pre-Buddhist religion of Tibet, since by the eleventh century the tradition of Tibetans coming to study and translate the major Buddhist texts at the feet of Indian masters was already well established.

17. It seems that leprosy had been a major health concern during the lifetime of the early Kadam masters such as Drom Tönpa and his immediate disciples in the eleventh and twelfth centuries in central Tibet. Thus, countering people's prejudices against lepers features prominently in their teachings. According to Tibetan sources, Drom Tönpa was so deeply affected by people's prejudices against those suffering from the disease that he dedicated the latter part of his life to nursing many lepers, eventually losing his own life to the illness.
18. *Rākṣasa*, or the Tibetan equivalent *sinpo* (*srin po*), refers to an ogrelike monster. The reference to Laṅka as the kingdom of rākṣasas draws from the Indian mythology found in the ancient Hindu Purāṇic literature.
19. This follows the Derge edition.
20. This mantra appears differently in all the various editions of the text, including the Lhasa Shol and Derge editions of *The Book of Kadam.*
21. Atiśa's full name is Dīpaṃkara Śrījñāna.
22. This reference is intriguing. If true, it suggests that there was communication between Tibet and Indonesia in the first millennium, something unheard of in the traditional Tibetan historical writings.
23. In opting for *monks* instead of *spiritual friends* (*geshe*), as found in the original Tibetan, we are following the Derge edition.
24. It's difficult to speculate what this monster is.
25. The expression *sky treasury (namkha dzö, nam mkha' mdzod*) alludes to a common legend in Buddhist literature of an inexhaustible treasure. It is said that the one who has mastered this wealth can pull material objects from the sky as if it were a treasury. This power is seen as one of the marks of a bodhisattva who has fully mastered the perfection of giving, which takes place on the first bodhisattva level.
26. This is an allusion to the meditators' failure to recognize Atiśa when he first arrived.
27. Known as *khakkhara* in Sanskrit and *kharsil* (*'khar gsil*) in Tibetan, this staff is one of the "thirteen articles of sustenance" of a fully ordained Buddhist monk. For a drawing and description of this staff, see Martin Willson and Martin Brauen, *Deities of Tibetan Buddhism: The Zurich Paintings of the Icons Worthwhile to See* (Boston: Wisdom, 2000), p. 568.
28. I was not able to clarify how large this is.
29. Since all the named monks are Indians, wherever possible I have attempted to reconstruct the probable Sanskrit name.

30. Meaning, perhaps, that it is disrespectful to the dharma to interrupt a teaching, even in order to pay respect to a noble one who has appeared unexpectedly.
31. *Abhisamayālaṃkāra* (*mNgon par rtogs pa'i rgyan*). This is a highly influential classical Buddhist text attributed to Maitreya (c. fourth century) that systematically expounds the themes of the *Perfection of Wisdom* scriptures.
32. The wording of this "colophon" is much shorter in the Derge edition of the text in *The Book of Kadam.*
33. This entire section, which is effectively a supplication to master Atiśa followed by an aspiration prayer, does not exist in *The Book of Kadam.* Most probably it was added by one of the editors of our present anthology.

17. Annotated Root Lines of Mahāyāna Mind Training

1. *Theg pa chen po'i blo sbyong gi rtsa tshig mchan bcas*, *DNZ*, vol. 3 (*ga*), pp. 421–26. For comments pertaining to the authorship of the "root lines" embedded in this annotated text and their relation to *The Root Lines* and the root text of the *Seven-Point Mind Training*, see the translator's introduction in *Mind Training: The Great Collection*, The Library of Tibetan Classics, vol. 1 (Boston: Wisdom, 2006).
2. In the Tibetan annotation system, the lines of the "root text" are in a larger font while the annotations are smaller. Similarly, to help maintain a clearer separation between the two, we have set the lines of the root text in italics, while interlinear notes are in a smaller font. My own additions, introduced to clarify the meaning, are provided within brackets. The Arabic numbers for the stanzas and Roman numerals for the prose are not part of the original text but have been inserted to make references easier.
3. Lines b, c, and d in this stanza are not found in the *Root Lines of Mahāyāna Mind Training without Annotations.*
4. The next two lines of this stanza are not found in the *Root Lines.*
5. Lines a, b, and c of this stanza are not found in the *Root Lines.*
6. In various commentaries, this line reads: "Relate to your meditation whatever you encounter right now." This variance is caused by a difference in the spelling of a single verb. When spelled with the suffix *b*, as is done here (*gang thub*) it gives the reading "whatever you can," and when spelled with the *g* suffix (*gang thug*), it gives the reading "whatever you encounter." Judging by its context, and more importantly, following the reading of the early commentarial literature, the second reading seems to be more accurate.
7. The next two lines of this stanza are not found in the *Root Lines.*
8. This line, though consonant with the *Seven-Point Mind Training*, reads in the *Root Lines* as follows: "Train in the five powers." This is due to a variation in a single letter of the verb. When written *jarwa* (*sbyar ba*), as is the case here, it means "to apply," whereas when written *jangwa* (*sbyang ba*), it means "to train."

9. This first line of the stanza is not found in the *Root Lines.*
10. Three general points are that your mind training does not contradict your pledges, that your behavior does not become sarcastic, and that it does not become biased.
11. A dzo, a cross between a yak and a cow, is a domestic animal capable of carrying heavy loads for long distances.
12. This line does not appear in the *Root Lines.*
13. This line does not appear in the *Root Lines.*
14. This line does not appear in the *Root Lines.*
15. Lines xi and xiii do not appear in the *Root Lines.*
16. The first two lines of this stanza are not found in the *Root Lines*, and the last two lines do not match up exactly. In the *Root Lines*, we read: "This proliferation of five degenerations is transformed into the path of enlightenment." This variant reading is, interestingly, due to a simple change in case. In the *Root Lines*, the case is genitive, while here the case is instrumental.
17. This entire stanza does not appear in the *Root Lines.*
18. This entire stanza does not appear in either the *Root Lines* or the *Seven-Point Mind Training.* "Fierce one" here refers to the mental afflictions that are powerful and vicious in their destructiveness.
19. Lines a, b, and d of this stanza do not appear in the *Root Lines.*
20. Lines b and c of this stanza do not appear in the *Root Lines.*
21. Lines xix to xxii are not found in the *Root Lines.*

18. Root Lines of Mahāyāna Mind Training without Annotations

1. *Theg pa chen po'i blo sbyong gi rtsa tshig mchan med*, *DNZ*, vol. 3 (*ga*), pp. 427–28. For problems pertaining to the authorship of this text, see the translator's introduction in *Mind Training: The Great Collection*, The Library of Tibetan Classics, vol. 1 (Boston: Wisdom, 2006). As indicated there, this root text sometimes diverges from the *Annotated Root Lines of Mahāyāna Mind Training*, the commentary that follows it in this anthology. The divergences are detailed in my notes to *Annotated Root Lines.*
2. The Tibetan original uses the instrumental case after the "two," giving the following reading: "Be upheld principally by the two witnesses." However, we have chosen here to follow the more established reading, which is consonant also with the version of the *Root Lines* found in the Derge edition of Jamgön Kongtrul's *Treasury of Precious Instructions.*

Bibliography

1. The Present Texts

The Source Volume

Jamgön Kongtrul Lodrö Taye, comp. *The Treasury of Precious Instructions. gDams ngag rin po che'i mdzod.* Vol. 3 (*ga*). Delhi: Shechen Publications, 1999. dnz.tsadra.org.

The Translated Texts

Atiśa (Dīpaṃkāra Śrījñāna). *Annotated Root Lines of Mahāyāna Mind Training. Theg pa chen po'i blo sbyong gi rta tshig mchan bcas. DNZ*, vol. 3 (*ga*), pp. 421–26.

———. *Bodhisattva's Jewel Garland: A Root Text of Mahāyāna Instruction from the Precious Kadam Scripture. Theg pa chen po'i man ngag bka' gdams glegs bam rin po che'i rtsa tshig byang chub sems dpa'i nor bu'i phreng ba. DNZ*, vol. 3 (*ga*), pp. 11–14. Second source: *Byang chub sems dpa'i nor bu'i phreng ba.* In *Blo sbyong glegs bam.* Lhasa: bshi sde par khang. n.d. BDRC W3CN22963. Third source: Dg.T. dbu ma, vol. 32 (*khi*), ff. 301b–302b. (Toh. 3951)

———. *A Lamp for the Path to Enlightenment. Byang chub lam gyi sgron ma. DNZ*, vol. 3 (*ga*), pp. 1–8. Second source: In T.PD. vol. 64, pp. 1641–48. Beijing: Krung go'i bod rig pa'i dpe skrun khang, 1994–2008.

———. *Root Lines of Mahāyāna Mind Training without Annotations. Theg pa chen po'i blo sbyong gi rtsa tshig mchan med. DNZ*, vol. 3 (*ga*), pp. 427–28.

———. *The Story of Atiśa's Voyage to Sumatra. Jo bo mnyam med gser gling pa dang mjal ba'i rnam thar. DNZ*, vol. 3 (*ga*), pp. 405–20.

Chenga Lodrö Gyaltsen. *Opening the Door to the Dharma: The Initial Method of Training One's Mind in the Mind Training Tradition of the Stages of the Path to Enlightenment. Byang chub lam kyi rim pa la blo sbyong ba la thog mar blo sbyong ba chos kyi sgo 'byed. DNZ*, vol. 3 (*ga*), pp. 429–544. Second source: In Collected Works, vol. 1. BDRC MW1KG2144.

Drom Tönpa Gyalwai Jungne. *How Atiśa Relinquished His Kingdom and Sought Liberation. Jo bo rjes rgyal srid spangs nas thar pa sgrub pa'i rnam par thar pa. DNZ*, vol. 3 (*ga*), pp. 379–404.

Gyalse Tokme Zangpo. *The Root Text of the Mahāyāna Instruction Known as the Seven-Point Mind Training. Theg pa chen po'i gdams ngag blo sbyong don bdun ma'i rtsa ba. DNZ*, vol. 3 (*ga*), pp. 8–11.

Jamgön Kongtrul. *The Brilliant Illumination of the Path to Enlightenment: A Commentary That Summarizes the Essence of A Lamp for the Path to Enlightenment. Byang chub lam gyi sgron ma'i 'grel pa snying por bsdus pa byang chub lam gyi snang ba rab tu gsal ba. DNZ*, vol. 3 (*ga*), pp. 15–61.

———. *A Guidebook for the Path to Great Awakening: The Ritual for Generating Enlightenment Mind according to the System Followed in the Lineage of the Profound View. Zab mo lta brgyud lugs kyi sems bskyed pa'i cho ga byang chub chen po'i gzhung lam. DNZ*, vol. 3 (*ga*), pp. 275–321.

Jamyang Khyentse Wangpo. *An Essential Summary of the Method of Practice in the System of the Stages of the Path to Enlightenment. Byang chub lam gyi rim pa nyams su len tshul gyi phyag bzhes snying por dril ba. DNZ*, vol. 3 (*ga*), pp. 161–79.

———. *The Excellent Path of the Bodhisattvas: A Ritual for Generating Enlightenment Mind and Accepting the Bodhisattva Vow according to the Mahāyāna System of Great Vastness. Theg chen shin tu rgyas pa'i sems bskyed dang sdom pa'i cho ga byang chub sems dpa'i lam bzang. DNZ*, vol. 3 (*ga*), pp. 323–75.

Jamgön Kongtrul Lodrö Taye. *A Listing of the Mahāyāna Works on Mind Training. Theg pa chen po'i blo sbyong gi dkar chag. DNZ*, vol. 3 (*ga*), pp. 377–78.

Losang Chökyi Gyaltsen, Fourth Paṇchen Lama. *The Easy Path That Leads to Omniscience: An Instruction Manual on the Stages of the Path to Enlightenment. Byang chub lam gyi rim pa'i khrid yig thams cad mkhyen par bgrod pa'i bde lam. DNZ*, vol. 3 (*ga*), pp. 111–60.

Sönam Gyatso, Third Dalai Lama. *The Nectar That Is Like Highly Refined Gold: An Instruction Manual on the Stages of the Path to Enlightenment. Byang chub lam gyi rim pa'i 'khrid gser gyi yang zhun. DNZ*, vol. 3 (*ga*), pp. 73–110.

Tāranātha. *The Essence of Nectar: A Manual of Instruction for the Three Types of Person on the Stages for Gaining Entry to the Victor's Teaching. rGyal ba'i bstan pa la 'jug pa'i rim pa skyes bu gsum gyi man ngag gi khrid yig bdud rtsi'i nying khu. DNZ*, vol. 3 (*ga*), pp. 181–273.

Tsongkhapa, Losang Drakpa. *The Flower Cluster of Spiritual Attainments: A Supplication Prayer to the Lineage Whose Blessings Are Near. Byin rlabs nye brgyud kyi gsol 'debs dngos grub kyi snye ma. DNZ*, vol. 3 (*ga*), pp. 71–72. Second source: *Byin rlabs nye brgyud kyi bla ma rnams la gsol ba 'debs pa / dNgos grub kyi snye ma.* In Collected Works, vol. 2 (*kha*), pp. 206–8. New Delhi: Mongolian Lama Guru Deva, 1978–1983. (Toh. 5275)

———. *A Verse Compendium of the Spiritual Practices of the Stages of the Path to Enlightenment. Byang chub lam gyi rim pa'i nyams len bsdus don gyi tshigs su bcad pa. DNZ*, vol. 3 (*ga*), pp. 63–69. Second source: *Byang chub lam gyi rim pa'i nyams len gyi rnam gzhag mdor bsdus te brjed byang du bya ba* (also known as *Lam rim bsdus don* and as *Nyams mgur*). In Collected Works, vol. 2 (*kha*). New Delhi: Mongolian Lama Guru Deva, 1978–1983. (Toh. 5275)

2. Canonical Works

The Ākāśagarbha Sūtra. Translated by the Sakya Pandita Translation Group. 84000: Translating the Words of the Buddha, 2014. *Ākāśagarbhasūtra.* Sanskrit text not extant. Tibetan text: *Nam mkha'i snying po'i mdo.* Dg.K. mdo sde, vol. 22 (*za*), ff. 264a–283b. (Toh. 260)

The Application of Mindfulness of the Sacred Dharma. Translated by the Dharmachakra Translation Committee. 84000: Translating the Words of the Buddha, 2021. Sanskrit text: *Saddharmasmṛtyupasthānasūtram.* In *A Less Traveled Path* (ch. 2 only). Edited by Daniel M. Stuart. Beijing and Vienna: China Tibetology Publishing House/Austrian Academy of Sciences Press, 2015. Tibetan text: *'Phags pa dam pa'i chos dran pa nye bar bzhag pa.* Dg.K. mdo sde, vol. 68 (*ya*), f. 82a–vol. 71 (*sha*), f. 229b. (Toh. 287)

The Array of Virtues of Mañjuśrī's Buddha Realm. Translated by the Dharmachakra Translation Committee. 84000: Translating the Words of the Buddha, 2021. Second English translation: "The Prediction of Mañjuśrī's Attainment of Buddhahood." In *A Treasury of Mahāyāna Sūtras*, translated by Garma C. C. Chang, pp. 164–88. University Park: Pennsylvania State University Press, 1983. *Mañjuśrībuddhakṣetraguṇavyūhasūtra.* Sanskrit text not extant. Tibetan text: *'Phags pa 'jam dpal gyi sangs rgyas kyi zhing gi yon tan bkod pa.* Dg.K. dkon brtsegs, vol. 3 (*ga*), ff. 248b–297a. (Toh. 59)

The Articles of Discipline. English translation of two sections, on medicine and on going forth, published by 84000: Translating the Words of the Buddha, 2018, 2021. Sanskrit text: *Mūlasarvāstivāda Vinayavastu.* Buddhist Sanskrit Texts, no. 16. 2 vols. Darbhanga, India: Mithila Institute, 1970. Tibetan text: *'Dul ba gzhi.* Dg.K. 'dul ba, vols. 1–4 (*ka–nga*). (Toh. 1)

The Aspirational Prayer for Excellent Spiritual Conduct. In *The Flower Ornament Scripture*, translated by Thomas Cleary, pp. 1511–18. Boston: Shambhala, 1993. Sanskrit text: *Bhadracaryapraṇidhāna.* In *Gaṇḍvyūhasūtra*, pp. 428–36. Darbanga, India: Mithila Institute, 1960. Tibetan text: *bZang po spyod pa'i smon lam gyi rgyal po.* Dg.K. phal chen, vol. 6 (*cha*), ff. 336b–341a. (Toh. 1105)

The Chapter on Truth. bDen pa po'i le'u. See *The Sūtra Teaching the Miracles in the Domain of Skillful Means That the Bodhisattvas Have at Their Disposition.*

Collection of Uplifting Sayings. Translated by W. Woodville Rockhill. Amsterdam: Oriental Press, 1975. First printed in 1884. Sanskrit text: *Udānavarga.* Edited by Franz Bernhard. Gottingen: Vandehoeck and Ruprecht, 1965. Tibetan text: *Ched du brjod pa'i tshoms.* Dg.K. mdo sde, vol. 28 (*sa*), ff. 209a–253a. (Toh. 326)

The Connected Discourses of the Buddha. Translated by Bhikkhu Bodhi. Boston: Wisdom, 2000. Pāli text: *Samyutta Nikāya.* https://tipitaka.org.

Descent into Laṅka Sūtra. Translated by D. T. Suzuki. London: George Routledge and Sons, 1932. Sanskrit text: *Saddharmalaṅkāvatārasūtram.* Buddhist Sanskrit Texts, no. 3. Darbanga, India: Mithila Institute, 1963. Tibetan text: *'Phags pa lang kar gshegs pa'i mdo.* Dg.K. mdo sde, vol. 5 (*ca*), ff. 87b–307a. (Toh. 107)

Detailed Explanations of Discipline. Vinayavibhaṅga, Sanskrit text not extant. Tibetan text: *'Dul ba rnam par 'byed pa* . Dg.K. 'dul ba, vol. 5 (*ca*), f. 21a–vol. 8 (*nya*), f. 269a. (Toh. 3)

Divine Stories (2 vols). Translated by Andy Rotman. Somerville, MA: Wisdom, 2008. Sanskrit text: *Divyāvadānam*. Buddhist Sanskrit Texts, no. 20. Darbanga, India: Mithila Institute, 1959.

The Flower Ornament Scripture. Translated by Thomas Cleary. Boston: Shambhala, 1993. *Avataṃsakasūtra*. Sanskrit text not extant. Tibetan text: *Sangs phal po che*. Dg.K. phal chen, vols. 1 (*ka*)–4 (*a*). (Toh. 44)

The Jewel Cloud Sūtra. Translated by the Dharmachakra Translation Committee. 84000: Translating the Words of the Buddha, 2019. *Ratnameghasūtra*. Sanskrit text not extant. Tibetan text: *dKon mchog sprin gyi mdo*. Dg.K. mdo sde, vol. 20 (*wa*), ff. 1b–112b. (Toh. 231)

Kālacakra Tantra (Ādibuddha Mahātantra). In *Kālacakra Tantra, Part 1*. Edited by Prof. Dr. Raghu Vira and Prof. Dr. Lokesh Chandra. New Delhi: International Academy of Indian Culture, 1966. Tibetan text: *mChog gi dang po'i sangs rgyas las phyung ba rgyud kyi rgyal po dpal dus kyi 'khor lo* (*Dus 'khor gyi rgyud*). Dg.K. rgyud, vol. 1 (*ka*), ff. 28b–186b. (Toh. 362)

The Kāśyapa Chapter. English translation in *A Treasury of Mahāyāna Sūtras*, ch. 20 "The Sūtra of Assembled Treasures." University Park: Pennsylvania State University Press, 1983, pp. 387–414. Sanskrit text: *Kāśyapaparivarta*. Edited by A. von Staël-Holstein. Shanghai: Commercial Press, 1926. Tibetan text: (*'Phags pa*) *'Od srung gi le'u shes bya ba theg pa chen po'i mdo*. Dg.K. dkon brtsegs, vol. 6 (*cha*), ff. 211a–260b. (Toh. 87)

The King of Samādhis Sūtra. 84000: Translating the Words of the Buddha, 2018. Translated by Peter Alan Roberts. Sanskrit text: *Samādhirājasūtram*. Buddhist Sanskrit Texts, no. 2. Darbanga, India: Mithila Institute, 1961. Tibetan text: *'Phags pa chos thams cad kyi rang bzhin mnyam pa nyid rnam par spros pa ting nge 'dzin gyi rgyal po zhes bya ba theg pa chen po'i mdo*. Dg.K. mdo mang, vol. 9 (*ta*), ff. 1–269b. (Toh. 127)

The Lion's Roar of Queen Śrīmala. Translated by Alex and Hikedo Weyman, pp. 57–113. Delhi: Motilal Banarsidass, 2007. *Śrīmaladevīsaṃhanādasūtra*. Sanskrit text not extant. Tibetan text: *Lha mo phreng gi seng ge'i sgra*. Dg.K. dkon brtsegs, vol. 6 (*cha*), ff. 255a–277b. (Toh. 92)

The Numerical Discourses of the Buddha. Translated by Bhikkhu Bodhi. Boston: Wisdom, 2012. *Aṅguttara Nikāya*. Pāli text: https://tipitaka.org.

The Perfection of Wisdom in Twenty-Five Thousand Lines. The Large Sūtra on Perfect Wisdom. Translated by Edward Conze. Berkeley: University of California Press, 1975. Sanskrit text: *Pañcavimśatisāhasrikāprajñāpāramitāsūtram*. 3 vols. Bibliotheca Indo-Tibetica Series, 61. Edited by Dr. Vijay Raj Vajracharya. Sarnath, India: Central Institute of Higher Tibetan Studies, 2006–2008. Tibetan text: *Shes rab kyi pha rol tu phyin pa stong phrag nyi shu lnga pa*. Dg.K. shes phyin, vols. 3–5 (*ga–ca*). (Toh. 3790)

The Play in Full Sūtra. Translated by the Dharmachakra Translation Committee. 84000: Translating the Words of the Buddha, 2013. Second English translation: *The Voice of the Buddha.* 2 vols. Translated from French by Gwendolyn Bays. Berkeley: Dharma Publishing, 1983. Sanskrit text: *Lalitavistara.* Buddhist Sanskrit Texts, no. 1. Darbanga, India: Mithila Institute, 1958. Tibetan text: *'Phags pa rgya cher rol pa zhes bya ba theg pa chen po'i mdo.* Dg.K. mdo sde, vol. 2 (*kha*), ff. 1–216b. (Toh. 95)

Samputa Tantra. No published Sanskrit edition available. Tibetan text: *dPal yang dag par sbyor ba zhes bya ba'i rgyud chen po.* Dg.K. rgyud, vol. 3 (*ga*), ff. 73b–158b. (Toh. 381)

The Stem Array. Translated by Peter Alan Roberts. 84000: Translating the Words of the Buddha, 2021. Second translation: In *Entry into the Realm of Reality*, pp. 1135–1518. Translated by Thomas Cleary. Boston: Shambhala, 1989. Sanskrit text: *Gaṇḍavyūhasūtra.* Buddhist Sanskrit Texts, no. 5. Darbanga, India: Mithila Institute, 1960. Tibetan text: *sDong po bkod pa'i mdo* (also *sDong po brgyan pa'i mdo*). Dg.K. phal chen, final chapter of sūtra, vol. 4 (*a*), ff. 24a–vol. 6 (*cha*). (Toh. 44)

Sūtra of Golden Light. Translated by R. E. Emmerick. Sacred Books of the Buddhists, no. 27. London: Luzac, 1970. Sanskrit text: *Suvarṇaprabhāsottamasūtram.* Buddhist Sanskrit Texts, no. 8. Darbanga, India: Mithila Institute, 1967. Tibetan text: *gSer 'od dam pa mdo sde'i dbang po'i rgyal po.* Dg.K. rgyud, vol. 11 (*da*), ff. 215b–405b. (Toh. 556)

The Sūtra on the Householder Vīradatta's Queries. In *The Questions of the Householder Vīradatta.* Translated by the University of Calgary Buddhist Studies Team. 84000: Translating the Words of the Buddha, 2022. *Vīradattagṛhapatiparipṛcchāsūtra.* Sanskrit text not extant. Tibetan text: *Khyim bdag dpas byin gyis zhus pa'i mdo.* Dg.K. dkon brtsegs, vol. 5 (*ca*), ff. 194a–204b. (Toh. 72)

Sūtra Inspiring Determination. Translated by the Blazing Wisdom Translation Group. 84000: Translating the Words of the Buddha, 2021. *Adhyāśayasaṃcodanasūtra.* Sanskrit text not extant. Tibetan text: *Lhag pa'i bsam pa bskul ba'i mdo.* Dg.K. dkon brtsegs, vol. 5 (*ca*), ff. 131a–153b. (Toh. 69)

Sūtra on the Inquiry of Avalokiteśvara on Seven Qualities. Translated by the University of Calgary Buddhist Studies Team. 84000: Translating the Words of the Buddha, 2014. *Avalokiteśvaraparipṛcchāsaptdadharmaka.* Sanskrit text not extant. Tibetan text: *'Phags pa spyan ras gzigs kyi dbyang phyug gis zhus pa'i chos bdun pa.* Dg.K. mdo sde, vol. 13 (*pa*), ff. 331a–331b. (Toh. 150)

Sūtra on Overcoming of Wrongful Conduct. Buddhapiṭakaduḥśīlanigraha. Sanskrit text not extant. Tibetan text: *Sangs rgyas kyi sde snod tshul khrims 'chal ba tshar gcod pa.* Dg.K. mdo sde, vol. 19 (*dza*), ff. 1a–77b. (Toh. 220)

Sūtra on Questions of the Bodhisattva Jñānottara. English translation: "On the Pāramitā of Ingenuity." In *A Treasury of Mahāyāna Sūtras*, pp. 427–68. University Park: Pennsylvania State University Press, 1983. *Āryasarvabuddhamahārahasyopāyakauśalyajñānottarabodhisattvaparipṛcchāparivarta.* Sanskrit text not extant. Tibetan text: *'Phags pa sangs rgyas thams cad kyi gsang chen thabs la mkhas pa byang chub sems dpa' ye shes dam pas zhus pa'i le'u*. Dg.K. dkon brtsegs, vol. 6 (*cha*), ff. 79a–139b. (Toh. 82)

Sūtra on Questions of Gaganagañja. Gaganagañjaparipṛcchāsūtram. Sanskrit text not extant. Tibetan text: *Nam mkha' mdzod kyis zhus pa'i mdo.* Dg.K. mdo sde, vol. 13 (*pa*), ff. 243a–330a. (Toh. 148)

Sūtra on Questions of Pūrṇa. Pūrṇaparipṛcchāsūtra. Sanskrit text not extant. Tibetan text: *Gang pos zhus pa'i mdo.* Dg.K. dkon brtsegs, vol. 4 (*nga*), ff. 168b–227a. (Toh. 61)

Sūtra Teaching the Four Factors. Translated by Adam Pearcey. 84000: Translating the Words of the Buddha, 2019. Sanskrit text: *Caturdharmanirdeśasūtra.* In *Dhiḥ Journal*, vol. 35. Sarnath: Central University of Tibetan Studies, 2003. Tibetan text: *'Phags pa chos bzhi bstan pa zhes bya ba'i theg pa chen po'i mdo.* Dg.K. mdo sde, vol. 22 (*za*), ff. 59a–59b. (Toh. 249)

Sūtra Teaching the Miracles in the Domain of Skillful Means That the Bodhisattvas Have at Their Disposition. Bodhisattvagocaropāyaviṣayavikurvāṇanirdeśa. Sanskrit text not extant. Tibetan text: *'Phags pa byang chub sems dpa'i spyod yul gyi thabs kyi yul la rnam par 'phrul ba bstan pa zhes bya ba theg pa chen po'i mdo* (also known as *The Chapter on Truth, bDen pa po'i le'u*). Dg.K. mdo mang, vol. 11 (*da*), ff. 57a–153b. (Toh. 146)

Sūtra of the Three Heaps. English translation: In *The Training Anthology of Śāntideva*, translated by Charles Goodman, pp. 167–68. New York: Oxford University Press, 2015. Sanskrit text: *Triskandhakasūtra.* In ch. 8, "Pāpaśodhanam." In *Śikṣāsamuccaya*, pp. 94–95. Buddhist Sanskrit Texts, no. 11. Darbhanga, India: Mithila Institute, 1960. Tibetan text: *'Phags pa phung po gsum pa zhes bya ba theg pa chen po'i mdo* (also *Byang chub sems dpa'i ltung ba bshags pa*). In Dg.K. mdo sde, vol. 24 (*ya*), ff. 57a–77a. (Toh. 284)

Tantra of the Procedures Common to All Maṇḍalas. Sarvamaṇḍalasāmānyavidhīnām guhyatantram. Sanskrit text not extant. Tibetan text: *dKyil 'khor thams cad kyi spyi'i cho ga gsang ba'i rgyud.* Dg.K. rgyud 'bum, vol. 20 (*wa*), ff. 141a–167b. (Toh. 806)

Vajraśekhara Tantra. Sanskrit text not extant. Tibetan text: *gSang ba rnal 'byor chen po'i rgyud rdo rje rtse mo.* Dg.K. rgyud, vol. 8 (*nya*), ff. 142b–274a. (Toh. 480)

The Verses That Summarize the Perfection of Wisdom. Incomplete English translation: In *The Perfection of Wisdom in Eight Thousand Lines and Its Verse Summary*, translated by Edward Conze, pp. 1–73. Bolinas: Four Seasons Foundation, 1973. Sanskrit text: *Ratnaguṇasaṃcayagāthā.* In *Mahāyāna Sūtra Saṃgraha*, pp. 352–98. Buddhist Sanskrit Texts, no. 17. Darbanga, India: Mithila Institute, 1960. Tibetan text: *'Phags pa shes rab kyi pha rol tu phyin pa sdud pa tsigs su bcad pa.* Dg.T. sher phyin sna tsogs, vol. 1 (*ka*), ff. 189–215a. (Toh. 13)

The White Lotus of Compassion Sūtra. Karṇāpuṇḍarīkasūtra. Sanskrit text not extant. Tibetan text: *'Phags pa snying rje padma dkar po zhes bya ba theg pa chen po'i mdo.* Dg.K. mdo sde, vol. 6 (*cha*), ff. 129a–297a. (Toh. 112)

3. Indian Treatises

Abhayākaragupta. *The Flower Cluster of Instruction. Śrīsaṃpuṭatantrarājaṭīkā Āmnāyamañjarī.* No published edition of Sanskrit text available. Tibetan text: *dPal yang dag par sbyor ba'i rgyud kyi rgyal po'i rgya cher 'grel pa man ngag gi snye ma.* Dg.K. rgyud, vol. 6 (*cha*), ff. 1b–316a. (Toh. 1198)

Āryadeva. *Four Hundred Verses.* English translation: *Aryadeva's Four Hundred Stanzas on the Middle Way with Commentary by Gyel-tsap.* Translated by Ruth Sonam with Geshe Sonam Rinchen. Ithaca: Snow Lion, 2008. Sanskrit text: *Catuḥśatakaśāstrakārikā.* Edited by P. L. Vaidya. Nagpur, India: Alok Prakashan, 1971. Tibetan text: *bsTan bcos bzhi brgya pa zhes bya ba'i tshig le'ur byas pa.* Dg.T. dbu ma, vol. 18 (*tsha*), ff. 1b–18a. (Toh. 3846)

———. *The Lamp That Integrates the Practice. Caryāmelāpakapradīpa.* English and Sanskrit text: Āryadeva's *Lamp That Integrates the Practices.* Edited and translated by Christian K. Wedemeyer. New York: American Institute of Buddhist Studies, 2007. Tibetan text: *sPyod pa bsdus pa'i sgron ma.* Dg.T. rgyud, vol. 34 (*ngi*), ff. 57a–106b. (Toh. 1803)

Āryaśūra. *Garland of Birth Stories.* English translation: *Garland of the Buddha's Past Lives* (2 vols). Translated by Justin Meiland. New York: New York University Press and JJC Foundation, 2009. *Jātakamālā.* Sanskrit text: *Garland of the Buddha's Past Lives.* 2 vols. New York: New York University Press and JJC Foundation, 2009. Tibetan text: *sKyes pa'i rabs kyi rgyud.* Dg.T. skyes rabs, vol. 89 (*hu*), ff. 1–135a. (Toh. 4150)

Asaṅga. *Collection of Determinations. Viniścayasaṃgrahaṇī.* No published edition of Sanskrit text available. Tibetan text: *rNam par gtan la dbab pa bsdu ba.* Dg.T. sems tsam, vol. 51 (*zhi*), ff. 1b–289a. (Toh. 4038)

———. *A Commentary on Recollection of the Buddha. Buddhānusmṛtivṛtti.* Sanskrit text not extant. Tibetan text: *Sangs rgyas rjes su dran pa'i 'grel pa.* Dg.T. mdo 'grel, vol. 34 (*ngi*), ff. 11b–15a. (Toh. 3982)

———. *The Compendium of Higher Learning.* English translation: *The Compendium of the Higher Teaching.* Translated from French by Sara Boin-Webb. Berkeley: Asian Humanities Press, 2001. Sanskrit text: *Abhidharmasamuccaya.* Edited by Prahlad Pradhan. Shantiniketan, India: Visva-Bharati, 1950. Tibetan text: *Chos mngon pa kun las btus pa.* Dg.T. sems tsam, vol. 55 (*ri*), ff. 44a–120a. (Toh. 4049)

———. *The Stage of a Bodhisattva.* English translation: *The Bodhisattva Path to Unsurpassed Enlightenment.* Translated by Artemus B. Engle. Boulder: Snow Lion, 2016. Sanskrit text: *Bodhisattvabhūmi.* Edited by Nalinaksha Dutt. Patna: K. P. Jayaswal Research Institute, 1978. Tibetan text: *rNal 'byor spyod pa'i sa las byang chub sems dpa'i sa.* Dg.T. sems tsam, vol. 50 (*wi*), ff. 1b–213a. (Toh. 4037)

———. *The Stage of a Śrāvaka.* Sanskrit text: *Śrāvakabhūmi.* Tibetan Sanskrit Works Series, vol. 14. Edited by Karunesha Shukla. Patna: K. P. Jayaswal Research

Institute, 1973. Tibetan text: *rNal 'byor spyod pa'i sa las nyan thos kyi sa*. Dg.T. sems tsam, vol. 49 (*dzi*), ff. 1b–195a. (Toh. 4036)

———. *The Stages of Spiritual Practice*. Sanskrit text (incomplete): *The Yogācārabhūmi of Ācārya Asaṅga* (parts 1–5), edited by Vidhushekhara Bhattacharya, pp. 1–232. Calcutta: University of Calcutta, 1957. *Buddhist Insight* (parts 8, 9, 11, and 14), pp. 327–31 and pp. 333–52. Delhi: Motilal Banarsidass, 1984 See *The Stage of a Śrāvaka* (part 13) and *The Stage of a Bodhisattva* (part 15). Tibetan text: *Sa mang po pa* (parts 1–12, 14, 16–17) Dg.T. sems tsam, vol. 48 (*tshi*), ff. 1–283a. (Toh. 4035)

Aśvaghoṣa. *A Collection of Words of Praise That Constitute Instruction for Meditating on the Conventional Form of Enlightenment Mind. Saṃvṛtibodhicittabhāvanopadeśavarṇasaṃgraha*. Sanskrit text not extant. Tibetan text: *Kun rdzob byang chub kyi sems bsgom pa'i man ngag yi ger bris pa*. Dg.T. dbu ma, vol. 31 (*ki*), ff. 13b–15a. (Toh. 3911)

Atiśa (Dīpaṃkāra Śrījñāna). *A Brief Arrangement of the Means by Which to Achieve the Mahāyāna Path. Mahāyānapathasādhanasaṃgraha*. Sanskrit text not extant. Tibetan text: *Theg pa chen po'i lam gyi sgrub thabs yi ger bsdus pa*. Dg.T. dbu ma, vol, 32 (*khi*), ff. 299a–302b. (Toh. 3954)

———. *A Commentary on the Difficult Points of "Entry into the Conduct That Leads to Enlightenment."* English translation: *A Lamp for the Path and Commentary*. Translated by Richard Sherbourne. S. J. London: George Allen and Unwin, 1983. *Bodhipathapradīpapañjikā*. Sanskrit text not extant. Tibetan text: *Byang chub lam gyi sgron ma'i dka' 'grel*. Dg.T. dbu ma, vol. 32 (*khi*), ff. 241a–293a. (Toh. 3948)

———. *Entry into the Two Truths*. In *Atiśa Dīpaṃkara: Illuminator of the Awakened Mind*. James B. Apple, pp. 126–131. Boulder: Shambhala, 2019. *Satyadvayāvatāra*. Sanskrit text not extant. Tibetan text: *bDen pa gnyis la 'jug pa*. Dg.T. dbu ma, vol. 30 (*a*), ff. 72a–73a. (Toh. 3902)

———. *Instruction on the Middle Way*. English translation: "Special Instructions on the Middle Way." In *Buddhist Spiritual Practices*, translated by James B. Apple, pp. 142–44. Berkeley: Mangalam Press, 2018. *Madhyamakopadeśa*. Sanskrit text not extant. Tibetan text: *dBu ma'i man ngag*. Dg.T. dbu ma, vol. 31 (*ki*), ff. 95b–96a. (Toh. 3929)

———. *Instruction on the Middle Way: A Chest of Jewels That Has Been Laid Open*. In *Jewels of the Middle Way: The Madhyamaka Legacy of Atiśa and His Early Tibetan Followers*. James B. Apple. Boston: Wisdom, 2019, pp. 63–113. *Ratnakaraṇḍodghāṭamadhyamakopadeśa*. Sanskrit text not extant. Tibetan text: *dBu ma'i man ngag rin po che'i za ma tog kha phye ba*, Dg.T. dbu ma, vol. 31 (*ki*), ff. 96b–116b. (Toh. 3930)

———. *A Lamp for the Path to Enlightenment. Bodhipathapradīpa*. Complete Sanskrit text not extant. Tibetan text: *Byang chub lam gyi sgron ma*. Dg.T. dbu ma, vol. 32 (*khi*), ff. 238a–241a. (Toh. 3947)

———. *The Ritual Method for Generating Enlightenment Mind and Receiving the*

Bodhisattva Vow. Cittotpādasaṃvaraviddhikrama. Sanskrit text not extant. Tibetan text: *Sems bskyed pa dang sdom pa'i cho ga'i rim pa.* Dg.T. dbu ma, vol. 33 (*gi*), ff. 245a–248b. (Toh. 3969)

Atiśa and Drom Tönpa (attributed to). *The Book of Kadam: The Core Texts.* Library of Tibetan Classics. Translated by Thupten Jinpa. Boston: Wisdom, 2008. Tibetan text: *bKa' gdam legs 'bam.* 2 vols. Kansu: Nationalities Press, 1993.

Bodhibhadra. *The Chapter on the Requisites for Cultivating Samādhi. Samādhisambhāraparivarta.* Sanskrit text not extant. Tibetan text: *Ting nge 'dzin gyi tshogs kyi le'u.* Dg.T. dbu ma, vol. 31 (*ki*), ff. 81b–93a. (Toh. 3924)

———. *A Commentary on the Difficult Points of the Twenty Verses on the Bodhisattva Vow. Bodhisattvasaṃvaravimśikāpañjikā.* Sanskrit text not extant. Tibetan text: *Byang chub sems dpa'i sdom pa nyi shu pa'i dka' 'grel.* Dg.T. sems tsam, vol. 58 (*si*), ff. 184b–217b. (Toh. 4083)

Candragomī. *Letter to a Disciple.* English translation: In *Invitation to Enlightenment,* translated by Michael Hahn, pp. 51–131. Berkeley: Dharma Publishing, 1999. Sanskrit text: *Śiṣyalekha.* In *Invitation to Enlightenment,* translated by Michael Hahn, pp. 51–131. Berkeley: Dharma Publishing, 1999. Tibetan text: *sLob ma la springs pa'i spring yig.* Dg.T. spring yig, vol. 94 (*nge*), ff. 46b–53a. (Toh. 4183)

———. *In Praise of Confession. Deśanāstava.* Sanskrit text not extant. Tibetan text: *bShags pa'i bstod pa.* Dg.T. bstod tshogs, vol. 1 (*ka*), ff. 204a–206b. (Toh. 1159)

———. *Twenty Verses on the Bodhisattva Vow.* English translation: *Candragomin's Twenty Verses on the Bodhisattva Vow and Its Commentary.* Translated by Mark Tatz. Dharamsala: Library of Tibetan Works and Archives, 1982. Sanskrit text: (vv. 1–9a, 11c, and 20cd): Kano Kazuo, Li Xueshu, and Ye Shaoyong, ed. "Sanskrit fragments of Candragomin's *Bodhisattvasaṃvaraviṃśikā.*" *Mikkyō Gakkaihō, The Annual Bulletin of the Esoteric Buddhist Society* 53 (March 2015): pp. 480–95. Tibetan text: *Byang chub sems dpa'i sdom pa nyi shu pa.* Dg.T. sems tsam, vol. 59 (*hi*), ff. 166b–167a. (Toh. 4081)

Candrakīrti. *In Clear Words.* English translation (ch. 1): *In Clear Words: The Prasannapadā Chapter One,* vol 2. Translated by Anne MacDonald. Vienna: Austrian Academy of Sciences Press, 2015. Sanskrit text: *Prasannapadā.* In *Madhyamakaśāstra of Nāgārjuna,* pp. 1–259. Buddhist Sanskrit Texts, no. 10. Darbhanga, India: Mithila Institute, 1960. Tibetan text: *dBu ma rtsa ba'i 'grel pa tshig gsal ba zhes bya ba.* Dg.T. dbu ma, vol. 23 (*'a*), ff. 1a–197a. (Toh. 3860)

———. *A Commentary on "Entry into the Middle Way." Madhyamakāvatārabhāṣyam.* Sanskrit text of chs. 1–5 in Candradrakīrti's *Madhyamakāvatārabhāṣya.* Edited by Horst Lasic, Xueshu Li, and Anne MacDonald. Beijing and Vienna: China Tibetology Publishing House and Austrian Academy of Sciences Press, 2015. Tibetan text: *dBu ma la 'jug pa'i bshad pa.* Dg.T. dbu ma, vol. 102 (*'a*), ff. 220b–348a. (Toh. 3862)

———. *A Commentary on the "Four Hundred Verses on a Bodhisattva's Spiritual Conduct."* English translation (chs. 1–4): *Four Illusions: Candrakīrti's Advice to Travelers on the Bodhisattva Path.* Translated by Karen C. Lang. Oxford: Oxford

University Press, 2003. Portions of Sanskrit text in Haraprasad Shastri, ed. "*Catuḥśatakaṭīkā.*" *Memoirs of the Asiatic Society of Bengal* 3, no. 8 (1914): pp. 449–514. Sanskrit text (portions of chs. 7–16): Additional Sanskrit reconstruction of portions of chs. 7–16 in *Catuḥśatakam.* Edited by P. L. Vaidya. Nagpur, India: Alok Prakashan, 1971. Tibetan text: *Byang chub sems dpa'i rnal 'byor spyod pa bzhi brgya pa'i rgya cher 'grel pa.* Dg.T. dbu ma, vol. 24 (*ya*), ff. 30b–239a. (Toh. 3865)

———. *Entry into the Middle Way.* English translation (root text verses): *Illuminating the Intent: An Exposition of Candrakīrti's Entering the Middle Way.* Translated by Thupten Jinpa. Somerville, MA: Wisdom, 2021. Sanskrit text (chs. 1–5): *Candradrakīrti's Madhyamakāvatārabhāṣya.* Edited by Horst Lasic, Xueshu Li, and Anne MacDonald. Beijing and Vienna: China Tibetology Publishing House and Austrian Academy of Sciences Press, 2015. Sanskrit text (ch. 6): Li Xuezhu, ed. "*Madhyamakāvatāra-kārikā* Chapter 6." *Journal of Indian Philosophy* 43, pp. 1–30 (2015). Tibetan text: *dBu ma la 'jug pa.* Dg.T. dbu ma, vol. 23 (*'a*), ff. 201a–219a. (Toh. 3861)

———. *Seventy Verses on the Triple Refuge.* English translation and Sanskrit text: *Triśaraṇasaptati.* Edited and Translated by Per K. Sorensen. Vienna: Arbetskreis fur Tibetische und Buddhistische Studien Universitat Wien, 1986. Sanskrit text: Kazuo Kano and Li Xuezhu, ed. "*Sanskrit Verses from Candrakīrti's Triśaraṇasaptati Cited in Munimatālaṃkāra.*" *China Tibetology* 1 (2014): pp. 4–11. Tibetan text: *gSum la skyabs su 'gro ba bdun cu pa.* Dg.T. dbu ma, vol. 33 (*gi*), ff. 262a–264b. (Toh. 3971)

Dharmakīrti. *Extensive Treatise on Knowledge.* Sanskrit text: *Pramāṇavārttika: The Kārikās with Manorathanandi's Vṛtti.* Varanasi: Bauddha Bharati, 1968. Tibetan text: *Pramāṇavārttikakārikā. Tshad ma rnam 'grel gyi tshig le'ur byas pa.* Dg.T. tshad ma, vol. 95 (*ce*), ff. 95b–151a. (Toh. 4210)

Dignāga. *A Compendium on Knowledge.* English translation (ch. 1): *Dignāga, on Perception.* Translated by Masaaki Hattori. Cambridge, MA: Harvard University Press, 1968. *Pramāṇasamuccaya.* Sanskrit text (ch. 1 vv. 1–44): *Dignāga's Pramāṇasamuccaya Chapter One.* Edited by Ernst Steinkellner. Vienna: Austrian Academy of Sciences Press, 2005. Tibetan text: *Pramāṇasamuccaya. Tshad ma kun las btus pa.* Dg.T. tshad ma, vol. 95 (*ce*), ff. 1b–13a. (Toh. 4203)

Dīpaṃkarabhadra. *The Guhyasamāja Mandala Ritual.* Sanskrit text: "*Guhyasamājamaṇḍalavidhi.*" *Dhīḥ: Journal of Rare Buddhist Texts* 42 (2006): pp. 109–54. Tibetan text: *dPal gsang ba 'dus pa'i dkyil 'khor gyi cho ga.* Dg.T. rgyud, vol. 34 (*ngi*), ff. 15b–35a. (Toh. 1798)

Haribhadra. *Illuminating the Ornament of Realization.* English translation: *Abhisamayālaṃkāra with Vṛtti and Āloka.* Translated by Gareth Sparham. 4 vols. Fremont, CA: Jain Publishing, 2006–2012. Sanskrit text: *Abhisamayālaṃkārāloka.* In *Aṣṭasāhasrikā Prajñāpāramitā*, pp. 267–558. Buddhist Sanskrit Texts, no. 4. Darbhanga, India: Mithila Institute, 1960. Tibetan text: *'Phags pa shes rab kyi pha rol tu phyin pa brgyad stong pa'i bshad pa mNgon par rtogs pa'i rgyan gyi snang ba.* Dg.T. shes phyin, vol. 6 (*cha*), ff. 1b–341a. (Toh. 3791)

Indrabhūti. *The Attainment of Transcendent Knowledge.* Sanskrit text: *Jñānasiddhi.* In *Guhyādyaṣṭsiddhisaṃgraha*, pp. 89–157. Rare Buddhist Text Series, no 1. Sarnath: Central Institute of Higher Tibetan Studies, 1987. Tibetan text: *Ye shes grub pa zhes bya ba'i sgrub pa'i thabs.* Dg.T. rgyud, vol. 50 (*wi*), ff. 36b–60b. (Toh. 2219)

Jetāri. *A Ritual for Generating Enlightenment Mind and Accepting the Bodhisattva Vow. Bodhicittotpādasamādānaviddhi.* Sanskrit text not extant. Tibetan text: *Byang chub kyi sems dang yi dam blang ba' cho ga.* Dg.T. dbu ma, vol. 33 (*gi*), ff. 241b–245a. (Toh. 3968)

Jinaputra. *A Commentary on the Compendium of Higher Learning.* Sanskrit text: *Abhidharmasamuccayabhāṣyam.* Edited by Nathmal Tatia. Patna, India: K. P. Jayaswal Research Institute, 1976. Tibetan text: *Chos mngon pa kun las btus pa'i bshad pa.* Dg.T. sems tsam, vol. 56 (*li*), ff. 1b–117a. (Toh. 4053)

Kamalaśīla. *Stages of Meditation* (first version). English translation: *Bhāvanākrama of Kamalaśīla.* Translated by Paramananda Sharma. Delhi: Aditya Prakashan, 1997. Sanskrit text: In *Minor Buddhist Texts, Part 2, Bhāvanākrama of Kamalaśīla, Sanskrit and Tibetan Texts with Introduction and English Summary by Giuseppe Tucci.* Rome: Istituto Italiano per il Medio ed Estremo Oriente, 1958. Tibetan text: *bsGom pa'i rim pa dang po.* Dg.T. dbu ma, vol. 31 (*ki*), ff. 22a–41b. (Toh. 3915)

———. *Stages of Meditation* (second or middling version). English translation: *Bhāvanākrama of Kamalaśīla.* Translated by Paramananda Sharma. Delhi: Aditya Prakashan, 1997. Reconstructed Sanskrit text: In *Bhāvanākrama*, pp. 231–52. Sarnath, India: Central Institute of Higher Tibetan Studies, 1997. Tibetan text: *bsGom pa'i rim pa bar pa.* Dg.T. dbu ma, vol. 31 (*ki*), ff. 56b–70a. (Toh. 3916)

Karṇakagomī. *A Subcommentary on [Dharmakīrti's] Autocommentary to [Chapter One of] The Extensive Treatise on Knowledge.* Sanskrit text: *Pramāṇavārttikavṛttiṭīkā.* Edited by Rahula Samkrtyayana. In *Karṇakagomin's Commentary on the Pramāṇavārttikavṛtti of Dharmakīrti.* Kyoto: Rinsen, 1982. First printed in 1943 in Allahabad. No Tibetan translation.

Kṛṣṇapāda. *Settling the Points That Are Difficult to Understand in "Entry into the Conduct That Leads to Enlightenment." Bodhicaryāvatāraduravabodhananirṇāya.* Sanskrit text not extant. Tibetan text: *Byang chub sems pa'i spyod pa 'jug pa'i rtogs par dka' ba'i gnas gtan la dbab pa.* Dg.T. dbu ma, vol. 27 (*sha*), ff. 90b–159a. (Toh. 3875)

Maitreya Nātha. *Distinguishing the Three Jewels and the Mahāyāna Spiritual Lineage.* English translation: *When the Clouds Part: The Uttaratantra and Its Meditative Tradition as a Bridge between Sutra and Tantra.* Translated by Karl Brunnhölzl. Boston: Snow Lion, 2014. *Ratnagotravibhāga* (a.k.a., *Mahāyānottaratantraśāstram*). Sanskrit text (root verses): *Ratnagotravibhāga Mahāyāno-*

ttaratantraśāstra. Edited by E. H. Johnston. Patna: Bihar Research Society, 1950. Tibetan text: *Theg pa chen po rgyud bla ma'i bstan bcos*. Dg.T. sems tsam, vol. 44 (*phi*), ff. 51a–69a. (Toh. 4024)

———. *The Ornament of Mahāyāna Sūtras*. In *A Feast of the Nectar of the Supreme Vehicle*. Translated by Stephen Gethin and the Padmakara Translation Group. Boulder: Shambhala, 2018. Sanskrit text: *Mahāyānasūtrālaṃkāra*. Buddhist Sanskrit Texts, no. 13. Darbhanga, India: Mithila Institute, 1970. Tibetan text: *Theg pa chen po mdo sde'i rgyan zhes bya ba'i tshig le'ur byas pa*. Dg.T. sems tsam, vol. 44 (*phi*), ff. 1–39a. (Toh. 4020)

———. *The Ornament of Realization*. English translation: *Abhisamayālaṃkāra with Vṛtti and Āloka*. Translated by Gareth Sparham. 4 vols. Fremont, CA: Jain Publishing, 2006–2012. Second English translation: *Abhisamaya Alaṃkāra*. Translated by Edward Conze. Rome: Serie Orientale Roma, 1954. Sanskrit text in *Abhisamayālaṃkāra*. Edited T. Stcherbatsky and E. E. Obermiller. Leningrad: Bibliotheca Buddhica, 1929. Tibetan text: *Shes rab kyi pha rol tu phyin pa'i man ngag gib stan bcos gi bstan bcos) mngon par rtogs pa'i rgyan zhes bya ba'i tshig le'ur byas pa*. Dg.T. shes phyin, vol. 1 (*ka*), ff. 1b–13a. (Toh. 3786)

———. *Root Verses on Distinguishing the Middle Way from Extremes*. English translation in *Seven Works of Vasubandhu*. Translated by Stefan Anacker. Delhi: Motilal Banarsidass, 1973. Sanskrit text: *Madhyāntavibhāgakārikā*. In *Madhyānta Vibhāga Śāstra*. Edited by Ramchandra Pandeya. Delhi: Motilal Banarsidass, 1971. Tibetan text: *dBus dang mtha' rnam par 'byed pa'i tshig le'ur byas pa*. Dg.T. sems tsam, vol. 44 (*phi*), ff. 40b–45a. (Toh. 4021)

Mātṛceta. *Letter to the Great King Kaṇiṣka*. English translation: In *Invitation to Enlightenment: Letter to the Great King Kaniṣka*, translated by Michael Hahn, pp. 5–49. Berkeley: Dharma Publishing, 1999. *Mahārājakaniṣkalekha*. Sanskrit text not extant. Tibetan text: *rGyal po chen po ka nis ka la springs pa'i spring yig*. Dg.T. spring yig, vol. 94 (*nge*), ff. 53a–56b.

Maudgalyāyana. *Discerning the World*. *Lokaprajñapti*. Sanskrit text not extant. *'Jig rten gzhag pa*. Dg.T. mngon pa, vol. 60 (*i*), ff. 1b–93a. (Toh. 4086)

Nāgārjuna. *A Compendium of Sūtra Passages*. *Sūtrasamuccaya*. Sanskrit text not extant. Tibetan text: *mDo kun las btus pa*. Dg.T. dbu ma, vol. 31 (*ki*), ff. 148b–215a. (Toh. 3934)

———. *A Drop of Nourishment for Beings: A Treatise on Political Ethics*. *Nītiśāstrajantupoṣaṇabindu*. Sanskrit text not extant. Tibetan text: *Lugs kyi bstan bcos skye bo gso ba'i thigs pa*. Dg.T. thun mong ba lugs kyi bstan bcos, vol. 94 (*ngo*), ff. 109a–112b. (Toh. 4330)

———. *Explaining Enlightenment Mind*. English translation: *A Commentary on the Awakening Mind*. Translated by Geshe Thupten Jinpa. Long Beach: Thupten Dhargye Ling, 2006. Sanskrit text: *Bodhicittavivaraṇam*. Misc. verses published by Ch. Lindtner (2003) and Kazuo Kano and Xueshu Li (2015). Tibetan text: *Byang chub sems kyi 'grel pa*. Dg.T. rgyud, vol. 34 (*ngi*), ff. 38a–45a. (Toh. 1800, 1801)

———. *The Jewel Garland.* English translation: *The Precious Garland and the Precious Song of the Four Mindfulnesses.* Translated by Jeffrey Hopkins and Lati Rinpoche with Anne Klein. New York: Harper and Row, 1975. Sanskrit text (incomplete): *Nāgārjuna's Ratnāvalī.* Edited by Michael Hahn. Bonn: Indica et Tibetica Verlag, 1982. Tibetan text: *rGyal po la gtam bya ba rin po che'i phreng ba.* Dg.T. spring yig, vol. 93 (*ge*), ff. 116a–135a. (Toh. 4158)

———. *Letter to a Friend.* English translation: *Nāgārjuna's Letter.* Translated by Geshe Lobsang Tharchin and Artemus B. Engle. Dharamsala, India: Library of Tibetan Works and Archives, 1979. Sanskrit text: *Suhṛllekha.* In *Ta la'i lo mar bris pa'i rGya dpe bris ma bshes springs skor gyi dpe bsdur zhib 'jug,* edited by dNgos grub tshe ring, pp. 133–84. Lhasa: bod ljongs bod yig dpe rnying dpe sprun khang, 2020. Tibetan text: *bShes pa'i spring yig.* Dg.T. spring yig, vol. 94 (*nge*), ff. 40b–46b. (Toh. 4182)

———. *Nāgārjuna's "Seventy Stanzas": A Buddhist Psychology of Emptiness.* Translated by Ven. Tenzin Dorjee and David Ross Komito. Ithaca, NY: Snow Lion, 1987. Reconstructed Sanskrit text: *Śūnyatāsaptati.* In *Śūnyatāsaptatiḥ with Auto-Commentary.* Bibliotheca Indo-Tibetica Series, vol 8. Sarnath, India: Central Institute of Higher Tibetan Studies, 1996, pp. 3–66. Tibetan Text: *sTong pa nyid bdun cu pa'i tshig le'ur byas pa.* Dg. T. dbu ma, vol. 17 (*tsa*), ff. 24a–27a. (Toh. 3827)

——— *Root Verses on the Middle Way.* English translation: *The Fundamental Wisdom of the Middle Way: Nagarjuna's Mulamadhyamakakarika.* Translated by Jay L. Garfield. New York: Oxford University Press, 1995. Sanskrit text: *Mūlamadhyamakaśāstra of Nāgārjuna.* Buddhist Sanskrit Texts, no. 10. Darbhanga, India: Mithila Institute, 1960. Tibetan text: *dBu ma rtsa ba'i tshig le'ur byas pa shes rab ces bya ba.* Dg.T. dbu ma, vol. 17 (*tsa*), ff. 1b–19a. (Toh. 3824)

———. *Sixty Verses on Reasoning.* English translation: *Nāgārjuna's Reason Sixty (Yuktiṣaṣṭikā), with Candrakīrti's Commentary Yuktiṣaṣṭikāvṛtti.* Translated by Joseph Loizzo. New York: Columbia University Press, 2007. *Yuktiṣaṣṭikākārikā.* Portions of Sanskrit text in: *Editions of the Sanskrit, Tibetan, and Chinese Versions, with Commentary and a Modern Chinese Translation.* Edited by Li Xuezhu and Ye Shaoyong. Shanghai: Zhongxi, 2014. Tibetan translation: *Rigs pa drug cu pa'i tshig le'ur byas pa.* Dg.T. dbu ma, vol. 17 (*tsa*), ff. 20b–22b. (Toh. 3825)

Pa Dampa Sangye (Pha Dam pa Sangs rgyas). *Hundred Verses of Advice to the People of Dingri.* English translation: In *The Hundred Verses of Advice.* Translated by the Padmakara Translation Group. Boston: Shambhala, 2006. Tibetan text: *Ding ri brgya tsa ma.* In *dKar rnying gi skyes chen du ma'i phyag rdzogs kyi gdams ngag gnad bsdus nyer mkho rin po che'i gter mdzod(rtsibs ri'i par ma),* vol. 27, pp. 429–39. Darjeeling: Kargyu Sungrab Nyamso Khang, 1978–1985.

Prajñākaramati. *A Commentary on the Difficult Points of "Entry into the Conduct That Leads to Enlightenment."* Sanskrit text: *Bodhicaryāvatārapañjikā.* Buddhist Sanskrit Texts, no. 12. Darbhanga, India: Mithila Institute, 1960. Tibetan text: *Byang chub kyi spyod pa la 'jug pa'i dka' 'grel.* Dg.T. dbu ma, vol. 26 (*la*), ff. 39a–287a. (Toh. 3872)

Prajñāvarman. *A Commentary on "Collection of Uplifting Sayings." Udānavargavivaraṇa.* Sanskrit text not extant. Tibetan text: *Ched du brjod pa'i tshoms kyi rnam par 'grel pa.* Dg.T. mngon pa, vol. 69 (*tu*), f. 46b–vol. 70 (*thu*), f. 221a. (Toh. 4100)

Ratnākarśānti. *An Ornament of Brilliant Jewels: A Commentary on "The Anthology of Sūtra Passages." Sūtrasamuccayabhāṣyaratnālokālaṃkara.* Sanskrit text not extant. Tibetan text: *Do kun la btus pa'i bshad pa rin po che snang ba'i rgyan.* Dg.T. dbu ma, vol. 31 (*ki*), ff. 215a–334a. (Toh. 3935)

Ratnarakṣita. *Samvarodayamahātantrarājapadminīnāmapañjikā.* First half of ch. 1 in "Ratnarakṣita's Padminī—A Preliminary Edition of and Notes on the First Half of Chapter 1." Edited by Ryugen Tanemura et al. *Journal of Kawasaki Daishi Institute for Buddhist Studies,* no. 1 (2016). Ch. 9. Edited by Junglan Ban and Kenichi Kuranishi. In *Annual of Institute for the Comprehensive Studies of Buddhism Taisho University,* no. 40 (March 2018). Tibetan text: *dPal sdom pa 'byung ba'i rgyud kyi rgyal po chen po'i dka' 'grel pad ma can.* Dg.T. rgyud, vol. 18 (*tsha*), ff. 1b–101b. (Toh. 1420)

Sai Tsalak (Sa'i rtsa lag). *A Commentary on "The Summary of the Five Heaps." Pañcaskandhaprakaraṇabhāṣya.* Sanskrit text not extant. Tibetan text: *Phung po lnga'i rab tu byed pa bye brag tu bshad pa.* Dg.T. sems tsam, vol. 58 (*si*), ff. 32a–139a.

*Samudramegha (*rGya mtsho sprin*). *A Commentary on "The Stage of a Bodhisattva," a Section from "The Stages of Spiritual Practice." Yogācārabhūmau bodhisattvabhūmivyākhā.* Sanskrit text not extant. Tibetan text: *rNal 'byor spyod pa'i sa las byang chub sems dpa'i sa'i rnam par bshad pa.* Dg.T. sems tsam, vol. 54 (*yi*), ff. 1b–338a. (Toh. 4047)

Śāntideva. *Compendium of Training.* English translation: *The Training Anthology of Śāntideva.* Translated by Charles Goodman. New York: Oxford University Press, 2015. Sanskrit text: *Śikṣāsamuccaya.* Buddhist Sanskrit Texts, no. 11. Darbhanga, India: Mithila Institute, 1960. Tibetan text: *bsLab pa kun las btus pa.* Dg.T. dbu ma, vol. 32 (*khi*), ff. 3a–194b. (Toh. 3940)

———. *Entry into the Conduct That Leads to Enlightenment.* English translation: *A Guide to the Bodhisattva Way of Life.* Translated by Vesna A. Wallace and B. Alan Wallace. Ithaca: Snow Lion, 1997. Sanskrit and Tibetan texts: *Bodhicaryāvatāra.* Edited by Vidushekhara Bhattacharya. Calcutta: The Asiatic Society, 1960. Tibetan text: *Byang chub sems dpa'i spyod pa la 'jug pa.* Dg.T. dbu ma, vol. 26 (*la*), ff. 1–40a. (Toh. 3871)

Sthiramati. *A Commentary on "The Five Heaps."* English translation: In *The Inner Science of Buddhist Practice,* pp. 245–369. Ithaca, NY: Snow Lion, 2009. Sanskrit text: *Pañcaskandhakavibhāṣā.* Edited by Jowita Kramer. Vienna: Austrian Academy of Sciences Press, 2013. Tibetan text: *Phung po lnga'i rab tu byed pa bye brag tu bshad pa.* Dg.T. sems tsam, vol. 57 (*shi*), ff. 195b–250a. (Toh. 4066)

———. *A Commentary on "Thirty Verses."* English translation: *Vasubandhu's Vijñapti Mātratā Siddhi with Sthiramati's Commentary.* Edited and translated by K. N. Chatterjee. Varanasi: Kishor Vidya Niketan, 1980. Sanskrit text: *Sthiramati's*

Triṃśikāvijñaptibhāṣya. Edited by Hartmut Buescher. Vienna: Österreichische Akademie der Wissenschaften, 2007. Tibetan text: *Sum cu pa'i bshad pa*. Dg.T. sems tsam, vol. 57 (*shi*), ff. 146b–171b. (Toh. 4064)

———. *A Subcommentary on "The Commentary on the 'Ornament of Mahāyāna Sūtras.'" Mahāyānasūtrālaṃkāravṛttibhāṣya*. Sanskrit text not extant. Tibetan text: *mDo sde rgyan gyi 'grel bshad*. Dg.T. sems tsam, vols. 46 (*mi*) and 47 (*tsi*). (Toh. 4034)

———. *A Subcommentary on "Distinguishing the Middle Way from Extremes."* Sanskrit text: *Madhyāntavibhāgaṭīkā*. In *Madhyānta-Vibhāga-Śāstra*, edited by Ramchandra Pandeya. Delhi: Motilal Banarsidass, 1971. Tibetan text: *dBu dang mtha' rnam par 'byed pa'i 'grel bshad*. Dg.T. sems tsam, vol. 45 (*bi*), ff. 189b–318a. (Toh. 4032)

Vasubandhu. *A Commentary on "Distinguishing the Middle Way from the Extremes."* English translation in *Seven Works of Vasubandhu*. Translated by Stefan Anacker. Delhi: Motilal Banarsidass, 1984. Sanskrit text: *Madhyānta-Vibhāga-Śāstra*. Edited by Ramchandra Pandeya. Delhi: Motilal Banarsidass, 1971. Tibetan text: *dBu dang mtha' rnam par 'byed pa'i 'grel pa*. Dg.T. sems tsam, vol. 45 (*bi*), ff. 1b–27a. (Toh. 4027)

———. *A Commentary on "The Ornament of Mahāyāna Sūtras."* English translation: *The Universal Vehicle Discourse Literature*. Translated by L. Jamspal, et al. New York: American Institute of Buddhist Studies, 2004. Sanskrit text: *Mahāyānasūtrālaṃkāravyākhyā*. Buddhist Sanskrit Texts, no. 13. Darbhanga, India: Mithila Institute, 1970. Tibetan text: *mDo sde'i rgyan gyi bshad pa*. Dg.T. sems tsam, vol. 44 (*phi*), ff. 129b–260a. (Toh. 4026)

———. *A Commentary on the Treasury of Higher Learning*. English translation: *Abhidharmakośabhāṣyam*. 4 vols. Translated by Leo M. Pruden. Berkeley: Asian Humanities Press, 1988. Sanskrit text: *Abhidharmakośabhāṣyam*. Sanskrit text edited By Prahlad Pradhan. Patna: K. P. Jayaswal Research Institute, 1975. Tibetan text: *Chos mngon pa'i mdzod kyi bshad pa*. Dg.T. mngon pa, vol. 61 (*ku*), f. 25a–vol. 62 (*khu*), f. 97b. (Toh. 4090)

———. *Five Heaps*. English translation: *The Inner Science of Buddhist Practice*, pp. 229–44. Ithaca, NY: Snow Lion, 2009. *Pañcaskandhaka*. Sanskrit text in *Vasubandhu's Pañcaskandhaka*. Edited By Li Xueshu and Ernst Steinkellner. Beijing and Vienna: China Tibetology Publishing House and Austrian Academy of Sciences Press, 2008. Tibetan text: *Phung po lnga'i rab tu byed pa*. Dg.T. sems tsam, vol. 57 (*shi*), ff. 11b–17a. (Toh. 4059)

———. *Root Verses of the Treasury of Higher Learning*. English translation: *Abhidharmakośabhāṣyam*. 4 vols. Translated by Leo M. Pruden. Berkeley: Asian Humanities Press, 1988. Sanskrit text: *Abhidharmakośakārikā*. Edited by G. V. Gokhale. *Journal of the Royal Asiatic Society* 22. Bombay: Royal Asiatic Society, 1946. Tibetan text: *Chos mngon pa mdzod kyi tshig le'ur byas pa*. Dg.T. mngon pa, vol. 61 (*ku*), ff. 1–25a. (Toh. 4089)

———. *Thirty Verses*. English translation: In *Seven Works of Vasubandhu*, translated by Stefan Anacker, pp. 181–90. Delhi: Motilal Banarsidass, 1998. Sanskrit text: In *Sthiramati's Triṃśikāvijñaptibhāṣya*. Edited by Hartmut Buescher. Vienna: Österreichische Akademie der Wissenschaften, 2007. Tibetan text: *Sum cu pa'i tshig le'ur byas pa*. Dg.T. sems tsam, vol. 57 (*shi*), ff. 1b–3a. (Toh. 4055)

Yaśomitra. *Clarification of the Meaning: A Subcommentary to "The Treasury of Higher Learning."* Sanskrit text: *Sphuṭārthābhidharmakośavyākhyā*. 4 vols. Edited by Swami Dwarikadas Shastri. Varanasi: Bauddha Bharati, 1970. Tibetan text: *Chos mngon pa'i mdzod kyi 'grel bshad*. Dg.T. mngon pa, vols. 142–43 (*gu–ngu*). (Toh. 4092)

4. Tibetan Works

Akuching Sherap Gyatso (A khu ching Shes rab rgya mtsho). *Opening the Door to the Realm of Immortality: Oral Instruction on "The Easy Path to Enlightenment," a Teaching That Contains the Entirety of the Teaching's Key Points.* Tibetan text: *bsTan pa'i gnad kun rdzogs pa'i gdams pa byang chub bde lam gyi zhal shes bdud rtsi'i dbyings gyi sgo 'byed.* In Collected Works, vol 4 (*cha*). Lhasa: Zhol par khang, d.u.

Akya Yongzin Yangchen Gawe Lodrö (A kyā yongs 'dzin dByang can dga' ba'i blo gros) (a.k.a., bLo bzang don grub). *A Mirror That Clarifies the Meaning of Obscure Terms in the Form of Answers to Questions Regarding "The Initial Method of Training One's Mind."* Tibetan text: *Thog mar blo sbyong gi dris lan brda don gsal ba'i me long*. In Collected Works, vol. 1. New Delhi: Lama Guru Deva, 1971.

Butön Rinchen Drup (Bu ston Rin chen grub). *History of Buddhism by Bu-ston.* Translated by E. E. Obermiller. Heidelberg: O. Harrassowitz, 1931. Reprint, Tokyo: Suzuki Research Foundation. *bDe bar gshegs pa'i bstan pa'i gsal byed chos kyi 'byung gnas gsung rab rin po che'i mdzod* (*Bu ston chos 'byung*). In Collected Works, vol. 24 (*ya*), pp. 633–1055. (Toh. 5197)

Chahar Geshe Losang Tsultrim (Cha har dge bshes blo bzang tshul khrims). *Answers to Questions Regarding "The Initial Method of Training One's Mind. Thog ma'i blo sbyong las brtsams pa'i dris lan*. In *sKyabs yul gyi khyad par shes pa las bratsams pa'i brjed byang*. In Collected Works, vol. 1., ff. 8b–17a. Reprint of *sKu 'bum byams pa gling*. Monastery wood-block edition, d.u.

Changkya Ngawang Losang Chöden (lCang skya Ngag dbang blo bzang chos ldan). *The Swift Path That Is a Great Secret: Notes Compiled from Oral Teachings Received from My Supreme Lama on the Unerring Meditations for Practicing the First Stage of the Glorious Guhyasamāja Tradition. dPal gsang ba 'dus pa'i rim pa dang po'i lam la slob tshul gyi dmigs rim 'khrul med bla ma dam pa'i zhal las byung ba zin thor bkod pa gsang chen myur lam*. In Collected Works, vol. 3, 32 ff. Lhasa: Zhol Par khang, d.u.

Chegompa Sherap Dorje (lCe sgom pa Shes rab rdo rje). *An Extensive Commentary on "The Jewel Heap of Edifying Similes." dPe chos rin chen spungs pa'i 'bum 'grel.* Delhi: T. Tshering, 1975. (Toh. 6964)

Chekawa Yeshe Dorje (mChad ka wa Ye shes rdo rje). *Root Text of the Seven-Point Mind Training Instruction. Theg pa chen po blo sbyong don bdun ma'i rtsa ba.* Aphorisms extracted from Gyalse Tokme Zangpo's commentary, titled *A Brief Explanation of the Orally Transmitted Root Text of the Seven-Point Mind Training Instruction. bLo sbyong don bdun ma'i snyan brgyud kyi tshig rnams yi ge nyung ngu'i sgo nas bkrol ba. DNZ*, vol. 4 (*nga*).

Chenga Lodrö Gyaltsen (sPyan snga bLo gros rgyal mtshan). *Becoming Well Restrained: Nectar from the Mouths of Holy Lamas. bLa ma dam pa'i zhal gyi bdud rtsi legs bsdams.* In Collected Works, vol. 1, 16 ff. New Delhi: Ngawang Gelek Demo, 1983.

Chim Jampai Yang (mChims 'Jam pa'i dbyangs). *Ornament of Abhidharma: A Commentary on Vasubandhu's Abhidharmakośa.* Translated by Ian Coghlan. Library of Tibetan Classics, vol. 23. Somerville, MA: Wisdom, 2018. Tibetan text: *Chos mngon mdzod kyi tshig le'ur byas pa'i 'grel pa mngon pa'i rgyan.* Lhasa: Khun grub zil gnon rje 'bum lha khang, n.d.

Chim Namkha Drak (mChims Nam mkha' grags). *The Mahāyāna Supreme Path. Theg chen lam mchog.* In *dGe slong nam mkha' grags kyis mdzad pa'i gsung phyogs bsdus.* Digital scans. BDRC W3CN18544.

Chone Drakpa Shedrup (Co ne Grags pa bshad sgrub). *A Brief Commentary Clarifying the Words of "The Compendium of the Stages of the Path." Lam rim bsdus don gyi tshig 'grel mdor bsdus gsal ba.* In Collected Works, vol. 9, pp. 15–38. Beijing: Krung go'i bod rig pa dpe skrun khang, 2009.

Dölpa Marzhurpa Sherap Gyatso, Geshe (dGe bshes Dol pa dMar zhur pa Shes rab rgya mtso). *Blue Udder.* English translation: *Blue Compendium* in *Stages of the Buddhas' Teachings.* Translated by Ulrike Roesler. In *Stages of the Buddha's Teachings: Three Key Texts*, pp. 37–117. Somerville, MA: Wisdom, 2015. Tibetan text: *Be'u bum sngon po.* In *bKa' gdams kyi man ngag be'u bum sngon po'i 'grel pa.* Bir, India: T. Tsondu Senghe, 1976.

Dragyap Jetsun Losang Norbu (Brag g.yab rJe btsun bLo bzang nor bu). *A Treasury of Precious Instruction: An Extensive Commentary on the Meanings Contained in "The Great Treatise on the Stages of the Path." Lam rim chen mo'i don rgya cher bshad pa man ngag rin chen bang mdzod.* In Collected Works, vols. 2 and 3. Brag g.yab: dGe ldan bshad sgrub chos skor gling, d.u. BDRC W1KG10787.

Drotön Dutsi Drak (Gro ston bdud rtsi grags). *The Precious Supreme Path That Is the Oral Commentary of the True Spiritual Teacher. Yang dag pa'i dge ba'i bshes gnyen gyi zhal gyi gdams pa lam mchog rin po che.* In Chim Namkha Drak, *The Mahāyāna Supreme Path.* In *dGe slong nam mkha' grags kyis mdzad pa'i gsung phyogs bsdus.* Digital scans. BDRC W3CN18544.

Gö Lotsāwa Zhönu Pel ('Gos lo tsā ba gZhon nu dpal). *The Blue Annals.* Translated by George N. Roerich. Delhi: Motilal Banarsidass, 1949. Tibetan text: *Deb ther sngon po.* New Delhi: International Academy of Indian Culture, 1974.

Gyalse Tokme Zangpo Pel (rGyal sras Thogs med bzang po dpal). *The Ritual for Generating the Aspirational and Active Forms of Enlightenment Mind according to the*

System of the Great Master Śāntideva. sLob dpon chen po zhi ba lha'i lugs kyi smon 'jug sems bskyed kyi cho ga. In Collected Works, ff. 74a–92a. Derge, d.u.

———. *Thirty-Seven Verses on the Practices of the Victors' Spiritual Offspring.* Translated as *The Thirty-Seven Practices of All the Bodhisattvas* by Adam Pearcy. Lotsāwa House, 2006. Tibetan text: *rGyal ba'i sras kyi lag len sum cu so bdun ma.* In Collected Works, ff. 38a–41a. Derge, d.u.

Kham Tongkor Jampel Gendun Gyatso (Khams stong bskor 'Jam dpal dge 'dun rgya mtsho). *Diamond Fragments: A Commentary on the Seventy Topics* (not translated into English). *Don bdun bcu'i rnam bshad bdud rtsi'i gzegs ma.* Bylakuppe, India: Sera Me College, 1969.

Khedrup Je Gelek Pelsang (mKhas grub rje dGe legs dpal bzang). *An Ocean of Spiritual Attainments: The Generation-Stage Practices of Guhyasamāja, the King of Tantras. rGyud thams cad kyi rgyal po dpal gsang ba 'dus pa'i bskyed rim dngos grub rgya mtso.* In Collected Works, vol. 7 (*ja*), pp. 3–381. New Delhi: Mongolian Lama Guru Deva, 1980. (Toh. 5481)

Khedrup Tenpa Dargye (mKhas grub bsTan pa dar rgyas). *An Overview of the Perfection of Wisdom. bsTan bcos mngon par rtogs pa'i rgyan rtza 'grel gyi spyi don rnam bshad snying po rgyan gyi snang ba* (*Phar phyin spyi don*). Reprint edition. New Delhi: Sermey Khensur Lobsang Tharchin, 1980.

Lechen Kunga Gyaltsen (Las chen Kun dga' rgyal mtshan). *A Lamp That Illuminates the History of the Kadam Spiritual Tradition. bKa' gdams kyi rnam par thar pa bka' gdams chos 'byung gsal ba'i sgron me.* Digital scan. BDRC bdr:MW23748.

Lhadri Gangpa (Lha 'bri sgang pa). *A Commentary on the Kadam Instruction Manual Titled "Blue Udder." bKa' gdams kyi man ngag be'u bum sngon po'i 'grel pa* (*Be'u bum sngon po'i 'grel pa*). Bir, India: T. Tsondu Senghe, 1976.

Lodrö Jungne (Gro lung pa bLo gros 'byung gnas). *A Commentary on the Stages of the Path for Gaining Entry to the Sugata's Precious Teaching. bDe bar gshegs pa'i bstan pa rin po che la 'jug pa'i lam gyi rim pa rnam par bshad pa* (*bsTan rim chen mo*). Mundgod, India: Library of Trijang Labrang, 2001.

Logönpa Sönam Lhayi Wangpo (Lo dgon pa bSod nams lha'i dbang po). *The Myriad Light Rays of the Sun: A History of the Precious Kadam Tradition. bKa' gdams rin po che'i chos 'byung rnam thar nyin mor byed pa'i 'od strong.* English translation (includes Tibetan text): Vetturini, Gianpaolo. "The bKa' gdams pa School of Tibetan Buddhism." PhD diss., London School of Oriental and African Studies, 2007.

Losang Chökyi Gyaltsen, Fourth Paṇchen Lama (Paṇ chen bLo bzang chos kyi rgyal mtshan). *The Jewel Garland: A Clear Presentation of Losang Chökyi Gyaltsen, a Bhikṣu and Dharma Teacher's Conduct. Chos smra ba'i dge slong blo bzang chos kyi rgyal mtshan gyi spyod tshul gsal bar ston pa nor bu'i phreng ba.* In Collected Works, vol. 1 (*ka*), pp. 7–456. (Toh. 5877)

———. *The Preeminent One's Joyful Feast: A Commentary on the Lamp for the Path to Enlightenment. Byang chub lam gyi sgron ma'i rnam bshad phul byung bzhad pa'i dga' ston*. In Collected Works, vol. 4 (*nga*), pp. 155–261. New Delhi: Mongolian Lama Gurudeva, 1973. (Toh. 5941)

Losang Yeshe, Fifth Paṇchen (Paṇ chen bLo bzang ye shes). *The Swift Path: A Meditation Manual on the Stages of the Path to Enlightenment.* Translated by Szegee Toh. Somerville, MA: Wisdom, 2023. Tibetan text: *Byang chub lam gyi rim pa'i dmar khrid thams cad mkhyen par bgrod pa'i myur lam* (*Myur lam*). In Collected Works, vol. 3 (*ga*), pp. 127–287. bKras Lhun Chos Sde Tshogs Pa, 199AD. BDRC MW1174. (Toh. 6980)

Ludrup Gyatso. *Guidance Manual of the Three Appearances. gSung ngag slob bshad snang gsum gyi khrid yig zla ba bdud rtsi'i thigs phreng skal bzang ku mud gsar pa'i kha 'byed.* In *Sa-skya Lam-'bras Literature Series*, vol. 15 (*ba*), 31–151 (ff. 1b–61a) Dehra Dun: Sakya Centre, 1983.

Naktso Lotsāwa Tsultrim Gyalwa (Nag tsho lo tsā ba Tshul khrims rgyal ba). *Eighty Verses in Praise of the Dharma King of the Three Realms, Dīpaṃkara Śrījñāna.* Tibetan text: *Khams gsum chos kyi rgyal po dpal ldan mar me mdzad ye shes la bstod pa'i rab tu byed pa tshigs bcad brgyad cu pa* (a.k.a., *bsTod pa brgyad cu pa*). In *Legs par bshad pa bka' gdams rin po che'i gsung gi gces btus nor bu'i bang mdzod*, pp. 30–39. Delhi: D. Tsondu Senghe, 1985. (Toh. 6971)

Ngawang Losang Gyatso, Fifth Dalai Lama (rGyal mchog lnga pa Ngag dbang blo bzang rgya mtso). *Mañjughoṣa's Oral Instruction: An Instruction Manual on the Stages of the Path to Enlightenment* (a.k.a., *Mañjuśrī's Oral Instruction*). *Byang chub lam gyi rim pa'i khrid yig 'jam pa'i dbyangs kyi zhal lung* (*'Jam dpal zhal lung*). Thimbu, Bhutan: Kun bzang stobs rgyal, 1976. (Toh. 5637)

Ngawang Tsering (Ngag dbang tshe ring). *A Collection of Several Notes on the Treatise Titled "The Initial Method of Training One's Mind." Thog mar blo sbyong gi gzhung 'ga'i tho yig btus te bkod pa.* In Collected Works, vol. 2, 22ff. New Delhi: Mongolian Lama Gurudeva, 1985.

Ngulchu Dharmabhadra (dNgul chu Dhar ma bha dra). *The Treasury of Jewels: Notes from Oral Teachings on "The Easy Path That Leads to Omniscience: An Instruction Manual on the Stages of the Path to Enlightenment." Byang chub lam gyi rim pa'i dmar khrid thams cad mkhyen par bgrod pa'i bde lam gyi zin bris rin chen bang mdzod.* In Collected Works, vol. 6 (*cha*), 133ff. (Toh. 6419) BDRC MW1KG1657

Pabongkhapa Jampa Tenzin Trinle Gyaltso, Kyabje (sKyabs rje Pha bong kha pa Byams pa bstan 'dzin 'phrin las rgya mtsho; a.k.a., sKyabs rje bDe chen snying po). *A Downpour of Auspicious Virtue: A Profound Instruction on the Recitation Text for the Preliminary Practices Titled "The Necklace for the Fortunate." sByor chos skal bzang mgrin rgyan gyi zab khrid man ngag bla ma'i zhal lung dge legs char 'bebs.* In *Three Records of the Oral Instructions of Pha bong kha pa bDe chen sñing po on the Essentials of the dGe-lugs-pa Approach to Buddhist Practice*, pp. 1–167. Delhi: Chophel Legden, 1977.

———. *The Essence of Ambrosia: A Complete, Unerring, and Profound Teaching That Delivers Liberation in Our Hands. The edited transcript of a practical instruction on the stages of the path to enlightenment, the doctrine that represents the inmost thought of the incomparable dharma king and contains the essence of all the scriptures.* English translation: *Liberation in Our Hands.* 3 vols. Translated by Serme Khensur Lobsang Tharchin with Artemus B. Engle. Howell, NJ: Mahayana Sutra and Tantra Press, 1990–2001. Tibetan text: *rNam grol lag bcangs su gtod pa'i man ngag zab mo tshang la ma nor ba mtshungs med chos kyi rgyal po'i thugs bcud byang chub lam gyi rim pa'i nyams khrid kyi zin bris gsung rab kun gyi bcud bsdus gdams ngag bdud rtsi'i snying po* (*rNam grol lag bcangs*). In Collected Works, vol. 11. New Delhi: Chophel Legdan, 1973.

Potowa Rinchen Sel (Po to ba Rin chen gsal). *Edifying Similes. dPe chos.* In *dPe chos rin chen spungs pa'i 'bum 'grel.* Delhi: T. Tshering, 1975. (Toh. 6964)

———. *An Extended Monologue. Chig lab ring mo.* In *bLo sbyong nyer mkho phyogs bsgrigs*, pp. 444–66. Lan khr'u': Kan su'u mi rigs dpe skrun khang, 2003.

Sakya Paṇḍita Kunga Gyaltsen (Sa skya paṇḍi ta Kun dga' rgyal mtshan). *A Treasury of Jewel-Like Excellent Sayings.* In *Ordinary Wisdom: Sakya Pandita's Treasury of Good Advice.* Translated by John T. Davenport, with Sallie D. Davenport and Losang Thonden. Boston: Wisdom, 2000. Tibetan text: *Legs par bshad pa rin po che'i gter.* In *The Complete Works of the Great Masters of the Sa Skya Sect of Tibetan Buddhism*, vol. 1, pp. 50–61. Tokyo: The Toyo Bunko, 1968.

Sharawa Yönten Drak (Sha ra ba Yon tan grags). *A Lamrim Text Composed by the Spiritual Teacher Zhang Sharwapa Yönten Drak. dGe ba'i bshes gnyen zhang shar ba pa yon tan grags kyis mdzad pa'i lam rim.* Lhasa: Ser gtsug nang bstan dpe rnying 'tshol bsdu phyogs bsgrigs khang, 2019.

Tāranātha. *The Jewel Mine of an Ocean of Tutelary Deities' Sādhana Rituals.* Tibetan text: *Yi dam rgya mtsho'i sgrub thabs rin chen 'byung gnas.* Collected Works, vol. 15. New Delhi: Choephel Lekden, 1974, 1975. BDRC MW12422.

Tepo Choktrul Yeshe Thupten Gyatso (The bo mchog sprul Ye shes thub bstan rgya mtsho). *The Oral Instruction of the Great Ascetic: A Brief Compilation of Notes from a Teaching on the Treatise Titled "Opening the Door to the Dharma: The Initial Method of Training One's Mind in the Mind Training System of the Stages of the Path to Enlightenment." Byang chub lam gyi rim pa la thog mar blo sbyong ba chos kyi sgo 'byed ces bya ba'i don rags bsdus tsam zhig zin bris su bkod pa drang srong chen po'i zhal lung* (a.k.a., *Drang srong chen po'i zhal lung*). Reprint of woodblock edition, d.u.

Tsangnyön Heruka Sangye Gyaltsen (gTsang smyon he ru ka Sangs rgyas rgyal mtshan). *The Hundred Thousand Songs: An Extensive Account of the Liberating Deeds of Milarepa.* English translation: *The Hundred Thousand Songs of Milarepa.* Translated by Christopher Stagg. Boulder: Shambhala, 2016. Tibetan text: *Mi la ras pa'i rnam thar rgyas par phye ba mgur 'bum.* Taipei: Corporate Body of the Buddha Educational Foundation, 2003.

———. *The Liberating Deeds of Milarepa, the Lord of Yogis, That Reveal the Path to Omniscience.* In *The Life of Milarepa.* Translated by Lobsang P. Lhalungpa. Boston: Shambhala, 1985. Tibetan text: *rNal 'byor gyi dbang phyug chen po mi la ras pa'i rnam par thar pa dang thams cad mkyen pa'i lam ston*. Varanasi: Kalsang Lhudup, 1968.

Tsangpa Gyare Yeshe Dorje (gTsang pa rgya ras Ye shes rdo rje). *A Lamp for the Eyes That Requires Little Difficulty: A Treatise for Those Who Mentally Abandon the World. 'Jig rten blos btang rnams kyi bstan bcos tshegs chung mig gi sgron me.* In Collected Works, pp. 259–69. Kathmandu: Ven. Khenpo Shedup Tenzin and Lama Thinley Namgyal, 1998.

Tsonawa Sherap Zangpo (mTsho sna ba Shes rab bzang po). *Excellent Sayings That Are Like Light Rays of the Sun: A Commentary on "The Aphorisms on Moral Discipline." 'Dul ba mdo rtsa'i 'grel pa legs bshad nyi ma'i 'od zer*. Beijing: Krung go'i bod kyi shes rig dpe skrun khang, 1993. (Toh. 6850A)

Tsongkhapa Losang Drakpai Pel, Je (rJe Tsong kha pa bLo bzang grags pa'i dpal). *The Flower Cluster of Spiritual Attainments: A Supplication Prayer to the Lineage Whose Blessings Are Near. Byin rlabs nye brgyud kyi bla ma rnams la gsol ba 'debs pa dngos grub kyi snye ma*. In Collected Works, vol. 2 (*kha*), pp. 206–8. New Delhi: Mongolian Lama Guru Deva, 1978–1983. (Toh. 5275)

———. *The Great Treatise on the Stages of the Path to Enlightenment*. 3 vols. Translated by Lamrim Chenmo Translation Committee. Ithaca, NY: Snow Lion, 2000–2004. Tibetan text: *Byang chub lam gyi rim pa chen mo* (*Lam rim chen mo*). In Collected Works, vol. 13 (*pa*). New Delhi: Mongolian Lama Guru Deva, 1978–1983. (Toh. 5392)

———. *A Guidebook for the Path to Enlightenment: A Commentary on the Morality of a Bodhisattva*. English translation: *Asanga's Chapter on Ethics with the Commentary of Tsong-Kha-Pa: The Basic Path to Awakening, the Complete Bodhisattva*. Translated by Mark Tatz. Lewiston/Queenston: The Edwin Mellon Press, 1986. Tibetan text: *Byang chub sems dpa'i tshul khrims kyi rnam bshad byang chub gzhung lam*. In Collected Works, vol. 1 (*ka*), 109 ff. New Delhi: Mongolian Lama Guru Deva, 1978–1983. (Toh. 5271)

———. *A Letter Establishing the Basis of Benefit and Happiness. 'Phrin yig phan bde'i gzhi 'dzin*. In Collected Works, vol. 2 (*kha*), pp. 554–56. New Delhi: Mongolian Lama Guru Deva, 1978–1983. (Toh. 5275)

———. *The Luminous Jewel Lamp: A Praise of the Exalted and Venerable Protector Maitreya. rJe btsun byams pa mgon po la bstod pa rin po che gsal ba'i sgron me*. In Collected Works, vol. 2 (*kha*), pp. 248–52. New Delhi: Mongolian Lama Guru Deva, 1978–1983. (Toh. 5275)

———. *Ocean of Reasoning: A Great Commentary on Nāgārjuna's Mūlamadhyamakakārikā*. Translated by Jay Garfield. New York: Oxford University Press, 2006. Tibetan text: *dBu ma rtsa ba'i tshig le'ur byas pa shes rab ces bya ba'i rnam bshad rigs pa'i rgya mtsho*. In Collected Works, vol. 15 (*ba*), 281 ff. New Delhi: Mongolian Lama Guru Deva, 1978–1983. (Toh. 5401)

———. *Opening the Door to the Supreme Path. Lam mchog sgo 'byed*. In Collected Works, vol. 2 (*kha*), pp. 202–6. New Delhi: Mongolian Lama Guru Deva, 1978–1983. (Toh. 5275)

Wensapa Losang Döndrup (dBen sa pa bLo bzang don grub). *The Stages of the Path Arranged as Supplication Prayers. Lam rim gsol 'debs su sgrigs pa.* In Collected Works, vol 1. Chengdu: Lho nub mi rigs par khang, 2000.

Yeshe Döndrup Gyaltsen (Ye shes don grub bstan pa'i rgyal mtshan), comp. *A Treasury of Jewels: An Anthology of Excellent Sayings from the Teachings of the Precious Kadam Tradition. Legs par bshad pa bka' gdams rin po che'i gsung gi gces btus nor bu'i bang mdzod* (*bKa' gdams bces btus*). Delhi: D. Tsondu Senghe, 1985. (Toh. 6971)

Zhönu Gyalchok (gZhon nu rgyal mchog) and Könchok Gyaltsen (dKon mchog rgyal mtshan), comps. *A Hundredfold Collection of Mind Training Works.* English translation: Thupten Jinpa, trans. *Mind Training: The Great Collection.* The Library of Tibetan Classics, vol. 1. Boston: Wisdom, 2006. Tibetan text: *bLo sbyong glegs bam.* Bir, India: D. Tsondu Senghe, 1983. BDRC WA12364.

5. Reference Works

A Catalogue of the Tohoku University Collection of Tibetan Works on Buddhism. Edited by Y. Kanakura et al. Sendai, Japan: Tohoku Imperial University, 1953.

A Complete Catalogue of the Tibetan Buddhist Canons. Edited by Hakuju Ui et al. Sendai, Japan: Tohoku Imperial University, 1934.

Bareau, André. *Les Sectes Bouddhiques du Petit Véhicule.* Paris: École Françise D'Extrême-Orient, 1955.

Beyer, Stephen. *The Cult of Tārā: Magic and Ritual in Tibet.* Berkeley: University of California Press, 1973.

Chattopadhaya, Alaka. *Atiśa and Tibet: Life and Works of Dīpaṃkara Śrījñāna in Relation to the History and Religion of Tibet.* Delhi: Motilal Banarsidass, 1999.

Edgerton, Franklin, ed. *Buddhist Hybrid Sanskrit Dictionary.* 2 vols. 1st ed. New Haven, CT: Yale University Press, 1953. Reprint, Delhi: Motilal Banarsidass, 1970.

The Great Tibetan-Chinese Dictionary. Bod rgya tshig mdzod chen mo. Beijing: Mi rigs dpe skrun khang, 1985.

The Great Tibetan Dictionary. Dun dkar tshig mdzod chen mo. Edited by Dungkar Losang Trinle. Pe cin: krung go'i bod rig pa dpe skrun khang, 2002.

The Inner Science of Buddhist Practice: Vasubandhu's "Summary of the Five Heaps" With Commentary by Sthiramati. Translated with an extended introduction by Artemus B. Engle. Ithaca: Snow Lion, 2009.

Jamgön Kongtrul Lodrö Taye. *The Catalog of "The Treasury of Precious Instructions."* Translated by Richard Barron. New York: Tsadra Foundation, 2013.

Keay, John. *India: A History.* Oxford: Oxford University Press, 2000.

Mahāvyutpatti. Bye brag tu rtogs pa chen po. Dg.T. sna tshogs, vol. 126 (*cho*), ff. 1b–131a. Reprint, Tokyo: Suzuki Gakujutsu Zaidan, 1962. (Toh. 4346)

McGovern, William Montgomery. *A Manual of Buddhist Philosophy.* Lucknow,

India: Oriental Reprinters, 1976. First published 1923 by E. P. Dutton and Co. (London).
Monier-Williams, Monier. *Sanskrit-English Dictionary*. 1st ed. London: Oxford University Press, 1899. Reprint, Delhi: Motilal Banarsidass, 1963.
Negi, J. S., ed. *Tibetan-Sanskrit Dictionary*. 16 vols. Sarnath, Varanasi: Central Institute of Higher Tibetan Studies, 1993–2005.
A Sanskrit-Tibetan Lexicon in Two Sections. sGra sbyor bam po gnyis pa. Dg.T. sna tshogs, vol. 126 (*cho*), ff. 131b–160a. (Toh. 4347)
Sarat Chandra Das, comp. *A Tibetan-English Dictionary*. Rev. ed. Delhi: Motilal Banarsidass, 1970.
Snellgrove, D. L., trans. *The Hevajra Tantra*. London: Oxford University Press, 1959.
Stein, Rolf Alfred. *Les tribus anciennes des marches sino-tibétaines: légendes, classifications et histoire*. Paris: Presses universitaires de France, 1961.
Willson, Martin, and Martin Brauen. *Deities of Tibetan Buddhism: The Zurich Paintings of the Icons Worthwhile to See*. Boston: Wisdom, 2000.

Index

Dampa Kunga, 580, 614, 909n510
Dampa Sangye, 793n127, 794n129
Dargye Zangpo, 526, 890n180
death, 15, 99, 106, 131, 547, 584
  certainty of, 173, 257–58, 261, 532
  factors contributing to, 260, 263
  of gods, signs of, 135–36, 296, 772n127
  recalling, 527–28
  spirits causing, 624–25
  suffering of, 293–94
  time of, as uncertain, 173, 259–60, 261–62, 553
  untimely, 263
  with unvirtuous mind, 263–64
  See also impermanence in form of death
deathless state, 609, 920n679
deceitfulness, 144, 202, 327–28, 368, 417, 468, 569–71, 734n128, 830n261, 905n457
dedication prayers, 103, 154, 243–45, 249, 779n196, 782n22
Deer Park, 928n815
defeats
  extreme, 12, 92, 143, 365, 418, 489–91, 607, 752n273, 774n149, 846n425, 859n167, 873n157, 918n653
  secondary offenses, 365
definitive meaning, 80, 87–88, 746n213
degenerate age, 163, 592, 781n19
deities
  Who Control Others' Magical Creations, 315, 826n219, 884n97
  Who Delight in Magical Creations, 315, 826n218
  See also desire-realm gods; worldly gods
deliberation, 17, 580, 583, 910n514, 912n530
demigods, 438
  "black faction," 295, 818n130
  domains of, 314, 315
  rebirth as, 252, 286
  suffering of, 135–36, 180, 295–98, 386, 459, 785n48
Dense Array Below None, 50
dependent origination, 80–82, 83, 84, 106, 308, 338, 349, 614, 633, 920n695
Deshin Shekpa, 616
desire, 304, 519
  antidote for, 184
  arising of, 568
  diminishing, 323
  failing to overcome, 354
  freedom from, 540, 586, 912n550
  having few, 570–71, 907n447
  results of, 526
  two types, 554
desire realm, 459, 826n220
desire-realm gods, 53, 826n219
  divine eye of, 818n139
  life span, 268
  rebirth as, 252, 296, 303
  suffering of, 135–36, 180, 297, 387, 459
Devadatta, 570
devotion, 16, 148, 206, 464, 501, 596, 615, 791n99
devotional works, xxxii, xxxiv, xxxv
dharma, 32, 590, 722n38
  accepting hardship for, 590
  advanced and fundamental, relationship of, 520, 527, 529–30, 531–33, 535, 552, 888n151
  and attachment to this life, incompatibility of, 524–26
  based on single aim, 15
  benefits of, 98, 547
  causes enabling, 628–30
  continuous, 625–28
  counterfeit, 489
  death and, 173, 260–62, 548–49
  discouragement in, 551, 592, 627
  as fetter, 566
  firmness about, 264–65
  generosity of, 204, 331–32
  happiness from, 539–41, 544
  as highest conduct, 539
  jewel, protection of, 277–78
  obstacles to, 530–32
  patience from reflecting on, 147–48, 335, 831n278
  progressive improvement in, 358
  repudiating, 112, 418, 500, 760n12
  starting point, 513, 514
  twofold, 29, 32, 722nn36–37, 760n19
  urgency of practicing, 258